THE QUESTION:

In a world of information overload, how do students become savvy, self-aware consumers of media?

THE ANSWER:

Instill proven media literacy principles and really show students how to:

- filter through the fluff
- indentify sources of bias
- distill and critically assess all media
- effectively navigate a media world

Ralph E. Hanson believes that armed with media literacy principles, students have the tools and critical thinking skills they need to be smart consumers of the media. Through 15 chapters, Hanson delivers comprehensive yet compact coverage, incisive analysis, and fun, conversational writing. While he delves into critical theory, and will take a critical stance on the media, he does not believe the media are something to be feared or demonized. Rather the media are an essential part of the way we live.

The Seven Secrets

Students are encouraged to think about what the media are, who controls the media, how media content is selected, why the media behave the way they do, and how society and the media interact with each other. Every time a secret is referenced, it's highlighted in yellow.

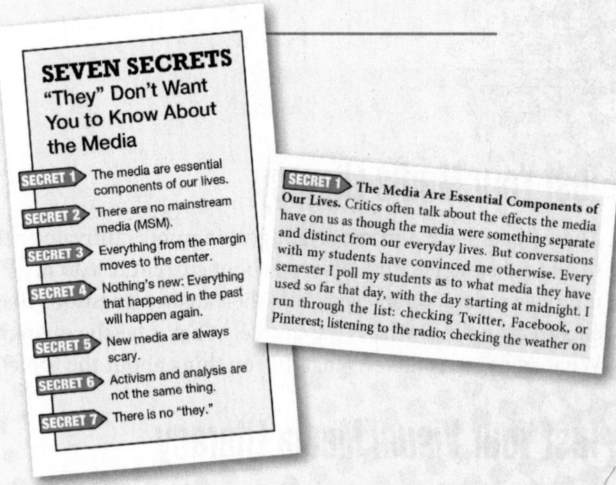

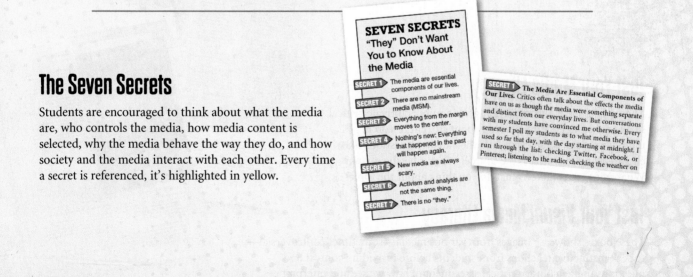

SEVEN SECRETS
"They" Don't Want You to Know About the Media

SECRET 1 The media are essential components of our lives.
SECRET 2 There are no mainstream media (MSM).
SECRET 3 Everything from the margin moves to the center.
SECRET 4 Nothing's new: Everything that happened in the past will happen again.
SECRET 5 New media are always scary.
SECRET 6 Activism and analysis are not the same thing.
SECRET 7 There is no "they."

SECRET 1 **The Media Are Essential Components of Our Lives.** Critics often talk about the effects the media have on us as though the media were something separate and distinct from our everyday lives. But conversations with my students have convinced me otherwise. Every semester I poll my students as to what media they have used so far that day, with the day starting at midnight. I run through the list: checking Twitter, Facebook, or Pinterest; listening to the radio; checking the weather on

Vignettes and Objectives

Each chapter kicks off with a compelling story about a figure or people at the center of a newsworthy event—the perfect way to hook students and exemplify chapter themes. Objectives call out key topics to encourage close, focused reading.

Chapter Timelines

Key events in the development of mass communication are placed within the context of other major historical dates.

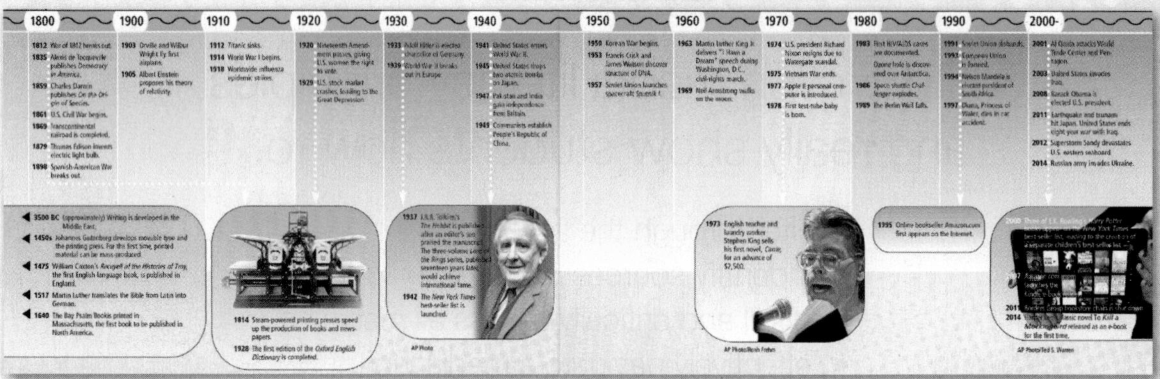

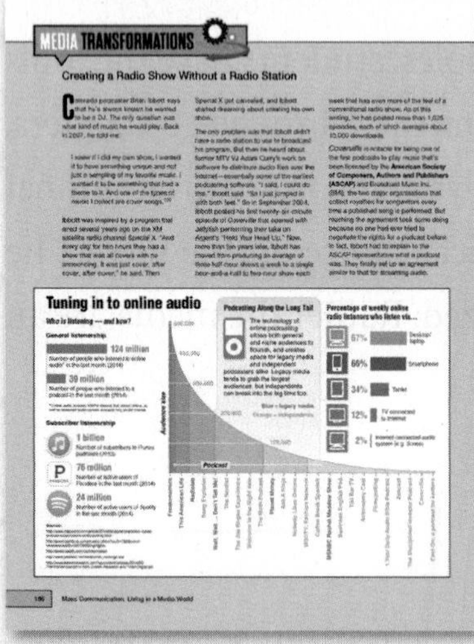

Media Transformations

This new set of boxes take an in-depth look at how media channels, use, and industries have transformed over recent decades. Each feature includes text telling the story of one transformation accompanied by an original infographic that gives the broader picure of the transformation.

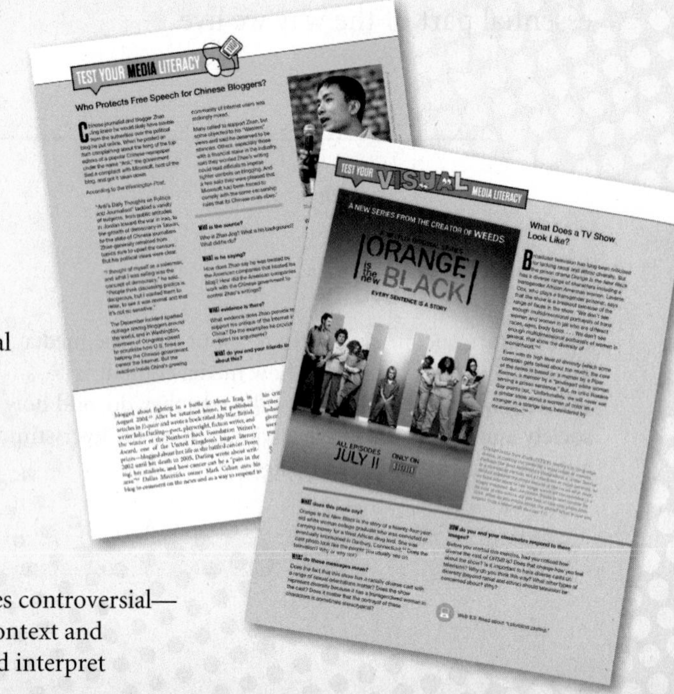

Test Your Media Literacy

These boxes have one important goal in mind: cultivate critical media consumers. Students read about current research, interviews, data, or an event, and then answer questions that elicit real analysis: who is the source? What is he/she saying? What evidence is there? What do you think about the topic?

Test Your *Visual* Media Literacy

These boxes showcase images from various media—sometimes controversial—to seek instinctive reactions from students before providing context and questions that encourage critical assessment of how we see and interpret images, and what more may be behind them.

Questioning the Media

These critical thinking questions, in the margin of every main section of the text, provide useful stop-and-think moments, addressing current media issues and encouraging students to consider how we use and consume media.

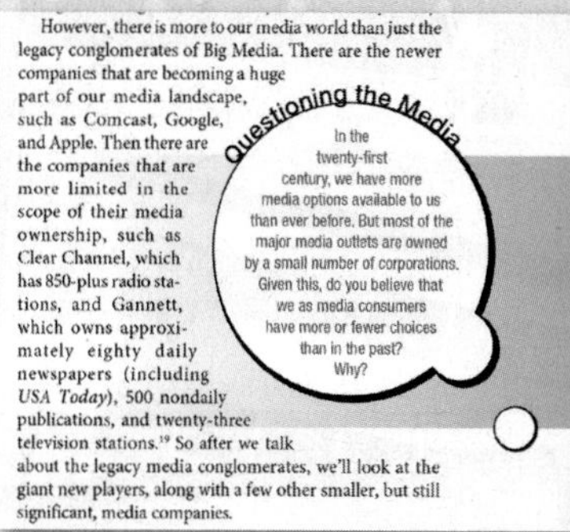

However, there is more to our media world than just the legacy conglomerates of Big Media. There are the newer companies that are becoming a huge part of our media landscape, such as Comcast, Google, and Apple. Then there are the companies that are more limited in the scope of their media ownership, such as Clear Channel, which has 850-plus radio stations, and Gannett, which owns approximately eighty daily newspapers (including *USA Today*), 500 nondaily publications, and twenty-three television stations.[19] So after we talk about the legacy media conglomerates, we'll look at the giant new players, along with a few other smaller, but still significant, media companies.

Community on the Net

Before the 1900s, it was relatively easy to define community: The community was made up of the people you interacted with every day. But the growth of the mass media led to changes in our understanding of community. People no longer need to be

Global Media Coverage

The global media icon, shown next to major headings in the text, cues readers to upcoming global media content.

The Receiver. The receiver is the audience for the mass communication message—that is, the people who are receiving and decoding the message. **Decoding** is the process of translating a signal from a mass medium into a form that

receiver: The audience for the mass communication message.

decoding: The process of translating a signal from a mass medium into a form that the receiver can understand and then interpreting the meaning of the message itself.

heterogeneous audience: An audience made up of a mix of people who differ in age, sex, income, education, ethnicity, race, religion, and other characteristics.

noise: Interference with the transmission of a message. This can take the form of semantic, mechanical, or environmental noise.

Marginal Glossary

Handy definitions at the foot of the page allow students to easily reference key terms.

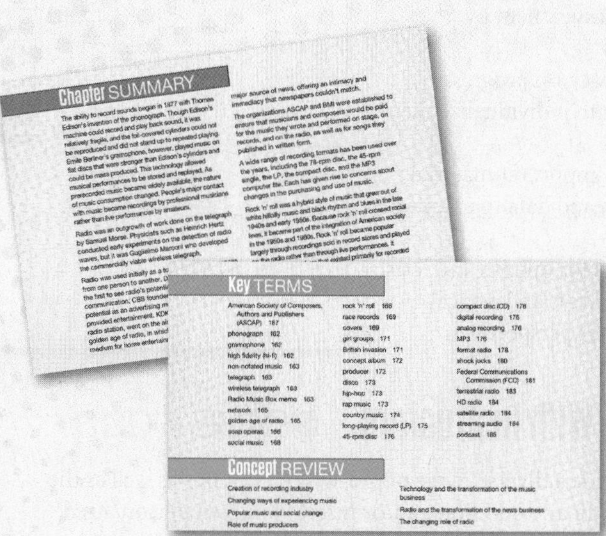

Chapter SUMMARY

Key TERMS

American Society of Composers, Authors and Publishers (ASCAP) 187
phonograph 162
gramophone 162
high fidelity (hi-fi) 162
non-notated music 163
telegraph 163
wireless telegraph 163
Radio Music Box memo 163
network 165
golden age of radio 165
soap operas 166
social music 168
rock 'n' roll 166
race records 169
covers 169
girl groups 171
British invasion 171
concept album 172
producer 172
disco 173
hip-hop 173
rap music 173
country music 174
long-playing record (LP) 175
45-rpm disc 176
compact disc (CD) 176
digital recording 176
analog recording 176
MP3 176
format radio 178
shock jocks 180
Federal Communications Commission (FCC) 181
terrestrial radio 183
HD radio 184
satellite radio 184
streaming audio 184
podcast 185

Concept REVIEW

Creation of recording industry
Changing ways of experiencing music
Popular music and social change
Role of music producers
Technology and the transformation of the music business
Radio and the transformation of the news business
The changing role of radio

Chapter Summaries

A brief recap of important points assists students in reviewing major themes, events, and concepts.

Key Terms List and Concept Review

An easy way to review and study, these lists provide page references.

Living Interactively

At no extra cost to students, they can access an interactive ebook version of the text when they buy a new print copy. Through a series of icons students link to multimedia content—including audio, video, articles (including *CQ Researcher* reports)—right where it matters most: on the page where a topic is discussed. Students take a deeper dive and explore a concept *while reading*. Students will have access to study tools such as highlighting, bookmarking, and note-taking. It's an enhanced, enriching, and interactive learning experience.

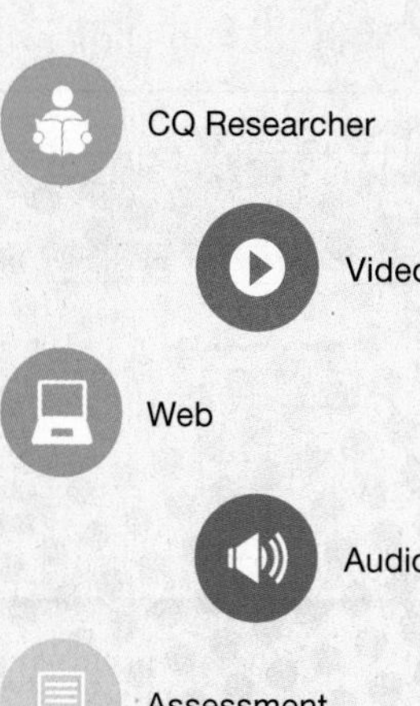

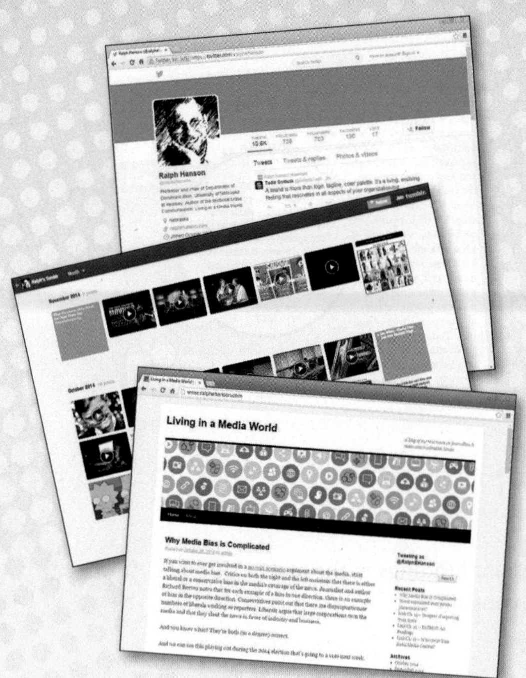

Living With Social Media

In addition to keeping his book fresh and current with frequent postings, Ralph Hanson ties his blog content to chapters so that videos, commentary, and articles are effectively framed with media literacy principles in mind. Check out a post or two, and Hanson's "Living in a Media World" blog (**http://ralphehanson.com**) will become your go-to resource for insightful and entertaining examples and cases relevant to the intro mass comm course—a great way to kick off a lecture or an in-class discussion.

Follow the author on Twitter (**http://twitter.com/@ralphehanson**) for daily links to media news.

Check out Ralph's Tumblr (**http://ralphehanson.tumblr.com**) for a trove of video clips that work well as a pre-class feature, along with photos and other images he's found online or created himself.

The book's **Facebook** page lets you share materials and find links to what Ralph's been posting on the blog and on Tumblr.

edge.sagepub.com/hanson5e

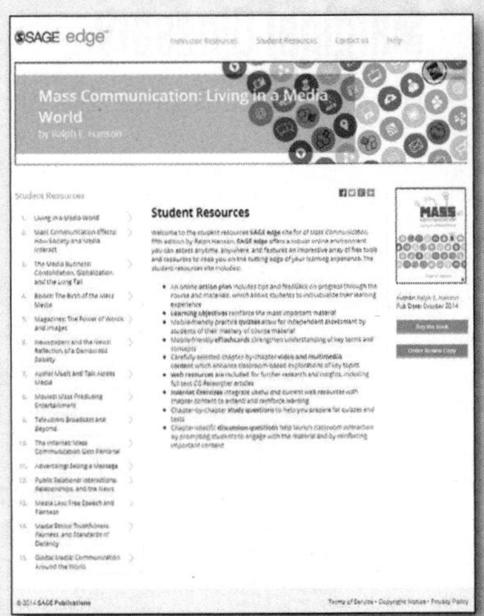

Living on the Web SAGE edge™

- Mobile-friendly **eFlashcards** strengthen understanding of key terms and concepts.
- Mobile-friendly practice **quizzes** allow for independent assessment by students of their mastery of course material.
- A customized online **action plan** includes tips and feedback on progress through the course and materials, which allows students to individualize their learning experience.
- Chapter-specific **learning objectives** reinforce the most important material.
- **Multimedia content** includes links to video, audio, web, and data that appeal to students with different learning styles.
- Chapter-by-chapter **study questions** to help you prepare for quizzes and tests.
- **Internet activities and exercises**, comprised of web resources and critical thinking questions to apply your knowledge of the chapter perspectives.

Living [Happily] With Instructors SAGE edge™

edge.sagepub.com/hanson5e

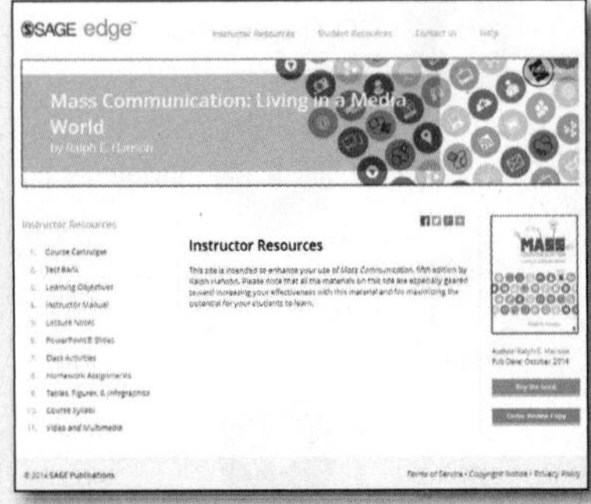

- **Test banks** provide a diverse range of pre-written options as well as the opportunity to edit any question and/or insert your own personalized questions to effectively assess students' progress and understanding.
- Editable, chapter-specific **PowerPoint®** slides offer complete flexibility for creating a multimedia presentation for your course.
- **Lecture notes** summarize key concepts on a chapter-by-chapter basis to help with preparation for lectures and class discussions.
- An **Instructor's manual** written by the author and offers chapter-by-chapter guidance.
- Carefully selected chapter-by-chapter **video links and multimedia content**, which enhance classroom-based explorations of key topics.
- **Exhibits from the printed book** are available in an easily-downloadable format for use in papers, hand-outs, and presentations.
- A **common course cartridge** includes all of the instructor resources and assessment material from the student study site, making it easy for instructors to upload and use these materials in learning management systems such as Blackboard™, Angel®, Moodle™, Canvas, and Desire2Learn™.

MASS
COMMUNICATION

EDITION
5

To Pam, Erik, and Andrew

SAGE was founded in 1965 by Sara Miller McCune to support the dissemination of usable knowledge by publishing innovative and high-quality research and teaching content. Today, we publish more than 750 journals, including those of more than 300 learned societies, more than 800 new books per year, and a growing range of library products including archives, data, case studies, reports, conference highlights, and video. SAGE remains majority-owned by our founder, and after Sara's lifetime will become owned by a charitable trust that secures our continued independence.

Los Angeles | London | Washington DC | New Delhi | Singapore | Boston

Mass Communication

Living in a Media World

EDITION 5

Ralph E. Hanson

University of Nebraska at Kearney

Los Angeles | London | New Delhi
Singapore | Washington DC | Boston

Los Angeles | London | New Delhi
Singapore | Washington DC | Boston

FOR INFORMATION:

SAGE Publications, Inc.
2455 Teller Road
Thousand Oaks, California 91320
E-mail: order@sagepub.com

SAGE Publications Ltd.
1 Oliver's Yard
55 City Road
London, EC1Y 1SP
United Kingdom

SAGE Publications India Pvt. Ltd.
B 1/I 1 Mohan Cooperative Industrial Area
Mathura Road, New Delhi 110 044
India

SAGE Publications Asia-Pacific Pte. Ltd.
3 Church Street
#10-04 Samsung Hub
Singapore 049483

Acquisitions Editor: Matt Byrnie
Associate Editor: Natalie Konopinski
Digital Content Editor: Gabrielle Piccininni
Editorial Assistant: Janae Masnovi
Production Editor: Laura Barrett
Copy Editor: Melinda Masson
Typesetter: C&M Digitals (P) Ltd.
Proofreader: Theresa Kay
Indexer: Will Ragsdale
Cover Designer: Janet Kiesel
Marketing Manager: Liz Thornton

Printed in Canada

Cataloging-in-publication data is available for this title from the Library of Congress.

ISBN 978-1-4833-4475-1

This book is printed on acid-free paper.

15 16 17 18 19 10 9 8 7 6 5 4 3 2 1

Brief Contents

Contents

PART II PRINT MEDIA

©iStockphoto.com/Andrew_ Howe

Courtesy of The Atlantic

©iStockphoto.com/FrankvandenBergh

PART III ELECTRONIC MEDIA

Film Magic/Getty Images

©iStockphoto.com/Davel5957

©iStockphoto.com/acprints

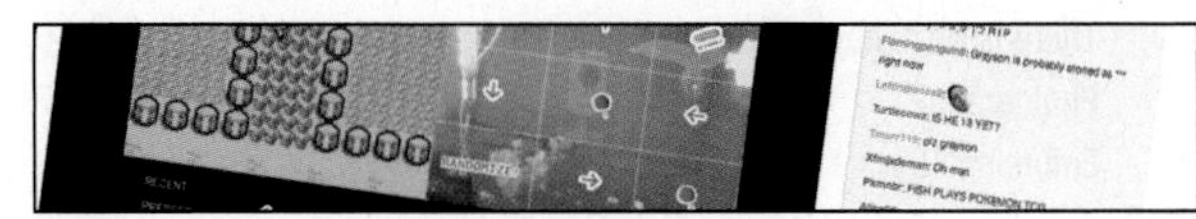

http://www.twitch.tv/fishplayspokemon

PART IV STRATEGIC COMMUNICATION

PSL Images/Alamy

©iStockphoto.com/malerapaso

PART V REGULATION AND CONTROL OF THE MEDIA

©iStockphoto.com/stepan popov

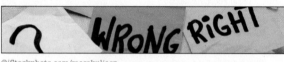

©iStockphoto.com/marekuliasz

©iStockphoto.com/alengo

Preface

Many of the defining moments of our lives come from our shared experiences with the media. It could be witnessing the death of a global terrorist through social media coverage, experiencing the thrill of a sports victory viewed streaming on the Internet, going to a blockbuster movie as the backdrop to a first date, or hearing a song from the summer you turned sixteen. For my generation, it was the moon walk. Parents all across the United States let their nine-year-olds stay up way past their bedtimes to watch on television the biggest show of their lives—*Apollo 11* astronaut Neil Armstrong setting foot on the moon. On September 11, 2001, my son and his fellow fifth-grade classmates sat mesmerized by news coverage of the airplanes crashing into the World Trade Center twin towers, the Pentagon, and a field in southwestern Pennsylvania. Some parents questioned whether their children ought to have watched these events, but my son said, “We begged the teacher to keep the TV on. We had to know.” As I write this, my former fifth-grader is a college graduate who has lived in Europe and Asia with a global perspective brought on in part by that fateful day in 2001. I’m starting to reach the point with my freshmen where their earliest major media memories are no longer 9/11. That horrible day remains the top media memory for many of them, but others are now including the start of the Iraq war, specific sporting events, or some kind of local news story.

Then there are the myriad trivial aspects of everyday life that come from our time with the media: the perfect pair of vintage Levi’s found in the shopping magazine *Lucky*, William Shatner’s version of the song “Common People” on the *Coverville* podcast, or arguments on the Internet about the merits of the Bowl Championship Series versus a college football playoff.

The media world we inhabit is constantly changing, as is our relationship with the media. In my first job as a college professor, I taught a course in media effects. On the first day of class, a student raised his hand and asked, “When do we get to the part where we talk about how television turns people into zombies?” His question has stayed with me through the years because it represents the view many people have about the media. The student’s attitude had been fostered by media critics with an agenda—getting elected to office, getting a regulation approved, promoting a product, or even pushing a moral choice. I have long taken the view that the successful study of mass communication is also a journey of self-awareness. We are students of media and also players in a media world.

Approach of the Book

A study conducted by the Kaiser Family Foundation shows that young Americans spend an average of seven hours and thirty-eight minutes a day interacting with mass media of one form or another. And because they are multitasking, teens actually consume close to eleven hours worth of media within that time. The media are a central aspect of our lives, and many worry about the influence of these institutions.

Mass Communication: Living in a Media World views the media in our world not as isolated institutions that somehow “do something” to us, but rather as forces that are central to how we live, work, and play. The media are not outside influences; they are part of who we are. From mobile media devices to streaming video, the pervasiveness of mass communication in our daily lives complicates our ability to understand the media’s rich history of technical, cultural, sociological, political, economic, and artistic achievements. *Mass Communication* reveals the forces that drive the industry, while at the same time motivating readers to think critically about how they consume media. It uses compelling stories and examples drawn from everyday life. Readers are encouraged to consider the media industry from the inside out and, in so doing, to explore the many dimensions of mass communication that operate in our society.

My students over the years have told me that they remember information better if it is presented as a story, and so I strive to be a storyteller. The narrative style of this book will help motivate students to do the reading and facilitate their recall of the material. Many of the Test Your Media Literacy exercises are based on writing assignments I’ve used in classroom settings, as well as in more writing-intensive online sections. These exercises connect the material from the book to the media that students use every day, and students say that these assignments make them really think about how they experience the media.

Organization

The book is organized into five parts, each examining critical dimensions that comprise the world of mass communication. *Part I: Introduction to the Media* presents the institutions, social effects, and business workings of the media in order to lay the foundation for understanding mass communication. *Part II: Print Media* explores the development of mass literacy and mass communication and what has traditionally been the paper-oriented print media, including newspapers, books, and magazines. *Part III: Electronic Media* covers the media of sound and motion, from radio and music to movies, television, and the Internet. *Part IV: Strategic Communication* delves into the advertising and public relations industries. *Part V: Regulation and Control of the Media* looks at the institutions, conventions, and rules that regulate and control the media in the United States and around the world, critiques normative theories of the press in various countries, and looks at how the media operate around the globe.

Most of the chapters about the individual print or electronic media (Parts II and III) are organized around the same basic structure. Following an opening vignette and chapter timeline come four major sections:

1. How the medium developed along with major changes in society and culture. More than just a history of the medium, this section considers how societal, cultural, and technological elements came together to create the medium we have today.
2. How the medium operates within the business and social world. This section looks at why the medium behaves the way it does within our economy.
3. Current issues and controversies between the medium and society. These often include issues involving media effects, such as the concern about the influence of fashion magazines on a young woman's body image or the influence of rock and rap lyrics on listeners.
4. The future of the medium, including the effects mobile technology and the long tail have had on it.

New to the Fifth Edition

We live in a media world that is constantly changing. My chief goal in writing this fifth edition, in addition to comprehensively updating the material, was to reflect the big changes taking place within the media industry while continuing to strengthen the book's media literacy focus. The fifth edition of *Mass Communication* deals with this period of rapid change with several new elements, including Media Transformations boxes and infographics, a strengthened focus on mobile and social media, new chapter opening vignettes, and an interactive e-book. Below are the details about these new offerings, as well as information on some returning features.

Revised chapter objectives—Learning objectives appear at the start of each chapter and call out key topics for close, focussed reading. Students can refer back to them for study guidance as well.

New Media Transformations boxes—These new boxes use a combination of text and visual graphics to help students understand the rapid rate of media changes over recent decades. Each Media Transformations feature includes text telling the story of one specific transformation such as how the transmission of news from disasters at Mt. Everest from the time of *Into Thin Air* in 1996 to the avalanche in 2014 changed, how e-books are changing the publishing industry, how podcasts are blurring the line between radio and online content, and how Netflix and other streaming services are transforming the way we define "watching television" in the twenty-first century. Many of these Media Transformations were inspired by changes that have happened since the first edition of his book came out about 10 years ago. Each story is accompanied by an original infographic that shows the broader picture of the transformation.

New chapter-opening vignettes—Ten brand new stories about key figures in the media provide a powerful narrative thread exemplifying the major themes of each chapter. These vignettes convey the excitement and relevance of media studies and critical enquiry by way of those whose lives have been profoundly affected by the media.

Mobile media—This edition includes a strengthened emphasis on the role the mobile media are playing in how we consume both legacy and new types of media. More than two-thirds of all Americans go online with mobile devices like smartphones or tablets. And this use of mobile media has moved us from the need-to-connect of dial-up service, to the always-on of broadband, to the access-everywhere of mobile Internet.

Social media—Throughout the book I take a more nuanced look at social media and how they are used not only on their own but as a tool for existing media to interact with their audiences. Social media has become increasingly relevant in today's media landscape: We get photos from astronauts and comments allegedly from NASA space probes from Twitter, and both Israeli and Palestinian military send out messages to the public through channels like YouTube. The role of social media across the various mediums is integrated throughout the book.

Global media—The fifth edition contains expanded global media coverage including a strengthened emphasis on the risks journalists face when reporting around the world. Reporters working in war zones in places like

Syria face not only the dangers of battle but also risk being kidnapped and beheaded in propaganda videos. As technology continues to change, so too do the boundaries on information that is available to media and consumers.

Updated chapters—Each chapter has been thoroughly updated to include new developments, new scholarship, and recent events in mass communication. Highlights of the revisions include:

Chapter 2, *Mass Communication Effects*, looks at new studies that give us fresh insight on classic areas of media effects studies such as the spiral of silence and cultivation theory.

Chapter 3, *The Media Business*, reflects the changing face of who provides media for our consumption, highlighting newer players like cable giant Comcast, which acquired NBC Universal, or revolutionary technology company Apple, with its high-volume hardware sales. A second emphasis is on how these companies are splitting up and recombining in new ways to dominate significant segments of the media marketplace.

Chapter 4, *Books*, looks at how e-books and e-book readers are changing the book marketplace both in terms of how books are distributed and how they are priced. There is also a look at how graphic novels have moved from being "mere" comic books into respected parts of the literary canon. (Not that there's anything wrong with comic books!)

Chapter 5, *Magazines*, includes a look at how social media are becoming integrated into legacy material features like magazine spreads. There is also a substantially updated look at magazine covers and race.

Chapter 8, *Movies,* looks at how digital media have transformed our movie watching experience. It now ranges from seeing movies in immersive digital IMAX theaters to viewing movies on the go using mobile devices and streaming services.

Chapter 10, *The Internet*, examines how video games have moved from being an individual pastime to something audiences will tune in across the country to watch.

Chapter 15, *Global Media*, looks at the risks journalists face carrying out their jobs, both from governments and from groups that don't want to be held up for examination.

Returning Favorites

While some of the book's new features were described above, the fifth edition contains many returning features and coverage that have been updated to enhance and improve upon the existing content.

The Seven Secrets—The Seven Truths have become the Seven Secrets in an effort to highlight the fun elements of these media literacy principles. Throughout all fifteen chapters, the Seven Secrets remind students about the principles of media literacy laid out in Chapter 1. These concepts deal with what the media are, who controls the media, how media content is selected, why the media behave the way they do, and how society and the media interact with each other. The Seven Secrets are as follows:

SECRET 1 The media are essential components of our lives.

SECRET 2 There are no mainstream media.

SECRET 3 Everything from the margin moves to the center.

SECRET 4 Nothing's new: Everything that happened in the past will happen again.

SECRET 5 New media are always scary.

SECRET 6 Activism and analysis are not the same thing.

SECRET 7 There is no "they."

The secrets are presented in depth in the last section of Chapter 1, and they recur, when relevant, in the subsequent chapters to remind students of these concepts and also to serve as a springboard for discussions or writing assignments. These important principals of media literacy are highlighted to call attention to where the Seven Secrets appear throughout the chapters, reminding readers to be attentive and thoughtful.

Illustrated chapter timelines—Updated timelines at the start of each chapter summarize major events in the development of mass communication and place them within the context of other major historical dates. This allows students to integrate their knowledge of world history with the parallel development of mass media. The timelines preview important dates in mass-media history that are detailed elsewhere in the chapter.

Test Your Media Literacy boxes—There's no better way to cultivate critical media consumers than by modeling critical thinking. These boxes present students with current research, interviews, and issues relating to the practice of mass communication, and ask questions that challenge students to evaluate and analyze the story being told. The readings are engaging and fun, but more important, the questions get students to do more than summarize what they've read—they encourage them to think.

Test Your Visual Media Literacy boxes—These boxes showcase images—sometimes controversial—from various media to seek instinctive reactions from students before providing context and questions that encourage critical assessment of how we see and interpret images, and what more may be behind them. Both media literacy boxes are supplemented with up-to-the-minute additions and further related information through my blog at http://ralphehanson.com.

Questioning the Media feature—This marginal feature poses critical-thinking questions that address current media issues and encourage students to consider how they use and consume media and develop their own opinions.

Global media icon— Globe icons next to major headings in the Table of Contents give a quick overview of where global media developments and issues are addressed throughout the books, and are shown next to the same headings in the text to cue readers to look for upcoming global media content.

Chapter summary—Each chapter concludes with a brief recap of important points to assist students in reviewing key themes, events, and concepts.

Key terms—Boldface terms are defined in the margins, and a list of key terms—with page references—appears at the end of each chapter to make the terms easy to locate.

Concept review—Central concepts are listed at the end of each chapter, providing students with a mini-study guide. The central concepts are ideas that go beyond one or two vocabulary words and may be developed throughout an entire section or chapter.

Living in a Media World's Social Media

Located at **http://ralphehanson.com,** my blog *Living in a Media World* covers the entire mass communication field and has been linked to by national Web sites, including FishbowlDC, Wonkette, Gawker, Eat the Press, and *USA Today*'s On Deadline. One of the blog's biggest benefits to you is that it provides a single destination for up-to-date material on the topics covered in this book. It also provides links to current multimedia features created by media outlets across the country. Think of it as a clearing house for current media news and features. You may also find examples of new assignments or early versions of new book features on the blog as well.

The *Living in a Media World* blog has now been joined by several other social media feeds. You can follow me on Twitter **(https://twitter.com/@ralphehanson)** for daily links to media news and whatever else I'm reading. I generally tag my tweets that tie most closely to this book with the hashtag #liamw (for Living In A Media World), as occasionally do other teachers and students. (Expect links to Web comics and motorcycle news to make an occasional appearance.) I also have a Tumblr **(http://ralphehanson.tumblr.com)** that will feature a lot of great video clips that work well as a pre-class feature, along with photos and other images I've found online or created myself. Typical content includes music clips, viral videos, memes, and commentary on geek culture. The Tumblr tends to be a bit less focused than the blog and sometimes includes photos I've taken. Finally, this book has a Facebook page **(https://www.facebook.com/livinginamediaworld)** where you can share materials and find links to what I've been posting about on the blog and on Tumblr.

Ancillaries

SAGE has created new student and instructor online resources customized to the text and featuring an array of tools for review, study, and further exploration.

SAGE edge™

SAGE provides comprehensive multimedia online resources at **http://edge.sagepub.com/hanson5e.** Instructors receive full access to the password-protected **SAGE edge Instructor Resources Site.**

SAGE edge for Instructors supports teaching by easily integrating quality content and creating a rich learning environment for students.

- **Test banks** provide a diverse range of pre-written options as well as the opportunity to edit any question and/or insert your own personalized questions to effectively assess students' progress and understanding.
- Editable, chapter-specific **PowerPoint® slides** offer complete flexibility for creating a multimedia presentation for your course.
- **Lecture notes** summarize key concepts on a chapter-by-chapter basis to help with preparation for lectures and class discussions.
- An **Instructor's manual** written by the author and offers chapter-by-chapter guidance.
- Carefully selected chapter-by-chapter **video links** and **multimedia content**, which enhance classroom-based explorations of key topics.
- **Exhibits from the printed book** are available in an easily-downloadable format for use in papers, handouts, and presentations
- A **common course cartridge** includes all of the instructor resources and assessment material from the student study site, making it easy for instructors to upload and use these materials in learning management systems such as Blackboard™, Angel®, Moodle™, Canvas, and Desire2Learn™

SAGE edge for students provides a personalized approach to help students accomplish their coursework goals in an easy-to-use learning environment. SAGE provide students with comprehensive multimedia online resources at **http://edge.sagepub.com/hanson5e.**

- Mobile-friendly **eFlashcards** strengthen understanding of key terms and concepts.
- Mobile-friendly practice **quizzes** allow for independent assessment by students of their mastery of course material.
- A customized online **action plan** includes tips and feedback on progress through the course and materials, which allows students to individualize their learning experience.
- Chapter-specific **learning objectives** reinforce the most important material.
- **Multimedia content** includes links to video, audio, web, and data that appeal to students with different learning styles.
- Chapter-by-chapter **study questions** to help you prepare for quizzes and tests.
- **Internet activities and exercises**, comprised of Web resources and critical thinking questions to apply your knowledge of the chapter perspectives.

About the Author

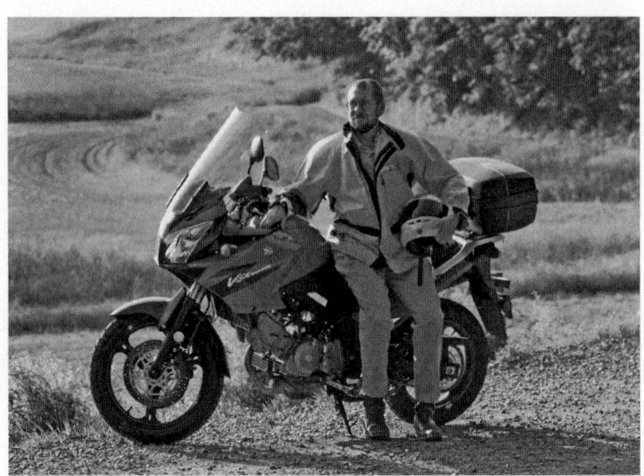

Ralph E. Hanson is professor and chair in the communication department at the University of Nebraska at Kearney, where he teaches courses in writing, blogging, reporting, and mass communication. Previously, he was on the faculty at West Virginia University and Northern Arizona University. He has been teaching introduction to mass communication for more than a decade, and he has worked extensively on developing online courses and degree programs. Hanson has a bachelor's degree in journalism and anthropology from Iowa State University, a master's degree in journalism from Iowa State, and a doctorate in sociology from Arizona State University. When Ralph is not out on his motorcycle, he is blogging on mass communication issues at http://ralphehanson.com. He Twitters as ©ralphehanson.

chapter 1

Living in a Media World

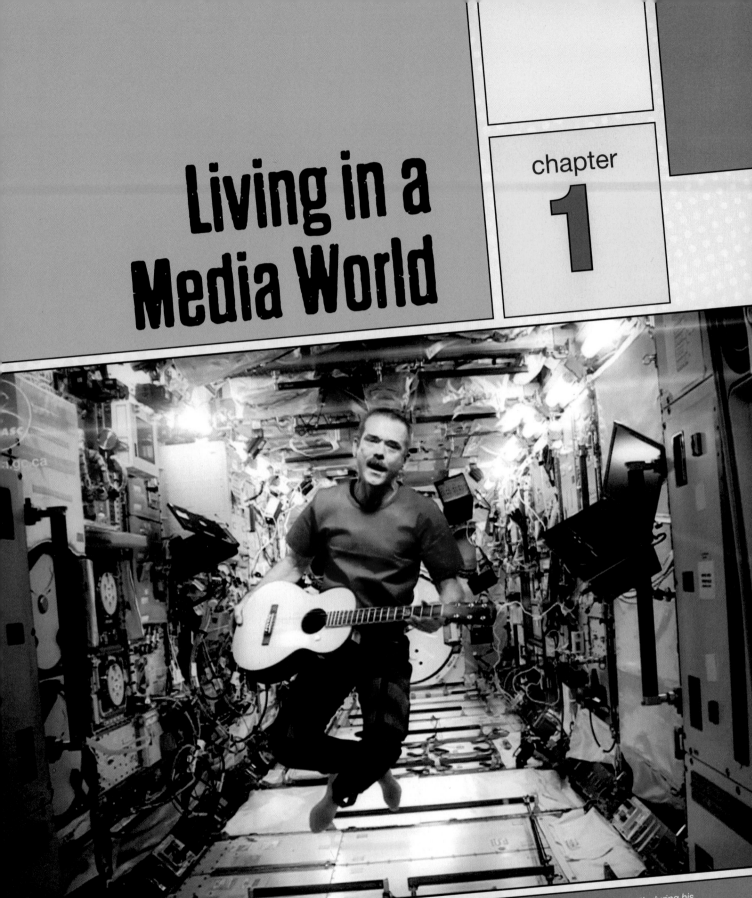

Canadian astronaut Chris Hadfield helped bring space science down to earth during his time on the International Space Station with his extensive social media presence. His most famous was a music video he recorded of David Bowie's 1969 hit "Space Oddity."

EPA/NASA/Landov

If you were asked to name an astronaut, chances are your first choice would be Neil Armstrong, the first man on the moon. Or you might go with Sally Ride, the first American woman in space. But you are not likely to come up with anyone who has flown since the early 1980s.

The only recent space traveler you might mention is retired Canadian astronaut Chris Hadfield, who showed the world what a magical place space could be and what a beautiful place Earth is spread out below his home in the International Space Station (ISS). During his five-month stay at the ISS in 2013, he demonstrated how social media can be used to bypass the traditional Big Media and communicate directly with millions of people across the globe.[1]

Even before going up to the ISS, he had an active presence on Twitter and YouTube, but following his tweets and videos from a low Earth orbit, he became a social media superstar with close to one million followers on Twitter.

While Hadfield did a great job of building a name for himself through social media during his time in space, that wasn't his real goal. Instead, he was trying to draw a whole new generation of young people into being interested in space exploration. So along with his space demonstration videos, he shared images of Earth, life in space, and the ISS itself.

Not long after he arrived at the ISS, Hadfield got started creating short videos about life in space that the Canadian Space Agency posted to YouTube. These showed Hadfield demonstrating how to use a treadmill, wash his hands, or even give a haircut. Toward the end of his stay at the ISS, Hadfield had approximately 681,000 followers on Twitter and more than 1.2 million followers across all of his social media accounts. Using the Internet from the International Space Station can be a bit of a challenge as the astronauts' connection speed is similar to what terrestrials had using dial-up Internet in the 1990s.[2]

But the thing that would really make Hadfield a global celebrity was when his son Evan convinced him to record the first music video in space—a somewhat edited cover of David Bowie's 1968 hit "Space Oddity." This video brought him to the forefront of popular culture, with nearly 21 million views as of March 2014. Hadfield does his own signing and guitar playing in the video, which was produced by Evan. This wasn't Hadfield's first foray into music, having previously recorded an Earth/space video with the Canadian band Barenaked Ladies, and while on Earth he has played with an all-astronaut rock band. Evan slightly rewrote the lyrics to include references to the space station and the Soyuz

LEARNING OBJECTIVES

After studying this chapter, you will be able to:

1 Identify the four levels of communication.

2 Explain the difference between mass communication and mass media.

3 Define three contemporary models of mass communication.

4 Explain the historical evolution of the media world.

5 Define what media literacy is.

6 Describe the "Seven Secrets" about the mass media.

Video 1.1: Watch some of Commander Hadfield's social media videos.

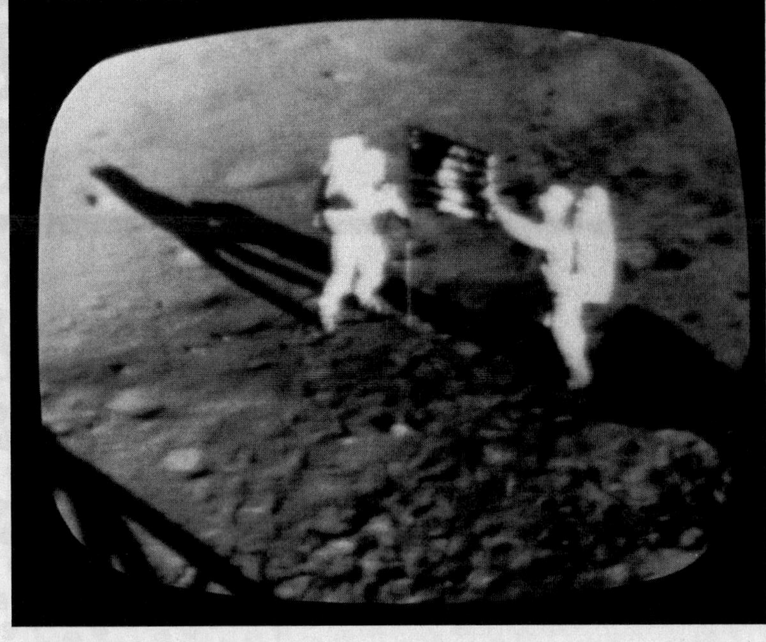

CBS Photo Archive/Getty Images

During the moon landing era of space exploration, all public communication by astronauts like Neil Armstrong and Buzz Aldrin was carefully controlled by NASA. Now, astronauts like International Space Station Commander Chris Hadfield can talk directly to the world through social media.

space capsule that would take Hadfield home, and he also gave the song a happy ending. (The astronaut dies in Bowie's version of the song.)

The evening before Hadfield was scheduled to return to Earth, the video was posted to YouTube. Hadfield himself had to do relatively little for the project. He had shot some video, recorded his vocal track, and strummed his guitar. So before he went to sleep on his last night in space, he logged onto YouTube. "I was shocked," Hadfield writes. "There had already been close to a million hits."[3] The next day after landing on Earth, he learned that it had reached more than 7 million views.

Hadfield's success with videos and other social media was not entirely self-made. His son Evan, whose specialty is social media marketing, helped his

Timeline

1800

1812 War of 1812 breaks out.

1835 Alexis de Tocqueville publishes *Democracy in America*.

1859 Charles Darwin publishes *On the Origin of Species*.

1861 U.S. Civil War begins.

1869 Transcontinental railroad is completed.

1879 Thomas Edison invents electric light bulb.

1898 Spanish-American War breaks out.

1900

1903 Orville and Wilbur Wright fly first airplane.

1905 Albert Einstein proposes his theory of relativity.

1910

1912 *Titanic* sinks.

1914 World War I begins.

1918 Worldwide influenza epidemic strikes.

1920

1920 Nineteenth Amendment passes, giving U.S. women the right to vote.

1929 U.S. stock market crashes, leading to the Great Depression.

1930

1933 Adolf Hitler is elected chancellor of Germany.

1939 World War II breaks out in Europe.

1940

1941 United States enters World War II.

1945 United States drops two atomic bombs on Japan.

1947 Pakistan and India gain independence from Britain.

1949 Communists establish People's Republic of China.

Pre-1800s Word of mouth and letters are the only means of transmitting messages.

1450s The first practical printing press is developed; printed material can be mass-produced.

1814 Steam-powered printing presses speed production of books and newspapers.

1844 Samuel Morse develops the telegraph; signals can be sent at a distance.

1887–1888 Emile Berliner develops the gramophone, which plays music on mass-produced discs.

1890s Nickelodeon movie theaters become popular.

1910 Thomas Edison (right) demonstrates first talking motion picture.

AP Photo

1939 Regularly scheduled television broadcasts begin in New York City.

AP Photo

father lose his "robotic" style of Twitter writing and cross-promoted his recordings, videos, and photos using a range of social media tools.

> **"I was shocked. There had already been close to a million hits."**
>
> —Chris Hadfield

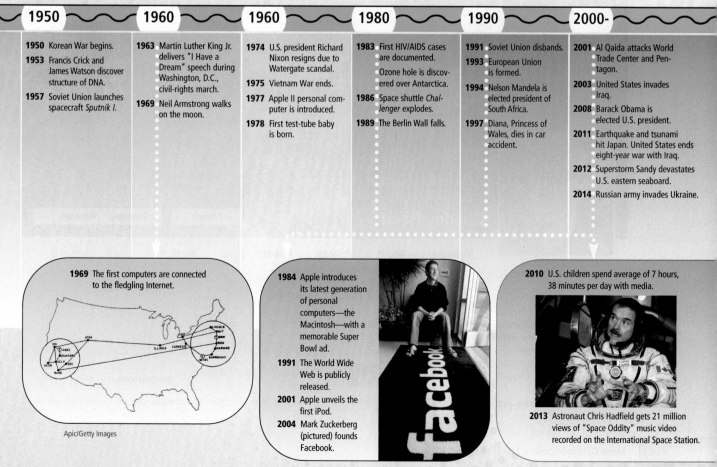

People your author's age are children of the space age. To us, the moon landing was a highlight of our childhood, not history. But now Commander Hadfield is bringing the space program to life for a new generation using interactive media that was barely in its infancy in 1969. For my generation, it was the heroic Neil Armstrong on television and the large-format photos from *Life* magazine announcing his historic first step on the surface of a globe that wasn't Earth. For my children, it's short messages, photos, and videos downloaded to a mobile phone or tablet from a permanent habit in space.

The story of how Chris Hadfield shared the wonder of space with people around the globe tells us much about what living in a media world is like. We have a lot of new social media channels that operate outside the rules of conventional journalism, and yet our so-called Big Media continue to dominate large segments of the business. We can get news as it happens from almost anywhere in the world if we only realize that it's available, and the distinctions between media audience members and media content creators are rapidly vanishing. ■

1950

- **1950** Korean War begins.
- **1953** Francis Crick and James Watson discover structure of DNA.
- **1957** Soviet Union launches spacecraft *Sputnik I*.

1960

- **1963** Martin Luther King Jr. delivers "I Have a Dream" speech during Washington, D.C., civil-rights march.
- **1969** Neil Armstrong walks on the moon.

1960

- **1974** U.S. president Richard Nixon resigns due to Watergate scandal.
- **1975** Vietnam War ends.
- **1977** Apple II personal computer is introduced.
- **1978** First test-tube baby is born.

1980

- **1983** First HIV/AIDS cases are documented.
- Ozone hole is discovered over Antarctica.
- **1986** Space shuttle *Challenger* explodes.
- **1989** The Berlin Wall falls.

1990

- **1991** Soviet Union disbands.
- **1993** European Union is formed.
- **1994** Nelson Mandela is elected president of South Africa.
- **1997** Diana, Princess of Wales, dies in car accident.

2000-

- **2001** Al Qaida attacks World Trade Center and Pentagon.
- **2003** United States invades Iraq.
- **2008** Barack Obama is elected U.S. president.
- **2011** Earthquake and tsunami hit Japan. United States ends eight-year war with Iraq.
- **2012** Superstorm Sandy devastates U.S. eastern seaboard.
- **2014** Russian army invades Ukraine.

1969 The first computers are connected to the fledgling Internet.

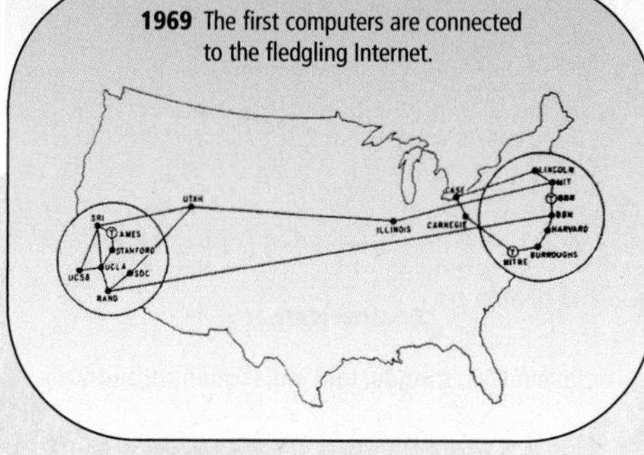

Apic/Getty Images

1984 Apple introduces its latest generation of personal computers—the Macintosh—with a memorable Super Bowl ad.

1991 The World Wide Web is publicly released.

2001 Apple unveils the first iPod.

2004 Mark Zuckerberg (pictured) founds Facebook.

Paul Sakuma/AP Photo

2010 U.S. children spend average of 7 hours, 38 minutes per day with media.

2013 Astronaut Chris Hadfield gets 21 million views of "Space Oddity" music video recorded on the International Space Station.

Alexander Nemenov/AFP/Getty Images

Levels of Communication

As the flow of social media from Chris Hadfield on the International Space Station shows, we no longer rely just on conventional media to engage in the various levels of communication. During the Apollo era, astronauts spoke with the public through carefully controlled television, newspaper, and radio events; and while these big media are still significant, they are increasingly being supplemented by channels that allow people to engage directly with these otherworldly newsmakers.

A 2010 graduate of the University of Nebraska at Omaha, Charley Reed is now the university's media relations coordinator. As such, he communicates a lot, and that communication is often flowing through social media like Facebook, Twitter, WordPress, and Tumblr. He uses these outlets to stay in touch with friends and colleagues, keep up on the news, teach his media class, and engage in personal journal writing. "A regular day for me essentially begins and ends with some sort of social media," Charley says.

> One of the first things I do when I get to work in the morning is check Facebook and Twitter to see what people are talking about. Knowing the day's trends helps me know how to pitch stories to Omaha's media outlets since many of them need help localizing national stories. I am definitely more of a Facebook user, though, since it's the closest to having a conversation. Twitter I check to see if anything new is happening that might pertain to the university because, anymore, news breaks on Twitter rather than in the paper or during the nightly news. I also use blogging sites like WordPress for the class I teach. That is where all of our class assignments are posted and where students go to find out any updates that might pertain to class. Tumblr is another site I use for personal writing that I want to share with others outside of work.[4]

When Charley is on social media, he's engaging in almost every possible level of communication, but before we try to analyze the levels of communication Charley is using, we need to define what communication is. Media scholar George Gerbner provides a simple definition: **Communication** is "social interaction through messages."[5] More plainly put, communication is how we interact with our entire world, whether through spoken words, written words, gestures, music, paintings, photographs, or dance. The important point is that communication is a *process*, not a static thing. Communication is an interaction that allows individuals, groups, and institutions to share ideas.

Media scholar and theorist Denis McQuail suggests that the various levels of communication can be viewed as a

---

communication: How we socially interact at a number of levels through messages.

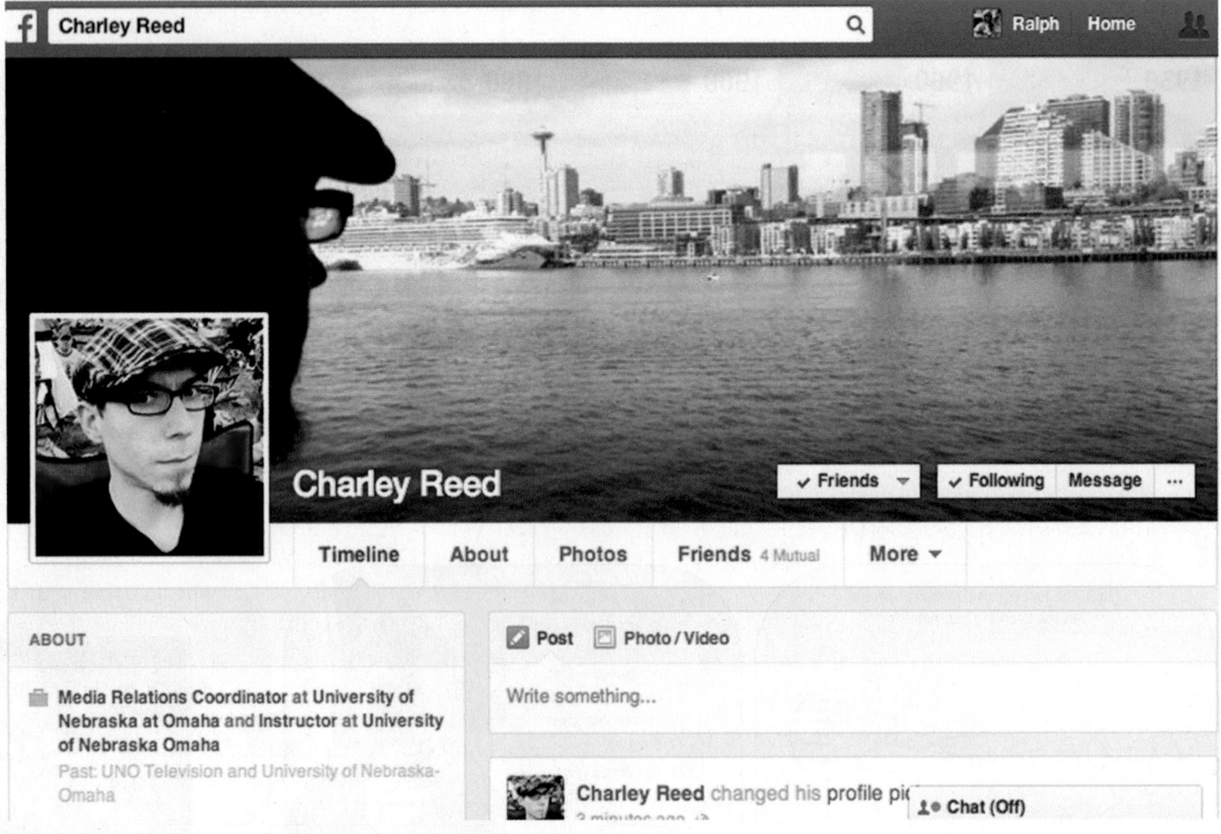

Courtesy of Charley Reed.

University media relations coordinator Charley Reed handles his own communication with his classmates, friends, and colleagues through his Facebook page.

pyramid with a large base of intrapersonal communication where everyone is sending messages, building up to a peak of mass communication at which a relatively small number of organizations or individuals are transmitting messages (see Figure 1.1).[6]

Figure 1.1 Levels of Communication

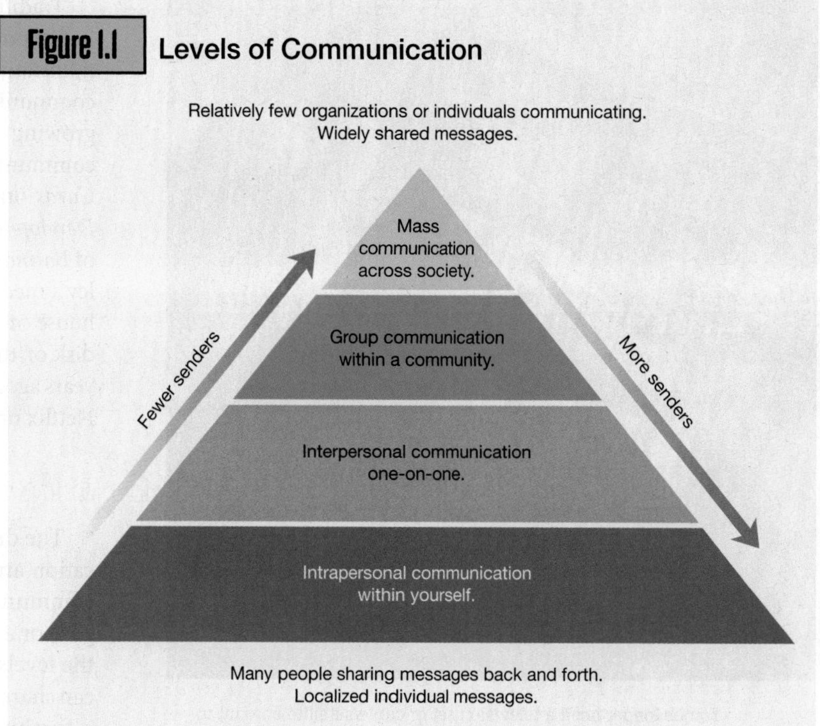

Source: Denis McQuail, *McQuail's Mass Communication Theory,* 6th ed. (London: SAGE Publications, 2010), 18. Reproduced by permission of Sage Publications. Copyright © Denis McQuail, 2005.

Intrapersonal Communication

Communication at its most basic level is **intrapersonal communication**, which is really communication within the self. This is how we think and how we assign meaning to all the messages and events that surround our lives. It ranges from the simple act of smiling in response to the smell of a favorite food coming from the kitchen to the complex reaction to an unexpected proposal of marriage. Feedback, or the response from the receiver of the message, is constant because we are always reflecting on what we have done and how we will react. Intrapersonal communication is the most prevalent form of communication and is, therefore, at the base of the pyramid. When Charley debates with himself as to whether something he is posting on Facebook reflects positively on the university, he's engaging in intrapersonal communication.

Interpersonal Communication

The next level on the pyramid is **interpersonal communication**, or one-on-one communication: "The intentional or accidental transmission of information through verbal or nonverbal message systems to another human being."[7] Interpersonal communication can be a conversation with a friend or a hug that tells your mother you love her. Like communication with the self, interpersonal communication is continual when others are around because we constantly send out messages, even if those messages consist of nothing more than body language indicating that we want to be left alone.

Interpersonal communication provides many opportunities for feedback. Your friend nods, raises an eyebrow, touches you on the arm, or simply answers your question. Not all interpersonal communication is done face-to-face, however. A telephone conversation, an SMS text message, an e-mail, or even a greeting card can be interpersonal communication, though at a somewhat greater emotional distance than in a face-to-face conversation. When Charley sends a personal message over Facebook, sends an e-mail to an editor about a possible story, or talks to his roommate over breakfast, he's engaging in interpersonal communication.

Questioning the Media

How many different ways have you engaged in interpersonal communication today? What techniques have you or your friends used to get messages (both verbal and nonverbal) across to each other? Do you prefer one technique over others? If so, why?

Group Communication

Group communication is near the top of the pyramid and has reached a level of unequal communication in which one person is communicating with an audience of two or more people. Group communication often has a leader and is more public than interpersonal communication. In a small group—for example, a family at the dinner table or a coach with a basketball team—each individual has an opportunity to respond to the leader and is likely to do so. In a large group—such as a 350-student lecture section of a university class—each individual still has an opportunity to respond but is unlikely to do so. Other situations test the boundaries of group communication, such as a Paul McCartney concert at a baseball stadium. With the amplifiers and multiple video screens, there is a high level of communication technology but limited possibilities for audience members to provide direct feedback to the performers. However, there is still interaction between Sir Paul and the audience.

---

intrapersonal communication: Communication you have with yourself. How you assign meaning to the world around you.

interpersonal communication: Communication, either intentional or accidental, between two people. It can be verbal or nonverbal.

group communication: Communication in which one person is communicating with an audience of two or more people. The roles of communicator and audience can be changing constantly.

Toronto Star via Getty Images

You no longer need a television set or cable/satellite account to watch video programming. Many people are turning to online streaming services like Netflix that they can view on their phone, tablet, or computer, as well as on a television set.

Charley engages in group communication when he participates in a class discussion, cheers at a hockey game, or leaves a status update on his Facebook page. For example, he once left an enthusiastic status update about the band Mastodon. His parents saw the update and bought him tickets to an upcoming Mastodon concert for his birthday.[8]

Mass Communication

Mass communication is the pinnacle of the communication pyramid; it is a society-wide communication process in which an individual or institution uses technology to send messages to a large, mixed audience, most of whose members are not known to the sender. Nationally broadcast speeches by politicians, stories about crime in the newspapers, and popular new novels are all forms of mass communication. These communications are fundamentally different from the forms described previously because the sender is separated in space, and possibly in time, from the receiver. Also, the audience is not really known to the communicator. When a communicator appears on television or writes an article for a newspaper, he or she doesn't know who will be listening or reading. What is more, the audience consists of many types of people. It might contain a young man in prison, an old woman in a nursing home, a child eating Cheerios for breakfast, or Charley as he's getting ready to go to the office. The message is communicated to all these people and to thousands or millions of others.[9]

Video 1.2: See footage from Paul McCartney's 2009 baseball stadium tour as well as the Beatles' 1965 tour.

Traditionally, mass communication has allowed only limited opportunities for feedback because the channels of communication are largely one way, but with the rise of interactive communication networks, the opportunities for feedback are growing rapidly. Charley consumes a wide range of mass communication during his day, including watching *House of Cards* on Netflix, watching the television series *Arrested Development* through Hulu, or reading DC Comics' reboot of *Batman*. You'll notice there's no traditional TV in Charley's media diet. Unless he's watching hockey at a friend's house or at a sports bar, all of his video comes to him via a disk or the Internet. "I got rid of cable and television four years ago," Charley says. "Anything I watch, I watch through Netflix or Hulu, on Amazon Prime, or on Blu-ray."[10]

A Mix of Levels

The distinctions among the various levels of communication are useful, but don't assume that every instance of communication can automatically be placed in one category or another. In reality, there are frequent crossovers in the levels of communication. Consider the Internet. You can share information with a friend via Snapchat. Through a Tumblr blog you can share your favorite images and videos. With a listserv, an employer can communicate with employees throughout the world. And through Web sites and podcasts, messages can go out to the entire world. The same is true of a newspaper, in which a classified ad can carry a proposal of marriage, a notice of a group meeting, or a political manifesto. When Charley goes out to dinner with friends, they cheer when the Stanley Cup hockey game being shown on the television gets exciting and talk about the game with each other, thus engaging in mass and group communication at the same time.

The purpose of this book is to help you better understand mass communication and the mass media. In the fifteen chapters of this book, we look at a variety of topics:

- The institutions that make up the media and how they function in and affect our society
- Who owns and controls the media business
- The media themselves, including books, magazines, newspapers, radio, recorded music, movies, television, and the Internet
- The industries that support the media, including advertising and public relations
- The laws and ethics that regulate and control the media
- The roles the media play in countries and cultures around the world

By the time you are finished, you will better understand what the media are, why they function as they do, and what roles they play in your life.

mass communication: When an individual or institution uses technology to send a message to a large, mixed audience, most of whose members are not known to the sender.

Elements of Mass Communication

Although people often use the terms *mass communication* and *mass media* interchangeably, they are significantly different concepts. Mass communication is a process, whereas the **mass media** are simply the technological tools used to transmit the messages of mass communication.[11] Earlier in this chapter we defined *mass communication* as a society-wide communication process in which an individual or institution uses technology to send messages to a large mixed audience, most of whose members are not known to the sender. Let's now take a closer look at all the players in the mass communication process and at several models that describe how these elements interact with each other.

The Players in the Mass Communication Process

There is an old way of describing mass communication known as the **Sender Message Channel Receiver (SMCR) or transmission model**. This transmission model does not do justice to the complexity of the mass communication process because it tends to portray mass communication as a largely one-directional flow of messages from the sender to the receiver, rather than as a complex interaction where senders and receivers are constantly changing places. But the model is still useful in helping to identify all the players we will be working with throughout this text.

The Sender. When critics talk about "the media" as a potent force, they are often talking about the ability of a few large corporations to control the messages that go out through the various channels of mass communication. These corporations, which are discussed in depth in Chapter 3, are the major senders in the mass communication process. They are the large, bureaucratic organizations that produce the complex messages we receive through the mass media, and they employ large numbers of people. If you look at the credits of a major movie, you'll see hundreds, if not thousands, of names listed. Even a relatively straightforward medium such as a newspaper requires a substantial staff of writers, editors, graphic artists, photographers, computer specialists, printers, truck drivers, delivery people, janitors, librarians, circulation clerks, accountants, advertising salespeople, business managers, and a publisher.

As you may have already figured out, there are many other senders besides the major corporations. For example, although the majority of the most frequently visited Web sites are produced by large media organizations, the Internet has given rise to smaller, more intimate media without the accompanying structure and staff. For example, *Six Until Me*, one of the leading blogs for persons with diabetes, is operated by patient and diabetes advocate Kerri Morrone Sparling, assisted by one other person. *Six Until Me* started back in 2005 with a total of two readers: Kerri's mother and her then-boyfriend. By 2011, her blog was reaching more than 90,000 visitors a month.[12] You may have acted as a "sender," too, just as Charley does when he writes an occasional guest post to your textbook author's blog.

Mass communication has generally been thought of as one-on-many communication, with few senders and many receivers, in contrast to interpersonal communication, which involves roughly equal numbers of senders and receivers. Sociologist C. Wright Mills wrote that the real power of the mass media is that they can control what topics are being covered and how much attention they receive. The most significant change brought about by the media in the United States, he said, was that public communication became a matter of sending information to a large number of receivers rather than a dialogue between roughly equal numbers of senders and receivers.[13]

The balance of power between senders and receivers in the mass media has started to change in recent years, however, with the rise of bloggers as a force in the news business. **Bloggers** are people who post their thoughts on a regularly updated Web site. We got a big reminder of the importance of blogs on Thursday, June 28, 2012, when the U.S. Supreme Court ruled that the Affordable Care Act, otherwise known as Obamacare, was constitutional. Everyone in the news media knew that this story would be breaking at 10 a.m. on Thursday, June 28. The decision coming down was definitely not a surprise.

And yet . . .

Both CNN and Fox News initially got the story wrong. In their effort to be the first to break the story, both cable news networks initially reported that the court had overturned the individual mandate requirement that everyone purchase health insurance or pay a fine/tax because the court rejected the argument that this was justified by the commerce clause of the Constitution—except that Chief Justice John Roberts's opinion went on to say that the mandate could be justified under Congress's authority to levy taxes. And so . . . two of our biggest sources of breaking news got the story flat-out wrong. Meanwhile, a little blog that typically draws a few thousand readers a day, SCOTUSblog, was the authoritative news site that everyone turned to for immediate and accurate news about the decision. And on a day that several bigger Web sites had trouble staying online because of heavy

---

mass media: The technological tools, or channels, used to transmit the messages of mass communication.

Sender Message Channel Receiver (SMCR) or transmission model: A dated model that is still useful in identifying the players in the mass communication process.

bloggers: People who post their thoughts, typically with the most recent posts at the top of the page, on a regularly updated Web site.

Web 1.1: Read why Kerri Sparling calls her blog *Six Until Me*.

Alex Wong/Getty Images

When news of the U.S. Supreme Court's decision on the constitutionality of the Affordable Health Act broke on June 28, 2012, competing cable news channels CNN and Fox News both got the story wrong. News consumers had to turn to the online SCOTUSblog to get an accurate report.

demand, SCOTUSblog had server capacity to spare despite drawing hundreds of times more traffic than normal.[14]

The Message. The **message** is the content being transmitted by the sender and reacted to by the receiver. Before a message can be transmitted, it must be encoded. **Encoding** requires at least two steps. First, the sender's ideas must be turned into a message: A script for a broadcast is drafted, a graphic is created, or a newspaper story is written. Then the message must be prepared for transmission: The script is taped and sent out over the air, the graphic is placed on a Web page, or the newspaper is printed.

Mass communication messages are transmitted rapidly to the receivers. Audience members can receive the message simultaneously, as they would in the case of a radio broadcast; at similar though not identical times, as in the case of a newspaper or magazine; or occasionally over an extended period, as in the case of a CD, movie, or video. In addition to being transmitted rapidly, mass communication messages are available to a wide audience. Mass communication messages also tend to be transient—here today and gone tomorrow. The newspapers and magazines are recycled, a new movie replaces the old at the theater, or a broadcast ends and a new one airs the next day. Even though the message can be stored in the form of a computer file or videotape, it is generally replaced when something new comes along. The receiver's attention fades even if the physical item remains.

Production of mass communication messages is generally expensive. The average cost of producing a studio movie in 2007 was $70.8 million, and advertising it added $25.7 million, according to figures from the Motion Picture Association of America.[15] Thirty seconds of commercial time during the 2012 Super Bowl cost as much as $3.5 million. (That's $116,000 per *second!*)[16] Sponsors for the Brazilian broadcasts of the 2014 World Cup soccer tournament paid $75 million each to get their message out on Brazil's *Rede Globo*. That's roughly the same as 20 thirty-second Super Bowl spots.[17] But, again, if people do not seek to make money with their messages, they can reach a large audience through the Internet at a relatively low cost.

What do all these messages mean? According to media scholar James Potter, the meaning of messages depends on who is receiving them and what kinds of media literacy skills the receivers can use to decode them. Potter writes that people with low levels of media literacy will look at the surface meanings in media content, whereas those with higher levels of media literacy can interpret messages from a wide range of perspectives with many choices of meanings.[18] For example, Jon Krakauer's book about the disaster that befell a group of Mount Everest climbers in 1996, *Into Thin Air*, can be read as a simple adventure story, an allegory of the battle between man and nature, or a study on obsession. (See box "Media Transformations: When Media Connect Us to the Most Remote Places on Earth.") Which of these interpretations is correct? Although *Into Thin Air* is most emphatically an adventure story, it also tells of Krakauer's struggle with the mountain and the weather, and it discusses why people are drawn to dangerous activities such as mountain climbing.

The Channel. The **channel** is the medium used to transmit the message. Recall that a mass medium is a technological tool. Think about a newspaper. It consists of black and colored ink printed on relatively low-quality paper. It

Web 1.2: Read how SCOTUSblog scooped both CNN and Fox News on coverage of the Obamacare Supreme Court decision.

Web 1.3: Get the latest on Super Bowl advertising and coverage.

message: The content being transmitted by the sender to the receiver.

encoding: The process of turning the sender's ideas into a message and preparing the message for transmission.

channel: The medium used to transmit the encoded message.

is portable, readily available, and cheap. An article can be clipped from the paper and placed in a pocket. A newspaper also provides local and regional news in greater depth than is possible with almost any other medium.[19]

Mehmet Kaman/Anadolu Agency/Getty Images

German soccer fans joined the world-wide television audience for the 2014 World Cup played in Brazil. The telecasts delivered huge audiences for the tournament's advertisers.

Print media include books, magazines, newspapers, billboards, and posters. Audiovisual media include radio, sound recordings, broadcast television, cable and satellite television, and video recordings. Interactive media include the Web, social media, mobile media, and video games.

What about mobile phones, faxes, letters, and e-mail? Do they fit in as channels of mass communication? Although e-mail is not generally considered to be a mass medium, an unsolicited commercial e-mail, known as *spam,* could satisfy at least part of the definition of mass communication, since spam is distributed widely to a large, mixed, and anonymous audience. News reports and sports scores arriving via SMS text messages on the small screen on a mobile phone would also seem to qualify. But our phone calls and e-mails from friends are generally considered to be interpersonal communications unless we post them to a blog or social media site for everyone to see.

The nature of the channel used to transmit a message can change the meaning of the message. Take, for example, the daily news. On the radio, the news is something happening in the background; read in a newspaper, news is something that demands your undivided attention. But can you call information news when it is presented by comedian Jon Stewart on *The Daily Show*? A dramatic speech given by a great orator on television will likely be much more influential than a transcript of the speech that's published on the Internet the next day.

The Receiver. The **receiver** is the audience for the mass communication message—that is, the people who are receiving and decoding the message. **Decoding** is the process of translating a signal from a mass medium into a form that the receiver can understand. The term *mass* can have at least two meanings when referring to audiences. In one sense, the term refers to the mix of ordinary people who receive the message—"the masses." In the second sense, the term refers to the size of the audience. The concept of mass, or popular, taste is an old one, but the concept of a massive, or large, audience developed in the twentieth century. The mass audiences reading major newspapers, listening to the radio, watching network television, or going to the movies are much larger than the crowds of people that gather for events such as political rallies or rock concerts. They form a **heterogeneous audience**—an audience made up of a mix of people who differ in age, sex, income, education, ethnicity, race, religion, and other characteristics. As with size, heterogeneity is a matter of degree. A small-town radio station is likely to reach an audience whose members are more similar than those listening to a station in a major urban area.

Receivers don't always get a clear message from the sender, however. Several types of **noise** can interfere with the delivery of the message. There is semantic noise, when the receiver does not understand the meaning of the message, such as when you can't understand the lyrics on a Latin music channel because you don't speak Spanish; mechanical noise when the channel has trouble transmitting the message, such as when a thunderstorm produces too much static for you to hear the score of a baseball game being broadcast on an AM radio station; and environmental noise, which occurs when the action and sounds surrounding the receiver interfere with the reception

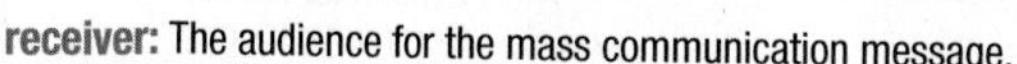

receiver: The audience for the mass communication message.

decoding: The process of translating a signal from a mass medium into a form that the receiver can understand and then interpreting the meaning of the message itself.

heterogeneous audience: An audience made up of a mix of people who differ in age, sex, income, education, ethnicity, race, religion, and other characteristics.

noise: Interference with the transmission of a message. This can take the form of semantic, mechanical, or environmental noise.

Video 1.3: Experience the difference between watching and reading two speeches.

MEDIA TRANSFORMATIONS

When Media Connect Us to the Most Remote Places on Earth

Jon Krakauer was out of his tent and on his way to the top of Mount Everest several hours before dawn on Friday, May 10, 1996. The journalist was just one of dozens of climbers trying to reach the summit at 29,028 feet. Climbing Everest had been a lifelong dream for Krakauer, and an assignment for *Outside* magazine had made it possible.

Krakauer reached the summit at 1:12 p.m., and after a brief stay at the top, he started on the long way back down. During his descent, a surprise snowstorm rolled in. At 6:45 p.m., just as it was getting dark, Krakauer stumbled back into camp and collapsed in his tent. Others in his party weren't so fortunate. By the time the storm cleared, eight of the climbers on the world's tallest mountain were dead, including guides Rob Hall and Scott Fischer.

Despite Mount Everest's remote location on the border between Nepal and Tibet, the world watched the tragedy unfold through Web sites, newspapers, television, magazines, and eventually even a major motion picture. In May of each year, Everest Base Camp becomes media central as climbers attempt to reach the summit and journalists show up to cover them, in part because of the high degree of risk involved. During a typical year, six to ten people will die on the mountain.[20]

To complete his assignment of researching and writing a story about the commercialization of Mount Everest, Krakauer climbed the peak as a paying customer of Hall. Krakauer was not the only journalist on the mountain the day of the snowstorm. Climber Sandy Hill Pittman was sending daily dispatches to NBC's Web site via satellite phone and yak courier; reporter Jane Bromet of *Outside Online,* a Web magazine, was covering the climb from Everest Base Camp; a South African newspaper was sponsoring another expedition; and an IMAX film crew was shooting a documentary about climbing the peak. The IMAX team, led by filmmaker and professional climber David Breashears, produced the movie *Everest*, which became the most successful large-format IMAX film ever and one of the top films of 1997.

Krakauer says that because of the media coverage, thousands of people around

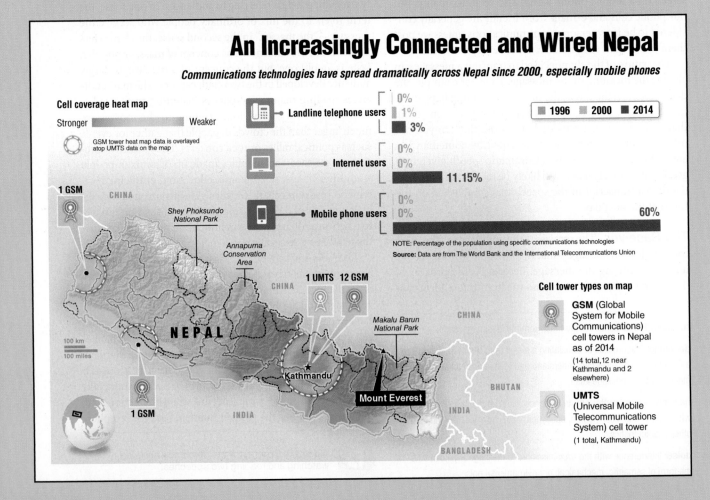

An Increasingly Connected and Wired Nepal

Communications technologies have spread dramatically across Nepal since 2000, especially mobile phones

	1996	2000	2014
Landline telephone users	0%	1%	3%
Internet users	0%	0%	11.15%
Mobile phone users	0%	0%	60%

NOTE: Percentage of the population using specific communications technologies

Source: Data are from The World Bank and the International Telecommunications Union

Cell coverage heat map
Stronger — Weaker
GSM tower heat map data is overlayed atop UMTS data on the map

1 GSM
CHINA
Shey Phoksundo National Park
Annapurna Conservation Area
CHINA
1 UMTS 12 GSM
CHINA
NEPAL
Makalu Barun National Park
100 km
100 miles
Kathmandu
Mount Everest
1 GSM
INDIA
BHUTAN
INDIA
BANGLADESH

Cell tower types on map

GSM (Global System for Mobile Communications) cell towers in Nepal as of 2014 (14 total, 12 near Kathmandu and 2 elsewhere)

UMTS (Universal Mobile Telecommunications System) cell tower (1 total, Kathmandu)

the world knew more about what was happening on the mountain than did the people who were climbing: "A teammate might call home on a satellite phone, for instance, and learn what the South Africans were doing at Camp Two from a spouse in New Zealand or Michigan who'd been surfing the World Wide Web."[21]

In the spring of 2014, an even worse disaster hit Everest, when a giant overhanging chunk of ice broke off and crashed down through a group of Nepalese workers climbing the Khumbu Icefall, killing 16 of them. Although there was a substantial media presence on Everest during the 1994 storm that Krakauer chronicled, climbers were even more connected to the outside world by the time of the 2014 disaster. From 2006 to 2009, famed Everest commercial guide Russell Brice had been featured in three seasons of a cable television series that documented attempts by his climbers to summit Everest. News from the 1996 disaster had to flow out via satellite phones. But by 2014, cell service, including 3G and 4G data service, was available from both base camp and the summit.[22] The Discovery Channel, which had aired Brice's Everest climbing series, had been planning to broadcast live Joby Ogwyn's attempt to summit Everest and then jump off the top of the mountain and fly down using a wing suit. But they canceled the show following the tragedy.[23] And as news of the 2014 disaster unfolded, legacy news channels such as the *Washington Post* were relying on bloggers such as climber Alan Arnette to relay the flood of news coming from the climbers, guides, and other bloggers at Everest.[24]

Media Transformations Questions

- **HOW** is a remote location like Everest changed when we have easy media access to it?
- **WHY** are people drawn to remote stories of adventure and danger from places like Everest that they are unlikely to ever visit?
- **HOW** has your life been changed by the fact that you have media around you constantly? Do you ever deliberately try to take time off from the media and communication technology?

Web 1.4: Read more on media access to Everest climbing and disasters.

of the message, such as when your roommate's loud stereo keeps you from concentrating on your introduction to mass communication textbook.

The receivers of a mass communication message have traditionally been seen as an **anonymous audience**. This means that the sender does not personally know all, or even most, of the people receiving the message. This doesn't mean that the audience consists of isolated people who have no connection to anyone else; audience members simply don't expect the sender to know who they are. But with the increasing number of channels available for audience members to send feedback to the senders—through the Web, social media, e-mail, faxes, text messages, and phone calls—audience members typically on the receiving end are becoming senders themselves and are becoming better and better known to the original senders. Sometimes, in the case of reality TV programs such as *The Voice*, audience members become active participants by voting on who should advance to the next level of the competition.

Contemporary Models of Mass Communication

Though the transmission model (SMCR) is useful for laying out the various elements of the mass communication process, it does not explain how mass communication works in our lives. It focuses primarily on the process of transmitting messages largely from the point

anonymous audience: An audience the sender does not personally know. These are not anonymous, isolated people who have no connection to anyone else; they simply are anonymous in their audience status.

Reuters/Jim Bourg

Members of the IMAX expedition filming the documentary *Everest* reach the summit after abandoning their first summit attempt in order to help rescue other climbers.

Table 1.1 Mass Communication Models

Models	Orientation of Sender	Orientation of Receiver
Transmission Model	Transfer of meaning	Cognitive processing
Ritual Model	Performance	Shared experience
Publicity Model	Competitive display	Attention-giving spectatorship
Reception Model	Preferential encoding	Differential decoding/ construction of meaning

Source: Denis McQuail, *McQuail's Mass Communication Theory,* 6th ed. (London: SAGE Publications, 2010). Reproduced by permission of SAGE Publications. Copyright © Denis McQuail, 2005.

of view of a sender trying to have an effect on the receiver. Media scholar Denis McQuail lays out three contemporary models that help us answer three different questions about the nature of mass communication[25] (see Table 1.1):

Ritual Model. Whereas the transmission model looks at how a message is sent, the ritual model puts audience members at the center of the equation. The **ritual model** looks at how and why audience members (receivers) consume media messages. This model suggests that we watch a program such as *The Voice* not so much to learn about aspiring singers or to receive advertising messages, but rather to interact in a shared ritual with family and friends. This ritual is then extended through television to other groups of people all across the United States. Media consumption thus goes beyond simply delivering messages and becomes a shared experience that brings us together as a people. For example, when news broke that Osama bin Laden had been killed on May 1, 2011, Twitter set what was then a record for sustained number of tweets being sent, with an average of 3,440 tweets per second between 10:45 p.m. and 12:30 a.m. Eastern Time. The tweeting peaked at 11 p.m. ET with 5,106 tweets per second. Audience members were obviously not just passively watching and reading the news; they were actively responding to it.[26]

Questioning the Media

Are you a media multitasker? Do you watch a single program from beginning to end, flip from channel to channel looking for something interesting, or watch two shows at once? Do you go online to chat about the show as you watch it? Could you even watch a single show from beginning to end without any other media? How does media multitasking enhance your experience?

Publicity Model. Sometimes media messages are not trying to convey specific information as much as they are trying to draw attention to a particular person, group, or concept. According to the **publicity model**, the mere fact that a topic is covered by the media can make the topic important, regardless of what is said about it. For example, when Janet Jackson displayed her breast for 9/16ths of a second during the 2004 Super Bowl, there were all sorts of charges that broadcast network CBS was lowering the moral standards of America's young people. The major effect of Jackson's stunt was that the Federal Communications Commission (FCC) adopted increasingly strict rules on broadcast decency. As a result, at least twenty ABC affiliates refused to air the World War II movie *Saving Private Ryan* the following November for fear that they would be fined for all the bad language contained in the movie. Concerns about changing television standards had existed for several years prior to Jackson flashing Super Bowl viewers, but the attention Jackson brought to the issue put broadcast decency in the limelight.[27]

Reception Model. The **reception model** moves us out of the realm of social science analysis and into the world of critical theory. Instead of looking at how messages affect audiences or are used by the senders or receivers, the reception model looks at how audience members derive and create meaning out of media content. Rather than seeing content as having an intended, fixed meaning, the reception model says that each receiver decodes the message based on his or her own unique experiences, feelings, and beliefs. You can take a single news story and show it to liberal and conservative observers, and both will claim that it is biased against their point of view. In fact, a 1982 study showed the more that journalists tried to present multiple sides of an issue, the more partisans on either side of the issue viewed the story as biased.[28]

Evolution of the Media World

Where did our media world come from? Is it just a product of the late twentieth century with its constant flow of

Web 1.5: Dealing with FCC decency rules in the years since Janet Jackson's wardrobe malfunction.

ritual model: A model of the mass communication process that treats media use as an interactive ritual engaged in by audience members. It looks at how and why audience members (receivers) consume media messages.

publicity model: A model of the mass communication process that looks at how media attention can make a person, concept, or thing become important, regardless of what is said about it.

reception model: A critical theory model of the mass communication process that looks at how audience members derive and create meaning out of media content as they decode the messages.

TEST YOUR MEDIA LITERACY

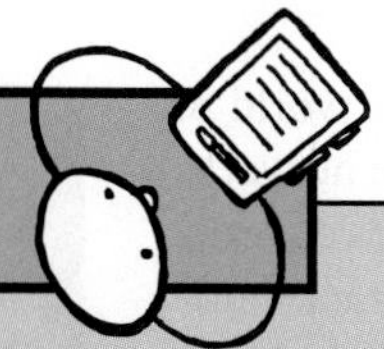

Can Television Take Anything Seriously?

In his book *Amusing Ourselves to Death,* media scholar Neil Postman argues that the primary effect of television is that it changes how people see the world; that is, with television, people start viewing everything as entertainment. Young people get their news in a comedy format, watching *The Daily Show* the same way they watch MTV. They learn about politics on the same channel that shows a professional football game.[1]

In an interview with Robert Nelson for the Civic Arts Review, Postman described the major point of *Amusing Ourselves to Death:*

> Television always recreates the world to some extent in its own image by selecting parts of that world and editing those parts. So a television news show is a kind of symbolic creation and construction made by news directors and camera crews. . . .
>
> Americans turn to television not only for their light entertainment but for their news, their weather, their politics, their religion, their history, all of which may be said to be their furious entertainment. What I'm talking about is television's preemption of our culture's most serious business. It is one thing to say that TV presents us with entertaining subject matter. It is quite another to say that on TV all subject matter is presented as entertaining and it is in that sense that TV can bring ruin to any intelligent understanding of public affairs. . . .
>
> And stranger still is the fact that commercials may appear anywhere in a news story, before, after, or in the middle, so that all events are rendered essentially trivial, that is to say, all events are treated as a source of public entertainment. How serious can an earthquake in Mexico be or a hijacking in Beirut, if it is shown to us prefaced by a happy United Airlines commercial and summarized by a Calvin Klein jeans commercial? Indeed, TV newscasters have added to our grammar a new part of speech altogether. What may be called the "now this" conjunction. "Now this" is a conjunction that does not connect two things but does the opposite. It disconnects. When newscasters say, "Now this," they mean to indicate that what you have just heard or seen has no relevance to what you are about to hear or see. There is no murder so brutal, no political blunder so costly, no bombing so devastating that it cannot be erased from our minds by a newscaster saying, "Now this." The newscaster means that you have thought long enough on the matter, let's say 45 seconds, that you must not be morbidly preoccupied with it, let us say for 90 seconds, and that you must now give your attention to a commercial. Such a situation in my view is not news. And in my opinion it accounts for the fact that Americans are among the most ill informed people in the Western world.[2]

WHO is the source?

Neil Postman (1931–2003), a prominent American educator, media theorist, and cultural critic, founded the media ecology program at New York University (NYU) and chaired the NYU Department of Culture and Communication. Postman wrote eighteen books and more than 200 magazine and newspaper articles for such periodicals as the *New York Times Magazine, Atlantic Monthly, Harper's,* and the *Washington Post.* He also edited the journal *ETC: A Review of General Semantics* and was on the editorial board of the *Nation.*

WHAT is he saying?

Postman argues that the primary effect of television is that it changes how people see the world; that is, with television, people start viewing everything as entertainment. In comparison, think about your own viewing habits. Do you watch the news the same way you watch MTV? Or learn about politics on the same channel that shows *Survivor*? Or see news about the war in Iraq, followed by a commercial for Domino's Pizza?

WHAT kind of evidence does the book provide?

What kind of data does Postman provide to support his arguments? What kind of evidence is needed to bolster these claims? Is there evidence that disputes his claims? How do you think Postman's background is likely to have shaped his view of television?

HOW do you or your classmates react to Postman's arguments?

What does the title *Amusing Ourselves to Death* mean to you? Do you feel that television trivializes important issues or makes them more palatable? Have you noticed similar effects in yourself as described by Postman? Do you notice differences in how news anchors make the transition from news to commercials and back again? Are the stories before and after the break any different from stories during the rest of the newscast?

DOES it all add up?

Do you believe that Postman's arguments are true today? In a study conducted in 2000, researchers found that 75 percent of television viewers under the age of thirty watched the news with the remote in their hands, ready to change channels if they got bored for a moment or two. Do you think that the data from this study support Postman's claims? Why or why not? Think back to when singer Michael Jackson died in 2009 and the cable news networks covered virtually nothing else for days on end. Do you think that Jackson's death was newsworthy enough to merit the coverage it received? Or were the cable news channels just trying to entertain their viewers?

---

[1]Neil Postman, *Amusing Ourselves to Death: Public Discourse in the Age of Show Business* (New York: Penguin Books, 1985).

[2]Robert Nelson, "Television and the Public Decline of Public Discourse," *Civic Arts Review,* vol. 3 (1990): 1. Excerpt used with permission.

Video 1.4: Neil Postman talks about his book *Amusing Ourselves to Death.*

print and electronic messages? Not really. The world of interconnected and overlapping communication networks that surrounds us has been evolving for hundreds of years. Before the advent of the mass media, people interacted primarily face-to-face. Most of the time, they interacted only with people like themselves and had little contact with the outside world. But people gradually created communication networks that used first interpersonal channels, then print media, electronic media, and, most recently, interactive media. This section examines how various communication networks have grown over the centuries to form the media world in which we now live.

Before Print: Pre–Mass Media Communication Networks

The first major communication network in the Western world predates the mass media and was developed by the Roman Catholic Church in the twelfth, thirteenth, and fourteenth centuries. During that period, messages flowed from the Vatican in Italy through the cardinals and bishops to priests in cathedrals and villages throughout Europe and finally to congregations through sermons from the pulpit.[29]

Print: Arrival of the Book

The first major expansion in communication beyond the Church was the development of the printing press—in particular, the invention of movable type in the 1450s—and the subsequent mass production of printed materials. Mass printing made it possible for major social changes, such as the Protestant Reformation, to spread from their country of origin to the rest of Europe and the world beyond.

©iStockphoto.com/nicoolay

Although the printing press allowed for the mass production of information, printing was still relatively slow, and publications remained fairly expensive. The addition of steam power to the printing press in 1814 dramatically increased the rate at which printed material could be reproduced.

Electronic Networks: Telegraph, Gramophone, Radio, Movies, and Television

The advent of electronic communication made the media world much more complex. This type of communication began in 1844 with the opening of the first telegraph line from Baltimore, Maryland, to Washington, D.C. In 1866, telegraph cables spanned the Atlantic Ocean, overcoming a seemingly insurmountable barrier that had long hindered transoceanic communication. Instead of sending a message on a two-week journey by boat across the ocean and waiting for a reply to come back the same way, two people on opposite sides of the ocean could carry on a dialogue via telegraph.

Everett Collection Historical/Alamy

By the 1880s, telegraph wires criss-crossed the New York City skyline, sending messages rapidly across the city, the country, and around the world.

In the 1880s, Emile Berliner invented the gramophone, or phonograph, which played mass-produced discs containing about three minutes of music. Just as printed books made possible the storage and spread of ideas, so the gramophone allowed musical performances to be captured and reproduced.

The invention of radio in the late nineteenth century freed electronic communication from the limits imposed on it by telegraph wires. Messages could come into the home at any time and at almost no cost to the receiver. All that was needed was a radio set to receive an endless variety of cultural content, news, and other programming.

Movies were first shown at nickelodeon theaters in the late 1890s and early 1900s and were produced by an entertainment industry that distributed films worldwide. Young couples on a date in London, Ohio, and London, England, could see the same movie, copy the same styles of dress,

Web 1.6: Read more on the first transatlantic telegraph cable.

and perhaps even practice the same kisses they saw in the movie. Due to radio and the movies, the media world became a shared entertainment culture produced for profit by major media corporations.

In 1939, patrons in New York's neighborhood taverns no longer had to settle for radio broadcasts of Yankees games being played at the Polo Grounds. Instead, a small black-and-white television set located on a pedestal behind the bar showed a faint, flickering image of the game. After a series of delays caused by World War II, television surpassed radio in popularity. It also became a lightning rod for controversy as people stayed home to watch whatever images it would deliver.

The Internet: Interactive Communication

After several decades of television, people had gotten used to the idea that news, information, and entertainment could be delivered almost magically into their homes, although they could do little to control the content of this medium other than change channels. Then a new medium emerged, one that made senders and receivers readily interchangeable. The Internet became a full-fledged mass communication network in the 1990s (though many people were unaware that the first nodes of this new medium were being linked together as far back as 1969). Rather than simply making it easier for individuals and organizations to send messages to a mass audience, the new computer networks were designed for two-way communication. Audience members were becoming message providers themselves.

The Internet's interactivity was the culmination of a trend toward giving audience members new control over their media. The growth of cable and satellite television, along with the videocassette recorder (VCR), had already given viewers more choices and more control, and the remote control allowed them to choose among dozens of channels without leaving their chairs.

The implications of interactivity are significant. Whereas the commercial media have come to be controlled by a smaller and smaller number of large corporations (see Chapter 3), an important channel of mass communication is open to ordinary people in ways that were never before possible. With a trivial investment in a computer and an Internet connection, individuals can grab the spotlight with news and entertainment on the World Wide Web.

Consider the example of artist Danielle Corsetto, creator of the popular Web comic *Girls With Slingshots.* Her comic started when she was in high school under the name *Hazelnuts,* but she took it online in October 2004 when fans of her sketches asked her when she was going to start publishing her comic. Corsetto explained to the *Frederick News-Post* that *Girls With Slingshots* (or GWS) is a slice-of-life comic that tells the story of "sour, grumpy girl" Hazel and her best friend, Jamie, a "bubbly girl who is very comfortable with herself."[30] One of the fascinating things about the comic is the level of diversity within its cast. There is Melody, who is deaf; Soo Lin, who is blind; Darren, who is gay; Erin, who is asexual; and McPedro, a cactus who talks when Hazel's been drinking. Anna Palindrome, writing for *Bitch Magazine* blog, says that her favorite thing about the comic is that it looks at disability from the point of view of a disabled person. "What I like about the jokes in this strip are that they are all over the place. Some are about how clueless people can be about blindness. Some are disability-related humour as told by people with disabilities."[31]

Corsetto explains, "It's more realistic and less stereotypical. All the characters have these unusual relations, both romantic and platonic . . . that are not what you would find in, say, a sitcom, but it's written like a sitcom. I'm kind of trying to normalize these things that are taboo."

Although the strip started out small, Corsetto's Web site now typically draws about 100,000 readers a day. And since 2007, she has made her living exclusively through drawing and writing comics. In addition to *Girls With Slingshots,* Corsetto works on a variety of side projects, including writing a graphic novel in the *Adventure Time* series. Given the subject matter, alcohol use, and language in *Girls With Slingshots,* Corsetto would not be able to publish her work in a legacy newspaper or magazine. Although the strip is distributed online, Corsetto makes her drawings using pen and ink on heavyweight paper, with the coloring being electronically added. She makes

Photo courtesy of The Frederick News-Post

Web cartoonist Danielle Corsetto works on her comic *Girls With Slingshots* in her studio in Shepherdstown, West Virginia. Although her comic is online, she still does her drawing by hand.

Image Source Plus/Alamy

One of the many reasons we go to the movies is to experience strong emotions such as fear, horror, surprise, or romance in a safe environment.

the majority of her income from advertising on her Web site, sales of self-published book collections of comics, and merchandise, such as a plush McPedro. She also gets income from her projects for legacy media, such as the *Adventure Time* book.[32]

Some critics would argue that the growth of cable television stations, Web sites, and magazines creates only an illusion of choice because a majority of the channels are still controlled by the same five or six companies.[33] Even so, it is a new media world, one in which audience members are choosing what media content they will consume and when they will consume it. It's a world that even media giants are being forced to adjust to.

Understanding the Media World

Most people have ambivalent feelings about their high levels of media use. The convenience of the mobile phone is offset by the fact that it makes a person available to others at all times. The wide selection of programming on cable television is wonderful, but the content on some of those channels can be disturbing. It is liberating to be connected to the entire industrialized world through the Internet, but the risk of invasion of privacy is troubling. This section discusses the concept of media literacy and examines some common misconceptions about the mass media. It also examines in detail "Seven Secrets" about mass media and mass communication that are at the center of this book's look at media literacy.

Questioning the Media

For as long as there have been media, there have been those who blame the media for society's ills. Others believe that critics are just trying to place the blame on a convenient target. How do you feel about this debate? Why?

Defining Media Literacy

The term **media literacy** refers to people's understanding of what the media are, how they operate, what messages they are delivering, what roles they play in society, and how audience members respond to media messages. Media scholar James Potter writes that people with high levels of media literacy have a great deal of control over the vision of the world they see through the media and can decide for themselves what the messages mean. In contrast, those with low levels of media literacy can develop exaggerated impressions of problems in society, even when those impressions conflict with their own experience. For example, media consumers who spend large amounts of time watching television often perceive society as far more dangerous and crime-ridden than it is because that's the image they see on television.[34] Potter says that too often consumers with low levels of media literacy assume that the media have large, obvious, and mostly negative effects on other people but little or no effect on themselves. Finally, those with low levels of media literacy tend to blame the media for complex social problems, such as teen pregnancy or school violence.

Potter has identified four basic dimensions of media literacy: cognitive, emotional, aesthetic, and moral.[35] Let's take a closer look at each of these dimensions.

The Cognitive Dimension. The cognitive dimension of media literacy deals with the ability to intellectually process information communicated by the media. This can involve interpreting the meaning of words on a printed page, appreciating the implications of ominous music in a movie, or understanding that a well-dressed character in a television show is wealthy. For example, the hardcover edition of Jon Krakauer's book *Into Thin Air* featured a series of ominous woodcuts at the beginning of each chapter. These illustrations may be viewed simply as decorations at the beginning of each chapter or interpreted as foreshadowing the suffering and peril to come.

The cognitive dimension also includes the skills necessary to access the media: using a computer, accessing high-definition programming on your new HDTV, or finding a book in the library. All of these are learned skills. We learn to read in school, learn the meaning of musical cues from movies we've seen, and learn how to navigate the Internet through repeated practice.

The Emotional Dimension. The emotional dimension of media literacy covers the feelings created by media

media literacy: Audience members' understanding of the media industry's operation, the messages delivered by the media, the roles media play in society, and how audience members respond to these media and their messages.

messages. Sometimes the emotions can be overwhelming; examples include the fear of a young child watching a scary movie or the joy of a parent watching a news story about a child in danger being rescued. People often spend time with songs, movies, books, and other media specifically to feel the emotions they generate.[36] *Titanic* became a box office champion in large part because of the young women who went to see the movie again and again to experience the emotional release it provided.[37] And it is unlikely that either the IMAX documentary *Everest* or Krakauer's *Into Thin Air* would have been such a commercial success were it not for the gut-wrenching emotions created by both the deaths and the dramatic rescues of the climbers on the mountain.

The Aesthetic Dimension. The aesthetic dimension of media literacy involves interpreting media content from an artistic or critical point of view. How well is the media artifact produced? What skills were used in producing it? How does it compare in quality to other, similar works? Understanding more than the surface dimensions of media content can require extensive learning. *Into Thin Air* was unquestionably a commercial success, and it was largely a critical success as well. But it was also controversial; several critics suggested that Krakauer had overdramatized the events that took place on Everest and unfairly portrayed one guide as a villain rather than a hero.[38] It is through such critical debate that alternative views and understandings of media content emerge.

The Moral Dimension. The moral dimension of media literacy consists of examining the values of the medium or the message. In a television situation comedy, for example, an underlying message might be that a quick wit is an important tool for dealing with problems or that a problem can be solved in a short time. In an action movie, the moral lessons may be that violence and authority are needed if one is to succeed and that the world is a mean and dangerous place. The moral message of most advertisements is that problems can be solved by purchasing something.[39] Among the many moral issues raised by *Into Thin Air* is the message that the presence of the media can change the nature of an event.

Seven Secrets About the Media "They" Don't Want You to Know

Media literacy is a tricky subject to talk about, because few people will admit that they really don't understand how the media operate and how messages, audiences, channels, and senders interact. After all, since we spend so much time with the media, we must know all about them, right? As an example, most students in an introduction to mass communication class will claim that the media and media messages tend to affect other people far more than they affect themselves. The question of media literacy can also become a political question, for which the answer depends on whether you are a liberal or a conservative, rich or poor, young or old. But the biggest problem in the public discussion of media literacy is that certain routine issues get discussed again and again, while many big questions are left unasked.

SEVEN SECRETS "They" Don't Want You to Know About the Media

- **SECRET 1** The media are essential components of our lives.
- **SECRET 2** There are no mainstream media (MSM).
- **SECRET 3** Everything from the margin moves to the center.
- **SECRET 4** Nothing's new: Everything that happened in the past will happen again.
- **SECRET 5** New media are always scary.
- **SECRET 6** Activism and analysis are not the same thing.
- **SECRET 7** There is no "they."

Consider some of the things we think we know about the media: "The news media are hopelessly liberal." "Watching too much television turns children into overweight zombies, or else it makes them violent. One or the other." "Reading too many fashion magazines makes young women anorexic." "The mainstream media cover up stories they don't want us to know about." "Our media are run by giant corporations that seek world domination." How do we know these things? Well, because people in the media tell us they are so! And they wouldn't say these things if they weren't true, would they?

But there are several things we don't hear about the media. Secret things. Perhaps it's because there is no one out there who can attract an audience by saying them. Or maybe it's because the ideas are complicated, and we don't like complexity from our media. Or maybe it's because "they" (whoever "they" may be) don't want us to know them.

So here are Seven Secrets about the media that "they" don't want you to know. These key issues of media literacy—which don't get the discussion they deserve—provide a foundation for the rest of the chapters in this book. (And just who are "they"? Wait for Secret Seven.)

SECRET 1 **The Media Are Essential Components of Our Lives.** Critics often talk about the effects the media have on us as though the media were something separate and distinct from our everyday lives. But conversations with my students have convinced me otherwise. Every semester I poll my students as to what media they have used so far that day, with the day starting at midnight. I run through the list: checking Twitter, Facebook, or Pinterest; listening to the radio; checking the weather on

Web 1.7: Read more on Web comics.

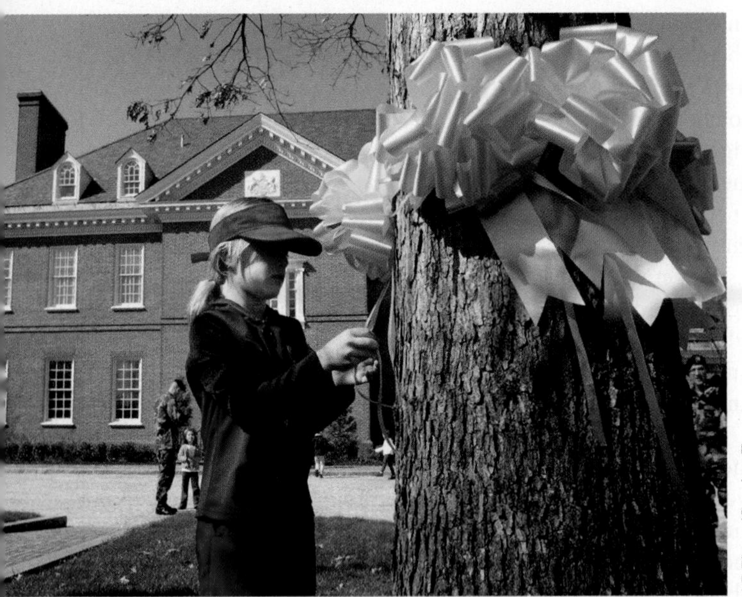

AP Photo/Carolyn Kaster

The meaning of yellow ribbons tied into a bow has transformed many times over the last several decades. Here nine-year-old Katie Lapp is tying ribbons on trees in front of the Pennsylvannia governor's mansion to show her support for America's troops serving overseas.

a mobile device; watching *The Colbert Report*; reading *Cosmopolitan*; reading a Nicholas Sparks novel; listening to an iPhone; and so forth. In fact, media use is likely to be the most universal experience my students will share. Surveys of my students find that more of my morning-class students have consumed media content than have eaten breakfast or showered since the day began at midnight. Are the media an important force in our lives? Absolutely! But the media are more than an outside influence on us. They are a part of our everyday lives.

Think about how we assign meanings to objects that otherwise would have no meaning at all. Take a simple yellow ribbon twisted in a stylized bow. You've seen thousands of these, and most likely you know exactly what they stand for—"Support Our Troops." But that hasn't always been the meaning of the symbol.

The yellow ribbon has a long history in American popular culture. It played a role in the rather rude World War II–era marching song "She Wore a Yellow Ribbon." The ribbon was a symbol of a young woman's love for a soldier "far, far away," and the lyrics mention that her father kept a shotgun handy to keep the soldier "far, far away." The yellow ribbon was also a symbol of love and faithfulness in the John Ford film *She Wore a Yellow Ribbon*. In the 1970s, the ribbon became a symbol of remembering the U.S. staff in the Iranian embassy that had been taken hostage. This meaning came from the song "Tie a Yellow Ribbon 'Round the Old Oak Tree," made popular by the group Tony Orlando and Dawn. The song tells about a prisoner coming home from jail hoping that his girlfriend will remember him. She can prove her love by displaying the yellow ribbon. The prisoner arrives home to find not one but 100 yellow ribbons tied to the tree. The display of yellow ribbons tied to trees became commonplace in newspaper articles and television news stories about the ongoing hostage crisis after the wife of a hostage started displaying one in her yard.

Later, during the 1990–1991 Persian Gulf War, Americans were eager to show their support for the troops fighting overseas, even if they did not necessarily support the war itself, and the stylized ribbon started to become institutionalized as a symbol of support. The yellow "Support Our Troops" ribbon was followed by the red ribbon of AIDS awareness, the pink ribbon of breast cancer awareness, and ribbons of virtually every color on other issues. And how do we know the meanings of these ribbons? We hear or see them being discussed through our media. The meaning is assigned by the creators of a ribbon, but the success of the ribbon depends on its meaning being shared through the media. So, do the media create the meanings? Not really. But could the meanings be shared nationwide without the media? Absolutely not. The media may not define our lives, but they do help transmit and disseminate shared meanings from one side of the country to the other.[40]

Web 1.8: See the actual list of my morning students' media use.

Web 1.9: Read more examples of Secret One.

SECRET 2 There Are No Mainstream Media (MSM). We often hear charges related to perceived sins of the so-called mainstream media. But who exactly are these mainstream media? For some, the MSM are the heavyweights of journalism, especially the television broadcast networks and the major newspapers, such as the *New York Times*. For others, the MSM are the giant corporations that run many of our media outlets. New York University journalism professor and blogger Jay Rosen says that the term *MSM* is often used to refer to media we just don't like—a "them."[41] It isn't always clear who constitutes the MSM, but in general we can consider them to be the old-line legacy big-business media—newspapers, magazines, and television.

But are these old media more in the mainstream than our alternative media? Look at talk radio. Afternoon talk radio is dominated by conservative political talk show hosts, such as Rush Limbaugh and Sean Hannity. Limbaugh, in particular, is fond of complaining about how the MSM don't "get it." But how mainstream are the MSM? On a typical evening, CNN will have approximately 568,000 viewers of its evening programming; Fox News will have 1.097 million; MSNBC will have 640,000; HLN (formerly CNN Headline News) will have 395,000; and the NBC, CBS, and ABC network newscasts will have a combined total of approximately 22.4 million viewers.[42]

(The Fox broadcast network does not have a network evening news broadcast.) The Rush Limbaugh show, on the other hand, averages just shy of 15 million listeners a week, and Fox host Sean Hannity's radio show draws about 14 million listeners per week.[43] (Note that television audiences and radio audiences are measured differently.) So which is more mainstream? A popular afternoon radio show with a large daily audience or a television news program with a much smaller audience? *Daily Kos*, a leading liberal political blog—and one of the most-read blogs on the Internet—attracts more than 6 million unique visitors per month.[44] Again, these numbers are not directly comparable with television ratings, but they are substantial. The Internet video site YouTube streams approximately 4 billion videos a day. No one video gets a particularly large viewership, but the combined total is massive.[45]

Even when important news breaks, it's likely we'll hear about it first through social media. When Navy SEALs killed Osama bin Laden in Pakistan in 2011, the news first broke on Twitter with a post by Keith Urbahn, chief of staff for former secretary of defense Donald Rumsfeld. His tweet read: "So I'm told by a reputable person they have killed Osama bin Laden. Hot Damn."[46] This was followed minutes later by a tweet from CBS news producer Jill Jackson reporting: "House Intelligence Committee aide confirms that Osama bin Laden is dead. U.S. has the body."[47]

Meanwhile, the big broadcast and cable news networks were struggling to confirm the story before declaring it to be true on the air. Even CBS, Jackson's own network, waited sixteen minutes more before officially announcing bin Laden's death. As Nicholas Jackson of the *Atlantic* reported it on the night of the announcement:

> With cable news anchors afraid to confirm the news of bin Laden's death before they had multiple sources of their own—Twitter quickly backed up with more confirmations, from senior administration officials and others—newspapers quickly jumped ahead of the story. As print reporters shared notes and confidential sources over Twitter, Wolf Blitzer stood in front of a green screen on CNN (he was at home when he got the news of Obama's press conference) and teased the audience: "We have strong suspicions of what this news might be."[48]

So it is largely meaningless to describe one medium as mainstream and another as nonmainstream. They are all significant presences in our world.

Can we distinguish between old and new media? Perhaps. Can we argue that our alternative sources of news and entertainment are any less significant than the traditional ones? Absolutely not.

SECRET 3 Everything From the Margin Moves to the Center. The mass media, both news and entertainment, are frequently accused of trying to put forward an extremist agenda of violence, permissiveness, homosexuality, drug use, edgy fashion, and nonmainstream values.

U.S. Government, http://www.flickr.com/photos/whitehouse/6599544015/sizes/l/in/photostream/

While President Barack Obama and his cabinet were watching the killing of Osama bin Laden unfold, news of the raid was already being reported live on Twitter.

People in the media business, be they entertainers or journalists, respond with the argument that they are just "keeping it real," portraying the world as it is by showing aspects of society that some people want to pretend don't exist. They have no agenda, the argument goes; they just want to portray reality.

Now it is true that much of what the media portray that upsets people is real. On the other hand, it is a bit disingenuous to argue that movie directors and musicians are not trying for shock value when they use offensive language or portray stylized violence combined with graphic sexuality. Think back to any of a number of recent horror movies. We all know that teenagers routinely get slashed to ribbons by a psycho killer just after having sex, right? Clearly movie producers are trying to attract an audience by providing content that is outside of the mainstream.

The problem with the argument between "keeping it real" and "extremist agenda" is that it misses what is actually happening. There can be no question that audiences go after media content that is outside of the mainstream. By the same token, the more nonmainstream content is presented, the more ordinary it seems to become. This is what is meant by Secret Three—one of the mass media's biggest effects on everyday life is to take culture from the margins of society and make it into part of the mainstream, or center. This process can move people, ideas, and even individual words from small communities into mass society.

Web 1.10: Read how news of Bin Laden's death spread.

Web 1.11: Read more examples of Secret Two.

http://cache.gawker.com/assets/images/13242/2010/10/main_still.png

Glee's Amber Riley played the part of Dr. Frank-N-Furter in the show's production of the gay-themed *Rocky Horror Picture Show*. The part was originally written for a man in drag.

We can see this happening in several ways. Take the popular Fox show *Glee*. Each week the members of the high school glee club perform pop songs as part of an ongoing plot in which an evil coach always tries to shut them down. For Halloween in 2010, the *Glee* kids were producing the *Rocky Horror Picture Show* as a high school musical. *Rocky Horror* tells the story of a gay male transvestite (Dr. Frank-N-Furter) who is building a boyfriend (Rocky) for himself. But the *Glee* version had actress Amber Riley playing the part of Dr. Frank-N-Furter, while the part of Rocky was still played by a male actor, Chord Overstreet. Thus, the central plotline went from being gay to straight. The *Glee* version also had Frank-N-Furter singing about being from "Sensational, Transylvania" instead of "Transsexual, Transylvania." With these changes, the *Rocky Horror Glee Show* became a perfect example of Secret Three. *Rocky Horror* started out as a camp musical in the 1970s that found enormous success in the counterculture community. But *Glee* sanitized it from a celebration of cross-dressing gay culture into a mass-market story of straight people playing with gay themes.

Glee has also made a habit of taking distinctive cover versions of popular songs that have been reimagined by independent artists and then performing them on the show without crediting the independent artist. For example, *Glee* did a version of Israel Kamakawiwoʻole's Hawaiian-styled cover of "Somewhere Over the Rainbow," and in another episode performed Jonathan Coulton's soft rock version of Sir Mix-A-Lot's rap "Baby Got Back." Even in the premiere episode of the series, the *Glee* singers performed an a cappella version of Journey's hit "Don't Stop Believin'" that was largely based on the work of singer Petra Haden. While it seems unlikely that there was a legal requirement that the producers compensate or even credit the artists for their creative covers, it would have certainly been nice for them to have noted how they had brought the work of obscure artists into the mainstream.[49] (You can find a link to these covers on the Secret Three link.)

An alternative approach is to look at how the media accelerate the adoption of activist language into the mainstream. Take the medical term *intact dilation and extraction*, which describes a controversial type of late-term abortion. A search of the LexisNexis news database shows that newspapers used the medical term only five times over a six-month period. On the other hand, *partial-birth abortion*, the term for the procedure used by abortion opponents, was used in more than 125 stories during the same time period. Opponents even got the term used in the title of a bill passed by Congress that outlawed the procedure, thus moving the phrase into the mainstream through repeated publication of the bill's name.

This process is not a product of a liberal or conservative bias by the news media. It's simply a consequence of the repeated use of the term in the press.

SECRET 4 Nothing's New: Everything That Happened in the Past Will Happen Again. Secret Four is a little different than the oft-repeated slogan, "Those who ignore the past are doomed to repeat it." Instead, it says that media face the same issues over and over again as technologies change and new people come into the business.

The fight between today's recording companies and file sharers has its roots in the battle between music publishers and the distributors of player piano rolls in the early 1900s. The player piano was one of the first technologies for reproducing musical performances. Piano roll publishers would buy a single copy of a piece of sheet music and hire a skilled pianist to have his or her performance recorded as a series of holes punched in a paper roll. That roll (and the performance) could then be reproduced and sold to anyone who owned a player piano without further payment to the music's original publisher.[50]

©iStockphoto.com/DNY59

Then, in 1984, Sony successfully defended itself against a lawsuit from Universal Studios by arguing that it had a right to sell VCRs to the public because there were legitimate, legal uses for the technology. Universal had protested the sales because the video recorders could be used to duplicate its movies. Before long, the studios quit trying to ban the VCR and started selling videocassettes of movies directly to consumers at reasonable prices. All of a sudden, the studios had a major new source of revenue.[51]

Web 1.12: Read more examples of Secret Three.

More recently, the recording industry has done its best to force consumers to buy its music on little plastic discs, having gotten the courts to levy large fines against consumers who "share" copyrighted music over the Internet. In the meantime, Apple sells millions of songs a week through its online iTunes music store for an average price of ninety-nine cents per song. And in the fall of 2006, Apple and Amazon started selling movie downloads through their online stores—a step that has the movie industry worried.

© Bettmann/CORBIS

Congressional hearings in the 1950s about horror comics, such as those pictured here, show how adults are always concerned about the possible effects of new media on children.

SECRET 5 New Media Are Always Scary. Concern about how new media will affect our lives is nothing new. Known as the legacy of fear, it dates back at least to the early twentieth century.

In the 1930s, there was fear that watching movies, especially gangster pictures, would lead to precocious sexual behavior, delinquency, lower standards and ideals, and poor physical and emotional health. The 1940s brought concern about how people would react to radio programs, particularly soap operas.[52]

Comic books came under attack in the 1950s. The notion that comic books were dangerous was popularized by a book titled *Seduction of the Innocent* by Dr. Fredric Wertham. Wertham also testified before Congress that violent and explicit comic books were a cause of teenage delinquency and sexual behavior. The industry responded to the criticism by forming the Comics Code Authority and ceasing publication of popular crime and horror comics such as *Tales From the Crypt* and *Weird Science.*

The 1980s and 1990s saw controversies over offensive rap and rock lyrics.[53] These controversies reflected widespread concern about bad language and hidden messages in songs. In 2009, pop star Britney Spears had a not-so-hidden allusion to the "*F* word" in her song "If U Seek Amy." If you speak the title aloud, it sounds like you are spelling out *F, U,* . . . well, you get the picture. Critics were, of course, shocked and dismayed at this example of a pop star lowering public taste. Of course, Spears didn't really create her naughty little lyric on her own. Aside from a host of rock and blues singers who have used similar lines, *Slate* writer Jesse Sheidlower notes that James Joyce used the same basic line in *Ulysses,* when he has a group of women sing:

> If you see kay
> Tell him he may
> See you in tea
> Tell him from me.

A careful reading of the third line will let you find a second hidden obscenity as well.[54]

Numerous media critics and scholars have argued that television and movies present a distorted view of the world, making it look like a much more violent and dangerous place than it is. More recently, mobile devices have been blamed for a range of social ills, from car accidents caused by distracted drivers to promiscuity caused by sexually explicit mobile phone text and photo messages.

The idea that new media are always scary applies as much to media companies as it does to audience members. Newspaper publishers were frightened that radio stations would

Web 1.13: Read more examples of Secret Four.

Web 1.14: Read more examples of Secret Five.

© Bettmann/CORBIS

While Britney Spears attracted controversy by including not-so-subtle naughty messages in her song "If U Seek Amy," author James Joyce (wearing the eye patch) included the same trick in his 1922 novel *Ulysses*.

©iStockphoto.com/LeeDaniels

steal away all their readers in the 1920s and 1930s. Record companies were also afraid that radio would steal away all the customers who were paying for record albums. And as we saw earlier in this chapter, the movie industry, the television industry, and the music industry are terrified of what the Internet is doing to their business.

Why has there been such long-running concern about the possible effects of the media? Media sociologist Charles R. Wright says that people want to be able to solve social ills, and it is easier to believe that poverty, crime, and drug abuse are caused by media coverage than to acknowledge that their causes are complex and not fully understood.[55]

Writing in 1948, sociologists Robert Merton and Paul Lazarsfeld identified four major aspects of public concern about the media:

- Concern that because the media are everywhere, they might be able to control and manipulate people. This is a large part of the legacy of fear.
- Fear that those in power will use the media to reinforce the existing social structure and discourage social criticism. When critics express concern about who owns and runs the media, this is what they are worried about.
- Fear that mass entertainment will lower the tastes and standards for popular culture by trying to attract the largest possible audience. Criticism of action movies, soap operas, and wrestling as replacements for healthier entertainment, such as Shakespeare's plays, is at the heart of this concern.
- The belief that mass entertainment is a waste of time that detracts from more useful activities. When your mother told you to turn off the television set and go outside, this was her concern![56]

SECRET 6 **Activism and Analysis Are Not the Same Thing.** The five secrets we've examined so far lead us to the conclusion of Secret Six: Critics of the mass media are not necessarily interested in giving an honest analysis of how the media affect the public at large. Instead, critics may have an agenda that has nothing to do with the nature of our mass media.

When senators hold hearings on violent video games and television programming, they may well be concerned about the effects of electronic violence on children. But they may also be trying to show that they are concerned about

TEST YOUR MEDIA LITERACY

Children's Media Use

Teens are significant media users. According to the 2010 study *Generation M2: Media in the Lives of 8–18 Year-Olds,* a follow-up to the 2005 study *Generation M*, children in the United States spend an average of seven hours and thirty-eight minutes a day using media—more time than they spend doing anything else other than sleeping.[1] There are also a lot of stereotypes about teen media use that may or may not be supported by evidence. The study, conducted by the Kaiser Family Foundation, surveyed teens and discovered that because teens are often engaged in media multitasking, they are actually consuming ten hours and forty-five minutes of media content within those seven and a half hours. Here are some of the study's major findings:

- Teens are big users of mobile devices: 66 percent of young people aged eight to eighteen have mobile phones, and 76 percent have an iPod or other MP3 player.
- Young people spend more time consuming media (forty-nine minutes per day) than they do talking on their phones (thirty-three minutes). And the biggest mobile phone activity? Seventh to twelfth graders spent an hour and a half per day texting, which was not counted as media use in this study.
- Few young people have rules controlling how much time they spend with media. But the approximately 30 percent who do have rules limiting their media consumption spend nearly three hours less per day with media.
- Young people are spending more time consuming video than in the past (four hours and twenty-nine minutes) but less time watching television (down by twenty-five minutes a day from 2004). How is this possible? They're watching video online and using mobile devices.

See the table for a summary of what the researchers found out about media use for children aged eight to eighteen over the last decade:

	Time Spent With Medium in a Typical Day		
Medium	2009	2004	1999
TV/Video	4:29	3:51	3:47
Music/Audio	2:31	1:44	1:48
Computer	1:29	1:02	0:27
Video Games	1:13	0:49	0:26
Print	0:38	0:43	0:18
Movies	0:25	0:25	0:18
Total Media Exposure	10:45	8:33	7:29
Multitasking Proportion	29%	26%	16%
Total Media Use	7:38	6:21	6:19

WHO is the source?

The Kaiser Family Foundation is a private, nonprofit foundation dedicated to researching and reporting on health-related issues. How do you think the Kaiser Family Foundation funded the study? How might this influence the findings and analysis? Who is the intended audience for this study?

WHAT is the report saying?

How has young people's media use changed over the last ten years? How can young people consume more than ten hours of media content in seven and a half hours?

WHAT kind of evidence does the study provide?

What kinds of data do the researchers use? Are those data sufficient to support the assumptions and thereby the recommendations?

HOW do you or your classmates react to the Generation M2 findings?

Do you think the results of the study accurately describe how you and your friends use media? How do you think your media use differs from how your parents use media? Who or what organizations may benefit from these findings? How might they change media usage in children? What questions are left unanswered? How does your media use compare with that of the young people in the study? How much time do you spend with the various media over the course of a week?

HOW were media used in your home?

What controls over media use did you have growing up? Did you have television or Internet access in your own room? Were any limits placed on how you could use your mobile phone? If so, what were they? Do you think these limits (or the lack of them) had any effect on how you use media or your mobile device now?

1. Victoria J. Rideout, Ulla G. Foehr, and Donald F. Roberts, *Generation M2: Media in the Lives of 8–18 Year-Olds* (Henry J. Kaiser Family Foundation, 2010).

Web 1.15: Read the entire *Generation M2* report.

PhotoAlto/Alamy

Young people today are spending more time viewing video and less time watching television than in the past. How is this possible? They are doing more of their viewing on mobile devices like phones and tablets.

America's children, or that they are getting tough on violence, or that they want to lend support to a cause that their contributors feel strongly about. Take as an example the following excerpts from a press release supporting a bill that would limit "gratuitous and excessive" television violence:

> "Increasing fines is an important way to tell broadcasters that we are serious about taking action against indecent material," [the senator] said. "For the sake of our children, we are not going to tolerate indecency, which seems to appear at all hours of the day on more TV channels than ever. We know from numerous studies that such gratuitous and graphic programming negatively affect our children.
>
> "But it's not enough to increase fines. We need to take on this problem in a truly comprehensive and systematic way that will enable us to diminish the appetite that television producers have for producing shows full of sex and violence. Instead of merely reacting to one or two high profile incidents, we need to preempt these incidents by fundamentally transforming the culture of programming. Only then will we be able to give parents more control of what their children are watching.
>
> "That's what . . . parents want. I hear over and over from them that they are very concerned about what their children are watching. I believe we have a moral imperative to meet this issue head on."
>
> [The senator's] bill enjoys wide support from a variety of groups, including: Parents Television Council, Benedum Foundation, Children Now, Children's Media Policy Coalition, Kaiser Family Foundation, National Association for Family and Community Education, National Coalition for the Protection of Children and Families, and the National Institute on Family and the Media.[57]

Look through the quotes for the signs of activism: "for the sake of our children," "that's what parents want," "the bill enjoys wide support from a variety of groups." Although the senator sponsoring the bill certainly is concerned about the issue of television violence, he has also—through this criticism of media violence—managed to ally himself with parents and several significant organizations in a way that is relatively safe.

As media consumers, whenever we hear criticism of the media, we ought to ask ourselves, "What is the critic's agenda?"

SECRET 7 **There Is No "They."** If you listen to media criticism for long, you will hear a pair of words used over and over again: *they* and *them.* It is easy to take potshots at some anonymous bogeymen—*they*—who embody all evil. I even engaged in it at the beginning of this section with the title "Seven Secrets About the Media 'They' Don't Want You to Know."

So who are *they?* No one. Everyone. A nonspecific other we want to blame. Any time I used "they" in a news story, my high school journalism teacher would always ask who "they" were. And that's what you need to ask whenever you hear criticism of the media. It isn't that the criticism is not accurate. It very well may be. But it probably applies to a specific media outlet, a specific journalist, a certain song, or a particular movie. But we can make few generalizations about an industry so diverse that it includes everything from a giant corporation producing the $220 million *Marvel's The Avengers* movie to young people posting on Facebook. There are a lot of media out there, but no unified *them.*

Web 1.16: Read more examples of Secret Six.

Web 1.17: Read more examples of Secret Seven.

Chapter SUMMARY

Communication takes place at a number of levels, including intrapersonal (within the self), interpersonal (between individuals), group (between three or more individuals), and mass (between a single sender and a large audience). Mass communication is a communication process that covers an entire society, in which an individual or institution uses technology to send messages to a large, mixed audience, most of whose members are not known to the sender. Mass communication can be examined in terms of the process of transmission; the rituals surrounding its consumption; the attention its messages draw to persons, groups, or concepts; or how audience members create meaning out of media content.

The first communication network was developed by the Roman Catholic Church, which could send messages reliably throughout Europe as early as the twelfth century. In the mid-fifteenth century, the development of printing made it possible for books and other publications to be mass produced for the first time, leading to numerous cultural changes. Books, magazines, newspapers, and other printed media forms became readily available, although they were expensive before steam-driven printing presses became common in the nineteenth century.

The electronic media emerged in the mid-nineteenth century with the invention of the telegraph, followed by recorded music, radio, movies, and television. These media allowed popular culture to be produced commercially and to be delivered easily and inexpensively into people's homes. The first interactive digital communication network, the Internet, was developed starting in the late 1960s but wasn't available to the general public until the 1990s. The Internet added a return channel to the mass communication process, initiating a much higher level of audience feedback. The Internet also allowed individuals to disseminate their own ideas and information without the costs of a traditional mass medium.

The rapid growth of the mass media has led the public and media critics to raise questions about the effects various media might have on society and individuals. Scholars have suggested that the best way to control the impact of the media in our lives is to develop high levels of media literacy—an understanding of what the media are, how they operate, what messages they are delivering, what roles they play in society, and how audience members respond to these messages. Media literacy includes cognitive, emotional, aesthetic, and moral dimensions.

Your text suggests that the following seven principles can guide your understanding of how the media operate: (1) the media are essential components of our lives, (2) there are no mainstream media, (3) everything from the margin moves to the center, (4) nothing's new—everything that happened in the past will happen again, (5) new media are always scary, (6) activism and analysis are not the same thing, and (7) there is no "they."

Keep up-to-date with content from the author's blog.

Take the chapter quiz.

Key TERMS

communication 4
intrapersonal communication 5
interpersonal communication 5
group communication 5
mass communication 6
mass media 7
Sender Message Channel Receiver (SMCR) or transmission model 7
bloggers 7
message 8
encoding 8
channel 8
receiver 9
decoding 9
heterogeneous audience 9
noise 9
anonymous audience 11
ritual model 12
publicity model 12
reception model 12
media literacy 16

Concept REVIEW

Levels of communication
Mass communication versus mass media
Elements of the mass communication process
Models of mass communication: transmission, ritual, publicity, and reception
Pre–mass media communication networks
Print media
Electronic networks
Interactive communication
Media literacy and its dimensions
Seven secrets about the media

Student STUDY SITE

Sharpen your skills with SAGE edge at **edge.sagepub.com/hanson5e**

SAGE edge for Students provides a personalized approach to help you accomplish your coursework goals in an easy-to-use learning environment.

Mass Communication Effects

How Society and Media Interact

chapter 2

AP Photo

Former National Security Agency contractor Edward Snowden shocked the world in 2013 by releasing thousands of documents to journalist Glenn Greenwald that he had smuggled out using a small flash drive. Prior to the digital age, taking that many documents out of an office would have required a busy photocopy machine and dozens of boxes.

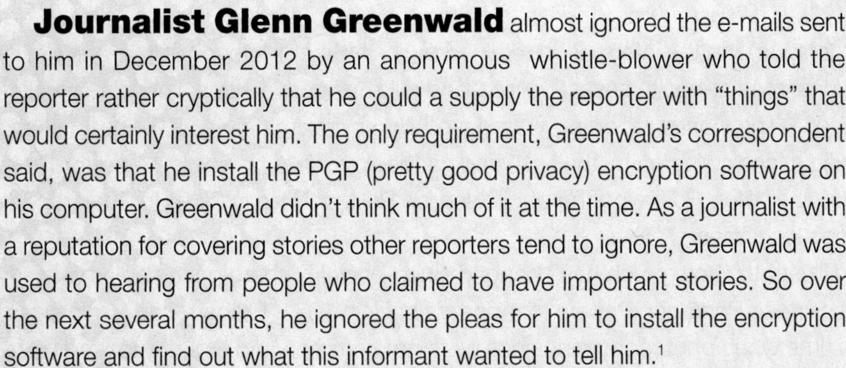

Journalist Glenn Greenwald almost ignored the e-mails sent to him in December 2012 by an anonymous whistle-blower who told the reporter rather cryptically that he could a supply the reporter with "things" that would certainly interest him. The only requirement, Greenwald's correspondent said, was that he install the PGP (pretty good privacy) encryption software on his computer. Greenwald didn't think much of it at the time. As a journalist with a reputation for covering stories other reporters tend to ignore, Greenwald was used to hearing from people who claimed to have important stories. So over the next several months, he ignored the pleas for him to install the encryption software and find out what this informant wanted to tell him.[1]

But six months after that first e-mail, Greenwald was convinced by documentary filmmaker Laura Poitras to install the software and exchange e-mail with the informant, who turned out to be former National Security Agency contract worker (and high school dropout) Edward Snowden.

Greenwald travelled to Hong Kong to meet with Snowden in May 2013 along with Poitras and another reporter from London's *Guardian* newspaper. Snowden, who was 29 years old at the time, had put together a huge collection of electronic copies of meticulously categorized top-secret documents that he believed would show the overreach of the NSA without endangering lives.[2]

Snowden told Greenwald that he wanted to see traditional journalism be done with the documents rather than just turn them loose on the world the way that Julian Assange did a couple of years earlier with the WikiLeaks Web site. "If I wanted the documents just put on the Internet en masse, I could have done that myself," Snowden said. "I want you [Greenwald] to make sure these stories are done, one by one, so that people can understand what they should know."[3]

The stories, written by Greenwald and others using the documents Snowden released, ended up telling Americans just what the NSA was doing with all the information it was collecting from the public. Snowden discovered that the NSA could:

- Track who is talking on a phone call, where the person is calling from, and to whom, when, and for how long
- Read text messages
- Know what you are watching on YouTube
- Know what you like on Facebook, as soon as you click on it
- Read your e-mail
- Recognize who is in your online photos
- Record your phone calls[4]

Snowden has been charged by the U.S. government "with theft of government property, unauthorized communication of national defense information and willful communication of classified communications intelligence." Each of

LEARNING OBJECTIVES

After studying this chapter, you will be able to:

1 Discuss the history and development of our understanding of media effects.

2 Name four types of effects the mass media can have.

3 Explain eight major communication theories and their uses.

4 Describe two ways in which political campaigns affect voters.

5 Identify Herbert Gans's eight basic journalistic values when reading a news story.

Web 2.1: Read more about Glenn Greenwald's reporting on Edward Snowden.

these charges carries a possible 10-year prison sentence.[5] He initially went to Hong Kong, where he met with journalists, and then moved on to Russia, which promised him asylum for a year. It was unknown as of this writing where he would move to once that year of asylum expired.

More than a year after Snowden handed over copies of secret NSA documents to the *Guardian* and the *Washington Post*, stories continue to emerge from the treasure trove of information. In July 2014, the *Post* reported that 90 percent of the people who had their communications collected by the NSA were ordinary Internet users from the United States and around the world who were not actual surveillance targets. Among the information retained by the NSA are "stories of love and heart-break, illicit sexual liaisons, mental-health crises, political and religious conversions, financial anxieties and disappointed hopes." The *Post*'s reporting was based on approximately 160,000 e-mail and instant-message conversations collected by the NSA and handed over by Snowden.[6] Reporters from the *Guardian* and the *Washington Post* won the public service Pulitzer Prize in 2014 for their reporting based on Snowden's documents.

The Snowden case illustrates how much has changed since Daniel Ellsberg gave copies of many of the volumes of the so-called Pentagon Papers to reporters back in 1971. Ellsberg had to physically photocopy pages at a time when photocopy machines were not common and typically locked down after hours. (You can read more about the Pentagon Papers case and Ellsberg in Chapter 13.) Snowden had to know how to bypass computer security, but beyond that, all he had to do was download the files to a flash drive. Ellsberg had to smuggle hundreds of physical pages out of the Pentagon.[7]

A blogger writing for the newsweekly the *Economist* says that whether you view people who leak top-secret electronic documents as heroes or traitors really doesn't matter. The writer argues that

Timeline

1800

1812 War of 1812 breaks out.
1835 Alexis de Tocqueville publishes *Democracy in America*.
1859 Charles Darwin publishes *On the Origin of Species*.
1861 U.S. Civil War begins.
1869 Transcontinental railroad is completed.
1879 Thomas Edison invents electric light bulb.
1898 Spanish-American War breaks out.

1900

1903 Orville and Wilbur Wright fly first airplane.
1905 Albert Einstein proposes his theory of relativity.

1910

1912 *Titanic* sinks.
1914 World War I begins.
1918 Worldwide influenza epidemic strikes.

1920

1920 Nineteenth Amendment passes, giving U.S. women the right to vote.
1929 U.S. stock market crashes, leading to the Great Depression.

1920s General concern arises about the effects of media on the public.

Library of Congress

1930

1933 Adolf Hitler is elected chancellor of Germany.
1939 World War II breaks out in Europe.

1934 George Herbert Mead introduces the concept of symbolic interactionism.
1940s Media scholars begin to believe that media effects are selective and indirect.
1940 Paul Lazarsfeld and colleagues conduct voter research for *The People's Choice* study.

AP Photo/Obed Zilwa

1940

1941 United States enters World War II.
1945 United States drops two atomic bombs on Japan.
1947 Pakistan and India gain independence from Britain.
1949 Communists establish People's Republic of China.

we are undergoing a major shift from a world with paper documents that are heavy and tied to a place to electronic documents that can be moved around the globe with the click of a mouse, and no amount of prosecuting cyberleakers will change that. The writer is not defending those who release electronic documents; rather, he's explaining the long-term impact that this change of media means. The blogger is essentially bringing to the forefront the ideas of Canadian economist Harold Innis, who believed that any given medium has a bias of lasting a long time or of being easy to distribute. Paper documents, which we are more used to, are heavy and hard to move. Electronic documents, on the other hand, don't have a physical form and thus can be moved about with incredible ease. As you will read later in this chapter, Innis was the scholar who inspired media theorist Marshall McLuhan's popular concept of "the medium is the message."[8]

As we think about Snowden and the transformations that electronic documents have brought to our society, remember that it is a key example of **SECRET 5** New media are always scary. In this chapter, we look at how our understanding of media and their effects have evolved over the past century and consider several approaches to studying these effects. Finally, we look at how media effects can be analyzed within the realm of politics. ■

> "I want you [Greenwald] to make sure these stories are done, one by one, so that people can understand what they should know."
>
> — Edward Snowden

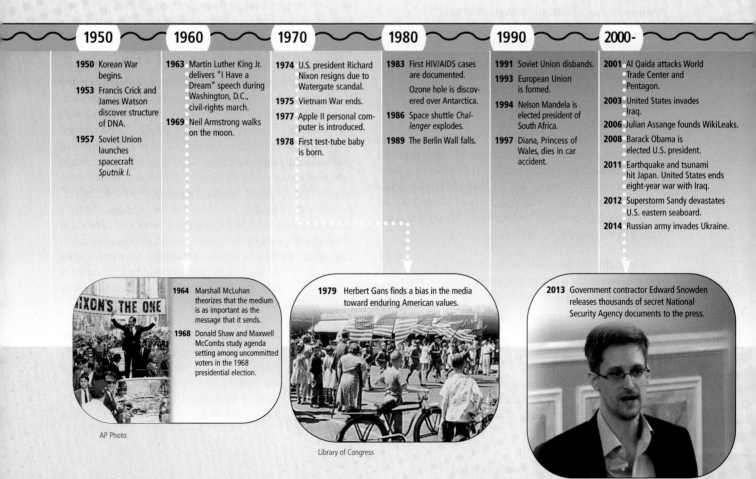

1950

1950 Korean War begins.

1953 Francis Crick and James Watson discover structure of DNA.

1957 Soviet Union launches spacecraft *Sputnik I*.

1960

1963 Martin Luther King Jr. delivers "I Have a Dream" speech during Washington, D.C., civil-rights march.

1969 Neil Armstrong walks on the moon.

1970

1974 U.S. president Richard Nixon resigns due to Watergate scandal.

1975 Vietnam War ends.

1977 Apple II personal computer is introduced.

1978 First test-tube baby is born.

1980

1983 First HIV/AIDS cases are documented.

Ozone hole is discovered over Antarctica.

1986 Space shuttle *Challenger* explodes.

1989 The Berlin Wall falls.

1990

1991 Soviet Union disbands.

1993 European Union is formed.

1994 Nelson Mandela is elected president of South Africa.

1997 Diana, Princess of Wales, dies in car accident.

2000-

2001 Al Qaida attacks World Trade Center and Pentagon.

2003 United States invades Iraq.

2006 Julian Assange founds WikiLeaks.

2008 Barack Obama is elected U.S. president.

2011 Earthquake and tsunami hit Japan. United States ends eight-year war with Iraq.

2012 Superstorm Sandy devastates U.S. eastern seaboard.

2014 Russian army invades Ukraine.

1964 Marshall McLuhan theorizes that the medium is as important as the message that it sends.

1968 Donald Shaw and Maxwell McCombs study agenda setting among uncommitted voters in the 1968 presidential election.

AP Photo

1979 Herbert Gans finds a bias in the media toward enduring American values.

Library of Congress

2013 Government contractor Edward Snowden releases thousands of secret National Security Agency documents to the press.

Associated Press

History of Media Effects Research

As we discussed in Chapter 1 in the section on media literacy, media consumers often assume that the media have large, obvious, and generally negative effects on people, and they look to blame the media for complex social problems.[9] In this section, we look at how our understanding of media effects has evolved and changed over the past 200 years.

Rise of Mass Society

Prior to the 1800s, most people in Europe and North America lived in rural communities where their neighbors were likely to be similar in ethnic, racial, and religious background. People knew their neighbors, and their neighbors knew them. There were only limited opportunities for people to change their station in life or to learn much about the outside world. But with the rise of the Industrial Revolution in the nineteenth century, we started to see massive migration from the rural areas into the cities and from various countries to the United States. As people moved into the cities, they started working for wages in factories with people who were quite different from them. With industrialization, people went from small, close-knit communities where they knew everyone to a mass society where they learned about the world from mass media sources, such as the new inexpensive newspapers, magazines, and paperback novels.[10]

SECRET 7 At the end of the nineteenth century, people came to believe that the traditional ties of church, community, and family were breaking down and losing their power to influence people. The comfortable local community was being replaced by something impersonal, complex, and removed from the traditions that had previously held people together. Concerned observers noted that people seemed to be alienated, isolated, and interchangeable members of a faceless mass audience, separated by the decline of the family and the growth of technology. So what held this new mass society together?[11] The increasingly frequent answer was that the mass media were replacing the church, family, and community in shaping public opinion.[12]

(For additional discussion of the growth of the mass media from its origins in the 1400s to the present day, see Chapter 1.)

Propaganda and the Direct Effects Model

Fears that media messages would have strong, direct effects on audience members grew out of propaganda efforts by all combatants during World War I and by Nazi Germany and Fascist Italy in the 1930s. Critics worried that mass media messages would overwhelm people in the absence of the influences of family and community. With traditional social forces in decline, it was inevitable, critics feared, that the media would become the most powerful force within society.

This argument viewed audience members as passive targets who would be hit or injected with the message, which, like a vaccine, would affect most people in similar ways. But research looking for powerful, direct effects leading to opinion and behavioral changes generally came up short. In fact, in the 1940s and 1950s, researchers sometimes doubted whether media messages had any effect on individuals at all.[13] Although most scholars now focus on the media's indirect effects on society rather than their direct effects on individuals, they remain concerned about how the media influence individuals.

The big problem is that the direct effects approach viewed media messages as a stimulus that would lead to a predictable attitudinal or behavioral response with nothing intervening between sender and audience. But although people have a shared biological heritage, they have different backgrounds, needs, attitudes, and values. In short, everyone has been socialized differently. The indirect effects approach still looks at the effects that messages have on individuals, but it accounts for the fact that audience members perceive and interpret these messages selectively according to individual differences. Because people's perceptions are selective, their responses to the messages vary as well. A person who is preparing to buy a car, a person who just bought a car, and a person who doesn't drive will each react differently to an automobile commercial.

Voter Studies and the Limited Effects Model

During the 1920s and 1930s, the decades when the Nazis, Italian Fascists, and Soviets were using propaganda, many critics worried that the media might be responsible for powerful direct effects on the public. Their general worries about the media extended to the possible effects of political campaign messages. Critics, considering recent urbanization and the decline of traditional institutions, feared that political media campaigns would "inject" people with ideas that would lead to the message creator's desired actions, such as supporting a particular candidate, ideology, or point of view. This model of powerful direct campaign effects was largely discredited by voter studies in the 1940s and 1950s, but it remains important because many people still believe that it is accurate.[14]

The People's Choice. One of the first large-scale social-scientific studies of campaign influences was *The People's Choice* study of the 1940 U.S. presidential election contest between Democrat Franklin D. Roosevelt and Republican Wendell Willkie.

A team of researchers led by Paul Lazarsfeld looked at how voters in Erie County, Ohio, decided which candidate to vote for. Lazarsfeld's team found that people who were highly interested in the campaign and paid the most attention to media coverage of it were the least likely to be influenced by the campaign. Why? Because they had decided whom they supported before the campaign had even begun.[15]

In contrast, voters who decided at the last minute usually turned to friends or neighbors, rather than the media, for information about the campaign. In general, they turned to people who followed the campaign closely, the ones whom Lazarsfeld called opinion leaders.

Opinion leaders are influential community members—friends, family members, and coworkers—who spend significant time with the media. Lazarsfeld suggested that information flows from the media to opinion leaders, and then from opinion leaders to the rest of the public. Keep in mind that the opinion leaders are ordinary people who are simply very interested and involved in a topic. Although this finding was not expected, it should not be terribly surprising that interpersonal influence is more important than the media. The idea here is fairly simple: People in groups tend to share opinions with one another, and when they want reliable information, they go to the people they know. With the lengthy campaigns today, people find it easier to turn to interpersonal sources than the wealth of media information. Yet this trend is nothing new. Although many people believe that our election campaigns are starting earlier and earlier every election cycle, presidential candidate William Jennings Bryan started his campaign for the 1900 election one month after the election of 1896![16] Even as early as the 1830s, when the penny press was just getting started, presidential campaigns could run as long as two years.

The People's Choice study, as well as other early voter studies, found that campaigns typically reinforced existing political predispositions and that few people changed their minds about whom they were going to support. There are several reasons for this:

- The voters who start off with strong opinions are unlikely to change them.
- The voters who pay the most attention to a campaign are those with the strongest political views; thus, they are the least likely to change their opinions.
- The most persuadable voters (those who are least informed) are not likely to pay attention to political communication and therefore are not strongly influenced by media coverage of the campaign.[17]

opinion leaders: Influential community members who invest substantial amounts of time learning about their own area of expertise, such as politics. Less well-informed friends and family members frequently turn to them for advice about the topic.

Library of Congress

Allied propaganda posters designed to build support for World War I weren't afraid to make use of strong negative stereotypes of the Germans.

The Importance of Meaning and the Critical/Cultural Model

Up through the 1940s, most of the research on the mass media focused on direct and indirect effects of media messages on the behaviors of groups and individuals. But another school of thought looks at how people use media to construct their view of the world rather than looking at how media change people's behaviors. Instead of using

Questioning the Media

Can you come up with a recent example of someone publicly making the argument that "the media" have powerful direct effects on people? How would you respond to his or her arguments?

Audio 2.1: Learn about the long presidential campaigns of the 1800s.

TEST YOUR VISUAL MEDIA LITERACY

When you ride ALONE you ride with Hitler !
Join a Car-Sharing Club TODAY !

National Archives

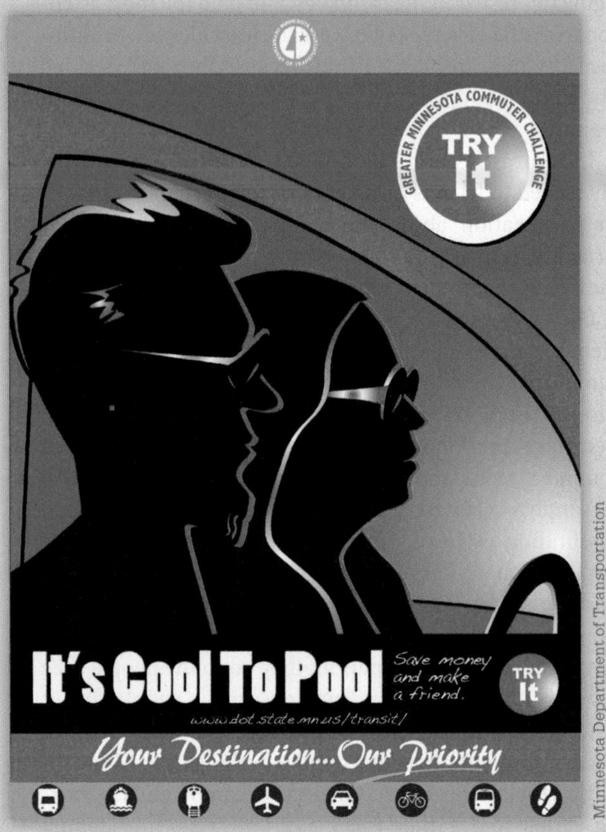

GREATER MINNESOTA COMMUTER CHALLENGE
TRY It
It's Cool To Pool
Save money and make a friend.
TRY It
www.dot.state.mn.us/transit/
Your Destination...Our Priority

Minnesota Department of Transportation

Are you surprised to see car sharing as a subject of propaganda? What's your reaction to each poster? How does looking at these images as propaganda, rather than as advertisements or marketing material, influence your view of their message? Would the message promoting car sharing have more influence on you if you were already considering doing it?

The Messages in Propaganda

There's an Internet meme known as Godwin's Law of Nazi Analogies that states: "As an online discussion grows longer, the probability of a comparison involving Nazis or Hitler approaches one."[1]

With the common use of Nazi name-calling these days, it's hard sometimes to remember that during World War II when people talked about Hitler and the Nazis, they were talking about actual Nazis. Hitler was a popular figure used by American and European government propagandists, as can be seen in the poster on the left promoting car sharing. Although it doesn't invoke Hitler, the Minnesota Department of Transportation also wants to get people carpooling with its Greater Minnesota Commuter Challenge and is promoting the cause using propaganda posters as well.[2]

WHAT are these posters saying?

What message is the World War II poster on the left trying to convey? What is the message of the poster on the right from the Minnesota Department of Transportation trying to say?

WHY are they sending the message?

Why are these two groups sending these messages? What is their goal in trying to persuade you to carpool?

HOW do you and your classmates interpret these messages?

How do you react to messages like these? How do arguments today comparing someone to Hitler differ from those made during the World War II era? How do the arguments for carpooling during World War II differ from arguments today? Do you think one is more persuasive than the other? Why?

[1]Mike Godwin, "Meme, Counter-Meme," *Wired*, October 1994, www.wired.com/wired/archive/2.10/godwin.if.html.

[2]Minnesota Department of Transportation, "The Greater Minnesota Commuter Challenge," 2012, www.dot.state.mn.us/transit/commuter/commute.html.

Web 2.2: Read more on Godwin's law.

the quantitative data analysis of the voter studies, the critical/cultural approach takes a more qualitative examination of the social structure in which communication takes place. It considers how meaning is created within society, who controls the media systems, and the roles the media play in our lives. Instead of looking at how messages affect people, it looks at how people use and construct messages.[18]

Under the critical/cultural approach, ordinary people are seen as moving from being information providers to information receivers, with only limited opportunities to answer back to the ideas being provided by the people in power. Thus the mass media become a tool for controlling the flow of information and the topics that can be discussed.[19] As we discuss in Chapter 3, with increasing media consolidation, more and more of our media are owned by fewer and fewer companies, so that there is an increasing level of control of what topics can be discussed and debated. Critical theorists would argue that the subjects that get covered are those in the best interests of the advertisers who support the media and the companies that own them.[20]

When Casey Anthony was acquitted of charges of murdering her daughter in 2011, cable news channels and social media devoted massive coverage to the verdict. Critics charge that when cases such as this don't involve an attractive white woman or girl, they get very little media attention.

An example of the critical/cultural approach is the charge, leveled by many critics, that the crime stories that deal with attractive, wealthy, white women and girls attract much more media attention than do disappearances of women of color or those who are poor. Consider the story of Casey Anthony. The attractive, young, white mother was accused of murdering her two-year-old daughter. During her trial in 2011, the news media, especially cable television, was obsessed with the case. When Anthony was found not guilty, Facebook, Twitter, and other social media sites were filled with outraged comments about the verdict. In addition, talk shows hosts such as Nancy Grace seemed to be obsessed with the case. Six months after the court acquitted Anthony, Google News still featured more than 1,500 links to news stories about the case. On the other hand, a Google search for Jahessye Shockley, a five-year-old African American girl from Arizona who disappeared in 2011, only turned up four news stories.[21]

A similar media silence characterized the 2004 disappearance of twenty-four-year-old Tamika Huston, an African American woman from Spartanburg, South Carolina. Her case received one or two mentions on Fox News, but it was noted mostly in stories about how disappearing black women are ignored while stories about white women and girls, such as the "runaway bride" and missing teenager Natalee Holloway, get story counts in the hundreds or thousands. Keith Woods, an expert on diversity issues at the Poynter Institute, a journalism think tank, says stories about minority women tend to receive less attention because reporters are more likely to report about people they see as being like themselves. And since most newsrooms tend to be disproportionately white and middle class, the disappearance of a white woman is seen as a bigger story. This control over which stories are reported means that the public at large is not aware that African American women are disproportionately more likely to disappear than white women.[22]

Effects of the Media in Our Lives

Media scholars throughout the twentieth century who studied the effects of the mass media on individuals and society questioned several aspects of the media, including the messages being sent, the media sending them, the owners of the media, and the audience members themselves.[23]

Message Effects

Not surprisingly, the earliest concerns about the effects of mass communication focused on how messages might change people's behaviors, attitudes, or beliefs. These message effects can take a variety of forms.

Cognitive Effects. The most common and observable message effect is on the short-term learning of information. This can be as significant as learning about a new medical treatment or as trivial as remembering the lyrics to a popular song. The amount of learning that takes place from media content depends largely on the motivation

Web 2.3: Read stories about media coverage on missing white women.

level of the person consuming the media. Political scientist Doris Graber found that people who want to be able to talk intelligently with others about media content (whether it be the news, a sporting event, or an entertainment program) learn much more from the media than people who are simply seeking entertainment. Research also shows that people learn more from people they identify with and pay more attention to political commentators they agree with than ones they dislike.[24] Hence the most popular political radio talk shows, such as those hosted by conservatives Rush Limbaugh and Sean Hannity, argue a single and consistent point of view rather than providing a range of views.[25]

©iStockphoto.com/mstay

Attitudinal Effects. People can develop feelings about a product, an individual, or an idea on the basis of media content. Viewers might decide that they like a new product, political candidate, or hairstyle because of what they have seen in a television commercial, a news broadcast, or a sitcom. Typically it is much easier to get people to form new opinions than to get them to change existing ones.[26] For example, political advertising generally tries to change the opinions of uncommitted voters rather than those of voters who already have strong political loyalties. In the 2008 presidential campaign, the Obama campaign frequently targeted young voters who had less established political loyalties with ads found on Comedy Central, VH1, or Xbox Live video games.[27] (For more on advertising in video games, see Chapter 10.)

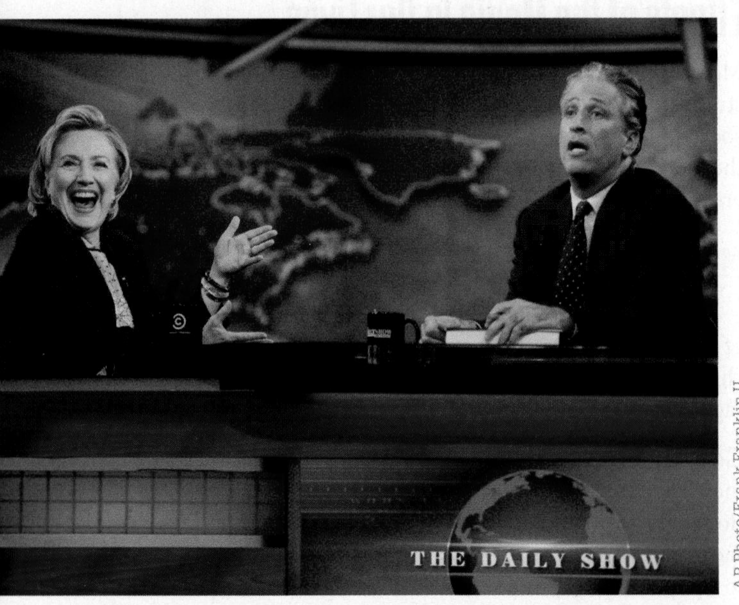

AP Photo/Frank Franklin II

Politicians like former U.S. Secretary of State Hillary Rodham Clinton often go on Comedy Central's *Daily Show* with host Jon Stewart as a way of reaching out to younger voters who would be hard to reach through more traditional news channels.

Behavioral Effects. Behavioral effects include actions such as clipping a coupon from a newspaper, buying a product, making a phone call, or voting for a candidate. They might also include imitating attractive behaviors (for example, dressing a certain way). Behavioral effects are in many ways the most difficult to achieve because people are reluctant to change their behavior. Sometimes, however, people go to the media deliberately looking for behavior to copy, as when a child watches an episode of *Batman* and then imitates it in play, or when a teenager watches a movie to learn how to behave on a date.[28]

Psychological Effects. Media content can inspire fear, joy, revulsion, happiness, or amusement, among other feelings.[29] A major psychological effect of media content, especially violent or erotic material, is arousal. Symptoms of arousal can include a rise in heart rate, adrenaline levels, or sexual response. Seeking a psychological response is a common reason for spending time with the media, whether the response sought is relaxation, excitement, or emotional release. Arousal can come from content (action, violence, sexuality, loud music or sound) and from style (motion, use of color, the rate and speed at which new images appear). Notice that music videos, which often offer little in terms of learning, provide many of these elements.[30] Contemporary composer John Adams talked about how his Pulitzer Prize–winning composition about the September 11, 2001, attacks, "On the Transmigration of Souls," makes people feel:

> Modern people have learned all too well how to keep our emotions in check, and we know how to mask them with humor or irony. Music has a singular capacity to unlock those controls and bring us face to face with our raw, uncensored, and unattenuated feelings. That is why during times when we are grieving or in need of being in touch with the core of our beings we seek out those pieces which speak to us with that sense of gravitas and serenity.[31]

Medium Effects

As mass media consumption grew in the 1950s, scholars also started paying more attention to the particular medium being used to transmit messages. Until the 1950s, most media effects research focused on the interactions among the sender, the message, and the receiver, ignoring the influence of the medium itself. But the medium used to communicate is crucial. Canadian communication researcher Marshall McLuhan argued that the medium used for transmission can be as important as the message itself, if not more so. McLuhan is best known for his statement "The medium is the message," by which he meant that the method of message transmittal is a central part of the message. For example, television does an excellent job of transmitting emotional messages because it includes both visual (explosions, luxury interiors) and audio (laugh tracks, scary music) cues along with words. And consider technology that enhances the sound of movies: Surround sound systems are designed to create a realistic experience by surrounding viewers with five distinct sound channels, as well as shaking them with a deep bass channel. The goal is not to transmit the message better, but to create a more overwhelming experience. (Think of how the impact of a summer blockbuster film would be diminished if the sound were turned down.) The same is true of large-screen high-definition television sets. Books and newspapers, in contrast, are much better at transmitting complex rational information because these media allow us to review the information and consider its meaning at our own pace.[32] The Web excels at providing obscure materials that appeal to a limited, widely dispersed audience, and it makes it easy for receivers to respond to what they've seen or heard.

©MGM/UA

Canadian media scholar Marshall McLuhan, right, is best remembered for his statement "The medium is the message." He became such a pop-culture figure in the 1970s that he had a cameo playing himself in Woody Allen's film *Annie Hall*.

SECRET 1 Media scholars now recognize that communication technology is a fundamental element of society and that new technologies can lead to social change.[33] (As Secret One points out, the media are essential components of our lives.) Media sociologist Joshua Meyrowitz, for example, argues that the existence and development of various media can lead to radical changes in society.

He writes that the development of publishing and books in the sixteenth century made it easy for new ideas to spread beyond the person who originated them and that this tended to undermine the control of ideas by both the monarchy and the Roman Catholic Church.[34] As can be seen by the Edward Snowden story discussed at the beginning of the chapter, the existence of digital documents, encrypted e-mail, and high-capacity thumb drives now allows a small group of technically skilled individuals to spread news and documents around the world, with governments powerless to stop them. Meyrowitz also identifies some social effects of particular media. In *No Sense of Place*, he argues that the major effect of print as a medium is to segregate audiences according to education, age, class, and gender. For example, a teenager needs to be able to read at a certain level to understand the content of a magazine targeted at young women or young men—content that a young child would be unable to comprehend. In contrast, electronic media such as television tend to cross the demographic boundaries. A child too young to read a magazine or book can still understand at least some of the information in a television program targeted at adults.[35] This is why parent groups and childhood educators push to have early-evening programming on television contain more "family-friendly" programs and why parents seek to restrict certain Internet sites on a family computer.

The importance of the particular medium used to convey a message applies at every level of communication, from intrapersonal (how is an audio journal different from a written one?) to interpersonal (how is a phone call different from an e-mail?) to mass (how is a book different from a movie?).

Ownership Effects

Instead of looking at the effects of media and their messages, some scholars examine the influence of those who own and control the media.[36] These critical scholars are concerned because owners of media determine which ideas will be produced and distributed by those media.

In the United States, the majority of media outlets are owned by a small number of giant multinational conglomerates and new media companies: Disney, News Corporation/21st Century Fox, Time Warner, Viacom/CBS, Bertelsmann, Comcast/NBCUniversal, and Google. Some

Audio 2.2: Listen to an interview with, and to the music of, John Adams.

Video 2.1: Watch clips of McLuhan speaking.

observers, such as German academic and sociologist Jürgen Habermas, fear that these corporations are becoming a sort of ruling class, controlling which books are published, which programs are aired, which movies are produced, and which news stories are written.[37] As we discuss in Chapter 3, Disney, News Corporation, and Google have all had to compromise at times with the Chinese government in order to keep doing business there. For example, Google had to agree to censor its search results about sensitive topics in China for the company to be allowed to operate there.[38]

Media critic and former newspaper editor Ben Bagdikian suggests that the influence of media owners can be seen in how the news media select stories to be covered. He argues that large media organizations will kill news stories and entertainment programs that don't reflect well on the corporation. The roots of this tendency go back to when captains of industry such as J. P. Morgan and the Rockefellers bought out magazines that criticized them in order to silence that criticism. What we end up with, Bagdikian says, is not the feared bogeyman of government censorship, but rather "a new Private Ministry of Information and Culture" that gives corporations control over what we will see, hear, or read.[39] Increasingly, however, the new alternative media are providing channels that allow consumers to bypass Big Media controls.[40] (See the section on long-tail media in Chapter 3 for more on how these new channels are enabling anyone who wants to distribute content to do so on a large scale.) Blogs such as *RedState* and *Daily Kos* give voice to issues from a partisan point of view with no controls at all other than those the authors choose to employ.

Active Audience Effects

Some of the early fears about the effects of the media on audience members arose from the belief that the audience truly was a faceless, undifferentiated mass—that the characteristics of the audience en masse also applied to the audience's individual members. Early critics viewed modern people as alienated and isolated individuals who, separated by the decline of the family and the growth of a technological society, didn't communicate with one another. After World War II, the concept of the mass audience began to change as scholars came to realize that the audience was made up of unique members who responded as individuals, not as undifferentiated members of a mass.[41]

Questioning the Media

Does the medium you use for mass communication change how you perceive the message? How does watching a movie at an IMAX theater differ from watching it on your television set? How does listening to a speech on the radio or on television differ from reading a copy of the speech online or in a newspaper? Are you more comfortable reading something disturbing than seeing a video about the same subject?

Today, communicators, marketers, and scholars realize that individuals seek and respond to different messages at different times and for different reasons. Therefore, they divide audiences on the basis of **geographics**, or where people live; **demographics**, or their gender, race, ethnic background, income, education, age, educational attainment, and the like; or **psychographics**, a combination of demographics, lifestyle characteristics, and product usage. Hence a young woman buying a small SUV to take her mountain bike out into the mountains will respond to a very different kind of advertising message than a mother seeking a small SUV so that she can safely drive her child to school during rush hour in the winter.

Audiences can also be classified by the amount of time they spend using media or by the purposes for which they use media. Each segment of the media audience will behave differently. Take television viewing as an example. Some people tune in daily to watch their favorite soap opera or talk show and won't change the channel for the entire hour. This is known as appointment viewing. Others surf through a number of channels using the remote control, looking for something that will capture their interest. Still others switch back and forth between two channels.

SECRET 7 With regard to television, the concept of a mass audience consuming the same content at the same time existed to some extent from the 1950s to the 1970s, when the vast majority of viewers had access to only three broadcast networks, but that concept broke down completely with the advent of cable, satellite, multiple broadcast networks, TiVo, DVDs, and VCRs. (This is an example of Secret Seven—There is no "they.")

Media scholar James Potter suggests that the media audience resembles a pyramid. (Remember the pyramid figure in Chapter 1?) At the peak of the pyramid we are all consuming the same messages, such as the horrifying reports of the September 11, 2001, terrorist attacks. At the base of the pyramid we are all different, consuming what interests us personally, such as when we surf the Internet. In between the narrow top and the wide base are the various audience segments that the media and advertisers are trying to reach.[42]

In addition to recognizing that different people use the media in different ways, scholars have realized that mass com-

Web 2.4: Check out the corporate sites of media giants.

Video 2.2: Watch commercials targeting different audiences.

geographics: The study of where people live; a method typically used to analyze potential markets for products and programs.

demographics: The study of audience members' gender, race, ethnic background, income, education, age, educational attainment, and the like; a method typically used to analyze potential markets for products and programs.

psychographics: A combination of demographics, lifestyle characteristics, and product usage; a method typically used to analyze potential markets for products and programs.

munication messages are generally mediated through other levels of communication. One reason this book discusses intrapersonal, interpersonal, and group communication in addition to mass communication is that these levels all come into play in how mass communication operates. People discuss political news with one another, cheer together for their favorite teams while watching a hockey game on television, and think about how stock market information is going to affect their investment plans. A young man's reaction to a love scene in a movie will differ depending on if he watches it with a group of friends, with his sweetie, or with his parents.[43]

Theories of Media and Society

There is a scene in *Star Wars Episode V: The Empire Strikes Back* in which Luke Skywalker is nervous about entering a cave beneath a tree in the Dagobah jungle. He asks Master Yoda, "What's in there?" Yoda replies, "Only what you take with you." And so it is with mass communication. What we find with mass communication research depends in large part on the theory base we take with us and the questions the theories suggest we pose. It's not so much that different approaches to research give us different answers—it's more that they take us to different questions. In this section, we look at several of the theoretical approaches to mass communication and the types of questions they raise.

Functional Analysis 

The effects of the media are not limited to those on individuals or groups. Some of the media's most significant effects reach society as a whole.

©iStockphoto.com/Nlshop

According to media scholar Harold Lasswell, the mass media are simply an extension of basic functions that society has always needed. Earlier societies had priests, town criers, storytellers, bards who sang ballads, and travelers who brought news from distant lands.[44] Communication can be functional or dysfunctional, but in either case it operates within the social system.[45] For example, some people respond inappropriately to the news of approaching danger. Instead of going to the basement during a tornado warning, a functional response, they go outside with their video cameras to get footage of the storm, a dysfunctional response. In both cases, they are responding to the news of the storm.

Lasswell wrote that the media perform three major social functions[46]:

1. Surveillance of the environment, looking for both threats and opportunities
2. Correlation of different elements of society, allowing segments of society to work together
3. Transmission of culture from one generation to the next

To these three, media sociologist Charles Wright adds the function of entertainment.[47] Let's look more closely at each of these functions.

Surveillance of the Environment. Much of what we know about the world we learn from the media through the process of **surveillance**. The media show us what is happening not only within our own culture, but in other societies as well. Our only other sources of knowledge about the world are our own direct experiences and the direct experiences that others share with us. For example, much of what we learned about the Arab Spring rebellions of 2011 came from social media, such as Facebook or Twitter. (We will discuss this in much more depth in Chapter 15, which focuses on global media.)

The constant flow of information from the media allows us to survey our surroundings. It can give us warnings of approaching danger—everything from changes in the weather to earthquakes to violence in the streets. This flow of information is essential for the everyday operation of society. The stock markets depend on the business news, travelers depend on weather forecasts, and grocery shoppers depend on knowing what's on special this week.

Surveillance can also serve to undermine society. For example, when people in poor nations see media images of what life is like in the United States and other industrialized Western nations, they may become dissatisfied with the conditions of their own lives, and this may lead to social unrest and violence. News about violence may also make people more fearful for their own safety.

Surveillance is not just for the masses. Government and industry leaders worldwide watch CNN or C-SPAN or read the *New York Times* or the *Financial Times* to know what other government leaders are saying and thinking.

News can also give status to individuals. Because media coverage exposes them to large audiences, they seem important. This process is known as **status conferral**. Thus, the U.S. president's press spokesperson becomes famous and important simply because he or she is speaking with

surveillance: How the media help us extend our senses to perceive more of the world surrounding us.

status conferral: The process by which media coverage makes an individual gain prominence in the eyes of the public.

Web 2.5: View tweets on the 2011 Egyptian revolution.

Web 2.6: Can social media move faster than an earthquake?

Web 2.7: Read about media coverage of big trial verdicts.

Bloomberg via Getty Images

Members of the Roberston family (Si, left; Willie, center; and Phil, right) became famous through the process of status conferral when they and their duck call company Duck Commander started being featured on the A&E Television Network show *Duck Dynasty*.

the media.[48] Think about the level of coverage the Casey Anthony not-guilty verdict (mentioned earlier in this chapter) received in the summer of 2011. According to the Project for Excellence in Journalism's news coverage index, during the week of the verdict the story filled 38 percent of the time on cable news channels. CNN's HLN channel, which is credited with bringing the trial to national attention through the efforts of talk show host Nancy Grace, had its ratings increase by 1,700 percent on the afternoon the verdict was announced.[49] No other trial since 2007 has even come close to this level of coverage. For example, the verdict in the murder trial for Dr. Conrad Murray, who was found guilty of involuntary manslaughter in the death of singer Michael Jackson, commanded only 8 percent of the cable news coverage that week.[50]

Correlation of Different Elements of Society.

Correlation is the selection, evaluation, and interpretation of events to impose structure on the news. Correlation is accomplished by persuasive communication through editorials, commentary, advertising, and propaganda. Through media-supplied correlation, we make sense out of what we learn through surveillance. It puts news into categories and provides cues that indicate the importance of each news item. Does it appear on the front page of the newspaper? Is it the first item on the broadcast? Is there a teaser on the magazine cover promoting the story?

Although many people say that they would prefer just the facts, virtually the only news outlet that provides no interpretation of events is the public affairs network C-SPAN, which has rigid rules governing how every event is covered. Far more viewers choose to go to the broadcast networks or cable news channels, which provide some interpretation, rather than watch the relatively dry, "just the facts" C-SPAN.[51]

It is often difficult to distinguish between communication that is informative and communication that is persuasive. Editorial judgments are always being made as to which stories should be covered and which should be omitted, which picture of a politician should be published, or what kind of headline should be written. Thus, it is useful to view surveillance and correlation as two functions that can be shared by a particular message.

Video 2.3: Watch C-SPAN coverage.

Socialization and Transmission of Culture.

Socialization is the process of integrating people within society through the transmission of values, social norms, and knowledge to new members of the group.

SECRET 1 It is through the media, as well as through our friends, family, school, and church, that we learn the values of our society. Socialization is important not only to young people as they are growing up, but also to immigrants learning about and assimilating into their new country, high school students heading off to college, and new graduates going to work.[52] (Another example of Secret One—The media are essential components of our lives.)

The media provide socialization in a variety of ways:

- Through role models in entertainment programming
- Through goals and desires as presented in media content

correlation: The process of selecting, evaluating, and interpreting events to give structure to the news. The media assist the process of correlation by persuasive communication through editorials, commentary, advertising, and propaganda and by providing cues that indicate the importance of each news item.

socialization: The process of educating young people and new members about the values, social norms, and knowledge of a group or society.

- Through the citizenship values portrayed in the news
- Through advertisements for products that may be useful to us in different stages of our lives

Entertainment. **Entertainment** is communication designed primarily to amuse, even if it serves other functions as well, which it almost always does. A television medical drama would be considered entertainment, even though it might educate a person about life in a hospital or the symptoms of a major illness. In fact, a major characteristic of all television programming, including entertainment programming, is to let people know what life outside their own world is like.[53]

Agenda Setting

Although explanations of powerful direct effects did not hold up under research scrutiny, people still had a hard time accepting that the news media and political campaigns had little or no effect on the public. **Agenda-setting theory** provides an alternative explanation that does not minimize the influence of the media on society.[54] This theory holds that issues that are portrayed as important in the news media become important to the public—that is, that the media set the agenda for public debate. If the media are not able to tell people what to think, as the direct effects model proposed, perhaps they can tell people what to think *about*. Agenda-setting theorists seek to determine whether the issues that are important to the media are also important to the public.[55] For example, the 2012 presidential election, and the Iowa caucuses in particular, received widespread discussion and attention in the United States following extensive coverage of campaigns and debates in 2012 and late 2011. The Project for Excellence in Journalism found that during the week of the Iowa first-in-the-nation caucuses, the election got 52 percent of all news space, overwhelming discussion of the economy and the ongoing conflict with Iran.[56]

The initial study of agenda setting was conducted in Chapel Hill, North Carolina, by Donald Shaw and Maxwell McCombs. The researchers found, among uncommitted voters in the 1968 presidential election, a strong relationship between the issues the press considered important and the issues the voters considered important. Since these voters had not already made up their minds about the upcoming election, their most likely source of cues, the researchers concluded, was the mass media. The study compared the content of the press and the attitudes of voters and found a strong correlation. Even though the researchers did not find evidence that the press persuaded people to change their opinions, they did find that the issues featured in the campaign and in the press were also the issues that voters felt were important.[57]

There are, however, some limits on the usefulness of the agenda-setting concept. If a story does not resonate with the public, neither the media nor the candidates will be able to make people care. For example, reports that Ronald and Nancy Reagan had conceived a child before they were married did not seem to do any damage to Reagan's image; nor was the Rev. Pat Robertson's campaign damaged by reports that the candidate and his wife had lied about the date of their wedding anniversary to hide the fact that their first child was conceived premaritally.

Uses and Gratifications Theory

Uses and gratifications theory turns the traditional way of looking at media effects on its head. Instead of looking at the audience as a sheep-like mass of receivers of messages, uses and gratifications theory views audience members as active receivers of information of their own choosing. Uses and gratifications theory is based on the following assumptions:

- Audience members are active receivers who have wants and needs. They then make decisions about media use based on those wants and needs. For example, in this approach, television doesn't *do things* to children, children *make use* of television.
- Media compete with many sources of gratification. I might watch television in the evening to relax. Television would be competing with reading a magazine, going for a walk, and playing with my son as alternative ways of relaxing.
- Audience members are aware of these choices and make them consciously.
- Our judgments about the value of various media uses must come from the audience's perspective.[58]

Questioning the Media

Can you name a story that has become an important issue primarily because it has received extensive coverage from the news media? What's an important issue that's been ignored or not covered enough by the news media? Considering both stories, why was one covered more extensively than the other?

The idea behind uses and gratification theory is that individuals are constantly seeking gratifications, and the media compete to provide them. Media scholar Arthur Asa

entertainment: Media communication intended primarily to amuse the audience.

agenda-setting theory: A theory of media effects that says that the media tell the public not what to think but rather what to think *about*—thus the terms of public discourse are set by what is covered in the media.

uses and gratifications theory: An approach to studying mass communication that looks at the reasons why audience members choose to spend time with the media in terms of the wants and needs of the audience members that are being fulfilled.

Berger says that among the gratifications that audience members might seek are to be amused, to experience the beautiful, to have shared experiences with others, to find models to imitate, and to believe in romantic love.[59] So someone who doesn't care about football might still watch a game on television and enjoy it because he wants to spend time with friends. Although he is consuming media, that's not the real point of his interaction with the television set.

Social Learning

At some point in your life, you've been told that experience is the best teacher. While experience may be a good teacher, it is also a harsh one, forcing us to suffer from our mistakes. Fortunately, we don't have to make all these mistakes ourselves, according to social psychologist Albert Bandura's **social learning theory**. Bandura writes, "If knowledge and skills could be acquired only by direct experience, the process of human development would be greatly retarded, not to mention exceedingly tedious and hazardous."[60] Instead, he says that we are able to learn by observing what others do and the consequences they face. Bandura says humans go through three steps to engage in social learning:

- We extract key information from situations we observe.
- We integrate these observations to create rules about how the world operates.
- We put these rules into practice to regulate our own behavior and predict the behaviors of others.

The media, by widening the information about the world that we are exposed to, play an important role in social learning. Think about a small boy who watches Batman defeat evil bad guys (EBGs) by physically fighting with them. Fighting with the EBGs proves to be a successful strategy and generally earns the superhero praise and the keys to Gotham City. Thus, while watching the animated show may not lead directly to the child engaging in violence, it could teach him that fighting is an effective way of solving problems and leads to social approval. He may then try out the practice by fighting with his sister, at which point he discovers it does not lead to social approval from his parents, and he stops the behavior. Or he might try it out by fighting with his friends and discover that it leads to his receiving respect. From this simplistic example, we can see how social learning theory can be applied to analyzing media. The content of the media can provide a large-scale source of content from which social learning can take place.[61] If the behavior being modeled is successful in achieving the person's goals, it may continue to be used. Think of the *Batman*-watching child who gains respect among his friends by fighting. If the behavior is unsuccessful in achieving results, the person may try other strategies. Think of the *Batman*-watching child who earns parental disapproval by fighting with his sister. He may instead sharpen his verbal or negotiating skills to gain the upper hand in conflicts with his sister.

Audio 2.3: Listen to Orson Welles's *War of the Worlds* broadcast.

Symbolic Interactionism

George Herbert Mead wrote back in 1934 that what holds us together as a culture is our common creation of society through our interactions based on language, or **symbolic interactionism**. We engage in symbolic interactions in which we continually attempt to arouse in others the feeling we have in ourselves by telling others how we feel.

SECRET 1 If our language is understood, we are able to communicate; if, on the other hand, we do not share common meanings, we will not be understood.[62] The mass media are by far the biggest source of shared meanings in our world. (Secret One—The media are essential components of our lives.)

If you think back to our discussion of the meaning of the yellow ribbon in Chapter 1, you can see how this works. We start with an arbitrary symbol: the yellow ribbon. We assign it meaning and then propagate that meaning through portrayal through the media. Eventually nearly everyone comes to have the same shared meaning of the looped ribbon, and the ribbon becomes a universal symbol of support—support for the troops, for disease sufferers, and for all kinds of social causes.

Sociologist W. I. Thomas provides us with one of the most quoted and understandable statements of symbolic interactionism: "If men define situations as real, they are real in their consequences."[63] If we ignore the outdated gender bias of the quote, there's a lot to analyze there. What Thomas is saying is that if people view a problem as being real, and behave as though a problem is real, it will have real consequences, even if the problem does not truly exist. Back in 1938, Orson Welles narrated a famous radio adaptation of H. G. Wells's *War of the Worlds*. The radio play was misinterpreted by some to be an actual news story, and there were many accounts at the time of people panicking and even committing suicide out of fear of the Martians invading New Jersey. Ever since then, broadcasters have been very careful to run extensive disclaimers on the air every time they run a *War of the Worlds*–style story, to make sure they don't panic their audience. There is also a widespread fear of powerful effects that the mass media can have on susceptible audience members. The only problem is that the research conducted at the time on the *War of the Worlds* panic was seriously flawed, and criticism of the research, which dates back to the 1940s, has largely been ignored, in part because the belief in the *War of the Worlds* effect is so strong. The truth is that there was far more perception of panic than

social learning theory: The process by which individuals learn by observing the behaviors of others and the consequences of those behaviors.

symbolic interactionism: The process by which individuals produce meaning through interaction based on socially agreed-upon symbols.

actual panic at the time. In summary, it doesn't matter much now whether the panic actually took place. What matters is that people believe that it did.[64]

Spiral of Silence 

German media scholar Elisabeth Noelle-Neumann, with her **spiral of silence**, has raised the question of why people become unwilling to express what they perceive to be a minority opinion. Noelle-Neumann became interested in this question in part from trying to find out why the Germans supported political positions that led to national defeat, humiliation, and ruin in the 1930s and 1940s, or why the French under German occupation were seemingly complacent as Jewish friends and neighbors were sent to concentration camps. Noelle-Neumann says that societies function on the basis of perceived consensus. We want to view ourselves as part of a majority and as holding the consensus opinion. Thus people will refrain from expressing opinions that they think will be at odds with those of their friends and neighbors, even though their neighbors might actually agree with them.[65]

So how do people receive the cues that indicate what popular public opinion is, so that they might agree with it? The media are important public institutions because they are often our best source of public opinion. Central to Noelle-Neumann's argument is that when people believe they are in the minority with their opinion, they will tend to stay quiet on the topic, thus feeding the sense that a particular opinion is held by a minority. Thus it becomes a death spiral of diversity of ideas, as more and more people come to believe that they hold a minority opinion.[66]

While the spiral of silence is a fascinating explanation of how public opinion functions, it is difficult to independently verify and prove whether it, in fact, works that way. Radicals will oftentimes speak up with unpopular opinions precisely because they are unpopular. And people who care deeply about an issue will speak out simply because they feel they are correct. As an example, think about the willingness of the country crossover group the Dixie Chicks to put themselves and their careers at risk by criticizing President George W. Bush in the early days of the Iraq war, at a time when they knew their views would be unpopular.[67] But a recent study from the Pew Research Internet Project found support for the spiral of silence when it comes to discussing controversial issues on social media. The researchers were attempting to find out whether social media such as Facebook or Twitter might make people more willing to express their opinions on political issues. The Pew study looked at how willing people were to express an opinion about Edward Snowden's release of classified documents as discussed in the opening vignette for this chapter. Not surprisingly, the study showed that Americans were split as to whether Snowden's leaks were a good idea and whether the surveillance policy was a good idea. But the study went on to show the following:

- People were less willing to discuss the Snowden case on social media than they were in person.
- People were more likely to share their opinions about Snowden if they thought their audience agreed with their point of view. This was true both in person and online.
- People who wouldn't share their opinion on Snowden in a face-to-face conversation were even less likely to share their opinion on social media.

Overall, the Pew study found a strong spiral of silence effect for controversial issues on social media.[68]

Media Logic

Media logic is an approach to analyzing the effects of mass media that was developed by David Altheide and Robert Snow. They argue that we live in a media world in which the dominant cultural forms are those defined by the media.[69] The media provide major types of content—news, sports, action, drama, comedy, and advertising—that follow standardized formats. When we turn on a television set, long before we can say what specific program is on, we can use format cues to tell what type of program it is, even if we've never seen it before. These standard formats become a lens through which we view our everyday life. For example, we may use the format of a sports broadcast to describe our presidential races and apply soap opera formats to describe ongoing political scandals. We also use these formats to shape our behaviors, especially when we want to get media attention. So when an organization has something important happening, its officials plan the event around the needs and schedules of the media they want to cover it.[70] Thus the event that the media covers is constructed especially to facilitate its being covered. Think about a group of protesters protesting the construction of a new power plant on a cold, rainy day. They huddle under their shelters with their signs until a news crew from a local television station shows up. Then the protesters come to life, marching and chanting for the benefit of the cameras. The mere fact that the cameras are there changes what's happening.

Cultivation Analysis

George Gerbner (1919–2005), the best-known researcher of television violence, did not believe televised violence has direct effects on people's behavior, but he was deeply concerned about its effect on society as a whole.[71] Gerbner

---

spiral of silence: A theory that suggests that people want to see themselves as holding a majority opinion and will therefore remain silent if they perceive that they hold a minority opinion. This tends to make the minority opinion appear to be less prevalent than it is.

media logic: An approach to studying the mass media that says the forms the media use to present the world become the forms we use to perceive the world and to create media messages.

Web 2.8: Read more about the Pew report on social media and the spiral of silence.

Alexandra Wyman/WireImage/Getty Images

Filmmaker Eli Roth, left, with Marilyn Manson, has drawn extensive criticism for the extreme torture violence in his *Hostel* horror film series.

developed an alternative to traditional message effects research called **cultivation analysis**. His argument was that watching large amounts of television cultivates a distinct view of the world that is sharply at odds with reality.[72]

Over the years, Gerbner and his colleagues analyzed thousands of network television programs for the themes they presented and the level of violence they included. In a series of studies beginning in 1967, Gerbner's team found high levels of violence on television. They defined violence as "the overt expression of force intended to hurt or kill."[73]

Network officials have been openly critical of Gerbner, saying that his studies weren't representative of television as a whole and that his definition of violence is not useful because it does not discriminate between the fantasy violence of a Road Runner cartoon and the more graphic gore of a *Saw* or *Hostel* movie.

Gerbner compared the rate of violence on television to the rate of it occurring in the real world. He concluded that television cultivates a view of the world that is much more violent than the world we live in. The nature of the violence is different as well, with most television violence occurring between strangers rather than between family members, as does real-life violence. Gerbner said that, because of this, people who watch a great deal of television perceive the world differently than do light viewers. Heavy television viewing cultivates a response that Gerbner calls the **mean world syndrome**. In an appearance before Congress, Gerbner testified:

> The most general and prevalent association with television viewing is a heightened sense of living in a "mean world" of violence and danger. Fearful people are more dependent, more easily manipulated and controlled, more susceptible to deceptively simple, strong, tough measures and hard-line postures. . . . They may accept and even welcome repression if it promises to relieve their insecurities. That is the deeper problem of violence-laden television.[74]

The effect of violent television, Gerbner argued, is not that it will program children to be violent; instead, the real harm is more complex:

- Violent programming pushes aside other ways of portraying conflict.
- Violent programming deprives viewers of other choices.
- Violent programming facilitates the victim mentality.
- Violent programming discourages production of alternative programming.[75]

Video 2.4: Watch ads from a variety of recent political campaigns.

Media, Politics, and Society

Our understanding of the media and the campaign process has evolved over the past hundred years. In the early decades of the twentieth century, scholars and critics worried that voters might be manipulated and controlled by campaign messages sent through the media, especially those that might be sent subliminally. This understanding changed in the 1940s and 1950s as scholars came to suspect that media effects might in fact be selective and indirect. Currently it is believed that an interactional relationship exists among politicians, the press, and the public in which each influences the others.

How Do Political Campaigns Affect Voters?

If, as *The People's Choice* study indicates, campaigns do not have strong direct effects on voters, what are candidates trying to accomplish with their campaigns? They may be trying to directly persuade voters with the content of the messages, but more likely they are trying to shape the campaign

cultivation analysis: An approach to analyzing the effects of television viewing that argues that watching significant amounts of television alters the way an individual views the nature of the surrounding world.

mean world syndrome: The perception of many heavy television watchers of violent programs that the world is a more dangerous and violent place than facts and statistics bear out.

MEDIA TRANSFORMATIONS

Cultivation Theory

By and large, most people who aren't media scholars would be hard pressed to name a single media theorist who isn't Marshall McLuhan. But the one possible exception would be George Gerbner because of his cultivation theory. Dr. Gerbner testified before Congress about televised violence in October 1981, and his cultivation theory is one of the top three cited theoretical approaches in communication research.

As you read in the section on cultivation analysis, one of the biggest areas of concern about media effects is how violence on television affects viewers, especially children. George Gerbner was one of the nation's leading researchers on televised violence. Gerbner explained what he considered to be major misconceptions about the effects of televised violence and what his research suggested the real effects were. He argued that watching large amounts of television cultivates a distinct view of the world that is at odds with reality.

Gerbner argued that, because of televised violence, heavy television viewers are more likely to

- overestimate their chances of experiencing violence,
- believe that their neighborhoods are unsafe,
- state that fear of crime is a very serious personal problem, and
- assume that the crime rate is rising, regardless of the actual crime rate.[76]

While Gerbner's developmental work on cultivation theory was done in the 1960s, '70s, and '80s back when most people had access to only three or four broadcast cable channels, it has continued to interest both audience members and scholars into the era of high definition and hundreds of cable channels.

Dr. Patrick E. Jamieson and Dr. Dan Romer at the University of Pennsylvania took a fresh look in 2014 at Gerbner's work to see how it would hold up to an examination of twenty-five years of data

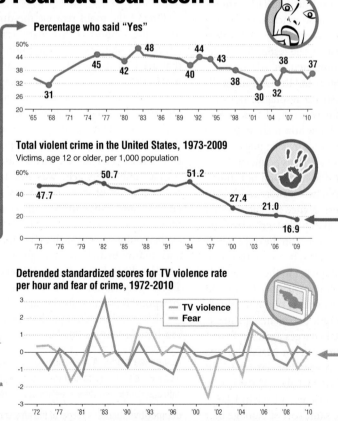

Nothing To Fear but Fear Itself?

● **As a way of measuring** the American public's perception of the threat of violence, in 1965 **Gallup** began asking Americans:

"Is there any area near where you live—that is, within a mile—where you would be afraid to walk alone at night?"

Responses show that the fear of violence increased over time until 1982. Perceptions then decreased to 30% in 2001, but have since gone back up to 37%.

Percentage who said "Yes"

50%, 44, 38, 32, 26, 20

31, 45, 42, 48, 40, 44, 43, 38, 30, 32, 38, 37

'65 '68 '71 '74 '77 '80 '83 '86 '89 '92 '95 '98 '01 '04 '07 '10

Total violent crime in the United States, 1973-2009

Victims, age 12 or older, per 1,000 population

60%, 40, 20, 0

47.7, 50.7, 51.2, 27.4, 21.0, 16.9

'73 '76 '79 '82 '85 '88 '91 '94 '97 '00 '03 '06 '09

Detrended standardized scores for TV violence rate per hour and fear of crime, 1972-2010

3, 2, 1, 0, -1, -2, -3

TV violence

Fear

'72 '77 '81 '83 '90 '93 '96 '00 '02 '04 '06 '08 '10

● **Yet over roughly the same period**, the actual rate of violent crime has dropped dramatically, falling from a high in 1994 of 51.2 victims per 1,000 to just 16.9 in 2009.

What explains the fact that the fear of violence doesn't rise and fall with the actual rate of violence?

● **Jamieson and Romer's** study measured the number of violent sequences per TV hour over roughly the same time frame, and their findings show that while the amount of violent content on television did not affect people's estimations of how dangerous the world around them was, it did make people more afraid of violence. The bottom graph here shows how instances of TV violence correlate to fear, using standardized scores that reflect how far above or below the overall average the scores are.

Jamieson and Romer give a more nuanced understanding of how cultivation may work. In their conclusion, they go back to one of Gerbner's chief concerns: that increasing amounts of televised violence could lead to increased fear, which could lead to people being supportive of authoritarian governance.

Sources: Patrick E. Jamieson and Daniel Romer, "Violence in Popular U.S. Prime Time TV Dramas and the Cultivation of Fear: A Time Series Analysis," Media and Communication (2014) 2.2: 31-41.

http://repository.upenn.edu/cgi/viewcontent.cgi?article=1365&context=asc_papers; Gallup,

http://www.gallup.com/poll/144272/nearly-americans-fear-walking-alone-night.aspx

(Continued)

(Continued)

about televised violence and people's fear of crime. Jamieson and Romer looked at 475 hours of television programming and Gallup interviews with more than 27,000 people. In their study, they found that while increased violent content on television did not change people's estimations of how dangerous the world around them was, it did make people more afraid of violence.[77]

Alyssa Rosenberg, writing for the Act Four blog at the *Washington Post*, says that shows like NBC's *Law & Order: Special Victims Unit* "create intense emotional bonds between viewers and on-screen characters," and Dr. Romer told her that shows like this might have distinctive effects: "Women report more fear of crime on surveys and the source of discrepancy is not clear. . . . Men are more likely to be victims of murder but women are more likely to be victims in domestic disputes and of course in rapes. So, these sorts of situations may loom larger in women's minds. Gerbner argued that movies and TV tend to show women as victims more than men, and this may also play a role."[78]

Media Transformations Questions

- **WHAT** is cultivation theory, and why has it remained so popular over the years?
- According to Gerbner, **WHAT** are the effects of television violence?
- **HOW** has the media world changed since Gerbner developed cultivation theory?
- **HOW** did reading about Gerbner's research and the follow-up to it by Jamieson and Romer change your understanding of the effects of media violence?

Web 2.9: Revisiting Dr. Gerbner and TV violence.

in more subtle ways. These are interactional models that say that the interaction among voters, the media, and the campaigns that are triggered by the ads are more important than any direct persuasion of voters. Here are two examples:

The **resonance model** says that the candidate's success depends in part on how well his or her basic message resonates with voters' preexisting political feelings. Thus, the candidate who does the best job of sending out messages that connect with target voters is the one most likely to win. The communication goal for the campaign is not so much to get people to change their minds as it is to get voters to believe that they share viewpoints with the candidate.[79] The resonance model was clearly used in the 2008 campaign in ads by both Democratic candidate Barack Obama and Republican candidate John McCain. Obama got strong resonance out of a commercial that claimed McCain was out of touch with ordinary people because he didn't know how many houses he owned. McCain got a similar resonance by charging Obama with being more of a celebrity than a serious politician.

The **competitive model** looks at the campaign not in isolation but as a competition between two or more candidates for the hearts and minds of voters. Hence the success of a campaign message, such as a speech that criticizes the candidate's opponent, depends as much on the opponent's reaction as it does on the message itself. Voter response can also depend on how the media react to the message. If the message attracts media attention, it may be played repeatedly on news broadcasts, as well as on political talk shows.[80] During the 2008 Democratic presidential primary, candidate Hillary Clinton leveled charges against Obama that he had lifted political rhetoric from Massachusetts governor Deval Patrick. Similar charges that Sen. Joe Biden had lifted a speech from the British Labor Party leader helped sink his campaign for the presidency back in 1988.[81]

But Obama did not suffer the same sort of damage that Biden did. Why not? First, Obama and Governor Patrick are friends, they share the same political adviser, and they have long shared a similar message. Second, Patrick did not object to the use of his words. Finally, Obama did not react particularly defensively to the charges of plagiarism. So, according to the competitive model, the public's direct reaction to the charges didn't matter as much as how the public reacted to Obama's reaction to the charges.

Media and Political Bias

One of the main reasons the direct effects model still has some support is that many critics believe the media affect the public's political opinions by presenting reports that are biased toward a particular candidate or political party. But, as we discuss in Chapter 6, in holding up detached, factual, objective journalism as an ideal for reporting, the press was making a commercial decision, not a moral one. During the penny press era of the 1830s to the 1860s, newspapers tried to appeal to the broadest possible audience. The best way to attract a large number of people, publishers felt, was not to take an identifiable political point of view, as had newspapers of the colonial era. The alternative to this supposedly objective style is a more opinionated form of reporting that takes on an explicit point of view, such as that found in *Time*, *Newsweek*, and many British or European newspapers, such as London's liberal *Guardian* or conservative (Tory) *Telegraph*. These publications have a clearly understood political viewpoint that is designed to appeal to a specific audience.[82]

This opinionated style has also been adopted by the brash cable channel Fox News, which rejects the traditional

resonance model: A model of political campaign effects that attributes a candidate's success to how well his or her basic message resonates with and reinforces voters' preexisting political feelings.

competitive model: A model of the effects of a political campaign that looks at the campaign as a competition for the hearts and minds of voters.

neutral style of CNN and the major broadcast networks.[83] Fox News commentator Bill O'Reilly says that part of his network's popularity comes from its willingness to think about what audience members want. "Unless your package is meaningful to the viewer, they're gone," he says. "The networks—and I include CNN in this—haven't figured that one out yet."[84] Erik Sorenson, former president of the MSNBC cable news channel, suggests that there is nothing wrong with taking a particular point of view. "I think a lot of people are beginning to ask, 'Is there something phony about pretending to be objective and reading off a teleprompter in the twenty-first century?'"[85] There can be no question that airing partisan news and commentary is a successful business strategy. Since 2002, Fox News has been the top-rated twenty-four-hour news network with its conservative point of view, attracting approximately 1.5 million prime-time viewers during the second quarter of 2014. MSNBC has had the second-largest audience, an average of 570,000 prime-time viewers, with its slate of liberal/progressive hosts. CNN, which takes a more neutral stand, is in third place with an average of 459,000 prime-time viewers. The audiences for all three of the major cable news networks have declined since the presidential election year of 2008, falling by an average of 13 to 16 percent, depending on the measure used.[86]

DON EMMERT/AFP/Getty Images

During the 2012 Republican presidential primary campaign, candidates (left to right) Ron Paul, Rick Santorum, Mitt Romney, and Newt Gingrich debated in Mesa, Arizona. The goal of the series of debates was not so much for the candidates to explain their viewpoints as it was an opportunity for them to show how they could interact and score points off each other and the moderators.

Liberal Versus Conservative Bias. Leaving aside the news media that take an explicit political viewpoint, is there a predictable bias in the American news media? Critics on both the right and the left maintain that there is either a liberal or a conservative bias in the media's coverage of the news. Journalist and author Richard Reeves notes that for each example of a bias in one direction, there is an example of bias in the opposite direction. For instance, Cokie Roberts at ABC News is the daughter of two Democratic members of Congress, but Diane Sawyer, anchor of ABC's *World News*, was on Republican president Richard Nixon's staff.[87] Although individuals and individual programs in the media clearly hold differing views about the news, does the argument of an overall bias within the news media hold up to scrutiny?

Liberals and conservatives trade arguments about media bias. Conservatives point out that there are disproportionate numbers of liberals working as reporters. Liberals argue that large corporations own the media and that they slant the news in favor of industry and business. The argument that there is a liberal bias in the news media often focuses on charges that reporters are more liberal than the public at large. According to the study *The American Journalist in the 21st Century*, which surveyed more than 1,150 journalists, 40 percent of journalists described themselves as having views from the left, or liberal, side of the political spectrum; 33 percent described themselves as "middle of the roaders"; and 25 percent described themselves as having views from the right, or conservative, side.[88] The study concluded that journalists were more likely to hold a range of liberal views than the public at large, especially on social issues.

The explanation for this finding may be that people who go into journalism tend to be concerned about injustices within society, a personality type that could tend toward liberal or progressive political views. Some observers argue that journalists have a "liberal and cosmopolitan" approach to the world, and this shapes journalistic views of good and bad.[89] A widely reported study in 2007 said that journalists who made political contributions were more likely to give to Democrats than Republicans. What wasn't reported nearly as often was that very few journalists made political contributions. In fact, the study found that less than two-tenths of 1 percent of all journalists made political contributions.[90] On the other hand, if one looks at the editorial pages of the major newspapers, a somewhat different bias might appear.

SECRET 6 Between 1948 and 1990, 78 percent of newspaper presidential endorsements were for Republicans, but Republican candidates for president received 51 percent of the popular vote, which would tend to suggest that the editorial pages of newspapers are somewhat more conservative than the public at large.[91] So when you hear charges of media bias being thrown about, remember Secret Six—Activism and analysis are not the same thing.

TEST YOUR MEDIA LITERACY

Bias in the News

No matter what the news media do, they are likely to be charged with being biased. How do critics know this bias exists? They just have to look at the news. It's perfectly obvious, "they" say. But a pair of research studies found that if you examine a news story about a partisan issue, readers or viewers from both sides will claim that it is biased against their point of view. The studies showed that as long as the story tried to present a nuanced view that presented multiple sides of an issue—that is, what journalists would call an unbiased view—partisans on either side of the issue viewed the story as hopelessly biased. On the other hand, if the story had a strong point of view—that is, it *was* biased—people tended to perceive it as less biased.[1]

WHO are the sources?

Who conducted the two studies written about in the story? Where do they work? What are their fields of study?

WHAT are they saying?

How do partisans react to stories that are supposedly neutral (or unbiased)? How do neutral observers react? How do members of the two groups react to stories that have an explicit point of view? How would you categorize this research in terms of being message, medium, ownership, or audience based? Can you categorize the type of theory base the researchers were using?

WHAT evidence exists?

How did the two researchers reach their conclusions? How did they conduct their research?

WHAT do you and your classmates think about media bias?

What stories do you or your classmates see as being biased? Do you ever think that stories are biased in your favor? How do you feel when a story is trying to be balanced by presenting information you disagree with? In light of these studies, how do you think the news media should respond to charges of being biased? Do you prefer neutral-style reporting or news with an explicit point of view? Why?

1. Shankar Vedantam, "Two Views of the Same News Find Opposite Biases," *Washington Post*, July 24, 2006, A02.

Web 2.10: Read the linked research study on bias in the news.

In a speech to college students, Karl Rove, former top adviser to President George W. Bush and a major Republican strategist, summed up the issue by saying that while he thinks the press is generally liberal,

> I think it's less liberal than it is oppositional. . . . Reporters now see their role less as discovering facts and fair-mindedly reporting the truth and more as being put on earth to afflict the comfortable, to be a constant thorn of those in power, whether they are Republican or Democrat.[92]

Gans's Basic Journalistic Values. There is more to the bias argument than the liberal-versus-conservative issue. For example, some observers charge that the media have a bias toward attractiveness or charisma. There can also be a bias toward making money or attracting an audience. Political scientist and media scholar Doris Graber argues that when it comes to selecting stories for coverage, the strongest bias is for those that will have the greatest appeal to the publication's or program's audience.[93]

Rather than looking for examples of bias in the news, media sociologist Herbert Gans set out to find the actual values exhibited within the stories themselves. He asked what the values—the biases—of journalism were. To find the answer, he studied the content of the CBS and NBC news programs, *Time* magazine, and *Newsweek*.

Gans found eight enduring values in the stories he studied: ethnocentrism, altruistic democracy, responsible capitalism, small-town pastoralism, individualism, moderatism, social order, and leadership. These values were not stated explicitly; rather, they emerged from what was presented as being good and normal and what was presented as bad.[94] Let's look briefly at each of Gans's values:

1. *Ethnocentrism* is the idea that your own country and culture are better than all others. This shows up in the U.S. media in stories that compare other countries' values to American values. To the degree that other countries live up to American ideals, they are good; if they are different, they are bad. Therefore, enemies of the United States are presented as evil because they don't conform to our values. Stories can be critical of the United States, but they are criticizing deviance from basic American values, not those values themselves.

2. *Altruistic democracy* is the idea that politicians should serve the public good, not their own interests. This leads to stories that are critical of corrupt politicians. By the

same token, citizens, as voters, have the same obligation to work for the public good and not for selfish interests. Special interest groups and lobbyists are suspect because they are not working for the common good. This was perhaps best illustrated by the Watergate hearings in the 1970s, which revealed the corrupt behavior that occurred in the White House so that President Richard Nixon could stay in power. President Bill Clinton was criticized for his affair with Monica Lewinsky in part because he was serving his own interests rather than working for the good of the American public.

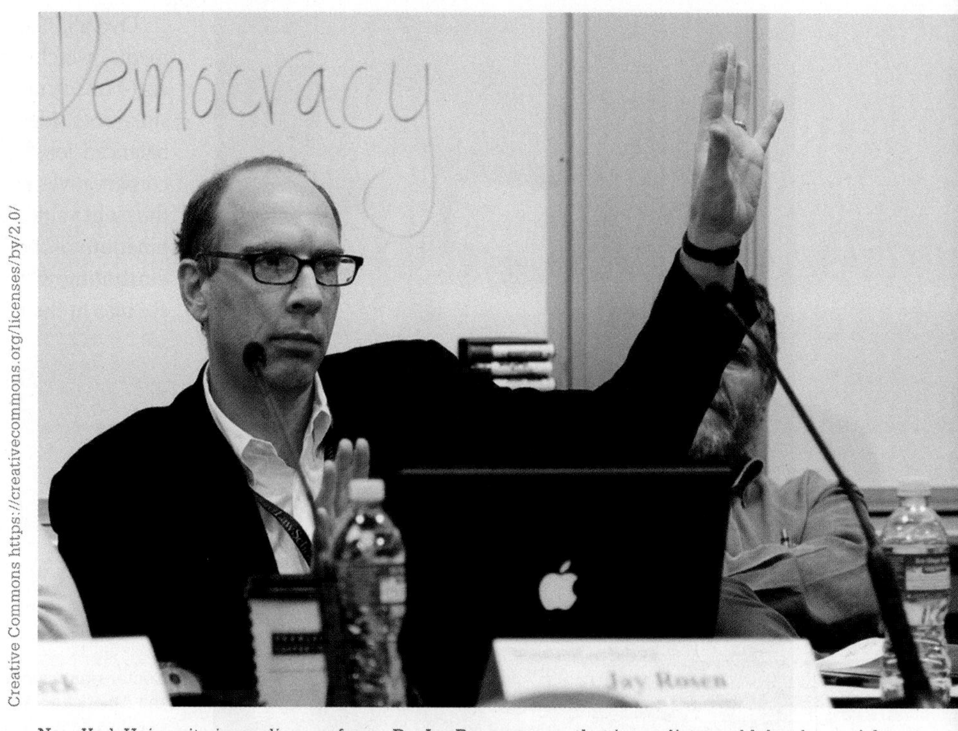

New York University journalism professor Dr. Jay Rosen argues that journalists could do a better job of reporting the news if they worked at covering multiple sides of issues rather than "both" sides. His arguments build on those of Dr. Herbert Gans on the values of the news media. The link below is to a conversation between Drs. Rosen and Gans.

3. *Responsible capitalism* is the idea that open competition among businesses will create a better, more prosperous world for everyone. But by the same token, businesses must be responsible and not seek excess profits. The same is true of labor unions. Hence the news media tend to be harsh in their coverage of greed and deception by big businesses, yet they still tend to praise people who develop and grow companies. This is why there has been so much negative coverage of banking and investment companies following the stock market crash and recession in the late 2000s.

4. *Small-town pastoralism* is nostalgia for the old-fashioned, rural community. The agricultural community is where all goodness is rooted, while big cities are dangerous places that suffer from numerous social problems. Suburbs, where many people live, tend to be overlooked entirely.

5. *Individualism* is the constant quest to identify the one person who makes a difference. People like the notion that one person can make a difference, that we are not all cogs in a giant machine. Reporters like to use a single person as a symbol. That explains in part why journalists focused on the murder of Neda Agha-Soltan during protests about the contested 2009 Iranian elections. Instead of trying to talk about the wide range of people involved in the protests, they used Agha-Soltan as a symbol to represent all the protesters.[95]

6. *Moderatism* is the value of moderation in all things. Extremists on both the left and the right are criticized. Although the media attempt to present a balance of opinions, they tend to report on views that are mildly to the left and right of center. One of the strongest criticisms the media can make is referring to an individual as an extremist.

7. The value of *social order* is seen primarily in the coverage of disorder. When journalists cover stories that involve disorder, such as protests, floods, disasters, or riots, the focus of the story tends to be on the restoration of order. This was one of the biggest issues in the media's coverage of the floods following Hurricane Katrina. The social order was in question for months following the storm, and the press focused heavily on how that order might be restored.[96]

8. Finally, the media value *leadership*. The media tend to look at the actions of leaders, whereas the actions of lower-level bureaucrats—which may well be more important—are ignored. This is in some ways an extension of the bias toward individualism, the difference one person can make.

Questioning the Media

Take a look at a recent news story from a major American news outlet. How many of Gans's news values can you find illustrated in it? Do you think Gans's eight news values still apply to what is being covered by American media? Why or why not?

Web 2.11: Read an interview with Herbert Gans.

Overall, Gans argues that there is reformist bias to the media, which tend to advocate "honest, meritocratic, and anti-bureaucratic government."[97] Journalists like to argue that since both sides criticize the press, they must be doing a good, balanced job.[98] Perhaps a better explanation for why both conservatives and liberals charge the media with bias is that the eight values Gans found within the media reflect a combination of both liberal and conservative values—again illustrating why people holding a particular viewpoint will see bias in the media's attempt to be neutral and balanced.

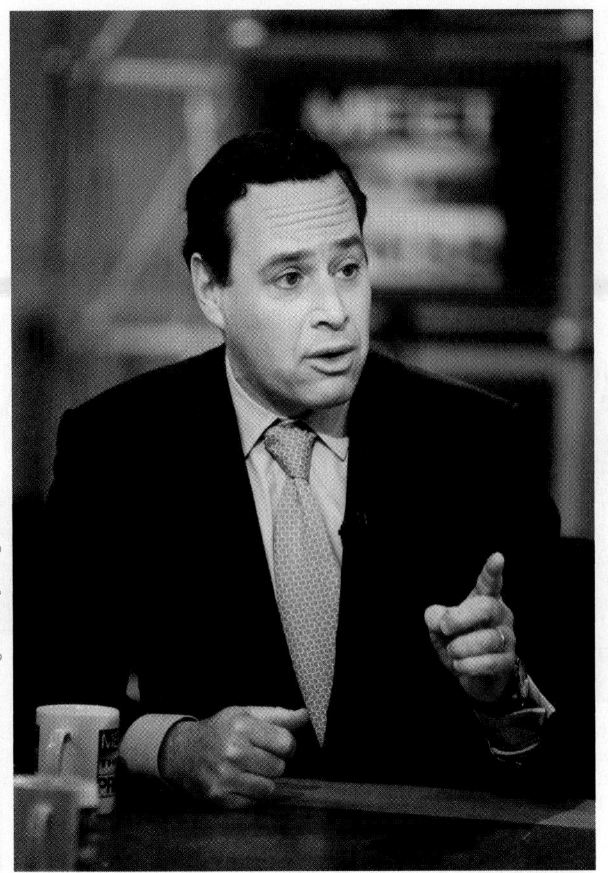

Brendan Smialowski / Stringer/Getty Images

Center-right media commentator David Frum resigned from the American Public Media business radio show *Marketplace* because he felt he could no longer reliably represent the views of mainstream conservatives. In general, the commentators in American media try to represent the mainstream liberal or conservative point of view. Very few represent an intermediate viewpoint. You can read more about why Frum resigned at www.ralphehanson.com/2011/10/12/david-frum-the-problem-with-balanced-commentary/.

Chapter SUMMARY

With the rise of mass society and the rapid growth of the mass media starting in the nineteenth century, the public, media critics, and scholars have raised questions about the effects various media might have on society and individuals. These effects were viewed initially as being strong, direct, and relatively uniform on the population as a whole. After World War I, critics were concerned that media-oriented political campaigns could have powerful direct effects on voters. This view, though still widespread, was largely discredited by voter studies conducted in the 1940s and 1950s. These studies found that the voters with the strongest political opinions were those most likely to pay attention to a campaign and hence were least likely to be affected by it. More recently, research has expanded to move beyond looking just at the effects that media and media content have on individuals and society to examinations of how living in a world with all-pervasive media changes the nature of our interactions and culture.

Understanding the effects of media on individuals and society requires that we examine the messages being sent, the medium transmitting these messages, the owners of the media, and the audience members themselves. The effects can be cognitive, attitudinal, behavioral, or psychological.

Media effects can also be examined in terms of a number of theoretical approaches, including functional analysis, agenda setting, uses and gratifications, social learning, symbolic interactionism, spiral of silence, media logic, and cultivation analysis.

Our understanding of the relationship among politicians, the press, and the public has evolved over the past half century. Recent studies have supported interactional approaches to understanding campaign effects, including the resonance and competitive models.

Many people claim that the media are biased toward one political view or another. Conservative critics argue that there is a liberal bias arising from the tendency of reporters to be more liberal than the public at large. The liberals' counterargument is that the press has a conservative bias because most media outlets are owned by giant corporations that hold pro-business views. Finally, some critics argue that the media hold a combination of values that straddle the boundary between slightly left and slightly right of center. The press in the United States began as partisan during the colonial period but adopted a detached, factual, objective style in the 1830s to appeal to a broader audience.

Keep up-to-date with content from the author's blog.

Take the chapter quiz.

Key TERMS

Concept REVIEW

Rise of mass society and mass communication
Message effects
Medium effects
Ownership effects
Active audience effects
Conceptions of media bias

Student STUDY SITE

Sharpen your skills with SAGE edge at **edge.sagepub.com/hanson5e**

SAGE edge for Students provides a personalized approach to help you accomplish your coursework goals in an easy-to-use learning environment.

The Media Business

Consolidation, Globalization, and the Long Tail

chapter

3

https://www.kickstarter.com/projects/spikelee/the-newestt-hottest-spike-lee-joint

Famed filmmaker Spike Lee turned to the crowdfunding site Kickstarter to finance his decidedly non-commerical movie Da Sweet Blood of Jesus. Lee descibed the movie as being about people who are "addicted to blood" but are not vampires.

Web Pix/Alamy

Famed African American filmmaker Spike Lee has a long record of producing independently minded films from his seminal movie *Do the Right Thing* to his biopic on Malcolm X, though he's also known for more commercial fare, like his thriller *Inside Man* starring Denzel Washington, Clive Owen, and Jodie Foster.

But during 2013 and 2014, he made an extremely low-budget, truly independent film for a little more than $1.25 million financed by more than 5,000 backers from the crowd-funding Web site Kickstarter.[1] *Da Sweet Blood of Jesus*, a movie Lee describes as a "bloody, funny, sexy movie" about people who are "addicted to blood" who are not vampires, was shot in 16 days in Brooklyn and Martha's Vineyard with a cast of unknowns.[2] Forrest Wickman, a movie reviewer for the Web site *Slate*, describes the movie as "veering wildly between pulpy exploitation . . . and art-house filmmaking," and notes that it is unlike anything that would ever get conventional funding.[3]

To get funding though Kickstarter, filmmakers (like everyone else seeking Kickstarter funding) put together a video pitch along with written details about their qualifications and the film they intend to make. Potential contributors pledge to fund projects they find interesting, but they only get charged if the project reaches the financial goal the creator set. If the project doesn't reach its funding goal, no money is exchanged.[4] Assuming the project does reach its goal and gets funded, the people who pledge do not get an investment in the movie as they might with conventional movie financing. Instead, they get the satisfaction of supporting the project and very often some kind of reward, such as a copy of the film or book produced by the project (though in the case of Spike Lee's film, the reward at the $10,000 level was getting to sit courtside with Lee at a Knicks NBA game).

At the time it was funded in August 2013, *Da Sweet Blood of Jesus* was the third largest movie project to be funded through Kickstarter (raising approximately $1.4 million), following behind a movie version of the cult TV series *Veronica Mars* ($5.7 million) and a Zach Braff film that raised $3.1 million.[5] Lee, along with Braff (a popular actor and the director of the film *Garden State*), has received criticism for funding his project through Kickstarter when he had other options available to him, with the presumption that the funding that went to him could have gone to other, more needy filmmakers.[6] The founders of Kickstarter, however, responded through their blog to defend the celebrity filmmakers:

LEARNING OBJECTIVES

After studying this chapter, you will be able to:

1. Describe how the media developed as a private industry in the United States from the colonial period to the present day.
2. Summarize how control of the media industry has changed from the 1950s to the present day.
3. Define what is meant by "media synergy" and illustrate it with at least three examples.
4. Explain why Apple, Google, and other tech companies may also be considered leading media companies.
5. Describe the concept of long-tail media and its implications for the future of the media industry.
6. Identify six groups that influence how the media behave and what content they present.

> “I’ve been doing KICKSTARTER before there was KICKSTARTER, there was no Internet.”
>
> —Spike Lee

Almost five million people have backed a project on Kickstarter, and more than a million have backed two or more projects. These repeat backers are responsible for 59% of the total money pledged to Kickstarter projects—a whopping $444 million. On average, 2,130 people a day have become new repeat backers this year. This is huge! Future creators will benefit from more and more people using Kickstarter.[7]

In his Kickstarter proposal, Lee says that using nontraditional funding to finance his films is nothing new to him:

> I’m an Indie Filmmaker and I will always be an Indie Filmmaker. Indie Filmmakers are always in search of financing because their work, their vision sometimes does not coincide with Studio Pictures. But I do put my own money in my films. I self-financed RED HOOK SUMMER. My fee for MALCOLM X was put back into the budget. The truth is I’ve been doing KICKSTARTER before there was KICKSTARTER, there was no Internet. Social Media was writing letters, making phone calls, beating the bushes. I’m now using TECHNOLOGY with what I’ve been doing.[8]

(Lee is also making the point of **SECRET 4** Nothing’s new: Everything that happened in the past will happen again.)

Kickstarter began in April 2009 and as of May 2014 had funded more than 60,000 projects. (Full disclosure: Your author has helped fund several music and Web comic projects through Kickstarter.)

Timeline

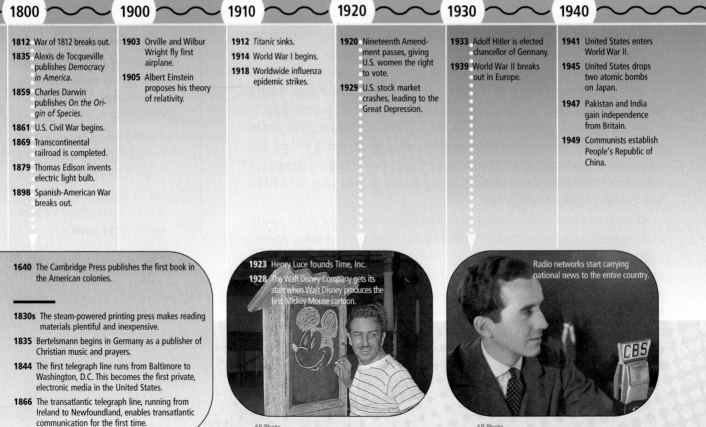

1800

1812 War of 1812 breaks out.
1835 Alexis de Tocqueville publishes *Democracy in America*.
1859 Charles Darwin publishes *On the Origin of Species*.
1861 U.S. Civil War begins.
1869 Transcontinental railroad is completed.
1879 Thomas Edison invents electric light bulb.
1898 Spanish-American War breaks out.

1900

1903 Orville and Wilbur Wright fly first airplane.
1905 Albert Einstein proposes his theory of relativity.

1910

1912 *Titanic* sinks.
1914 World War I begins.
1918 Worldwide influenza epidemic strikes.

1920

1920 Nineteenth Amendment passes, giving U.S. women the right to vote.
1929 U.S. stock market crashes, leading to the Great Depression.

1930

1933 Adolf Hitler is elected chancellor of Germany.
1939 World War II breaks out in Europe.

1940

1941 United States enters World War II.
1945 United States drops two atomic bombs on Japan.
1947 Pakistan and India gain independence from Britain.
1949 Communists establish People’s Republic of China.

1640 The Cambridge Press publishes the first book in the American colonies.

1830s The steam-powered printing press makes reading materials plentiful and inexpensive.
1835 Bertelsmann begins in Germany as a publisher of Christian music and prayers.
1844 The first telegraph line runs from Baltimore to Washington, D.C. This becomes the first private, electronic media in the United States.
1866 The transatlantic telegraph line, running from Ireland to Newfoundland, enables transatlantic communication for the first time.

1923 Henry Luce founds Time, Inc.
1928 The Walt Disney Company gets its start when Walt Disney produces the first Mickey Mouse cartoon.

AP Photo

Radio networks start carrying national news to the entire country.

AP Photo

Of the more than 14,000 film and video projects that have been funded as of the summer of 2014, 70 have been screened at Sundance, and more than 100 have been screened at the SXSW festival in Austin, Texas.[9]

Beyond being a new source of funding for filmmakers, Kickstarter represents a new way of the movie industry looking at the Internet and the people who inhabit it. As *New York Times* media blogger David Carr points out, the legacy movie industry, represented through the Motion Picture Association of America and the National Association of Theatre Owners, sees the online world as a scary place where movie pirates reside, while independent filmmakers view it as an exciting source of support to make movies Hollywood isn't interested in making. And this makes Kickstarter an example of both *Secret Five*—New media are always scary—and *Secret Two*—There are no mainstream media.

In recent years, ownership of newspapers, book and magazine publishers, recording labels, movie companies, and Internet companies has become increasingly concentrated, moving from the hands of the families that started them into the hands of a small number of very large corporations. However, entrepreneurs are able to use digital technologies to create new media that can turn upside-down Big Media's focus on using traditional tools to deliver media using the same techniques they have for years. Instead of looking at "the media" as a unified whole, we look at who owns and controls the varied mass media and how new channels are emerging rapidly. ■

Video 3.1: Learn more about how even big-name filmmakers are using crowdfunding to finance their movies.

1950

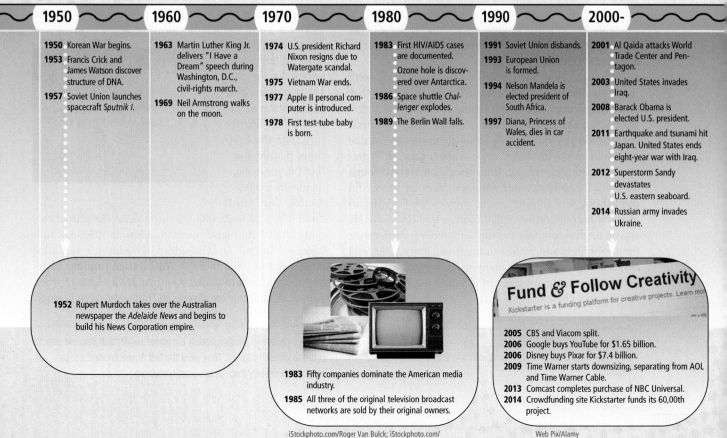

- **1950** Korean War begins.
- **1953** Francis Crick and James Watson discover structure of DNA.
- **1957** Soviet Union launches spacecraft *Sputnik I*.

1960

- **1963** Martin Luther King Jr. delivers "I Have a Dream" speech during Washington, D.C., civil-rights march.
- **1969** Neil Armstrong walks on the moon.

1970

- **1974** U.S. president Richard Nixon resigns due to Watergate scandal.
- **1975** Vietnam War ends.
- **1977** Apple II personal computer is introduced.
- **1978** First test-tube baby is born.

1980

- **1983** First HIV/AIDS cases are documented.
  Ozone hole is discovered over Antarctica.
- **1986** Space shuttle *Challenger* explodes.
- **1989** The Berlin Wall falls.

1990

- **1991** Soviet Union disbands.
- **1993** European Union is formed.
- **1994** Nelson Mandela is elected president of South Africa.
- **1997** Diana, Princess of Wales, dies in car accident.

2000-

- **2001** Al Qaida attacks World Trade Center and Pentagon.
- **2003** United States invades Iraq.
- **2008** Barack Obama is elected U.S. president.
- **2011** Earthquake and tsunami hit Japan. United States ends eight-year war with Iraq.
- **2012** Superstorm Sandy devastates U.S. eastern seaboard.
- **2014** Russian army invades Ukraine.

1952 Rupert Murdoch takes over the Australian newspaper the *Adelaide News* and begins to build his News Corporation empire.

1983 Fifty companies dominate the American media industry.
1985 All three of the original television broadcast networks are sold by their original owners.

iStockphoto.com/Roger Van Bulck; iStockphoto.com/Gino Santa Maria; iStockphoto.com/Pali Rao

Fund & Follow Creativity
Kickstarter is a funding platform for creative projects.

2005 CBS and Viacom split.
2006 Google buys YouTube for $1.65 billion.
2006 Disney buys Pixar for $7.4 billion.
2009 Time Warner starts downsizing, separating from AOL and Time Warner Cable.
2013 Comcast completes purchase of NBC Universal.
2014 Crowdfunding site Kickstarter funds its 60,00th project.

Web Pix/Alamy

The Development of the Media Business in the United States

The U.S. media are unique in the world in that they are almost entirely privately owned and operated for profit. Even the broadcasting industry, which in most countries is tightly controlled by the government, is run by private businesses.[10]

A Tradition of Private Ownership

The media in the United States have a long tradition of private ownership that dates back to the 1640s. The media industry was among the first in the American colonies: The first printing press came to the Massachusetts Bay Colony in 1638. It was used to establish the Cambridge press, publisher of *The Whole Booke of Psalmes*, better known as the Bay Psalm Book. This became the colonies' first best-seller and was even exported back to Great Britain and Europe. Most of the early published works consisted of religious tracts, such as sermons, and were printed under license of the colonial government.[11]

Newspapers were published throughout the colonial and revolutionary period, but they were not the large, general-appeal publications we are familiar with today. Instead, they provided commentary and gossip that would appeal to members of a particular political group. Benjamin Harris, who published the first newspaper in the colonies in 1690, also ran a coffeehouse, and the content of his paper, *Publick Occurrences Both Forreign and Domestick*, resembled the talk in his coffeehouse. Only one issue of the paper appeared, in part because Harris had failed to obtain a license to publish.

Although the newspapers of the colonial period were much smaller than those to come during the 1800s, they could nevertheless be quite profitable. Publisher and statesman Benjamin Franklin became relatively wealthy publishing his *Pennsylvania Gazette*—although his success was due at least in part to his ability, as postmaster general, to prevent competing newspapers from being distributed through the mail.[12] Franklin, along with several other successful publishers, was able to use his paper's profitability to improve his publications and thus increase his success. He was an intense competitor, vying with other publishers for the top writers and editors in the book, newspaper, and magazine businesses.[13] In many ways, he established the pattern that media moguls would follow for the next two and a half centuries.

Web 3.1: Learn more about the Bay Psalm Book.

Even though print media were widespread in America in the 1700s, subscription prices were high, and publications were subsidized by political parties. It wasn't until the development of **penny press** newspapers in the 1830s that the news industry really got started. These inexpensive, widely circulated papers were published in large numbers and were the first American newspapers to be supported primarily through advertising revenue and read by large numbers of people.[14] The same model of advertising-supported media guided the development of the magazine industry in the 1800s.

In the United States, unlike most other countries, the electronic media have always been privately owned, beginning with the telegraph line between Washington, D.C., and Baltimore, Maryland, in 1844. By 1849, the telegraph was being used to transmit news on a regular basis. Although it was replaced by newer technology in the twentieth century, the telegraph set the stage for private ownership of electronic media.[15] Today the broadcasting industry is primarily a private business in the United States, although it is regulated by the government. In contrast, while Britain has a thriving commercial broadcasting industry, the publicly funded British Broadcasting Corporation (BBC) has a much bigger presence than the U.S. Public Broadcasting Service (PBS). And while the Internet, the most recent of the electronic media, began as a partnership between the military and universities in the 1960s and 1970s, it was fully opened to business and the public in the 1990s.

The Growth of National News

Nationally circulated magazines provided news and entertainment in the nineteenth and early twentieth centuries, and radio networks carried national news from the 1930s on, but it was the growing popularity of television networks in the 1950s that gave the United States a true national media culture. For the first time, people routinely depended on nationally available media for their news. The CBS and NBC television networks started carrying a half-hour nightly news broadcast in 1963; ABC followed suit in 1967, and CBS added its weekly newsmagazine *60 Minutes* in 1968. In 1979, ABC started running a late-night news update called *America Held Hostage* when American embassy employees in Iran were taken hostage.

©iStockphoto.com/derrek

penny press: Inexpensive, widely circulated papers that became popular in the nineteenth century. They were the first American media to be supported primarily through advertising revenue.

As the hostage crisis dragged on for 444 days, the update evolved into the program now known as *Nightline*.

Public affairs network C-SPAN began broadcasting on cable in 1979. It carried full coverage of the U.S. House of Representatives live and unedited; coverage of the Senate was added in 1986. CNN went on cable in 1980, promising not to go off the air until "the end of the world." CNN subsequently went worldwide with CNN International and CNN en Español.

All this means that, even though a relatively limited number of companies own the media outlets, Americans have access to a wide range of competing news sources. The absolute number of independent sources has declined, but their availability is vastly improved.[16] In addition to these giants, several slightly smaller companies are extraordinarily influential on how our media operate. While the focus in this chapter is on the media in the United States, we take a much broader look at global media in Chapter 15.

Big Media: The Conglomerates

Media journalist Ken Auletta notes that massive changes have taken place in the media industry during the past forty years. In 1980, the videocassette recorder (VCR) was a scarce luxury, cable television was just starting to become popular, the personal computer was for hobbyists, the Internet was available only to academics and the military, *USA Today* had yet to be published, MTV and CNN were not yet on cable, there were only three broadcast television networks, you couldn't buy a compact disc (CD), and mobile phones were connected to large boxes and used only by the wealthy and people with mobile offices.

By 2011, digital video recorders (DVRs) were in almost 40 percent of all U.S. homes with television, basic cable was in more than 52 percent of homes and was available to over 95 percent of them, direct broadcast satellite television was in 24 percent, radio was universally available, over 90 percent of American teens had access to the Internet at home, the *Wall Street Journal* sold 2.1 million copies a day, there were at least six national broadcast networks, and over 85 percent of Americans had mobile telephones.[17] In Europe, there were approximately 4,000 television channels available, and in Western Europe, approximately 86 percent of all adults had a mobile phone.[18]

Since corporations control so much of what is available to the public, it is worth examining who they are and what they control, as well as how they have had to change to react to the new media environment of the twenty-first century.

synergy: Where the combined strength of two items is greater than the sum of their individual strengths. In the media business, synergy means that a large company can use the strengths of its various divisions to successfully market its content.

Companies that had counted on consolidation to bring in profits from synergy were likely to be disappointed as often as they were pleased. In general, the word **synergy** refers to a combination of effects that is greater than the sum of the individual effects. For example, two medications given together may do more than twice as much good as the two medicines given separately. In the media business, synergy means that a combined company can offer more value, cost savings, or strength than two companies could separately.

Questioning the Media

Is America better off having privately owned media? Would you rather see government-owned or -controlled media replace the privately owned media? Why or why not? How would this change our media?

However, there is more to our media world than just the legacy conglomerates of Big Media. There are the newer companies that are becoming a huge part of our media landscape, such as Comcast, Google, and Apple. Then there are the companies that are more limited in the scope of their media ownership, such as Clear Channel, which has 850-plus radio stations, and Gannett, which owns approximately eighty daily newspapers (including *USA Today*), 500 nondaily publications, and twenty-three television stations.[19] So after we talk about the legacy media conglomerates, we'll look at the giant new players, along with a few other smaller, but still significant, media companies.

Questioning the Media

In the twenty-first century, we have more media options available to us than ever before. But most of the major media outlets are owned by a small number of corporations. Given this, do you believe that we as media consumers have more or fewer choices than in the past? Why?

Disney: The Mouse That Grew 

The Walt Disney Company, popularly known as the Mouse, may be the world's most famous media company, due to its wealth of recognizable characters, such as Mickey Mouse and Donald Duck (see Box 3.1). It is also the largest of the legacy media conglomerates. In 2010, it had revenue

Video 3.2: Search the C-SPAN archive to find a streaming copy of every program the public affairs network has ever aired.

Web 3.2: Read an interview with Ben Bagdikian.

Web 3.3: Take a peek at the corporate Web sites for several of the most dominant media corporations.

Box 3.1 What Does Disney Own?

Book Publishing

- Hyperion Books
- Disney Publishing Worldwide

Magazine Publishing

Numerous magazines, including:

- *Biography*
- *Discover*
- *Us Weekly* (partial)
- *ESPN The Magazine*
- *Marvel Comics*

Broadcast Network

- ABC

Broadcast Television Stations

Disney owns eight ABC affiliates in major cities, including Chicago, Los Angeles, San Francisco, New York City, and Houston.

Cable Networks

Many cable networks (either partially or in full), including:

- Disney Channel (plus multiple international versions)
- ESPN Inc. (includes 15 separate properties)
- A&E Networks
- ABC Family
- Lifetime (at least three versions as part of the A&E Networks)

Movie Studios and Distributors

- Walt Disney Pictures
- Touchstone Pictures
- Buena Vista
- Pixar
- Marvel Entertainment
- Lucasfilm

Other Properties

- Theme parks in China, Japan, France, and the United States
- A cruise line business
- Disney stores
- Numerous international television broadcasting and production companies

Sources: "Who Owns What," *Columbia Journalism Review*, http://www.cjr.org/resources/?c=disney; *Hoover's Company Records—In-Depth Records: The Walt Disney Company* (Austin, Texas: Hoover's Inc., 2014).

Video 3.3: Comedian Paint gives a musical parody of what happens to several Disney princesses after the movie ends.

Web 3.4: Who owns the media you're consuming?

of $45 billion, with $34 billion coming from the United States and Canada and more than $3 billion from Asia and the Pacific.[20] (Comcast, which owns NBCUniversal, is about one-third bigger than Disney. We'll talk about that more later on.)

From Mickey Mouse to Media Giant. The Disney Company got its start in 1928 when Walt Disney started producing Mickey Mouse cartoons. The first two silent Mickey cartoons came and went with little fanfare, but the third, which featured synchronized music and sound effects, was a huge hit. Walt Disney produced more than one hundred short animated cartoons featuring Mickey and his friends. In 1937, he took animation to the next level by releasing the first feature-length cartoon, *Snow White and the Seven Dwarfs*. A major success for the studio, the film held the box-office record of $8 million until *Gone With the Wind* was released in 1939.

In the 1950s, the Disney Company started producing live-action feature films and wildlife documentaries.[21] It was also in the 1950s that Disney opened its first theme park, in California.

Walt Disney was among the first Hollywood movie producers to see the potential of television, for which he produced and hosted a weekly program for more than a decade.[22] He understood the concept of synergy very early and used his television show to promote his movies and theme park. The Disney Company has also been licensing merchandise longer than almost any other media company. In 1930, the company signed its first international licensing contract for Mickey Mouse products, and the famous Mickey Mouse watch went on sale in 1933. By 1954, the company was selling more than 3,000 Disney items, ranging from pajamas to school supplies.[23]

After Walt Disney's death in 1966, the company lost much of its direction.[24] But in 1984, Michael Eisner, formerly of ABC Television and Paramount Pictures, took over as head of the studio, a job he held until 2005. Under Eisner's leadership, the Disney Company produced a series of popular animated films; formed new movie companies, including Touchstone Pictures (which has produced films for adults, such as *Pretty Woman*); and moved into television.[25]

In addition to being a significant force in American media, the Disney Company has been developing a presence throughout Europe and Asia. As of 2013, approximately 25 percent of Disney's earnings came from outside North America, but the quest for an international audience has not always gone smoothly.[26] For example, Disneyland Paris, which opened in 1992, went through four name changes and numerous cultural changes before it became profitable. Tokyo Disneyland, which opened in 1983, started off slowly but was soon busier than the California Disneyland. But the market Disney is most interested in is China, with its 1.3 billion potential consumers.[27]

Disney had been doing business in China for several years before the communists came to power in 1949. But for the next thirty-five or so years, Disney and other Western businesses were barred from the country. By the mid-1980s, China was becoming more open to Western business and culture, so in 1985 Disney began negotiations with Chinese broadcast media to bring Mickey Mouse and Donald Duck cartoons to Chinese television.[28]

In 1996, Disney's relationship with China hit a rough period when Touchstone released the movie *Kundun*. The film, which deals with Tibet and the Dalai Lama, outraged the Chinese government. (China controls Tibet and has attempted to suppress the teachings of the Dalai Lama.) After *Kundun*'s release, Disney programming was banned briefly in China.[29]

XINHUA/Gamma-Rapho via Getty

The Walt Disney Company has worked extensively in recent years to expand its offerings in China, including a theme park in Shanghai.

By 2002, Disney had successfully distanced itself from *Kundun* and was airing its cartoons on *Dragon Club*, which reaches 60 million Chinese households, and by 2005 it had twenty-three programming blocks on Chinese television. The company also had more than 1,800 Disney Corners in Chinese department stores.[30]

Disney opened Hong Kong Disneyland in 2005. Despite some early problems, including overcrowding and cultural misunderstandings, the park has been growing, and Disney invested $800 million into expanding the park in 2009.[31] Since that expansion, the Hong Kong park has been moderately successful, with rising attendance and profits.[32] Chinese visitors don't seem to be bothered by the fact that the rides have English soundtracks. One Chinese guest told the *Washington Post*, "I don't expect to see many Chinese things in Disneyland. I came to see different things, fresh things."[33] Disney has continued to work on a $5.5 billion theme park in Shanghai in conjunction with a Chinese corporation. Brooks Barnes, writing for the *New York Times*, says Disney is counting on the Chinese becoming more interested in Western-style entertainment and media.[34]

Disney's reach extends far beyond its children's programming and theme park operations. Central to the Disney Company today is the ABC broadcast network and the ESPN cable networks. ABC had been an independent company until 1985, when it was bought by Capital Cities Communications. Ten years later, Disney bought Capital Cities and acquired ABC as part of the deal.[35] Unlike Viacom and Time Warner, Disney is primarily a content company—a producer of programming. Although it owns ten television stations and a number of radio stations, it has not (as of this writing) invested heavily in local cable companies, theaters, or an Internet service provider. It also has invested in retail stores and theme parks.[36]

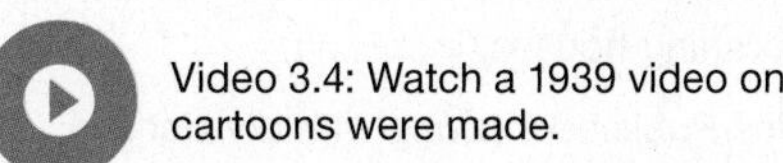
Video 3.4: Watch a 1939 video on how Walt Disney cartoons were made.

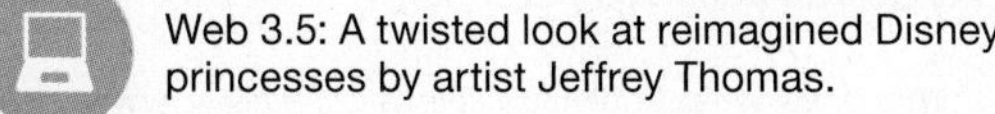
Web 3.5: A twisted look at reimagined Disney princesses by artist Jeffrey Thomas.

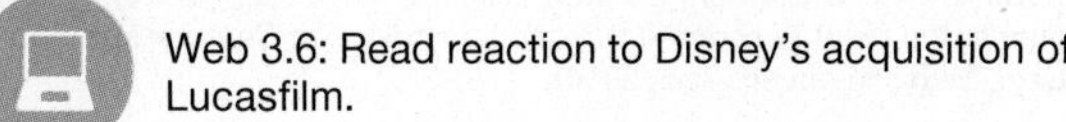
Web 3.6: Read reaction to Disney's acquisition of Lucasfilm.

The Twenty-first Century at Disney. Disney has had a series of ups and downs over the past several years, sometimes in the same areas of the company. These include:

- Animation—Disney's animation studio suffered a string of failures starting in 2000 with traditional, hand-drawn animation, but the company revitalized its cartoon offerings by acquiring Pixar, the studio responsible for the three *Toy Story* movies, *WALL-E*, and *Up*. In 2013 and 2014, Disney animation had its biggest hit ever (not counting the Pixar-branded movies) with *Frozen*.[37]
- Synergy at Disney—Synergy isn't just a good idea at Disney; it's a corporate passion. Two or three times a year, the company runs a "boot camp" for executives called Disney Dimensions. For eight days, executives play a costumed character at a theme park and learn how meals are cooked and beds are made, how movies are animated, how the finance and legal departments are run, and how the television networks do business.[38] While Disney still uses synergy to cross-market consumer products, theme parks,

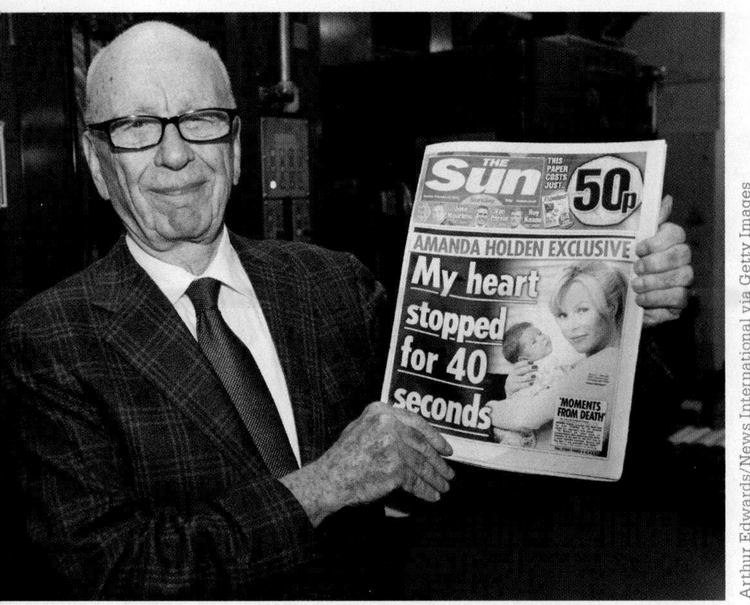

THE Sun
50p
AMANDA HOLDEN EXCLUSIVE
My heart stopped for 40 seconds
MOMENTS FROM DEATH

Arthur Edwards/News International via Getty Images

Australian Rupert Murdoch, shown here in 1985, heads News Corporation, which owns, among many other media properties, the *Wall Street Journal*, the *New York Post*, Fox News, and Fox Broadcasting.

and media content, the company has taken the concept much farther than that.[39]

- Media convergence at Disney—Just as Disney saw the potential for bringing together movie and television properties back in the 1950s and 1960s, in recent decades it has understood how to bring together other popular sources of media entertainment such as Marvel Entertainment (home of Iron Man and the rest of the Avengers) and Lucasfilm (home of the *Star Wars* series). The company has also moved into using online media as a partial owner of the online streaming video service Hulu and uses it to provide viewers with additional opportunities to watch shows from ABC, ABC Family, Disney Channel, and SOAPnet. Disney was also among the first of the Big Media companies to make its movies and television shows available through Apple's online iTunes store.[40]

News Corporation and 21st Century Fox: A Worldwide Giant Splits in Two 

In 2013, Rupert Murdoch's worldwide news and entertainment giant News Corporation became the latest media conglomerate to break itself into two parts. News Corporation retained Murdoch's newspapers, information services, and book publishing business. It publishes the *Wall Street Journal* and the *New York Post* in the United States, along with the *Times* and the *Sun* in London. (Its biggest paper, the *News of the World*, was shut down following a phone hacking scandal in 2011. You can learn more about this in the "Test Your Media Literacy" box.) 21st Century Fox took on his cable, broadcast, film, pay television, and satellite properties. Interestingly, the entertainment-oriented 21st Century Fox owns Fox News rather than the news-oriented News Corp. Murdoch has a worldwide presence in nine different media: newspapers, magazines, books, broadcasting, direct-broadcast satellite television, cable networks, a movie studio, home video, and the Internet. (See Boxes 3.2 and 3.3.) In fact, the only continent on which Murdoch doesn't own media properties is Antarctica.[41] In fiscal year 2012, News Corporation had sales of $8.6 billion, and 21st Century Fox had sales of $27.7 billion, for a total of $36.3 billion, making the two companies together about 25 percent smaller than Disney.[42]

From Australia to the World. Rupert Murdoch's father owned two Australian newspapers, but when the elder Murdoch died in 1952, the younger Murdoch had to sell one of the papers to cover inheritance taxes. So Murdoch's News Corporation empire grew out of a single newspaper, the *Adelaide News*, which had a circulation under 100,000.[43]

By 1964, Murdoch had put together a major newspaper chain and had begun publishing the *Australian*, a national newspaper. In 1969, he moved to Britain, taking over the Sunday tabloid *News of the World* and eventually acquiring four more tabloids. In 1977, he moved to the United States, where he acquired the *New York Post* and transformed it into a lively, politically conservative paper.

In the 1980s, Murdoch bought the 20th Century Fox movie studio and a number of U.S. television stations and used them to create the Fox television network. He also became an American citizen at this time because the United States does not permit foreign ownership of a television

Box 3.2 What Does News Corporation Own?

Newspapers

More than 275 newspapers worldwide, including:

The Wall Street Journal

The *New York Post*

The Times (of London)

The Sun (London tabloid)

The Australian (national daily)

Magazines

All or part of four Australian magazines

Book Publishing

Multiple book publishing houses, including:

- HarperCollins Publishers (along with divisions in England, Australia, and Canada)
- Zondervan (religious publisher)

Sources: "Who Owns What," *Columbia Journalism Review*, www.cjr.org/resources/index.php; *Hoover's Company Records—In-Depth Records: News Corporation* (Austin, Texas: Hoover's Inc., 2014); *Hoover's Company Records—In-Depth Records: 21st Century Fox* (Austin, Texas: Hoover's Inc., 2014).

Box 3.3 What Does 21st Century Fox Own?

Broadcast Television Networks

- Fox Broadcasting
- MyNetworkTV (broadcast network launched in 2006)

Broadcast Television Stations

21st Century Fox owns at least twenty-five television stations in at least seventeen cities, including New York City; Los Angeles; Minneapolis; Washington, D.C.; and Phoenix.

Cable/Satellite Networks

Numerous cable networks, including:

- Fox News Channel
- Fox Sports Net
- Fox Sports Europe, Africa, Asia, and Latin America
- Fox Sports 1 (formerly the Speed Channel)
- FX

Global Channels

- Fox International Channels (300 channels across Latin America, Europe, Asia, and Africa, in forty-four languages)
- STAR India (network of more than thirty channels in seven languages)

Direct Broadcast Satellite Companies (all or partial ownership)

Multiple DBS services, including:

- British Sky Broadcasting (BSkyB)
- Sky Deutschland
- Sky Italia

Movie Studios

- 20th Century Fox (including at least seven spin-off studios)
- Fox Interactive

Sources: "Who Owns What," *Columbia Journalism Review*, www.cjr.org/resources/index.php; *Hoover's Company Records—In-Depth Records: News Corporation* (Austin, Texas: Hoover's Inc., 2014); *Hoover's Company Records—In-Depth Records: 21st Century Fox* (Austin, Texas: Hoover's Inc., 2014).

network. The Fox News cable network was launched in 1996 and has for years been the most popular of the cable news operations. In 2011, it had the fourth-highest ratings of any cable network (USA, ESPN, and TNT were higher) and was the top-rated cable news channel.[44] In addition to its more than twenty-five broadcast television stations, book publishing operations, and broadcast and cable networks, News Corporation is the world's dominant player in the direct broadcast satellite business, owning a large portion of BSkyB (Britain), Sky Italia (Italy), and Sky Deutschland (Germany). It also owns a stake in China's state-owned telecommunications company.[45] The Murdoch family owns approximately 40 percent of both News Corporation and 21st Century Fox, and Murdoch runs his business using the same hands-on style he employed when it was a small family-owned company.

By far the biggest news surrounding News Corporation in recent years was its 2007 purchase of the *Wall Street Journal* and its parent company, Dow Jones & Company Inc. Murdoch paid a substantial premium for the paper to buy it from its longtime controlling owners, the Bancroft family. Although the *Journal* has always had a politically conservative editorial page, the paper's news coverage has generally been considered evenhanded. When Murdoch first expressed interest in the *Journal*, there were concerns in the news industry that he would apply the same partisan style to the paper that he used with the Fox News Channel. To date, that doesn't seem to have happened. Murdoch has been active in the paper's management, but he has not made substantial change in the paper's style or approach to news.[46]

The Twenty-first Century at News Corporation and 21st Century Fox. News Corporation split into two separate companies in 2013. Rupert Murdoch's media corporations seem to have figured out the rapidly changing media world of the new century. They have experienced growing revenue throughout the recent recession, rising from annual sales of $16 billion in 2002 to more than $36 billion in 2012.[47] How have his corporations managed to be so successful?

- Being willing to change to match the new media environment—News Corporation split into two separate companies in 2013 for a number of reasons, not the least of which was the toxic environment surrounding the *News of the World* phone hacking scandal. The split also allowed for the more profitable entertainment-oriented 21st Century Fox to follow a separate path from the news and publishing News Corporation.[48]
- Giving consumers what they want—Although Murdoch is known for his politically conservative newspapers and cable news channel, his companies are generally pragmatic about delivering what audiences want. Fox Broadcasting carries shows such as *The Simpsons*, *Family Guy*, and *American Dad*, which frequently make the lists of the most objectionable shows on television, and News Corporation's British tabloids can get quite racy—the London *Sun* includes a photo of a topless woman as a daily feature.
- Wise use of multiple platforms—21st Century Fox produces a wide range of content that can be distributed through multiple platforms. For example, a movie produced by 20th Century Fox can be shown in theaters, sold on a disc by 20th Century Fox Home Entertainment, aired on Fox Broadcasting, shown again on the FX cable channel, and finally used as an

Web 3.7: Read more about the split of News Corporation here.

TEST YOUR MEDIA LITERACY

News of the World Hacking Scandal

The *News of the World* was for many years the biggest circulating British tabloid newspaper (8.4 million copies an issue), and it long had a reputation for cutting ethical corners to report the sordid details of crimes and celebrity gossip. But it really outdid itself when reporters for the paper hacked into the phone of a murdered thirteen-year-old girl to listen to her voice mail messages. On other occasions, the paper's reporters were accused of hacking into the phones of British terrorism victims, making payoffs to members of the Scotland Yard police force, and having improper connections to prominent British politicians.

Matters got bad enough that former editors and reporters at the paper were arrested or even sent to jail over the scandals. There was even talk for a time that News Corporation officials could be prosecuted in the United States for violating the Foreign Corrupt Practices Act for bribing British officials. The scandal finally became so intense that News Corporation shut down the embattled tabloid that had been published since 1843. This was all shocking, but should it have been, given that the *NOTW*'s sister paper, the *Sun*, runs a topless pinup on page 3 of every issue?

The fact that the *News of the World* was also owned by Rupert Murdoch's News Corporation made this a big story within the press. After all, News Corporation is a major world news organization and a major media owner in the United States. It owns one of the most respected and largest-circulating newspapers in the United States, the *Wall Street Journal*.

SECRET 4 Through all this, it's worth remembering Secret Four—Nothing's new: Everything that happened in the past will happen again. The behavior of Mr. Murdoch's tabloids is nothing new. As you will read about in Chapter 6, if you go back to the rise of the yellow press in New York City back in the late 1800s, about the time that modern standards of journalism were being established, you will see that Joseph Pulitzer's *New York World* and William Randolph Hearst's *Evening Journal* engaged in very similar escapades. In one case, the two papers battled over covering a spectacular murder case that involved dismemberment and a love triangle. One newspaper publisher even leased the apartment where the murder took place in order to keep competing reporters away.

WHO is the source?

Rupert Murdoch has been in the newspaper business in various areas around the world since the 1950s and is one of the most powerful people in the news industry. What news outlets does he control? How do you think his background shaped how the *News of the World* behaved?

WHAT were the reporters doing?

Follow the link and read several of the supporting articles that go with the post. What were reporters at the *News of the World* accused of doing?

WHAT have other newspapers done?

How does the behavior of the reporters at the *News of the World* compare to that at the yellow papers of the late 1800s? Would you expect reporters from contemporary American newspapers or broadcasters to behave like the reporters at the *News of the World* did? Why or why not?

HOW do you and your classmates react to the behavior of tabloid reporters?

Do you think that the press cared more about this story than the general public did? Why do you think so? Are you surprised at the behavior of the reporters at the *News of the World*? Are reporters ever justified in doing things like hacking people's voice mail accounts? Why or why not?

Sources: Nick Davies and Amelia Hill, "Missing Milly Dowler's Voicemail Was Hacked by *News of the World*," *Guardian*, July 4, 2011, www.guardian.co.uk/uk/2011/jul/04/milly-dowler-voicemail-hacked-news-of-world; Bob Garfield and Brooke Gladstone, "*News of the World* Folds: Transcript," July 8, 2011, http://www.onthemedia.org/2011/jul/08/news-world-folds/transcript/; Brooke Gladstone, "Muted U.S. Public Reaction to British Tabloid Scandal: Transcript," July 22, 2011, http://www.onthemedia.org/2011/jul/22/muted-us-public-reaction-british-tabloid-scandal/transcript/; Bob Garfield, "The Love Triangle, Murder and Missing Head That Sparked a Tabloid War: Transcript," July 22, 2011, http://www.onthemedia.org/2011/jul/22/love-triangle-murder-and-missing-head-sparked-tabloid-war/transcript/.

Web 3.8: You can read more about the hacking scandal with this blog post.

---

afternoon or late-night program on a 21st Century Fox–owned television station.[49] This multiplatform approach then leads to global synergy.

- Global synergy at News Corporation—News Corporation's direct broadcast satellite systems currently cover much of the globe. Due to his various studios, Murdoch also owns the means to produce content to flow out over these channels. He has, in the words of media journalist Ken Auletta, both content and the pipeline. Owning every step of the process is important according to Murdoch, who says, "We'd like to be **vertically integrated** from the moment

---

vertical integration: Controlling all aspects of a media project,. including production, delivery to consumers in multiple formats, and the promotion of the product through other media.

of creation through to the moment of delivery into the home."[50] Although News Corporation owns media properties around the world, Murdoch does not take a one-size-fits-all approach in providing content to these varied channels. "You would be very wrong to forget that what people want to watch in their own country is basically local programming, local language, local culture," Murdoch says. "I learned that many, many years ago in Australia, when I was loading up [News Corporation's network] with good American programs and we'd get beat with second-rate Australian ones."[51]

UPI/News International/Yue Mok/LANDOV

News of the World's final edition, published on July 10, 2011. The paper had at one time been the highest-circulating newspaper in Britain and was known for its lurid covers and headlines, but News Corporation shut down the paper following its phone hacking scandal.

Time Warner: Starting the Trend That Smaller Is Better

At one point, Time Warner was the world's largest media conglomerate; with 2008 sales of almost $47 billion, it brought in $9 billion more than Disney did that year. But in 2010, Time Warner was down to annual revenue of $26.9 billion. Why did the company have such a gigantic drop in revenue over just a two-year period? Well, hold on just a moment. It's also worth noting that in 2008 Time Warner lost $13.4 billion, but in 2010, it turned a profit of $2.6 billion. What happened? The decline in the company's size and growth of profitability came from its selling off of several assets, including Internet provider AOL in 2009 and cable TV provider Time Warner Cable. (That's right. Time Warner Cable is not owned by Time Warner. Just so that's clear. We'll talk about that a little bit further on.) Since then, Time has continued to spin off properties and grow in profitability, with 2013 revenue of $29.8 billion and a profit of $3.7 billion. Time Warner is a major player in film, television, cable TV, publishing, and online content, and it is the home to many iconic media characters, such as Scooby-Doo, Harry Potter, and Batman (see Box 3.4).[52]

Box 3.4 What Does Time Warner Own?

Cable Networks

- HBO (at least sixteen channels)
- CNN (at least six channels)
- WTBS
- TNT Drama
- truTV
- Turner Classic Movies
- Cartoon Network (at least four channels)

Broadcast Television Network

- The CW Television Network (co-owned with CBS)

Movie and TV Studios

- Warner Bros.
- DC Entertainment (Marvel's main rival for comic book–based movies)
- New Line Cinema
- Castle Rock Entertainment
- Hanna-Barbera Cartoons

Sources: "Who Owns What," *Columbia Journalism Review*, http://www.cjr.org/resources/?c=timewarner; *Hoover's Company Records—In-Depth Records: Time Warner Inc.* (Austin, Texas: Hoover's Inc., 2014).

Note: This table lists only a sample of Time Warner's holdings. The company also owns multiple television and movie production companies.

Time, Warner Bros., and Turner Broadcasting. Media giant Time Warner started out as the publisher of *Time* magazine, founded in 1922 by Henry Luce and his prep-school friend Briton Hadden. *Time* quickly prospered, and by 1930, Luce had started the business magazine *Fortune*, which was followed by the photo magazine *Life* in 1936. By the 1980s, Time Inc. had added multiple magazines, book publishers, local cable companies, and the Home Box Office (HBO) cable movie channel to its holdings. In 1989, Time merged with Warner Communications, which had grown out of the Warner Bros. movie studio. This merger combined a major movie studio with the nation's largest magazine publisher.

Web 3.9: Visit Time Warner's corporate site.

Among Time Warner's businesses were a large number of **local cable television systems**, which delivered programming to individual homes (these have since been spun off as the separate company Time Warner Cable), and HBO, one of the first premium cable networks. In 1996, Time Warner vastly expanded its stable by purchasing cable pioneer Ted Turner's group of channels, which included the CNN networks, WTBS, TNT, Turner Classic Movies, and the Cartoon Network. Along with his cable properties, Turner also sold his Internet operations and movie studio. When Time Warner took over Turner Broadcasting System (TBS), Turner became a vice president of the new company and its largest stockholder. More significantly, the Turner networks had passed from the control of a single individual to that of a publicly owned company, in much the same way that Robert Johnson's BET would later be bought by Viacom.[53]

The Twenty-first Century at Time Warner. Although Time Warner is the biggest of the Big Media, that bigness has been a mixed blessing for the company since 2000.

- In 2001, the big news was that AOL, then known as America Online, was merging with (some said buying) Time Warner. At the time of the merger, AOL was valued at $124 billion; when the companies separated in 2009, AOL's value was below $3 billion. The goal of the merger was to have greater synergy between AOL's online offerings and Time Warner's older legacy media. The only problem? The AOL–Time Warner synergy never really worked. The new company soon cut more than 4,000 jobs and sold off numerous properties, including its sports teams, its book division, and the Warner Music Group.[54]
- In 2014, Time Warner took its magazine publishing arm, Time Inc., and made it into its own, independent company. This means that the part of the media giant that gave Time Warner half of its name is no longer a part of the company. Time Inc. publishes more than ninety magazines and forty-five Web sites. Magazine publishing has been going through a difficult time since the Great Recession of 2007–2009, and *New York Times* reporters David Carr and Ravi Somaiya say they were not surprised to see Time Warner cutting the magazine division loose in much the same way it previously had with Time Warner Cable and AOL.[55]
- Legacy synergy—There are examples, however, of synergy working among the longtime elements of Time Warner. Owning multiple channels allows a company to repackage media content for different audiences. Warner Bros. can first show a movie in theaters, then sell it through Time Warner Cable's pay-per-view division, then market DVDs of it through the company's home video division, air it on the HBO premium movie channel, and broadcast it on the WTBS or TNT basic cable channels.

Viacom and CBS: Two Companies, Same Management

The relationship between media conglomerate Viacom and established broadcast network CBS has been a long-term on-again, off-again one. Although they are currently two separate corporations with separate stocks, the ownership and management of the two companies heavily overlap. The companies had combined revenue for 2012 of almost $28 billion. Of that $28 billion, $13.9 billion came from Viacom and $14 billion from CBS. CBS owns the CBS broadcast network, half of the CW broadcast network, a number of television production companies, approximately thirty broadcast television stations, and the Simon & Schuster publishing group. Viacom owns the movie studio Paramount and numerous cable channels, including Comedy Central, BET, and the various MTV and Nickelodeon channels (see Box 3.5).[56]

The Child Buys/Sells the Parent. CBS became a force in broadcasting when William S. Paley and his father bought United Independent Broadcasters and turned it into the Columbia Broadcasting System (CBS). In the mid-1980s, when all three of the original broadcast networks changed ownership, CBS was bought by investor Laurence Tisch and his Loews Corporation. Westinghouse bought Tisch's company in 1995, and by 1997 it had sold all its nonmedia businesses and was simply CBS Inc.

Then, in one of the strangest twists in media history, CBS was bought by Viacom in 1999. What made this transaction so unusual was that Viacom had begun as a small film production unit within CBS. Later, in 1971, the federal government became concerned that the broadcast networks were becoming too powerful, so it forced them to sell their content production units. As an independent company, Viacom grew into a major producer of cable television programming; its products included MTV and Nickelodeon.

In 1987, theater owner Sumner Redstone bought Viacom. Under Redstone's leadership, the company became a dominant media corporation in the 1990s. It acquired the Blockbuster video store chain, the Paramount

Web 3.10: Visit Viacom's corporate site.

Web 3.11: Visit the CBS corporate site.

local cable television systems: The companies that provide cable television service directly to consumers' homes.

movie studio, and the start-up television network United Paramount Network (UPN). (In 2006, UPN was merged with the WB network to become the CW.) Finally, Viacom bought CBS, the television network that had given birth to it decades before.[57] But then in 2005, Viacom and CBS split back into two separate corporations with separate stocks being traded. So they are no longer a single Big Media company, right? Well, sort of. Sumner Redstone and his daughter Shari were, as of 2014, still top executives of both companies, though Les Moonves, who is not part of the Redstone family, was CEO of CBS.[58]

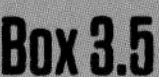

Box 3.5 What Do Viacom and CBS Own?

Viacom and CBS split into separate corporations in 2005, though they are still largely owned and managed by the same people. In general, CBS owns broadcasting and publishing properties while Viacom owns cable and movie properties.

CBS

Broadcast Television Networks (CBS)

- CBS television network
- The CW television network (co-owned with Time Warner)

Broadcast Television Stations

CBS owns approximately thirty television stations in at least twenty-seven cities, including New York City, Los Angeles, Chicago, Philadelphia, and San Francisco.

Radio Properties

- CBS Radio operates numerous radio stations, most of which are in the top fifty U.S. markets.

Book Publishing

- Simon & Schuster

Viacom

Viacom owns numerous cable channels, including:

- Viacom Media Networks (seventeen channels, including MTV, VH1, Nickelodeon, Country Music Television, and four varieties of BET)
- Comedy Central (partial owner)

Movie Studios

- Paramount Pictures
- MTV Films
- Nickelodeon Movies

Source: "Who Owns What," *Columbia Journalism Review*, www.cjr.org/resources/index.php; *Hoover's Company Profile Database: Viacom* (Austin, Texas: Hoover's Inc., 2014); *Hoover's Company Profile Database: CBS Corporation* (Austin, Texas: Hoover's Inc., 2014).

Video 3.5: See what all the fuss was about with the Janet Jackson indecency case.

Fatih Saribas/Reuters/Landov

Sumner Redstone, speaking here to guests at a television studio in Istanbul, Turkey, turned the small content-production company Viacom into a media industry giant.

The Twenty-first Century at Viacom and CBS.

The split of Viacom and CBS into separately traded companies was the most visible change at Redstone's companies, but other, more significant, changes have happened there as well:

- Indecency—CBS and Viacom have been at the center of the debate on broadcast indecency that came out of Janet Jackson's infamous "wardrobe malfunction" during the 2004 Super Bowl broadcast. (For more on the issue of broadcast indecency, see Chapter 13.) Radio stations owned by CBS have also drawn fire from critics and the Federal Communications Commission (FCC) for sexually explicit broadcasts by shock jocks Howard Stern and Opie and Anthony, all of whom have since left CBS. Viacom has paid more than \$3.5 million in fines and promised to suspend and possibly fire anyone who makes an indecent broadcast over the company's properties.[59]
- Music videos—Viacom continues to be the dominant force in music videos, owning BET (rap and hip-hop), MTV (music appealing to teens and twenty-somethings), VH1 (music appealing to people who were teens a long time ago), and Country Music Television.
- The split was more than just finance—Common wisdom held that the split of Viacom and CBS was purely a financial move, but the two companies seem to be reacting very differently to the new media environment. While Viacom, with its cable and movie studio properties, has been vehemently opposed to video-sharing services, such as YouTube, posting Viacom-owned content to the Web without a licensing agreement, CBS, on the other hand, was able to reach an agreement with YouTube to share advertising revenue raised from clips posted from CBS-owned programs. Why this different response? Media

Paul A. Herbert/Invision/AP Photo

American Idol, produced by a subsidiary of German media giant Bertelsmann, is a global phenomenon with versions of the show creating new stars like Caleb Johnson on television networks all around the world.

journalist Ken Auletta has written that the most likely reason is that Viacom has always been in the business of licensing content while CBS was in the business of selling advertising time. YouTube was a good match to the CBS model and a bad match for Viacom. It may also be that Viacom is suffering more from Secret Five—New media are always scary—than is CBS.[60]

Bertelsmann: The World's Largest Publisher

Although the German media corporation Bertelsmann has historically been known for its book and music publishing and management business, it also has a major presence in magazines, newspapers, and Internet and broadcast properties (see Box 3.6). Bertelsmann is both the world's largest publisher and the largest publisher of English-language books. In 2009, it had sales of $22 billion.[61]

Books Still Matter. Bertelsmann started out in 1835 as a publisher of Christian music and prayers. It was also the original publisher of the fairy tales of the Brothers Grimm in the nineteenth century. After World War II, the company was run by Reinhard Mohn, a former German Luftwaffe officer who learned to speak English while in a prisoner-of-war camp in Kansas.[62]

Web 3.12: Visit the Bertelsmann corporate site.

Unlike most of the other media giants, Bertelsmann is a privately held company—it is owned by a German foundation that mandates that the company not only earn a profit but also operate for the benefit of its employees and various social causes.[63] Bertelsmann sees book publishing as one of the key media of the twenty-first century and, having purchased the major American publisher Random House for $1.4 billion in 1998, has a much stronger presence in this area than the other media giants. It also owns the RTL Group, Europe's largest television broadcaster, and a large number of magazines through its Gruner + Jahr division.[64]

The Twenty-first Century at Bertelsmann. As a publisher and European broadcaster, Bertelsmann is not in the public eye the way Time Warner, Viacom, and Disney are. It does not have Scooby-Doo, SpongeBob, or Mickey Mouse as a mascot, but it has quietly made its presence felt by utilizing the following methods[65]:

- Returning to core strengths—Up until 2002, under the leadership of CEO Thomas Middelhoff, Bertelsmann looked like it was preparing to become a generalized media giant on the scale of Time Warner or Disney. But members of the Mohn family forced Middelhoff out and returned the company to its core business of book and magazine publishing. Ever since, the company has been gradually selling off peripheral businesses and buying back its stock.[66]
- Broadcasting in Europe—Bertelsmann is big in European television, owning 90 percent of the RTL Group, Europe's largest broadcaster. In addition to operating more than forty-five television channels in a dozen countries, it also produces the wildly popular *American Idol* and a wide range of other *Idol* versions around the world.[67]
- Adapting to the changing music business—Bertelsmann has long been in the music business, first with the Bertelsmann Music Group (BMG) and later with its partnership with Sony BMG Music Entertainment.[68] But with the massive changes that file sharing and digital downloads have brought to the music industry, Bertelsmann has taken a new approach. It sold out its interest in Sony BMG to Sony, and it's now involved with pressing CDs for other publishers and managing the song catalogs of more than 200 artists without being their publisher. So Bertelsmann has gotten out of the business of selling music and is now in the business of assisting companies that do sell it.[69]

Box 3.6 What Does Bertelsmann Own?

Book Publishing

- Random House (including Bantam, Dell, and Ballantine)
- WaterBrook Mulnomah
- Knopf
- Fodor's Travel

Magazines

- Gruner + Jahr (publisher of numerous trade magazines)
- More than two dozen European magazines, including the German publication *Stern*
- Multiple North American magazines (partially or in full), including *National Geographic*

Broadcasting

- Numerous European television stations (partially or in full), including RTL Group, Europe's largest television company
- Multiple television production companies
- Multiple radio services throughout Europe
- FremantleMedia (multiple international versions; producer of *Idol* singing competition series)

Sources: "Who Owns What," *Columbia Journalism Review*, http://www.cjr.org/resources/?c=timewarner; *Hoover's Company Records—In-Depth Records: Time Warner Inc.* (Austin, Texas: Hoover's Inc., 2014).

Big Media: The New Players

SECRET 2 The conglomerates have long been seen as the unquestioned rulers of the American media. But trying to rank the biggest media companies has gotten to be harder and harder with the rise of new media companies. Look at Disney, generally considered to be the largest of the media conglomerates with annual income of just over $45 billion. Then compare it to cable giant Comcast, which now owns NBCUniversal (NBCU). For 2013, Comcast had annual revenue of $64.6 billion, up from $37.9 billion in 2010. Or consider search giant Google. In 2012, it had annual sales of $50.2 billion, most of which came from advertising. That would put it right between Comcast and Disney in terms of income.[70] So let us now look at the other contenders in the Big Media business. Remember Secret Two—There are no mainstream media. There is a wide range of media out there, all of which are significant.

Comcast/NBCUniversal: Cable Buys Broadcaster

NBCUniversal is one of the oldest broadcasters in the United States. It was founded in 1926 by the Radio Corporation of America (RCA), the original monopoly in the broadcast business. Initially, the federal government established RCA to consolidate all the patents required to start the radio business. RCA formed the National Broadcasting Company (NBC) to provide radio programming across the country. As is described in more detail in Chapter 7, NBC had two networks, the "Red" and the "Blue." In the 1940s, it sold the Blue network, which became ABC, now owned by Disney.[71] In the 1930s, RCA began developing television technology and was the first network with regularly scheduled television broadcasts.

In 1985, General Electric (GE) bought both NBC and RCA. The purchase was controversial from the very beginning because GE's primary business is not media but manufacturing and financial services. GE makes consumer electronics, electric generating plants, and aircraft engines. Critics questioned whether a major defense contractor ought to be allowed to own a broadcast network.[72]

Up until the fall of 2009, cable, Internet, and phone service provider Comcast wasn't on anyone's list of American media giants. Sure, it was the largest single supplier of cable television and Internet services in the United States, but it wasn't talked about in the same breath as Disney, Viacom, or Fox. But then the news started breaking that the cable giant was in negotiations to purchase 51 percent of NBCUniversal from GE, which would give the Philadelphia-based company controlling ownership of the network/movie studio. In January 2011, the FCC approved Comcast's purchase of majority ownership of NBCU.[73] The transition of complete ownership of NBCUniversal from GE to Comcast had been expected to be an extended process, with the new owner gradually acquiring the entertainment company's stock. But that changed in February 2013 with the announcement that Comcast would be completing its purchase of NBCU by the end of March of that year. Amy Chozick and Brian Stelter of the *New York Times* report a variety of reasons for the faster pace of the acquisition, including a conflict between the corporate cultures of Comcast and GE, Comcast's desire to control programming sources as well as channels for distribution, and the fact that Comcast could afford to complete the transaction.[74] Purchasing NBCUniversal made Comcast the nation's most valuable pure-media company. (Apple is often considered the world's most valuable company, depending on its stock price, but it is only partially a media company.)[75] For 2013, Comcast had revenue of $64.6 billion, making it almost a third bigger than Disney.[76]

Comcast makes the majority of its revenue by selling cable television, Internet, and phone services to its more than 17 million subscribers. Along with its media-related properties, Comcast owns an interest in professional sports teams and arenas in Philadelphia. The purchase of NBCU gave it the NBC broadcast network, the number-two Spanish-language broadcast network Telemundo, ten NBC affiliate stations, and more than twenty cable networks. These cable networks include the top-rated USA Network, along with Bravo, Syfy, and the Weather Channel. On the film side, the deal gave Comcast control of the major film studio Universal Studios and small-picture/indie studio Focus Features. And, finally, the deal included the Universal Studios theme parks in Florida and California.[77]

Although Comcast is a publicly owned corporation, one-third of the company's voting stock is controlled by CEO Brian Roberts, son of the company's founder. Comcast got its start in the cable business in Mississippi in 1963 and got its name in 1969. After acquiring cable systems in Pennsylvania, it moved to Philadelphia. Throughout the 1980s, Comcast grew by buying up local cable service throughout the United States. In the late 1980s and early 1990s, Comcast started buying up mobile phone companies as well. In 2004, Comcast made its first bid at buying a Big Media company with an offer for Disney. While that deal was not successful, it did set the stage for the cable giant making the play for NBCUniversal (see Box 3.7).

Critics of the merger were concerned that giving control of the NBCU twenty-plus major cable networks to one of the nation's leading Internet and cable providers could lead to a "walled garden" Internet, where only Comcast subscribers would have access to NBCU programing. The agreement Comcast made with the FCC on the merger requires Comcast to give up management control of the Hulu streaming video service (though it can still be an investor). Also, the FCC can require Comcast to make its shows widely available on the Internet if its competitors start doing so first.[78] Those concerns grew when in February 2014 Comcast announced that it had reached an agreement to buy Time Warner Cable for more than $45 billion in stock. This is controversial because Comcast is the nation's largest cable provider and Time Warner Cable is the nation's second largest. If the transaction is approved by the FCC and the U.S. Department of Justice, Comcast would have control of the programming going out to as many as 33 million cable subscribers. (Why is that number in doubt? There are roughly 100 million cable subscribers in the United States. If Comcast controls more than 30 percent of those subscriptions, it could run into regulatory problems. So if the merger goes through, Comcast is likely to sell off approximately 3 million subscribers to fall below that magical 30 percent figure.)

Before we go any further, let's make one thing clear. Time Warner Cable is a company that provides cable TV and Internet services to subscribers in New York, Dallas, Los Angeles, North Carolina, Maine, and Ohio. It is not the general media giant Time Warner that owns the Turner Broadcasting properties and Warner Bros. movie studio. So why the *Time Warner* in Time Warner Cable? That's easy. Time Warner the media company owned Time Warner Cable up until 2009, when it spun off the cable/Internet provider into its own company.[79]

Media reporter Ken Auletta says the purchase would give Comcast a couple of key advantages[80]:

- More subscribers would give Comcast more negotiating power with both television program providers and Internet program providers.
- It would give Comcast access to Time Warner Cable's powerful video-on-demand service that lets consumers have access to programming they want to see without being able to skip commercials.

One thing the deal probably won't do is make you like your cable company any better. The merger won't give customers any more choices in whom they can buy cable service from. Local service will continue to be a monopoly negotiated between a single service provider and the municipality. And consumer advocates argue that the

Box 3.7 What Does Comcast/NBC Universal Own?

Broadcast Television Networks

- NBC broadcast network
- Telemundo Spanish-language broadcast network

Broadcast Television Stations

NBCU owns twenty-eight television stations, some of which are NBC affiliates and some of which broadcast the Spanish-language Telemundo network.

Cable Networks

Numerous cable networks (partially or in full), including:

- CNBC (financial news)
- MSNBC (news)
- Bravo
- Syfy
- USA Network
- The Weather Channel

Movie Studios

- Universal Pictures
- Focus Features

Online Properties

- Weather.com
- Hulu (streaming video)

Cable/Internet/Phone Services

Comcast is a major cable/Internet/phone services provider with more than 17 million subscribers.

Sports Teams and Facilities

Comcast owns partial interest in Philadelphia-area professional sports teams and arenas.

Sources: "Who Owns What," *Columbia Journalism Review*, www.cjr.org/resources/index.php; *Hoover's Company Records—In-Depth Records: Comcast Corporation* (Austin, Texas: Hoover's Inc., 2014); *Hoover's Company Records—In-Depth Records: NBCUniversal Media, LLC* (Austin, Texas: Hoover's Inc., 2011).

Web 3.13: Read more about Comcast's accelerated purchase of NBCUniversal from GE.

Web 3.14: Read more about Comcast's attempt to buy Time Warner Cable.

merger will likely lead to higher prices to consumers.[81]

Google: Making Search Mass Media

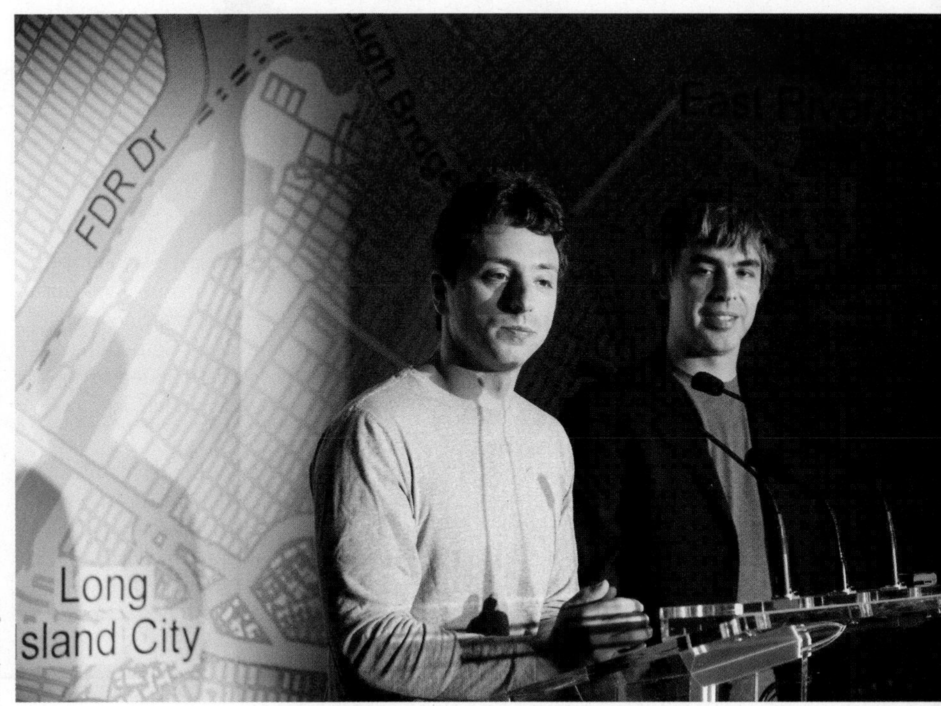

Getty Images

Google founders Sergey Brin and Larry Page took their company from being a search engine start-up in 1998 to being the world's leading online advertising company.

In previous editions of this book, I raised the question "Are search engines a new part of mass communication?" Certainly the Internet and the World Wide Web are a part of our mass media, and search engines, such as Google and Bing, are the tools we use to find information on the Web. They might even be considered news media. Think about Google News. It's in essence a search tool that decides what the major news stories of the day are, collects links to them on a single page, and presents them to the reader. According to Google, Google News draws stories from more than 4,500 English-language news sources from around the world. The articles are evaluated by Google's computers as to how often and on what sites the stories appear. Google claims this leads to an unbiased presentation of the news.[82]

In 2012, Google had worldwide sales of $50.2 billion, including $23.5 billion from the United States. This places Google, like Comcast, ahead of all of the legacy media conglomerates in terms of revenue. Of this income, the vast majority of it came from advertising sales. Not only is Google bringing in a lot of income; it is among the most profitable of the media companies as well. Given all this, Google has to be considered one of the major new players in the media business.[83]

Although Google was founded as a search engine, it also offers an e-mail service (Gmail), blogging (Blogger), photo sharing (Picasa), video (YouTube), and a mobile device operating system (Android). Unlike so many other media companies, Google does not try to sell its products to consumers. Instead, it sees each of these as a way of delivering highly targeted advertising to consumers whom it attracts by providing free services.

Google was founded in 1998 by two engineers who didn't even suspect they were going into the advertising business. Sergey Brin, the child of Jewish Russian immigrants, learned to program at age nine when his parents gave him a Commodore 64 computer. He partnered with Larry Page, whose father was a professor of computer science at Michigan State and whose mother was a database consultant. Brin and Page met each other while in graduate school at Stanford. One night, Page explains, he had a dream: "I was thinking: What if we could download the whole Web, and just keep the links."[84]

The two classmates created a search system based on that idea that worked by analyzing the quality of links to a topic and then scored them according to a system known as PageRank, which stood for both Larry Page's name and the rank of the Web page itself. Google was initially launched not in a garage (though it would later move into a garage), but in graduate housing at Stanford. Google was founded without a business plan or a strategy for making money. But what the founders did have was a strategy for creating the most simple, clean search system.

While Brin and Page were quite happy to burn through investors' money without worrying about generating any, the venture capitalists who were bankrolling the company did want a return on their investments. It was in 2002 that Google finally figured out that to make money for its investors, it had to be in the advertising business. What Google's engineers came up with was the AdWords system, where advertisers bid on the rights to advertise next to search results. The advertisers buy certain keywords that they want their ads to appear next to. But Google requires that the ads that appear be relevant to the people doing the search. So, for example, advertisers can't buy the word *chocolate* and use it to put up links selling cars. But the words "helicopter parts" would be perfect for someone wanting to sell tools for repairing helicopters. Advertisers are only charged when audience members click on their ads.

Google's second big advertising product was AdSense, which places ads on blogs and Web sites that match the ads with the content of the site. Then Google splits the revenue, with about two-thirds of the money going to the owner of the Web site. This put Google in the position

Web 3.15: Visit Google's corporate site.

MEDIA TRANSFORMATIONS

Who Are Our Media?

Although consumers have vastly more media choices than they did in the past, the number of companies providing those choices has declined substantially.

Media critic and Pulitzer Prize–winning journalist Ben Bagdikian wrote that in 1983 the media business was dominated by fifty corporations that controlled more than half the newspaper, magazine, television, radio, and music output in the United States. By 1987, this number had shrunk to twenty-nine companies, and as of 2004, only five companies controlled a majority of the media output in the United States: Time Warner, Disney, Viacom, Bertelsmann, and News Corporation. A sixth company could be added to this list: General Electric, which until recently owned NBCUniversal.[85]

But that picture of six conglomerates controlling American media does not work anymore. To be sure, Disney and Bertelsmann are still single-corporation media giants. But News Corporation has now split into News Corporation and 21st Century Fox; Time Warner has split off several divisions and is now a much smaller company than it was in 2008; and Viacom split into two corporations—Viacom and CBS—back in 2005, with CBS handling broadcasting and Viacom handling movies and cable. In the most dramatic change, cable giant Comcast acquired NBCUniversal from General Electric, so one of the original Big Three broadcast networks is now being run by a company whose major business is running local cable systems. And as this

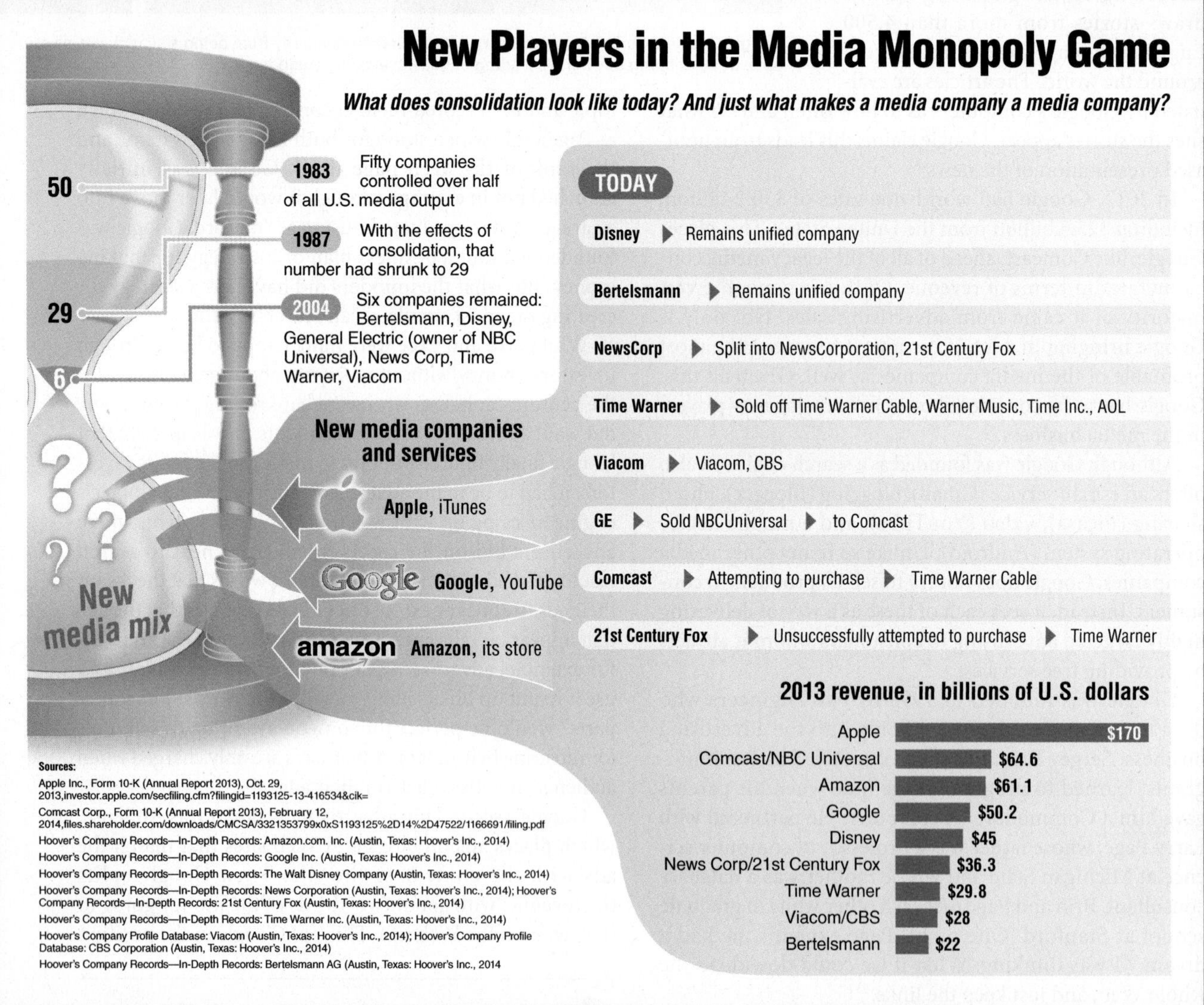

New Players in the Media Monopoly Game
What does consolidation look like today? And just what makes a media company a media company?
50
29
6
1983 Fifty companies controlled over half of all U.S. media output
1987 With the effects of consolidation, that number had shrunk to 29
2004 Six companies remained: Bertelsmann, Disney, General Electric (owner of NBC Universal), News Corp, Time Warner, Viacom
New media companies and services
Apple, iTunes
Google, YouTube
Google
amazon
Amazon, its store
New media mix
TODAY
Disney ▶ Remains unified company
Bertelsmann ▶ Remains unified company
NewsCorp ▶ Split into NewsCorporation, 21st Century Fox
Time Warner ▶ Sold off Time Warner Cable, Warner Music, Time Inc., AOL
Viacom ▶ Viacom, CBS
GE ▶ Sold NBCUniversal ▶ to Comcast
Comcast ▶ Attempting to purchase ▶ Time Warner Cable
21st Century Fox ▶ Unsuccessfully attempted to purchase ▶ Time Warner
2013 revenue, in billions of U.S. dollars
Apple $170
Comcast/NBC Universal $64.6
Amazon $61.1
Google $50.2
Disney $45
News Corp/21st Century Fox $36.3
Time Warner $29.8
Viacom/CBS $28
Bertelsmann $22
Sources:
Apple Inc., Form 10-K (Annual Report 2013), Oct. 29, 2013,investor.apple.com/secfiling.cfm?filingid=1193125-13-416534&cik=
Comcast Corp., Form 10-K (Annual Report 2013), February 12, 2014,files.shareholder.com/downloads/CMCSA/3321353799x0xS1193125%2D14%2D47522/1166691/filing.pdf
Hoover's Company Records—In-Depth Records: Amazon.com. Inc. (Austin, Texas: Hoover's Inc., 2014)
Hoover's Company Records—In-Depth Records: Google Inc. (Austin, Texas: Hoover's Inc., 2014)
Hoover's Company Records—In-Depth Records: The Walt Disney Company (Austin, Texas: Hoover's Inc., 2014)
Hoover's Company Records—In-Depth Records: News Corporation (Austin, Texas: Hoover's Inc., 2014); Hoover's Company Records—In-Depth Records: 21st Century Fox (Austin, Texas: Hoover's Inc., 2014)
Hoover's Company Records—In-Depth Records: Time Warner Inc. (Austin, Texas: Hoover's Inc., 2014)
Hoover's Company Profile Database: Viacom (Austin, Texas: Hoover's Inc., 2014); Hoover's Company Profile Database: CBS Corporation (Austin, Texas: Hoover's Inc., 2014)
Hoover's Company Records—In-Depth Records: Bertelsmann AG (Austin, Texas: Hoover's Inc., 2014

is being written, Comcast is now attempting to purchase Time Warner Cable, which is the second largest cable provider in the country.

Perhaps the biggest changes of all have been with new media companies coming to the forefront. Search giant Google, which draws 96 percent of its revenue from advertising, makes more money than Disney, the biggest of the old media companies. In addition to being in the search business, Google also distributes an almost unimaginable amount of video through YouTube. And how does one even attempt to classify a company like Apple? While it clearly generates most of its income selling hardware, much of that hardware is related to media consumption and production. Apple is also the largest music retailer in the United States. It's no accident that Apple dropped *Computer* out of its corporate name back in 2007.[86]

All this brings us back to Secret Two: There are no mainstream media. We have lots of different media out there, ranging from the legacy corporations, to new media giants, to individuals sharing their work through services like YouTube. And they are all our media.

Media Transformations Questions

- **DO** you think of Apple as a media company? Why or why not?
- **SHOULD** we be concerned that one company might control cable access for one-third of all subscribers in the United States?
- **WHICH** companies do you think of as major media? Do you think much about where you get your media?
- **DO** you worry about who controls the media you consume?

of collaborating with a lot of smaller, independent sites and being seen as a benefactor. This not only made Google quite profitable; it allowed lots of small sites to make money as well.

While in retrospect using search as an advertising medium seems really obvious, Google was founded on the idea of making the best possible search engine, not making money. The founders figured that if they built a great product, they would eventually come up with a good source of revenue.

SECRET 5 Secret Five says new media are always scary, and we should remember that the scariness is oftentimes bigger for the media industry than it is for consumers. This is why Google's approach to the media business is so different from that of legacy media. At a time when the music and movie industries are terrified of their fans/users/customers and are taking them to court for being "pirates," Google is trying to figure out how to better serve them. Google co-founder Larry Page told media journalist Ken Auletta, "[Thinking that] your customers or users are always right, and your goal is to build systems that work for them in a natural way is a good attitude to have. You can replace the system. You can't replace the user."[87]

Apple: Reinventing the Media

Although Apple is best known as a technology company, it has done as much as any corporation to change the media business in the twenty-first century. A quick check of Apple's balance sheet shows that in 2013 the California company sold $91 billion worth of iPhone products; $32 billion worth of iPads; $21 billion worth of more conventional computer equipment; $16 billion worth of iTunes, software, and other services; $4.4 billion worth of iPods; and $5.7 billion worth of accessories. Apple also has gone through incredible levels of growth. Apple had $66 billion in revenue for 2010, which grew to $170 billion in 2013. That's close to tripling its income over three years.[88] And if you look carefully at the numbers, computers are only a small part of the company's business. That's why these days the company's name is Apple, not Apple Computer.

Steve Jobs co-founded Apple back in 1976 with his friend Steve Wozniak. "Woz" was the inventor, and Jobs was the businessman and visionary. Wozniak left the company in 1983, and Jobs was forced out by Apple's board of directors in 1985.[89] After leaving Apple, Jobs founded NeXT Inc., which built an innovative UNIX-based computer that was used by Tim Berners-Lee to create the World Wide Web.[90] (You can read more about Berners-Lee in Chapter 10.)

Then in 1997 Apple had a change of heart, bought out NeXT Inc., and brought Jobs back as its interim CEO. The NeXTSTEP software morphed into OS X, Apple's radical and successful remake of its computer operating system. By 2001, Jobs had dropped *interim* from his title and started Apple on the path to its current success, in which the Mac is not just a computer, but rather a "digital hub" for all types of media and entertainment content. It was also in 2001 that Apple introduced its iconic media player, the iPod.[91]

With the iPod, and its accompanying iTunes software, Jobs solidified his company as a player in the new media business. Jobs did numerous things people told him he couldn't do. He persuaded the major recording labels to offer their music through Apple's iTunes store. He persuaded the major broadcast and cable networks to sell their television shows through the iTunes store. He persuaded major movie studios to sell and rent their movies through . . . oh, you get the picture.[92]

In addition to running Apple, Jobs took Pixar, a computer graphics company he bought for $10 million from *Star Wars* director George Lucas, and turned it into America's leading animation studio, valued in excess of $7 billion when he sold it to Disney in 2006.[93] Upon the sale of Pixar, Jobs became Disney's biggest stockholder and a member of the company's board of directors, thus cementing an already strong relationship between Apple and Disney.[94] Disney CEO Robert Iger depended on Jobs for

AP Photo/Noah Berger

Apple CEO Tim Cook introduces the iPad Air and a new version of the iPad Mini at one of the company's highly anticipated media events. While Apple is primarily in the hardware business, they've transformed how people consume media in the 21st century.

guidance on how his company could avoid the problems the music industry faced in dealing with the Internet. Iger's response was to license his studio's content to Apple's iTunes store so that customers could legally buy and watch Disney entertainment on their computers and mobile devices.[95]

When Jobs lost his long battle with pancreatic cancer in 2011, the response from fans and the news media—from Facebook to cable news—was at a level you might have expected from the death of Joan Rivers or Robin Williams, not from the head of one of the world's most valuable corporations. But then few companies inspire the level of intense loyalty that Apple does, and few companies have been more associated with the personality and identity of its founder.[96] Tim Cook took over as Apple's CEO in 2011 after Jobs stepped down due to his illness, and Apple has continued its rapid growth under Cook's leadership. Although some question whether Apple can continue to thrive without Jobs at the helm, Cook has overseen Apple's expansion into the Chinese market, as well as the purchase of Dr. Dre's headphone and music company Beats Electronics for $3.2 billion.[97]

Web 3.16: Read a remembrance of Apple co-founder Steve Jobs.

Other Major Players

Although they do not challenge any of the cross-media giants for size and scope, there are at least fifty more major players in the American media market. A complete list of these companies can be found on the "Who Owns What" page at *Columbia Journalism Review*'s Web site (www.cjr.org/resources/index.php).

Let's take a brief look at two of these companies that illustrate the strong concentration of ownership in individual media.

Gannett Co. Inc. Gannett is the biggest newspaper publisher in the United States, owning approximately eighty daily newspapers and the second-largest single paper, *USA Today*. Gannett also owns the Army Times Publishing Company, British newspaper publisher Newsquest, television stations in sixteen U.S. states, nine printing plants, and a direct marketing division.

USA Today has a daily circulation of 1.7 million, and the rest of Gannett's approximately eighty American daily papers deliver a total of 5 million copies a day. In addition, Gannett owns approximately 500 nondaily publications in the United States and 200 papers in the United Kingdom.[98] Gannett started out in 1906 with a single newspaper, the *Elmira Star-Gazette* in New York. Gannett then bought out the competing paper in town, the *Evening Star*, and merged it in with the *Gazette*, thus eliminating the competition. The company repeated this pattern—buying up the competition and shutting it down—across the country.[99] The Gannett newspaper chain grew steadily through the 1970s and early 1980s, but it gained the most attention in 1982 when it launched *USA Today* as a national newspaper. Starting a new national paper was an expensive, long-term project; the paper didn't turn a profit until 1993.

There is widespread concern that the newspaper industry as a whole is in a major circulation and advertising sales decline, and Gannett is no exception. For 2013, Gannett had earnings of $5.2 billion and turned a 7.5 percent profit.[100]

Clear Channel Communications, Inc./iHeartMedia. No company illustrates better the rapid move to consolidation of ownership than Clear Channel Communications. Up until 1996, Clear Channel was a significant, though not large, player in the radio business, owning thirty-five radio stations and nine television stations. But in 1996 the FCC lifted most of the restrictions on the number of stations a single company could own. By 2005, Clear Channel owned, operated, or programmed more than 1,200 radio stations in the United States. After reaching that peak, the owners took the company private and sold off a number of stations so that, as of 2014, Clear Channel owned approximately 860 stations reaching more than 239 million people.[101] The company also owns more than 840,000 outdoor advertising billboards. Although it is by far the dominant radio company in the United States, it does face substantial competition from the new satellite

TEST YOUR MEDIA LITERACY

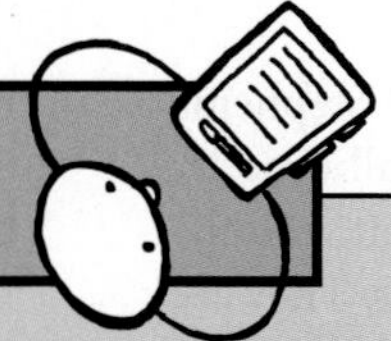

Google's Core Principles

Google has long been known as the company with the unofficial slogan of "Don't be evil." While that was really intended to be more of a rule for working with colleagues than a business philosophy, the company does have a statement of ten core principles that are supposed to guide its actions.[1] They are:

1. Focus on the user and all else will follow.
2. It's best to do one thing really, really well.
3. Fast is better than slow.
4. Democracy on the Web works.
5. You don't need to be at your desk to need an answer.
6. You can make money without doing evil.
7. There's always more information out there.
8. The need for information crosses all borders.
9. You can be serious without a suit.
10. Great just isn't good enough.

You can see the full explanation of these principles at http://www.google.com/about/company/philosophy/.

In addition to its "Don't be evil" culture of excellence, Google is also famous for its worker-friendly environment. It has masseuses on staff not just for executives, but for the engineers who write code. It has free meals served out of a kitchen that is supervised by the Grateful Dead's former chef. An employee can get his or her hair cut or car washed, visit the dentist, go for a workout, or receive child care, all without leaving the Google campus.

Are all these benefits to be nice to employees? Or are they just a way of getting more productivity out of them?

Douglas Edwards, who was the fifty-ninth employee hired by Google back in 1999, wrote in his book *I'm Feeling Lucky* about how the free food that the company offered cut the time people spent eating:

> Like most googlers, I spent less than half an hour at lunch. . . . Without the café, I would have lost twenty minutes getting to a restaurant, half an hour eating, and another twenty minutes getting back. I would have stopped thinking about Google as I cleared the front door.[2]

WHO is the source?

Who are the founders of Google? How do they differ from the founders of other media companies? How does Google differ from other Big Media companies?

WHAT are they saying?

Google's founders brought a distinct philosophy to their business. How would you describe it from what you've read? How does it differ from other major companies? (Feel free to follow the link above to get more details.)

WHAT is the lasting impact?

Has Google's approach to doing business affected its success? Is Google trying to be supportive of its employees, or is it just trying to keep them at work longer by offering lots of services at the office? Does Google live up to its principles? Why or why not?

HOW do you and your classmates react to Google's approach to doing business?

Do you and your classmates think that Google truly tries to avoid being evil? Can a company succeed in a world market when it tries to uphold American values of freedom of information and speech? Would you want to work for Google? Why or why not?

[1] Google, "Our Philosophy," September 2009, http://www.google.com/about/company/philosophy/.

[2] Douglas Edwards, *I'm Feeling Lucky: The Confessions of Google Employee Number 59* (New York: Houghton Mifflin, 2011).

CQ Researcher 3.1: Read a report on Google's success and dominance.

Video 3.6: Douglas Edwards talks about his time with Google.

radio services.[102] In September 2014, Clear Channel Communications changed its name to iHeartMedia to better reflect the fact that the company does business as a streaming audio provider in addition to being an owner of hundreds of radio stations.[103]

Media Economics and the Long Tail

Lists of major media companies generally include companies such as cable television company Comcast, magazine publisher Meredith, or the movie and music divisions of Sony. What don't show up as often are the independent artists, writers, and videographers whose works appeal to a relatively small group of consumers. But when those many small groups are added together, they become an audience big enough to rival those being attracted by Big Media.

The world of Big Media is the world of blockbusters—selling a lot of copies of a limited number of products. Blockbusters include the big summer movies that cost more than $100 million to produce and require the sale of millions of tickets to be a financial success. They are novels

Questioning the Media

Do you think that these new players in the media world have more or less influence on us than the traditional media companies we previously discussed? Why? Before reading this chapter, did you view Google or Apple as media companies? Why or why not?

by Nicholas Sparks and Stephenie Meyer. They are albums by Jay-Z, Taylor Swift, and the Black Eyed Peas. They are the common media products, the common culture we all share.

Despite the consolidation of the media business and the ever-growing emphasis on the importance of blockbusters to Big Media, a strange phenomenon has been taking place. The annual box office has been falling for movies, broadcast television has lost one-third of its audience, and sales of CDs are plummeting, yet people seem to be consuming more media content than ever.

The Short Head Versus the Long Tail

Chris Anderson, in his book *The Long Tail*, argues that we are leaving the era of mass culture and entering one that is vastly more individualistic and much less mass oriented. He writes that, when he was growing up, the only alternatives to Big Media were the library and the comic book store. But today there are vastly more choices at both the commercial and noncommercial levels. Take Apple's iTunes music and video store. Through it, you can buy current blockbuster songs, movies, and television shows, but you can also find rather obscure materials, such as the songs of indie music duo Pomplamoose (*pamplemousse* means "grapefruit" in French), who have built a following through videos on YouTube. Or an EP by the Arizona-based band Calexico. Or the crowd-sourced dance film *Girl Walk // All Day* that was posted serially online over a month and a half. Or you could take a look the gross-out horror film *The Human Centipede* from mail-order DVD rental/streaming video company Netflix.

This is how Anderson describes the shift that has taken place as consumers turn from the mass content produced by broadcasters and publishers to the more focused content provided by broadband connections to the Internet:

> The great thing about broadcast is that it can bring one show to millions of people with unmatchable efficiency. But it can't do the opposite—bring a million shows to one person each. Yet that is exactly what the Internet does so well. The economics of the broadcast era required hit shows—big buckets—to catch huge audiences. The economics of the broadband era are reversed. Serving the same stream to millions of people at the same time is hugely expensive and wasteful for a distribution network optimized for point-to-point communication.[104]

In short, our mass communication is becoming less mass, and we have new media companies that specialize in providing narrowly focused content. Anderson uses the statistical term the **long tail** to refer to this phenomenon.

Figure 3.1 depicts this phenomenon as a distribution curve showing that a relatively limited number of media products—books, songs, DVDs—sell the most copies. This area of a limited number of products and high sales on the left—the **short head**—is where Big Media companies like to live. When a movie comes to a local theater, it needs to attract about 1,500 people over a two-week period for the run to be a success. That means that you won't see a lot of the more obscure movies in your local theater. A CD has to sell at least four copies a year to justify the shelf space it takes up—that is, to pay the rent on its shelf space. Even if it sells 5,000 copies nationwide, if it can't sell four copies in your local store, your local store can't pay the rent on the half-inch of shelf space the CD takes up. So Big Media are all about finding the limited number of hits that will appeal to the most people. As Anderson observes, that's what they have to do to survive.[105]

To see the short-head portion of the demand curve, look at Walmart, the United States' biggest music retailer. The discount giant carries about 4,500 different CDs in its stores. Of those, 200 CDs account for more than 90 percent of their sales. But what about the remaining thousands and thousands of songs that a limited number of people are

Figure 3.1 The New Media Marketplace

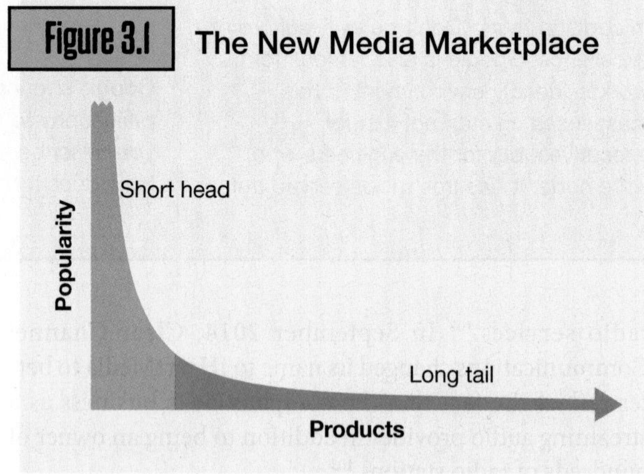

Video 3.7: See and hear Pomplamoose, Calexico, and *Girl Walk // All Day.*

Web 3.17: Read Chris Anderson's article on long tail.

long tail: The portion of a distribution curve where a limited number of people are interested in buying a lot of different products.

short head: The portion of a distribution curve where a large number of people are interested in buying a limited number of products.

interested in buying? They constitute the long-tail portion of the graph that extends off to the right. This is where a limited number of people are interested in buying a lot of different products (as opposed to the short head, where a lot of people are interested in buying a limited number of products).

In contrast to Walmart, Anderson uses online music service Rhapsody as an illustration of the long-tail portion of the demand curve. As of 2011, Rhapsody offered approximately 13 million different music tracks to download. Not surprisingly, the big hits sell a lot of copies. But if you move beyond the big hits—the top 25,000 tracks—you find that Rhapsody still sells a lot of music. From the 25,000 best-selling tracks to the 100,000th best-selling track, sales of each song are at least 250 copies a month and make up nearly a quarter of Rhapsody's downloads. From the 100,000th to the 800,000th most popular songs—and that's a long way down the popularity chart—Rhapsody is still selling enough to make up 16 percent of its business. How can Rhapsody afford to do this? Two factors come into play: (1) Its cost of inventory is minimal—it just has to store the songs on a big array of hard drives; it doesn't have to physically stock the music, and (2) it does business over the entire country with a single store, so it doesn't need a lot of consumers in a single location who want to buy something. If they live anywhere in the United States, that's good enough.[106]

Characteristics of the Long Tail

Anderson writes that the biggest players in the long tail include Rhapsody, which lets subscribers download songs; Apple, the largest seller of legal music downloads; Netflix, which offers hundreds of thousands of different movies by DVDs sent through the mail or through online streaming; and Amazon, the dominant online seller of books, movies, and CDs. These companies can offer selection far beyond the current hits. Anderson argues that there are six principles that drive the success of the long-tail portion of the media marketplace:

- High number of goods—There are far more niche goods than hits. This means that if you can sell enough different niche goods, you can get as many sales as if you were selling a limited number of hits.
- Low cost of reaching markets—The cost of reaching niche markets is falling dramatically, thanks to the ease of access provided by the Internet and the ability to—in many cases—sell a digital download rather than a physical product.
- Ease of finding niche products—Consumers need to be able to find these niche products. This means there need to be tools—Anderson calls them filters—that allow consumers to search through a huge selection of media content to find the particular material they are looking for. This is something Internet movie rental store Netflix excels at. Netflix has consumers rate a series of movies and then provides recommendations based on those ratings.
- Flattening of the demand curve for mainstream hits—Once consumers can find their niche products, the demand curve tends to flatten. Now that consumers can find the full range of products available, there will be relatively less demand for the hits and more demand for the niche products. This will make the long tail longer and lower the demand for the hits.
- Size of collective market—There are so many niche products that they collectively can have as big a market as the hits do. In other words, you can sell as much focusing on the long tail as on the short head if you can offer enough choices.
- Tailoring to personal tastes—Once niche products become available, findable, and affordable, consumers will choose to go with media content that fits their personal wants and needs rather than consuming the hits that hold a mild appeal to so many. Media hits will become less important because consumers can get what they want rather than what happens to be available locally.[107]

Consequences of the Long Tail

Anderson says that a number of consequences arise out of a shift to the long tail from traditional mass media:

- Democratization of the means of production—It used to be that to record a CD you needed a big, expensive recording studio. Now anyone with a laptop computer and some inexpensive software can put together a multitrack recording or edit a short video. You can publish a professional-looking book without the benefit of a major publisher using a laser printer and a local copy shop. The development of the powerful home computer has made it possible for anyone to be a media producer.
- Democratization of the means of distribution—Through the Internet and sites such as eBay and Amazon, anyone can open a national, or even international, sales channel. YouTube gives ordinary people a place to distribute their home-produced videos. I even run a tiny media-oriented bookstore using an Amazon partnership. As Anderson puts it, "The PC made everyone a producer or publisher, but it was the Internet that made everyone a distributor."[108]
- Greatly reduced cost of connecting suppliers and consumers—Sellers and consumers can now find each other through tools such as Google search, iTunes, YouTube, and blogs.

Our twenty-first-century media world has room for a wide range of distribution channels. For the hits, there is nothing like Big Media for distribution. Movie theaters, book stores, big-box retailers (such as Walmart), broadcast network television, and magazines do a great job of selling or distributing media content that appeals to a large group of people. Second are the hybrid retailers—companies such as Amazon and Netflix that have no brick-and-mortar retail stores but have to send out a physical product, such as books, CDs, or DVDs. The hybrid retailers can have national distribution and serve niches, but they still deliver a physical product. Finally, the digital retailers, such as Apple iTunes and Rhapsody, sell downloads with no physical product. Any store that sells a virtual rather than a physical product handles the farthest end of the long tail.[109]

Questioning the Media

What kinds of long-tail media content do you consume on a regular basis? Are there any long-tail artists/authors you like better than short-head/mainstream media? How did you discover them?

One of the most successful providers of long-tail content has been Google's video service YouTube. While YouTube started as a way to make video easy to share, it quickly grew into a major alternative source of video entertainment. "We are providing a stage where everyone can be seen. We see ourselves as a combination of *America's Funniest Home Videos* and *Entertainment Tonight*," cofounder Chad Hurley told Associated Press reporter Michael Liedtke.[110]

Unlike the infamous site Napster, which used to share music files, YouTube has not been confrontational with Big Media. It has always promptly removed any content at the request of corporate copyright owners, but it has also pursued extensive revenue-sharing projects with those same companies. It also limits clips by users to ten minutes, which helps prevent large-scale copyright infringement from users posting entire movies or television shows.[111] (YouTube has entered into contracts with Big Media companies to stream longer videos of professionally produced content.)[112]

As of July 2014, YouTube reported showing 6 billion hours of video per month. (Yes, that's *billion* with a "b.") The company also reported 100 hours of new videos being uploaded to the site per minute.[113]

SECRET 1 With 128.4 million unique viewers in the United States per month, YouTube has a bigger audience than most cable channels.[114] But YouTube differs significantly from cable television. A television channel decides to put up a limited amount of programming each day and hopes that an audience will look at it, whereas YouTube puts up lots of content produced by both professionals and amateurs and then sees what the audience decides to look at. Unlike traditional television, YouTube is capable of delivering programming that reaches audiences that range in size from dozens to millions. "We accept everyone that uploads video to our site, and it's the community that decides what's entertaining," Hurley says.[115] YouTube's expansive approach is a prime example of Secret One—The media are essential components of our lives. YouTube combines the roles of creator, program manager, and viewer into a single person. YouTube is an expression of the audience's interests with almost unlimited levels of choice.

AP Photo/Noah Berger

Steven Chen (left) and Chad Hurley launched the video-sharing Web site YouTube in 2004. It has since become one of the top locations on the Internet for user-generated video.

Diane Mermigas of the *Hollywood Reporter* sees the merger of Google and YouTube as "the first viable new-media successor to broadcast and cable television."[116] She says the combination provides the tools needed to post, view, find, and place advertising on both amateur and professional video programming over broadband channels. She sees the pair leading the charge to have the "eyeballs, ad dollars and creative content that have sustained traditional television" move over to Internet video.[117] This is also why the late Steve Jobs succeeded in making Apple a success in the online media world. Apple understood that consumers needed an easy way to find and then use digital content, providing both the online iTunes music store and the various iPods and iPhones to play back the downloads. Using Apple's products, a consumer can download, transport, and access content anywhere and at any time.[118] The new media companies that are becoming significant and growing players understand the nature of the long tail and will deliver what consumers want.

Who Controls the Media?

Despite the growing presence of the long tail, the news and entertainment business is still dominated by a small number of highly profitable big businesses. This is clearly a source of concern for those who worry that only a limited number of interests control what is being presented to the public at large. But media scholar Michael Schudson argues that, even though the media are run by profit-seeking capitalists, the media do a good job of providing responsible journalism. The *New York Times* still views its primary responsibility as providing readers with an accurate reporting of the day's news. Furthermore, the media present a variety of viewpoints, even if they tend to focus on the middle ground rather than the extreme left or right.[119]

SECRET 7 It is easy to view the media giants as powerful forces (the "they" of Secret Seven—There is no "they") that control the lives of their audiences. While it is true that there is no "they," reality is far more complex than that. Numerous pressures on the media influence what they deliver—pressures that come from owners, stockholders, advertisers, or even the audiences. Companies seek profits, but they must also seek credibility, largely because their credibility gives value to the product they are selling. As long as a wide range of audiences exists, the media will strive to carry a diversity of content.

Bob Herbold of Microsoft told *Advertising Age* that the media landscape is being changed radically by the rise of **broadband networks**, which are high-speed channels for sending data and video into the home via cable or wireless connections. No longer can the networks dictate what people will view. As Herbold puts it, "One of the things that will be dramatically different than the past is that your ability to capture the individual for a period of time and almost force them to watch something will be greatly diminished."[120]

Consumers now have the option of going to traditional Big Media companies or viewing events directly. Those with the time and inclination can watch the actions of the U.S. government on three separate C-SPAN networks. Anyone who can afford a high-speed Internet connection can receive virtually an unlimited array of media choices.

SECRET 1 Critics often ask whether Big Media control society. This is a worthy question, but it is overly simplistic because it assumes that a single force runs these powerful institutions. The media-literate consumer will remember Secret One—The media are essential components of our lives—and ask a somewhat different question: "Who controls the media and their content?" It's not an easy question to answer. The influence of media owners is limited. If people don't want to watch a certain movie, no amount of promotion can get them to go see it. If a television show is offensive, few major companies will want to advertise on it. So the list of those who control the media needs to include advertisers, governments, pressure groups, news sources, and audience members themselves.

---

broadband networks: High-speed channels for transmitting multimedia content into the home via cable or wireless connections.

Owners

Owners of the media have ultimate control over the content their newspapers, Web sites, or television stations carry. Critics charge that corporate owners may attempt to control the news that is reported by the news organizations they own. There is rarely a direct order from headquarters to kill a story, but that doesn't mean the owners don't exercise control over content, either directly or indirectly. In the late nineteenth and early twentieth centuries, financiers such as J. P. Morgan and the Rockefeller family bought controlling ownership of magazines that had been harassing them, such as *Harper's*, *Scribner's*, and *Century*, and simply stopped the unflattering exposés. It wasn't so much censorship as new owners taking the magazines in safer directions.[121]

Perhaps the biggest issue is how news organizations cover stories involving their owners. In the case of ABC News, that owner is the Walt Disney Company. Disney's tight control of all aspects of its properties is legendary. For example, in 2011 Johnny Depp's contract for *Pirates of the Caribbean 4* prohibited ABC affiliates from interviewing or videotaping the actor at the premiere of his non-Disney movie *The Rum Diary*.[122] Former Disney president Michael Eisner told National Public Radio, "I would prefer ABC not to cover Disney. . . . I think it's inappropriate for Disney to be covered by Disney. . . . ABC News knows that I would prefer them not to cover [Disney]."[123]

But the potential for conflicts of interest may be more hypothetical than real. General Electric, former owner of the NBC broadcast network, was frequently cited as an example of a company that might try to control how its news operation would cover its parent company. In a story about consumer boycotts, NBC made no mention of boycotts against its parent company, GE. Nor did it mention GE in a story about defective bolts in nuclear reactors. But media critic Todd Gitlin writes that since 1990 NBC News has "routinely" covered scandals involving General Electric.[124]

Advertisers

With the exception of books, CDs, and movies, American commercial media are supported largely by advertising revenue. As a result, advertisers have a major influence on the types of news and entertainment presented in the media. They can threaten to withdraw their advertising if they don't like a story; they might even suggest that a particular topic should be covered or not covered. Some companies simply don't want to have their ads associated with controversial material, whereas others may be trying to stop the media from running stories that would be directly damaging to the company.[125] Tobacco companies have long punished magazines that run antismoking stories by withholding ads from those publications. But the influence of advertisers can be subtler. For a period during the 1990s, automaker Chrysler asked magazines to alert the company if controversial articles would be appearing near its ads.[126]

There is no question that television programming is produced to attract the specific audiences that advertisers

Photo by CNN via Getty Images

This image of a man standing up to the tanks in Tiananmen Square came to symbolize to the world the protesters against the Chinese government. A Google search of images from the Tiananmen Square protests will bring up this photo most anywhere in the world other than China.

want to reach. A group of advertisers has even established a fund to promote the development of "family-friendly" television programs—that is, programs designed to attract the kind of audience the advertisers want to target.[127] For further discussion on this, see Chapter 11.

Government 

Governments around the world influence how media companies operate. When Comcast made its bid for NBCUniversal, it had to go through more than a year of governmental review before it was allowed to complete the deal, and when AOL and Time Warner merged, they faced eleven months of review by the U.S. Federal Trade Commission.[128] The companies had to deal with a similar review by government regulators in Europe as well.

Rupert Murdoch's News Corporation and 21st Century Fox, whose satellite services provide television to much of Europe and Asia, have had to make compromises in the content they provide. For example, objections by the Chinese government led Murdoch to drop the BBC from his Star satellite system in China. Although he wasn't happy with the decision, he says it was the only way he could sell television services in China.[129] Similarly, Google has faced extensive criticism for censoring its search results on the Chinese version of its search and news sites. For example, a search for pictures of Tiananmen Square on Google in London will produce the iconic photo of a man in a white shirt blocking the path of a tank headed toward the protesters. The same search in China produces a photo "of happy smiley tourists."[130]

While the United States has a relatively unregulated media marketplace, the government still places numerous controls on the broadcast industry. These are discussed in depth in Chapter 13.

Special Interest Groups

Special interest groups often put pressure on the media either to avoid dealing with particular topics in what they consider to be an offensive manner or to stay away from certain topics altogether. For example, when the *Philadelphia Inquirer* made the decision to reprint controversial Danish cartoons that portrayed the prophet Muhammad in an offensive way, Muslims in the Philadelphia area responded by picketing the paper. The cartoons also ran in the University of Illinois student paper, the *Daily Illini*. Publishing the cartoons sparked a debate about the issue on campus, prompted peace protests, and started a public dispute by the staff of the paper as to whether the cartoons should have run.[131] For more on the Danish cartoons, see Chapter 15.

News Sources

Among the strongest influences on the news media are the people who provide stories. Those who are available to provide information or be interviewed will determine what kinds of stories are reported. In general, the views that are most likely to be reported come from people who are in positions of authority or have institutional connections. These people are often government officials, business executives, or experts in a specialized field. They can choose with whom they will speak, and they are able to negotiate ground rules for interviews.

In contrast, ordinary people, poor people, and the disadvantaged typically have little influence on the media or how stories are covered.[132] For example, in 1992 Zoë Baird was nominated to be attorney general of the United States. It soon became known, however, that she had hired two Hispanic domestic workers to take care of her children and had not paid Social Security taxes for them. Baird eventually had to withdraw her name from nomination. The story received extensive coverage both because of the political implications and because of the likelihood that other professional women would run into similar problems. But most of the news media ignored the plight of Latino domestic workers who weren't receiving Social Security benefits. Because they were not in positions of power, domestic workers such as those Baird had employed weren't seen as sources and hence had no influence. The one exception was the Spanish-language television network Univision, which reported the story from the point of view of low-paid immigrant workers.[133]

When a magazine is planning to run a story about a major celebrity, it must negotiate who the photographer will be, who the writer will be, and how much control the source will have over photo selection and article content. The negotiations involve not just the particular story being run, but also whether the celebrity will be available for future articles for that magazine and other publications handled by the same company. Since many magazines depend on newsstand sales, and having a top celebrity on the cover can make the difference in an issue's success, the magazines are often willing to negotiate. Not all magazine editors are satisfied with the practice, however. Bob Guccione Jr., founder of *Spin*, says, "Access to stars today is so controlled. In the '60s and '70s, there was a fresh reporting that was honest and frank. Today, readers can sense this is propaganda, just a stage in a marketing campaign."[134]

In 2007, the magazine *GQ* killed a lengthy, unflattering story about the Hillary Clinton presidential primary campaign. At about the same time, the magazine was also working on a story about the charitable work being done by former president Bill Clinton—a story that was scheduled to run on the cover. According to the Washington, D.C., news Web site Politico, the Clinton campaign "pulled a page from the book of Hollywood publicists and offered *GQ* a stark choice: Kill the piece, or lose access to . . . Bill Clinton."[135] Why would the magazine agree to do this? Primarily because the former president's face "is viewed within the magazine industry as one that can move product."[136] *GQ* editor Jim Nelson denies that there was a connection between the killing of one story and the former president's willingness to pose for the magazine's cover.

Audiences

The power of audiences comes primarily from their willingness to read a particular book, watch a particular movie, or listen to a particular CD. Nothing can make audience members pay attention to media content. If the audience is not there, the media are not likely to carry the programming.

Questioning the Media

Who do you believe controls the media? What evidence do you have of their influence? Has this chapter changed your understanding of who runs the media?

In an attempt to gauge their audiences' interests, the major media companies conduct continual research. *Sports Illustrated* used a Facebook poll to have fans from around the world pick the cover for the 2011 end-of-the-year issue. This was the first time that the cover was picked by fans rather than by *SI* editors. (In case you were wondering, the cover featured injured Rutgers football player Eric LeGrand returning to the field in a motorized wheelchair.)[137]

Movie producers and directors routinely make changes in their films on the basis of test audience research. The 2006 independent film *Little Miss Sunshine* grossed eight times its cost of production after incorporating edits to the movie based on the results of a small test screening. Audience members had liked the movie but had been confused about where the family was traveling in the road trip at the center of the film.[138]

Focus group research sometimes affirms what the director already wanted to do. When Warner Bros. questioned whether young people would sit still for a two-and-a-half-hour version of the movie *Harry Potter and the Sorcerer's Stone*, producers showed it to a children's focus group. Members of the test audience reported that the length was not a problem; in fact, they wanted to see more details from the book in the film.[139]

Chapter SUMMARY

The American media industry, the largest in the world, is run by private business with only minor government control. Having gotten its start in the 1640s, it was among the first industries in the American colonies. However, media business did not become big until the 1830s, when high levels of literacy and the development of the steam-powered printing press allowed for the mass production of newspapers, books, and magazines. The growth of the electronic media in the second half of the twentieth century helped create a national media culture, as the same content became available simultaneously throughout the country.

For many years, six large media conglomerates dominated the American and much of the global media. They own the major television networks, broadcast stations, cable channels and providers, newspapers, magazines, record labels, movie studios, and Internet services. These companies tend to be vertically integrated—producing, promoting, and delivering content to the consuming audience. But there are a number of new players in the media business who are also significant. They provide cable television and Internet services, online search and content, and integrated media content and hardware. Among the biggest media companies operating in the United States are Time Warner, Disney, News Corporation, 21st Century Fox, Viacom/CBS, Bertelsmann, Comcast/NBCUniversal, Google, and Apple.

Widespread access to the Internet has brought about the rise of smaller-scale new media companies that specialize in providing a wide range of media content that appeals to relatively small numbers of consumers. When combined, these niche markets, known as the long tail of media, can rival the size of the markets for blockbuster media content.

While the media industry is dominated by a limited number of companies, these companies have to please a wide range of groups in order to operate successfully. Those groups include the companies' owners, advertisers, government, special interest groups, news sources, and audience members.

Keep up-to-date with content from the author's blog.

Take the chapter quiz.

Key TERMS

penny press 54

synergy 55

vertical integration 60

local cable television systems 62

long tail 72

short head 72

broadband networks 75

Concept REVIEW

American tradition of private ownership of media

Growth of Big Media

Revenue sources for the media

Media synergy

Long-tail media

Forces that control the mass media (owners, advertisers, government, special interest groups, news sources, and audiences)

Student STUDY SITE

Sharpen your skills with SAGE edge at **edge.sagepub.com/hanson5e**

SAGE edge for Students provides a personalized approach to help you accomplish your coursework goals in an easy-to-use learning environment.

chapter

4

Books

The Birth of the Mass Media

Boston Globe/Getty Images

Rainbow Rowell (left, posing for photo) is the author of the young adult novel Eleanor & Park. The book has attracted controversy for its portrayal of bullying and the use of rough language.

Omaha author (and former newspaper columnist) Rainbow Rowell did not grow up well-off. She grew up primarily in Omaha, Nebraska, but spent several years living in rural areas, getting by at times without phone service, electricity, or gas. In an early column, she discussed having her family circumstances improve:

> We went from desperate to poor. And poor felt so good. My mother went on Aid to Families with Dependent Children—welfare. . . . We had food, real food. Milk and oranges and yogurt. Pasta, apples, cheese. Hamburgers. Potatoes. Bread and cereals. And beans.[1]

Rowell understood what it meant to grow up poor. She had to be talked into taking the ACT college entrance exam by her high school principal because she didn't think she could afford to go to college.[2]

Rowell also understood what it meant to be teased, to be bullied. In one of her first columns written for the *Omaha World-Herald*, she talked about growing up with the first name Rainbow. The teasing wasn't even always intentional. Adults would hear her say her name was Rainbow and reply, "Isn't that sweet. But what's your real name?" Children could do more, chanting "Rambo, Rambo, Rainbow Bright." The final question that everyone eventually came to was, "So, were your parents, like, hippies?" And, as much as she would like to deny it, she has to plead guilty. She was named after the Jimi Hendrix album *Rainbow Bridge.*[3]

To Rowell, writing about children who live in and deal with poverty is a big deal because it was a part of her life. As a college student, she wrote about how she felt about growing up poor: "Sometimes I think that no matter how hard I study and smile and struggle, the poverty is still in me, rotting on my breath, devouring my stomach, burning in the back of my throat. In my eyes."[4]

Her experiences growing up poor help shape the story Rowell tells in her award-winning novel for teens, *Eleanor & Park.* The book tells the story of a poor, overweight girl who connects with a Korean American boy who loves indie music. As John Green put it in his *New York Times* review of the book, "The world cannot allow Eleanor a boyfriend of any kind, because she's poor and fat and dresses funny. The world cannot allow Park a girlfriend because he likes wearing eyeliner, and everyone knows that's gay."[5]

LEARNING OBJECTIVES

After studying this chapter, you will be able to:

1 Discuss the development of the book from earliest pictograph to mass-produced publication.

2 Describe two major cultural changes that took place with the development of the typemold and printing press.

3 Explain the functions of each of the three major players in the book publishing and distribution business.

4 Discuss the tension between "popular" books and "great" books.

5 Describe three ways in which the long tail is transforming the book business.

> **“**The world cannot allow Eleanor a boyfriend of any kind, because she’s poor and fat and dresses funny.**”**
>
> —John Green

The language in *Eleanor & Park* is raw. The other kids on the school bus are cruel to the two misfits, and the bullies use crude and offensive language as they mock the two friends. Because of these disturbing elements, Rowell was uninvited from doing a reading in an Anoka County, Minnesota, library, and a group called the Parents Action League asked the school district to remove its seventy copies of the book from the Anoka-Hennepin school libraries. Members of the group “also called for the librarians who chose *Eleanor & Park* for the district’s voluntary summer reading program to be punished.”[6]

The Anoka-Hennepin school board decided that the book was inappropriate for the summer reading program, writing that the book would be “R-rated” if it were a movie, based on adult content and profanity in the story. Once the school board removed *Eleanor & Park* from the summer reading list, it also decided to not finalize its contract with Rowell to come to a reading at the library.[7]

Rowell told *World-Herald* columnist Erin Grace that it seemed to her that the people opposed to her book wanted to close their eyes to a part of the world that is real. “When these people call *Eleanor & Park* an obscene story, I feel like they’re saying that rising above your station isn’t possible. . . . That if you grow up in an ugly situation, your story isn’t even fit for good people’s ears. That ugly things cancel out everything that is beautiful.”[8]

Timeline

1800

1812 War of 1812 breaks out.
1835 Alexis de Tocqueville publishes *Democracy in America*.
1859 Charles Darwin publishes *On the Origin of Species*.
1861 U.S. Civil War begins.
1869 Transcontinental railroad is completed.
1879 Thomas Edison invents electric light bulb.
1898 Spanish-American War breaks out.

1900

1903 Orville and Wilbur Wright fly first airplane.
1905 Albert Einstein proposes his theory of relativity.

1910

1912 *Titanic* sinks.
1914 World War I begins.
1918 Worldwide influenza epidemic strikes.

1920

1920 Nineteenth Amendment passes, giving U.S. women the right to vote.
1929 U.S. stock market crashes, leading to the Great Depression.

1930

1933 Adolf Hitler is elected chancellor of Germany.
1939 World War II breaks out in Europe.

1940

1941 United States enters World War II.
1945 United States drops two atomic bombs on Japan.
1947 Pakistan and India gain independence from Britain.
1949 Communists establish People’s Republic of China.

◀ **3500 BC** (approximately) Writing is developed in the Middle East.
◀ **1450s** Johannes Gutenberg develops movable type and the printing press. For the first time, printed material can be mass-produced.
◀ **1475** William Caxton’s *Recuyell of the Histories of Troy,* the first English-language book, is published in England.
◀ **1517** Martin Luther translates the Bible from Latin into German.
◀ **1640** The Bay Psalm Bookis printed in Massachusetts, the first book to be published in North America.

1814 Steam-powered printing presses speed up the production of books and newspapers.
1928 The first edition of the *Oxford English Dictionary* is completed.

Wikimedia Commons

1937 J.R.R. Tolkien’s *The Hobbit* is published after an editor’s son praised the manuscript. The three-volume *Lord of the Rings* series, published seventeen years later, would achieve international fame.
1942 The *New York Times* best-seller list is launched.

AP Photo

Despite the school district's decision to cancel Rowell's reading, the Omaha author still visited the area, when the Saint Paul Public Library and the Avalon Charter School gave her a fresh invitation to come visit. Rowell participated in both a reading and a forum on controlling access to young adult books.[9]

Books are a source of entertainment, culture, and ideas for society and have given rise to more lasting controversies than almost any other medium. Book publishing is also a major business that is supported by the people who buy books. In this chapter, we look at how books developed from a hand-copied medium for elites into a popular medium consumed by millions, how society was revolutionized by the development of printing, how the publishing business operates, the conflict between literary and popular writing, and efforts to censor writers. ■

Web 4.1: Read more about the attempts to keep Rainbow Rowell's novel *Eleanor & Park* out of a Minnesota public library reading program.

> "When these people call *Eleanor & Park* an obscene story, I feel like they're saying that rising above your station isn't possible.... That if you grow up in an ugly situation, your story isn't even fit for good people's ears."
>
> —Rainbow Rowell

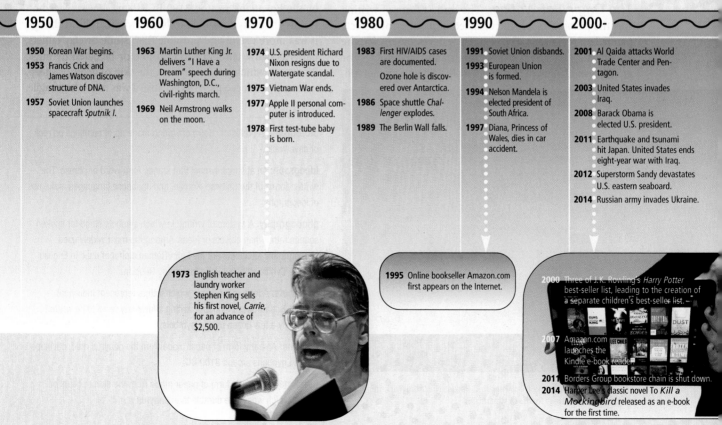

1950

1950 Korean War begins.

1953 Francis Crick and James Watson discover structure of DNA.

1957 Soviet Union launches spacecraft *Sputnik I*.

1960

1963 Martin Luther King Jr. delivers "I Have a Dream" speech during Washington, D.C., civil-rights march.

1969 Neil Armstrong walks on the moon.

1970

1974 U.S. president Richard Nixon resigns due to Watergate scandal.

1975 Vietnam War ends.

1977 Apple II personal computer is introduced.

1978 First test-tube baby is born.

1980

1983 First HIV/AIDS cases are documented.

Ozone hole is discovered over Antarctica.

1986 Space shuttle *Challenger* explodes.

1989 The Berlin Wall falls.

1990

1991 Soviet Union disbands.

1993 European Union is formed.

1994 Nelson Mandela is elected president of South Africa.

1997 Diana, Princess of Wales, dies in car accident.

2000-

2001 Al Qaida attacks World Trade Center and Pentagon.

2003 United States invades Iraq.

2008 Barack Obama is elected U.S. president.

2011 Earthquake and tsunami hit Japan. United States ends eight-year war with Iraq.

2012 Superstorm Sandy devastates U.S. eastern seaboard.

2014 Russian army invades Ukraine.

1973 English teacher and laundry worker Stephen King sells his first novel, *Carrie*, for an advance of $2,500.

AP Photo/Ronh Frehm

1995 Online bookseller Amazon.com first appears on the Internet.

2000 Three of J.K. Rowling's *Harry Potter* best-seller list, leading to the creation of a separate children's best-seller list.

2007 Amazon.com launches the Kindle e-book reader.

2011 Borders Group bookstore chain is shut down.

2014 Harper Lee's classic novel To *Kill a Mockingbird* released as an e-book for the first time.

AP Photo/Ted S. Warren

The Development of the Book and Mass Communication 

Books, consisting of words printed on paper, were the original medium of mass communication (although the Roman Catholic Church had previously achieved a degree of mass communication through sermons, as discussed in Chapter 1). Books allowed ideas to spread, encouraged the standardization of language and spelling, and created mass culture. Books and other printed materials also helped bring about such major social changes as the Protestant Reformation.

Early Books and Writing

Before there could be books, there had to be writing. Writing is thought to have originated around 3500 BC in the Middle East, in either Egypt or Mesopotamia. This means that written language is around 5,500 years old; spoken language, in comparison, is thought to be at least 40,000 years old. The great advantage offered by writing was that information could be stored. No longer did people have to memorize enormous amounts of information to maintain it. Stories could be written down and preserved for generations. However, early writing was not yet a form of mass communication. Reading and writing were elite skills held by people called scribes; their rare abilities gave them power within religious institutions and governments (which were often one and the same).[10]

The Origins of Writing. The earliest form of writing was the **pictograph**, which consisted of pictures of objects painted on rock walls. The next major development was the **ideograph**—an abstract symbol that stands for an object or an idea. An ideograph is more formalized than a pictograph, with one symbol for each object or idea. Languages such as Chinese, Korean, and Japanese still make use of ideographs. The major challenge created by having one symbol for each word is that people have to learn thousands of individual symbols. For example, literary Chinese has 50,000 or more symbols, and everyday written Chinese has between 5,000 and 8,000 symbols.

DeAgostini/Getty Images

The Newspaper Rock petroglyphs from Petrified Forest National Park in Arizona are among the earliest forms of writing.

Ideographs are often used as international symbols, such as those seen on street signs. They are particularly useful in areas where many languages are spoken. Imagine a traveler in Europe looking for a place to take a bath. With an ideograph, a single symbol can stand for *bain* in French, *bad* in Danish, or *baño* in Spanish.

Sometime after 2000 BC, phonographs (not to be confused with record players) were first used. **Phonography** is a system of writing in which symbols stand for spoken sounds rather than for objects or ideas. **Alphabets**, in which letters represent individual sounds, were developed between 1700 BC and 1500 BC. Sound-based alphabet writing, with only a few dozen symbols, was relatively easy to learn compared to the earlier systems of ideographs. Being a scribe thus became less of an elite position. Among the earliest surviving written works are the Greek poet Homer's *Iliad* and *Odyssey*.[11]

The Development of Paper. Once people had a way to record ideas in writing, they needed something to write on. The earliest documents were written on cave walls, rocks, and clay tablets, but these media had limited usefulness. Imagine taking notes on slabs of wet clay that had to be taken back to your dorm room to dry. Something light, portable, and relatively inexpensive was needed. **Papyrus**, a primitive form of paper made from the papyrus reed, was developed by the Egyptians around 3100 BC. Papyrus was placed on twenty- to thirty-foot-long rolls known as scrolls. Although it was more useful and portable than stone or clay tablets, papyrus had a tendency to crumble or be eaten by bugs. **Parchment**, which was made from the skin of goats or sheep, eventually replaced papyrus because it was much less fragile.

---

pictograph: A prehistoric form of writing made up of paintings on rock or cave walls.

ideograph: An abstract symbol that stands for a word or phrase. The written forms of the Chinese, Korean, and Japanese languages make use of ideographs.

phonography: A system of writing in which symbols stand for spoken sounds rather than objects or ideas. Among the most widely used phonographic alphabets are the Latin/Roman alphabet used in English and the Cyrillic alphabet used for writing Russian.

alphabets: A form of writing in which letters represent individual sounds. Sound-based alphabet writing allows any word to be written using only a few dozen unique symbols.

papyrus: An early form of paper made from the papyrus reed, developed by the Egyptians around 3100 BC.

parchment: An early form of paper made from the skin of goats or sheep, which was more durable than papyrus.

World History Archive/Alamy

The Egyptians developed papyrus, an early form of paper made from the papyrus reed, around 3100 BC. These hieroglyphics are from a papyrus scroll of The Egyptian Book of the Dead.

Paper, made from cotton rags or wood pulp, was invented by the Chinese between 240 BC and 105 BC.[12] Knowledge of papermaking was brought from China to Baghdad by the Muslims in the late 700s, and then to Europe by way of Spain in the mid-eleventh century. Papermaking spread throughout Europe during the 1300s, but it didn't replace parchment until printing became common in the 1500s.

Books Before the Era of Printing. Throughout the early medieval period (400–800 AD), most books in Europe were religious texts hand-copied by monks in the **scriptoria**, or copying rooms, of monasteries. Because of the difficulty of preparing parchment, monks sometimes scraped the writing off old parchments to create new books. This led to the loss of many Greek and Latin texts. Books that had lasted hundreds of years and survived the fall of Rome were lost simply because they were erased!

With the rise of literacy in the thirteenth century, the demand for books increased. It soon exceeded the output of the monks, and the production of books shifted to licensed publishers, or stationers. Books were still copied by hand one at a time from a supposedly perfect original (or *exemplar*). One title from this era was Geoffrey Chaucer's *Canterbury Tales*, which is still in print today.

By the fourteenth century, books were becoming relatively common. Religious texts known as illuminated manuscripts were embellished with pictures and elaborately decorated calligraphy, in part to help transmit the message to nonliterate audiences.[13]

The Development of the Printing Press

Printing was invented in China toward the end of the second century. Images were carved into blocks of wood, which were inked and placed on sheets of paper, thereby reproducing the image. However, woodcuts saw limited usage because materials could not be reproduced rapidly. Between 1050 and 1200, both the Chinese and the Koreans developed the idea of movable type, but with thousands of separate ideographs, printing was not practical.

Gutenberg and Early Typesetting. Johannes Gutenberg (1394–1468), a metalworker living in Mainz, Germany, in the mid-1400s, became the first European to develop movable type. Although he developed the first practical printing press (using a modified winepress), Gutenberg's most significant invention was the **typemold**, which enabled printers to make multiple, identical copies of a single letter without hand-carving each.

The most famous of Gutenberg's printed books was his edition of the Bible published in 1455. Approximately 120 copies of this Bible were printed, of which 46 are known to survive. In the 1980s, one of Gutenberg's Bibles sold for $5.39 million at Christie's auction house.[14]

Typesetting was a difficult task in Gutenberg's day. The printer selected a type case containing all the characters of a typeface in a particular size and style known as a **font**—from a font or fountain of type. (Today the word *font* has become largely synonymous with *typeface* and is no longer restricted to mean a particular size and style—for example, bold or italic.) The printer then took from the case the letters needed to spell the words in a line of type and placed them on a type stick, which looked something like the rack used to hold letters in a Scrabble game. Once an entire line had been set, the printer placed it in a printer's frame, which held the type down.

Italics were invented in 1501 by the Italian printer Aldus Manutius (c. 1450–1515), from whom the early desktop publishing firm Aldus took its name. By the 1600s, printers could purchase mass-produced type rather than making their own typemolds. Many popular typefaces originated in the seventeenth and eighteenth centuries and are named after the printers who devised them: Claude Garamond, William Caslon, John Baskerville, and Giambattista Bodoni. A quick check of a computer's font menu will show how many of them are still in use.[15]

The Invention of Mass Culture

Gutenberg's development of the typemold and printing press signaled the invention of mass communication and massive cultural changes. Culture was moving from something that was produced in the local community to something that could have a regional, national, or even international scope by being transmitted through the new mass media.

paper: A writing material made from cotton rags or wood pulp; invented by the Chinese between 240 BC and 105 BC.

scriptoria: Copying rooms in monasteries where monks prepared early hand-copied books.

typemold: A mold in which a printer would pour molten lead to produce multiple, identical copies of a single letter without hand-carving each.

font: All the characters of a typeface in a particular size and style. The term *font* is typically used interchangeably today with the word *typeface*.

Video 4.1: Check out a video history on the development of modern alphabets.

Video 4.2: Was Johannes Gutenberg the most influential person of the second millennium?

TEST YOUR MEDIA LITERACY

How Do Words Get Into the Dictionary?

Putting together the definitive English dictionary was a big job, and one that never really ended. Work on the first edition of the *Oxford English Dictionary* (*OED*) began in 1857 with the goal of finding the origin of every word in the English language. When the authors started the project, they thought it might take ten years. Instead, the first edition, all ten volumes of it, was not completed until April 1928.

Today the *OED* has been through two editions and several supplements. In the 1990s, work began on an electronic version of the dictionary. In December 2011, the editors completed their most recent updating of the dictionary and started over again with the letter *A*.[1] Each month, contributors to the *OED* submit more than 18,000 new words to be considered for inclusion. The following words are among those added to the electronic edition in 2013[2]:

- *Emoji*—A word borrowed from Japanese that refers to "small digital images or icons that are used in texting and other electronic communications to express ideas and emotions."
- *Buzzworthy*—"Likely to generate enthusiastic interest and attention, especially in the popular media."
- *Dad dancing*—"An awkward, unfashionable, or unrestrained style of dancing to pop music, as characteristically performed by middle-aged or older men."

E+/Getty Images

These stylized smiley faces are examples of *emoji*, small digital icons used in electronic communication to express feelings. *Emoji* is a Japanese word that has just recently become part of the English language.

WHAT is the source?

What makes the *OED* different from the dictionary you have on your desk? Why would hundreds of lexicographers contribute entries to its first edition? Is there a need for so many sources? How might their background(s) influence the inclusion of new words?

WHAT is the purpose of this work?

Why do the precise meanings of words matter? If the first edition of the *OED* took more than seventy years to create, and the process of updating it is ongoing, is having an accurate and complete dictionary worth all this effort?

HOW do you and your classmates use the dictionary?

When was the last time you looked up the meaning of a word in the dictionary? Did it mean what you thought it did? What new words would you or your friends add to the dictionary? Does anyone worry about whether a word is being used correctly anymore? Do the uses or meanings of words change too fast for a dictionary to keep up with them? Does the dictionary have a purpose other than to record definitions?

1 "Latest Online Update: December 2011," Oxford English Dictionary, http://public.oed.com/the-oed-today/recent-updates-to-the-oed/previous-updates/december-2011/.

2 "New Word Notes: December 2013," Oxford English Dictionary, public.oed.com/the-oed-today/recent-updates-to-the-oed/december-2013-update/new-words-katherine-martin/; "September 2013 Update," Oxford English Dictionary, public.oed.com/the-oed-today/recent-updates-to-the-oed/previous-updates/september-2013-update/; "June 2013 Update," Oxford English Dictionary, public.oed.com/the-oed-today/recent-updates-to-the-oed/previous-updates/june-2013-update/.

Video 4.3: Watch an interview with author Simon Winchester.

Standardized Books and Language. The first of the changes wrought by movable type was the printing of standardized books. The printing press allowed text to be stored in multiple "perfect" copies. No longer could copyists insert mistakes when they reproduced a book. Printing thus gave students identical copies of books to study. The printing press also made books available in greater numbers and at lower cost. Although printing did not make books inexpensive, it did make them affordable to people besides priests and the wealthy, especially due to the growth of libraries. The printing press also made new types of books available, particularly those written in a country's common language, such as German, instead of Latin, which was spoken only by the highly educated.

English printer William Caxton (c. 1422–1491) helped establish the rules for English, standardizing word usage, grammar, punctuation, and spelling. He accomplished much of this simply by publishing books in English rather than in the more scholarly Latin.[16] The standardization of the English language came about gradually, though. For example, in his journals written in the early 1800s, explorer William Clark notes that he and Meriwether Lewis set out "under a jentle brease."[17] It's not so much that Clark didn't know how to spell these words; at the time, there was still no single "correct" spelling.

Dissemination of Ideas and the Reformation. By far the most important effect of the printing press was that it allowed ideas—such as those of the Protestant Reformation—to spread easily beyond the communities where they originated. Although the printing press did not cause the Protestant Reformation, it certainly helped it take root.

Martin Luther, the German monk who founded the Lutheran Church, clearly understood how the printing press could be used to spread his ideas throughout Europe. In 1522, Luther translated the New Testament of the Bible into German so that ordinary people might be able to read it.

Library of Congress

German metalworker Johannes Gutenberg, depicted here, developed the typemold and printing press that led to the first mass-produced books.

Books in the New World

The first printing press in the New World was set up by the Spanish in Mexico City in 1539; by 1560, the press had issued more than thirty-seven titles. This was a full century before the British in the Massachusetts Bay Colony would start printing. Unfortunately, none of the books from the Spanish press survive today.[18]

Printing in North America began in 1640 with the publication of *The Whole Booke of Psalmes,* known familiarly as the **Bay Psalm Book**. Put together by Puritans who were unhappy with existing translations of the psalms, the first edition sold 1,700 copies, a spectacular accomplishment when one considers that only 3,500 families lived in New England at the time. (Book historian James D. Hart suggests that some of these copies were exported back to England.[19]) Over the next 125 years, the Bay Psalm Book went through at least fifty-one editions in the colonies and Europe. (You can read more about how the Bay Psalm Book played a role in the establishment of the media business in the new world in Chapter 3.)

SECRET 1 **SECRET 5** The advent of the printing press and the publication of books in the language of everyday life helped doom Latin as a spoken language and put literacy—and the ability to interpret religious texts—within the reach of common people for the first time in history.

The creation of a literate mass society also helped spread scientific ideas, such as Copernicus's claim that Earth was not the center of the universe. Books made it possible for people to learn individually, thus allowing new ideas to break into an otherwise closed community. This is also why every government since Gutenberg's time has wanted at least some control over the mass media.[20] So with the advent of mass media barely begun, we see the first examples of Secret One—The media are essential components of our lives—and Secret Five—New media are always scary.

Bay Psalm Book: The first book published in North America by the Puritans in the Massachusetts Bay Colony. The book went through more than fifty editions and stayed in print for 125 years.

In 1731, Benjamin Franklin established one of the colonies' earliest circulating (or subscription) libraries in Philadelphia. Patrons had to pay forty shillings initially, then ten shillings a year to continue borrowing volumes. Franklin's patrons were businessmen and tradesmen. Franklin's name occurs repeatedly in discussions of the media of the colonial era. He was an important book, magazine, and newspaper publisher—the Ted Turner or Rupert Murdoch of his day.

What did people in the American colonies read? Among the best-known authors was Franklin himself, whose *Poor Richard's Almanack* sold nearly 10,000 copies per year, far more to date than any other books at the time in North America.[21] Nonreligious books that sold well in New England included those on agriculture and animal husbandry, science, surveying, and the military.

But not everything was of serious interest. In the 1680s, Boston's leading bookseller attempted to order two copies of the book *The London Jilt, or, the Politick Whore; shewing all the artifices and stratagems which the Ladies of Pleasure make use of, for the intreaguing and decoying of men; interwoven with several pleasant stories of the Misses' ingenious performances,* a title not that different from what might be ordered today.[22]

Questioning the Media

Are books more influential than television or movies? Why do you think so? Which medium has caused the most change and turmoil in the world? Can you name some examples of this? Are there any books that have changed the world?

Samuel Richardson's *Pamela*, published in 1740, was the first English novel. It was a book for the middle class, with characters and situations that ordinary people could identify with. Franklin published a

Kit Carson on the War-Path, published by Munro's Ten Cent Novels, was one of the many dime novels read by the newly literate public in the nineteenth century.

colonial edition of the novel in 1744, but it would be forty-five years until the first American novel was published.

The Development of Large-Scale, Mass-Produced Books

The industrial prosperity of the mid-1800s spurred the growth of cities and the emergence of the middle class. During this time, the number of people who attended public schools grew as well. Education up to the high school level, although still not universal, was becoming common.[23] It was also a period of growth for libraries; the number of subscription libraries tripled between 1825 and 1850. American industrialist Andrew Carnegie financed the construction of nearly 1,700 public libraries from 1900 to 1917; since then, the number of public libraries has continued to grow and was estimated at 10,000 in 2011.[24] Mass culture in the United States expanded throughout the nineteenth century, disseminated widely through penny press newspapers, magazines, Sunday School tracts, and inexpensively produced books.

Serial novels, which were published in installments, were popular in the 1830s and 1840s. Charles Dickens published *The Pickwick Papers* as a serial novel. Serial publication made each section of the book less expensive than a whole book, which appealed to readers, and brought in a steady flow of income, which appealed to publishers.[25] (Serial novels got a boost again in the 1990s when Stephen King published his novel *The Green Mile* in paperback serial form.) The first paperbacks, the so-called **dime novels** (which, despite their name, often sold for as little as a nickel), were heroic action stories, popularized by authors such as Bret Harte, and they generally celebrated democratic ideals. The Civil War was a big time for sales of dime novels, with copies being shipped to Union soldiers as a morale booster.

The 1800s saw massive changes on the business side of publishing, too. Hand-powered flat-bed presses could print no more than 350 pages a day, but the new steam-powered **rotary press** (invented in 1814) could print as many as 16,000 sections (not just pages) in the same amount of time. Through all this, type still had to be set by hand, much as it was in Gutenberg's day. But 1885 saw the introduction of the Mergenthaler **Linotype** typesetting machine, which let a compositor type at a keyboard rather than pick each letter out by hand, thus speeding up the printing process once again. The Linotype was the standard for typesetting until the age of computer composition.

The nineteenth century thus brought the first real mass media that could be recognized today, with books, newspapers, and magazines being printed and distributed in forms that anyone could afford. With the growth of democracy and mass-produced reading materials came the growth of mass literacy.

Buying and Selling Books

In the twentieth century, the writing and selling of books became big business, with a huge variety of books being published. The numbers have continued to grow in the early twenty-first century. In 1995, 1.2 million separate books were available, and by 2005, Amazon.com claimed to have more than 3.7 million titles available. Of

serial novels: Novels published and sold in single-chapter installments.

dime novels: Inexpensive paperback books that sold for as little as five cents (despite their name). They were especially popular during the Civil War era.

rotary press: A steam-powered press invented in 1814 that could print many times faster than the older, hand-powered flat-bed presses.

Linotype: A typesetting machine that let an operator type at a keyboard rather than pick each letter out by hand. The Linotype was the standard for typesetting until phototypesetting became common in the 1970s.

course, most bookstores don't carry anywhere near that number; still, the giant superstores typically carry 50,000 to 150,000 titles.[26]

Getting all those books from the authors' computers or typewriters into the hands of readers is what the publishing business is all about. It involves three major players: publishers, writers, and booksellers.

Publishers

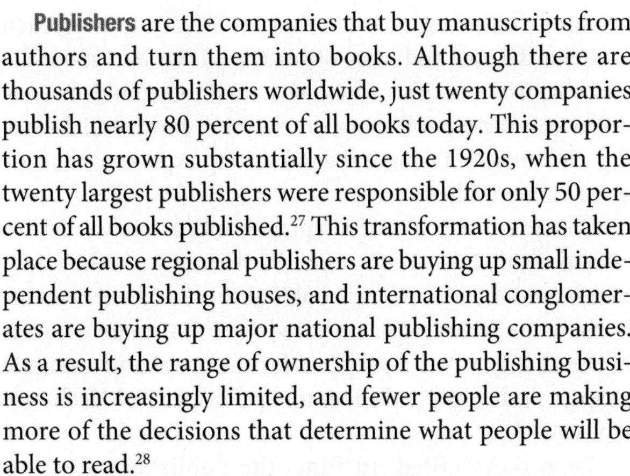

Publishers are the companies that buy manuscripts from authors and turn them into books. Although there are thousands of publishers worldwide, just twenty companies publish nearly 80 percent of all books today. This proportion has grown substantially since the 1920s, when the twenty largest publishers were responsible for only 50 percent of all books published.[27] This transformation has taken place because regional publishers are buying up small independent publishing houses, and international conglomerates are buying up major national publishing companies. As a result, the range of ownership of the publishing business is increasingly limited, and fewer people are making more of the decisions that determine what people will be able to read.[28]

The process of consolidation in the publishing industry can be seen in the story of American publisher Random House. Random House was founded in 1925. After years of growth, in 1960 the company acquired another major American publishing house, Alfred A. Knopf. In 1965, Random House was bought by media conglomerate RCA, and throughout the 1970s and 1980s, Random House continued to grow, buying up a host of publishers. Finally, in 1998, German media giant Bertelsmann bought Random House and combined it with its existing publishing holdings.[29]

Random House has continued to grow by acquiring smaller publishers. In 2009, it acquired Ten Speed Press, an independent alternative publisher of titles such as *What Color Is Your Parachute?* and the *Moosewood Cookbook*. This acquisition brings to mind another, when News Corporation, through its HarperCollins division, bought out literary publisher Ecco Press. Daniel Halpern, founder of the press, told the *Washington Post*:

> People will say, "There goes another independent press, isn't it too bad." The short answer is, "Yes, it's too bad." But that's the reality. Let's not be sentimental about this stuff. This is not a time when the small press can survive.[30]

---

publishers: The companies that buy manuscripts from authors, turn them into books, and market them to the public.

university and small presses: Small-scale publishers that issue a limited number of books covering specialized topics. They are often subsidized by a university or an organization.

The World's Top Publishers. The publishing business is a global industry, with owners in the United States, Germany, Britain, Canada, and the Netherlands. These companies publish a variety of books, ranging from best-selling fiction to textbooks to technical references. The following table reports the companies' revenue only from book publishing. (Fans of the *Fifty Shades of Grey* trilogy might be interested to know that strong sales of the BDSM trilogy moved Random House from number eight on the list in 2011 to number five in 2012.[31])

Table 4.1 Top Global and U.S. Publishers

Top five global publishers		Revenue	Ownership
1.	*Pearson*—Major education publisher	$9.1 billion	United Kingdom
2.	*Reed Elsevier*—Professional publications	$5.9 billion	United Kingdom/ Netherlands/ United States
3.	*Thomson Reuters*—Financial publications	$5.4 billion	Canada
4.	*Wolters Kluwer*—Financial publications	$4.8 billion	Netherlands
5.	*Bertelsmann—Random House*	$3.3 billion	Germany
Top U.S. publishers		**Revenue**	
1.	*McGraw-Hill*—Textbook giant	$2.29 billion	
2.	*Scholastic*—Harry Potter's American publisher	$2.15 billion	
3.	*Cengage*—Major education publisher	$1.99 billion	
4.	*Wiley*—Technical publisher	$1.78 billion	
5.	*Houghton Mifflin Harcourt*—Special interest books	$1.29 billion	

Source: Adapted by the author from "The World's 60 Largest Book Publishers, 2013," *Publishers Weekly*, July 19, 2013, www.publishersweekly.com/pw/by-topic/industry-news/financial-reporting/article/58211-the-global-60-the-world-s-largest-book-publishers-2013.html.

University and Small Presses. Not all publishing is done by large corporations; a substantial number of **university and small presses** issue a limited number of books and may not be in the business for profit. Among their titles are books that serve a limited geographic or subject area or an academic discipline—mostly scholarly books or textbooks. An example of a small press is Interweave Press, which publishes books about knitting, weaving, and crafting. But academic presses occasionally print breakout books. The late Norman Maclean, an English professor at the University of Chicago, had his memoir about growing up in Montana and fly fishing published by the University of Chicago Press. The book, *A River Runs Through It*, was an enormous success (and was made into a movie directed by Robert Redford and starring Brad Pitt).[32]

No small publisher has had more surprising success than the Naval Institute Press (NIP). It's a nonprofit publisher that produces, for the most part, books about naval history and strategy. Typical titles include *Destroyer Captain*, *Stealth Boat*, and *Combat Fleets of the World*. But it has also published military fiction titles, two of which became major best sellers. The first of these was Tom Clancy's *Hunt for Red October*. Clancy, who was working as an insurance agent at the time he wrote the story, had peddled his manuscript about a Russian submarine captain to just about every major publisher in the United States, but none expressed any interest in the book. Finally he submitted it to the NIP. Although the publisher had never handled a work of fiction before, it eagerly put Clancy's book into print. During the months following publication, the book's sales increased gradually as people talked about this great novel from an obscure little publisher. Finally, six months after it was published, *The Hunt for Red October* was at the top of the best-seller lists, just due to word of mouth.

The NIP's second big success was Stephen Coonts's *Flight of the Intruder*. Coonts had queried thirty-six publishers about his Vietnam War novel; thirty of them refused to even look at the manuscript, and four rejected it. He was waiting to hear from the last two when Clancy's success encouraged him to submit it to the NIP. *Flight of the Intruder* made it onto the *New York Times* best-seller list seven weeks after publication, helped in part by a blurb from Clancy and by the fact that book reviewers were now familiar with the NIP. *Flight of the Intruder* spent six months on the best-seller list and sold 230,000 copies in hardback.[33]

Questioning the Media

Do authors still need conventional publishers in the age of long-tail distribution of e-books? Are readers able to sort through the huge number of indie-published books to find the kind of books they want to read? Have you ever bought an indie-published book? If so, what was it? Who benefits the most from indie publishing?

The Government Printing Office. Surprisingly, the federal government is one of the nation's biggest publishers. The U.S. Government Printing Office (GPO) has been producing government documents and books in a variety of forms since it was founded back in 1861. While most of its titles are dry government reports, the GPO has published occasional best sellers, including the *9/11 Commission Report*, the Warren Commission's report on the Kennedy assassination, and the so-called Pentagon Papers (discussed in Chapter 13). To mark the fiftieth anniversary of the Warren Commission report, the GPO published a digital edition, including the 888-page report along with the twenty-six volumes covering the hearings. As of this writing, Congress was considering changing the name of the Government Printing Office to the Government Publication Office to better reflect the fact that so many of its documents are now in electronic form.[34]

Authors

The next group of players in the publishing business is composed of the authors—the people who write the books. Most media attention goes to blockbuster authors, such as Suzanne Collins and Stephen King, or literary authors, such as Richard Russo and Alice Munro; less is written about the vast majority of authors who write without multimillion-dollar contracts, book tours, or television commercials during *The View*. But what is the publishing experience like for an ordinary author?

Consider the story of a typical book, a science fiction romance titled *Moon of Desire*. Pam Hanson (a first-time author and the wife of this book's author) and her mother, Barbara Andrews (who authored several romance novels in the 1980s), wrote a proposal for the novel and a sample chapter and submitted them to a publisher in March (see Figure 4.1).

Then they waited. In June, the publisher agreed to acquire the manuscript. The authors received a contract for the book, which called for the manuscript to be delivered by December 1. With the contract signed, the authors were paid the first half of their advance. This did not mean, however, that they got rich. Advances for first novels are typically between $1,000 and $5,000, and this advance was typical.

Then came the work of writing the book—90,000 words, or about 360 typed, double-spaced pages. The mother and daughter traded drafts back and forth between their computers. A week before the deadline, they sent the finished book to their editor at the publishing company. If the authors had missed their deadline, the publisher would have had the right to reject the book and cancel the contract.

A few weeks later, in early January, the editor sent revisions to the authors. Manuscript revisions may consist of anything from trivial changes in punctuation or grammar to major changes in characterization or plot. In this case, the only major change was that the mutant cannibals menacing the heroine in one chapter had to be toned down a bit. Once the manuscript was accepted, the authors received the second half of the advance. But keep in mind that advances are against royalties (a percentage of the selling price of each book paid to the author), meaning that the advance payments will be deducted from the author's royalty payments.

After a manuscript has been accepted and revised, the book goes into production. An artist creates a cover illustration on the basis of information from an "art fact sheet" that suggests possible scenes for the cover and describes what the hero and heroine look like. The *Moon of Desire* cover featured the hero and heroine on a raft floating on a

Figure 4.1 Ten Steps in the Book Publishing Process

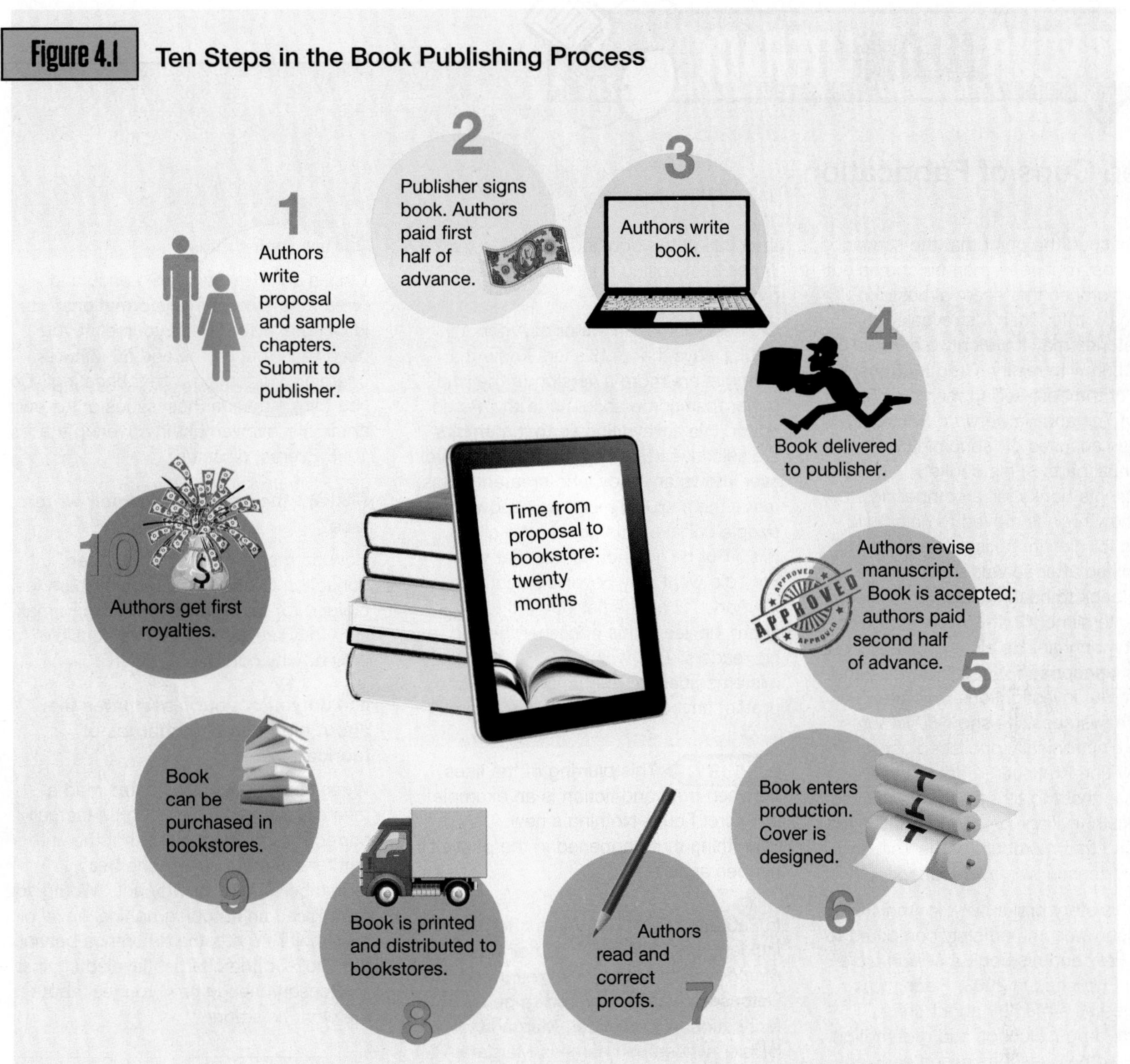

1
Authors write proposal and sample chapters. Submit to publisher.
2
Publisher signs book. Authors paid first half of advance.
3
Authors write book.
4
Book delivered to publisher.
Time from proposal to bookstore: twenty months
APPROVED
Authors revise manuscript. Book is accepted; authors paid second half of advance.
5
Book enters production. Cover is designed.
6
Authors read and correct proofs.
7
Book is printed and distributed to bookstores.
8
Book can be purchased in bookstores.
9
10
Authors get first royalties.

©iStockphoto.com/penfold; ©iStockphoto.com/julichka; ©iStockphoto.com/5455586; ©iStockphoto.com/frender; ©iStockphoto.com/LonelySnailDesign; ©iStockphoto.com/milosluz; ©iStockphoto.com/Warchi; ©iStockphoto.com ©iStockphoto.com/4x6; ©iStockphoto.com/tashka2000;

flaming sea. A book designer lays out the rest of the book, deciding what the pages will look like, what typeface will be used, and how big the book will be. (These can be serious considerations. Stephen King was required to cut 150,000 words, nearly half its length, from the original edition of *The Stand* to make it more marketable.[35])

Once the book is set in type, a copy of the ready-to-print pages—known as **proofs**—is sent to the authors. Authors are supposed to correct only blatant errors in proofs, although some have been known to start rewriting the book at this point. As is usual in popular fiction, Hanson and Andrews had about a week to read the proofs of their book and send them back to the publisher; after the corrections were made, the proofs were sent to a printer to produce the finished book.

At this point, it's time to start marketing the book. This may include placing advertisements in newspapers, in fan magazines, or even on television and scheduling a book tour and media appearances. But Andrews and Hanson, like most first-time novelists, had to make do with virtually no marketing support. Twenty months after the original proposal was submitted, the book was available in bookstores.

Book publishing can be lucrative for some, but the majority of writers make very little money. Tom Clancy's multimillion-dollar advances are exciting but not typical. According the U.S. Bureau of Labor Statistics, the median income for writers and authors was $55,940 per year in 2012.[36] Hanson and Andrews, who wrote their book under a single pseudonym, Pam Rock, saw their first royalties

---

proofs: The ready-to-print typeset pages sent to book authors for final corrections.

TEST YOUR MEDIA LITERACY

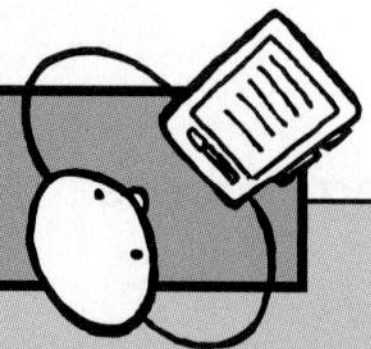

Three Cups of Fabrication

It's reached the point that the scenario is almost routine. A memoir comes out telling stories that seem almost too good to be true. Then it's revealed that those stories may have only a minimal connection with reality. Greg Mortenson, author of the best-selling memoirs *Three Cups of Tea* and *Stones Into Schools*, has been accused of fabricating substantial parts of his books. Mortenson's books tell a compelling story about how he was moved to help build schools for girls in Pakistan and Afghanistan after he was rescued and nursed back to health following a failed attempt to climb K2, the world's second highest mountain. He also discusses how he was kidnapped for seven days by the Taliban. But investigations reported by the TV newsmagazine show *60 Minutes* and an electronically published short book by Jon Krakauer (of *Into Thin Air* fame) say that Mortenson actually visited the Pakistani village a year after his failed climb and that members of the Taliban deny Mortenson was ever kidnapped.[1]

When this story broke back in April 2011, Mortenson was immediately compared to James Frey and his book *A Million Little Pieces*. Published in 2003, *Pieces* was presented as a memoir about crime, violence, drugs, alcohol, and redemption. Despite some questions raised early on about its essential truthfulness, it was a wildly popular best seller, and many readers deeply identified with Frey.[2]

But in January 2006, the muckraking investigative Web site The Smoking Gun (TSG) reported that the book was filled with exaggerations and "a million little lies."[3] TSG investigated Frey after the site had trouble finding a mug shot from one of Frey's numerous arrests portrayed in the book. (TSG has a big section devoted to celebrity mug shots.) What the site's researchers found in their investigation was that Frey either fabricated or grossly embellished the accounts of his involvement in a train accident that killed a girl, the time he spent in jail, and the details of a friend's suicide.[4]

Memoirs are the hot literary property of the twenty-first century. In February 2006, right after the Frey scandal, more than half of the books on the *New York Times* best-selling nonfiction list were memoirs.

Charles Adams, an editor at Algonquin Books, says that publishers know that memoirs are more a version of the truth rather than some absolute truth: "As an editor, I've always known that memoirs are selective truth. I don't know that I've ever known anybody who created things, made them up, so much as I know that people edit their memories. We all do this." But he goes on to say that what Frey did went way beyond selective memory: "Look, he flat-out lied to his agent, he lied to his publisher, he lied to his readers. This was not misremembering, or changing things to protect anybody."[5]

SECRET 4 This blurring of the lines between truth and fiction is an example of Secret Four—Nothing's new: Everything that happened in the past will happen again.

In February 2008, two years after the Frey incident, the Holocaust memoir *Misha: A Mémoire of the Holocaust Years* by Misha Defonseca was discovered to be a fabrication. A week later, Margaret Seltzer, whose pen name is Margaret B. Jones, was outed for fabricating her gang-life memoir *Love and Consequences*, which was about growing up as a half-white, half–Native American foster child in Los Angeles. In reality, Seltzer is all white and grew up in an upper-middle-class Los Angeles neighborhood where she attended private school.[6]

Before answering the questions below, read several of the suggested readings linked to in Web 4.2.

WHO are the sources?

Who is Greg Mortenson? How do you think his experiences in central Asia shaped what he wrote in *Three Cups of Tea*? Who is James Frey? Could he have honestly turned an autobiographical novel into a memoir?

WHO are their critics?

Who is Jon Krakauer? (Go back and reread the "Media Transformations" box in Chapter 1 to refresh yourself if you need to.) What are he and *60 Minutes* charging Mortenson with fabricating? Do you think Krakauer has issues of his own about his involvement in covering the 1996 Everest disaster?

WHAT are the problems memoir writers face?

How do memoirs differ from other nonfiction books? Should publishers feel obliged to "fact-check" memoirs to make sure they are as accurate as possible? Why or why not?

HOW do you or your classmates feel about memoirs and charges of fabrication?

When you or your classmates read a memoir, do you expect it to be factually correct, or do you accept that the author can tell a story as he or she best remembers? Why or why not? Would you rather read an autobiographical novel or a memoir? What's the difference between the two? Do the charges leveled against Mortenson change how you feel about the work he's done?

---

[1] Howard Kurtz, "Another Memoir Meltdown," April 18, 2011, blogs.thedailybeast.com/spin-cycle/2011/4/18/60-minutes-expose-of-greg-mortenson-book-highlight; Jon Krakauer, *Three Cups of Deceit* (San Francisco: Byliner, Inc. 2011).

[2] Adam Kirsch, "He Wrote What They Wanted," *New York Sun*, January 11, 2006; The Smoking Gun, "A Million Little Lies," January 8, 2006, www.thesmokinggun.com/jamesfrey/0104061jamesfrey1.html.

[3] Ibid.

[4] Scott Eyman, "It's My Story (and I'll Lie If I Want to)," *Palm Beach Post*, February 21, 2006.

[5] Eyman, "It's My Story (and I'll Lie If I Want to)"; Motoko Rich, "Gang Memoir, Turning Page, Is Pure Fiction," *New York Times*, March 4, 2008.

[6] Rich, "Gang Memoir, Turning Page, Is Pure Fiction."

Web 4.2: Read more on Frey and an update on the Mortenson case.

beyond the initial advance more than two and a half years after the initial proposal was sent in.

Booksellers

The last major players in the book business are the book wholesalers and retailers—the companies that take the book from the publisher to the book-buying public.

Bookseller and Distributor Consolidation. The Ingram Book Company, the nation's largest book wholesaler, distributes approximately 1.4 million of book titles to more than 35,000 retail, library, and educational outlets. In essence, Ingram and its smaller competitors are the sources from which bookstores buy their books.[37]

The buyers at Ingram are among the most important in the book business; they determine how many copies of a book will be stocked in the company's warehouses. This can, in turn, determine the size of a book's press run. Ingram's buyers are respected not only by bookstore owners but also by scholarly presses.[38]

Reuters/Central Asia Institute

Greg Mortenson poses with a group of students from a school in northeastern Afghanistan. Mortenson has been accused of fabricating parts of his memoirs about building schools in central Asia.

Among booksellers, Barnes & Noble is the one big chain still standing. The company's revenue totaled $6.81 billion for 2013, and it operates 675 superstores and 686 college bookstores throughout the United States. It is also an online bookseller thanks to its BarnesandNoble.com site, and the company has its own line of Nook e-readers, though it discontinued its color Nook in 2013, leaving the company with just a black-and-white e-reader. Barnes & Noble has struggled financially over the last several years, posting a loss of $157 million for 2013.[39]

The alternative to these big stores—which frequently offer book clubs, live music, book events, and even in-store cafés—are the independent bookstores, which are represented by the American Booksellers Association (ABA). The ABA currently represents 1,200 independent bookstores, down from 5,200 in 1991.[40]

A major alternative to both the chain and the independent bookstores are online bookstores, most notably Amazon.com, discussed later in the section on the future of books.

Another type of bookseller is the mail-order book club. The Book-of-the-Month Club is the nation's oldest and largest book club. Its books were originally selected by an elite group of readers, but they are now chosen by the club's marketing directors. The judges were eliminated in mid-1994, by which time their role had become essentially ceremonial. The club focuses on marketing best sellers rather than highlighting books by new authors whom readers may not appreciate. A former book club judge argued in the *New York Times* that the placing of a marketing manager in the number-two position at the club transformed it from a literary organization into a mail-order store that could just as easily sell kitchen supplies or clothes.[41]

In recent years, book clubs have faced increased competition from book superstores and online bookstores. However, in addition to sales, book clubs generate mailing lists that can be used to market other products. Book clubs are also important because, when they are operated by a publisher, they produce a high level of revenue by cutting out the intermediate bookstore. For example, romance publisher Harlequin has a book club for each of its major imprints. Recently, book clubs have started operating online, believing that this will help them attract young readers.

The Textbook Business

Textbooks are different from other books in one major respect—the people who select the books aren't the same as the end users, the people who have to buy and pay for them. Students charge that, because of this disconnect, faculty members don't take price sufficiently into account when picking books for their courses.

Estimates on how much students spend per year on textbooks vary widely, but a Government Accountability Office study estimated costs at $900 per year. The same report showed that textbook prices increased at more than twice the overall rate of inflation between 1986 and 2004.[42] Retail

CQ Researcher 4.1: Read a report on how digital technologies are changing learning in schools.

Figure 4.2 A Comparison of Publisher and Bookseller Income and Costs From Student Course Material Expenditures

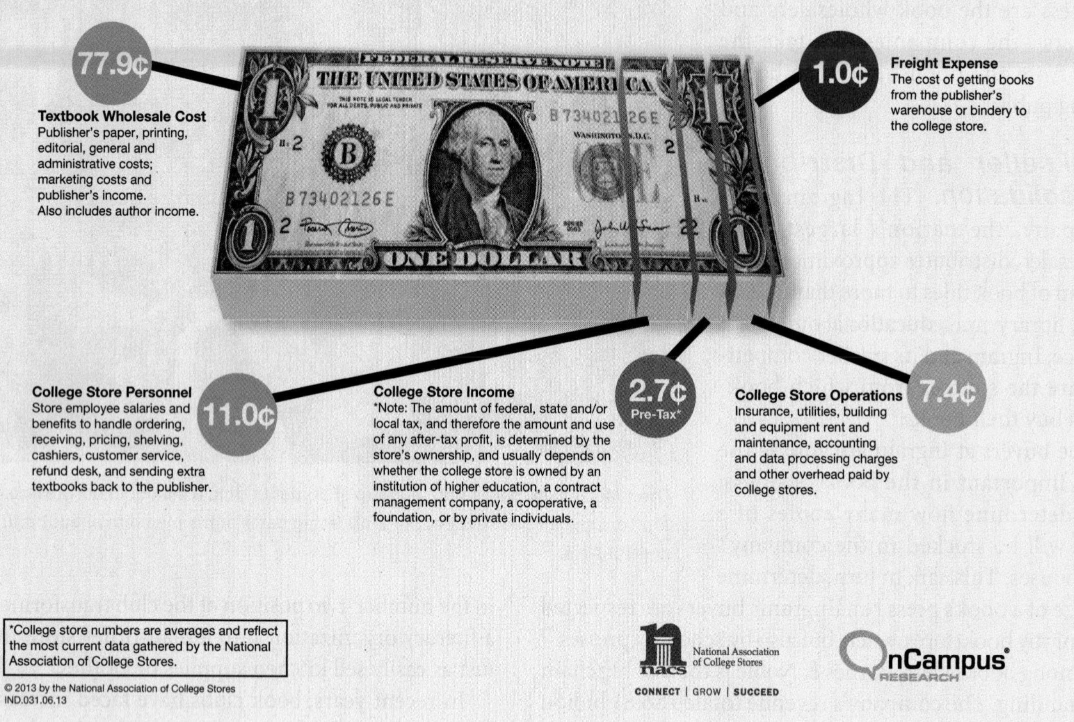

Where the New Textbook Dollar Goes*...
77.9¢
Textbook Wholesale Cost
Publisher's paper, printing, editorial, general and administrative costs; marketing costs and publisher's income. Also includes author income.
1.0¢
Freight Expense
The cost of getting books from the publisher's warehouse or bindery to the college store.
College Store Personnel
Store employee salaries and benefits to handle ordering, receiving, pricing, shelving, cashiers, customer service, refund desk, and sending extra textbooks back to the publisher.
11.0¢
College Store Income
*Note: The amount of federal, state and/or local tax, and therefore the amount and use of any after-tax profit, is determined by the store's ownership, and usually depends on whether the college store is owned by an institution of higher education, a contract management company, a cooperative, a foundation, or by private individuals.
2.7¢
Pre-Tax*
College Store Operations
Insurance, utilities, building and equipment rent and maintenance, accounting and data processing charges and other overhead paid by college stores.
7.4¢
*College store numbers are averages and reflect the most current data gathered by the National Association of College Stores.
© 2013 by the National Association of College Stores
IND.031.06.13
National Association of College Stores
CONNECT | GROW | SUCCEED
OnCampus RESEARCH

Source: National Association of College Stores, http://www.nacs.org/LinkClick.aspx?fileticket=_Jz-tFOW7oM%3D.

bookseller giant Barnes & Noble also has a separate division devoted to selling textbooks that did more than $1.7 billion in business in 2011 through its more than 630 campus bookstores. Along with making money for the company itself, the stores also give the school they're associated with a cut of the sales.[43] John Frederick, provost of the University of Nevada at Reno, attributes some of the high costs to the bundling of CDs and Web site passwords with new textbooks. When students buy the books used, they often do not get access to the Web site or have the CDs. "The publishers engage in a lot of tactics to limit the used-book market," Frederick said. "It is a real problem, but until universities band together to create policies that would control the price of textbooks or exert some kind of market pressure to reduce the cost, there won't be any easy solutions."[44] To be fair to the publishers, they have high fixed costs compared to the booksellers, including development, permissions, royalties, marketing, design, typesetting, and printing, which they must incur to put out even one copy of a new or revised edition. Figure 4.2 compares the profits and costs of publishers and authors from new editions to the profits of booksellers from new and used editions.

Students have tried a variety of methods to control their books costs. Some simply download pirated scans of textbooks from peer-to-peer file sharing sites in much the same way as they download illegal copies of music, TV shows, or movies. Other students go online and buy less-expensive black-and-white international editions. Still others go to social media sites to find out which professor uses the least expensive book. Perhaps the most pervasive change has been the growth of textbook rental plans. Under them, students pay a rental fee that is between two-thirds and one-half the cost of either a new or used book, then they turn the book back in to the bookstore at the end of the semester. In essence, it's a guaranteed buy-back plan.[45]

Other schools are trying out electronic textbooks, which are delivered using portable devices called **e-book readers**. But while students like e-textbooks in principle, when forced to choose between a printed book and an e-book, most choose a printed textbook.[46]

Apple got a lot of attention in January 2012 when it launched its iBooks 2 electronic textbook system, targeted

---

e-book reader: A portable device for viewing, and sometimes selling, electronic books and other texts. Among the most popular are the Amazon Kindle and the Barnes & Noble Nook.

primarily at high schools. Apple combined new reader software with a user-friendly authoring system and an online store to sell the books. The way the system works is that each student buys his or her own copy of the book at a cost of about $15 and installs it on an iPad. Over the life of the book, students or the school district pay roughly the same amount as the book in paper format would cost. (A printed book is typically used for five years; students would have to own an iPad and buy copies of all their books for themselves each year.) Apple's authoring system can only be used for the iBooks 2 software, and if the book is sold (as opposed to being given away for free), it has to be sold through Apple's online store. While there is no doubt that Apple's new system can be used to create interesting alternatives to traditional textbook buying, it's unclear at this point how popular the closed system will be. As of the spring of 2014, the iBooks authoring and sales system had not made a big splash in the world of commercial textbooks.[47]

(More on e-books can be found in the "Future of Books" section at the end of this chapter.)

Students also try to cut their textbook costs by buying used books. The manager of the Oregon State University bookstore notes that more than 40 percent of the textbooks sold at the store are used.[48] Of course, with used textbooks, neither the publisher nor the author gets a cut of the sales, only the bookstore.

Library of Congress

Famed photographer Mathew Brady took this portrait of celebrated American author Nathaniel Hawthorne in the mid-nineteenth century. Brady's role in the development of photojournalism is discussed in Chapter 5.

Books and Culture

For all the attention that movies, television, CDs, and video games get from social critics, books continue to be a major source of excitement, controversy, money, and even violence.

©iStockphoto.com/Andrew_Howe

The Importance of Blockbuster Books

A continual tension exists between blockbuster books that make large amounts of money for publishers and so-called important books that have lasting literary value. But this tension is nothing new—it dates back at least to the middle of the nineteenth century.

Great Books Versus Popular Books. As noted earlier in this chapter, the mid-1800s were a period of strong growth for the publishing business, with the number of serious novels and popular fiction titles increasing rapidly. Americans wrote almost 1,000 novels from 1840 to 1850, up from the 109 books of American fiction published between 1820 and 1830.[49]

The 1850s saw the publication of Nathaniel Hawthorne's *Scarlet Letter*, Herman Melville's *Moby-Dick*, and Walt Whitman's *Leaves of Grass*, but none of these "great books" sold nearly as well as popular novels written by and for women. Hawthorne resented losing sales to popular women authors. He once became so frustrated that he commented, "America is now wholly given over to a d——d mob of scribbling women, and I should have no chance of success while the public taste is occupied with their trash—and should be ashamed of myself if I did succeed."[50]

The **domestic novels** that Hawthorne was complaining about told of women who overcame tremendous problems through their Christian strength, virtue, and faith, ending up in prosperous middle-class homes. One of the best known of Hawthorne's "scribblers," at least today, is Sarah Josepha Hale. She was well known not only as a novelist, but also as a writer of children's books (she was the author of "Mary Had a Little Lamb") and the editor of *Godey's Lady's Book*, a popular women's magazine of the day (see Chapter 5).[51]

Women authors of popular fiction continue to sell well today. According to the Romance Writers of America, romantic fiction had annual sales of $1.08 billion in 2013,

---

domestic novels: Novels written in the nineteenth century by and for women that told the story of women who overcame tremendous problems to end up in prosperous middle-class homes.

Video 4.4: Watch a demonstration of Apple's e-textbooks.

the majority of which was written and read by women. Nearly 40 percent of the sales of romances were as e-books, the rest were spread among mass-market paperbacks, **trade** paperbacks, and hardbacks.[52]

Hawthorne's complaints about popular fiction outselling serious writing are often echoed today. Major publishers work hard to promote a limited number of blockbuster books—in part because only a small percentage of books make a profit. For example, in 2000 romance publisher Harlequin recorded a dramatic increase in profits primarily because of two best-selling titles.[53] Typical among the best-selling authors whom publishers love is mystery writer Janet Evanovich. She started writing romance novels for Bantam, then branched out into the wildly successful Stephanie Plum bounty hunter novels. Evanovich's novels mix humor, adventure, mystery, and romance. "I wanted to write the book that made people feel good. If you are having a bad day, you could read my book and I might make you smile," she has said.[54] Why did Evanovich choose to write about a somewhat inept female bounty hunter? According to her, she saw a space for it in the marketplace: "So I took what I loved about the romance genre and squashed it into a mystery format."[55] The first printing of her 2009 novel *Finger Lickin' Fifteen* was 2 million copies, and 30 million copies of her books are in print. In contrast, Marilynne Robinson's Pulitzer Prize–winning novel *Gilead* sold only 345,000 copies. Good sales, to be sure, but nowhere near the levels of popular fiction.[56]

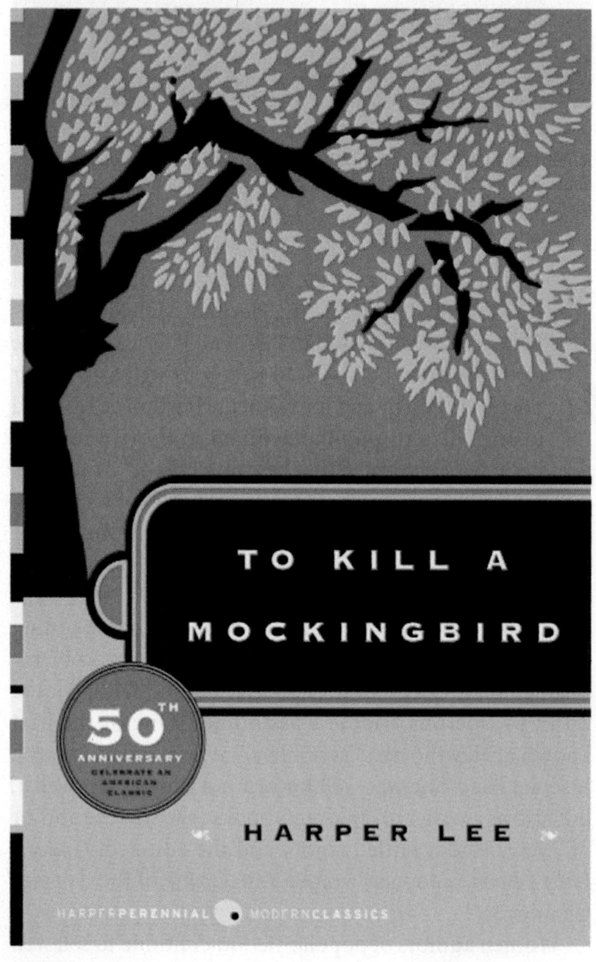

AP Photo/Harper Collins Publishers

Harper Lee's classic novel *To Kill a Mockingbird* was issued as an e-book for the first time in 2014.

Web 4.3: You can get a daily quote from C. S. Lewis from the @CSLewisDaily Twitter feed.

Not every best-selling book is popular fiction, however. Harper Lee's classic *To Kill a Mockingbird*, which has stayed in print for more than fifty years, continues to sell nearly 1 million copies a year.[57]

These blockbuster authors illustrate the main thrust of the publishing business today—finding writers who can turn out one big hit after another. Harry Hoffman, a former bookstore chain CEO, points out that books have to compete with Nintendo and television. In essence, publishing no longer views itself as being in the literature business; instead, it considers itself to be in the entertainment business.[58]

Of course, popular fiction and literature can sometimes intersect. Among the most influential best sellers of the past fifty years is John Ronald Reuel (J. R. R.) Tolkien's epic-length fantasy trilogy, *The Lord of the Rings.* Initially published in England in 1954 and 1955, the story has remained continuously in print and has now sold more than 100 million copies—11 million during 2002 alone. (The sales boost in 2001 and following years can be attributed in part to the popularity of the movie series based on the books.)

Tolkien, an English professor at Oxford, was a colleague of C. S. Lewis, author of the popular *Chronicles of Narnia*, which also formed the basis for a popular movie series. A veteran of World War I, Tolkien specialized in the history of language and literature, and his passion was European myths and sagas. He started work on *The Hobbit*, his first book set in the fictional Middle Earth, in 1930, telling the story of Bilbo Baggins and his adventures. *The Hobbit* was written initially to entertain Tolkien's four children, but the book was published in 1937 after the ten-year-old son of an editor read the manuscript and liked it. The book was a success, and the publisher asked for a sequel. Seventeen years later, the first part of *The Lord of the Rings* was published.

Tolkien wrote the story as a single book, but the publisher divided it into three volumes to make it more practical to print and sell. In fact, the story was so long that even Tolkien didn't know what to do with it. In a letter to his publisher, Tolkien wrote, "My work has escaped from my control, and I have produced a monster: an immensely long, complex, rather bitter, and rather terrifying romance, quite unfit for children (if fit for anybody)."[59]

trade books: General-interest fiction and nonfiction books that are sold in hardback or large-format paperback editions.

Although Tolkien died in 1973, his books have had a lasting influence on American popular culture. *The Lord of the Rings* strongly influenced rock groups such as Yes and Led Zeppelin, and it inspired Gary Gygax to quit his job as an insurance salesperson and devote himself to developing his role-playing game Dungeons & Dragons. The online game EverQuest, which is based on fantasy themes created in *The Lord of the Rings*, receives more than $5 million a month in subscription revenue from its fans. There is even an academic journal devoted to Tolkien's Middle Earth and its linguistics. Most important, the entire genre of contemporary fantasy literature owes its existence to Tolkien. The fantasy sections in bookstores and the whole genre of swords-and-sorcery movies would not exist but for the inspired writings of a British professor.[60]

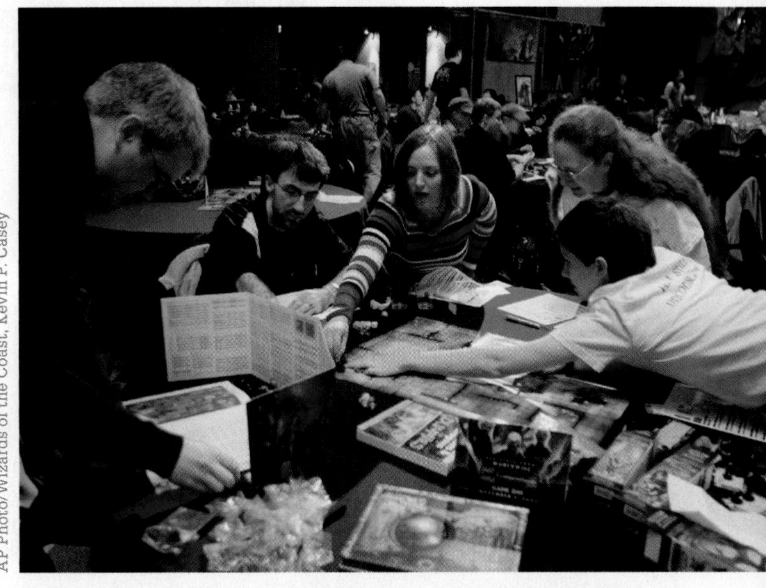

AP Photo/Wizards of the Coast, Kevin P. Casey

J.R.R. Tolkien's epic *Lord of the Rings* trilogy inspired legions of fantasy writers as well as the creation of the role-playing game Dungeons & Dragons.

Young-Adult Series Break the Best-Seller Lists. The biggest publishing phenomena in recent years have been young-adult novels set in supernatural or dystopian worlds: J. K. Rowling's magical *Harry Potter* books, the *Twilight* vampire series by Stephenie Meyer, and the dystopian worlds of Suzanne Collins's *Hunger Games* and Veronica Roth's *Divergent* series. These series deal with worlds inhabited by young people who suffer from normal teen angst, as well as all the conflicts brought about by vampires, werewolves, wizards, and reality show battles to the death. Rowling's seven-volume *Harry Potter* series has 143 million copies in print in the United States. Meyer's teen-vampire romance series has had four volumes published to date and has sold 40 million copies.[61] And the newcomer, Collins's three-volume *Hunger Games* series, which tells the story of a young woman who becomes a rebel leader after being forced to fight to the death with other teens in a televised arena, has sold more than 65 million copies with one of the four movies based on the books yet to be released.[62]

In addition to bringing the joy of reading to millions of young people (and adults, for that matter), the authors have upset the major best-selling book lists. Prior to the publication of *Harry Potter and the Goblet of Fire*, the fourth book in the series, the *New York Times* had been ranking books by sales in four categories: fiction and nonfiction, paperback and hardback.

But in February 2000, *Harry Potter* was threatening to take up four spots on the *Times* hardback fiction list.[63] This dominance spurred complaints by publishers who felt that the children's books were keeping their authors who wrote for adults from being recognized.[64] So before *Goblet of Fire* was released, the *New York Times* created a separate best-seller list for children's books. Some people in the industry praised the new list, saying that it gave children's books the attention they deserved, whereas others claimed that it had been created just to keep the young wizard from taking up four slots on the fiction list.

According to Caron Chapman of the Association of Booksellers for Children, the top books on the children's best-seller list will not change as often as those on the adult list:

> Adults constantly want the newest and the latest. But in children's bookselling it's not the newest or the latest, but the best that teachers and parents are looking for. Adult bestseller lists have nothing to do with the best book, but which title has the most marketing support that week.[65]

By 2009, Meyer's *Twilight* books were occupying four of the top ten spots on the *USA Today* best-seller list, which combines all books (hardback, paperback, fiction, and nonfiction) into a single list. But *Breaking Dawn*, the fourth book in the series, does not appear on any of the *New York Times* best-seller lists. Instead, the story of Bella and Edward—along with that of Harry, Hermione, and Ron, as well as that of Katniss, Peeta, and Gale—inhabits the Children's Series books list. This list treats the entire series as essentially a single entity rather than individual titles.

Children's books can appeal to adults as well. Carl Davies, who works in educational publishing, says:

> There seems to be a big crossover between what children like and what adults like, and Harry Potter is the best example of that. But it's not just adults reading the modern favorites, because what's clear is that children are also reading the classics of the past that their parents read.[66]

Web 4.4: Check out the four separate *New York Times* best-seller lists featuring books targeted at children and young adults.

TEST YOUR VISUAL MEDIA LITERACY

Comics Don't Have to Be Funny

The story of Holocaust victim Anne Frank is known to most young people who went through American schools. Her teen diary that tells the tale of the two years she and her family spent hiding in a small apartment from the Nazis is a standard part of our middle school or high school English curriculum. But parts of her story don't come through her famous diary. For example, Anne wasn't interested in the fact that the apartment she hid in was located above a jam warehouse. As a teenage girl, Anne was far more interested in Peter, the teen boy who was hiding with her, or fighting with her mother.

When the folks who run the Anne Frank House in Amsterdam decided to commission a new biography of Anne, instead of turning to conventional biographers, they contacted comic book creators Ernie Colón and Sid Jacobson.[1] While the pair had worked on such light titles as *Casper the Friendly Ghost* and *Richie Rich,* they had also collaborated on the graphic novel treatment of the U.S. government's *9/11 Commission Report* on the September 11 terror attacks. Their graphic novel/biography of Frank covers a much wider time period than the diary, going from Anne's parents' lives before she was born and extending until the publication of the diary years after Frank's death.

HOW does a graphic novel differ from a novel that just has text?

For decades, high school students have been reading the story of Anne Frank in the format of a teenaged girl's diary. How does telling the story with drawings transform the experience?

WHY are they sending this message?

What is the publisher trying to accomplish with the graphic novel? Is it appropriate to tell a serious story like that of Anne Frank or the 9/11 attacks in comic book format? Have you ever read the graphic novel *Maus* by Art Spiegelman that tells the story of the Holocaust with the Jews as mice and the Germans as cats? If so, what was your reaction?

HOW do you and your classmates interpret graphic novels?

Do you or your classmates read graphic novels/comic books? Would you be more likely to read a graphic novel than a text novel on a serious subject? What can you do with a graphic presentation that you can't do with text?

[1]Jamie Katz, "A New Look at Anne Frank," *Smithsonian.com,* January 25, 2011, www.smithsonianmag.com/arts-culture/a-new-look-at-anne-frank-108812/?no-ist=.

Web 4.5: Read more about how Anne Frank's famous diary has been in the news.

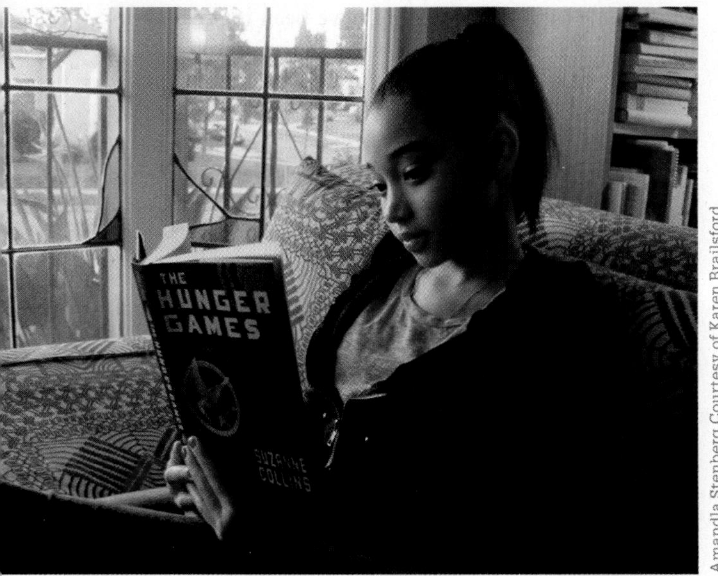

Amandla Stenberg Courtesy of Karen Brailsford

Actress Amandla Stenberg was a big fan of the *Hunger Games* series of books before she was cast as the "tribute" character Rue. She told *Publishers Weekly* that she has read the first book five times.

Books and Censorship 

Books are capable of exciting great passion in readers who love them and those who hate them. Wherever there are books, there are people who will want to ban or control them for one reason or another. Attempts at control can range from removing the book from a school library to threatening to kill the author.

Book Banning. In the United States, most book censorship efforts are local rather than national in scope. Book banning is generally limited to removing specific titles from school libraries or reading lists. Typically such efforts involve books thought to contain sexually explicit material, offensive language, violence, a portrayal of homosexuality, or offensive treatment of religion. (*Eleanor & Park*, which we discussed at the beginning of the chapter, has had complaints about the language, adult content, and bullying within the story.) Other reasons given are for being "unsuited" for a given age group or for being "anti-family."[67] Occasionally, though, a book's publisher will instigate the censorship. Ray Bradbury's novel *Fahrenheit 451* tells the story of a "fireman" whose job is to burn books rather than put out fires. (Fahrenheit 451° is the temperature at which book paper starts to burn.) The book was originally published in 1953, but in 1967 Ballantine Books brought out an edition for high schools that modified seventy-five passages in the text to eliminate such words as *hell*, *damn*, and *abortion*. This was done without Bradbury's knowledge or consent. When he found out about it thirteen years later, he demanded that the edited version be withdrawn.[68]

Different titles show up on various lists of banned or challenged books, but a few appear repeatedly. Maya Angelou's *I Know Why the Caged Bird Sings* has had its position on many school reading lists challenged because of its description of the rape of the author as a child. Other frequently challenged books include the *Goosebumps* series by R. L. Stine, J. D. Salinger's coming-of-age novel *The Catcher in the Rye*, and Kurt Vonnegut's account of the firebombing of Dresden, *Slaughterhouse-Five*.[69]

Box 4.1 Most-Challenged Books of 2013

1. *Captain Underpants* (series), by Dav Pilkey
   Reasons: Offensive language, unsuited for age group, violence
2. *The Bluest Eye,* by Toni Morrison
   Reasons: Offensive language, sexually explicit, unsuited to age group, violence
3. *The Absolutely True Diary of a Part-Time Indian,* by Sherman Alexie
   Reasons: Drugs/alcohol/smoking, offensive language, racism, sexually explicit, unsuited to age group
4. *Fifty Shades of Grey*, by E. L. James
   Reasons: Nudity, offensive language, religious viewpoint, sexually explicit, unsuited to age group
5. *The Hunger Games,* by Suzanne Collins
   Reasons: Religious viewpoint, unsuited to age group
6. *A Bad Boy Can Be Good for a Girl,* by Tanya Lee Stone
   Reasons: Drugs/alcohol/smoking, nudity, offensive language, sexually explicit
7. *Looking for Alaska,* by John Green
   Reasons: Drugs/alcohol/smoking, sexually explicit, unsuited to age group
8. *The Perks of Being a Wallflower,* by Stephen Chbosky
   Reasons: Drugs/alcohol/smoking, homosexuality, sexually explicit, unsuited to age group
9. *Bless Me Ultima,* by Rudolfo Anaya
   Reasons: Occult/Satanism, offensive language, religious viewpoint, sexually explicit
10. *Bone* (series), by Jeff Smith
   Reasons: Political viewpoint, racism, violence

Source: Adapted from American Library Association, "Frequently Challenged Books of the 21st Century," http://www.ala.org/bbooks/frequentlychallengedbooks/top10#2013.

The American Library Association has been tracking the most-challenged books for several years. Challenged books are those that some individual or group has attempted to remove or restrict. The challenger does not need to have been successful in getting the title banned for it to appear on the list. See Box 4.1 for the most-challenged books of 2013.

Not all banned books are contemporary. A number of classics have been banned as well. According to the American Library Association, the following books are frequently challenged[70]:

- *The Scarlet Letter* by Nathaniel Hawthorne, because a book about adultery conflicts with a community's values

Web 4.6: Read more about challenged books.

Questioning the Media

Should parents be able to get books removed from school libraries or reading lists because they find ideas or language in them objectionable? What arguments can you make for or against this?

- *Of Mice and Men* by John Steinbeck, because it contains profanity
- *Twelfth Night* by William Shakespeare, because the comedy is perceived as promoting homosexuality

The Adventures of Huckleberry Finn, Mark Twain's classic, has, for a range of reasons, been in trouble ever since its publication in 1885. *Little Women* author Louisa May Alcott said of *Huck Finn*, "If Mr. Clemens cannot think of something better to tell our pure-minded lads and lasses, he had best stop writing for them." Mark Twain was not bothered by Alcott's comments in the least, responding, "That will sell 25,000 copies for us, sure."[71] The town library of Concord, Massachusetts, banned the book as unfit, while others described it as "rough, coarse, and inelegant."[72] The basic complaint was that the novel was disrespectful and contained profanity. More recently, *Huck Finn* has been criticized as being racist. While Pulitzer Prize–winning novelist Jane Smiley does not want to see *Huck Finn* banned, she suggests that it does not deserve its position in the canon of great American literature.[73] This is, of course, an example of Secret Four—Nothing's new: Everything that happened in the past will happen again.

Judy Blume. American writer Judy Blume is a perennial member on lists of banned authors because of her novel *Forever*, a story about a teenager's discovery of her sexuality. What does Blume write about that is so upsetting? Wet dreams, wanting to belong, death, divorce, the cruelty of kids, masturbation, and menstruation.[74]

Blume was a New Jersey housewife when she wrote her first picture book in 1969. Ten of her books are on *Publishers Weekly*'s list of the top 200 children's paperbacks of all times, and two are in the top ten. More than 65 million copies of her novels have been sold, and her books have been translated into twenty languages.[75]

While Judy Blume is upset that her books are banned, she is more upset about what the banning does to her readers:

> It upsets me much more for the message that it sends to young people, which is, there is something in these books that we do not want you to know. And if you do not read about it, you never know about it. And that something, for the most part, is puberty, anything to do with sexuality. And, you know, they are all going to go through puberty whether their parents want them to or not.[76]

Most attempts at censoring books in the United States result in at most a book's being removed from a school library, but that is not always the case in the rest of the world. Few cases of censorship have been quite as spectacular as the efforts to suppress Indian-born novelist Salman Rushdie's intensely controversial novel *The Satanic Verses*, a religious satire/allegory that is extremely offensive to Muslims. Rushdie's book was first banned in India in the fall of 1988 and caused rioting in Pakistan in 1989. At that time, Iran's Ayatollah Khomeini placed a religious ruling, or *fatwa*, on Rushdie for the book's blasphemous content and called for the author's death.

In the early days of the *fatwa,* Rushdie went into hiding and moved from house to house daily. According to some sources, the *fatwa* played a role in eventually breaking up his marriage.[77] Khomeini died several months after issuing the *fatwa*, making it difficult to remove the death sentence and leaving Rushdie in a kind of lifelong limbo. One of the reasons why the book offends Muslims is that it contains a dream sequence in which prostitutes pretend to be wives of the prophet Muhammad in order to increase their business. Additionally, it refers to Muhammad as Mahound, a Christian demon.[78] The text also contains trilingual puns that require an understanding of Hindu, Muslim, and British culture.

After the death threat, several major chain bookstores did not carry *The Satanic Verses*, but most independent booksellers continued to sell it. The chain stores eventually relented, and *The Satanic Verses* ended up at the top of the *New York Times* best-seller list.

In the fall of 1998, the Iranian government, through its foreign minister, Kamal Kharrazi, said that it would give no reward or assistance for killing Rushdie. However, as of this writing, militant Islamic organizations are still allegedly offering bounties of as much as $3 million on the author's life.[79] Despite the lifting of the official government death threat, Rushdie is not allowed to fly on British Airways planes.[80] Rushdie was fifty-one when the nine-year-old *fatwa* was lifted, and although he still sees a continued need for caution, he views the threat as ended. Rushdie had this to say to the *New York Times* about what it was like living under the *fatwa*:

> It's an extraordinary thing to see people walking down the streets of foreign cities, carrying your picture with the eyes poked out and calling for your death. It's as if somebody were to break your picture of the world, and everything you think about somehow ceases to be true.[81]

Although Rushdie himself was never attacked, several other individuals with connections to his book were killed or injured. Hitoshi Igarashi, the Japanese translator of *The Satanic Verses*, was stabbed to death in Tokyo in July 1991; Italian translator Ettore Capriolo was beaten and stabbed by a man demanding Rushdie's address; and William Nygaard, Rushdie's Norwegian publisher, was shot and wounded in October 1993. As recently as January 2012, Rushdie had to cancel an appearance at a major literary festival in India because of death threats against him. He was rescheduled to speak via television, but threats of violence against the festival organizers led to even that being cancelled.[82]

Web 4.7: Read about the controversy surrounding Judy Blume's books.

Courtesy of Beaufort Books

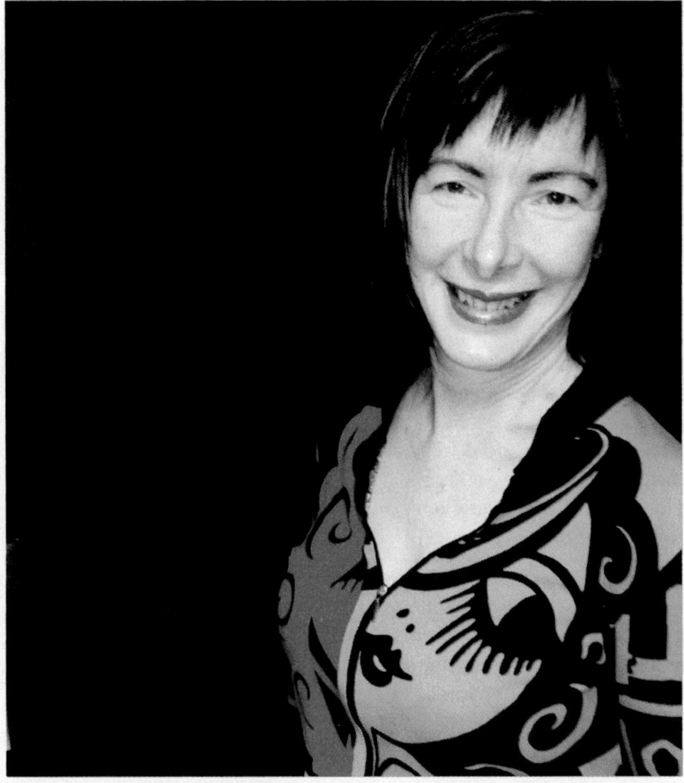
Zoe Boysen

The Jewel of Medina, written by Sherry Jones (right), generated international controversy when extremists attempted to firebomb the offices of its British publisher.

Rushdie is not the only author to face threats. In 2008, Britain's Scotland Yard stopped an attempt to firebomb the publisher of *The Jewel of Medina*, a controversial book about the prophet Muhammad and his child bride by American author Sherry Jones. The attack targeted Jones's Dutch publisher, Martin Rynja. The American publisher of *Jewel*, Random House, canceled its publication because the company feared it might incite violence. (Random House is the largest English-language publisher and is owned by German publishing giant Bertelsmann.) Random House has been accused of canceling publication of the book after having the manuscript criticized by an associate professor of Islamic history at the University of Texas. Jones was able to replace Random House with Beaufort Books as her American publisher.[83]

Other authors who have received death threats include Bangladeshi doctor, poet, and novelist Taslima Nasrin; Nigerian poet Ken Saro-Wiwa; and Nobel Prize–winning Nigerian author Wole Soyinka.[84]

The Future of Books

As we discussed in Chapter 3, the digital media and the Internet are bringing big changes to the media business, providing consumers with alternatives to blockbuster books. Instead, a limited number of consumers spread out across the country can access far more specialized content than they could find in even the biggest **brick-and-mortar** bookstore. This phenomenon is known as the long tail. The long tail recognizes that we are no longer limited by geography as to what media we will buy and whom we will talk to. As Chris Anderson, the author of *The Long Tail*, explains, "We are turning from a mass market back into a niche nation, defined now not by our geography but by our interests."[85]

Books and the Long Tail

The Internet launched the long-tail segment of the media by allowing a company to produce a catalog that is available to everyone with very little marginal cost for each additional viewer. Amazon.com founder Jeff Bezos started selling books on the Internet because the Web was the only practical way to offer the variety that he sought:

> It . . . turns out that you can't have a big book catalog on paper; it's totally impractical. There are more than 100,000 new books published every year, and even a superstore can't carry them all. The biggest superstores have 175,000 titles and there are only about

brick-and-mortar stores: Brick-and-mortar stores are those that have a physical presence at which you can shop.

Web 4.8: Read more about threatened authors.

MEDIA TRANSFORMATIONS

Can paper books and e-books coexist?

After several years of being the perpetual "next big thing," electronic books have finally hit the mainstream. Classic books such as *Treasure Island* are being posted to the Internet, best-selling crime novels and romances are being released in electronic form, and so-called indie books, such as those by best-selling fantasy author Amanda Hocking, are being sold directly to readers by the authors.

Consumers have been justifiably nervous about jumping into e-books for technical and logistical reasons. And then there is the whole question of "Why?" What do you get out of an e-book that you can't get from a traditional paper book?

Superstar author Jonathan Franzen, famous for his novels *The Corrections* and *Freedom*, came out in 2012 solidly opposed to e-books. Why? It would seem that Franzen's main objection to e-books is their lack of permanence. Commenting at the Hay cultural festival in Colombia, he said:

> The technology I like is the American paperback edition of *Freedom*. I can spill water on it and it would still work! So it's pretty good technology. And what's more, it will work great 10 years from now. So no wonder the capitalists hate it. It's a bad business model. . . . I think for serious readers, a sense of permanence has always been part of the experience. Everything else in your life is fluid, but here is the text that doesn't change.[86]

Central to Franzen's critique is that books ought to be in a fixed format that doesn't need to be updated; therefore, they don't need to be delivered on a platform that lets them be changed.

Author and commentator Jonathan Segura admits that there are limitations to e-books. As he writes at the blog *Monkey See*: "I am a scribbler, and you cannot scribble in the margins of an ebook. Not all books are available in digital editions. . . . E-books do not allow you to advertise your literary affectedness on the subway."[87] But Segura does not buy the argument that there is a conflict between traditional paper books and e-books:

> You can choose to have your text delivered on paper with a pretty

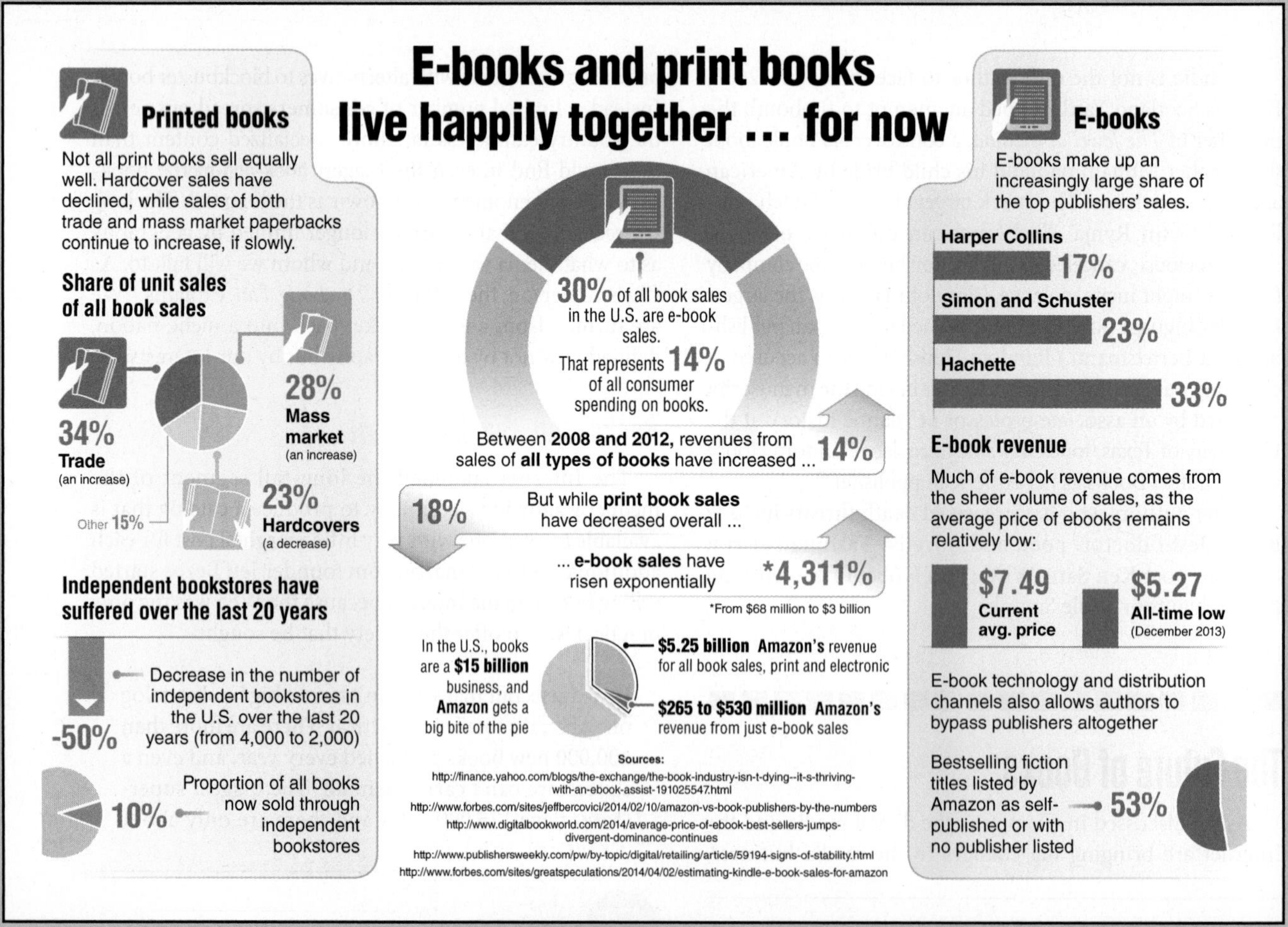

E-books and print books live happily together . . . for now

Printed books

Not all print books sell equally well. Hardcover sales have declined, while sales of both trade and mass market paperbacks continue to increase, if slowly.

Share of unit sales of all book sales

34% Trade (an increase)
28% Mass market (an increase)
23% Hardcovers (a decrease)
Other 15%

Independent bookstores have suffered over the last 20 years

-50% Decrease in the number of independent bookstores in the U.S. over the last 20 years (from 4,000 to 2,000)

10% Proportion of all books now sold through independent bookstores

30% of all book sales in the U.S. are e-book sales.

That represents 14% of all consumer spending on books.

Between **2008 and 2012**, revenues from sales of **all types of books** have increased ... 14%

But while **print book sales** have decreased overall ... 18%

... **e-book sales** have risen exponentially *4,311%

*From $68 million to $3 billion

In the U.S., books are a **$15 billion** business, and **Amazon** gets a big bite of the pie

$5.25 billion **Amazon's** revenue for all book sales, print and electronic

$265 to $530 million **Amazon's** revenue from just e-book sales

Sources:

http://finance.yahoo.com/blogs/the-exchange/the-book-industry-isn-t-dying--it-s-thriving-with-an-ebook-assist-191025547.html

http://www.forbes.com/sites/jeffbercovici/2014/02/10/amazon-vs-book-publishers-by-the-numbers

http://www.digitalbookworld.com/2014/average-price-of-ebook-best-sellers-jumps-divergent-dominance-continues

http://www.publishersweekly.com/pw/by-topic/digital/retailing/article/59194-signs-of-stability.html

http://www.forbes.com/sites/greatspeculations/2014/04/02/estimating-kindle-e-book-sales-for-amazon

E-books

E-books make up an increasingly large share of the top publishers' sales.

Harper Collins 17%
Simon and Schuster 23%
Hachette 33%

E-book revenue

Much of e-book revenue comes from the sheer volume of sales, as the average price of ebooks remains relatively low:

$7.49 Current avg. price
$5.27 All-time low (December 2013)

E-book technology and distribution channels also allows authors to bypass publishers altogether

Bestselling fiction titles listed by Amazon as self-published or with no publisher listed 53%

cover, or you can choose to have it delivered over the air to your sleek little device. You can even play it way loose and read *in both formats*![88]

Aside from the reasons discussed in these debates, why would you want an e-book reader, other than to have the latest gadget? Some other justifications include:

- Instant gratification—The moment you decide you'd like a specific book, you can buy and download it to your e-reader.
- You can always have several books with you—Even the cheapest Kindle can hold hundreds of books at a time.
- Availability of titles—There are a growing number of books, either out-of-print titles or independently published books, that are available only in electronic format.

The appeal of the Kindle has grown significantly in recent years. Many public libraries are now "checking out" books to Kindles, allowing the borrower to keep the book on his or her device for a limited checkout time. And Amazon reports that it is now selling more books in Kindle format than in paperback or hardback formats combined.

Journalist Ezra Klein sums up the conflict book lovers feel when they start using e-books instead of paper books:

> I like books. And I feel guilty every time I look up from my iPad and see the hundreds of books lining my walls, looking at me like Woody and Buzz watching Andy discover video games. But it's getting easier and easier for me to see how they get replaced by eBooks, and harder and harder for me to come up with arguments about why that's a bad thing.[89]

Media Transformations Questions

- **WHAT** advantages does an e-book have over a printed book? Why would you prefer a printed book over an e-book?
- **DO** publishers sell e-books because it is easy to change the content of them?
- **DO** printed books still have any advantage in the twenty-first century?
- **MANY** of my students tell me they prefer to do recreational reading using an e-book reader, but that they prefer their textbooks to be printed books. How do you feel about this? Would you prefer to get your textbooks and college readings as an e-book or paper book? How about your recreational reading? Would you trust a tablet or e-book reader to store your books and notes?

three that big. So that became the idea: let Amazon .com be the first place where you can easily find and buy a million different books.[90]

SECRET 2 And this was the radical notion—instead of offering a selection of books, why not offer every book, all 5.6 million or so English-language books in print? Amazon can keep the most popular books in stock in its warehouses and seamlessly order books from publishers if they are in smaller demand. It can even offer out-of-print books from private stores that partner with Amazon or custom-publish them through arrangements it's made with publishers. (This is a prime example of Secret Two—There are no mainstream media. Due to long-tail retailers like Amazon, consumers are no longer limited to just the biggest books from the biggest publishers.)

The online bookstore began operations in July 1995, and by December 1998, it had served more than 4.5 million customers. Why is it called Amazon? Because it begins with an *A* and therefore will appear first on alphabetical lists. In 1998, Amazon started selling videos and CDs, and since 1999, it has added toys, clothing, kitchen equipment, and other merchandise.

A key feature of Amazon is that it tracks customers' interests by recording what they've already bought on Amazon.com. Each time a buyer enters the site, a personalized home page shows related books that the customer might not have known about otherwise. Shoppers looking at the description of Jimmy Buffett's autobiography, *A Pirate Looks at Fifty*, for example, also see a recommendation for Herman Wouk's *Don't Stop the Carnival*, which tells the tale of a man running a hotel on a tropical island and is one of Buffett's favorite books.

Online bookstores are among the most successful businesses in electronic commerce. One reason for their initial success was that in the early days of the commercialized Internet, people who owned computers were also likely to read books. Also, well-educated people, who tend to read for pleasure and entertainment, are likely to work in offices where they have Internet connections and thus can buy books online. Finding books online can be easier than finding them in a bookstore, especially if the title is obscure. A former Random House executive notes that online bookstores provide instant gratification.

Questioning the Media

Where did you buy your last book? If you bought it online, when was the last time you were in a brick-and-mortar bookstore? Do you worry about the decreasing presence of brick-and-mortar bookstores, or do you think the industry will eventually abandon print books? Do you like the computer-generated recommendations from online stores like Amazon.com, or do you find them dehumanizing and creepy? Explain your answer.

Marketing partnerships are an important element of online bookstores. Anyone who wants to can set up an online bookstore on his or her Web site in partnership with Amazon and receive a small commission for every book sold. In the past, BarnesandNoble.com had partnerships with the *New York Times* and *USA Today*'s Web sites that let readers purchase the books being written about in the papers. Of course, such partnerships raise questions about objectivity: Can a book review be objective when the newspaper that's reviewing the book is also selling the book?[91]

Electronic Publishing and Print on Demand

In the past few years, a new form of publishing has emerged: electronic books. These can be classic books that have been placed on the Internet, best sellers designed to be read on an electronic viewer, or new books published only in electronic format. Electronic distribution has become a popular format for self-publishing as well. Although some electronic titles are designed to be read on a computer, the most exciting development is the e-book reader, which is a small handheld device with a screen that can hold hundreds of separate titles. Whereas many people are reluctant to give up paper and ink, others think that being able to carry an entire library in a device the size of a single paperback sounds pretty good.[92]

We've been hearing about e-books replacing standard books, or at least becoming commonplace, for several years now. Franklin offered an e-book reader; Sony has had a variety of them. Books have been sold that can be read on PDAs and smartphones, Project Gutenberg has been putting public domain books online, and there are multiple publishers out there pushing their online book wares.

At least one alternative e-book format has been successful for many years, and that's the audiobook. For an audiobook, a voice actor, famous or not, reads books (or even magazine articles) aloud so that they can be listened to on a cassette player, a CD player, or (more recently) an MP3 player. In 2008, audiobooks accounted for $331 million in sales, according to the Audio Publishers Association.[93]

Unlike electronic print books, audiobooks have found a market among commuters and those who exercise. They provide a distinct value to consumers in that they allow readers to consume books and similar material in environments where they can't easily read. Audiobooks also have the advantage of being readily understandable—everyone knows what "books on tape" are, even if most people buy them on CDs or as digital downloads. Finally, even though special equipment is required to use them, you likely already own the equipment or can buy it for very little money. This means there's very little risk in adopting this new technology.

When most people talk about e-books, however, they're referring to books in the form of a text file that can be read on a computer screen or some other media device.

CQ Researcher 4.2: Read about the changing face of book publishing.

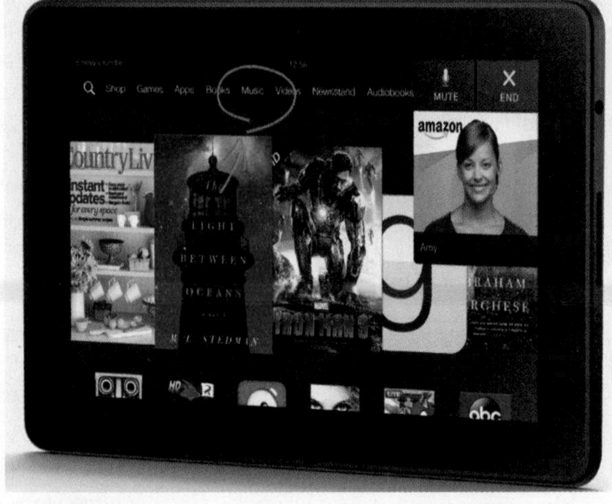

AP Photo/Mark Lennihan

E-book readers, such as the iPad, allow consumers to download books, magazines, and newspapers to take with them anywhere.

A big barrier to the widespread adoption of e-books is that consumers are hesitant to buy an expensive device that could be left orphaned with no new content. Other people are concerned that the devices are just too complicated to use: How do you get the books downloaded? Where do you find them? How do you operate the thing?

Finally, there's the whole question of whether e-books provide a compelling advantage to readers. What do they get out of the device that they don't get out of a traditional paper book?[94] For those of us who are big readers, we generally like books and see no reason to go to one more gizmo.[95]

Slate writer Jacob Weisberg is typical among fans of Amazon's Kindle, which has become the dominant e-book reader on the market for a variety of reasons, not the least of which is that you can buy the books from Amazon.com and have them downloaded directly to your e-book reader without any connection to a computer.[96]

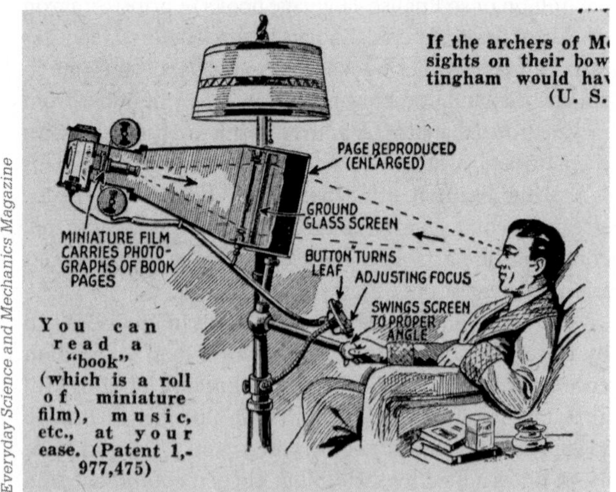

Everyday Science and Mechanics Magazine

We think we're pretty modern these days if we're reading the latest best seller on a Kindle, Nook, or iPad. But what was state-of-the-art for e-readers back in the 1930s? Matt Novak, a curator for the Smithsonian Institution, found this illustration in the April 1935 issue of *Everyday Science and Mechanics* for a microfilm-based book reader that could be mounted next to your favorite chair. Wonder why it never caught on . . .

Amazon founder Jeff Bezos, in an interview on *the Charlie Rose show*, said that a successful e-book reader should be cheap enough that everyone can own one and that every book in the world should be available on it.[97] But he might have added that e-books need to guarantee users that once they buy a book for their reader, they'll be able to keep it.

That was the problem faced by readers who purchased George Orwell's *Nineteen Eighty-Four* or *Animal Farm* in 2009.[98] During that summer, people who purchased copies of the two classic novels discovered that Amazon had erased the books from their Kindles and refunded the purchase price. It turned out that the publisher offering the two books through Amazon did not have the legal right to sell them in the United States. So Amazon used its electronic connection to take the text off the e-book readers.

To its credit, Amazon realized that erasing the titles was a bad mistake. As consumers pointed out, if you bought an illegal paperback copy of a book, Amazon wouldn't be able to take it back, and it should be no different for e-books.

Amazon founder Jeff Bezos posted an unambiguous apology on the company's Web site shortly afterward:

> This is an apology for the way we previously handled illegally sold copies of *1984* and other novels on Kindle. Our "solution" to the problem was stupid, thoughtless, and painfully out of line with our principles. It is wholly self-inflicted, and we deserve the criticism we've received. We will use the scar tissue from this painful mistake to help make better decisions going forward, ones that match our mission.[99]

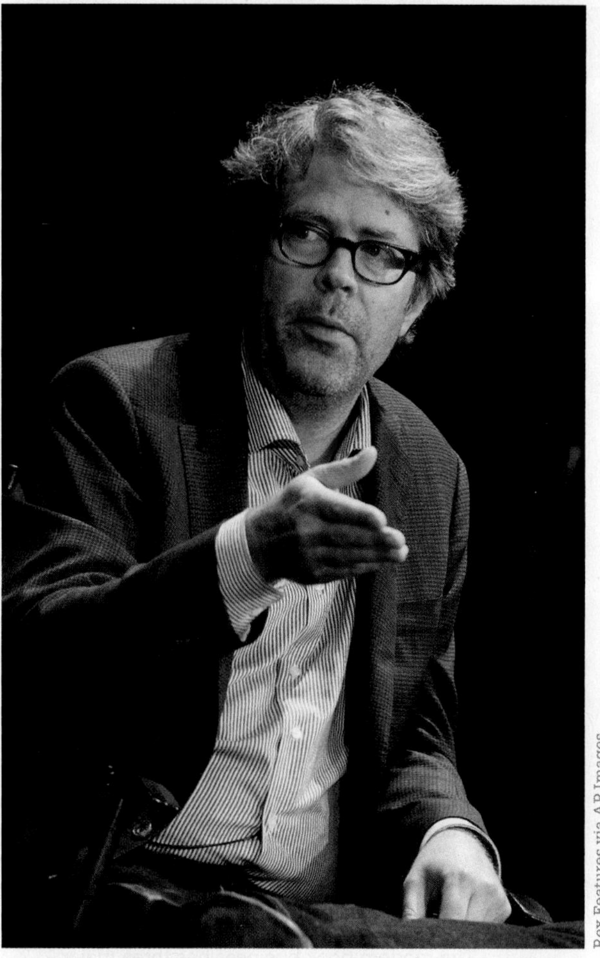

Rex Features via AP Images

Best-selling author Jonathan Franzen has been outspoken in his criticism of e-books, claiming that they lack permanence.

Print on Demand. The other side of electronic publishing is **print on demand**, in which the physical book is not printed until it's ordered or when the distributor of the book prints additional copies in small batches. This is how Amazon supplies some of its smallest-selling titles. The company has banks of large-capacity laser printers that can turn out fresh copies of books from digital copies stored on a computer. This allows the company to stock books at a cost that approaches zero until the book is ordered.[100] Book wholesaler Ingram also does print on demand through its subsidiary Lightning Source, which can print 100,000 different titles from more than 2,300 publishers.[101]

---

print on demand: A form of publishing in which the physical book is not printed until it's ordered, or until the distributor of the book prints additional copies in small batches.

Chapter SUMMARY

Early forms of writing first appeared in the Middle East about 3500 BC. Over the next 2,000 years, writing evolved from simple pictographs to highly developed ideograms and the sound-based alphabet system. Modern rag-based paper was developed in China between 240 BC and 105 BC. In medieval Western Europe, early hand-copied books were created primarily by monks and other religious figures. Because they were difficult to produce, these books were expensive and rare.

In the mid-fifteenth century, Johannes Gutenberg developed the typemold. Printing presses using Gutenberg's movable type allowed books and other publications to be mass produced for the first time, leading to numerous cultural events, including the Protestant Reformation, the rise of literacy, and standardization of grammar and spelling.

In the New World, publishing began soon after European settlement, first in Mexico City by Spanish settlers and later by British colonists in the Massachusetts Bay area. As literacy and education spread throughout the growing middle class during the nineteenth century, improvements in printing technology made inexpensive popular reading materials, such as dime novels and serials, readily available. The first comprehensive dictionary of the English language also was produced during the nineteenth century.

The modern book business has three major participants: publishers, authors, and booksellers. The book business, like the rest of the media industry, has been characterized by rapid consolidation, with a limited number of companies controlling a substantial portion of the publishing, distribution, and retail business.

Publishers produce a wide range of books, but most of the industry's profits come from a limited number of best-selling titles from authors such as Stephen King, Tom Clancy, and Janet Evanovich. Young-adult authors such as J. K. Rowling and Stephenie Meyer have been extremely popular and have dominated the best-seller lists in recent years. The textbook industry has come under increased scrutiny by both legislators and consumers for high costs. Responses have included textbook rental, electronic editions, and lowered costs of production.

Although books rarely attract the degree of controversy that movies, television, or video games do, they are occasionally banned in the United States, typically by an individual library or school district. The most common reason for restricting books is that they contain offensive language, racial bias or stereotypes, sexual material, or offensive comments about religion. Outside of the United States, some controversial authors have faced threats of violence or even death, most notably Salman Rushdie, author of *The Satanic Verses.* Such bans and threats almost never prevent the books from being sold, however.

The Internet has become an important marketplace for books, especially those for which demand is limited. Online bookstores such as Amazon.com can keep books available by selling them as digital downloads or as print-on-demand titles. E-book readers are becoming increasingly popular as a means of distributing books, especially textbooks.

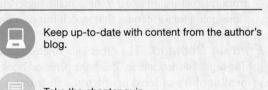

Keep up-to-date with content from the author's blog.

Take the chapter quiz.

Key TERMS

pictograph 84
ideograph 84
phonography 84
alphabets 84
papyrus 84
parchment 84
paper 85
scriptoria 85
typemold 85
font 85
Bay Psalm Book 87
serial novels 88
dime novels 88
rotary press 88
Linotype 88
publishers 89
university and small presses 89
proofs 91
e-book reader 94
domestic novels 95
trade books 96
brick-and-mortar stores 101
print on demand 105

Concept REVIEW

Development of paper and writing

Impact of standardized books

The publishing business

Censorship

Book-banning

Fatwa

Memoir

Popular fiction/literature

Mass market/trade publications

Long-tail book sales

e-books

Student STUDY SITE

Sharpen your skills with SAGE edge at **edge.sagepub.com/hanson5e**

SAGE edge for Students provides a personalized approach to help you accomplish your coursework goals in an easy-to-use learning environment.

chapter 5

Magazines

The Power of Words and Images

Photo by Evan Agostini/ Invision/AP, file

Lena Dunham—the creator, executive producer, and actress in the HBO series Girls—is no stranger to controversy; and her cover story from the February 2014 issue of Vogue was no exception. Critics were concerned that the images by famed photographer Annie Leibovitz had been excessively Photoshopped.

The level of Photoshopping going on at fashion/beauty/lifestyle magazines has been an ongoing controversy, with performers such as Adele, Kelly Clarkson, and Kate Winslet being made almost unrecognizable as photographers and photo editors try to make the curvy stars' bodies comply with fashion magazine standards of beauty.

So it should come as no surprise that when Lena Dunham, the unconventional star of the HBO series *Girls*, posed for famed photographer Annie Leibovitz for the cover of *Vogue* magazine that questions would start being raised as to how authentic her images were. Dunham, in case you've missed the story, is famous for being naked in *Girls*—a lot—and her tattooed, un-toned body is both celebrated and criticized for being an alternative to conventional standards of Hollywood beauty.

When the Dunham issue of *Vogue* came out, the blog *Jezebel*—which tends to be very critical of Photoshopped images of women—offered $10,000 to anyone who would supply it with the original, unedited images of the photos *Vogue* published. It didn't take long for someone to provide *Jezebel* with the photos. As it turns out, the photos themselves were highly manipulated: New backgrounds were added, locations were changed, and a bird was placed on Dunham's head. But surprisingly little was done to Dunham herself. On the cover photo, for example, her neck was made thinner, her head was made smaller (which makes her eyes look bigger), and her jawline was made narrower. The bigger manipulations included taking a studio image of Dunham, adding a pigeon to her head, and then placing her on a street in Brooklyn.[1]

Dunham told *Slate* following *Jezebel's* publication of the unedited images that she had no problem with how Leibovitz had digitally altered her, and that she understands and appreciates the difference between reality and what is published in a fashion magazine:

> A fashion magazine is like a beautiful fantasy. *Vogue* isn't the place that we go to look at realistic women, *Vogue* is the place that we go to look at beautiful clothes and fancy places and escapism and so I feel like if the story reflects me and I happen to be wearing a beautiful Prada dress and surrounded by beautiful men and dogs, what's the problem? If they want to see what I really look like go watch the show that I make every single week.[2]

Dunham goes on to say that she didn't feel like anyone pressured her into doing anything that she didn't want to do. "I never felt bullied into anything," she said. "I felt happy because they dressed me and styled me in a way that really reflects who I am. And I felt that was very lucky and that all the editors understood my persona, my creativity and who I am. . . . I know some people have been very angry about the cover and that confuses me a little. I don't understand why, Photoshop or no, having a woman who is different from the typical *Vogue* cover girl could be a bad thing."[3]

LEARNING OBJECTIVES

After studying this chapter, you will be able to:

1 Explain the importance of the *Saturday Evening Post* in the development of the mass media in the United States.

2 Describe the key characteristics of trade, literary, and consumer magazines.

3 Illustrate how magazines have given a voice to different groups of people.

4 Discuss the role that magazines and magazine ads play in defining people's body image.

5 Describe what is meant by "native advertising" and why it is controversial.

6 Discuss the major trends in twenty-first-century magazine publishing.

Web 5.1: Links to some of the controversial images of Lena Dunham.

The controversy surrounding Leibovitz's cover featuring Dunham is nothing new. The photographer has long been known for her controversial magazine covers and images. From her 1981 *Rolling Stone* cover featuring a nude John Lennon taken the day he was murdered, to the 1991 *Vanity Fair* cover featuring a nude and very pregnant Demi Moore, to her 2008 implied-topless photo of a then-underage Miley Cyrus, Leibovitz's work has always been able to get people talking.

Leibovitz started out wanting to be a painter, but she submitted a photo she had taken of beat poet Allen Ginsberg to *Rolling Stone* magazine. Her photo was accepted, and she went to work for the publication full-time at age twenty. The photo that put her on the map was a cover portrait for *Rolling Stone* of a naked John Lennon clinging to Yoko Ono. The photo was taken just hours before Lennon was murdered.[4]

It was during her time at *Rolling Stone* that Leibovitz learned the practical details of shooting successful magazine covers: The subject of the photo has to be recognizable, there has to be something worthy of notice in the picture, and there has to be room for the magazine's name and a few lines of type.

Leibovitz went on to shoot for *Vanity Fair*, creating many of its best-known covers, including the infamous one that featured a nude Demi Moore, who was eight months pregnant at the time. The Moore cover sold an extra 500,000 copies of the magazine, and former editor Tina Brown notes that *Vanity Fair* picked up about 75,000 new subscriptions as a result.

Ad man and designer George Lois, who produced many of the most memorable covers of *Esquire* magazine back in the 1960s, says that whatever else it was, the Moore photo was a great magazine cover.

"A truly great magazine cover surprises, even shocks, and connects in a nanosecond," Lois wrote in *Vanity Fair*.

Timeline

1800

1812 War of 1812 breaks out.

1835 Alexis de Tocqueville publishes *Democracy in America*.

1859 Charles Darwin publishes *On the Origin of Species*.

1861 U.S. Civil War begins.

1869 Transcontinental railroad is completed.

1879 Thomas Edison invents electric light bulb.

1898 Spanish-American War breaks out.

◀ **1704** Daniel Defoe founds the Review, the first magazine in England.

1821 The Saturday Evening Post, the first truly national magazine in the United States, starts publication.

1828 The Spectator, the oldest continuously published magazine in the English language, publishes its first issue in England.

1837 Sarah Josepha Hale becomes the editor of Godey's Lady's Book and creates the modern women's magazine.

1840 Mathew Brady gains reknown as a portrait photographer and later becomes famous for his Civil War photos.

1900

1903 Orville and Wilbur Wright fly first airplane.

1905 Albert Einstein proposes his theory of relativity.

1910

1912 *Titanic* sinks.

1914 World War I begins.

1918 Worldwide influenza epidemic strikes.

1910 W. E. B. DuBois founds the Crisis as the NAACP's official magazine.

Library of Congress

1920

1920 Nineteenth Amendment passes, giving U.S. women the right to vote.

1929 U.S. stock market crashes, leading to the Great Depression.

1920s Harold Ross founds the New Yorker, which becomes a home for highbrow magazine writing.

1923 Henry Luce founds Time magazine, the eventual centerpiece of the Time Warner media empire.

AP Photo

1930

1933 Adolf Hitler is elected chancellor of Germany.

1939 World War II breaks out in Europe.

1940

1941 United States enters World War II.

1945 United States drops two atomic bombs on Japan.

1947 Pakistan and India gain independence from Britain.

1949 Communists establish People's Republic of China.

A glance at the image . . . depicting a famous movie star beautifully bursting with life and proudly flaunting her body, was an instant culture buster—and damn the expected primal screams of those constipated critics, cranky subscribers, and fidgety newsstand buyers, who the editors and publishers surely knew would regard a pregnant female body as "grotesque and obscene."[5]

SECRET 3 Looking at Leibovitz's long career in magazine journalism, you can see a prime example of Secret Three—Everything from the margin moves to the center. Leibovitz started shooting counterculture figures for the upstart magazine *Rolling Stone* and progressed to shooting A-list celebrities for *Vanity Fair* and *Vogue* in the 1990s, 2000s, and 2010s.[6] In fact, over the last five decades, you would be hard pressed to not find a year where one or more of the most talked-about magazine covers was shot by Leibovitz.

> "A truly great magazine cover surprises, even shocks, and connects in a nanosecond."
>
> —George Lois

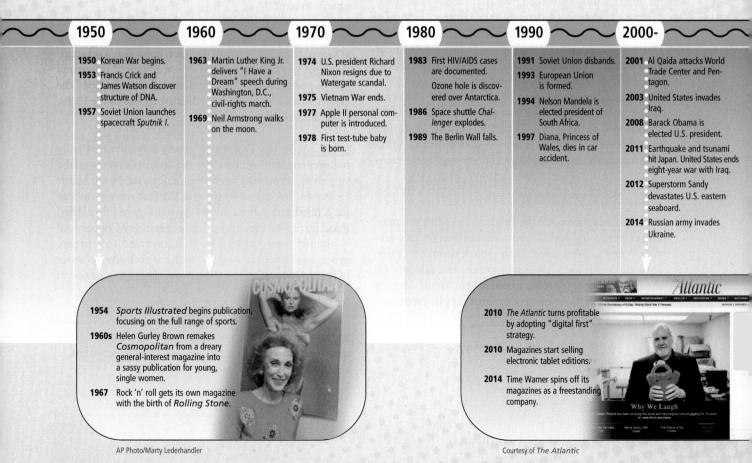

Provocative covers by photographers such as Annie Leibovitz help draw readers into magazines that cover every imaginable topic, from fashion to sports to news. In this chapter, we look at how the magazine industry grew from a general national medium into one that serves a wide range of narrow interests. We look at the types of magazines published today, some controversies that surround magazine articles and advertisements, how the magazine industry operates, and what the future of the magazine industry holds. ■

1950

1950 Korean War begins.
1953 Francis Crick and James Watson discover structure of DNA.
1957 Soviet Union launches spacecraft *Sputnik I.*

1960

1963 Martin Luther King Jr. delivers "I Have a Dream" speech during Washington, D.C., civil-rights march.
1969 Neil Armstrong walks on the moon.

1970

1974 U.S. president Richard Nixon resigns due to Watergate scandal.
1975 Vietnam War ends.
1977 Apple II personal computer is introduced.
1978 First test-tube baby is born.

1980

1983 First HIV/AIDS cases are documented.
Ozone hole is discovered over Antarctica.
1986 Space shuttle *Challenger* explodes.
1989 The Berlin Wall falls.

1990

1991 Soviet Union disbands.
1993 European Union is formed.
1994 Nelson Mandela is elected president of South Africa.
1997 Diana, Princess of Wales, dies in car accident.

2000-

2001 Al Qaida attacks World Trade Center and Pentagon.
2003 United States invades Iraq.
2008 Barack Obama is elected U.S. president.
2011 Earthquake and tsunami hit Japan. United States ends eight-year war with Iraq.
2012 Superstorm Sandy devastates U.S. eastern seaboard.
2014 Russian army invades Ukraine.

1954 *Sports Illustrated* begins publication, focusing on the full range of sports.
1960s Helen Gurley Brown remakes *Cosmopolitan* from a dreary general-interest magazine into a sassy publication for young, single women.
1967 Rock 'n' roll gets its own magazine with the birth of *Rolling Stone.*

AP Photo/Marty Lederhandler

2010 *The Atlantic* turns profitable by adopting "digital first" strategy.
2010 Magazines start selling electronic tablet editions.
2014 Time Warner spins off its magazines as a freestanding company.

Courtesy of *The Atlantic*

The Development of a National Culture

Before radio and television, magazines were people's primary source for in-depth news, ideas, and pictures. In 1704, Daniel Defoe, later famous for writing *Robinson Crusoe*, founded the first real magazine in England—a weekly periodical called the *Review*. Physically, the *Review* looked just like the newspapers of the era. But newspapers focused exclusively on news, whereas Defoe's magazine covered public policy, literature, and morals. Edward Cave's *Gentleman's Magazine* was the first publication to use the word *magazine*, which was derived from the original meaning of the word as a place where goods or supplies are stored.[7]

What is a **magazine**? It is a periodical that contains articles of lasting interest. Typically, magazines are targeted at a specific audience and derive income from advertising, subscriptions, and newsstand sales. Magazines are also intended for a broader geographic area than newspapers, and in the nineteenth century, they increased in both number and circulation as the demand for nationwide advertising grew. (For more about the connection between the growth of advertising and magazines, see Chapter 11.)

Early Magazines

In 1740, Benjamin Franklin announced his plan to publish the *General Magazine*, with lawyer John Webbe as editor. But in a story that could rival any of today's headlines, Webbe was stolen away by publisher Andrew Bradford to edit his *American Magazine*. As a result, Bradford's magazine was published three days before Franklin's. The magazine industry in the New World was less than a week old, and it had already had its first battle.[8]

The hundred magazines published prior to 1800 contained many reprints from newspapers around the colonies, as well as items from British magazines. Magazines were free to reprint whatever they wanted because at the time there were no copyright laws or copyright protections.

The *Saturday Evening Post*

Just as television and the Internet do today, the magazines of the eighteenth and nineteenth centuries provided news, education, and entertainment. Their collections of humor, verse, and stories were designed for the small amounts of leisure time people had in the early 1800s. Because libraries were in short supply, magazines often were the only regular source of high-quality written entertainment.

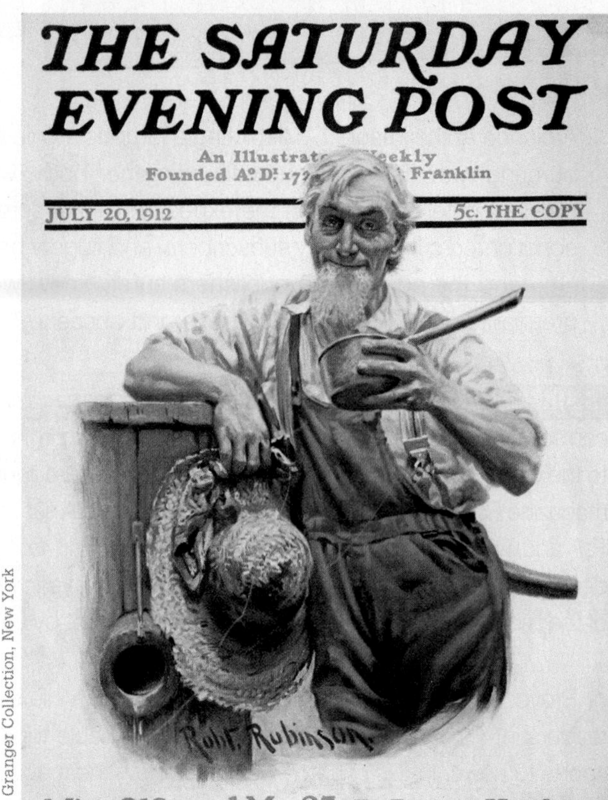

THE SATURDAY EVENING POST
JULY 20, 1912
5c. THE COPY
Miss 318 and Mr. 37—By Rupert Hughes

The Granger Collection, New York

For more than a century, the *Saturday Evening Post* was one of the dominant magazines in the United States.

The most significant of the early magazines was the *Saturday Evening Post*, first published on August 4, 1821. It looked like a four-page newspaper, and a year's subscription cost two dollars, half payable in advance.[9] It featured essays, poetry, obituaries, stories, and a column called "The Ladies' Friend." It contained advertising, and by the 1830s, it was illustrated as well.

SECRET 1 The *Post* was in many ways the first truly national medium—unlike the newspapers that covered a single city, it was read in every American state from Maine to Florida. For at least forty years, the *Post* was *the* voice of the United States. It published the writings of Edgar Allan Poe, Harriet Beecher Stowe, James Fenimore Cooper, and Nathaniel Hawthorne. The *Post* appealed to a broad, general audience rather than the more exclusive audience of literary magazines. By 1848, it was the leading weekly in

Web 5.2: Read what the *Saturday Evening Post* is like today.

magazine: A periodical that contains articles of lasting interest. Typically, magazines are targeted at a specific audience and derive income from advertising, subscriptions, and newsstand sales.

The Granger Collection, New York

The Granger Collection, New York

War photography hasn't changed that much since its beginnings during the American Civil War. This image of the Battle of Gettysburg (left) was taken in 1863 by photographer Timothy H. O'Sullivan, who initially trained under Mathew Brady. The photo on the right was taken in August 2009 in Kabul by Massoud Hossaini and is of three gunmen killed by Afghan security forces after they attacked a bank building in the Afghan capital.

the United States, and even as late as 1937, it had a circulation of more than 3 million.

In 1928, Leon Chipple described the *Post* as follows:

> This is a magic mirror; it not only reflects, it creates us. What the [*Saturday Evening Post*] is we are. Its advertising helps standardize our physical life; its text stencils patterns on our minds. It is a main factor in raising the luxury-level by teaching us new wants. . . . But it does more than whet our hunger; by blunt or subtle devices it molds our ideas on crime, prohibition, Russia, oil, preparedness, immigration, the World Court. . . . This bulky nickel's worth of print and pictures is a kind of social and emotional common denominator of American life.[10]

This is an early statement, though not a unique one, that speaks to Secret One—The media are essential components of our lives. It does not imply that magazines are the creators of our world. Rather, it claims that the magazine is an integral, inseparable part of who we are in the media world.

With the coming of television, the *Post* found its preeminent position in American culture fading. The world was changing, but the *Post* did not change with it. It was stuck in the middle-class America of the pre–World War II era that it depicted in its Norman Rockwell covers. Following a series of editorial and advertising missteps, the *Post* gradually became a monthly publication, and as of 2001, it was being published only bimonthly as a nostalgia and health magazine. The coming of television also forced magazines in general to change from appealing to broad audiences to focusing on narrower, more specific ones.

Questioning the Media

In the 1800s, magazines were our major national-level medium. Which media serve that role today? Are magazines still a "magic mirror" of our culture? If not, what's replaced them? Is this new medium a more interactive mirror? Why or why not?

The Birth of Photojournalism

In addition to providing the first national source of news and commentary, magazines were the first source of **photojournalism**—the use of photographs to portray the news in print. At first, pictures were printed in periodicals by using hand-engraved plates copied from photographs. Then in the 1880s came the invention of the **halftone**, an image produced by a process in which photographs are broken down into a series of dots that appear in shades of gray on the printed page. The halftone allowed the photograph to be reproduced directly in the publication rather than being copied into a drawing.

photojournalism: The use of photographs to portray the news in print.

halftone: An image produced by a process in which photographs are broken down into a series of dots that appear in shades of gray on the printed page.

Web 5.3: View the Library of Congress's collection of Civil War era photos.

Photographer Mathew Brady is often credited with inventing photojournalism in the mid-nineteenth century. In 1845, Brady began to become famous for his portraits of noted Americans. He attempted to sell printed reproductions of his photographs, and though the effort failed because the costs were too high, he set the stage for later celebrity photographers, such as Annie Leibovitz. Brady also realized that much of the value of his photographic portraits came from their being reproduced as engravings, woodcuts, lithographs, and the like. The original was valuable, but so were the reproductions. Today Brady is best remembered for his pictures of the American Civil War, the first war to be photographed from beginning to end.

During the war, Brady was as much a studio operator as a photographer. He supervised the work of a number of talented photographers, and he made sure that the photos found their way into magazines and newspapers. By 1863, *Harper's Weekly* was reproducing Brady's Civil War photos, which horrified American audiences. The photographers followed the Union Army in wagons filled with their equipment and portable darkrooms. Many of the photos credited to Brady, whose eyesight was failing, were likely shot by his assistants. Photographers working for Brady often got extremely close to the line of fire. Thomas C. Roche, who often worked for Brady, got so close that he was seen shaking dirt off himself and his camera after shells hit nearby. In fact, some of Brady's best photographers left his employ so that they might get the credit they thought they deserved for taking pictures under such dangerous conditions. Brady's greatest contribution was not so much the individual war photographs that he may or may not have taken, but what evolved from the photographs: the idea that photographs are published documents preserving history.[11]

The Magazine Business

After the American Civil War, the number of magazines and their circulation grew rapidly. This growth was fueled by a number of factors, such as the emergence of a new middle class, whose members had learned to read in public schools and were now starting to read magazines. Also, a growing number of national advertisers saw the magazine as an efficient means by which to reach their target audiences. Magazine distribution was aided by the **Postal Act of 1879**, which allowed periodicals to be mailed across the nation easily and inexpensively. Improvements in printing, typesetting, and illustration engraving also contributed to the growth of magazines.

Web 5.4: Read the latest on magazine statistics.

The Economics of Magazine Publishing

The post–Civil War era saw the introduction of several magazines, including *Popular Science*, *Good Housekeeping*, *National Geographic*, *Vogue*, and *Outdoor Life*, that are still in existence. From the start, these magazines provided news, ideas, advice for the home, and entertainment. They are all examples of **consumer magazines**—publications targeting an audience of like-minded consumers. As of 2012, there were approximately 7,390 consumer magazines.[12] Of those, 231 were new magazines launched in 2012.

Consumer magazines cover a wide range of topics, but if it seems to you that the most popular subject is celebrities, you aren't far off. An analysis of the content of top consumer magazines found that the largest number of pages (14.6 percent) were devoted to entertainment and celebrity coverage. This was followed by apparel and accessories with 13.1 percent of the pages and food and nutrition with 8.5 percent of the pages. You can see the full analysis in Table 5.1.[13]

Deriving their revenue from subscriptions, newsstand sales, and advertising, consumer magazines tend to be the most visible and profitable segment of the industry. Their continued success is due to their focus on specific audiences; they stand in contrast to the many general-interest magazines that have failed as new media took their places. Top magazine advertisers include toiletries and cosmetics, food and food products, pharmaceuticals, apparel and accessories, retail, and media and advertising.

Trade Magazines

The second major category of periodicals consists of **trade magazines** (also known as business-to-business magazines), which are published for people who work in a particular industry or business. Trade magazines tend to be smaller, less colorful, and more specialized than consumer

Postal Act of 1879: Legislation that allowed magazines to be mailed nationally at a low cost. It was a key factor in the growth of magazine circulation in the late nineteenth century.

consumer magazines: Publications targeting an audience of like-minded consumers.

trade magazines: Magazines published for people who work in a particular industry or business.

magazines. While there are about twice as many trade magazines as consumer magazines, they account for only about 17 percent of the industry's revenue.[14] Trade magazines vary radically in circulation, scope, and the degree to which people outside of the industry know about them. For example, *Women's Wear Daily* is routinely quoted in the mainstream press and talked about by anyone interested in fashion. On the other hand, *Practical Accountant*, which covers all aspects of public accounting, is unlikely to be heard of outside of its very specialized field. The biggest topics for trade magazines are the computer industry, agriculture, medicine, and manufacturing.[15] Whereas some trade magazines are available by subscription, many have *controlled* circulation, meaning that people have to qualify in order to subscribe. For example, the grocery trade magazine *Refrigerated & Frozen Foods* is sent free of charge to people who work as frozen food producers, processors, and marketers. Subscribers have to fill out a survey form once or twice a year to continue qualifying for their free subscription. Advertisers know that most of the people who receive the magazine actually buy the products being advertised.[16] Trade magazines have suffered during the recent recession, with ad revenues down more than 30 percent in 2009.[17]

Literary and Commentary Magazines

Although today in the United States there are relatively few **literary magazines**—publications that focus on serious essays and short fiction—they were part and parcel of the magazine market of the 1800s. Two that still survive are *Harper's* (not to be confused with *Harper's Bazaar*) and the *Atlantic*.

The literary magazines helped to establish authors such as American writers Edgar Allan Poe and Mark Twain, as well as British writers such as Joseph Conrad and Thomas Hardy. *Harper's* magazine was founded in 1850 and was known for its illustrations, especially during the American Civil War. By 1863, *Harper's Weekly* was reproducing Mathew Brady's portraits and Civil War photos. *Harper's* continues today as an influential publication, best known for its monthly "Index" of loosely connected facts and statistics.

In recent years, the *Atlantic* (known in the past as *Atlantic Monthly*) has gained a reputation for publishing provocative nonfiction by authors such as Tracy Kidder, and it still occasionally publishes poetry and short fiction. (Take a look back at Table 5.1 to see how small a role fiction plays in magazine content these days.) Despite the overall trend toward specialization, the *Atlantic* has been doing well in the twenty-first century. It cut back from twelve to ten issues a year in 2007 but has had a steady increase in circulation, and in 2010, it turned its first profit in decades, based in large part on its increase in revenue from digital editions.[18] This trend continued through 2012, with the *Atlantic* seeing modest growth in magazine circulation and much larger growth with its online properties.[19] (You can read more about how the *Atlantic* turned profitable through its digital strategy in the section on the future of magazines at the end of the chapter.)

Political journals also flourished in the late nineteenth and early twentieth centuries. The *Nation* and the *New Republic* are examples of progressive political opinion still being published today. The *Nation*, founded in 1865,

literary magazines: Publications that focus on serious essays and short fiction.

Table 5.1 Top Magazine Topics by Page Count, 2013

Type of content	Pages	Percent
Entertainment/Celebrity	18,724	14.6%
Wearing apparel/Accessories	16,902	13.1%
Food and nutrition	10,913	8.5%
Business and industry	9,079	7.1%
Home furnishings/Management	8,765	6.8%
Culture	7,464	5.8%
Travel/Transportation	6,975	5.4%
Miscellaneous	6,258	4.9%
Beauty and grooming	6,233	4.8%
Sports/Recreation/Hobby	5,738	4.5%
National affairs	4,919	3.8%
General interest	4,502	3.5%
Health/Medical science	4,134	3.2%
Self-help/Relationships	3,921	3.0%
Personal finance	2,996	2.3%
Fitness/Beauty	2,455	1.9%
Building	2,380	1.9%
Global/Foreign affairs	2,132	1.7%
Gardening and farming	1,415	1.1%
Children	1,246	1.0%
Consumer electronics	1,098	0.9%
Fiction	403	0.3%

Sean Gearhart/Getty Images

Source: Adapted by the author from *Magazine Media Factbook* 2013/2014 (New York: Association of Magazine Media, 2013).

discussed current affairs, improving the lot of the working class, and civil rights. The *New Republic*, founded in 1914, promoted labor, civil rights, and antifascism. Both magazines featured letters from readers as an interactive forum for discussion. More than just filler, these letters were central to the magazines' content. The idea of reader feedback as a central component of a publication has reached its full potential on Internet magazines that feature elaborate discussion boards.

The *Nation* and the *New Republic* depend on subsidies from the capitalist system they often criticize. Although the *Nation* claims to be the oldest continuously published American weekly, it loses money every year.[20] According to publisher Victor Navasky, the magazine's poor financial showing is due to a combination of factors, including small circulation and the fact that the magazine is not "advertiser friendly":

> At *The Nation*, we're in the business of attacking the companies that more financially successful magazines are in the business of soliciting for advertising, most notably tobacco. But these titles of opinion are at the core of what journalism should be about, and at their best, they can set the standard for the profession.[21]

William F. Buckley's *National Review* was founded in 1955 as a conservative response to these magazines. In terms of circulation, it is the largest of the three discussed here (more than 178,000 copies per month). Although it is technically a for-profit venture, which means it can endorse candidates and legislation, its leading source of income remains donations from readers. As is typical for opinion magazines, the conservative *National Review* gains readership when Democrats are in power and loses readership when Republicans win elections. (That pattern is reversed for the liberal *New Republic* and *Nation*, which lose circulation when Democrats win elections.[22]) Founder Buckley died in 2008, and his son Christopher left the board of directors of the magazine after endorsing Barack Obama for president.

AP Photo/ The Journal Gazette, Ed Breen

William F. Buckley Jr. founded the *National Review* as a conservative response to magazines such as the *New Republic* and the *Nation*.

The Crisis*: *Giving African Americans a Voice. One of the most important functions of a magazine of ideas is to offer a voice to those who otherwise would be kept silent. That was the purpose of W. E. B. Du Bois's journal, the *Crisis*. Du Bois, a Harvard-educated civil rights leader, started the *Crisis* as the official voice of the National Association for the Advancement of Colored People (NAACP) in 1910. At first, the magazine had only 1,000 subscribers, but by 1920, it had a monthly circulation of 100,000. The *Crisis* became as successful as other political journals, such as the *Nation* and the *New Republic*, with almost as many white readers as black readers.

At its inception, the journal was one of a very few outlets for black writers. "Up until [1910] there were only five black writers who'd been published. The NAACP saw a need for art and literature," said Manie Barron, who edited an anthology of writings from the *Crisis*.[23] The *Crisis* was the leading voice against segregation in the South. It published debates between Du Bois and African American educator and leader Booker T. Washington over the proper role of black education and featured the first appearance of many of Langston Hughes's poems.[24]

Du Bois edited the *Crisis* until 1934. After he stepped down, the journal gradually became more of an African American consumer magazine than an independent journal of black intellectual writing. To address the problem, the NAACP suspended publication of the magazine for

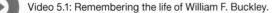

Video 5.1: Remembering the life of William F. Buckley.

Web 5.5: Read issues of the *Crisis* from 1910 to 1922.

about a year in the mid-1990s to work on giving it a new focus. According to civil rights leader Julian Bond, who oversaw the remake of the magazine, "[The *Crisis*] was once the place where you read about race, and the new board wanted to make it that again." In 2008, the magazine moved from being a monthly publication to quarterly in order to control costs, and in 2010, the *Crisis* celebrated its hundredth anniversary.[25]

The Muckrakers. Investigative reporting was made famous by the Watergate political scandal of the early 1970s, but it began in the late 1800s at several newspapers and magazines. The most lasting examples came from the so-called muckraking magazines. The term **muckrakers** was coined by President Theodore Roosevelt to describe socially activist investigative journalists publishing in progressive-minded magazines in the early years of the twentieth century. Although Roosevelt favored the social and political reforms that the exposés clearly indicated were necessary, he suggested that the investigative reporters who published such stories were "muckraking"—that is, they were digging up dirt without stopping to see the good things in the world.

The most famous of the muckrakers was Samuel S. McClure, who led the fight at the beginning of the twentieth century for "business, social, and political reform."[26] Although McClure was a reformer, he also sought to make a profit through the investigative articles he published in his magazine, *McClure's*. Although the writing in *McClure's* was sensationalistic, it was based on fact. Circulation skyrocketed, and it was hard to find copies of the magazine on newsstands. Advertisers liked the magazine for the attention it attracted and its high readership.

McClure's took on the insurance industry, the railroads, and urban problems. Two of the most prominent writers at *McClure's* were Lincoln Steffens and Ida Tarbell. Steffens started work at *McClure's* in 1902 and was quickly sent out into the field to report on municipal government corruption. Over the next two years, his reporting on the misdeeds of officials in St. Louis, Minneapolis, Pittsburgh, Philadelphia, Chicago, and New York led to indictments and reform. The resulting six articles were eventually collected in the classic book *The Shame of the Cities*.[27] But the magazine's most famous target was Standard Oil. Tarbell had been assigned to write a series of stories that would showcase the oil giant's achievements. Working with the full cooperation of company officials, Tarbell spent five years writing the fifteen-article series, which revealed that the company had achieved its incredible success through the use of bribes, fraud, and violence.[28]

By 1908, the muckraking movement had played itself out. The original talented and committed muckrakers had moved on to other pursuits, and they were replaced by people who were more concerned with sensationalism than with accuracy.

Newsmagazines

Henry Luce, through the now-enormous Time Warner media empire, has probably done more to shape the American media environment than virtually anyone else. Luce was born in China, the son of a Christian missionary, and he graduated from Yale in 1920. He conceived the idea of *Time* magazine while in prep school with his friend Briton Hadden.

The two founded the magazine in 1923 as a reaction against the journalism of the time. They wanted a magazine that would keep readers up-to-date on current events in a single weekly magazine. Organized around news departments, *Time* was written in a style that put the news in context and told the reader how to think about the issues—a style that the magazine maintains to this day. While *Time* presents multiple sides of a story, it also indicates which side the magazine thinks is correct, rejecting the notion of objectivity as impossible.

Luce later took on the world of business with *Fortune*, a glossy magazine featuring the photography of Margaret Bourke-White. The magazine's purpose was to "reflect industrial life as faithfully in ink and paper and word as the finest skyscraper reflects it in stone, steel, and architecture."[29] Luce also was convinced that Americans wanted to get their news through pictures, so he started *Life* magazine in 1936. A success from the start, *Life* had 230,000 subscribers for its first issue and a print order for 466,000 copies. Within four months, the print order was for more than 1 million copies.[30]

When *Life* was launched, the big star at the magazine was neither the editor nor a writer; it was photographer Margaret Bourke-White. Bourke-White was more than just a photographer—she became a cultural icon. Bourke-White's greatest love was industrial photography. Smokestacks, trains, steam pipes, bursts of flame—these were the subjects she most wanted to shoot. In 1929, Henry Luce, the founder of *Time*, saw Bourke-White's photos of the Otis Steel mill and foundry and decided that she was the photographer he wanted to take pictures for his new magazine, *Fortune*. Bourke-White shot photos using such daring methods as hanging off the stone gargoyles at the tops of skyscrapers. She also photographed in Russia at a time when most foreigners were not allowed to take pictures of Soviet industry.[31]

---

muckrakers: Progressive investigative journalists typically publishing in magazines in the early years of the twentieth century.

Web 5.6: See famous images from *Life* magazine.

Margaret Bourke-White rests her camera on a steel gargoyle at the top of New York's Chrysler Building in 1934.

In 1936, Bourke-White journeyed across the South with writer Erskine Caldwell, who had written the controversial novels *God's Little Acre* and *Tobacco Road.* At the time, Caldwell was America's most banned writer because of his sexually explicit (for the time) descriptions of relationships between men and women. Together Caldwell and Bourke-White documented the poverty of the South in the book *Have You Seen Their Faces?*

Following Bourke-White's work at *Fortune*, Luce put her to work on *Life* two months before it started publication. Her first assignment for the new magazine was photographing the dams of the Columbia River basin. But she also shot pictures of people living in Montana—the taxi dancers in the bars, the prostitutes, the customers bowling. The cover photo was typical of Bourke-White's industrial photography: the monumental Fort Peck Dam with a couple of tiny figures included to indicate scale. But her photo essay about the people in the bar, which included a picture of a four-year-old who sat there at night while her mother waited tables, created an uproar among *Life*'s readers and brought the magazine a tremendous amount of attention.[32]

During World War II, Bourke-White became the first woman photographer accredited by the U.S. Army. The army even designed a uniform for her that became the model for those worn by all women correspondents. During the war, she was on an American ship in the Mediterranean Sea that was torpedoed by a German U-boat. As she left the ship on a lifeboat in the middle of the night, Bourke-White's biggest frustration was that the darkness prevented her from taking photographs:

> I could think of nothing but the magnificent pictures unfolding before me, which I longed to take and could not. I suppose for all photographers their greatest pictures are their untaken ones, and I am no exception. For me the indelible untaken photograph is the picture of our sinking ship viewed from our dangling lifeboat.[33]

Luce went on to create *Sports Illustrated*, which debuted on August 12, 1954. Critics suggested that the magazine would face an early demise because no one would be interested in it. After all, football fans wouldn't want to read about basketball or hockey. But by 1968, *Sports Illustrated* had a circulation of 1.5 million, and it currently sells more than 3.1 million copies a week.[34]

As of this writing in the spring of 2014, Time Warner was preparing to spin off its magazine properties, including *Time, Sports Illustrated,* and *People,* as a freestanding company.[35] (See Chapter 3 for more on this change.)

Women's Magazines 

One of the biggest categories of consumer magazines is those targeted at women. Women's magazines got their start in 1830, when Louis Godey began publishing *Godey's Lady's Book*. Edited by Sarah Josepha Hale from 1837 to 1877, *Godey's* was one of the most influential magazines dealing with American life, even though it was much more lowbrow than *Harper's* or *Atlantic Monthly.* According to magazine historian James Wood,

> Godey's became an American institution in the nineteenth century. It affected the manners, morals, tastes, fashions in the clothes, homes, and diet of generations of American readers. It did much to form the American woman's idea of what she was like, how she should act, and how she should insist that she be treated.[36]

Godey's also was a place where women writers could be published alongside established male authors. Hale took

Web 5.7: See the complete text and picture plates of *Godey's* January 1851 issue.

responsibility for openly promoting women writers. Previously, women writers had to use initials or male pseudonyms, or they had to publish in unsigned columns. Hale, however, boldly printed the names of women authors. In the same way that the *Crisis* gave voice to African American writers, *Godey's* gave women a forum. (Black women's magazines existed then as well. For example, *Ringwood's Afro-American Journal of Fashion* was being published in Cleveland in the 1890s.)

Hale also campaigned for education and exercise for women, so it isn't surprising that illustrations in *Godey's* frequently showed women carrying books, magazines, and letters. Hale argued that women needed to receive an education for their own sakes, not just to make them better wives and mothers. The fiction Hale published in *Godey's* even portrayed single women leading satisfying lives.

Hale wrote a column for fourteen years, and her last editorial appeared in *Godey's* in December 1877. She was eighty-nine years old. Hale died in 1879, and though the magazine lived on without her for a while, it was never the same.

Why does Hale still matter to us today? It is because women's magazines continue to follow in her footsteps. They provide a place for women to come together apart from men and provide material that is of specific interest to women, such as articles about women's health. They also celebrate women artists and writers.[37]

The "Seven Sisters." Following in the tradition of *Godey's Lady's Book* were the mainstream women's **service magazines**—magazines that primarily contain articles about how to do things in a better way. These articles cover such topics as health advice, cooking tips, employment help, and fashion guides. The top service magazines were once known as the "seven sisters": *Good Housekeeping, McCall's, Redbook, Ladies' Home Journal, Woman's Day, Better Homes and Gardens*, and *Family Circle*. Each is distinctive, but they all deal with a concern for home, family, and quality of life from a traditional woman's perspective.

Cyrus H. K. Curtis founded the *Ladies' Home Journal* in 1883, and in many ways, it was essentially the same magazine then that it was when it shut down in 2014. It promoted a traditional view of a woman's role in the home; it told her how to dress, what to cook, how to raise children, and how to decorate the house. But it also dealt with issues that were controversial at the time, such as venereal disease and premarital sex. In 1906, the magazine argued against the so-called double standard, in which young men were allowed to sow their wild oats while women were expected to remain virgins. Women and children were paying the

service magazines: Magazines that primarily contain articles about how to do things in a better way. These articles cover such topics as health advice, cooking tips, employment help, and fashion guides.

Fashions for December 1842

The Granger Collection, New York

Godey's Lady's Book, under editor Sarah Josepha Hale, featured hand-colored fashion plates of the latest styles from Europe, such as those pictured here from 1842.

price, the magazine argued, because parents would not discuss the implications of sexual promiscuity with their sons, and the young men who were most promiscuous and likely to carry disease were those most likely to appeal to women. Similar concerns about AIDS and other sexually transmitted diseases appear in magazines today.[38]

The "seven sisters" were reduced to six in 2001 when *McCall's*, founded in 1876, ceased publication. It was reformulated and renamed *Rosie*, after television talk show host and movie star Rosie O'Donnell. The new magazine was successful, experiencing growing circulation and ad pages, until O'Donnell quit her talk show and publicly came out as a lesbian, at which point she started having trouble with her publisher. The feud over editorial direction and the choice of editor led to the magazine's folding in December 2002. *Rosie* was the first major women's service magazine to cease publication since 1957.[39]

Pierre Suu/Getty Images

Anna Wintour shows off the style she promotes as editor of *Vogue*—the fashion bible.

Then, in the summer of 2014, *Ladies' Home Journal* ceased publication as a monthly, moving to being a "quarterly, newsstand-only publication with 'a robust digital presence.'" According to reporting from industry publication *Ad Age*, though the *Journal* had held onto its circulation well with 3.2 million subscribers, it had had serious declines in advertising revenue. A spokesperson for Meredith, the *Journal's* publisher, told *Ad Age*, "You've got a women's lifestyle field that has expanded from the original Seven Sisters to a much broader field competing for limited ad dollars."[40]

Fashion/Beauty/Lifestyle Magazines. The fashion/beauty/lifestyle (FBL) magazines are read by about 40 million women every month. This number includes the readers of women's service magazines, as well as those who read the more youth-oriented magazines, such as *Glamour* and *Cosmopolitan*.

Compared to service magazines, the fashion books (magazines are often called books in the trade) focus more on clothes and style and less on lifestyle. Prominent among them are *Vogue* and *Harper's Bazaar*. *Vogue*, which we discussed in the opening vignette, was established in 1892 and has long been the leading fashion magazine. Edna Woolman Chase started working for *Vogue* in the 1890s, became its editor in 1914, and remained there until 1952, thus becoming one of the longest-tenured voices in fashion. *Vogue* has some editorial content about people, culture, and ideas, but it is devoted primarily to fashion, both in its editorial content and in its advertising. *Vogue* has long been an international presence, with Paris, Milan, and London editions, and it started publishing a Russian edition in 1998.

Each of the FBLs claims that it has a unique editorial focus. Such protestations aside, the magazines may be more alike than they are different. Paula Span of the *Washington Post*, a former freelance writer for *Glamour*, says,

> [These magazines] take a remarkably narrow view of women's interests. The proverbial visitor from space would conclude that earthling women in their twenties and thirties care only about their bodies and what to put in them and on them, their relationships with men and, to a far lesser extent, their jobs; the rest of the world is largely absent.[41]

Cosmopolitan. If the "seven sisters" were the most venerable members of the women's magazine family, *Cosmopolitan* is the naughty cousin. Until 1996, *Cosmo* spoke with the voice of its longtime editor, Helen Gurley Brown. Brown took over at *Cosmo* in 1965 and turned the "insipid, faintly intellectual" magazine into *the* magazine for young women, with a peak circulation of 3 million in 1985. (As of 2013, *Cosmo* had a monthly circulation of just over 3 million.[42]) Brown coined the term *mouseburger* to describe the quiet, introverted "girl" *Cosmo* was out to help. Under Brown, readers were "*Cosmo* girls," though more recently the magazine has updated its image to "fun, fearless, and female."

Cosmo has always focused on practical advice about relationships, work, fashion, health, beauty, and sex. But when acclaimed women's magazine editor Bonnie Fuller took over the helm, the magazine started dealing with issues such as AIDS and sexual harassment. Fuller told the *New York Times*, "I wanted to make it more seductive, not so much in a sexual sense, but in a sense that the reader just couldn't wait to get it and then just couldn't possibly put it down."[43] Fuller also eliminated the occasional male pinups that have appeared in *Cosmo* over the years. (The most famous pinup was the one of Burt Reynolds published in 1972. His nude photo in *Cosmo* may have cost him the Oscar for the movie *Deliverance*.)

Web 5.8: Take a look back at *Ladies Home Journal* over the years.

Video 5.2: Get to know famed women's magazine editor Bonnie Fuller.

Cosmopolitan has a presence that extends far beyond the United States, with fifty-six international editions published in locations such as Britain, Thailand, Poland, Indonesia, and Malaysia. Its British edition has a circulation in excess of 400,000 copies a month. Critics charge that *Cosmo* is exporting American culture and values to the rest of the world. Helen Gurley Brown, who remained as editor of the international editions after stepping down as editor of the U.S. edition, had this to say to the *South China Morning Post*:

> People have very flatteringly said that *Cosmo* is like Coca-Cola or McDonald's, and I say "Glory Hallelujah!" There is nothing bad about Coca-Cola—unless you drink too much of it—and McDonald's makes delicious hamburgers. We are exporting what people want. . . . We're not trying to change Asian culture. . . . It's a magazine for women who love men, who love children and motherhood, and who have a choice of doing work. Now, that doesn't sound so heinous or reprehensible, does it?[44]

Kevin Foy/Alamy

This collection of women's magazines for sale in China illustrates the incredible diversity in the magazine market. Among them are a Chinese edition of the American magazine *Fitness*, a Japanese manga, and several Chinese magazines.

Men's Magazines

Many men's magazines, such as *Field & Stream* and *Motor Trend*, appeal to men through their hobbies. Women might read them, but the target audience is male. There are also men's magazines featuring provocative photos of women, such as *Playboy* and (originally) *Esquire*. The most recent trend in men's magazines is toward lifestyle magazines that resemble women's magazines but are intended for men; these include *Maxim* and *Men's Health*.

Esquire: *A Morale Booster for the Troops.*

Esquire was founded in 1933, and though it published original work by writers such as Ernest Hemingway and F. Scott Fitzgerald, it was also known for its risqué pinups by artists Alberto Vargas and George Petty. These airbrushed drawings of impossibly perfect women frequently got the magazine into legal trouble for violating obscenity laws, but the pictures would be considered extremely mild by today's standards. (The University of Kansas houses the *Esquire* archives of pinup art, some of which is quite valuable. The collection's estimated value is between $10 and $20 million.) *Esquire*, due in no small part to its pinups, was considered an important morale booster during World War II and the Korean conflict, with comedian Bob Hope quoted as saying, "Our American troops are ready to fight at the drop of an *Esquire*."[45]

In recent years, *Esquire* has suffered from an identity crisis and experienced declining circulation and advertising revenue. It has changed ownership at least twice in recent decades, and it has changed its look and formula several times. Despite its problems, *Esquire* always has room for fine writing. Jim Harrison's *Legends of the Fall* first appeared there, as did many of Tom Wolfe's most influential nonfiction articles in the 1960s. In the early 2000s, *Esquire* returned to its roots and started placing greater emphasis on good writing and, as a result, picked up advertisers who want to reach a more upscale audience and more subscribers.[46]

Playboy: *A Magazine and a Lifestyle.*

Playboy first appeared in 1953 as a competitor to *Esquire*, and it made no pretense about what it was really about—pictures of nude women—though, like *Esquire*, it publishes articles by many noted writers. But in addition to the photos and the articles, *Playboy* promoted a lifestyle: the sexually free good life.

Founder Hugh Hefner started out doing circulation promotion for *Esquire* at $60 a week. He wanted to create a magazine that would appeal to young urban males much like himself. He started by paying $200 for color printing plates and the rights to publish a nude photo of Marilyn Monroe. He obtained permission to reprint stories and articles by well-known writers, as well as cartoons and dirty jokes. After collecting subscriptions from around the country, he started *Playboy* for less than $7,000.[47] Hefner says that he would like to be remembered for changing attitudes toward sex: "I would like to be remembered as someone who has had a significant impact in changing sexual values, in changing the repressive attitudes toward sexuality."[48]

Although *Playboy* still goes out to 1.3 million readers every month (it sold 7 million copies a month at its peak of popularity in 1972 and was down to 2.6 million readers in 2008), it gets very little attention compared to newcomers such as *Maxim*. In September 2002, *Playboy* hired away

Maxim's executive editor in an attempt to bring a more modern attitude to the aging magazine.[49]

Maxim: *The Rebirth of Men's Magazines.* The top men's magazine is *Maxim*, which offers a blend of sex, sports, and humor. Launched in April 1997 as a spin-off of the British version, it has been highly influential, and *Details*, *GQ*, and *Esquire* have all mimicked its style. As of 2013, *Maxim* had a monthly circulation of 2 million copies, enough to make it the thirty-first-largest circulation magazine in the United States (see Table 5.2 for a list of the top ten magazines). As recently as 1998, it wasn't even in the top 200. (For comparison, *Men's Health* is the number-two men's magazine, coming in at thirty-fifth on the circulation list.) If you measure magazine success by number of ad pages, however, the more fashion- and current events–oriented *GQ* is at the top.[50]

Questioning the Media

How do magazines appealing to men and women differ from each other? What do the articles in each tell you about the audiences? Are these magazines getting more alike or more different over time? What accounts for the change, or lack of it, in a magazine's content over the years?

Table 5.2 What Are the Top Ten Magazines?

Magazine	Circulation***
1. *AARP The Magazine*	21,931,184*
2. *Game Informer*	7,829,179**
3. *Better Homes and Gardens*	7,624,505
4. *Reader's Digest*	5,241,484
5. *Good Housekeeping*	4,396,795
6. *Family Circle*	4,014,881
7. *National Geographic*	4,001,937
8. *People*	3,542,185
9. *Woman's Day*	3,394754
10. *Time*	3,301,056

Source: "Magazines by Circulation for Six Months, Ended June 30, 2013." *Advertising Age*, adage.com/datacenter/datapopup.php?article_id=244466. Reprinted with permission from Advertising Age/American Demographics. © Crain Communications Inc., 2014.

**AARP The Magazine* may be a bit of a surprise as the top magazine in the country, but as the magazine of AARP, it goes out to every member.

***Game Informer* was the number-eleven magazine in 2008, with a circulation of 3,517,598.

****Sports Illustrated* comes in at thirteen (3.1 million), *Cosmopolitan* at fourteen (3 million), *O, The Oprah Magazine* at eighteen (2.4 million), *Maxim* at thirty-one (2 million), *Rolling Stone* at fifty (1.5 million), and *Playboy* at fifty-nine (1.3 million).

Web 5.9: Read more about magazines, media, and body image.

Former editor Mark Golin, one of the few men to have been on the staff at *Cosmopolitan*, says that *Maxim* stands out among men's magazines because it is not about a single topic, such as cars, clothes, or computers. Instead, it tries to meet the needs of the "inner guy." "There's a guy inside all men," Golin told the *New York Times*, "and whether you're pumping gas in Iowa or you're working on Wall Street, you can't ignore your inner guy."[51]

The *Times* has referred to *Maxim* as "the *Playboy* of the 1990s," and its cleavage-laden covers and sexy humor would seem to support that label. Why the adolescent focus on women? Golin explained it this way: "I think if you are going to have a general-interest magazine for men, well—surprise, surprise, one of men's general interests is women."[52]

One reason magazines such as *Maxim* are so profitable is that they attract a great deal of fashion and gadget advertising. They feature scantily clad women, reviews of electronics, entertainment, fashion, and humor. Moreover, they tend to feature "quick tidbits" of information rather than full-fledged articles.[53]

In Britain, *Maxim* and competitors *FHM* and *Loaded* have seen sharp declines in circulation in recent years, as have the weekly magazines for men, *Zoo* and *Nuts*. The weeklies feature the same raunchy sexual content but have more up-to-date humor and sports gossip.[54] What has taken their place as the most popular men's magazine? *Men's Health*, which features articles on improving your diet, drinking less, and exercising more.[55]

Adventuring is another important area for men's magazines. Some men like to go looking for danger, and magazine articles give readers a chance to do so—but safely. For example, an issue of *Men's Journal* contained an article titled "Climb Mount Rainier: A Serious Mountaineering Challenge With Minimal Risk of Headline-Making Deaths. Call It Everest for Everyman."[56]

The magazine industry has recently tapped men as a major new audience for service magazines such as *Men's Health* and *Men's Journal*. The editors of these magazines have been featured in gossip columns and are getting the kind of high-profile media attention that was formerly limited to the editors of leading women's magazines such as *Vogue* and *Harper's Bazaar*.[57]

Magazines and Modern Society

Magazines may not hold the dominant place in the media market today that they did in the late nineteenth and early twentieth centuries, but they are still a critical component of our culture. One reason magazines remain important is that they are able to reach narrow, specific communities with a slickly produced message. Among the major controversies surrounding magazines today are the images of women they present, the blurring of editorial and advertising content, the level of reality in editorial content, and the appropriateness of material aimed at teenagers.

Magazines and Body Image

It's no secret that a significant number of girls and young women suffer from eating disorders as a result of their quest to find beauty through thinness. The trend toward excessive thinness as a standard of beauty has become more prominent in recent decades. In 1972, 23 percent of U.S. women said that they were dissatisfied with their overall appearance. By 1996, that figure had grown to 48 percent. Critics frequently charge that the thin models in fashion magazines (both in ads and in editorial content) are at least partially responsible for promoting extreme thinness as attractive. In 1953, when Marilyn Monroe was featured in the debut issue of *Playboy*, she was a size twelve with measurements close to the then-ideal of 36-22-35, which by today's standard would make her a **plus-sized model**. Today, the much-photographed Jennifer Aniston is an impossible (for most women) size zero.[58]

British Calvin Klein model Kate Moss was known in the 1990s for her waif-like look that was dubbed "heroin chic" because of her resemblance to an emaciated heroin addict. After Moss admitted she had been drunk on the job for ten years, Calvin Klein ended his long-running contract with the super-thin model, though the designer claimed the separation had nothing to do with her confession.[59] The controversy surrounding Moss went beyond her drinking, alleged drug usage, heroin-chic look, and posing nude in slick magazine advertisements for jeans and underwear. The big source of criticism was that she presented an unrealistic and unobtainable image of what an attractive woman should look like. A teenage girl who ran track, weighed ninety-five pounds, and was five feet tall told *People* magazine,

> I'm not happy if I think I look fat in what I'm wearing. Kate Moss looks so cool in a bathing suit. I don't know if I'm conditioned [to think this way] or if it's just me, but I don't think anything could make me abandon my desire to be thin.[60]

SECRET 3 Advertisers of products other than clothing have become concerned about the thin image being presented in fashion magazines. When photos of model Trish Goff appeared in the British edition of *Vogue* in 1996, Omega Watches pulled its ads from the magazine, saying that the magazine was portraying skeletal, anorexic-looking models.[61]

By 2006, criticism of overly thin models was coming from no less than former Victoria's Secret model Frederique van der Wal. The Fashion Week shows that year in Madrid, Spain, banned models whose body mass index was too low.[62] In 2007, Madrid's Fashion Week shows again banned super-thin models, as did the Milan shows.

plus-sized model: A female fashion model who wears an average or larger clothing size.

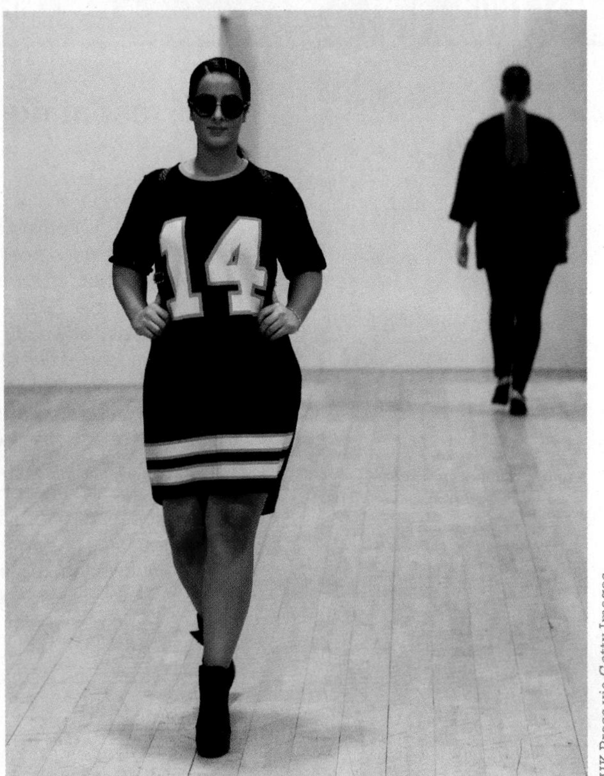

UK Press via Getty Images

A model walks the runway at the British Plus Size Fashion Weekend show during London Fashion Week. Plus size models are becoming more common in magazines as the publications try to feature a full range of size in their fashion spreads.

Remember Secret Three—Everything from the margin moves to the center? It's possible that the willingness of women's magazines to use models of differing sizes is becoming more commonplace than it was several years ago.

It all started back in 2005 with the Dove Campaign for Real Beauty and its so-called Lumpy Ladies. That ad campaign, featuring attractive women of a variety of sizes posing in their underwear for photographer Annie Leibovitz, helped open up a dialogue about size, beauty, and magazine content. Were we going to see more images of "realistic-looking" women in magazine features and advertisements?[63] (That, of course, begs the question as to what constitutes "real women." Are size-two women not real? Or is it more that average-sized women are ignored by the media?)

The campaign paved the way for differently sized models (although they are still the exception rather than the rule, as can be seen in several examples from 2011). The cover of the June 2011 issue of Italian *Vogue* featured scantily clad plus-sized models Tara Lynn, Candice Huffine, and Robyn Lawley sitting around a table set with bowls of pasta as part of an effort to fight anorexia among fans of fashion magazines. The inside photos went considerably further, featuring sexually charged images shot by photographer Steven Meisel, who became famous for shooting singer Madonna's book *Sex*.[64]

TEST YOUR VISUAL MEDIA LITERACY

Presenting a Broader Range of Beauty

Walter Chin/Trunk Archive

How do you react to this "*unconventional*" photo of a model showing a belly pooch? Do you think it's unattractive, a great realistic image, or no big deal? Why do you think you have this instinctive reaction?

Glamour magazine set off something of an Internet uproar with a small photo it ran in its September 2009 issue. It was a nearly nude image of model Lizzie Miller sitting on a bench with a big smile on her face. As FBL magazine photos go, it's not a shocker. Certainly other photos in the magazine, either editorial or advertising, showed more skin. So why did this photo garner so much attention? Because Ms. Miller has a small belly pooch.

Glamour editor-in-chief Cindi Leive wrote on her blog:

> It's a photo that measures all of three by three inches in our September issue, but the letters about it started to flood my inbox literally the day *Glamour* hit newsstands. . . . "I am gasping with delight . . . I love the woman on p 194!" said one . . . then another, and another, and another and another and another. So . . . who is she? And what on earth is so special about her?
>
> Here's the deal: The picture wasn't of a celebrity. It wasn't of a supermodel. It was of a woman sitting in her underwear with a smile on her face and a belly that looks . . . wait for it . . . *normal*.[1]

The photo went with a story by Akiba Solomon about women feeling comfortable in their own skin. The photo had no caption, no mention of who the model was, no mention of the fact that she wore a size twelve or fourteen and weighed 180 pounds.

The response to this small photo was big. In less than two weeks, more than 770 comments about the photo were posted to Leive's blog, not to mention the many e-mails. Most of the comments were laudatory. One woman called it "the most amazing photograph I've ever seen in any women's magazine," while another wrote, "Thank you Lizzie, for showing us your beauty and confidence, and giving women a chance to hopefully recognize a little of their own also."[2]

Not everyone loved the photo and what it stood for, however. One commenter wrote, "I must say I have to agree that the normalization of obesity is a disturbing trend today." Another commented, "We have enough problems with obesity in the US and don't need your magazine promoting anymore of it. Shame on *Glamour* for thinking this was sexy!"[3]

Mary Pipher, author of *Reviving Ophelia*, a book about teen girls and body image, says the new emphasis on diverse images of beauty in fashion magazines is a good, if limited, step. "Presenting a broader range of beauty, even if it's under the guise of selling cosmetics, gives girls more permission to think they too are attractive."[4]

Miller told journalist Lydia Slater of London's *Daily Mail* that she initially felt embarrassed when the photo was published because it showed her stretch marks and a tummy roll. "I said to myself: 'OK, It's not the best picture, but it's not a big deal. And anyway, nobody's going to see it.'"[5] But more than a year after the photo was published, Miller had become a superstar of the modeling world and says she has become much more accepting of her own size. "We need to be celebrating skinny girls, curvy girls, tall girls, short girls, black girls, Asian girls, and all nationalities," Miller said. "I think that would make women feel a lot better about themselves. We have a long way to go until a girl who's curvy can be in a magazine without a lot of attention being drawn to her."[6]

WHO is the source?

Who is Lizzie Miller? What does she do?

WHAT makes her photo from *Glamour* magazine stand out?

Look at the Lizzie Miller photo from *Glamour* magazine. What makes it differ from the typical photo in fashion/beauty/lifestyle magazines for women? What makes it differ from photos in special "size" issues of magazines?

WHAT do people say about the photo?

How does Miller describe her feelings about the photo? What did it do for her career? How did *Glamour*'s readers react to the photo? What did critics of the photo have to say?

HOW do you and your classmates react to the Miller photo?

What do you and your friends think about the Miller photo? Why do you think the photo drew such strong reactions? Is it important for fashion magazines to publish photos of models of different sizes? Will plus-sized models find a place in fashion spreads that aren't devoted to "curvy" models?

Web 5.10: Find out about model Lizzie Miller and "the photo."

---

[1]Cindi Leive, "On the C.L.: The Picture You Can't Stop Talking About: Meet 'The Woman on p. 194,'" *Glamour*, August 17, 2009, www.glamour.com/health-fitness/blogs/vitamin-g/2009/08/on-the-cl-the-picture-you-cant.html.

[2]Ibid.

[3]Ibid.

[4]Associated Press, "Fashion Magazines Showing More Body Types," *USA Today*, August 9, 2005.

[5]Lydia Slater, "The Spare Tyre That Started a Revolution: Model Lizzie Miller on the 'Embarrassing' Picture That Made Her a Star," *The Daily Mail*, September 20, 2010, www.dailymail.co.uk/femail/article-1313462/Plus-size-model-Lizzie-Miller-embarrassing-picture-star.html.

[6]Ibid.

The contrast between plus-sized models and more conventionally sized magazine models was highlighted with a story in *PLUS Model Magazine* (an online magazine at http://plus-model-mag.com/) that had relatively tame naked photos of plus-sized model Katya Zharkova next to an unnamed "straight-sized" model. *PLUS Model* editor in chief Madeline Figueroa-Jones explained the magazine's photo spread thusly:

> The answer to the question is this, there is nothing wrong with our bodies. We are bombarded with weight-loss ads every single day, multiple times a day because it's a multi-billion dollar industry that preys on the fear of being fat. Not everyone is meant to be skinny, our bodies are beautiful and we are not talking about health here because not every skinny person is healthy.
>
> What we desire is equality to shop and have fashion options just like smaller women. Small women cannot be marketed to with pictures of plus-size women, why are we expected to respond to pictures of small size 6 and 8 women? We don't! When the plus size modeling industry began, the models ranged in size from 14 to 18/20, and as customers we long for those days when we identify with the models and feel happy about shopping.[65]

Figueroa-Jones worked as a plus-sized model and now runs a photo agency in addition to editing *PLUS Model Magazine*. Although the article makes a number of unsupported claims about the average weight of women and models, there can be little doubt that models are significantly smaller than typical women.[66] The popular blog *Jezebel* notes that there are growing numbers of plus-sized models being featured in magazines, and not just in "the usual 'Love Your Body' special issues."[67]

Typical of the "Love Your Body" features that *Jezebel* was referring to is one from *V* magazine from its "size" issue, in which one story compared a "straight-sized" model with a plus-sized model, while a second story featured several plus-sized models, including Tara Lynn, in varying states of dress. Lynn also had the cover of the "curvy" issue of *Elle* France. But this may be starting to change, at least a little. In March 2014, as we discussed in the opening vignette, unconventional actress Lena Dunham was on the cover of *Vogue* as a celebrity, not as a part of a "special" issue.

Who's in Control? Advertising Versus Editorial

One of the biggest conflicts in the magazine business is the separation between the editorial and advertising departments. Articles attract readers, but advertisements pay many of the bills. So a continual struggle exists between editors and advertisers to keep content separate from advertisements, to please advertisers, and to make money for the publishers.

Synergy and Magazines. We're used to seeing massive synergy in the movie and television business due to product placement and product-themed shows. But *Shape* magazine seems to have hit a new high—or low—with the practice. The September 2005 issue of the women's fitness magazine featured the cover line, "Win Liz Hurley's Cover Look." Hurley is on the cover wearing a bikini from her own line of clothing, and she's wearing makeup credited to Estée Lauder, for whom Hurley is a paid endorser. This all goes with a two-page ad inside the cover from the cosmetic maker. So Hurley is promoting her clothing line and the cosmetics she endorses, and *Shape* is getting a major ad from the cosmetics manufacturer. Hurley and *Shape* magazine said that there is no connection between the ad and the editorial feature. Magazine expert Samir A. Husni told the *New York Times* that what *Shape* did was nothing new. "It's more a reflection of the entire industry."[68]

Questioning the Media

Do popular consumer magazines pander too much to advertisers? Do you have trouble telling the difference between advertisements and articles? Or does it matter as long as the advertising is interesting?

Fashion/beauty/lifestyle magazine *W* is working to extend synergy to its social media channels as well. The magazine's 2014 spring fashion issue was built around an "Instaglam" theme, playing off the name of the photo-sharing Instagram social media site. Lucy Kriz, publisher of *W* magazine, told *Luxury Daily*, "As March was our social media issue, we wanted to highlight the synergy between magazine, digital and social content. From coordinating tweets, Instagrams and Facebook posts with those feature in the issue . . . we drove the biggest traffic spike on the site since its relaunch, delivering click-through rates above industry average to our brand partners."[69]

What does she mean with that "marketing speak"?

W coordinated its social media posts to go with the articles in the magazine and the social media of its advertisers with the goal of increasing the number of readers visiting both *W*'s Web site and the advertisers' sites.

The Blurring of Advertising and Editorial Content. The often strong connection between advertisers and editorial content at fashion magazines does not necessarily carry over to other periodicals, but that doesn't mean that advertisers don't try to make their ads look like magazine articles. This used to be known as "advertorial content"—combining the words *advertising* and *editorial*—but has now

Web 5.11: Check out controversial magazine covers.

Web 5.12: Learn more about the *studies* of race and magazine covers.

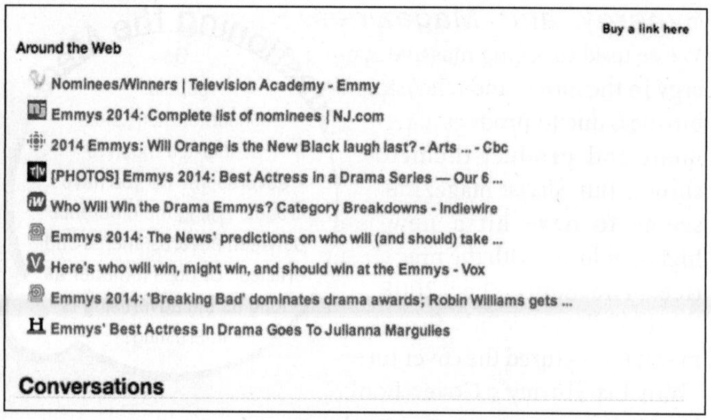

Buy a link here

Around the Web

Nominees/Winners | Television Academy - Emmy

Emmys 2014: Complete list of nominees | NJ.com

2014 Emmys: Will Orange is the New Black laugh last? - Arts ... - Cbc

[PHOTOS] Emmys 2014: Best Actress in a Drama Series — Our 6 ...

Who Will Win the Drama Emmys? Category Breakdowns - Indiewire

Emmys 2014: The News' predictions on who will (and should) take ...

Here's who will win, might win, and should win at the Emmys - Vox

Emmys 2014: 'Breaking Bad' dominates drama awards; Robin Williams gets ...

Emmys' Best Actress In Drama Goes To Julianna Margulies

Conversations

Retrieved from http://www.huffingtonpost.com/2014/08/25/emmys-best-actress-drama_n_5698762.html

These links to stories about the 2014 Emmy Awards look like standard links that appear following a Huffington Post story, but they are there as paid "native ads" designed to look like regular editorial content. Note the link at the upper right corner that says "Buy a link here."

come to be known as **native advertising**. This is where paid content is created by the staff of the publication on behalf of paid clients. This content often looks just like the "real" articles on the pages with only minimal labeling.[70] One women's magazine featured a "senior merchandising editor" wearing a beautiful new coat in a feature called "Hot Shot of the Month." However, the "editor" was really an advertising staffer, and the "hot shot" was really a free promotion for a favored advertiser.[71] Such **native ads** are nothing new, but they have generally been accompanied by a disclaimer saying that the item is an advertisement or a special advertising section.

The *Atlantic*, which now considers itself as much an online publication as a magazine, frequently posts native ads to its various Web sites. In fact, native ads were responsible for 59 percent of the company's online revenue in 2012.[72]

The Importance of Magazine Covers

As Annie Leibovitz has demonstrated time and again, what (and who) appears on a magazine's cover can make or break its newsstand sales. With the steady fall of magazine circulation since 2008, publishers have been eager to find ways to make their publications stand out from the crowd.[73] For example, *Family Circle* magazine decided that it would try to stand out in the displays near supermarket checkout lines by using soothing, homey images rather than celebrity covers.

Dick Stolley, one of the founding editors of *People* magazine, established the following rules for covers:

- Young is better than old.
- Pretty is better than ugly.
- Rich is better than poor.
- Music is better than movies.
- Movies are better than television.
- Nothing is better than a dead celebrity.[74]

Janet Chan, who has served as editorial director of parenting publications for Time Inc., says,

> You'll follow a lot of rules and you could say that's the science, but I think a lot of it is gut. For me, thinking of designing a cover is looking for the image that says, "You want to take this puppy home."[75]

Covers and Race. The fear of losing sales can make editors reluctant to take chances, and one result of this editorial caution is that relatively few nonwhites appear on the covers of men's, women's, teen, and entertainment magazines. *New York Times* reporter David Carr notes that in 2002 less than 20 percent of American magazine covers featured people of color and five years earlier only 12.7 percent of people appearing on magazine covers were nonwhite.[76] (This survey did not include fashion magazines, such as *Vogue*.)

Since then, things have not changed much. A survey of magazines that typically feature women on the cover found that between September 2012 and September 2013, 18 percent of the covers featured women of color, while 82 percent featured white women. Of the 16 magazines analyzed, *Teen Vogue* was the most diverse, featuring a 50/50 split with four white women and four women of color. On the other hand, the men's magazine *Maxim* was the least diverse, featuring 12 covers with white women and none with women of color.[77] If you compare those figures to the most recent census data, women of color make up 36.3 percent of the United States' female population.[78]

One of the clearest examples of the segregation of magazine covers can be seen with the ever-controversial *Sports*

PRNewsFoto/David's Bridal/AP Photo

One magazine that always has an African American model on the cover is *O, The Oprah Magazine*. The publication always features Oprah Winfrey on the cover—in this case she's wearing a Vera Wang gown that extends across two aditional pages.

native advertising: Advertising materials mixed in with articles and written by staff writers designed to look like editorial content rather than paid advertising.

Illustrated swimsuit issue. Over its first fifty years, the swimsuit issue featured only two women of color on the cover—Tyra Banks in 1996 and 1997, and Beyoncé in 2007. Even in 2006, when the cover featured eight models wearing swimsuit bottoms, all of them were white, and most were blond. (It is worth noting that *Sports Illustrated* has had at least five Hispanic cover models over the years.[79]) On a television special celebrating the fiftieth anniversary of the *Sports Illustrated* swimsuit issue, Banks thanked the magazine for putting her on the cover, saying, "I want to thank *Sports Illustrated* . . . for being daring and for making every little black girl that year that saw that issue go 'oh my God, mama, I think I'm pretty because a black girl's on the cover just like me.'"

According to Carr, editors at the top consumer magazines believe that, all things being equal, covers with white models sell better than those with a minority model. However, *O*, which always features Oprah Winfrey on the cover, has a largely white readership. And singer-actress Jennifer Lopez, golfer Tiger Woods, and tennis-playing sisters Venus and Serena Williams have increasingly appeared on magazine covers. Teen magazines, which often focus on the multiracial music business, are also quite likely to show people of color on their covers. Of course, since Barack Obama was elected president, first lady Michelle Obama has been on numerous magazine covers, including *Vogue, O, Us Weekly, People,* and *Glamour.*

Cover Lines. Along with the cover image, cover lines have to draw readers into the publication. **Cover lines** are teaser headlines used to shock, intrigue, or titillate potential buyers. Keep in mind that it is important for cover lines to interest subscribers, as well as drive newsstand sales. If a subscriber is going to renew a magazine, he or she must want to read it, preferably as soon as it arrives. The goal is for cover lines to appeal to as many readers of the magazine as possible. "I would say 85 percent of your cover has to appeal to 100 percent of the audience," says magazine editor Susan Kane.[80] Numbers are often used in cover lines because they suggest value ("79 beat-stress ideas. Rush less, work smarter, find happiness and balance now!")—in other words, they imply that a great deal of good material is to be found inside the magazine.[81]

One thing that makes FBL magazines stand out in the checkout line is their distinctive cover lines. The first issue of *Glamour* under editor Bonnie Fuller had the cover line "Doing it! . . . 100 women's secret sexual agendas—Who wants what, how bad and how often." The same month, *Cosmopolitan* had the cover line "Sex Rules! 10 Make-Him-Throb Moves So Hot You'll Need a Fire Hose to Cool Down the Bed." Even *Redbook*, a service magazine targeted at mothers approaching middle age, proclaims "Sex every night: can it deepen your love? Yes! Yes! Yes!" "Put 'orgasm' on the cover and it will sell," says former *Glamour* editor Ruth Whitney.[82] Of course, some of these covers are *too* hot for grocery stores, which may place blinders over them to avoid offending their customers.[83]

cover lines: Teaser headlines on magazine covers used to shock, intrigue, or titillate potential buyers.

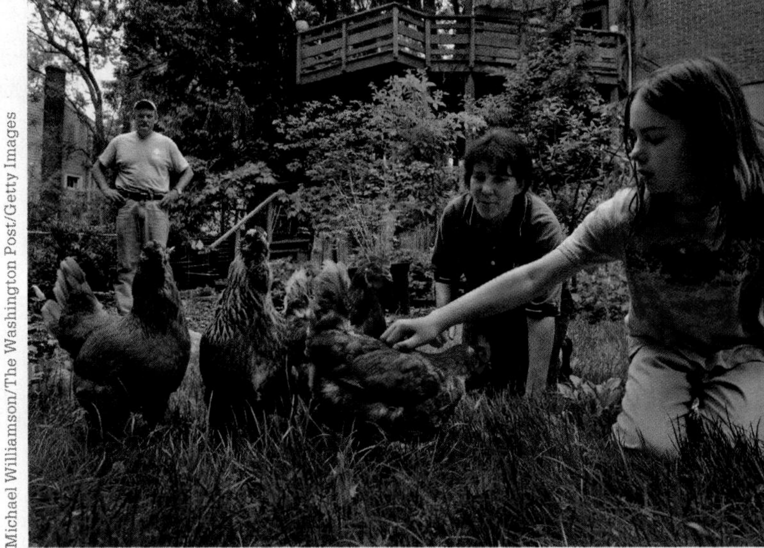

Michael Williamson/The Washington Post/Getty Images

There is a magazine for almost every imaginable group. There's even *Backyard Poultry* for people who raise chickens, ducks, or geese in their yards in urban settings. This family raises chickens in the backyard of their Takoma Park, Maryland, home.

The Future of Magazines

SECRET 4 Although the magazine industry has gone through massive changes, in many ways it is still the same as it was when it was founded in 1741 (providing another example of Secret Four—Nothing's new: Everything that happened in the past will happen again).

Magazines for the Twenty-first Century

According to media scholar Leara D. Rhodes, the American magazine industry has been a series of "launches and failures, new magazines, and revitalization of old ones."[84]

Rhodes says that successful magazines have traditionally shared a number of characteristics, including the following:

- Building a relationship between the magazine and its readers
- Providing information readers can't easily find other places

Questioning the Media

What magazines (if any) do you read regularly? Which of the characteristics noted by Rhodes do they share? How have the magazines you read changed over time, and why do you think those changes were made? Did they lead to a better magazine?

MEDIA TRANSFORMATIONS

Going From Paper to Digital

When the iPad was first released in 2010, it was clear that this new tablet computer had the potential to be a successful delivery system for electronic editions of magazines. The big question that remained was whether traditional magazine publishers would be willing to put out the effort to create tablet versions of their magazines that were easy to use and that provided readers with something of value.

The *New Yorker*, the magazine your author reads as a tablet edition, is available through Apple's App Store for the iPad, the Amazon Appstore for Android for the Kindle Fire, and Next Issue Media for the Galaxy Tab. There is also an edition for the regular e-ink Kindle and a stripped-down version for the iPhone.

The *New Yorker*'s tablet edition went live for the iPad in October 2010, and debuted on the Kindle Fire a little over a year later. The magazine also offers a complete archive online. The *New Yorker* has been somewhat of a pioneer in electronic offerings, as it initially sold its electronic archive as an engraved portable hard drive.[85]

The *New Yorker* has done particularly well in the transition to a tablet era. The Pew foundation reports that the magazine has successfully raised its basic subscription price and has many subscribers paying for both the print and the tablet versions of the magazine. It's also brought in new online humor content that isn't behind the paywall to help draw people in to the magazine's Web site. "We decided that this was a serious

Steve Rhodes

The *New Yorker* offers their magazine in a variety of tablet formats, including Apple's iPad and Amazon's Kindle.

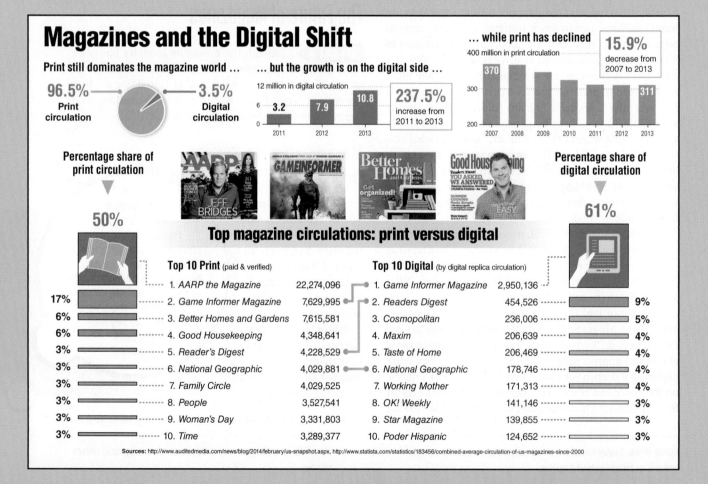

Magazines and the Digital Shift

Print still dominates the magazine world ...

96.5% Print circulation — 3.5% Digital circulation

... but the growth is on the digital side ...

12 million in digital circulation

2011	2012	2013
3.2	7.9	10.8

237.5% increase from 2011 to 2013

... while print has declined

400 million in print circulation

2007	2008	2009	2010	2011	2012	2013
370						311

15.9% decrease from 2007 to 2013

Percentage share of print circulation 50%

Percentage share of digital circulation 61%

Top magazine circulations: print versus digital

Top 10 Print (paid & verified)

Share	Rank	Magazine	Circulation
50%	1.	*AARP the Magazine*	22,274,096
17%	2.	*Game Informer Magazine*	7,629,995
6%	3.	*Better Homes and Gardens*	7,615,581
6%	4.	*Good Housekeeping*	4,348,641
3%	5.	*Reader's Digest*	4,228,529
3%	6.	*National Geographic*	4,029,881
3%	7.	*Family Circle*	4,029,525
3%	8.	*People*	3,527,541
3%	9.	*Woman's Day*	3,331,803
3%	10.	*Time*	3,289,377

Top 10 Digital (by digital replica circulation)

Rank	Magazine	Circulation	Share
1.	*Game Informer Magazine*	2,950,136	61%
2.	*Readers Digest*	454,526	9%
3.	*Cosmopolitan*	236,006	5%
4.	*Maxim*	206,639	4%
5.	*Taste of Home*	206,469	4%
6.	*National Geographic*	178,746	4%
7.	*Working Mother*	171,313	4%
8.	*OK! Weekly*	141,146	3%
9.	*Star Magazine*	139,855	3%
10.	*Poder Hispanic*	124,652	3%

Sources: http://www.auditedmedia.com/news/blog/2014/february/us-snapshot.aspx, http://www.statista.com/statistics/183456/combined-average-circulation-of-us-magazines-since-2000

business for us," *New Yorker* publisher Lisa Hughes told the Pew Research Center. "It was the moment to invest in NewYorker.com; to build it out and make it a real game changer."[86]

Hearst, which publishes a range of popular magazines, has taken to selling "continuous-service" electronic subscriptions that cost $1.99 a month, billed to a credit card. This results in an annual subscription rate of about $24 a year, more than the publisher typically gets for a paper subscription. Hearst, like many other publishers, is finding that electronic editions are a great way to sell back issues of the magazine. In fact, Hearst reports that 40 percent of its single-copy electronic sales are made after the paper copy is off the newsstand.[87]

Owners of tablets are not abandoning print, however, and a study from consumer research group GfK MRI showed that tablet owners were 66 percent more likely than the average U.S. adult to be heavy users of printed magazines. (In case you were wondering, the study defined a heavy magazine user as someone who read thirteen or more magazines, on average, per month.[88])

When Apple's iPad first was released, magazines were trying to sell electronic single issues for the same (high) price as newsstand copies. Then, in 2011, Apple started selling online subscriptions, but took its usual cut of 30 percent on each sale. More problematic to magazine publishers, Apple also kept all of the information about who the subscribers were—information potentially as valuable as the subscription revenue itself.[89]

Magazines have responded to this by selling combined subscriptions that include both the print and digital versions. These digital versions may include a PDF version that will display on any device or a platform-specific app version that will run on an Apple or Google Android device.

Media Transformations Questions

- **WHY** is the switch to digital publishing, and especially "digital first" (discussed later in this chapter), so scary for magazines? (Remember Secret Five—New media are always scary—applies especially to media companies!) Why would the *New Yorker* be willing to take the chance?
- **WHAT** makes offering tablet editions of magazines along with print editions difficult for publishers?
- **HOW** have magazines benefited by adopting digital-first and tablet-publishing strategies? What problems have they had to accept?

- Adapting to social changes
- Being supported by advertisers
- Adjusting to economic changes and limitations
- Shaping public discourse by defining the major issues of society[90]

Just as *McClure's* led to reform of the oil industry at the turn of the previous century, Seymour Hersh's *New Yorker* articles about the abuses at Abu Ghraib prison in Iraq led to investigations of the way prisoners were being treated.

The total circulation of magazines in the United States has risen as the population's overall level of education has increased, thus raising the level of literacy. From 1970 to 2005, the annual paid circulation of all magazines measured by the Audit Bureau of Circulation grew by 67 percent. (The Audit Bureau of Circulation certifies to advertisers how many copies of the largest consumer magazines are actually sold.[91]) Rhodes says that, as educational availability and literacy rise in Asia and Latin America, it seems likely that they will also see a substantial growth in magazine circulation. While overall circulation for magazines dipped starting with the recession of 2008, that decline appears to have leveled out by 2013. Keep in mind, however, that magazines can boost their circulation by offering deeply discounted subscriptions.[92]

Atlantic Media/Richard A. Bloom

The *Atlantic*, a literary/political magazine that dates back to the 1800s, has been successful at adopting a "digital-first" strategy that has helped it start turning a profit for the first time in years.

We can identify several current trends in magazine publishing:

- Magazines are targeting narrower audiences—Unlike the general-interest magazines of the nineteenth century and first half of the twentieth century, contemporary magazines are targeted at specific audiences. While *Maxim* has successfully targeted young men, a group the magazine industry ignored previously, the niches can be much smaller. For example,

Backyard Poultry targets readers interested in raising chickens and other poultry on a small scale. It publishes six times a year and has 60,000 subscribers along with 35,000 copies distributed on newsstands. *All About Beer* (which is all about beer) has been in print for more than thirty years, publishes eight times per year, and distributes about 35,000 copies per issue.[93] Says magazine executive Kevin Coyne, "It's the Me Generation saying, 'I have tastes and preferences, and now I can seek them out in various forms.' It's all about the consumer exercising his choices."[94]

- Presentation is important—The layout and graphics of magazines are critical in determining how people will respond to them. Journalist Michael Scherer writes that magazines today "are filled with color, oversized headlines, graphics, photos, and pull quotes."[95]
- Articles are short—Magazines such as *Maxim*, *InStyle*, and *Us Weekly* have replaced many of their full-fledged articles with text boxes that look like extended captions. According to Keith Blanchard of *Maxim*,

> If you are trying to reach cranky retirees, maybe six-thousand-word rants are appropriate. [*Maxim*] readers are busier today than they will ever be in their lives; they have shorter attention spans than any previous generation; they are chronically over-stimulated and easily bored.[96]

Magazines in the Digital Age

The twenty-first century has been challenging for the magazine industry, to say the least. The economic collapse in 2008 and 2009 led to a 25 percent drop in ad pages sold in 2009 accompanied by a 2.2 percent drop in circulation.

The field of newsmagazines in particular has been suffering, with *U.S. News & World Report* going totally online and discontinuing its print version. *Newsweek*, formerly owned by the Washington Post Company, sold for $1. In 2013, the new owners suspended publication of the paper edition to go totally online, but they then resumed paper publication in March 2014. As recently as 2007, *Newsweek* had had more than 3 million subscribers, but that number fell off the cliff that year, declining by half as of 2010, with the number of ad pages declining by a similar amount.[97]

Time magazine has had declines both in readership and in advertising pages. *Time*'s circulation dropped to 3.3 million copies in 2012, down 1.7 percent from the year before, and suffered a 12 percent drop in advertising pages.[98]

One magazine that has done relatively well during this period of transition is the *Atlantic*. The Pew Research Center's "State of the News Media" report estimated the *Atlantic*'s 2010 profits at $1.8 million. This is from a company that had long been financially marginal and had been losing money for at least a decade. (At its lowest point in 2005, the magazine was losing close to $7 million a year.) What made the difference? Jeremy Peters, writing for the *New York Times*, said the magazine "needed to kill itself to survive."[99] According to Justin Smith, president of the *Atlantic*'s parent company, "[We] brainstormed the question, 'What would we do if the goal was to aggressively cannibalize ourselves?'"[100]

Instead of fighting the Internet and all the changes it has wrought, the *Atlantic* adopted a **digital-first strategy**, in which online and electronic editions are the first priority, not preserving the print edition. In October 2011, the magazine's digital revenues topped its print revenues, but not because the print revenues fell. In fact, in that same month the print edition had one of its best ad sales months in years.[101]

The *Atlantic* had a number of advantages that aided its move to a digital-first strategy. It's a small organization, which makes change simpler. It also targets an upscale, well-educated audience, which also facilitated the change. Overall, the *Atlantic* gets about half of its revenue from advertising, and 40 percent of that revenue comes from digital advertising. Advertising representatives working for the company were told not to worry about the platform they sold for. Digital ads and print ads were of equal importance.

Web 5.13: Read magazine reports for the last several years.

digital-first strategy: An approach to magazine publishing where online and electronic editions are more important than preserving circulation and revenue from print editions.

Chapter SUMMARY

Magazines were the first media to become national in scope rather than appealing to a limited geographic area. They also contained articles designed to be of lasting appeal. Although there were magazines available during the colonial period, the first significant American magazine was the *Saturday Evening Post*. Espousing conservative, middle-class values, the *Post* was seen as a reflection of American society. Literary and commentary magazines flourished in the nineteenth century, and several of them survive today. These magazines provided a forum for important authors and were among the first to feature the work of pioneering photojournalists such as Mathew Brady.

W. E. B. Du Bois expanded the range of commentary magazines with the founding of the *Crisis* as the official magazine of the NAACP. The *Crisis* became the first magazine to provide a forum for black writers. The early twentieth century saw a trend in investigative magazine reporting known as muckraking. The work of the muckrakers set the stage for much of the investigative reporting done today by newspapers and television news.

Henry Luce founded *Time* magazine in 1923, creating what would become one of the nation's largest media companies—Time Warner. Luce's publishing empire grew to include not just the news in *Time*, but also photojournalism in *Life,* sports journalism in *Sports Illustrated,* and personality and celebrity journalism in *People.*

Women's magazines got their start with *Godey's Lady's Book* under the editorship of Sarah Josepha Hale. In addition to editing the magazine, Hale established many of the principles of modern magazines: copyrighting the stories, running original material, and paying authors for their work. The "seven sisters" women's service magazines followed in much the same tradition as *Godey*'s and were concerned mainly with the home, family, and quality of life. An alternative to the traditional values of service magazines is offered by the more youth-oriented fashion/beauty/lifestyle magazines, such as *Glamour* and *Cosmopolitan.*

Many magazines targeted at men appeal to them through their hobbies, but the two most influential men's magazines are *Esquire* and *Playboy.* Although *Playboy* was initially more explicit with its pinup photography, both it and *Esquire* now feature men's fashion, lifestyle coverage, and articles by well-known writers. In recent years, a new type of men's magazine focusing on adventure, fashion, health, and sex has appeared; the most popular of these magazines is *Maxim.*

Trade publications are magazines that cover a particular industry rather than being designed for consumers. Although they often are more serious and feature less photography and color than the consumer magazines, they make up a substantial portion of the magazine market.

Fashion magazines have been criticized in recent years for featuring extremely thin models in both ads and editorial content. Critics argue that the unrealistic image promoted by these models can contribute to the development of eating disorders in young women. Several magazines and advertisers have bucked this trend and featured plus-sized models and even ordinary people. Other conflicts in the magazine industry can involve the blurring of editorial content and advertising, as well as the photos and headlines used on covers.

Magazines in the twenty-first century are continuing many of the trends that made them successful throughout their history, including building relationships with readers, adapting to change, being supported by advertisers, and defining major issues in society. Magazines continue to be successful in their print formats but are expanding their content with tablet versions and other digital offerings.

Keep up-to-date with content from the author's blog.

Take the chapter quiz.

Key TERMS

magazine 112
photojournalism 113
halftone 113
Postal Act of 1879 114
consumer magazines 114
trade magazines 114
literary magazines 115
muckrakers 117
service magazines 119
plus-sized model 123
native advertising 126
cover lines 127
digital-first strategy 130

Concept REVIEW

Development of the magazine industry

The influence of magazines on national culture

The development of photojournalism

The difference between consumer and trade magazines

The role magazines play in giving voice to groups

The controversy over the influence of magazine content on body image

The battle between advertising and editorial content

Function and controversy of magazine covers and cover lines

Relationship between magazines and their readers

The growth of digital publishing

Student STUDY SITE

Sharpen your skills with SAGE edge at **edge.sagepub.com/hanson5e**

SAGE edge for Students provides a personalized approach to help you accomplish your coursework goals in an easy-to-use learning environment.

Newspapers and the News

Reflection of a Democratic Society

chapter 6

Amazon founder and CEO Jeff Bezos announced his plans to buy The Washington Post for $250 million in August of 2013.

AP Photo/Reed Saxon

The news started breaking on Twitter on the afternoon of August 6, 2013, that there was a big meeting scheduled at the *Washington Post.* Not long after, word came that Amazon founder and space memorabilia collector Jeff Bezos had purchased the paper for $250 million from the Graham family, who had run the paper for four generations. Although Bezos founded and is the largest stockholder in book sales and media giant Amazon.com, he bought the paper out of his own personal fortune (and with a fortune estimated at $26 billion, the *Post* cost less than 1 percent of his net worth). When Bezos does things, he doesn't do them in a small way. As an example, not long before buying the *Washington Post*, he funded and led an expedition to recover two of the massive F-1 Saturn V moon rocket engines from the bottom of the Atlantic Ocean.[1]

The fact that this is a personal purchase is important. *Washington Post* reporter Paul Farhi pointed out at the time of the purchase that under Bezos the paper will be privately owned, so he will not be accountable to shareholders or other investors. He'll be allowed to take a long-term approach, something he has a track record of doing. Although the *Post* reported being profitable at the time of the sale, it has been suffering a steady decline in revenue over the past several years and has had declining print circulation as well.[2]

At a time when the common wisdom says that newspapers are a dying medium from the last century, why would one of the wealthiest men in the world purchase a paper that has had declining revenue for six years? Bezos told the *Post*'s Farhi that he does not see any magic answer to the problems metropolitan newspapers are facing:

> The *Post* is famous for its investigative journalism.. . . It pours energy and investment and sweat and dollars into uncovering important stories. And then a bunch of Web sites summarize that [work] in about four minutes and readers can access that news for free. One question is, how do you make a living in that kind of environment? If you can't it's difficult to put the right resources behind it.[3]

When the Graham family decided to sell the *Washington Post*, they were looking for an investor who could pay the $250 million asking price and not demand an immediate return on the investment. And that's when CEO Don Graham thought about his friend Bezos. Despite dealing with cutting-edge

LEARNING OBJECTIVES

After studying this chapter, you will be able to:

1 Discuss the development of the colonial and early American press.

2 Explain how tabloid newspapers differ from broadsheet newspapers.

3 Describe the four major types of newspapers today, with examples.

4 Name six basic news values used by journalists.

5 Discuss the risks that reporters take to cover the news.

6 Explain how the Internet and mobile technology have changed the news and newspaper business.

technology, Bezos has a reputation for taking the long-range view of business.[4] Back in 2011 in an interview with longtime tech journalist Steven Levy, Bezos talked about the fact that his companies have always taken a long view. Bezos says:

> Our first shareholder letter, in 1997, was entitled, "It's all about the long term." If everything you do needs to work on a three-year time horizon, then you're competing against a lot of people. But if you're willing to invest on a seven-year time horizon, you're now competing against a fraction of those people because very few people are willing to do that. Just by lengthening the time horizon, you can engage in endeavors that you could never otherwise pursue.[5]

One of Bezos's first innovations after buying the paper was providing subscribers to other metropolitan papers, including the *Dallas Morning News*, the *Honolulu Star-Advertiser*, and the *Minneapolis Star-Tribune*, unlimited free access to the *Post*'s Web site and mobile apps. Normally, people who want to view more than a limited number of articles at the *Post* have to pay a monthly subscription fee (your author among them). The goal of Bezos's plan is to bring people in to the site who are outside of the paper's print circulation area and who are unlikely to be good candidates for being paying customers, but who still have a documented interest in news. Bezos might also look at bundling access to the *Post* with other online subscription services, such as Amazon Prime or Spotify.[6] In another action, the *Post* actually has been hiring people, adding fifty new staffers during the first half of 2014. This is in sharp contrast to the years of buyouts of senior employees that had cut the size of the newsroom over previous years.[7]

Timeline

1800

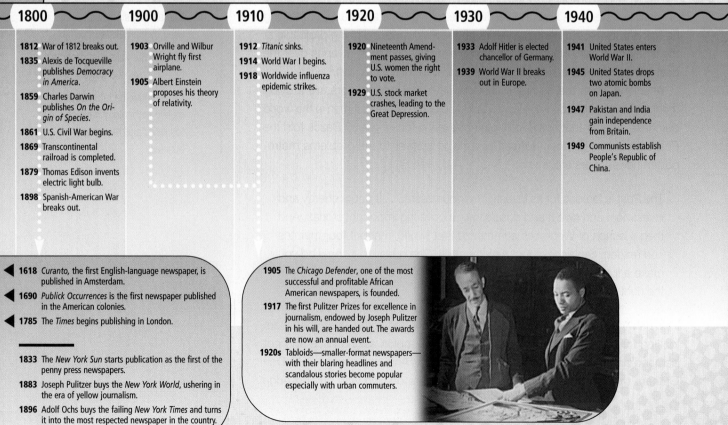

1812 War of 1812 breaks out.
1835 Alexis de Tocqueville publishes *Democracy in America*.
1859 Charles Darwin publishes *On the Origin of Species*.
1861 U.S. Civil War begins.
1869 Transcontinental railroad is completed.
1879 Thomas Edison invents electric light bulb.
1898 Spanish-American War breaks out.

1900

1903 Orville and Wilbur Wright fly first airplane.
1905 Albert Einstein proposes his theory of relativity.

1910

1912 *Titanic* sinks.
1914 World War I begins.
1918 Worldwide influenza epidemic strikes.

1920

1920 Nineteenth Amendment passes, giving U.S. women the right to vote.
1929 U.S. stock market crashes, leading to the Great Depression.

1930

1933 Adolf Hitler is elected chancellor of Germany.
1939 World War II breaks out in Europe.

1940

1941 United States enters World War II.
1945 United States drops two atomic bombs on Japan.
1947 Pakistan and India gain independence from Britain.
1949 Communists establish People's Republic of China.

1618 *Curanto*, the first English-language newspaper, is published in Amsterdam.
1690 *Publick Occurrences* is the first newspaper published in the American colonies.
1785 The *Times* begins publishing in London.

1833 The *New York Sun* starts publication as the first of the penny press newspapers.
1883 Joseph Pulitzer buys the *New York World*, ushering in the era of yellow journalism.
1896 Adolf Ochs buys the failing *New York Times* and turns it into the most respected newspaper in the country.

1905 The *Chicago Defender*, one of the most successful and profitable African American newspapers, is founded.
1917 The first Pulitzer Prizes for excellence in journalism, endowed by Joseph Pulitzer in his will, are handed out. The awards are now an annual event.
1920s Tabloids—smaller-format newspapers—with their blaring headlines and scandalous stories become popular especially with urban commuters.

Library of Congress

Although Bezos has said he hasn't figured out how to make a major metropolitan paper into a growing, profitable media outlet, he does know that the paper's readers have to be at the company's core. "I'm skeptical of any mission that has advertisers at its centerpiece. Whatever the mission is, it has news at its heart."[8]

Some media observers have questioned whether newspapers, the oldest of news media, have any future. They have suggested that words and pictures on paper will be replaced by news and images flowing out over digital channels. The newspaper industry is clearly going through an intense period of change, but it is far from dying. In this chapter, we look at how journalism and the press developed in the United States, how newspapers operate today, whom newspapers large and small are now serving (that is, their audiences), and how newspapers are being transformed in the digital age. ■

Web 6.1: Read more about Jeff Bezos and the businesses he owns.

> "The *Post* is famous for its investigative journalism… It pours energy and investment and sweat and dollars into uncovering important stories. And then a bunch of Web sites summarize that [work] in about four minutes and readers can access that news for free."
>
> —Jeff Bezos

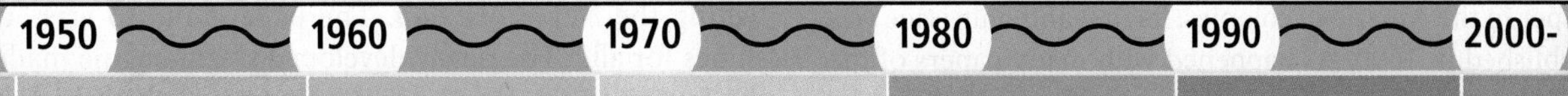

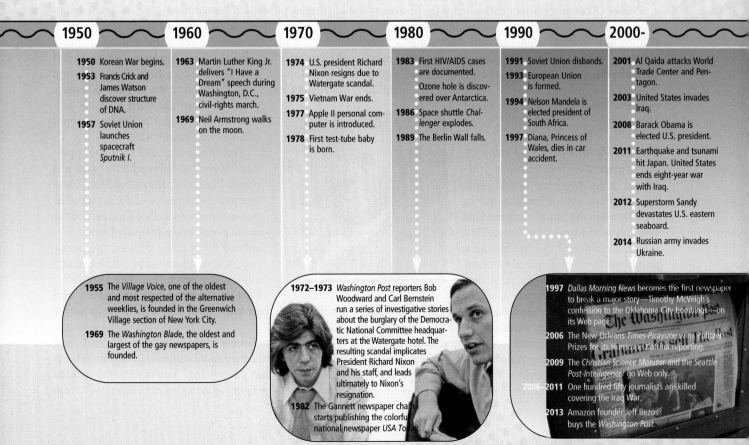

1950 Korean War begins.
1953 Francis Crick and James Watson discover structure of DNA.
1957 Soviet Union launches spacecraft *Sputnik I*.

1963 Martin Luther King Jr. delivers "I Have a Dream" speech during Washington, D.C., civil-rights march.
1969 Neil Armstrong walks on the moon.

1974 U.S. president Richard Nixon resigns due to Watergate scandal.
1975 Vietnam War ends.
1977 Apple II personal computer is introduced.
1978 First test-tube baby is born.

1983 First HIV/AIDS cases are documented. Ozone hole is discovered over Antarctica.
1986 Space shuttle *Challenger* explodes.
1989 The Berlin Wall falls.

1991 Soviet Union disbands.
1993 European Union is formed.
1994 Nelson Mandela is elected president of South Africa.
1997 Diana, Princess of Wales, dies in car accident.

2001 Al Qaida attacks World Trade Center and Pentagon.
2003 United States invades Iraq.
2008 Barack Obama is elected U.S. president.
2011 Earthquake and tsunami hit Japan. United States ends eight-year war with Iraq.
2012 Superstorm Sandy devastates U.S. eastern seaboard.
2014 Russian army invades Ukraine.

1955 The *Village Voice*, one of the oldest and most respected of the alternative weeklies, is founded in the Greenwich Village section of New York City.
1969 The *Washington Blade*, the oldest and largest of the gay newspapers, is founded.

1972–1973 *Washington Post* reporters Bob Woodward and Carl Bernstein run a series of investigative stories about the burglary of the Democratic National Committee headquarters at the Watergate hotel. The resulting scandal implicates President Richard Nixon and his staff, and leads ultimately to Nixon's resignation.
1982 The Gannett newspaper chain starts publishing the colorful national newspaper *USA Today*.

AP Photo

1997 *Dallas Morning News* becomes the first newspaper to break a major story—Timothy McVeigh's confession to the Oklahoma City bombings—on its Web page.
2006 The New Orleans *Times-Picayune* wins Pulitzer Prizes for its Hurricane Katrina reporting.
2009 The *Christian Science Monitor* and the *Seattle Post-Intelligencer* go Web only.
2006–2011 One hundred fifty journalists are killed covering the Iraq War.
2013 Amazon founder Jeff Bezos buys the *Washington Post*.

Saul Loeb/AFP/Getty Images

Inventing the Modern Press

Newspapers first appeared soon after Johannes Gutenberg's invention of movable type. The first English-language newspaper was *Curanto,* which was published in Amsterdam in June 1618. This was not a newspaper as we would recognize it today, but rather a single broadsheet filled with both British and foreign news. By 1622, similar papers (or newsbooks, as they were called) were being published in Britain. The government attempted to control these papers, which were empowering the new capitalist class at the expense of the aristocracy, but the papers were still distributed through places such as coffeehouses.[9]

SECRET 4 If you look ahead to the 1960s and 1970s in the United States, this is not all that different from how the early gay and alternative newspapers were distributed, thus illustrating Secret Four—Nothing's new: Everything that happened in the past will happen again.

Among those publishing broadsheets were church reformers Martin Luther and John Calvin, and their religious writings also helped bring about some of the earliest attempts at censorship.[10]

Colonial Publishing: A Tradition of Independence

Publick Occurrences is frequently cited as the first newspaper in the American colonies; its first and only issue was published in 1690. As happened with many papers of the era, the government promptly shut it down. In this case, the government objected to the paper's disparaging remarks about the king of France. The first paper to publish multiple issues was the *Boston News-Letter,* which was founded in 1704.

©iStockphoto.com/joecicak

Benjamin and James Franklin. Just as media dynasties exist today, they existed in the American colonies, with Benjamin and James Franklin having their hands in just about every medium available at the time. Starting in 1721, James, the elder of the two brothers, published the *New-England Courant,* the first newspaper to be published without the explicit approval of the British Crown. When James was thrown into prison for irritating the authorities, sixteen-year-old Benjamin, who had been working as a printer's apprentice, took over the paper. By 1729, he had purchased the *Pennsylvania Gazette* and began turning it into the most influential paper in the colonies. Franklin published the colonies' first political cartoon, the oft-reprinted "Join, or Die" cartoon, and he introduced the weather report as a regular feature.[11]

The Penny Press: Newspapers for the People

The newspapers of the American colonies had little in common with newspapers today. Before the 1830s, daily papers contained shipping news and political essays. Designed primarily for the wealthy elite, these papers were often underwritten by political parties, and their content was determined by the editors' opinions. Although we might consider this biased coverage, these early papers made no pretense of objectivity. Why should they? Each political party had its own paper, and the small number of subscribers (2,000 at most) tended to share similar viewpoints. Battles between rival newspapers could get quite heated, even extending to physical violence.

Colonial newspapers were quite expensive, costing as much as six cents a day at a time when a worker might make eighty-five cents a day. Papers were typically available only by annual subscription, which had to be paid in advance. These papers showed their business bias with names like the *Advertiser* or the *Commercial.* They typically consisted of four pages, with the front and back filled primarily with advertising and the inside pages with news and editorial content.[12]

***Benjamin Day and the* New York Sun.** In the 1830s, Benjamin Day conceived a new type of newspaper, one that would sell large numbers of copies to the emerging literate public. On September 3, 1833, he started publishing the *New York Sun.* The paper's motto was "It shines for all." The newly developed steam engine made the *Sun* possible. Hand-powered presses, which hadn't changed much since Gutenberg's time, could print no more than 350 pages a day, but a steam-powered rotary press could print as many as 16,000 sections (not just pages) in the same amount of time (see Chapter 4).[13]

The *Sun* emphasized facts over opinion. Papers that followed in its wake had names like *Critic, Herald,* or *Star.* These inexpensive papers sold for a penny or two on the street, so they soon earned the name penny press. Instead of being subsidized by political parties, the penny papers were supported by circulation and advertising revenues. They also didn't have to worry about subscribers who wouldn't pay their bills, since they were all sold on the street for cash.[14]

Now that publishers could economically print large numbers of papers, they could command a big enough circulation to attract advertising. As a result, their profits came primarily from advertising revenues, not from subscriptions or subsidies. The makers of patent medicines, which often consisted largely of alcohol or narcotics, were the biggest advertisers. Want ads (today's classifieds) also became a prominent feature of the papers.

Penny papers were typically independent rather than being the voice of a particular political party. In fact, they tended to ignore politics altogether because their readers weren't interested in political issues. As an example, one day the *Sun*'s congressional news column reported: "The proceedings of Congress thus far, would not interest our readers."[15]

The concept of "news" was invented by the penny press: These papers emphasized news—the newest developments from the police, courts, and the streets. The traditional papers called the penny papers sensationalistic, not because they ran big headlines or photos—neither existed at the time—but because they were printing "news" instead of political arguments or debates. The penny press also moved toward egalitarianism in the press. The affairs of ordinary people were as much news as accounts of rich aristocrats.[16]

Library of Congress

Newsboys sold newspapers on the streets of New York and other major cities for one or two cents a copy during the penny press era of the nineteenth century.

The British press went through a similar period of change, moving from the highly partisan press of the 1700s to a more "objective" focus on news by the end of the nineteenth century—again a change largely in response to the rise of a literate working class and the desire to reach a large audience for the paper's advertising.[17]

A Modern Democratic Society. The 1830s were a period of intense growth for the United States—in industry, in the economy, and in political participation. The penny newspaper was a vital part of this growth, providing the information the public needed to make democracy work. In 1830 there were 650 weeklies and sixty-five dailies in the United States, but in just ten years those numbers had doubled: to 1,241 weeklies and 138 dailies.[18] It was a period when more people were working for wages outside the home and were starting to use consumer goods purchased with cash. The penny press provided a means for advertising these goods, which in turn expanded the market for them.

The United States was being transformed from a rural community to an urban society, from an agricultural nation to an industrial one, from self-sufficient families to a market-based economy. Michael Schudson argues that the penny papers were a strong force in this change:

> These papers, whatever their political preferences, were spokesmen for egalitarian ideals in politics, economic life, and social life through their organization of sales, their solicitation of advertising, their emphasis on news, their catering to large audiences, their decreasing concern with the editorial.
>
> The penny papers expressed and built the culture of a democratic market society, a culture which had no place for social or intellectual deference.[19]

SECRET 1 During the Civil War era, the press continued its move toward being independent from political parties. The press provided people with news about the war and whether the nation would continue to exist. Following the war, newspapers continued to grow and began to be an important part of people's everyday lives. This was the establishment of Secret One—The media are essential components of our lives. Hazel Dicken-Garcia, in her history of the nineteenth-century press, wrote,

> The press became a "habit" as Americans, perhaps for the first time, recognized a vital need for it and established it as [a] part of their lives in a way that was unprecedented. Families sought news of relatives fighting in the war, and national leaders needed information about events as a basis for making decisions and forming policies for conducting the war. . . . Since everyone had a stake in the war and thus a driving need to know about events, the newspaper became primary reading material as never before.[20]

The Granger Collection, New York

Pioneering woman journalist Nellie Bly created a sensation in the late 1800s with her "stunt journalism" written for Joseph Pulitzer's *New York World.*

Pulitzer, Hearst, and the Battle for New York City

If the penny papers of the first half of the nineteenth century gave birth to modern journalism, the battles between New York publishers Joseph Pulitzer and William Randolph Hearst in the 1880s and 1890s provided journalism's turbulent adolescence.

Pulitzer and the New York World. Joseph Pulitzer came to the United States from Austria in 1864 at the age of seventeen to fight in the Civil War. He survived the war, studied law, and went on to become a reporter for a German-language newspaper. In 1878, he bought the *St. Louis Post and Dispatch* and became its publisher, editor, and business manager.

In 1883, Pulitzer bought the failing *New York World*, and in just three years, he boosted its circulation from 15,000 to more than 250,000. High circulation was critical because large readership numbers attracted advertisers who were willing to pay premium prices. Twelve years after Pulitzer bought the paper, it had a daily circulation of 540,000.[21]

Pulitzer changed the appearance of the paper's front page, replacing dense type with huge multicolumn pictures and big headlines. He brought to journalism a sense of drama and style that appealed immensely to his turn-of-the-century audience. Author and press critic Paul Weaver credits Pulitzer with the invention of the modern newspaper's front page. Before Pulitzer, the front page was no different from any other page in the paper. Pulitzer started the practice of giving the most important story the biggest and widest headline and running that story above the fold of the paper, where it would be immediately visible to anyone looking at the paper on a newsstand. Thus, **above the fold** came to refer to a prominent story.

Pulitzer made many other innovations. He changed headlines so that they said something more specific about the story. For example, a pre-Pulitzer New York paper ran the story about President Lincoln's assassination under the headline "Awful Event." Pulitzer required his editors to use headlines containing a subject and an active verb, so that the Lincoln assassination might have run under the headline "Lincoln Shot." Pre-Pulitzer stories told readers what they needed to know in a formal, structured way. Pulitzer presented the news as a story that people wanted to read; journalists went from just being reporters to being storytellers as well.[22]

New Readers: Immigrants and Women. The New York City of the 1880s and 1890s was a city of immigrants—people who wanted to learn to speak and read English—and the city's newspapers were important teachers. Pulitzer's *New York World* used big headlines, easy words, and many illustrations, all of which helped the paper appeal to the immigrant community. This was also the period when the modern Sunday paper got its start. In 1889, half of all New Yorkers bought Sunday papers. To make his Sunday editions more appealing, Pulitzer started trying out illustrations, comic strips, and color Sunday comics.

Pulitzer also tailored his newspaper to women readers by publishing women's pages and romantic fiction. He had a difficult time balancing the interests of women against those of male readers. He didn't want to offend working-class male

Video 6.1: Watch an interview with Paul Weaver.

Web 6.2: Read about Nellie Bly's visit to an insane asylum.

above the fold: A term used to refer to a prominent story; it comes from placement of a news story in a broadsheet newspaper above the fold in the middle of the front page.

readers by making the paper too feminist in content, but he couldn't ignore the independent women who were now reading papers. Women were the primary purchasers of household items, and advertisers wanted to reach them. So the newspaper needed to tailor its content to reach these "new women" while still appealing to its working-class male readers.

No one epitomized the journalism of Pulitzer's *New York World* better than "stunt journalist" Nellie Bly, who proved that women could go to the same extremes as men when trying to get a story. From her first act at the *World* (pretending to be insane in order to get an insider's report on a women's lunatic asylum) to her most famous stunt (traveling around the world in under eighty days), she always did things more extravagantly than anyone else.[23]

Bly, who lived from 1864 to 1922, authored hundreds of newspaper articles, which were generally long and written in the first person, for the *Pittsburg Dispatch*, the *New York World*, and the *New York Evening Journal.* She was born Elizabeth Jane Cochran but went by the nickname Pink (probably for the pink dresses she wore). It was at the *Dispatch* that she started using the pen name Nellie Bly. In addition to covering women's stories for the *Dispatch*, Bly wrote a travelogue of a journey to Mexico under the headline "NELLIE IN MEXICO." She also made a name for herself covering the plight of young women working in factories.

In 1887, Bly moved to New York in the hope of finding a job at one of the city's vibrant daily papers. First on her list was Pulitzer's *New York World.* She eventually was able to see John Cockerill, managing editor of the *World.* It was Cockerill who suggested that Bly go undercover to write a story about the women's lunatic asylum. If her story was good, he told her, she would get the job.

The asylum had been charged with abusing inmates, but none of the stories written about it had the power of Bly's insider account. To gain access, Bly moved into a rooming house and proceeded to act erratically so as to be committed to the asylum. Once inside, she wrote articles describing patients being fed rotten food and being choked and beaten by nurses. After ten days, an attorney for Pulitzer came to rescue her. The series of stories she produced was a masterpiece.

With this series, Bly proved that a woman could find success in sensationalistic journalism and that she could tell a great story under dangerous circumstances. Today many people would consider it unethical for reporters to pretend to be someone they aren't, and many major papers would reject their work. But in the New York of Hearst and Pulitzer, Bly's stunts were wildly successful and were imitated by other reporters.[24]

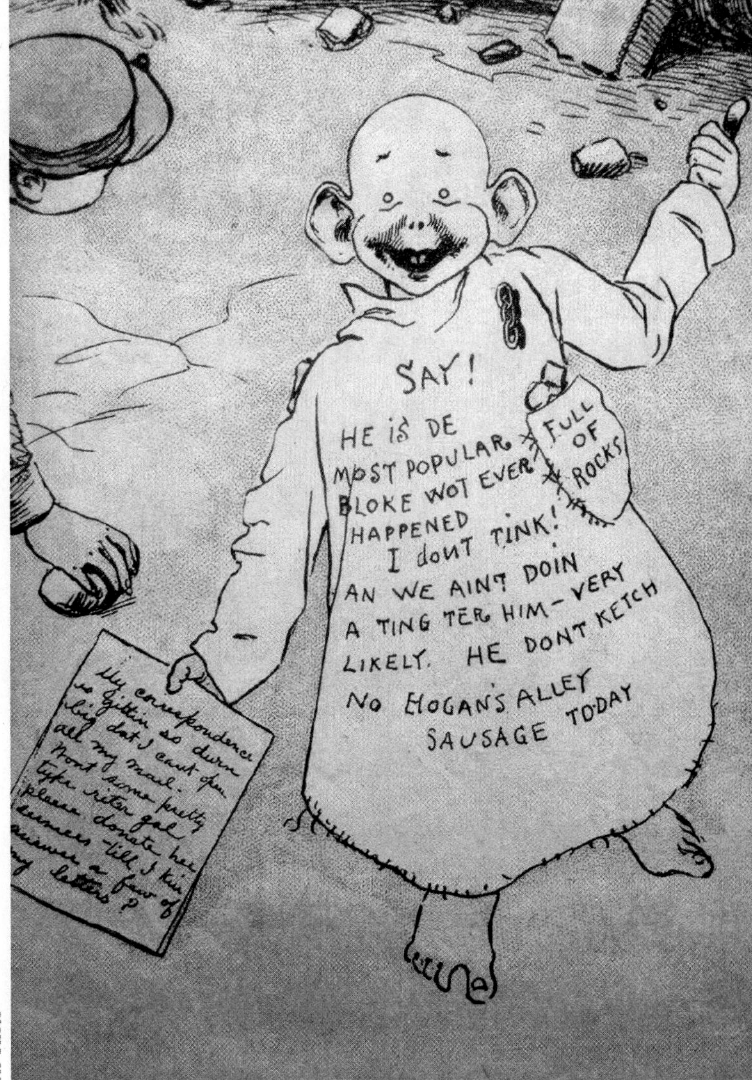

AP Photo

"The Yellow Kid" was such a popular early comic strip character that both the *New York Journal* and the *New York World* had separate versions of the feature drawn by two different artists.

The Era of Yellow Journalism. William Randolph Hearst came from a wealthy family and began his newspaper career as editor of the *San Francisco Examiner*, which was owned by his father. Having dominated the San Francisco newspaper market, Hearst followed Pulitzer into the New York market by purchasing the *New York Journal.* Soon he was using Pulitzer's own techniques to compete against him. Hearst and Pulitzer became fierce rivals, each trying to outdo the other with outlandish stories and stunts. This style of shocking, sensationalistic reporting came to be known as **yellow journalism**. Why yellow? At one point, the two papers fought over which one would publish the popular comic strip "The Yellow Kid," which featured a smart-aleck character and could be considered the "Doonesbury" of its day. Eventually, both papers featured their own "Yellow Kid" drawn by different artists.

yellow journalism: A style of sensationalistic journalism that grew out of the newspaper circulation battle between Joseph Pulitzer and William Randolph Hearst.

Web 6.3: Learn more about "The Yellow Kid."

Average net paid circulation of THE NEWS, Dec., 1927: Sunday, 1,357,556 Daily, 1,193,297

DAILY NEWS

NEW YORK'S PICTURE NEWSPAPER

EXTRA EDITION

Vol. 9. No. 173 66 Pages — New York, Friday, January 13, 1928 — 2 Cents IN CITY LIMITS

DEAD!

Story on page 3

(Copyright: 1928: by Pacific and Atlantic photos)

RUTH SNYDER'S DEATH PICTURED!—This is perhaps the most remarkable exclusive picture in the history of criminology. It shows the actual scene in the Sing Sing death house as the lethal current surged through Ruth Snyder's body at 11:06 last night. Her helmeted head is stiffened in death, her face masked and an electrode strapped to her bare right leg. The autopsy table on which her body was removed is beside her. Judd Gray, mumbling a prayer, followed her down the narrow corridor at 11:14. "Father, forgive them, for they don't know what they are doing?" were Ruth's last words. The picture is the first Sing Sing execution picture and the first of a woman's electrocution. Story p. 3; other pics. p. 28 and back page.

Tom Howard/NY Daily News Archive via Getty Images

One of the most shocking and sensationalistic tabloid covers of all time ran when the *New York Daily News* snuck a photographer into the execution of murderer Ruth Snyder in 1928.

Nowhere was yellow journalism more exaggerated than in the *World*'s and *Journal*'s attempts to drum up fury over the events taking place in Cuba that led to the Spanish-American War. War, then as now, sold a lot of newspapers, and Hearst did his best to sensationalize the conflict in Cuba. He sent reporter Richard Harding Davis and artist Frederic Remington to Havana, Cuba, to cover the possible hostilities between the Spaniards and the Cubans. But there was little to report, and Davis and Remington were kept away from the fighting. According to a popular story, Remington became so discouraged that he telegraphed Hearst asking permission to return to New York: "Everything is quiet. There is no trouble here. There will be no war. Wish to return." Hearst's supposed reply? "Please remain. You furnish the pictures and I'll furnish the war."[25] It's uncertain whether this story is true, but there is no doubt that Hearst used the power of the press to sway public opinion.

Web 6.4: Read more on the New York *Daily News*'s "DEAD!" cover.

Pulitzer eventually repented for his excesses during the era of yellow journalism by endowing a school of journalism at Columbia University. He also endowed the Pulitzer Prizes that every year honor the best reporting, photography, and commentary in journalism.

The Tabloids

Reading newspapers isn't the sort of thing people ever feel a need to apologize for—unless they are reading one of the tabloids. These include not only weekly supermarket tabloids, such as the *Star* and the *National Enquirer*, but also a substantial number of daily tabloids, such as the *New York Daily News* and the *Chicago Sun-Times,* that present the news in a lively style that makes people want to read them.

***The* New York Daily News.** Tabloids first became popular during the 1920s. **Tabloid newspapers** are printed in a half-page (11- by 14-inch) format and usually have a cover rather than a traditional front page. They stand in contrast to **broadsheet newspapers**, which are the standard size of 17 by 22 inches. Riding a resurgence of sensationalism that hadn't been seen since the yellow journalism days of Hearst and Pulitzer, the papers of the 1920s became known for a lively, illustrated style known as **jazz journalism**.

One of the great early tabloids was the *New York Daily News*, which is still popular today.[26] The paper features big photos, huge headlines, and sensationalistic stories. Its most famous cover ran on January 13, 1928. Ruth Snyder had been convicted of murdering her husband and had been sentenced to electrocution. Then, as now, executions of women were rare. Although photographers were excluded from the execution, the *Daily News* sent in a Chicago photographer (because he wouldn't be recognized by anyone present) who had strapped a camera to his ankle. At the moment of the execution, he pulled up his pant leg and took the picture. The photo ran the next day under the headline "DEAD!"[27]

Today's tabloids are no less cutthroat and competitive than Hearst's and Pulitzer's papers in the late 1800s or the tabloids in the 1920s. The *Daily News* continues to do battle on the streets of New York with its rival, the *New York Post.* They compete not only to be the primary paper of working-class New Yorkers, but also to be the tabloid that readers of the more serious *New York Times* pick up for their gossip stories, sometimes referred to as "twinkies."[28]

How fierce is the competition between these two papers? On one occasion the *New York Post* ran an

tabloid newspapers: Newspapers with a half-page (11- by 14-inch) format that usually have a cover rather than a traditional front page like the larger broadsheet papers.

broadsheet newspapers: Standard-sized newspapers, which are generally 17 by 22 inches.

jazz journalism: A lively, illustrated style of newspapering popularized by the tabloid papers in the 1920s.

Associated Press photo of a girl competing in a spelling bee. But because she was sponsored by the *Daily News*, the *Post*'s biggest rival, the *Post* used a computer to edit out the *Daily News* logo from the sign she was wearing.[29] Of course, competition among the American tabloids is nothing compared to that of the British working-class papers. Those tabloids, such as the *Sun* and the *Daily Mirror*, are intensely sensationalistic, and the *Sun* even features a daily topless pinup on its page three. The tabs substantially outsell the more responsible papers.

Broadcast News

In the 1920s, newspapers started facing competition from new outlets. Broadcast media began to provide up-to-the-minute news delivered with a speed and immediacy that newspapers could not match.

Radio News. SECRET 4 News was a part of radio programming from the very start. KDKA demonstrated the power of radio news with its 1920 nighttime broadcast of the Harding-Cox presidential election results—before the newspaper stories appeared the next morning. The newspapers, understandably, were upset by radio's apparent poaching on their territory. In fact, in the 1930s, they threatened to cut off radio stations' access to Associated Press news and even threatened to stop running radio program listings. The newspapers insisted that unless the news was of "transcendent importance," radio shouldn't broadcast it until the newspapers were available. Not surprisingly, the radio networks didn't think much of this idea. Although various restrictions were tested for a short while, in the end, radio news could not be stopped. As we will see again and again, old media usually try unsuccessfully to hold back the development of new media, providing yet another example of Secret Four—Nothing's new: Everything that happened in the past will happen again. Yet the old media do not go away. Instead, after a period of resistance, they change and adapt to the new environment.[30] Radio eliminated the extra editions of newspapers that used to be published whenever dramatic news occurred, but newspapers as a whole suffered only a slight decline in circulation.[31]

One place where radio held clear superiority over newspapers was in the realm of live news. Radio could, for the first time, bring news from around the world to people "as it happened." At no time was this more apparent than during World War II. When Adolf Hitler's army marched into Austria in 1938, CBS was on the air from Europe with immediate news and up-to-the-minute commentary. No radio correspondent of the era stood out more than CBS's European director, Edward R. Murrow. When Germany declared war on England in 1939, Murrow reported it from London in a voice that became familiar to all Americans. During the bombing of London, Americans listened to his live reports, which contained not just the news but also the sounds of everyday life: the air raid sirens, the anti-aircraft guns, and the explosions of bombs. Murrow spoke directly to listeners from London rooftops and made them feel as if they were there with him.[32]

Television News Goes 24/7. Television news started with brief coverage of the 1940 Republican national convention on an experimental NBC television station in New York City. By 1948, both the Democratic and Republican conventions were covered extensively for the still-tiny television audience. Documentary programs, such as *See It Now*, which was hosted by former CBS radio newsman Edward R. Murrow, took on lightweight topics, as well as intensely controversial issues, such as Wisconsin senator Joseph McCarthy, who had accused numerous people of being communists. The program also aired notable segments on the Korean War. In 1947, NBC started TV's longest-running news and commentary program, *Meet the Press*, which is still on today.

In August 1948, the *CBS-TV News* started airing for fifteen minutes every weeknight, setting the standard length for network news until the 1960s. When the ocean liner *Andrea Doria* sank in 1956, a CBS camera crew on a seaplane got footage of the ship going down, which was broadcast promptly. Journalist and broadcast professor Edward Bliss Jr. noted that with the film of the *Andrea Doria*, "Television had demonstrated that it could take the public to the scene of a major story more effectively than any other news medium."[33]

Questioning the Media

How do you get your news? Do you read a newspaper, go to a legacy media site online, watch television, or listen to the radio? What advantages do you experience from using this news source? What is the downside of relying on that source?

Television started playing a major role in presidential elections starting in 1960 with the famous Kennedy-Nixon debates.

In 1963, CBS expanded its nightly news show to half an hour, with Walter Cronkite at the anchor desk. Along with the news, the program featured commentary from veteran newsman Eric Sevareid. NBC soon followed the new format, joined four years later by ABC. During this time, videotape, satellite communication, and color started coming into common use, giving television news more immediacy and impact than ever before. With correspondents bringing into American homes graphic news from the war in Vietnam, as well as spectacular coverage of the moon landing in 1969, television news rose in importance as the way to see what was happening in the world.

On November 3, 1979, the staff of the American Embassy in Tehran was taken hostage by Iranian militants, and ABC started a nightly news update at 11:30 p.m. Eastern Time.

Audio 6.1: Listen to one of Edward R. Murrow's broadcasts.

That news update eventually turned into *Nightline* with anchor Ted Koppel, and it became one of the most respected news shows on television. The following year, Ted Turner's CNN went on the air with news twenty-four hours a day and the promise that the station would not sign off until the end of the world.[34] By the time the Gulf War began in January 1991, viewers were turning to CNN, not the networks, for news.[35] But CNN's dominance was not to last. By 2003 and the war in Iraq, CNN was facing competition in the twenty-four-hour news business from Fox News and, to a lesser extent, MSNBC. As early as 2002, the year after the September 11 terrorist attacks, Fox News was getting consistently higher ratings than the more established CNN. Fox did a number of things to distinguish itself from its rival. Most significantly, it was willing to take a point of view. While CNN and the broadcast networks followed the traditional objective, or neutral, style of reporting, Fox took an opinionated view in the manner of the major newsmagazines and European newspapers.[36] According to the Nielsen ratings, Fox News has fewer unique viewers than does CNN, but they watch the channel for a longer period of time.[37]

The News Business

The newspapers during the era of yellow journalism were the primary source of news at the time. They faced competition from magazines, but heavyweights such as *Time* and *Newsweek* had yet to weigh in. Radio news was a decade or two away, television news would have to wait half a century, and CNN was nearly a hundred years in the future. Although newspapers today owe a huge debt to the great papers of the past, they are operating in a substantially different media environment, one that is saturated with fast, up-to-the-minute competition.

Newspaper Conglomerates—Consolidation and Profitability

Unlike those of Hearst and Pulitzer, today's newspapers typically face little competition from other newspapers. There are 1,382 daily newspapers currently being published, down about 25 percent from one hundred years ago. This doesn't mean that cities are going without newspapers, however; it means only that there are relatively few cities (less than 1 percent) that have competing papers.[38] Also, most newspapers today are owned by large **chains**, corporations that control a significant number of newspapers or other media outlets. Former journalist Ben Bagdikian notes in his book *The Media Monopoly* that before World War II more than 80 percent of all American newspapers were independently owned. Today that picture has reversed, with chains owning more than 80 percent of all papers. The British press has had a longer tradition of concentration of ownership, with three lords owning 67 percent of the daily circulation as early as 1910.[39]

Why is the consolidation in the publishing business taking place? Sometimes family owners just want to get out of the newspaper business. In many cases, inheritance laws virtually force the sale of family-owned papers after they have been passed down through three generations. The chain with the largest circulation is Gannett, the publisher of *USA Today*, which owns approximately eighty-five daily newspapers that have a combined circulation of more than 6.5 million.[40] In addition to Gannett, other major publishers include Thomson Newspapers, Cox Media Group, the New York Times Company, Advance Publications (formerly Newhouse), the Tribune Company, and Dow Jones & Company. In Britain, the largest single owner of newspapers is Rupert Murdoch's News Corporation, which publishes the tabloid the *Sun* as well as the more respected broadsheets the *Times* and the *Sunday Times*. News Corporation publishes more than 175 newspapers in five countries and is the largest publisher of English-language newspapers.

Until recently, newspaper publishing was one of the most profitable businesses in the United States. The Gannett newspaper chain had earnings as high as 30 to 40 percent profits from its papers.[41] The average profit for

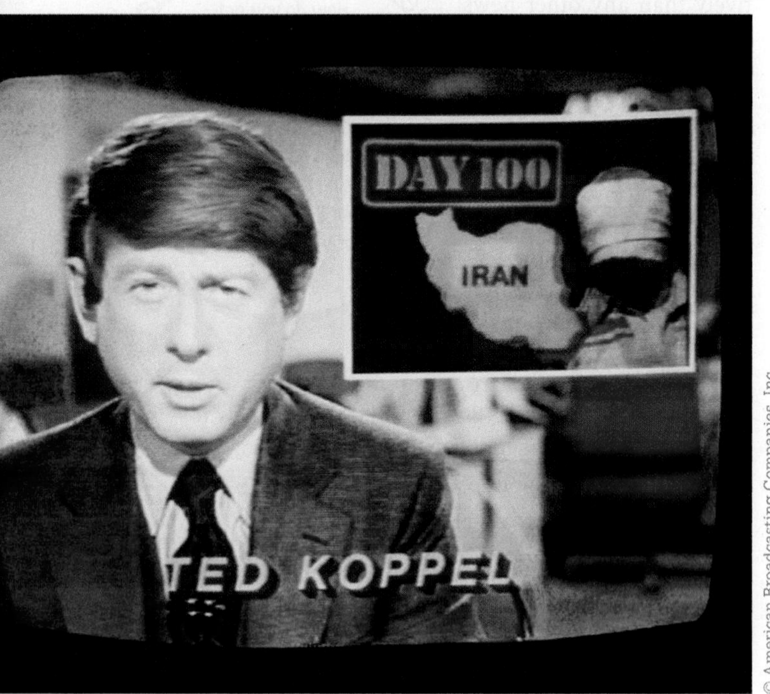

© American Broadcasting Companies, Inc.

Ted Koppel anchored a nightly news update on ABC about the American Embassy staff taken hostage in Iran in 1979. That news update eventually became the long-running late-night news show *Nightline*.

Video 6.2: Watch excerpts from the early days of *Nightline*.

chains: Corporations that control a significant number of newspapers and other media outlets.

publicly owned newspaper chains in 2005 was nearly 20 percent, noticeably higher than that for companies in the Fortune 500.[42] But all that changed in the late 2000s. Annual newspaper advertising revenue fell by 58 percent from its peak in 2000 until 2013.[43] The drops in income were the worst at metropolitan dailies, whereas the national newspaper the *Wall Street Journal* performed relatively well. While the stock prices of newspaper companies have stabilized somewhat since 2010, overall they are down anywhere "between a half and a tenth of their value" from the mid-2000s, according to the Pew 2010 "State of the Media" report.[44] For more on what these economic changes mean to the newspaper industry, see the section titled "The Future of Newspapers" at the end of this chapter.

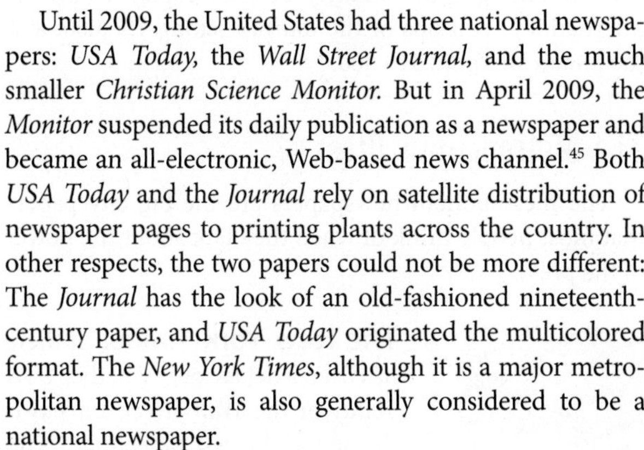

National Newspapers

Until 2009, the United States had three national newspapers: *USA Today,* the *Wall Street Journal,* and the much smaller *Christian Science Monitor.* But in April 2009, the *Monitor* suspended its daily publication as a newspaper and became an all-electronic, Web-based news channel.[45] Both *USA Today* and the *Journal* rely on satellite distribution of newspaper pages to printing plants across the country. In other respects, the two papers could not be more different: The *Journal* has the look of an old-fashioned nineteenth-century paper, and *USA Today* originated the multicolored format. The *New York Times,* although it is a major metropolitan newspaper, is also generally considered to be a national newspaper.

***The* Wall Street Journal.** The nation's premier newspaper for business and financial news has been doing well recently and experiencing increases in both its print circulation and digital revenues. At a time when other papers have been cutting newsroom staff size and budgets, the *Journal* has been hiring staff and producing new features. The *Journal* stands out in contrast with its major competition, *USA Today.* The *Journal* was the last major paper to start using color, and it has still not fully embraced photography. Instead, it uses pen-and-ink drawings for the "mug shots" that accompany its stories. The *Journal* has cultivated a traditional look that deliberately evokes the newspaper layouts of the pre-Pulitzer era.[46] It did undergo a substantial redesign in 2006, primarily to make the paper narrower so that it didn't use as much newsprint, and it has continued a slow movement toward a more modern look. The *Journal*'s circulation is the largest of any American newspaper, with a combined print/digital circulation of 2.38 million.[47] It is the definitive source of financial news, it is highly regarded for its national and international news from reporters such as the late Daniel Pearl, and its editorial page is one of the nation's leading conservative voices. As was discussed in Chapter 3, the *Wall Street Journal,* along with its parent Dow Jones & Company Inc., was acquired by Rupert Murdoch's News Corporation. To date, this has not resulted in substantial changes to the paper.[48]

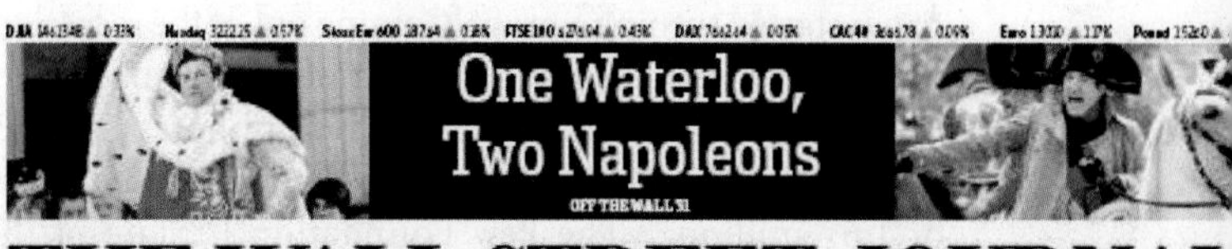

One Waterloo, Two Napoleons

THE WALL STREET JOURNAL

EUROPE EDITION · DOW JONES · VOL. XXXI NO. 47 · TUESDAY, APRIL 9, 2013

'You turn if you want to. The lady's not for turning.' October 1980

'We have ceased to be a nation in retreat.' July 1982, following victory in the Falklands conflict

'Who is society? There is no such thing! There are individual men and women and there are families.' September 1987

'We have not successfully rolled back the frontiers of the state in Britain, only to see them reimposed at a European level.' September 1988

Britain Loses Its Iron Lady

Japan's Stimulus Stretches To Europ

Thatcher's Legacy

Inside

Rex Features via AP Photo

The *Wall Street Journal* is the United States' biggest circulation newspaper with a mix of business, national and international news, along with a conservative editorial focus.

USA Today: *News McNuggets.* When the Gannett newspaper chain founded *USA Today,* journalists made fun of the new national paper, calling it McPaper. They claimed that the brightly colored paper full of short stories was serving up "news McNuggets" to an audience raised on television news. John Quinn, a former editor of the paper, once joked that *USA Today* was "the newspaper that brought new depth to the meaning of the word shallow."[49] Critics of the paper warned that starting a national newspaper was a good way for Gannett to lose a lot of money in a hurry, and the critics were right. In its first decade, *USA Today* reportedly lost more than $800 million, but by 1993, the

Web 6.5: Links to the top ten U.S. newspapers.

paper started turning a profit. Coming out of the recession, *USA Today* had declining circulation, and it had fewer "sponsored" copies being bought in bulk by hotels; in 2013, it had an average daily combined print/digital circulation of 1.67 million.[50] The Pew Foundation's "State of the Media" report for 2011 speculated that some of the decline for the national paper could be in part because travelers are now getting their news via their laptops, smartphones, or tablets.[51] We'll have more on that topic in the "Future of Newspapers" section at the end of the chapter.

The paper now has strengthened its national news section, increased its international news section, and begun running in-depth stories. The paper also tries to get stories other papers don't have rather than just providing an easy-to-understand product. In addition, it has beefed up its foreign staff and hired outside reporters from prestigious newspapers and magazines.

One reason *USA Today* has become more influential is that it is found everywhere. A traveler is much more likely to find *USA Today* in a hotel than the *Washington Post* or the *New York Times*. Even the critics have started coming around in recent years. Ben Bagdikian, who once described the paper as "a mediocre piece of journalism," recently said, "It has become a much more serious newspaper. They have abandoned the idea that every person who picks up the paper has an attention span of 30 seconds. . . . I don't think it's a joke anymore."[52]

©iStockphoto.com/FrankvandenBergh

What influence has *USA Today* had on the newspaper industry as a whole? First and foremost, *USA Today* changed the look of newspapers. It drove color onto the front page and made black-and-white papers look drab in comparison. Second, it was organized clearly by section, thus initiating a trend in which papers began imposing more structure on the news. Finally, and most controversially, *USA Today* has led the trend toward shorter stories.[53]

The most important effect of *USA Today* is that it has forced industry professionals to reconsider what business they are in. The publication's Web site describes *USA Today* as a "multi-platform news and information media company . . . Through its unique visual storytelling, USA TODAY delivers high-quality and engaging content across print, digital, social and video platforms."[54]

English-Language International Newspapers. There are three major English-language international newspapers. The best known of these is the *International New York Times* (formerly the *International Herald Tribune*), which is published in Paris and distributed in 180 countries. Formerly owned in partnership by the *Washington Post* and the *New York Times*, it is now owned exclusively by the *New York Times*.[55] The paper was founded in 1887 as a European edition of the now-defunct *New York Herald*. Traditionally, the *Tribune* reprinted articles from a variety of papers, but it is now based more directly on the *New York Times* content.[56]

Financial Times, owned by British media conglomerate Pearson, is primarily a business newspaper. Its one-time editor Gordon Willoughby told *Ad Age Global* magazine, "We see ourselves as an international window on the business world. There is a global business engine, and it is becoming increasingly outward looking, and that plays to what we're good at."[57]

Although the *Wall Street Journal* is thought of primarily as a U.S. paper, it also publishes European and Asian editions. "We aspired to be the global newspaper of business and the newspaper of business globally. We don't aspire to overtake local newspapers in the U.K., Germany, or Japan," says Richard Tofel of the *Journal*.[58]

None of these papers has a large circulation, with the *Tribune* selling approximately 217,000 copies a day, the international editions of the *Journal* selling 156,000, and the *Financial Times* 319,000.[59]

The Metropolitan Press

The metropolitan newspapers are the big-city papers that most people think of when they talk about the power of the press.

***The* New York Times.** If there has been a debate over whether *USA Today* or the *Wall Street Journal* is the nation's biggest paper, there is no question about which paper is most influential. When people in the United States refer to the *Times* without naming a city, they are almost certainly referring to the *New York Times*. According to at least one definition, news is what is "printed on the front page of the *New York Times*." News stories in the United States often don't become significant until they have been covered in the *New York Times*. The front page of the *New York Times* has as much news on it as is contained in an entire half-hour network newscast. The Sunday *New York Times* is huge: In September 1998, the paper published an Arts and Leisure section with 124 pages, a record for the *New York Times*—and that was just one section![60]

According to *Time* magazine,

> A *Times* morning-after analysis of a presidential debate can set the agenda for days of campaign coverage and punditry. Its decision to feature, say, a murder in Texas on Page One can prompt hordes of reporters to hop a plane south. Its critics can make or break a Broadway play or turn an obscure foreign film into tomorrow's hot ticket.[61]

While the company's longtime motto is "All the News That's Fit to Print," the Hoover's business report suggests that a better choice would be "All the News That's Fit to

Print and Post Online."[62] While the *Times* is classified here as a metropolitan paper, it has as much in common with the major national papers as with the city papers. More than one-third of its readership is located outside New York City. For a list of the top ten newspapers in the United States, see Table 6.1.

The *New York Times* has been a respected newspaper ever since Adolph Ochs bought the failing penny press paper in 1896 and gave it an emphasis on serious national and international news. Its stodgy look, with long columns of type, earned it the nickname "Gray Lady." However, on October 16, 1997, the *Times* started running color photos on its front page, joining virtually every other paper in the country in this practice. Yet even with color the paper doesn't look like *USA Today.* As the *American Journalism Review* put it, "Don't expect the Gray Lady to step out in any gauche dress just to show off."[63] The *Times* is basically a black-and-white paper with color used as accents, according to newspaper design expert Mario Garcia.[64]

The Washington Post. The *New York Times* set the standard for newspaper journalism in the twentieth century and continues to do so today, but in the 1970s, the *Washington Post* inspired a generation of young journalists with its coverage of the **Watergate scandal**, the subsequent cover-up, and the downfall of President Richard Nixon. Watergate was a story that shook the nation and transformed the *Post* from a big-city paper to one with a national reputation.

The scandal started with a "third-rate burglary" of the Democratic National Committee headquarters in the Watergate office and apartment complex on June 16, 1972. When the five Spanish-speaking burglars were arrested, one was found carrying an address book that contained the number for a phone located in the White House.

Among those assigned to cover the story were two young reporters, Bob Woodward and Carl Bernstein. They soon realized that this was no ordinary burglary. As weeks and then months went by, their painstaking reporting connected the burglars to the White House and eventually to the president himself. They further discovered that the White House had been systematically sabotaging the Democratic presidential candidates and attempting to cover up these actions.

During the summer of 1973, Americans were spellbound by the Senate hearings into the Watergate scandal. Finally, with impeachment seeming a certainty, Nixon resigned as president on August 8, 1974.[65] Watergate was no doubt a high point for the *Washington Post*, but the Janet Cooke story was likely one of its lowest. Cooke was hired by the *Post* to improve its coverage of the African American community. She was a young African American woman who claimed to have a degree from Vassar, and she was a fantastic writer. On Sunday, September 28, 1980, Cooke delivered just the kind of story she had been hired to write—a compelling account of an eight-year-old boy named Jimmy who was a heroin addict being shot up by his mother's boyfriend. Although the story was compelling, it wasn't

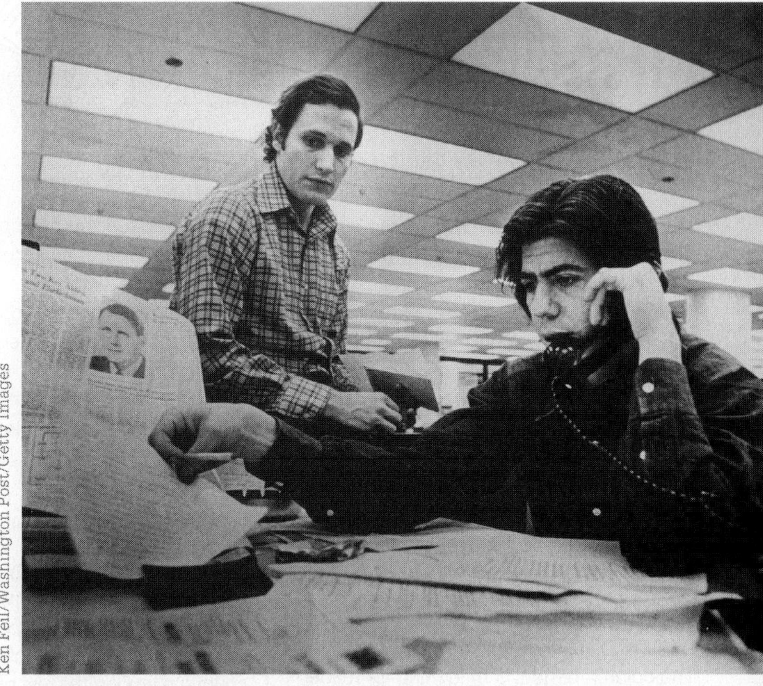
Ken Feil/Washington Post/Getty Images

Bob Woodward (left) and Carl Bernstein helped bring the *Washington Post* to national prominence in the 1970s with their coverage of the Watergate break-in and the subsequent cover-up.

TABLE 6.1 Top Ten Daily Newspapers in Terms of Average Weekday Circulation, March 2013

Paper	Print	Digital	Total
1. *Wall Street Journal*	1,480,725	898,102	2,378,827
2. *New York Times*	731,395	1,133,923	1,865,318
3. *USA Today*	1,424,406	249,900	1,674,306
4. *Los Angeles Times*	432,873	177,720	610,593
5. *New York Post*	299,950	200,571	500,521
6. *Washington Post*	431,149	42,313	473,462
7. *Chicago Sun-Times*	184,801	77,660	262,461
8. *Denver Post*	213,830	192,805	406,635
9. *Chicago Tribune*	368,145	46,785	414,930
10. *Dallas Morning News*	190,613	65,912	256,525

Source: Average Circulation at the Top 25 U.S. Daily Newspapers, Alliance for Audited Media, March 2013, www.auditedmedia.com/news/research-and-data/top-25-us-newspapers-for-march-2013.aspx.

Watergate scandal: A burglary of the Democratic National Committee headquarters in the Watergate office and apartment building that was authorized by rogue White House staffers. Its subsequent cover-up led to the resignation of President Richard Nixon in 1974. Bob Woodward and Carl Bernstein, two reporters from the *Washington Post,* covered the Watergate scandal.

TEST YOUR MEDIA LITERACY

Truth-Telling as a Journalistic Priority

In January 2012, *New York Times* public editor Arthur Brisbane set off a disturbance on the Internet and Twitterverse when he asked, apparently seriously, whether reporters ought to be calling out sources for claiming things as "facts" that are demonstrably not true. (The public editor at the *Times* is a position some papers call the reader representative or the ombudsman. Brisbane is a longtime print journalist who has worked for the *Kansas City Times*, the *Washington Post*, and the *Kansas City Star*.) The column appeared under the headline "Should *The Times* Be a Truth Vigilante?"

The column began, "I'm looking for reader input on whether and when *New York Times* news reporters should challenge 'facts' that are asserted by newsmakers they write about."[1] In other words, he was asking, "Should reporters call out sources for lying?"

He went on to write that there is no question that columnists on the opinion pages of newspapers can point out lies, but should reporters do this?

Brisbane was prompted to write the column based on a message he got from a reader:

> My question is what role the paper's hard-news coverage should play with regard to false statements—by candidates or by others. In general, the *Times* sets its documentation of falsehoods in articles apart from its primary coverage. If the newspaper's overarching goal is truth, oughtn't the truth be embedded in its principal stories? In other words, if a candidate repeatedly utters an outright falsehood . . . shouldn't the *Times* coverage nail it right at the point where the article quotes it?[2]

Brisbane's online column drew a huge range of comments, many of which could be paraphrased as, "Well, duh!"

A commenter from Pennsylvania gave a typical response: "If you genuinely do not know whether or not the paper of record should act as a stenographer for liars, then count me among the rest of the commenters who is incredulous that you had to ask."[3]

Another commenter, this one from Seattle, posted sarcastically, "I'm a pharmacist. Do you think it is absolutely imperative that the next time you come to me for medication I actually give you what your doctor ordered or will just any old medication be just fine? . . . This whole article is about the dumbest thing I have ever read in ANY newspaper."[4]

Among the hundreds of comments were accusations that the paper was printing lies from President Obama, the government of Israel, or the Bush administration during the lead-up to the war in Iraq.

But the answer to Brisbane's question is not necessarily so simple. Greg Sargent, writer of the *Washington Post*'s political blog *Plum Line*, says that trying to fact-check everything before it gets printed would be difficult. On the other hand, Sargent points out that the *Times* prints misleading statements from candidates repeatedly, to the point that a reasonable person reading the paper would think those claims were true.[5]

Journalists, of course, always want to be reporting "the truth," but knowing what is true, what is false, and what is opinion can be challenging. One response to this has been the so-called fact-checking movement in journalism. The Annenberg Public Policy Center's FactCheck.org, begun in 2003, was the first project to address the issue. It monitors the accuracy of articles and ads about political figures. The *Washington Post* has its own version of this system called "The Fact Checker," which rates claims by politicians on a scale of one to four Pinocchios. PolitiFact.com, sponsored by the *Tampa Bay Times*, has sometimes caused controversy with its "Truth-O-Meter," which rates political claims from "true" to "pants-on-fire false." All of these Web sites publish fact-checking stories online as freestanding stories.

Rem Rieder, editor of *American Journalism Review*, writes that incorporating fact-checking into regular news stories would be a big improvement. He says, "Allowing a politician to get away with nonsense day after day lets false statements seep into the public consciousness. Once that happens, it can be hard to dislodge them."[6] He writes that journalists need to be sure to hold all politicians to account,

true—something that was not discovered until the story was awarded the Pulitzer Prize in 1981. Days after Cooke won the award, reporters learned that her college credentials had been fabricated, and soon she confessed that Jimmy's story had been made up as well.[66]

Cooke obviously had not behaved ethically in fabricating the story and her credentials. But Bob Woodward, who was one of Cooke's editors, also accepted responsibility for printing the story. Woodward explained the journalistic and moral lapse in an interview with *Washingtonian* magazine:

> When we found [the story] was a fraud, we exposed it ourselves, putting all the information, very painfully, in the paper. We acknowledged a lapse of journalism.
>
> It took me a while to understand the moral lapse, which was the more unforgivable one. I should have tried to save the kid and then do the story. . . . If it happened now, I'd say, "Okay, where's this kid who's being tortured to death?"

Web 6.6 Read more about the fact-checking controversy.

regardless of political party, without falling into the trap of false equivalency: "If Democrats are prevaricating more than Republicans, or vice versa, don't succumb to the temptation to be equally tough on both sides."[7]

Jill Abramson, the now former executive editor for the *New York Times,* responded to Brisbane's column by arguing that the paper does "rigorous fact-checking and truth-testing" on a daily basis in a variety of ways, including in-depth stories, commentaries, and blogs. "Can we do more?" she asks. "Yes, always. And we will."[8]

One of the strongest reactions to Brisbane's column came from New York University journalism professor Dr. Jay Rosen. Rosen, who has been an outspoken critic of the approach mainstream journalists take to objectivity, says that the need to ask Brisbane's question comes out of an increasing desire for journalists to seem "unbiased." He wrote on his blog *Press Think*,

> Something happened in our press over the last 40 years or so that never got acknowledged and to this day would be denied by a majority of newsroom professionals. *Somewhere along the way, truthtelling was surpassed by other priorities the mainstream press felt a stronger duty to.* These include such things as "maintaining objectivity," "not imposing a judgment," or "refusing to take sides" . . . Journalists felt better, safer, on firmer professional ground—more like pros—when they stopped short of reporting substantially untrue statements as false.[9]

WHO are the sources?

Arthur Brisbane is the former public editor for the *New York Times* (August 2010–August 2012), and Jay Rosen is a professor of journalism for New York University. How do you think their backgrounds shaped their responses to the question about real-time fact-checking? Does it make a difference that one is a professional journalist and the other a professional academic?

WHAT are they saying?

Go online and read what Brisbane and Rosen have to say on the issue of real-time fact-checking. What are their central arguments? What do they disagree about? What do they agree on?

WHAT do others say about their reporting?

Read some of the comments from readers on Brisbane's posts. What are they saying? What kinds of criticism are they leveling against the *Times?* Are they criticizing Brisbane's question or the way the *Times* covers issues? Is anyone supportive of his question?

HOW do you and your classmates react to the issues Brisbane and Rosen raise?

Do you and your classmates think that reporters need to call out sources, especially politicians, when they say things that aren't true? Do you think that it's possible to do so? Will calling out sources for lying make reporters appear to be biased? Is it bad if you know what point of view a reporter holds about a topic?

---

[1]Arthur Brisbane, "Should *The Times* Be a Truth Vigilante?" January 12, 2012, *New York Times*, publiceditor.blogs.nytimes.com/2012/01/12/should-the-times-be-a-truth-vigilante/.

[2]Ibid.

[3]Ibid.

[4]Ibid.

[5]Greg Sargent, "What Are Newspapers For?" *Washington Post*, January 12, 2012, www.washingtonpost.com/blogs/plum-line/post/what-are-newspapers-for/2012/01/12/gIQAuUCqtP_blog.html.

[6]Rem Rieder, "Real Time Fact-Checking," *American Journalism Review*, February 2012, ajr.org/Article.asp?id=5237.

[7]Ibid.

[8]Arthur Brisbane, "Update to My Previous Post on Truth Vigilantes," *New York Times*, January 12, 2012, publiceditor.blogs.nytimes.com/2012/01/12/update-to-my-previous-post-on-truth-vigilantes/.

[9]Jay Rosen, "So Whaddaya Think: Should We Put Truthtelling Back Up There at Number One?" January 12, 2012, pressthink.org/2012/01/so-whaddaya-think-should-we-put-truthtelling-back-up-there-at-number-one/.

> My journalistic failure was immense, but the moral failure was worse. And if I had worried about the kid, I would have learned that the story was a fraud. There would have been no journalistic failure.[67]

Fourteen years after Cooke's story was written, retired *Post* editor Ben Bradlee was still haunted by the story and by the blow it delivered to the paper's credibility: "That was a terrible blot on our reputation. I'd give anything to wipe that one off."[68]

In more recent years, as discussed in the opening vignette, the *Washington Post* has become known for its national presence through its online presence and for the fact that it was recently purchased by Amazon founder Jeff Bezos.

***The* Los Angeles Times.** When people talk about the press in general, they are usually speaking of the major East Coast papers such as the *Washington Post* and the *New York Times.* In the early 2000s, the *Los Angeles Times* established a national presence as well. While it may not have "push[ed] the *New York Times* off its perch,"[69] it has been one of the most respected papers on the West Coast, winning three Pulitzer Prizes in 2003, five in 2004, two in 2005, and one each in 2007 and 2009.

Lately, however, the *Los Angeles Times* has been in the news more often for the controversy surrounding cost-cutting by its owner, the Tribune Company, which also owns the *Chicago Tribune* and superstation WGN.

Since 2003, the paper has cut more than 500 people from its newsroom, reducing the number of journalists working for it from more than 1,100 to approximately 550. In addition, the paper's last four respected editors and a publisher either quit or were fired over disputes about the newsroom cuts.[70]

As of this writing in the summer of 2014, Tribune Company was in the process of spinning off the newspaper publishing wing of the company into its own new company—Tribune Publishing. The new company would own the Tribune Company's publishing assets, including the *Chicago Tribune* and the *Los Angeles Times*.[71]

The paper had previously attracted controversy over its requirement in the late 1990s that reporters attempt to include quotes from women and minorities in their stories. This wasn't so much political correctness as it was marketing correctness. Just as the penny papers started running less politically biased stories to attract the largest possible audience, so the *Los Angeles Times* is now quoting more women and Latinos to boost that segment of the paper's readership.[72] Publisher Mark Willes, who ran the paper from 1995 to 2000, set goals for increasing the number of quotes from women and minorities and made those goals a factor in determining editors' raises.[73]

Reporters at the paper have raised several questions about the new requirement: (1) Should they always identify people by race and/or sex to make sure each source gets counted as a woman or minority? What if the race or sex of a person isn't relevant to the story? (2) What if the reporter is interviewing someone over the phone and doesn't know the race of the interviewee? Does he or she have to ask? (3) What categories constitute diversity? Women, blacks, Native Americans, gays and lesbians, Hispanics? Certainly. But what about a Russian immigrant, a Jew, or a Muslim? (4) Does interviewing one African American guarantee that all black viewpoints have been covered? Some reporters have questioned whether specific minority groups even have a unified point of view.[74]

Questioning the Media

Should news outlets identify a source quoted in a story as being female or a minority even if the source's race or sex has no bearing on the story? Why or why not? Does having women and minority sources improve the quality of the news?

Editors refer to building diversity by quoting minorities and women in stories that aren't about minority issues as **mainstreaming**. Mainstreaming has extended far beyond the *Los Angeles Times*. The *San Jose Mercury News* uses the process in its food section to include material on Eastern Europeans, Southeast Asians, and African Americans and how they are cooking. Keith Woods, former diversity coordinator for the Poynter Institute, writes that mainstreaming is a problem when "people with little expertise and less to say have been forced into stories simply because they fit a demographic quota."[75] Yet when the process brings in a wider range of sources and allows journalists to learn more about their community, then it is successful. Quotas for mainstreaming by quotes are currently in a decline, but the principle—making newspapers more inclusive—is still very much alive.[76]

Web 6.7: Learn more about community newspapers.

Community and Suburban Papers

The **community press** consists of weekly and daily newspapers serving individual communities or suburbs instead of an entire metropolitan area. These papers make extensive use of the Web. While there are more than 1,400 daily newspapers being published in the United States, there are also more than 7,000 nondaily community newspapers, according to the National Newspaper Association.[77]

One of the reasons community papers are important is that they publish news that readers can't get anywhere else. Journalism professor Eric K. Meyer points out that community newspapers "have the most loyal audiences and the news that you can't get elsewhere. A local newspaper won't get scooped by CNN."[78]

Readers often go to a local newspaper, either in the paper format or on the Web, when they feel that the national press isn't covering a story in enough detail. According to the Pew Research Center's Project for Excellence in Journalism, for the past twenty years about 90 percent of newspaper readers have gone to the local paper for news about where they live. During Hurricane Katrina, the New Orleans *Times-Picayune* went from 80,000 page hits a day to 30 million as people around the world tried to find out what was happening in the Crescent City. While the *Times-Picayune* is generally considered a metropolitan paper, in the days, weeks, and months following Hurricane Katrina, it was functioning very much as a community paper.[79]

News and Society

What is news? Ask ten different journalists, and you'll come up with ten different definitions. One way of defining news is to list its characteristics, the values

mainstreaming: The effort by newspapers such as the *Los Angeles Times* to include quotations by minorities and women in stories that aren't about minority issues.

community press: Weekly and daily newspapers serving individual communities or suburbs instead of an entire metropolitan area.

journalists use when they select which stories to report. These include the following:

- Timeliness—An earthquake that happened last night is more newsworthy than one that happened two months ago.
- Proximity—An auto accident in your town in which two people are injured is more likely to make it into the paper than an auto accident 300 miles away in which two people are killed.
- Prominence—When two movie stars have lunch together, it's news. When you have lunch with your mother, it's not.
- Consequence—A $50 billion tax cut is more newsworthy than a $5,000 one.
- Rarity—The birth of an albino tiger is news.
- Human interest—Events that touch our hearts, such as the birth of octuplets, often make the news.

AP Photo/Ivor Prickett Sunday Times

Sunday Times reporter Marie Colvin, shown here in Egypt's Tahrir Square during the Arab Spring protests, covered the world's most dangerous places for more than two decades before she was killed in 2012 while covering the fighting in Syria.

Another way to define news is to look at the wide range of ways newspaper editors think of it. Charles Dana, editor of the New York *Sun* in the late 1800s, defined news as "anything that will make people talk."[80] John B. Bogart, a city editor of the *Sun*, gave us a classic definition: "When a dog bites a man, that is not news. But when a man bites a dog, that *is* news." As mentioned earlier in the chapter, news is often defined as "that which is printed on the front page of the *New York Times*."[81] Noted journalist Walter Lippmann defined news as a "picture of reality on which men can act."[82] And there are cynics who say that the perfect news story is one that deals with "pets, tits, or tots."[83]

Sources, Advertisers, and Readers—Whom Do You Please?

Traditionally, newspapers have maintained a figurative wall between the business department and the newsroom, sometimes jokingly called the "separation of church and state." Reporters and editors are supposed to be concerned not with profits, but rather with reporting the news as best they can. But the barrier is coming down, and editors are increasingly looking at their newspaper as a product that should appeal to advertisers as well as readers.

John Oppedahl, who has served as editor and publisher of the *Arizona Republic*, as well as publisher of the *San Francisco Examiner*, says that editors must be concerned about the business health of their papers:

> Editors have to become more interested and more involved in how their enterprises make money. . . . If you take the view that editors really have been marketers all along, and maybe never wanted to say it, now I think they need to admit that they are.[84]

However, sometimes publishers go from printing news that *readers* want to publishing news that *advertisers* want. For example, many newspapers now publish advice and news about personal investing in addition to the traditional stock reports. While these features are undoubtedly popular with readers, they are even more popular with advertisers, who want their ads for financial services surrounded by stories telling readers that they ought to be investing.

The Project for Excellence in Journalism annual report for 2006 stated the situation fairly baldly: "At many old-media companies, though not all, the decades-long battle at the top between idealists and accountants is now over. The idealists have lost."[85]

Patriotism and the Press—Reporters Risk Their Lives to Report the News

Covering the news, especially from a war zone, can be a dangerous occupation. Journalist deaths in Iraq peaked in 2006 and 2007, with thirty-two journalists dying each of those years. Between March 2003, when the United States invaded Iraq, and December 2011, when the war ended, 150 journalists were killed covering the conflict. According to statistics compiled by the Committee to Protect Journalists, more than 60 percent of the journalists who died during the Iraq war were deliberately murdered as opposed to dying in battles or on dangerous assignments. In addition, fifty-four media workers were killed, including translators, drivers, guards, fixers, and administrative workers.[86]

"The deaths in Iraq reflect the utter deterioration in reporters' traditional status as neutral observers in wartime," said Committee to Protect Journalists executive director Joel Simon. "When this conflict began . . . , most journalists died in combat-related incidents. Now, insurgents routinely target journalists."[87] This continues a trend that started with the murder of popular *Wall Street Journal* reporter Daniel Pearl back in 2002. A videotape discovered on February 25, 2002, showed Pearl being stabbed to death and then decapitated. Pearl had been kidnapped in Pakistan on January 23 while attempting to reach a radical Islamic cleric for an interview.[88] The story he was chasing, however, was apparently a trap designed by a group calling itself the National Movement for the Restoration of Pakistani Sovereignty.[89] Four men were eventually captured and convicted in Pakistani courts for his kidnapping and murder. Pearl and his wife, Mariane, a freelance broadcast journalist, had arrived in Pakistan shortly after the September 11, 2001, attacks. He was covering the country as part of his job as the *Journal*'s South Asia bureau chief.

Mariane Pearl says that her husband's kidnapping was not a typical one, in which the goal is ransom or exchange. "My feeling is that the killing of Danny was more of a declaration of war."[90] Why Pearl was murdered is not clear. His widow speculates that it could have been for a story he had written or something he was working on. He may have simply been seen as a symbol of the West.

In 2013, at least seventy journalists were killed around the world in direct connection to their work, according to the Committee to Protect Journalists. Of those deaths, twenty-eight came from reporters covering the civil war in Syria. The Committee to Protect Journalists reports that deteriorating security conditions have "made it virtually impossible for foreign journalists to work in Syria." Among the dozens of journalists who have been kidnapped, there was NBC's chief foreign correspondent Richard Engel and his crew. The journalists were captured by a Syrian militia group while traveling with a group of Syrian rebels. Although Engel and his team were not physically harmed, they were subject to repeated mock executions. The news team was finally freed when the militia members holding them got into a fire fight at a rebel checkpoint. Iraq was the number-two country for journalism fatalities in 2013 with ten, Egypt with six, Pakistan with five, and Somalia with four.[91]

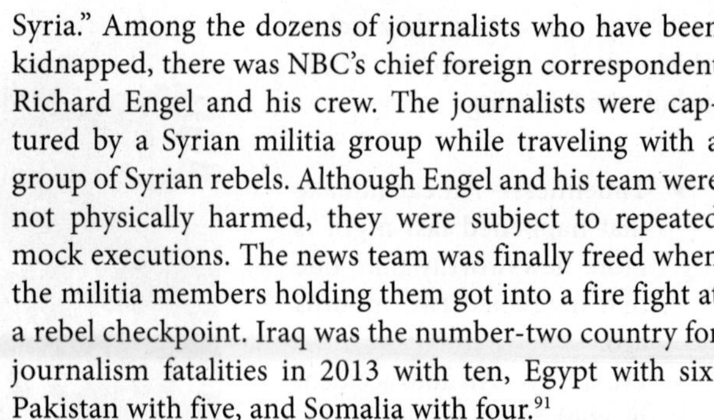

Terry Anderson, an Associated Press reporter who was kidnapped in Lebanon in 1985 and held hostage for seven years, asks, "Why would anyone undertake this kind of work?" He finds the answer within Pearl's life. At the time of his kidnapping, Pearl was determined to try to understand why a man would pack his shoes with explosives before boarding an airplane. Anderson says that correspondents like Pearl put themselves at risk because they believe in reporting the truth:

> They believe it is better for you to know that such things happen than not to know. They believe it is better for you to see the faces of the victims, almost always innocent children and women, and to hear their voices than to let them die ignored and unrecognized. They believe that if they can just make you pay attention, your horror and anger and outrage will match theirs, and you will demand that such things stop. And sometimes, they are right.[92]

Video 6.2: Learn about the career of Associated Press war correspondent George Esper.

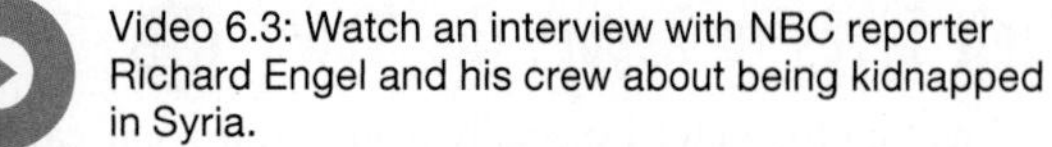

Video 6.3: Watch an interview with NBC reporter Richard Engel and his crew about being kidnapped in Syria.

Web 6.8: Read more on the risks journalists face.

The Alternative Press

Throughout this chapter we have emphasized mainstream, corporate-run, big-city newspapers. But there are also a wide range of **alternative papers** that serve specialized audiences such as racial and ethnic minorities, gays and lesbians, and young people.

Contemporary Minority/Ethnic Papers. The African American press has had a significant presence in the United States since at least 1827. Nearly 4,000 black newspapers have been published in the United States at one time or another.[93]

Freedom's Journal was among the first black newspapers; it was founded in 1827 to show all readers, white and black, that "black citizens were humans who were being treated unjustly."[94] Many black editors of the era faced great danger when they printed articles that contained fact-based accusations against whites. Mobs would destroy the newspaper's

alternative papers: Weekly newspapers that serve specialized audiences such as racial minorities, gays and lesbians, and young people.

offices, and editors who had not left town might be murdered.

Editors of black papers faced further difficulties because much of the intended audience for the papers was illiterate. Moreover, because the majority of the audience was poor, relatively little advertising was available. These editors put their lives and livelihoods at risk publishing a paper that few might read and that probably would lose money.

A variety of emancipation papers followed in the footsteps of *Freedom's Journal*, but none had as great an impact as the *North Star*, which published its first issue in Rochester, New York, on December 3, 1847. Its editor, Frederick Douglass, was known as a gifted writer, and his new paper let readers know that it would be fighting for an end to slavery and the recognition of the rights of blacks. The *North Star* was read and noticed, but it faced the same problems as earlier black papers, including antiblack violence, a shortage of qualified staff, and a chronic lack of money. What it did have was a clear mission and a distinctive journalistic style. The *North Star* was published from 1847 until 1860.[95]

Library of Congress

John Sengstacke, part owner and manager of the *Chicago Defender*, a leading African American newspaper with a national circulation in the middle of the twentieth century, reviews layouts with an assistant.

Another important African American paper is the *Chicago Defender*. Founded in 1905, the *Defender* was considerably less serious than the *North Star*, modeling its style on the yellow journalism of William Randolph Hearst. It was designed to be a black paper with a mass following rather than a publication for black intellectuals and white elites. It was also designed to appeal to advertisers and even make money for its publisher.

Clearly, the *Defender*'s goals included profit as well as advocacy. The paper was sensational, with large red headlines trumpeting stories of crime. By 1920, the *Defender* had a circulation of more than 280,000, a spectacular number at the time. It reached far beyond Chicago, with two-thirds of its readers located outside the city.[96]

The *Defender* encouraged southern blacks to move north to find jobs in Chicago and, not coincidentally, become loyal subscribers to the paper. In retaliation, it was banned throughout the South, and at least two of the paper's distributors were murdered. *Defender* editor Robert Abbott fought for civil rights and an end to lynchings. Abbott, born in 1868, has been credited with founding "the modern Negro press."[97] He demonstrated that black papers could be profit-making institutions, as well as activist publications.

In the 1950s, the *Defender* became a daily tabloid. For a while it provided extensive, day-by-day coverage of the civil rights movement. In 2003, following the death of longtime publisher and editor John H. Sengstacke in 1997, the *Defender* and three other papers owned by relatives of Abbott were sold to Real Times Media. In 2011, the *Defender* laid off its executive editor, news editor, and several staffers in an attempt to cut costs.[98]

What makes a black paper authentically black? In his book *The Black Press, U.S.A.*, Roland Wolseley suggests several qualifications: The paper must be owned and managed by blacks, it must be intended for black readers, and it must be an activist for the black community.[99]

Spanish-language newspapers are also doing well. While their circulation is declining—as is the case with newspapers across the board—their advertising revenue is growing, most of which comes from local advertising.[100] *El Nuevo Herald*, published as a companion to the *Miami Herald*, is the United States' largest Spanish-language paper, with a circulation in excess of 80,000. But the two papers differ in many more ways than just the language. Journalist Dan Grech, speaking on the NPR radio show *On the Media*, said, "The *Miami Herald*, like most U.S. newspapers, prizes objectivity. *El Nuevo Herald* is more like papers in Latin America and Europe that push for social change."[101]

Web 6.9: Check out several alternative papers.

MEDIA TRANSFORMATIONS

From Newspapers to News Brands

Newspapers may not be selling as many sheets of newsprint as they did in the past, but they are certainly not going away as a place that people turn to for news. Consider the *New York Times*. Over the past several years, *New York Times* owner and publisher Arthur Sulzberger has been talking about how the paper will be changing. He set off a storm of controversy in spring 2007 with a comment at the World Economic Forum in Switzerland: "I really don't know whether we'll be printing the *Times* in five years, and you know what? I don't care either . . . The Internet is a wonderful place to be, and we're leading there."[102]

This statement generated comments on almost every major press blog, but what few people noticed was that Sulzberger had been saying the same thing for at least eight years. When he was part of an *Advertising Age* roundtable in 1999, Sulzberger was asked about the future of the *Times.* He answered,

> I don't care how they get it 100 years from now. And the key is not caring. It goes back to knowing the audience, and being, not ambivalent, but agnostic, rather. Agnostic about the methods of distribution. Because we can't afford to be tied to any production process . . . There will still be communities of interest. There will still be a need, both socially and politically, for common and shared experiences.[103]

Now there is a big difference between "I don't care how they get it 100 years from now" and "I really don't know if we'll be

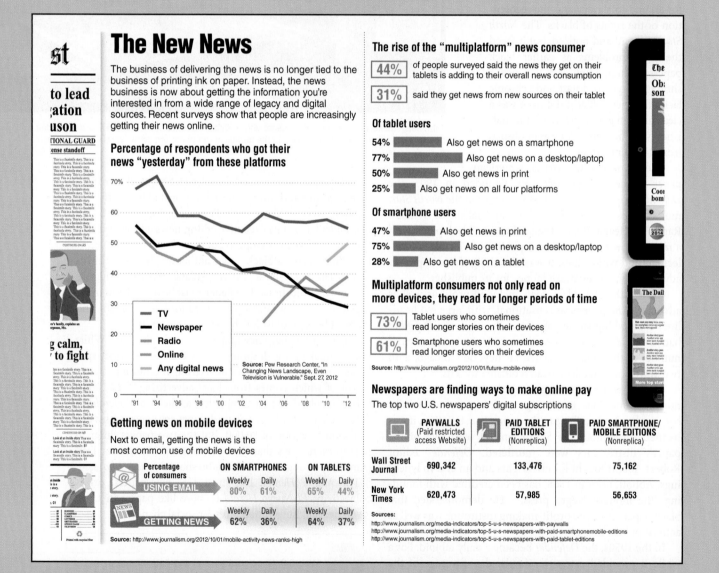

The New News

The business of delivering the news is no longer tied to the business of printing ink on paper. Instead, the news business is now about getting the information you're interested in from a wide range of legacy and digital sources. Recent surveys show that people are increasingly getting their news online.

Percentage of respondents who got their news "yesterday" from these platforms

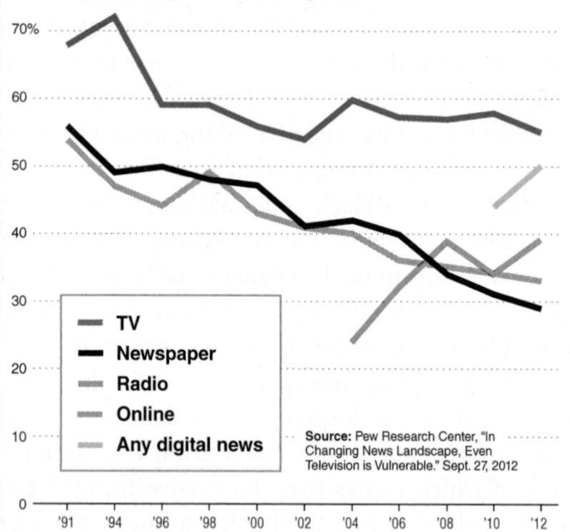

Source: Pew Research Center, "In Changing News Landscape, Even Television is Vulnerable." Sept. 27, 2012

Getting news on mobile devices

Next to email, getting the news is the most common use of mobile devices

Percentage of consumers	ON SMARTPHONES Weekly	ON SMARTPHONES Daily	ON TABLETS Weekly	ON TABLETS Daily
USING EMAIL	80%	61%	65%	44%
GETTING NEWS	62%	36%	64%	37%

Source: http://www.journalism.org/2012/10/01/mobile-activity-news-ranks-high

The rise of the "multiplatform" news consumer

44% of people surveyed said the news they get on their tablets is adding to their overall news consumption

31% said they get news from new sources on their tablet

Of tablet users

- 54% Also get news on a smartphone
- 77% Also get news on a desktop/laptop
- 50% Also get news in print
- 25% Also get news on all four platforms

Of smartphone users

- 47% Also get news in print
- 75% Also get news on a desktop/laptop
- 28% Also get news on a tablet

Multiplatform consumers not only read on more devices, they read for longer periods of time

73% Tablet users who sometimes read longer stories on their devices

61% Smartphone users who sometimes read longer stories on their devices

Source: http://www.journalism.org/2012/10/01/future-mobile-news

Newspapers are finding ways to make online pay

The top two U.S. newspapers' digital subscriptions

	PAYWALLS (Paid restricted access Website)	PAID TABLET EDITIONS (Nonreplica)	PAID SMARTPHONE/ MOBILE EDITIONS (Nonreplica)
Wall Street Journal	690,342	133,476	75,162
New York Times	620,473	57,985	56,653

Sources:
http://www.journalism.org/media-indicators/top-5-u-s-newspapers-with-paywalls
http://www.journalism.org/media-indicators/top-5-u-s-newspapers-with-paid-smartphonemobile-editions
http://www.journalism.org/media-indicators/top-5-u-s-newspapers-with-paid-tablet-editions

printing the *Times* five years from now." But the basic thought, the real point of his comments, is the same—the *New York Times* is no longer in the business of putting black ink on white paper. Instead, the *Times* is in the news business and the ad sales business, and it is going to be delivering news and advertising in whatever forms will turn a profit.

Under its new ownership by Amazon founder Jeff Bezos, the *Washington Post* is now moving from a strategy of being "for and about Washington" to building a national and international readership, where its targeted audience is the English-speaking world. As *Columbia Journalism Review*'s Michael Meyer wrote in June 2014, Bezos's main objective for the *Washington Post* is "reaching the maximum number of customers by putting the *Post*'s journalism in a package (a tablet, a mobile site) that will draw the greatest number of readers. As it has been with Amazon, his obsession at the *Post* is finding a way to integrate product into millions of people's lives in a way they haven't yet experienced."[104]

The world that Sulzberger and Bezos are talking about is already well on its way to being a reality. Data from the Pew Research Journalism Project shows that while a majority of readers still consume their newspaper news exclusively as ink on paper, many others do at least some of their consumption in digital formats as well. For a complete look, see Table 6.2.

TABLE 6.2 Newspaper Audience by Platform

Platofrm	Percentage of Circulation
Print	55 percent
Print/web	15 percent
Print/web/mobile	10 percent
Web-only	7 percent
Web/mobile	5 percent
Print/mobile	4 percent
Mobile only	3 percent

Source: Newspaper Audience by Platform, Pew Research Journalism Project, March 26, 2014, www.journalism.org/media-indicators/newspaper-audience-by-platform.

Media Transformations Questions

- **IS** a newspaper still a newspaper if a majority of its readers access it online or with a mobile device? If so, what makes it a newspaper?
- **DO** metropolitan papers (or even local newspapers) become national media like cable news networks if the adopt a digital first strategy?
- **DOES** it matter to you whether your favorite news source exists in a form other than digital? (That is, do you care whether there is a newspaper, magazine, or broadcast operation connected with it?)

The Gay Press. The question of authenticity is a difficult one for the entire alternative press, not just for ethnic papers. How can a paper represent the interests and concerns of a particular group yet still operate as a profitable commercial venture? This question has been particularly problematic for the gay press.

The *Washington Blade* was the oldest and biggest gay weekly paper in the country.[105] It was started in 1969 as a one-page mimeograph that was distributed in several gay bars at a time when such establishments were routinely raided by police. More recently, a typical edition of the *Blade* ran to more than a hundred pages and included news about health, as well as legal and political issues. In the early 1990s, one of the key features of the *Blade* was the large number of obituaries of men who had died of AIDS; these have become much less numerous in recent years. The *Blade* became such a success that it expanded outside the District of Columbia in 1997 with the *New York Blade*.

But in 2009, the recession hit the media industry hard, including the lesbian/gay/bisexual/transgender (LGBT) press. The most prominent of the gay papers to be affected was the *Washington Blade*. Just weeks after the *Blade*'s fortieth anniversary party, the paper's parent company, Window Media, shut down after investors were unable to meet financial requirements from their Small Business Administration financing. With the closing of Window Media, a number of gay papers across the country were shuttered along with the *Blade*. The *New York Blade* also ceased publication in 2009, when its parent company, HX Media, closed.[106] While many of these papers stayed closed, the *Washington Blade* did manage a revival under new management in April 2010, and as of 2012 was back to publishing both on paper and online on a regular basis.[107]

Although the *Washington Blade* has revived itself, it is the exception rather than the rule. Why did these previously successful publications fail? There are several likely reasons:

- Like many media companies in the late 2000s, the owners of LGBT newspapers were facing severe financial problems. Even though the *Washington Blade* was reportedly turning a profit up until the time it closed, its parent company was not.
- The audiences for LGBT media were early adopters of online social media and Web-based publications.

SECRET 3 Gay culture has moved into the mainstream. Remember Secret Three—Everything from the margin moves to the center. When gay and lesbian papers were founded in the 1960s and 1970s, reporters at the papers

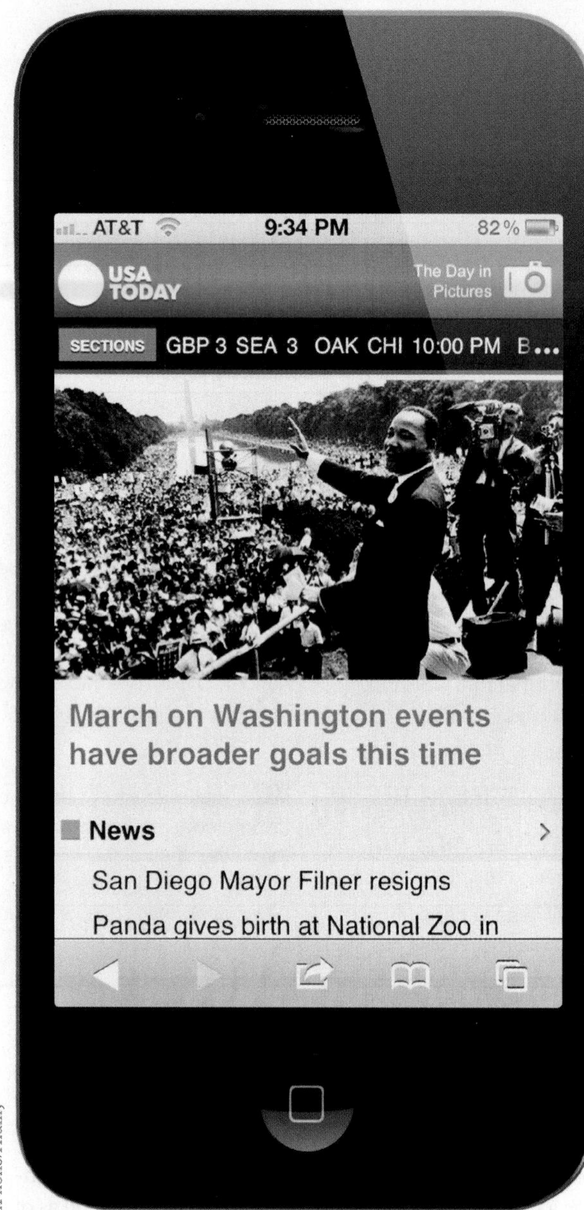

iPhone/Alamy

National newspaper *USA Today* is known as much for its online and mobile content as for its print edition. The paper optimizes its sites for display on phones, tablets, and computers.

feared for their personal safety. Reporter Lou Chibbaro Jr., an employee of the *Blade* since 1976, told the *Washington Post* that, over the course of his career there, he had gone from writing under an assumed name in the 1970s to sitting in the front row at a presidential press conference in 2009. With gay and lesbian issues increasingly being covered by Big Media, there may not be the same demand for gay-specific newspapers now.[108]

The trend of gay publications moving to the mainstream has been an ongoing one. In the 2000s, there was an extensive debate in New York over whether straight-owned papers could adequately cover the LGBT community. In a 1997 interview with *Editor & Publisher* magazine, Troy Masters, the former publisher of a gay-owned New York newspaper, laid out the issue clearly in a way that could apply equally well to culture- or community-specific alternative papers outside the gay community:

> There needs to be a hard look at whether or not a publication that serves a specific group of people—whether they're of a certain race, nationality, sexual orientation, or whatever—can be owned and run by people who are not from that place. Do they truly understand the culture they're getting involved with, to treat the business the way it needs to be treated and to be sensitive to those they're trying to reach? It's very important, I think, for those kinds of publications to be treated first as a culture, and lastly as a marketplace.[109]

Questioning the Media

What makes an alternative paper authentic? Does a gay newspaper need to have a gay publisher or editor? Can a newspaper serving the African American community be owned by a white newspaper chain?

"Underground Papers." A third kind of alternative paper is the so-called alternative weekly. When these papers got started in the 1960s and 1970s, they were known first as underground newspapers, then as alternative weeklies. Today some prefer to be called just weeklies.[110] Among the popular weeklies now are the Chicago *Reader*, the Boston *Phoenix*, and the New Times chain.

Alternative weeklies present a stark contrast to the traditional urban newspapers in that they continue to grow in circulation. Among the Association of Alternative Newsmedia, average circulation reached 7.64 million in 2005.[111]

Although much of the content of these papers is relatively mainstream, the advertising often includes personals and ads for phone sex lines and massage parlors. Many of these papers, which depend solely on ad revenues, are distributed for free. They attract young people who have left behind daily newspapers and network news in favor of CNN, MSNBC, Fox News, and the Internet.

Just as mainstream newspapers are bought up by corporate newspaper chains, so are alternative papers being consolidated in alternative chains. This trend raises the question of whether these feisty papers will retain their independence and unique voice after becoming part of corporate America, or whether they will lose the qualities that made them popular in the first place. For example, in some cases, new owners have blocked potentially offensive cartoons and April Fools' Day editions. However, advertisers like the young, affluent readership these weekly papers can deliver, and they have expressed concern that watered-down content will lead to reduced reader interest.[112]

TEST YOUR MEDIA LITERACY

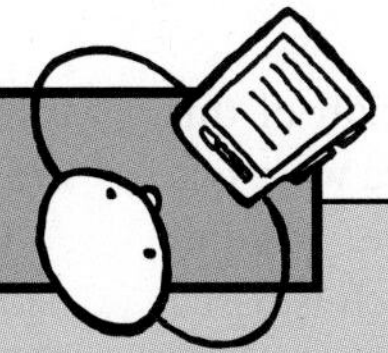

Can Journalists Be on Social Media?

Everyone needs to be careful about revealing too much personal information through social media such as Twitter or Facebook, but journalists see this as a particularly difficult issue because of fears of alienating sources and readers.

Wall Street Journal reporters are not supposed to post about how a story was reported. The paper's code of conduct says: "Let our coverage speak for itself, and don't detail how an article was reported, written, or edited." Reporters are also required to get their editor's permission before friending a confidential source.[1]

The BBC has fairly elaborate guidelines on using social media, especially in cases when its workers identify themselves as BBC employees. One rule suggests that BBC employees should not include a political identification online, even if they don't indicate that they work for the BBC.[2]

The *Toronto Star* also has a reasonably extensive social media policy that, among other things, bans reporters from offering opinions about the stories the paper covers. It also tells reporters and editors that they can't respond to reader comments: "As well, journalists should refrain from debating issues within the *Star*'s online comments forum to avoid any suggestion that they may be biased in their reporting."[3]

Mathew Ingram, writing for the blog *Gigaom*, says that this policy, which keeps reporters from engaging with the public, completely misses the point of social media. He writes,

> [The] main point being missed is that social media is powerful precisely *because it is* personal. . . . The best way to make social media work is to allow reporters and editors to be themselves, to be human, and to engage with readers through Twitter and Facebook and comments and blogs.[4]

Even tweets intended for a limited, private audience can be problematic. Raju Narisetti, one of two managing editors for the *Washington Post*, discontinued his personal Twitter account after questions about his tweets were raised by *Post* staff members. One of the tweets in question read, "We can incur all sorts of federal deficits for wars and what not, but we have to promise not to increase it by $1 for healthcare reform? Sad."[5] Another read, "Sen Byrd (91) in hospital after he falls from 'standing up too quickly.' How about term limits. Or retirement age. Or commonsense to prevail."[6]

The *Washington Post* issued guidelines in fall 2009 about what editorial employees ought to be posting online. The guidelines read, in part:

> When using [social networks], nothing we do must call into question the impartiality of our news judgment. We never abandon the guidelines that govern the separation of news from opinion, the importance of fact and objectivity, the appropriate use of language and tone, and other hallmarks of our brand of journalism.
>
> What you do on social networks should be presumed to be publicly available to anyone, even if you have created a private account. It is possible to use privacy controls online to limit access to sensitive information. But such controls are only a deterrent, not an absolute insulator. Reality is simple: If you don't want something to be found online, don't put it there.
>
> *Post* journalists must refrain from writing, tweeting, or posting anything—including photographs or video—that could be perceived as reflecting political, racial, sexist, religious, or other bias or favoritism that could be used to tarnish our journalistic credibility.[7]

WHO are the sources?

You have looked at codes of conduct for journalists using social media at several major news organizations from around the world. What are these news organizations? How do they differ from each other?

WHAT are they saying?

These codes of conduct tell reporters under what circumstances they can make posts on social media such as Twitter and Facebook. What kinds of rules do they expect reporters to follow? What happens to journalists who violate these standards?

WHAT kind of evidence indicates that journalists misuse social media?

What examples do the news organizations give to illustrate the problem of journalists misusing social media? What harm do they say this will bring to the news organization?

HOW do you and your classmates react to journalists using social media?

Do you or your classmates follow the social media feeds of any journalists? What do you discover about them from their tweets or Facebook posts? Do you think that journalists risk appearing biased by what they post to their social media feeds? Do you think it is right for news organizations to restrict how journalists use their social media accounts?

---

[1]Diane Brady, "What's the Right Corporate Policy for Twitter, Facebook and Blogs?" *Businessweek*, May 14, 2009, www.businessweek.com/careers/managementiq/archives/2009/05/whats_the_right.html.
[2]BBC, "Editorial Guidelines," www.bbc.co.uk/guidelines/editorialguidelines/advice/personalweb.
[3]Mathew Ingram, "Newspapers and Social Media: Still Not Really Getting It," April 5, 2011, gigaom.com/2011/04/05/newspapers-and-social-media-still-not-really-getting-it/.
[4]Ibid.
[5]Andrew Alexander, "*Post* Editor Ends Tweets as New Guidelines Are Issued," *Washington Post*, September 25, 2009, voices.washingtonpost.com/ombudsman-blog/2009/09/post_editor_ends_tweets_as_new.html?wprss=ombudsman-blog.
[6]Ibid.
[7]Ibid.

Questioning the Media

What do you think is the future for newspapers? Do you or your parents read newspapers? If newspapers die off in the "dead tree" format, what will replace them?

When the first edition of this book came out, there were two major alternative chains: New Times, which is based in Phoenix, Arizona, and publishes at least ten papers, and Stern Publishing of New York. Stern, which produces the most established alternative newspaper, the *Village Voice*, publishes at least seven papers. The *Village Voice*, founded in 1955, has a weekly circulation of 247,502, by far the largest of all the alternative weeklies in the country. *Phoenix New Times*, established in 1970, has a weekly circulation of 132,000. In 2005, New Times merged with the *Village Voice* chain. The new combined company controls about 14 percent of the circulation of alternative weekly papers.[113]

The Future of Newspapers

SECRET 2 Trying to make sense of what is happening to the newspaper business is difficult, in part because of Secret Two—There are no mainstream media. Some of the most visible segments of the newspaper business are facing major challenges, which critics are fond of pointing out. But other portions of the business, especially the more rural community papers, are thriving. So to understand the changing newspaper market we have to look at it as several media, not just one.

Are Newspapers a Dying Medium?

There can be no doubt that the business of the major urban newspapers is changing. Newspapers have been among the slowest media to recover from the 2008 recession. While things are not getting better for newspapers, they have been getting worse at a much slower pace recently. Advertising dollars and circulation numbers are continuing to decline, but at radically slower rates than in the previous couple of years. And Pew's 2011 "State of the News Media" report says that newspapers are still profitable. As was mentioned earlier in the chapter, the difference is that they are now averaging a profit of about 5 percent a year, as opposed to the 20 to 25 percent that was the norm in the 1990s. Keep in mind that in the not-so-distant past, newspapers were among the most profitable businesses in America.[114]

On the other hand, the newspapers that can be seen as national in scope (the *Wall Street Journal* and the *New York Times* in particular) are holding tight in terms of paid circulation and readership. And smaller newspapers in more rural areas are also doing well. The big problem is with the major urban papers.

The afternoon dailies were the first to feel the effects of the changing media landscape. Afternoon papers, especially the giant papers published by Hearst and Pulitzer, were enormously popular in the early 1900s. These papers were bought by factory workers who started their jobs too early to read a paper in the morning and preferred to buy papers on their way home. Today, however, afternoon papers don't fit neatly into most people's schedules. Morning papers are still convenient and valued, but afternoon papers have to compete with the evening television news. Also, it is easier for morning papers to provide up-to-date coverage. Not much happens overnight as the morning paper is being put together, but the afternoon paper's news is already old. Distribution is also difficult because of heavy traffic during the day, something that morning papers, which go out between midnight and four in the morning, don't have to worry about.[115]

Most of the job losses have been at the major urban papers. According to the 2006 Project for Excellence in Journalism report, the top three newspapers lost no circulation, and the loss at the smaller newspapers was "modest." The big-city papers that have to cover a large metro area and a host of suburbs are the ones in trouble. And with the loss of staff, it becomes harder for these big papers to serve "as watchdogs over state, regional, and urban institutions, to identify trends, and to define the larger community public square."[116] A good example of a paper undertaking this watchdog function is the *Washington Post*'s stories about the substandard conditions and care for injured Iraq war veterans at Walter Reed military hospital. In addition to being an important national story, it was also an important local story for the Washington, D.C., area.

A few of these papers have suspended their print editions and become exclusively digital publications. Among the most prominent of these was the *Christian Science Monitor*, which went all digital in April 2009.[117] Another paper to go digital-only was the *Seattle Post-Intelligencer*, which stopped publication in March 2009 but retained an online presence dominated by commentary.[118]

The change at the *Monitor* to all-electronic distribution is not as radical as some observers are claiming. Although the *Monitor* has had a substantial online presence for some time, its daily circulation of approximately 50,000 copies was relatively small compared to either *USA Today* or the *Wall Street Journal*, both of whom measure their circulation with the word *million* attached. The *Monitor*'s importance comes not from its size, but rather from its overall reputation as one of the country's best papers. Its Web site attracts about 1.5 million page views per month.[119]

Audio 6.2: Learn more about *Bloomberg News.*

Chapter SUMMARY

The first newspapers were published in Europe in the seventeenth century. Numerous papers were published in the American colonies, but they faced extensive censorship from the British government. Newspapers printed before the nineteenth century tended to be partisan publications that were supported through high subscription fees and political subsidies. This changed with the rise of the penny press in the 1830s. The penny papers were mass produced on steam-powered printing presses and contained news of interest to ordinary people. The papers cost one or two cents and were supported by advertisers who wanted to reach the papers' large numbers of readers.

The late nineteenth and early twentieth centuries were characterized by the yellow journalism of the New York newspapers published by Joseph Pulitzer and William Randolph Hearst. The two publishers tried to attract circulation and attention by running comic strips, advice columns, and sensational stories about sex, crime, and scandal. This was also the time when newspapers started running extensive headlines and illustrations.

The major classes of newspapers today include

- national papers that attempt to cover issues of interest to the entire country, such as *USA Today* and the *Wall Street Journal*;
- metropolitan papers that cover a particular city, such as the *New York Times* and the *Washington Post*;
- community papers that serve a particular town or suburb and provide news that readers cannot get elsewhere; and
- alternative newspapers that serve specialized populations rather than a broad, general audience. These can serve ethnic populations within a community, groups such as gays and lesbians, or even young people that are not interested in traditional newspapers.

Evolving technology has brought changes to the newspaper business. The rise of television news resulted in a decline in the number of afternoon newspapers, and changes in news-consumption patterns have drawn audiences and advertisers away from both newspapers and broadcast television news. Digital media have given newspapers new opportunities to update the news rapidly and fresh ways to deliver the news. Whatever the method of delivery, reporters struggle with the issue of objectivity, especially when the story is close to home and when they are risking their lives to report the news.

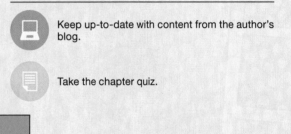

Keep up-to-date with content from the author's blog.

Take the chapter quiz.

Key TERMS

above the fold 138
yellow journalism 139
tabloid newspapers 140
broadsheet newspapers 140
jazz journalism 140
chains 142
Watergate scandal 145
mainstreaming 148
community press 148
alternative papers 150

Concept REVIEW

Reporter objectivity and detachment
Tradition of journalistic independence
Advertising-supported media
Changing newspaper market
Consequences of corporate ownership of newspapers
Determining the proper role for the alternative press
Balancing serving investors, advertisers, and readers
Risks of reporting from a war zone
New media versus old sources of news

Student STUDY SITE

Sharpen your skills with SAGE edge at **edge.sagepub.com/hanson5e**

SAGE edge for Students provides a personalized approach to help you accomplish your coursework goals in an easy-to-use learning environment.

chapter 7

Audio

Music and Talk Across Media

Film Magic/ Getty Images

Mash-up Artist Gregg Gillis of Girl Talk performs in San Francisco during the 2011 Outside Lands Music and Arts Festival. Gillis is known for mixing together hundreds of music clips to create a sonic collage.

Anne Marsen dances the part of "The Girl" in the feature-length Girl Walk // All Day video interpretation of the Girl Talk mash-up album All Day. The video was filmed in New York City and features a small cast of dancers and passers-by that the dancers interact with.

Jacob Krupnick Productions

Trying to explain what Gregg Gillis, a.k.a. Girl Talk, does to someone who grew up in the days of the Doors or the Ramones can be a bit challenging. He's a disc jockey who plays clips from multiple songs at the same time. Put more elegantly, Gillis is a mash-up artist—someone who combines two or more pieces of music to create something new.[1]

As an example, one of the most famous mash-ups is DJ Danger Mouse's *Grey Album*, a combination of the vocals from rapper Jay-Z's *Black Album* and samples from the Beatles' 1968 album *The Beatles* (better known as the *White Album*). While Jay-Z had created the a cappella version of his album specifically for mash-up use, Beatles publisher EMI was not amused and attempted to get the *Grey Album* suppressed.[2]

As great as the work by people such as Danger Mouse may be, nothing really compares to the level of mash-ups done by Pittsburgh's Gillis. Gillis has a degree in biomedical engineering, but several years ago he quit his day job to create the incredible mixes that have gone into his five albums. His 2010 album *All Day* reportedly contains 400 different samples—typically some kind of rapping combined with samples of pop, rock, or soul music from the last forty or fifty years. The artists he uses include the Doors and the Ramones.

Both Danger Mouse and Girl Talk have given away their albums online, and none of the samples have been licensed or paid for use. Capitol/EMI, the Beatles' publisher, sent out a cease-and-desist letter telling Danger Mouse and the Web sites hosting his work to take down the album because it infringed on the Beatles' copyright. But when the album remained online, nothing happened to those distributing the content. And so far no one has sued Girl Talk's Gillis for his massive sampling.

Were he to attempt to license the music, Gillis estimates that it would cost several million dollars and that many of the songs wouldn't be available at any price. According to Duke law professor James Boyle, speaking on NPR's *On the Media*, there may be a range of reasons no one has gone after Gillis:

> There is the story that the labels learned from DJ Danger Mouse and don't want to risk creating the Che Guevara of the digital sampling age, the lost hero to which all of us will offer reverence and thus make him even more popular.
>
> Another story is, they're going, hmm, this is really interesting. Let's let him run a bit, and when we finally see how things are playing out then we'll figure out a way of getting a revenue stream out of this. A third story is they realize it's actually fair use and they don't want a bad precedent brought against them. And then a fourth one is that they are gibbering in terror and are so scared by this new phenomena, they're incapable of rational action of any kind and so are caught in a kind of fugue state, as the digital music scene develops.[3]

LEARNING OBJECTIVES

After studying this chapter, you will be able to:

1 Describe how major developments in audio technology changed how people experience music.

2 Explain how rock 'n' roll developed out of two different music traditions.

3 Explain how radio transformed from a channel for interpersonal communication to mass communication.

4 Describe how different recording formats have given rise to concerns about the purchasing of music.

5 Discuss how long-tail audio technology is changing the radio and recording industry for everyone from music fans to international stars.

Video 7.1: See or download Girl Talk's albums.

Video 7.2: Learn more about *Girl Walk // All Day*.

Gillis told *Wired* that artists are still coming to terms with the implications of remix and collage culture. "Sharing ideas and being influenced by those who come before you has always been the foundation of progress in art and music," he said. "I think it's become a lot more obvious in the internet age, though. People are more directly interactive with what they consume. . . . It's commonplace now for people to take pre-existing media, recontextualize it and show it to the world."[4]

There's also an argument to be made that sampling can even help the career of artists who have had their music "recontextualized." As an example, in 2000 rapper Eminem sampled trip-hop artist Dido's song "Thank You" in his single "Stan." "Stan" became a hit for Eminem and led to Dido becoming an international star. (To be fair, Dido was credited on the album and was featured in the video that went with "Stan."[5])

The most impressive outgrowth of Girl Talk's *All Day*, however, is a full-length dance film called *Girl Walk // All Day* directed by indie filmmaker Jacob Krupnick. Krupnick, working with a cast of three principal dancers (The Girl, The Gentleman, and The Creep), tells the story of a young woman's day in Manhattan as she rebels against the restrictions of her dance class and attempts to get everyone else in the city moving with her. Since the film is based around an album that uses hundreds of unlicensed music samples, it's being distributed for free using streaming media online. It is also being shown as part of a multimedia dance party experience held in a range of venues, including a church in Manhattan, an upscale restaurant in Seattle, and the SXSW festival in Austin, Texas. The movie itself was funded through Kickstarter, an online service that raises start-up capital from the public.

Gillis released *All Day* using a Creative Commons license that said other people could make use of his work as long as they attribute it back to him, so Krupnick tells *Wired* he figured he was allowed to freely use the music. (You can read more about Creative Commons in Chapter 13, "Media Law.") He says, "I just heard this album that you have to download immediately. Wouldn't it be wild if we danced all over New York and made a music video to the whole thing?"[6]

Timeline

1800

1812 War of 1812 breaks out.
1835 Alexis de Tocqueville publishes *Democracy in America*.
1859 Charles Darwin publishes *On the Origin of Species*.
1861 U.S. Civil War begins.
1869 Transcontinental railroad is completed.
1879 Thomas Edison invents electric light bulb.
1898 Spanish-American War breaks out.

1900

1903 Orville and Wilbur Wright fly first airplane.
1905 Albert Einstein proposes his theory of relativity.

1910

1912 *Titanic* sinks.
1914 World War I begins.
1918 Worldwide influenza epidemic strikes.

1920

1920 Nineteenth Amendment passes, giving U.S. women the right to vote.
1929 U.S. stock market crashes, leading to the Great Depression.

1930

1933 Adolf Hitler is elected chancellor of Germany.
1939 World War II breaks out in Europe.

1940

1941 United States enters World War II.
1945 United States drops two atomic bombs on Japan.
1947 Pakistan and India gain independence from Britain.
1949 Communists establish People's Republic of China.

1844 Samuel Morse develops the telegraph; electronic signals can be sent over long distances.
1897 Guglielmo Marconi develops ship-to-shore radio.

villorejo/Alamy

1912 The sinking *Titanic* sends distress call by radio.
1916 David Sarnoff writes the Radio Music Box memo.
1920 KDKA, broadcasting out of Pittsburgh, Pennsylvania, becomes the first commercial radio station.
1922 The BBC is created as a public broadcasting service in England.

F. G. O. Stuart/Wikimedia Commons

1938 Orson Welles's 60-minute live radio broadcast of the H. G. Wells novel *War of the Worlds* creates a panic among listeners who believed that Martians attacked the United States.
1949 Dewey Phillips's program, *Red, Hot, & Blue,* becomes one of the first rock 'n' roll and R&B music shows on the air.

Looking at all this creativity and the attention that Girl Talk and *Girl Walk // All Day* have attracted, we see a couple of the Seven Secrets coming into play:

SECRET 2 There are no mainstream media. Neither Girl Talk's album *All Day* nor the *Girl Walk // All Day* film were released through traditional "mainstream" media operations. Yet both have been highly acclaimed and consumed by people across the country.

SECRET 5 New media are always scary. Both the album and the film are upsetting to the existing media industry. At a time when major media companies and advocacy groups are making a big noise about file sharing and piracy, two separate artists are working at putting together completely different models for economic success. As you will see later on in this chapter, there are accusations that the audio industry is dying, while others respond that it is merely changing. Either way, change and new media are always scary.

In this chapter, we look at how the recording industry and radio developed together as our first electronic media. We then examine how society has changed, how cultures have grown and merged, and how audience members have responded to the production of shared music and talk. Finally, we look at where the industries are headed in the twenty-first century. ■

"People are more directly interactive with what they consume. . . . It's commonplace now for people to take pre-existing media, recontextualize it and show it to the world."

—Gregg Gillis, a.k.a. Girl Talk

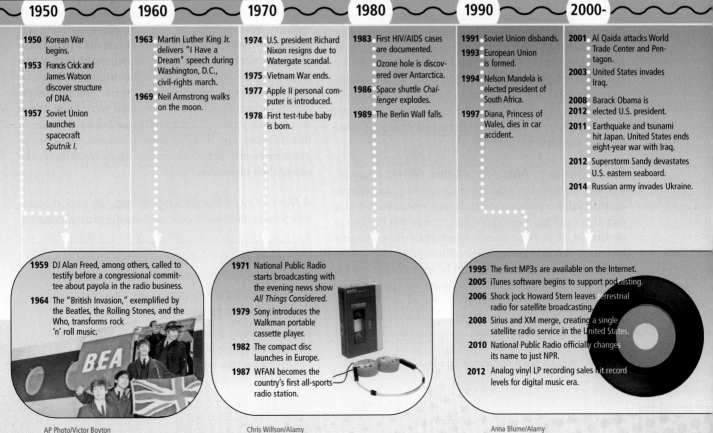

1950

1950 Korean War begins.

1953 Francis Crick and James Watson discover structure of DNA.

1957 Soviet Union launches spacecraft *Sputnik I*.

1960

1963 Martin Luther King Jr. delivers "I Have a Dream" speech during Washington, D.C., civil-rights march.

1969 Neil Armstrong walks on the moon.

1970

1974 U.S. president Richard Nixon resigns due to Watergate scandal.

1975 Vietnam War ends.

1977 Apple II personal computer is introduced.

1978 First test-tube baby is born.

1980

1983 First HIV/AIDS cases are documented.

Ozone hole is discovered over Antarctica.

1986 Space shuttle *Challenger* explodes.

1989 The Berlin Wall falls.

1990

1991 Soviet Union disbands.

1993 European Union is formed.

1994 Nelson Mandela is elected president of South Africa.

1997 Diana, Princess of Wales, dies in car accident.

2000-

2001 Al Qaida attacks World Trade Center and Pentagon.

2003 United States invades Iraq.

2008 2012 Barack Obama is elected U.S. president.

2011 Earthquake and tsunami hit Japan. United States ends eight-year war with Iraq.

2012 Superstorm Sandy devastates U.S. eastern seaboard.

2014 Russian army invades Ukraine.

1959 DJ Alan Freed, among others, called to testify before a congressional committee about payola in the radio business.

1964 The "British Invasion," exemplified by the Beatles, the Rolling Stones, and the Who, transforms rock 'n' roll music.

AP Photo/Victor Boyton

1971 National Public Radio starts broadcasting with the evening news show *All Things Considered*.

1979 Sony introduces the Walkman portable cassette player.

1982 The compact disc launches in Europe.

1987 WFAN becomes the country's first all-sports radio station.

Chris Willson/Alamy

1995 The first MP3s are available on the Internet.

2005 iTunes software begins to support podcasting.

2006 Shock jock Howard Stern leaves terrestrial radio for satellite broadcasting.

2008 Sirius and XM merge, creating a single satellite radio service in the United States.

2010 National Public Radio officially changes its name to just NPR.

2012 Analog vinyl LP recording sales hit record levels for digital music era.

Anna Blume/Alamy

History of Sound Recording and Transmission

Before there could be mass consumption of popular music, there had to be a means of recording and distributing it. Those means evolved through the decades via Thomas Edison's early efforts with the phonograph, the development of the gramophone, and the creation of the LP and the compact disc. The recording industry changed the way people consumed music. Before the phonograph and gramophone, the only way to experience music was to perform it yourself or go to a concert. The invention of the record meant that recordings of professional musicians became the standard way to listen to music.

Storing Musical Performances: The Development of the Recording Industry

A variety of stories have been told about Thomas Edison and his invention of an early sound-recording machine, the **phonograph**, in 1877. One version has Edison giving a sketch of the phonograph to employee John Kruesi with the instruction, "the machine must talk."[7] Another has Edison sketching the phonograph, with a note at the bottom telling his assistant to "build this."[8]

Edison's First Recordings. These stories do not do justice to Edison's true genius or to the difficulties of creating a machine that could record and play back the voice. Running through these myths is the mistaken notion that Edison came up with an idea for sound recording that worked perfectly the first time it was tried. In reality, Edison and his assistants probably worked as long as ten months on the problem of the phonograph before they finally succeeded in recording Sarah Josepha Hale's children's rhyme, "Mary Had a Little Lamb." This famous first recording lasted no more than ten seconds.[9]

Emile Berliner: Mass-Produced Music. As with so many media inventions, no one was quite sure what to do with Edison's phonograph. Edison envisioned it as a dictation machine. Reproducing music was only the fourth on his list of possible uses.[10] The biggest flaw with his invention was that Edison's foil cylinders did not hold up to repeated playing and could not be reproduced. It took the work of a young German immigrant to make the phonograph a truly practical device.

Web 7.1: More on Thomas Edison.

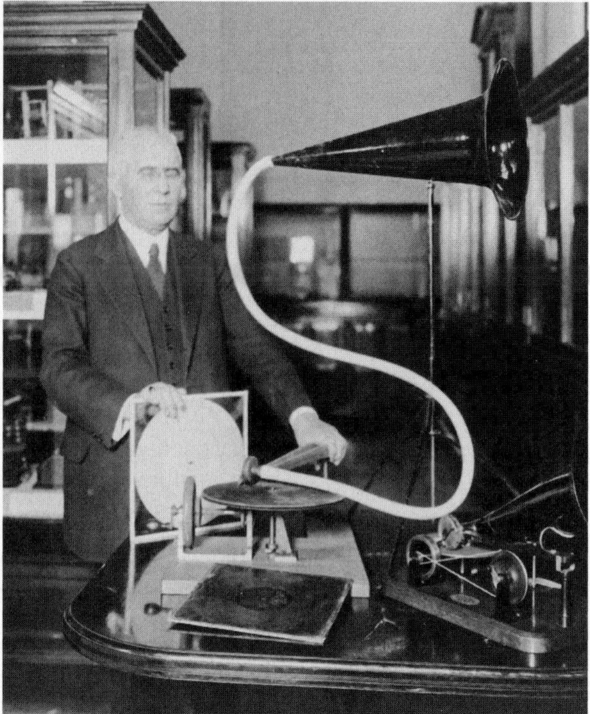

Library of Congress

Emile Berliner was able to turn Thomas Edison's idea for a phonograph into a commercially viable product that lasted in one form or another for more than one hundred years.

Emile Berliner arrived in the United States in 1870 at the age of nineteen. By 1888, he had developed a method for recording sound on flat discs rather than on cylinders. Berliner's disc recordings (or records) were louder and more lifelike than the cylinder recordings of Edison or Bell. Berliner called his device the **gramophone**. Eventually, however, all record players were called phonographs.

Berliner also helped develop the idea of the recording industry. With Edison's phonograph, every recording was an original. Berliner viewed his invention not as a business dictating machine, but as an entertainment device. His discs could be reproduced from the original etched-zinc master, allowing publishers to mass produce high-quality—at least for the time—musical recordings almost as easily as printers could reproduce books. Because of this, Berliner saw that "prominent singers, speakers, or performers may derive an income from royalties on the sale of their phonautograms."[11]

A New Way of Publishing Music. By 1935, the term **high fidelity (hi-fi)** was being used to refer to a combination

phonograph: An early sound-recording machine invented by Thomas Edison; the recorded material was played back on a cylinder.

gramophone: A machine invented by Emile Berliner that could play prerecorded sound on flat discs rather than cylinders.

high fidelity (hi-fi): A combination of technologies that allowed recordings to reproduce music more accurately, with higher high notes and deeper bass, than was possible with previous recording technologies.

of technologies that allowed recordings that reproduced music more accurately, with higher high notes and deeper bass, than previous forms of recording had allowed. One of the developments that helped pave the way for hi-fi was the electric phonograph (along with the amplifier and loudspeakers), which began replacing the all-mechanical gramophone. By 1949, magnetic tape recorders were commonplace in recording studios. Musicians no longer had to record directly onto discs.

The phonograph changed the face of music. Previously, there were only two ways to store music. The first, and oldest, was for parents to teach their children the traditional songs of their culture. The alternative was written music, or musical scores, that contained symbols for the musical notes to be played. The phonograph provided a revolutionary way of storing the actual music, not just the symbols written down by the composer. It also made possible the storage of **non-notated music**, such as folk songs or jazz solos, which did not necessarily exist in written form. Music scholar Charles Hamm has compared the phonograph to a musical time machine that allows listeners to go back and hear the actual sounds.[12]

Transmitting Music and Talk: The Birth of Radio

Around the time the recording industry was getting started, radio was under development as one of the first media to break through the barrier of space. With print media such as books, magazines, and newspapers, the message being transmitted was always on a piece of paper that had to be carried from one place to another. Thus, the fastest form of transportation at the time was also the fastest channel of communication. This meant that it could take weeks for a message to cross the Atlantic or Pacific Ocean, or even to get from New York to California or from London to Moscow. But in the nineteenth century, several inventions separated communication and transportation, starting with the wired media of the telegraph and telephone and moving on to the wireless technology of radio.

MARCONI FIRST WIRELESS MESSAGE 1895

©iStockphoto.com/the_guitar_mann

Samuel Morse's invention of the **telegraph** in 1844 allowed messages to be sent electrically, so that they didn't have to be carried from place to place. No longer did transportation set limits on communication. Messages could travel at the same speed as electrons traveling along a wire.[13] By 1866, a telegraph cable extended across the Atlantic Ocean, so that even that giant barrier had been conquered.

But the wire itself was a serious limitation. Telegraph wires could break (or be cut, as they frequently were during the American Civil War). To communicate with ships at sea, a *wireless* telegraph was necessary.

In 1888, German physicist Heinrich Hertz found that he could detect the signal created by an electrical spark on one side of a room with a small loop antenna on the other side. What he had created was essentially the simplest possible radio transmitter and receiver. In 1894, Guglielmo Marconi read about Hertz's work and concluded that he could create a **wireless telegraph**, a point-to-point communication tool that used radio waves to transmit messages. Over a period of several years, he developed a system to send and receive radio signals, with the distance traveled by his signals expanding from the length of his attic to the width of the Atlantic Ocean.[14]

Radio as Mass Communication. In 1901, physicist Reginald Fessenden started sending voice signals over a radio in his laboratory. On Christmas Eve in 1905, he broadcast poetry and Christmas carols. Since his continuously modulated voice signals could be received by the same equipment that received Morse code, wireless operators up and down the Atlantic coast heard Fessenden's amazing broadcast. Though it would be years before regularly scheduled commercial broadcasts would begin, Fessenden had set the stage for broadcasting something more than just Morse code.

Up until 1905, it was the scientists who were driving the radio business with their new technologies, but it was a young American Marconi employee who saw that radio could be much more than just a way to send messages from one person to another. David Sarnoff, born in 1891, was a good student, but the need to help support his Russian-immigrant family led him to leave school after the eighth grade to work full-time. In a story that seems almost too good to be true, the fifteen-year-old Sarnoff went to the *New York Herald* to try to get a job as a journalist. As luck would have it, the first person he met at the *Herald* building worked for a telegraph company. Sarnoff went to work for the Commercial Cable Company, and from that point on, he never left electronic media.[15]

The Radio Music Box Memo. In 1915, Sarnoff addressed to the director of American Marconi a document that he considered the most important of his career. The so-called **Radio Music Box memo** outlined radio's

non-notated music: Music such as a folk song or jazz solo that does not exist in written form.

telegraph: The first system for using wires to send messages at a distance; invented by Samuel Morse in 1844.

wireless telegraph: Guglielmo Marconi's name for his point-to-point communication tool that used radio waves to transmit messages.

Radio Music Box memo: David Sarnoff's 1915 plan that outlined how radio could be used as a popular mass medium.

Web 7.2: Learn more about Guglielmo Marconi.

Listening to music over headphones is nothing new, but in the 1920s, this farmer needed a wheelbarrow to move the radio set (left) from place to place.

potential as a popular mass medium. While Sarnoff did not invent the technology of radio and was not the first person to send out entertainment over the radio, he did summarize what radio could, and indeed did, become. Sarnoff's insight was that radio could be more than a point-to-point medium, a one-on-one form of communication. As Sarnoff saw it, what was then perceived as the great disadvantage of radio as a telegraph tool—that everyone who listened could hear the message—could be turned into an enormous advantage if one wanted to send out messages that everyone was *supposed* to listen to. In his memo, Sarnoff wrote,

> I have in mind a plan of development which would make radio a household utility in the same sense as the piano or phonograph. The idea is to bring music into the houses by wireless.
>
> While this has been tried in the past by wires, it has been a failure because wires do not lend themselves to this scheme. With radio, however, it would be entirely feasible. For example, a radio telephone transmitter having a range of, say, 25 to 50 miles can be installed at a fixed point where instrumental or vocal music or both are produced. . . . The receiver can be designed in the form of a simple "Radio Music Box" and arranged for several different wave lengths, which should be changeable with the throwing of a single switch or pressing of a single button.[16]

Web 7.3: Read and see more about broadcasting pioneer David Sarnoff.

With this memo, Sarnoff essentially invented radio as a social institution. But this new medium would have to wait, because on the eve of U.S. involvement in World War I, the navy was buying all of Marconi's transmitters. Although American Marconi did not act on Sarnoff's memo, the young immigrant did not forget the ideas for radio's potential that he had laid out so clearly.

More Receivers Than Transmitters. One of the biggest surprises of the radio business was that so many more receivers were sold than transmitters. Manufacturers had assumed at the start that there would be almost as many people sending as receiving messages.[17] In reality, however, electronic communication was following in the footsteps of print. The earliest books had been copied by hand and passed from one person to another. But just as the printing press provided books, magazines, and newspapers to the masses, radio was now becoming a mass medium.

The RCA Radio Monopoly. During World War I, the navy had taken control of all radio technology, including the patents, and it wanted to maintain control after the war. But civilian government officials in the United States, in keeping with the U.S. tradition of independent media, rejected the idea of all-government control. In an attempt to avoid anarchy in the new medium, the navy advocated creating a private monopoly to control radio development.

The Radio Corporation of America (RCA) was formed as a consortium of four major companies: General Electric, AT&T, Westinghouse, and United Fruit Company. General Electric was included because it made radio transmitters and owned what had formerly been American Marconi. AT&T was the world leader in wired communication, and Westinghouse owned many critical patents. But why was United Fruit Company a part of RCA? United Fruit had used radios to connect its boats to banana plantations in South America and while doing so had developed improved technology that the monopoly needed. These four companies brought together the 2,000 or so patents that were needed to make the radio business work. RCA not only became a major producer of radio equipment, but it also founded NBC, the first of the major broadcasting networks.[18]

Westinghouse employee and self-educated engineer Frank Conrad started making Sarnoff's dream of the Radio Music Box come true. In 1920, with Westinghouse's support, Conrad started broadcasting music on Sunday afternoons. Westinghouse then built Conrad a more powerful transmitter and put together a broadcast schedule.

Pittsburgh's radio station KDKA was licensed for broadcast on October 27, 1920. Others soon followed. Over in Britain, the British Broadcasting Company was created in 1922. It was initially a privately run company owned by the manufacturers of broadcasting equipment, and its first station was licensed in 1923. In 1927, the company became the British Broadcasting Corporation, a public, noncommercial monopoly for broadcasting in the United Kingdom.[19]

Radio Advertising. Although KDKA was the first commercial radio station, it was not the first station to run a commercial. KDKA existed to provide programming with the goal of getting people to buy radio sets. But WEAF, broadcasting in New York City, was the first station to sell airtime to advertisers. The modest success of these commercials soon led to radio advertising by oil companies, department stores, and American Express.

©iStockphoto.com/robas

The radio industry considered several possibilities for making money. One possibility was to support radio broadcasting with a "tithe" (a specified percentage) of revenues from sales of radios by all manufacturers. Another possibility was to support it with a substantial public endowment. The problem was that neither of these schemes would provide enough money to pay for the high-priced entertainers that listeners wanted to hear. This meant that radio stations were going to need advertising revenue. Ultimately, the rest of the media industry would accept advertising as the main source of income for broadcasting. In Britain, by contrast, the original BBC was supported by revenue from selling radio receivers and radio-receiving licenses, and it was prohibited from selling commercials.[20]

Radio Networks. By 1923, more than 600 radio transmitters were broadcasting in the United States. These stations were limited to the programming they could produce locally. How did these stations fill their broadcast day? In big cities, this was no problem because there were plenty of concerts, lectures, and sporting events to put on the air, but rural areas or small towns were limited in their selection of locally produced culture and entertainment. In another of his famous memos, Sarnoff suggested that RCA form a new company, a **network**, to provide programming to a large group of broadcast stations, thus making a wider selection of programming available to smaller stations.

RCA established the National Broadcasting Company (NBC) on July 22, 1926. It was the United States' first major broadcasting network, and it survives today in the form of the NBC television network. NBC was actually two networks, the "Red" and the "Blue." (See Figure 7.1.) (Due to an antitrust ruling, RCA was eventually forced to sell the Blue network, which then became ABC.)

William Paley and the Power of Radio Advertising. With the growing demand for radio programming, the two NBC networks soon faced new competition, none more significant than William Paley's Columbia Broadcasting System (CBS). Although Paley was born in the United States, his parents were Russian immigrants. He grew up in a wealthy household, and his family owned a successful cigar company. William Paley's father, Sam, had been approached about advertising his cigars on the fledgling United Independent Broadcasters (UIB) network. Sam Paley was not interested, but William was.

William Paley bought his first radio ads while his father was away on business, and although Sam initially chastised his son for wasting money, he soon heard people talking about the wonderful show his company sponsored. That was enough to convince him. William then developed a program called *La Palina Smoker* that featured an orchestra, a singer, and a comedian. It also resulted in increased cigar sales. Before long William, who was not quite twenty-seven years old, had the opportunity to buy UIB, which he did with help from his father. Once he became president of the network, he promptly renamed it the Columbia Broadcasting System.[21]

Paley understood better than anyone else that broadcasting was a business that had to make a profit on its own. NBC believed that its mission was to develop programs for the benefit of its listeners, but CBS realized that its real clients were the advertisers who sponsored the programs. Its programs were designed and produced specifically to attract the kind of audience a particular advertiser was looking for. For CBS, the "product" was the audience its programs attracted.

From the Golden Age to the Television Age

The 1920s, 1930s, and 1940s came to be known as the **golden age of radio**, an era in which radio played the same role that television does today. Radio was the mass medium that served as the primary form of entertainment in the household. This was a big change. It meant that people were getting most of their entertainment from outside the home rather than from within. Instead of being entertained by Aunt Martha's and Cousin Sue's piano duets, they were listening to Bing Crosby's crooning or Bob Hope's comedy on the radio.

network: A company that provides common programming to a large group of broadcast stations.

golden age of radio: A period from the late 1920s until the 1940s, during which radio was the dominant medium for home entertainment.

Audio 7.1: Check out the KDKA all-news station.

Figure 7.1 The Early Red and Blue NBC Radio Networks

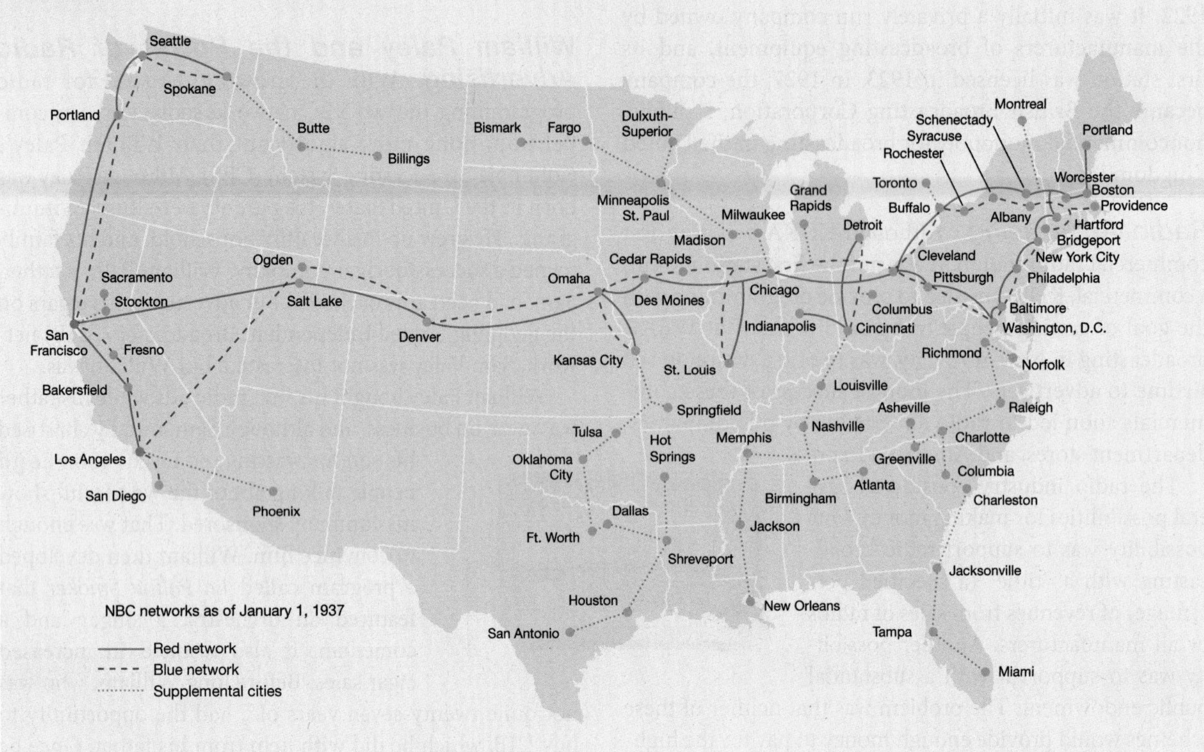

Source: Library of Congress.

Golden Age Radio Programming. A wide range of programming was available on the radio during the golden age. Live music, both popular and classical, was a staple. NBC even had its own orchestra that performed on a regular basis. There were also dramas and action programs, including *Little Orphan Annie*, *The Lone Ranger*, and *The Shadow*.

Some radio programs from the golden age survive today as television programs, most notably **soap operas**. The soaps, as they are called for short, are daytime dramas targeted primarily at women; they got their name from the commercials for soap and other cleaning products that ran during the shows. For better or worse, soaps were the first programs targeted specifically at women, a key audience for advertisers. It wasn't until the advent of television in the 1950s that soaps ceased to be a major part of radio programming.[22] CBS's *Guiding Light* started on the radio in 1937, moved over to television in 1952, and finished its seventy-two-year run on September 18, 2009.

Amos 'n' Andy. Despite the popularity of soap operas, no radio show attracted a bigger audience than *Amos 'n' Andy,* the first nationally broadcast daily drama.[23] *Amos 'n' Andy* began in January 1926 on Chicago radio station WGN as *Sam 'n' Henry*. The show was a fixture on the radio, in one form or another, for nearly thirty-five years. Starring on the show were two white actors—Charles Correll and Freeman Gosden—who played the roles of two African Americans, Sam and Henry, who owned the Fresh Air Taxi Company. Correll and Gosden wrote all the scripts themselves and furnished the voices for the title characters and the members of their fraternal lodge, the Mystic Knights of the Sea. Their names were later changed to Amos and Andy when Correll and Gosden syndicated the show nationally, since WGN owned the characters of Sam and Henry. At the peak of its popularity, *Amos 'n' Andy* was played in restaurants and in movie theaters between shows so that people wouldn't have to stay home to listen.

For the history of radio news, see Chapter 6, "Newspapers and the News."

The BBC: Voice of the Old Empire. Although in the United States radio is generally seen as an entertainment medium, the British Broadcasting Corporation (BBC) has been broadcasting news and culture worldwide for more than seventy years.

Audio 7.2: Listen to the BBC World Service.

soap operas: Serialized daytime dramas targeted primarily at women.

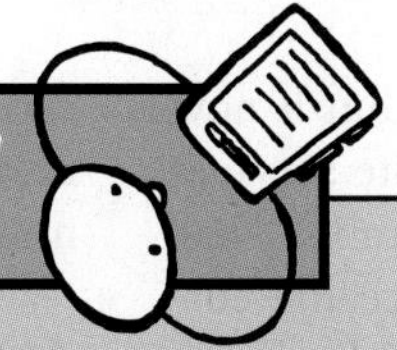

TEST YOUR MEDIA LITERACY

When Is a Radio Show Racist?

Amos 'n' Andy has been both praised and criticized. It was condemned as racist by many groups, including the National Association for the Advancement of Colored People (NAACP), that saw the humor in the show as demeaning and the characters as uneducated and ignorant of city life. The most lasting criticism of the show, however, was that it was produced by whites predominantly for the entertainment of whites. One of my African American students summed up the issue clearly: "So what you are telling me is that the most popular show in the country was about white people making fun of black people?" Clearly a show created under these parameters wouldn't be acceptable today.

But *Amos 'n' Andy* may not have been as racist as it seemed. Freeman Gosden and Charles Correll were guests of honor at an annual picnic hosted by the *Defender*, Chicago's leading weekly black newspaper in 1931. In addition, several members of the black press had good things to say about the show in its early days. It was also one of the few programs that showed African Americans (even if played by whites) in everyday life. The supporting characters in the fictional lodge were middle-class blacks, a social phenomenon many whites at that time didn't even know existed.[1]

WHO is the source?

Who wrote, acted in, and produced the show? Who were the critics of the program?

WHAT are they saying?

What are the central criticisms of the program? What are the arguments in support of it?

WHAT kind of evidence is provided?

What evidence is provided that the show had support in the African American community at the time it was aired? What is the evidence that the program was racist? How did these views change over time?

HOW do you and your classmates react to Amos 'n' Andy?

Was it the fact that the stars were white and the characters were black that made the show racist? If you say yes, why do you think this is so? Is it possible for a program to make jokes about racial issues without being racist? How could it do this?

NBC/NBCU PhotoBank via Getty Images

One of the most popular, and controversial, programs of the golden age of radio was *Amos 'n' Andy*, which featured white performers Freeman Gosden (l) and Charles Correll playing the part of two African Americans.

[1]Melvin Patrick Ely, *The Adventures of Amos 'n' Andy* (New York: Free Press, 1991).

Audio 7.3: Listen to excerpts from *Amos 'n' Andy*.

As mentioned earlier, the BBC was created as a public service in the 1920s. In the 1930s, it started broadcasting on the shortwave radio band, which allowed its signals to extend around the world. During World War II, the BBC was the international voice of opposition to the Nazis, broadcasting in more than forty languages, including French, Danish, and Hindi.[24] Listening to BBC broadcasts in Nazi-occupied Europe was a punishable offense.

Today the BBC's World Service radio network has an audience of approximately 150 million people. According to the BBC's Caroline Thomson, the goal of the World Service is to reach approximately 95 percent of the world's population.[25] The logistics of doing this become complicated when the BBC is broadcasting in a dozen or more different time zones. When do you broadcast a morning show on a network heard around the world?

BBC's international reach can be seen with the program *Focus on Africa*. For a continent that depends on radio as its primary medium of mass communication (for more on media in Africa, see Chapter 15), the BBC provides a reliable source of news that is not censored by local governments. To avoid charges of being a colonial voice of white Britain in black Africa, most of the reporting on the show is done by African journalists. *Focus on Africa* is such an important source of news that it is often rebroadcast on local African stations, sometimes just by taking a shortwave radio and holding it up to the station's microphone.[26]

While the BBC has long been known for its shortwave broadcasts, it has been changing in recent years. It still broadcasts by shortwave in Asia and Africa, but it now relies on webcasting, FM stations, and satellite services to reach the United States, Canada, Australia, New Zealand, and the Pacific Islands.[27] Also, since the collapse of communism in Eastern Europe and the rising conflict in the Middle East, the BBC has closed a number of its Eastern European–language radio services and has been working on launching an Arabic-language television service.[28]

Becoming a Companion Medium. As television began claiming more and more of the broadcast audience, radio was forced to change. No longer were people sitting down in their living rooms to listen to programs on the radio. Instead, they turned on the radio while they did other things: working, washing dishes, driving. Yet radio did not fade away; instead, it reinvented itself as companion radio, a medium that would always be there to keep listeners company. Radio host Julius Lester put it this way:

> Radio is so integral a part of us now that we do not consciously notice its presence; it is a member of the family, a companion, and the voices issuing through its speakers are those not of strangers but of friends.[29]

Changing the Musical Experience: From Social Music to Personal Soundtracks

Being able to store and transmit musical performances was extremely important, but that may not have been the biggest change brought about by the invention of the phonograph and radio. Rock historian James Miller writes that the phonograph (and eventually radio) represented a vast expansion of people's access to music: "Symphonies that a person living in the nineteenth century would have been lucky to hear once were available for repeated listening on home phonographs."[30] Before the invention of the phonograph or radio, people had to go to a concert hall, theater, or club to hear music if they didn't play it themselves.

Questioning the Media

How do personal music players, such as smartphones, iPods, and Walkmans, change how we interact with people? Does walking around with headphones on isolate us from each other? Do you use your headphones or earbuds to keep people at a distance?

The Death of "Social Music." The phonograph and radio brought a wider range of music into the household, but this led to the loss of so-called **social music**, or music that people play and sing for one another in the home or in other social settings. Prior to the new technology, people had to play an instrument or sing to have music in the home. Sheet music was a popular feature in magazines like *Godey's Lady's Book*, along with recipes and sewing patterns. For most people, there was little social distance between the performer and the audience, and musical instruction played a greater role in the education of the upper and middle classes. With advances in technology over the years, however, the social connections available through a shared musical experience changed profoundly.

Akio Morita's "Personal Soundtrack." Akio Morita is not a household name, but the Japanese engineer who invented the Sony Walkman has influenced how people listen to music as much as anyone since Thomas Edison and Emile Berliner.

When the Walkman was introduced in 1979, it was available in two versions—either as a tiny tape player or as a stereo FM radio. They were relatively expensive, with the tape player version costing upwards of $200, but they allowed each person to live in his or her own "personal musical cocoon."[31]

Until 1979, the only way to take music away from home was with either a poor-quality pocket AM radio or a giant boom box. Writer RiShawn Biddle points out that the Walkman was more than just a way to protect your fellow bus passengers from your choice of music: "It's also been a coach, concert hall, and personal reader for millions of workout warriors, housewives, and retirees. For travelers, it is a trusty companion, something to ward off talkative salesmen and grandmothers loaded with wallet-size photos."[32]

Media scholar Michael Marsden notes that the Walkman gives people privacy in public areas: "It's your personal space that you've created, in a world in which we don't have a lot of personal space. It's a totally private world."[33]

Not everyone is so enthralled with the effects of the Walkman, however. Critic John Zerzan argues that the Walkman is one of a number of technologies that lead to a "sort of withdrawal from social connections."[34] One thing the Walkman has clearly done, however, is contribute greatly to the trend of personalized media use characterized by iPods, MP3 players, music downloads, and podcasts.

Music, Youth Culture, and Society

Though recorded music was on the market long before there was **rock 'n' roll**, rock 'n' roll was born alongside modern recording technology and flourished on the radio. It was amplified from the start, featured new instruments such as the solid-body electric guitar, and brought together a host of traditions from white hillbilly music to black

---

social music: Music that people play and sing for one another in the home or other social settings. In the absence of radio, recordings, and, later, television, this was the means of hearing music most readily available to the largest number of people.

rock 'n' roll: A style of music popularized on radio that combined elements of white hillbilly music and black rhythm and blues.

rhythm and blues. World War II spurred the development of rock 'n' roll as a cross-cultural phenomenon because blacks and whites mixed socially during the war more often than they had before and because the Armed Forces Radio played a range of white and black musical styles.

"Rock 'n' Roll" and the Integration of Music

Before 1948, recordings by popular black musicians were referred to as **race records** and included everything from blues to gospel to jazz. But in 1949, the editors of *Billboard* magazine, which ranks sales of all types of records, started calling the genre rhythm and blues (R&B).[35] It was at the same time that "folk" records began to be called "country and western."[36]

Why did R&B emerge when it did? There are a number of reasons. One is that the big bands that played jazz and swing (popular in the 1930s and 1940s) were expensive because there were so many musicians. An amplified blues band with a singer, an electric guitar, an electric bass, and a drummer could make a lot of sound, and great dance music could be built around the strong bass beat.[37] Also, African American musicians gained respect when white artists recorded cover versions of black songs.[38]

On December 28, 1947, a black R&B singer named Wynonie Harris recorded "Good Rockin' Tonight" in a studio in Cincinnati, Ohio. The song would become a big hit on black jukeboxes and radio stations. Was this the first rock 'n' roll song? Entire books have been devoted to answering that question, but "Good Rockin'" is as likely a candidate as any. It was a jukebox hit for Harris, and later became a radio hit when **covered** by young Elvis Presley. It certainly helped give this new kind of music its name. The following year brought a series of songs with the word *rock* in the title, including "We're Gonna Rock, We're Gonna Roll," "Rockin' at Midnight," "Rock the Joint," and "Rock and Roll."

By and large, these songs were not played on white radio stations. The problem wasn't the color of the musicians; it was the meaning of the word *rock*. As record promoter Henry Glover put it,

> We were restricted with our possibilities of promoting this song because it was considered filth. . . . They had a definition in those days of the word "rock," meaning the sex act, rather than having it known as "a good time," as they did later.[39]

race records: A term used by the recording industry prior to 1949 to refer to recordings by popular black artists. It was later replaced by more racially neutral terms such as *R&B*, *soul*, and *urban contemporary*.

covers: Songs recorded (or covered) by someone other than the original artist. In the 1950s, it was common for white musicians to cover songs originally played by black artists, but now artists commonly cover all genres of music.

Library of Congress

Rhythm and blues records produced by African American artists were more likely to be played on jukeboxes in clubs than on the radio in the 1940s.

Elvis Presley and Chuck Berry: Blending Black and White Musical Traditions. While Harris and numerous other R&B singers were performing rock 'n' roll in the late 1940s and early 1950s, two stars—one white, the other black—would put rock 'n' roll on the national and international map. Elvis Presley and Chuck Berry demonstrated what could be done with the blending of hillbilly (or country) and R&B.[40]

Elvis Presley made his first recording in 1953, although no one knows the exact date. Marion Keisker, the woman behind the desk at Memphis Recording Service, remembered a young man who recorded a couple of songs on a ten-inch acetate disc for his mother. When she asked Presley whom he sounded like, his response was "I don't sound like nobody."[41] Keisker had the good sense to make an extra copy of Presley's recording and file it under the heading "good ballad singer." "The reason I taped Elvis," she explained, "was this: Over and over I remember Sam [Phillips, Keisker's boss] saying, 'If I could find a white

Web 7.4: Learn more about the history of rock 'n' roll.

Video 7.3: Watch Swedish dance music star Robyn and American folk singer Lucy Wainwright Roche preform very different versions of "Call Your Girlfriend."

Keystone Pictures USA/Alamy

Elvis Presley became the "king" of rock 'n' roll by combining elements of hillbilly and R&B music.

man who had the Negro sound and the Negro feel, I could make a billion dollars,' this is what I heard in Elvis."[42]

The man who would become known as "the king" soon started performing hillbilly music in Memphis and recording for Phillips, starting with "Good Rockin' Tonight." To Presley, performing was almost a religious experience: "It's like your whole body gets goose bumps," Presley said. "It's like a surge of electricity going through you. It's almost like making love, but it's even stronger than that."[43]

Just as hillbilly singer Elvis Presley borrowed from R&B, so blues guitarist Chuck Berry borrowed from the white hillbilly singers. The song "Maybellene" was based on an old fiddle tune called "Ida Red" and supposedly got its name from a mascara box. Others claim that Maybellene was the name of a cow in a third-grade reading book. Either way, the song combined a hot guitar, a hot car, and a hot woman.

Berry wanted to break out of some of the restrictions of traditional blues. While his audience at the clubs wouldn't stand for any change in the basic blues style, they had no problem with Berry's original rendition of an old white fiddle tune. Berry's unconventional style made people sit up and take notice. Berry recalls people talking about his music at an African American club:

> Some of the clubgoers started whispering, "Who is that black hillbilly at the Cosmo?" After they laughed at me a few times, they began requesting the hillbilly stuff and enjoyed trying to dance to it. If you ever want to see something that is far out, watch a crowd of colored folk, half high, wholeheartedly doing the hoedown barefooted.[44]

Presley started playing "Maybellene" in Louisiana while Berry was playing it in New York. This illustrates a key feature of the birth of rock 'n' roll: Two previously segregated types of music were coming together and becoming a new musical form—one that teens couldn't get enough of.

Rock Radio. Another reason for rock 'n' roll's growing popularity was that disc jockeys such as Alan Freed and Dewey Phillips were playing rock 'n' roll and R&B records on their radio shows.

On October 29, 1949, Dewey Phillips started a show on WHBQ in Memphis called *Red, Hot & Blue* that played R&B records. The show became an instant hit and quickly went from forty-five minutes in length to three hours. WHBQ's program director remembered it this way: "He got something like seven requests his first night. Well, the next night, I don't know the exact amount, but it was more like seventy requests. Then, even more incredible, the next night, it was closer to seven hundred."[45] Although Phillips was white, he played music by black artists and had a substantial audience of black radio listeners in Memphis. This

Michael Ochs Archives/Getty Images

Chuck Berry's music, played on rock 'n' roll stations in the 1950s and early 1960s, appealed to African American and white listeners alike.

was unusual at a time when most stations appealed either to the white or the black community, but not to both.

Motown Records put together a number of African American girl groups, including the Supremes (pictured) and Martha and the Vandellas.

The Changing Face of Popular Music

The 1950s were a period of transition for popular music, with tastes shifting from the Tin Pan Alley songs of an Irving Berlin or Cole Porter to the songs of a Chuck Berry or Buddy Holly that were rooted in R&B. Already firmly established through concerts and radio airplay, rock 'n' roll now took center stage with records produced by artists ranging from **girl groups** to the Rolling Stones.

Motown: The Sound of Young America. No record label was more important in bringing R&B to the masses than Detroit's Motown Records. Motown, founded by Berry Gordy Jr., was the most successful of the independent record labels and one of the most successful black-owned businesses.

SECRET 3 Popular culture scholar Gerald Early says that the real importance of Motown was that it took black music and sensibilities and made them important for the public at large. He also credits Motown with establishing a black popular culture at a time when jazz—especially the improvisational work of Miles Davis and John Coltrane—was becoming highbrow culture. One of the big accomplishments of Motown was that it no longer published songs by black artists for white artists to cover, as was common practice in the 1950s and early 1960s. Instead, the African American Motown artists themselves turned out the hits. Motown moved black music into the mainstream and out of the world of race records, thus illustrating Secret Three—Everything from the margin moves to the center.[46]

The move of African American music and artists into the mainstream mirrored larger changes in society. In May 1961, African American Freedom Riders staged sit-ins to desegregate restrooms and lunch counters in bus stations in the South. In October 1962, the Motown Revue was doing its part to promote desegregation with such established acts as the Marvelettes, Marvin Gaye, and the Supremes. While the Motown artists were not Freedom Riders, they broke some of the same ground on their tour. Mary Wilson of the Supremes put it this way:

> Our tours made breakthroughs and helped weaken racial barriers. When it came to music, segregation didn't mean a thing in some of those towns, and if it did, black and white fans would ignore the local customs to attend the shows. To see crowds that were integrated—sometimes for the first time in a community—made me realize that Motown truly was the sound of young America.[47]

Motown's years as an independent company came to an end in 1988 when Gordy sold the label to Boston Ventures for $61 million. Motown was subsequently sold to PolyGram in 1993 for $301 million. It still exists, but it is now a small unit within media giant Universal Music Group.

The lasting effect of Motown artists can be seen with the huge outpouring of affection for Michael Jackson following his death in 2009.

The British Invasion: A Rougher Rock. In the 1960s, rock underwent a number of changes. The most significant of these were brought about by groups that came to the United States from England. The so-called **British invasion** began in 1964 and brought a rougher edge to white rock 'n' roll with the music of the Beatles, Dusty

girl groups: A musical group composed of several women singers who harmonize together. Groups such as the Shirelles, the Ronettes, and the Shangri-Las, featuring female harmonies and high production values, were especially popular in the late 1950s and early 1960s.

British invasion: The British take on classic American rock 'n' roll, blues, and R&B transformed rock 'n' roll and became internationally popular in the 1960s with groups such as the Beatles and, later, the Rolling Stones and the Who.

Video 7.4: Take a video walk through rock 'n' roll history from Elvis to hip-hop.

Audio 7.4: Use Spotify to listen to this playlist of one hundred great Motown songs.

Michael Ochs Archive/Getty Images

The Beatles' album *Sgt. Pepper's Lonely Hearts Club Band,* along with The Beach Boys' *Pet Sounds* and Frank Zappa's *Freak Out,* was among the first rock concept albums that brought together a set of songs on a common theme.

Springfield, the Hollies, the Who, and, of course, the Rolling Stones. To appreciate the influence of these British bands, one need only look at the charts. In 1963, only one British band made it onto *Billboard*'s charts; in 1964, thirty-four did so.[48]

Traditionally, recorded music by popular groups was a means of promoting their live shows. But by 1966, it had become almost impossible for the Beatles to perform live because their screaming fans drowned them out. In fact, Beatles scholar Allan Moore notes that by 1966 the band had ceased touring because they couldn't hear themselves play. Instead, they became a studio band whose music was heard primarily on records and the radio.[49] In 1967, the Beatles recorded an album, *Sgt. Pepper's Lonely Hearts Club Band,* that transformed rock in a number of ways: It was one of rock's first **concept albums**—an album that brought together a group of related songs on common themes. It was also one of the first rock albums that was more than a collection of hit singles and their flip sides.[50]

What exactly is the concept of this album? Many of the songs have autobiographical themes derived from John Lennon's and Paul McCartney's childhood memories of Liverpool, England. Also, the songs are supposedly being played by the fictional band of the title.[51]

Interpretations of the songs on this album have varied. Some claim that "Lucy in the Sky With Diamonds" is about the drug LSD. Lennon said that the song was based on a picture his son Julian drew when he was four years old. Others say that McCartney's song "Fixing a Hole" is about injecting himself with heroin, though McCartney's own account claimed that it was about renovating an old farmhouse he had recently purchased. In 2004, McCartney acknowledged publicly that there are, indeed, drug references in many Beatles songs, including in "Lucy in the Sky With Diamonds."[52] Part of what makes *Sgt. Pepper* so successful, however, is that it doesn't matter which interpretation the listener supplies. They all work. The members of the band were more concerned about how the songs sounded than what they meant.

Sgt. Pepper gave rise to albums that were designed to be played from beginning to end, though these two-sided vinyl records had to be turned over at the twenty-three-minute mark. The seamless presentation of seventy minutes of music would have to wait for the 1980s and the advent of the CD.

Sgt. Pepper highlights a change that was starting to take place in the music business: The long-playing record (LP) was replacing the single as rock music's main format. Moore notes that in 1967 bands still relied primarily on singles to promote themselves and albums were of secondary importance. But that was changing with groups such as Cream and Led Zeppelin focusing on albums. Led Zeppelin's greatest hit, "Stairway to Heaven," was never released as a single, probably because it wouldn't fit the short format of the 45.[53]

The Growing Importance of Producers. As popular music increasingly became a studio creation, the albums' **producers** became as important as the artists themselves. The main job of a producer is to put together the right songs, songwriters, technicians, and performers in the creation of an album.

Rock historian Charlie Gillett argues that the producer is the person who is responsible for making hit records. Producer Rick Rubin revitalized Johnny Cash's career near

Web 7.5: An in-depth look at super-producer Rick Rubin.

concept album: An album by a solo artist or group that contains related songs on a common theme or even a story, rather than a collection of unrelated hits or covers.

producer: The person who puts together the right mix of songs, songwriters, technicians, and performers to create an album; some observers argue that the producer is the key catalyst for a hit album.

the end of his life with a series of albums that included songs by U2, Nine Inch Nails, and Tom Petty, among others. Producer Kenneth "Babyface" Edmonds has created or revived the careers of such artists as Aretha Franklin, Toni Braxton, Whitney Houston, Boyz II Men, and TLC. Unlike the producers and writers of the Motown era, Edmonds occasionally goes into the studio himself. Although he has produced at least fifty-seven top hits, Edmonds is quick to give praise to the artists who perform his songs.[54]

With rock, the producer shapes the sound and becomes an integral part of the musical process. Few albums demonstrate this as clearly as Pink Floyd's *Dark Side of the Moon.* Starting in 1973, *Dark Side of the Moon* spent 741 weeks on the *Billboard* Top 200 album chart, far longer than any competitor (though other albums have sold more copies). Alan Parsons produced the album, released in 1973, which paints a bleak picture of "alienation, paranoia, schizophrenia." But more than any message of the songs, *Dark Side of the Moon* presents an incredible sonic picture. It uses stereo to its fullest extent, sending sounds swirling around the listener's head. Parsons recorded a wide variety of voices talking, laughing, and screaming, which were mixed in at various times and speeds.[55] Pink Floyd continued the direction of the Beatles' *Sgt. Pepper* album, in which rock was music made to be recorded and constructed as much as performed.

The role of the producer continued to grow throughout the 1970s with the advent of **disco** and a range of heavily produced club music, including rap, house, and techno. Disco was primarily a means of getting people to dance. It came out of the gay male subculture in New York City and was popularized in the 1977 hit movie *Saturday Night Fever.* Disco was in many ways the ultimate producer music, in which the beat and the overall sound created by the producer mattered more than the vocals or talents of the instrumentalists.

Why does disco matter today? First and foremost, it was an entire genre of music that depended on technology and the producer, building on trends started by bands such as Pink Floyd and the Beatles. It also made black and Latino music more important commercially and led the movement toward the splintering of pop music into a range of genres.[56]

Hip-Hop Brings Together DJing, Dancing, Rapping, and Art. While the terms *hip-hop* and *rap* are often used interchangeably, rapping is really just a single facet of the larger world of hip-hop. According to English professor Mickey Hess, the hip-hop sound got started in the 1970s, when DJs began name-checking where they were from, including their cities, streets, or even neighborhoods. Although the music went national, it was still local in its orientation and was a statement of pride about the rapper's home. As Mr. Cheeks from the Lost Boyz put it, "It's only right to represent where I'm from."[57]

disco: The name of the heavily produced techno club dance music of the 1970s, which grew out of the urban gay male subculture, with significant black and Latino influences. In many ways, disco defined the look and feel of 1970s pop culture, fashion, and film.

hip-hop: A cultural movement that originated in the 1970s and 1980s that features four main elements: MCing, or rapping over music; DJing, or playing recorded music from multiple sources; B-boying, a style of dancing; and graffiti art.

Mohamed El Deeb, a 28-year-old North African hip hop singer, poses in front of a wall decorated with graffiti near Tahrir Square in Cairo, Egypt, during pro-democracy protests in the summer of 2012. El Deeb writes and performs songs inspired by the protests in Egypt.

Where did hip-hop begin? Many sources point to a block party in the Bronx, New York, on August 11, 1973, at which DJ Kool Herc is credited with inventing the breakbeat, "using two turntables and two copies of the same record to loop the same instrumental break over and over."[58] But Hess argues that it wasn't so neat and clear-cut of a start. He claims instead that credit goes to a series of DJs working in Harlem nightclubs using similar techniques along with doing "call-and-response" from the audience. Hess lists four main elements of **hip-hop** culture:

- MCing—The spoken word or rapping over recorded music
- DJing—Playing recorded music from multiple sources, oftentimes overlapping
- B-boying—Physical movement, a style of hip-hop dancing, often referred to as breakdancing
- Graffiti art—The visual images of the culture

These separate elements show how hip-hop evolved from a variety of areas of the country, with DJing coming out of New York, graffiti art growing out of styles popularized in Philadelphia, and the dancing coming from both New York and Los Angeles. The MCing, or rhyming, is credited as coming from the work of a variety of rhyming radio hosts in cities such as Detroit, Philadelphia, New Orleans, and Austin.

SECRET 3 **Rap music** started to spread out of the Bronx via cassettes that were passed from person to person. Remember, however, that these were analog recordings that couldn't be copied repeatedly like digital recordings can today. There was also a high level of borrowing/stealing/remixing going on even at the very beginning. Sugar Hill Gang's "Rapper's Delight," which introduced rap and hip-hop into the mainstream, used lyrics from a Bronx MC who hadn't released a record. Blondie's rap hit "Rapture," which came out in 1980, was among the first rap songs to receive radio airplay on stations that appealed to white audiences[59] (thus showing us another example of Secret Three—Everything from the margin moves to the center).

Understanding the importance of a rapper's roots and locale is key to understanding how hip-hop has spread around the world. Global rappers give shout-outs to homes as varied as Norway, Japan, Egypt, and Korea. Linguistics professor Marina Terkourafi talks about how hip-hop has followed in the footsteps of rock and jazz in moving out of the United States and then blending with traditional and regional musical styles from around the world.[60] She writes that while the central themes of hip-hop in the United States have typically centered on race and gender, globally it has been used to protest against the status quo and raise awareness of local issues.

Libyan exile Abdulla Darrat told NPR's *On the Media* how North African hip-hop was used to fuel rebellion against oppressive political leaders such as former Libyan strongman Moammar Gadhafi during the Arab Spring movement of 2011. Given that these artists could not perform openly, their videos got distributed through social media such as Facebook or YouTube. Darrat says that these songs give voice to protesters who otherwise would not be heard: "What the world really needs to understand about the struggle in these regions is there is a youth that has hope. They have optimism about the future, but they see lots of obstacles in their way."[61]

Questioning the Media

Do you listen to hip-hop or other sampled music? Do you think hip-hop artists are stealing from the musicians who created the sampled music? Why or why not? Is music created with samples something original?

Audio 7.5: Learn about the role of hip-hop in the Arab Spring revolts of 2011.

Video 7.5: See *Billboard*'s complete Top 25 Country Artist List.

Fernando Salazar/Wichita Eagle/MCT via Getty Images

Country singer George Strait has had more hit records over more years than anyone else in the music business.

Country: Pop Music for Adults

Country music was born in the late nineteenth century, evolving out of a range of musical forms that included Irish and Scottish folk music, Mississippi blues, and Christian gospel music.[62] It was originally called "old-timey" or hillbilly music. Country grew in the 1950s and 1960s with the so-called Nashville sound that was popularized by musicians such as Jim Reeves, Eddy Arnold, and Patsy Cline. It was at about this time that Elvis Presley took the hillbilly sound in another direction with early rock 'n' roll, but country never disappeared.

In 1980, many Americans rediscovered country music due to the hit film *Urban Cowboy*, starring John Travolta, and the 1990s and 2000s saw the further growth of country music thanks to songs from artists such as Rascal Flatts, the late Johnny Cash, and Carrie Underwood, as well as the soundtracks of movies such as *O Brother, Where Art Thou?* and *Walk the Line*.[63] According to research done by *Billboard* magazine prior to its 2011 Country Music Summit, the top five country acts from 1985 to 2011 were:

5. Tim McGraw, who had twelve number-one albums;
4. Alan Jackson, who had twenty-six number-one hits;

rap music: This genre arose out of the hip-hop culture in New York City in the 1970s and 1980s. It emerged from clubs where DJs played and remixed different records and sounds and then spoke (or rapped) over the top.

country music: Originally referred to as hillbilly or "old-timey" music, this genre evolved out of Irish and Scottish folk music, Mississippi blues, and Christian gospel music and grew in the 1950s and 1960s with the so-called Nashville sound.

3. Reba McEntire, the only woman on the list to have number-one country singles in four consecutive decades;

2. Garth Brooks, who has been the top-selling country album artist;

and, in the number-one spot,

1. George Strait, the legendary country singer who is the only artist in Billboard history to have a top-ten single every year for thirty-one consecutive years.[64]

Why does country music continue to be so popular? "Country music is about lyric-oriented songs with adult themes," according to Lon Helton, a music journalist. "You've probably got to be 24 or 25 to even understand a country song. Life has to slap you around a little bit, and then you go, 'Now I get what they're singing about.'"[65] Unlike the sex and drugs of rock 'n' roll, country deals with suburban issues like "love, heartache, family ties, and middle-aged renewal."[66]

Concerns About Effects of Music on Young People

Some of the biggest controversies surrounding rock have involved not the music but the words—from 1950s lyrics dealing with "rocking and rolling" to references to drugs in the 1970s to derogatory comments about women in contemporary rap.

It is difficult to know what the influence of a song's words will be. Adults often read metaphorical meanings into a song while young people see only the literal meaning of the lyrics. Understanding music also goes beyond the content of the lyrics. Listeners pay as much attention to the melody, rhythm, and style of music as they do to the lyrics. Finally, songs are often as much about feelings as they are about rational thought. They set a mood rather than transmit a specific message.[67]

SECRET 5 Since rock's inception, parents and other concerned adults have wondered about the effects of its lyrics on impressionable listeners, thus illustrating Secret Five—New media are always scary. This questioning has led to product liability trials, congressional hearings, and movements to label and/or ban certain albums for objectionable content.

Few music formats have engendered as much controversy as rap and hip-hop. Rap can be partially understood as an outgrowth of several trends, dating back to the Beatles' *Sgt. Pepper* and Pink Floyd's *Dark Side of the Moon.* With the advent of multitrack recording, producers were adding layers of talk and ambient sound to the music created by band members. Rap simply extended this process, making the DJ part of the music and sampling from a range of already completed musical recordings. There was no longer a single "correct" mix of the various tracks; instead, the final version was constructed by whoever wanted to work with it.

Among the controversies surrounding rap is the complaint that it is misogynistic and violent. Rappers defend the violence in their recordings by noting that we live in a violent world; the violence in the recordings is simply "keeping it real." Michael Fuchs, a former executive of media giant Time Warner, says that he sees some of the criticism of rap as racist:

> It's a fact that white kids are buying black music and are being influenced by it, and that frightens their parents. It's not very different than the feeling my parents had thirty years ago when rock and roll came out—about the influence of black music.[68]

The Importance of Pop Music. Popular music today goes well beyond just the composition; it is an entire social statement. Besides the music, there are the photos on the cover of the CD, the text within the booklet inside the CD, the music video, the interviews on *Entertainment Tonight*, the posters, the Web site, and the fashion. It is through popular music that young people often have their first contact with much of our culture. It provides young people not just with music, but with an entire identity.[69] Our identification with the music of our youth is something that sticks with us throughout adulthood. Alternative rocker Liz Phair points out:

> There's something that happens to people as they reach adulthood. They spend a lot of time trying to figure out what first hit them about rock 'n' roll. It's like the first time you took a drug. You want that first time back.[70]

From Singles to Digital Downloads: Making Money in the Recording Industry

For as long as there have been methods for recording and playing back sounds, there have been debates over how to make money selling music. Berliner's 78-rpm discs were fragile, held only three and a half minutes of music, and had only marginal sound quality by today's standards. So while there was no question that 78s needed to be replaced, there was no consensus on what the new format should be.

LPs Versus 45s

The **long-playing record (LP)** was developed by Columbia Records and introduced in 1948. The discs were labeled unbreakable; this was not quite true, but the vinyl LPs were much less delicate than the 78-rpm discs. More importantly, an LP could reproduce twenty-three minutes of high-quality music on each side. CBS demonstrated the

---

long-playing record (LP): A record format introduced by Columbia Records in 1948. The more durable LP could reproduce twenty-three minutes of high-quality music on each of two sides and was a technological improvement over the 78-rpm.

Burak Cingi/Redferns via Getty Images

Vinyl records have had a resurgence in sales in recent years as listeners, such as these at Rough Trade East in London, rediscover the sound and artwork on the larger format discs.

system to RCA president David Sarnoff and offered to let RCA, its competitor, use the system. But RCA declined the offer and put out its own format, the **45-rpm disc**. It had high-quality sound, but the 45 could play only about four minutes of music at a time.[71] Eventually, record players were sold that could play both 45s and LPs, and both formats existed side by side, with the LP used for longer compositions and the 45 for single popular songs.

Vinyl LPs have staged a resurgence in recent years, as both artists and consumers have latched onto the twelve-inch discs containing analog music. Sales of vinyl recordings grew by 19 percent in 2012, according to a *Billboard* report, while digital download sales increased by only 14 percent. CD sales, in contrast, fell by 13 percent for the year. That's not to say that vinyl sales are a big part of the market, making up only 2.3 percent of all physical sales of music for the year. Why are LPs regaining their popularity? Part of it is their size. The discs come with big covers that have plenty of room for dramatic art and liner notes. Recording artists, from big names like Justin Timberlake and Pink to obscure indie acts, like the prestige and "specialness" that a vinyl release brings. And consumers often get a code for a free digital download with the premium-priced analog recording so they can still listen to the music on their computer, phone, or iPod.[72]

Compact Discs and Digital Recording

Work on the **compact disc (CD)** was started by Philips Electronics physicist Klaas Compaan as early as 1969. Compaan had the idea of photographically recording music or video on discs that could be read with a laser. Not wanting to get into the kind of format war that raged between the 45 and the LP in the 1940s, Philips joined with Sony to create a standard for the compact disc. The CD was launched in Europe in 1982 and in the United States in 1983.

SECRET 5 While we have generally talked about new media being scary to consumers (Secret Five), **digital recording** (a method of recording sound that involves storing it as a series of numbers) has been the scariest of the new media to people in the music industry. With **analog recording** (the original method of recording that involved cutting a groove on a record or placing a magnetic signal on a tape that was an image of the sound wave being recorded), copies were not as good as the originals, and copies of copies showed further degradation in quality. Thus, the prospect of home digital recordings, which are exactly the same as the originals without loss of quality, upset companies whose livelihood depended on the sales of original recordings.

For several years, home digital copying was held up by the recording industry, which wanted CD players to include security chips that would stop people from making copies. Of course, as soon as the industry came up with a way to stop people from copying digital music, hackers responded with ways of breaking the system. Ultimately, home CD copying emerged from the computer industry rather than the music industry. People wanted to be able to "burn" CDs with their own data, programs, and music.[73]

Music on the Internet

The most recent format for music is a compressed music file known as an **MP3** (short for Moving Picture Experts Group audio layer 3). MP3s can be played on a computer or on a portable MP3 player, such as an iPod, or they can be burned onto a recordable CD. The files can be easily shared over the Internet by e-mail, on Web sites, or through music-sharing services.

SECRET 2 Aside from allowing people to share music files, one of the biggest effects of this new distribution channel has been to allow new groups to publicize their

---

45-rpm disc: This record format was developed in the late 1940s by RCA. It had high-quality sound but held only about four minutes of music per side. It was the ideal format for marketing popular hit songs to teenagers, though.

compact disc (CD): A digital recording medium that came into common use in the early 1980s. CDs can hold approximately seventy minutes of digitally recorded music.

digital recording: A method of recording sound—for example, that used to create CDs—that involves storing music in a computer-readable format known as binary information.

analog recording: An electromechanical method of recording in which a sound is translated into analogous electrical signals that are then applied to a recording medium. Analog recording media included acetate or vinyl discs and magnetic tape.

MP3: Short for Moving Picture Experts Group audio layer 3; a standard for compressing music from CDs or other digital recordings into computer files that can be easily exchanged on the Internet.

TEST YOUR MEDIA LITERACY

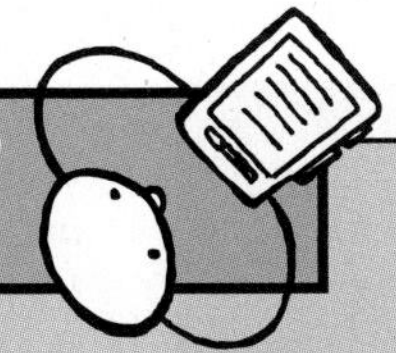

Who Is Being Hurt by Declining Sales of Recorded Music?

SECRET 6 The recording industry has had more than a decade of declining sales. In 2000, American music fans bought 785.1 million albums. By 2006, that number had dropped to 588.2 million (including both CDs and digital downloads). And in 2008, that number had reached 428.4 million.[1] That's a 45 percent drop in sales over eight years. The industry has blamed consumers for the decline because of file sharing, piracy, and easy home duplication of CDs. What the industry has not done is come up with a coherent response to the massive change that's taking place in the music business, whether it likes it or not. But as you think about this, remember Secret Six—Activism and analysis are not the same thing.

The decline in the sales of prerecorded music is not imaginary. Take a look at Figure 7.2 on page 179, a graph put together by tech writer Michael DeGusta based on sales data from the Recording Industry Association of America (RIAA). The graph shows the sales in inflation-adjusted dollars of recorded music in the United States from 1973 to 2009. As DeGusta points out in his explanation of the graph, U.S. recorded music sales in 2009 were down 64 percent from their peak in 1999 and down 45 percent from where they were in 1973. Why have these sales declined so much? Common wisdom suggests that it's illegal sharing/copying (commonly called piracy) and a general lack of interest in buying complete albums. Some of it also may be that in the 1990s people were re-buying music on CDs that they had bought years earlier on vinyl. People converting from CDs to digital players such as iPods simply had to scan in their CDs to convert them to the new format.[2]

There have even been suggestions made that the music industry as a whole is dying. But as journalist-blogger Matthew Yglesias explains, it's really the recording industry that's dying, not the music business. He writes in his blog, "People still listen to music. People still play music. People who play music even still earn money. But the business of *selling recordings of music* is shrinking."[3]

Take, for example, the eclectic country singer-songwriter Lyle Lovett. Lovett tells *Billboard* that while he has sold 4.6 million albums over the last twenty years, he's made all of his money from performing and touring. "I've never made a dime from a record sale in the history of my record deal," he said. "I've been very happy with my sales, and certainly my audience has been very supportive. I make a living going out and playing shows."[4] So why does Lovett still record and sell albums? "Records are very powerful promotional tools to go out and be able to play on the road." (Note from your author—if you get the chance to see Lovett in concert, do so. He puts on a great show!)

WHO is the source?

Who is Lyle Lovett? What has he done in the music industry?

WHAT is he saying?

How much money has Lovett made selling albums? Is he worried about the problem of file sharing or "record piracy"? Why does he record albums?

WHAT kind of evidence is there?

According to tech writer Michael DeGusta, what does the evidence say has happened to recorded music sales since 1973? How does he explain the changes? What are the causes?

HOW do you and your classmates feel about the music industry?

How often do you and your friends pay for music compared to "sharing" it over the Internet? Why do you pay for or not pay for music? What could record labels do that would make you more willing to buy CDs or legal downloads? Do you think declining sales of record music have hurt artists such as Lyle Lovett?

---

[1]James Callan, "U.S. Album Sales Decline 14% While Online Track Sales Surge," Bloomberg.com, January 1, 2009, www.bloomberg.com/apps/news?pid=20601103&sid=aC7ekniUw9Fs&refer=us; Brian Hiatt and Evan Serpick, "The Record Industry's Decline," *Rolling Stone*, June 28, 2007.

[2]Michael DeGusta, "The REAL Death of the Music Industry," *Business Insider*, February 18, 2011, www.businessinsider.com/these-charts-explain-the-real-death-of-the-music-industry-2011-2.

[3]Matthew Yglesias, "The Death of the Recordings-Sale Industry," February 19, 2011, thinkprogress.org/yglesias/2011/02/19/199969/the-death-of-the-recordings-sale-industry/.

[4]Reuters/Billboard, "Lyle Lovett Sells Millions, Earns Nothing," July 10, 2008, www.reuters.com/article/2008/07/10/us-lovett-idUSN1030835920080710.

Web 7.6: Check out Jon Bon Jovi's claim against Apple and its co-founder Steve Jobs.

Web 7.7: Read more about what Michael DeGusta has to say about the decline of music sales.

Video 7.6: Watch Lyle Lovett in concert.

© Everett Collection Inc / Alamy

Singer Katrina Leskanich was the namesake of the '80s band Katrina and the Waves, but these days she's performing on her own and releasing her music independently using long-tail tools.

music by delivering it directly to the consumer through the Internet, either through their own Web site or social networking sites, thus illustrating Secret Two—There are no mainstream media.

Questioning the Media

Do you listen to independent artists or big recording stars? If you listen to independent artists, who are they? How did you find out about them? How did you find their music? What makes independent artists more interesting to you? Do you think long-tail distribution of indie artists makes it harder to find their work? Why or why not?

Take the example of Katrina Leskanich. If you lived through the 1980s, you likely remember the Katrina and the Waves summer anthem "Walking on Sunshine." And even those too young to have noticed it the first time around have probably heard it in movie soundtracks and on TV shows. The band had several other modest hits in the United States and the United Kingdom.

But now Ms. Leskanich, the band's lead singer, is fifty-plus years old, and fresh-faced stars of the 1980s aren't going to get a lot of attention from the music industry twenty-five years later. Her latest album, *Walking on Sunshine*, was released independently in February 2009. It's received little, if any, radio airplay, but it was featured on the popular podcast *Coverville*. You won't find a copy of the CD at your local music retailer, but you can find it on Amazon.com as either a download or a burn-to-order CD, or you can buy a download from iTunes.[74] An alternative version of the album was released through CD Baby, which sells music through its own Web site, as well as other online channels.

What has happened is that Leskanich has made the move from the short head to the long tail of the music industry, as we talked about back in Chapter 3.

Some independent or maverick musicians and bands might applaud the increased exposure they get from the Internet, but the music industry is intensely concerned about music file "sharing," preferring to call it theft, piracy, or copyright violation. What worries publishers is that no one is paying for these files.[75] Publishers have tried various copy protection schemes to stop consumers from making digital copies, some going so far as to put software on their CDs that spies on consumers and reports back to the publisher how the music is being used.[76] And, as is discussed in Chapter 10, the recording industry for the past several years has been filing suit against consumers who have been downloading unlicensed copies of music from the Internet.[77]

The Business of Radio

With the coming of television, radio was forced to change and no longer tried to be all things to all people. Instead, each station now appeals to a particular audience. Teenagers don't have to listen to the same programs as store clerks; stockbrokers don't have to listen to the same programs as college students. Want rock 'n' roll? There's a station for it. Oldies? Another choice or two. News? Talk? Classical music? Soul? If you live in an urban area, chances are you can find stations providing all these different radio formats. Over the past decade, radio has continued to change, undergoing a massive change of ownership and seeing the growth of numerous new competitors.

Finding a Niche: Popular Radio Formats

The most popular radio format in 2012 in the United States was country and new country, with 14.2 percent of stations carrying it (see Table 7.1), followed closely by news/talk, which commands 11.4 percent of the national audience. Pop Contemporary Hits **format radio** is what used

Web 7.8: Wondering what all those different radio formats are? Wonder no more.

format radio: A style of radio programming designed to appeal to a narrow, specific audience. Popular formats include country, contemporary hits, all talk, all sports, and oldies.

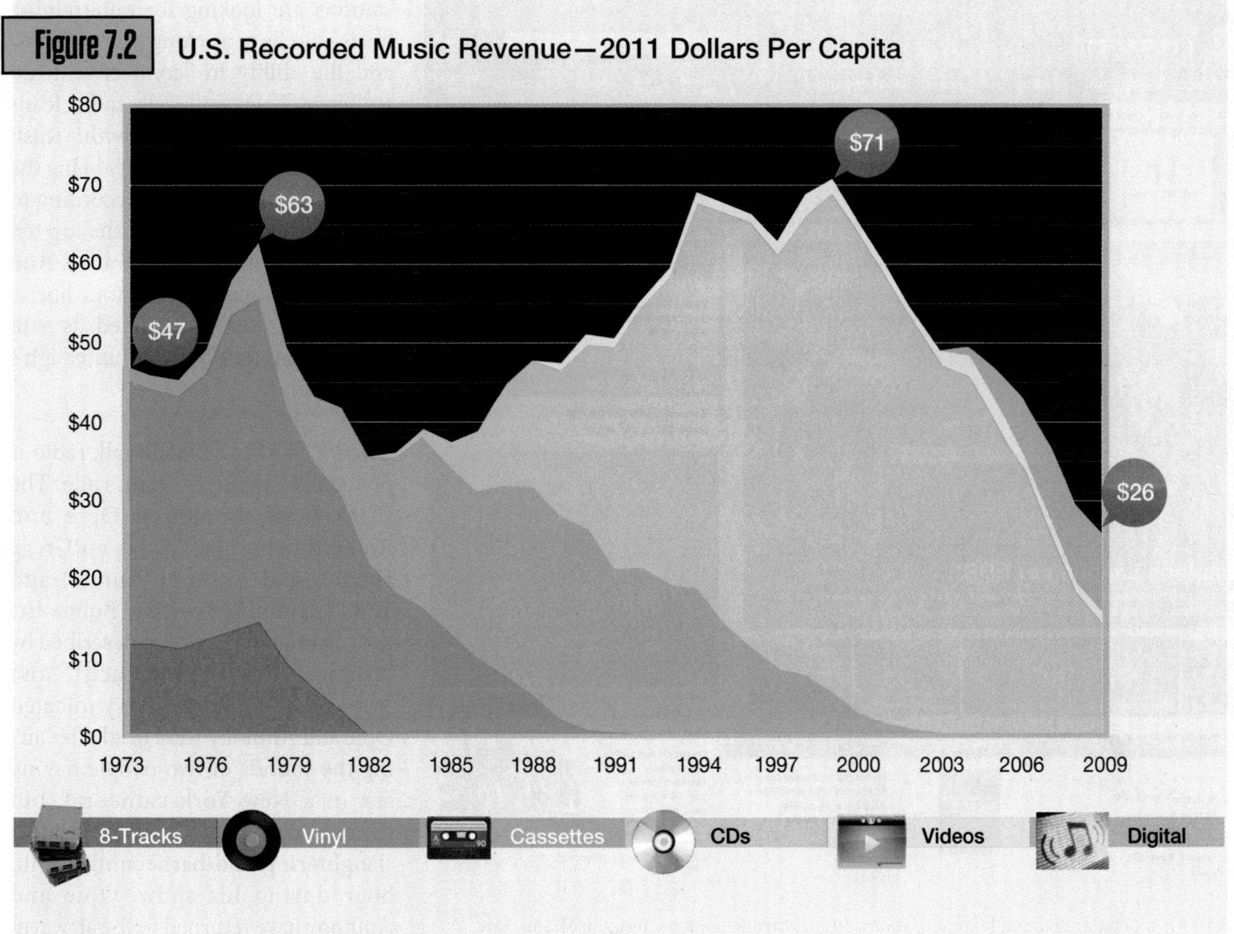

Source: Reprinted with permission of Michael DeGusta.

to be known as Top 40 and is made up of a range of current hits; while it would seem to be primarily a teen format, more than half of its audience is older than twenty-five. It draws 8.2 percent of the radio audience. Adult Contemporary and Soft AC consist of light and soft rock and are designed to appeal to listeners aged twenty-five to forty, especially women; it draws about 8.1 percent of the audience. While audience members might call lots of what they listen to oldies, the radio business breaks it down into a variety of categories, including Classic Hits (5.2 percent), Classic Rock (5.2 percent), and Oldies (1.2 percent). Rhythmic CHR was a format developed to appeal to the United States' changing ethnic makeup, with listeners spread fairly evenly among black, Hispanic, and "other."[78]

Spanish-Language Broadcasting. As the Hispanic population in the United States, especially in the Southwest and Florida, continues its rapid growth, Spanish-language stations are increasing in popularity and drawing high ratings. As of fall 2009, more than 1,300 Spanish-language stations were broadcasting in a variety of formats.[79] This is a huge growth from the 533 that were broadcasting in 1998. Spanish-language formats include multiple styles of music, news/talk/information, and religious programming.[80] The top-rated stations in Los Angeles frequently broadcast in Spanish and play either Mexican or adult contemporary music. The Los Angeles Dodgers baseball team has two sets of play-by-play announcers, one for English broadcasts, and the other for the team's Spanish-language network. And ESPN has a Spanish-language, all-sports radio network based out of Miami that focuses heavily on soccer games and news.[81]

Spanish-language stations are getting strong support from advertisers who want to reach the Hispanic community, and evidence indicates that Spanish-speaking consumers respond better to advertisements in their own language than to those in English.[82]

Talk Radio: Politics, News, Shock Jocks, and Sports

As mentioned earlier, news/talk is one of the top radio formats. Talk radio has exploded during the past twenty-five years. In 1985, only 200 stations carried the format; by 1995, that number had grown to more than 1,000. Marvin Kalb, formerly with CBS News, credits talk radio with providing a sense of community that people don't find anywhere else: "If we still gathered at town meetings, if our churches were still community centers, we wouldn't need talk radio. People feel

http://www.espndeportes.com/espndeportesradio/

ESPN Deportes is a popular Spanish-language sports radio network headquartered in Miami. Not surprisingly, ESPN Deportes's major focus is on soccer, or as they would say, "futbol."

increasingly disconnected, and talk radio gives them a sense of connection."[83] Talk radio is also important to the radio industry as more and more young people turn away from broadcasting to digital sources of music.[84]

Political Talk. Talk radio is a major source of political information for 44 percent of Americans, and the political information they are getting from talk radio is largely conservative.[85] Although journalism generally values balanced coverage, New York radio host Brian Lehrer notes that such coverage doesn't mesh well with the nature of talk radio:

> Some people's views don't fit neatly into traditional conservative or liberal labels. But that's not what's wanted in the media these days, especially in talk radio. They want you to be 100 percent confident that you have the truth and 100 percent predictable in your views.[86]

Carl Anderson, senior vice president for programming and distribution for ABC Radio Networks, says that radio stations are looking for entertaining hosts who have a strong point of view and the ability to "connect with an audience."[87] Overall, talk radio leans strongly conservative, with Rush Limbaugh and Sean Hannity being the two most popular hosts. According to *Talkers* magazine, eight of the top ten talk show hosts are conservative. And the listenership of the top four liberal talk show hosts combined is still smaller than that of Rush Limbaugh's show alone.[88]

Shock Jocks. Not all talk radio is political; some is just plain rude. The **shock jocks**, including Opie and Anthony (whose real names are Gregg Hughes and Anthony Cumia) and Todd Clemm (known as "Bubba the Love Sponge"), have been described by critics as "disgusting," "racist," and "repulsive."[89] Nationally syndicated Opie and Anthony were fired after airing the sounds of two people having sex in a New York cathedral, but Clemm was kept on the air after slaughtering and barbecuing a wild boar during his show. Opie and Anthony have returned to the airwaves with a slightly toned-down show. Howard Stern, the most controversial of the shock jocks, left terrestrial radio in 2006 for satellite broadcasting, where he has a multiyear contract worth $500 million.[90]

All-Sports Radio. Sports programming occupies a growing segment of the talk format. The cable television network ESPN now provides sports radio programming and even has its own station in Chicago.[91] Some stations have gone so far as to adopt what has been called a "guy" radio format. "This isn't sports radio, it's guy radio," says forty-something radio host Glenn Ordway of Boston's WEEI. "It's what guys our age talk about in bars and on golf courses. . . . This is not broadcasting we're doing, it's narrowcasting."[92]

Although it's a narrow segment of the radio-listening public, the dedicated, loyal, and fanatic fans are very attractive to advertisers. "What separates sports radio from other radio is the passion of its listeners, and that makes it fertile hunting ground for us," says one major guy radio advertiser. "These are men who scream at their radios instead of punching the dial looking for the next cool song."[93]

Web 7.9: Check out the latest on Rush Limbaugh.

shock jocks: Radio personalities, such as Howard Stern, who attract listeners by making outrageous and offensive comments on the air.

Radio Consolidates and Goes High Tech

Prior to 1985, broadcast owners were restricted nationally to seven AM radio, seven FM radio, and seven television stations.[94] During the 1980s, with the growth of cable and satellite television, the **Federal Communications Commission (FCC)** relaxed some ownership rules, which resulted in greater consolidation of ownership through media mergers. The trend toward broadcast deregulation was accelerated greatly with the Telecommunications Act of 1996. Although most of the law dealt with the cable television and telephone industries, the law lifted the restrictions on overall broadcast ownership. A single company could now own unlimited numbers of radio stations, with up to eight stations in a single market.[95]

The impact on radio was almost immediate. Within a year and a half, radio ownership had become far more concentrated and far less diverse. By 2003, the number of radio stations on the air had grown by 5.9 percent, but the number of station owners had fallen by 35 percent.[96] Clear Channel used the rule change to buy up $30 billion worth of radio stations nationwide, going from owning forty-two stations in 1995 to more than 1,200 stations by 2003.[97] As of 2014, Clear Channel was still the largest station owner in the United States, with 860 stations reaching more than 239 million listeners. In addition to owning all those stations, Clear Channel also provides syndicated programming for more than 5,000 stations through its Premiere Networks. It also sells advertising spots for about 4,000 radio stations (and 600 television stations) through Katz Media.[98] As an amazing side note, in 2014 Clear Channel changed its name to iHeartMedia to highlight the company's streaming audio business along with its legacy radio stations.[99]

Many stations now operate with virtually no staff other than a few people to sell and produce advertising. The music, news, weather, and talk all come from either a satellite service or a computer hard drive, with automation software serving up the local commercials, announcements, and programming. If it sounds like programming on the radio is the same from one side of the country to the other, it could be because the stations you are listening to all get their programs from the same centralized source.[100]

Table 7.1 Popular Radio Formats

Although the ratings of various radio formats vary from month to month, here is an overall picture of the audience percentage of the various top formats. Note that the report of number of stations includes FM, AM, HD, and Internet streaming.

FORMAT	AUDIENCE PORTION	# OF STATIONS
Country + New Country	14.2%	2,893
News/Talk/Information	11.4%	3,984
Pop Contemporary Hit Radio (Top 40)	8.2%	1,012
Adult Contemporary + Soft AC	8.1%	1,390
Classic Hits	5.2%	883
Classic Rock	5.2%	944
Hot Adult Contemporary	4.7%	810
Urban Adult Contemporary	4.1%	336
Rhythmic Contemporary Hit Radio	3.4%	370
All Sport	3.1%	1,274
Urban Contemporary	3.0%	274
Contemporary Christian	2.9%	1,691
Mexican Regional	2.9%	550
Adult Hits + 80's Hits	2.2%	395
Active Rock	2.1%	356
AOR + Mainstream Rock	2.0%	336

Source: "Radio Today 2013: How America Listens to Radio" (Arbitron, Fall 2012 survey period).

Note: Among the other formats are Alternative, Oldies, Spanish Contemporary, All News, Classical, Religious, Album Adult Alternative, Classic Country, Spanish Adult Hits, Gospel, Contemporary Inspirational, Spanish Religious, and Tejano. *Audience Portion* is of 12+ persons. *# of Stations* includes AM, FM, HD radio, and streamed stations.

Public Radio

With approximately 11,000 commercial stations, radio is a big business in the United States. But for all the power and reach of the commercial radio business, public radio provides a significant alternative.

NPR. Public radio was authorized by the 1967 Public Broadcasting Act, which was designed primarily to create educational television. The act allocated stations at the lower end of the FM dial for noncommercial broadcasting, and most of the station licenses went to colleges and universities. In 1971, National Public Radio (NPR) went on the air with its first program, the evening newsmagazine *All Things Considered.*[101]

One thing *All Things Considered* can do that other news shows can't is present the news in depth. Eight-minute-long stories are not unusual, and twenty-minute stories are broadcast when the topic

Questioning the Media

Do you listen to any shock jocks? If so, who? Should shock jocks such as Opie and Anthony be allowed on broadcast radio, or should they be forced onto alternative audio channels such as satellite broadcasting or the Internet? Why or why not?

Federal Communications Commission (FCC): The federal agency charged with regulating telecommunications, including radio and television broadcasting.

AP Photo/Richard Drew

News commentator Juan Williams was fired by NPR in 2010 over controversial comments he made on Fox News.

merits the length. This occurs in a medium in which thirty seconds is considered a long story.

The public radio network remained relatively small until two major developments occurred. The first was the growth of the satellite delivery of network programming. Satellite allows good signals go out to all stations no matter how remote they are. The second development was the installation of FM radios in most private cars. Since public radio was almost exclusively on the FM band, the advent of FM car radios made it possible to reach interested people with enough time to pay attention. Not surprisingly, NPR's biggest audiences are in cities whose workers have long commutes.[102] By 2013, there were 835 NPR member stations reaching a monthly audience of 27.3 million.[103]

NPR launched the two-hour news program *Morning Edition* in 1979, and since then it has become the most-listened-to morning news show in the country, with 7.6 million listeners tuning in daily. This is about one-third larger than the *Today* show's audience and 60 percent higher than that of ABC's *Good Morning America.*[104] Of course, this isn't a completely fair comparison because *Morning Edition* is on radio and the other two shows are on television. Americans also view NPR as being a particularly credible source of news, with people rating the radio network as having a higher level of believability than CBS, NBC, ABC, MSNBC, and Fox News.[105]

Although NPR is widely respected for the depth and quality of its reporting, it has become embroiled in a series of partisan controversies. In 2010, the network fired contributor Juan Williams over comments he made on Fox News about some people feeling anxiety when they see Muslims on airplanes. NPR president Vivian Schiller later said that Williams was fired for a long series of comments that violated NPR guidelines. The firing, and the way it was handled, led to extensive criticism of NPR by conservative media hosts and politicians. This led to calls in Congress to discontinue all federal funding of the network. Eventually Schiller resigned over the controversy, as did NPR's vice president for news.[106]

One of the major challenges facing public radio is funding. For 2014, NPR had expected revenue of $178.1 million and projected expenses of $183 million, leading to a deficit of $6.1 million.[107] Of that money, approximately 25 percent came from sponsorship, which allows corporations, organizations, and individuals to run short messages during programs. While most of these underwriting announcements promote the companies themselves as institutions, there are also announcements promoting particular books or television programs. NPR's news division had a yearly budget of about $70.7 million and a staff of about 365 people in 2012, not counting the reporters working for all the affiliated stations. The largest sources of revenue for NPR are programming fees paid by local member stations (37 percent of the budget) and the above-mentioned sponsorship fees (25 percent). While NPR gets relatively little money directly from the federal government, it does get funds from it indirectly through the programming fees paid its member stations, which do get federal funds.[108]

You may have noticed that this section of the chapter was headed as "NPR" and not "National Public Radio." That's because in 2010 the network changed its name from National Public Radio to just NPR to reflect the fact that much of its programming is delivered over the Web or via apps for mobile devices and tablets. So to understand the full reach of NPR, it should be noted that in addition to its 27.3 million radio listeners, it has 28.6 million podcast programs downloaded per month and 20.8 million unique visitors to its Web site, NPR.org. As NPR's new chief executive said in a tweet, "We need to reach audience in ways convenient and accessible to them in emerging and traditional platforms."[109]

Web 7.10: The many ways to consume NPR using mobile technology.

Audio 7.6: Find out more about *Mountain Stage* and listen to podcasts.

Live Music on the Radio. Not all music broadcast on the radio today is prerecorded on CDs. One of public radio's most popular shows is Garrison Keillor's *Prairie Home Companion*, which features a range of live music, skits,

Table 7.2 Digital Audio Audiences, 2014

According to Triton Digital and Edison Research, consumers get audio programming from a wide range of sources. Here are a few examples.

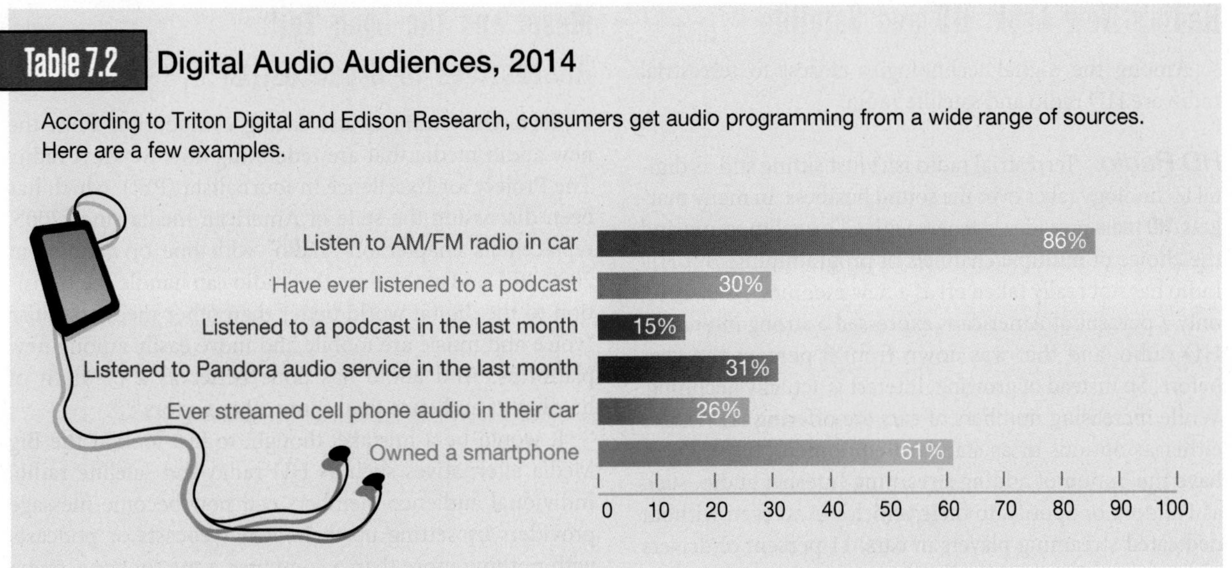

Source: "The Infinite Dial 2014: Navigating Digital Platforms" (Triton Digital, Edison Research, 2014), www.edisonresearch.com/home/archives/2014/03/the-infinite-dial-2014.php.

guests, and the centerpiece of the show, Keillor's monologue delivery of the news from Lake Wobegon, a mythical town in Minnesota that represents the stereotypical small Midwestern town "where the women are strong, the men are good looking, and all the children are above average." *Mountain Stage,* produced by West Virginia Public Radio, has been broadcasting live performances by a variety of artists since 1984. In addition to country, bluegrass, and folk artists, the show has featured performers such as Crash Test Dummies, Sheryl Crow, Sarah McLachlan, Counting Crows, and They Might Be Giants. Although *Mountain Stage* does not generally carry stadium show headliners, R.E.M. did do an acoustic segment on the show.[110]

Former producer Andy Ridenour told *Billboard* magazine that the show's greatest strength is that it exposes audience members to different artists and types of music: "One of the most common complaints we hear is that people don't get to hear anything new on the radio. Here, they get a chance to hear an artist they like and maybe two artists they never heard of."[111]

The Future of Sound

For the past hundred years or so, the recording industry has been making money off the sale of little packages, either discs or cartridges of some sort. The coming of radio created the first blip in the market, leaving sellers wondering why people would buy records when they could get the music for free on the radio. The record companies soon learned that they could earn revenue from licensing the music to the radio stations and from promoting their records by having them played on the radio. Then came computers and the Internet, which allowed people to burn copies of CDs on blank media or transmit them to other people as MP3 files.

Now radio—the recording industry's old nemesis—is facing new competition and transformations of its own. Radio started with AM broadcasting as the primary medium for news and entertainment. Then, in the late 1940s and early 1950s, television displaced radio and transformed it into a companion medium that people listened to in the background rather than something that dominated their attention. A third round of change came when FM broadcasting became popular in the 1970s, bringing stereo and high fidelity to broadcasting. FM eventually surpassed AM in popularity, especially in the realm of music, leaving AM radio to be dominated by sports, talk, and news—formats that don't suffer from low fidelity and the lack of stereo.[112]

People used to listen to radio predominantly in their cars and at home. Now people are listening in the office using radio stations' Web streams. They also download audio podcasts or go to pay satellite services. Despite the new options, analog broadcasting remains by far the most popular choice—93 percent of Americans age twelve or older still listen to **terrestrial radio** every week. But traditional radio is facing stiff competition. According to the Pew Foundation's "State of the News Media 2012" report, up to 38 percent of Americans listen to audio on digital devices every week.[113] (See Table 7.2.)

There is no question of whether the entire sound industry is going through a massive change. The only real question is what will emerge.

terrestrial radio: AM and FM broadcast radio stations.

Radio's New Look: HD and Satellite

Among the digital technologies closest to terrestrial radio are HD radio and satellite radio.

HD Radio. Terrestrial radio isn't just sitting still as digital technology takes over the sound business. In many markets, **HD radio** provides listeners with CD-quality sound and the choice of multiple channels of programming. But HD radio has not really taken off as a new medium. As of 2010, only 7 percent of Americans expressed a strong interest in HD radio, and that was down from 8 percent the year before. So instead of growing, interest is actually declining. While increasing numbers of cars are offering HD radios either as options or as standard equipment, buyers now have the option of adding streaming Internet audio, such as Pandora or Spotify, to their vehicles. And even without dedicated streaming players in cars, 11 percent of drivers report using their mobile devices to stream music in their vehicles.[114]

Satellite Radio. In 2008, the two competing **satellite radio** services, Sirius and XM, merged to become SiriusXM. The two services still offer separate programming but have overlap between them. They've also united their efforts to promote the idea of subscription radio. Sirius XM ended 2013 with more than 24 million subscribers.[115] Neither of the two companies turned a profit as independents, and the newly merged company came close to filing for bankruptcy in February 2009, saved only by an infusion of cash provided by Liberty Media, the owner of major pay TV services.[116]

The biggest name on satellite radio is former broadcast shock jock Howard Stern, who moved over to Sirius after his protracted and very public battle with Viacom, which syndicated him, and the FCC, which fined his stations more than $2.5 million over a ten-year period.[117] Stern seems to be thriving on satellite radio with no corporate or FCC censors to put limits on him. In an interview with the *New York Times*, Stern said, "We're talking about the stuff you can't talk about. The show on terrestrial radio in the last ten years had been so watered down."[118]

Satellite radio also provides news and public affairs channels, such as CNN, Fox News, BBC World Service, and NPR. One advantage of satellite radio over regular radio is that travelers are able to tune in to a channel in New York and listen to it all the way to California. The disadvantage, other than the cost, is that these services provide no local content, such as traffic reports, local news, or weather forecasts—the staples of car radio.[119]

Web 7.11: Look at recent audio industry reports.

Audio 7.7: Listen to the University of Nebraska at Kearney's student radio station KLPR.

Music and the Long Tail: Alternatives to Broadcasting

Terrestrial radio is also facing competition from the new audio media that are redefining how we view radio. The Project for Excellence in Journalism (PEJ), which has been discussing the state of American media since 2005, replaced its chapter on "radio" with one on "audio" in 2009. PEJ said at the time that radio can handle the transition to the digital world better than other media because "voice and music are mobile and move easily among new platforms. And audio has done better as a medium of holding its audience than some other sectors."[120]

It would be a mistake, though, to just look at the Big Media alternatives such as HD radio and satellite radio. Individual audience members can now become message providers by setting up their own Webcasts or podcasts with nothing more than a computer, a microphone, and a connection to the Internet. With these technologies, even programming that extends deep into the long tail of media content can be distributed easily.

Streaming Audio. The original online alternative to radio was **streaming audio**, also known as webcasting, or Internet radio. This can take a wide range of forms. Some content is tied to a terrestrial station; others are Internet only, such as Pandora or Spotify. Pandora, for example, was started in 2005, and as of 2014, 31 percent of Americans age 12 or older listen to Pandora at least monthly, and 50 percent of all smartphone owners have downloaded the Pandora app.[121] In essence, smartphones and other mobile devices are becoming the new portable radio, as well as being players for your personal collection of recorded music.

Streaming audio also greatly extends the reach of stations, especially small ones with low-powered transmitters. A 3,800-watt student station that can barely cover fifteen miles over the air can reach an entire city, not to mention the world, through streaming. In essence, streaming can do for a small radio station what cable did for Ted Turner's local Atlanta television station, WTBS—turn it into a radio superstation that anyone in the world can receive.

The Infinite Dial 2014 study from Triton Digital and Edison Research found that an estimated 124 million

HD radio: Sometimes also referred to as high-definition radio, this technology provides listeners with CD-quality sound and the choice of multiple channels of programming, but it is not yet commonly available in mass-market outlets or as standard equipment in cars.

satellite radio: The radio service provided by digital signal broadcast from a communications satellite. Supported by subscribers, this service covers a wider area than terrestrial radio and offers programming that is different from corporate-owned terrestrial stations. However, it is costly and doesn't provide local coverage, such as traffic and weather reports.

streaming audio: Audio programming transmitted over the Internet.

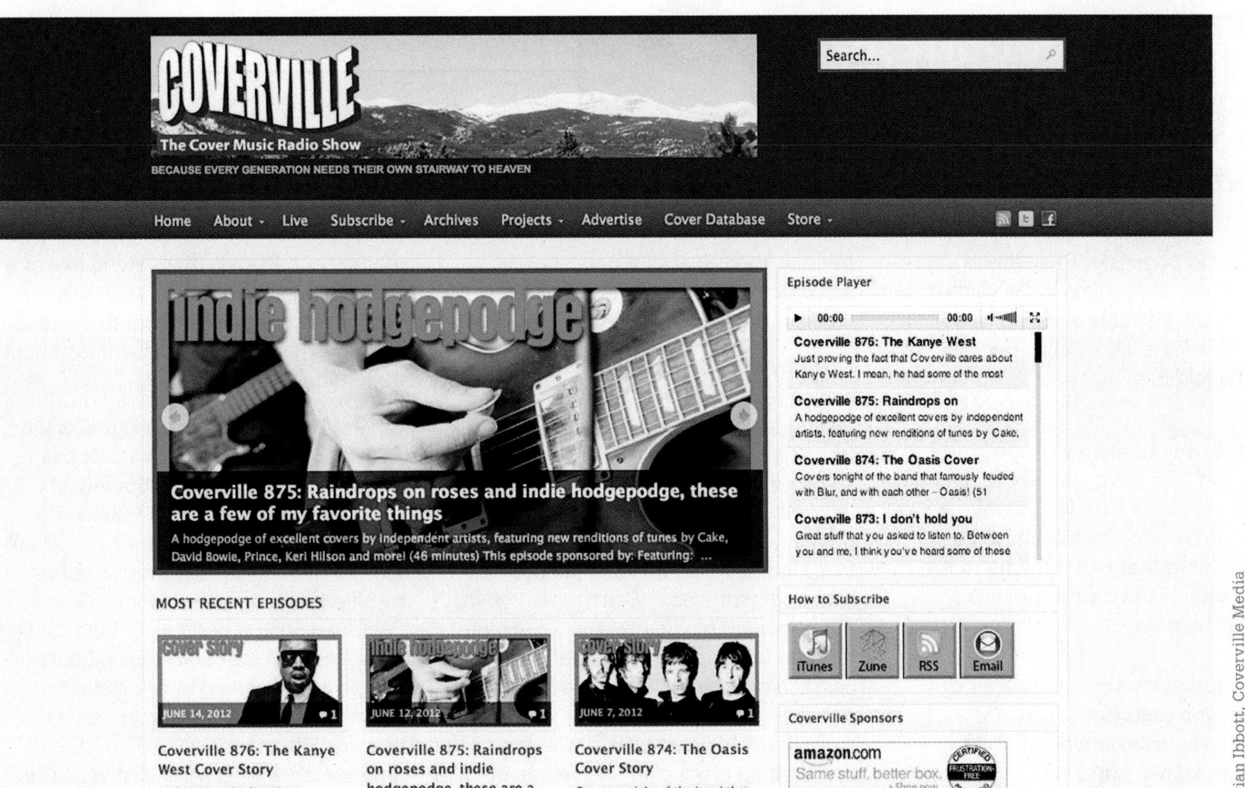

Brian Ibbott, Coverville Media

Brian Ibbott's *Coverville* podcast generally airs three times a week and can feature such unusual songs as the Norwegian version of "Time Warp" from *The Rocky Horror Picture Show.*

Americans listen to an online radio station or other streaming audio service on a monthly basis.[122]

Podcasting. A long-tail alternative to terrestrial radio and prerecorded music is the **podcast**. Podcasts are audio programs distributed over the Internet as MP3 compressed music files that can be listened to online or downloaded to a computer or an MP3 player. They open up distribution of audio programming to anyone with a basic computer and an online connection.

It is difficult to say exactly when podcasting got started, but summer 2004 is the commonly held period because that's when RSS 2.0, which could handle enclosures (essentially attachments) along with straight text, was released. It's also when former MTV VJ Adam Curry and software developer Dave Winer wrote the program iPodder. It was one of the first programs available that could download a podcast off the Internet and transfer it to an iPod. It's much easier to say when podcasting became widely known—February 9, 2005, when *USA Today* ran two articles about the new medium and phenomenon in the paper.[123]

In May 2005, podcasting became easier when Apple's iTunes software started supporting subscriptions to podcasts. You don't need an iPod to listen to a podcast (any computer or MP3 player will do), but iPods have a huge portion of the market, and iTunes support means that even those with low levels of technical sophistication are able to listen to podcasts.[124]

Questioning the Media

How do you listen to audio programs? Do you listen to terrestrial radio? Satellite radio? Podcasts? Streaming services such as Spotify or Pandora? Why do you use these sources?

That's not to say that podcasting is anywhere nearly as popular as radio. As of 2011, 45 percent of Americans said they were aware of podcasts, up only marginally from the 43 percent who were aware of them in 2009. Twenty-five percent of all Americans have listened to an audio podcast, and 12 percent (approximately 35 million) listen to them on a monthly basis. But podcasts have a long way to go to come even close to terrestrial broadcasting in popularity, as 93 percent of Americans aged twelve and older report using AM/FM radio at least once a week.[125]

podcast: An audio program produced as an MP3 compressed music file that can be listened to online at the listener's convenience or downloaded to a computer or an MP3 player. Podcasts sometimes contain video content as well.

Audio 7.8: Listen to several classic episodes of *Coverville*.

MEDIA TRANSFORMATIONS

Creating a Radio Show Without a Radio Station

Colorado podcaster Brian Ibbott says that he's always known he wanted to be a DJ. The only question was what kind of music he would play. Back in 2007, he told me:

> I knew if I did my own show, I wanted it to have something unique and not just a sampling of my favorite music. I wanted it to be something that had a theme to it. And one of the types of music I collect are cover songs.[126]

Ibbott was inspired by a program that aired several years ago on the XM satellite radio channel Special X. "And every day for two hours they had a show that was all covers with no announcing. It was just cover, after cover, after cover," he said. Then Special X got canceled, and Ibbott started dreaming about creating his own show.

The only problem was that Ibbott didn't have a radio station to use to broadcast his program. But then he heard about former MTV VJ Adam Curry's work on software to distribute audio files over the Internet—essentially some of the earliest podcasting software. "I said, I could do this," Ibbott said. "So I just jumped in with both feet." So in September 2004, Ibbott posted his first twenty-six-minute episode of *Coverville* that opened with Jellyfish performing their take on Argent's "Hold Your Head Up." Now, more than ten years later, Ibbott has moved from producing an average of three half-hour shows a week to a single hour-and-a-half to two-hour show each week that has even more of the feel of a conventional radio show. As of this writing, he has posted more than 1,025 episodes, each of which averages about 10,000 downloads.

Coverville is notable for being one of the first podcasts to play music that's been licensed by the **American Society of Composers, Authors and Publishers (ASCAP)** and Broadcast Music Inc. (BMI), the two major organizations that collect royalties for songwriters every time a published song is performed. But reaching the agreement took some doing because no one had ever tried to negotiate the rights for a podcast before. In fact, Ibbott had to explain to the ASCAP representative what a podcast was. They finally set up an agreement similar to that for streaming audio.

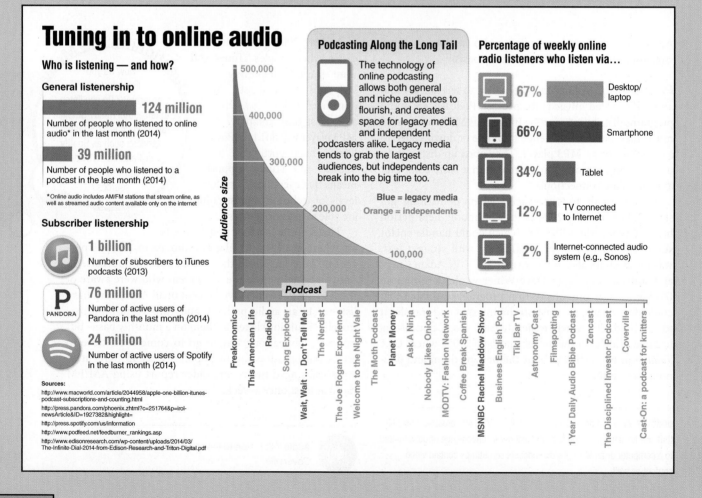

Tuning in to online audio

Who is listening — and how?

General listenership

124 million
Number of people who listened to online audio* in the last month (2014)

39 million
Number of people who listened to a podcast in the last month (2014)

*Online audio includes AM/FM stations that stream online, as well as streamed audio content available only on the internet

Subscriber listenership

1 billion
Number of subscribers to iTunes podcasts (2013)

PANDORA
76 million
Number of active users of Pandora in the last month (2014)

24 million
Number of active users of Spotify in the last month (2014)

Podcasting Along the Long Tail

The technology of online podcasting allows both general and niche audiences to flourish, and creates space for legacy media and independent podcasters alike. Legacy media tends to grab the largest audiences, but independents can break into the big time too.

Blue = legacy media
Orange = independents

Audience size
500,000
400,000
300,000
200,000
100,000
Podcast

Freakonomics
This American Life
Radiolab
Song Exploder
Wait, Wait ... Don't Tell Me!
The Nerdist
The Joe Rogan Experience
Welcome to the Night Vale
The Moth Podcast
Planet Money
Ask A Ninja
Nobody Likes Onions
MODTV: Fashion Network
Coffee Break Spanish
MSNBC Rachel Maddow Show
Business English Pod
Tiki Bar TV
Astronomy Cast
Filmspotting
1 Year Daily Audio Bible Podcast
Zencast
The Disciplined Investor Podcast
Coverville
Cast-On: a podcast for knitters

Percentage of weekly online radio listeners who listen via...

67% Desktop/laptop
66% Smartphone
34% Tablet
12% TV connected to Internet
2% Internet-connected audio system (e.g., Sonos)

Sources:
http://www.macworld.com/article/2044958/apple-one-billion-itunes-podcast-subscriptions-and-counting.html
http://press.pandora.com/phoenix.zhtml?c=251764&p=irol-newsArticle&ID=1927382&highlight=
http://press.spotify.com/us/information
http://www.podfeed.net/feedburner_rankings.asp
http://www.edisonresearch.com/wp-content/uploads/2014/03/The-Infinite-Dial-2014-from-Edison-Research-and-Triton-Digital.pdf

After producing so many episodes, Ibbott has a good handle on what makes for a great cover song:

> It has to be unique. It has to sound like the band covering it and not try to be a note-by-note reproduction f the original. It has to be a good song. It has to stand on its own even if it weren't a cover. It doesn't have to be recognized, but it helps.[127]

Ibbott plays some highly unusual covers, such as William Shatner's version of Pulp's "Common People," but he does have limits. He has a few that he sets aside for a worst-cover-ever show and others that he just won't play. "I stay away from covers done by current pop stars who get enough airplay. There's nothing clever about the cover. It's like their agent said, 'I really like this song. Why don't you do a cover of this?'"[128]

Just as podcasts grew out of combining radio-style programing with Internet distribution of shows that can be listened to on an MP3 player or smartphone, Ibbott's alternative broadcasting efforts continue to grow. Ibbott now has his own twenty-four-hour streaming Coverville Radio that plays covers all day and night with a Web page that tells what songs are going out; he's produced 292 episodes of his *Lyrics Undercover* podcast that gives the story behind popular songs; he co-hosts a four-day-a-week show called *The Morning Stream*; and he has his own record label, Coverville Records.

Media Transformations Questions

- **HOW** have podcasts and streaming media transformed who can create radio-style programming?
- **HOW** do podcasts and streaming media programming differ from what you can get on radio? Think about both content and how you listen.

New Economic Models for the Music Industry

SECRET 5 There can be no question that the many sectors of the sound industry are currently facing a heavy dose of Secret Five—New media are always scary. The issues of file sharing, user-generated content, and music videos (topics also covered in Chapter 9 and Chapter 10) are forcing changes in how radio and the recording industries can make money.

Computer technology has made it easy to manufacture pirate editions of CDs that can be sold on the street at a deep discount. (For that matter, it has made it easy for consumers to "burn" copies of their CDs for their friends for free.) The industry charges that this is stealing from artists and that the new media for distributing music are going to destroy the recording industry. These new technologies are certainly changing the music business, but they probably aren't destroying it.

USA Today's technology writer Kevin Maney points to the example of China, where the music business is thriving even in the face of rampant piracy. Maney argues that in China, most CDs on the market are pirate editions, so artists have no choice but to make an income through live performances, sale of merchandise, and commercial endorsements.[129]

It can be argued that piracy and file sharing hurt the record labels more than they do the musicians. File sharing may even help musicians. Roger McGuinn, former front man of the 1960s band the Byrds, says that he received only a fraction of a cent per record on the early Byrds albums and never saw any royalties at all on a solo album that sold 500,000 copies. How did he make his money? Touring. Now McGuinn gives away tracks on his Web site and sells

AP Photo/Dave Martin

Nine Inch Nails' Trent Reznor, left, and Robin Finck perform during the Bonnaroo Arts and Music Festival in Manchester, Tenn. Reznor offers his recordings as everything from free downloads to autographed deluxe $300 packages.

American Society of Composers, Authors and Publishers (ASCAP): The original organization that collected royalties on musical recordings, performances, publications, and airplay.

CDs that he's recorded at a home studio straight to fans at concerts and online. He tells *USA Today* that these home-produced CDs are the only ones that have made him money.[130] Classical and jazz banjo player Béla Fleck, of Béla Fleck and the Flecktones, makes the majority of his income touring across the United States in the summer. Fleck says his band makes 70 percent of its income from concerts, 20 percent from album sales, and 10 percent from merchandise. The CDs are mostly made to help fans discover his music.[131] Trent Reznor of Nine Inch Nails offers his recordings as free downloads online to save his fans from having to go to file sharing sites. He also helps them share fan videos through his Web site. But according to Techdirt's Mike Masnick, Reznor also offers his music for sale in a variety of packages. With his album *Ghosts I-IV,* fans wanting to pay for the music could buy everything from a pair of CDs for $10 to an autographed "Ultra-Deluxe Limited Edition Package." The $300 edition sold out in thirty hours. Now, granted, Reznor is not a typical musician, but he does illustrate how by interacting with fans in a meaningful way he can make them want to pay him for his music.[132]

Media technology journalist Mark Glaser writes that record labels and artists don't have a "god-given right" to sell CDs for $13 to $18 apiece. He outlines the wide range of choices consumers have now:

> As music lovers, we now have many more choices for how we can get our music fix. We can listen to the radio, to satellite radio, to Internet radio, or hear new music on TV shows like American Idol or on commercials. We can download free music from file-sharing networks [though that can be illegal]. We can hear music straight from the websites of artists, and even get their tracks from MySpace pages. We can buy physical albums from the dwindling number of retail music stores or Wal-Mart and Target, or buy digital tracks or albums from iTunes or other online outlets.[133]

Chapter SUMMARY

The ability to record sounds began in 1877 with Thomas Edison's invention of the phonograph. Though Edison's machine could record and play back sound, it was relatively fragile, and the foil-covered cylinders could not be reproduced and did not stand up to repeated playing. Emile Berliner's gramophone, however, played music on flat discs that were stronger than Edison's cylinders and could be mass produced. This technology allowed musical performances to be stored and replayed. As prerecorded music became widely available, the nature of music consumption changed. People's major contact with music became recordings by professional musicians rather than live performances by amateurs.

Radio was an outgrowth of work done on the telegraph by Samuel Morse. Physicists such as Heinrich Hertz conducted early experiments on the detection of radio waves, but it was Guglielmo Marconi who developed the commercially viable wireless telegraph.

Radio was used initially as a tool for sending messages from one person to another. David Sarnoff was among the first to see radio's potential as a tool for mass communication; CBS founder William Paley saw its potential as an advertising medium that incidentally provided entertainment. KDKA, the first commercial radio station, went on the air in 1920, ushering in the golden age of radio, in which radio was the dominant medium for home entertainment. Radio was also a major source of news, offering an intimacy and immediacy that newspapers couldn't match.

The organizations ASCAP and BMI were established to ensure that musicians and composers would be paid for the music they wrote and performed on stage, on records, and on the radio, as well as for songs they published in written form.

A wide range of recording formats has been used over the years, including the 78-rpm disc, the 45-rpm single, the LP, the compact disc, and the MP3 computer file. Each has given rise to concerns about changes in the purchasing and use of music.

Rock 'n' roll was a hybrid style of music that grew out of white hillbilly music and black rhythm and blues in the late 1940s and early 1950s. Because rock 'n' roll crossed racial lines, it became part of the integration of American society in the 1950s and 1960s. Rock 'n' roll became popular largely through recordings sold in record stores and played on the radio rather than through live performances. It evolved into an art form that existed primarily for recorded playback rather than live performance.

In the 1960s and 1970s, rock music became more heavily produced, and there was a shift from hit singles to albums. Music by groups such as the Beatles and Pink Floyd brought the role of the producer to the forefront, a move that accelerated with the development of disco and rap. Hip-hop culture brought together playing music, talking over the songs, dancing, and a distinctive graffiti art style.

Parents and other adults have expressed concern about lyrics that include profanity, references to suicide and violence, and sentiments that are derogatory toward women.

As television displaced radio as the dominant broadcast medium, radio was transformed into a companion medium with a wide range of formats designed to appeal to narrow, specific audiences. These formats include many types of music, Spanish-language broadcasting, talk, news, and sports.

FM has gradually replaced AM as the dominant radio band. Although FM has a shorter broadcast range, it has much higher-quality sound (higher fidelity).

Although the majority of radio stations are commercial, public radio—a staple of FM radio programming—provides an important alternative. Terrestrial radio is still the dominant sound medium; however, it faces growing competition from digital alternatives such as HD radio, satellite radio, streaming audio, and podcasting.

Keep up-to-date with content from the author's blog.

Take the chapter quiz.

Key TERMS

phonograph 162
gramophone 162
high fidelity (hi-fi) 162
non-notated music 163
telegraph 163
wireless telegraph 163
Radio Music Box memo 163
network 165
golden age of radio 165
soap operas 166
social music 168
rock 'n' roll 168
race records 169
covers 169
girl groups 171
British invasion 171
concept album 172
producer 172
disco 173
hip-hop 173
rap music 174
country music 174
long-playing record (LP) 175
45-rpm disc 176
compact disc (CD) 176
digital recording 176
analog recording 176
MP3 176
format radio 178
shock jocks 180
Federal Communications Commission (FCC) 181
terrestrial radio 183
HD radio 184
satellite radio 184
streaming audio 184
podcast 185
American Society of Composers, Authors and Publishers (ASCAP) 187

Concept REVIEW

Creation of recording industry

Changing ways of experiencing music

Popular music and social change

Role of music producers

Technology and the transformation of the music business

Radio and the transformation of the news business

The changing role of radio

Student STUDY SITE

Sharpen your skills with SAGE edge at **edge.sagepub.com/hanson5e**

SAGE edge for Students provides a personalized approach to help you accomplish your coursework goals in an easy-to-use learning environment.

chapter 8

Movies

Mass Producing Entertainment

AP Photo/Rebecca Blackwell

Mexican filmmaker Alfonso Cuarón had a huge hit with his movie Gravity, which featured sparse dialog, a small cast, and dramatic 3D cinematography.

Warner Bros./Photofest

Sandra Bullock stars in the Alfonso Cuarón 3D film Gravity. Although George Clooney co-stars in the movie, most of the movie has Bullock on her own, trying to survive a space disaster.

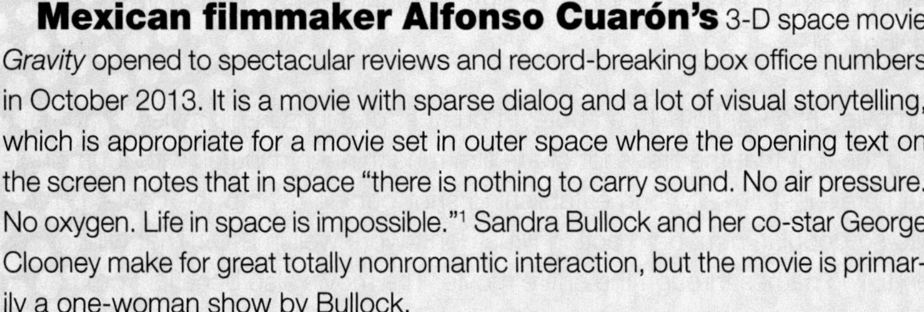

Mexican filmmaker Alfonso Cuarón's 3-D space movie *Gravity* opened to spectacular reviews and record-breaking box office numbers in October 2013. It is a movie with sparse dialog and a lot of visual storytelling, which is appropriate for a movie set in outer space where the opening text on the screen notes that in space "there is nothing to carry sound. No air pressure. No oxygen. Life in space is impossible."[1] Sandra Bullock and her co-star George Clooney make for great totally nonromantic interaction, but the movie is primarily a one-woman show by Bullock.

Gravity was Cuarón's seventh film, and he tells *Vulture* that he can't quite believe he could pull it off. "We got away with it. That's the thing. It's a very unlikely film, first of all, to put together. It's basically one character floating in space."[2] This movie wasn't Cuarón's first well-regarded science fiction/fantasy story—he'd also made *Harry Potter and the Prisoner of Azkaban* (which many, including your author, consider to be the best of the Harry Potter movies) and the dystopian *Children of Men*.

Cuarón grew up in Mexico City, and knew at a young age that he wanted to direct movies. Alfonso's younger brother Carlos remembers when Alfonso first got a camera at age twelve. "He was a huge pain in the ass, shooting everything. My sister and I became his prop, his stunt, whatever. It was unbearable. He would repeat that he was going to be film director again and again."[3]

Cuarón continued his tradition of being unbearable in film school, where he got expelled prior to graduation. He then finished learning his craft by working as everything from a microphone carrier to an assistant director.

Cuarón co-wrote the movie with his son Jonas, who describes the movie they wanted to make this way:

> Basically we wanted to make a 90-minute movie that would grip the audience with suspense and tension. It would be like a roller coaster ride but at the same time it would be a film that also connects with the audience on an emotional level. . . . We also wanted to speak about different themes without stopping the action with dialogue. We wanted to use the action to bring the themes that interested the two of us.[4]

Like most great movies, *Gravity*'s success wasn't an accident. It was conceived and shot as a 3-D movie from the very beginning. Cuarón planned *Gravity* as a 3-D movie even before *Avatar* was busy showing the world what could be done with really great 3-D in 2010. (I know, I know—many of you absolutely hated the derivative *Dances With Wolves* storyline and rehashing of the human villains from *Aliens* in *Avatar*, but that doesn't change the fact that it had extraordinary visual storytelling.)

Every shot in *Gravity* was planned around how it would look in 3-D. Eric Eisenberg writes at the *CinemaBlend* blog that Cuarón uses 3-D to create "deep, immersive environments."[5] What makes this 3-D movie so fascinating

LEARNING OBJECTIVES

After studying this chapter, you will be able to:

1. Explain what the studio system was like and why it ended.
2. Discuss how the growth of television and home video transformed the movie industry.
3. Explain what is meant by the "blockbuster era" in the movie industry and how movies have become brands.
4. Explain how digital production and projection have changed filmmaking.
5. Discuss the evolution of the ratings system using examples of different movies.
6. Explain how the Internet and other long-tail tools have changed the movie promotion and distribution process.

is that for the most part neither director/co-screenwriter Cuarón nor co-star George Clooney particularly likes 3-D, especially when it is tacked on just to generate higher ticket prices.[6] Cuarón is quoted at Complex.com as saying:

> The problem now is that they make all these films that are not designed for 3D and then convert them as a commercial afterthought—and they are crap. They don't follow the rules of 3D of what does and doesn't work. There are a handful of films that have used 3D in a proper way so it can be an amazing tool.[7]

Los Angeles Times movie critic Kenneth Turan notes a number of things in his review that make *Gravity* special, including the fact that the first shot of the film runs thirteen minutes without a single cut.[8] No rapid-fire edits here—just a really long establishing shot putting us into the context of the film. (The rapid-fire edits so popular in modern action films don't work well in 3-D.) That willingness to engage in brave storytelling carries through the entire movie. The movie also benefits from having a unified voice. The screenplay was written by Alfonso Cuarón and his son Jonas. This means that the movie did not suffer from endless second-guessing from the studio about the script. It also means that the director and his son had a really good idea of what they were going to do from the very beginning.

Cuarón's fellow director Brad Bird, famous for *Mission Impossible: Ghost Protocol, The Incredibles*, and the woefully underappreciated *Iron Giant*, sent out a series of tweets about what makes *Gravity* important, and what kind of an influence Cuarón's work will have on the movie industry. He wrote:

> GRAVITY is a master class in film direction, as harrowing as it is haunting & beautiful. Bullock & Clooney are Terrific. Cuaron CRUSHES IT.

Timeline

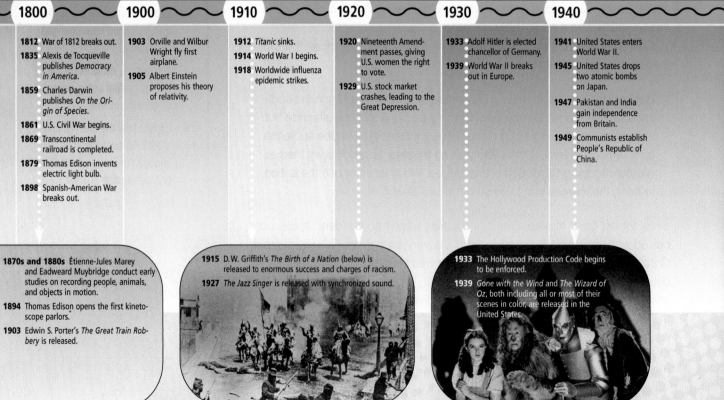

1800

1812 War of 1812 breaks out.
1835 Alexis de Tocqueville publishes *Democracy in America*.
1859 Charles Darwin publishes *On the Origin of Species*.
1861 U.S. Civil War begins.
1869 Transcontinental railroad is completed.
1879 Thomas Edison invents electric light bulb.
1898 Spanish-American War breaks out.

1870s and 1880s Étienne-Jules Marey and Eadweard Muybridge conduct early studies on recording people, animals, and objects in motion.
1894 Thomas Edison opens the first kinetoscope parlors.
1903 Edwin S. Porter's *The Great Train Robbery* is released.

1900

1903 Orville and Wilbur Wright fly first airplane.
1905 Albert Einstein proposes his theory of relativity.

1910

1912 *Titanic* sinks.
1914 World War I begins.
1918 Worldwide influenza epidemic strikes.

1915 D.W. Griffith's *The Birth of a Nation* (below) is released to enormous success and charges of racism.
1927 *The Jazz Singer* is released with synchronized sound.

AP Photo

1920

1920 Nineteenth Amendment passes, giving U.S. women the right to vote.
1929 U.S. stock market crashes, leading to the Great Depression.

1930

1933 Adolf Hitler is elected chancellor of Germany.
1939 World War II breaks out in Europe.

1933 The Hollywood Production Code begins to be enforced.
1939 *Gone with the Wind* and *The Wizard of Oz*, both including all or most of their scenes in color, are released in the United States.

AP Photo

1940

1941 United States enters World War II.
1945 United States drops two atomic bombs on Japan.
1947 Pakistan and India gain independence from Britain.
1949 Communists establish People's Republic of China.

More than most films, GRAVITY . . . is visual storytelling, like a silent film. The shots are deeply thought out.

In answer to the question "But does the 3D in GRAVITY help improve the narrative or just the visuals?" Bird makes his most important point: "In GRAVITY, the visuals ARE the narrative."

Bird warns, however, that Hollywood will likely miss the important message of *Gravity*:

GRAVITY's $ucce$$ will lead to a new round of 3D films NOT conceived for 3D, as DARK KNIGHT's success led to "IMAX" films NOT shot in IMAX.[9]

Regardless of the size of a movie's budget, profits, or spectacle, we still go to the movies for the same basic reason: to escape from the world around us. We spend a couple of hours in a darkened room with a group of people and share a created experience—a bit of excitement, sentiment, or romance. In this chapter, we look at how the movie industry developed from peep show kinetoscopes to today's IMAX theaters. We examine the roles of movies in society, public concerns about movies, and efforts by government and industry to regulate the content of films. ■

> "The problem now is that they make all these films that are not designed for 3D and then convert them as a commercial afterthought—and they are crap."
>
> —Alfonso Cuarón

Web 8.1: Read more about what made *Gravity* such a success.

Video 8.1: See animation and early movie examples from Muybridge, Edison, and Porter.

1950

1950 Korean War begins.
1953 Francis Crick and James Watson discover structure of DNA.
1957 Soviet Union launches spacecraft *Sputnik I*.

1960

1963 Martin Luther King Jr. delivers "I Have a Dream" speech during Washington, D.C., civil-rights march.
1969 Neil Armstrong walks on the moon.

1970

1974 U.S. president Richard Nixon resigns due to Watergate scandal.
1975 Vietnam War ends.
1977 Apple II personal computer is introduced.
1978 First test-tube baby is born.

1980

1983 First HIV/AIDS cases are documented.
Ozone hole is discovered over Antarctica.
1986 Space shuttle *Challenger* explodes.
1989 The Berlin Wall falls.

1990

1991 Soviet Union disbands.
1993 European Union is formed.
1994 Nelson Mandela is elected president of South Africa.
1997 Diana, Princess of Wales, dies in car accident.

2000-

2001 Al Qaida attacks World Trade Center and Pen-tagon.
2003 United States invades Iraq.
2008 Barack Obama is elected U.S. president.
2011 Earthquake and tsunami hit Japan. United States end seight-year war with Iraq.
2012 Superstorm Sandy devastates U.S. eastern seaboard.
2014 Russian army invades Ukraine.

1947–1950s Committee hearings on communism in Hollywood begin the blacklist era.
1968 Movie ratings replace the Production Code.

1947– House Un-American Activities

AP Photo

1976 The first movies are released on home video.

©iStockphoto.com/Ju-Lee

1999 *The Blair Witch Project* demonstrates that a small-budget film can be enormously successful.
2005 U.S. box office revenues decrease for the first time since 1991.
2007 Oscar-nominated short films are sold as downloads from Apple's iTunes store.
2010 James Cameron's *Avatar* replaces *Titanic* as movie box office champion.
2012 Silent, black and white film *The Artist* wins Oscar for Best Picture.
2012 More people are streaming movies than watching DVDs or other physical media.
2014 Alfonso Cuarón wins Oscar for best director for his 3-D blockbuster *Gravity*.

©James Leynse/Corbis

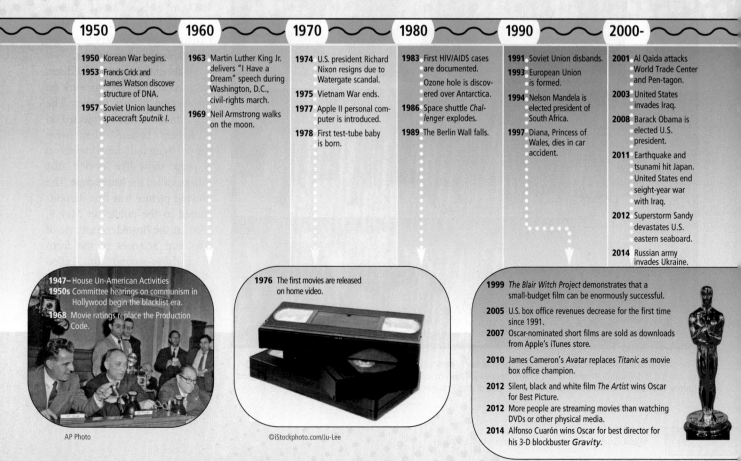

The Development of Movies

The movie industry has its roots in the 1880s, but it wasn't until the early twentieth century that movies became a major public entertainment. In the late 1920s and early 1930s, movies gradually grew from ten-minute silent films into talking films up to two hours long. Although movie attendance peaked in the 1940s, viewing movies in theaters remains popular today, despite competition from television and home video.

The First Moviemakers 

Thomas Edison is generally credited with developing the American motion picture industry, but like other media, movies came into being because of the work of many people; Edison was just one of several scientists and engineers who created the new medium of film.

Edison, Marey, and Muybridge. In the 1870s and 1880s, at least two people were working on the problem of capturing and portraying motion. The first was Étienne-Jules Marey. Trained in medicine, Marey sought to measure and transcribe motion, starting with blood and the heart and then progressing on to how animals move. While Marey was never able to project moving pictures, he did help develop systems for taking repeated photos of people and animals in motion.[10]

British photographer Eadweard Muybridge was the second major influence on Edison. Muybridge, like Marey, wanted to capture the motion of animals on film. To settle a bet, the governor of California hired him to establish whether all four hooves of a horse leave the ground when it is galloping.[11] Muybridge set up twenty-four cameras at evenly spaced locations around a racetrack. Tripwires allowed the passing horse to trigger the cameras. Muybridge then projected the images using a type of zoetrope, a child's toy that put a series of images on a spinning cylinder. He was thus able to establish that all four hooves do leave the ground during a gallop.

Muybridge eventually photographed both animals and humans moving against a black-and-white grid; his photos were published in 1887 in a book titled *Animal Locomotion.* He became a celebrity, touring the country to lecture and display his photographs.

At about the same time, Edison assigned an employee to work on the motion picture project. The first movies were not projected on a screen; instead, they were viewed by an individual viewer on a peep show–like device that Edison called the **kinetoscope**. The moving picture was first demonstrated to the public on May 9, 1893, at the Brooklyn Institute of Arts and Sciences in the form of a thirty-second film called *Blacksmith Scene.* Other early films showed a man sneezing,

Eadweard Muybridge/George Eastman House via Getty Images

The photos of a woman in motion in this collection are typical of the images Eadweard Muybridge created for his book *Animal Locomotion.* With these repeated photographs, Muybridge demonstrated that you could create an illusion of motion by displaying a series of still images.

kinetoscope: An early peep show–like movie projection system developed by Thomas Edison that could be used only by an individual viewer.

"Sandow the Strong Man" displaying his muscles, and Annie Oakley riding her horse.

The kinetoscope was soon replaced by a system in which films were projected on a screen, and the viewing of movies was transformed from a solitary activity to a group experience. The first American theaters grew out of the penny arcades where kinetoscopes had been located. These early theaters came to be known as "nickelodeons" because tickets cost five cents. By 1900, the nickelodeon theaters were a popular form of entertainment throughout American cities.

Library of Congress

Young people in the 1940s dressed a little more formally when they went to the movies than do today's movie audiences, but these Chicago moviegoers were still looking to have fun away from parental supervision for an afternoon or evening.

Early French Filmmakers. In France, brothers Auguste-Marie and Louis-Jean Lumière started working with Edison's motion picture ideas in 1894. They created what they called a *cinématographe*, a portable movie camera that could also be used as a projector. The brothers also set the standards for the speed at which film would be shot and for the format of the film, details that Edison would eventually adopt. On December 28, 1895, they opened their first theater, where they showed short movies portraying everyday life in families, at factories, and on the street.

One of the earliest films to tell a story rather than record everyday life was created by another Frenchman, Georges Méliès. His most famous film was the 1902 *A Trip to the Moon*, which featured special effects such as a spaceship hitting the man in the moon in the eye. But although it told a story, it was essentially a stage show captured on film.[12]

Edwin S. Porter: Telling a Story With Film. Edwin S. Porter expanded on Méliès's ideas to create one of the first hit movies in the United States. While working as a projectionist for Edison, Porter saw Méliès's *Trip to the Moon* many times. He soon started making movies for Edison, most notably the 1903 film *The Great Train Robbery.* Porter laid out almost every element of the action in the film, which tells the story of a group of outlaws who get on a train, rob the strongbox and the passengers, kill everyone who gets in their way, and are eventually shot and killed by the posse hunting them down. The movie, containing twelve separate scenes shot in a variety of locations, tells a realistic story. *The Great Train Robbery* helped establish how stories could be told through film. It is also an early example of Secret Five—New media are always scary. After all, Porter's film showed audiences exactly how to go about robbing a train.[13]

D. W. Griffith: The Birth of the Blockbuster. Director D. W. Griffith was the George Lucas or Steven Spielberg of the silent-movie era, creating epic films that captured the entire nation's imagination. At a time when most directors were making movies that ran for twenty-five minutes at most, Griffith produced films that ran for an hour or more. In essence, Griffith created the first modern **feature-length film**. Griffith's most significant film—*The Birth of a Nation,* released in 1915—tells the story of the rise of the Ku Klux Klan in the years following the Civil War. The film runs for over three hours and, at a cost of more than $110,000, was the most expensive movie to date. It also cost audiences more to see it; tickets were $2 in the big cities at a time when admission to most pictures was less than a dollar.

Based on Thomas Dixon's book *The Clansman*, Griffith's film is blatantly racist. At the time of its release, the film was criticized for a range of reasons, including its portrayal of African Americans as "nothing but beasts" and its attack on the North. One critic, referring to the three miles of film used in making the movie, called it "three miles of filth."[14]

Griffith soon outdid himself with another movie, *Intolerance*, which ran even longer than *The Birth of a*

feature-length film: A theatrical movie that runs more than one hour.

Video 8.2: Watch a nearly three-hour cut of *Intolerance*.

Nation. It cost nearly $500,000 to make and tells four separate stories spread out over a period of 2,500 years. It is a bold, dramatic film, but it was a financial failure, costing Griffith the fortune he had made with *The Birth of a Nation*.

Intolerance marked the point at which outside financial backing became necessary for a movie to get produced. Today the only exceptions to this are low-budget movies, such as *The Blair Witch Project*, and movies made by very wealthy directors, such as George Lucas. (Lucas financed the *Star Wars* prequel series, Episodes I, II, and III, in part with profits from *Star Wars* merchandise and his special-effects house, Industrial Light and Magic. He eventually sold his company Lucasfilm to Disney in 2012.)

Outside financing means that directors are accountable to the people who control the purse strings. Few directors today have the right to a "final cut," or final version, of the movie. That right is generally reserved by the people who control the money.[15]

Movie Stars. In the early days of the movie industry, studios were reluctant to give actors screen credit for fear that this would encourage them to ask for more money. But the studios soon discovered that the public liked some actors and actresses better than others and were more likely to go to a movie featuring one of their favorites.

Directors such as D. W. Griffith employed a group of regular players in all their films. Florence Lawrence was one of the first to break out of this anonymous group; Griffith's studio, Biograph, paid her a stunning (for the time) $25 a week. Linda Griffith, D. W.'s wife, wrote in a memoir, "[Florence's] pictures became tremendously popular, and soon all over the country Miss Lawrence was known as 'The Biograph Girl.'"[16] After Lawrence left Biograph for a rival studio, Independent Motion Picture, she became one of the first actresses to receive a screen credit.[17]

The Studio System

Why are so many movies made in Hollywood? Although the earliest movies were filmed in New Jersey and New York, the appeal of southern California soon became apparent. One argument for going west was to get away from Thomas Edison's "patent police," who tried to control the use of movie technology. But California also offered almost constant sunlight, as well as the varied settings of ocean, desert, and mountains. In addition, the new movie studios needed a great deal of space, and at the beginning of the twentieth century, land in California was still relatively cheap.

At about the same time, the movie studios figured out that the most effective way to produce movies was with a factory-like process known as the **studio system**, in which all of the talent worked directly for the movie studios. Paramount Pictures, MGM, Warner Brothers, and other major studios controlled every aspect of the production process, from writing to editing. They employed a number of writers, directors, and actors ("stars") who were under contract to work for a weekly salary. The movies were put together in assembly-line fashion. The studios also had almost absolute control of the distribution system.

Distribution was carried out in two ways. The first way was **block bookings**, in which theater owners were required to book a whole series of movies in order to get a few desirable films. The studio package might offer four headliner movies with big-name stars, ten mid-range pictures, ten more low-level films, and twelve no-star, bottom-of-the-line pictures. Sometimes salespeople insisted that theaters take the studio's entire package of fifty-two films, one for each week of the year. The second, and even more effective, way for studios to guarantee that their movies would be shown was to buy up theaters.[18]

United Artists. Actors and directors soon rebelled against the controls placed on them by the studio system. Despite being pampered and well paid, they had to make the movies the studios told them to make. By 1919, several of the most popular performers and directors, including D. W. Griffith, Charlie Chaplin, Mary Pickford, and Douglas Fairbanks, joined forces to create their own company, United Artists.

Instead of producing movies as the other major studios did, United Artists acquired and distributed movies after independent film producers had completed them. United Artists was essentially a model for the modern film studio—not a maker of films but a distributor and a source of financing.

United Artists remained a significant independent force in the movies until 1981, when one of its movies, Michael Cimino's *Heaven's Gate*, managed to lose almost its entire cost of production—$44 million—forcing the nearly bankrupt studio to merge with MGM. (*Heaven's Gate* is a dusty, confusing, and depressing western that was relatively expensive for the time it came out.[19])

Talking Pictures. In terms of technological developments in the movies, color and black-and-white movies coexisted for many years, but movies with sound replaced silent films almost immediately. Once people had both seen and heard their favorite stars, there was no turning back.[20]

Video 8.3: Watch the documentary *Final Cut: The Making and Unmaking of* Heaven's Gate.

studio system: A factory-like way of producing films that involved having all of the talent, including the actors and directors, working directly for the movie studios. The studios also had almost total control of the distribution system.

block bookings: Requiring a theater owner to take a whole series of movies in order to get a few desirable, headliner films. This system was eventually found to violate antitrust laws.

Although many people point to *The Jazz Singer*, released in 1927, as the first talking film, it was actually a silent film with two talking (and singing) segments. The first successful demonstration of the talking picture was a series of short films that accompanied the feature *Don Juan* in 1926. *Don Juan* was a silent film, but it had a **synchronized soundtrack** (wherein sounds are synchronized with the pictures in a movie) with musical accompaniment, and the accompanying films demonstrated the equipment that would make talking films possible. This set of short films included performances by opera singers and a talk by Will H. Hays, president of the Motion Picture Producers and Distributors of America.

Library of Congress

The silent movie stars "sweet" Mary Pickford and "swashbuckling" Douglas Fairbanks were one of the first Hollywood power couples and were two of the founders of the United Artists movie studio.

The Jazz Singer was called a **talkie**—a movie with synchronized sound—but it was the singing as much as the talking that impressed most people. In the movie, Al Jolson, talking to his mother, delivered one of the cinema's most prophetic lines, "Come on, Ma. Listen to this."[21] The public loved it. It was talking pictures such as *The Jazz Singer* that helped build Warner Bros. into one of the nation's premier movie studios. Until then, Warner Bros. had been a relatively small player. The studio's breakthrough came with the realization that talkies were about more than talk. As Harry Warner put it, "If it can talk, it can sing."[22]

SECRET 5 The movie industry as a whole was leery of talking pictures for a couple of reasons. On the simplest level, talking pictures in the early days required that stars be able to speak well while acting, something that wasn't necessarily easy to do. (In the contemporary movie industry, much of the dialogue is rerecorded after the photography is finished.) A bigger problem was that talking pictures were expensive. Not only did theaters have to upgrade their equipment, but the noisy movie projectors had to be muffled in soundproof booths. Sound issues existed during the filming process as well, as noisy equipment that allowed cameras to swoop around the actors couldn't be used. This problem restricted the camera's mobility in the early talkies and kept them from being as visually interesting as the best of the silent films, such as *Metropolis* or *Nosferatu*. There was also the problem of noise in the vicinity of the studios (such as the roar of passing trains). Even the bright arc lights used to light the sets made a sizzling sound that had to be eliminated. As one industry observer noted, "It was easy to make pictures, easy to make records; but another matter to make them together."[23] (And this is another example of Secret Five—New media are always scary . . . especially to the media industry.)

The influence of talking films soon gave rise to concerns like those familiar to us today. One newspaper columnist complained,

> The talkies will make Hollywood the slang center of the United States. . . . A wisecrack recorded in Hollywood will be heard in all corners of the country months before the same quip could travel from town to town across the continent with a road show or a vaudeville troupe.[24]

It took awhile for the talking movies to find their way. As one critic pointed out in *Harper's* in 1929, the talkies were neither plays nor silent movies. They were something new, and Hollywood had to determine what that was. Writers, directors, and actors had to figure out what could be done with the new medium. Animation pioneer Walt Disney, for example, saw sound more as a way to add music and sound effects to his cartoons than as a way to make them talk.[25] In recent years, the quality of sound has become increasingly important, both in theaters and at home. George Lucas's *Star Wars*, released in 1977, broke new ground not only with its visual effects, but also with its sound effects. It was among the first movies to fully exploit the Dolby sound system, and the Lucas-developed THX theater sound system has become a standard for high-quality movie sound.

---

synchronized soundtrack: Sound effects, music, and voices synchronized with the moving images in a movie.

talkie: A movie with synchronized sound; these quickly replaced silent films.

AP Photo

The congressional hearings on communists in Hollywood extended over a several-year period. This photo shows actor Lionel Stander testifying before the House Un-American Activities Committee in 1953.

The End of the Studio System. By 1938, the U.S. Department of Justice was starting to view the movie studio system as a monopoly that needed to be brought under control. It decided to make a test case of Paramount Pictures. Paramount and the other major studios were charged with conspiring to set the terms for theaters renting their films—requiring them to charge certain minimum prices and to accept block booking—and discriminating in favor of certain theaters. The studios also worked to keep independent films out of theaters they owned.

An early portion of the settlement of what became known as the "Hollywood Antitrust Case"[26] required studios to show theater owners films before booking them, limit block bookings to five movies at a time, and no longer force theaters to book short films. But the power of the studios was not truly dismantled until 1948 when the U.S. Supreme Court ruled that the studios must sell their theaters. This final portion of the case's settlement led to the system in use today, in which the studios primarily finance and distribute films produced by independent companies rather than make movies themselves with their own staff.[27]

Video 8.4: The cast of *Singing in the Rain* attempts to shoot their first "talking" scene.

Video 8.5: Watch a short 1950 documentary on the Hollywood Ten.

The Blacklist

SECRET 5 The years following World War II were a dark time for the movie industry. The studios' power was diminished by the Supreme Court's rulings in the antitrust case, and some politicians had an overwhelming fear that Hollywood and its movies might be playing a role in spreading communism. In 1947, a congressional committee known as the **House Un-American Activities Committee**, under the leadership of Parnell Thomas, held hearings on possible communist influences in Hollywood.

In his introductory remarks, Thomas laid out the fears quite clearly:

> We all recognize, certainly, the tremendous effect which moving pictures have on their mass audiences, far removed from the Hollywood sets. We all recognize that what the citizen sees and hears in his neighborhood movie house carries a powerful impact on his thoughts and behavior.
>
> With such vast influence over the lives of American citizens as the motion-picture industry exerts, it is not unnatural—in fact, it is very logical—that subversive and undemocratic forces should attempt to use this medium for un-American purposes.[28]

It is this legacy of fear—fear that the movies and other media could have undesirable effects on unsuspecting audience members (remember Secret Five—New media are always scary)—that led to the research and controls on the movie industry. (This topic is discussed in depth later in this chapter.)

Two weeks of committee hearings were held, the most divisive of which involved ten "unfriendly witnesses" who questioned the right of the committee to ask them about their associations and beliefs. The committee repeatedly asked the question, "Are you now, or have you ever been, a communist?" Instead of answering, the witnesses, known as the **Hollywood Ten**, challenged the constitutionality of the hearings. They were jailed for contempt of Congress, and the movie industry instituted a **blacklist** that banned anyone from working in Hollywood who was a known communist, a suspected communist, or a communist sympathizer.[29]

House Un-American Activities Committee: A congressional committee chaired by Parnell Thomas that held hearings on the influence of communism on Hollywood in 1947. These activities mirrored a wider effort to root out suspected communists in all walks of American life.

Hollywood Ten: A group of ten writers and directors who refused to testify before the House Un-American Activities Committee about their political activities. They were among the first people in Hollywood to be blacklisted.

In December 1949, Parnell Thomas was convicted of padding his payroll and went to jail himself. But hearings continued under new leadership in the early 1950s, and by 1953, the blacklist contained the names of as many as 324 suspected communists. The contracts of those who were blacklisted could be canceled; if they were freelancers, the studios simply wouldn't buy their work.[30]

The hearings tore Hollywood apart. Some of the unfriendly witnesses had to move. The uncooperative witnesses lost their jobs and were ostracized, and those who had provided names were viewed as informers.

©Johannes Eisele/dpa/Corbis

German director Wim Wenders (left) and German chancellor Angela Merkel are wearing 3-D glasses at a screening of the film *Pina* at the 61st Berlin International Film Festival.

While the blacklist was in place, several writers continued to sell screenplays under assumed names or wrote screenplays without receiving any credit at all. In 1956, Dalton Trumbo, writing under the name Robert Rich, won an unclaimed Academy Award for his screenplay for *The Brave One*. In 1957, David Lean's epic movie *The Bridge on the River Kwai* won an Oscar for best screenplay. The script, written by Carl Foreman and Michael Wilson, was based on a novel by the French author Pierre Boulle. But since the scriptwriters were blacklisted, the credit went to Boulle, who could not write or speak English.[31] (And in case you were wondering, Boulle also wrote the novel that inspired the *Planet of the Apes* movie series.) The blacklist was finally broken in 1960, when Trumbo received screenwriting credits for the films *Spartacus* and *Exodus*.

Television and the Movies

In the 1950s, people began turning to television rather than movies for routine entertainment. The exodus of families to the suburbs also contributed to a decline in movie audiences, especially in the old urban Art Deco movie palaces. Sports, both professional and collegiate, started drawing audiences away from the movies as well.[32]

In 1946, movie audiences reached their peak, and 80 million tickets were sold every week. But by 1953, ticket sales had dropped by almost half, to 46 million a week. It was clear that Hollywood would have to do something to reverse this trend.

Larger-Than-Life Movies. One thing Hollywood did to entice viewers away from television was to make the movies shown in theaters bigger and better than before. Hollywood tried three-dimensional (3-D) movies, but they required special projection equipment and 3-D glasses. The gimmick started out successfully, but people soon became bored with the novelty, which ultimately added little to the movie experience. Almost the only serious movie to be released in the 3-D format in its first incarnation was Alfred Hitchcock's *Dial M for Murder*. The 3-D format experienced a revival in the 2000s, especially with movies targeted at children, such as Pixar's *Up* and Brendan Fraser's *Journey to the Center of the Earth*.[33] But now many big-budget action movies get a 3-D release as well, whether they were designed for 3-D or not, with goal of drawing in the higher ticket prices that 3-D movies command. And, of course, there are the rare films envisioned as 3-D movies from the start, such as James Cameron's *Avatar*, Ridley Scott's *Prometheus*, and Alfonso Cuarón's *Gravity*.

After the first effort to popularize 3-D films fizzled out, more successful were attempts to project a larger picture on the screen. The most extreme of these was the Cinerama process, in which each scene was filmed from three slightly different angles and projected on a huge curved screen using three projectors. The purpose was to create the feeling of realism through the use of peripheral vision. The Cinerama theaters could also handle smaller wide-screen systems such as CinemaScope.

Along with the larger screens came larger movies, including epics such as *The Ten Commandments* and the gladiator movie *Spartacus*. Today, wide-screen technology is starting to find its way into television through the use of digital video discs and high-definition digital broadcasts.

The Advent of Color. Television also helped bring about the conversion to color movies. During the 1950s, television was almost exclusively black and white. Color was first used in Hollywood in the 1920s at about the same time that sound came in, but it was expensive, the studios were

blacklist: A group of people banned from working in the movie industry in the late 1940s and 1950s because they were suspected of being communists or communist sympathizers. Some of them, such as a few screenwriters, were able to work under assumed names, but others never worked again in the industry.

Web 8.2: Learn more about the current 3-D movie revival.

Questioning the Media

Why do you go to the movies? Do you feel that the experience of going to the movies is worth the cost? Why or why not?

focusing on the conversion to sound, and black-and-white film was easier to work with. Still, there are some important color movies from this era. Both *Gone With the Wind* and *The Wizard of Oz* made effective use of color: Think of the vivid images of Dorothy's ruby red slippers—silver in the original L. Frank Baum books—and Scarlett O'Hara's green velvet dress made from the parlor drapes.

Dimension Films/Photofest

Eva Green and Josh Brolin star in *Sin City: A Dame to Kill For,* a movie that is mostly presented mostly in black and white with occasional splashes of color.

One factor that delayed the conversion to color movies was that they initially required a complex camera that shot simultaneously on three separate reels of film (one for each of the three additive colors—cyan, magenta, and yellow). After World War II, American studios adopted a process used in Germany to shoot in color using a single reel of film, which made color filming much easier. Competition from television forced Hollywood to start using color in virtually every film from the 1950s on.[34]

Occasionally, period-piece movies will be released in black and white for effect—think of 2011's multiple-Oscar-winning *The Artist* (which was also largely a silent film with a musical soundtrack); the 2005 Oscar-nominated *Good Night, and Good Luck*; or *Schindler's List,* which won the Oscar for best picture in 1993. (Come to think of it, maybe shooting a movie in black and white is a good way to get an Oscar . . .) Other movies are shot predominantly in black and white such as the live-action/computer-animation blend *Sin City* and Tim Burton's animated *Frankenweenie.* More recently, Alexander Payne's *Nebraska,* which is set in the present day, was done completely in black and white.

The Growth of Multiplex Theaters. In recent decades movie theaters themselves have been changing to meet the needs of a changing audience. As large numbers of people moved from cities to suburbs, the vast Art Deco movie palaces that seated as many as 2,000 people were no longer being filled. Gradually, these megatheaters have been replaced by smaller theaters grouped together in what is known as a **multiplex**. These have a single box office and concession stand, but contain anywhere from three to twenty screens. Each of the auditoriums is relatively small, but when a major movie is released, it can be shown in several of the theaters.[35] The number of theater screens declined in 2000 and 2001 to approximately 25,000 but has grown in recent years to almost 39,000. Many of these new theaters feature stadium seating, improved sound systems, and premium refreshments, such as real butter on the gourmet popcorn.[36]

Video 8.6: Watch the trailer for *The Artist*.

Web 8.3: Check out Gordon McAlpin's Multiplex Web comic *A Night in the Patio*.

The Movie Business

If the early 1900s were the silent-film era and the 1930s and 1940s were the studio era, then the period from the late 1970s to the present day is the **blockbuster era**, in which studios try to make relatively expensive movies with a large, predefined audience. These movies are packaged with cable deals and marketing tie-ins, such as McDonald's Happy Meal toys.

The Blockbuster Era

Steven Spielberg is generally credited with creating the blockbuster era with the release of his 1975 summer hit *Jaws.* It was the first movie to gross more than $200 million, and it set the stage for the big summer movies. Prior to *Jaws*, it was believed that a movie had to be released during the Christmas season to be a major success. *Jaws*

multiplex: A group of movie theaters with anywhere from three to twenty screens that share a common box office and concession stand. Largely a suburban phenomenon at first, they replaced the old urban Art Deco movie palaces.

blockbuster era: A period from the late 1970s to the present day in which movie studios make relatively expensive movies that have a large, predefined audience. These movies, usually chock-full of special effects, are packaged with cable deals and marketing tie-ins, and they can be extremely lucrative if they are able to attract large repeat audiences.

had a number of things going for it: It was directed by one of the most popular directors of the late twentieth century, it featured a compelling musical score by John Williams, and it was based on a best-selling novel by Peter Benchley.

Jaws was accompanied by a giant television advertising campaign that began three days before the movie's release. But the marketing of the movie had started two years earlier with an announcement that the movie rights had been acquired and speculation about who the stars might be. Journalists were taken to the production site in record numbers to keep the stories flowing. The movie's release was scheduled to occur within six months of the publication of the paperback book, and the book's cover included a tie-in to the movie. As the release date for the movie approached, copies of the paperback were sent out to waiters, cab drivers, and other ordinary people to build word of mouth. Finally, the movie was given a summer release date to capitalize on the beach and swimming season.

The *Jaws* campaign was designed to get people to the movie and talk about it. If the talk had been negative, all the advertising in the world couldn't have saved the movie. But with everyone talking up the movie, *Jaws* took off.[37]

The success of *Jaws* started a tradition of larger-than-life summer movies that continued with the *Star Wars* trilogies, the *Indiana Jones* series, Christopher Nolan's *Batman: Dark Knight* trilogy, and the *Pirates of the Caribbean* series. Some observers have gone so far as to describe the summer blockbuster movie as "a wide-screen, color, stereophonic *ride*."[38] The description is apt, because by the 1990s, many of the studios had followed Disney's lead and produced theme parks with rides based on movies. In some cases, the ride has cost more to produce than the movie itself. The most recent example is the Wizarding World of Harry Potter attraction at the Universal Orlando theme park in Florida, which opened in the spring of 2010 and cost an estimated $265 million to construct. As of this writing, the Orlando park has just opened Diagon Alley, a second major section of the attraction, Universal Studios Japan has opened its new $422 million Harry Potter attraction, and the Universal Studios Hollywood Park has its Harry Potter attraction under construction. (Interestingly enough, there's a huge amount of cross-corporate partnerships going on here. The rights to the books are owned by Scholastic; the rights to just about everything else are owned by Warner Bros., a unit of Time Warner. But the theme park was constructed by Universal, a unit of NBCUniversal, which has cable giant Comcast as its owner. Got that?[39])

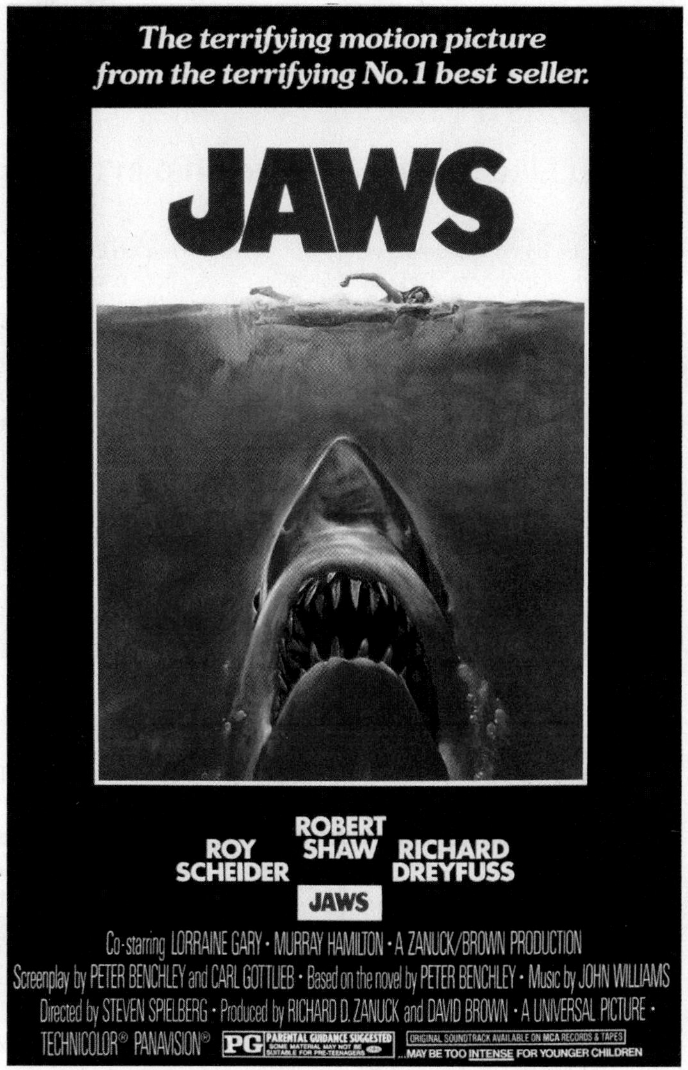

Pictorial Press Ltd/Alamy

Steven Spielberg created the summer blockbuster film with *Jaws*. The 1975 film was the first movie to gross more than $200 million.

Due to the growing size of the home video market and the problem of movie piracy, moviemakers are working to maximize their initial audience. In July 2011, *Harry Potter and the Deathly Hallows: Part 2* set a record by opening in 4,375 theaters. It brought in more than $169 million on its opening weekend in the United States and made more than $273 million in its first ten days.[40]

Avatar may be the most commercially successful movie in history (see Table 8.1), but it didn't have the biggest audience. That honor belongs to the Civil War epic *Gone With the Wind*, which sold more than 100 million tickets in 1939 and countless more for multiple rereleases over a decades-long period (see Table 8.2).[41] One reason the 2009 *Avatar* is at the top of the box office charts is that tickets for it cost much more than the Depression-era tickets for *Gone With the Wind*. Adjusted for inflation, *GWTW* ticket prices would have brought in a total of $1.62 billion, considerably more than the domestic box office receipts of *Avatar*.

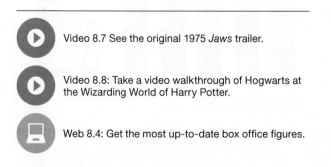

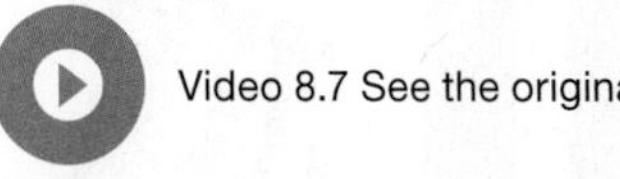
Video 8.7 See the original 1975 *Jaws* trailer.

Video 8.8: Take a video walkthrough of Hogwarts at the Wizarding World of Harry Potter.

Web 8.4: Get the most up-to-date box office figures.

MEDIA TRANSFORMATIONS

As You Like It: Movie Viewership in the Digital Era

Even in the age of streaming video, tablets, smartphones, DVD and Blu-ray players, pay-per-view cable, and home theater systems, going to the movies is something special. People go for a variety of reasons—to learn things, to escape from everyday life, to enjoy a pleasant activity, to pass the time, to avoid feeling lonely, to fit in with others, or to learn about themselves.[42] Young people who are dating may go to the movies for no other reason than to be alone in the dark away from parental supervision.

But there are other things that make going to the movies unique. Movies are typically "edgier" than what is shown on television, although cable and home video have changed this substantially. There is also the larger-than-life aspect of movies such as the *Harry Potter* or *James Bond* or *Hobbit* series, which bring people into theaters for an overwhelming visual and sonic experience. While the giant screen Cinerama system has died out, large-format IMAX theaters that were traditionally used for science and nature films at museums are now screening popular releases on their screens that can be several stories tall. Action and science fiction movies such as *Avatar, The Dark Knight Rises,* and *Gravity* all brought in more than $100 million globally each from

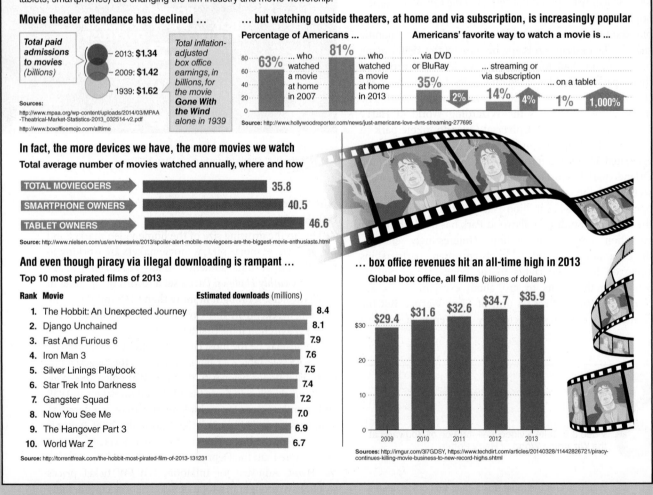

As You Like It: Movie Viewership in the Digital Era

New viewing platforms and technologies (online subscription, streaming, DVD, tablets, smartphones) are changing the film industry and movie viewership.

Movie theater attendance has declined ...

Total paid admissions to movies (billions)

- 2013: **$1.34**
- 2009: **$1.42**
- 1939: **$1.62**

Total inflation-adjusted box office earnings, in billions, for the movie ***Gone With the Wind*** *alone in 1939*

Sources:
http://www.mpaa.org/wp-content/uploads/2014/03/MPAA-Theatrical-Market-Statistics-2013_032514-v2.pdf
http://www.boxofficemojo.com/alltime

... but watching outside theaters, at home and via subscription, is increasingly popular

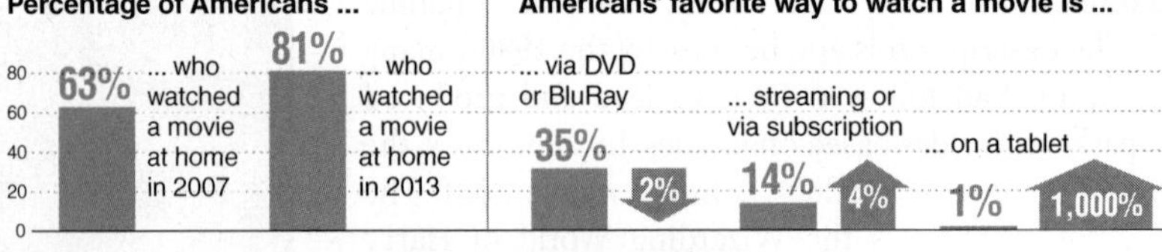

Source: http://www.hollywoodreporter.com/news/just-americans-love-dvrs-streaming-277695

In fact, the more devices we have, the more movies we watch

Total average number of movies watched annually, where and how

Source: http://www.nielsen.com/us/en/newswire/2013/spoiler-alert-mobile-moviegoers-are-the-biggest-movie-enthusiasts.html

And even though piracy via illegal downloading is rampant ...

Top 10 most pirated films of 2013

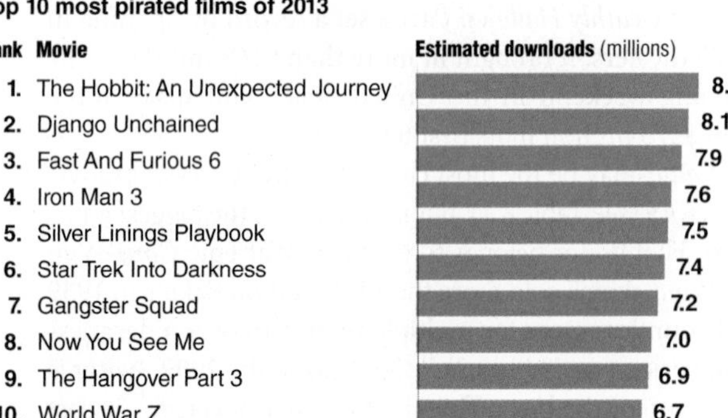

Rank	Movie	Estimated downloads (millions)
1.	The Hobbit: An Unexpected Journey	8.4
2.	Django Unchained	8.1
3.	Fast And Furious 6	7.9
4.	Iron Man 3	7.6
5.	Silver Linings Playbook	7.5
6.	Star Trek Into Darkness	7.4
7.	Gangster Squad	7.2
8.	Now You See Me	7.0
9.	The Hangover Part 3	6.9
10.	World War Z	6.7

Source: http://torrentfreak.com/the-hobbit-most-pirated-film-of-2013-131231

... box office revenues hit an all-time high in 2013

Global box office, all films (billions of dollars)

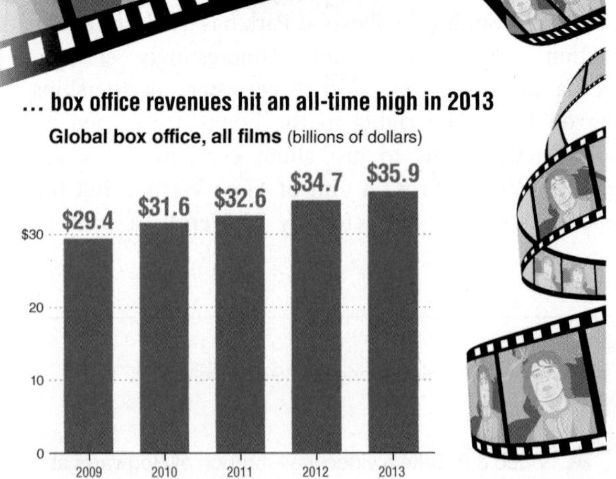

Sources: http://imgur.com/3I7GDSY, https://www.techdirt.com/articles/20140328/11442826721/piracy-continues-killing-movie-business-to-new-record-highs.shtml

IMAX showings, in part because IMAX theaters can charge $15 a person (or more!) for tickets.[43] (Your author has a history of driving up to 180 miles to see a movie at a large-format theater.)

Movies can also be a group experience. People watching the *Paranormal Activity* horror movies at home may not have the overwhelming sense of dread that comes from being in a theater full of terrified people.

According to movie scholar Garth Jowett,

> Teenagers and young adults will probably always want to escape the confines of the home, and others will more than likely continue to be motivated to seek out an experience which allows intense individual involvement with little risk within an appealing social context.[44]

As noted elsewhere in this chapter, movie theater attendance has stayed relatively stable over the last several years, averaging between 1.3 and 1.4 billion tickets sold per year. The size of the box office varies from year to year, but is trending slightly upward, due primarily to increased ticket prices. According to a study by the industry group the Motion Picture Association of American (MPAA—the same people who produce movie content ratings), two-thirds of Americans went to the movies at least once in 2013.[45]

But movies are no longer exclusively, or even primarily, a theatrical experience. As of 2012, 42 percent of Americans aged fourteen to seventy-five have streamed a movie to their television set, computer, or mobile device. While people still watch movies using Blu-ray or DVD discs, the percentage of them who do so has dropped from 37 to 35 percent.[46] And it's really important to remember that it isn't an either/or situation for movie viewing. A study by media measurement firm Nielsen found that smartphone owners attend 9 percent more movies than the population at large, and tablet owners view 20 percent more movies.[47] The same study found that mobile device users also watched more paid and free movies at home. And the MPAA study showed that frequent moviegoers were also more likely than the general population to own computers, disc players, smartphones, tablets, video game systems, and video streaming devices.

IMAX CEO Richard Gelfond told *USA Today* that the blockbuster movies will tend to draw audiences in to see movies in theaters, while smaller movies will appeal to people viewing at home or on the go: "When you have blockbuster movies, people are still going to want to go to a theatre and see them. When you have more independent movies, or movies that rely on plot than on special effects, I think people will see them on devices."[48]

Media Transformations Questions:

- **HOW** many times did you go see a movie in a theater over the last 12 months? Were any of them at a large-format (i.e., IMAX) theater?
- **HOW** did you decide to see a movie at the theater?
- **DO** you deliberately wait to see certain movies at home? What kind of movies are they?
- **DO** you ever watch movies on a mobile device? Why or why not?

Home Video

Home videocassette recorders (VCRs) started becoming an important source of movies in the 1980s, and by 1994, over 85 percent of all U.S. homes had one. However, by about 2005, digital video discs (DVDs) and high-definition Blu-ray discs had largely displaced the VCR. As of 2006, nearly 81 percent of all households had a DVD player, whereas 79 percent had VCRs. This was a big change from 1999, when 89 percent of households had VCRs, and fewer than 7 percent had DVD players.[49] DVDs provide a higher-quality image and dramatically better sound than videocassettes, and they have popularized the letterbox (or wide-screen) format. Pixar's *Incredibles* brought in $261 million in theaters, making it one of the most successful films of 2004. When it was released on DVD, it made an additional $368 million.[50] By 2012, more people were streaming movies over the Internet using services such as Netflix, Hulu, and Amazon than were playing DVDs or other physical media. Of course, consumers were still paying much more for the movies on physical media than for streaming. A study by research firm IHS Screen Digest estimated that Americans would stream 3.4 billion movies over the Internet in 2012, but they would spend only $1.72 billion on those movies, compared to $11.1 billion on discs.[51]

In addition to making more money for the studios, home video opened up a world of older movies and foreign movies to today's audiences. Previously, movie lovers could see a film only when it first came out or was re-released, when it was shown in 16-mm format on a college campus or in a revival house, or when it finally appeared on late-night television. With the wide range of home video options now available, people can watch movies again and again, whenever they want.

Digital Production and Projection

The revolution that started with desktop publishing—which enabled people to produce books, newspapers, and magazines on their computers and laser printers—has begun transforming the production of movies.

Computers first came to Hollywood in a big way with *Star Wars* (Episode IV for those of you geeky enough to care). Director George Lucas used a computer-controlled camera to shoot the space battle scenes. He was able to create multiple layers of images more easily because he could make the camera move exactly the same way on each shot.

Video 8.9: Watch the trailer for *Sky Captain and the World of Tomorrow*.

Table 8.1 Box Office Receipts of Top Movies (Actual Domestic Revenue)

Rank	Movie	Year of release	Box office receipts
1	*Avatar*	2009	$760 million
2	*Titanic*	1997	$659 million*
3	*Marvel's The Avengers*	2012	$623 million
4	*The Dark Knight*	2008	$534 million
5	*Star Wars: Phantom Menace*	1999	$474 million**
6	*Star Wars*	1977	$461 million
7	*The Dark Knight Rises*	2012	$448 million
8	*Shrek 2*	2004	$441 million
9	*E.T. The Extra-Terrestrial*	1982	$435 million
10	*The Hunger Games: Catching Fire*	2013	$425 million
149	*Gone With the Wind*	1939	$199 million

Source: "Domestic Grosses," *Box Office Mojo*, July 22, 2014. Available from http://boxofficemojo.com/alltime/domestic.htm. Used with permission.
*Includes $58 million in revenue from a 2012 3-D re-release.
**Includes more than $40 million in revenue for a 2012 3-D re-release. Prior to the 3-D version, it had been at the number-seven spot.

More recently, Lucas's *Star Wars: Attack of the Clones* (Episode II) was the first big-budget feature to be shot entirely using high-definition video.

Sky Captain and the World of Tomorrow, released in 2004, was the first mainstream American movie in which all the backgrounds and sets were computer animated in an otherwise live-action movie.[52] Director Kerry Conran wrote his own software to create computer-generated backgrounds that would meld with the live-action footage of the actors shot before a blue screen, in much the same way that computer special effects are added into movies. In this case, though, without the computer-generated backdrops, there would be nothing other than the actors. There were no "sets" to speak of. The only "real" things in the film were the actors, their costumes, and the props they were holding.

Conran told the *Washington Post* back in 2004 that he believed his technology would allow filmmakers more freedom to pursue their visions:

> The studios today are in this awkward and horrible position where films cost so much money to make, they have to be cautious so they can appeal to the broadest possible audience, so that is half the point of this experiment, to see if independent filmmakers and studios can both take chances again, to think differently.[53]

While the technology might have allowed Conran to make a movie he couldn't have otherwise, the film did not come cheap, costing a reported $70 million. But Conran saw that $70 million price tag as a bargain compared to the much more expensive action thrillers, such as the *Spider-Man* franchise.

At the time the film came out, no one had seen anything quite like it, and veteran movie producer Jon Avnet proclaimed the process "a version of the virtual studio" and "unquestionably the wave of the future."[54]

Unfortunately for the film's creators, audiences in neither the United States nor anywhere else in the world were particularly interested in the film. With a domestic gross of only about $38 million and a worldwide gross of $58 million, the film did not make back its production costs through ticket sales.[55]

Conran predicted correctly back in 2004 that his techniques would find their way into action, fantasy, and science fiction movies. "In a romantic comedy, where you have the people walking through a park, it makes less sense to go to the effort to completely create this park than go outside and shoot it," he told the *Pittsburgh Post-Gazette*.

Table 8.2

Box Office Receipts of Top Movies (Adjusted for Inflation)

Rank	Movie	Year of release	Box office receipts
1	*Gone With the Wind*	1939	\$1.61 billion
2	*Star Wars*	1977	\$1.42 billion
3	*The Sound of Music*	1965	\$1.13 billion
4	*E.T. The Extra-Terrestrial*	1982	\$1.13 billion
5	*Titanic*	1997	\$1.08 billion
6	*The Ten Commandments*	1956	\$1.04 billion
7	*Jaws*	1975	\$1.02 billion
8	*Doctor Zhivago*	1965	\$998 million
9	*The Exorcist*	1973	\$880 million
10	*Snow White and the Seven Dwarfs*	1937	\$868 million

Source: "Domestic Grosses: Adjusted for Inflation," *Box Office Mojo*, July 22, 2014. Available from http://boxofficemojo.com/alltime/adjusted.htm. Used with permission.
Note: Avatar is ranked fourteenth on the inflation-adjusted list as of July 2014, falling between *Ben Hur* (1959) and *Return of the Jedi* (1983).

"It's probably not suited for everything, but it could be used for anything."[56]

SECRET 3 The surprise hit *300*, based on a graphic novel, would likely never have been made if not for the budget economies of digital production. The movie, which features an over-the-top recreation of the Battle of Thermopylae with all-digital sets and backgrounds, cost only \$65 million to produce, cheap compared to the recent sword-and-sandal epic *Troy*, which cost \$175 million, and *Gladiator*, which cost \$103 million. With that low cost of production, *300* was able to earn back its basic budget the first weekend of release, and it eventually earned more than \$210 million domestically and \$456 million worldwide.[57] What made the film so cheap? First, it was shot in Canada, where production and labor costs are lower. Second, it was shot completely on high-definition video on a blank sound-stage using the technology pioneered in *Sky Captain*. With the success of *300*, we see avant-garde techniques becoming mainstream, providing yet another instance of Secret Three—Everything from the margin moves to the center.[58]

Star Wars creator George Lucas wrote in 1999 that he believed that film and projectors would soon be replaced by digital computer projection. Aside from questions about the quality of the images, digital projectors give a better 3-D image than do conventional projectors, and they drastically lower the cost of distributing prints to theaters.[59] The six major movie studios of the MPAA have written standards, known as the Digital Cinema Initiative, so that theaters have a consistent set of rules for how digital projection will be handled. The biggest challenge for the conversion to digital projection is expected to be cost, with estimates varying from \$20,000 to close to \$100,000 per screen, depending on the theater's size and the desired quality.[60] As of 2014, more than 90 percent of all commercial theaters were capable of projecting digitally, and with its release of the Will Ferrell comedy *Anchorman 2: The Legend Continues*, the Paramount movie studio was reportedly ending its distribution of most of its movies on 35-mm film. When the Oscar-nominated *Wolf of Wall Street* came out, it was the first major studio movie to be released exclusively in digital form, according to the *Los Angeles Times*. The only exceptions to this policy will be a few high-profile movies, such as Christopher Nolan's science fiction movie *Interstellar.*[61]

Web 8.5: Check out the box office and estimated costs of recent movies.

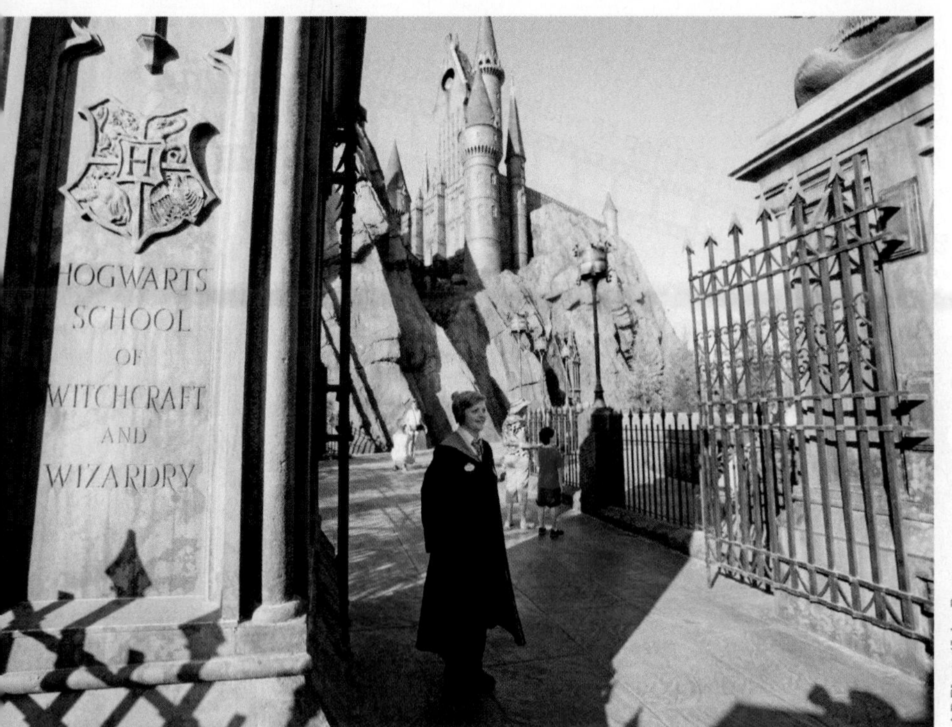

AP Photo/John Raoax

The Wizarding World of Harry Potter at the Universal Orlando theme park includes a variety of attractions, including Hogwarts castle.

What Makes a Movie Profitable?

Although a blockbuster movie can be enormously profitable, a relatively low percentage (20–30 percent) of movies actually make money. Movies can be financial failures even if they make $40 million and can be successful even if they make only $2 million—it all depends on how much the movie cost to produce and promote.[62]

The best-known way to make money in the movies is to produce a big-budget blockbuster with big stars and a big-name director, have a giant domestic and international box office, sell lots of licensed products, sell millions of DVDs, and generally turn the movie into a Fortune 500 corporation. Sometimes this process even produces a pretty good film. Look at the movie *Inception* as an example. It took in more than $292 million domestically and $532 million from the foreign box office on a budget of $160 million.[63] When you spend that much money making a movie, it has to be a success. Of course, with talent such as director Christopher Nolan, actor Leonardo DiCaprio, and a score by Hans Zimmer, it was bound to be a success. Another example is the movie version of the best-selling young adult novel *The Hunger Games*. Produced for the relatively low budget of $78 million and starring the well-regarded Jennifer Lawrence, it brought in a near-record $152 million on its opening weekend.[64]

Sometimes the international box office can help redeem a domestic stinker. That was the case with director Andrew Stanton's first live action film, *John Carter*. Stanton had a successful track record of directing hit animated films for Pixar, so when he made his live-action debut, he was given a relatively free hand. This involved spending approximately $250 million on the film, which was based on the Edgar Rice Burroughs Mars novels. *John Carter* had a $30 million opening weekend, which was considered disastrous for such a high-budget film. Over its 2012 run, it brought in only $73 million domestically, but almost three times that—$211 million—on the international market. The global box office still didn't keep the movie from being labeled an economic failure, but it did help it considerably.[65] Gore Verbinski, who directed the wildly successful *Pirates of the Caribbean* series, suffered a similar fate with his 2013 version of *The Lone Ranger*, which stared Johnny Depp. Made for $215 million, the action comedy brought in only $89 million in the United States, though like *John Carter* it was somewhat redeemed by an international box office of $171 million.[66]

The alternative approach is to make a movie with a tiny-to-small budget that has a clear target audience, have a modest box office, and make a great return on investment. A good example of this is 2014's *Fault in Our Stars*. The movie started with a built-in audience of fans of the best-selling young adult novel that tells the story of two teens who fall in love while suffering from cancer. The movie was filmed for $12 million and had huge social media buzz from its target audience of teen and twenty-something women. The film had a spectacular opening, earning $48.2 million over its first weekend, and it went on to earn more than $120 million in the United States, and a similar amount internationally. The movie will likely not be one of the top-ten grossing movies of 2014, but it will almost certainly be the most profitable, earning more than ten times its cost of production.[67]

On a smaller scale was the Christian-themed *Fireproof*. Produced for a budget of $500,000, it was promoted through churches and grossed more than $33 million. Now *Fireproof* did not make a large amount of money, but any movie that can bring in sixty-six times its cost of production has to be seen as a success.[68]

(For lists of top movies, by revenue, refer back to Tables 8.1 and 8.2.)

The problem for studio executives, of course, is figuring out in advance which movie can support a large budget and which one can't. It's easy to figure out the big-budget movies that are likely to be blockbusters (well, maybe, at least those that *ought* to be blockbusters, if they are done right). But why do little movies like *Bridesmaids*, the *Paranormal Activity* series, or *Slumdog Millionaire* break out to become hits?

According to *USA Today* movie critic Susan Wloszczyna, these movies, and others like them, are ones that "grab the people who actually part with money to see movies."[69] The basics are pretty straightforward: Make an interesting film that doesn't fit a big-budget mold, keep its costs under control, and be savvy about how you promote it. If it does well, the upside is almost unlimited. If you miss, the movie is still likely to make back its cost through video, cable, and broadcast rights.

Walt Disney Studios Motion Pictures/Courtesy Everett Collection

The Marvel Comics movie *Guardians of the Galaxy* was one of the biggest hits of 2014 with its big budget production, comic book sensibilities, and a great 1970s classic rock soundtrack.

Take, for example, two movies starring Natalie Portman: *V for Vendetta* and *Garden State.* Neither movie had a large box office; both are quirky, idiosyncratic films. However, both turned a profit. *V for Vendetta* is a dark, worrisome movie in which the main character, V, is a terrorist. While he is fighting fascism, he's also killing innocent people. What gave the filmmakers the freedom to make such an interesting film? The budget. *Vendetta* had a production budget of $54 million and brought in a domestic box office of $70 million and an international box office of $62 million. Not a big success, but not a big budget either, especially for a sci-fi action flick. Or let's get a little more personal in scale, with Zach Braff's *Garden State.* This story of a young man coming home to New Jersey for a funeral after trying to make it in Hollywood brought in more than ten times its production budget of $2.5 million. It had a charming script, good actors working for low salaries, and a great alternative pop soundtrack, with tracks by Coldplay, Zero 7, and Thievery Corporation.[70]

Noted director Spike Lee, whom we talked about back in Chapter 3, says that he has maintained his independence as a moviemaker largely by keeping costs under control:

> I've been very comfortable, for the most part, in that I view myself as an independent filmmaker—as one of the few directors that has final cut. And the deal's always been this: "Spike, we're not willing to give you so much money, so make do with what you've got." You can't argue with that.[71]

Movies and Society

The possible negative effects of movies have long been a source of concern. Although movies are attended by people of all ages, they appeal most strongly to adolescents and young adults, who are perceived as particularly vulnerable to media influences. But as film critic Glenn Kenny points out,

> Since film is by and large a popular (and terribly expensive) art, the vast majority of moviemakers want to give the audience the pictures they think the audience wants to see, or the pictures that preview cards and focus groups tell moviemakers the audience wants to see. This kind of give-and-take makes it difficult to tell the dancer from the dance, as it were; add to that the fact that certain movies affect the way we look at other movies, and the puzzle of how we're changed by them becomes more complex.[72]

How Much Influence Do Movies Have? 

The debate over how movies affect people is contentious, even today. Moviemakers claim that they don't shape society, they just reflect it. But this ignores the fact that movies are a central part of society, and even mirrors have effects. Movie historian Gerald Mast notes that

> movies have . . . been an immensely powerful social and cultural force. . . . They have produced social changes—in ways of dress, patterns of speech, methods of courting. And they have mirrored social changes—in fashion, sexual mores, political principles.[73]

A well-known example of the purported effects of the movies comes from the 1934 Clark Gable and Claudette Colbert movie *It Happened One Night.* Counter to the standard of dress for men at the time, Gable's character took off his shirt and exposed a bare chest; he wore no undershirt. After the movie was released, sales of undershirts reportedly plummeted because of Gable's example,[74] though whether this fall-off ever really happened is a matter of some debate.[75]

IN ORDER FOR A MOVIE TO PASS THE BECHDEL TEST, IT HAS TO SATISFY THREE RULES: ONE, IT HAS TO HAVE MORE THAN ONE NAMED FEMALE CHARACTER; TWO, THEY HAVE TO TALK TO EACH OTHER; AND, THREE, THEIR CONVERSATION CAN'T BE ABOUT A MAN.

OBVIOUSLY, DOROTHY'S MOVIE CHOICE OF PERSEPOLIS PASSES THE TEST.
HOWEVER, SO DOES JOYCE'S CHOICE OF TWILIGHT: ECLIPSE.

THE BECHDEL TEST ISN'T A STRICT INDICATOR OF WHETHER A MOVIE IS FEMINIST OR NOT.
WHAT? IT PASSES? THAT'S ABSURD.

MAN, I BET NOBODY AT YALE LIKES TWILIGHT.
TAKE THAT, LIBERAL ELITE!

David Willis

The Web comic *Dumbing of Age* tells the story of a group of students at a Midwestern college. In this strip, the characters are discussing movies in a women's studies class.

Research Results. As movies grew in popularity in the 1920s, people became concerned about their effects on viewers, especially young people. The Payne Fund, a private foundation, sponsored a series of thirteen studies, several of which analyzed the content of movies, who was going to the movies, and what, if any, effects the movies were having on the audiences. The researchers found that a small number of basic themes appeared in movies over and over again: crime, sex, love, mystery, war, children, history, travel, comedy, and social propaganda. More than three-fourths of all movies dealt with crime, sex, or love.

Questioning the Media

If you wanted to be a successful movie producer in Hollywood, what kind of movies would you make? How much influence do budget and promotion have on a movie's success? Why do some big-budget movies fail and micro-budget movies make it big?

A second major finding was that people could remember a surprising amount of what they had seen in movies, even six months after seeing them. Why such a high level of recall? Perhaps it was because movies were novel at the time, but another explanation was that movies gave people something to talk about, thus stimulating recall.

Some critics had suggested that movies might be responsible for moral decay, and one of the studies looked at whether the morals portrayed in movies were at odds with those of the viewing public. Not surprisingly, the moral standards of characters in movies tended to be lower than those of viewers. After all, people who behave differently from us are the most interesting to watch.

Herbert Blumer, a noted social psychologist, conducted a major study that examined the diaries of young people who recorded how they thought they had been influenced by movies. He found that participants reported imitating the behaviors they saw in movies and copying the actions of their favorite stars in their games and play. Young people reported that they saw movies as a source of ideas about action, romance, and standards of beauty. In essence, they were using the movies to learn how to behave as an adult.[76]

Video 8.10: Learn more about Bollywood films and watch a great movie clip.

Hooray for Bollywood: India's Movie Industry. The biggest source of movies in the world is not California or even the United States as a whole. That honor belongs to Bollywood—the filmmakers of India, especially the city of Mumbai (formerly Bombay). Although Bollywood films are popular worldwide, they are not seen frequently in the United States. But 2009's Oscar winner for best picture may help change that. *Slumdog Millionaire*, a British movie set in India that makes use of a lot of the stylistic conventions of Bollywood, won eight Oscars and made more than $140 million in the United States.[77]

Each year Bollywood produces more than 1,000 films that are distributed throughout Africa, China, and the rest of Asia. A 2002 BBC News online poll found that the world's most popular movie star at that time was not Harrison Ford or Julia Roberts; it was Indian actor Amitabh Bachchan, who has starred in more than one hundred Bollywood movies.[78] (And, as a little bit of movie trivia, in *Slumdog Millionaire* the young Jamal escapes from a locked room by jumping into an outhouse pit in order to get an autograph from Bachchan.)

Typical of India's films are the *masala*, or spice, movies. They feature several musical numbers, a strong male hero, a coy heroine, and an obvious villain.[79] The movies have as many as ten separate storylines—a contrast to American movies, which typically tell one or two stories.

One reason for the musical numbers in Indian films is that they help break through language barriers. India alone has more than twenty-five languages. Anupam Sharma, who works in the Indian movie industry, says that Bollywood movies touch people throughout the world: "Because of the distances and different dialects in India, music is the universal language."[80] When it comes to

TEST YOUR VISUAL MEDIA LITERACY

Photofest

TM & Copyright © 20th Century Fox Film Corp./courtesy Everett Collection

Both of these movies came out within a year of each other in the late 1980s. Based on what you see on the posters, what would you expect from each movie? According to what you see, which probably had stronger roles for women in it? Do these posters offer any clues about whether the female characters in the movies interact with one another?

Does It Look Like Women Have Major Film Roles?

There are lots of movies that feature great relationships between men. There are a number of movies with interesting roles for women. But how many movies out there feature multiple major female characters that interact with each other? That's the question the Bechdel Test for Women in Film tries to answer.

The Bechdel Test, named after cartoonist and graphics novel artist Alison Bechdel, attempts to test whether women have a meaningful presence in a movie.[1] It does so by asking three questions:

1. Are there two or more women who have names in the movie?
2. Do they talk to each other?
3. Do they talk to each other about something other than a man?

Not surprisingly, male-centric movies such as *Fight Club*, *42*, and *Moneyball* don't pass. Movies focusing on the activities of multiple women, such as *Bridesmaids,* the *Sex in the City* movies, and the action-oriented *Hunger Games* and *Aliens*, clearly do pass. But as media critic Anita Sarkeesian points out, some not-so-obvious fails include:

- The original *Shrek*
- *The Big Lebowski*
- *Slumdog Millionaire*
- And even *The Princess Bride*

Remember, the Bechdel Test doesn't judge the quality of the movie or whether it treats women with respect. It only requires that the movie have two or more women who talk to each other about something other than a man.

WHO is the source?

What is the Bechdel Test? By whom was it developed?

WHAT are they saying?

What is the goal of the Bechdel Test? What does it tell us? What doesn't it tell us?

WHAT evidence is there?

Watch a recently released movie and take notes on the Bechdel questions. Which of the questions does your movie pass? What are some examples of why the movie does or does not pass the Bechdel Test?

WHAT do you and your classmates think?

Were you surprised by how your analysis turned out? Does thinking about the Bechdel Test change how you view movies? Does the Bechdel Test address an issue we should be concerned about? Why or why not?

[1]Lisa Katayama, "The Bechdel Test for Women in Movies," July 22, 2010, www.boingboing.net/2010/07/22/the-bechdel-test-for.html; Rachel Sklar, "The Bechdel Test for Movies (and Media?)," July 22, 2010, www.mediaite.com/online/the-bechdel-test-for-movies-and-media/.

Video 8.11: Read several blog posts on the Bechdel Test and watch a great video explanation of it.

romance and sex, Bollywood films tend to be far more conservative than American films. "India is still clinging on to its social values, which explains Bollywood's success everywhere but in America," said Priya Joshi, an Indian cinema scholar. "Bollywood films don't have any kissing in them or tend not to. Warner Bros. used to make movies like this in the past. . . . If it's ready to return to its roots, then it's ready for Bollywood."[81]

Movie critic Roger Ebert wrote that American audiences could enjoy these films:

> It is like nothing [Americans] have seen before, with its startling landscapes, architecture and locations, its exuberant colors, its sudden and joyous musical numbers right in the middle of dramatic scenes, and its melodramatic acting (teeth gnash, tears well, lips tremble, bosoms heave, fists clench).[82]

©iStockphoto.com/Davel5957

If that sounds similar to the musical movie *Moulin Rouge*, that's no accident. Director Baz Luhrmann acknowledges he was inspired in part by the Bollywood moviemaking style.[83] (As a side note, Nigeria claims to be the world's second largest producer of movies, though its movies all are direct-to-video and do not typically see theatrical release.[84])

The Production Code: Protecting the Movies From Censorship

Movies are somewhat different from other media in that their producers have always been conscious of the need for limits on what they can portray. In 1909, theater owners formed the National Board of Censorship to establish a national standard for movies. The idea was that the board would ban offensive films, with the implication that approved films were suitable to be shown. Ironically, the board was formed primarily to protect the theater owners from trouble rather than to protect their audiences from offensive films.[85]

What was considered objectionable content in movies of this era? Prostitution, childbirth, and masturbation were all decried in the 1920s, as was drug use.[86] One critic argued that there was no question that censorship was necessary. The only question was whether the censors should be controlled by the industry or by the government.[87]

Hollywood and Morality. One of the factors prompting censorship efforts was that the behavior of stars off screen was considered as immoral as some of the movies themselves. When Mary Pickford, a silent-movie star who made a specialty of heroines with ringlets, such as Rebecca of Sunnybrook Farm, quietly divorced her husband to marry her costar Douglas Fairbanks, her behavior became the talk of the nation. Actor Fatty Arbuckle became entangled in scandal after it appeared that he had bribed a district attorney to cover up the presence of a dozen "party girls" at one of his parties. He was later accused of murdering one of his guests—a young aspiring actress—at another party. Although he was eventually acquitted after three trials, the public never fully forgave him, and he didn't appear on screen for over a decade.[88] A 1922 pamphlet charged that Hollywood was a mass of "wild orgies," "dope parties," "kept men," and "kept women."[89]

The Birth of the Production Code. The motion picture industry began formalizing its morality rules with "The Don'ts and Be Carefuls," a set of guidelines passed in 1927. The impetus for this action was a series of hearings by the Federal Trade Commission and the threat of government regulation.[90] As has generally been the case with the movie industry, censorship of the movies came from within the industry for economic reasons. Movie historian Gerald Mast described the moral dilemma in which the moviemakers found themselves:

> Because the movies have sold sex and violence from the beginning (what extremely popular and public art ever sold anything else?), and because they were created within and supported by a society that condoned neither the doing nor the display of sex and violence, the motion picture industry has been in the paradoxical position of trying to set limits on how much it would let itself sell.[91]

Facing a range of accusations of immorality, the studios looked for someone who could improve the industry's image. They found that person in Will H. Hays, who had been U.S. postmaster general from 1921 to 1922. Hays was named president of the Motion Picture Producers and Distributors of America and became famous for his development of the **Production Code**, which controlled the content of movies from the 1930s until movie ratings came into use in 1968. The purpose of the code, in its early days, was primarily to convince people that Hollywood was doing something about morality in the movies. But by 1933, Hollywood was forced to start living up to the standards it professed to support.[92]

Among other things, the code required that evil not be made to look alluring and that villains and lawbreakers not go unpunished: "Crime shall never be presented in a way that might inspire others with a desire for imitation. Brutal killings are not to be presented in detail." Also, there could be no profanity or blasphemy in the movies. The code was also fairly strict about sex, noting that

---

Production Code: The industry-imposed rules that controlled the content of movies from the 1930s until the current movie ratings system came into use in 1968.

scenes of passion needed to be handled carefully: "Excessive and lustful kissing, lustful embraces, suggestive postures and gestures, are not to be shown." Interracial romance was also forbidden.[93]

Only occasionally could anything "immoral" get past the code, and big-budget movies from major studios were more likely to get away with pushing the edge of acceptability. Rhett Butler's closing line in *Gone With the Wind*, "Frankly, my dear, I don't give a damn," was shocking to audiences in 1939 because nothing so raw had previously been allowed by the censors.[94]

The Ratings System

By the 1960s, many movies were violating provisions of the Production Code, and some were even released without the code's approval. This forced a reevaluation of how movies were judged. Otto Preminger's 1953 movie *The Moon Is Blue* was the first major American movie to be released without code approval. Although it was controversial at the time, it would be considered mild today—imagine a movie causing a stir for including the words *virgin* and *mistress*.

In 1968, under the direction of its new president, Jack Valenti, the MPAA scrapped the increasingly outdated Production Code. The code was replaced with a system of voluntary ratings indicating the audience for which the movie was most appropriate.

How Are Movies Rated? Movie ratings are assigned by a panel of ten to thirteen parents who live in the Los Angeles area. In 1999, the panel consisted of seven women and five men ranging in age from twenty-eight to fifty-four. It included homemakers, carpenters, a teacher, a food and beverage manager, and a manicurist. On a typical workday, the raters screen and discuss three movies. They then assign each movie one of the following ratings:

- G: General audiences. All ages admitted.
- PG: Parental guidance suggested. Some material may not be suitable for children.
- PG-13: Parents strongly cautioned. Some material may be inappropriate for children under age 13.
- R: Restricted. Persons under age 17 will not be admitted unless accompanied by a parent or adult guardian.
- NC-17: No one under age 17 will be admitted.

This system evolved from the original system of four ratings: G, M, R, and X. The rating of M (mature audiences) was soon changed to GP (general audiences, parental guidance suggested) and then to PG (parental guidance).

Certain kinds of content usually prompt particular ratings. Drug use generally requires at least a PG-13 rating. Sexually oriented nudity results in an R rating. (*Titanic* got by with a PG-13 rating because its nudity occurred when an artist sketched his model, and not in a later love scene.) Violence that is rough and persistent requires an R. A single use of the "F word" requires a PG-13. If that word is used more than once, or used in a sexual sense, the movie is supposed to be rated R, though the board may override that rule by a two-thirds vote. (As an example, the Julia Roberts movie *My Best Friend's Wedding* used the "F word" in a sexual sense and still received a rating of PG-13.)

Some critics charge that gay sex is more likely than heterosexual sex to receive a severe rating. It appears likely that the 1969 Oscar-winning movie *Midnight Cowboy* was given an X rating primarily because actor Jon Voight portrayed a male prostitute who serviced male clients. Others have charged that female sexuality is more likely to receive restrictive ratings than is male sexuality; interracial sex is also considered inflammatory.

Some movies get submitted for ratings in early versions to see how far directors can go and still get the desired R rating. *Bruno*, a mockumentary by the creator of *Borat*, got a rating of NC-17 the first time it was submitted. Several scenes implying gay sex were removed before the film was granted an R. Sacha Baron Cohen, the film's writer and star, was required to deliver an R-rated version of the movie for theatrical release. One movie executive told the Hollywood blog *The Wrap*, "A guy like Sacha shoots what he wants, and then he negotiates."[95] (Editing the movie down to an R rating didn't end up making the movie a success—*Bruno* brought in less than half the box office revenue as did *Borat*.[96]) Cohen had similar battles over his 2012 film *The Dictator*. While it had an R rating for its run in theaters, the home video was released as *The Dictator: BANNED & UNRATED Version*.

Indiana Jones *and PG-13.* In the mid-1980s, it became clear that the rating system had a weakness. Movies were being released with a PG rating that did not merit an R but nevertheless included content that went beyond a PG rating. A new rating was proposed, PG-13, which would inform parents of the content of the film but not set limits on who could be admitted.

The rating change was supported strongly by director Steven Spielberg, who forced the issue with *Indiana Jones and the Temple of Doom* and *Gremlins*. Both movies were attacked for being too violent and intense for preteens, although they did not include content that would require an R rating. Spielberg observed ironically, "I've never made an R movie and hope never to make one, so I've been one of the first to appeal for a ratings change that would take the onus off the filmmaker as parent to America. That's not our role."[97] (This was back when Spielberg was making youth-oriented summer blockbuster action films rather than his more serious films dealing with World War II, the Holocaust, and terrorism.)

Media mogul Barry Diller, head of Paramount Studios in the 1980s, summed up the problem with the rating

Video 8.12: See some samples of movies before restrictions of the Production Code.

system, which at the time contained four ratings, even though only two could be used on a regular basis:

> It became apparent some time ago that only the PG and R ratings mattered much anymore. Nobody anticipated it, but both the G and X acquired negative associations—one for being innocuous, the other for being pornographic. There was a growing difference between what seemed appropriate content for teens and preteens.[98]

Today, PG-13 is seen as the most desirable rating because teenagers see these movies as more sophisticated than those rated G or PG.[99] Between 1995 and 2009, PG-13 movies had the highest average gross box office, with 1,711 movies earning an average of just under $40 million. Movies with G and PG ratings were close behind at $35 million. But the average box office for R-rated movies was only $14.5 million, and NC-17 movies grossed an average of $3.4 million.[100]

The X Problem. A second major problem with the rating system had to do with the X rating. The trouble began when the MPAA did not trademark the X rating and therefore could not control its use. The pornography industry began labeling its unrated films XXX on the theory that if X was adult, XXX would be *really* adult. Because the X rating became associated with pornography, many newspapers and television stations refused to carry advertisements for X-rated movies, and many theaters pledged not to show such movies, despite the artistic merit that some movies receiving the rating might have.

©iStockphoto.com/CG-CREATIVE

In 1990, the MPAA threatened to assign an X rating to *Henry & June*, which portrayed the relationship between writer Henry Miller, his wife, and writer Anaïs Nin. The producers protested, and the MPAA responded by creating a new rating, NC-17, which supposedly was less prejudicial than X. In reality, little changed; theaters and media outlets treat the new rating as equivalent to X.

Movies that receive the dreaded NC-17 rating often must be reedited to qualify for the more commercially viable R rating. But the producers of *Midnight Cowboy*, the first and only X- or NC-17-rated movie to win an Oscar for best picture, decided against reediting the film. Producer Jerome Hellman notes that after the movie won the Oscar, the film board offered to give the film an R rating if the producers would cut one frame from the movie so that it could be advertised as a "re-cut" version. The producers refused, but the board relented and changed the movie's rating to R.[101]

Some people in the movie industry have speculated that Steven Spielberg's World War II film *Saving Private Ryan* should have received an NC-17 for the violence in the opening scene, which depicts the D-Day invasion of France, but avoided it because of Spielberg's reputation. Filmmaker Spike Lee, speaking at the Cannes Film Festival, said,

> The MPAA has two different standards: one for violence, one for sex. I mean, I like *Saving Private Ryan* very much, especially the first hour. But if that's not an NC-17 film, I don't know what is. That's the way war should be depicted. But when people walk around picking up their severed arms and stuff like that, that's an R?[102]

Former MPAA president Jack Valenti defended *Private Ryan*'s R rating:

> *Saving Private Ryan* was a reenactment of one of the most crucial days in American history. I think every 13-year-old in the country ought to see it, even though it was rated R, to understand that the freedom you take for granted was paid for in blood.[103]

In 2007, the MPAA made some slight revisions to the rating scheme. These include a new warning to discourage parents from bringing young children to more intense R-rated movies. The ratings board now reveals the demographics of the people who do the ratings. There have also been calls to expand the acceptability of the NC-17 rating so that the R rating is not applied to movies that children shouldn't be allowed to see. But the updates to the rating system did not go so far as to create an official "hard R" rating that would ban all viewers under the age of seventeen from attending the movies.[104]

Regardless of the criticisms, parents appreciate the rating system. A 1999 survey showed that three-fourths of U.S. parents find the ratings useful in deciding what their children should be allowed to see.[105]

The Future of Movies

The movie business is facing an uncertain future. In 2005, the U.S. box office was down by 6 percent from the year before.[106] There were a lot of explanations for what caused the downturn. Conservative critics claimed that Hollywood was too liberal and was making movies that didn't appeal to the American public.[107] Others claimed that the problems were too many sequels and remakes. While sequels, remakes, and raunchy movies have continued to draw big audiences, the total size of the movie audience has stayed below the 1.58 billion ticket level it hit in 2002. (Keep in mind that audience size peaked back in the 1940s, with sales of just over 4 billion tickets a year.[108]) Since 2005, movie ticket sales have hovered in the area of 1.3–1.4 billion tickets per year.[109] Although the Hollywood box office has continued its climb in dollars earned, that has been driven more by increased ticket prices than by an increase in audience size.

Why are movie audiences declining, or staying the same? The sharp decline in movie audiences back in the

Web 8.6: Examine the challenges Hollywood faces in attracting audiences.

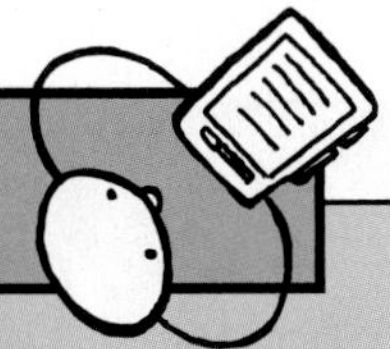

TEST YOUR MEDIA LITERACY

Movie Ratings

As we have discussed, the movie rating scheme is controversial for a number of reasons. Christopher Dodd, chairman of the MPAA and a former United States senator, says that the rating scheme exists to help parents pick appropriate movies for their children rather than to comment on the quality of the movie.[1] Dan Glickman, a former chair of the movie industry council, said in a 2008 speech,

> Ratings do not exist to cast judgment on whether a movie is "good" or "bad." The system is not a gatekeeper of society's morality and values. It does not require artists to promote behavior and beliefs deemed socially or morally upright. Some, from time to time, try to pressure the system into taking on these inappropriate roles in a free society. But the primary mission is transparency for parents—clear information about the content of films.[2]

But sometimes ratings keep an intended audience away from a movie with admittedly difficult content. Such was the case when the documentary *Bully* was released in 2012. The movie is about the problem of the bullying of teenaged children, and it contains scenes containing harsh language and cruelty. The MPAA gave the documentary a rating of R for bad language, but movie stars like Johnny Depp, as well as other advocates who oppose bullying, fought the rating so that teens could see the movie without their parents accompanying them.[3]

Cynthia Lowen, *Bully*'s producer, chose to give the movie an initial unrated release rather than saddle it with the R rating, but that means that many, though not all, movie theaters will refuse to show it because they never show unrated movies. Another frequent response for theaters is to treat unrated movies as though they are NC-17. In late March 2012, *Bully* had a limited release in which many of the theaters took a flexible approach about admitting teens, including letting young people in with notes from their parents.[4]

Bully was also released with an alternative "Common Sense" rating of "Pause 13+," the same rating the group—Common Sense Media—gave *The Hunger Games*. The rating means that for age thirteen and older, parents should "know your child, some content may not be right for some kids."[5] According to the organization's Web site,

> Common Sense Media is dedicated to improving the lives of kids and families by providing the trustworthy information, education, and independent voice they need to thrive in a world of media and technology.
>
> We exist because our nation's children spend more time with media and digital activities than they do with their families or in school, which profoundly impacts their social, emotional, and physical development. As a non-partisan, not-for-profit organization, we provide trustworthy information and tools, as well as an independent forum, so that families can have a choice and a voice about the media they consume.[6]

Eventually, the producers of *Bully* and the MPAA came to an agreement to release the film with a PG-13 rating if three instances of the "F word" were taken out.[7]

WHO is the source?

What is the MPAA? What is the MPAA's primary responsibility? Who is Common Sense Media? What is its primary responsibility?

WHAT are they saying?

According to the MPAA, what is the function of the movie rating system? What do the critics that you've read about elsewhere in this chapter say is wrong with it? How does Common Sense Media differ from the MPAA?

WHAT evidence is there?

Why was the movie *Bully* given an R rating from the MPAA? Why was it given a Pause 13+ from Common Sense Media? How do these ratings differ?

WHAT do you and your classmates think?

How well do you and your friends think the rating system is working? Did it keep you out of R-rated movies when you were younger? Do you believe parents use the rating system as intended? Should harsh language, such as repeated use of the "F word," require that a movie receive an R rating? Should movies be released with alternative ratings from groups such as Common Sense Media when the filmmakers don't like the rating from the MPAA? Should theaters be willing to show movies based on "Common Sense" ratings? Why or why not? Do you think the MPAA and producers did the right thing by editing the movie down to a PG-13?

1The Reliable Source, "'Bully' Debate Comes to Washington as Chris Dodd and Harvey Weinstein Debate at MPAA," *Washington Post*, March 15, 2012, www.washingtonpost.com/blogs/reliable-source/post/bully-debate-comes-to-washington-as-chris-dodd-and-harvey-weinstein-debate-at-mpaa/2012/03/15/gIQAFOHJFS_blog.html.

2Dan Glickman, *40 Years of Freedom: A Progress Report on the Modern Movie Ratings System* (Washington, D.C.: Media Institute, 2008), www.motionpictureassociation.org/press_releases/glickman%20speech%20--%20media%20institute%20--%20sept%2010%202009.pdf.

3Brendan Sasso, "Weinstein to Release 'Bully' Unrated to Avoid MPAA System," March 27, 2012, thehill.com/blogs/hillicon-valley/technology/218365-weinstein-to-release-bully-unrated-to-avoid-mpaa-system.

4Sarah Anne Hughes, "'Bully' Will Be Shown to Minors at AMC Theaters With Permission Slip, Carry a Common Sense Rating," *Washington Post*, March 28, 2012, www.washingtonpost.com/blogs/celebritology/post/bully-will-be-shown-to-minors-at-amc-theaters-with-permission-slip-carry-a-common-sense-rating/2012/03/28/gIQAnucRgS_blog.html.

5Common Sense Media, "Behind the Common Sense Media Ratings System," 2012, www.commonsensemedia.org/about-us/our-mission/about-our-ratings.

6Common Sense Media, "Our Mission," 2012, www.commonsensemedia.org/about-us/our-mission.

7ABC News, "'Bully' Film Rating Lowered to PG-13 After Public Pressure," April 6, 2012, abcnews.go.com/blogs/entertainment/2012/04/bully-film-rating-lowered-to-pg-13-after-public-pressure/.

Web 8.7: Find links to the source material for this Test Your Media Literacy box and ratings on *Bully*.

While Steven Spielberg's World War II movie *Saving Private Ryan* has been widely acclaimed, some (including director Spike Lee) have said that the movie clearly deserved an NC-17 rating for the extreme battlefield violence in the film's first hour.

1940s and 1950s was clearly a function of the rise of television as a new medium.[110] Currently movie audiences have many more alternatives than they did in the 1950s, due to cable/satellite television, home video, pay-per-view, and Internet sources.

Regardless of the reasons for it, the movie industry has to react to this changing economic reality. The studios are doing so by building up their big-release summer movies as major brands, using the Internet to promote their products, and finding new ways to distribute small movies to a dispersed audience.

Movies as a Brand

In the 1980s, domestic box office receipts accounted for more than 50 percent of movie income for studios; by 1995, this figure had fallen below 15 percent. Today studios earn as much or more from **ancillary, or secondary, markets** as they do from domestic ticket sales. These are movie revenue sources other than the domestic box office. For example, home video rights may be worth twice the theatrical box office total.[111] Ancillary markets include the following:

- International distribution rights
- Pay-per-view rights
- Premium cable channel rights
- Network television
- Home video
- Book rights
- Toys and clothes
- Product placement

Summer and holiday blockbuster movies have evolved into more than just films. They've become entire cottage industries—brands, if you will—in and of themselves. Take the 2009 hit movie *Transformers: Revenge of the Fallen.* It was one of the highest-grossing movies for the year, producing $369 million in domestic box office in its first four weeks of release. It also did $404 million in international ticket sales over the same time period.[112] Electronics company LG created a limited-edition *Transformers* phone. *Transformers* director Michael Bay then directed a thirty-second television commercial for the phone, using the talents of Digital Domain, the same special-effects company that brought the robots to life in the movie. Digital Domain also did the effects for *Transformer*-themed commercials for fast-food company Burger King.[113] Prior to the movie's release, Kmart had a promotional tie-in giving away free tickets to the movie to people who bought at least $50 in menswear, as well as a promotion of *Transformers* toys, video games, and clothing. The 7-Eleven convenience store chain offered *Transformers* Slurpee cups, character straws, and movie-themed flavors.[114] On a much larger scale, the 2010 Chevy Camaro was featured in the movie as the *Transformer* called Bumblebee. Bumblebee served as a major character in video games developed for the Sony Playstation 3, Microsoft X-Box 360, and the Nintendo Wii. And if the toy version wasn't enough, Chevrolet built a special-edition Camaro with Bumblebee paint and a *Transformers* badge.[115]

The *Transformers: Revenge of the Fallen* brand example illustrates how important marketing tie-ins can be for a big-name movie and how the brand can become as important—and lucrative—as the movie itself.

Movie Promotion on the Internet

When Daniel Myrick and Eduardo Sánchez headed out into the Maryland woods in October 1997 to film *The Blair Witch Project*, they had no idea they were creating what would become one of the big hits of 1999 or that they would change how movies are promoted.

Blair Witch purports to be a documentary filmed by three students investigating the legend of a murderous witch who lived in the woods near Burkittsville, Maryland. The movie did not even have a script; instead, the actors started with only a thirty-five-page plot outline. The actors were also the film crew, using an old 16-mm film camera and a $500 High-8 video camera. The total cost of filming the movie was between $35,000 and $60,000, although some critics wonder how it could have cost even that much.[116] The movie eventually grossed more than $250 million worldwide.

---

ancillary, or secondary, markets: Movie revenue sources other than the domestic box office. These include foreign box office, video rights, and television rights, as well as tie-ins and product placements.

The performers shot twenty hours of film and tape over an eight-day period while wandering about in the woods. The directors left notes for the actors each day, but the performers were given a lot of latitude. "We let [them] do what they wanted to do," Myrick says. "We gave them little clues as to where we wanted the scenes to go, but most of it was improvised."[117]

Myrick and Sánchez, along with production company Artisan, promoted *Blair Witch* in the same low-budget way in which it had been filmed, making use of cable television and the Internet rather than mainstream media. The pair created a mock documentary about the making of the movie, *The Curse of the Blair Witch*, which aired on the Syfy channel, and many viewers took this as evidence that the events recorded in the film had actually occurred. The promotional campaign capitalized on the confusion over whether the movie was fact or fiction, and many people who saw the film during the first week or two after its release thought that it might be real.[118]

Ten years after the movie scared movie fans and producers alike, *Los Angeles Times* blogger Glenn Whipp argued that the biggest impact of *The Blair Witch Project* was the effectiveness of the Web-based viral marketing campaign put together for the movie. The movie had good buzz coming out of showings at the Sundance and Cannes film festivals, and marketing materials made it sound like the footage for the film was real footage that had been found. Horror film director Scott Derrickson told Whipp, "The blurb on the poster said this was 'found footage,' and there was nothing in the marketing to lead you to believe it was anything but that."[119]

Web sites are now being used to court fans months or even years before a movie comes out. In many cases, the site is designed to maintain awareness of the movie even after the advertising is done and to build awareness once again when the movie is released on video. Independent film producer Mark Duplass (*The Puffy Chair*) says that in addition to changing how movies are promoted, *Blair Witch* also changed how movies look, with "the semi-improvised nature, the hand-held digital camera work, the naturalistic acting inside a genre piece, the idea of 'We don't have a [lot] of money, so let's build a budget that's appropriate, so we can execute it correctly.'"[120]

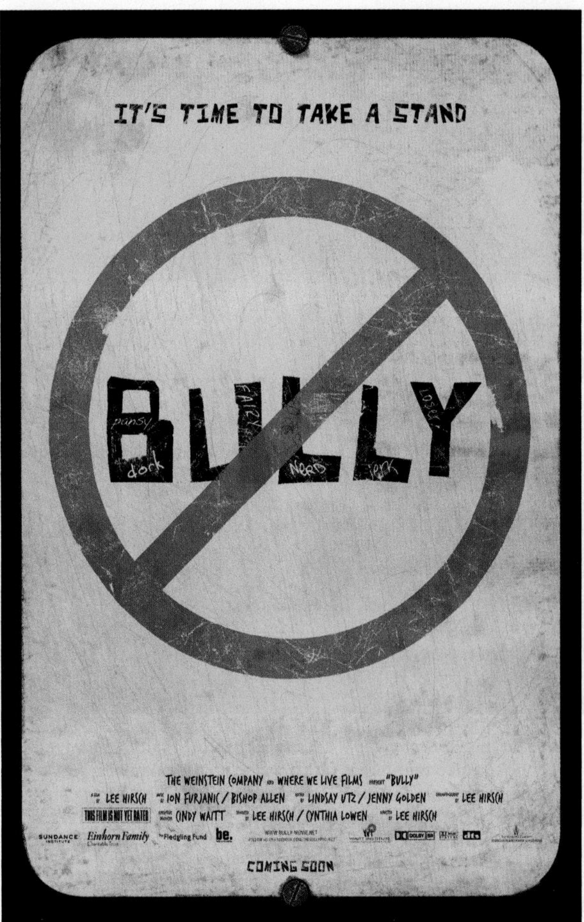

Michael Dwyer/©Weinstein/Courtesy Everett Collection

The producers of the documentary *Bully* had an extended battle with the MPAA's ratings board over whether the film on school bullying should have an R or a PG-13 rating.

Movies and the Long Tail

The long tail is going to have a bigger and bigger effect on the movie industry in the years to come, but 2007 marked the point at which it jumped to the forefront. Before then, unless you lived in New York or Los Angeles, you were not likely to have seen the Oscar winners for best animated short film and best live-action short. But in 2007 the films were available as digital downloads from Apple's iTunes store for $1.99 each. This means that for less than the price of a movie ticket in an urban market, you could download and view all five nominated films in either category, even if you live in Kearney, Nebraska. What you are seeing here is nothing less than the full impact of the long tail hitting the mainstream movie industry.

When *Long Tail* author Chris Anderson tries to explain the central concepts of his book, he often points to the online DVD rental store Netflix as a prime example. In 2012, Netflix carried 100,000 different DVD and Blu-ray titles. It also had more than 12,000 titles available for immediate viewing over either a computer or a streaming video box that connects the subscriber's television set to the Internet. Netflix has, of course, Sofia Coppola's 2006 version of *Marie Antoinette* starring Kirsten Dunst. But it also has the 1938 version of the film starring Norma Shearer in the title role, with John Barrymore as King Louis XV and Tyrone Power as Marie Antoinette's lover. For those

Questioning the Media

Movies can make a significant income through both product placement and merchandise based on the movie. Do you buy products with movie tie-ins? (Be honest—Star Wars and Disney toys?) Can you give an example where product placements were intrusive in the movie? Are some movies really just feature-length commercials?

Twientieth Century Fox Film Corporation/Photofest

The Fault in Our Stars was a big success in 2014 with a relatively low budget and a tear-jerker script based on the popular novel of the same name that tells the story of a young couple facing cancer treatment together. The movie benefited from a built-in audience from fans of the book.

Questioning the Media

What movies do you watch at home? How do you find them? Does the easy access to movies from Netflix or Amazon affect the number and types of movies you watch?

who really want to delve deeply into the topic, Netflix also offers at least three documentaries on the ill-fated queen: *Marie Antoinette*; *Marie Antoinette: The Scapegoat Queen*; and *Marie Antoinette: Queen of Versailles.* Anderson found that audiences aren't just interested in a few big hits; they are interested in a deep pool of choices. The problem has always been distribution. Movie theaters are great for showing a limited number of movies to a lot of people. That's why theater owners love the summer blockbusters. But when you can draw from audiences nationwide, even movies with a limited appeal can be successful. As you can imagine, the tiny and dedicated cadre of Marie Antoinette fans is spread out all over the country.

Netflix reports that about 30 percent of its disc rental business comes from new releases and 70 percent comes from older films. Why? Netflix provides the tools on its Web site to help its customers find these older movies. Netflix tracks the movies you've rented previously and how you've rated them. It then uses that information to recommend other movies you would probably like. Anderson says that if Netflix can use consumer data to recommend films, the cost of marketing small movies to consumers is lowered to almost zero:

> Advertising and other marketing can represent more than half of the costs of the average Hollywood blockbuster, and smaller films can't play in that game. Netflix recommendations level the playing field, offering free marketing for films that can't otherwise afford it, and thus spreading demand more evenly between hits and niches.[121]

Four years after its initial release, *Hotel Rwanda*, a serious drama about the Rwandan genocide, was still number fourteen on the Netflix Top 100 list, although it grossed only $25 million in its original theatrical release. Netflix allowed an audience to find this movie through its customer recommendation system even though it hasn't had a giant advertising budget and a potato chip tie-in. Also, Netflix provides distribution for foreign films that might not be shown all that often in the United States, such as the films of Hungarian director Béla Tarr or the avant-garde art films of artist Stan Brakhage.

Famed film critic Roger Ebert found that on his Web site, www.rogerebert.com, no one posted review accounts for more than 1 percent of the page views. Instead of the blockbusters dominating the traffic, almost all of the 10,000-plus reviews on the site are attracting some level of attention.[122]

Chapter SUMMARY

Ways of recording motion on film were first developed by photographers Étienne-Jules Marey and Eadweard Muybridge in the 1880s. Inventor and entrepreneur Thomas Edison applied their ideas in building the first practical motion picture display system, the kinetoscope. In France, the Lumière brothers invented the first portable movie camera and the first projector that could be used to display movies to a crowd.

Early directors such as Edwin S. Porter developed movie storytelling techniques that were expanded eventually into the feature-length film by D. W. Griffith. Griffith demonstrated that the public was interested in and willing to pay for larger-than-life films with longer running times. Griffith was also one of the first directors to seek outside financing for his movies.

From the 1920s through the 1940s, the studio system dominated moviemaking in the United States. Under the studio system, all the talent—from writers to directors to actors—was under contract to the studios. The major studios, such as Paramount and Warner Brothers, ran the movie industry like a factory assembly line, controlling which movies were made and how they were distributed. The studio system ended when the U.S. Supreme Court broke up the studios' monopoly in 1948.

A troubled time followed for the movie industry. The 1950s brought new competition from television and a controversial blacklist of writers, directors, and actors who were suspected of being communists. Hollywood responded by producing bigger, more spectacular movies; making almost all movies in color; and breaking up giant theaters into smaller, multitheater complexes known as multiplexes.

The movie industry is currently dominated by high-budget blockbuster movies with a large, predefined audience and marketing tie-ins. Although the initial domestic box office receipts are still important, movies often make more income from ancillary, or secondary, markets, such as foreign rights, video rights, and cable television rights. Blockbuster movies are now seen as a brand of interrelated products rather than just a movie. Yet smaller, low-budget movies often carry less risk of failure because they don't have to make nearly as much money to be profitable. Movies targeted at niche audiences can also be profitable if they have a controlled budget.

Moviemakers are increasingly relying on digital technology to make and promote movies. In addition to being used for special effects, digital technology makes it possible to shoot and edit low-budget movies using digital video rather than more expensive film. Directors can even shoot the movie on a blank soundstage and insert the sets and backgrounds digitally. Digital technology in the form of the Internet is also being used to promote movies directly to consumers.

Since the 1920s, there have been concerns about the effects that movies may have on young viewers. Hollywood has attempted to protect itself from criticism, initially by limiting the content of movies through its Production Code and more recently with age-based ratings.

Theatrical movies are facing increased competition from home video. While the total box office has risen in recent years, the number of people attending the movies has declined. Moviemakers are responding with innovative new ways of promotion and by finding audiences for movies of more limited interest.

Keep up-to-date with content from the author's blog.

Take the chapter quiz.

Key TERMS

kinetoscope 194
feature-length film 195
studio system 196
block bookings 196
synchronized soundtrack 197
talkie 197
House Un-American Activities Committee 198
Hollywood Ten 198
blacklist 199
multiplex 200
blockbuster era 200
Production Code 210
ancillary, or secondary, markets 214

Concept REVIEW

Digital filmmaking
The idea of moving pictures
The rise and fall of the studio system
The blacklisting of suspected communists in the 1940s and 1950s
The changes television forced on the movie industry
How movies can make profits from being big or being small
The effects of movies on society
How Hollywood has responded to threats of censorship
How Hollywood has responded to the changing nature of the movie market

Student STUDY SITE

Sharpen your skills with SAGE edge at **edge.sagepub.com/hanson5e**

SAGE edge for Students provides a personalized approach to help you accomplish your coursework goals in an easy-to-use learning environment.

chapter

9

Television

Broadcast and Beyond

Jorge Ramos moved to the United States from Mexico in 1973, and he's now the anchor of one of the most watched television news shows in Spanish in the United States.

AP Photo/Alan Diaz

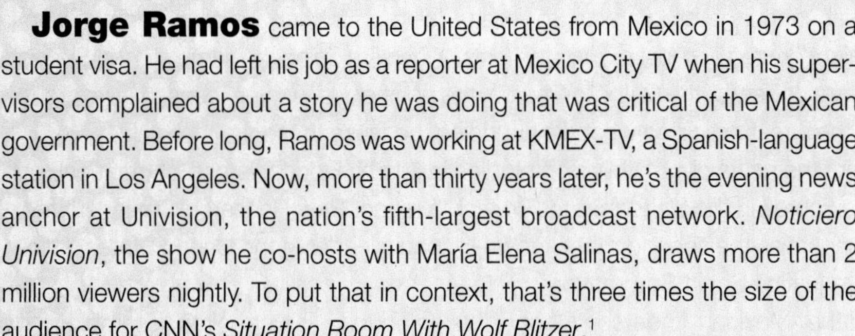

Jorge Ramos came to the United States from Mexico in 1973 on a student visa. He had left his job as a reporter at Mexico City TV when his supervisors complained about a story he was doing that was critical of the Mexican government. Before long, Ramos was working at KMEX-TV, a Spanish-language station in Los Angeles. Now, more than thirty years later, he's the evening news anchor at Univision, the nation's fifth-largest broadcast network. *Noticiero Univision*, the show he co-hosts with María Elena Salinas, draws more than 2 million viewers nightly. To put that in context, that's three times the size of the audience for CNN's *Situation Room With Wolf Blitzer*.[1]

While he has been compared to the legendary CBS news anchor Walter Cronkite, who in the 1960s established the basic format for evening network news, he actually follows a very different model—one that has more in common with the clear point of view of Latin American and European journalism than that of the more detached objective American reporting.

Ramos has been criticized for engaging in advocacy journalism by the conservative media watchdog group Media Research Center, and he's been accused of being a "Democratic pundit," but Ramos defends himself, saying that he is a tireless advocate for Latino and immigrant groups.

"Our position is clearly pro-Latino or pro-immigrant. We are simply being the voice for those who don't have a voice," Ramos told the *Los Angeles Times*.[2] When he interviewed President Barack Obama during his 2012 reelection campaign, Ramos confronted he president on his policies that have led to the deportation of more than 1.4 million undocumented immigrants. And he did that confrontation in English so clips from it could be easily replayed on English-language stations. "I am emotionally linked to this issue," Ramos told the *LA Times*. "Because once you are an immigrant, you never forget that you are one."[3]

Ramos argues that it is vital for the Spanish-language media to speak up on issues like immigration because Hispanics don't have many other advocates. In an interview on NPR's *On the Media*, he said,

> The big difference is that without looking for that we are representing a group of people who have no political representation. We are 17% of the population, but we only have three senators, only three. Where are the other 14 senators that we need to represent the Hispanic community? And that, historically, has been—relied on Univision and Spanish-language journalists.[4]

In addition to his shows in Spanish on Univision, he appears on Univision's English-language *Fusion* network done in partnership with ABC. Although he now speaks excellent English, Ramos says that when he first came the United States to study journalism at work at the Los Angeles station KMEX-TV, his English skills were poor. "My English was—I couldn't even understand myself."

LEARNING OBJECTIVES

After studying this chapter, you will be able to:

1 Discuss the development of television from its invention to HDTV today.

2 Explain how cable/satellite television, recorders such as VCRs and DVRs, and the adoption of digital television have transformed the television industry.

3 Discuss the issue of racial and ethnic diversity on television.

4 Identify three key reasons why viewers watch television.

5 Discuss the problem of broadcast decency, using examples.

6 Explain how streaming video services are changing TV in the twenty-first century.

To Ramos, broadcasting in English is becoming increasingly important because that's how he connects with people who are in power in the United States. He tells *New York* magazine that he likes broadcasting in English on the Fusion network. "What I really like is that for the first time, I don't need translation. And without translation, there's an immediate impact. And definitely the language of power is English."[5]

Ramos told NPR's Brooke Gladstone that there can be a big difference between reporting in English and reporting in Spanish because the audience for his English-language programs skews much younger than that for his Spanish-language programs. "So, yeah, doing a story about gays and abortion in English, I would go straightforward and just explain the facts. When I'm doing the same story in Spanish, I will always have the point of view of the Catholic Church, the point of view of very conservative groups, even some people on the street criticizing what we are doing, because those are their values."[6]

Ramos, who anchors the news out of Univision studios in Miami, Florida, is one of the most well-known Hispanic media figures in the United States. In fact, a recent Pew Research Center survey of Latinos found that Ramos was the second most known Hispanic leader in the United States, following only Supreme Court justice Sonia Sotomayor.[7]

He has been called the "Mexican Anderson Cooper," referring to his silver-haired resemblance to the CNN anchor. Ramos is also part of a transition from neutral reporting, or a "view from nowhere," to an anchor with a knowable point of view.

Frank Sesno, a former CNN journalist and director of the George Washington University School of Media and Public Affairs, told Politico.com, "What we would or would not have accepted years ago has changed as more broadcast personalities and bloggers especially have assumed more opinionated/lead roles in the conversations. The candidates will know that, but they'll still want Jorge—as last time—to reach the powerful demographic of Hispanic voters, which may be the key to success or failure for both parties in 2016."[8]

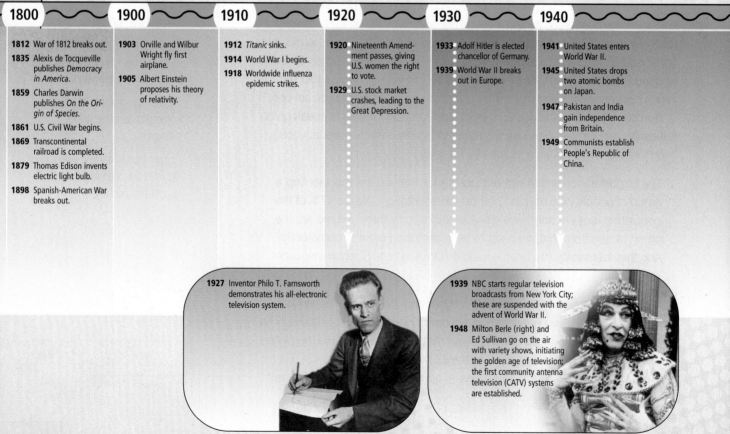

Timeline

1800

- **1812** War of 1812 breaks out.
- **1835** Alexis de Tocqueville publishes *Democracy in America*.
- **1859** Charles Darwin publishes *On the Origin of Species*.
- **1861** U.S. Civil War begins.
- **1869** Transcontinental railroad is completed.
- **1879** Thomas Edison invents electric light bulb.
- **1898** Spanish-American War breaks out.

1900

- **1903** Orville and Wilbur Wright fly first airplane.
- **1905** Albert Einstein proposes his theory of relativity.

1910

- **1912** *Titanic* sinks.
- **1914** World War I begins.
- **1918** Worldwide influenza epidemic strikes.

1920

- **1920** Nineteenth Amendment passes, giving U.S. women the right to vote.
- **1929** U.S. stock market crashes, leading to the Great Depression.

1930

- **1933** Adolf Hitler is elected chancellor of Germany.
- **1939** World War II breaks out in Europe.

1940

- **1941** United States enters World War II.
- **1945** United States drops two atomic bombs on Japan.
- **1947** Pakistan and India gain independence from Britain.
- **1949** Communists establish People's Republic of China.

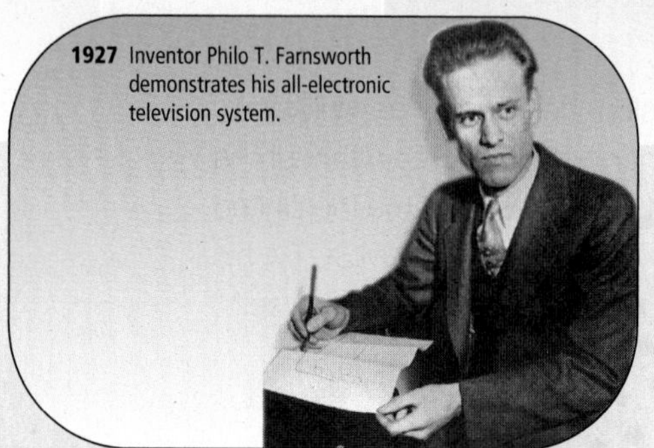

1927 Inventor Philo T. Farnsworth demonstrates his all-electronic television system.

AP Photo

1939 NBC starts regular television broadcasts from New York City; these are suspended with the advent of World War II.

1948 Milton Berle (right) and Ed Sullivan go on the air with variety shows, initiating the golden age of television; the first community antenna television (CATV) systems are established.

AP Photo

One thing that politicians of all stripes have learned is that Ramos never stops asking pointed questions and never pulls his punches. And this has earned Ramos respect. Matt Drudge, who runs the essential conservative news Web site *Drudge Report*, has called Ramos "the last journalist standing." In a tweet, Drudge wrote, "Warning to politicians. If you see him . . RUN!"[9]

> "Our position is clearly pro-Latino or pro-immigrant. We are simply being the voice for those who don't have a voice."
>
> —Jorge Ramos

The television environment today has radically changed from the time when CBS news anchor Walter Cronkite was the most respected broadcaster in America. We've gone from three nationwide broadcast networks to at least six, gone from no cable-only stations to hundreds, and gained multiple formats for viewing prerecorded movies and shows at home. In this chapter, we look at how this new television world came about and how it has influenced society. We start with the development of broadcast television and then cable/satellite television. We then consider who controls the television industry, how the world portrayed on television compares to the "real" world, and how television is becoming more interactive. We look at the roles television plays within society as a major recreational activity, a view of the world, and an influence on young people. And, finally, we look at where television is headed. ■

Audio 9.1: Listen to *On The Media's* Brooke Gladstone interview Univision anchor Jorge Ramos.

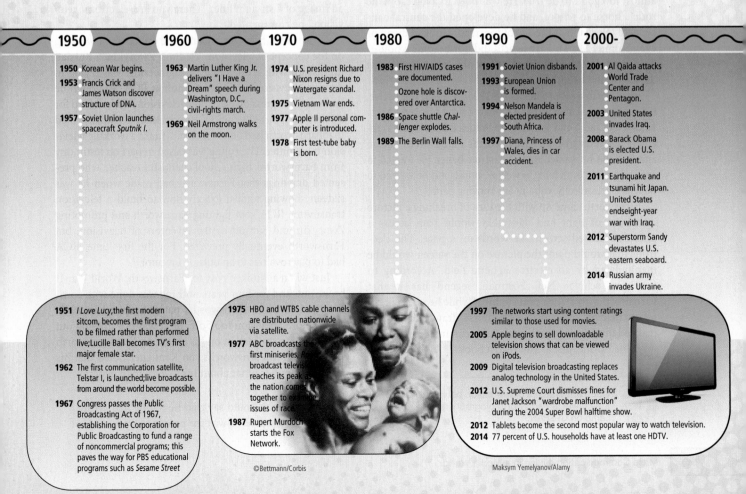

1950

- **1950** Korean War begins.
- **1953** Francis Crick and James Watson discover structure of DNA.
- **1957** Soviet Union launches spacecraft *Sputnik I*.

1960

- **1963** Martin Luther King Jr. delivers "I Have a Dream" speech during Washington, D.C., civil-rights march.
- **1969** Neil Armstrong walks on the moon.

1970

- **1974** U.S. president Richard Nixon resigns due to Watergate scandal.
- **1975** Vietnam War ends.
- **1977** Apple II personal computer is introduced.
- **1978** First test-tube baby is born.

1980

- **1983** First HIV/AIDS cases are documented.
  Ozone hole is discovered over Antarctica.
- **1986** Space shuttle *Challenger* explodes.
- **1989** The Berlin Wall falls.

1990

- **1991** Soviet Union disbands.
- **1993** European Union is formed.
- **1994** Nelson Mandela is elected president of South Africa.
- **1997** Diana, Princess of Wales, dies in car accident.

2000-

- **2001** Al Qaida attacks World Trade Center and Pentagon.
- **2003** United States invades Iraq.
- **2008** Barack Obama is elected U.S. president.
- **2011** Earthquake and tsunami hit Japan. United States endseight-year war with Iraq.
- **2012** Superstorm Sandy devastates U.S. eastern seaboard.
- **2014** Russian army invades Ukraine.

- **1951** *I Love Lucy*,the first modern sitcom, becomes the first program to be filmed rather than performed live;Lucille Ball becomes TV's first major female star.
- **1962** The first communication satellite, Telstar I, is launched;live broadcasts from around the world become possible.
- **1967** Congress passes the Public Broadcasting Act of 1967, establishing the Corporation for Public Broadcasting to fund a range of noncommercial programs; this paves the way for PBS educational programs such as *Sesame Street*

- **1975** HBO and WTBS cable channels are distributed nationwide via satellite.
- **1977** ABC broadcasts the first miniseries, *Roots*; broadcast television reaches its peak as the nation comes together to examine issues of race.
- **1987** Rupert Murdoch starts the Fox Network.

©Bettmann/Corbis

- **1997** The networks start using content ratings similar to those used for movies.
- **2005** Apple begins to sell downloadable television shows that can be viewed on iPods.
- **2009** Digital television broadcasting replaces analog technology in the United States.
- **2012** U.S. Supreme Court dismisses fines for Janet Jackson "wardrobe malfunction" during the 2004 Super Bowl halftime show.
- **2012** Tablets become the second most popular way to watch television.
- **2014** 77 percent of U.S. households have at least one HDTV.

Maksym Yemelyanov/Alamy

Television: Broadcast and Cable/Satellite

Television has gone through massive changes since its birth in the 1930s. Initially, it provided a limited number of options that were broadcast at no cost to viewers. Viewers could watch only the programs offered by the major networks, and only at the times when those programs were being broadcast. But in the 1980s, the balance of power between audience and broadcasters began to change. Not only did videocassette recorders (VCRs) allow viewers to choose when they would watch programs, but a range of broadcast, cable, and satellite channels allowed viewers a wider choice of what programs to watch. Television has in effect become two media: broadcast and cable/satellite.

AP Photo

Philo T. Farnsworth developed the central principles of television broadcasting at age fourteen, and by the age of twenty-one he had produced a working television transmission system.

Broadcast Television

Broadcast television in the United States is based on the idea that programming should be available to all viewers and should be paid for through advertising. Although today broadcast television is just one part of our TV diet, for many years it was the only item on the menu.

The Invention of Television. The story of Philo T. Farnsworth, the man who invented electronic television, is almost too good to be true. He was born in a log cabin, he rode a horse to school, and he developed the central concepts of television at the age of fourteen. Unlike Edison or even Samuel Morse, Farnsworth did not become a household name, yet he invented one of the most significant devices of the twentieth century.

Farnsworth was born in Utah in 1906. When he was twelve, his family settled in Idaho, and in their new house were magazines about radio and science, which fueled Farnsworth's creativity and imagination.[10] Farnsworth's heroes were Edison and Bell, but he wanted to do them one better. He wanted to send out moving pictures as well as sound, and he wanted to do it all electronically, without any moving parts.

Farnsworth came up with the idea of breaking a picture into lines of light and dark that would scan across a phosphor-coated screen like words on a page. The electrons that would paint the picture on the screen would be manipulated by an electromagnetic field. According to television scholar Neil Postman, legend has it that Farnsworth's great idea came to him "while he was tilling a potato field back and forth with a horse-drawn harrow and realized that an electron beam could scan images the same way, line by line, just as you read a book."[11]

Video 9.1: Watch a conversation between Daniel Stashower, a Farnsworth biographer, and Brian Lamb on C-SPAN.

By age twenty-one, Farnsworth had developed an all-electronic system for transmitting an image using radio waves. On September 7, 1927, he successfully transmitted an image of a straight line. "There you are, electronic television," he commented.[12]

Farnsworth, however, was not the only person working on the concept of television. Vladimir Zworykin, a Russian immigrant with a doctorate in engineering, was trying to develop television for David Sarnoff at RCA. Although he had made progress on electronic television and had filed for a patent on it in 1923, the U.S. Patent Office eventually ruled that Farnsworth had been the first to make a working television transmitter. The ruling was based in part on testimony from Farnsworth's high school chemistry teacher, who presented drawings that Farnsworth had made when he was sixteen showing almost exactly how to build a television transmitter. RCA kept fighting Farnsworth and promoting Zworykin and Sarnoff as the inventors of television, but Farnsworth eventually prevailed. For the first time, RCA had to pay royalties to an outside inventor.[13]

Just when all looked rosy for Farnsworth, World War II broke out, and for four years nothing was done with commercial television. Farnsworth's patents expired in 1947, right before television took off. Yet it was not missing out on the chance to cash in on his invention that Farnsworth came to regret. Farnsworth's son Kent later noted that his father was rather bitter about his invention in general:

> I suppose you could say that he felt he had created kind of a monster, a way for people to waste a lot of

their lives. Throughout my childhood his reaction to television was "There's nothing on it worthwhile, and we're not going to watch it in this household, and I don't want it in your intellectual diet."[14]

The Beginning of Broadcasting. The first significant television broadcasts using all-electronic systems occurred in 1939, when NBC started sending out television broadcasts from the New York World's Fair. But American involvement in World War II halted the manufacture of television sets in 1942, and most stations went off the air. Peace came in 1945, and by 1946 RCA had television sets back on the market.

From 1948 to 1952, the licensing of new television stations was frozen to give the Federal Communications Commission (FCC) and television producers time to figure out how the technology should be used and controlled. Because of the freeze, only some cities had television. The television cities saw drastic drops in attendance at movies and sporting events. Restaurant owners hated the popular variety program *Your Show of Shows*, which aired on Saturday nights, because customers rushed home to watch television instead of staying out to eat and drink.[15] During the same period, the Supreme Court issued its ruling in *United States v. Paramount* that broke the studios' control over the movie industry (see Chapter 8). Television was ready to take over the entertainment industry.

A number of shows characterized this early period of television. Milton Berle, host of the *Texaco Star Theatre*, came to be called "Mr. Television" and was known for his funny costumes and physical humor. The *Ed Sullivan Show* (originally called *Toast of the Town*) became the place to see new and innovative talent. In later years, Sullivan would feature the Beatles and Elvis Presley. The 1950s also saw a number of anthology dramas, essentially short plays or movies, with a new cast and story each week. One show that made a successful leap from radio to television was Edward R. Murrow's CBS news documentary series *Hear It Now*, which became *See It Now* on the new visual medium.

Lucy, Desi, and the End of Live Television. No other entertainment program of the 1950s would have a longer, more lasting impact than one produced by a brash redheaded actress and her Cuban American husband.

When Lucille Ball and Desi Arnaz created their groundbreaking sitcom *I Love Lucy* in 1951, they had to overcome two major obstacles. The first was persuading CBS to let Arnaz play Lucy's television husband. At that time, this was controversial because Ball was white and Arnaz Hispanic. The second challenge was that most television shows at the time were being broadcast live from New York City studios, but Lucy and Desi wanted to continue to live in California. Their solution was to film the show before a studio audience, edit the program like a movie, and ship it to New York to be broadcast. Within a year, *I Love Lucy* was the most popular show on television.

CBS Photo Archive/Getty Images

Lucille Ball and her husband, Desi Arnaz, created the modern situation comedy in 1951 with their show *I Love Lucy*, which was filmed rather than performed live.

Being filmed rather than performed live meant that there were high-quality copies of *I Love Lucy* that could be shown again and again. Arnaz held the rerun rights to the show, which gave the couple the money to build their own television production company, Desilu Studios. More than fifty years after *Lucy* first went on the air, audiences are still laughing at the show.

The format Ball and Arnaz created, a half-hour comedy filmed with three cameras before a live studio audience, became a mainstay of television programming. Today, the situation comedy remains one of the most popular program formats.[16]

The Arrival of Color Television. The networks started experimenting with color television as early as 1954, but by 1959, only three shows were regularly being shown in color. (The familiar NBC peacock logo was initially created to show black-and-white viewers that they were missing programs in color.) It wasn't until 1965 that all three of the original television networks were broadcasting in color. One reason for the slow acceptance of color was the price of the television sets. The *Boston Globe* notes that in 1965 color televisions cost the equivalent of what a midline HDTV set cost in 2000 (between $2,500 and $5,000).[17] The switch to color was not completed until the early 1970s.[18]

Cable and Satellite Television 

Today, cable and satellite television constitutes almost a separate medium from broadcast television, but initially

 Video 9.2: Watch classic *I Love Lucy* episodes online.

AP Photo/Saurabh Das

Local cable television companies offer a variety of programming choices via satellite.

cable was designed as nothing more than a delivery system for broadcast channels.

Community Antenna Television. In the early days of television, people in remote areas or in communities sheltered by mountains frequently could not receive the new signals. Among these was Mrs. L. E. Parsons of Astoria, Oregon. Parsons wanted to have television, but the nearest station was 125 miles away. Her husband solved the problem by placing an antenna on top of a local hotel and running a cable into their apartment. Once word got out that the Parsons family had television, the hotel, local bars, and even the neighbors started asking for connections to their antenna. This early form of cable television, which simply retransmitted broadcast channels, came to be known as **community antenna television (CATV)**.[19]

Connecting to these early cable systems was expensive; the cost ranged from $100 to $200. Although there were isolated experiments with subscription channels, for the most part cable remained a way to serve areas with poor reception, and the FCC devised restrictive rules to keep it that way. Until the 1970s, cable was primarily a way to get a good TV signal, not additional programming.[20]

Satellite Distribution and the Rebirth of Cable. By 1975, the face of cable television was beginning to change. The FCC began loosening the rules on cable companies, and new channels were being distributed via satellite.[21]

Home Box Office (HBO) was the first service to make the leap from merely providing access to providing programming. In 1975, it requested permission from the FCC to start sending out its programming nationwide via satellite. Surprisingly, not one of the **Big Three networks** (NBC, CBS, and ABC) objected to the upstart service as it gained access to their viewers across the country. After all, HBO was just an office, some videotape machines, and a satellite uplink. It had no affiliates, had no stations, and could reach only people who were on cable, a small fraction of the viewing market. But the satellite system had a key advantage. Five hundred cable systems could obtain the programming as cheaply as one. They just had to put up a dish to bring in the signal.

Although HBO was the first to go nationwide, no one has done more than Ted Turner to create modern cable television. After his father's suicide in 1963, the twenty-four-year-old Turner inherited a billboard company that was in financial trouble.[22] Turner was not content with running one of the nation's largest billboard companies, so in 1970, he bought Channel 17 in Atlanta. The UHF station was in serious financial trouble, largely because it was located on a part of the broadcast band that many television sets couldn't receive and many people didn't bother to look at. Turner promptly renamed the station WTCG, which stood for Turner Communication Group.

Turner's next big step was buying the last-place Atlanta Braves baseball team and the Atlanta Hawks basketball franchise, thus guaranteeing him exclusive rights to a pair of shows (the teams' games) that would run more than 200 episodes a year. It was also programming that would motivate Atlantans to make the effort to find Channel 17.

When RCA launched a television satellite in 1976, Turner saw his next big opportunity. He realized that he could use the satellite to send his station nationwide and provide programming to the growing number of cable systems. On December 27, 1976, WTCG became Superstation WTBS (Turner Broadcasting System). With that step, Turner became one of the first of a new breed of television entrepreneurs who were turning local stations into national powerhouses.

At this point, Turner made the riskiest move of his career: He created Cable News Network (CNN), the first

Video 9.3: Watch Ken Auletta talk about Ted Turner's career.

community antenna television (CATV): An early form of cable television used to distribute broadcast channels in communities with poor television reception.

Big Three networks: The original television broadcast networks: NBC, CBS, and ABC.

twenty-four-hour news channel. In its early years, CNN had many technical problems and no reputation to speak of. Critics, in fact, referred to CNN as the "Chicken Noodle Network" because it paid its employees poorly and was run amateurishly.[23] Despite the network's problems, however, viewers soon discovered that if they wanted breaking news, they could find it immediately on CNN. Unlike ABC, NBC, and CBS, CNN did not have to interrupt soap operas or sitcoms to put news on the air.

When ABC and Westinghouse tried to start a competing cable news service in 1982, Turner launched his second news network, CNN Headline News, which featured round-the-clock, half-hour newscasts. Since then, CNN has expanded to provide CNN Radio, CNN International, CNN Airport Network, and CNN en Español.

Turner took his idea of repackaging material a step further by buying up the MGM movie library and the Hanna-Barbera cartoon library, which gave him control of the Flintstones, the Jetsons, and Scooby-Doo. He used these pop-culture figures, along with additional sports broadcasting rights he acquired, to program WTBS, along with Turner Network Television (TNT), the Cartoon Network, and Turner Classic Movies.

In 1996, Turner Broadcasting was acquired by media giant Time Warner, and although Turner lost direct control of his networks, he did get access to the Warner Bros. library of movies and classic cartoons. When *Time* magazine's editors declared Turner their "Man of the Year" in 1991, they wrote that he had fulfilled Marshall McLuhan's ideal of the global village. CNN has not made all people brothers and sisters, but *Time* said that the network has given people a window on the world:

> In 1991, one of the most eventful years of this century, the world witnessed the dramatic and transforming impact of those events of live television by satellite. The very definition of news was rewritten—from something that *has happened* to something that is *happening* at the very moment you are hearing of it. A war involving the fiercest air bombardment in history unfolded in real time—before the cameras.[24]

Before long, numerous channels were available to cable companies via satellite, including Black Entertainment Television (BET) and the children's network Nickelodeon. In 1978, amid much ridicule, the Entertainment and Sports Programming Network (ESPN) was launched as a twenty-four-hour-a-day sports channel carrying such little-known sports as Australian-rules football and curling. But ESPN quickly grew into one of the most popular channels on cable.[25]

During this period, nine out of ten viewers were watching prime-time programs on the networks, which were still controlled by the people who had started the first radio networks: William Paley at CBS, David Sarnoff at NBC, and Leonard Goldenson at ABC.[26]

Jude Domski/Wire Image/Getty Images

Cable television pioneer and CNN founder Ted Turner created a media empire with global reach that goes a long way to fulfilling the ideal of the global village.

However, the 1980s saw the growth of a new kind of cable—a service that brought new channels into the household along with the original networks. Cable television viewers now have access to a wide range of programming, most of which can be grouped into a few major categories:

Questioning the Media

In the home where you grew up, did you have cable/satellite television or just broadcast television? If you had cable/satellite, do you know how much your bill for it was per month? If you had to give up one, which would it be, and why?

- Affiliates of the Big Four broadcast networks (ABC, NBC, CBS, and Fox)
- Independent stations and smaller network affiliates
- Superstations—Local independent stations that broadcast nationwide via satellite (WTBS, WGN, etc.)
- Local-access channels—Channels offering local government programming and community-produced shows
- Cable networks—Advertiser-supported networks that may also receive small fees for each subscriber on a particular cable system (MTV, CNN, BET, etc.)
- Premium channels—Extra-cost channels that don't carry advertising (HBO, Showtime, etc.)

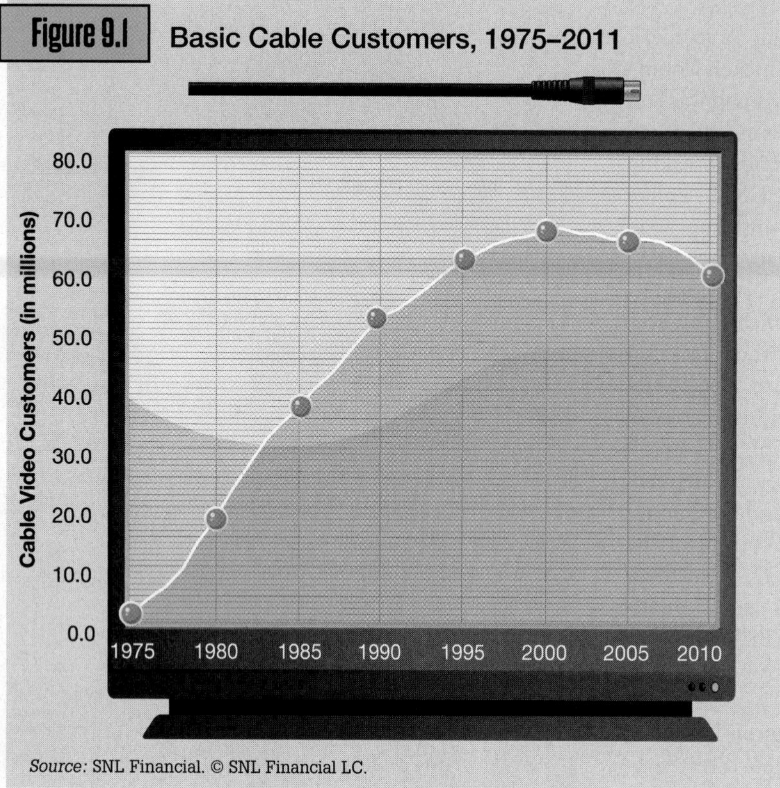

Source: SNL Financial. © SNL Financial LC.

- Pay-per-view channels—Channels showing special events, concerts, and movies that subscribers pay for on an individual basis
- Audio services—High-quality music services[27]

Cable services offered massive competition to the broadcasters and created a new television landscape. Approximately 50 percent of all American households (about 58 million) subscribe to cable service. And 48 million of those subscribers also get the extended digital video service.[28] By way of comparison, in the United Kingdom, cable was in 13.1 percent of all homes by the end of 2011. (Direct broadcast satellite service is much more popular in the UK than cable, reaching roughly 39 percent of TV viewers there.[29]) (See Figure 9.1.)

Hollywood and the VCR. Although videotape has been used in television studios since the 1950s, it was not until the late 1970s that the **videocassette recorder (VCR)** became a household appliance that allowed viewers to make permanent copies of television shows. VCRs took time to catch on. Initially, there were two incompatible formats (VHS and Beta), and the machines themselves were expensive, costing $800 or more. In 1985, only two out of ten U.S. homes had VCRs, but by 1991, they could be found in seven out of ten homes.

Consumers loved the fact that they could record programs and watch them later, but movie and television producers were upset that people were recording—and keeping—programs without paying for them. They were also concerned that movies and programs would be duplicated and resold around the world. Universal and Disney sued Sony over its promotion of the VCR for recording movies, but in 1984, the U.S. Supreme Court ruled that television viewers had the right to record copyrighted programs for their own personal use. Piracy of the programming was clearly illegal, but this was not the fault of the equipment manufacturers.[30]

Direct Broadcast Satellites. Satellite programming providers have been competing with cable since the 1980s, but their success was limited initially because of the rapid growth of cable, the large dish antennas required, and the limited number of channels consumers could receive. All this changed in the 1990s with the advent of the low-earth-orbit **direct broadcast satellite (DBS)**. Several DBSs were launched to deliver programming through a new kind of antenna about the size of a pizza.

As of December 2011, approximately 29 percent of U.S. households had satellite television. Satellite service in the United States grew rapidly from the mid-1990s until about 2007, when adoption of the new delivery system stabilized at current levels.[31] In Europe, which has less of a tradition of cable television than the United States, DBS services are very popular. 21st Century Fox's Sky Italia has almost 5 million subscribers in Italy, offering approximately 190 channels of programming through satellite and mobile delivery.[32]

DBS is now competing head-to-head with cable. A problem the satellite services face in this competition is that their subscribers still have to put up an old-fashioned antenna to get local broadcast stations. To address this drawback, in major markets DBS companies provide local stations via satellite as well.[33]

Digital Television

Just as sound recording has moved to digital formats with CDs and MP3 files (see Chapter 7), so is television

Web 9.1: Get the scoop on HDTV presence in U.S. homes.

videocassette recorder (VCR): A home videotape machine that allows viewers to make permanent copies of television shows and, thus, choose when they want to watch programs.

direct broadcast satellite (DBS): A low-earth-orbit satellite that provides television programming via a small, pizza-sized satellite antenna; DBS is a competitor to cable TV.

shifting from the analog technology of Farnsworth and Zworykin to computerized digital technology. All television broadcasting in the United States was scheduled to be digital by February 17, 2009, but in January 2009, the federal government decided that people weren't ready for the transition, despite several years of warnings that the change would be taking place. Critics of the move to digital broadcasting pointed out that many of the households that rely on broadcast signals for television have incomes under $30,000 and may have trouble affording the set-top box that converts digital broadcast signals into analog signals that old-fashioned television sets can display. To help solve this problem, the government issued coupons to help poor families buy the converters. In fact, a shortage of the coupons was among the reasons that the conversion was delayed.

SECRET 4 VCR ownership peaked in 1999, with nearly 89 percent of households owning a VCR. By the end of 2006, that proportion had fallen ten points to 79 percent. VCRs were replaced predominantly by DVD players, which are now in 79 percent of all homes.[34] VCRs are also facing competition from the new digital video recorders (DVRs), such as TiVo, that record television programs on a computer hard disk. The DVR lets a viewer jump in to start watching a recorded show fifteen minutes after it comes on the air. The viewer can then fast-forward through the commercials, and by the time the show is over, the viewer has caught up with the "live" broadcast. DVRs are seen as easier to use than VCRs but typically require a monthly subscription fee to use. As of December 2013, DVRs were in 47 percent of American households, up from 40 percent in 2010 and 23 percent in 2007.[35] (This gives us another example of Secret Four—Nothing's new: Everything that happened in the past will happen again.)

As you may have noticed from those figures, the rate of growth of DVR adoption has slowed dramatically in the last few years. Why? It's probably not that people don't want to be able to watch shows on their own schedule. Instead, people have many more options now than just prerecording shows to watch. For example, a 2013 study shows that 61 percent of cable subscribers have access to video on demand (VOD), with which they can just call up a missed show without doing any recording. They may also have access to a streaming service like Netflix that lets them pick from an enormous library of movies, television shows, and original content.[36] (We'll come back to this at the end of the chapter.)

On Friday, June 12, 2009, the last of the analog television broadcast stations was shut off. That doesn't mean that everyone started using new digital sets, however. Instead, many people will continue to get their television from a digital cable or satellite box, or get a converter box. On the two days following the shutdown of analog broadcasting, the FCC received approximately 400,000 calls to its hotline, considerably below the 600,000 to 3 million calls it was expecting.[37] There are two distinct digital formats. **High-definition television (HDTV)** is in a wide-screen format (like a theater movie) and features an ultra-clear high-resolution picture with superior sound. The other digital format is **standard digital television**, which makes it possible to broadcast up to six channels on the same frequency space that now carries one channel. (However, the picture is no better than that produced by existing signals.[38]) Using standard digital, a PBS station can choose to put out a single HDTV program or four digital programs at the current resolution, giving children a choice at any given time between *Arthur*, *Barney*, *Sesame Street*, and *Wishbone*.

high-definition television (HDTV): A standard for high-quality digital broadcasting that features a high-resolution picture, wide-screen format, and enhanced sound.

standard digital television: A standard for digital broadcasting that allows six channels to fit in the broadcast frequency space occupied by a single analog signal.

REUTERS/Aman Mehinli/Landov

Although cable television remains the largest alternative to broadcast programming in the United States, satellite delivery is much more common throughout much of the world, as is illustrated by this block of apartments in the Turkmen city of Türkmenabat.

The development of HDTV began in the 1980s, and on November 1, 1998, the launch of the space shuttle *Discovery* was the first event to be covered in a nationwide broadcast using a digital television signal. The broadcast was viewed by a tiny audience of just a few hundred people in twenty cities, with forty-two stations carrying digital signals.[39] As of March 2014, approximately 77 percent of U.S. homes had at least one HDTV set, and 46 percent of U.S. homes had more than one HDTV. Overall, 59 percent of the televisions in use in the United States in 2014 were HDTVs, up from 34 percent in 2010 and just 18 percent in 2008.[40]

Richard Levine/Alamy

Since all television broadcasting went digital in 2009, HDTVs have become increasingly popular. Viewers need either a cable/satellite connection or a converter box if they want to keep using analog sets.

From Broadcasting to Narrowcasting: The Changing Business of Television

Television got its start with the three networks that dominated the radio industry in the 1940s: NBC, CBS, and ABC. There were some independent stations as well, such as WGN in Chicago and WOR in New York, which had grown out of major independent radio stations, but for the most part, everyone in the country was watching NBC, CBS, or ABC. This would remain the status quo until cable and VCRs exploded in popularity in the 1980s.

Networks and Affiliates

The Big Three **television networks** are the companies that have provided programs to local stations around the country since the start of the television industry. These affiliate stations require a license from the FCC, equipment, and a local staff. The choice of what shows to carry is up to the local station. If a station carries a particular program, the station receives a fee from the network, along with the revenue from selling local commercials during the show. The network makes its money from the national commercials that run during the program. If an individual station decides that it could make more money running a locally produced program, such as a college basketball game, or a program from an independent producer, it can do so. In that case, the station pays for the program but keeps all the advertising revenue. The only exceptions are the dozen or so stations that each network owns and operates; although they have a certain amount of independence, these stations must please their network owners.[41]

Educational Broadcasting Becomes Public Broadcasting

Noncommercial broadcasting in the United States was conceived as a way of delivering educational programming. Then Congress passed the Public Broadcasting Act of 1967, which established the Corporation for Public Broadcasting to provide funds for a wide range of noncommercial programs, including public service and educational programs. The noncommercial, or public, stations came to share programming through a new network, the **Public Broadcasting Service (PBS)**. This nonprofit broadcast network is funded by government appropriations, private industry underwriting, and support from viewers.[42]

While PBS stations eventually became widely available, they tended to have small audiences except for their daytime children's programming, which included the groundbreaking *Sesame Street*.[43] *Sesame Street*'s creator, Joan Ganz Cooney, says that the goal of the show was to give disadvantaged inner-city children a head start on school: "We argued that it would make all the psychological difference in their success in school if [disadvantaged children] came in with the same kind of skills as a middle-class child."[44] *Sesame Street* was also designed to have a slick, fast-paced, commercial look. It even had "sponsors," such as the number 5 and the letters *Q* and *U*.

When the show premiered on November 8, 1969, it immediately grabbed a significant audience, and even now it is among the most watched of all children's shows. But was it a success at helping disadvantaged children develop reading and math skills? That question is difficult to answer. At least one major study found that *Sesame Street* was successful in preparing children for school, but that "advantaged" children gained fully as much from it as disadvantaged students; thus, the show was not closing the gap between the haves and the have-nots.

In the 1990s, PBS started attracting a significant audience with programming such as the Ken Burns documentaries *The Civil War* and *Baseball*. Those larger audiences, in

---

television network: A company that provides programs to local stations around the country; the local affiliate stations choose which programs to carry.

Public Broadcasting Service (PBS): A nonprofit broadcast network that provides a wide range of public service and educational programs. It is funded by government appropriations, private industry underwriting, and viewer support.

turn, led to support from a number of large corporations that hoped their brief underwriting announcements would reach the upscale audiences who watch PBS. These announcements are not quite commercials, but they do allow corporations to present a short message to viewers. Among recent PBS underwriters are oil giant BP, GMC Trucks, AT&T, and State Farm Insurance. More recently, PBS has been attracting big audiences with British imports such as *Downton Abbey* and *Sherlock*.

AP Photo/Richard Drew

Sesame Street features guests from a wide range of backgrounds, including Colombian musician Juanes, posing here with Muppets Rosita (left) and Elmo (right).

The Fox Network

The 1980s brought numerous changes to the broadcasting market. Not only were VCRs and cable becoming popular, but there was also a new broadcast network. Australian newspaper publisher Rupert Murdoch started the Fox broadcast network after buying 20th Century Fox and incorporating it into his mammoth global media empire (see Chapter 3). He put the new network on the air in 1986 by buying stations in six of the top ten television markets. Although companies had tried to set up alternative broadcast networks before, none had really succeeded. Murdoch had an advantage in that during the 1980s people were becoming accustomed to watching cable channels, which meant they were no longer wed to regular network programming.

Fox was able to attract independent stations because it was offering them free programming rather than making them rely on syndicated material, most of which consisted of network reruns. The offerings were initially limited, with a late-night talk show starring Joan Rivers followed by Sunday-evening programming beginning in 1987.

While Fox managed to attract viewers with shows such as *The Simpsons* and *Married With Children,* what put it on the map was stealing NFL football away from the Big Three. NFL football was a show that people were accustomed to watching; now they just had to watch it on a new network. Fox also brought in the under-thirty viewers coveted by advertisers with hit programs such as *The X-Files* and *Melrose Place*.[45] The Big Three broadcast networks were becoming the **Big Four networks**.

More recently, Fox has been attracting large audiences with hit shows such as *American Idol, Family Guy,* and *The Simpsons* (which as of this writing has been on the air more than twenty-five years!).

Defining Ratings

One of the biggest concerns for television networks, whether broadcast or cable, is the size of their audiences. Rates for commercials, which provide all the income for broadcast networks and a substantial portion of the income for cable services, are determined by how many people are viewing a show at a given time.

Measuring television audiences used to be pretty simple, at least in principle. You found out how many people watched a given show at a given time on one of three major networks, and you had your answer. The fact that you depended on a limited sample of people who had to fill out complex diaries or use a set-top "people meter" may have complicated things a bit, but basically it was simple. But now we have four major English-language broadcast networks, the Univsion Spanish-language broadcast network, PBS, several minor broadcast networks, dozens of major cable networks, and hundreds of specialized cable networks. There is also the issue of measuring the alternative methods for viewing these programs, the most important of which is delayed viewing on DVR.

Due to the expansion of viewing choices, the ratings required for a show to be a success have gotten smaller. In 2011, the top-rated singing competition show *American Idol* attracted an average of 29 million viewers per week. In 1996, *ER* was the top-rated drama, and it drew an audience of more than 30 million viewers per week.[46]

Now that DVRs are in more than 47 percent of all homes, the number of people watching shows on a

Big Four networks: The broadcast landscape we know today: the Big Three networks plus the Fox network.

Video 9.4: Watch a segment of *Sesame Street* featuring *Star Trek*'s Patrick Stewart.

Video 9.5: Watch puppets explain how the Nielsen ratings system works.

delayed basis has become more important. Nielsen, which measures television audiences, now considers:

- Live only—People who are watching the program live as it happens.
- Live + SD—People who watch the program the same day as it airs. If you record a program on your DVR and start watching it fifteen minutes after it starts, this is you.
- Live + 3—People who watch the program live or within three days of airing.
- Live + 7—People who watch the program within seven days of its airing. This is the most complete measure of a show's popularity. (It does not, however, account for the episode of the Food Network's competition show *Chopped* that I recorded three months ago but finally watched last night.[47])

The major provider of viewership data, known as *ratings*, is Nielsen Media Research. The company keeps track of the shows watched in 9,000 homes located across the United States. Although the Nielsen families receive a token payment for their participation, they are essentially volunteering to keep track of all their television viewing. Nielsen uses a combination of methods to measure audience size. In the largest urban markets, the company uses a device called the **PeopleMeter.** Viewers push buttons on the machine to record who is watching programs at specific times. In smaller markets, viewers fill out daily diaries, listing what they watched.

©iStockphoto.com/acprints

While Nielsen tracks overall network viewership throughout the year, the company looks at the audience size of individual stations four times a year (November, February, May, and July) during periods known as **sweeps**. Networks and individual stations often schedule their best—or at least most popular—programming during sweeps periods to attract the highest possible ratings. These higher ratings allow them to charge more for commercials. Nielsen also tracks the ages and sex of audience members, and advertisers are oftentimes as concerned about the demographics of their audience as they are about the absolute size of it.

Nielsen provides networks and stations with several different measurements. The most important of these is the **rating point**, the percentage of the total potential television audience actually watching the show. For example, Nielsen estimated that there were 114.5 million households with televisions in use in 2008. If 1,145,000 homes viewed a particular program, that would produce a rating of 1 (1,145,000 / 114,500,000 = .01, or 1 percent of the total potential audience). A program viewed in 15 million households would have a rating of 13.1.[48]

The second major measurement Nielsen provides is the **share**, the percentage of television sets in use that are tuned to a particular show. Instead of telling producers how many households are watching the show, the share measures how popular a particular show is compared to everything else that is broadcast at the time. Although a show that airs at 1:00 a.m. might have a relatively low rating (say, 3 or 4), it could have a high share (30 or 40) because a large portion of a small audience is watching it.[49]

An Earthquake in Slow Motion

Fox, cable, and the VCR changed everything for the television industry—a set of changes that media writer Ken Auletta has called "an earthquake in slow motion." In 1976, the prime-time viewing audience belonged to the Big Three, with nine out of ten viewers watching network programming. By 1991, the Big Three had lost a third of their viewers. These viewers hadn't stopped watching television; they had just moved to other channels. In 1976, the typical home had a choice of seven broadcast channels; by 1991, it had a choice of thirty-three cable channels.[50] Today, homes with digital cable programming can have access to more than one hundred channels.

Another part of the earthquake was that the original Big Three networks were sold to new owners in 1985. NBC was taken over by General Electric, CBS was purchased by investor Larry Tisch, and ABC was purchased by Capital Cities Communications. Since that time, ABC has been acquired by Disney, CBS has been purchased and spun off by Viacom, and Comcast has bought NBC. The networks are no longer controlled by the people who started them.[51]

The earthquake also affected profits. Revenues for the broadcast networks plummeted in the 1990s, whereas cable network revenues grew. Cable channels typically make more profit than the broadcast networks. Cable channels are the most profitable part of Walt Disney Co., NBCUniversal, News Corporation, and Time Warner. ESPN, despite spending more than $5.2 billion on content in 2011, was the most profitable part of Disney.[52]

Despite their lower profitability, the broadcast networks generally have much bigger audiences than cable services. Popular cable shows such as professional wrestling or reality programs such as *Swamp People* typically attract an audience

---

PeopleMeter: An electronic box used by the ratings company Nielsen Media Research to record which television shows people watch.

sweeps: The four times during the year that Nielsen Media Research measures the size of individual television station audiences.

rating point: The percentage of the total potential television audience actually watching a particular show. One rating point indicates an audience of approximately 1.14 million viewers.

share: The percentage of television sets in use that are tuned to a particular show.

of, at most, 5 million viewers, whereas top-rated network shows such as *NCIS* typically attract three to four times as many viewers.

Why, then, are cable channels making more money than the broadcast networks? Traditionally, cable programs have cost less to produce than network programs, but spending on cable shows has been growing rapidly over the last several years. But the biggest difference is that broadcasters have a single source of revenue—advertising—whereas most cable channels have both a subscription fee and advertising revenue. In 2010, cable networks brought in nearly $48 billion in revenue. Of that, $22.3 billion came from advertising revenue, but $25 billion came from fees from cable and satellite operators.[53]

Diversity on Television

Broadcast television and the major cable networks have been roundly criticized for presenting a distorted view of reality. Aside from the issue that people on television comedies and dramas are not only attractive and funny, but they also resolve problems in less than an hour, there are complaints that television presents a world that is overwhelmingly white, male, and middle class.

In 1999, the Big Four networks introduced twenty-six new shows; not one of them featured a nonwhite lead character. This led to protests and threats of boycotts by African American and Latino groups. Ralph Farquhar, an African American television producer, told the *Arizona Republic*,

> I don't believe they're intentionally [excluding minority talent]. But people have to pay attention, you know? The makeup of America . . . has changed radically over the past 20 or 30 years, and yet TV doesn't necessarily reflect the diversity and the composition of the American population.[54]

Scott Sassa, a Japanese American network television executive, recalls being upset as a child when he saw an Anglo playing an Asian character. "I've got to tell you, growing up, seeing David Carradine as a Chinese guy [ticked] you off," Sassa said, referring to the martial arts series *Kung Fu*. Sassa says that the networks will have to reach out to nonwhites in a meaningful way if they want to hold on to their audiences:

> You not only want to see someone that looks like you on TV—you want to see someone that is a role model, someone that you want to aspire to be. That's what we need to do—create role models that are diverse, that make people in these minority groups feel good.[55]

Huffington Post pop culture blogger Meron Mogos notes that most recent shows on television have at least one supporting ethnic character, but few have nonwhites in starring roles. The exception to that is the ABC show *Scandal*, the first show in four decades to have an African American woman as the lead.[56] The show staring Kerry Washington was created by Shonda Rhimes, who also did *Grey's Anatomy*. Washington's character is based on real-life African American woman Judy Smith, who was a communication director for the George W. Bush White House and then went to work as a crisis management expert.

Questioning the Media

Do you use a DVR to time shift your television viewing? Do you skip commercials when you watch programs on the DVR? If you are skipping commercials, how should television networks make money?

Washington told CNN in an interview that her character Olivia "is someone who happened to be born female and black and those elements add to who she is as a human being. Do I think another person of another race could play her? Yes. Do I think it would change the story a little bit? Do I think it would change the character a little bit? Yes."[57]

Writer/producer Rhimes told *Entertainment Weekly* that although she has seen progress in casting diversity, she thinks there is room for improvement:

> Do I want to see any more shows where someone has a sassy black friend? No, because I'm nobody's sassy black friend. I just want to see shows in which people get to be people and that look like the world we live in. The world is changing, and television will have to follow.[58]

One channel that manages to have a higher level of diversity is the Food Network. While its hosts are not that different from the rest of television, the contestants in the chef competitions, such as *Chopped* and *Cutthroat Kitchen*, have a wide range of racial and ethnic diversity.

One of the things that cooks on the Food Network need to be good at is telling the story of their food, and people of differing backgrounds generally have interesting stories to tell, whether that of being an immigrant, growing up facing adversity, or simply being a determined young person trying to succeed.

Huffington Post Black Voices blogger Deborah Plummer notes that as of 2012, *Chopped* had nine judges, three of whom were women, one of whom was Ethiopian, one of whom was Mexican, and one of whom was Indian. The shows also feature competitors who are of varying sizes, accents, and sexual orientation.[59]

A major research project at UCLA's Ralph J. Bunche Center for African American Studies found that despite some recent improvements, minorities are still radically underrepresented on television, ranging from one-twelfth to one-half their actual share of the population. Not including sports, minorities appeared at about half the

Video 9.6: Watch Ken Auletta talk about his book *Three Blind Mice*.

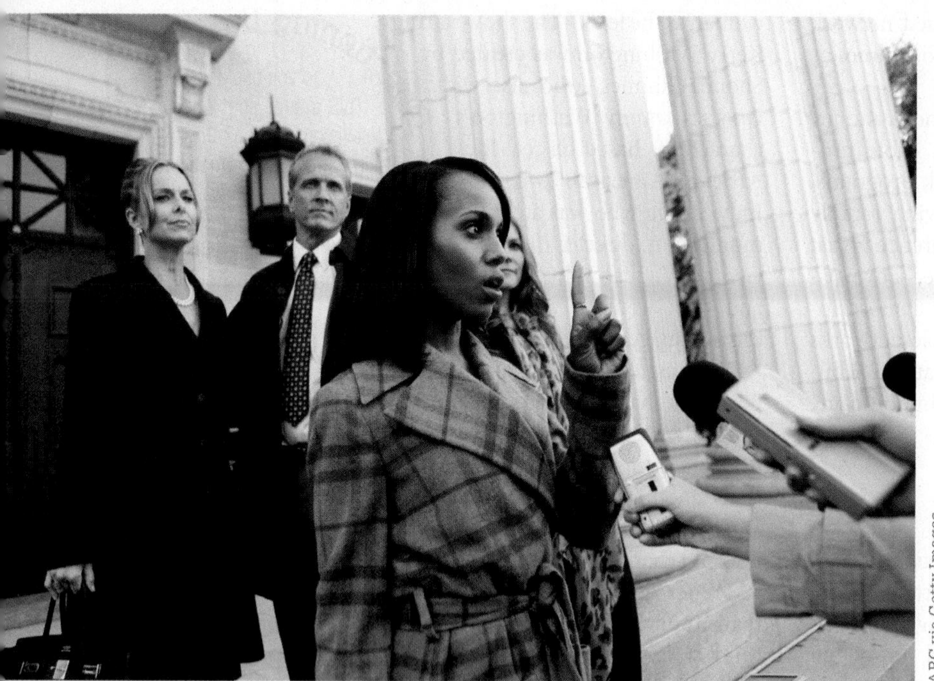

The ABC television series *Scandal* staring Kerry Washington is the first show in four decades to have an African American woman as the star of the show.

expected rate on cable TV and reality shows, but on broadcast scripted shows, they were underrepresented by a factor of seven to one.[60]

If you want to make some comparisons on your own, 2010 U.S. Census Bureau estimates break down the current population as follows:

White, not Hispanic—64%
Hispanic—16%
African American—13%
Asian—5%
More Than One Race—3%
American Indian—0.9%
Pacific Islander—0.2%

(These values add up to more than 100 percent because some people overlap in categories.)[61]

Univision and Spanish-Language Broadcasting. Although Latinos are seriously underrepresented on the Big Four English-language networks, there has been substantial growth in Spanish-language television. As discussed at the beginning of this chapter, Univision, a Spanish-language broadcast network, is actually the fifth-largest network, something it trumpeted in a 2005 full-page ad in the *New York Times*. Univision tends to do particularly well in the highly prized eighteen- to thirty-four-year-old demographic. The network's popular telenovela *Mañana es para siempre* (*Tomorrow Is Forever*) routinely takes second place in its time slot among the younger demographics.[62] In 2013, Univision got the critical fourth place in the Nielsen February sweeps period among the prized audience demographic of adults aged eighteen to forty-nine. Part of this success came from Univision's growing popularity, and some of it came from NBC having a particularly bad year; but while Univision can't count on holding onto that fourth-place spot in the ratings, it does have a strongly growing audience.[63]

In addition to Univision, the Spanish television market includes the much smaller Telemundo network, along with a host of independent stations. Most markets offer no more than two Spanish-language television stations, but Phoenix, Arizona, has at least five.

The most popular programs on Spanish television are the **telenovelas**, or soap operas, which make up fifteen of the top twenty Spanish programs and are popular in both Latin America and the United States. Produced primarily in Mexico and Brazil, the telenovelas are exceedingly detailed and involved miniseries, with each story lasting six months to a year.[64] In December 2010, Univision drew 7.3 million viewers for the final episode of its six-month-long telenovela *Soy tu dueña* (*Woman of Steel*). The series drew an average audience of 5.4 million viewers per episode—an audience that was often better than those for shows airing against it on Fox or NBC. The only shows to defeat the series finale that night were a rerun of the comedy *Two and a Half Men* and ESPN's *Monday Night Football*.[65]

The telenovelas are at the heart of the criticism of Spanish-language networks. Latino critics say that the networks need to do more than just rerun Latin American programs; they need to make programs about Hispanics living in the United States. (Approximately half of Univision's programming comes from outside the United States.) There have also been complaints that the U.S. networks do not show dark-skinned Hispanics.

In an interesting twist, telenovelas have started making the jump over to English-language television. In the 2006–2007 season, ABC had a big hit with *Ugly Betty*, which is based on the hit Colombian telenovela *Yo soy Betty, la fea*. However, *Ugly Betty*'s ratings faded during the 2009–2010 season.[66]

To address the criticisms, Univision has started producing its own American-based sitcom, and it scored major hits by airing live broadcasts of the FIFA World Cup soccer tournaments.[67] It has taken cues from other American networks and created a game show called *A Millón*, which

Web 9.2: Read about a controversial article from the *New York Times* that calls Rhimes an "angry black woman."

telenovelas: Spanish-language soap operas popular in both Latin America and the United States.

TEST YOUR VISUAL MEDIA LITERACY

Netflix/Photofest
A NEW SERIES FROM THE CREATOR OF WEEDS
A NETFLIX ORIGINAL SERIES
ORANGE is the new BLACK
EVERY SENTENCE IS A STORY
ALL EPISODES JULY 11
ONLY ON NETFLIX

What Does a TV Show Look Like?

Broadcast television has long been criticized for lacking racial and ethnic diversity. But the prison drama *Orange Is the New Black* has a diverse range of characters including a transgender African American woman. Laverne Cox, who plays a transgender prisoner, says that the show is a breakout because of the range of faces in the show. "We don't see enough multidimensional portrayals of trans women and women in jail who are different races, ages, body types. . . . We don't see enough multidimensional portrayals of women in general, that show the diversity of womanhood."[68]

Even with its high level of diversity (which some complain gets talked about too much), the core of the series is based on a memoir by a Piper Kerman, a memoir by a "privileged white woman serving a prison sentence." But, as critic Roxane Gay points out, "Unfortunately, we will never see a similar show about a woman of color as a stranger in a strange land, bewildered by incarceration."[69]

Orange Is the New Black (OITNB), Netflix's cutting-edge drama, is making the news for a wide range of reasons. Perhaps the most noteworthy thing about it is that Netflix is a streaming service, not a broadcast or cable network, so Netflix releases the entire season of the series all at once, so fans who want to can binge watch all the episodes in a single weekend. But the prison drama is also notable for its cast of characters. As you look at this cast photo from 2014, what do you notice about the photo? What would you expect from a show with this cast?

WHAT does this photo say?

Orange Is the New Black is the story of a twenty-four-year-old white woman college graduate who was convicted of carrying money for a West African drug lord. She was eventually imprisoned in Danbury, Connecticut.[70] Does the cast photo look like the people you usually see on television? Why or why not?

WHAT do these messages mean?

Does the fact that this show has a racially diverse cast with a range of sexual orientations matter? Does the show represent diversity because it has a transgendered woman in the cast? Does it matter that the portrayal of these characters is sometimes stereotypical?

HOW do you and your classmates respond to these images?

Before you started this exercise, had you noticed how diverse the cast of *OITNB* is? Does that change how you feel about the show? Is it important to have diverse casts on television? Why do you think this way? What other types of diversity (beyond racial and ethnic) should television be concerned about? Why?

Web 9.3: Read about "colorblind casting."

Steve Mort/AFP/Getty Images

Spanish-language soap operas, known as telenovelas, have been very popular, both on Univision and the much smaller Telemundo. This photo shows members of the cast of *Mi Corazan Insiste* working on the program for Telemundo.

follows the same basic format as *Who Wants to Be a Millionaire?* The network has also followed the lead of VH1's *Behind the Music* and produced a series highlighting the downfalls of popular music stars.[71]

In 2005, ABC became the first network to start offering its prime-time programs either dubbed or closed-captioned in Spanish. The translation takes considerable effort to make sure that the jokes still work. Ruben Veloso, who heads the company that translated *Desperate Housewives* and *Lost* for ABC, says that sometimes they have to massage the script to keep it true to the storyline and to keep the innuendos and double entendres in the dialogue.[72]

Black Entertainment Television. Cable television also has networks that attempt to appeal to nonwhite audiences. The most significant is Black Entertainment Television (BET). The twenty-four-hour network reaches 60 million households, including 12.5 million black households.[73] When BET was acquired by media giant Viacom, it was already a $2 billion corporation that included restaurants, magazines, books, music, and cable networks.[74]

Started in 1980 as a local Washington, D.C., channel, BET was the nation's first black-owned cable network.[75] Although BET carries primarily talk shows and music videos, the network has also produced a series of made-for-television movies based on the Arabesque line of African American romance novels.[76]

Video 9.7: Check out which telenovelas are currently popular.

SECRET 3 Aside from the network's success in attracting viewers, BET became profitable because major advertisers such as General Motors were looking for media to reach nonwhite consumers. The *New York Times* says that this is part of an ongoing trend of multicultural marketing aimed at African American, Hispanic, and Asian American consumers, which account for increasing segments of the U.S. population. BET's Louis Carr says that nonwhite consumers have to be taken much more seriously, not as a secondary target but as a primary target. In places like New York, Chicago, Los Angeles, Detroit, and Philadelphia, if you add up the African American population, the Hispanic population, and the Asian population, they're not minorities anymore. They're majorities.[77]

(Another example of Secret Three—Everything from the margin moves to the center.)

Audience Members as Programmers: Public Access Cable. Among the greatest voices for diversity on television are the **public access channels** carried on many cable systems. Such channels air public affairs programming and other locally produced shows; these include community bulletin boards, educational programming, coverage of government meetings, and programs created by members of the community. Public access channels allow people to deliver their ideas directly to the public without going through a gatekeeper such as a journalist or another third party. At its best, public access is a soapbox that goes beyond the town square and all the way into a majority of homes in the community.[78]

More than 15,000 hours of public access programming are produced each year at more than 2,000 locations. Following are some examples of public access programming:

- In Greensboro, North Carolina, several African American churches use the public access channel to bring sermons to house-bound people.
- A public access station in Massachusetts carries a weekly show, *Haiti Tele-Magazine Network*, for Haitian immigrants.
- In Dallas, Texas, a weekly program focuses on the local Iranian community.[79]

Public access television doesn't always live up to the standard of the public good, however. According to Laura Linder, who has studied public access television extensively, most programming on these channels is fairly conventional, but some of it is controversial. Unsuccessful experimental

public access channels: Local cable television channels that air public affairs programming and other locally produced shows.

films, exhibitionism, and racist hate speech can find their way onto public access channels. For example, viewers in one community complained about an animated film that they believed promoted drug use. On another controversial program, the host butchered and cooked iguanas. (He was eventually arrested for cruelty to animals.) Controversial programs often lead to calls for eliminating public access channels, but the courts have generally ruled that public access cable is a free-speech forum and therefore is protected as long as nothing illegal is broadcast.

How important are local access cable channels? It depends in large part on local activists. According to independent public access television producer Chris Hill, "If there's good public access, it's a result of grassroots organizing by people who see this as an important public resource."[80]

NBC/Photofest

NBC's hit series *The Blacklist* makes income both from airing on broadcast TV and from being shown on the streaming service Netflix.

Linder says that public access programming differs from other forms because it is produced by audience members, not by media professionals. Public access cable is part of the trend toward more interactive media, such as the Internet and local talk radio. It transforms viewers into media producers rather than just audience members.

Television and Society

Few new social institutions have become an integral part of society faster than television did in the late 1940s and early 1950s. In 1948, there were fewer than 100,000 televisions in use; a year later, that number was more than 1 million, and by 1959, there were 50 million sets in use. In less than ten years, television had become a part of everyday life in the United States. Television viewership tended to grow more slowly in the highly regulated European market, something we talk about in depth in Chapter 15.

As television became commonplace, people started to worry about its effects on viewers: How much time were people spending viewing television? What activities would it replace? Why were people watching television? Most important, what effect, if any, would the content of television programs have on viewers? Would it lead to violence and juvenile delinquency? Would it take children into the world of adults too early? Would it transform society?

Television as a Major Social Force

In *Tube of Plenty*, Erik Barnouw argues that television had a revolutionary impact on society:

> The advent of television was widely compared, in its impact, with that of the Gutenberg printing press centuries earlier. Television was beginning to be seen as the more revolutionary innovation. The reasons were so obvious that they had seldom been discussed. Television viewing required no skill beyond normal human functions. Reading, on the other hand, was a skill acquired over years via effort and drilling—and not acquired by everyone. It generally involved the mediation of father, mother, grandfather, grandmother, teacher, priest, and others, a factor favoring social continuity, a transmittal of values. Television short-circuited all this. It could begin in cradle or playpen, and often did. It could bypass father, mother, grandfather, grandmother. It reached the child long before teacher and priest. Their role in the acculturation process had been sharply reduced. They had sporadically, fitfully, sought to recapture a more decisive role by seeking to control the images on the tube—but that control had slipped elsewhere, to the world of business. In a development of historical significance, the television's messages had become dominant social doctrine.[81]

Questioning the Media

When and why do you watch television? Do you watch specific shows or just whatever is airing? Do you think it's possible to watch "too much" television? Why or why not? What did you watch last night?

Barnouw is arguing that although television audiences have fragmented with the growth of cable, satellite, and

Web 9.4: Read the Kaiser Family Foundation study "Generation MC2: Media in the Lives of Eight- to Eighteen-Year-Olds"

Actress Mary Tyler Moore raised havoc with network censors in 1961 when she danced on *The Dick Van Dyke Show* wearing capri pants. Moore defended her outfit, saying, "I'll dress on the show the way I dress in real life."

home video, television is still the dominant shared experience in the modern world, reaching more people than schools, families, and churches.

Time Spent Watching Television. One reason social critics have been so concerned about the influence of television is that Americans spend a lot of time watching it. Estimates of the amount vary. Nielsen Media Research says that the average person watches about four hours of television a day.[82] According to another estimate, Americans spend fifteen hours a week actively watching television and have the TV turned on for an additional twenty-one hours a week while doing other things.

Television viewing can also be looked at in terms of how it dominates our free time. A study of the functions of television in everyday life notes that on average Americans spend half of their leisure time watching television. The same study showed that at any given moment in the evening more than one-third of the U.S. population is watching television; in the winter that proportion rises to over 50 percent.[83]

A study by the Kaiser Family Foundation found that children spend an average of four and a half hours a day watching television content. This is despite the fact that they are spending less time in front of a television set. How is this possible? While television sets are still the most popular media device among young people, the TV set is gradually losing ground to video they can watch on their computer screens, tablets, or phones.[84] (For more on these figures, turn back to Chapter 1.)

Television as Competition for Other Activities. Although television viewing is often reported in terms of average amounts of time spent viewing, such figures don't always give a complete picture. The differences between heavy and light television viewers can be significant. A 1990 study found that people who watch a lot of television tend to spend more time home alone than light viewers. The study also showed that light viewers spend more time walking than heavy viewers.

Unfortunately, these studies usually cannot determine why people behave in these ways. Do heavy viewers stay home specifically to watch television, or are they unable to get out of the house for one reason or another? Perhaps busy people who like to walk don't have time to watch television. One finding that is not difficult to interpret was that people who watch sports on television also tend to participate in sports. The study also found that the amount of time people spend reading does not seem to be affected by how much television they watch.[85]

How Do Viewers Use Television?

In addition to examining how much television people are watching, researchers have studied how and why people watch television. These uses and gratifications studies seek to determine what uses people make of television viewing and what gratifications (or benefits) they gain from it. The central premise of these studies is that television (like other media) is not an actor that does things to viewers. Instead, audience members are active participants who select programming to meet particular needs.

What might these needs be? The study *Television in the Lives of Our Children* found that children watch television for many of the same reasons that adults do:

- To be entertained.
- To learn things or gain information. In many cases, this information relates to socialization: how to act like an adult, how to be a better athlete, how other people live.
- For social reasons. The content of TV doesn't matter so much as the fact that they watch it with friends or talk about it at school the next day.

The researchers also found that different children watched the same program for different reasons. One child might watch a cartoon show because he was lonely and the show provided company, another might watch it because it made her laugh, and a third might watch it because his friends were watching it.[86]

While Janet Jackson's 2004 Super Bowl "wardrobe malfunction" resulted in eight years of legal wrangling and threatened fines, when cable news host Nancy Grace exposed her nipple on *Dancing With the Stars* in 2011, it caused little controvery.

Standards for Television

In the 1950s and 1960s, networks and advertisers imposed strict controls on what could be shown on television. For example, Mary Tyler Moore and Dick Van Dyke played the married couple Laura and Rob Petrie on *The Dick Van Dyke Show*, which aired from 1961 to 1966. Although married, the Petries had to sleep in separate twin beds. Sponsors also raised their eyebrows when Moore wore jeans and capri pants on the show because these garments might be considered suggestive. Moore fought the sponsors and won, saying, "I'll dress on the show the way I dress in real life."[87] This was the era when comedian Lucille Ball had to use the word *expecting* rather than *pregnant* on her show when she was obviously carrying a child.[88]

What could be shown was determined by each network's own standards and practices department. The goal of these departments, which at one time had as many as sixty people working in them, was to make sure the network did not lose viewers or sponsors because of offensive content. Since the 1980s, they have decreased in size by 50 percent or more. This change is due partly to a loosening of societal standards throughout the 1970s, but it is also a response to the more explicit content of cable television programming.[89]

Alfred Schneider, who served as a censor for ABC television for more than thirty years, observes that the networks feel freer to deal with difficult topics today than in earlier decades:

> Sometimes the quality of a particular program allows you to do things that you would not permit in other programs. I once said that in my lifetime there would never be full frontal nudity on network television. I was wrong. I lived to see *War and Remembrance*, where I permitted full frontal nudity in the concentration camp scenes. I finally justified it by saying that this was not nudity, this was death.
>
> As we see the growth of more distribution systems, the growth of independents, my position will have to change. As the populace becomes more educated, more inquisitive, more concerned about issues, I will be more comfortable taking greater risks knowing that people will seek out their choices.[90]

In 1997, broadcasters fundamentally changed their programming controls; instead of placing an occasional warning before programs considered inappropriate for children, they implemented a two-part rating system modeled after the one used for movies. There is an age-appropriateness rating that closely matches the movie system, with ratings of G, PG, TV-14 (for fourteen-year-olds and older), and TV-MA (for mature audiences). Many networks also provide a content rating of S (sexual content), V (violence), L (crude language), and/or D (adult dialogue).[91] It was also in 1997 that the so-called V-chip, an electronic device allowing parents to block programs with certain content ratings, began to be included in television sets.

Television producers were initially concerned that shows with ratings for violence or sexual content might be harder to market. But rather than restricting television content, broadcasters have used the ratings to warn viewers that material on a program will be explicit. As Robert Thompson, director of Syracuse University's Center for Television and Popular Culture, has noted,

Video 9.8: Watch Mary Tyler Moore dancing in capri pants.

TEST YOUR MEDIA LITERACY

No Sense of Place

Media scholar Joshua Meyrowitz, in his book *No Sense of Place,* argues that the very existence of television is an influence on society because it breaks down the physical barriers that separate people. In the past, he says, people were limited to interacting with those whom they could see and hear face-to-face. Meyrowitz describes how the coming of electronic media, and television in particular, changed this:

> The boundaries marked by walls, doors, and barbed wire, and enforced by laws, guards, and trained dogs, continue to define situations by including and excluding participants. But today such boundaries function to define social situations only to the extent that information can still be restricted by restricting physical access.[1]

These boundaries can be broken at many levels. A child watching television can see people talking about adult topics such as infidelity, pregnancy, or cross-dressing. A teenager in New York City can see the impact of drought on people in Iowa. Young men can listen in on what women say on a "girls' night out." In each of these cases, in the pretelevision era, the viewer would have been isolated because of his or her "place," whether it was geographic location, age, sex, or socioeconomic status. But television gives everyone an equal view into these formerly separate worlds.

This breakdown of place has occurred not just within the United States, but throughout the industrialized world. As we discussed in Chapter 3, the United States is the world's largest supplier of entertainment programming; it is also the largest supplier of imagery to the world. The most important effect of CNN and other satellite-based television news services is that they give people everywhere in the world access to the same information at the same time, whether those people are heads of state, diplomats, soldiers, or citizens. The late Don Hewitt, longtime producer of the CBS newsmagazine *60 Minutes*, has said that this global sharing of information is changing the world:

> When there was a disaster, it used to be that people went to church and all held hands. Then television came along, and there was this wonderful feeling that while you were watching Walter Cronkite, millions of other Americans were sharing the emotional experience with you. Now the minute anything happens they all run to CNN and think, "The whole world is sharing this experience with me."[2]

WHO is the source?

Who is Joshua Meyrowitz? What book has he written?

WHAT is he saying?

According to Meyrowitz, how has television transformed society? What does Meyrowitz mean when he says television and other electronic media break down the barriers of place? What kind of barriers does Meyrowitz suggest are being broken by television?

WHAT evidence is there?

What examples of this process does Meyrowitz provide? When and where does this process take place?

WHAT do you and your classmates think about Meyrowitz's arguments?

List some examples of how television has let you see aspects of everyday life that would normally remain hidden from you. Does television take you "places" you couldn't go to otherwise? If so, list some examples. Do you ever use television to deliberately watch worlds you wouldn't be able to see otherwise?

[1]Joshua Meyrowitz, *No Sense of Place* (New York: Oxford University Press, 1985).
[2]William A. Henry III, "History as It Happens; Linking Leaders as Never Before, CNN Has Changed the Way the World Does Its Business," *Time,* January 6, 1992, 24–27.

Web 9.5: Read an interview with Joshua Meyrowitz.

The people who wanted ratings to put the brakes on this new explosion of raunchy television saw just the opposite happen. Anybody should have seen this coming. If you give producers the opportunity to use a TV-MA rating, it's an invitation to make TV-MA programs.[92]

Video 9.9: Watch both the Janet Jackson and Nancy Grace wardrobe malfunctions.

Web 9.6: Read the latest about the settlement of the Janet Jackson indecency case before the Supreme Court.

For the most part, the R-equivalent TV-MA rating has been confined to cable television shows such as Comedy Central's raunchy cartoon *South Park.* The Big Four broadcast networks have rarely aired programs with the TV-MA rating, the most notable exceptions being uncut broadcasts of serious R-rated movies such as *Schindler's List* and *Saving Private Ryan.*

The Problem of Decency

The line of what was acceptable on broadcast television was redrawn following the 2004 Super Bowl halftime show on CBS when Justin Timberlake exposed Janet Jackson's breast for nine-sixteenths of a second. The FCC received more than 500,000 complaints.[93] Immediately following the broadcast, the FCC started talking about the problem of indecency on television. References to sexual or bodily functions are considered to be indecent. FCC rules say that broadcast radio and television stations can't air indecent material between 6:00 a.m. and 10:00 p.m., when children are most likely to be watching. This differs from obscene programming (discussed further in Chapter 13), which "describes or shows sexual conduct in a lewd and offensive way" and has no "literary, artistic, political, or scientific value."[94] Obscene material is not protected by the First Amendment. Rules about indecency apply to broadcast materials but not to cable or satellite material. On June 29, 2012, the case regarding CBS finally came to a conclusion with the U.S. Supreme Court declining to review a lower court decision throwing out the fine.[95] As a side note in this case, cable news host Nancy Grace also exposed her nipple on the reality show *Dancing With the Stars*, this time for almost an entire second. But so far the FCC has not acted on any complaints, and it appears unlikely to lead to any fines or other legal action.[96]

There is no single standard for what constitutes broadcast indecency, and this standard clearly changes over time. During the 1990s and early 2000s, bare bottoms became common on shows such as *NYPD Blue*. But since the Janet Jackson fuss, even this minimal nudity has been digitally blurred when shown on broadcast television, and reality programs such as *Survivor* have become careful to digitally blur any hint of nudity that occurs during the programs' competitions as well.

There has been some serious fallout from the Janet Jackson stunt as well. Several CBS affiliates hesitated to rebroadcast the documentary *9/11* because of the rough language used by firefighters in the film.[97] In 2004, sixty-six ABC affiliate stations refused to air the R-rated movie *Saving Private Ryan* for fear they would be fined for the movie's graphic violence and extensive profanity.[98] (Congress raised the fines from $32,500 to $325,000 per "incident" following the Jackson case, which is why smaller stations are cautious about any program that might trigger an FCC response.) Broadcast standards in Europe are far more likely to regulate hate speech, advertising, and materials that are harmful to children than to control nudity.[99]

Gene Policinski, executive director of the First Amendment Center, questions whether television can really tell the story of events such as the 9/11 attacks or the invasion of Normandy during World War II within the limits of decency rules:

> War is a bloody hell, and *Private Ryan* brought home the terror and anguish, as well as the heroics and sacrifices, of the heralds of the "greatest generation" who stormed ashore at Normandy in a manner no sanitized depiction had done previously. Who can view any veteran of that invasion in the same manner after seeing that film?[100]

The Future of Television

Whether it is delivered by broadcast, cable, or satellite, television is changing so quickly that it might be unrecognizable to Philo T. Farnsworth. The cable industry, for example, is in the process of replacing copper wire with fiber-optic cable that uses light rather than electricity to send out video and other types of signals. Fiber-optic cable has the advantage of being able to carry much more information than copper wire can, but more importantly, it has the capacity to allow audience members to send signals back to the program providers.[101]

Interactive Television

This new control of television by consumers is available at a number of levels. As the number of available channels increases, cable providers can offer multiple versions of single channels. Cable movie provider HBO offers multiple channels, each of which has movies starting at different times. The same is happening with pay-per-view channels, on which movies start at fifteen-minute intervals.

©iStockphoto.com/Jitalia17

Consumers themselves can add to their degree of control. As mentioned earlier in the chapter, with DVRs, viewers are able to not only record programs and view them whenever they wish; they can also pause a program to take a phone call or get a snack and restart it when they return. In essence, the digital recorders give viewers the same control over "live" television that they have over prerecorded programs.

Video on Demand. One service that has really taken off in the past several years and has the potential to change the

video on demand: Television channels that allow consumers to order movies, news, or other programs at any time over fiber-optic lines.

Web 9.7: What do students mean when they say they are watching television?

MEDIA TRANSFORMATIONS

Defining Television in the Twenty-first Century

Until the mid-2000s, we had a pretty good idea of what watching television meant. You would sit down in front of your television set, which would receive signals over the air from a cable or satellite service or from some kind of media player, such as a VCR or DVD player.

Then, in 2005, Apple started selling an iPod that could play video, and it offered current television shows the day after they aired for $1.99 an episode through the iTunes store. At first, it was primarily ABC programming, owned by Disney, that was available on iTunes.[102] (Remember, at the time of his death, Apple founder Steve Jobs was a member of the Disney board of directors and the company's biggest single stockholder.) But by 2007, all of the Big Four networks were selling episodes through iTunes, as were many cable powerhouses. So Apple got broad acceptance of the idea that people would pay cash to download current television shows and that they could use portable devices to view those shows almost anywhere.

That was also the year that DVD rental service Netflix started streaming movies and TV shows over the Internet. Initially, the streaming was just to computers, but it soon expanded to devices such as the Roku box, Blu-ray players, and video game consoles that could play Netflix programming instantly on a television set.

Now Netflix and other streaming services, such as Amazon Instant Video, Hulu, and Hulu Plus, can be accessed on smartphones and tablets.[103] In fact, tablets are now the second-most-popular way to watch television programming, according to research by media giant Viacom. The company's study showed that as of 2012, 15 percent of American's television viewing is done on tablets.[104]

All of these developments raise the question as to whether people are ready to **cut the cord**—disconnect from a traditional pay video service such as cable or satellite and replace it with content streamed over the Internet. Do you really need a cable or satellite subscription to watch a wide range of television programming anymore? Nielsen estimates that approximately 5 percent of television viewers have cut the cord, going exclusively to broadband delivery of video.[105] Among those who have cut the cord is famed media blogger Jim Romenesko, who writes that he made the change when his cable bill hit $203 a month in February 2011. At that point, he says he sold his three flat-screen TVs and took to doing all of his television viewing on his iPad. He says he has no regrets about making the switch, though he might feel differently if he were a big sports fan.[106]

AP Photo/Damian Dovargoanes

Netflix is a major provider of streaming movies and television shows that can be played on a computer, a mobile device, or a television set.

Media Transformations Questions:

- **WHAT** does it mean to say you are "watching television" now?
- **DO** you watch video programming on your computer or mobile device? Why or why not?
- **WHAT** kind of programming do you watch on your computer or mobile device?
- **DO** you pay for it or is it free? If it's free, would you pay for the service if free options went away? Why or why not?
- **HAVE** you cut the cord or considered cutting the cord? Why or why not?

cutting the cord: Replacing traditional paid video services, such as cable or satellite television, with Internet-based streaming video services.

Defining Television in the 21st Century

Netflix recently jumped ahead of HBO with a spike in subscribers due in large part to its new content offerings and the increasing ease of streaming content. Both companies have developed new delivery and content strategies in the race to redefine the business model.

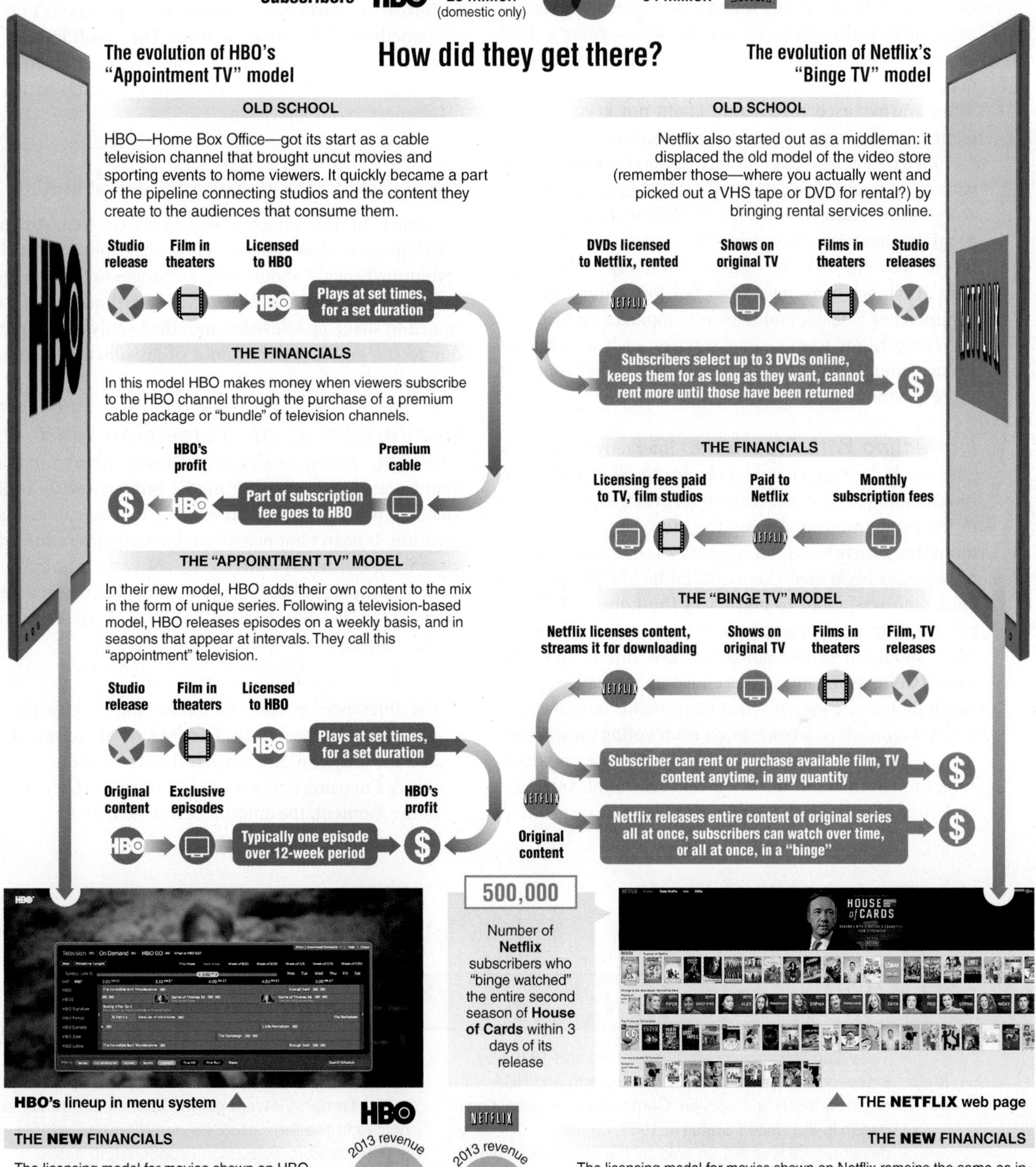

Subscribers
HBO
28 million
(domestic only)
34 million
NETFLIX
The evolution of HBO's "Appointment TV" model
How did they get there?
The evolution of Netflix's "Binge TV" model
OLD SCHOOL
HBO—Home Box Office—got its start as a cable television channel that brought uncut movies and sporting events to home viewers. It quickly became a part of the pipeline connecting studios and the content they create to the audiences that consume them.
Studio release
Film in theaters
Licensed to HBO
Plays at set times, for a set duration
THE FINANCIALS
In this model HBO makes money when viewers subscribe to the HBO channel through the purchase of a premium cable package or "bundle" of television channels.
HBO's profit
Premium cable
Part of subscription fee goes to HBO
THE "APPOINTMENT TV" MODEL
In their new model, HBO adds their own content to the mix in the form of unique series. Following a television-based model, HBO releases episodes on a weekly basis, and in seasons that appear at intervals. They call this "appointment" television.
Studio release
Film in theaters
Licensed to HBO
Plays at set times, for a set duration
Original content
Exclusive episodes
HBO's profit
Typically one episode over 12-week period
OLD SCHOOL
Netflix also started out as a middleman: it displaced the old model of the video store (remember those—where you actually went and picked out a VHS tape or DVD for rental?) by bringing rental services online.
DVDs licensed to Netflix, rented
Shows on original TV
Films in theaters
Studio releases
Subscribers select up to 3 DVDs online, keeps them for as long as they want, cannot rent more until those have been returned
THE FINANCIALS
Licensing fees paid to TV, film studios
Paid to Netflix
Monthly subscription fees
THE "BINGE TV" MODEL
Netflix licenses content, streams it for downloading
Shows on original TV
Films in theaters
Film, TV releases
Subscriber can rent or purchase available film, TV content anytime, in any quantity
Netflix releases entire content of original series all at once, subscribers can watch over time, or all at once, in a "binge"
Original content
500,000
Number of Netflix subscribers who "binge watched" the entire second season of House of Cards within 3 days of its release
HOUSE of CARDS

HBO's lineup in menu system ▲

▲ THE NETFLIX web page

THE NEW FINANCIALS

The licensing model for movies shown on HBO remains the same as in the original model, but as content creators, HBO pays for creation and production and reaps the revenues exclusively. Since they've been in the business for a while and have an international audience, the revenues by now far outweigh the costs to them.

HBO — 2013 revenue — Operating profit: **$1.8 billion**

NETFLIX — 2013 revenue — Operating profit: **$228 million**

THE NEW FINANCIALS

The licensing model for movies shown on Netflix remains the same as in the original model, but as content creators, like HBO, Netflix pays for creation and production and reaps the revenues exclusively. But unlike HBO, because Netflix releases its content all at once rather than at set times, viewers can at least in theory consume much more since there are no limits to how much they watch. But since Netflix's model is relatively new, it is currently spending more in investments than it is making in profits.

Sources: http://www.nytimes.com/2014/02/17/business/media/punching-above-its-weight-upstart-netflix-pokes-at-hbo.html, http://www.thestreet.com/story/12438231/1/netflix-and-house-of-cards-vs-hbo.html

entire industry is **video on demand**. This service consists of television channels that allow viewers to order movies, news, or other programs that are digitally delivered at any time over fiber-optic lines. Time Warner began experimenting with such a system in 1993 and made its Full Service Network available to subscribers in Orlando, Florida. During the experiment, the company found that people liked having more choices, that they wanted to be able to pause a show and continue it later, and that young people adapted better to new technology than did older people. But the technology Time Warner used in Orlando could not keep up with demand as the number of subscribers increased.[107]

Video on demand has now moved into the mainstream, with more than 60 percent of all cable subscribers having access to it. These systems allow consumers to pick the program they want to watch and to pause, rewind, and fast-forward through the content. But many of these systems also block consumers from fast-forwarding through commercials.[108] Cable and satellite companies are also seeing competition from online services such as Amazon Prime, Hulu, Hulu Plus, and Netflix. We'll talk about that more in a moment.

Interacting With Programs. Interactive television goes beyond giving viewers a chance to select their own programming. It involves making them active participants in the programming. Among the most famous (or infamous) interactive television episodes was one that appeared on *Saturday Night Live*. Comedian Eddie Murphy played a cook who was about to boil Larry the Lobster. Viewers could call in on special phone lines to vote on whether Larry should or should not get cooked at the end of the show. (Compassionate viewers ended up saving Larry that night, though the lobster's final fate remains unknown.) It is not that much of a reach to go from voting on whether to save Larry the Lobster to calling in to vote on which singer to eliminate from the current season of *American Idol*. According to Brian Garden of MTV, "You are growing up with a generation that is almost overly empowered. They aren't satisfied with anything less than full control."[109] John Pavlik of the Center for New Media at Columbia University sees interactivity as becoming a standard part of television:

> When you transform people from couch potatoes into active participants, you turn TV programs into something like a sticky website. They want to keep playing along. Every program can have an interactive component. I think it will become the main way we connect to our televisions.[110]

The Earthquake in Slow Motion Continues

Earlier in this chapter, we discussed Ken Auletta's "earthquake in slow motion"—how the cable and satellite revolution brought about massive changes to the television business in the 1980s and 1990s. This earthquake has continued to shake up television into the twenty-first century due to the growing importance of broadband video and alternative viewing devices.

Convergence of Television and the Internet. Media analysts have been talking for years about convergence in the media industry with audio, video, still images, and text coming together in a single medium. It hasn't happened yet, but computers and television are definitely starting to converge, though not always in the ways that people were expecting. In a 2006 interview, Mike Bloxham of Ball State University told *Media Post* that

> the difference between the TV and the PC is getting less almost by the month. They're kind of morphing, and the only real difference is the size of the screen, where I'm using it, my need state or mind state, and, at the moment, the amount of interactivity.[111]

Chapter SUMMARY

Television was developed in the 1920s and 1930s by independent inventor Philo T. Farnsworth and RCA engineer Vladimir Zworykin. Commercial broadcasting began in the United States in 1939, but its development was put on hold by the outbreak of World War II. By the early 1950s, television was established as the dominant broadcast medium. Color television broadcasts came into widespread use in the 1960s.

Although primitive forms of cable television existed in 1948, cable did not become a significant medium until the early 1980s when satellite distribution of channels became common. Among the early cable channels were a number of networks created by Ted Turner. Viewers gained access to additional choices in the form of VCRs and direct broadcast satellite service. Television broadcasting has switched from analog signals to multiple digital formats, and VCRs have almost completely been replaced by DVRs, DVDs, video on demand, and streaming technology.

Television networks have been criticized for failing to include women and minorities in their programming, but cable channels have delivered more programming that addresses diverse interests. Networks have also been criticized for carrying too much violent and sexually explicit programming. But television has been praised for breaking down geographic and social barriers. Broadcast television is currently going through a cycle in which "indecent" content is being suppressed by the government.

Television is changing rapidly, with audience members getting many new options to control how and when they receive programming. With VCRs, DVRs, interactive television, and broadband video, viewers can choose what they watch and when they watch it. They are also able to interact with the programming through online and mobile resources.

Keep up-to-date with content from the author's blog.

Take the chapter quiz.

Key TERMS

community antenna television (CATV) 224
Big Three networks 224
videocassette recorder (VCR) 226
direct broadcast satellite (DBS) 226
high-definition television (HDTV) 227
standard digital television 227
television networks 228
Public Broadcasting Service (PBS) 228
Big Four networks 229
PeopleMeter 230
sweeps 230
rating point 230
share 230
telenovelas 232
public access channels 234
video on demand 239
cutting the cord 240

Concept REVIEW

The differences between broadcast television and cable/satellite television

Ted Turner's ideas for repackaging programming for cable and distributing it nationwide

How Hollywood and other content providers have resisted changes in television technology

The impact that digital broadcasting will have on the television industry

Ken Auletta's "earthquake in slow motion"

The changing face of diversity on television

How standards of decency change on television

How audience members are taking control of how they interact with television

Student STUDY SITE

Sharpen your skills with SAGE edge at **edge.sagepub.com/hanson5e**

SAGE edge for Students provides a personalized approach to help you accomplish your coursework goals in an easy-to-use learning environment.

chapter 10

The Internet

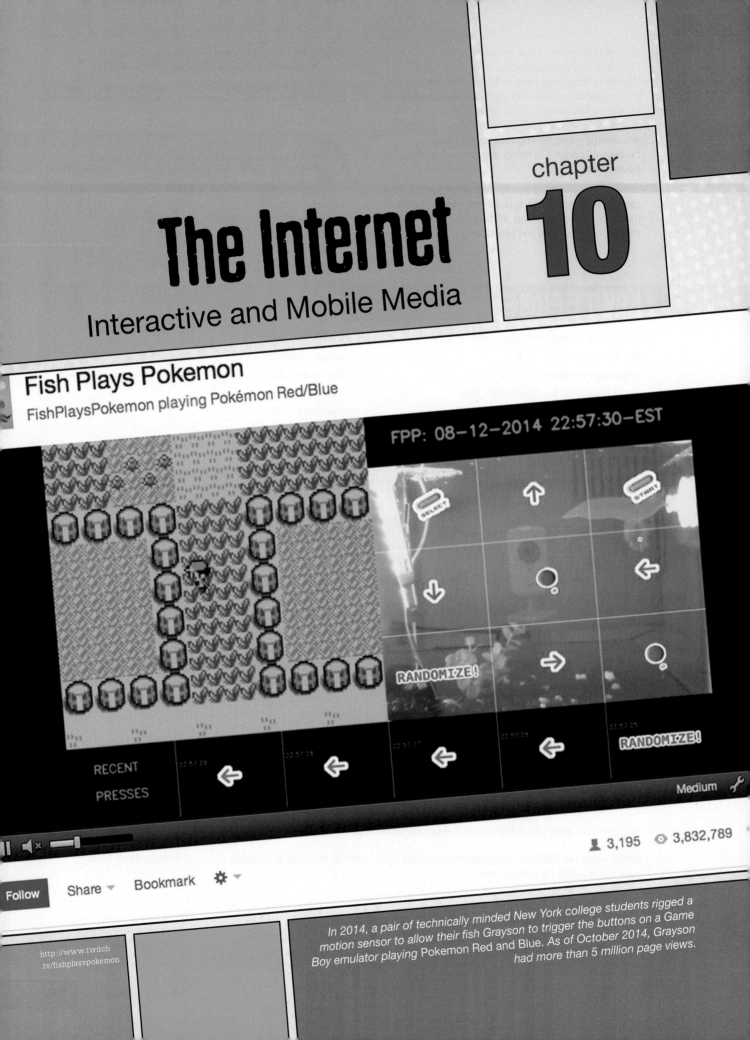

Interactive and Mobile Media

Fish Plays Pokemon

FishPlaysPokemon playing Pokémon Red/Blue

FPP: 08-12-2014 22:57:30-EST

SELECT

START

RANDOMIZE!

RECENT PRESSES

22:57:29

22:57:28

22:57:27

22:57:26

22:57:25

RANDOMIZE!

Medium

3,195 3,832,789

Follow Share Bookmark 

http://www.twitch.tv/fishplayspokemon

In 2014, a pair of technically minded New York college students rigged a motion sensor to allow their fish Grayson to trigger the buttons on a Game Boy emulator playing Pokemon Red and Blue. As of October 2014, Grayson had more than 5 million page views.

As I sit at my computer in the summer of 2014, a fish named Grayson is playing the video games *Pokémon Red and Blue* on a Game Boy emulator using a motion sensor aimed at his fish tank. Each area of the tank is assigned to a different Game Boy button, and as he swims into the area, the button is triggered. That a pair of technically oriented college students in New York would rig some equipment to allow their fish to randomly play a video game is not surprising. It's the kind of hack that might seem reasonable on a late Friday night. The fact that as many as 22,000 people at a time would watch the fish play *Pokémon* using the video game streaming service Twitch is kind of amazing.[1]

Should you join in on the party, you will see a divided screen showing the Pokémon game on the left, the swimming fish with the control grid imposed over it in the center, and a chat session on the right where viewers either try to kibitz the fish or proclaim that he is dead. (The fish's owners point out continually that Grayson isn't dead; he's just sleeping.)

Catherine Moresco and Patrick Facheris, Grayson's owners, were likely inspired by the efforts of an anonymous Australian gamer who rigged the fifteen-year-old Game Boy game *Pokémon Red* to be played by the inhabitants of the stream's chat room. At its peak, as many as 75,000 people at a time were inputting controller commands with text comments. The stream differs from most of the video game viewing that takes place on Twitch because it combines the sport of watching someone play a video game on Twitch.tv with actually participating in the progress of the game.[2]

Streaming video games seems, on the surface, relatively straightforward, but the legal complications are . . . complicated.

After some initial uncertainty, video game manufacturers have gotten on board with their games being streamed and viewed. In fact, the latest consoles from Sony and Xbox (Microsoft) are designed to stream on Twitch. But the music contained within the video games, along with music the player or streamer might be listening to, is not licensed. For example, the music that plays on the radio station in the car within the *Grand Theft Auto* games is licensed for use in the game, but may not be legal for use over streaming video.[3]

LEARNING OBJECTIVES

After studying this chapter, you will be able to:

1 Explain how Internet technology developed.

2 Identify the three levels of communication on the Internet.

3 Describe three defining components of the World Wide Web and the nine principles on which it is based.

4 Describe five characteristics of social media.

5 Explain how legacy media are reacting to the growth of new online media.

6 Describe the four elements of the hacker ethic and how they apply to the contemporary Internet.

7 Discuss conflicts over content, intellectual property, and privacy on the Web.

This problem of unlicensed music leads to the audio for the game recordings being automatically blocked by software looking for violations, in much the same way that content gets blocked on YouTube. The problem is that the same sound blocking that cuts out the music also gets rid of all the video game sounds. Oddly enough, this is only an issue on videos that have been recorded and stored on Twitch's servers, not the music that comes up on live streams. This is also an example of Secret Five—New media are always scary . . . especially to people who own other media.

In May 2014, stories originating in the entertainment press came out saying that Google was preparing to buy video game streaming service Twitch, but in the end, online retail giant Amazon bought the company for $970 million.[4] The streaming service Twitch was founded in 2011 as an outgrowth of the live-streaming video site Justin.tv, and it has more than 50 million users. *Businessweek* reports that the site has 7 million users per day, and more than 1 million people posting or streaming videos from the site.[5] Amazon's purchase of the video game streaming service is part of its larger commitment to gaming. It has an in-house gaming studio, and is one of the largest video game vendors in the world. (Note that while Amazon paid close to $1 billion for Twitch, legacy news provider *The Washington Post* sold for only $250 million to Amazon founder Jeff Bezos.)

Timeline

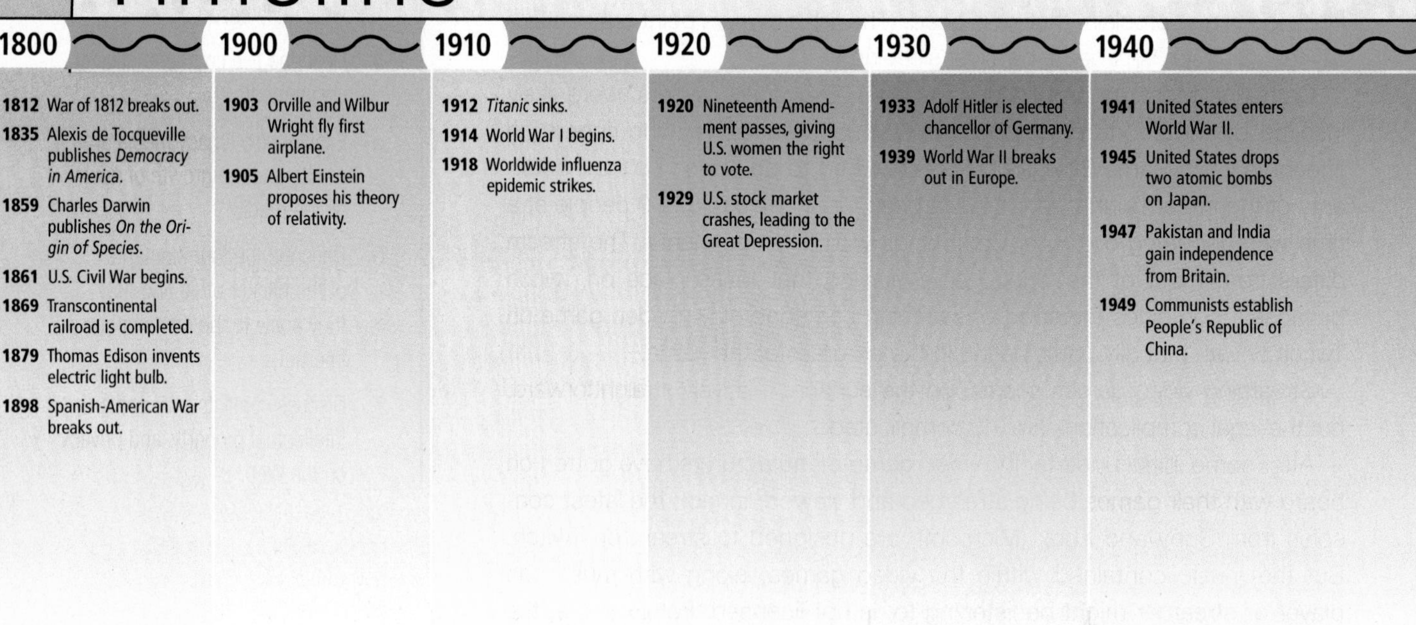

1800
1812 War of 1812 breaks out.
1835 Alexis de Tocqueville publishes *Democracy in America*.
1859 Charles Darwin publishes *On the Origin of Species*.
1861 U.S. Civil War begins.
1869 Transcontinental railroad is completed.
1879 Thomas Edison invents electric light bulb.
1898 Spanish-American War breaks out.
1900
1903 Orville and Wilbur Wright fly first airplane.
1905 Albert Einstein proposes his theory of relativity.
1910
1912 *Titanic* sinks.
1914 World War I begins.
1918 Worldwide influenza epidemic strikes.
1920
1920 Nineteenth Amendment passes, giving U.S. women the right to vote.
1929 U.S. stock market crashes, leading to the Great Depression.
1930
1933 Adolf Hitler is elected chancellor of Germany.
1939 World War II breaks out in Europe.
1940
1941 United States enters World War II.
1945 United States drops two atomic bombs on Japan.
1947 Pakistan and India gain independence from Britain.
1949 Communists establish People's Republic of China.

The Internet is in the process of establishing itself not just as a new medium of mass communication, but also as one where old types of media can find new ways of content. Not only can you play video games online; you can watch other people play video games, and you can even watch a fish play video games! In this chapter, we look at the origins of the Internet, how it has changed from its original government roots, how it has evolved from a tool for computer sharing into a major new mass medium, and how it has caused social change everywhere from the corporate boardroom to the Middle East. ■

> **“Is the fish dead?**
> No, the fish is not dead.
> He just sleeps sometimes
> **I really think the fish is dead.**
> Seriously, it's okay guys.
> *He's just sleeping.”*
> —FishPlaysPokemon FAQ

Video 10.1: Watch fish and fans play *Pokémon* online through Twitch.

1950

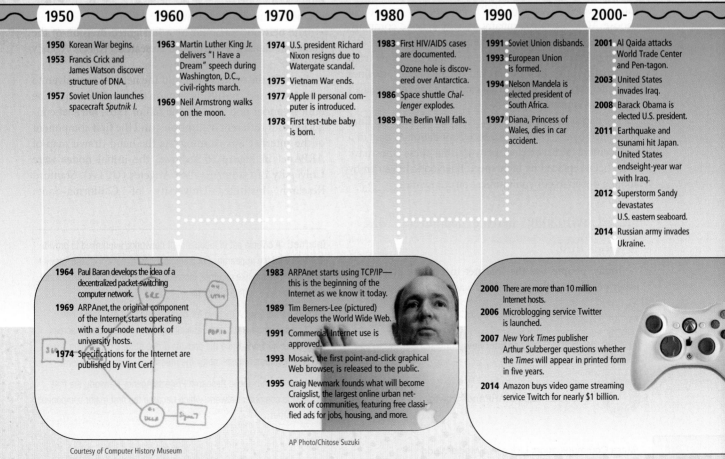

1950 Korean War begins.
1953 Francis Crick and James Watson discover structure of DNA.
1957 Soviet Union launches spacecraft *Sputnik I*.

1960

1963 Martin Luther King Jr. delivers "I Have a Dream" speech during Washington, D.C., civil-rights march.
1969 Neil Armstrong walks on the moon.

1970

1974 U.S. president Richard Nixon resigns due to Watergate scandal.
1975 Vietnam War ends.
1977 Apple II personal computer is introduced.
1978 First test-tube baby is born.

1980

1983 First HIV/AIDS cases are documented.
Ozone hole is discovered over Antarctica.
1986 Space shuttle *Challenger* explodes.
1989 The Berlin Wall falls.

1990

1991 Soviet Union disbands.
1993 European Union is formed.
1994 Nelson Mandela is elected president of South Africa.
1997 Diana, Princess of Wales, dies in car accident.

2000-

2001 Al Qaida attacks World Trade Center and Pen-tagon.
2003 United States invades Iraq.
2008 Barack Obama is elected U.S. president.
2011 Earthquake and tsunami hit Japan. United States endseight-year war with Iraq.
2012 Superstorm Sandy devastates U.S. eastern seaboard.
2014 Russian army invades Ukraine.

1964 Paul Baran develops the idea of a decentralized packet-switching computer network.
1969 ARPAnet,the original component of the Internet,starts operating with a four-node network of university hosts.
1974 Specifications for the Internet are published by Vint Cerf.

Courtesy of Computer History Museum

1983 ARPAnet starts using TCP/IP—this is the beginning of the Internet as we know it today.
1989 Tim Berners-Lee (pictured) develops the World Wide Web.
1991 Commercial Internet use is approved.
1993 Mosaic, the first point-and-click graphical Web browser, is released to the public.
1995 Craig Newmark founds what will become Craigslist, the largest online urban network of communities, featuring free classified ads for jobs, housing, and more.

AP Photo/Chitose Suzuki

2000 There are more than 10 million Internet hosts.
2006 Microblogging service Twitter is launched.
2007 *New York Times* publisher Arthur Sulzberger questions whether the *Times* will appear in printed form in five years.
2014 Amazon buys video game streaming service Twitch for nearly $1 billion.

Arterra Picture Library/Alamy

The Development of the Internet

SECRET 4 The Internet is the most recent of the mass media. It is still rapidly evolving and changing, just as radio did in the 1920s and television did in the 1950s. (Remember Secret Four—Nothing's new: Everything that happened in the past will happen again.) Like radio, the Internet was not conceived initially as a mass medium. Instead, the first wide-area computer networks were designed to enable academics and military researchers to share data. But these early users soon found that the most useful benefit of the network was being able to send electronic mail to one another instantly.

Although the earliest components of the Internet were in use by 1969, the Net was limited largely to interpersonal communication until 1991, when Tim Berners-Lee released the World Wide Web as an easy and uniform way to access material on the Internet. Since then, the Internet has become a medium unlike any other because it is the only one that incorporates elements of interpersonal, group, and mass communications.

So what is the **Internet**? A national panel on the future of the Internet defines it this way: "The Internet is a diverse set of independent networks, interlinked to provide its users with the appearance of a single, uniform network."

The Net starts with the link from your computer to an Internet service provider (ISP). For an ISP, you might choose AOL, a cable company, your telephone company, or possibly a small local company that sells Internet service in one or two counties. The messages then flow from the smaller links into bigger and bigger digital pipelines (the Internet's "backbone") that carry millions of messages across the country.

The backbone was initially a set of high-speed data lines controlled by the National Science Foundation as part of a replacement of its original network, but these lines have since been replaced by high-speed fiber-optic lines run by about a dozen major communication companies.

Packet Switching: Letting Computers Talk to Each Other

Today, people use the Internet to communicate with other people, but the technology was originally developed to let computers talk to one another. In the early 1960s, researchers on both sides of the Atlantic Ocean were working on the problem of how to transfer information stored on one computer to another.

In 1964, engineer Paul Baran was designing a military communication network that could survive a nuclear strike. He sought to design a network in which every computer was connected to several other computers so that if one computer failed, an alternative route using different computers could be established. Baran's second insight was that computers could break large messages into a number of smaller message blocks, or packets, which could be sent independently across the network. **Packet switching**, as Baran's scheme came to be known, cuts messages into little pieces and sends them along the easiest route to their final destination (see Figure 10.1). The receiving computer starts reassembling the messages and asks for any missing packets to be resent.[6]

The U.S. Air Force was initially willing to implement Baran's network, but AT&T, which had a monopoly on long-distance phone service at the time, refused to cooperate, so Baran put his idea on hold.[7] Meanwhile, in England, researcher Donald Davies was working on a proposed public communication network. Davies and Baran, working independently, came up with remarkably similar notions for packet switching.[8]

ARPAnet

Eventually the U.S. military built the first nationwide packet-switching network. However, the network that was built was intended to serve the needs of academic researchers, not to survive nuclear war.

The network was built by a farsighted division of the Pentagon called the Advanced Research Projects Agency (ARPA).[9]

In 1968, the contract to build the network was given to a Boston-based consulting firm on the condition that it be built in under one year. By the fall of 1969, **ARPAnet** connected four different institutions, and the first component of the Internet was running. As the hand-drawn map of ARPAnet in Figure 10.2 shows, the initial nodes were University of California–Los Angeles (UCLA), Stanford Research Institute, University of California–Santa

Web 10.1: Read an interview with Paul Baran.

Web 10.2: Maps of ARPAnet growth.

Internet: "A diverse set of independent networks, interlinked to provide its users with the appearance of a single, uniform network"; the Internet is a mass medium like no other, incorporating elements of interpersonal, group, and mass communications.

packet switching: A method for breaking up long messages into small pieces, or packets, and transmitting them independently across a computer network. Once the packets arrive at their destination, the receiving computer reassembles the message into its original form.

ARPAnet: The Advanced Research Projects Agency Network; the first nationwide computer network, which became the first major component of the Internet.

Figure 10.1 Packet-Switching Networks

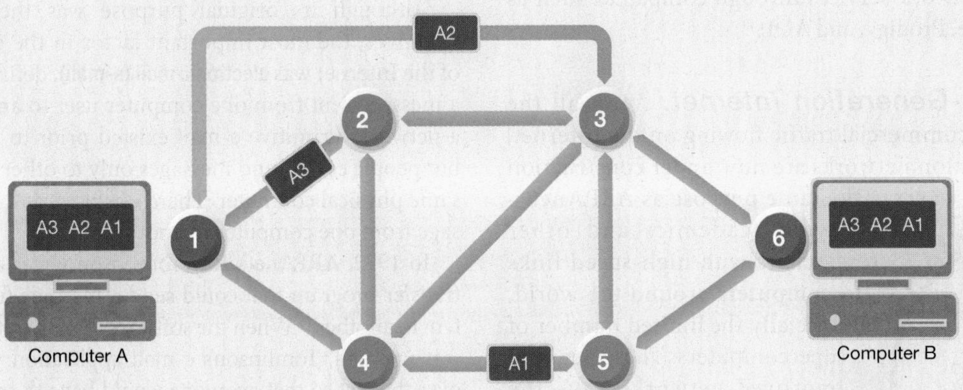

Packet switching is at the core of how wide-area computer networks operate. The sending computer breaks down the message into a number of smaller pieces, or packets, that can be sent separately across the network. These packets each follow their own routes to the destination computer, where they are reassembled into the original message.

Barbara, and University of Utah. ARPAnet came online at about the same time as the first moon landing. Whereas Neil Armstrong's "one small step" was noted throughout the world as one of the great achievements of humanity, no one outside of ARPA was aware that a new, world-changing medium had just been born.[10]

Connecting Incompatible Networks

As ARPAnet expanded to more and more universities, other networks were formed. Each of these small networks worked well in its own limited and defined sphere, but they couldn't communicate with one another. How could they be linked together?

Creating the Internet's Protocols. The answer came from work done by Bob Kahn and Vint Cerf. The pair envisioned a box, or gateway, that would serve as a translator for all the various incompatible networks. The individual networks would talk to the gateways using a common set of rules, or "protocols." Their protocol was known as **TCP/IP**. TCP stands for Transmission Control Protocol, which controls how data are sent out on the Internet. IP stands for Internet Protocol, which provides the address for each computer on the Internet. The term *Internet* was coined in 1973 as an abbreviation for "inter-networking of networks."

TCP/IP: TCP stands for Transmission Control Protocol, which controls how data are sent out on the Internet; IP stands for Internet Protocol, which provides the address for each computer on the Internet. These protocols provided common rules and translations so that incompatible computers could communicate with each other.

Figure 10.2 Drawing of Four-Node Network

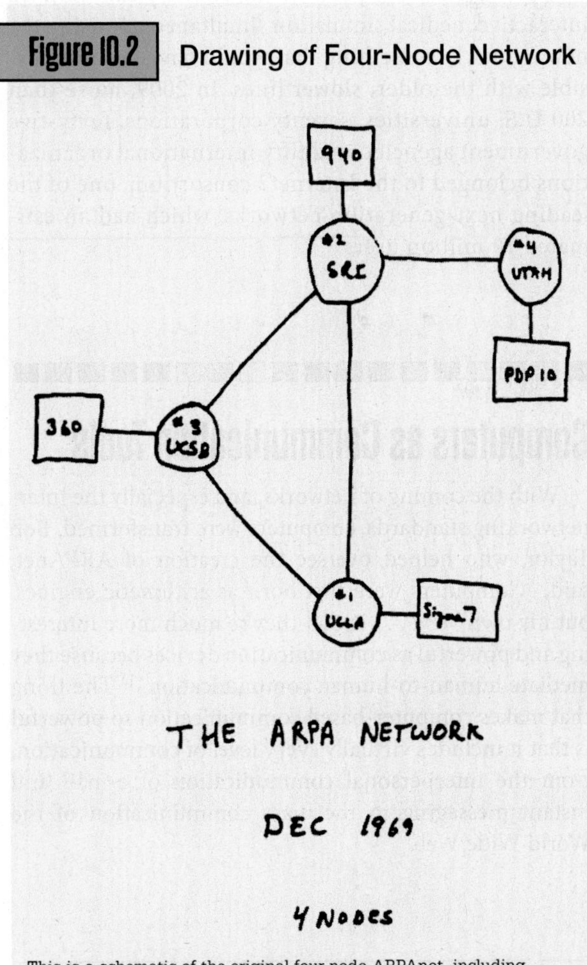

This is a schematic of the original four-node ARPAnet, including University of California–Los Angeles, Stanford Research Institute, University of California–Santa Barbara, and University of Utah.

Source: Courtesy of Computer History Museum.

Commercial Networks. As academics started making personal use of the Internet, nonacademics became interested in computer communication and started buying access to network services through companies such as CompuServe, Prodigy, and AOL.[11]

The Next-Generation Internet. With all the public and commercial traffic flowing on the Internet, next-generation networks are now under construction to serve the same purpose as ARPAnet—to provide academics and other researchers with high-speed links to computers around the world, especially the limited number of supercomputers. These new and improved networks have the potential to move data ten to twenty times faster than the conventional Internet, given ideal conditions. Their primary advantage is that they make possible video and interactive applications that are of much higher quality. For example, students at medical schools in different parts of the country can view an interactive medical simulation simultaneously using the new network, something that would have been impossible with the older, slower lines. In 2009, more than 200 U.S. universities, seventy corporations, forty-five government agencies, and fifty international organizations belonged to the Internet2 consortium, one of the leading next-generation networks, which had an estimated 10 million users.[12]

Questioning the Media

Let's see how well you know the newest medium: What is the Internet? Who owns and controls it? Where did it come from?

Computers as Communication Tools

With the coming of networks, and especially the internetworking standards, computers were transformed. Bob Taylor, who helped oversee the creation of ARPAnet, said, "Computers were first born as arithmetic engines, but my own view . . . is that they're much more interesting and powerful as communication devices because they mediate human-to-human communication."[13] The thing that makes computer-based communication so powerful is that it includes virtually every level of communication, from the interpersonal communication of e-mail and instant messaging to the mass communication of the World Wide Web.

Web 10.3: Quotes from Vint Cerf, the "father of the Internet."

Interpersonal Communication: E-mail and Instant Messaging

Although its original purpose was the sharing of resources, the most important factor in the development of the Internet was **electronic mail (e-mail)**, defined simply as a message sent from one computer user to another across a network. Primitive e-mail existed prior to the Internet, but people could send messages only to other users on the same physical computer. There was no way to send a message from one computer to another.

In 1972, ARPAnet's Ray Tomlinson wrote a simple file-transfer program that could send a message from one system to another.[14] When the software that operated ARPAnet was updated, Tomlinson's e-mail application was sent out over the Net so that everyone would have the same materials. Tomlinson also created the form of address using the @ symbol. It was a way of saying, "This is a message for a person 'at' a particular computer." The other reason was that the @ symbol did not appear in users' names or locations. It was the one symbol that meant what Tomlinson wanted it to mean and that was not already in use.[15] Even with all the growth the World Wide Web has undergone throughout the decades, e-mail continues to be the most important Internet application for the largest number of people, even if it isn't as trendy as newer technologies.

Interpersonal communication on the Internet has expanded beyond e-mail through a variety of "chat" services, most notably **instant messaging (IM)** programs, which are e-mail systems that allow users to chat with one another in real time, hold virtual meetings that span multiple cities or even countries, and keep track of which of their "buddies" are currently logged on to the system.[16]

Group Communication: Listservs and Newsgroups

E-mail and instant messaging can act as a vehicle for group as well as individual communication. This occurs through listservs and newsgroups.

Listservs are Internet discussion groups that use e-mail to exchange messages between as few as a dozen people or as many as several thousand. A listserv subscriber sends a message to a central address, where it is duplicated and sent out to all the members of the group.[17] The distinguishing characteristic of a listserv is that users must subscribe to the

electronic mail (e-mail): A message sent from one computer user to another across a network.

instant messaging (IM): E-mail systems that allow two or more users to chat with one another in real time, hold virtual meetings that span multiple cities or even countries, and keep track of which of their "buddies" are currently logged on to the system.

listservs: Internet discussion groups made up of subscribers that use e-mail to exchange messages between as few as a dozen people or as many as several thousand.

group. In some cases, it is limited to people who work in a particular office; in other cases, anyone who is interested in the topic may join.

Newsgroup bulletin boards are the next step. Newsgroups allow people to post and reply to messages from anywhere in the world. They may have a definite list of subscribers or be open to anyone who wants to stop by for a look.[18] Since the birth of the World Wide Web (discussed in the next section), a huge number of Web-based discussion groups have arisen. Frequently associated with media Web sites, these groups often blur the lines between newsgroups and listservs, allowing subscribers to choose between viewing the messages on a central Web site and receiving them via e-mail.

Tim Berners-Lee, the British physicist who created the World Wide Web software, was a part of the opening ceremony of the London 2012 Olympic Games.

Mass Communication: The World Wide Web

Until 1990, using the Internet for anything more than e-mail was a challenge. Information was scattered about in various places, with no easy way to access it. All that changed with the invention of the World Wide Web by British physicist Tim Berners-Lee. Berners-Lee, who built on the ideas of several Internet pioneers, created the software that allows the Internet to work as a medium of mass communication. He developed a system that is easy to use, allows users to access any type of information, and has a simplified single addressing system for accessing any document located on the Web anywhere in the world.

Predecessors of the Web. The idea of the Web dates back to the 1960s. In 1968, Stanford researcher Doug Engelbart staged a demonstration of his vision of an interactive computer. He used a pair of computer terminals in an "online" session that included word-processing documents, hypertext documents, and live video images (sent over closed-circuit analog lines). Engelbart was ahead of his time and largely ignored, but his work was the first expression of what would come with the Macintosh, Microsoft Windows, and videoconferencing.[19]

Another early vision of the Web, more philosophical than technical, came from Ted Nelson. Nelson described a form of "nonsequential writing" that he called **hypertext**—material formatted to contain links that allow the reader to move easily from one section to another and from document to document. The most commonly used hypertext documents are Web pages.

Tim Berners-Lee and the Birth of the World Wide Web. When Tim Berners-Lee was a child, his parents owned a Victorian-era advice book called *Enquire Within Upon Everything.* What would it be like, Berners-Lee wondered, if there really was a book that contained everything you might want to know? In 1980, he made his first attempt to create such a resource by writing a program called Enquire to organize documents, lists of people, and projects on his computer. The hypertext program would let him find and connect any of his documents. Although Enquire was limited to Berners-Lee's computer, the young British physicist thought about the possibilities of the program extending beyond his own computer to every computer in the world:

> Suppose all the information stored on computers everywhere were linked . . . Suppose I could program my computer to create a space in which anything could be linked to anything? All the bits of information in every computer . . . on the planet would be available to me and to anyone else. There would be a single, global information space.[20]

---

hypertext: Material in a format containing links that allow the reader to move easily from one section to another and from document to document. The most commonly used hypertext documents are Web pages.

Video 10.3: Watch an interview with Tim Berners-Lee.

Web 10.4: Visit the first World Wide Web site.

Berners-Lee was never asked to create the Web; he simply thought it would be a good idea for researchers to be able to find documents they needed regardless of which computer those documents resided on. In 1989, he returned to his Enquire idea and started writing the software for a system he called the **World Wide Web**, which allows users to view and link documents located anywhere in the world using standard software.

By 1990, the European Organization for Nuclear Research (CERN), where Berners-Lee was working at the time, had the first Web server and a simple browser. (A Web server is a program that makes Web pages available on the Internet. A browser is a program for viewing Web pages.)

The World Wide Web has three major components:

1. The **uniform resource locator (URL)**—the address of content placed on the Web. An example is www.mysite.com.
2. The **hypertext transfer protocol (http)**—the standard set of rules used by Web servers and browsers for sending and receiving text, graphics, or anything else on a Web site. When you type http://, you are telling your Web browser to use this protocol, or set of rules.
3. The **hypertext markup language (HTML)**—the programming language used to create Web pages. It consists of all the tags (brief computer commands) that say how text ought to be presented, where graphics should be placed, and what links should be included.

©iStockphoto.com/ahlobystov

Although the Web has grown immensely in complexity since it was invented, these three basic elements remain central to how it operates.

Berners-Lee released the Web software in the summer of 1991 on several Internet newsgroups. These early users helped him test and debug the program and made suggestions for improvement, and the Web started spreading around the world.

Whereas Berners-Lee developed the Web on a NeXT computer system, the development of browsers for a wide range of computers was done on a volunteer basis by people around the world. These individuals were willing to share their work, but language barriers sometimes posed a problem. One of the early browsers had documentation only in Finnish. (You can read more about Steve Jobs and the NeXT computers at the beginning of Chapter 3.)

The most surprising thing about the World Wide Web may be that it was developed almost entirely as a collaborative, nonprofit venture. "What amazed me during the early days was the enormous amount of free energy that went into developing that technology," says Michael Folk, one of the early Web developers. "People from all over the world contributed huge amounts of time and ideas in a surprisingly noncompetitive, collaborative way."[21]

A Vision for the Web. Although the World Wide Web has grown far beyond what anyone could have imagined and has changed immeasurably, it is still shaped by the basic vision of Tim Berners-Lee. His goal was to create a completely decentralized system for sharing information that would have no central hub. With no central control, the whole system could scale—that is, grow almost indefinitely—yet still work properly. Berners-Lee was looking for a system in which any computer could link to any other computer: "The power of a hypertext link is that it can link to absolutely anything. That's the fundamental concept."[22]

The success of the World Wide Web illustrates one of the major strengths of the Internet: Although users can buy a Web browser or Web server, the basic technology is free. According to Dave Walden, who worked on the original ARPAnet software,

> [Berners-Lee] brought out something, he gave it to a few of his friends, they tried it, they saw that it was good, and he gave it away. It went all over the world. That's how the World Wide Web standard came on the world.[23]

The next time you go surfing on the Web, look for evidence of the principles—openness and accessibility—on which it is based:

- Information of all kinds should be available through the same window, or information space. This means that you don't have to use one program to look up phone numbers and another to find the news.
- All documents on the Web must be equally accessible.
- There must be a single address that will take users to a document.

World Wide Web: A system developed by Tim Berners-Lee that allows users to view and link documents located anywhere in the world using standard software.

uniform resource locator (URL): One of the three major components of the Web; the address of content placed on the Web.

hypertext transfer protocol (http): A method of sending text, graphics, or anything else over the Internet from a server to a Web browser.

hypertext markup language (HTML): The programming language used to create and format Web pages.

- Users should be able to link to any document at any space.
- Users should be able to access any type of material from any type of computer.
- Users should be able to create whatever types of relationships between information that they want to. It should be possible to link a document to any other document.
- The Web should be a tool not just for information, but also for collaboration. It is designed for interaction, as well as publication.
- There is no central control of the Web.
- The Web software should be available free to anyone who wants to use it.

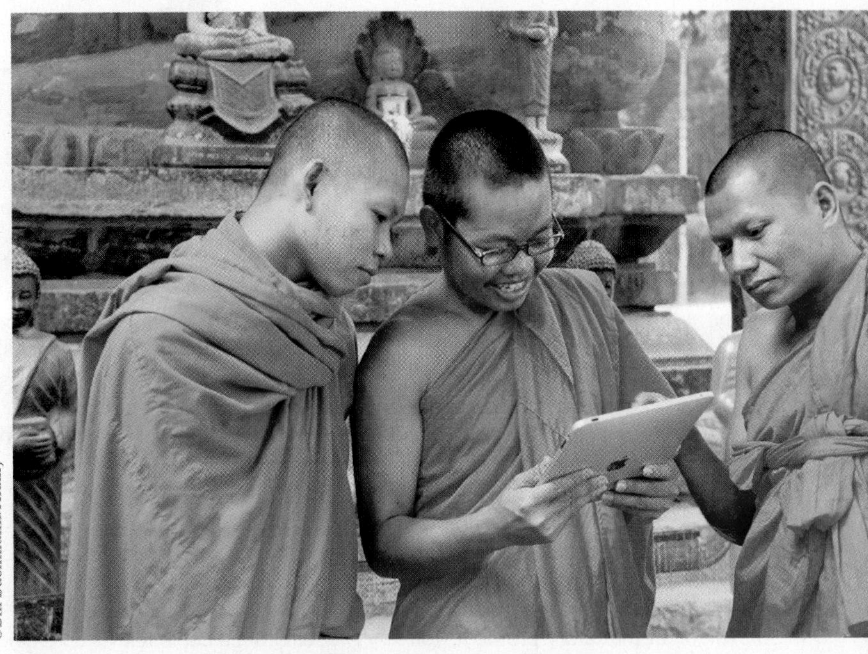

©Bill Bachmann/Alamy

Mobile devices, such as the iPad being used by these young Cambodian monks, bring Internet access to developing areas without easy access to traditional computers.

Bringing the Net to the Public

Before 1993, the Internet and the World Wide Web belonged primarily to university and military personnel who had used ARPAnet. But in his history of the Internet, *Nerds 2.0.1*, Stephen Segaller notes that three things happened during the early 1990s to turn the Internet into a significant social force: The World Wide Web code was posted to the Internet, commercial users were allowed onto the Net for the first time, and the first easy-to-use graphical Web browser was written and posted to the Net. With these changes, the Internet outgrew its military and research origins and became a public medium.

Mosaic. Although Berners-Lee had created a browser as part of the original World Wide Web, it was limited in terms of the computers it would run on, and it could not display anything other than text. **Mosaic**, the first easy-to-use graphical Web browser, was created by a group of student programmers led by Marc Andreessen at the University of Illinois at Urbana-Champaign. The developers wanted to create a tool that would make it easier to find things on the Internet and that would provide an incentive to put information on the Web. As with the original Web software, Mosaic was posted on the Internet, free for users to download. More than 1 million users downloaded Mosaic in 1993 (the year it was released), and Andreessen, then twenty-one and a graduate, founded Netscape Communications.[24]

Mosaic: The first easy-to-use graphical Web browser, developed by a group of student programmers at the University of Illinois at Urbana-Champaign.

social media: Web sites that allow users to generate content, comment, tag, and network with friends or other like-minded people.

Social Media: Sharing Our Lives Online

Like so much of the media, social networks (also known as **social media**) are a central part of how we live (Secret One). While time and distance used to be barriers to communication, these can now be crossed with relative ease if you have access to some basic online technology, whether through desktop computers or mobile devices. We think of mobile phones as being a transformational technology, but the social networks we can access through these phones can transform things even further.

What is a social network? According to researchers M. Chethan and Mohan Ramanathan, "Social networks connect individuals or groups over a common platform. Once connected, the human tendency to share information or chat (talk?) trivia becomes the driving force, creating a mind-boggling amount of information and traffic."[25]

What do social media have that makes them social? Chethan and Ramanathan write that there are five basic characteristics that make social media social:

- **User-created generated content**—Social networks aren't Web sites where you go just to consume content; you go there to create it. This content can include written words, photos, podcasts, and streaming audio and video.
- **Comments**—The communication doesn't just flow from one creator to other consumers. Everyone who is active on the social network is commenting on what others are posting. This interaction can range from

MEDIA TRANSFORMATIONS

Going Mobile

The World Wide Web, which even in the age of mobile apps is still a major part of how we go online, turned twenty-five years old in 2014. And over that time, our access to computers and computer-based media has changed dramatically. If we go back to 1983 in the years before the World Wide Web, a Harris poll found that 10 percent of adults had a home computer and that 14 percent of that small number had a modem to go online using a slow landline phone connection. (If you solve out that story problem, you find that 1.4 percent of American adults were online that year.) Berners-Lee launched the earliest version of the Web in 1989, and by 1995, 14 percent of American adults had Internet access, primarily using dial-up. But perhaps more significantly, 42 percent of Americans had not even heard of the Internet.[26]

By the year 2000, 37 percent of us were online, but only 3 percent had the fast, always-on broadband connection. **Broadband service**, such as a cable modem from a cable television provider or a digital subscriber line (DSL) from a phone company, offers connections that are many times faster than dial-up service. But broadband offers more than just increased connection speed. With a broadband connection, subscribers are connected to the Net whenever their computer is turned on. This means that they don't have to download their e-mail;

broadband service: A high-speed continuous connection to the Internet using a cable modem from a cable television provider or a digital subscriber line from a phone company.

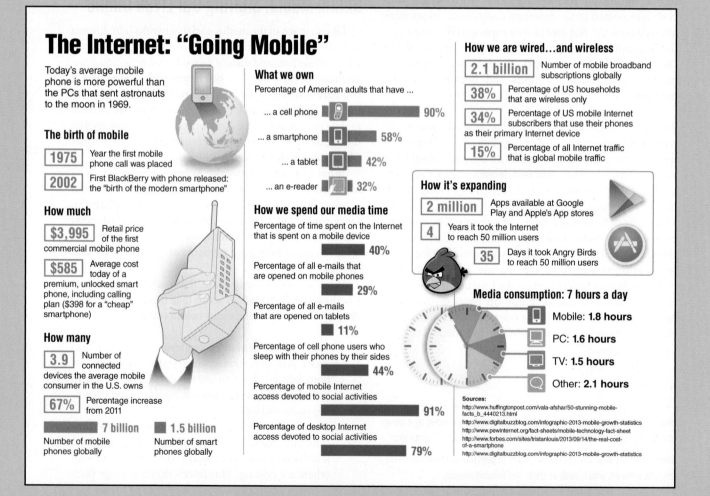

The Internet: "Going Mobile"

Today's average mobile phone is more powerful than the PCs that sent astronauts to the moon in 1969.

The birth of mobile

1975 Year the first mobile phone call was placed

2002 First BlackBerry with phone released: the "birth of the modern smartphone"

How much

$3,995 Retail price of the first commercial mobile phone

$585 Average cost today of a premium, unlocked smart phone, including calling plan ($398 for a "cheap" smartphone)

How many

3.9 Number of connected devices the average mobile consumer in the U.S. owns

67% Percentage increase from 2011

7 billion Number of mobile phones globally

1.5 billion Number of smart phones globally

What we own

Percentage of American adults that have ...

... a cell phone 90%

... a smartphone 58%

... a tablet 42%

... an e-reader 32%

How we spend our media time

Percentage of time spent on the Internet that is spent on a mobile device 40%

Percentage of all e-mails that are opened on mobile phones 29%

Percentage of all e-mails that are opened on tablets 11%

Percentage of cell phone users who sleep with their phones by their sides 44%

Percentage of mobile Internet access devoted to social activities 91%

Percentage of desktop Internet access devoted to social activities 79%

How we are wired...and wireless

2.1 billion Number of mobile broadband subscriptions globally

38% Percentage of US households that are wireless only

34% Percentage of US mobile Internet subscribers that use their phones as their primary Internet device

15% Percentage of all Internet traffic that is global mobile traffic

How it's expanding

2 million Apps available at Google Play and Apple's App stores

4 Years it took the Internet to reach 50 million users

35 Days it took Angry Birds to reach 50 million users

Media consumption: 7 hours a day

Mobile: **1.8 hours**

PC: **1.6 hours**

TV: **1.5 hours**

Other: **2.1 hours**

Sources:
http://www.huffingtonpost.com/vala-afshar/50-stunning-mobile-facts_b_4440213.html
http://www.digitalbuzzblog.com/infographic-2013-mobile-growth-statistics
http://www.pewinternet.org/fact-sheets/mobile-technology-fact-sheet
http://www.forbes.com/sites/tristanlouis/2013/09/14/the-real-cost-of-a-smartphone
http://www.digitalbuzzblog.com/infographic-2013-mobile-growth-statistics

it's always there. It means that things such as online radio, instant messaging, and streaming video are easily accessible.

By 2014, the Web's twenty-fifth birthday, 87 percent of American adults were online in one way or another. But it's that "another" that is transformative. More than two-thirds of Americans (68 percent) go online with mobile devices like smartphones or tablets. Beyond that, one-third of all cell phone owners say their mobile device is their primary way of going online. And in its own way, the move to mobile connectivity is just as revolutionary as the move from dial-up to broadband. For while broadband gave us "always on" connections, mobile Internet gives us "anytime-anywhere" access to information.[27]

Media Transformations Questions

- **HOW** many ways do you have to connect to the Internet? What are they?
- **HOW** long can you last without going online?
- **DO** you have a smartphone or tablet? What do you use them for?
- **IF** you do have a mobile device, how is working with it different from using a laptop or desktop computer?

Web 10.5: Read about how social and mobile technology has transformed our online experience.

extensive online debates to things as simple as "liking" a photo on Facebook.

- **Tagging**—People tag, or mark, photos and text in which they are featured. They can also tag ideas or keywords within their posts, such as the "hashtags" in Twitter.
- **Social networking**—People are able to share what they post online with groups of friends or like-minded people. These can be groups of friends on Facebook, "circles" on Google+, or followers on the simple blogging service Tumblr.
- **Customization**—Everyone can make their social network pages unique to them. For example, on your Facebook page you get to choose a small profile photo and a larger "cover" photo. On your Twitter page you get a small "avatar" image, and you can set the colors and background on your Twitter feed page.

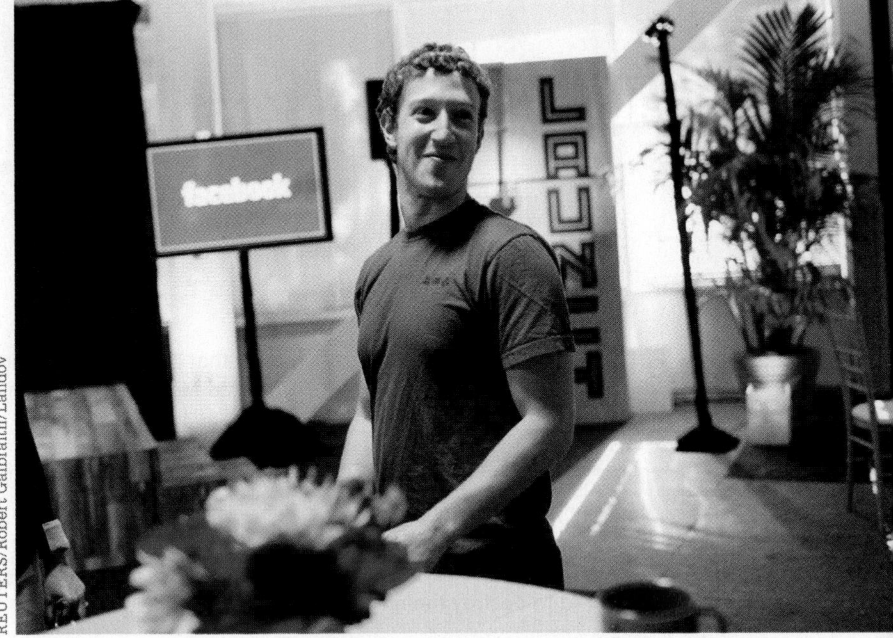

REUTERS/Robert Galbraith/Landov

Facebook founder Mark Zuckerberg (above) has become a celebrity not only through Facebook but by being portrayed by Jesse Eisenberg in the Oscar-winning film *The Social Network*.

Among the most popular social networks are Facebook, the giant of the field; microblogging site Twitter; and pinboard site Pinterest.

While we often think about social media as being primarily for recreational or social purposes, they can also be used by businesses and organizations for collaboration, public relations, and crowdsourcing—a fancy term for getting other people to do your homework.

The big shift in social networking currently is the move to mobile platforms, whether those be smartphones, tablets, or small media devices such as the iPod touch.

Facebook

As anyone who has seen the movie *The Social Network* knows, Mark Zuckerberg created Facebook while he was a student at Harvard back in 2004. As a child, Zuckerberg created a simple messaging program that solved the problem of how his father's front office could announce that a dental patient had arrived. Instead of playing computer games, he created them, according to a profile of him that ran in the *New Yorker*.

While there is controversy as to who developed the idea of Facebook, there can be little doubt that Zuckerberg turned the concept into an incredibly popular tool for

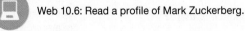

Web 10.6: Read a profile of Mark Zuckerberg.

Web 10.7: Six new facts about Facebook from the Pew Research Center.

Web 10.8: Working with social media.

TEST YOUR VISUAL MEDIA LITERACY

ONE DOES NOT SIMPLY
WALK INTO MORDOR WITH GOOGLY EYES

Dwain Smith

Have you seen this image of actor Sean Bean with the caption that starts "One does not simply . . ."? Where have you seen it? What are some of the versions of it you've seen? Where do this image and quote come from?

One Does Not Simply Create a Meme . . .

What you are looking at is an Internet meme based on the scene in the *Lord of the Rings* trilogy where Prince Boromir tells the group gathered to destroy the ring of power that "One does not simply walk into Mordor." This still from the movie has been repeatedly captioned with a variety of comments, including

- "One does not simply catch all the Pokémon";
- "One does not simply read the terms and conditions";
- "One does not simply leave a Marvel movie before the end of the credits"; and
- a range of topics not suitable for reprinting in your textbook.

The term *meme* was coined by author Richard Dawkins in his book *The Selfish Gene* to describe a "unit of cultural transmission."[1] Memes generally take an established cultural "text" (which can actually be words, video, audio, art, or photography) and use it in repeated ways to make some kind of commentary and create a common bond between those who understand it. Among the most popular memes are the "Hitler Finds Out About" video meme using the bunker scene from the German movie *Downfall*. The meme takes an emotional scene from the movie featuring German dialogue and then adds English subtitles to tell a very different humorous story.

Although the owners of the copyrights on the source materials for memes would often like to prevent the use of their content in such parodies, copyright law generally protects the memes as "fair use," a concept we will talk about more in Chapter 13 on media law.

WHO is the source?

Who came up with the concept of memes? Where do memes come from? Who produces them?

WHAT are they saying?

What is a meme? What do memes tell us about our culture?

WHAT evidence is there?

Follow the video link to the "Hitler Finds Out About" video meme. Watch the original clip from *Downfall* and at least one of the memes based on the clip. How does the meme re-create and change the meaning of the original clip? How do the creators use the movie about Hitler to comment on contemporary society?

WHAT do you and your friends think about this?

What are your favorite memes? Have you ever taken an established meme and created a new version of it? (For example, your author and this book's multimedia editor created the "One does not simply walk into Mordor with googly eyes" example shown above.) Do you think that memes violate the rights of the people who created the original text (cultural material) that the meme is based on?

[1]Alexia Tsotsis, "What Is a Meme?" November 11, 2010, techcrunch.com/2010/11/11/share-me/.

Video 10.4: Watch the "Hitler Finds Out About" meme.

communicating with friends. He told journalist Jose Antonio Vargas (whom we will talk about further in Chapter 14) that when he was in college, he and his friends would speculate about how people would use the Internet. "We'd say, 'Isn't it obvious that everyone was going to be on the Internet?'" he said. "'Isn't it, like, inevitable that there would be a giant social network of people?' It was something that we expected to happen."[28] As of 2013, more than 70 percent of the American adults who were online were on Facebook, and more than 1.23 billion people were active on Facebook worldwide, making it far and away the biggest social network.[29]

Facebook differs from much of the Web and has more in common with the old AOL than with the Web in general. It is a "walled garden" where people can play games, share articles, and post cute videos of cats. Central to Facebook is the idea that advertisers will be able to reach exactly the consumers that they want to based on information people have shared on Facebook. I can't be certain, but I'm pretty suspicious that the ad offering a good deal on the Blu-ray set of the *Alien* movies was targeted at people like me who are tagged as fans of director Ridley Scott. In any event, the ad worked. I ordered the set.

Twitter

In 2006, three college dropouts developed Twitter, a medium that combines elements of mobile text messaging, online instant messaging, and a good dose of blogging. By 2012, it had more than 182 million people answering the question, "What are you doing?" in 140 characters or less.[30]

Evan Williams, Jack Dorsey, and Biz Stone started the microblogging Twitter service as a project while they were working for the podcasting company Odeo.[31] Twitter is designed to let people communicate with their friends, family, and coworkers using messages no longer than 140 characters. The little messages, known as "tweets," can be delivered to your friends, your acquaintances, or anyone in the world who can be bothered to read them. You can send and receive tweets as e-mails, on Facebook, through a widget on a Web page, or on your cell phone as text messages.

Social networking expert Clay Shirky told NPR's *On the Media* that the 140-character limit of Twitter is essential to its success:

> There's a certain relief . . . in being forced to write in short form. When you're writing an email . . . you can end up agonizing over it and so forth. But if you can only say one thing, if you can only, you know, manage a sentence or even a sentence fragment, it really makes you concentrate on what it is you're wanting to say.[32]

Although much of Twitter's content is made up of reports of ordinary daily activities, it can move beyond the mundane. During the 2008 terror attacks in Mumbai, India, much of the news coming out of the country was through social networking tools such as Twitter. For many people, this was their first exposure to Twitter.[33]

Technology consultant Charlene Li told the *Sunday Times* of London that Twitter can be valuable to businesses because they can use it to set up a two-way relationship with their customers, creating a sense of interaction. At a time when many consumers decide not to watch television commercials by fast-forwarding through them using their DVRs, they are still willing to receive messages such as electronic coupons. "Twitter is a great platform to push out those messages," Li said. "I don't mind Starbucks making an announcement on my Twitter page but I don't want them in my inbox."[34]

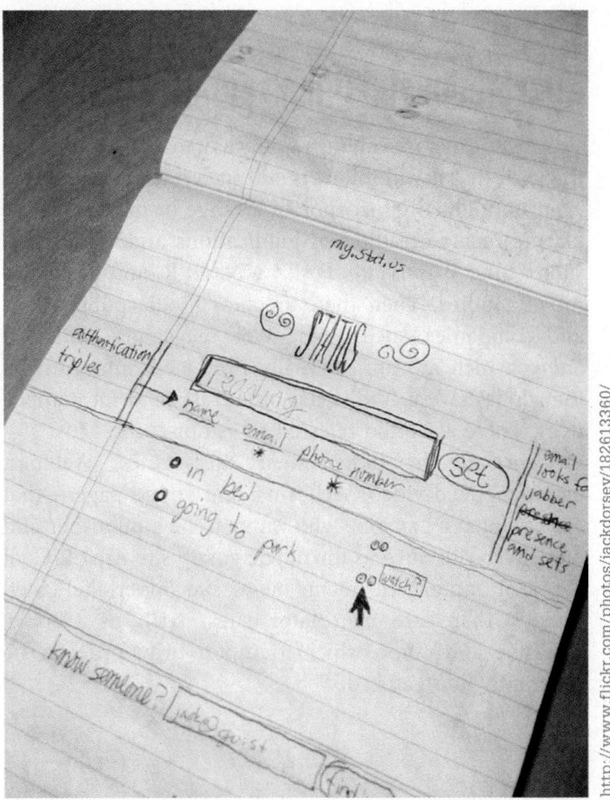

http://www.flickr.com/photos/jackdorsey/182613360/

Jack Dorsey's original sketch of what would become Twitter. In this version, he called it stat.us.

Questioning the Media

How many different social media accounts do you have? Whom are they with? With whom do you communicate using social media? Do you ever think you share too much through social media? Why or why not?

Web 10.9: Twitter feeds to follow.

New Media and Online Entertainment

The Internet is evolving rapidly as a mass medium, and the path that it will follow is still uncertain. It will, however, undoubtedly incorporate a range of players. These players include traditional publications and companies, such as the *Washington Post*, CNN, NPR, and the major movie studios. Then there are new media publications and companies, such as the Web magazines *Slate* and *Salon*, which are professionally produced online media that don't have a traditional broadcast or print component. These are often referred to as dot-coms. Most significant are the independent sites—zines, Weblogs, user-generated video, Webcams, and gossip pages—that are operated by anyone who wants to be a publisher and has a Web site, such as the movie gossip site Ain't It Cool News or motorcycle racing news site SuperbikePlanet. Finally, there are aggregator sites, such as Google, YouTube, and Yahoo, which attempt to bring order to the inherently unorganized Web.

Legacy Versus New Media

Legacy media companies that publish news online are sometimes called *click and mortars*. They have larger economic and journalistic resources than do the dot-coms and include existing media companies such as Gannett (publisher of *USA Today*), NBC, and Disney.[35]

Along with reprinting news that is printed or broadcast by traditional media, these sites may include supplementary material that cannot appear in the original publication. For example, the Web version of a profile of author Hunter S. Thompson in *Atlantic Monthly* was accompanied by audio excerpts from the Thompson interview.

News sites from traditional media are particularly effective when there is breaking news. The Web site can provide immediate updates in much the way that television does, but the Web can reach workers at their desks. The other advantage of Internet news is that heavy coverage of a breaking story does not prevent the Web site from covering the rest of the news. Television is more limited because covering one major story prevents stations from devoting time to other stories.[36]

Newspapers have been able to create good Web sites in part because they already have the staff to gather news. In Internet terms, they have a good source of content. In some ways, newspaper Web sites have come to resemble miniature television networks.

Web 10.10: See some media Web site examples.

Video 10.5: Watch the short film *405*.

Despite the name World Wide Web, one reason newspapers succeed is that they are local. Most people work, buy cars, and rent or buy housing in the city in which they live, making local classified ads an important component of the newspaper. When news Web sites were first launched, they were expected to lose money, but the media conglomerates that control many of the most popular sites now expect to make profits. Whereas banner advertising is the most prominent form of advertising on the Web, employment ads (want ads) and classified ads are the most important source of revenue for newspapers.[37]

The main advantage that online media offer consumers is that they can customize the site to deliver only the news they want. Your sports page leads with the teams you follow, your weather forecast is local, and you don't have to wade through the international news if you aren't interested in it. Cyberpunk author William Gibson likes the idea of being able to control the information coming in to him, but he is also concerned about how such limits will affect him:

> We have access to so much information, the problem is really valving it down and selecting the bits. Eventually we'll all have very specialized software agents that spend their time pre-sorting that stuff for us. That worries me a bit because I know if I had one of those, there are things I would utterly ignore that I should know about. There's something to be said for a certain amount of randomness in your news intake.[38]

Movies, TV, and the Net. The first use of the Internet by the movie industry was to promote films through brochure-like Web pages. Then came *The Blair Witch Project*, which showed how interaction on the Web could draw in viewers. Finally, the Internet started being used as the screening venue for short films. Film sites on the Web have become the minor leagues of the movie and television industry. Aspiring filmmakers first establish themselves with a short, low-cost Internet film in the hope that someone in the industry will notice them.[39] Of course, on user-generated content sites, such as YouTube, the short films can be beyond low budget.

Another thing the Internet can do is air films that may be too avant-garde for conventional media. The Web site UbuWeb, for example, is a repository of a wide range of avant-garde and experimental films, interviews, and e-books. According to Dave Garrett, who broke into Hollywood with an Internet film about elderly women playing Russian roulette,

> The Internet is not the place to look for mainstream fare; that's something you can find on television or at the movies. Our film was perfect for the Internet. You couldn't see it on TV because it had old women shooting themselves.[40]

Among the first big hits on the Internet was *405*, a short film that tells the story of an airliner landing on a highway, which was downloaded more than 2 million times in 2000. The film was created by Bruce Branit and Jeremy Hunt, who worked during the day at the special-effects house Digital Muse. *405* had no budget—allegedly the only significant expense was the traffic ticket the moviemakers got for filming illegally on the highway—though it did make use of Branit and Hunt's special-effects skills and some of the software and equipment to which they had access at work.[41]

As we discussed in Chapter 9, audience members, especially younger ones, are moving away from regarding television sets as the primary way to view video. They can now get both video podcasts and digital downloads of movies and television shows through online services such as iTunes or Amazon.com, or from streaming video services such as Netflix. From there, they can view their video on computers, smartphones, tablets, or other portable video players. Back in 2000, Martin French, who worked for the Internet film site MeTV, put it this way: "Let's be honest, nobody wants to sit in front of the PC and [watch movies]. It's not a comfortable position."[42] Obviously, people *are* willing to view video on their computers, tablets, and even smartphones. It is true that alternative devices have gotten better, but there is an ongoing cultural change on how people view video.

The Internet is also being used as a promotional tool for mainstream media content. We saw this early on with *The Blair Witch Project* Web site, followed by the *Lost Experience* alternate reality game. Consider, too, the online scavenger hunt for the 2007 Nine Inch Nails album *Year Zero*, which featured thumb drives containing downloads of CD tracks located around the country, a mysterious Web site located at iamtryingtobelieve.com, and comments on a blog. Music industry trade magazine *Billboard* suggested that all these elements were not so much a promotional campaign for the album, but rather additional components of "a new entertainment form."[43]

http://www.405themovie.com, screenshot

405, created on home computers with specialized video software, was one of the first successful films to be produced for distribution over the Internet.

New Media. Competing with the traditional media on the Web are the Web magazines—publications that look a lot like traditional magazines but don't have a print or broadcast counterpart. The two leading Web magazines are *Slate* and *Salon*, which publish articles similar to those in glossy literary magazines such as the *Atlantic* or the *Nation*.[44]

How do these differ from "real" magazines? On the one hand, the Web magazines have low publishing costs and can be updated without the long lead time required for printed magazines. On the other hand, readers expect Web publications to be updated daily, and most of these magazines have no subscription revenue to supplement advertising. Although articles in Web magazines can be of any length, they rarely run longer than 2,000 words, primarily because that's how much people are willing to read.[45] One thing the Web magazines offer that print and broadcast magazines cannot is the opportunity for readers to respond to articles through a message board.

Aggregator Sites. The biggest challenge facing Web surfers is the enormous amount of content on the Internet. How do people find what they are looking for? An easy first step is to rely on sites produced by traditional media companies. But how do people find specialized information? That's where the **aggregator sites** come in. Aggregator sites provide surfers with easy access to e-mail, news, online stores, and many other sites. Among the earliest of these was Excite, which started out as a service for litigation-support departments, political campaigns, and public relations agencies. Its product evolved gradually into a navigation aid—something that would help people to find their way around the Internet. Excite co-founder Joe Kraus said, "Basically, we call ourselves Publishing on Steroids. Devoid of print, paper, or ink, we do what a publisher does, or a cable provider does. We aggregate consumers around our programming and then we sell that demographic back to advertisers."[46]

Web10.11: Check out UbuWeb.

Web 10.12 Who plays video games?

aggregator site: An organizing Web site that provides surfers with easy access to e-mail, news, online stores, and many other sites.

With companies such as Google, Yahoo, AOL, and Netscape all providing newspaper- or magazine-like content, the Web has turned into a commercial mass medium supported by advertising, just as television, radio, or magazines might be.

Video Games as Mass Communication. In my own media literacy class, I used to raise the question as to whether video games and video game consoles count as mass communication and whether they are a new mass medium. I think the answer is a definite yes, for a number of reasons[47]:

- Video game consoles are media content delivery devices. The PlayStation 2 was a DVD player as well as a game console, and the PlayStation 3 was among the early Blu-ray players. Microsoft's Xbox One is now pitching itself as a general-purpose media entertainment hub that can be used to stream television programs and movies, play video games, and stream video game play back onto the Internet.[48]
- Video games, like television shows or movies, have stars. They have mascots. The most prominent of these is Super Mario, who has been a force in the gaming world for Nintendo since 1981, but the list also includes characters such as Sonic the Hedgehog for Sega and *Halo*'s Master Chief for the Microsoft Xbox.
- Video games are a new venue for advertising. Just like newspapers, magazines, and Web sites are funded by ad revenue, many game publishers are turning to the advertising world to help manage costs. Companies such as IGA Worldwide are devoted entirely to securing deals for companies to advertise in games, which have a near-perfect saturation in the eighteen- to thirty-four age market. As was mentioned in Chapter 2, Barack Obama advertised in video games during his election campaign—the first presidential candidate ever to do so.[49]
- Video games, now more than ever, are the site of entire communities. One needs only to look to online-specific games, such as *World of Warcraft*, or to online versions of console games, such as the *Halo* or *Call of Duty* series. The concept of online communities has become commonplace today. Now, instead of gathering around the water cooler to discuss the latest news or entertainment item, people are using Bluetooth headsets to talk to friends and family while playing capture the flag or fighting bosses to help their character rise to the next level.[50]
- Video games can be more profitable than the movies. In the summer of 2008, the controversial video game *Grand Theft Auto IV* was released at about the same time as the hit movie *Iron Man*. In its first two weeks of release, *Iron Man* grossed approximately $200 million, whereas *Grand Theft Auto IV* grossed $500 million over the same amount of time.[51]

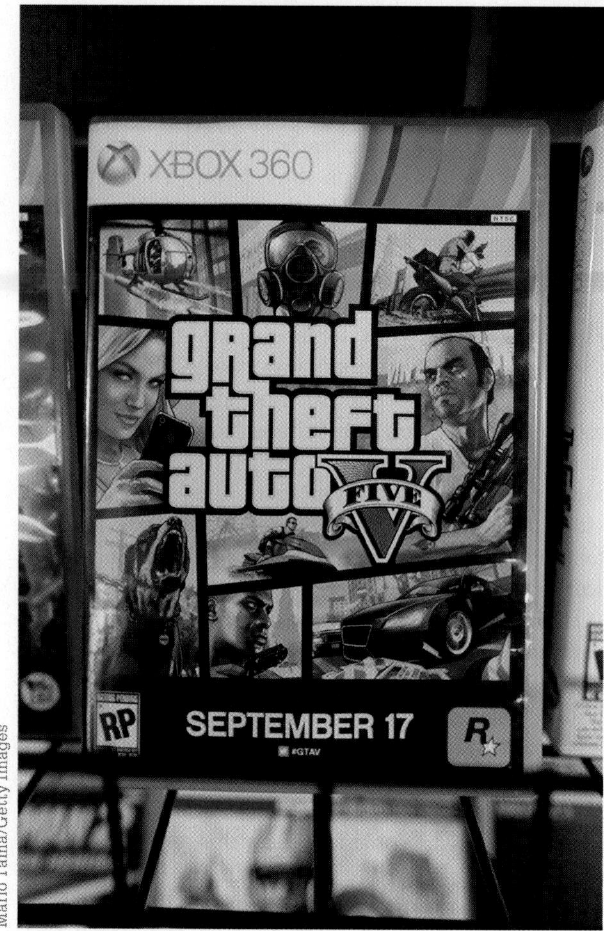

Mario Tama/Getty Images

Video games like *Grand Theft Auto* can cost as much as a major movie to produce, but they also have enormous potential to make money for the publisher. When *Grand Theft Auto V* was released, it racked up more than $800 million the first day it was on sale.

- Video games have become a central part of the synergy used to promote and profit from popular movies, books, and television programs. When the latest *Batman* or *Harry Potter* movie is released, it is almost a given that tie-in video games will be on the shelves, sometimes weeks before the movie comes out, in addition to the expected surge in comic or regular book sales. Even some television shows, such as *Survivor*, have games, and game characters such as Sonic and Mario have had their own Saturday morning cartoon show.[52]

Given all this, it's hard not to see video games as a mass medium or a form of mass communication. According to the Pew Internet and American Life Project, 97 percent of teens aged twelve to seventeen play video games in one form or another, with fully 50 percent reporting having played "yesterday." Of those who play video games, 86 percent play on consoles, 73 percent play on computers, and 60 percent play on portable game systems. As of 2008, the most frequently played games were *Guitar Hero*, *Halo 3*, *Madden NFL*, *Solitaire*, and *Dance Dance Revolution*.[53] Among adults aged eighteen and older, 53 percent play video games, and 21 percent play daily. Computers are the most popular place for older users to play video games; consoles are more common among younger players.[54]

Giving Individuals a Voice

Ultimately the most interesting thing about the Web as a communication medium is that it opens up the world of publishing and broadcasting to anyone who has a computer, an Internet account, and something to say. The line between traditional journalism and newsletter publishing is changing because people no longer need to have a printing press or broadcast station to win national attention for their ideas. If what they write is compelling enough, people will pay attention.

Lawrence K. Grossman, former president of NBC News and PBS, wrote in the *Columbia Journalism Review* that

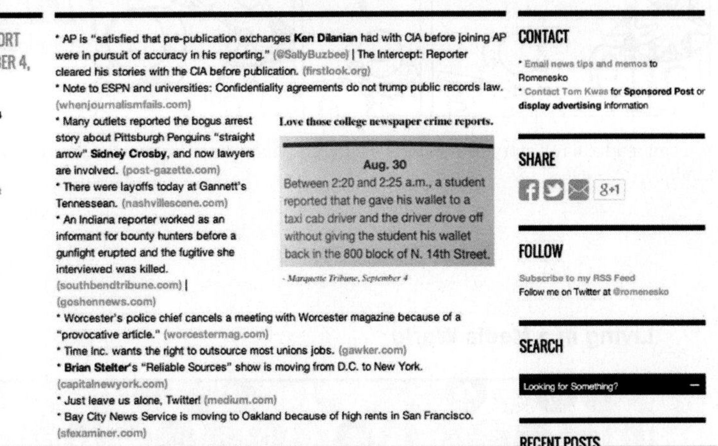

jimromenesko.com

JimRomenesko.com is a leading blog on press and media issues. Romenesko also ran for many years a blog covering gossip about Starbucks coffee (http://starbucksgossip.typepad.com).

> Gutenberg made us all readers. Radio and television made us all first-hand observers. Xerox made us all publishers. The Internet makes us all journalists, broadcasters, columnists, commentators, and critics. To update A. J. Liebling's classic crack about freedom of the press belonging to those who own one: In the next century freedom of the press could belong to everyone, at least everyone who owns a modem.[55]

The Changing Nature of News. There is a vast flood of information of dubious quality on the Web, and distinguishing what is good from what is nonsense can be difficult. As Internet chronicler Stephen Segaller wrote, information on the Internet is "unregulated and uncensored, and its providers are largely unaccountable."[56] The point here is that the information is truly free. Although people with large amounts of money can have a greater presence on the Internet than can poor people, the Net is open to everyone. An example of this can be seen in the online, user-written encyclopedia Wikipedia. Wikipedia was founded in 2001 by Jimmy Wales. Its 1 million articles are among the most viewed pages on the Web. Like the Web as a whole, the entries in this free encyclopedia are of varying quality. A recent *New Yorker* article says that Wikipedia has excellent articles on major topics such as author Franz Kafka or the ships of the U.S. Navy, but it frequently gets bogged down with trivia and political debates.[57]

Because such large amounts of information, accurate and otherwise, are being posted to the Web, the Internet has become a major news source. Many stories start out on the Internet and then creep into the mainstream media. Rumors can start spreading on the Internet and be reprinted without attribution at several sites. Although each version may have the same original source, they can appear to be multiple instances of reporting; thus, the story starts to acquire significance.[58]

When Bill Clinton's White House aide Vince Foster committed suicide, rumors about his death started circulating in politically conservative newsletters. The stories were then discussed on the Internet and spread from there to conservative newspapers and then to more middle-of-the-road media. As media scholar and critic James Fallows says, "Editors in the mainstream press have sometimes acted as if any fact posted on a Web site were . . . part of the public record, ending all arguments about whether to discuss it in newspapers or on the evening news."[59]

Questioning the Media

Before you read this chapter, would you have considered video games to be a form of mass communication? Why or why not? In your mind, what does or does not make video games a mass medium?

Blogs. When Tim Berners-Lee created the World Wide Web, he viewed it not just as a convenient and inexpensive place to access published materials, but also as a forum

Web 10.13: Read about Wikipedia.

Web 10.14: Read more about Dan Rather and the Pentagon memos.

Dave Kellet and Small Fish Studios, Inc.

You can read the full story of Sheldon's visit with Wikipedia at www.sheldoncomics.com/archive/071209.html.

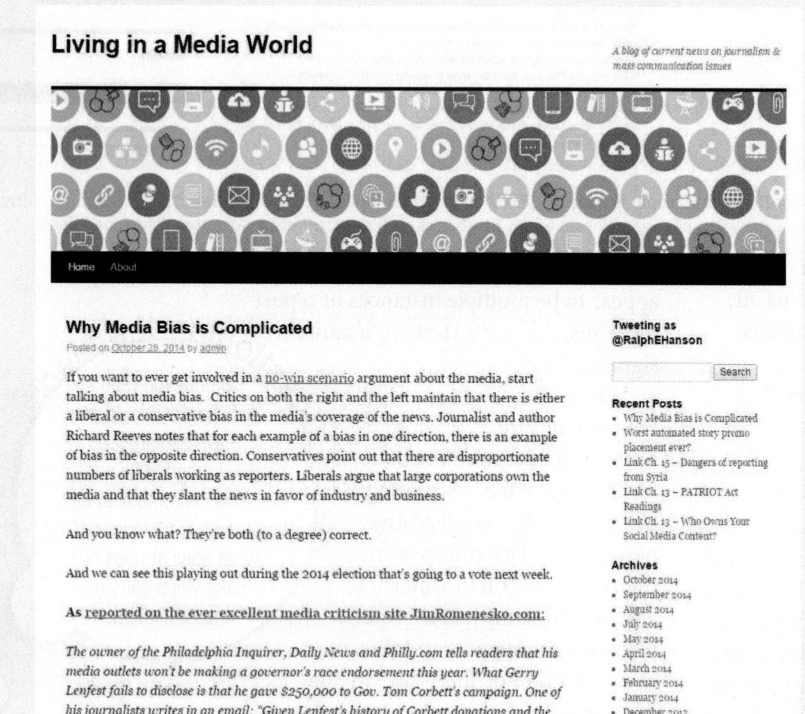

http://ralphehanson.com

Blogs have exploded in popularity in recent years, allowing anyone with a computer and an Internet connection to publish his or her thoughts on virtually any subject. (This includes the author of this text, at http://ralphehanson.com.)

where people could interact and create their own materials. "We ought to be able not only to find any kind of document on the Web, but also to create any kind of document, easily," he wrote in his history of the Web. "We should be able not only to follow links, but to create them—between all sorts of media. We should be able not only to interact with other people, but to create with other people."[60]

Berners-Lee's original idea was that every Web browser would also be an editor that ordinary people could use to create content as well as to view it—a vision that the early Web browsers did not support. But the late 1990s brought a new development called the **Weblog** (or **blog** for short), which is a collection of links and commentary in hypertext that can be created and posted on the Internet with relatively little effort. Blogs can be public diaries, collections of photos, or commentaries on the news. They often also allow readers to comment on and annotate what the owner has posted.

SECRET 2 Blogs are in many ways a throwback to the early days of magazine publishing, when authors wrote without expecting to be paid. While there are subsidized blogs, the vast majority are run simply to give the writers a forum.[61]

I made the case earlier in this book that blogs can be almost as mainstream as what we consider to be the mainstream media. (Remember Secret Two—There are no mainstream media.) One test of the importance of a news source is whether it is included in the LexisNexis online news database. LexisNexis is part of a giant subscription service that gives clients access to the full text of major newspapers, magazines, financial reports, and court documents. As of 2006, LexisNexis started including text from selected blogs, including the political gossip site *Wonkette*.

A prominent example of the influence of bloggers came when Dan Rather, on the CBS newsmagazine *60 Minutes II*, reported on a set of memos that seemed to show that President George W. Bush's superior officer had been critical of his service in the Air National Guard. The story ran a couple of months before the 2004 election, and it drew immediate criticism from the conservative blogs *Power Line* and *Little Green Footballs*. The bloggers pointed out inconsistencies in the typefaces used in the memos, suggesting that they looked more like the product of a modern word processor than that of a 1970s vintage typewriter. They also raised questions about the motives and honesty of the source of the documents. Criticisms coming from these and other blogs led to Rather stepping down as the anchor of the *CBS Evening News*.[62]

Blogs have also given readers different perspectives on stories than they might receive otherwise. Army Spc. Colby Buzzell came to national attention when he

Weblog (blog): A collection of links and commentary in hypertext form on the World Wide Web that can be created and posted on the Internet with relatively little effort. Blogs can be public diaries, collections of photos, or commentaries on the news.

TEST YOUR MEDIA LITERACY

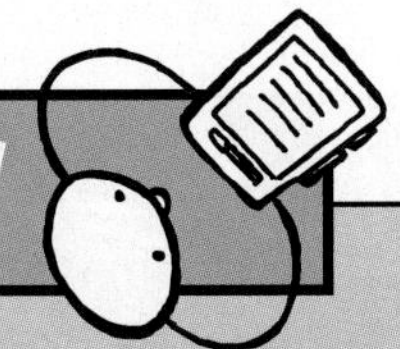

Who Protects Free Speech for Chinese Bloggers?

Chinese journalist and blogger Zhao Jing knew he would likely have trouble from the authorities over the political blog he put online. When he posted an item complaining about the firing of the top editors of a popular Chinese newspaper under the name "Anti," the government filed a complaint with Microsoft, host of the blog, and got it taken down.

According to the *Washington Post*,

> "Anti's Daily Thoughts on Politics and Journalism" tackled a variety of subjects, from public attitudes in Jordan toward the war in Iraq, to the growth of democracy in Taiwan, to the state of Chinese journalism. Zhao generally refrained from topics sure to upset the censors. But his political views were clear.
>
> "I thought of myself as a salesman, and what I was selling was the concept of democracy," he said. "People think discussing politics is dangerous, but I wanted them to relax, to see it was normal and that it's not so sensitive."
>
> The December incident sparked outrage among bloggers around the world, and in Washington, members of Congress vowed to scrutinize how U.S. firms are helping the Chinese government censor the Internet. But the reaction inside China's growing community of Internet users was strikingly mixed.
>
> Many rallied to support Zhao, but some objected to his "Western" views and said he deserved to be silenced. Others, especially those with a financial stake in the industry, said they worried Zhao's writing could lead officials to impose tighter controls on blogging. And a few said they were pleased that Microsoft had been forced to comply with the same censorship rules that its Chinese rivals obey.[1]

WHO is the source?

Who is Zhao Jing? What is his background? What did he do?

WHAT is he saying?

How does Zhao say he was treated by the American companies that hosted his blog? How did the American companies work with the Chinese government to control Zhao's writings?

WHAT evidence is there?

What evidence does Zhao provide to support his critique of the Internet in China? Do the examples he provides support his arguments?

WHAT do you and your friends think about this?

Zhao Jing.

What do you and your classmates think about international Internet controls? Should American Internet companies be willing to do business in countries that censor the Net? Why or why not? Have you ever had to deal with controls or censorship of what you can post or search for online? If so, what kind of problems have you experienced?

[1]Philip P. Pan, "Bloggers Who Pursue Change Confront Fear and Mistrust," *Washington Post*, February 21, 2006, www.washingtonpost.com/wp-dyn/content/article/2006/02/20/AR2006022001304.html.

Web 10.15: Read Zhao Jing's full story.

blogged about fighting in a battle at Mosul, Iraq, in August 2004.[63] After he returned home, he published articles in *Esquire* and wrote a book titled *My War*. British writer Julia Darling—poet, playwright, fiction writer, and the winner of the Northern Rock Foundation Writer's Award, one of the United Kingdom's largest literary prizes—blogged about her life as she battled cancer. From 2002 until her death in 2005, Darling wrote about writing, her students, and how cancer can be a "pain in the arse."[64] Dallas Mavericks owner Mark Cuban uses his blog to comment on the news and as a way to respond to his critics and those who report on him. But he also writes about digital music and the RIAA (the Recording Industry Association of America)—not surprisingly, given his background in the high-tech industry.[65] He also uses his blog to speak out on issues as diverse as capital punishment and pay for interns.

Search as a Medium

The question of whether the Internet's search capability is a news medium is significant because various

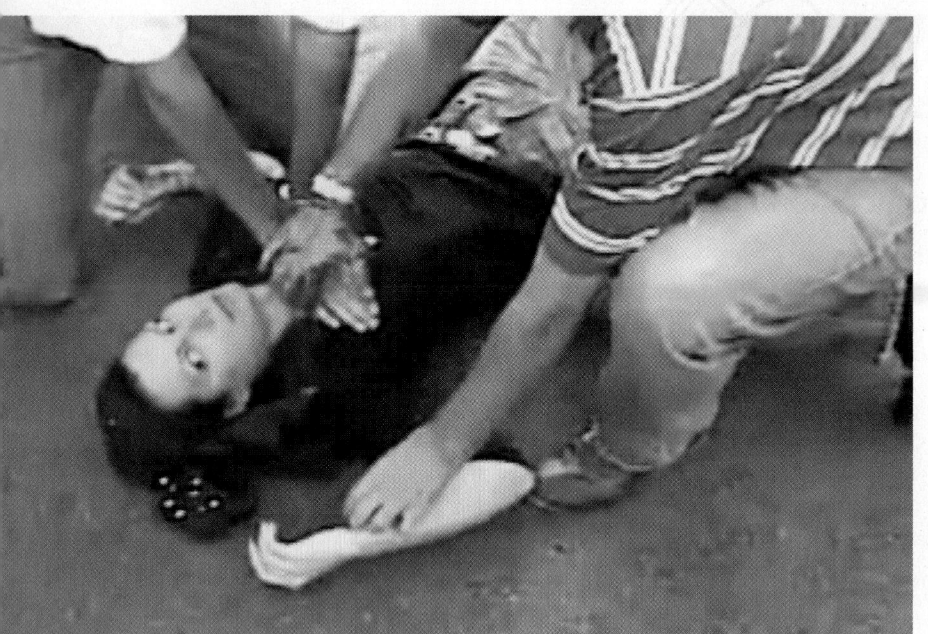

This still image of the murder of Neda Agha-Soltan during the election protests of 2009 in Iran was captured by mobile phone video and distributed worldwide via Facebook and other social media.

governments around the world want to put limits on Internet searching. And companies such as Google, Microsoft, and Yahoo all seem willing to build limits into their portals as part of the price of doing business in countries that have more restrictions on free speech than the United States. Sometimes the censorship of searches is relatively noncontroversial, such as France's attempts to make Yahoo filter out all references to Nazi paraphernalia.[66] But the collaboration of the search companies with the Chinese government has started to raise major questions in the United States. Yahoo gave up the name of blogger Zhao Jing to the Chinese government after the government required the company to do so. Yahoo defended its actions by saying that it had no choice but to comply with local law.[67] Yahoo also says that the Chinese are better served by a censored Internet than by no Internet at all. Google, which operates with the unofficial motto of "Don't be evil," censors its searches in China, but the company does inform users that it has removed items from their searches.

The Long Tail of Internet News

The Internet, through blogs, podcasts, and user-video sites such as YouTube, has opened up the options for long-tail news that doesn't get out through legacy (or mainstream) channels. Take the concept of **citizen journalism**. Often when we talk about citizen journalism, we're talking about a newspaper-like blog that posts reports about hyperlocal issues, such as neighborhood events or elementary school sports. These provide valuable alternatives to stories carried in traditional newspapers or on local television news. But they have more in common with the old-time community newspapers that ran stories about who-had-dinner-with-whom than with cutting-edge journalism.

But news video posted through sites such as YouTube can lead to amateur cell phone video having international implications. Following the disputed elections in Iran during the summer of 2009, a large number of protesters took to the streets. These protests were suppressed by police, who did not allow journalists to cover the events taking place. But that didn't stop people from shooting cell phone video and then posting it to the Internet.

One of the most dramatic examples of this was the news about the murder of Neda Agha-Soltan, a twenty-six-year-old Iranian woman who was studying philosophy and vocal music. Though accurate details about Agha-Soltan are scarce, the *New York Times* reported that she was engaged, valued freedom, and was killed while stopping to get some fresh air after driving home from a singing lesson.[68] When she got out of the car near where protesters were marching, she was shot by a sniper. Her death was captured on cell phone video. The person who captured the video e-mailed it to a friend, who then forwarded it to the Voice of America, the British newspaper the *Guardian*, and several other friends. One of those friends, who lives in the Netherlands, posted the video to Facebook. From there, it moved on to a report on CNN.[69] All of this allowed the person who shot the video to bypass official Iranian censorship efforts to block Internet, cell phone, and text message traffic.[70]

Video 10.6: Watch video of Neda Agha-Soltan and read more about her case.

The Internet and Society

Despite having its roots in the world of military research, the Internet works primarily to permit the independent use of computers. The earliest users of time-sharing computer systems, in which several people on separate terminals could share a single computer, started seeing these large institutional computers as "theirs." Stewart Brand, author of the *Whole Earth Catalog*, said that users soon began to understand how they could use computers for their own purposes:

citizen journalism: Journalism created by people other than professional journalists, often distributed over the Internet.

Kennedy had said, "Ask not what your country can do for you. Ask rather what you can do for your country"... Basically we were saying, "Ask not what your country can do for you. Do it yourself." You just tried stuff and you did it yourself. You didn't ask permission.[71]

This would become the rallying cry of the Internet: Take control of it for yourself. This attitude sent shock waves throughout the media industry because it transformed the model of mass communication from one in which a minimal number of producers delivered news, entertainment, and culture to a public whose choices were limited. Instead it became one in which consumers can choose for themselves what news they want to learn about, what movies they want to see, what music they will listen to, and when they will do so.

This environment of uncontrolled information is not all bliss, however. Some critics point out that the same giant media companies that dominated the older forms of media produce much of the content available on the Internet. Others complain that information on the Internet is uncontrolled, unreliable, and often unsuitable for young people to view.

Questioning the Media

Do you agree with the hacker ethic that "information wants to be free"? If media content is going to be free, who will pay the content creators? Should the government be stopping people from sharing copyrighted materials? Why or why not?

The Hacker Ethic

As a young man, Steve Jobs saw programming computers as a way of rebelling against and controlling an increasingly technological world. Jobs and Steve Wozniak, the co-founders of Apple, built electronic "blue boxes" that let them place long-distance phone calls for free by bypassing AT&T's control system. Beyond allowing the two to steal phone service and play an occasional prank, the boxes taught Jobs that technology could empower individuals:

What we learned was that we could build something ourselves that could control billions of dollars' worth of infrastructure in the world. . . . We could build a little thing that could control a giant thing. That was an incredible lesson.[72]

Jobs's attitude embodied what is known as the **hacker ethic**. The ethic is summed up in Steven Levy's book *Hackers*, originally published in 1984, before the Internet was a public medium and before many of the major Internet tools, most notably the World Wide Web, had been developed. (Levy uses the term *hackers* to refer to people who like programming computers and using them to their fullest potential. He prefers using *digital trespassers* to refer to people who break into institutional computers. It appears, however, that many of the "true" hackers are often also digital trespassers.)

Courtesy of O'Reilly Media

Author and journalist Steven Levy laid out the principles of hacker culture in a book he wrote in 1984, *Hackers*, many years before the Internet became a popular mass medium.

SECRET 3 Understanding the hacker ethic is critical to understanding the development of the Internet because its values shaped so many of the new medium's developers. Levy lists four key principles of the hacker ethic[73]:

1. "Access to computers—and anything which might teach you something about the way the world works—should be unlimited and total." Hackers want to obtain programs, data, and computers, and they do not respect rules that keep them from these tools. They believe that they should be able to directly control any computer system they can find; what's more, they believe that they can probably do a better job of running the system than the people who own it.

2. "All information wants to be free." This translates into a disregard for copyright law. Hackers believe that all

hacker ethic: A set of values from the early days of interactive computing that holds that users should have absolute control over their computer systems and free access to all information contained on those computers. The hacker ethic shaped much of the development of the Internet.

information should be available to anyone who wants to make use of it. This was at the heart of file-sharing pioneer Napster and user-video site YouTube. If you have music, photographs, artwork, writings, or programs on your hard drive, why shouldn't you be able to share them? And if those same things exist on other computers, why shouldn't you be able to access them? This idea of universally shared information is at the heart of Berners-Lee's design of the World Wide Web. The problem, as the Napster and YouTube cases show, remains how the creators of these works are going to be paid for the digital copies that users share. Ironically, Steven Levy got a taste of the "information wants to be free" movement in 2001, when he found the entire text of his book *Hackers* posted on a Web site at Stanford University.

3. "Mistrust authority—promote decentralization." The hacker culture distrusts centralized bureaucratic authority. Bureaucracies hide information and make rules controlling who can have access to it. So the best way to keep information free is to keep it out in the open.

4. You should be judged by your skills and not by "bogus criteria such as degrees, age, race, or position." On the Internet, traditional measures of individuals, such as age, education, sex, or income, matter less than they do under most other conditions because people are able to create identities for themselves that may or may not correspond with their actual identities. In essence, this is an extension of the multiple roles and identities people have always had. You can simultaneously be a teacher, a parent, a spouse, and a child. On the Internet, users can further extend their identities, changing their sex, race, and background. On a listserv or newsgroup, people can construct entirely new identities for themselves. When all anyone knows about you is your e-mail address, you are free to be whoever you want to be.

The application of the values of the hacker ethic to the Internet in general provides an example of Secret Three—Everything from the margin moves to the center.

The Notion of Cyberspace

The word *cyberspace* is used extensively to describe the Internet and the interactions that take place there. But the word predates common use of the Internet and the shared culture it has created. The word *cybernetics* (from the Greek *kybernetes*, meaning "pilot" or "governor") has been in use since 1948 to refer to a science of communication and control theory. Science-fiction writer William Gibson is generally credited with coupling the prefix *cyber* to the word *space* in his 1984 novel *Neuromancer*, although the authoritative *Oxford English Dictionary* (see Chapter 4) notes that Gibson originally used the word in a magazine story in 1982. Gibson defines cyberspace in this way: "Cyberspace is where the bank keeps your money. It's where a long-distance telephone call happens. It's this ubiquitous, non-physical place where increasingly a lot of what we think of as our civilization takes place."[74]

Gibson sees cyberspace and the culture of the Internet as an expression of the hippie ideals of freedom and self-expression: "Tired as I am with all the hype about the Internet and the info highway, I suspect that from a future perspective it will be on a par with the invention of the city as a force in human culture."[75]

In addition to coining the word *cyberspace*, Gibson is credited with coming up with the idea of cyberpunk. That word was originally used in the late 1980s to describe the hardboiled style of science fiction that deals with the interface between humans and machines, which Gibson created with *Neuromancer*. In his novels, Gibson paints a picture of the future in which nations are in a decline, international corporations are growing in importance, and the world is dominated by consumerism.[76] The word *cyberpunk* has since been extended to describe movies—most notably the *Matrix* series, *Blade Runner*, and *Total Recall*—that raise questions about the differences between humans and machines. For all his talk about the influence of cyberspace, do not assume that Gibson is enamored of high technology. He wrote *Neuromancer* using a 1927-model portable typewriter. By 1995, he had switched to writing on a computer, but it was a castoff from one of his children.

Dimitri Vervitsiotis/Getty Images

Do you have any photos up on social media sites such as Facebook that would bring you unwanted attention? How would you feel if your parents or a potential employer saw them?

Community on the Net

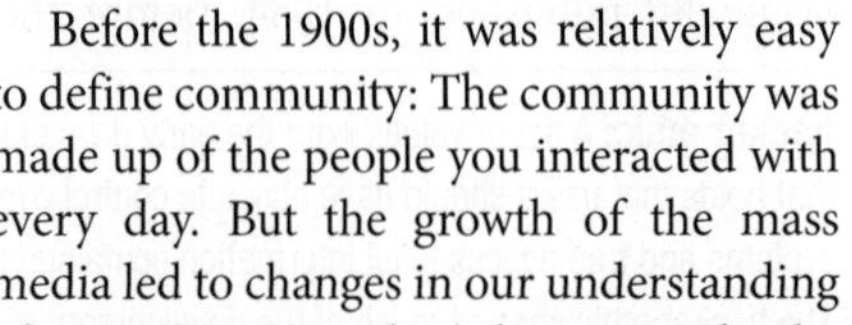

Before the 1900s, it was relatively easy to define community: The community was made up of the people you interacted with every day. But the growth of the mass media led to changes in our understanding of community. People no longer need to be

TEST YOUR MEDIA LITERACY

How Much Privacy Do You Have With Your Social Media Accounts?

The point of having social media accounts such as Facebook, Twitter, Foursquare, and the like is to be able to share aspects of your life with your friends and the rest of the world.

Which is fine when you are going out to dinner with your parents or working on a class project.

But what about when you are sharing pictures of the party you went to last night? The party where you were drinking and you are under age? The party that violated the rules of your athletic scholarship? The photo that shows you passed out as an example of how you acted in college five years ago might be one that an employer wants to look at today.

There's been considerable talk lately about how much privacy you actually have with your social media. Start with the notion that anything that you don't make private is by definition public. So anything that you post to social media that you don't hide can be seen by everyone. Including your parents, your future employers, reporters, and the police.

But what about the things you hide behind a password and privacy settings? Consider the following:

- A Minnesota middle school girl says she was forced to reveal her Facebook password to police and school officials.
- Government agencies and colleges are asking for applicants' Facebook passwords.
- Student athletes are being forced to "friend" coaches if they want to stay on the team.
- Revolutionaries in the Middle East are being forced to give up social media passwords upon arrest.[1]

WHO is the source?

What social media accounts do you have? Are you on Facebook? Twitter? LinkedIn? Foursquare? Pinterest? Any others?

WHAT are they saying?

What do you have posted there? What kind of pictures? Personal information? Comments or status updates?

WHAT evidence is there?

What would your friends be able to see about you? What would someone who is not your "friend" see? If an employer, your parents, the police, a reporter, or a potential date were to look you up online, what would they learn about you? Would letting them "friend" you change what they would find?

WHAT do you and your friends think about this?

1 Do you think that it's an invasion of your privacy to have someone investigate you online without your permission? Why or why not?

2 What would you look for if you were investigating someone online?

3 How would you feel about being asked to let an employer, coach, teacher, or the like into your accounts? Why do you feel that way?

4 Can anything you put online be considered private? Why or why not?

5 What have you done to protect the image of your profile online?

[1]Bob Sullivan, "Up Against the Wall! Should District Be Allowed to Demand Middle-Schooler's Facebook Password?" *MSNBC*, March 13, 2012, http://www.nbcrightnow.com/story/17146660/up-against-the-wall-should-district-be-allowed-to-demand-middle-schoolers-facebook-password; Bob Sullivan, "Govt. Agencies, Colleges Demand Applicants' Facebook Passwords," *MSNBC*, March 6, 2012, redtape.msnbc.msn.com/_news/2012/03/06/10585353-govt-agencies-colleges-demand-applicants-facebook-passwords; Kashmir Hill, "Hey Teacher (And Employer), Leave Those Facebook Passwords Alone," Forbes, March 7, 2012, www.forbes.com/sites/kashmirhill/2012/03/07/hey-teacher-and-employer-leave-those-facebook-passwords-alone/; "Watch What You Type: Social Media a Tool for Revolutionaries, and Increasingly, for Security Agencies," *Knowledge @ Wharton*, March 5, 2012, knowledge.wharton.upenn.edu/arabic/article.cfm?articleid=2793&language_id=1.

Web 10.16: Read articles on social media privacy invasion.

face-to-face with each other to interact. Larry Tesler, who helped develop the idea of computer communities at the Xerox PARC research center and at Apple Computer, has said that

> when we were human beings in small tribes hunting and gathering, everybody you had to deal with was somebody you saw every day. We're a species that's based on communication with our entire tribe. As the population grew and people had to split up into smaller tribes and separate, they got to the point where they would never see each other for their whole lives. The Internet is the first technology that lets us have many-to-many communication with anybody on the planet. In a sense, it's brought us back to something we lost thousands of years ago. So one reason I think the Internet's taken off so fast is that we always needed it. And we finally have it.[77]

Web 10.17: The World Wide Web turned twenty-five in 2014. How well is it aging?

Sipa via AP Images

A Kenyan woman checks her cell phone at the Dandora dumpsite, one of the largest and most toxic in Africa. Located near slums in the east of the Kenyan capital Nairobi, the open dump site was created in 1975 and covers 30 acres. People in developing countries in areas like Africa are most likly to go online using moble devices like phones.

Is It Really a World Wide Web? When Tesler claims that the Internet allows people to interact with others anywhere on the planet, he overstates the case. Worldwide, approximately 40 percent of the population has Internet access. In developing countries, that number can average 30 percent, compared to 75 percent of the population in developed nations.[78] But the spread of mobile technology is helping bring change. Africa has the lowest percentage of people online, with only 20 percent having access, but that's up from 2 percent in 2010. This growth is coming because people are now getting access via phones using mobile broadband. And that technology is allowing for the 40 percent growth rate in Africa. Companies like Facebook and Google are putting substantial effort into bringing inexpensive over-the-air Internet services to poorer areas.

The Digital Divide. Even in the United States, access to a high-quality Internet connection is not universal. Although there are not large systemic differences in access based on race and ethnicity, research by Pew shows that access to high-speed broadband connections go up as people's education levels and income increase. Urban people are also more likely to have broadband than people in rural settings.[79]

Conflicts Over Digital Media

For all the benefits associated with the Web, the new medium has been criticized on a number of fronts. For one thing, a great deal of material on the Web is inappropriate for children. Another criticism is that Web surfers give up their privacy when they visit certain sites. Finally, it is argued that people spend so much time with their virtual communities and friends that they forget about their real lives.

Web 10.18: Read the whole Pew report on home broadband access.

Controlling Content on the Web. The World Wide Web differs from all other media in that it is essentially an open forum where anyone can publish anything. More importantly, anyone can access anything he or she wants to. Because of this lack of control, unsupervised Web surfing is not particularly suitable for children. As computers and the Internet came to classrooms in the 1990s, parents and teachers became concerned about the possibility of students viewing pornography, hate speech, or even instructions on how to build a homemade bomb.

One solution to this problem is the use of filtering software, which can block access to certain kinds of material. This approach has been successful to a degree, but no filtering scheme can block all offensive material and still allow access to a full range of sites. For example, in 1998, the Loudoun County, Virginia, public libraries installed filtering software. The software successfully blocked pornographic material, but it also blocked sites with information on sex education, breast cancer, and gay rights.[80]

The fundamental problem with trying to control information on the Net is that the network of networks was designed specifically to overcome blocks and breakdowns. Once information is on the Net, it is virtually impossible to stop it from spreading. Net pioneer John Gilmore summed up the issue neatly: "The Net interprets censorship as damage and routes around it."[81]

Protecting Intellectual Property on the Web. **SECRET 6** Secret Six tells us that activism and analysis are not the same thing, and that is clearly seen in the discussion over how much control there should be to protect intellectual property online. The year 2012 brought intense debate over two laws before the U.S. Congress: SOPA and PIPA. The Stop Online Piracy Act and the Protect IP (intellectual property) Act were designed to allow the government to shut down Web sites that traffic in unlicensed media content and to prohibit American companies from doing business with Web sites that carry unlicensed media content. Big media companies argued that they need the protection such laws provide to protect them from massive economic losses from online piracy. But many tech companies, including Google, and individuals who make a living selling their own media content online claimed that laws such as SOPA and PIPA would stifle legal online media and hand over complete control of the Web to big media companies. While Congress was debating these laws, numerous Web sites, including online encyclopedia Wikipedia, went dark for the day, blacking out their pages in protest of the proposed controls.[82] Eventually, both laws were withdrawn from consideration.[83]

The advocacy group Public Knowledge has provided suggestions for a more balanced approach that protects the rights of both consumers and producers. These ideas can be reviewed at *Wonkblog*, the policy blog of the *Washington Post*'s Brad Plumer[84]:

- Ways to punish companies that demand material be taken off the Web without any justification need to exist. As the law stands now, any request made that demands that material be taken down for copyright violation must be complied with. The person who posted the offending material can appeal, but in the interim, the content is down.
- Copyright terms need to be shortened. (You can read more about the development of modern copyright law in Chapter 13.)
- "Fair use" law needs to be simplified and have penalties limited to actual damages suffered by the copyright holder.
- Companies need to be stopped from making overreaching copyright claims. Public Knowledge uses as an example the disclaimer that runs before NFL games. It prohibits "any pictures, descriptions, or accounts of the game without the NFL's consent."
- Consumers should be allowed to bypass electronic copy protection for legal uses of the media. As an example, most DVDs and Blu-ray discs have software in place that keeps consumers from making copies of the discs they have purchased. According to copyright law, consumers are allowed to make backup copies of media they own. At the same time, the Digital Millennium Copyright Act makes it illegal to break the copy protection that keeps you from making a legal copy of the media.

Privacy and the Web. A consumer walking into a conventional bookstore can wander from aisle to aisle, picking up titles of interest. After leaving the store, no one knows what books the consumer looked at. But when that same consumer shops at the online bookstore Amazon .com, the store keeps track of everything looked at. The Amazon software will then make recommendations to the shopper according to previous searches and purchases. Is this a great convenience or a serious loss of privacy?

Web users give up their privacy every time they go online. Each time they fill out a form, join a group, or buy something, information (name, address, interests, etc.) is stored so that the owner of the site will know more about its visitors. Web sites create tiny files called **cookies** to identify Web site visitors and potentially track their actions on the Web. Cookies may identify users so that they don't have to reenter their names and passwords. Or, as Amazon's cookies do, they might keep track of which types of items a visitor likes to look at. Cookies are generally designed to assist users as they visit one particular Web site, but they can also be used to track users' Web-surfing habits or to provide evidence of what sites they have visited.

©iStockphoto.com/Anatoliy Babiy

Web site developers can use cookies to tailor sites to a particular visitor. For example, a news site could use information from a cookie to provide the scores of your favorite teams, quotes for the stocks in your portfolio, or reviews of the style of music you like. This tailoring to individual tastes could take a more sinister cast, however. Web creator Tim Berners-Lee speculates that cookies could even be used to tailor propaganda to match the biases of the viewer:

> Imagine an individual visiting the Web page of a political candidate, or a controversial company. With a quick check of that person's record, the politician or company can serve up just the right mix of propaganda that will warm that particular person's heart—and tactfully suppress points he or she might object to.[85]

Convergence of Old and New Media

There is lots of talk these days about convergence and new media, such as why the Web will replace the old dead-tree media (newspapers and magazines), broadcast media, and other formats as the main source for news. New media synergy, we are told, will bring together the depth of text with an abundance of photos, audio, and video. You get all of the advantages of the old media in one package.

There are signs that this is happening. NPR (formerly National Public Radio) launched its new NPR.org Web site in July 2009 with the goal of enabling journalists to present photos, video, audio, and written stories to go with streaming copies and transcripts of all the stories that have aired on NPR since May 2005. The site also makes these resources available on mobile media such as the iPhone and Android.[86]

---

cookies: Tiny files that Web sites create to identify visitors and potentially track their actions on the site and the Web.

Web 10.19: Read the full post on Public Knowledge's arguments here.

Convergence is also delivering media that wouldn't be available otherwise. As will be discussed in Chapter 15, the Arab news channel Al Jazeera started its English-language service in November 2006, but it had trouble finding any U.S. cable or satellite services willing to carry it. For the time being, Americans who are interested in watching Al Jazeera must do so primarily over the Internet or using a mobile device app, though a few cable services started carrying it following the Arab Spring movement in 2011.

Reverse Synergy **SECRET 7** Sometimes you get reverse synergy—the worst of the old and new media in one new package. A prime example of reverse synergy happened in 2008 when Bloomberg's online financial news service posted a six-year-old news story about United Airlines (UAL) filing for bankruptcy. The story was true—it was just six years out of date. What happened was this: An undated story about UAL's 2002 bankruptcy filing showed up on a Google search on "bankruptcy 2008" done by a reporter working for *Income Securities Advisor*. The story from the *South Florida Sun-Sentinel* dated back to December 10, 2002, when UAL did file for bankruptcy. The reporter who performed the search posted the story to Bloomberg News. In response to the story, investors started dumping their shares in UAL, dropping the stock from $12.17 a share to approximately $3 a share. Not realizing what had happened, United Airlines was baffled by the tanking of its stock, but it quickly posted an online denial of the story. By the time the market closed, UAL stock was back up to $10.92.[87]

Web 10.20: Read about another "oops" article republished—this one from 1918 reprinted in 2012 as news.

What can we learn from this? Think about Secret Seven—There is no "they." The story that sent the stock price crashing was a single story from a single Web site. Wouldn't you think that if a major corporation had filed for bankruptcy twice in six years the story would be playing on every major news site, not just a single Florida paper that had no local connection to the story? At the risk of oversimplifying things, the story was posted because someone—a "they"—said it was so. This resulted in a huge destruction of wealth, albeit a temporary one, because of a story that had no truth value and apparently was posted completely by accident.

Chapter SUMMARY

The Internet arose in the late 1960s out of efforts to share expensive computer resources provided by the military to universities across the United States. The initial network, called ARPAnet, went online for the first time in the fall of 1969. The network operated using packet switching, a method of transferring information that breaks down messages into small packets that are transmitted separately across the network and reassembled once they are received. Through e-mail and file sharing, ARPAnet soon became a tool used by academics to collaborate and communicate across the country.

As the number of incompatible networks grew in the 1970s, Bob Kahn and Vint Cerf developed the TCP/IP protocols that allowed the networks to communicate with each other. In 1983, ARPAnet started using the TCP/IP protocols. This is commonly seen as the true beginning of the Internet.

The Internet is unique among the mass media in allowing interpersonal communication through e-mail and instant messaging; group communication through listservs, newsgroups, and discussion boards; and mass communication through the World Wide Web.

The World Wide Web was developed in 1989 by British physicist Tim Berners-Lee while he was working at the European Organization for Nuclear Research in Switzerland. His goal was to produce a decentralized system for creating and sharing documents anywhere in the world. The Web has three major components: the uniform resource locator (URL), the hypertext transfer protocol (http), and the hypertext markup language (HTML). Berners-Lee published the code for the World Wide Web on the Internet in 1991 for anyone in the world to use at no cost.

The Internet in general and the Web in particular were based on a set of values known as the hacker ethic. This ethic holds that information should be freely distributed and that individuals should have as much control over computers as possible.

The World Wide Web has turned the Internet into a major mass medium that provides news, entertainment, and community interaction. The Web offers a mix of content providers, including traditional media companies, new media companies offering publications available only on the Web, aggregator sites that offer help in navigating the Web, and individuals who have something they want to say.

The Web has been criticized for elevating rumors to the level of news, making inappropriate material available to children, collecting private information about users, and creating a false sense of intimacy and interaction among users.

Over the past several years, users have moved increasingly from slow dial-up connections to high-speed "always on" connections to mobile "access everywhere" connections that have changed how people view and use the Internet. Media are making use of these high-speed and mobile connections to deliver content that includes a rich mix of video, audio, photos, and text.

Keep up-to-date with content from the author's blog.

Take the chapter quiz.

Key TERMS

Internet 248
packet switching 248
ARPAnet 248
TCP/IP 249
electronic mail (e-mail) 250
instant messaging (IM) 250
listservs 250
hypertext 251
World Wide Web 252
uniform resource locator (URL) 252
hypertext transfer protocol (http) 252
hypertext markup language (HTML) 252
Mosaic 253
social media 253
broadband service 254
aggregator sites 259
Weblog (blog) 262
citizen journalism 264
hacker ethic 265
cookies 269

Concept REVIEW

The merging of the different levels of communication
Tim Berners-Lee's idealistic conception of the World Wide Web
How the Internet gives voice to individuals
The long-term effect of the hacker ethic
How convergence is changing the media industry

Student STUDY SITE

Sharpen your skills with SAGE edge at **edge.sagepub.com/hanson5e**

SAGE edge for Students provides a personalized approach to help you accomplish your coursework goals in an easy-to-use learning environment.

chapter
11
Advertising
Selling a Message

THE POWER OF HABIT

WHY WE DO WHAT WE DO IN LIFE AND BUSINESS

Charles Duhigg

AP Photo/Random House

Earl Wilson/The New York Times/ Redux

Charles Duhigg, author of The Power of Habit: Why We Do What We Do in Life and Business.

In the age of online shopping and digital information, it's easy to get paranoid about how much vendors know about us. You want to get creeped out? Start paying attention to the recommendations that Amazon makes to you based on what you've previously looked at and purchased.

But taking all your shopping to a brick-and-mortar department store won't help preserve your privacy. Exhibit number one? Target figured out that a high school girl was pregnant and started sending her direct-mail coupons for maternity products before her father knew anything was going on.[1]

How did Target know the young woman was preggers? It seems that pregnant women have very predictable buying patterns. Sometime during the second trimester, four to six months into the pregnancy, pregnant women start buying things such as prenatal vitamins and maternity clothing. Once a woman starts buying these products, she's likely to be giving birth in three to six months.

According Charles Duhigg, author of the book *The Power of Habit: Why We Do What We Do in Life and Business,* Target tracks every consumer who comes to its stores with a unique number tied to his or her credit/debit card. Using this number, Target knows what pattern of products every consumer buys. This information is then paired with data about the consumer that is purchased by the store, says Target statistician Andrew Pole. Before long, the store knows a lot of information about a customer, including preferred purchases, address, income, race, and even estimated earnings.[2]

So our high school student was buying the right combination of cocoa butter lotions, soaps, and mineral supplements that told Target there was an 86 percent likelihood she was pregnant. So Target started sending her coupons for the products people expecting babies are likely to buy.

When these coupons showed up in the mail, the young woman's father got upset and called the manager of his local Target to complain. "My daughter got this in the mail!" the father told the manager. "She's still in high school, and you're sending her coupons for baby clothes and cribs? Are you trying to encourage her to get pregnant?"

The manager apologized repeatedly to the father. Then the father had an interesting discussion with his daughter and called Target back to apologize. His daughter *was* pregnant, but she hadn't told him.

Obviously, Pole's system of evaluating the young woman's purchases worked as intended. But how were he and his employer going to deal with the backlash from consumers who just figured out how much the company knew about them?

LEARNING OBJECTIVES

After studying this chapter, you will be able to:

1 Describe two major reasons why advertising grew dramatically in importance during the nineteenth century.

2 Define what "advertising" is using examples of six different types of advertisements.

3 Describe the four major groups in the advertising business and the key characteristics of each.

4 Explain how advertisers use demographics and psychographics to target their audience.

5 Name four common misconceptions about the advertising industry.

6 Discuss the controversies surrounding advertising directed at children.

7 Discuss how companies are using integrated marketing communication (IMC) to promote their brands.

"If we send someone a catalog and say, 'Congratulations on your first child!' and they've never told us they're pregnant, that's going to make some people uncomfortable," Pole told Duhigg. This led Target to work on figuring out how to get its ads delivered to pregnant women without the women knowing they were being targeted. As Duhigg puts it, "How do you take advantage of someone's habits without letting them know you're studying their lives?"

The solution ended up being fairly simple. Target mails out coupon books to consumers based on their purchasing history all the time. Usually, those coupons don't upset people. So the secret, according to a Target executive, was to mix the pregnancy product coupons in with a collection of other innocuous coupons that hid the fact that Target knew the woman was pregnant.

"We found out that as long as a pregnant woman thinks she hasn't been spied on, she'll use the coupons," the executive said. "As long as we don't spook her, it works."

What the Target department store is doing in this example is not so different from what every major U.S. advertiser is trying to do: figure out who its prime audience members are and what motivates them and then reach those members with a persuasive message at the time they are ready to buy or make up their mind about a purchase. As we will see later in this chapter, that's why Godiva chocolates target upscale adult women, Miller Lite hires celebrity spokespeople with whom beer drinkers would like to sit down at a bar, and a Minnesota medical center targeted people who were interested in and could afford cosmetic surgery.

Communication professor Joseph Turow told NPR's *On the Media* that this kind of targeting raises all sorts of ethical questions for the companies doing it. "So I think the issue here is how much do people know about what's going on, and do they have any control over it?" he said.

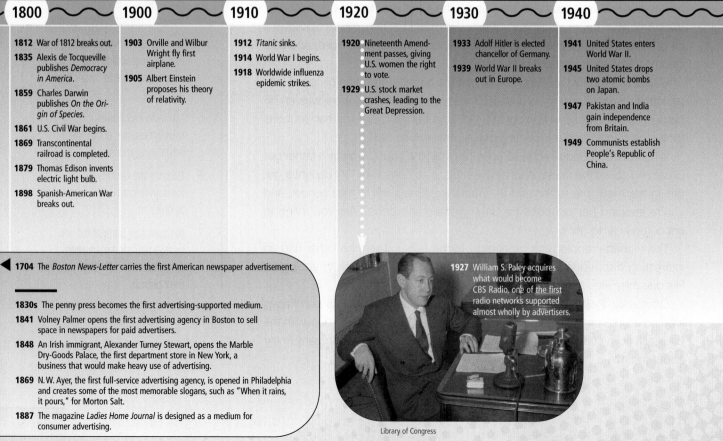

Timeline

1800

1812 War of 1812 breaks out.
1835 Alexis de Tocqueville publishes *Democracy in America*.
1859 Charles Darwin publishes *On the Origin of Species*.
1861 U.S. Civil War begins.
1869 Transcontinental railroad is completed.
1879 Thomas Edison invents electric light bulb.
1898 Spanish-American War breaks out.

1900

1903 Orville and Wilbur Wright fly first airplane.
1905 Albert Einstein proposes his theory of relativity.

1910

1912 *Titanic* sinks.
1914 World War I begins.
1918 Worldwide influenza epidemic strikes.

1920

1920 Nineteenth Amendment passes, giving U.S. women the right to vote.
1929 U.S. stock market crashes, leading to the Great Depression.

1930

1933 Adolf Hitler is elected chancellor of Germany.
1939 World War II breaks out in Europe.

1940

1941 United States enters World War II.
1945 United States drops two atomic bombs on Japan.
1947 Pakistan and India gain independence from Britain.
1949 Communists establish People's Republic of China.

1704 The *Boston News-Letter* carries the first American newspaper advertisement.

1830s The penny press becomes the first advertising-supported medium.
1841 Volney Palmer opens the first advertising agency in Boston to sell space in newspapers for paid advertisers.
1848 An Irish immigrant, Alexander Turney Stewart, opens the Marble Dry-Goods Palace, the first department store in New York, a business that would make heavy use of advertising.
1869 N.W. Ayer, the first full-service advertising agency, is opened in Philadelphia and creates some of the most memorable slogans, such as "When it rains, it pours," for Morton Salt.
1887 The magazine *Ladies Home Journal* is designed as a medium for consumer advertising.

1927 William S. Paley acquires what would become CBS Radio, one of the first radio networks supported almost wholly by advertisers.

Library of Congress

So, for example if you get an ad, say from NewYorkTimes.com and it's tailored to you, it would be great if there were a way that you could know, a) that it's tailored for you, b) where did they get those data from, c) how does it fit into a larger picture of you that advertiser or that periodical has? And can you do anything about it?[3]

> “How do you take advantage of someone's habits without letting them know you're studying their lives?”
>
> —Charles Duhigg

It's worth noting here that Turow made these comments nearly three years before the Target pregnancy advertising case came to light. Later on in the chapter, we'll continue looking at how data targeting can go wrong when companies make incorrect assumptions about their customers' pregnancies.

Although advertising has been a part of American media since the 1700s, the challenge today is to get consumers to pay attention to the messages that pay for so much of the media we receive. In this chapter, we look at the development of the advertising industry in the United States, the major players in the advertising process, and the influence advertising has had on contemporary culture. ■

Web 11.1: Read more about Target's targeting.

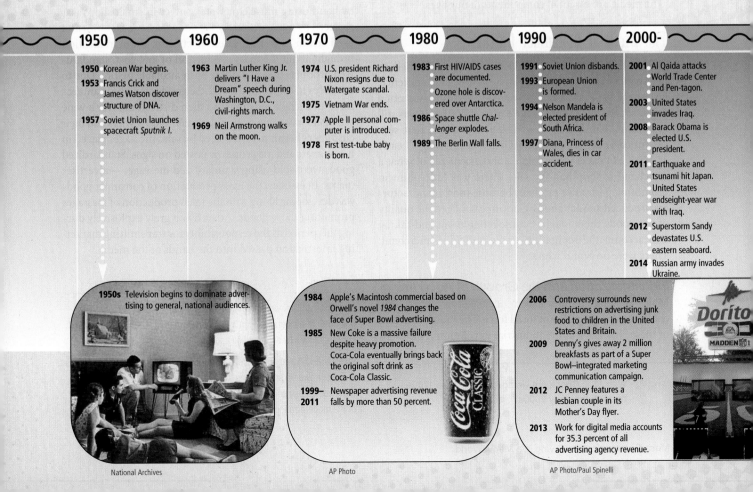

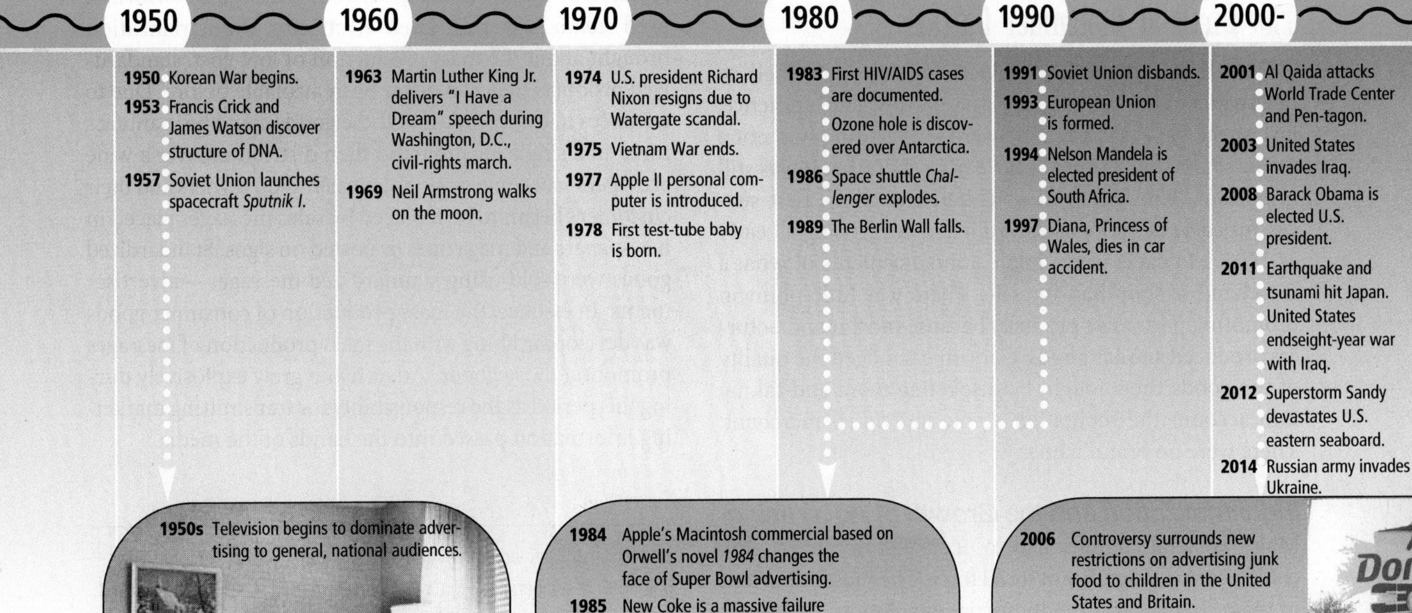

1950
1950 Korean War begins.
1953 Francis Crick and James Watson discover structure of DNA.
1957 Soviet Union launches spacecraft *Sputnik I.*
1960
1963 Martin Luther King Jr. delivers "I Have a Dream" speech during Washington, D.C., civil-rights march.
1969 Neil Armstrong walks on the moon.
1970
1974 U.S. president Richard Nixon resigns due to Watergate scandal.
1975 Vietnam War ends.
1977 Apple II personal computer is introduced.
1978 First test-tube baby is born.
1980
1983 First HIV/AIDS cases are documented.
Ozone hole is discovered over Antarctica.
1986 Space shuttle *Challenger* explodes.
1989 The Berlin Wall falls.
1990
1991 Soviet Union disbands.
1993 European Union is formed.
1994 Nelson Mandela is elected president of South Africa.
1997 Diana, Princess of Wales, dies in car accident.
2000-
2001 Al Qaida attacks World Trade Center and Pen-tagon.
2003 United States invades Iraq.
2008 Barack Obama is elected U.S. president.
2011 Earthquake and tsunami hit Japan. United States endseight-year war with Iraq.
2012 Superstorm Sandy devastates U.S. eastern seaboard.
2014 Russian army invades Ukraine.

1950s Television begins to dominate advertising to general, national audiences.

National Archives

1984 Apple's Macintosh commercial based on Orwell's novel *1984* changes the face of Super Bowl advertising.

1985 New Coke is a massive failure despite heavy promotion. Coca-Cola eventually brings back the original soft drink as Coca-Cola Classic.

1999–2011 Newspaper advertising revenue falls by more than 50 percent.

AP Photo

2006 Controversy surrounds new restrictions on advertising junk food to children in the United States and Britain.

2009 Denny's gives away 2 million breakfasts as part of a Super Bowl–integrated marketing communication campaign.

2012 JC Penney features a lesbian couple in its Mother's Day flyer.

2013 Work for digital media accounts for 35.3 percent of all advertising agency revenue.

AP Photo/Paul Spinelli

The Development of the Advertising Industry

One element of the media that is almost inescapable is advertising. The American Marketing Association defines **advertising** as "any paid form of nonpersonal communication about an organization, product, service, or idea by an identified sponsor."[4] Advertisements are the commercial messages that pay for an article about cardiovascular health in *Prevention*, an editorial about foreign policy in the *New York Times*, and the block of Rolling Stones hits on the local classic rock radio station.

SECRET 1 Advertising makes possible the vast array of inexpensive media available worldwide. But there is more to advertising than just cheap media. Advertising drives the size and diversity of the world's economy by telling consumers the multimedia functions they can perform by using a new computer, the image they will project by wearing a brand of clothing or driving a particular car, or the eating pleasure and health benefits they will experience by sampling a new variety of breakfast cereal. Advertising has been a key element of the American economy and culture of consumption and acquisition for more than one hundred years and has existed since before the United States was a nation. With the pervasiveness and importance of advertising in our society, we see once again Secret One—The media are essential components of our lives.

Library of Congress

Due to the advent of transcontinental railroads in the late nineteenth century, products such as beer went from being predominantly locally produced to being national brands produced for a larger market.

The Birth of Consumer Culture

The earliest American advertising was published in newspapers and was targeted at a narrow, elite audience, just as the papers themselves were. Advertising was not a major source of income for the early papers, but it was still important. The *Boston News-Letter*, one of the first successful colonial newspapers, solicited advertising as early as 1704. Most ads were simple announcements of what a merchant or shop had for sale. There was little point in promoting particular products because most manufacturers produced similar goods. Consumers judged the quality of the goods they bought by inspecting them and taking into account the reputation of the individual merchant. There were no brand names.[5]

Industrialization and the Growth of Advertising. Major societal changes had to occur before advertising could become a significant social force. The most important of these changes was the Industrial Revolution. The 1800s were a period of rapid **industrialization**, in which work done by hand using muscle or water power in small shops was replaced by mass production of goods in large factories that used steam power or, later, electricity. Industrialization brought about the mass production of low-cost, standardized products that had never been available before. Due to advances in transportation, these goods could be manufactured in a single location and then distributed over a wide area. Personal conversations between shop owners and their customers began to be replaced by sales messages placed in newspapers and magazines or posted on signs. Standardized goods were sold using standardized messages—advertisements. In essence, the mass production of consumer goods was developing along with the mass production of messages promoting those goods. Advertising grew explosively during this period as the responsibility for transmitting marketing information passed into the hands of the media.[6]

Web 11.2: Check out vintage ads from the 1700s through the early 2000s.

advertising: Defined by the American Marketing Association as "any paid form of nonpersonal communication about an organization, product, service, or idea by an identified sponsor."

industrialization: The movement from work done by hand using muscle or water power in small shops to mass production of goods in factories that used energy sources such as steam power or electricity. It was part of the modernization process.

Modernization: Satisfying Needs Through Shopping. Along with industrialization, the nineteenth century was characterized by **modernization**, the social process by which people go from being born with an identity and a role in life to being able to decide who they want to be, where they want to live, what they want to do, and how they want to present themselves to the world.

As more products became available, advertising was used to promote them and what they stood for. People could now adopt a certain style and purchase the items necessary to portray that style to others—the clothes they wore, the food they served, the soap they washed with, and so forth. Each of these goods was associated with an image that was supposed to rub off on its user. How did people learn about these meanings? Through the advertising that gave meaning to the products.[7]

Media historian Michael Schudson has written that in modern societies people believe they can satisfy their social needs by buying and using mass-produced goods.[8] The late 1800s brought department stores that received new merchandise frequently and then sold it quickly, in contrast to the older dry-goods and clothing stores, which might receive new goods twice a year. As people moved into new communities where their old family identities had little meaning, they could create a new identity for themselves through the products they chose. For example, in the 1920s, people started to buy more ready-made clothes rather than sewing clothes for themselves. This ready-made clothing, which they learned about through advertisements, allowed them to be fashionable and "modern" and to "put on" the identity that went with the clothes.

The Growth of Brand Names

With the growth of industry allowing more production and the construction of transcontinental railroads and steamships making possible better distribution, more and more prepackaged consumer goods came on the market, ready to be promoted through advertising. Among the first were patent medicines—manufactured remedies that often consisted primarily of alcohol and laudanum (opium). Instead of being shipped to stores in large containers and bottled at the point of sale, these products arrived bottled and ready to be sold to the consumer. These were the first products of the **economy of abundance**, in which there are as many or more goods available as there are people who want to buy them.[9]

Brand-name goods became popular at the end of the nineteenth century. A **brand name** is a word or phrase attached to prepackaged consumer goods so that they can be better promoted

Library of Congress

Manufacturers of patent medicines promising cures for almost anything—internal ailments, weight gain or weight loss, debility, the common cold—were among the biggest of the early national advertisers.

Questioning the Media

With modernization, we can try on new personas by using products that are marketed to help us create our identities. What are some advertised products you use because they say something about who you are? How are these products advertised? What do they tell others about you?

modernization: The process of change from a society in which people's identities and roles are fixed at birth to a society where people can decide who they want to be, where they want to live, what they want to do, and how they want to present themselves to the world.

economy of abundance: An economy in which there are as many or more goods available as there are people who want to or have the means to buy them.

brand name: A word or phrase attached to prepackaged consumer goods so that they can be better promoted to the general public through advertising and so that consumers can distinguish a given product from the competition.

Pears'
Soap.
YOU DIRTY BOY!
You Dirty Boy!
ALL THE LEADING DRUGGISTS SELL PEARS' SOAP.

Library of Congress

Pears' Soap was one of the earliest national brands. Pears' ads encouraged consumers to ask not for soap, but for Pears'.

to the general public through advertising. In a highly mobile society, these standardized, branded products became a source of stability for consumers. The idea of stability coming from a brand-name product has persisted into the twenty-first century. For example, wherever they are, weary travelers are likely to stop for a meal at a familiar and comfortable landmark such as a McDonald's or a Pizza Hut.[10]

The development of brand-name goods was a driving force behind the growth of advertising. Brands were necessary to distinguish the new mass-produced products from one another. The names made it possible for people to ask for goods produced by a specific manufacturer, and advertising let people know what these brands were and what they stood for.

Quaker Oats, which was among the first prepackaged cereals, was typical of early brand-name products. It was sold in a multicolored box illustrated with the trademarked "man in Quaker garb." The cereal was a product of consistently high quality that was manufactured in Cedar Rapids, Iowa, and distributed to the entire country. Wherever you purchased the product, it would be the same. Quaker Oats promoted its trademark everywhere, including "on billboards, streetcars, newspapers, calendars, magazines, blotters, cookbooks, Sunday church bulletins, metal signs on rural fences, company-sponsored cooking schools, free samples given away house-to-house, booths at county fairs and expositions."[11]

Thomas J. Barratt developed the first branded soap. "Any fool can make soap," he commented. "It takes a clever man to sell it."[12] Barratt created the Pears' Soap brand and promoted it with outdoor and newsprint ads asking, "Have you had your Pears' today?" Other versions included "How do you spell soap? Why, P-E-A-R-S', of course," and "GOOD MORNING! Have you used Pears' Soap?" Pears' became one of the most talked-about brands of its era and was even mentioned by prominent writers such as Mark Twain. The Pears' Soap catchphrases were the "Where's the beef," "Keeps on going and going," or "Just do it" of their day.

Advertising-Supported Media

The growth of products that needed advertising to succeed brought about a similar growth in advertising-supported media. Beginning in the 1830s, newspapers became much easier and cheaper to produce due to the availability of inexpensive wood-pulp paper and the steam-powered rotary press. The new penny papers (see Chapter 6) were sold to large numbers of people. These large audiences appealed to advertisers, so newspapers moved from depending on subscription revenue to advertising revenue as their primary form of support. The change was dramatic. Instead of merely tolerating advertising, newspapers began to encourage it and even created special advertising sections to seek it out.

Magazines also started out with an uneasy relationship with advertising. In the 1800s, publications such as *Harper's* ran only limited advertising in an attempt to preserve their elite image. Another reason early magazines carried little advertising was that their circulation was national, whereas most advertising was done in local publications. Because there were few national brands at the time, few companies wanted or needed to reach a national audience.

Once manufacturers needed to reach the magazines' national audiences, the economics of magazine publishing changed. No longer were publishers selling magazines to subscribers; instead, they were selling subscribers to advertisers. The *Ladies' Home Journal*, which published from 1887 to 2014, was designed specifically as a medium

Web 11.3: See "Larry" and ads for Quaker Oats.

Video 11.1: Check out commercials with a list of famous advertising catchphrases.

for consumer advertising.[13] Publisher Cyrus H. K. Curtis put it this way in a speech to advertisers:

> Do you know why we publish the *Ladies' Home Journal*? The editor thinks it is for the benefit of American women. That is an illusion, but a very proper one for him to have. But I will tell you; the real reason, the publisher's reason, is to give you people who manufacture things that American women want and buy a chance to tell them about your products.[14]

Curtis also used advertising to promote his magazine and build its circulation. When *Ladies' Home Journal* closed in 2014, it was not for lack of circulation—it still had more than 3 million subscribers—but the fact that advertisers had lost interest in the magazine's somewhat older readership.

©iStockphoto.com/CurvaBezier

Although the radio industry flirted with revenue options such as taxes and profits from selling radios, it soon became clear that the only way to make enough money to pay for top-notch entertainers and make a profit was to sell advertising. William Paley founded the CBS radio network after he saw how successful radio advertising was for his family's cigar company (see Chapter 7). Paley understood that good programming could attract a large audience that advertisers would want to reach. Sponsors frequently bought not just advertising time, but the entire program. This gave rise to shows such as the *Maxwell House Coffee Time*, the *Lucky Strike Dance Orchestra*, and the *General Motors Family Party*.

There was never any debate about whether television would be driven by advertising. Television grew quickly in the 1950s, and advertisers recognized its potential as a powerful tool for reaching all Americans. By 1960, 90 percent of all homes had television sets.[15] As with the rest of the media, television's "product" is the audience watching its programs. Thus, the primary purpose of the Super Bowl, from television's point of view, is not to choose a professional football champion but rather to deliver 45 percent of the American audience to advertisers for one evening each year. Robert Niles, a network marketing executive, echoed Cyrus Curtis's promise to deliver an audience to American manufacturers almost a century earlier when Niles stated, "We're in the business of selling audiences to advertisers. [The sponsors] come to us asking for women 18 to 49 and adults 25 to 54 and we try to deliver."[16]

Consumer Advertising.

Local advertising attempts to induce people to go to a local store or business to buy a product or service, whether it be a new Toyota truck, a gallon of milk, or a travel agent's services. These ads announce the product or service and its price and tell consumers where they can buy it. The local ad is also looking for immediate, direct action. Thus, a **direct action message** is designed to get consumers to purchase a product or engage in a behavior. For example: "Hurry down, these prices won't last, buy today!"

National advertising is designed to build demand for a nationally available product or service, but it does not send consumers out to a particular store to buy a can of Pepsi, a movie video, or a bag of cat food. National advertising assumes that the consumer knows where to buy the product or service or can be told in a local ad where and how to do so. The national advertiser is also more patient and can wait for consumers to take action. Thus, an **indirect action message** is designed to build the image of and demand for a product. Perhaps a consumer won't buy a new washing machine this week, but he will eventually, and that's when he should buy a Maytag.

Advocacy Advertising.

Advocacy ads are intended to promote a particular point of view rather than a product. In 1993, for example, the state of California ran a $28 million antismoking campaign financed through a cigarette tax. U.S. unions and businesses have fought foreign competition with advocacy ads. Companies express their concerns directly to the public through advocacy ads, bypassing traditional news channels. Such advertising has a long history in the United States, dating back to 1908, when AT&T ran a campaign arguing that it was natural that the phone company should be a monopoly.

Public Service Advertising.

Some of the most iconic advertising in the United States comes not from

---

local advertising: Advertising designed to get people to patronize local stores, businesses, or service providers.

direct action message: An advertising message designed to get consumers to go to a particular place to do something specific, such as purchasing a product, obtaining a service, or engaging in a behavior.

national advertising: Advertising designed to build demand for a nationally available product or service and that is not directing the consumer to local retail or service outlets.

indirect action message: An advertising message designed to build the image of and demand for a product, without specifically urging that a particular action be taken at a particular time and place.

advocacy ads: Advertising designed to promote a particular point of view rather than a product or service. Can be sponsored by a government, corporation, trade association, or nonprofit organization.

Video 11.2: See a collection of national ads.

Video 11.3: View examples of the classic ads.

WHY?
SMOKEY
remember–
only you can PREVENT FOREST FIRES!

AP Photo/USDA

Smokey Bear has been getting the word out about fire safety for more than sixty-five years. This poster dates from the 1960s. One change is that he is now working to prevent "wildfires" instead of "forest fires."

business, but from long series of **public service ads** created by the Advertising Council. The Ad Council got its start as the War Advertising Council back in 1942 with such memorable messages as the Rosie the Riveter "We Can Do It" campaign, which was designed to promote women working in factories producing goods for the war effort. The best-known creation of the Ad Council is likely Smokey Bear, who has stayed on message for more than sixty-five years, telling members of the public that only they can prevent forest fires. He is the second-most-recognized image in the United States, falling just behind Santa Claus. What is more, generations of children have taken great joy in delivering his basic message of fire prevention to their parents and other adults. Other prominent Ad Council campaigns include the 1971 "Crying Indian" antipollution campaign, support for the United Negro College Fund, and McGruff the Crime Dog taking "a bite out of crime."[17]

The editorial and opinion pages of the prestigious national newspapers are popular spots for placing advocacy ads. This is partly due to the credibility associated with appearing on those pages and partly because it's a good place to reach the target audience of influential decision makers. These ads might, for example, support or oppose a piece of legislation. Sometimes the target of an advocacy ad in the *Washington Post* might be senators or representatives who are being reminded of the support they have received in the past from a given company or industry.[18]

Trade Advertising. **Business-to-business (trade) ads** promote products directly to other businesses rather than to the consumer market. Business-to-business advertising is a critical part of the advertising industry. Consider the fact that General Electric earns 80 percent of its revenue from nonconsumer business.[19] Business customers can be reached through trade magazines, such as *Electronic Engineering Times*; business-oriented cable news channels, such as CNBC; or local weekly business newspapers.

The Advertising Business

Advertising is a multifaceted business that involves four major groups. First, there's the *client*, the person or company that has a product or an idea to promote. Then there's the *advertising agency or department* that researches the market, creates the advertising, and places it in the media. Next, there's the *medium*, be it television, the Internet, a newspaper, a magazine, or some other medium, that carries the advertisement. Finally, there's the *audience*, the people who see or hear the advertisement, whom the client hopes to influence.[20]

For a product to be successful in the marketplace, all four of these groups must work together successfully. There must be a good product backed by advertisements that have a strong sales message delivered through well-chosen media to an appropriate audience. If any part of this process is flawed or seriously miscalculated, the product is likely to fail.

The Client

The first component of advertising is the client, the company with something to sell. The client may want to increase awareness of a new product, encourage people to use an existing product more often, build a positive image of a product, convince users of competitors' products to

public service ads: Advertising designed to promote the messages of nonprofit institutions and government agencies. The messages are typically produced and run without charge by advertising professionals and the media. Many of these ads are produced by the Ad Council.

business-to-business (trade) ads: Advertising that promotes products and services directly to other businesses rather than to the general consumer market.

switch brands, promote a benefit of a product, or demonstrate some new use for a product. The 3M Company increased sales of its Scotch brand cellophane tape by suggesting other uses for the product beyond repairing torn paper. Arm & Hammer baking soda's original purpose was to make cakes rise, but the company also increased sales by promoting the product as a cleaner and deodorizer. One of Arm & Hammer's best ads tells consumers to buy a box of baking soda and pour it down the drain to clean and deodorize the sink. In essence, the company was suggesting that people buy its product to throw it away! Arm & Hammer's research showed that people used baking soda to freshen laundry and to brush their teeth, so the company introduced detergent and toothpaste enhanced with baking soda.[21] Begun in 1993 on behalf of the California Milk Processor Board, the "Got Milk?" advertising campaign succeeded at boosting milk sales and has become one of America's longest-running and most celebrated ad series. The "Got Milk" ads ran both in California and nationally until 2014, when the national milk promotion board decided to focus on milk's protein content in its advertising. But the campaign does still live on in California more than twenty years after it started.[22]

For details on America's top advertisers, take a look at Table 11.1.

For a product to be successful, it needs more than a good advertising campaign. It also needs to be a good product at the right price and has to be available for consumers to buy. When Sony launched its PlayStation 2 video game system, it did relatively little initial advertising and held off releasing popular games because it couldn't manufacture enough of the consoles to satisfy public demand. Customers were ready and willing to buy, but the product simply was not available.[23] Once there was a sufficient quantity of the product, Sony started advertising.

SECRET 4 No amount of advertising can save a product that the public just doesn't want to buy, as Coca-Cola discovered when it launched New Coke in 1985. Coca-Cola spent $4 million on research that seemed to indicate that consumers would like the new formula better than the original recipe. But consumers reacted to the change with anger and frustration, and Coca-Cola eventually had to bring back the old drink under the name Coca-Cola Classic.[24] The research may have shown what people liked best in blind taste tests, but it didn't take into account how people felt about the product, what meaning they assigned to it, and the fond memories they associated with it.[25] What the research missed was "the abiding emotional attachment" Coke drinkers had for the product in its familiar form. One Coke executive told *Advertising Age* magazine, "We obviously tried to do psychological research, but it wasn't adequate."[26]

Casual-wear retailer Gap experienced a similar reaction in 2010 when it rolled out a new logo to replace its two-decades-old iconic blue square with white capital letters without testing it with customers first. The response on the Internet was instant and negative. In a matter of days, Gap management brought back the old logo and issued a statement that said, "O.K. We've heard loud and clear that you don't like the new logo." A second statement, this one from company president Marka Hansen, went on to say, "We've learned a lot in this process. And we are clear that we did not go about this in the right way. We recognize that we missed the opportunity to engage with the online community."[27] (This is also an example of Secret Four—Nothing's new: Everything that happened in the past will happen again.)

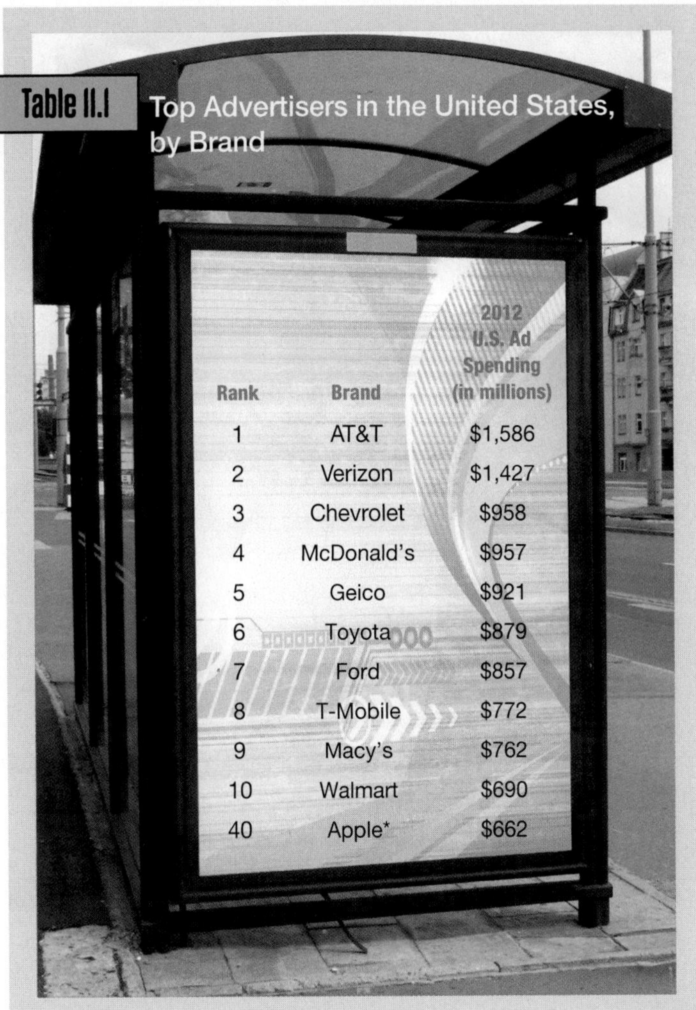

Table 11.1 Top Advertisers in the United States, by Brand

Rank	Brand	2012 U.S. Ad Spending (in millions)
1	AT&T	$1,586
2	Verizon	$1,427
3	Chevrolet	$958
4	McDonald's	$957
5	Geico	$921
6	Toyota	$879
7	Ford	$857
8	T-Mobile	$772
9	Macy's	$762
10	Walmart	$690
40	Apple*	$662

*For comparison, Apple is the world's highest-valued corporation. It is ranked number twelve in terms of advertising spending.

Source: Data from the *Advertising Age Top 200 Megabrands.* Reprinted with permission from *Advertising Age/American Demographics.* Copyright, Crain Communications Inc., 2014.

The Agency

The advertising profession originated in the 1840s when agents started selling ad space to clients in the new

Web 11.4: Find out more about how milk is being promoted.

got milk?
HOUSE OF DERÉON
Home bodies.
Growing up I always wanted to be just like my mom. So I drank milk. Some studies suggest that women who drink enough milk tend to weigh less and have less body fat than those who don't. So drink 24 ounces of lowfat or fat free milk every 24 hours as part of your healthy diet and see for yourself. Who says father knows best?
24/24 milk your diet. Lose weight!

AP Photo/Milk Processors of America

Singer Beyoncé has been featured in the long-running "Got Milk?" campaign aimed at promoting the consumption of a wide range of milk and dairy products.

advertising-supported newspapers. At first, the advertising agents worked directly for the newspapers, but before long, they became more like brokers dealing in advertising space for multiple publications. George Rowell, the leading advertising agent of the 1860s and 1870s, was the first agent to buy large amounts of newspaper advertising space wholesale and sell it to his customers as they needed it. Rowell was also the first to publish a directory of newspaper circulation numbers, thus providing clients with an independent source of this vital information. Before Rowell's innovation, newspapers could, and did, lie about the size of their circulation.

The early agents earned a 15 percent commission on the space they sold for the newspapers. This is why advertising agencies were traditionally paid by commission on the media space and time they sold; initially, that was all they were selling.[28]

Before long, advertising agents moved beyond just selling space in the media. Their clients wanted help developing the ads for the space they were purchasing. In 1868, twenty-one-year-old Francis W. Ayer opened N. W. Ayer and Son (giving his father a 50 percent share in the company and the lead name), one of the first agencies to write copy, put together the artwork for an ad, and plan campaigns. The agency recognized that providing the associated services that would make advertising easier for clients would help the agency sell more space for the media.

Gradually, ad agencies came to represent their clients rather than the media in which they sold advertising space. This shift resulted from the **open contract**, which enabled the agency to provide advertising space in any publication (and eventually on broadcast outlets as well) rather than only a few. The agent was now handling the advertising services for the client, not selling space for the media.[29]

In the 1920s and 1930s, advertisers increasingly recognized that there were different market segments and that ads should be tailored to those segments. Agencies also realized that they needed to use a different mix of media for each of their target audiences. Eventually, they began offering clients three major services: research, creative activity, and media planning.

Research and Planning. Agencies typically use research throughout the entire advertising campaign. The initial research activity is aimed at identifying the characteristics of the target audience and what those people are looking for in a product. Ads are then tested to see how well members of the target audience respond to them. After the campaign, the agency will evaluate its success. How many people remembered seeing the ad? How many people clipped the coupon or called the phone number? How much did sales go up or down?

The process starts with objectives. What does the client want to accomplish with the ads? These objectives could be increasing sales, increasing awareness, or getting people to clip a coupon or make a phone call. The agency may also study characteristics of the product's target audience, a process that is discussed later in the chapter.

Finally, the agency may test the ads itself, either as a pretest before the ads are run or as a recall test after the campaign. One problem advertising researchers face is that the people they want to reach may be unwilling to participate in the research. And the people who are willing to participate may be trying to give the agency the answers they are looking for. Although advertising research continues to be a powerful tool for reducing uncertainty, it is still a difficult process at best.[30]

Creative Activity. There is more to marketing a product than advertising, but advertising is the most visible aspect of marketing, and it has to provide what legendary advertising executive David Ogilvy called **the big idea**—an advertising concept that will grab people's attention, make them take notice, make them remember, and—most important—make them take action. Leo Burnett, founder of one of the nation's biggest agencies, agrees with Ogilvy:

---

open contract: An arrangement that allows advertising agencies to sell space in any publication (and eventually on broadcast outlets as well) rather than just a limited few.

the big idea: The goal of every advertising campaign—an advertising concept that will grab people's attention and make them take notice, remember, and take action.

The word "idea" is loosely used in our business to cover anything from a headline to a TV technique. [But] I feel that a real idea has a power of its own and a life of its own. It goes beyond ads and campaigns. Properly employed, it is often the secret of capturing the imagination of great masses of people and winning "the battle for the uncommitted mind," which is what our business really is about.[31]

AP Photo/Keith Srakocic

Young adult clothing manufacturer and marketer American Apparel has long used provocative and controversial ads to promote their clothes.

In advertising, a tension often exists between creativity and salesmanship. An ad may do a great job of grabbing people's attention and generating talk, but if the ad doesn't have a solid sales message, consumers will not remember the product or give serious thought to buying it. There have been a number of ads that have done a great job of grabbing the public's attention. But have they done a good job of promoting the product? Have they built the value of the brand?

Consider Anheuser-Busch back in 2009. Its brand Bud Light (the most popular beer in the United States) was launching its Bud Light Lime beer in cans. (Previously it had only been available in bottles.) Anheuser-Busch promoted the launch with an online ad that had people talking about "getting it in the can"—as in a suburban housewife confessing, "I never thought I'd enjoy getting it in the can as much as I do." The crude sex joke attracted a lot of talk and attention from the advertising press. But it's not clear what the message did to promote the brand or increase sales.[32]

American Apparel has long been known for producing explicit ads for its line of young adult clothing that have featured nudity and provocative poses. One recent campaign promoted its knitwear, bodysuits, and stockings with poses that made women appear "vulnerable and overtly sexual," according to Britain's Advertising Standards Authority. American Apparel executives defended their ads, saying they had tried to create "authentic, honest and memorable images relevant to their customer base."[33] There can be no question that American Apparel has been successful with its shock-style ads. The problem comes in figuring out what the company can do next to grab attention.

Irish brewer Guinness, on the other hand, has been successful in grabbing attention, generating talk, and building its brand image with an ad that features a group of men playing wheelchair basketball in a gym. As the ad comes to an end, all but one of the men stand up and then join their one wheelchair-bound friend in a bar for a round of Guinness. The ad has all the standard elements of a beer ad—guys playing sports and then going out to drink beer together afterward. But it adds the unexpected twist that gives it a huge dose of heart.[34]

Adman Hank Seiden puts it this way: "All good advertising consists of both idea and execution. All bad advertising consists of just execution."[35]

Ogilvy believed that all advertising should be created to sell a product or promote a message. It does not exist to be innovative, exciting, creative, or entertaining. Good ads may be all of those things, but the central principle is that they must achieve the client's goals:

> A good advertisement is one which sells the product *without drawing attention to itself.* It should rivet the reader's attention on the product. Instead of saying, "What a clever advertisement," the reader says, "I never knew *that* before. I must try this product."[36]

For products that are similar, the **brand image** attached to them is often critical. This image gives a brand and the

brand image: The image attached to a brand and the associated product that gives the product a personality or identity that makes it stand out from similar products and stick in the mind of the consumer.

Video 11.4: See the ads from American Apparel, Bud Light, and Guinness.

Video 11.5: Find out more about advertising legend David Ogilvy.

associated product a personality or identity and helps it stand out from the pack. Ogilvy once headed a campaign to give Hathaway shirts a personality when the company's competitor, Arrow, was spending almost a hundred times more on advertising than Hathaway, a smaller company, could. Ogilvy's solution was to buy a black eye patch in a drugstore for $1.50. A model wearing the eye patch was shown conducting an orchestra, driving a tractor, and sailing a boat. This simple bit of brand identity boosted Hathaway out of 116 years of obscurity and turned it into a leading brand.

Ogilvy argues that at the heart of all advertising is an appeal based on facts that are of interest to consumers. As he wrote in the early 1960s, "The consumer isn't a moron. . . . You insult her intelligence if you assume that a mere slogan and a few vapid adjectives will persuade her to buy anything. She wants all the information you can give her."[37]

For print ads, the most important element is the headline, because five times as many people read the headline as read the rest of the copy. This means that 80 percent of the ad's effectiveness comes from the headline. The headline must tell readers whom the ad is for, what the product is, what the product does for the consumer, and why he or she should buy it. That's a lot of responsibility for eight to fifteen words. Ogilvy says that the most powerful headline words are *free* and *new*. Other words favored by Ogilvy are

> how to, suddenly, now, announcing, introducing, it's here, just arrived, important development, improvement, amazing, sensational, remarkable, revolutionary, startling, miracle, magic, offer, quick, easy, wanted, challenge, advice to, the truth about, compare, bargain, hurry, *[and]* last chance.[38]

Although these phrases are overused, they do work. Look at what Ogilvy considered to be the greatest headline he ever wrote: "At Sixty Miles an Hour the Loudest Noise in the New Rolls-Royce Comes from the Electric Clock." It uses the word *new*, it contains a fact that also sells a benefit, and it is true.

Media Planning.

Media planning involves figuring out which media to use, buying the media at the best rates, and then evaluating how effective the purchase was. It is the least glamorous part of the advertising business, but it is central to a successful campaign. No matter how brilliant the idea or how beautiful the execution, if the ad doesn't reach the target audience, it can't accomplish anything. Typically, advertisers try to pick a mix of media that will deliver the highest percentage of the target audience at the lowest cost per thousand views, or **CPM**. (M is the Roman numeral for 1,000.) Selecting the right media involves identifying the audience for the ad and knowing which media they use.[39]

Web 11.5: Find out more about these advertising agencies.

Agency Size and Income.

Advertising agencies have grown immensely since their modest start selling newspaper advertising space. According to *Advertising Age*'s 2014 advertising agency report, the 900-plus agencies studied had their income grow in 2013 by 3.7 percent from the previous year to reach a total of $39.1 billion. (That figure included advertising, media, digital marketing services, health care communication, and public relations.) Work for digital media now dominates the business, accounting for 35.3 percent of all advertising agency revenue in 2013.[40] Keep in mind that this is just the portion of the income that goes to the agency. This figure doesn't include the amount that goes to pay the media for advertising time and space. According to *Advertising Age*'s 2014 annual report, advertisers in 2014 were on track to spend $167.3 billion on advertising in the United States using media for which the size of the audience is measured. (This does not include, for example, direct-mail advertising.) Of that, television accounted for the largest share with 38.3 percent, followed by online with 24.6 percent, newspapers with 12.1 percent, radio with 10 percent, magazines with 9.8 percent, and outdoor and cinema with 5.2 percent. Overall, advertising spending among the hundred top national advertisers increased by 2.8 percent in 2012 for a total of $104.5 billion, a number still below that of the 2009 recession.[41]

Several major trends have emerged in the agency business since the 1980s. One trend is toward the purchase of independent agencies and small groups of agencies by larger holding companies. The biggest of these are WPP, Omnicom Group, Publicis Groupe, and Interpublic Group of Companies.[42] A second trend is a shift toward greater specialization of agency functions. One agency may do research and creative work, whereas another agency (known as a media buyer) develops the media plan and buys the time and space. Because of this specialization, agencies are moving from the commission structure to charging fees for their services. After all, if an agency is just doing creative work, it can't charge a commission on media space that it isn't buying.[43]

The Media

The third group in the advertising business is made up of the media that carry advertisements. These include newspapers, magazines, radio, television, outdoor sites such as billboards and metro buses, and digital. The two media that do not receive large amounts of advertising revenue are movies and books, although movies are increasingly using paid product placements and theaters run advertisements before showing movies. Books initially did not carry ads because advertising was not common when books were first published. In the nineteenth century,

media planning: The process central to a successful ad campaign of figuring out which media to use, buying the media at the best rates, and then evaluating how effective the purchase was.

CPM: Cost per thousand exposures to the target audience—a figure used in media planning evaluation.

when advertising became popular, there were other, cheaper media in which to advertise. Postal regulations also pose a barrier to advertising in books: Materials containing advertising can't be shipped using the post office's inexpensive book rate. But advertising scholar James Twitchell suggests that as delivery options expand through companies such as FedEx and UPS, advertising in books may become commonplace, especially in expensive academic books.[44] This textbook doesn't yet contain advertisements in its pages, but you probably found a few advertising pieces for credit cards or magazine subscriptions in the bag the bookstore clerk gave you. In Table 11.2, you can see the relative importance of different media to the top hundred leading national advertisers in the United States.

PSL Images/Alamy

Digital billboards with changing messages, such as these in New York City's Times Square, have revitalized the outdoor advertising business.

Newspapers. Newspapers were the original advertising medium, but they have been suffering major declines in advertising revenue. Between 1999 and 2011, ad revenue declined by more than 50 percent, with classified advertising falling off by 75 percent. Some of this was due to the recent recession, but advertising analyst Ken Doctor says that much of it is coming from newspapers failing to make the digital transformation: "Despite uneven digital ad results reported by newspaper and magazine companies, it's not that the money isn't there—they just haven't transitioned their businesses enough to compete for it."[45] According to the Newspaper Association of America, newspaper print advertising fell 8.6 percent from 2012 to 2013, but newspaper digital advertising increased by 1.5 percent.[46]

Nevertheless, newspapers remain an advertising medium, carrying a majority of local advertising and a significant amount of national advertising. They allow advertisers to present detailed information (such as grocery prices) that would be confusing on radio or television, and they give audience members plenty of time to interpret the information. Newspaper ads make it easy to include coupons, Web addresses, and 800 numbers that readers can clip and save. They also allow advertisers to target not only specific cities, but also specific areas of the city (this is known as **zoned coverage**). Cities typically have only one or two newspapers, so advertisers can cover the entire market with a single purchase. Finally, newspapers allow advertisers to buy space at the last minute.[47]

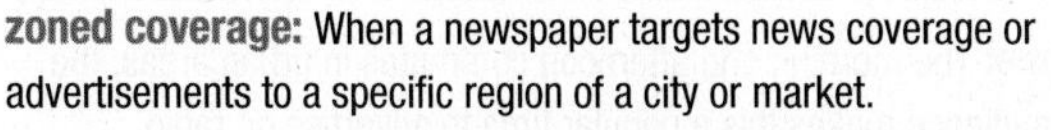

zoned coverage: When a newspaper targets news coverage or advertisements to a specific region of a city or market.

Magazines. Magazines are an excellent medium for reaching a specific niche audience. Before the 1950s, general-interest magazines were the best way to reach a mass, national audience. Since the 1960s, however, that role has fallen to television. The response of magazines has been to seek ever narrower audiences—there are magazines for motorcyclists, computer users, young women, retired people, knitters, and video game players. Whatever audience an advertiser wants to reach, it is likely to find a magazine to help it do so. For business advertisers, magazines may be the only alternative to direct mail for reaching their target audiences. Magazines offer higher print quality than newspapers do but have a much longer lead time, so magazine advertising requires careful planning. The advertising market for magazines has been changing over the last decade. While the number of ad pages sold has been falling, the revenue from digital sources, such as Web sites and mobile apps, has been growing.[48] Go back to the chapter on magazines (Chapter 5) and reread the section about the *Atlantic* and its "digital-first" strategy as a reminder.

Outdoor Advertising. Outdoor ads (also known as "out of home advertising") catch people in a captive environment—such as in a car surrounded by slow-moving traffic on the way to work—but they are limited to short, simple messages. The biggest change to have happened to outdoor advertising is the advent of the digital billboard. Essentially giant video screens, digital billboards display a static image that stays up for six to eight seconds before shifting to a new image. Digital billboards can include changing information, such as time or temperature, or even the day's television schedule for a local station.[49] In major cities, there are transit

Table 11.2 U.S. Ad Spending Totals by 100 Leading National Advertisers in Measured Media[50]

Medium	2012 spending Medium (in millions)
Network TV	$27,434
Cable TV network	$24,373
Magazines (consumer, Sunday, B-to-B, local)	$23,825
Newspapers (national to local, inserts)	$18,878
Spot TV	$17,091
Internet display	$10,279
Radio (network, national spot, local)	$8,361
National syndicated TV	$5,133
Outdoor	$4,221

signs—posters on bus-stop shelters, on subway platforms, and on the buses and in the subway cars themselves. Ads have also been placed in the bottom of golf holes so that you see them when you pick up your ball. Overall, $6.38 billion was spent on outdoor advertising in 2011, with billboards accounting for 65 percent of the spending, transit signs making up 17 percent, street furniture 6 percent, and alternative outdoor advertising 12 percent.[51] New York City's Times Square is one of the most valuable places in the United States for outdoor advertisements because of the large number of people who pass through it each day, its frequent coverage on television, and the nearly constant presence of tourists who are photographing the area.[52]

Radio. Radio enables advertisers to broadcast their message repeatedly and to target a narrow audience. Advertisers can choose stations with programming aimed at teens, women ages twenty-five to fifty-four, young adult males, Spanish speakers, or almost any other demographic group. Like outdoor advertising, radio ads can be very effective in big cities where advertisers can reach a captive audience in their cars during the morning and afternoon commutes, which are known as **drive time**. Radio also offers a short lead time and relatively low costs.

Television. Although the most popular television shows remain an appealing place to advertise to a general, national audience, the remote control, the mute button, and the proliferation of cable channels have made it difficult to get viewers to pay attention to commercials. The audience for broadcast television has been declining, but the Big Four networks (see Chapter 9) can still reach a mass audience quickly and effectively. Television offers sound, motion, and visuals. A drawback, however, is that many of the best advertising time slots on the networks, such as those during the Super Bowl, are sold nearly a year in advance. There is also the problem of viewers channel surfing during commercial breaks or skipping commercials using the fast-forward button on their digital video recorders (DVRs).

The new television environment allows targeted advertising, such as ads aimed at the youth market on MTV or CW, the Hispanic market on Univision, or the African American market on BET. For local television advertising, there are independent stations along with the network affiliates. In many communities, local advertisers can buy time on a range of cable stations with local commercial breaks as well. The biggest problem facing television advertisers is that of clutter, which is discussed later in this chapter.

Digital. Digital advertising has been the fastest-growing segment of the advertising market, increasing by double-digit percentages for several years. During the recession in 2009, online advertising saw its first decline since the dot-com bubble burst in 2002 and sent numerous Web properties into bankruptcy.[53] But since then, online advertising has resumed its rapid growth. A study by eMarketer found that in 2013 American consumers spent more time with digital media than with television for the first time. The study estimated that they would spend an average of four hours and twenty-eight minutes a day with television, but that they spent five hours and forty-six minutes with all digital media combined. eMarketer defines digital media as all online, mobile, and streaming services. The growth of use of digital media comes almost exclusively from the growth of mobile devices, with their daily amount of use growing by 23 percent between 2013 and 2014.[54] eMarketer is reporting that mobile advertising spending is growing between 50 and 100 percent per year while desktop ad spending is growing by just single digits.[55]

Digital advertising has the advantage of being able to closely target consumers. As an example, when your author visits Web sites that contain advertising, ads for

Web 11.6: Check out the selection of outdoor ads.

drive time: The morning and afternoon commutes in urban areas; the captive audience makes this a popular time to advertise on radio.

motorcycle accessories often appear because the cookies in his browser history tell the ad server that he's interested in motorcycles. And we all expect that kind of behavior with online ads. But sometimes, as marketing professional David Berkowitz points out, that level of knowledge about us seems a little creepy. Berkowitz asks you to suppose you are searching for a camera using the Web browser on your smartphone. You bring up an ad from Target for a camera you're interested in. The ad can tell that you already have the Target shopping app on your phone, so it automatically sends you the appropriate page on the app to view the camera you are searching for. The question then becomes: Are you creeped out by the fact that an ad on a Web page knows what apps you have installed on your phone? Or do you like the fact that the ad is smart enough to redirect you to an app you already have on your phone?[56] (For more on digital advertising, look ahead to the section of the chapter on long-tail advertising.)

https://twitter.com/Oreo/status/298246571718483968

When the lights went out on the New Orleans Super Bowl in 2013, the big television advertisers like Coke and Pepsi didn't like having their carefully planned series of ads disrupted. On the other hand, Oreo's agency quickly put together a social media ad that they delivered almost immediately. Oreo's spur of the moment social media ad got the company more attention than they could have gotten out of elaborate computer preparations. (The ad quickly picked up more than 15,000 retweets and 5,400 favorites.)

The Audience

As we talked about in the opening vignette of this chapter, the audience is made up of the people advertisers want to reach with their messages. The audience is also the central "product" that media sell to advertisers. In yet another example of **targeting**, advertisers try to make a particular product appeal to a narrowly defined group. Ads for Starburst candies, for example, target the teen and preteen audiences, whereas ads for Godiva chocolates target upscale adult women. The people appearing in an ad are chosen carefully to make members of the target audience say, "This is a product made for someone like me." Advertising executive Robert Meury notes that his agency carefully selects the celebrities who appear in Miller Lite ads: "We make sure our stars are guys you'd enjoy having a beer with. And the locations we film in are always real bars."[57]

As with other types of media, such as radio and television, audience members for advertising are often defined by the "graphics": demographics, geographics, and psychographics. As you may recall from Chapter 2, demographics are the measurable characteristics of the audience, such as age, income, sex, and marital status, whereas geographics involve measurements of where people live. Psychographics combine demographics with measurements of psychological characteristics, such as attitudes, opinions, and interests.

Psychographics and VALS®. In advertising, it's not enough to know the demographics of the client's target audience (age, income, sex, etc.). Advertisers also want to know what the target audience dreams about, aspires to, and feels. These are the topics covered by psychographic research.

The term *psychographics* was first used in the 1960s to refer to a measure of consumer psychology. Depending on the project, researchers may look at a person's lifestyle, relationship to the product, and personality traits.[58]

Questioning the Media

Can you name several advertisers who are targeting people like you? Who are they? How can you tell they are targeting you? How do you feel about this?

Emanuel Demby, one of the first users of the term, defines *psychographics* as the use of psychological, sociological, and anthropological data to segment a market into relevant groupings. The way the income variable is conceived is more sophisticated than just grouping markets by income levels. Demby argues that it is just as important to know whether someone's income is increasing, decreasing, or remaining stable as it is to know the person's actual income. Why? Because how things are going in people's lives will say something about how they see

targeting: The process of trying to make a particular product or service appeal to a narrowly defined group. Groups are often targeted using demographics, geographics, and psychographics.

Figure 11.1 The VALS Types

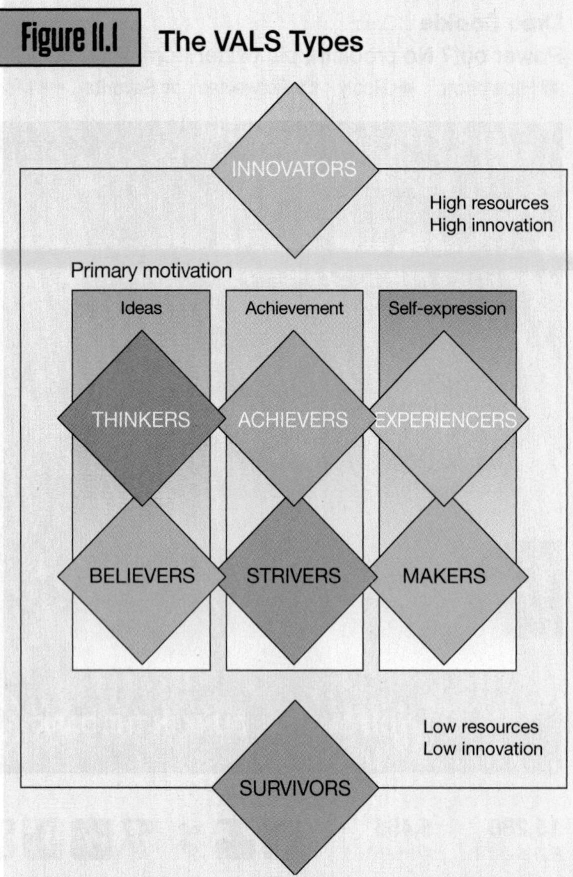

To Receive an Accurate VALS Type:
By design, the questions are for use by people whose first language is American English. If you are not a citizen of the United States or Canada, residency should be for enough time to know the culture and its idioms. **If you do not meet these conditions, your VALS type will not be valid.**

Source: Strategic Business Insights (SBI), www.strategicbusinessinsights.com/vals. Reprinted by permission.

themselves. If advertisers understand how members of the target audience see themselves, they can craft ads that will more readily appeal to the target.[59]

The best-known psychographic system, VALS™, was developed by SRI International and is currently owned and operated by Strategic Business Insights. VALS places people in one of eight consumer groups according to their primary motivation and level of resources (see Figure 11.1). Resources are the tangible and intangible things that people have to draw on as they seek success: their education, income, health, and self-confidence, among other factors. Primary motivation is the person's approach to life. Ideals-motivated consumers ("Thinkers" and "Believers") are guided by knowledge and principles; achievement-motivated consumers ("Achievers" and "Strivers") look for products that will demonstrate their status and success to others; and Self-Expression-motivated consumers ("Experiencers" and "Makers") seek action, variety, and risk.

Web 11.7: Want to know your own VALS category? Take the survey!

Web 11.8: Here are several ads from mainstream companies supporting gay marriage.

At the top of the VALS framework are the innovators, described as being "successful, sophisticated, take-charge people with high self-esteem." These are people who have established careers and value the image of a product as "an expression of their taste, independence, and personality." At the bottom of the VALS framework are the survivors, who have few resources and believe "the world is changing too quickly." VALS describes them as cautious consumers with little to spend but with high brand loyalty.[60]

How might a company use psychographics and these personality types to target its advertising? As an example, a Minnesota medical center used VALS to identify and understand consumers who were interested in and able to afford cosmetic surgery. The resulting ad campaign targeted to these individuals was purportedly so successful that the clinic was fully booked.[61]

To see targeting in action, we can look at some real-world examples. The first example discusses the targeting of a product (Mountain Dew); the second, a particular audience (gays and lesbians); and the third, some instances of targeting failures.

Targeting a Product: Mountain Dew. Advertising soft drinks can be a particular challenge because all the drinks are basically the same thing—sweetened carbonated water and a small amount of flavoring—with just a few variations, such as regular or diet, caffeinated or caffeine free. Since the products are so similar, the key to promoting the brand is selling not just a drink but an entire attitude and approach to life, thus making the product appeal to a particular audience. Television scholar Joshua Meyrowitz describes the basic message of a diet soda commercial as "Drink this and you'll be beautiful and have beautiful friends to play volleyball with on the beach."[62]

Mountain Dew has existed as a product since the 1940s and has always projected a rebellious and irreverent image, according to Scott Moffitt, who was director of marketing:

> We have a great unity of message and purpose that has been consistent over time about what we are and what we aren't. The brand is all about exhilaration and energy, and you see that in all that we do, from advertising and community to grassroots programs and our sports-minded focus. We have a very crystal clear, vivid positioning.[63]

In keeping with its young, energetic image, Mountain Dew sponsors events such as ESPN's X Games because they project the same image the soft drink does. It also goes after heavy consumers who drink three or more cans of Mountain Dew a day.

Mountain Dew now holds a coveted spot among the top four or five soft drinks, behind Coke, Pepsi, and Diet Coke, but it started out as a bar mix consisting of lemon-lime juice, orange juice, low carbonation, and caffeine. It cultivated a hillbilly image and logo and was billed as "zero-proof hillbilly moonshine." In the 1960s, Pepsi bought the brand and started giving it more of a hip image. Following a period of confused advertising images in the 1980s, Mountain Dew came into its own in 1992. Bill Bruce, who was the creative director on the Mountain Dew account, describes Mountain Dew's coming-of-age process:

> Seattle grunge music was happening at the time. Extreme sports were happening. So there was this subculture that we wanted to tap into. The idea was to show the most extreme things. We created these four characters, the Dew Dudes, who represented what was happening at the time musically and culturally.[64]

This approach was first used with Diet Mountain Dew, but given its success, it eventually became the central theme of the entire campaign.

The ongoing challenge to Mountain Dew as it grows in popularity is to maintain its edginess and youth appeal so that it can maintain both its sales and its image. Most recently, Mountain Dew has been trying to engage young urban consumers. (In marketing speak, urban marketing means reaching out to African American and Latino consumers. We'll talk more about that in a bit.) The company's goal is to go beyond the rural markets where Mountain Dew has been enormously successful into the cities where it has traditionally sold less well. Mountain Dew is doing this by featuring hip-hop performers Lil Wayne; Tyler, The Creator; and Rick Ross. (It should be noted that some of the ads to come out of this campaign have backfired for the soft drink maker by offending virtually everyone with racist and misogynistic storylines.[65])

Photo by Casey Rodgers/Invision for Mountain Dew/AP Photo

Mountain Dew has reached out to young, active people by using spokesmen such as professional snowboarder Danny Davis.

Targeting an Audience: Advertising to the Gay Market. One audience that advertisers are increasingly targeting is the gay and lesbian market. Gays are desirable as a market to advertisers because they are perceived to be relatively upscale and highly educated.[66] "Because they primarily don't have children and there is one income for each person in the household, you are talking about a population with large sums of disposable income that non-gay families with children wouldn't have," says Rick Dean of the research firm Overlooked Opinions.[67] Media company Rivendell Media estimates that the gay and lesbian market has an annual buying power of $641 billion.[68]

As early as 1994, vodka producer Absolut was among the first major companies to place ads in gay publications, including *Out* and the *Advocate*.[69] In addition to advertising in gay publications, companies are using gay couples in ads. Some advertisers have gone further, experimenting with gay-specific ads. Hyatt Hotels and Resorts has targeted the gay and lesbian market since the late 1990s and has depicted same-sex couples in its messages.[70] Advertising to the gay community carries the risk of antigay groups organizing boycotts of companies that do so, but the effectiveness of such boycotts has been limited.[71]

SECRET 3 The gay advertising market has grown considerably in the twenty-first century, due in part to the launch of at least three gay-themed cable television channels, including Viacom's Logo TV. These join 145 separate gay and lesbian publications, including both newspapers and magazines.[72] Advertising targeted at gay audiences is also showing up increasingly outside of gay media. Bud Light, the most popular beer in the United States, re-created the red equal sign (signifying support for same-sex marriage equality) using a red background and two cans for Bud Light) as a social media avatar. And travel site Expedia has a three-minute online ad that tells the story of a father overcoming his attitudes and traveling to his daughter's same-sex wedding. The ad is unique in being told completely from the questioning father's point of view.[73] This continued growth of advertising in gay publications and of gay-themed ads is another example of Secret Three—Everything from the margin moves to the center.

Web 11.9: See how Mountain Dew's add featuring Felicia the Goat went terribly wrong.

TEST YOUR MEDIA LITERACY

Advertising to Targeted Markets

It's pretty obvious, given demographic trends, that major corporations are going to need to target racial and ethnic communities if they want to stay relevant in today's market. The census estimates that approximately 65 percent of Americans identify themselves as "white only." The exact figures get a bit confusing, given that Hispanic is an ethnic category, not a racial category. But that means if companies make their advertising primarily relevant to white people, they're leaving 35 percent of the market out there on the table.

As companies try to market to Hispanic, African American, and Asian American audiences, they need to appeal to their target and avoid offensive and dated stereotypes. McDonald's, for example, has targeted the African American market though efforts often called "urban marketing." One ad that has attracted both positive and negative attention for the fast-food chain is an ad called "McNuggets Love," which features an R&B singer crooning about his lady sneaking out at night to meet with her true love—a ten-piece box of Chicken McNuggets. The campaign was a major success for McDonald's, increasing McNuggets sales by 20 percent.[1] But some consumers found the ad offensive or annoying, with one saying, "It's sad that this is how the marketing execs at the McDonald's corporate office think they can attract the urban consumer."[2] In 2012, McDonald's featured African American actress Teyonah Parris from the AMC show *Mad Men* in a more traditionally themed urban-targeted ad. McDonald's spokesperson Danya Proud had this to say about the company's urban marketing efforts:

> We have a responsibility to all of our customers to effectively reach them. We certainly take pride in all of our advertising and try to make it relevant and appealing.
>
> We work with a dedicated African-American advertising agency that works with us to develop relevant, contemporary creative for our brand, that will resonate with this demographic. Again, as with all our advertising, these commercials reflect a light-hearted, fun approach to our brand, our menu, and our customers' experience with our brand.[3]

WHO are the sources?

What kind of a company is McDonald's? Who is it trying to reach with its urban marketing campaign?

WHAT are they saying?

How is McDonald's attempting to reach the urban audience? What does McDonald's mean by "urban marketing"?

WHAT evidence is there?

Why is McDonald's trying to target ethnic and racial minority groups? What can it gain? What can it lose? Do ads targeting specific minority groups appeal to the wider population as a whole?

WHAT do you and your classmates think?

How do you and your friends feel about companies advertising to targeted audiences? Watch the "McNuggets Love" ad online. Do you find it appealing? Insulting? Offensive? Funny? Why or why not? Do you think this ad appeals to a broad or narrow audience? How does it compare with the Teyonah Parris ad?

[1] Laurel Wentz, "'McNuggets Love' a Multicultural Ad Winner," *Chicago Business,* October 6, 2009.

[2] Geoffrey Bennett, "McDonald's Going Too Far to Market Their McNuggets?" *NPR*, December 3, 2008, www.npr.org/blogs/newsandviews/2008/12/mcdonalds_going_too_far_to_mar.html.

[3] Ibid.

Video 11.6: View several urban McDonald's ads.

Failures of Targeted Advertising. Efforts to target specific audiences are not always successful. When Hornell Brewing launched its western-themed Crazy Horse malt liquor, the company thought it had a product to complement its Dakota Hills Black Sunday brand. The beer was targeted not at Native American groups, but rather at people on the East Coast who were interested in western culture. But Native American groups expressed outrage at the use of the venerated chief's name to sell alcohol.[74] Crazy Horse, a leader of the Oglala Sioux in the nineteenth century, was opposed to drinking.[75] Objections by the Native American community eventually led the U.S. Commerce Department to refuse Hornell a trademark on the product; in addition, the beer was banned in Minnesota and Washington, and its sale was discouraged in Nebraska.[76]

As we saw with the opening vignette about Target reaching out with coupons to women who are pregnant, people expecting a child are highly valued by marketers. What gets people to spend more money than having a baby? Photo-sharing site Shutterfly thought it had a sure winner with a campaign that sent out an e-mail to people it thought had new babies, based on the photos they had posted. But unfortunately for Shutterfly, not everyone it reached out to had actually had a baby, and some of the recipients had had a miscarriage, had a child die, or were dealing with infertility. Following the social media

Web 11.10: See how Shutterfly missed with their campaign targeting new parents.

backlash, Shutterfly sent out a sincere apology for its mistake, which helped the company some with the folks who had received the e-mail in error. But that wasn't the end of the problem. Some of the Shutterfly customers who were properly targeted because they had had new babies were freaked out by the fact the company knew they had a baby. The lesson here? Always be careful when you target people to talk about their babies![77]

Richard Milnes/Demotix/Corbis

Coca Cola has embraced marketing its soft drink to the gay community with their display of the rainbow flag at their store in Sydney, Australia.

Advertising in Contemporary Culture

Advertising is much more than a part of the marketing and media business; it is a central element of American culture. Children sing advertising jingles the way they once sang nursery rhymes. In the 1970s, the music from a Coca-Cola commercial even became a hit single, "I'd Like to Teach the World to Sing."

Critics argue that advertising places a burden on society by raising the cost of merchandise and inducing people to buy things they don't need. The American Association of Advertising Agencies has defended the ad business, claiming that there are four common misconceptions about the industry[78]:

1. Advertising makes you buy things you don't want—The industry responds by saying that no one can make you buy things you don't want. People are free to do as they please.
2. Advertising makes things cost more—Advertisers claim that advertising builds demand for products, which can then be manufactured in larger quantities, more efficiently, and at a lower cost. (This defense ignores the idea of the prestige brand, however. Advertising does not make a bar of Clinique soap cost more to produce, but the premium image attached to the soap allows the company to charge more for it. Consumers apparently want to be able to buy better, more expensive products.)
3. Advertising helps sell bad products—The industry responds that a good ad may lead people to buy a product once, but it won't sustain demand for a product they don't like. In fact, the industry argues that good advertising for a bad product will kill the product faster than if it hadn't had a good campaign behind it. M. Night Shyamalan, director of the movies *The Sixth Sense* and *Signs*, says that with enough advertising studios can buy a good opening weekend for a movie, but only good word-of-mouth reports by fans will make the movie a long-term success.[79]
4. Advertising is a waste of money—The ad industry counters that advertising strengthens the economy by helping to move products through the marketplace and supporting the mass media.

SECRET 6 Throughout this section of the chapter, you will see numerous examples of Secret Six—Activism and analysis are not the same thing. In many of the following cases, you will see activism and analysis continually intertwined. See if you can sort out the two from each other.

The Problem of Clutter 

When critics complain that there are too many ads on television, few would be quicker to agree than advertising agencies and their clients. They are very concerned about the huge number of commercials and other messages—collectively referred to as **clutter**—that compete for consumer attention between programs.

Advertisers dislike clutter because the more ads and nonprogram messages there are on television, the less attention viewers will pay to any given message. A study conducted by the Cabletelevision Advertising Bureau found that viewers are much more likely to remember the first ad in a group (called a *pod*) than the fourth or fifth.[80]

clutter: The large number of commercials, advertising, and other nonprogramming messages and interruptions that compete for consumer attention on radio, television, and now the Internet.

Video 11.7 Watch Coca-Cola's famous vintage commercial (and a new one from the 2014 Super Bowl).

Susanne Doepke/Geisler-Fotopress/picture-alliance/dpa/AP Images

Movie director M. Night Shyamalan argues that while movie studios can spend enough on advertising to buy themselves a good opening weekend, only good word-of-mouth can bring a movie long-term box-office success.

The clutter problem is not limited to television; each day the average American adult is exposed to 150 advertisements in one form or another.

According to a study commissioned by advertising agencies and their clients, clutter is reaching record levels. In 2005, U.S. network television averaged about fifteen minutes of advertising and promotional clutter per hour during prime time.[81] Cable television rates were even higher, with MTV averaging sixteen minutes and thirteen seconds of clutter per hour. In 2010, cable channel Spike may have set a record for clutter with a single commercial pod running ten minutes during an episode of *Entourage*.[82]

Clutter is generally defined as anything that is not part of the program itself: ads, public service announcements, network promotions, and other gaps between programs. In the spring of 2009, Fox Broadcasting experimented with what the network called "Remote-Free TV," in which the network cut the commercial load during shows such as *Fringe* and *Dollhouse* to only ten minutes as a way of keeping viewers from channel surfing or fast-forwarding through the breaks. The network charged advertisers a 40 to 50 percent premium for spots that ran during Remote-Free TV. The experiment proved to be a mixed success for Fox. Both sponsors and viewers liked the reduced commercial load. So what made the response mixed? Fox earned less money and so abandoned the experiment at the end of the 2009 spring television season.[83]

Despite the problems of higher clutter, lower-rated network programs, and increasing CPM rates, networks continue to sell advertising time, and advertising experts say that clutter won't disappear until clients stop buying time from the networks.

Advertising clutter in the United Kingdom has also grown dramatically over the past several years, though it's still nowhere near the level seen in the United States. In 2001, the average Briton saw 258 television commercials per week. By 2005, that total had risen to 311. But this was still dramatically lower than the 789 ads per week seen by typical U.S. viewers. Ad clutter in the United Kingdom is lower partly because of legal restrictions on the number of minutes of commercials per hour and because the BBC, a state-supported media entity, doesn't carry ads.[84]

Breaking through the clutter is a continuing challenge for advertisers, who have come up with a variety of solutions to the problem. Tire company Goodyear breaks through the clutter by putting its message on the Goodyear Blimp, which flies over sporting and other entertainment events that draw large audiences.[85] Drug companies fight clutter by using celebrities in their advertisements. Former senator and presidential candidate Bob Dole served as an early spokesman for the impotence drug Viagra; NBA star Alonzo Mourning talked about the anemia drug Procrit, which is used to treat a kidney disorder that almost ended his career; and actress Lorraine Bracco, who played a psychiatrist on *The Sopranos*, discussed depression in ads for drugs manufactured by Pfizer Inc.[86]

Debunking Subliminal Advertising

With all the concern about advertising clutter, it is ironic that there is substantial public concern about **subliminal advertising**—messages that are allegedly embedded so deeply in an ad that they cannot be perceived consciously. The concept has been popularized by several writers, but no research has ever been done to demonstrate that advertising audiences can be influenced by messages they don't perceive consciously.

SECRET 3 Although there is no evidence that it works and little evidence that any advertisers try to create ads with

Web 11.11: Check out claims of subliminal advertising.

subliminal advertising: Messages that are allegedly embedded so deeply in an ad that they cannot be perceived consciously. There is no evidence that subliminal advertising is effective.

hidden messages, much of the public believes that subliminal advertising is used and is effective. A survey published in 1993 found that among people who were familiar with the concept of subliminal advertising, 72 percent thought it was effective.[87] The concept of subliminal advertising came to public attention in 1957, when Jim Vicary, a market researcher, claimed to have exposed movie audiences to the commands "*drink Coca-Cola*" and "*eat popcorn*" flashed on the screen so quickly (less than .03 of a second) that they could not be perceived consciously. Vicary claimed that popcorn sales increased by an average of 57.5 percent and Coke sales went up 18.1 percent. Vicary claimed that people could be influenced strongly by things they didn't see. It turned out, however, that Vicary had not conducted the tests but had simply made up the statistics on increased sales of popcorn and Coke. Throughout 1957 and early 1958, Vicary collected more than $4 million in consulting fees; in June 1958, he disappeared.

In 1970, Wilson Bryan Key, a university professor in Canada, revived the idea of subliminal advertising. While looking at a photo in an article in *Esquire*, he thought he saw an image of a phallus. Key has since been arguing that Madison Avenue hides images of death, fear, and sex in advertisements to increase sales.[88] It is unclear how these hidden images are supposed to influence viewers, who presumably are ignoring the clutter of overt advertising.

When Advertisements Are More Important Than the Program

Sometimes television ads are as interesting as the programs during which they appear. Commentators have even argued that people sometimes stay tuned to a boring Super Bowl broadcast just to see the commercials. Ridley Scott, best known as the director of blockbuster movies such as *Gladiator*, *Hannibal*, and *Black Hawk Down*, made a name for himself by directing the 1984 Super Bowl commercial that introduced Apple's Macintosh computer. Scott's commercial, known as "1984," changed the world of advertising. Not only was it one of the most talked-about commercials of all time, but it also showed that good commercials can be more memorable than the shows they accompany.[89]

©iStockphoto.com/iqoncept

The commercial, created by the Chiat/Day agency, was a success on a number of levels. It portrayed a dramatic image of a young woman athlete rebelling against an Orwellian "Big Brother" situation. It generated talk among the 100 million viewers who saw it, and it transmitted the central message that Apple wanted to get across: that there was an alternative to what was perceived at the time as the all-encompassing power of IBM (a role that has since been taken over by Microsoft).[90]

The commercial aired once on network television during the third quarter of the Super Bowl. After the Super Bowl, the commercial was broadcast free on the Big Three network news shows, and the trade magazine *Advertising Age* named it the commercial of the decade. Steve Hayden, who wrote the spot while employed at Chiat/Day, says that the agency wanted to sum up the whole philosophy of the computer in one commercial: "We thought of it as an ideology, a value set. It was a way of letting the whole world access the power of computing and letting them talk to one another."[91]

Ironically, the commercial almost didn't run at all. When it was previewed for Apple's board of directors, several members were horrified by it and wanted the spot scrapped. John O'Toole, former president of the American Association of Advertising Agencies, explained the significance of the ad as follows:

> What "1984" as a commercial for Apple really signified was the first time somebody could put a great deal of production money into a single commercial and run it only once and get tremendous benefit from running it only once. It took great coordination with PR. It was really event marketing, with sales promotion and PR built in. That was the beginning of the new era of integrated marketing communications.[92]

Advertising to Children 

Few aspects of advertising raise more concerns than commercials targeted at children. Yet children (and through them, their parents) are a highly desirable audience and market for advertisers. If your parents tell you that there weren't as many commercials targeted at children when they were young, they're right. In 1983, companies were spending $100 million a year to reach children. But by 2008, spending on advertising directed at children had grown to $17 billion a year. That means that marketers are spending 170 times more today to reach children than they were a generation ago.[93]

Television Advertising to Children. A U.S. Federal Trade Commission study published in 1978 under the title "Television Advertising to Children" found that children between the ages of two and eleven see approximately 20,000 television commercials a

Questioning the Media

Do you watch the Super Bowl every year for the ads? What are your favorite Super Bowl ads? What makes you like them?

Web 11.12: See the latest on Super Bowl advertising.

Video 11.8: Apple's "1984" Super Bowl commercial.

year—that's the equivalent of about three hours a week, or slightly less than half an hour per day. The study was highly controversial at the time because it called for bans (never implemented) on all advertising in programs for which a "significant" portion of the audience was under the age of eight and on television ads for sugary foods targeted at children ages eight to eleven.[94]

Marketing to children in the twenty-first century goes far beyond the traditional print and thirty-second television ads. Companies are instead pouring money into product placement, in-school programs, mobile phone ads, and video games.[95] In 2006, the advertising industry revised its guidelines for advertising to children for the first time in thirty-two years. The new guidelines require companies to distinguish between advertising and programming content, show mealtime foods as part of a single balanced meal rather than as part of a larger balanced diet, and identify when online games contain advertising.[96]

Food Ads Directed at Children. In recent years, the biggest criticism of advertising directed at children has moved from cigarettes to junk food. The U.S. federally chartered Institute of Medicine says that there is "strong evidence that exposure to television advertising" is connected with obesity, which can lead to numerous illnesses, including diabetes.[97] The institute goes on to say that ads for junk food targeted at children under age eight can help establish a lifetime of poor eating patterns.[98] Of course, what constitutes healthy food is subject to some debate. Would a high-fiber granola bar with significant levels of sugar qualify as health food or junk?

Richard Martin, a spokesman for the Grocery Manufacturers Association, said at a U.S. Federal Trade Commission hearing that the association does not believe there are bad foods: "Any food can be responsibly consumed by everyone, including kids."[99]

The advertising industry has been critical of the report's recommendations to regulate food ads targeted at children. Daniel L. Jaffe, an executive with the Association of National Advertisers, told the *Washington Post* that

> the government stepping in and saying what should be in messages on TV is a very radical proposal. . . . If you do it for food, there's no reason it can't be done for other controversial product categories. People are already trying to restrict the advertising for prescription drugs.[100]

In response to the report and other criticism from activist groups, the U.S. advertising and food industries say they are working to limit the advertising of junk food to children. A group of ten of the largest food and beverage companies—including Kraft, Coca-Cola, PepsiCo, and Hershey's—has pledged to use at least half of its ads directed at children under age twelve to promote healthier foods or encourage healthy lifestyles. It will also take junk food promotions out of online interactive games.[101]

Televised advertising of junk food to children has been a major issue in the United Kingdom as well, with the government putting in place strong new regulations of the practice. The new restrictions limit the promotion of high-fat, high-sugar, and high-salt foods to children under age sixteen to certain hours of the day. The ban has been controversial in Britain because these food ads provide funding for popular children's programming, such as *Bob the Builder* and *My Parents Are Aliens.* Producers argue that without the revenue from food ads, the commercial broadcast networks will stop producing high-quality children's content.[102] Critics of the ban say that this would leave British children with the choice of commercial-free BBC programming or imported satellite programming from companies such as Disney.[103] Anne Wood, creator of the popular *Teletubbies* series, told the *Guardian,*

> I am horrified and, believe me, it's not from a personal or self-interested position. . . . The health lobby seems to have won the day, but what about the other cultural side, protecting the rights of children to have television made for them, as adults do?[104]

Because the restrictions include ads targeted at children under sixteen, the ban will also affect MTV, costing the network as much as 8.8 percent of its income.

The Future of Advertising

With the rise of new advertising media, including computers connected to the Internet, mobile phone screens, and video games, the older media, such as television, newspapers, and magazines, are going to be facing substantial challenges.

Integrated Marketing Communication

One response to the rapidly changing marketing environment advertisers are facing is **integrated marketing communication**, or IMC. The idea is that there should be an overall communication strategy for reaching key audiences and that this strategy can be carried out using advertising, public relations, sales promotion, and interactive media. Dating back to the 1980s and 1990s, IMC is a long-term approach to building the value of a brand or an organization.[105]

We can see how IMC gets used to build a brand by looking at how Denny's worked to "re-introduce" the restaurant to America and to bring "light and lapsed" Denny's customers back into the fold in the winter of 2009.[106] At the center of the IMC campaign was a creative ad that ran during the Super Bowl featuring a group of "wise guy" gangsters planning a hit while a waitress delivers clown-faced pancakes. The message? Serious people deserve a serious breakfast. The ad then closed out with the announcement

---

integrated marketing communication: An overall communication strategy for reaching key audiences using advertising, public relations, sales promotion, and interactive media.

TEST YOUR MEDIA LITERACY

Limits on Advertising Food to Children

Advertising to children in general has been controversial for years, but as of late the criticism has become more focused on children's food ads. As mentioned earlier in this chapter, the controversy is a great example of Secret Six—Activism and analysis are not the same thing. In a nutshell, a recent research study conducted by the Institute of Medicine found the following, in respect to food preferences and diets:

- There is strong evidence that television advertising influences the food and beverage preferences of children aged two to eleven years. There is insufficient evidence about its influence on the preferences of teens aged twelve to eighteen years.
- There is moderate evidence that television advertising influences the food and beverage beliefs of children aged two to eleven years. There is insufficient evidence about its influence on the beliefs of teens aged twelve to eighteen years.
- There is strong evidence that television advertising influences the short-term consumption of children aged two to eleven years. There is insufficient evidence about its influence on the short-term consumption of teens aged twelve to eighteen years.
- There is moderate evidence that television advertising influences the usual dietary intake of younger children aged two to five years and weak evidence that it influences the usual dietary intake of older children aged six to eleven years. There is also weak evidence that it influences the usual dietary intake of teens aged twelve to eighteen years.[1]

WHO are the sources?

You have read about groups in the United States and the United Kingdom that have both advocated for and opposed advertising food products to children. Who are these groups?

WHAT are they saying?

Why do critics oppose food advertisements targeted at children? What types of food ads do they object to? How have supporters of this advertising responded? How have the responses in the United Kingdom and the United States differed?

WHAT evidence is there?

What evidence has been presented that food advertising directed at children is harmful? What evidence has been presented that it is benign or even helpful? Who is sponsoring and funding the studies?

WHAT do you and your classmates think about food advertisements directed at children?

What kinds of effects do you think food advertisements have on children? Do you think that the arguments that advocates and opponents are presenting are sincere? Or are the advocates just trying to advance their own agendas?

[1]J. Michael McGinnis, Jennifer Appleton Gootman, and Vivica I. Kraak, *Food Marketing to Children and Youth: Threat or Opportunity?* (Washington, D.C.: Institute of Medicine of the National Academies, 2005), books.nap.edu/openbook.php?record_id=11514&page=1.

Web 11.13: Read the Institute of Medicine report on advertising food to children.

that the chain was giving away a free breakfast to everyone who came to Denny's on the following Tuesday between 6 a.m. and 2 p.m.[107]

The result? Roughly 2 million people came in for their free Grand Slam breakfast of two eggs, two strips of bacon, two sausages, and two pancakes. That's an effective message. Especially when you consider that most of the people who took advantage of the free food also paid for a drink that came close to covering the cost of the meal.[108]

Brian Quinton, an editor at large for *Promo* magazine, sees the Denny's campaign as a mixed success from an IMC point of view. Denny's had a clever ad that ran twice during the Super Bowl, a full-page ad that ran in *USA Today*, an e-mail sent out to Denny's customers, and a compelling promotional offer. Denny's also sent out press kits about the promotion, placed signs within the stores, and highlighted the promotion on the company Web site. The campaign was discussed on NBC's *Today Show*, and it received extensive media attention elsewhere.[109] But while the Denny's campaign was a success, the integration of it was not as well done as it could have been. The biggest problem was that the company did not have enough capacity on its Web site to handle the sudden 1,700 percent increase in viewership during the game. The Web site crashed as soon as the first ad ran and stayed down throughout the game. The company also didn't include its Web address in the commercials.[110]

Despite these difficulties, Denny's IMC campaign would have to be considered a success from a results point of view. Denny's estimated that the promotion, including the ads and food, cost $5 million and claimed it generated $50 million in publicity, though it did not elaborate on how that was measured.[111] The Super Bowl ads were seen by 98 million viewers, and millions more saw local news stories generated by

Video 11.9: Watch the Denny's IMC ads and read more about the campaign.

MEDIA TRANSFORMATIONS

From Advertorials to Native Advertising

Back in 1950, legendary adman David Ogilvy created one of the best examples of an ad trying to masquerade as magazine editorial content. "The Guinness Guide to Oysters" gave readers a delicious look at Atlantic oysters and suggested that a Guinness Extra Stout would go great with them. As Brian Clark wrote in his advertising column at the Web site *Say Daily,* "I don't even like oysters, and this sounds amazing right now."[112] Ogilvy's Guinness and oysters ad is oftentimes held up as the real start of the **advertorial**—a paid message where the advertisement blends in with the surrounding materials in the magazine, newspaper, or Web site. While advertorials have been around for more than sixty years, a new version known as *native advertising* has emerged. Native ads are essentially a more sophisticated form of sponsored content that "matches a publication's editorial standards while meeting the audience's expectations."[113] (They are also an example of Secret Four—Nothing's new: Everything that happened in the past will happen again.) Lots of prestige media companies—including the *Atlantic,* the *Washington Post,* and the *New York Times*—are making use of native ads, especially on their Web sites.[114]

While ads designed to look like editorial content are nothing new, having the publication's editorial staff producing articles appearing as sponsored content is breaking down the old barrier between "church and state"—the blurred line between the business side and the content side of a publication.[115] The big challenge to both the advertiser and the publication is that the content of native ads needs to really match the style and standards of the hosting publication. This called for a fair amount of bravery for Southwest Airlines when it partnered with the news parody Web site *The Onion*. The airline's basic message is that it offers great fares and is loyal to its customers. The message in its native ad video on *The Onion* gets that message across, but in the sarcastic and crude *Onion* style. Microsoft used an *Onion* video to get across the message

advertorial: Advertising materials in magazines designed to look like editorial content rather than paid advertising.

The Anatomy of a Native Advertisement

Native ads work best when they match both the style of the publication they appear in and the tastes of the target audience. Case in point: the Onion Lab's successful minute and a half long video ad campaign called "Loyalty Goes Both Ways" for Southwest Airlines.

- Presented as a fake news report on ONN, the video parodies Southwest's loyalty program and captures the brand's well-known sense of humor, but with the Onion's legendary satirical "fake news" bite.
- The reporter introducing the story says:

"For years Southwest Airlines has boasted having the most loyal customers in the industry; now the low-cost airline is calling on its most frequent customers to finally do something in return for the airline, after years of selflessly offering inexpensive flights ..."

And a member of Southwest's ground crew is shown saying,

"You said you wanted free checked bags, and we listened. *Now you listen to us.*"

Parody of marketing message banners from airport

Typical b-roll (or background action) footage for news story about airlines

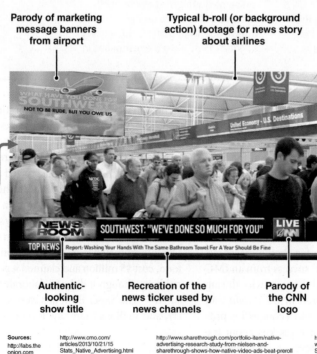

WHAT HAVE YOU DONE FOR SOUTHWEST? NOT TO BE RUDE, BUT YOU OWE US

United Economy · U.S. Destinations

NEWS ROOM | SOUTHWEST: "WE'VE DONE SO MUCH FOR YOU" | LIVE ONN

TOP NEWS | Report: Washing Your Hands With The Same Bathroom Towel For A Year Should Be Fine

Authentic-looking show title

Recreation of the news ticker used by news channels

Parody of the CNN logo

Why native advertising works

101,463 Number of YouTube views of Southwest "Loyalty Goes Both Ways" advertisement, 5 months since posting.

90% Percentage of U.S. publishers who have offered native ads or who plan to offer native ads on their websites.

38.9% Percent of all paid social advertising on social media sites that is spent on native ads.

32% The likelihood that a consumer will share a native ad with others.

19% The likelihood that a consumer will share a conventional banner ad with others.

2.1% Percentage of "brand lift" generated by viewers toward a brand after watching pre-roll ad.

82% Percentage of "brand lift" generated by viewers toward a brand after watching native ad.

85% Percentage of consumers who have never heard of native ads.

Sources: http://labs.theonion.com; http://www.cmo.com/articles/2013/10/21/15 Stats_Native_Advertising.html; http://www.sharethrough.com/portfolio-item/native-advertising-research-study-from-nielsen-and-sharethrough-shows-how-native-video-ads-beat-preroll; http://25h4pl1p8r9f2fc6of24zpt71dz2.wpengine.netdna-cdn.com/wp-content/uploads/2014/04/Native_Advertising_Infographic_Sharethrough_Nielsen.pdf that Internet Explorer, "the web browser you love to hate, just got better."[116]

Native ads can go horribly wrong, however, when the content of the article/ad doesn't match the standards of the hosting publication. One of the most notorious examples came from 2013 when the *Atlantic* ran a sponsored article on its Web site extolling the opening of twelve new Scientology churches. Along with the article, which seemed to be at odds with content from the *Atlantic,* the comments section following the article appeared to have nothing but positive comments about Scientology. Comments on most articles at the site are both positive and negative. After the article was up less than twelve hours, it was pulled from the Web site, and the next day an apology was posted that began:

> We screwed up. It shouldn't have taken a wave of constructive criticism—but it has—to alert us that we've made a mistake, possibly several mistakes. We now realize that as we explored new forms of digital advertising, we failed to update the policies that must govern the decisions we make along the way.[117]

The *Atlantic* followed up that apology two weeks later with new guideless for how it would handle sponsored content in the future.[118]

Media Transformations Questions:

- **DO** you think that native advertising or sponsored content lowers the reputation of publications that sell it?
- **HOW** do you feel about reading articles that are sponsored by the people being written about? Would you find them as interesting as articles that were not sponsored? Why or why not?

Video 11.10: Take a look at some of the native ads discussed above.

the promotion on the two days following the ads.[119] What's more, it appears Denny's did a good job of hitting its target audience of light and lapsed customers, as follow-up research showed that approximately 60 percent of the customers for the Tuesday promotion fell into that group.[120]

Is Anyone Watching Television Ads? 

There is only a fixed amount of money available for advertising and marketing products. And as companies move their advertising dollars to new media—online for ads and streaming content and to mobile phone screens—there will be less money for older media, such as television. If that were not enough, television is grappling with declining audience sizes and new technologies, such as DVRs, which allow viewers to skip watching commercials altogether. As of 2011, DVRs were in nearly 40 percent of American households.[121]

The broadcast networks are responding to this threat in various ways. CBS is selling Web ads as a package with broadcast ads. These aren't the simple banner ads of the 1990s; they are video ads that come before streaming Web content. Sneaker manufacturer Converse used its broadcast ads to get consumers to generate short videos featuring Converse sneakers, and the company then featured the videos on its Web site.[122]

Mobile Advertising. Mobile devices like smartphones and tablets have become the latest frontier for advertising, with their bright color screens and their ubiquitous use among the notoriously hard-to-reach population of adults aged eighteen to thirty-four. Although many companies are simply using banner ads to go with wireless Web content, others are creating interactive apps to promote their products.

Despite having small screens, cell phones have several key advantages to advertisers. They are always on, they are always with the person who owns them, and the phone belongs to an identifiable individual. This lets advertisers send out highly targeted messages that can contain time-sensitive offers. Another popular use of mobile phone advertising is to get consumers to participate in activities such as voting for contestants on reality shows.[123]

Advertising consultant Kathryn Koegel said she learned a lot about mobile advertising being done around the world when she served as a judge of the GSMA Global Mobile Awards. What did she discover? That folks are doing much more interesting and creative things globally using simpler tools than marketers are in the United States.[124]

The problem, Koegel claims, is that in the United States advertisers are obsessed with fancy iPhone apps that really don't do much to promote the brand. What Koegel found globally was that companies promoted involvement using simple SMS text messages and creative approaches that led to publicly visible activity.

She points to a Japanese campaign that uses the GPS and motion sensor in the iPhone to lead people to try to catch virtual butterflies by waving their phones about in public areas. "Catching" the butterflies leads to delivery of coupons to participants. So not only are the participants collecting coupons using the app, they're doing it in a way that's bound to get the people around them talking about it.

As a second example, she discusses the winning mobile campaign from the competition—one that sells Cornetto ice cream in Turkey through the use of a video game projected on the wall of a building in Taskim, Turkey's answer to Times Square. People compete by controlling game characters on the side of the building using text messages from their phones. If they complete the task, they win free ice cream that is collected on the spot.

The lesson from Koegel isn't that there is anything wrong with mobile apps, you just want to make sure that

AP Photo/Alan Diaz

Denny's used a complete IMC campaign to bring in light and lapsed customers that included Super Bowl advertising, a free breakfast giveaway promotion, and extensive contacts with the press around the country.

you have clear goals for what you are trying to accomplish with them.

What kind of mobile marketing could you think up?

Product Placement

Product placement has long been with us. When Paul Newman drank a beer in the 1981 movie *Absence of Malice*, it was a Budweiser. And when Steve McQueen played cop Frank Bullitt back in 1968, he chased criminals through San Francisco in a Ford Mustang GT. But in recent years, product placement has gotten considerably more sophisticated, rising occasionally to the level known as plot placement, branded entertainment, or **product integration**, in which the product or service being promoted is not only seen, but is central to the story.[125]

Questioning the Media

How do you feel about television programs featuring sponsored products within the shows? Do you find product placement more annoying in scripted programs than in reality shows? Why or why not?

One of the forces driving the growth of this expanded form of product placement is that multitasking consumers are increasingly ignoring television ads by skipping past them on the DVR, surfing other channels during commercial breaks, or leaving the room to get a snack.[126]

The biggest challenge to product placement is making it seem natural rather than intrusive, as intrusive placement tends to put off consumers, according to *New York Times* advertising columnist Stuart Elliott. That may be why so much of the product placement is in reality shows, where the use of products as rewards and prizes makes them fit in better.

There seem to be no limits now to which products can get placed in prime-time programs. Pregnancy was an unmentionable topic on television in the 1950s, but pregnancy tests are showing up frequently in product placements in shows ranging from *Gossip Girl* to *Sex and the City*.[127]

Television and movie writers have rebelled against product integration, complaining that it interferes with their creative integrity; they've also called for getting a cut of the placement income if they're going to be writing the placements into the stories. Patric Verrone, president of a movie and broadcast writers' union, explained why writers are concerned about product integration: "Product placement is simply putting a branded box of cereal on the kitchen table in a show. Product integration is having the characters talk about the crunchy deliciousness of the cereal."[128]

The Long Tail of Advertising

For all the talk about the importance of Internet advertising, it remains a relatively small part of advertising spending, accounting for only 6.9 percent of all advertising spending in the United States. Despite recent declines in spending, online advertising is expected to resume growth and should be more and more important in the years to come.[129]

Among the best known of the long-tail advertising tools are Google's AdWords and AdSense programs. Rather than buying a particular Web site, advertisers instead buy certain keywords, which place their ads next to particular content. Under AdWords, when surfers do a Google search that includes the keyword, the ad appears next to the search result. With AdSense, Web sites have a code on them that searches the content of the site and puts ads relevant to the subject matter next to the content

Video 11.11: Take a look at Kathryn Koegel's analysis of successful mobile advertising efforts, including the iButterfly campaign.

Video 11.12: Check out examples of both punk polka and techno polka.

product integration: The paid integration of a product or service into the central theme of media content. This is most common in television programming or movies, but it can be found in books, magazine articles, Web pages, or even songs.

posted there. So if I had AdSense on my site and wrote about DVDs in a blog entry, ads for retailers that sold DVD players would start coming up. The advertisers pay for each person who clicks on the served-up ad, with a portion of the money going to the owner of the site where the ad appeared.[130] Although this tool can be used to market any product, it is especially useful for advertising long-tail media. If I were trying to sell punk polka CDs, for example, I would try to maximize the return on my advertising money by reaching only people who were already reading about punk polka bands. Google also supports its Android mobile device operating system software with advertising sales.[131]

One of the big problems with Internet advertising is documenting how many people have actually clicked on the ad. Major advertisers have complained that "click fraud" drives up their cost of online advertising. The owner of a Web site with online ads may pay friends to click on the ads repeatedly to generate more page views and hence more income.[132] Or competitors of a particular advertiser will click on that advertiser's ad to run up his bill.[133] There are even automated programs known as clickbots or hitbots that will click away twenty-four hours a day, running up the bill for advertisers.

In an interesting move, in 2006, Google started selling advertising space in newspapers using the same program the company uses to sell advertising on its search engine and on Web pages.[134] As discussed in Chapter 3, Google is rapidly moving into becoming more and more of a general purpose media company, once more illustrating Secret Three—Everything from the margin moves to the center.

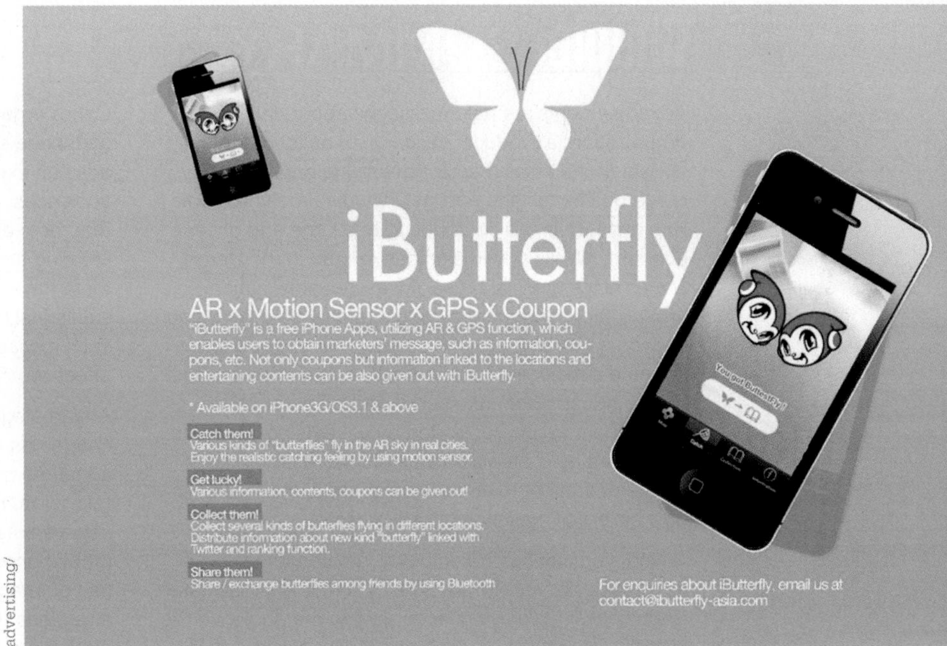

http://www.ralphehanson.com/2011/02/16/finding-success-through-mobile-advertising/

The iButterfly mobile advertising campaign in Japan had consumers waving their smartphones around in the air to catch virtual butterflies and receive electronic coupons.

Mario Perez/CBS via Getty Images

Microsoft has used product integration in the crime series *Hawaii Five-0* to feature the company's Surface tablet computer.

Chapter SUMMARY

Advertisements are paid messages about an organization, a product, a service, or an idea that appear in the mass media. Advertising provides numerous benefits to society, including making media less expensive and contributing to a large and diverse economy. While advertising has existed in the United States since colonial times, it was industrialization, urbanization, and the growth of national transportation networks in the nineteenth century that allowed it to become a major industry. Advertising transformed the media industry from one supported primarily by subscribers to one supported by advertising revenues. Publishers (and later broadcasters) were no longer sellers of content to audience members; they were now sellers of audiences to advertisers.

Advertising can be broken down into consumer advertising, advocacy advertising, and trade (business-to-business) advertising, according to the audience the client is attempting to reach and the idea or product it is trying to sell. The advertising industry encompasses four main groups: the client who has something to advertise, the advertising agency or department that creates the advertising, the media that carry the ads, and the audiences targeted by the advertisements.

Advertisers use a variety of strategies to reach their audiences. They may attempt to understand the needs, wants, and motivations of audience members through psychographic research. They also target products to specific demographic groups.

Critics argue that advertising raises the cost of merchandise, that many ads are tasteless, and that ads can exploit young people and other vulnerable audiences. Advertisers join the critics in complaining that there are too many advertisements in the media, creating the problem referred to as clutter. Although there have been complaints of advertisers embedding subliminal messages in ads, there is no evidence that such messages have been used or that they are effective.

Advertising is going through a period of significant change as new technology emerges that allows consumers to bypass viewing commercials on television. But technology is also providing numerous new venues for advertising, including the Internet and mobile phones. Companies are increasingly making use of integrated marketing communication strategies that bring together multiple forms of marketing communication to promote their brands. Advertisers are also looking at promoting their products through elaborately developed product placement schemes.

Keep up-to-date with content from the author's blog.

Take the chapter quiz.

Key TERMS

- advertising 276
- industrialization 276
- modernization 277
- economy of abundance 277
- brand name 277
- local advertising 279
- direct action message 279
- national advertising 279
- indirect action message 279
- advocacy ads 279
- public service ads 280
- business-to-business (trade) ads 280
- open contract 282
- the big idea 282
- brand image 283
- media planning 284
- CPM 284
- zoned coverage 285
- drive time 286
- targeting 287
- clutter 291
- subliminal advertising 292
- integrated marketing communication 294
- advertorial 296
- product integration 298

Concept REVIEW

Industrialization, modernization, and the growth of consumer advertising

The importance of brands

Advertising-supported media

Types of advertising

The players in advertising: clients, agencies, media, and audiences

Advantages and dangers of targeted advertising

The use of demographics and psychographics in targeting markets

The challenge of advertising in a cluttered market

The growth of integrated marketing communication

Student STUDY SITE

Sharpen your skills with SAGE edge at **edge.sagepub.com/hanson5e**

SAGE edge for Students provides a personalized approach to help you accomplish your coursework goals in an easy-to-use learning environment.

chapter 12

Public Relations

Interactions, Relationships, and the News

Kraft turned a small shortage of Velveeta into an opportunity to promote the popularity of the cheese product for making queso dip during the football playoffs season.

AP Photo/Paul Sakuma, File

The news broke the first week of January 2014. Football fans in the heat of the NFL playoffs were facing potential disaster. It wasn't a potential strike of NFL players or a lockout by management. And it wasn't a dispute between a cable company and the network broadcasting the big game, threatening a blackout of the Super Bowl over a major urban area. No, this was something really serious, the Cheesepocalypse—a shortage of Velveeta with which to make queso dip for Super Bowl and playoff watch parties.

It started when *Advertising Age* magazine contacted Kraft Foods after news reports surfaced of shortages at East Coast grocery stores. Kraft spokeswoman Jody Moore told *Ad Age*, "Given the incredible popularity of Velveeta this time of year, it is possible consumers may not be able to find their favorite product on store shelves over the next couple of weeks."[1]

And with that, Kraft had a minor crisis on its hands. In some ways, it was a good problem to have—consumers wanted more of its iconic product than the company could supply, which demonstrated that its marketing efforts promoting making salsa and cheese dip were successful. But how would the company respond to its customers and stores? How would they interact with their publics?

There were charges that the Velveeta shortage was some kind of a marketing ploy, but Kraft spokespeople insist that the shortage was real, caused by a combination of some "minor manufacturing challenges" and heavy seasonal demands.[2]

As word of the shortage spread, Twitter users started lamenting it. Among the early tweets collected by *People* magazine's Great Ideas blog were these[3]:

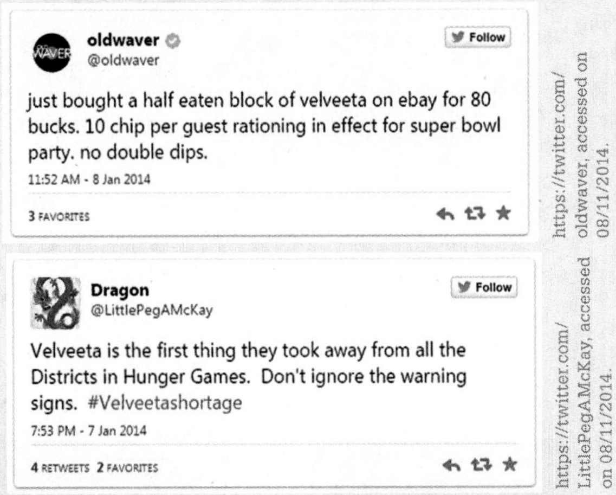

oldwaver
@oldwaver
Follow
just bought a half eaten block of velveeta on ebay for 80 bucks. 10 chip per guest rationing in effect for super bowl party. no double dips.
11:52 AM - 8 Jan 2014
3 FAVORITES
Dragon
@LittlePegAMcKay
Follow
Velveeta is the first thing they took away from all the Districts in Hunger Games. Don't ignore the warning signs. #Velveetashortage
7:53 PM - 7 Jan 2014
4 RETWEETS 2 FAVORITES
https://twitter.com/oldwaver, accessed on 08/11/2014.
https://twitter.com/LittlePegAMcKay, accessed on 08/11/2014.

Fans of Velveeta got online to talk about the spot shortages of the product using hashtags on Twitter. One of the most popular ones was #Velveetashortage.

Kraft built on this social media response in a number of ways. The company promoted the use of the #cheesepocalype hashtag, and built a Cheesepocalpyse Web site that mapped out reports of Velveeta shortages using Twitter reports from across the country. The company also used its Tumblr blog, which normally suggested humorous uses for Velveeta, to officially announce the shortage.[4]

LEARNING OBJECTIVES

After studying this chapter, you will be able to:

1. Discuss how public relations developed from press agentry to a profession.
2. Describe the three major functions of public relations.
3. Explain the five components of the ROPES public relations process.
4. Explain how a PR professional should deal with a crisis.
5. Explain how the Internet has changed the public relations process.
6. Discuss how public relations shapes the news we receive and our view of politicians.
7. Describe how political activists use public relations to promote their causes.

So what did Kraft and Velveeta get out of the Cheesepocalypse social media campaign? According to *Ad Age*'s Jack Neff, the brand got a huge amount of free publicity—publicity that was likely out of proportion to the "crisis." (The shortage was only of one packaging size.) But Kraft marketing executive Cannon Koo points out the #cheesepocalypse hashtag helped the company identify its so-called "super-consumers," the people who consume the most of the brand. Super-consumers are the folks who make up about 10 percent of the buyers for any brand, but account for anywhere from 30 to 70 percent of the brand's sales. Information about how these super-consumers use Velveeta has let the company increase its sales.[5]

Greg Gallagher, marketing director at Kraft, told the *Harvard Business Review*, "The previous thinking was that the quickest, easiest path to growth was to identify light users or lapsed users. But when we waked to super-consumers, we learned that in fact they wanted to use Velveeta more—they were starving for it."[6] Another benefit of the Cheespocalypse publicity was that a recall of a limited number of Velveeta products for being mislabeled went almost completely unnoticed—not because Kraft engaged in any kind of cover-up, but rather because the press and consumers were more engaged in a more compelling story line.[7]

Beyond the social media content itself, the active discussion drew a large amount of news media and blog coverage of Velveeta. Web sites from Michigan to Alabama wrote about the Cheesepocalypse. The publicity generated was not always positive, with the aforementioned Alabama news blog mocking the Kraft Velveeta shortage map, saying, "Hopefully folks in severe areas of Alabama and across the country will learn to function without Velveeta. If they use it to make dips, mac and cheese casseroles, melt on burgers etc., maybe they will rethink those recipes and substitute a healthier, real food option."[8]

But given that this was about Super Bowl food, I doubt too many people were worried about the health bit . . .

Timeline

1800

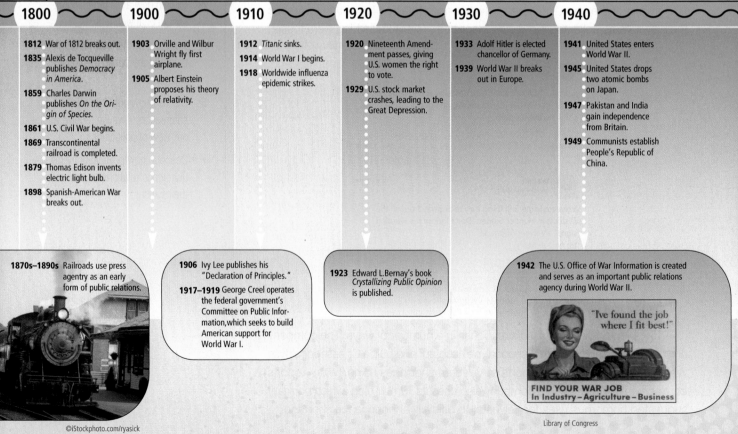

1812 War of 1812 breaks out.
1835 Alexis de Tocqueville publishes *Democracy in America*.
1859 Charles Darwin publishes *On the Origin of Species*.
1861 U.S. Civil War begins.
1869 Transcontinental railroad is completed.
1879 Thomas Edison invents electric light bulb.
1898 Spanish-American War breaks out.

1870s–1890s Railroads use press agentry as an early form of public relations.

©iStockphoto.com/ryasick

1900

1903 Orville and Wilbur Wright fly first airplane.
1905 Albert Einstein proposes his theory of relativity.

1906 Ivy Lee publishes his "Declaration of Principles."
1917–1919 George Creel operates the federal government's Committee on Public Information, which seeks to build American support for World War I.

1910

1912 *Titanic* sinks.
1914 World War I begins.
1918 Worldwide influenza epidemic strikes.

1920

1920 Nineteenth Amendment passes, giving U.S. women the right to vote.
1929 U.S. stock market crashes, leading to the Great Depression.

1923 Edward L.Bernay's book *Crystallizing Public Opinion* is published.

1930

1933 Adolf Hitler is elected chancellor of Germany.
1939 World War II breaks out in Europe.

1940

1941 United States enters World War II.
1945 United States drops two atomic bombs on Japan.
1947 Pakistan and India gain independence from Britain.
1949 Communists establish People's Republic of China.

1942 The U.S. Office of War Information is created and serves as an important public relations agency during World War II.

"I've found the job where I fit best!"
FIND YOUR WAR JOB
In Industry – Agriculture – Business

Library of Congress

Kraft's promotion of the Cheesepocalypse is at the core of how social media can be effectively used in public relations. Social media are not just new ways to push marking information; they are a great tool for interacting with and getting to know the people who love a product best. In the case of Velveeta, Kraft got to know the product's super-consumers better and helped them share recipes and new ways to use the soft cheese product. (Kraft's effective use of social media to interact with its consumers and turn what could have been a problem into a big plus for the brand is a great example of Secret Two—There are no mainstream media. In this case, interactive social media were far more important to Kraft than legacy media were.) The Cheesepocalypse highlights many of the key issues we look at in this chapter. In addition to examining the development of the public relations industry, we discuss how the public relations process works, the various publics that organizations need to work with, and how public relations professionals have used public relations to protect and advance their employers' interests. ■

> "The previous thinking was that the quickest, easiest path to growth was to identify light users or lapsed users. But when we waked to the super-consumers, we learned that in fact they wanted to use Velveeta more—they were starving for it."
>
> —Greg Gallager, Kraft Foods

Web 12.1: Get the whole story on the Cheesepocalypse.

1950

1950 Korean War begins.

1953 Francis Crick and James Watson discover structure of DNA.

1957 Soviet Union launches spacecraft *Sputnik I*.

1960

1963 Martin Luther King Jr. delivers "I Have a Dream" speech during Washington, D.C., civil-rights march.

1969 Neil Armstrong walks on the moon.

1970

1974 U.S. president Richard Nixon resigns due to Watergate scandal.

1975 Vietnam War ends.

1977 Apple II personal computer is introduced.

1978 First test-tube baby is born.

1980

1983 First HIV/AIDS cases are documented.

Ozone hole is discovered over Antarctica.

1986 Space shuttle *Challenger* explodes.

1989 The Berlin Wall falls.

1990

1991 Soviet Union disbands.

1993 European Union is formed.

1994 Nelson Mandela is elected president of South Africa.

1997 Diana, Princess of Wales, dies in car accident.

2000-

2001 Al Qaida attacks World Trade Center and Pentagon.

2003 United States invades Iraq.

2008 Barack Obama is elected U.S. president.

2011 Earthquake and tsunami hit Japan. United States ends eight-year war with Iraq.

2012 Superstorm Sandy devastates U.S. eastern seaboard.

2014 Russian army invades Ukraine.

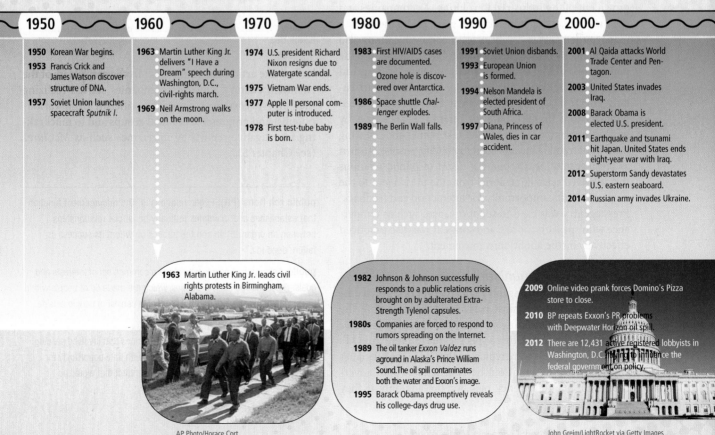

1963 Martin Luther King Jr. leads civil rights protests in Birmingham, Alabama.

AP Photo/Horace Cort

1982 Johnson & Johnson successfully responds to a public relations crisis brought on by adulterated Extra-Strength Tylenol capsules.

1980s Companies are forced to respond to rumors spreading on the Internet.

1989 The oil tanker *Exxon Valdez* runs aground in Alaska's Prince William Sound. The oil spill contaminates both the water and Exxon's image.

1995 Barack Obama preemptively reveals his college-days drug use.

2009 Online video prank forces Domino's Pizza store to close.

2010 BP repeats Exxon's PR problems with Deepwater Horizon oil spill.

2012 There are 12,431 active registered lobbyists in Washington, D.C., trying to influence the federal government on policy.

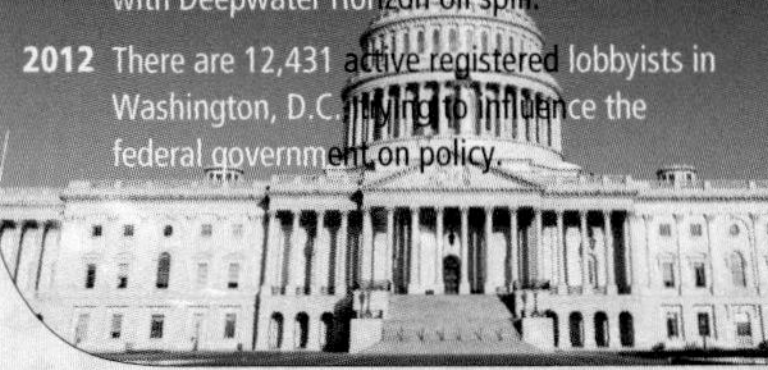

John Greim/LightRocket via Getty Images

From Press Agentry to Professionalism

The field of **public relations** (also called **PR**) has had an uneven image in the United States. (The term *public relations* is discussed more extensively later in this chapter.) In his book on corporate public relations, Marvin Olasky noted that practitioners have been called "high-paid errand boys and buffers for management."[9] Other names have been less flattering. Despite such criticisms, public relations is critical to industry, government, and nonprofit organizations. These organizations need to deal with the people who work for them, invest in them, are served by them, contribute to them, regulate them, or buy from them. They need to interact with the world. Ultimately, that's what public relations is all about—relating with a wide range of publics. A **public** is a group of people who share a common set of interests. An *internal public* is made up of people within the organization. An *external public* is made up of people outside the organization.

The Origins of Public Relations

The origins of public relations go back as far as the American Revolution, with pamphlets like Thomas Paine's *Common Sense*, which built up the case for the colonies' break with England. In the early 1800s, author Washington Irving used publicity to build excitement for his latest book. But the PR profession is generally seen as having grown out of the Industrial Revolution. As companies and their accompanying bureaucracies grew, so did the need to manage their image.[10] Advances in communications also made publicity campaigns more feasible. It wasn't until the penny press of the 1830s and 1840s produced widespread newspaper circulation that publicity began to be particularly effective. Circus entrepreneur P. T. Barnum raised publicity to a fine art, building interest in his shows by writing letters to the editor under fake names and accusing himself of fraud. Thus, this early publicity process, known as **press agentry**, was a one-way form of public relations that involved sending material from the press agent to the media with little opportunity for interaction and feedback. Press agentry was used to support causes such as temperance with speakers, books, and songs. It was also practiced effectively by the abolitionist movement.

One-Way Communication. As noted in the preceding section, press agentry consisted of one-way communication. For the most part, press agents before the 1920s worked at building publicity for their clients rather than managing or creating a specific image. Standard Oil's efforts in the 1890s were typical of the time. The oil giant's advertising agency sent out news articles as paid advertisements, but the agency paid for the ads only if they looked like articles or editorials.[11] In the early years of the twentieth century, however, companies started realizing that they needed to respond to criticism from various populist and progressive political groups and to muckraking investigative reports by magazines such as *McClure's* (see Chapter 5).

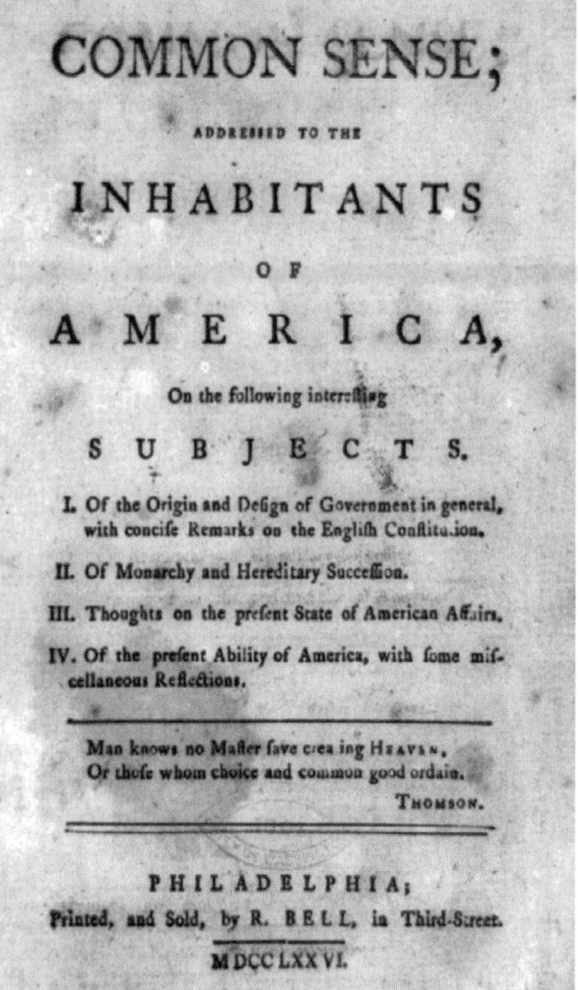

COMMON SENSE;

ADDRESSED TO THE

INHABITANTS

OF

AMERICA,

On the following interesting

SUBJECTS.

I. Of the Origin and Design of Government in general, with concise Remarks on the English Constitution.

II. Of Monarchy and Hereditary Succession.

III. Thoughts on the present State of American Affairs.

IV. Of the present Ability of America, with some miscellaneous Reflections.

Man knows no Master save creating HEAVEN,
Or those whom choice and common good ordain.

THOMSON.

PHILADELPHIA;

Printed, and Sold, by R. BELL, in Third-Street.

MDCCLXXVI.

Library of Congress

Thomas Paine's famous *Common Sense* pamphlet is an example of an early PR effort. It was used to build the case for the American Revolution.

---

public relations (PR): Public relations is "the management function that establishes and maintains mutually beneficial relationships between an organization and the publics on whom its success or failure depends."

public: Any group of people who share a common set of interests and goals. These include *internal publics*, which are made up of people within the organization, and *external publics*, which consist of people outside the organization.

press agentry: An early form of public relations that involved sending material from the press agent to the media with little opportunity for interaction and feedback. It often involved conduct that would be considered deceptive and unethical today.

The Beginnings of Image Management. The first major users of public relations were railroads, which had numerous reasons for working on their images.[12] In the 1870s, many railroads wanted to divide freight traffic among themselves according to predetermined percentages so as to avoid competition. The railroads did not want criticism of their monopolistic practices in the press, so they bribed reporters and editors, either by making cash payoffs or, more subtly, by giving free passes for travel on the railroad to cooperative members of the press. The Illinois Central Railroad realized that praise of the railroads coming from academics would do more good and be more persuasive than puffery coming from the industry itself, so it funded university research on the railroads, the findings of which could then be quoted by the press.

Like the railroads, the utility and telephone industries saw the value of public relations. Chicago Edison argued to both the government and the public that providing electricity was a "natural monopoly" and should not be open to competition. In the early 1900s, AT&T required newspapers in which it advertised to run positive articles about its actions. Both the utilities and the phone company used publicity firms to write articles and editorials promoting the companies' points of view that were placed in newspapers around the country.

Library of Congress

Circus promoter P. T. Barnum built publicity for his shows through posters such as this one, as well as by staging protests and complaints about his circus.

Ivy Lee. Ivy Lee, one of the two key founders of modern public relations, brought to the business a strong understanding of both economics and psychology. Lee recognized that the public often reacted more strongly to symbols and phrases than to rational arguments, and he built his campaigns around the importance of symbolism.[13] He also saw that it was important to put a human face on corporations.[14]

Lee was the first PR professional to deal with crisis management, and although *spin control* did not become a popular term until the 1980s, he was practicing it as early as 1910. Lee wanted to do much more for his clients than just send out favorable publicity; he wanted to manipulate public opinion in favor of his clients. That meant actively working with the press.

Among the problems faced by the railroads was reporting on accidents. The accepted practice of the industry in the late 1800s was either to cover up accidents or to bribe reporters not to write about them. Lee suggested that it might be in the railroads' best interests to deal with the press openly. When his client, the Pennsylvania Railroad, had a wreck, Lee invited reporters to visit the scene of the accident at the company's expense. After they arrived, he helped them report on the story. Company officials were amazed to see that the publicity they received when they cooperated with the press was a vast improvement over what they received when they fought with it.[15]

Lee also recognized the importance of telling the truth. Although the arguments he presented clearly supported his clients' viewpoints, Lee was always careful to be accurate in any factual claims. This was not so much because telling the truth was right or moral as because doing so was effective.[16] Lee once told oil giant John D. Rockefeller Jr., "Tell the truth because sooner or later the public will find it out anyway. And if the public doesn't like what you are doing, change your policies and bring them into line with what the people want."[17]

Questioning the Media

Back in the early 1900s, Ivy Lee said that PR professionals needed to deal with publics "openly and honestly." Do you think modern PR professionals live up to this ideal? Why or why not?

In 1902, American coal mine operators were facing a strike. The mine owners ignored the press, but the unionized miners worked with reporters to their advantage, and due to this the public strongly supported the workers. When the mine owners faced another strike in

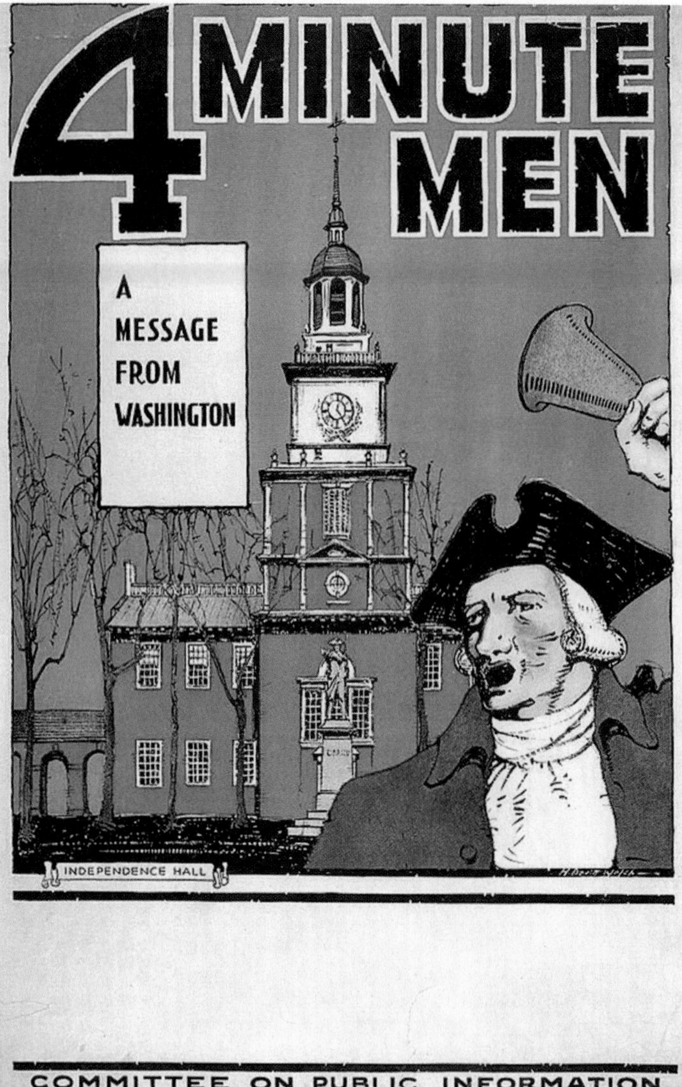

The Committee on Public Information had 75,000 "Four-Minute Men" who gave brief speeches about the war to churches and civic groups across the United States.

1906, they hired Lee's publicity firm, Parker and Lee.[18] Lee convinced the mine operators that they could no longer ignore public opinion. A former business reporter, he started giving newspapers all the information they asked for. Supplied with clear and accurate statements from the mine owners, reporters started writing stories that were considerably less antagonistic to the mine owners.

At about this time, Lee developed his "Declaration of Principles," which outlined how he thought public relations ought to be carried out. These principles can be summarized quite simply: Openly and honestly supply accurate and timely news to the press.[19]

Lee himself suffered from bad public relations late in his career: In the 1930s, he was accused of being a Nazi propagandist because he had worked for the German Dye Trust. The damage to his reputation from this association came at least in part from the many enemies he had made over the course of his career.[20]

Edward L. Bernays. Along with Ivy Lee, the other founder of public relations was Edward L. Bernays, who was the first person to apply social-scientific research techniques to the field. Bernays, a nephew of Sigmund Freud, promoted the use of psychology to manipulate public opinion, a technique that he called "**engineering consent**":

> This phrase means, quite simply, the use of an engineering approach—that is, action based only on thorough knowledge of the situation and on the application of scientific principles and tried practices in the task of getting people to support ideas and programs. Any person or organization depends ultimately on public approval and is therefore faced with the problem of engineering the public's consent to a program or goal.[21]

In addition to promoting his clients, Bernays actively promoted the concept of public relations as a profession. To that end, he wrote the first books on the practice, *Crystallizing Public Opinion* (1923) and *Propaganda* (1928). In 1923, Bernays taught the first course in public relations, which he offered at New York University.

Like Lee, Bernays recognized the importance of the crowd in modern life. He found that the best way to influence the public was to arrange for messages to be delivered by credible sources. "If you can influence the leaders, either with or without their conscious cooperation, you automatically influence the group which they sway," he commented.[22] While the guaranteed influence of leaders over groups may be a bit of an overstatement, the use of credible or admired individuals to speak on behalf of a company is certainly central to public relations.

To Bernays, the chief characteristic distinguishing public relations from the press agentry of the past was that public relations was a two-way interaction between individuals or organizations—communication that involved listening as well as speaking. Bernays wrote that by the 1920s it had became clear to practitioners that words alone did not constitute public relations; there had to be actions to go with the words.

World War I: The Federal Government Starts Using Public Relations

The years 1914–1918 were a period of major growth for public relations. According to Bernays, during this time governments figured out how important persuasive

Video 12.1: Learn more about Edward L. Bernays.

engineering consent: The application of the principles of psychology and motivation to influencing public opinion and creating public support for a particular position.

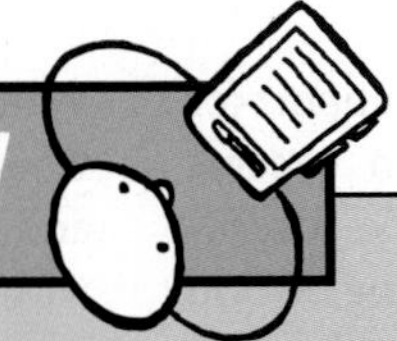

TEST YOUR MEDIA LITERACY

False Reports Garner Publicity

Back in 1939, a young actress by the name of Rita Hayworth was trying to become a household name, and her press agent, the legendary Henry Rogers, was willing to do whatever it took to make her a Hollywood star. One of these efforts was putting out a made-up press release naming Hayworth the winner of a nonexistent "best-dressed off-screen actress" contest held by a nonexistent group. That story landed Hayworth a big photo story in *Look* magazine (a competitor of *Life*) and launched the buxom actress's career.[1]

Why do we care? Because it's happened again.

George Hurrell/John Kobal Foundation/ Getty Images

Emporio Armani, 2011 Fall-Winter Campaign

Truthfulness is not always the first priority when it comes to entertainment publicity. Actress Rita Hayworth in the 1930s and singer Rihanna in the 2010s had their publicity agents pull similar stunts and claim that the performers had won imaginary awards for their appearances.

SECRET 7 More recently, the British newspaper the *Daily Mail* ran a story proclaiming that singer Rihanna's ad campaign for Armani undies had won an award from *Advertising Age* magazine for being the sexiest of the year. It even quoted *Ad Age* as saying: "It's Rihanna at her sexiest. She's never looked this good." They also added: "She's in amazing shape and the pictures are stunning."[2] (As a side note, the "they" in the attribution should have been a tip-off that there was not really a source behind the story. Remember Secret Seven—There is no "they.")

Even Rihanna tweeted about the award.

The only problem? As press blogger Jim Romenesko points out, *Ad Age* didn't actually give out an award for the sexiest ad. That's why none of the stories about it (including those from the *Huffington Post,* the *Hindustan Times*, the *Global Grind*, and others) had links back to *Ad Age*.[3]

The actual source of the story? A company called TNI Press Ltd. that writes stories for British tabloids and is the source for a number of recent stories extolling Rihanna's sexiness. In his *New York Times* obituary, Henry Rogers was quoted as saying in 1987, "If I did now what I did then, I'd be barred from every news media outlet."[4]

Hmmm . . . maybe not. Think about **SECRET 4** Nothing's new: Everything that happened in the past will happen again.

As a side note, at the time this story was spreading, your author ran a Google search on Rihanna's Armani ad and found twenty-four media stories about it but only one link to the actual correction. When it comes to celebrity gossip—gossip likely put forward by the celebrity himself or herself—do we really care whether it's true?

WHO are the sources?

What is the *Daily Mail*? What kind of stories does it run? Who was Henry Rogers?

WHAT are they saying?

What did Henry Rogers do for Rita Hayworth? What did the *Daily Mail* do for Rihanna? What connection is there between Henry Rogers and the Rihanna story?

WHAT evidence is there?

What evidence did the *Daily Mail* have that the Rihanna story was true? How about the news sites that reprinted the story? What could these publications have done to check the story before they published it?

WHAT do you and your classmates think about fabricated celebrity stories?

Why do you think that the *Daily Mail* ran the story with photos about Rihanna? Do you think that it cared whether or not the story was true? Was there any difference between what the *Daily Mail* did for Rihanna and what Henry Rogers did for Rita Hayworth? Do you and your friends have any faith in the truth of tabloid stories about celebrities?

---

[1] Robert McG. Thomas Jr., "Henry Rogers, 82, Press Agent Who Built Hollywood Stars," *New York Times*, May 1, 1995, www.nytimes.com/1995/05/01/obituaries/henry-rogers-82-press-agent-who-built-hollywood-stars.html?src=pm.

[2] Deborah Arthurs, "Rihanna's Steamy Armani Adverts Voted the Sexiest of 2011 (and Let's Not Forget Miranda Kerr's and Kate Moss Too)," *Daily Mail*, December 28, 2011, www.dailymail.co.uk/femail/article-2079455/Rihannas-steamy-Armani-adverts-voted-sexiest-2011.html.

[3] Jim Romenesko, "Ad Age *Did Not* Name Rihanna's Armani Ad Year's Sexiest," December 30, 2011, jimromenesko.com/2011/12/30/ad-age-did-not-name-rihannas-armani-ad-years-sexiest/.

[4] Thomas Jr., "Henry Rogers, 82, Press Agent Who Built Hollywood Stars."

Web 12.2: Read the original story about Rita Hayworth and Rihanna.

communication could be to mobilize popular support for a major war: "Ideas and their dissemination became weapons and words became bullets."[23] The U.S. government used public relations extensively during World War I. Within a week of the U.S. entry into the war, President Woodrow Wilson established the Committee on Public Information (CPI) under the direction of George Creel, the former editor of the *Rocky Mountain News*. The committee operated from April 6, 1917, until June 30, 1919, building American support for the war. Although the committee lacked many of the modern tools of mass communication—radio was still in its infancy, and the movie industry was just taking its first steps—it was still able to use advertising, billboards, and posters, as well as newspaper opinion pieces, articles, and pamphlets.

The committee also used interpersonal channels. It enlisted 75,000 "Four-Minute Men" who took the committee's messages to churches and civic groups by delivering four-minute speeches. Research conducted in the 1940s later proved the effectiveness of this technique by confirming that people often turn to individuals they know and trust when they are looking for guidance about an important topic. So if an organization wants to influence a particular public, the best way may be to use influential local individuals, along with the mass media.[24] Bernays referred to this process as **opinion leadership**—using "journalists, politicians, businessmen, scientists, professional men, authors, society leaders, teachers, actors, women of fashion and so on" to deliver influential messages to the public.[25]

Woodrow Wilson's use of public relations was not limited to the war effort. He was the first president to hold regular television screenpress conferences, and under Wilson the Federal Trade Commission used publicity to force the food industry to adopt more sanitary practices.

The federal government turned to public relations once again during World War II. The Office of War Information served much the same purpose that the CPI had during World War I. The main difference was that the new group was able to use talking films and radio to supplement the print and interpersonal communications used by the CPI.

Public Relations Becomes a Profession

During the 1940s and 1950s, public relations continued to grow as a profession, and colleges and universities began offering degrees in the field. Advances in polling made it easier to measure public opinion, and clients began to realize that PR firms could help shape how people felt about companies and issues. Clients were also looking for help in making use of the emerging medium of television.

Throughout the 1960s, the media became more critical of both business and government as the United States became caught up in the Vietnam War, the civil rights movement, the student and women's movements, environmentalism, and consumerism (for example, groups such as Ralph Nader's consumer activist organization). This trend continued into the 1970s with the rise of Watergate-inspired investigative reporting. It was a time when institutions had to actively manage their images, and they realized the importance of communicating with individuals, businesses, governments, and social organizations.[26]

The Business of Public Relations

There is a popular misconception among students that public relations primarily involves talking and meeting with people. Although it certainly includes these elements, there is much more to the profession. Public relations involves managing an organization's image through planning, research, communication, and assessment.

What Is Public Relations?

Edward Bernays described three major functions of public relations[27]:

1. Informing—Sending out information to a variety of publics, ranging from the people who work in a company's office to its customers on the other side of the world. An example of information would be a press release announcing a new product line to stores that sell the company's products.

2. Persuading—Attempting to induce members of various publics to change their attitudes or actions toward an idea, product, or institution. An example of persuasion would be a lobbying campaign to persuade the government to remove a tax on the company's product.

3. Integrating—Attempting to bring publics and institutions together with a shared set of goals, actions, and attitudes. An example of an integrative event would be a charity auction designed to raise funds for a park in the city where the company has its offices as the company works to become a vital part of the community.

Bernays saw public relations as a public good, necessary for the proper functioning of society. He argued that society was moving too fast and becoming too complex for the average person to cope with and that the only hope for a functional society was to merge public and private interests through public relations.

This two-way model of interaction between the institution and its publics is the central notion of modern public relations, which can be defined as "the management function that establishes and maintains mutually beneficial

opinion leadership: A two-step process of persuasion that uses respected and influential individuals to deliver messages with the hope of influencing members of a community, rather than just relying on the mass media to deliver the message.

relationships between an organization and the publics on whom its success or failure depends."[28]

This definition has three basic segments:

1. Public relations is a *management function*. This means that it is central to the running of a company or organization and not merely a tool of the marketing department.

2. Public relations establishes *mutually beneficial relationships*. This means that public relations is an interaction that should benefit both sides—the organization and the public(s).

3. Companies depend on *various publics* to succeed. One of the primary reasons PR campaigns fail is that they neglect these relationships and consider only the company's point of view.

One mistake companies must avoid is to assume that glib communication can be a substitute for real action when solving a public problem. This can be seen clearly in the case of the film industry in the 1920s and 1930s. As discussed in Chapter 8, during that period movies were being criticized for their immorality. Industry leaders responded by hiring former U.S. postmaster Will Hays to supervise the moral content of movies. Throughout the 1920s, Hays preached a message of corporate responsibility to the press, but the industry made no significant changes in response to criticism of the portrayal of sex, violence, and drug use in the movies.[29]

©iStockphoto.com/malerapaso

By 1934, critics had had enough of soothing words without action, and the Catholic Legion of Decency started a movie boycott. With the threat of government censorship growing, the movie industry finally adopted a production code that put strict limits on what directors could portray. Public relations historian Marvin Olasky argues that if the movie industry had dealt with its critics in a meaningful way in the 1920s, it might have avoided the restrictions forced on it in the 1930s.[30]

The Public Relations Process

Although there are a number of different ways of looking at the PR process, we are going to look at it using a model known as ROPES: research, objectives, programming, evaluation, and stewardship.[31]

1. Research—Researching the opportunities, problems, or issues the organization is facing.
2. Objectives—Setting specific and measurable objectives for the PR campaign.
3. Programming—Planning and implementing the activities necessary to carry out the objectives.
4. Evaluation—Testing the messages and techniques before using them, monitoring the programming while it's being delivered, and measuring the results of the programming.
5. Stewardship—Maintaining the relationships created through the previous steps.

Central to the ROPES process is the notion that public relations is concerned primarily with creating, developing, and nurturing relationships between an organization and its key publics.[32] To see how this process is carried out, let's look at how Breathe Right used public relations both to build awareness of its nasal strips and to promote alternative uses of the product.

Research. CNS, the original parent company of Breathe Right, was looking to broaden the market for its nasal strips, and through research it found that customers were using the product in new ways. Breathe Right strips were initially designed to hold people's nostrils open while they slept to help prevent snoring. But athletes, especially professional football players, soon began using the nasal strips to get more air into their lungs during competitions. At the 1995 Super Bowl, players wearing Breathe Right strips scored eight of the game's ten touchdowns.[33] CNS wanted to capitalize on this positive publicity, so the company commissioned research to measure various publics' initial perceptions of its product. Such research can include the following elements:

- Public opinion research—Finding out how the public views the company or product, its actions, and its image.
- Content analysis—Analyzing what is being written or said about the company in the media.
- Focus groups—Bringing together members of a particular public to talk about how they perceive an organization, a product, or an issue.[34]

Through consumer research, Breathe Right's manufacturer found that the visibility of the strips during the 1995 Super Bowl had helped build public awareness of the product. According to marketing manager Kirk Hodgdon, "After the game, three out of every four adults had heard of Breathe Right, compared to one in four a year earlier."[35]

Objectives. A successful PR campaign depends on a clear definition of what the client wants to accomplish.

Web 12.3: The Public Relations Society of America defines public relations.

Matthew Stockman/Getty Images

Breathe Right nasal strips have long depended on unpaid endorsements from professional athletes to promote their product. But they got an unexpected boost from racehorse California Chrome when its owner refused to enter him in one of the Triple Crown races if he couldn't have the horse wear nasal strips to help him breathe.

This depends on having clearly measurable objectives for the campaign. In the case of Breathe Right, CNS wanted to build awareness of the product and identify it with athletic performance. Among the objectives CNS set was raising the percentage of the target public that was aware of the Breathe Right brand and raising the percentage of the audience that knew athletes used the strips to improve athletic performance.

Programming. The company decided to build on its campaign of working with NFL trainers. In 1996, it advertised during the Super Bowl, gave strips to everyone attending the game, and publicized its advertising and promotion. CNS combined advertising, promotion, and media relations to build awareness of its product. The promotion involved building relationships directly with football fans by distributing the Breathe Right strips at the game. The company also advertised during the game to highlight the product so that fans would be likely to notice the players wearing the strips.[36] The media relations campaign emphasized the players who wore the strips and publicized the company's status as one of the smallest Super Bowl advertisers.

Evaluation. Evaluation of the campaign happened at every stage of the process. Campaign materials were tested during development, while they were being delivered, and at the conclusion of the campaign. This involved seeing how well the campaign met the objectives that had been set earlier in the campaign.

Breathe Right's evaluation showed that CNS had gained a great deal from its 1996 Super Bowl campaign. Not only did it reap the advertising benefit of reaching the big game's massive audience, but it also generated a significant amount of good publicity for the company. Breathe Right received coverage on the front page of *USA Today*'s money section, which mentioned it as one of the smallest companies to advertise during the Super Bowl.[37] The product also received unpaid endorsements from athletes who said that the product improved their performance by giving them more oxygen, a claim the company itself did not make.

Stewardship. Breathe Right's communication campaign based on working with professional football players and football fans has continued. In 2001, Breathe Right created limited edition colored nasal strips honoring Super Bowl competitors Green Bay Packers and Dallas Cowboys.[38] And, in 2010, Breathe Right had a partnership with the New York Giants. Breathe Right produced Giants-themed nasal strips and had an interactive Web page where fans could post their "game face" wearing the strip.[39] (By this point, Breathe Right's parent company CNS had been acquired by pharmaceutical giant GlaxoSmithKline.)

As a side note, in 2014, nasal strips for horses, produced by a former subsidiary of CNS, brought the perceived performance benefits of nasal strips back to national attention when a controversy emerged over whether star horse California Chrome would be allowed to wear the strips in the Belmont Stakes race in his attempt to be only the twelfth horse ever to win the Triple Crown in thoroughbred racing. And along with the news about California Chrome came the inevitable mention that many NFL athletes have found success using the Breathe Right strips.[40]

Who Are the Publics?

The term *public relations* seems to imply that there is a single monolithic group of people—"the public"—with whom the client needs to communicate. But, in reality,

Web 12.4: Get the rest of the story on California Chrome and the nasal strips.

there are many such groups, since a public is any group of people who share a common set of interests.[41] These could include a company's employees, customers, stockholders, government regulators, or even people who live in the community where a new factory is to be built. In general, however, these publics can be divided into two main groups: internal publics and external publics, as mentioned earlier.

Internal Publics. An important audience for companies, and one that is easy to forget, is the internal public—the people who work for the company. Not only are good relations with employees important for morale and responsiveness, but employees are also an important informal source of news about the company. Through e-mail, chat rooms, phone calls, and media contacts, employees are a central part of a company's communication environment.[42] When Cannon Koo at Kraft makes plans to communicate with his internal publics, he first looks at the food giant's marketing staff.

Corporations use a variety of media to communicate with their internal publics. In the case of employees and managers, this communication can be done through something as simple as a weekly e-mail or as elaborate as a four-color company newspaper. But internal communication is not limited to simple written materials. Web video, closed-circuit television, and even satellite conferences can be used to bring important news to employees. When the Three Mile Island nuclear plant suffered a major accident in 1979, a neighboring utility used videotaped programs to help its employees learn more about nuclear power. This form of education decreased the likelihood that the employees would spread misleading information when they talked with friends and family members.[43]

©iStockphoto.com/alex-mit

Many organizations have started **intranets**, which are computer networks that are open only to members of that organization. Such a network can be used as an internal news source, a collection of corporate documents, or even an interactive communication channel. Canadian public relations agency Thornley Fallis uses an intranet-based video chat service to help employees avoid the flood of e-mails. CEO Joseph Thornley writes, "For us, video is the best communications channel. Unlike e-mail and text, it enables us to read facial expressions, posture, and all the physical clues that add nuance to communications."[44]

Intranets can also go beyond being a channel for important internal communications to serve as a hub for social interaction within the company or organization. These functions could include photo albums, an online swap meet, or even a store featuring company-branded products.[45]

External Publics. Whereas internal publics are well known to an organization, the range of external publics is far larger and relatively less well known. The press is one of the most important external publics because it is through the press that organizations communicate to many of their publics. Building a good relationship with the press is critical. Public relations practitioners as early as Ivy Lee and Edward Bernays found that working with the press during good times would lead to better relations during bad times.[46] Ian Monk, a British journalist turned PR practitioner, says that the relationships he built up as a reporter help him immensely in the PR business: "I deal with former colleagues and protégés all the time, and the relationships I have already built with them are invaluable."[47] For Kraft, external publics would include Velveeta buyers, super-consumers, and anyone who eats macaroni and cheese.

Media relations can be defined as two-way interactions with members of the press. Typically, media relations involve the placement of unpaid messages within the standard programming or news content of the medium. Good media relations, ultimately, are good relations with the public at large. A positive image with the press will often become a positive image with the general public. And a company that the public likes to begin with tends to weather a crisis much better than one that is disliked. According to PR practitioner Susanne Courtney, "Corporate PR is about building up an 'equity' account with groups like the investment community, customers, media, employees and others that a company may need to draw on in a time of need."[48]

Presenting a company to the press is the most visible part of public relations. Press conferences, feature stories for the trade press, photographs, news releases, and streaming video are all tools that PR practitioners use to help manage the messages they send out to various publics through the media. Sometimes the press activities of an agency may be subtler. A PR firm may encourage a prominent leader to write an opinion piece favorable to its client's point of view for publication on the editorial page of a major newspaper. Or it may arrange for a reporter to interview a company president. Or it may simply provide useful background material to reporters.

For Kraft, communication with the professional media is an ongoing relationship. In addition to holding press events, Kraft spokesperson Jody Moore communicated with the advertising trade press through e-mail to make sure that *Ad Age* fully understood the company's Cheespocalypse campaign.[49]

---

intranets: Computer networks designed to communicate with people within an organization. They are used to improve two-way internal communication and contain tools that allow for direct feedback. They are a tool for communicating with internal publics.

media relations: Two-way interactions between PR professionals and members of the press. These can involve press conferences, press releases, video news releases, or interviews. Typically, media relations involve the placement of unpaid messages within the standard programming or news content of the medium.

These unpaid messages gain credibility because they come through the press rather than directly from the corporation. When a company wants to directly control the message it sends to the public, it uses advertising as a part of its PR plan.

Crisis Communication 

Nothing tests an organization's PR ability more than a **crisis**, an event perceived by the public as being damaging to the organization's reputation or image. Al Tortorella, an executive with the PR firm Burson-Marsteller, claims, "A crisis is what the media says it is."[50] What he means is that a problem can be defined as a crisis when it becomes public and begins to be perceived as a crisis. This means that it is possible to prevent a problem from becoming a crisis, but companies should never count on problems being kept secret; they need to have a plan for handling them if they turn into crises.

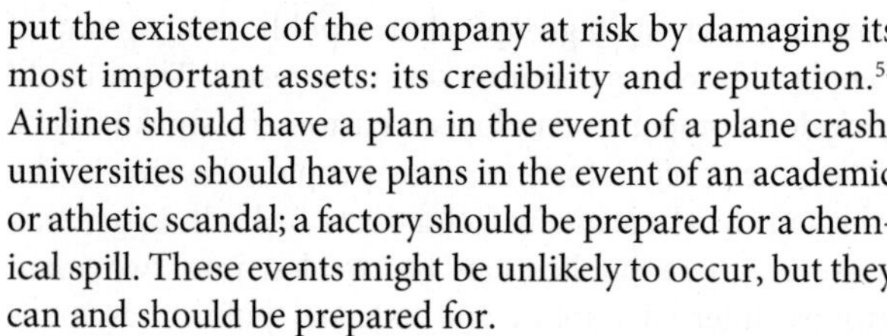

©iStockphoto.com/hb5800

For example, in 1994, computer programmers discovered that the Pentium computer chip designed by Intel could, in certain rare cases, compute a wrong answer. The flaw in the chip was a minor problem affecting only a very few scientists, but no one wanted to have a computer that "made mistakes." Public relations consultant Susan Thomas says that the flurry of negative publicity about the flaw created a crisis for the company:

> What Intel learned from the original Pentium crisis is [that] the difference between the perceived size and actual size of a problem is irrelevant. Just because the chance of the miscalculation happening was slim, it didn't matter. Customers were upset. They wanted responsiveness and answers. . . . When Intel said "only a very small percentage would be affected," it sounded like the company was saying "this isn't worth bothering about."[51]

Intel eventually resolved the crisis by offering all of its customers a "no-questions-asked" replacement chip.

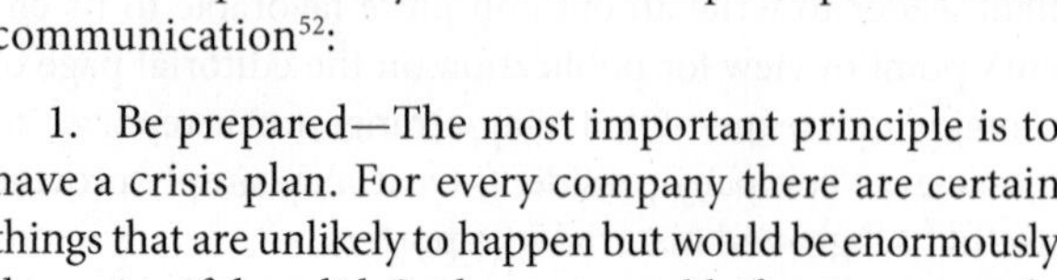

Principles of Crisis Communication. What should a company do when it faces a crisis? In general, it should communicate promptly and honestly with all its publics. More specifically, there are five principles of crisis communication[52]:

1. Be prepared—The most important principle is to have a crisis plan. For every company there are certain things that are unlikely to happen but would be enormously damaging if they did. Such events could, if serious enough, put the existence of the company at risk by damaging its most important assets: its credibility and reputation.[53] Airlines should have a plan in the event of a plane crash; universities should have plans in the event of an academic or athletic scandal; a factory should be prepared for a chemical spill. These events might be unlikely to occur, but they can and should be prepared for.

2. Be honest—One of the problems with lying is that liars are often caught. Cover-ups almost always end up being exposed, and the cover-up looks worse than the original problem. Instead, get the story out and over with quickly. President Richard Nixon's lies about the break-in at the Democratic Party's headquarters in the Watergate building created far more problems for him than did the actual burglary itself. For President Bill Clinton lying about his relationship with Monica Lewinsky was infinitely more damaging to his reputation than was the affair itself.[54] Public relations consultant Bob Wilkerson says, "The truth is going to get out. I want it out of my lips. It's bad enough I've had an incident. It's even worse if it looks like I was trying to cover up."[55]

3. Apologize, and mean it—The company should respond with real action, not just words. In 2006, motorcycle manufacturer Yamaha got caught claiming that its new middleweight sport bike had an engine that would rev up to 17,500 RPM. This was significantly higher than any competing motorcycle. It turned out that both the tachometer and the marketing department were a little optimistic because the motorcycle's true redline was 16,200 RPM. In real life, this discrepancy probably doesn't matter much. But when complaints about the overstated redline started surfacing on the Internet, Yamaha made a simple decision to completely neutralize the crisis. The company sent a letter to everyone who had bought the motorcycle, apologized for the discrepancy, and offered to buy back the bike—including tax, setup, and interest—no questions asked.[56] In addition to having done the right thing, Yamaha squelched the crisis immediately and kept it from damaging the company's otherwise good reputation with motorcyclists.

4. Move quickly—Public relations critics say that how a company reacts in the first few hours after a crisis occurs will determine how the crisis is perceived from that point on. "All crises have a window of opportunity to gain control of 45 minutes to 12 hours," says crisis communication expert Paul Shrivastava.[57] Beyond that point, people will have already decided what they think about the crisis, and once they have made up their minds, they are reluctant to

Web 12.5: How Yamaha effectively handled its public relations problem.

crisis: Any situation that is perceived by the public as being damaging to the reputation or image of an organization. Not all problems develop into crises, but once a situation develops into a crisis, it can be damaging to an organization's reputation even if information change them. In the past, companies could build their response around the time the morning newspapers were published or the nightly news was broadcast, but cable news channels and newspaper Web sites can publish news at any time, and social media will spread unfounded and unverified speculations that traditional news outlets might avoid. Bad news can also spread rapidly over the Internet.[58] Even when things move quickly, the company still needs to act carefully. Crisis management decisions are much more difficult to make than conventional decisions because they deal with things that have important consequences. They also need to be made quickly, while the whole world watches.[59]

5. Communicate with the press and other constituencies—These include the company's own employees and management, stockholders, government regulators, and customers, as well as the press. It was immediate communication with all publics that helped minimize Yamaha's problems with its advertising misinformation.

The application of these principles can be seen in two examples of crisis communication that are discussed in the following subsections. In the first, the company handled both the physical response and the communication response almost perfectly and emerged from the crisis with a good market position and a stronger image than it started with. In the second, mishandled communications led to a blot on the company's reputation that has endured for more than twenty years.

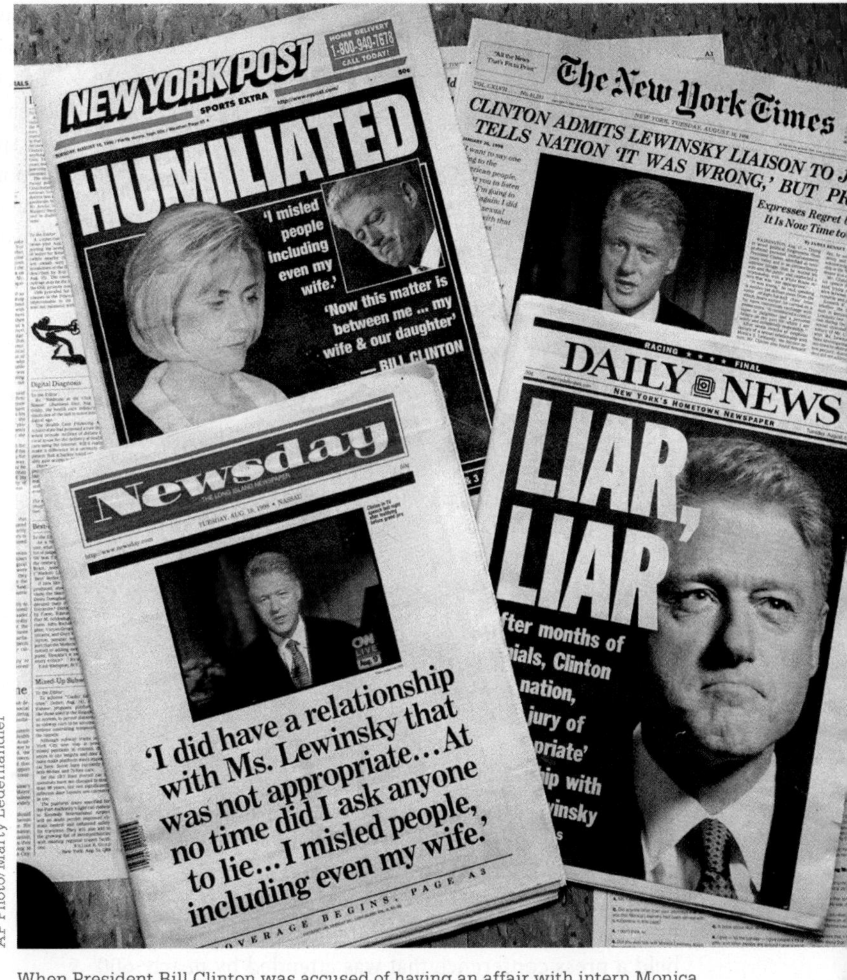

AP Photo/Marty Lederhandler

When President Bill Clinton was accused of having an affair with intern Monica Lewinsky, he initially denied that it had taken place. Months later, he finally admitted that he had lied about the affair. In the long run, critics say Clinton was damaged more by his denials than by the news of the affair itself.

The Tylenol Scare. In September 1982, the consumer products giant Johnson & Johnson faced a crisis that could have destroyed one of its most important brands, Tylenol. Seven people in the Chicago area died after taking cyanide-laced Extra Strength Tylenol capsules. The deaths set off what the *New York Times* called "the biggest consumer product scare in history."[60] (The perpetrator was never caught.) But Johnson & Johnson, with the help of PR agency Burson-Marsteller, managed to preserve the brand and the company's reputation with a combination of appropriate ethical action and good public relations.

The first thing the company did right was to be entirely honest with the media and public. The praise it subsequently received for its openness improved its image.[61]

The next thing the company did right was to take immediate action in response to the tampering. As soon as Johnson & Johnson learned of the problem, it immediately stopped advertising the product and took it off the market in Chicago.[62]

Throughout the crisis, Burson-Marsteller conducted nightly telephone surveys to measure public opinion. When those polls showed that the public feared that other Tylenol capsules might be tampered with, Johnson & Johnson took the product off the market nationwide.[63] The company was perceived as acting responsibly, and in fact it *was* acting responsibly.

Johnson & Johnson had clearly won the first PR battle and was being perceived as a responsible company that had been the victim of a vicious attack. The second battle was the campaign to rebuild trust in the Tylenol brand.

In November 1982, Johnson & Johnson announced the relaunch of Extra Strength Tylenol with the news that the product would now be sold in a triple-sealed container. Along with the expected marketing support, Johnson & Johnson engaged in an extensive PR campaign that utilized educational advertising, media appearances, and personal contacts.

The company sent out more than 2,000 sales representatives to meet with major retailers and doctors. An advertising campaign informed people about the new tamper-resistant packaging, and Johnson & Johnson announced the relaunch of the brand in a thirty-city

Web 12.6: In the fall of 2014, the NFL had a crisis with star players committing violence against women.

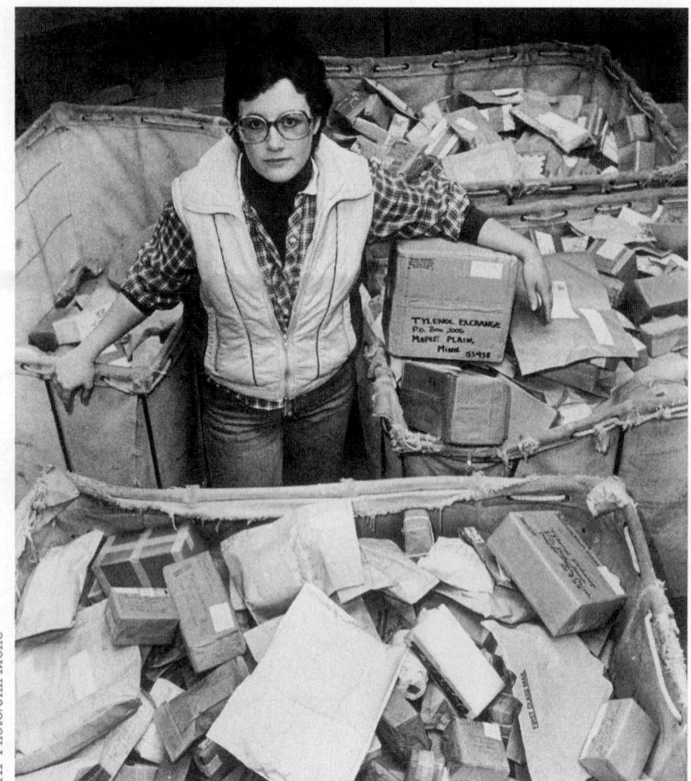

AP Photo/Jim Mone

Johnson & Johnson had to handle the recall of millions of containers of Tylenol in 1982 after tainted capsules led to the deaths of seven people in the Chicago area.

teleconference delivered via satellite. Simultaneously, it held a press conference that was attended by nearly 600 journalists. Finally, Johnson & Johnson's CEO, James Burke, appeared on both *60 Minutes* and the daytime talk program *The Phil Donahue Show.*

The campaign was a success. Before the crisis, Tylenol had had a 37 percent share of the pain reliever market; this number dropped to 7 percent during the tampering scare. But within a month of the relaunch Tylenol was back to 28 percent of the market, and it eventually regained its status as the industry leader.[64]

Johnson & Johnson succeeded in protecting its brand and reputation for a number of reasons. First, few people blamed the company for the tampering; the fault appeared to lay with an individual beyond the span of the company's control. Second, the company acted quickly and responsibly in the interests of consumers. It was also open with its various publics, freely admitting what it did and didn't know. Finally, the company actively worked through the difficult situation and engaged the press by viewing it as an ally instead of as an adversary.

The* Exxon Valdez *and BP Oil Spills. On March 24, 1989, the oil tanker *Exxon Valdez* ran aground in Alaska's Prince William Sound, spilling 240,000 barrels of crude oil into the ocean. This oil soon washed up on shore, coating beaches, birds, and sea life in an environmentally sensitive area. Exxon spent more than $2 billion on the cleanup of the oil spill, but it still ended up with a tarnished image. Former reporter and network news president William Small notes that no company ever spent as much as Exxon did following the oil spill and still came out looking so bad.[65]

Exxon's post-spill image problem had numerous causes that illustrate the difference between Johnson & Johnson's response to a crisis and Exxon's:

- Perception of fault—Unlike the Tylenol tampering case, Exxon was considered at fault for the oil spill. Exxon's first problem was that it was the company's tanker that had run aground. It is difficult from a PR point of view to defend a company that has done something wrong.[66]
- Lack of effective crisis plan—Exxon never developed a crisis plan for dealing with such a serious oil spill. Although Exxon shared responsibility with the Coast Guard for the lack of proper facilities, the fact that it did not have cleanup equipment in Alaska forced it to shoulder the blame after the spill.[67]
- Failure to take immediate control—Exxon did not take immediate control of the flow of information. Not until a week after the spill did Exxon's CEO, Lawrence Rawl, make public comments. Meanwhile, numerous heartbreaking images of fouled wildlife started coming from the area. Almost all the press coverage of the spill was negative. In fact, Exxon made it actively difficult for reporters to get the company's point of view. The company's initial response was reportedly handled by a one-person PR office in Houston that had trouble coping with all the requests for information. Moreover, Exxon held all its news briefings for reporters in Valdez, Alaska, which had limited communication channels, instead of in a more accessible location, such as New York.[68]
- Failure to accept responsibility immediately—Exxon didn't initially accept ethical responsibility for the spill and apologize. The company started off by trying to spread the blame, claiming that the Coast Guard, Alaska environmental officials, and the weather were also responsible. Whether or not these claims were valid, the press and the public saw Exxon as responsible. As one Alaska official put it, "I would suggest it's Exxon's tanker that ran up on the rocks."[69]

The final blow to Exxon's image came in the fall after the oil spill, when a memo from a company official was leaked to the press. The memo said that Exxon would end the cleanup effort whenever it chose to, that it would do nothing in the winter, and that it did not promise to return in the spring. The memo made the company look arrogant and uncaring.[70] Exxon eventually accepted responsibility for the oil spill and the cleanup, but by then the company's image was damaged irrevocably.

Web 12.7: Examine how Exxon and BP handled public relations during the major spills.

SECRET 4 Even twenty-five years after the accident, the *Exxon Valdez* remained the standard to which environmental disasters were compared. When the Deepwater Horizon oil rig that was drilling for the London-based BP PLC exploded and sank in the Gulf of Mexico during the summer of 2010, triggering the world's largest oil spill, people immediately began comparing it to the Exxon spill. Critics contrasted BP's cleanup efforts to Exxon's, but they also compared public relations responses. Of course, the current media world full of online social media, blogs, and multiple 24/7 cable channels that faced BP was very different from the one Exxon had to deal with. Yet the issues facing the two oil companies remained similar: Both tried to focus on technological issues rather than the effects on people, and both companies tried to shift blame away from themselves and onto others. But most of all, it appears that neither company had a plan to deal with a major oil spill. Communications professor Kathleen Fearn-Banks told the *New York Times* blog *Greenwire*, "BP never had a plan in place for the worst-case scenario or they would have put it in place. I don't think it's a question of money . . . They absolutely don't know what to do at all."[71] (This is a prime example of Secret Four—Nothing's new: Everything that happened in the past will happen again.)

AP Photo/Dave Martin

Despite the lessons learned after the catastrophic *Exxon Valdez* oil spill that had occurred twenty-one years earlier, the BP oil company seemed ill prepared to deal with its wide range of publics following the 2010 Deepwater Horizon spill in the Gulf of Mexico.

Public Relations and the Internet

In the late 1980s and early 1990s, the PR industry acquired a new friend and enemy—the Internet. The Internet gave PR practitioners a new way to research and to distribute information, but it also provided a powerful new channel for the spreading of rumors that had the potential to develop into crises.

A New Information Channel. Among many other things, the Internet has given the PR industry a new tool. Now companies can distribute press releases, background information, and photos to the media through e-mail and Web sites. If a company's Web site or social media feed has a good reputation, it can become the first place reporters go to for information. Since reporters often start by going online to research articles, placing statistics and facts on a Web site can affect the way a company is covered.

The Internet has also given companies a means of bypassing the traditional media and communicating directly with various publics. Customers, stockholders, and even critics may go to a company's Web site in search of information. A Web site also ensures that a company's point of view is being presented the way the company intends it to be. Along with having a good Web site, companies need to make sure that their site will show up at the top of the list of search results for their company. It can be embarrassing if a company's critics appear above the company itself in a Web search.[72]

The Internet also allows companies to find out what people are saying about them. Many organizations monitor Web sites and social media to see what complaints and kudos are coming their way. Public relations practitioners may join chats and discussion groups to help shape what is being said about their clients. Of course, with millions of Web sites and social media accounts in existence, just finding out what is being said about a company can be a massive undertaking.[73]

Crisis management consultant Jonathan Bernstein says that online media create significant new PR challenges. He writes that organizations need to consider the following:

SECRET 5 The Internet gives critics access to the world without the checks and balances of traditional journalism. Prior to the Internet, the only way to reach a broad, general audience was through the professional media, which might not always be a fan of your company but would probably treat you fairly. Many Internet sites can be biased or don't engage in editorial oversight or fact-checking.

- Once a crisis hits the Internet, it can't be contained. It used to be that a local news story would stay local. Now, once a story is posted to a newspaper's or television station's Web site, it's gone national.
- The Internet makes it easy for critics to leak confidential information. This can include not just reports of confidential information, but also images of original documents or recordings of phone calls.
- In the absence of good information, rumors will flourish on the Internet. Of course, this problem isn't unique to the Internet. Anytime an organization

Screenshot: The Today Show 04/16/2009

Domino's Pizza faced an enormous image crisis in 2009 when two employees at a North Carolina store posted a prank video of themselves tampering with pizzas and subs.

doesn't provide creditable information, rumors and gossip will fill the gap.[74] But the Internet can accelerate the process by which rumors travel.

- These considerations illustrate perfectly the importance of Secret Five—New media are always scary.

Coming to Terms With Social Media. One of the great challenges that online media bring to the public relations business is that they are a continually moving target. Just when PR professionals think they have blogs and the Web figured out, along comes the rise of social media such as Facebook, Twitter, Pinterest, and Instagram. Social media expert Pamela Seiple has written that PR professionals need to realize that social media are an opportunity for interactions with various publics, not just a channel to send out information. She notes that, through social media, stories about your company's brand can spread and mutate at a much faster rate than in the past. According to her, "If your company is not participating in social media today, it's missing an opportunity to spread its message and missing valuable—and even damaging—conversations that could be taking place about your brand." One of the most important uses for social media, according to Seiple, is building ongoing relationships with publics, including customers, vendors, opinion makers, and the press.[75]

UCB is a pharmaceutical company that makes drugs to treat epilepsy. Trish Nettleship, as its director of social media, wanted to work with a social media service that could help epilepsy patients have a reliable source of information and connect with other people suffering from the same problems. So she had UCB partner with a medical social media site called PatientsLikeMe. In addition, UCB continued to develop Epilepsy Advocate, its presence on Facebook. But these social media sites wouldn't help UCB communicate back and forth with patients if its social media managers had to go through a lengthy approval process before posting anything to the sites. In the past, every social media post from the company had to go through a two-week-long approval process with visits to the medical, legal, and regulatory departments. But by the time the response had been approved, the original poster would have lost interest. So UCB trained its in-house managers on what they could or couldn't post online, and then gave them the authority to respond immediately. As Leigh Householder reported for *Health Care Communication News*, "the team was able to refocus . . . on actively supporting patients and increasing the general amount of discussion (online and in the exam room) about partial-onset seizures."[76] This gets at the heart of what companies need to do as they move into interacting with publics through social media. The old rules simply won't keep up with the new tools.

Video 12.2: Find out how Domino's and Pizza Hut reacted to ugly videos created by rogue employees.

Web 12.8: Read the backstory on UCB and social media.

Domino's: Fighting Back Against Social Media. It used to be that the worst media a company had to worry about was a scathing story by an investigative journalist on a program such as *60 Minutes*. But today a corporation's worst PR nightmare can come from amateur-produced video posted on video-sharing sites, such as YouTube, and then publicized through social media sites, such as Twitter and YouTube. That's what Domino's Pizza discovered in April 2009 when two employees in Conover, North Carolina, posted a video showing one of them putting cheese up his nose and then placing it on a sandwich, blowing his nose on a sandwich, and farting on a sandwich. The other employee narrated the video with comments:

> In about five minutes it'll be sent out on delivery where somebody will be eating these, yes, eating them, and little did they know that cheese was in his nose and that there was some lethal gas that ended up on their salami.[77]

Once the video was posted on YouTube, word about it spread rapidly online through Twitter and other social media, and the video quickly racked up more than 1 million views.

The Domino's Pizza chain attempted to respond quickly and responsibly, but it may have spoken out too late in the rapidly changing environment of the Internet. The company responded publicly to the video within forty-eight hours of finding out about it, delaying its response reportedly to keep from drawing further attention to the video. Domino's eventual response included a YouTube video featuring company president Patrick Doyle, a complete cleaning of the store where the video was shot, and a revision of the company's hiring practices. The company also started a Twitter account with which to respond to customers.[78]

Richard Levick of the PR firm Levick Strategic Communications told *Advertising Age* that Domino's handled the crisis well after its initial delay in responding: "After the first 24 hours, they were largely textbook. They started a Twitter account, separated themselves from the villains, shut down the store, apologized, went to their demographic, went to YouTube—I think all of that is great."[79]

Levick said that companies need to do several things to prepare for online crisis communication:

- Identify your crisis team—This includes PR professionals, lawyers, and digital communication specialists.
- Imagine your nightmare scenarios—Make sure that you have the online resources so that when a crisis hits and people start searching for information, they come to your Web site first.
- Track the blogosphere and other social media—Make sure you know what people are saying about you, and be responsive to the people who are talking about your company.
- Don't wait—You have a very limited time to respond.[80]

SECRET 2 Following the posting of the video, the two employees were identified by bloggers, arrested, and charged with distributing prohibited foods. Although the Domino's Pizza chain has largely recovered from the crisis created by the video, the North Carolina store where the video was shot has not. After closing briefly for cleaning following the posting of the video, the store closed for good five months later.[81] Note that while this story was covered by legacy media, it really moved through social media, thus illustrating Secret Two—There are no mainstream media. The Domino's story is also an illustration of **SECRET 4** Nothing's new: Everything that happened in the past will happen again. How so? In February 2014, a Pizza Hut in Kermit, West Virginia, had to explain why a security video had surfaced of one of its district managers urinating in a dish-washing sink at the restaurant. The video was subsequently posted to YouTube where it accumulated more than 600,000 views in three months. The video, and subsequent news coverage of it, resulted in the manager being fired, the restaurant being first temporarily and then permanently closed, and the parent company apologizing and pointing out to the news media that it doesn't tolerate the sort of behavior depicted in the video.[82]

Rumors on the Internet. Controlling the spread of rumors has always been a problem for the PR industry, but the growth of the Internet has allowed rumors to spread faster and more frequently than ever before.

Seattle-based coffee giant Starbucks faced an Internet rumor that the company did not support the war in Iraq or anyone who was fighting in it. According to the *Seattle Times*, the rumor got started when a Marine sergeant sent an e-mail to friends. In the e-mail, he claimed that Starbucks had written a letter saying the company did not support the troops or the war in response to another Marine who had asked for free coffee. The e-mail then circulated extensively on the Internet. Several months later, the sergeant sent out an e-mail apologizing for the incorrect statement, but the apology didn't get nearly the amount of attention that the initial accusation did. Starbucks responded to the rumor through a rumor-control page on its Web site and through an entry on Snopes.com, the urban legend debunking site. Despite the company's active response, the rumor continued to circulate for more than two years after it got started. As a precautionary measure, Starbucks monitors blog and Web coverage of the company, but it doesn't respond to every rumor.[83]

Questioning the Media

How do social media change the public relations process? Can you think of an example of how social media content has helped or hurt an organization? Why do you think this happened?

Public Relations and Society

This chapter has so far looked at public relations largely from the point of view of either PR firms or their clients. But it is also useful to look at it from the public's perspective. Public relations shapes the news we receive through newspapers, magazines, television, radio, and even the Internet. In the form of "spin control," it attempts to shape our view of politicians and public policy, and it is also a central component of social movements.

Public Relations Supports the News Business

Public relations plays a significant role in what is presented as news in the media. Sociologists David Altheide and Robert Snow argue that public relations is an integral part of the news business because most of the events—including crime and disaster reporting—covered by the media were created by PR practitioners to obtain coverage for their clients.[84] Just how much of the news originates with public relations?

Depending on how it is measured, anywhere from 40 to 90 percent of all news starts out as public relations. The *Columbia Journalism Review* (*CJR*) tried to narrow this down by studying an issue of the *Wall Street Journal*. The researchers selected 111 stories from the paper. The companies mentioned in the stories were then contacted and asked to send a copy of their original press releases. *CJR* found that 72 percent of the stories they were able to analyze were based almost exclusively on material from a press release. The

MAI/Greg E. Mathieson/Landov

Press secretary Josh Earnest is responsible for making sure that President Barack Obama gets his message out to reporters in a way that portrays the administration in the best possible light.

study estimated that 45 percent of all the stories in the *Wall Street Journal* that day had been based on press releases, and that 27 percent of the actual news space was devoted to press releases.[85] The newspaper's executive editor estimated that 90 percent of the stories in the paper started with a company's announcement.

Questioning the Media

What do spin doctors do? Do our news media pay too much attention to spin doctors? Why or why not? Whom do spin doctors help?

How does this happen? Think about a typical news day. Most news coming from Washington, D.C., involves a press conference, a speech, a press release, or an event created specifically to be covered by the media. A scientific report on an environmental issue is published, and both environmentalists and industry groups hold press conferences to provide background information. A bank robber is arrested, and the police hold a media briefing. Even a basketball game will be reported using statistics provided by the sports information office and quotes from an official post-game interview session hosted for the media.

Although a lot of news may originate in PR efforts, executives and other individuals covered by the media sometimes have an exaggerated sense of what public relations can accomplish. One movie studio boss reportedly told an applicant for a PR position, "Your responsibility will be, if I step out of my limousine and my pants fall down, you make sure that no one gets a photo to the press."[86] That's a guarantee no PR practitioner can make.

Public Relations and the Government

Along with the general public and media, the various levels of government are major external publics. Through their government relations departments, PR firms represent their clients before the federal government, federal agencies, state legislatures, and even municipal bodies. As businesses face increasing government regulation, they have increased their efforts to work with government to shape legislation and regulations that are favorable to their interests.[87] Government relations includes lobbying for laws that will best meet the needs of the organization, as well as simply building goodwill with legislators and regulatory bodies. The Center for Responsive Politics, a nonpartisan research group that studies the influence of money on elections and public policy, estimates that, in 2012, there were 12,431 active, registered lobbyists in Washington who spent approximately $3.23 billion trying to influence the federal government on policy issues.[88] But that figure, as big as it is, only tells part of the story. Work by the Sunlight Foundation, another nonprofit focused on open government, found that for every dollar spent on reported lobbying, another dollar was spent on influencing activities that didn't meet the narrow legal definition of lobbying that was required to be reported. Thus, they estimate the total amount spent on "government relations" in 2012 to be $6.7 billion.[89]

The government itself is a major practitioner of public relations. All elected federal officials have a press secretary, and many have a communications director. The various agencies themselves have PR offices. The role of the political press secretary is a challenging one, as the spokesperson has to serve his or her boss while still dealing honestly with the press and the public. Sometimes this involves being evasive. As one congressional press secretary told the Washington, D.C., paper the *Hill*,

> It is a matter of practice and experience and being able to steer a conversation toward issues you are looking to advance . . . The golden rule is you don't answer the question you are asked, you answer the question you want to answer.[90]

Lanny Davis, who advised President Bill Clinton on damage control, says that when the press and the public are interested in an issue, the spokesperson only has one option: "Tell the truth, tell it all, tell it early, tell it yourself."[91] During the Monica Lewinsky sex scandal, President Clinton ignored the "tell the truth" rule, and the scandal stuck with him throughout the remainder of his second term in office. Had he acknowledged the affair when the story first broke rather than denying it, the story might well have blown over quickly. That's what happened when President Barack Obama

Box 12.1 "Tricks of the Trade" for Government Press Secretaries

The *Hill* reporter Betsy Rothstein lists the following common "tricks of the trade" press secretaries use in dealing with reporters they don't want to talk to:

Say "I will call you back" and then don't.

Repeat the same phrase over and over.

Try to talk the reporter out of writing the story.

Act brusque and distant.

Don't return phone calls until the day after the deadline.

Talk in short sentences.

Act as though you are in a hurry and need to get off the phone as soon as possible.

Source: Betsy Rothstein, "Capital Living: The Fine Art of Flacking," *The Hill*, February 22, 2006.

revealed his college-days drug use in his 1995 memoir, *Dreams From My Father*. The book allowed him to time the revelation of his drug use early in his political career and kept others from using it against him.[92]

The U.S. military has been actively involved in public relations since World War I. Although the military's initial PR efforts were intended to recruit volunteers, they were also interacting with the press. Today the Armed Forces Radio and Television Service provides internal public relations in the form of radio and television broadcasts for service people overseas. There are also public information activities and community relations for the areas surrounding military bases.[93]

Spin Control: A More Personal Form of Public Relations

A new kind of public relations, known as spin control, has risen to the forefront since the 1970s. Rather than simply providing press releases, events, and background information, so-called spin doctors attempt to influence how a story will be portrayed and discussed. Newspaper columnist and former speechwriter William Safire suggests that the word *spin* came from the idea of spinning a yarn—that is, telling a story. It may also have a sports connotation, as in putting a spin on a tennis or billiard ball.[94]

John Scanlon, a New York City publicist, is often cited as a top spin doctor. He is acquainted with many members of the national press corps and will call them when he considers a story unbalanced—or at least contrary to his client's interests. He also sends out frequent mailings to influential people in which he presents his point of view regarding events in the news. Scanlon's goal is not so much to give information to the press as to influence how stories are interpreted—that is, to control the spin put on them.

Here are some of the things spin doctors do:

- Selectively leak information in advance, hoping that reporters will pay more attention to it than to information received later.
- Contact members of the press immediately after an event in an effort to get them to adopt the desired spin or interpretation of the event.
- Push the idea that there are always two sides to every story. As Scanlon notes, "What seems to be true is not necessarily the case when we look at it and we dissect it and we take it apart, and we turn it around and we look at it from a different perspective."[95]

Public Relations and Political Activism

Not all public relations is practiced by professionals working for large agencies. As numerous political activists have shown, public relations can be an effective tool for social change as well. In 2005, the farm labor group Coalition of Immokalee Workers won a battle with Yum Brands, the parent company of Taco Bell, over rights and pay for migrant workers. The laborers engaged in a work boycott against Taco Bell's produce farmers, held an extended hunger strike to draw attention to their cause, carried out a 230-mile protest walk, and organized a consumer boycott against Taco Bell. Despite the fact that migrant farmworkers are typically seen as a relatively powerless group, the workers were able to force a change in the fast-food business.[96]

Public Relations and the Civil Rights Movement

Civil rights leader Martin Luther King Jr. displayed a brilliant understanding of public relations throughout the campaign to integrate the South in the 1950s and 1960s. King knew that it would take a combination of action, words, and visibility in the media to eliminate segregation laws and integrate lunch counters, restrooms, water fountains, and businesses. He practiced public relations in churches, hotel rooms, and even jail.

In 1963, King and the Southern Christian Leadership Conference, a civil rights group, wanted to do something highly visible that would let the entire nation see the evils of segregation. The goal of the campaign was to hold nonviolent demonstrations and acts of resistance that would force segregated stores and businesses to be opened to African Americans.

King and his colleagues picked Birmingham, Alabama, as one of their targets, in part because the city's police commissioner was Eugene "Bull" Connor. Connor was a

Web 12.9: Learn how Dr. King demonstrated his understanding of public relations.

MEDIA TRANSFORMATIONS

Old and New Tools for Integrated Marketing Communication

When West Virginia University wants to reach out to its many publics, it needs to use a wide range of tools, ranging from old-school techniques like newsletters and press releases all the way to interactions through social media.

The biggest challenge WVU's integrated marketing communication (IMC) staff faces is the wide range of publics with which it needs to communicate and build relationships. WVU is a big institution, with approximately 10,000 employees across all of its campuses, 5,000 employees at its hospital and in its health

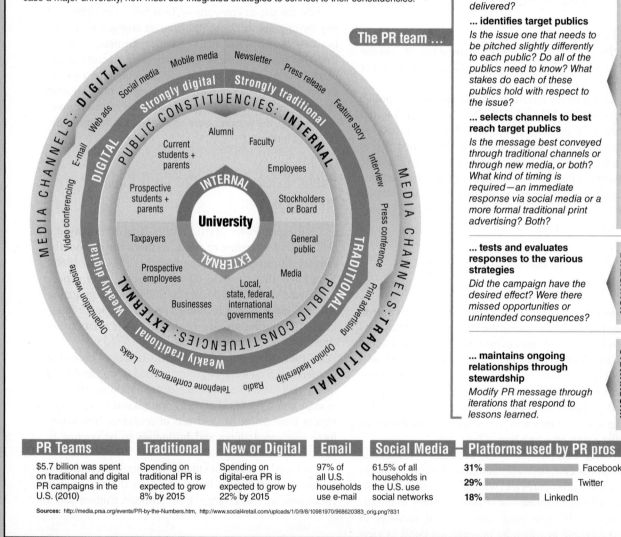

A University's Integrated Communication Strategy for the Digital Age

Various media channels available to public relations teams have changed. Organizations, in this case a major university, now must use integrated strategies to connect to their constituencies.

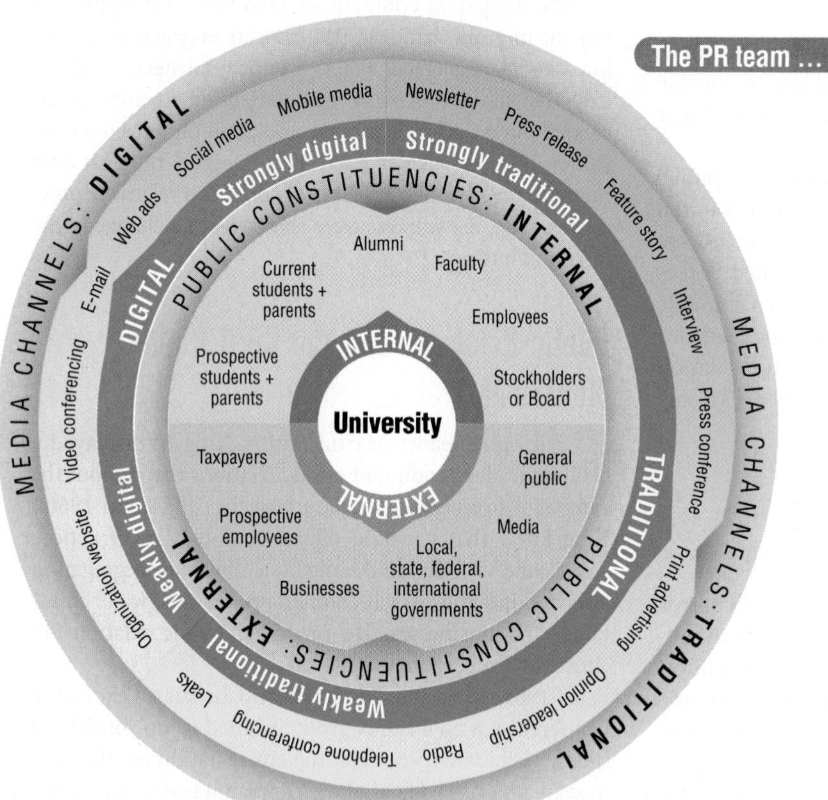

The PR team ...

PROGRAMMING

... researches, analyzes need, crafts message

Is there a problem or crisis to respond to, or some kind of special message or information that needs to be delivered?

... identifies target publics

Is the issue one that needs to be pitched slightly differently to each public? Do all of the publics need to know? What stakes do each of these publics hold with respect to the issue?

... selects channels to best reach target publics

Is the message best conveyed through traditional channels or through new media, or both? What kind of timing is required—an immediate response via social media or a more formal traditional print advertising? Both?

EVALUATION

... tests and evaluates responses to the various strategies

Did the campaign have the desired effect? Were there missed opportunities or unintended consequences?

STEWARDSHIP

... maintains ongoing relationships through stewardship

Modify PR message through iterations that respond to lessons learned.

PR Teams	Traditional	New or Digital	Email	Social Media
$5.7 billion was spent on traditional and digital PR campaigns in the U.S. (2010)	Spending on traditional PR is expected to grow 8% by 2015	Spending on digital-era PR is expected to grow by 22% by 2015	97% of all U.S. households use e-mail	61.5% of all households in the U.S. use social networks

Platforms used by PR pros

31%	Facebook
29%	Twitter
18%	LinkedIn

Sources: http://media.prsa.org/events/PR-by-the-Numbers.htm, http://www.social4retail.com/uploads/1/0/9/8/10981970/968620383_orig.png?831

sciences program, and nearly 30,000 undergraduate and graduate students. And that's just the beginning of university's list of publics. There are the parents for these students and more than 160,000 alumni supporters, not to mention prospective students and opinion leaders throughout the state.[97]

The central goal for the IMC office is telling the story of the university to that long list of publics. "The exciting part of this job is that as a public university we are at ground zero of telling the story of the American dream for many people," according to Chris Martin, the former vice president for university relations at WVU. "We are a nexus of journalism, multimedia storytelling, and traditional communication."

The IMC staff at West Virginia University is filled with people who have journalistic talent who understand storytelling and content marketing and who have communication strategy skills and technical skills. "WVU needs people who can tell stories on various platforms," Martin says, pointing out that it's no longer enough to send out press releases to legacy media and hope the stories get broadcast or published.

Increasingly, WVU is communicating directly with its publics. This means it has to establish a relationship of trust with its wide-ranging audiences. It means the university has to be willing to talk openly and honestly about the bad news as well as the good. One issue Martin had to deal with while at WVU was when a crew for the *I'm Shmacked* college-partying documentary showed up in Morgantown on a sunny and warm St. Patrick's Day to shoot video of WVU students drinking more than their recommended share of alcohol. When the video hit YouTube, there was a lot of chatter about it on social media sites such as Twitter and Facebook.

"We were prepared to deal with occasions where students will have an alcohol-fueled situation," Martin said. "But this one caught us somewhat by surprise because of the good weather." So while WVU's IMC office did have to deal with some fallout from the video, Martin says people have to keep things in perspective. "Look at what people were calling viral video. It initially had about 200,000 hits, but a viral video of the WVU marching band on Veterans Day had more than 2 million views."

Martin says her greater concern at the time was a story she missed getting out:

> The day after the *I'm Shmacked* video went online, I went to a presentation by a Nobel Prize winning physicist that had 400 people trying to get into a 350 seat theater. And I thought, "Shame on us for not getting press here for this story." We have all these students packed in here for a lecture on the origins of the universe. Why didn't we anticipate this? Why didn't we have a crew here?
>
> That's really where you have to be vigilant. Stereotypes exist because the total volume of narrative is so thin. So you need to tell a bigger story. And that's how you really have to handle an issue like *I'm Shmacked*.

Media Transformations Questions

- **WHAT** tools does a university IMC office use to communicate with its various publics?
- **HOW** should an IMC office respond to negative material showing up on social media? Is it too late to respond when the material actually shows up?
- **CAN** an IMC office just get rid of old tools in the era of social media?

Video 12.3: Watch how WVU communicates with its publics.

racist who could be counted on to attack peaceful marchers. King's campaign was called Project C, for confrontation, and it included press conferences, leaflets, and demonstrations in front of hundreds of reporters and photographers. Starting in April 1963, African American volunteers marched in the streets, held sit-ins at segregated lunch counters, and boycotted local businesses. As the protests started, so did the arrests. The story was covered by the *New York Times* and the *Washington Post.* King and his colleagues knew that all the protests in the world would be ineffective if they were not covered by the press and that being beaten up by police would accomplish little if no photographers were present to document the event.

David Halberstam, who was a newspaper reporter in the South at the time, commented on the civil rights leaders' understanding of public relations:

> The key was to lure the beast of segregation out in the open. Casting was critical: King and his aides were learning that they needed to find the right venue, a place where the resistance was likely to be fierce, and the right local official to play the villain. Neither was a problem: King had no trouble finding men like . . . Bull Connor, who were in their own way looking for him, just as he was looking for them.[98]

On Good Friday, King and Ralph Abernathy joined in the marching so that they would be arrested. While King was in jail, he wrote the "Letter from Birmingham Jail," which was smuggled out and published as a brochure. His eloquent words, given added force by having been written in jail, were reprinted across the country.

After King was released, he and his followers raised the stakes. Adults would no longer march and be arrested;

AP Photo/Bill Hudson

In 1963 Americans were shocked by images, such as this one from photographer Bill Hudson, of police attacking civil rights marchers with dogs, fire hoses, and clubs.

instead, children became the vanguard of the movement. The images, which appeared in print media throughout the world, were riveting. In his biography of King, Stephen Oates wrote, "Millions of readers in America—and millions overseas—stared at pictures of police dogs lunging at young marchers, of firemen raking them with jet streams, of club-wielding cops pinning a Negro woman to the ground."[99]

King faced criticism for allowing young people to face the dangers of marching in Birmingham. But he responded promptly by criticizing the white press, asking the reporters where they had been "during the centuries when our segregated social system had been misusing and abusing Negro children."[100]

Although there was rioting in Birmingham and King's brother's house was bombed, the campaign was ultimately successful. Business owners took down the "WHITE" and "COLORED" signs from drinking fountains and bathrooms, and African Americans were allowed to eat at the lunch counters and sit on the buses. The successful protest in Birmingham set the stage for the march on Washington in August 1963, during which King gave his famous "I Have a Dream" speech.[101]

Chapter SUMMARY

Public relations (PR) developed out of the press agentry of the late 1800s. Publicity firms used one-way communication, deceptive techniques, and bribery. By the beginning of the twentieth century, large corporations such as railroads and utilities realized that they needed to develop more sophisticated relationships with the press if they hoped to control their images.

Ivy Lee and Edward L. Bernays are generally considered to be the founders of public relations as a profession. Lee was among the first press agents to recognize that dealing with the press promptly and truthfully was the best way to obtain positive coverage for his clients. In 1906, he codified this approach in his "Declaration of Principles." Bernays wrote the first book about public relations and taught the first college course on the subject.

During World War I, the federal government realized the value of public relations and used a variety of techniques to build support for U.S. participation in the war. Public relations continued to grow as a profession as businesses became increasingly regulated and the public began to distrust both businesses and the government.

Public relations can be seen as performing three main functions: informing, persuading, and integrating (bringing together) publics, both internal and external. Among the most important publics are the media. Effective public relations generally includes both communication and action. The PR process consists of four steps: (1) defining the problem, (2) planning, (3) communicating, and (4) evaluating. Successful companies work at communicating with their publics during both good times and times of crisis. The rise of the Internet and instantaneous communication not controlled by major media has forced the public relations industry to speed up its rate of response to problems and to deal with a wider range of problems. Public relations is used by a wide range of organizations, including corporations, the government, and activist groups.

Keep up-to-date with content from the author's blog.

Take the chapter quiz.

Key TERMS

public relations (PR) 306
public 306
press agentry 306
engineering consent 308
opinion leadership 310
intranets 313
media relations 313
crisis 314

Concept REVIEW

One-way versus two-way communication

The professionalization of public relations

The public relations process

Managing a public relations crisis

The impact of the Internet on public relations

The relationship between public relations and the news business

The uses of public relations by the government and government officials

The uses of public relations by advocacy groups

Student STUDY SITE

Sharpen your skills with SAGE edge at **edge.sagepub.com/hanson5e**

SAGE edge for Students provides a personalized approach to help you accomplish your coursework goals in an easy-to-use learning environment.

chapter

13

Media Law

Free Speech and Fairness

Library of Congress

Barbara Ringer, the only woman in the room at this hearing in the 1960s on copyright revision, sued the Library of Congress successfully for sex discrimination after she was passed over for the top position in the Copyright Office.

When you record a television show on your digital video recorder (DVR), include a quote from a book in a newspaper review, or register the copyright of an article you have written, chances are you are benefiting from the work of Barbara A. Ringer. Ringer, who went to work for the Copyright Office in the Library of Congress in 1949, right after she graduated from law school, has had as much influence on U.S. copyright law as anyone in the twentieth century.

The copyright laws Ringer faced when she started at the Library of Congress were written in 1909, not long after Mark Twain fought for international copyright protection for his books. As Matt Schudel of the *Washington Post* has pointed out, the 1909 version of the law was written before there was television, commercial radio, copying machines, or the recording industry.[1] This was an era in which the hot new music distribution technology was the player piano. There were no DVRs, no iPods, no file sharing.

Although her work predated the Internet and digital distribution, Ringer could see new media technology was coming. In a 1975 speech, she said, "The basic human rights of individual authors throughout the world are being sacrificed more and more on the altar of . . . the technological revolution."[2] Ringer worked with a simple premise: Authors, songwriters, and performers ought to be protected. As an example of the kind of policies that Ringer was seeking to change, the Copyright Act of 1909 exempted owners of coin-operated music boxes from having to pay royalties to composers and performers. As a result, when the jukebox came on the scene, composers and performers were cut out of royalties from that source as well.[3]

Ringer also fought to make sure that the law would protect authors and artists even if they didn't follow every proper step in registering their copyright. "My philosophy has always been to reward authors for what they do, not to punish them for what they don't do," she said.[4]

Ringer worked for twenty-one years on the legislation that became the Copyright Act of 1976. Among the provisions Ringer put into the law were the following:

- The concept of fair use—Authors and reviewers could quote briefly from works without having to secure permission.

LEARNING OBJECTIVES

After studying this chapter, you will be able to:

1 Describe the development of a free press in the United States.

2 Discuss the limits that have been placed on free expression and other First Amendment rights, including those put in place since September 11, 2001.

3 Explain the three elements that must be present for libel to occur and the four major defenses against libel.

4 Name the four major forms of invasion of privacy.

5 Discuss the issue of whether the press can be legally required to behave ethically using three Supreme Court case examples.

6 Explain how the media industry is controlled through copyright law, broadcast, and Internet regulation.

- Extension of copyright—Copyright protection for an individual would last fifty years after the author's death (previously, the copyright term was twenty-eight years).
- Protection for new media—Copyrighted works were protected from duplication by "means not yet devised."[5]

Law professor Pamela Samuelson called Ringer "one of the most important contributors to copyright law during the 20th century."[6] How important was she? Samuelson noted that Ringer, testifying before Congress in 1971, told a representative "that his son wouldn't infringe on copyright if he recorded a song from the radio." That comment became part of the U.S. Supreme Court ruling in 1984 that it was legal for people to record television shows on their videocassette recorders for home use.

In addition to being a pioneer on copyright law, Ringer was an ardent defender of women's and minority rights.[7] She was passed over for promotion to be the head of the Copyright Office in 1971, despite stellar evaluations and the recommendation of the retiring head. Instead, a man with much less experience was named as register of copyrights. At the encouragement of her friends, Ringer filed and won a sex and racial discrimination suit. The reasoning behind the sex discrimination was fairly obvious. But the racial discrimination was a bit more complicated, given that Ringer was white. The federal hearing examiner in her case ruled that Ringer had been discriminated against because she had been an outspoken supporter of African Americans at the Copyright Office and the Library of Congress.[8]

In 1977, three years before she retired, Ringer was given the President's Award for Distinguished Federal Civilian Service, the highest honor for a federal worker. Ringer returned briefly to the Library

Timeline

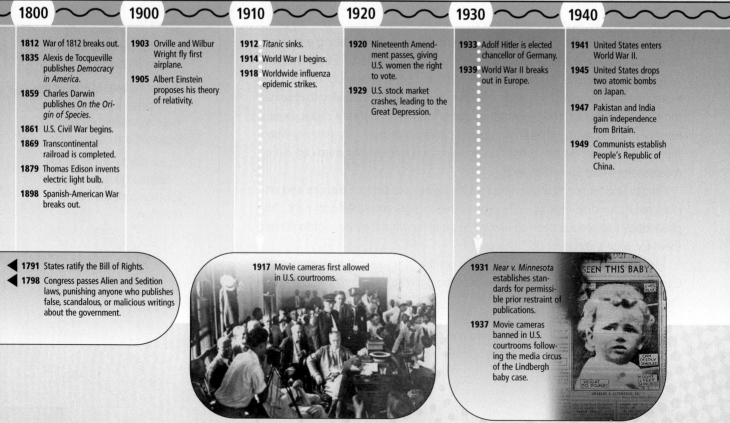

1800

1812 War of 1812 breaks out.
1835 Alexis de Tocqueville publishes *Democracy in America*.
1859 Charles Darwin publishes *On the Origin of Species*.
1861 U.S. Civil War begins.
1869 Transcontinental railroad is completed.
1879 Thomas Edison invents electric light bulb.
1898 Spanish-American War breaks out.

1900

1903 Orville and Wilbur Wright fly first airplane.
1905 Albert Einstein proposes his theory of relativity.

1910

1912 *Titanic* sinks.
1914 World War I begins.
1918 Worldwide influenza epidemic strikes.

1920

1920 Nineteenth Amendment passes, giving U.S. women the right to vote.
1929 U.S. stock market crashes, leading to the Great Depression.

1930

1933 Adolf Hitler is elected chancellor of Germany.
1939 World War II breaks out in Europe.

1940

1941 United States enters World War II.
1945 United States drops two atomic bombs on Japan.
1947 Pakistan and India gain independence from Britain.
1949 Communists establish People's Republic of China.

◀ **1791** States ratify the Bill of Rights.
◀ **1798** Congress passes Alien and Sedition laws, punishing anyone who publishes false, scandalous, or malicious writings about the government.

1917 Movie cameras first allowed in U.S. courtrooms.

AP Photo

1931 *Near v. Minnesota* establishes standards for permissible prior restraint of publications.
1937 Movie cameras banned in U.S. courtrooms following the media circus of the Lindbergh baby case.

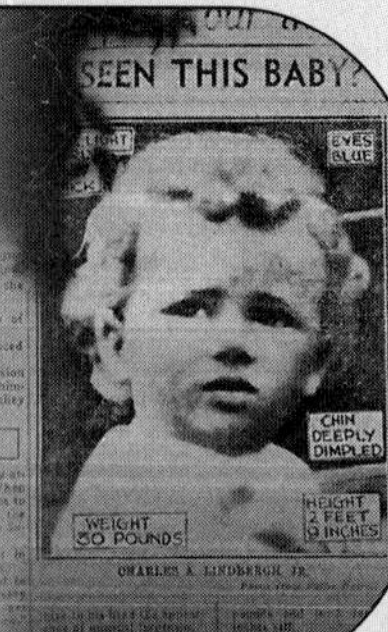

AP Photo

of Congress to be the interim register of copyrights from 1993 to 1994. At the time, she recognized the enormous changes taking place due to the rise of digital media and urged the Copyright Office to embrace digital records that could be accessed freely by all interested persons.[9]

Ringer retired at age fifty-five from the Copyright Office and joined a Washington, D.C., law firm. She also bought land in rural Virginia, where she built her home. During her retirement, she volunteered at her local library, cataloguing the new books that came in. Following an extended illness, Barbara Ringer died in 2009 at the age of eighty-three.[10]

In this chapter, we look at the laws that both protect and restrict the press. We start by examining the First Amendment to the U.S. Constitution, which established a minimally restrictive system of media law. We then look at media law in terms of how it protects individuals through laws governing libel, invasion of privacy, and the right to a fair trial. Next, we look at the controls that can be placed on the press, including requirements that the press tell the truth, restraints on publication, and regulation of obscenity. Finally, we look at how the broadcast industry is regulated by the government in a somewhat stricter fashion than the rest of the media. ■

> "My philosophy has always been to reward authors for what they do, not to punish them for what they don't do."
>
> —Barbara A. Ringer, U.S. Copyright Office

Web 13.1: Remembrances of the first woman to head the U.S. copyright office.

1950

1950 Korean War begins.

1953 Francis Crick and James Watson discover structure of DNA.

1957 Soviet Union launches spacecraft *Sputnik I.*

1960

1963 Martin Luther King Jr. delivers "I Have a Dream" speech during Washington, D.C., civil-rights march.

1969 Neil Armstrong walks on the moon.

1970

1974 U.S. president Richard Nixon resigns due to Watergate scandal.

1975 Vietnam War ends.

1977 Apple II personal computer is introduced.

1978 First test-tube baby is born.

1980

1983 First HIV/AIDS cases are documented.

Ozone hole is discovered over Antarctica.

1986 Space shuttle *Challenger* explodes.

1989 The Berlin Wall falls.

1990

1991 Soviet Union disbands.

1993 European Union is formed.

1994 Nelson Mandela is elected president of South Africa.

1997 Diana, Princess of Wales, dies in car accident.

2000-

2001 Al Qaida attacks World Trade Center and Pentagon.

2003 United States invades Iraq.

2008 Barack Obama is elected U.S. president.

2011 Earthquake and tsunami hit Japan. United States endseight-year war with Iraq.

2012 Superstorm Sandy devastates U.S. eastern seaboard.

2014 Russian army invades Ukraine.

1957 *Roth v. the United States* establishes the standard for obscenity.

1964 *New York Times v. Sullivan* establishes the standard for libel of public officials.

1971 The Pentagon Papers case leads to first instance of prior restraint of a specific newspaper article; the Supreme Court later overturns the lower court's ban on publication.

AP Photo

1994 Intense media attention during the O.J. Simpson murder trial highlights the conflict between the right to a free press and the right to a fair trial.

1996 The Communications Decency Act attempts to prohibit pornography on the Internet; the Supreme Court strikes down most of its provisions.

1998 The Digital Millennium Copyright Act expands protection of movies music, and software.

2010 U.S. Supreme Court allows unlimited contributions to political action committees in Citizens United case.

2011 Congress passes 4-year extension to the 2001 USA Patriot Act, permitting domestic surveillance and wiretapping to combat terrorism.

2011 U.S. Supreme Court upholds free speech protections for Westboro Baptist Church pickets.

2014 First libel case based on tweet settled.

Ingvar Björk/Alamy

The Development of a Free Press

The First Amendment to the U.S. Constitution is at the core of all U.S. laws concerning the media. It says simply that

> Congress shall make no law respecting an establishment of religion, or prohibiting the free exercise thereof; or abridging the freedom of speech, or of the press; or the right of the people peaceably to assemble, and to petition the Government for a redress of grievances.

Although the First Amendment states that "Congress shall make no law," the U.S. Supreme Court has long upheld certain limits on both speech and the press. People do not have "the right to say anything they please, any way they please, anywhere or under any circumstances."[11] In this section, we look at how the notion of freedom of expression and of the press has developed and what regulations and restrictions the government can place on that freedom.

The First Amendment: "Congress Shall Make No Law"

According to First Amendment scholar Fred Cate, the First Amendment is an essential component of a representative democracy because a democracy cannot function unless the people have the right to freely and openly discuss matters of public concern. It is through free and open speech that change takes place within society. The First Amendment does not just protect popular or conventional ideas; it protects all forms of expression, including offensive ideas. Even some level of false expression is allowed because the truth is not always clear. Thus, the solution to the expression of dangerous ideas is to permit more, rather than less, communication.[12]

The most basic right guaranteed by the First Amendment is freedom of speech without constraint by the government. The right of freedom of the press is an extension of the rights of individuals to express themselves.[13] In addition to its explicit mention of the press and speech, the First Amendment provides a wide range of other rights, including freedom of religious practice, the right to assemble, and the right to petition the government.

The Roots of American Free Speech

Speech was not always free in the American colonies. Colonial newspapers were published under licenses granted by the British colonial government, with the phrase "Published by Authority" printed at the top of each edition. This notice implied that the British government approved of what was being published, and editors violated that approval at their peril.

The Granger Collection, New York

The Bill of Rights, ratified in 1791, established protection for all forms of expression, not just popular ideas.

The Zenger Case. John Peter Zenger and his wife, Anna Catherine Zenger, were independent editors, printers, and small-business owners in the American colonies. Zenger started his *New York Journal* in 1733 and, like many editors of that time, was soon in trouble with the authorities. Zenger accused Gov. William Cosby of political corruption for replacing New York Supreme Court justices with whom he disagreed.[14] The governor retaliated by throwing Zenger in jail on a charge of seditious libel (writing things critical of the government). When the case went to trial in 1735, Zenger, who was represented by prominent lawyer Andrew Hamilton, defended himself against the charge by claiming that what he had written was the truth. The shocked judge argued that the truth of the statement didn't matter. But Zenger and Hamilton refused to back down, and the jury found Zenger not guilty, thus establishing truth as a defense against libel.

While her husband was in prison, Anna Catherine took over the operation of the paper, thus becoming one of the first women newspaper publishers in the country.[15]

Limits on Free Speech. In 1791, the states ratified the first ten amendments to the Constitution, commonly known as the Bill of Rights. But making the Bill of Rights a part of the Constitution did not end the government's efforts to limit people's right to freedom of expression.

SECRET 4 In 1798, just seven years after the ratification of the Bill of Rights, Congress passed, and President John Adams signed, the **Alien and Sedition Acts**. These laws punished anyone who published "false, scandalous, or malicious writings against the government of the United States, or either house of the Congress of the United States, or the President of the United States" with substantial fines, jail time, or deportation. One editor went to prison for accusing Adams of corruption, and a second went to prison for supporting the critical editor. All those charged under the acts were eventually pardoned by Thomas Jefferson when he became president.[16]

Sedition became a crime once again during World War I, when more than 1,900 people were prosecuted under sedition statutes for criticizing the government, the military draft, or American involvement in the war. Following the war, some but not all of the anti–free speech provisions were repealed.[17] Then, in 1940, during the run-up to American involvement in World War II, Congress passed the Smith Act, which made it a crime to advocate the violent overthrow of the government or to belong to a group that advocated the violent overthrow of the government. The central purpose of the act was to suppress the Communist Party of the United States.[18]

Cagle Cartoons, Inc.

The National Security Agency (NSA) has used a broad understanding of the PATRIOT Act Section 215 to justify collecting voice and e-mail data on almost any American citizen.

Limits on Free Speech in the Post-9/11 Era

Forty-five days after the September 11, 2001, terrorist attacks, Congress passed the USA PATRIOT Act, its name an acronym that stands for "Uniting and Strengthening America by Providing Appropriate Tools Required to Intercept and Obstruct Terrorism." The PATRIOT Act follows in the tradition of previous wartime laws in changing the balance point between maximizing our civil liberties and protecting the United States from perceived threats. The act is one more example of Secret Four—Nothing's new: Everything that happened in the past will happen again.

The law permitted a host of activities by the Justice Department, including the placing of wiretaps and increased domestic surveillance, and it also widened the definition of what constitutes terrorism. Most of the objections to the act fall under the Fourth Amendment to the U.S. Constitution, which protects against "unreasonable searches and seizures." But there are First Amendment implications as well. One of the biggest is that Section 215 of the act allows the Federal Bureau of Investigation (FBI) to examine individuals' media use by obtaining "library records, health-care records, logs of Internet service providers and other documents and papers."

Jameel Jaffer of the American Civil Liberties Union (ACLU) says that the fact that people may be watched can keep them from looking at things they might otherwise view: "If people think that the government is looking over their shoulders to see what books they are reading or what Web sites they are visiting, many are not going to read those books or visit those Web sites." The law also makes it a crime for anyone to provide "expert assistance" to any group designated as being a terrorist organization, even if there is no evidence that the advice leads to further terrorism.

Most controversial was the provision that those people served with PATRIOT Act warrants couldn't tell anyone that they had received them. That is, anyone served with a PATRIOT Act warrant lost his or her free speech rights when it came to discussing the warrant. Since the act was originally passed in 2001, it has undergone changes that have scaled back the limits on free speech. The most important of these changes is that people served with warrants under the act now have permission to consult an attorney.

The PATRIOT Act has also been used to identify journalists' confidential sources. Brian Ross and Richard Esposito of ABC News wrote in their blog, the *Blotter*, that the federal government was tracking the phone numbers they called after they reported on the Central Intelligence Agency's (CIA's) secret prisons in Romania and Poland. Ross charges that this tracking of his calls was done under Section 215 of the act. "It's a provision of the Patriot Act designed to fight terrorism—and it's being used to fight journalists," Ross said. "That's what it really comes down to."

Alien and Sedition Acts: Laws passed in 1798 that made it a crime to criticize the government of the United States.

Web 13.2: Read more about PATRIOT Act implications.

While there had been a variety of reports about potential misuse of Section 215 similar to those from Brian Ross, the world learned the extent of the collection of "metadata" in a series of stories from the *Guardian* newspaper based on documents leaked by former National Security Agency contractor Edward Snowden. Snowden revealed that the NSA had been collecting bulk information that showed "who called whom, the date, time, duration and frequency of calls for millions of Americans who are not suspected of any crimes."[19] These data do not include the content of the calls, but just the metadata alone could establish someone's political activities, health issues, or personal relationships. As of this writing, Congress was working on versions of the USA FREEDOM (Uniting and Strengthening America by Fulfilling Rights and Ending Eavesdropping, Dragnet-Collection and Online Monitoring) Act that would attempt to put controls on how the NSA collects and uses this type of information.[20] (You can read more about Snowden and how he leaked thousands of confidential documents to the press in the opening vignette of Chapter 2.)

Questioning the Media

Does the First Amendment go too far in its protections of the press and of individuals? Why or why not? Why do you think the government periodically tries to limit our First Amendment rights?

Although the PATRIOT Act has undergone revisions since it was passed in 2001, Congress approved and President Obama signed a four-year extension of key provisions of the law in May 2011.[21]

Protection of Individuals

Although the press is censored only rarely in the United States, individuals do have a right to protect themselves from being harmed by the media. Rather than exercising prior restraint to prevent the press from printing or broadcasting potentially damaging material, U.S. law allows individuals to sue the press for any damage they feel they have suffered. Protection of individuals from the press focuses on three main issues: libel, invasion of privacy, and the right to a fair trial.

Libel

Although in general the press cannot be restricted from publishing something, it can be held accountable for what it does publish. This is accomplished primarily through libel law. **Libel** is any published statement that unjustifiably exposes someone to ridicule or contempt. In general, for a statement to be libelous, it needs to contain three elements: defamation, identification, and publication.

1. Defamation—To defame is to damage a person's reputation in some way. This can involve calling someone, for example, a criminal, a communist, or a drunk. If a student newspaper ran an article falsely accusing Dr. Smith, a journalism professor, of selling an A grade in his Introduction to Mass Communication class for $100, Dr. Smith would probably have been defamed.

2. Identification—No person can sue for libel unless the defamation can be proved to apply to him or her; another reader or viewer must agree that the comment applies to the person who is suing. Just leaving that person's name out of the article isn't enough. If a person can be identified, he or she can sue. Going back to the example of Dr. Smith, suppose that the article did not mention his name but merely said that the teacher of the Introduction to Mass Communication course at Big State University was taking bribes for grades. If Dr. Smith was the only person teaching the course at Big State U, he would have been identified.

3. Publication—To be libelous, the statement must be published or broadcast and seen by someone other than the author and the person who was defamed.[22]

How can the media defend themselves against libel suits? After all, much of what gets printed or broadcast in the news has the potential to damage a person's reputation. There are at least two approaches. When an article is genuinely false and defamatory, the media look to a landmark 1960s case, *New York Times Co. v. Sullivan*, which is discussed later in this chapter. First, let's look at approaches that are used when the material in an article is true, privileged, or a statement of opinion.

The Defense of Truth. The Zenger case from the early 1700s established truth as an absolute defense against libel. It is not always an effective defense, however, because the truth is not always clear. In the article about Dr. Smith, it may well be true that a student accused Dr. Smith of selling grades, but it would be much more difficult to prove that Dr. Smith actually sold the grades.

The Defense of Privilege. Asserting privilege is a much better defense than truth in a libel case. As a legal defense against libel, **privilege** is the idea that statements made in government meetings, in court, or in government documents cannot be used as the basis for a libel suit. What is more, any fair and accurate report of what happened at the meeting, in court, or in a government document is also protected from libel.[23] For example, the privilege defense protects a reporter who is covering a murder trial. The journalist is privileged to give a fair and accurate report of any testimony, no matter how inflammatory, without fear of being sued.

---

libel: A published statement that unjustifiably exposes someone to ridicule or contempt; for a statement to be libel, it must satisfy the three elements of defamation, identification, and publication.

privilege: A legal defense against libel that holds that statements made in government meetings, in court, or in government documents cannot be used as the basis for a libel suit.

Opinions. Opinions are neither true nor false, so a statement of opinion cannot be used as the basis of a libel suit. Calling someone an idiot or a jerk would probably not be considered libelous; both words are expressions of opinion. Editorial cartoons, parodies, and reviews are all generally considered to be opinion and are given fairly broad latitude in their protection from libel. But remember that, to be protected, statements need to be clear expressions of opinion. An article that states "Dr. Smith, in my opinion, is selling grades" would most likely be considered libelous: Claiming that a fact is a statement of opinion does not protect the writer.

New York Times Co. v. Sullivan. The defenses of truth, privilege, and opinion arise from the notion that the press has published something it is entitled to publish. But there are times when the press gets a story wrong, runs an advertisement containing factual errors, or makes a mistake in a headline. In these cases, the press is likely to look to the 1964 case of *New York Times Co. v. Sullivan.*[24]

The 1960s were a period of racial unrest in the United States, marked by protests and rioting over efforts to integrate schools, lunch counters, and other public facilities. White segregationists claimed that the national media were interfering with local issues that were none of their business,[25] a prime example of Secret Six—Activism and analysis are not the same thing.

On March 29, 1960, a civil rights group ran a full-page ad in the *New York Times* to raise money for Dr. Martin Luther King Jr. The ad included the names of numerous well-known individuals, such as Harry Belafonte, Marlon Brando, Nat King Cole, Jackie Robinson, and former first lady Eleanor Roosevelt, and was paid for by the Union Advertising Service for the Committee to Defend Martin Luther King and the Struggle for Freedom in the South.[26]

Among the sections of the ad that created trouble was the following:

> In Montgomery, Alabama, after students sang "My Country 'Tis of Thee" on the State Capitol steps, their leaders were expelled from the school, and truck-loads of police armed with shotguns and tear-gas ringed the Alabama State College Campus. When the entire student body protested to state authorities by refusing to reregister, their dining hall was padlocked in an attempt to starve them into submission.[27]

This passage contained several false statements. The students did not sing "My Country 'Tis of Thee," and the police did not literally surround the building.

Although Montgomery police commissioner L. B. Sullivan, who was in charge of the police department, was not mentioned by name in the advertisement, he felt that any accusations against the police department were accusations against him. He also charged that the advertisement contained numerous factual errors. He asked the

Jon Kopaloff/FilmMagic/Getty Images

Hole lead singer Courtney Love won the United States' first Twitter libel case because the jury ruled she didn't realize the statement she posted online about her lawyer was false.

Times to retract the ad, but the paper responded that it did not see how the ad reflected negatively on Sullivan's reputation. So Sullivan filed suit, joining eleven other libel cases that were pending against the *Times*.[28]

In the initial three-day trial, the *Times* admitted that the ad contained errors, but friends of Sullivan testified that they did not think less of him as a result because they did not believe what they had read in the ad. Nevertheless, the judge instructed the jury that they could presume that the material in the ad was libelous and that it had damaged Sullivan's reputation. The jury returned a verdict in favor of Sullivan, awarding him $500,000 in damages. The verdict was upheld by the Alabama Supreme Court.

The case then went before the U.S. Supreme Court, which reversed the lower courts with a sweeping ruling in favor of the *Times*. The Court could have overturned the lower court judgment simply by ruling that Sullivan had not been identified in the ad or by saying that Sullivan's reputation had not suffered any damage. But it decided instead to use the case to consider whether the public had the right to criticize the government.[29] The Court ruled that it was not enough to protect true statements; false statements against public officials made in good faith should also be protected.

With the *Sullivan* case, the Court established a new standard for libel. It ruled that public officials would have to show that the media had acted with **actual malice** and displayed a reckless disregard for the truth or falsity of a published account. In the *Sullivan* case, the Court ruled, the paper had not acted with malice; at worst it had been negligent. One of the goals of the Court's judgment was to help protect against self-censorship—to prevent publications from being so afraid of making a mistake that they would not print anything that might be controversial. The Court was attempting to balance the right of a public official to protect his or her reputation versus a critic's right to speak out against that official.

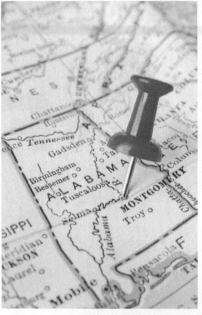

Libel and Public Figures. In 1967, the Supreme Court extended the actual malice standard to apply to public figures as well as public officials. The theory behind this extension of the *Sullivan* standard was that these people have voluntarily exposed themselves to public scrutiny and thus to the threat of being libeled.

The standard was settled by the case of *Gertz v. Robert Welch, Inc.* in 1974.[30] The John Birch Society's magazine had run an article accusing Elmer Gertz of being a communist. The question was whether Gertz, an attorney, was a public figure. The Court ruled that private individuals deserve more protection because they have not voluntarily submitted themselves for public attention and because they are less able than public figures to defend themselves.[31]

Libel and Social Media. In general, there are few differences in the standard for libel between legacy media and social media. The big difference is that legacy media have a legal staff to advise writers when they are writing or broadcasting something that could be problematic; people on Twitter or Facebook rarely do. Also, as attorney Ellyn Angelotti points out, social media like Twitter make publishing potentially defamatory content much easier.[32] Finally, while newspapers or broadcasters are typically responsible for what they publish because they actively control what goes out in their name, social media sites themselves are not responsible for what people post using their service. As of this writing, the Twitter libel case to be settled dealt with a tweet posted by singer/celebrity Courtney Love that suggested "one of her attorneys had been 'bought off.'" The jury in the case ruled in favor of Love and against her attorney. The jury ruled that Love's tweet contained false information but that she didn't know that it was false.[33] (Note to students: Don't assume that other juries would rule the same way!)

Invasion of Privacy 

What magazines do you subscribe to? What books do you check out from the library? How much money do you have in the bank? What movies have you rented from the video store? What do you buy at the grocery store? Why did you see the doctor last week? Are you uncomfortable with these questions? Most people would like to keep such information private.[34]

With all this information potentially available, what legal expectation do people have of maintaining a private life in the information age? The Constitution offers no explicit protection of privacy, but a right to privacy has been implied, and the issue shows up in a number of ways. The "freedom to associate" clause of the First Amendment prevents the government from requiring a group to release its membership list to the public. It also protects the right of an individual to possess any type of literature in the privacy of his or her own home. The Fourth Amendment limits searches and seizures, and the Fourteenth Amendment limits disclosure of personal information. In cases involving privacy, the courts try to balance an individual's right to protect his or her privacy and reputation versus the public's interest in a news or feature story that the press might publish.

In general, legal protection exists for four types of invasion of privacy: intrusion, embarrassment, false light, and misappropriation. Let's look briefly at each of these.[35]

Intrusion. **Intrusion** is invasion of privacy by physical trespass into a space surrounding a person's body or onto property under his or her control. Reporters and photographers are not allowed to go onto private property to collect news without the permission of the owner, but in some cases, the news-gathering function and the right of the public to know can conflict with the rights associated with private property. For example, a reporter and a photographer were sued for intrusion when they pretended to be patients at a private California medical clinic that was being

Video 13.1: Hear journalist Anthony Lewis discuss the *Sullivan* case.

Web 13.3: Learn more about libel, privacy, and social media.

actual malice: A reckless disregard for the truth or falsity of a published account; this became the standard for libel plaintiffs who were public figures or public officials after the Supreme Court's decision in *New York Times Co. v. Sullivan.*

intrusion: Invasion of privacy by physical trespass into a space surrounding a person's body or onto property under his or her control.

run by a plumber practicing medicine without a license. Their visit to the clinic was ruled to be trespass, but the story won numerous prizes and resulted in the clinic's being shut down.[36]

The courts have generally held that undercover reporting is legal, if not necessarily ethical, as long as it does not involve trespass. (For more about intrusion, see the section on *Food Lion v. ABC* later in this chapter.)

Embarrassment. Sometimes reporters come across true information that is so embarrassing and private that a person has reason to expect that it will not be published, especially if he or she is not well known. In general, embarrassment cases are difficult to win. If the information is true, it will often be considered newsworthy, which is the press's strongest defense in privacy cases.

One of the best-known embarrassment cases arose in 1975, when Oliver "Bill" Sipple, a former U.S. Marine, helped save President Gerald R. Ford by knocking aside Sara Jane Moore's gun as she attempted to shoot the president. Two days later, a columnist for the *San Francisco Chronicle* implied that Sipple was gay. Sipple sued the *Chronicle* for giving unwanted publicity to that information. The court ruled against Sipple, however, because he had been written about in gay magazines and had marched in gay pride parades. The court also ruled that the information about Sipple was legitimate news.

So when is something that is private *not* newsworthy? On October 13, 1961, an Alabama woman went into a fun house at the local county fair. As she came out, an air jet blew her skirt up, exposing her underwear, and a photographer from the local newspaper took her picture. The woman was recognized by friends and relatives, who teased her about the picture. She called the paper at least twice but received no sympathy. The paper's editor says that had he apologized at that point, the case would have likely ended. But he didn't, and the woman sued and won.[37] What distinguishes this case from the Sipple case? Sipple had just saved the president's life and hence was a part of the news. In the Alabama case, however, the woman had done nothing to make herself newsworthy.

False Light. **False light** is similar to libel, and people who file libel suits often simultaneously file false light suits. False light doesn't really seem to be an invasion of privacy, but that's how the law treats it.[38] False light occurs when a journalist publishes untrue statements that alter an individual's public image in a way that he or she cannot control. The Cleveland *Plain Dealer* lost a false light suit when reporter Joe Eszterhas (who later became famous for writing the screenplay for the movie *Basic Instinct*) described

false light: Invasion of privacy in which a journalist publishes untrue statements that alter a person's public image in a way that he or she cannot control.

misappropriation: Invasion of privacy by using a person's name or image for commercial purposes without his or her permission.

AP Photo/San Francisco Examiner, Gordon Stone

In 1975, Oliver "Bill" Sipple (left) helped save President Gerald R. Ford by foiling an assassination attempt by Sara Jane Moore. After the *San Francisco Chronicle* revealed Sipple was gay, he sued the paper, but the courts ruled that information about Sipple was newsworthy and, therefore, not an invasion of his privacy.

a poverty-stricken widow whose husband had been killed in a bridge collapse several months earlier in West Virginia—even though he had neither met or spoken with the woman. He wrote:

> Margaret Cantrell will talk neither about what happened nor about how they are doing. She wears the same mask of non-expression she wore at the funeral. She is a proud woman. Her world has changed. She says that after it happened, the people in town offered to help them out with money and they refused to take it.[39]

Regardless of whether the woman's reputation was damaged, the portrayal was clearly false because Eszterhas had never been in contact with her.

False light often arises more from context than from a deliberate attempt to deceive. For example, a television story about street prostitution might show men and women walking down the street, with the implication that the women are prostitutes and the men are their customers. ABC television settled multiple lawsuits over just such a story (though without admitting guilt).

Questioning the Media

Does the press go too far in revealing private details about celebrities? Why or why not? Given that celebrities benefit from positive coverage, should they be given more power to control negative coverage?

Misappropriation. The final form of invasion of privacy is quite different from the preceding three. **Misappropriation** is using a person's name or image for commercial purposes without his or her permission. The right to control the commercial use of their names and images is of great importance to athletes and celebrities, who may make more money from endorsements than they do from competing or acting. For example, in 1997, basketball legend Michael Jordan earned $31.3 million in pay from the Chicago Bulls but over $40 million from endorsements.[40] Clearly, it is in Jordan's economic and financial interest to control the use of his name and image.

©iStockphoto.com/Syldavia

What of the paparazzi armed with telephoto lenses that make a business out of stalking celebrities? Television and movie star Jennifer Aniston has filed numerous invasion-of-privacy lawsuits to stop distribution or publication of topless photos taken of her. It is not clear how a court would rule on her cases, as most of them have been settled out of court. Aniston has used a range of legal strategies in her cases, including copyright infringement, intrusion, and misappropriation.[41] (She apparently did not have a problem with her officially sanctioned topless photo that ran on the cover of *GQ* magazine in 2005, at the same time one of her lawsuits was in progress.[42]) In 2009, California governor Arnold Schwarzenegger signed a bill into law that allows lawsuits against media outlets that publish photos shot illegally. In general, freelance photographers can be sued for violating privacy laws, but the publications that buy their photos have been shielded from liability. Free-speech advocates argue that California's new law could interfere with legitimate news gathering. Legal experts have questioned whether California's law is enforceable because it can be difficult to prove when and where a photo was taken.[43]

Social Media and Privacy. If we were to go ask Captain Obvious whether we had any right to privacy with things we post to social media sites, he would immediately reply, "Duh, no, it's meant to be shared, obviously." And from a practical point of view, he would be correct—once anything is posted to the Internet, it's bound to go public. If you want to keep something secret, don't post it. But from a legal point of view, you do have some protection. According to a 2012 ruling by the District Court of New Jersey, if you post something that is available only to a select group of people (i.e., "friends"), you may have a reasonable expectation of privacy. On the other hand, a 2009 California Court of Appeals ruling found that someone who posted a series of complaints about her hometown on MySpace had no grounds to sue for invasion of privacy when her comments were republished in a local newspaper.[44]

Privacy Law in Europe. When Britain's beloved Princess Diana died in a car crash on August 30, 1997, the entire world mourned, and many people in Europe and the United States blamed the accident on overly aggressive photographers chasing the car in which she was riding. Although evidence soon came to light that Diana's driver had been drunk at the time, the high-speed chase through the streets of Paris brought the privacy rights of the rich and famous to the forefront of the public's attention.[45]

France has relatively strict privacy laws that proclaim "each individual has the right to require respect for his private life. . . . Privacy revolves around the secrecy of one's intimate life and the right to oppose investigation and revelation of this domain."[46] This protects against coverage of a person's family life, sexual activity or orientation, illness, and private leisure activities. The person suing does not need to show that he or she has been damaged; the law presumes that invasion of privacy, by its very nature, is damaging.

Despite the strength of the restrictions, the penalties for violating the laws are relatively mild.[47] Most fines are under $50,000, and the French press view them largely as a cost of doing business. Although the law also allows the courts to confiscate the publications containing the offending photographs, in practice the courts almost never do so.[48]

Whereas France has relatively strict laws, until recently, British law did not recognize an individual's right to privacy. For example, in 1987, British actor Gorden Kaye suffered a serious head injury in an accident. Kaye was subsequently interviewed while he was semiconscious and recovering from brain surgery. The British courts ruled that the only thing legally wrong with the article was that it implied that the actor had consented to the interview. Thus, the article was published without penalty.[49]

In 2000, the British Parliament put into law the Human Rights Act, which requires the press to observe a "proper balance" between privacy and publicity.[50] It is too soon to tell exactly how the vague standard set out in this new law will be applied. So far, actors Michael Douglas and Catherine Zeta-Jones have sued under the act to prevent a magazine from running photos of their wedding. (The celebrity couple had sold exclusive rights to the wedding pictures to a competing publication for a reported £1 million.) The British courts finally ruled seven years later that Douglas and Zeta-Jones had the right to sell photo access exclusively to a single publication.[51] Model Naomi Campbell won her case against the *Mirror* tabloid for running a picture of her leaving a Narcotics Anonymous meeting, while singer Elton John lost a case claiming a newspaper photo taken on the street made him look bald.[52] How much protection the law will provide and what balance it will strike between the rights of the press and the rights of individuals remain to be seen, however. According to the British newspaper the *Guardian,* the Human Rights Act may be repealed, but it would likely be replaced with a very similar new law.[53]

At the other end of the spectrum, neither Spain nor Germany has laws governing the actions of the press

Web 13.4: More on privacy laws and photographers.

Web 13.5: Read about French privacy protections.

regarding the private lives of public officials and celebrities. Italy, which gave the world the word *paparazzi*, has limited privacy laws, but they are not enforced with significant penalties.[54]

Free Press/Fair Trial

The right to a free press often conflicts with the right to a fair trial. The Sixth Amendment to the U.S. Constitution guarantees accused individuals the right to be tried by an impartial jury, and the Fourteenth Amendment requires that criminal defendants be tried fairly before an unprejudiced jury. Supreme Court justice Hugo Black wrote that "free speech and fair trials are two of the most cherished policies of our civilization, and it would be a trying task to choose between them."[55]

Tim Graham/Alamy

Paparazzi, such as these in Milan, are independent photographers who shoot pictures of celebrities and public figures, often in embarrassing situations.

Over the years, there have been repeated charges that pretrial publicity interferes with the ability to select an impartial jury and that media coverage turns trials into circuses. These complaints became particularly loud during O. J. Simpson's 1994 murder trial, which attracted an inordinate amount of media attention. Media scholar Matthew D. Bunker argues that the conflict between a free press and a fair trial does not require that one right be sacrificed for another. Instead, he suggests that creative decisions by judges can lead to fair trials and open media coverage at the same time.[56] The general rule is that the First Amendment must be upheld unless there is a compelling state interest in regulating the speech. If speech is regulated, it must be done in the least restrictive way possible. The reasoning is that there should be no official version of the truth. Instead, people should be able to put forward contrasting ideas that compete for attention.

The Case of Dr. Sam Sheppard. One of the most spectacular collisions between the right to a free press and the right to a fair trial involved the murder trial of Dr. Sam Sheppard. The case, later fictionalized in the television series and movie *The Fugitive*, involved the murder of Sheppard's wife, Marilyn, who was found beaten to death in their home in 1954. In his defense, Sheppard, a prominent Cleveland doctor, claimed to have been awakened by his wife's screams and to have fought with his wife's attacker, who left him unconscious.

Sheppard's story did not convince the police, and he soon became the leading suspect in his wife's murder. Reporters found out that Sheppard had been having an affair with a woman named Susan Hayes. A newspaper headline demanded "Why Isn't Sam Sheppard in Jail?" As the trial began, the Cleveland newspapers printed the names and addresses of prospective jurors, along with their pictures. Jurors were also allowed to view the media during the trial, despite a "suggestion" by the judge that they avoid doing so.

Sheppard was convicted of murder, but his conviction was overturned by the U.S. Supreme Court, and he was given a new trial. This time he was acquitted. The Court, in *Sheppard v. Maxwell*,[57] said that the "carnival atmosphere" surrounding Sheppard's trial had denied him due process. But the Court also noted that it was the judge's responsibility to make sure the defendant received a fair trial. If stopping coverage of the trial was not an option, what could the courts do to avoid this problem? The Court suggested a number of possibilities[58]:

- Put a gag order on participants in the trial to keep them from talking to the press in the first place (although the press would be free to report on anything that happened in the courtroom itself).
- Sequester the jury.
- Postpone the trial until the publicity dies down.
- Change the venue for the trial.
- Order a new trial.

United States v. Noriega. Can the press ever be stopped from printing information about a court case? In general, the Supreme Court has held that it is the government's job, not the job of the press, to protect a defendant's right to a fair trial. The only major case that the press has been restricted from covering was *United States v. Noriega*,[59] which occurred in the fall of 1990. In this case, the court issued a temporary restraining order against CNN to

Web 13.6: Read about *United States v. Noriega*.

Web 13.7: Read more on cameras in the courtroom.

TEST YOUR VISUAL MEDIA LITERACY

What's your first reaction to this photo? Does it shock and anger you? Why or why not? Should members of groups such as the Westboro Baptist Church have the right to picket near a soldier's funeral?

Should Legal Protections Extend to Offensive Speech?

The Westboro Baptist Church (WBC) of Topeka, Kansas, has made itself infamous over the last decade by picketing the funerals of American servicemen and women, as well as at other high-profile funerals, carrying signs proclaiming "GOD HATES FAGS" and "THANK GOD FOR DEAD SOLIDERS." The church, which is not connected to any other Baptist denomination, is generally described as being mainly composed of the extended family of its founder and former leader, the late Fred Phelps. The church argues that God is punishing the United States for homosexuality, and its members picket the funerals to draw attention to their group.[1] (Fred Phelps died in March 2014, but the WBC has continued with its pickets reportedly under the leadership of non-relative Steve Drain.[60])

In 2006, the Phelps family brought their pickets to the funeral of Lance Cpl. Matthew Snyder, who was killed in Iraq. The protesters were reportedly kept approximately 1,000 feet away from the church where the funeral was being held. Then, a week later, a member of the Westboro church posted an "epic" to the church's Web site that told a disparaging story about Snyder and his family, claiming that Snyder's parents raised him to "defy his creator" and that they taught him that "God was a liar." Albert Snyder, Matthew's father, sued Phelps for intentional infliction of emotional distress and invasion of privacy. He was initially awarded an $11 million judgment, but that judgment was later reduced to $5 million by the judge. The case was then reversed by the federal appeals court, based in part on the Supreme Court's ruling in *Falwell v. Flynt* that even speech that was "gross and repugnant in the eye of most" was still protected.[2]

When the case of *Snyder v. Phelps* reached the U.S. Supreme Court, there was an extensive public debate over the rights of the Phelps family to free speech versus the rights of the Snyder family to bury their son in peace.

During arguments before the court, the attorney for the Snyder family testified, "We're talking about a funeral. If the context is ever going to matter, it has to matter in the context of a funeral. Mr. Snyder simply wanted to bury his son in a private, dignified manner."[3] In response, Margie J. Phelps, daughter of Fred Phelps, argued that there is no constitutional law to keep her from exploiting a funeral for her cause. She told the court that "when I hear the language of 'exploiting the bereavement,' I look for: What is the principle of law that comes from this court? This notion of exploiting, it has no definition in a principle of law that would guide people as to when they could or could not."[4]

The Court eventually ruled in favor of the Phelps family's right to protest in an 8–1 decision, holding that the Phelps family had followed local laws and stayed the required 1,000 feet away from the funeral. Chief Justice John Roberts, writing for the majority, said that "speech is powerful. It can stir people to action, move them to tears of both joy and sorrow, and—as it did here—inflict great pain. On the facts before us, we cannot react to that pain by punishing the speaker. As a Nation we have chosen a different course—to protect even hurtful speech on public issues to ensure that we do not stifle public debate."[5]

WHO are they?

Who is Fred Phelps? Who is Albert Snyder?

WHAT did they say?

Why did Albert Snyder sue Fred Phelps and the Westboro Baptist Church? Why do Phelps and his family picket veterans' funerals?

WHAT evidence is there?

What grounds would the Court have had for ruling in favor of Snyder? What grounds did the Court have for ruling in favor of Phelps?

WHAT do you and your classmates think?

Do you agree with how the Court ruled in the Phelps case? Why or why not? What would the consequences be for free speech if the Court had ruled against Phelps? What can communities do (if anything) about the Westboro Baptist Church protests? Do you think people have a right to protest at or near funerals?

[1]Garrett Epps, "Westboro Baptist Church's Surreal Day in Court," *Atlantic*, October 6, 2010, www.theatlantic.com/national/archive/2010/10/westboro-baptist-churchs-surreal-day-in-court/64167/.

[2]Stuart Taylor Jr., "Court, 8–0, Extends Right to Criticize Those in Public Eye," *New York Times*, January 25, 1988, www.nytimes.com/1988/02/25/us/court-8-0-extends-right-to-criticize-those-in-public-eye.html.

[3]Robert Barnes, "Court Considers Westboro Baptist Church's Anti-Gay Protests at Military Funerals," *Washington Post*, October 6, 2010, www.washingtonpost.com/wp-dyn/content/article/2010/10/06/AR2010100603950.html.

[4]Ibid.

[5]John G. Roberts, "*Snyder v. Phelps* Excerpt: Robert's Majority Opinion in Westboro Church Case," *Washington Post*, March 2, 2011, www.washingtonpost.com/wp-dyn/content/article/2011/03/02/AR2011030203069.html.

Video 13.2: More details on *Snyder v. Phelps*.

Web 13.8: Read more about *Falwell v. Flynt*.

prevent the network from broadcasting tapes of former Panamanian leader Manuel Noriega talking with his lawyers. The judge felt that broadcasting the tapes would unduly benefit the government in designing its strategy for prosecuting the former leader on drug charges. Nevertheless, CNN did broadcast one of the conversations. The restraining order was lifted eventually, but CNN was found guilty of contempt of court for broadcasting the original tape.[61]

Cameras in the Courtroom. While there is no question that reporters and the public are entitled to view trials, there has been considerable debate over whether television and other cameras ought to be allowed in the courtroom.

The central argument in favor of allowing cameras is that the right to an open trial belongs to the public, not to the participants in the trial. Steven Brill, founder of the cable network Court TV, argues that television coverage of trials

> offer[s] the public the chance to see the legal system at work and to judge with their own eyes whether it has performed properly. [It] can heighten public understanding of the system, counter rumors and speculation, and provide important insurance against abuses of defendants' rights.[62]

Movie cameras were first allowed in courtrooms in 1917. But in 1935, when Bruno Richard Hauptmann was on trial for the kidnapping and murder of aviator Charles Lindbergh's baby, the trial became a media circus. As a result, in 1937, a general ban was placed on movie and still photography in courtrooms. The fraud trial of the flamboyant Texas financier Billie Sol Estes in 1965 led to a Supreme Court decision that the time had not yet come for cameras to be allowed in the courtroom. But the Court went on to say that this might change when cameras became smaller and less intrusive.

In the 1970s and 1980s, electronic technology led to small, remote-controlled cameras. In 1977, the Florida Supreme Court started experimenting with allowing televised coverage of state court proceedings; by 1981, twenty-nine states had laws allowing partial television access.[63] By 1999, the vast majority of states had begun to allow cameras in their courtrooms under certain circumstances, although the judge generally retained the discretion to control when they could be used. Most states limit coverage of jurors, and many allow witnesses to refuse to be shown on television.[64] Experiments conducted in Illinois and Minnesota in the 2010s found that in general television cameras in the courtroom were not particularly disruptive. In fact, a Minnesota judge reported that she forgot the cameras were there.[65] A judge in Illinois commented that the courts couldn't use what happened in the circus-like televised O. J. Simpson murder trial because that case was "an aberration."[66] The one place cameras have not been allowed into is the U.S. Supreme Court. However, members of Congress and the judiciary have argued that the public should be able to watch the Supreme Court hear oral arguments on important cases such as the constitutionality of President Obama's health care reform law.[67]

Controlling the Press

SECRET 4 Despite the First Amendment, Congress has repeatedly placed restrictions on speech and the press. These restrictions include bans on false advertising, libel, perjury, obscenity, reporting troop movements during time of war, and solicitation of murder.[68] This section looks at some of these limits in detail as illustrations of Secret Four—Nothing's new: Everything that happened in the past will happen again.

Honesty and the Press

The law clearly states that the press can be held responsible for printing material that is libelous or invades a person's privacy, but can it require that the press behave ethically? Journalists certainly should behave ethically, but can the law require them to keep a promise or tell the truth? This question has been tested in a number of cases.

Cohen v. Cowles Media. In 1982, Republican Wheelock Whitney was running for governor of Minnesota. With just one week to go before the election, the campaign discovered that the Democratic candidate for lieutenant governor had been arrested and convicted of a minor theft eleven years earlier. What could Whitney's campaign managers have done with this information? Simply revealing it to the public would have made them look as if they were engaging in a smear campaign. Instead, they hired local public relations practitioner Dan Cohen to leak the information to the press. Cohen spoke to a series of reporters, offering them a deal:

> I have some documents which may or may not relate to a candidate in the upcoming election, and if you will give me a promise of confidentiality—that is, that I will be treated as an anonymous source, that my name will not appear in any material in connection with this, and you will also agree that you're not going to pursue with me a question of who my source is—then I'll furnish you with the documents.[69]

Four reporters from the Minneapolis/St. Paul media agreed to Cohen's terms, and all received copies of the court documents. But once they had the documents, the media responded in three different ways. Television station WCCO decided not to run a story at all. The Associated Press distributed a brief story outlining the charges against the candidate that did not identify Cohen as the source of the story. But against the wishes of their reporters, both the *Star Tribune* and the *Pioneer Press*, the Twin Cities' leading newspapers, ran stories that identified Cohen as the source of the story. In the end, the Democratic candidates won handily, and the information about the lieutenant governor seemed to have no effect on the election.

There was, however, fallout for Cohen: He was immediately fired by his employer, who did not want to risk offending the new administration that Cohen had helped attack.

Cohen then sued the newspapers. He argued that the newspapers had entered into a verbal contract with him, exchanging a promise of confidentiality in return for the information he provided. The newspapers argued that they had done nothing wrong by printing Cohen's name. Instead, they had simply printed a true and accurate story about dirty tricks during a political campaign. Although the papers clearly broke an agreement with Cohen, they said that they were entitled to do so because they were printing the truth, which was protected by the First Amendment.

SECRET 4 The trial court found in favor of Cohen and awarded him $200,000 in damages for being fired, as well as punitive damages of $500,000. The state court of appeals, however, struck down the punitive damages. When the case reached the U.S. Supreme Court, the justices ruled by a 5–4 vote that the First Amendment did not excuse the media from having to live up to the contracts into which they entered.[70]

Controversy over the verdict arose within the press. Although it was the source who sued the press, the conflict lay primarily between editors and reporters. Could editors overrule promises made by reporters? The local reporters' union started urging reporters not to reveal their confidential sources to their editors unless the sources agreed to it. The newspaper publishers argued that the courts ought not to make judgments about journalistic ethics.

©iStockphoto.com/On-Air

Food Lion v. ABC. In some instances, the courts have not punished the press for deceptive behavior. In 1992, the ABC television newsmagazine *Primetime Live* sent undercover reporters Lynn Dale and Susan Barnett to apply for jobs as food handlers at a Food Lion grocery store. The network had been tipped off by disgruntled union officials that the store had been cleaning, bleaching, and repackaging beef, chicken, and fish that had passed its freshness date. The reporters (who did not reveal their true occupation) wore hidden microphones and cameras to document the store's misconduct. When the story ran, ABC charged that Food Lion had mixed old hamburger with new, sold improperly packaged chicken, and engaged in other unsanitary practices.[71]

SECRET 4 Food Lion sued ABC, but not for libel as might be expected. Instead, it sued the network and producers for résumé fraud and trespass. Although the story was substantially true, Food Lion was trying to punish ABC for its aggressive—some would say unethical—reporting techniques. In the initial trial, Food Lion won its case and was awarded $5.5 million in damages. (We'll talk more about the ethics of reporters lying in Chapter 14.) But the judge reduced the award to $316,402, saying that $5.5 million was excessive for lying on a job application and entering a closed area of the store.

The U.S. Court of Appeals for the Fourth Circuit reduced the damages to a symbolic $2: $1 for trespass and $1 for breach of loyalty (not serving their employer properly).[72] The court made it clear that this was not really a résumé fraud or trespass case, but a libel suit in disguise (in which truth would be an absolute defense). Food Lion argued that the broadcast had damaged its reputation and that it deserved compensation, but the court held that the reporters' only offense was lying on their résumés. The judgment, although technically ruling against ABC with the award of symbolic damages, preserved the right of journalists to report truthful information.

Prior Restraint

The most extreme and least accepted form of control of the press in the United States is **prior restraint**, a judicial order that stops a media organization from publishing a story or image. In the American colonies, prior restraint was the rule rather than the exception. All newspapers were published by the approval of the Crown; if they did not have that permission, they could not publish. But since the ratification of the First Amendment, in only a handful of cases have stories been barred from being published or broadcast.

Near v. Minnesota. The landmark case on prior restraint is the 1931 case of *Near v. Minnesota.* Jay Near was the publisher of the *Saturday Press*, a racist, anti-Semitic newspaper. Among other things, Near used his paper to charge that the police were controlled by a "Jewish gangster" and therefore were not going after gamblers and bootleggers. A Minnesota court stopped publication of the paper, using a state law allowing prosecutors to suppress publications that were "malicious, scandalous, and defamatory."

SECRET 4 On appeal, the U.S. Supreme Court ruled that the government did not have the right to suppress an entire publication merely because it was offensive. Instead, the Court said that the government could engage in prior restraint only to suppress the publication of military information during time of war, incitement to overthrow the government, or obscenity. Since none of Near's material fell into those categories, he could not be restrained from publishing it. The case established a major precedent: Although obscenity and publication of military secrets were not protected by the First Amendment, virtually everything else, no matter how offensive, was.[73]

---

prior restraint: A judicial order that stops a media organization from publishing or broadcasting a story or image.

The Pentagon Papers. The second major case of prior restraint arose in 1971, when the federal government tried to suppress newspaper stories about a top-secret, forty-seven-volume report with the irresistible title "History of U.S. Decision-Making Process on Vietnam Policy." The report, which came to be known as the Pentagon Papers, contained extensive background information about how America had become involved in the Vietnam War, going as far back as the Truman administration's assistance to France in its colonial war in Indochina. Along with this lengthy commentary were copies of the original documents on which the report was based.[74]

©iStockphoto.com/Phototreat

Daniel Ellsberg (left) was cleared of espionage charges for leaking copies of a top-secret Pentagon report to the press after it was revealed that the Nixon administration had authorized a break-in of Ellsberg's psychiatrist's office.

One of the authors of the report was Daniel Ellsberg, a former U.S. Marine who worked for the Rand Corporation think tank. Although he made only minor contributions to the massive report, he was one of the few familiar with its entire contents. Ellsberg became convinced that if the report was publicized, the public outcry would bring the war to a quicker end. So he started leaking copies of the papers to members of Congress and a few academics. Finally, in March 1971, he gave *New York Times* reporter Neil Sheehan nearly 7,000 pages from the report, withholding only the four "diplomatic" volumes, which he thought should be kept confidential.

Sheehan headed a team of reporters from the *New York Times* that read and verified what was in the papers. There was considerable debate at the *Times* about the ethics of publishing the papers.

On June 13, 1971, after three months of work, the *New York Times* started publishing stories about the Pentagon Papers. On June 14, President Richard Nixon's attorney general asked the paper to stop publishing the information, but it politely declined to do so. On June 15, the third installment of the series was published, and the Justice Department obtained a restraining order against the *Times* to prevent it from publishing any additional stories. It was, as journalist Sanford Ungar put it, "the first time in the nation's history that a newspaper was restrained in advance by a court from publishing a specific article."[75]

Ellsberg started looking for another news organization to cover the story. All three of the major broadcast networks turned him down, but the *Washington Post* was eager to obtain a copy of the papers. Lawyers for the *Post* cautioned the paper not to run the stories because the *Times* had already received a court order not to publish. But to *Washington Post* managing editor Ben Bradlee, not publishing was unthinkable—a violation of what journalism was all about: "Not publishing the information when we had it would be like not saving a drowning man, or not telling the truth."[76] So on Friday, June 18, the *Post* published its first Pentagon Papers story, and on June 19, the government obtained a restraining order against the *Post*.

At this point, the documents and stories were spreading across the country. Although approximately twenty newspapers published articles based on the Pentagon Papers, only four were taken to court: the *New York Times*, the *Washington Post*, the *Boston Globe*, and the *St. Louis Post-Dispatch*.[77]

SECRET 6 The U.S. Supreme Court heard arguments on the restraining orders on Saturday, June 26, and voted 6–3 to allow the newspapers to resume publishing their stories. Justice Potter Stewart raised the central issue in the case: Did the publication of the Pentagon Papers pose "such a grave and immediate danger as to justify prior restraint?" Stewart said that it did not: "The only effective restraint upon executive policy and power . . . may lie in an informed and enlightened citizenry—in an informed and critical public opinion which alone can here protect the values of democratic government."[78]

Justice William O. Douglas wrote that one of the primary goals of the First Amendment is to stop the government from covering up embarrassing information. In fact, the reason the First Amendment was ratified in the first place was to put a stop to random charges of seditious libel against people who were exposing embarrassing information about the government. The court pointed out that the government had been engaging in activism, not analysis, when it sought to control the release of the Pentagon Papers; in other words, this was an illustration of Secret Six—Activism and analysis are not the same thing.

Now, nearly forty years later, the lessons of *New York Times Co. v. United States*[79] (informally known as the Pentagon Papers case) are still relevant. While the Pentagon Papers were classified "top secret," the secrets they contained were embarrassing political secrets, not dangerous military secrets.[80] In 1989, Erwin Griswold, who had argued the government's case before the Supreme Court, said that he had "never seen any trace of a threat to the national security" from publication of the papers.[81]

But what about Daniel Ellsberg, the man who leaked copies of the Pentagon Papers to the press? The legality of Ellsberg's releasing the documents was never really resolved. Ellsberg was indicted on charges of conspiracy, misappropriation of government property, and violating the Espionage Act. But the court eventually declared a mistrial and dismissed the charges against him after it was revealed that the Nixon administration had Ellsberg's psychiatrist's office burglarized and made illegal recordings of the sessions there. In recent years, Ellsberg has spoken out against the Persian Gulf War and the invasion of Iraq.[82]

The* Progressive *Case. In the Pentagon Papers case, the newspapers were desperately trying to publish their articles. But eight years later, author Howard Morland and the *Progressive* magazine *wanted* to have an article censored. Morland was an Air Force pilot turned antinuclear activist who maintained that the government was concealing details about how hydrogen bombs operate—not for security reasons but to stifle public opposition to the weapon. Morland used unclassified documents and interviews with scientists to write an article explaining how these weapons of mass destruction worked. Morland and the *Progressive* knew that censorship would transform the article from an obscure piece in a radical magazine into a cause célèbre that would receive nationwide publicity.

©iStockphoto.com/Phototreat

They got their wish. A former professor of Morland's submitted an early draft of the article to the U.S. Department of Energy (DOE), which manages nuclear material in the United States. In addition, the magazine's editor sent the article and drawings to the DOE to have them checked for accuracy. On March 1, 1979, a district court judge in Wisconsin issued a temporary restraining order against the *Progressive* because the article presented a "clear and present danger" to the United States.

It initially appeared that the government might have a good case against Morland and the *Progressive*. The *Near* case (discussed earlier in this chapter) had established that the government could censor a publication that published "the sailing dates of transports or the number and location of troops." Although the types of information involved in national security had changed since *Near*, the same argument might be made—that the article would compromise national security by giving away military secrets. (It should be noted that although the article explained how a hydrogen bomb worked, it did not provide instructions for building one.)

Central to the *Progressive*'s defense was the argument that there were no secrets in the article because all the material it contained was available from nonclassified sources. The government argued that Morland's organization of the material into an article made it a security problem.[83] While the *Progressive* case was under appeal, a number of people started working on similar articles. *Milwaukee Journal Sentinel* reporter Joe Manning re-created Morland's research and published a two-part story that covered the three "secrets" from Morland's article in fairly simple terms. Then nuclear hobbyist Charles Hansen wrote an eighteen-page letter to the editor of the *Madison Press Connection* that outlined much the same information as Morland's article. On September 17, 1979, the day after the Hansen letter appeared, the government dropped its case, declaring that its attempt to suppress the information was "meaningless, superfluous, unnecessary, inconsequent."[84]

The *Progressive* finally ran Morland's article in November 1979 under the headline "The H-Bomb Secret: How We Got It, Why We're Telling It," but it was a somewhat hollow victory for the magazine.[85] Its editors had gotten the attention they sought, but unfortunately for them, everyone saw the case as a freedom-of-the-press issue—not the important debate over nuclear weapons they were hoping for.

The Pentagon Papers and *Progressive* cases have two important implications. The first is that much information that the government would like to believe is secret is actually public knowledge. The second is that in a free and open society it is very difficult to keep information secret that determined people want to make public. And with the addition of the Internet to the range of available media, virtually anyone is able to publish any information widely and easily. Although it is still possible to punish individuals and media corporations after the fact for publishing or broadcasting inappropriate material, prior restraint is becoming virtually impossible in the United States and the Western democracies.

Free Speech and Students

Do the rights that protect adult journalists also protect student reporters working on high school newspapers? More than twenty-five years ago, the U.S. Supreme Court decided the answer is no. In 1988, a group of high school students in Hazelwood, Missouri, sued the school system because their principal had barred articles about pregnancy and divorce from the student newspaper. The Supreme Court in *Hazelwood v. Kuhlmeier*[86] ruled that a

Web 13.9: Read about students getting expelled for posting online.

Web 13.10: What are the implications of the *Hazelwood* decision twenty-five years later?

principal could censor a student newspaper when it was produced as part of a class. It wrote:

> The First Amendment rights of students in the public schools are not automatically co-extensive with the rights of adults in other settings . . . A school need not tolerate student speech that is inconsistent with its "basic educational mission," even though the government could not censor similar speech outside the school.[87]

The Court ruled that the student newspaper is a classroom exercise rather than a vehicle for free speech, and hence administrators may censor any content that is "reasonably related to legitimate pedagogical concerns."[88]

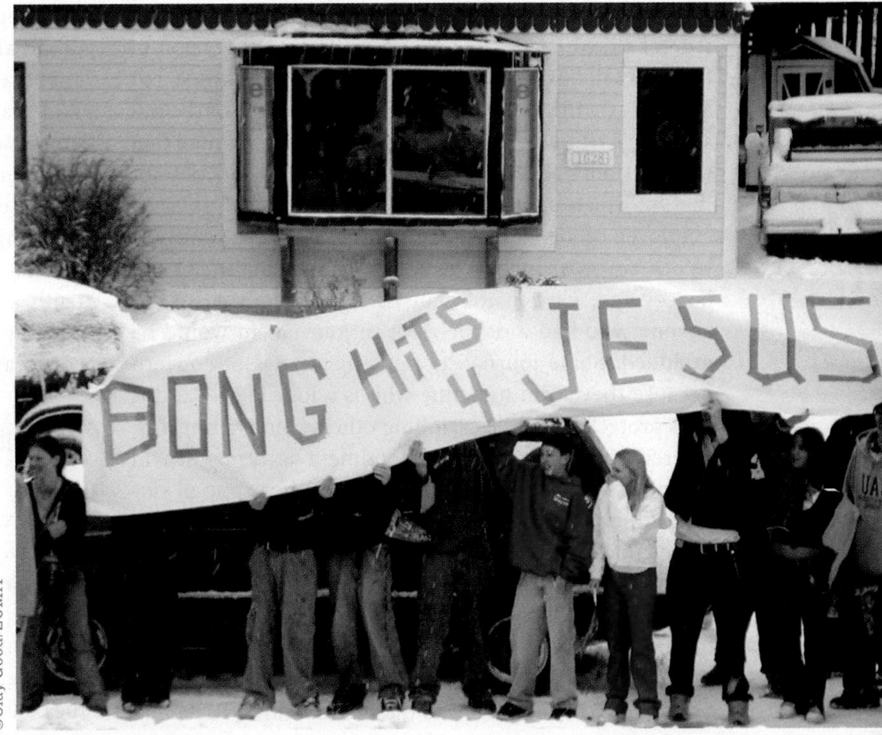

©Clay Good/ZUMA

Student Joseph Frederick was suspended from his high school in 2002 for displaying a sign reading "BONG HiTS 4 JESUS" across the street from the school when the Olympic torch came through his town of Juneau, Alaska. The U.S. Supreme Court supported his suspension in a 5–4 ruling.

One way students have reacted against this censorship is by starting Web-based newspapers that are not sponsored by the school. In addition, at least six states have passed laws that restore to high school students the rights they had prior to the *Hazelwood* decision. These laws limit the circumstances under which student newspapers can be censored, generally allowing articles to be banned only if they are "libelous, obscene, or will create a substantial disruption of school activities."[89]

There have also been several cases that dealt with schools trying to limit the free speech of students in other venues. Some schools have attempted to limit what students can post to either blogs or social networking sites such as Facebook and MySpace. Three middle school students in the Chicago area were suspended after they posted "obscene and threatening" comments about a teacher in their blog. Schools in the Washington, D.C., area have banned students from using their school-provided e-mail accounts to register with Facebook.[90] And a student in Indiana was expelled from high school for a grammar joke laced with the "*F* word" that he tweeted late at night from what he claims was his own computer.[91]

Student Joseph Frederick was suspended from a Juneau, Alaska, high school in 2002 by the principal, Deborah Morse, for holding up a giant sign saying "BONG HiTS 4 JESUS" across the street from his high school as the Olympic torch passed through his town.[92] The school district in the case claims that the student was promoting drug use. The student responded, "I wasn't trying to say anything about drugs. I was just trying to say *something*. I wanted to use my right to free speech, and I did it."[93] The case, known as *Morse v. Frederick*, was heard by the U.S. Supreme Court in 2007. The Court ruled on June 25, 2007, that principals could punish speech that could "reasonably be viewed" as promoting the use of illegal drugs.[94]

Questioning the Media

Do students lose their First Amendment rights when they enter the schoolhouse door? Why or why not? Should school administrators be able to freely censor student publications?

Interestingly enough, the student received support from the ACLU, gay rights advocates, and the Christian Legal Society (CLS). (The CLS and gay rights groups were concerned that other school districts might use the case as a way of limiting speech about religious or gay rights issues.)

Many students may not be aware that their rights are being limited or what their rights entail. A survey of more than 100,000 high-school-aged students found that three-fourths of them believed incorrectly that flag burning was a crime. The survey also found that 36 percent of students said newspapers should get government permission before publishing stories and that 32 percent said the press has "too much freedom to do what it wants."[95]

Journalists Going to Jail

Many states have **shield laws** that protect journalists from having to testify in court (and divulge sources) under certain circumstances, but there is currently no federal shield law in place. Many journalists are lobbying strongly for one.

---

shield laws: Laws that give journalists special protection from having to testify in court about their stories and sources.

The U.S. Senate has been considering bills creating a federal shield law for several years. The 2014 version of the bill easily passed out of the Judiciary Committee, but as of this writing had not been put up for a vote of the full senate.[96] Critiques of earlier versions of the bill noted that it would only cover a reporter or blogger who "obtains the information sought while working as a salaried employee of, or independent contractor for, an entity."[97] In other words, only professional, paid journalists would be covered. Citizen journalists, student journalists, or anyone who had a day job not in journalism would be excluded. Some journalists find shield laws of concern because they seem to define who is a journalist—and is thus protected—while excluding others who are not considered journalists. First Amendment attorney David Bodney says, "Any attempt to legislate the scope of our First Amendment rights is unsettling business."[98] Despite these concerns, Bodney does support the proposed federal law.

Since the 1960s, a number of journalists have either been fined or sent to jail for refusing to testify in federal courts. These have included journalists who witnessed drug crimes or the actions of the Black Panther Party and some who interviewed murder suspects.

More recently, journalists Matt Cooper and Judith Miller faced fines and jail time for refusing to testify to a federal grand jury about who had leaked information to them about the identity of a covert CIA officer. Both were eventually granted permission to testify by the source they sought to protect, vice presidential adviser I. Lewis "Scooter" Libby Jr. *Time* magazine's Cooper testified without serving jail time after his employer ordered him to do so. *New York Times* reporter Miller went to jail for eighty-five days for refusing to testify in the same case. Miller finally accepted the release by Libby from her promise of confidentiality and testified.[99]

Are Bloggers Protected? As concerned journalists are aware, the big question is who is entitled to shield law protection. There is no question that shield laws protect newspaper, television, and radio reporters, but what about independent bloggers? Are they considered journalists too? Possibly, but this isn't a certainty. A California judge ruled that three blogging sites had to reveal their sources of company secrets about Apple Inc., but that decision was overturned on appeal, when the court ruled that bloggers were protected by California's shield law.[100]

San Francisco blogger Josh Wolf spent close to eight months in jail after refusing to testify about an anarchists' demonstration he witnessed, the longest sentence to date served by a member of the media. Wolf answered two questions for prosecutors and released a copy of videotape he had shot, something he had been willing to do all along. What he was *not* willing to do was testify about all he had seen at the demonstration.[101] While Wolf was in jail, a debate raged as to whether he deserved protection as a journalist. He had not made a promise of confidentiality, nor was he employed by a mainstream media outlet. But Wolf maintained that when he was shooting video, he was acting as a journalist. "It was journalism to the extent that I went out to capture the truth and present it to the public," Wolf said. "It has nothing to do with whether or not I'm employed by a corporation or I carry a press pass."[102]

Web 13.11: An example of why bloggers matter.

Obscenity

The *Near* case, in addition to allowing prior restraint of sensitive military information, established that obscene material is not protected by the First Amendment. The term **obscenity** describes sexually explicit material that is legally prohibited from being published. This raises the question of what kinds of material can be considered obscene. Finding the answer has proved difficult, both for the courts and for society.[103]

Roth v. United States. The Supreme Court made its first contemporary attempt to answer the question of what constitutes obscenity in 1957 in *Roth v. United States.*[104] Samuel Roth, who ran a business selling sexually explicit books, photos, and magazines, had been convicted of mailing obscene material through the U.S. Postal Service. He appealed his case to the U.S. Supreme Court, which eventually upheld his conviction. But more important, the Court used the case to start establishing standards for what was and was not protected by the First Amendment. The *Roth* case reaffirmed that the courts could regulate obscenity and that obscenity is not protected by the First Amendment. But the justices also cautioned that "sex and obscenity are not synonymous."[105]

With *Roth*, the court established a three-part test to help determine whether something is obscene: "Whether to the average person, applying contemporary community standards, the dominant theme of the material taken as a whole appeals to prurient interests."[106] The three parts of this test can be analyzed as follows:

1. The standard for obscenity is set by individual "community standards" using the view of an "average person." This means that neither the most liberal nor the most conservative view should be used, nor should there be a national standard.

2. The work must be "taken as a whole." It's not enough for there to be a single sexually explicit section; the work as a whole must be explicit to be obscene.

obscenity: Sexually explicit material that is legally prohibited from being published.

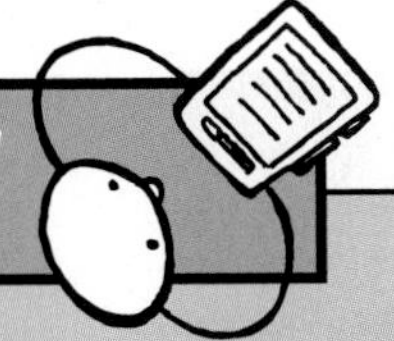

TEST YOUR MEDIA LITERACY

Citizens United v. Federal Election Commission

Is spending money on behalf of a candidate or an issue the same as speaking out in favor of or in opposition to it? According to the case of *Citizens United v. Federal Election Commission*, it is.[1]

In the case, a nonprofit company sued to be able to run a documentary film on cable television that some saw as a thinly disguised anti–Hillary Clinton political ad. The Federal Election Commission (FEC) said the film couldn't be aired because the McCain-Feingold public law dealing with campaign financing prohibited corporate-funded commercials for or against a presidential candidate from being aired less than thirty days before the election.

Citizens United appealed the ruling, and the U.S. Supreme Court ruled that organizations such as corporations and labor unions, as well as individuals, could give money in unlimited amounts to political action committees (PACs). These so-called super PACs can bundle together contributions to either support or oppose a particular candidate or issue. The one caveat is that the committees are not allowed to directly coordinate their activities with those of a candidate's official campaign.

How separate these are is a matter of some debate, with top campaign officials oftentimes being on the steering committees for the associated super PAC.

James Bopp, a conservative activist lawyer, argues that the Court's decision makes it possible for individuals and organizations to create more political speech through their spending. As an example, multimillionaire Sheldon Adelson helped keep Newt Gingrich's primary run for the Republican nomination going in 2012 by making a $10 million donation to Gingrich's super PAC. Other supporters of the decision argue that the ads supported by the super PACs create a better informed public.[2]

Before the *Citizens United* case, an individual could spend unlimited money directly on advertising that supported or attacked a candidate, but he or she couldn't give that money to a political action committee.[3]

AP Photo/Dana Verkouteran

Photographers aren't allowed to take pictures of the U.S. Supreme Court in action, so news outlets use sketch artists to portray the action there. This sketch from 2009 shows then–U.S. solicitor general Elena Kagan arguing the case of *Citizens United v. Federal Election Commission*. Kagan went on to become an associate justice of the court in 2010.

Critics of the ruling argue that it puts almost unlimited political power in the hands of those who have the most money to spend.[4]

WHAT is the source?

What is the case of *Citizens United v. Federal Election Commission*? What was Citizens United arguing?

WHAT was the ruling?

How did the U.S. Supreme Court decide in this case? What were the Court's other options?

WHAT evidence is there?

Read the linked articles for more on the *Citizens United* case, then answer the following question: How has the *Citizens United* case changed politics in the United States? How did the justices make their ruling?

WHAT do you and your classmates think about the *Citizens United* case?

Is the spending of money the same as political speech? How do you view the *Citizens United* case? Does it free up the political process or put too much power in the hands of a few individuals?

[1]Jeffrey Toobin, "Annals of Law: Money Unlimited," *New Yorker*, May 21, 2012, www.newyorker.com/reporting/2012/05/21/120521fa_fact_toobin.

[2]Terry Gross, "Understanding the Impact of Citizens United," NPR.org, February 12, 2012, www.npr.org/2012/02/23/147294511/understanding-the-impact-of-citizens-united.

[3]Richard L. Hasen, "The Numbers Don't Lie," *Slate*, March 9, 2012, www.slate.com/articles/news_and_politics/politics/2012/03/the_supreme_court_s_citizens_united_decision_has_led_to_an_explosion_of_campaign_spending_.html.

[4]Joan Walsh, "John Roberts' Gilded Age SCOTUS," *Salon*, May 14, 2012, www.salon.com/2012/05/14/john_roberts_gilded_age_scotus/singleton/.

Audio 13.1: Listen to more on the *Citizens United* case.

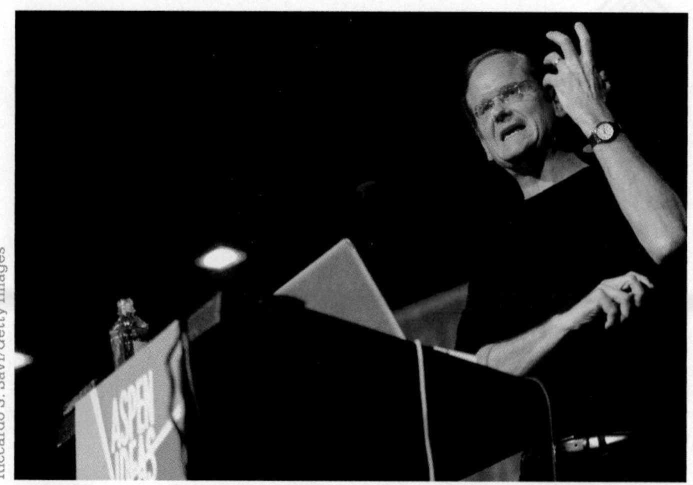
Riccardo S. Savi/Getty Images

Stanford University law professor Lawrence Lessig led the group that created the alternative copyright licenses known as Creative Commons.

3. The work must appeal to "prurient interests." This is the most difficult point. Prurient interest means, according to the Court, an "exacerbated, morbid or perverted" interest in nudity, sex, or excretory functions.[107]

Miller v. California. The standards established in the *Roth* case were refined with the Supreme Court's ruling in *Miller v. California*. Like Roth, Miller had been convicted of sending obscene material through the mail. The *Miller* case upheld the basic standard from *Roth* but had further impact in two key areas. The first is that states have used this ruling to ban child pornography, and many states have added laws that ban other types of content.

The second key aspect of *Miller* is it held that material that has "serious literary, artistic, political, or scientific value" cannot be banned. This protects, for example, information about sexual health and birth control. It also protects erotic literature, such as D. H. Lawrence's novel *Lady Chatterley's Lover. Miller* also reaffirmed that local communities could set their own standards. There is not an expectation, the Court said, that "the people of Maine or Mississippi accept public depiction of conduct found tolerable in Las Vegas or New York City."[108]

Obscenity in the Information Age. The *Roth* and *Miller* standards both assume that obscene material is being sold at a particular location in a particular community. Neither case anticipated the problems raised by the growth of the Internet and satellite television. What can the courts do about sexually explicit material that is located on a Web server in New York City but is viewed by a person in Morgantown, West Virginia? Attorney Rieko Mashima's piece in *Computer Lawyer* explains the problem: "On the Internet, which is available to a nationwide audience, a sender of information can neither control where it will be downloaded or through which places it will travel, nor tailor contents for different communities."[109]

Web 13.12: Is this the copyright law revision we need?

Pay-per-view cable and satellite television provide a similar problem. In 1999, Larry W. Peterman, owner of a video store in Provo, Utah, was charged with renting obscene films and appeared to be headed to jail. Then his lawyer came up with the idea of recording all the erotic movies that could be seen on pay-per-view at the Provo Marriott Hotel across the street from the courtroom. A little more research found that far more people in Provo were buying adult movies from cable and satellite providers and in hotels than from Peterman's video store. The jury promptly acquitted Peterman on all charges.[110]

The courts have yet to rule definitively on how to handle local control of pornography delivered by satellite or Internet, although Congress made an attempt to do so with the Telecommunications Act of 1996, discussed later in this chapter. And as of 2004, the Federal Communications Commission (FCC) started cracking down on what it called "indecent" communication on broadcast television, as discussed in Chapter 9.

Regulation of the Media Industry

The print media have been largely unregulated throughout the history of the United States beyond copyright and fair use provisions. But broadcast media have been necessarily controlled from the beginning, for two reasons: Radio and television stations have to meet certain technical standards to keep from interfering with each other's broadcasts, and the government has an interest in making sure that the limited number of broadcast frequencies available are used in the public interest. In this section, we look at how these controls of the media industry have been applied.

Copyright and Fair Use

Creators of books, newspapers, magazines, music, and other media products have been protected from having their works appropriated by others since the first U.S. copyright law was passed in 1790. In the law's original form, works were protected for fourteen years, and copyright could be renewed for an additional fourteen years. This protection was extended only to American authors and artists, however. It wasn't until the 1890s that copyright was extended to works by authors and artists from other countries. Under the leadership of Barbara Ringer in the 1960s and 1970s (discussed at the beginning of this chapter), the length of copyright was increased from the original twenty-eight years to fifty years after the creator's death for an individual copyright. In 1998, the Copyright Term Extension Act extended individual copyright to seventy years after the creator's death, and extended corporate copyright to ninety-five years. Why ninety-five years for the corporate copyright? If not for that extension, Mickey Mouse would have entered the public domain in 2003.[111] The 1998 Digital Millennium Copyright Act expanded the copyright on materials that are recorded digitally, such as electronic books, CDs, and DVDs. It has long been illegal to distribute duplicate copies of electronic material without permission, but the act also makes it a crime to produce software or hardware designed to break the copy protection on movies, music, or other software. The act leaves users in an odd position: It is legal to make a backup copy of a DVD movie for personal use, but it is illegal to use a computer program that will make a copy of the protected movie.[112] In 2002, a group led by Sanford University law professor Lawrence Lessig created an alternative set of copyright licenses known as Creative Commons that allow authors and artists to reserve a limited set of rights for a creative work without using all the restrictions of a conventional copyright. For example, a photographer can license his or her photo so that anyone can use the image without permission as long as he or she attributes the photo to the original creator. The main advantage of Creative Commons is that it allows creators a middle ground between full copyright and placing their work in the public domain.[113]

©iStockphoto.com/ Stepan Popov

The Rise and Fall of Broadcast Regulation

Broadcast regulation began with the Radio Act of 1912, passed immediately after the sinking of the *Titanic*. But this regulation dealt only with point-to-point communication, such as ship-to-shore radio. Meanwhile, commercial broadcasting got its start in 1920 when radio station KDKA went on the air in Pittsburgh. By 1925, broadcasters were calling for regulation by the government to bring stability to the new industry.

The Radio Act of 1927 created the Federal Radio Commission. This act was also the first to charge broadcast stations with acting in the "public interest, convenience, and necessity." With the Communications Act of 1934, the Radio Commission evolved into the Federal Communications Commission. The 1934 act brought all electronic communication, wired and wireless, under the control of the FCC, but the basic tenets of the 1927 act remained in place:[114]

- The airwaves are licensed to broadcasters, but the broadcasters do not own them.
- The FCC has the power to regulate broadcasters to ensure that they act in the public interest.
- The FCC can tell broadcasters what frequencies and power to use and where their transmitters can be located.

Mandating Fairness on the Air

In addition to attempting to regulate the murky area of indecency, the FCC has regulated how broadcasters handle political campaigns and controversial issues.

The Equal Time Provision. The FCC's **equal time provision** requires broadcast stations to make equivalent amounts of broadcast time available to all candidates running for public office. The rule does not require stations to provide time to candidates; it requires them only to ensure that all candidates have equal access. So if a station sells time to one candidate, it must be willing to sell an equal amount of similarly valuable time to all candidates who can afford it. The rule also states that if a station gives free non–news time to one candidate, it must provide similar amounts of free time to all candidates. The purpose of the rule is to prevent stations from favoring one candidate over another while making use of a valuable public resource.[115]

The equal time provision has been subject to controversy in cases where candidates have sought to run ads that are either offensive or libelous. Because stations cannot edit or censor anything in political advertisements, the FCC has ruled that broadcasters are not responsible for libelous statements made in political ads. There has also been conflict over explicit antiabortion ads. In 1992 and 1994, some stations channeled the graphic messages and images contained in such ads to a "safe harbor" time between midnight and 6 a.m., when children were unlikely to see them. Indiana congressional candidate Michael Bailey objected to the channeling, saying that the explicit ads were an essential part of his campaign; he persuaded stations to run the ads during prime time, although the stations ran disclaimers before many of them. The FCC has since said that ads dealing with abortion could be channeled into the "safe harbor" time periods.[116]

There are limits to what candidates can do. When *Hustler* publisher Larry Flynt declared that he would run for president and would broadcast pornographic campaign commercials under the equal time provision, the FCC said that the "no censorship" clause would not apply to "obscene or indecent political announcements."

The Fairness Doctrine. More controversial than the equal time provision was the **fairness doctrine**. Under this 1949 rule, stations were required to cover controversial issues of public interest and to present contrasting views on those issues. The fairness doctrine required not that stations give the same amount of time to all sides of an

equal time provision: An FCC policy that requires broadcast stations to make equivalent amounts of broadcast time available to all candidates running for public office.

fairness doctrine: A former FCC policy that required television stations to "afford reasonable opportunity for the discussion of conflicting views on issues of public importance."

MEDIA TRANSFORMATIONS

Who Owns Your Social Media Content?

You've posted a lot of material on social media. You've got several hundred photos of you and your friends, all tagged with your names and locations. You've got stories about your vacation, a political rant or two, and tons of birthday wishes you've handed out. Most of those photos you post or tweet are of interest only to you, your family, or your friends. But suppose you share a photo you've taken of breaking news on your Twitter feed, and a couple of legacy media outlets publish the photo without payment to you. Is that OK?

The question of who owns what you've posted to social media sites is complex, and it has big implications on how we pay for the sites with access online. The exact uses that a social media site can make of your content depend in part on its terms of service (TOS) agreement—the endlessly long document you clicked off on agreeing with to use the service.

Social media sites almost certainly are not allowed to provide or resell your content to other publishers. Freelance photographer Daniel Morel successfully sued for payment from both the photo agency Agence France-Presse (AFP) and the *Washington Post* for reprinting or distributing photos Morel had tweeted of the 2010 Haitian earthquake. AFP argued that because Morel had posted high-resolution images of his photos to Twitter he was allowing any use of his images.[117]

It's Your Selfie...But Is It Facebook's Property?
Most companies agree that user generated content (UGC) is the posters' intellectual property, but users often do not understand that many companies also have explicit rights to use, alter, or even sell that content once it has been posted.
Pieces of UGC shared on Facebook in one year
360 billion
Photos uploaded to Facebook per year, at the current rate
36 billion
To Flicker
130 million
Number of videos watched per month on YouTube
60 million
35 Hours of video uploaded to YouTube every minute
84% Millenials reporting that UGC influenced their purchasing decisions
74% Boomers who responded similarly
Are you oversharing with your favorite social media site?
You own the content you post on the site, as long as it is your intellectual property.
And, technically, you can control how the content is shared on the site.
But does the site have the explicit right to adapt your content? Can it redistribute it?
facebook
Yes, both. Any material you post in publicly accessible areas can be sub-licensed by Facebook, including to sites other than Facebook, and may be adapted.
flickr
Yahoo!, owner of Flickr, can distribute and adapt your images "solely for the purposes for which Content was submitted" but that right applies only to Yahoo! sites. Yahoo! does not grant the right to third parties to use your content.
Google+
Yes, Google has the right to adapt your content for "the purposes of operating, promoting and improving [their] services and to develop new ones" and they can continue to do that even after you stop using the service. Google does not claim the right to redistribute your content.
Instagram
Instagram may "use" your content, including via sub-licensing agreements, though the terms of service do not explicitly say your content may be adapted.
twitter
Yes, both. Twitter can sub-license and adapt your content, including to third parties.
Source: Data are from Kathy E. Gill, spreadsheet associated with the article "Who Really Owns Your Photos in Social Media? (Updated 2013 Edition)." Mediashift, PBS.org https://docs.google.com/spreadsheet/ccc?key=0AnXSzfUpz7nXdFd6UlBkTjd4MWRkU3JOT2lkWHdqQVE#gid=0
Sources:
http://www.poynter.org/latest-news/top-stories/241949/who-owns-ellen-degeneres-oscar-selfie
http://www.fastcompany.com/3021749/work-smart/10-surprising-social-media-statistics-that-will-make-you-rethink-your-social-stra
http://socialnewsdaily.com/1185/infographic-revenue-from-user-generated-content-on-social-media
http://video-commerce.org/2012/02/how-user-generated-video-reviews-are-convincing-millennials-to-buy-more-of-your-stuff
http://blog.bazaarvoice.com/2012/01/24/infographic-millennials-will-change-the-way-you-sell
25% Facebook users who don't bother using privacy settings
Revenues from User Generated Content
Twitter $645 million
LinkedIn $1.5 billion
YouTube $1.5 billion
Facebook $7.8 billion
Sources: http://www.statista.com/statistics/271582/revenue-of-selected-social-media-companies
http://www.businessinsider.com/youtubes-2013-revenue-2014-7

But if you post photos to a sharing service like Tumblr or Pinterest, other users of the service are allowed to reblog or pin what you've put up as long as they don't claim the work as their own. And once you've posted an image, you have no guarantee that deleting the photo will ever get it completely off the social network.[118]

The one thing social media sites are absolutely able to do is target advertising at you based on the content you post or respond to online—which is why your author continues to get ads for science fiction and action movies on his Facebook page.

Media Transformations Questions

- **HAVE** you ever posted something to a social media site that could have commercial value? What was it? What did you do to protect it?
- **HOW** have you made use of photos, artwork, or other content you've found on social media sites?
- **WHY** might legacy news outlets want to use materials that initially show up through social media channels?

Web 13.13: Have you read your social media Terms of Service lately?

issue, but rather that they "afford reasonable opportunity for the discussion of conflicting views on issues of public importance."[119]

The major objection to the fairness doctrine was that stations might avoid covering controversial issues because they did not want to present extreme viewpoints or cover every aspect of an issue. For example, stations would argue that they did not want to cover issues dealing with racism for fear of having to give the Ku Klux Klan an opportunity to participate. Critics argued that the public suffered because they received no coverage of issues rather than every possible variation.

A 1985 study by the FCC found that the fairness doctrine tended to inhibit free speech and was no longer needed because of new media outlets such as cable television. Moreover, the FCC had had to deal with thousands of complaints filed under the rule each year. Following publication of the 1985 study, the FCC essentially stopped enforcing the fairness doctrine, and it was repealed in 1987.[120] Despite this, radio talk show hosts such as Rush Limbaugh continued to argue that the federal government was considering bringing back the fairness doctrine in order to silence conservative commentators.[121] In a strange footnote, the FCC announced in the summer of 2011 that it was finally taking the language that authorized the fairness doctrine out of its regulation book. Why was it still listed there despite being repealed in 1987? Technically, it was still the rule even though the FCC had voted against its enforcement nearly twenty-five years earlier.[122]

The Telecommunications Act of 1996

The Telecommunications Act of 1996 has been called the biggest reform of broadcast regulation since the formation of the FCC in 1934.

Revising Broadcast Regulation. The section of the Telecommunications Act that attracted the most attention was the one calling for the creation of the V-chip, which allows parents to electronically block material with a particular content rating. But the greatest impact the act has had is that it relaxed most of the rules that restricted how many broadcast stations a particular company can own. This led to the rapid turnover of many broadcast properties and an increasing concentration of ownership, completing a trend that began in the 1970s and 1980s.[123] (For more about concentration of media ownership, see Chapter 3.)

Regulation of the Internet. In addition to calling for the V-chip, the Communications Decency Act provision of the Telecommunications Act of 1996 attempted to regulate the Internet in a similar way to the regulation of broadcasting.

Figuring out what kind of medium the Internet is from a legal standpoint has been a problem for both Congress and the courts. On the one hand, the Internet looks something like television because it comes in over a wire and is displayed on a screen, and many Web sites are maintained by the same companies that operate television networks. On the other hand, the Internet can be seen as more like a newspaper or magazine. There's a great deal of print on the Internet, and newspapers have a strong presence there. Also, the number of channels on the Internet is not limited, as is the case with broadcast or even cable television. But, unlike both television and print, the Internet has strong elements of interpersonal communication, resembling the telephone network in this respect. There is no central authority controlling what can and cannot be said on the Internet. Some observers argue that perhaps regulation of the Internet should model regulation of the telephone system. Others say the Internet might qualify as an open public forum, without any need for regulation at all.[124]

In reality, the Internet has elements of all these media—radio, broadcast and cable television, telephone,

Web 13.14: Read about the death of the fairness doctrine.

Questioning the Media

Given that we can access huge amounts of video and audio online, is there any good reason for the government to continue regulating broadcast content? Why or why not?

newspapers, and magazines. The companies that provide high-speed Internet service to the home are regulated to a degree, as are phone or cable television companies. First Amendment protection for media sites on the Web is similar to that given to print media. Individuals have the same levels of responsibility for what they say through the Internet as they do anywhere else. In general, Internet bulletin boards and chat rooms are treated in much the same way as telephone communication. The people posting to the bulletin boards, not the company providing Internet access, are responsible for what they say, just as a phone company is not responsible for a libelous or defamatory phone call or fax sent over its lines.

In the fall of 2009, the FCC started working on writing rules on **Net neutrality**, rules that would require Internet providers to provide equal access to content from all providers. Under Net neutrality, telecommunication providers could not favor their own products over those of others. For example, without Net neutrality regulations, a company that provided its own online video service could slow down access to video provider YouTube. Internet providers argue that forcing such companies to give unlimited bandwidth to applications such as streaming video could slow down access for the majority of their customers who don't use such services.[125]

The many levels of communication on the Internet make it extremely difficult to control. The Communications Decency Act attempted to ban Internet messages that are "obscene, lewd, lascivious, filthy, or indecent." The law was opposed by the American Library Association, the Electronic Frontier Foundation (an electronic communication rights group), and the ACLU, among others. Although the law banned only the transmission of indecent messages to minors, it seemed impossible to keep minors out of discussions involving adults.

In 1997, the Supreme Court struck down the Communications Decency Act as an unconstitutional limit on the free speech of adults. It ruled that the possibility of a minor being present in a chat room did not remove the adults' First Amendment rights. Justice John Paul Stevens wrote in the majority opinion, "The interest in encouraging freedom of expression in a democratic society outweighs any theoretical but unproven benefit of censorship."[126] The only certainty is that Congress will continue to consider how to regulate communication on the Internet.

Since 1997, attempts have been made to pass new legislation that would control "indecent" content on the Web without infringing on the free speech of adults. As of this writing, the Child Online Protection Act (a follow-up law that attempts to deal with weaknesses in the Communications Decency Act) was still working its way through the courts.[127] You can read more about regulation of the Internet in Chapter 10.[128]

Net neutrality: Rules that would require Internet service providers to give equal access to all online content providers.

Chapter SUMMARY

The First Amendment to the U.S. Constitution says that

> Congress shall make no law respecting an establishment of religion, or prohibiting the free exercise thereof; or abridging the freedom of speech, or of the press; or the right of the people peaceably to assemble, and to petition the Government for a redress of grievances.

This statement is at the core of all media law in the United States. The purpose of the amendment is to protect the free and open discussion necessary to a democratic society. Although the First Amendment guarantees the right of free speech, Congress has passed several laws that limit this freedom. These include the Alien and Sedition Acts of 1798; the Espionage Act of 1917; the Smith Act of 1940; the USA PATRIOT Act of 2001; and laws controlling libel, invasion of privacy, publication of military secrets, and obscenity.

The rights of individuals are protected from actions of the media through libel law, invasion of privacy law, and guarantees of a fair trial. Libel is a statement that unjustifiably exposes someone to ridicule or contempt. For a statement to be libelous, it must include defamation, identification, and publication. In general, the media are allowed to publish defamatory material that is true, privileged, or a statement of opinion. *New York Times Co. v. Sullivan* established that public officials seeking to win a libel suit must show that the media acted with actual malice in publishing a false defamatory statement.

There are four basic forms of invasion of privacy: intrusion, embarrassment, false light, and misappropriation. In some cases, journalists can defend themselves against charges of invasion of privacy by showing that the story in question was newsworthy. There is often a conflict between an individual's right to a fair trial and the press's right to cover that trial. The Supreme Court has generally ruled that the judge, not the press, is responsible for guaranteeing the defendant a fair trial. The Court has also ruled that protection of the right to a fair trial should require as few limits on the freedom of the press as possible. This can be done by imposing gag orders, sequestering the jury, postponing or changing the venue of a trial, or ordering a new trial.

Since 1977, courts in the United States have been experimenting with allowing cameras in the courtroom. Proponents of such a policy argue that televising trials allows the public to better understand how the justice system works. Opponents argue that cameras are intrusive and turn trials into media circuses.

Although the press is subject to the same laws as society as a whole, it is protected from censorship in most cases. The government is allowed to prevent publication of certain information only if the material is obscene or gives away military secrets during time of war. There have been only three major cases involving prior restraint: *Near v. Minnesota*, the Pentagon Papers case, and the *Progressive* H-bomb story. High school newspapers published as a classroom activity are not afforded the same level of protection, however. The courts have ruled that obscenity is not protected by the First Amendment, and they have established that the standard for obscenity will be set using state law and local community standards.

The broadcast media traditionally have been regulated much more heavily than the print media because they make use of the public airwaves. They are regulated both for technical reasons and to ensure that they serve the public interest. Major legislation controlling the broadcast media was passed in 1927, 1934, and 1996. Standards for regulating the Internet are still evolving, but they appear to be more similar to print regulations than to broadcast ones.

Keep up-to-date with content from the author's blog.

Take the chapter quiz.

Key TERMS

Alien and Sedition Acts 331
libel 332
privilege 332
actual malice 334
intrusion 334
false light 335
misappropriation 335
prior restraint 340
shield laws 343
obscenity 344
equal time provision 347
fairness doctrine 347
Net neutrality 350

Concept REVIEW

Conflict between the right of free speech and the protection of individuals' reputations

Elements of the First Amendment

Defenses against libel

Defenses against invasion of privacy suits

Conflict between the right to a free press and the right to a fair trial

Obligations of the press

Ways in which the press may be controlled

Students' rights to free speech

Differences between obscenity and indecency (see also the discussion in Chapter 9)

Changes in broadcast regulation

Student STUDY SITE

Sharpen your skills with SAGE edge at **edge.sagepub.com/hanson5e**

SAGE edge for Students provides a personalized approach to help you accomplish your coursework goals in an easy-to-use learning environment.

chapter 14

Media Ethics

Truthfulness, Fairness, and Standards of Decency

Veronika Lukasova/ ZUMA Press/Corbis

AP photographer Richard Drew (right) shot many iconic images in downtown Manhattan on September 11, 2001, including this image of the World Trade Center's north tower collapsing.

AP Photo/Richard Drew

Photographer Richard Drew got up on September 11, 2001, to work the 7:00 a.m. to 4:30 p.m. shift covering New York City for the Associated Press. His assignment for the morning was to photograph a maternity fashion show featuring pregnant models. Around 9:00 a.m., his cell phone rang, and his editor told him, "Bag the fashion show—you have to go." An airplane had hit the south tower of the World Trade Center. No one yet knew that this was the start of a day of terrorist attacks on the United States that would include two planes hitting the twin towers of the World Trade Center in New York, a plane crashing into the Pentagon near Washington, D.C., and a plane crash landing in a field in rural Pennsylvania.[1]

When Drew got to the World Trade Center, he faced a chilling sight. People who were trapped in the towers above the floors where the airliners had struck the buildings faced an impossible choice: flames and jet fuel explosions behind them, or a plunge of eighty stories or more from the windows in front of them. Drew said, "I saw people coming down from the building. We were watching people falling from the building."[2]

He did what any news photographer had to do—he started taking pictures. By the end of the day, he had shot 215 frames.

Among those frames were dozens of images that would become all too familiar to Americans in the ensuing days and weeks: the buildings collapsing in a cloud of dust, the explosions and flames, a person clinging to debris as it fell from the collapse.

As long as he could, Drew kept shooting pictures of what would come to be known as Ground Zero. He was pulled back by emergency workers when the first tower collapsed. When the second tower collapsed, Drew finally left the area, running from the cloud of ash that enveloped the site.

Drew recalled taking photos of a dozen or more people falling from the World Trade Center towers. But none attracted the attention or created the controversy of his "falling man" photo. The photo showed a man in a white jacket and black pants falling headfirst from the tower. It appeared on page seven of the *New York Times* and in hundreds of papers around the world. Drew told a reporter for Yahoo News that he didn't think the photo was too explicit for the public. "To me, it's a real quiet photograph," he said. "There's no violence in it."[3]

Drew says that too many of the photos taken on September 11 were sterile, showing buildings and wreckage but not people. The photos he shot of people falling gave viewers a sense of what had really happened. "It has to

LEARNING OBJECTIVES

After studying this chapter, you will be able to:

1. Define five major ethical principles affecting journalism.
2. Explain the Bok model for ethical decision making.
3. Explain the kinds of difficulties journalists and media writers have encountered in attempting to be truthful.
4. Discuss the ethical issues related to sensationalism in the news.
5. Explain how journalists can get into trouble trying to report on rapidly breaking stories.
6. Explain how and why advertisers attempt to control the media in which they place their ads.
7. Discuss the ethical conflict in PR between serving the client and serving the public.

AP Photo/Richard Drew

Have you seen Richard Drew's photo of "the falling man" before? What is your reaction to this photo? Does a photo like this belong on the front page of the newspaper? Why or why not?

do with putting a human element with this story. My recollection of watching these buildings fall was like a movie. And all the pictures we've seen don't show the human element except for these people falling."[4]

In the days following the attacks, Drew continued to shoot Ground Zero, taking pictures of the piles of flowers, the many dozens of teddy bears people left behind, and the hundreds of pictures people posted of their missing friends and loved ones. Two days passed before Drew slowed down enough to feel the impact of the attacks and their aftermath. He got a call on his mobile phone from his four-year-old daughter, who said, "I just want to tell you I love you." Molly Gordy, Drew's wife, said that his daughter's call broke through Drew's emotional wall. He called the office, said he had to take a day off, and went to see his family. "[He] accepted the fact that in order to take a moving picture, you have to be moved," Gordy said.[5]

Drew says that he records history every day, although some days contain more history than others. He was one of the first photographers on the scene when presidential candidate

Timeline

1800

1812 War of 1812 breaks out.

1835 Alexis de Tocqueville publishes *Democracy in America*.

1859 Charles Darwin publishes *On the Origin of Species*.

1861 U.S. Civil War begins.

1869 Transcontinental railroad is completed.

1879 Thomas Edison invents electric light bulb.

1898 Spanish-American War breaks out.

1900

1903 Orville and Wilbur Wright fly first airplane.

1905 Albert Einstein proposes his theory of relativity.

1910

1912 *Titanic* sinks.

1914 World War I begins.

1918 Worldwide influenza epidemic strikes.

1920

1920 Nineteenth Amendment passes, giving U.S. women the right to vote.

1929 U.S. stock market crashes, leading to the Great Depression.

1930

1933 Adolf Hitler is elected chancellor of Germany.

1939 World War II breaks out in Europe.

1940

1941 United States enters World War II.

1945 United States drops two atomic bombs on Japan.

1947 Pakistan and India gain independence from Britain.

1949 Communists establish People's Republic of China.

350 BC (approximately) Aristotle writes about ethics in ancient Greece.

1781 Immanuel Kant publishes the *Critique of Pure Reason,* his treatise on the categorical imperative.

1863 John Stuart Mill publishes *Utilitarianism,* in which he refines his ideas of morality as "the greatest good for the greatest number."

1947 The Hutchins Commission examines the role the press play in American society.

AP Photo/Robert Kradin

Robert Kennedy was assassinated in 1968, and he photographed the first World Trade Center bombing in 1993. But nothing he had ever experienced was as monumental as September 11:

> My peers have told me that I photographed the death of these people. But I feel that I've captured a piece of these people's lives. I photograph what happened, and, in turn, I record and document history, and this is what happened. This is history.[6]

Media ethics are a difficult subject because the news media are not always polite or nice, nor should they be. Their job is to keep the public informed, increase people's understanding of the world, and aid the functioning of a democratic society. And as photographer Richard Drew has pointed out, journalists sometimes must show things that are uncomfortable, disturbing, and upsetting.

In this chapter, we look at and attempt to understand why media practitioners behave the way they do and how their behavior can be judged by the media-consuming public. ■

> **"I photograph what happened, and, in turn, I record and document history, and this is what happened. This is history."**
>
> —AP Photographer Richard Drew

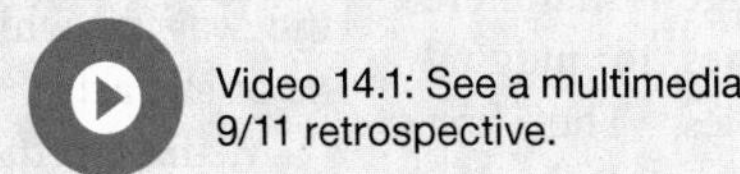

Video 14.1: See a multimedia 9/11 retrospective.

1950

- **1950** Korean War begins.
- **1953** Francis Crick and James Watson discover structure of DNA.
- **1957** Soviet Union launches spacecraft *Sputnik I*

1960

- **1963** Martin Luther King Jr. delivers "I Have a Dream" speech during Washington, D.C., civil-rights march.
- **1969** Neil Armstrong walks on the moon.

1970

- **1974** U.S. president Richard Nixon resigns due to Watergate scandal.
- **1975** Vietnam War ends.
- **1977** Apple II personal computer is introduced.
- **1978** First test-tube baby is born.

1980

- **1983** First HIV/AIDS cases are documented. Ozone hole is discovered over Antarctica.
- **1986** Space shuttle *Challenger* explodes.
- **1989** The Berlin Wall falls.

1990

- **1991** Soviet Union disbands.
- **1993** European Union is formed.
- **1994** Nelson Mandela is elected president of South Africa.
- **1997** Diana, Princess of Wales, dies in car accident.

2000-

- **2001** Al Qaida attacks World Trade Center and Pentagon.
- **2003** United States invades Iraq.
- **2008** Barack Obama is elected U.S. president.
- **2011** Earthquake and tsunami hit Japan. United States endseight-year war with Iraq.
- **2012** Superstorm Sandy devastates U.S. eastern seaboard.
- **2014** Russian army invades Ukraine.

1954 Media coverage of the Army- McCarthy hearings investigating conflicting accusations between Joseph McCarthy and the U.S. Army contributed to McCarthy's decline in popularity.

Bettmann/Corbis

1981 *Washington Post* reporter Janet Cooke's Pulitzer Prize–winning story is found to be a fabrication.

1994 *Time* magazine runs a digitally altered photograph of O.J. Simpson, which is widely regarded to be prejudicial; editor James Gaines issues an apology statement the next week.

AP Photo

- **1998** Several reporters at *Rolling Stone* and the *Boston Globe* are accused of fabricating news stories.
- **2001** Journalists face many ethical challenges covering the September 11 Al Qaida attacks.
- **2011** Pulitzer Prize–winning journalist Jose Vargas reveals he's an undocumented alien who entered the U.S. illegally as a child.
- **2012** Radio host Rush Limbaugh loses multiple advertisers after calling a law student and birth control advocate a "slut" on the air.
- **2014** Your presence on Facebook is worth $7 a year to the social network.

Anatolii Babii/Alamy

Ethical Principles and Decision Making

The words *morality* and *ethics* are often used interchangeably, but they are distinctly different concepts. Media ethics scholars Philip Patterson and Lee Wilkins explain that **morals** refer to a religious or philosophical code of behavior that may or may not be rational. **Ethics**, by contrast, come from the ancient Greek study of the rational way to decide what is good for individuals or society. A moral decision depends on the values held by a particular individual, but an ethical decision should be explainable to others in a way that they will appreciate, regardless of whether they accept it. In short, ethics consist of the ways in which we make choices between competing moral principles.[7]

Journalists in the United States have a wealth of competing ethical principles to draw upon beyond the basic Judeo-Christian values that constitute the core of American morality. (This is not to deny that there are many other significant religious traditions in the United States. But a recent survey of journalists showed that they come overwhelmingly from either Christian or Jewish households.[8]) Franklin Foer, writing in the *New Republic*, suggests that there are two approaches to judging journalistic ethics. The first considers the journalist's process of producing the product. If the process has moral failings, such as conflicts of interest, then the product will be flawed. The other approach, which he advocates, suggests that the product itself should be judged. Apart from the process of production, what can be said about the ethical quality of the outcome?[9] In this section, we examine the major ethical principles affecting journalism (all of which fall within Foer's two categories), consider how they might be applied to journalistic decision making, and look at a contemporary model for deciding between competing ethical principles.

Questioning the Media

What is the difference between making an ethical decision and making a moral decision? How can it be problematic to make a moral decision? Can a decision be ethical without being moral?

Aristotle: Virtue and the Golden Mean

The Greek philosopher Aristotle was a student of Plato and the tutor of Alexander the Great. Although he lived more than 2,300 years ago (approximately 350 BC), his writings on ethics, logic, natural science, psychology, politics, and the arts contain insights that are still relevant, especially his comments on ethics and human endeavor. Aristotle argued that the ultimate goal of all human effort is "the good," and the ultimate good is happiness. To Aristotle, achieving happiness involved striking a balance, a "just-right point between excess and defect."[10] Popularizers have labeled this valued midpoint the **golden mean**.

The classic example of the golden mean is courage, which strikes a balance between the inaction and timidity of cowardice and the recklessness of foolhardiness, both of which are unacceptable behaviors. The example of courage also illustrates how the acceptable ethical middle ground is not a single defined place, but its parameters depend on the abilities and strengths of the individual.[11]

To behave ethically, according to Aristotle, individuals must

- know what they are doing,
- select their action with a moral reason, and
- act out of good character.

©iStockphoto.com/PanosKarapanagiotis

In other words, Aristotle emphasized the character and the intent of the actor and how those determine the way in which he or she acts.

Media ethics scholar David L. Martinson cautions journalists not to take an overly simplistic view of the golden mean and assume that it refers only to compromise. Instead, they must recognize that finding the mean requires virtue. Martinson writes:

> A virtuous journalist is one who communicates truthfully in a manner which will enable the reader or listener to better understand the reality of the

---

morals: An individual's code of behavior based on religious or philosophical principles. Morals define right and wrong in ways that may or may not be rational.

ethics: A rational way of deciding what is good for individuals or society. Ethics provide a way to choose between competing moral principles and help people decide in cases where there is not a clear-cut right or wrong answer.

golden mean: Aristotle's notion that ethical behavior comes from hitting a balance, a "just-right point between excess and defect."

TEST YOUR VISUAL MEDIA LITERACY

John McDonnell/The Washington Post/Getty Images

Have you seen photos of horrific sports injuries like this one that Washington Redskins quarterback Robert Griffin III suffered to his knee during a 2013 playoff game against the Seattle Seahawks? What is your reaction to this photo? Does a photo like this belong on the front of the sports page of the newspaper? Why or why not?

Horrific Sports Injuries

The television audience for the Redskins vs. Seahawks NFL playoff game was huge on Sunday, January 6, 2013. And everyone watching was horrified when they saw Redskins quarterback Robert Griffin III twist his knee in a direction that no knee is supposed to go. The next morning, readers of the *Washington Post* saw the incredibly clear image of RGIII's injury, taken by *Post* photographer John McDonnell, spread out across the top of the sports section.[13]

A longtime friend of mine (and journalism grad) was bothered by the photo and questioned the need for the paper publishing it. I tweeted about the photo and got an almost immediate response from a student in Iowa who also really didn't think the photo should have been published, saying, "I'm not good with seeing things like that—makes me cringe. I can't look at it!"[14]

Similar debates have emerged over video being shown over and over again on television of basketball players getting hurt during games, such as when Louisville's Kevin Ware suffered a compound fracture of his tibia and fibula playing against Duke in 2013, or when Indiana Pacers' Paul George suffered a horribly broken leg during a Team USA showcase.[15]

WHAT does this photo say?

What does this photo of Robert Griffin III say? What news value does it have? Does it tell you anything important about football and about that Sunday's game?

WHY was this photo published?

Why do you think the *Washington Post* published this photo? Why would editors decide not to publish the photo?

HOW do you and your classmates interpret this photo?

How does this photo make you feel? Does it change your understanding of professional football? Are still images any better or worse than video? Does it matter whether the photo or video has explicit gore? Does that make it any less disturbing? You will have the opportunity to think about this photo and revisit these questions as you work your way through the first portion of this chapter.

Web 14.1: See coverage of a variety of sports injuries here.

community, nation, and world in which he or she lives. In that communication, the journalist will show respect for human dignity and individual circumstances.[12]

To test this principle, consider the photo of Washington Redskins quarterback Robert Griffin III (RGIII) injuring his knee in a playoffs game, discussed in the nearby "Test Your Media Literacy" box. A newspaper editor trying to decide whether to run a sports injury photo might want to hit a mean between sensitivity and the need to report what happened. One extreme would be not running the photo at all; the other would be running a graphic image of the athlete writhing in pain. A possible middle ground would consist of running the photo of the hit taking place. Other forms of balance might be reducing the size of the photo so that it would have less impact than a large photo and placing it on an inside page rather than on the front of the sports page. The decision to run the photo could also be justified by the argument that the editor was acting out of good character by feeling an obligation to help readers understand the dangers of professional football.

Kant: The Categorical Imperative

The German philosopher Immanuel Kant published his most important writings during the final decades of the eighteenth century. Kant differed from Aristotle in that Kant suggested that morality lies in the act itself and not in the character of the actor or the intent behind the action. He also put forward the Judeo-Christian value of seeing people as ends, never as a means to an end. In short, Kant emphasized that you can't use people to achieve your goals.

Kant's ethics begin with the notion that we have the ability to reason and hence are able to base our actions on moral reasoning. Because of this, people are responsible for their own actions and are obliged to act in a moral way.

The basic summary of Kant's **categorical imperative**, written in the 1780s, states: "Act as if the maxim of your action were to become through your will a universal law of nature."[16] In simpler terms, Kant asks people to consider what would be the result of everyone acting the same way they themselves wish to act. Kant does not worry particularly about the consequences of an action; rather, he looks at the act itself. This does not mean that Kant doesn't consider outcomes important; it means only that he believes unethical behavior cannot be justified by its possibly desirable outcomes.

In the case of the sports injury photo, the philosopher might ask what moral decision the photographer made. The photographer's decision was to tell the truth about what happened during the game. Would we be willing to accept the consequences of everyone telling the truth? What problems might arise out of a position of absolute truth?

John Stuart Mill: The Principle of Utility

In the movie *Star Trek II: The Wrath of Khan*, the emotionless Spock performs a rational yet selfless act. He saves the crew of the starship *U.S.S. Enterprise* by entering a reactor room to prevent an explosion that would have killed everyone on board the ship. But in doing so he absorbs a lethal dose of radiation. As he dies, he justifies his actions to his friends with the maxim, "The good of the many outweighs the good of the few, or the one." In this moment, Spock sums up the central tenet of the nineteenth-century ethical philosopher John Stuart Mill's **principle of utility**: the greatest good for the greatest number.

Mill did not create the idea of utility, but he did do a great deal to refine and promote the philosophy known as utilitarianism. Mill wrote that the consequences of actions are important in deciding what is ethical: "An act's rightness is [a] desirable end."[17]

Looking back to the Aristotelian notion of happiness as the ultimate public good, utilitarianism holds that which is virtuous is that which provides the greatest happiness for the greatest number. Or, looked at another way, that which causes the least pain is best. The challenge in applying this principle is that the same act can cause both happiness and pain. NBC News faced extensive criticism when it decided to air excerpts from a multimedia disk created by Seung-hui Cho, who shot and killed thirty-two students and faculty at Virginia Tech in April 2007. Family and friends of the victims said that they felt victimized all over again when they saw the video. NBC News president Steve Kapas said the network ran the excerpts from the disk so that the public might better understand what had happened. "This is as close as we'll ever come to being in the mind of a killer," he said.[18] The network accepted the additional suffering it caused a smaller number of people who knew the victims in order to accomplish the greater good of informing the public at large.

Mill also held that some forms of pleasure or happiness are morally superior to others. He suggested that actions and decisions that improve the lot of society as a whole may be superior to those that merely provide the most physical or emotional pleasure.[19]

Employing utilitarian reasoning, an editor might decide not to run the photo of a badly injured athlete because of all the pain it would cause viewers of the image. Since the photo would likely cause a great deal of pain, there is a strong argument against running it.

John Rawls: The Veil of Ignorance

The contemporary philosopher John Rawls builds on the ideas of utilitarianism. His argument is that which is just is also that which is fair:

> First: Each person is to have an equal right to the most extensive basic liberty compatible with a similar liberty for others. . . . Second: Social and economic inequalities are to be arranged so that they are both (a) reasonably expected to be to everyone's advantage, and (b) attached to positions and offices open to all.[20]

To decide what is fair, the journalist must hide behind Rawls's **veil of ignorance**, a principle of ethics that says that justice emerges when we make decisions without considering the status of the people involved and without considering where we personally fall in the social system. In other words, we shouldn't ask, "How does this affect me?" Behind this veil, everyone is equal. Journalists following

Video 14.2: Watch Spock explain the principle of utility.

categorical imperative: Kant's idea of a moral obligation that we should act in a way in which we would be willing to have everyone else act; also known as the principle of universality.

principle of utility: John Stuart Mill's principle that ethical behavior arises from that which will provide the greatest good for the greatest number of people.

veil of ignorance: John Rawls's principle of ethics that says that justice comes from making decisions that maximize liberty for all people and without considering which outcome will give us personally the biggest benefit.

this principle would not question whether they or their subjects were powerful or powerless, rich or poor, black or white, male or female.

Reporters deciding how to treat sources should make the same decision whether they like or dislike the person. They should imagine how they would want to be treated if they were the source and would have to live with the outcome of the story. The value of freedom of the press must be considered on an equal level with the protection of individual privacy, as reporters behind the veil of ignorance do not know whether they are a reporter or a source.[21]

It is difficult to say what a photo editor would decide to do with a sports injury photo using the veil of ignorance. On the one hand, taking the perspective of the family of the person in the photo, he or she might decide that publicizing the athlete in agony is an invasion of the athlete's privacy. On the other hand, the editor might say that the photo will generate sympathy and support for the athlete.[22]

Hutchins Commission: Social Responsibility Ethics

In 1947, widespread concerns about the ethical behavior of the press led Henry Luce, the founder of *Time* magazine, to form a commission to study the responsibility of the press in the United States. Chaired by scholar Robert M. Hutchins, the commission concluded that the First Amendment, by itself, might not be enough to protect the free speech rights of the public because a small number of corporations controlled a large number of the available communication outlets. Although the government might not be limiting free speech, corporations might do so. The report reached two major conclusions:

1. The press has a responsibility to give voice to the public and to society.
2. The free press was not living up to that responsibility to the public because of its need to serve its commercial masters.

The social responsibility theory of the press, holding that the press has an ethical obligation to society, arose from the Hutchins report. (This theory is discussed further in Chapter 15.) The Hutchins Commission listed five requirements for a responsible press:

1. The media should provide a truthful, comprehensive, and intelligent account of the day's events in a context that gives them meaning.
2. The media should serve as a forum for the exchange of comment and criticism (that is, the press should present the full range of thought and criticism).
3. The media should project a representative picture of the constituent groups within the society.
4. The media should present and clarify the goals and values of the society.
5. The media should provide full access to the day's news.

SECRET 2 Today, the range of long-tail media, including blogs and podcasts, allows both professional and citizen journalists to bypass legacy media (traditional big media) and go directly to the public, though it is hard for the long-tail news outlets to have the impact that a newspaper or television station can. Nevertheless, this is one more example of Secret Two—There are no mainstream media.

Using a social responsibility approach, running the photo of Robert Griffin's injury can be defended, assuming that it is run with the goal of giving readers a better understanding of the risks and dangers of professional football.

©iStockphoto.com/marekuliasz

The Bok Model for Ethical Decision Making

Given the many competing ethical principles journalists have to consider, it can be difficult to decide what is right or wrong, as our consideration of the decision about running a disturbing photo illustrates. But contemporary ethicist Sissela Bok provides a fairly straightforward three-step model for analyzing an ethical situation:

1. Consult your conscience—How do you feel about the action? What does your conscience tell you is right?
2. Seek alternatives—Is there another way to achieve the same goal that will not raise ethical issues? Is there an expert to whom you can turn for advice?
3. Hold an imaginary ethical dialogue with everyone involved—Ask, "How will my action affect others?" Discuss the issues involved from the point of view of each of the people whom it will affect. Think about who will be involved: the source, the news consumer, the public at large, a special interest group, and so forth.[23]

In her book *Lying: Moral Choice in Public and Private Life*, Bok suggests consulting experts and holding a public dialogue. It may not be practical for a working reporter or editor to apply her method fully, but the basic approach of consulting one's conscience, considering alternatives, and taking the point of view of all affected parties is reasonable.[24]

Ethics and News

Journalists only rarely face ethical dilemmas on the scale of those surrounding the September 11 attacks, but they face many smaller choices every day. These can involve deciding how to report information from an authoritative source that the journalist knows to be lying, balancing the rights of various individuals, deciding how to present a story, or deciding which photograph to run. Some of these decisions are routine, but all of them require ethical choices. Of course, journalists and the people with whom they work don't always live up to high ethical standards, so we look here at how news organizations deal with those problems.

Truthfulness

Journalists have always claimed that they feel obliged to report the truth,[25] and reporters or editors who violate this commitment to truth have paid dearly. As was discussed in Chapter 6, the *Washington Post*'s credibility suffered a major blow when the paper discovered in 1981 that a Pulitzer Prize–winning story by reporter Janet Cooke was fabricated. In the spring of 2003, young *New York Times* reporter Jayson Blair created shock waves throughout the news business when it was revealed that he had fabricated or plagiarized at least thirty-six stories for the nation's most prestigious newspaper. The controversy concerns not only the poor behavior of particular journalists, but also the implications of that behavior for the publication and the resulting lack of trust in the institution. At issue, too, is the lack of commitment to the truth on the part of publications and editors that put exciting stories ahead of making sure those stories are true.

In her book on the nature of lying, Bok states that there are at least two factors to weigh when considering a lie. The first is whether the speaker is intending to transmit the truth or attempting to deceive people. The second is whether the statement itself is true or false. Bok argues that the major ethical problem related to truth-telling is intentionally deceiving someone to "make them believe what we ourselves do not believe."[26]

Media ethics scholar David Martinson argues that telling the truth entails more than just stating facts that are not false. Instead, the press needs to report "the truth about the fact." In the early 1950s, when Sen. Joseph McCarthy—without any evidence—started accusing people of being communists, the press reported his charges without giving any indication that the charges he was making might be false or without conducting independent verification. It was true that McCarthy had made the statements, but the statements themselves were not true. Martinson suggests that the press too often asks whether the story is factually true instead of asking whether the story helps the public understand the truth.

Video 14.3: Read and watch about the Frey fabrication.

Web 14.2: Read about Stephen Glass and law school.

As we discussed in Chapter 4, the truthfulness of nonfiction books has also been called into question. The instances of fabrication have gone beyond such notable cases as James Frey's memoir, *A Million Little Pieces*. In another memoir, a former U.S. secretary of labor fabricated testimony that he supposedly had given before Congress.[27] And a prominent writer admitted including imagined conversations in a biography of Ted Kennedy. Presidential biographer Edmund Morris went so far as to insert himself as a fictional character in his biography of Ronald Reagan (a fact that he acknowledged in the introduction to the book).

Catching Fabrications: How Stephen Glass Fooled the Fact-Checkers. With the exception of tabloid stories about a space alien having Elvis's baby, articles in magazines and newspapers are generally assumed to be true, or at the very least based on fact. But occasionally that basic assumption is called into question.

Consider the following case: A twenty-five-year-old writer named Stephen Glass had written incredible stories for the *New Republic*, *Rolling Stone*, *George*, and *Harper's*. Other writers—some would say jealous colleagues—thought Glass's stories, with their customary "wow" opening paragraphs that set the scene, were too good to be true. Unfortunately, they were. In 1998, Glass was caught fabricating an article for the *New Republic* about teenage hackers, and his subsequent firing sent shock waves throughout the magazine industry.[28] Follow-up investigations suggested that Glass had fabricated material for dozens of articles without the magazines' fact-checkers catching on.

Said Charles Lane, then the editor of the *New Republic*, "I don't wish [Glass] ill. . . . I just don't want him to be in journalism."[29] After becoming the poster boy for bad journalism, Glass left the magazine business, went to law school, and wrote a novel. Following the critical and commercial failure of his novel, Glass has reportedly worked as a paralegal and as an occasional member of a Los Angeles comedy troupe.[30]

How did Glass get away with his fabrications? First, the magazines didn't conduct fact-checking as well as they should have. Second, Glass would submit articles late so that they couldn't be checked, and he would fabricate substantiation for them, such as a phony Web page and voice mail message for the beleaguered high-tech company in the hacker story.[31] In an article for the political magazine *George*, Glass wrote a description of presidential advisor Vernon Jordan based on anonymous sources. He avoided the fact-checking by saying that his sources would be fired if they were contacted at work. After editors found out that Glass had been fabricating articles, fact-checkers discovered that the sources he had cited didn't exist. To be fair to the fact-checkers, their procedures were designed to catch mistakes, not outright fabrications.[32]

One result of the fallout from Glass's fabrications was a renewed commitment to fact-checking at magazines; another was increased skepticism toward sensational stories, especially by young writers.

Lying About Who You Are. Former *Washington Post* reporter Jose Vargas was a successful young journalist. He was part of a reporting team that won a Pulitzer for covering the Virginia Tech massacre, he wrote a well-regarded profile of Facebook founder Mark Zuckerberg for the *New Yorker*, and he's written for numerous outlets around the country, including the *Huffington Post* and the *San Francisco Chronicle*.

The secret that Vargas kept until the summer of 2011 was that he is an undocumented immigrant who entered the United States illegally from the Philippines.

Vargas outed himself in a first-person article for the *New York Times Magazine*. In it, he told the story of how he came to the United States as a twelve-year-old boy to live with his grandparents in California. He did not know that he had entered the country on forged papers until he took his supposed immigration status card to the Department of Motor Vehicles at age sixteen to get his driver's permit. There he was told that his card was fake and that he should not come back again.[33]

Justin Sullivan/Getty Images

Pulitzer Prize–winning reporter Jose Vargas revealed in the summer of 2012 that he was an undocumented immigrant who entered the country illegally from the Philippines when he was a child.

As he told MSNBC's Rachel Maddow, Vargas's parents and grandparents intended for him to work shadow economy jobs until he could find an American citizen to marry and get a permanent residency permit that way. Only one problem: When Vargas was in high school, he came out publicly as being gay. So while he was out of the closet as a gay male, he remained secretive about his immigration status.[34]

Vargas initially offered his story to the *Washington Post*, but the paper turned him down. Vargas then shopped it to the *New York Times Magazine*, which jumped at the chance. The editors went so far as to "tear up" the completed magazine and put the Vargas story on the cover.[35]

The story of Vargas and his outing of himself caused a fair amount of controversy in journalistic circles because Vargas had been lying about his immigration status for his entire adult life.[36] Phil Bronstein, who had hired Vargas to write for the *San Francisco Chronicle*, writes that he felt duped by Vargas, especially since Vargas wrote about the experiences of undocumented workers without mentioning that he was one himself. On the other hand, Bronstein hopes that Vargas's story may lead to meaningful immigration reform:

> But if he can come out, the force of his story—both good reaction and bad—and his project just might lubricate the politically tarred-up wheels of government and help craft sane immigration policy. If it has that effect, we should forgive him his lies.[37]

At the heart of Vargas's story is this central ethical conflict: A journalist lying about his or her identity is always troubling for any reason, but if Vargas had not lied about who he was, he could not have been a reporter. This is, at its core, the definition of an ethical problem. Because ethics are all about what you do when no answer seems right, when all answers are problematic, when telling the whole truth stands in the way of telling *any* truth.

Corporate Conflict of Interest

Being fair and balanced are core journalistic values that have been discussed extensively in earlier chapters. At times, however, other factors can overwhelm that value, especially when the interests of the news organization's owners are in conflict with the values of balance and fairness. This problem of a conflict of corporate interest extends beyond suppressing stories; it also involves actively promoting the company's interests.

At the peak of the Internet boom in the late 1990s, for example, one of the highest-profile dot-com Web sites was Pets.com, a seller of pet supplies. The site's "spokesthing" was a sock puppet that appeared on a number of programs, including *Good Morning America* and ABC's *Nightline*, to eulogize comic strip artist Charles Schulz. The puppet was introduced on *Good Morning America* as the Pets.com sock puppet. This widespread use of the Web site's name was likely the result of Disney, the owner of the ABC broadcast network, also owning 5 percent of Pets.com. The appearance of the puppet on the shows led to coverage of the appearance in the *New York Times*, as well as in several other media outlets.[38] The promotion of Pets.com by a major media channel that co-owns the site is a clear example of synergy (discussed in Chapter 3), but it also illustrates a conflict of interest.

Traditionally, such conflicts of interest are recognized when reporters give favorable coverage to a company in which they have an interest or to a person who is their friend. Or a conflict could involve the negative coverage of

Video 14.4: Watch an interview with Jose Vargas.

TEST YOUR MEDIA LITERACY

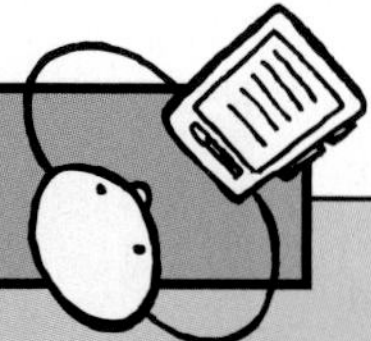

When Is Deception by Reporters Acceptable?

There's been quite a fuss made recently about a journalist from an alternative news publication. This alt-journalist called a conservative politician on the phone and pretended to be someone the politician would feel comfortable talking to. The alt-journalist then took the material from his ill-gained interview and used it to embarrass the politician. Once the interview was published, the Society of Professional Journalists issued a statement about how unethical the deception was. Meanwhile, the rest of the news media talked on and on about the deception, and the original prankster got a big laugh over all the attention he gained by flouting journalistic convention.

You would be excused if you thought I was talking about how radical journalist Ian Murphy, editor of the *Buffalo Beast,* impersonated billionaire conservative political activist David Koch in order to get an embarrassing interview with Republican Wisconsin governor Scott Walker during the 2011 lead-up to the recall campaign against the governor. And you would be right.[1]

But this could also describe a similar situation that took place more than twenty years ago.

In the spring of 1990, Arizona governor Jan Brewer, then a state senator, proposed a bill that would require the labeling of record albums that portrayed sexual content in a violent context, violence, Satanism, murder, morbid violence, or the use of illegal drugs. It would also have made it crime to sell these offensive albums to minors.

David Koen, music reviewer for the Phoenix-area alternative newspaper *New Times* (which you can read about in Chapter 6), taped a series of interviews with the senator while pretending to be a columnist from the *Mesa Tribune*, a local conservative daily newspaper.

Using Senator Brewer's recorded comments from the taped interviews, Koen constructed a rap tape based on the group W.A.S.P.'s song "F*** Like a Beast." He then played this tape over a sound system at noon at the state capitol. For several weeks, stories about the conflict continued to surface across Arizona and national media. The fuss finally died down when Brewer withdrew her bill from consideration.[2]

SECRET 4 Journalists occasionally "go undercover" in order to collect news about people who are breaking the law or abusing the public trust; sometimes they even win awards for the stories that come out of this impersonation. (Think back to Chapter 13 and the story about *Food Lion v. ABC.*) Much less often they go undercover in order to create a satirical story to draw attention to a particular issue.

The punkings of Governors Brewer and Walker and the subsequent media agitation over them serve as a great reminder of Secret Four—Nothing's new: Everything that happened in the past will happen again.

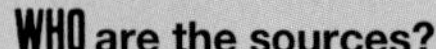

WHO are the sources?

Who are Ian Murphy and David Koen? Where do they work? How do the papers they work for differ from more mainstream newspapers?

WHAT did they do?

How did Murphy and Koen report their stories? Who did they claim to be? How did their sources and the public react to what Murphy and Koen did?

HOW does what they did compare to the ABC Food Lion reporters?

Go back to Chapter 13, page 340, to read about the case of ABC producers lying about their work history to get jobs working in a Food Lion store. How did the actions of Murphy and Koen differ from those of the ABC producers investigating Food Lion? How did their motivations for being deceptive about their identities differ?

HOW do you and your friends feel about deception by reporters?

AP Photo/Ross D. Franklin

Back when she was still a state senator, Arizona Governor Jan Brewer was punked by a music critic from a local alternative newspaper.

Do you think that reporters are ever justified in being deceptive about who they are? Is it acceptable for a reporter to be deceptive for a serious story? How about for a satirical story? Why or why not? Is there a difference between the two?

---

[1]Jim Romenesko, "SPJ Scolds *Buffalo Beast* for Call to Wisconsin Governor," *Poynter*, February 23, 2011, www.poynter.org/latest-news/mediawire/120621/spj-scolds-buffalo-beast-for-call-to-wisconsin-governor/; Peter Wallsten, "The Blogger Behind the Scott Walker Prank Call," *Washington Post*, February 23, 2011, voices.washingtonpost.com/44/2011/02/the-blogger-behind-the-scott-w.html; Ezra Klein, "What a Prank Call Proves About Wisconsin," *Washington Post*, February 23, 2011, voices.washingtonpost.com/ezra-klein/2011/02/what_a_prank_call_proves_about.html.

[2]Ralph E. Hanson, "F*** Like a Beast: Arizona Governor Jan Brewer's First Brush With National News," *Living in a Media World*, April 28, 2010, ralphehanson.com/blog/archive_10_01.html#042810_brewer.

Web 14.3: Read stories of journalistic impersonation.

someone they dislike. With the growth in size and concentration of media companies in the past decade, an increasing issue is conflict of interest by the owners themselves.

Conflicting investments don't just occur with megacorporations. Newspapers have been investors in local professional sports teams, which can also raise conflict-of-interest issues. The best-known case of a newspaper investment in a sports team is that of the *Chicago Tribune*, which purchased the Chicago Cubs in 1981 and then sold the team in 2009. Even though the paper owned the team for close to three decades, the *Tribune*'s sports staff were often hard on the Cubs. (Of course, some observers argue that, given the Cubs' performance over the past hundred years, it would be hard *not* to be critical of the team.[39])

Newspapers always claim that they keep the business side of their operations separate from that of the newsroom, but it is sometimes hard for the public to see things that way.

Sensationalism

Along with political, international, economic, and other significant news, journalists sometimes focus on news that may not be important but is certainly interesting, largely because that's what audience members seem to enjoy. Cable television commentator Chris Matthews defends such news coverage on the basis of what he calls "the watercooler principle." He says, "If people are talking about it at the office around the watercooler, then it should be on the show."[40] Pulitzer Prize–winning reporter Edna Buchanan describes it this way:

> The best day is one when I can write a lead that will cause a reader at his breakfast table the next morning to spit up his coffee, clutch at his heart, and shout, "My God! Martha, did you read this?" That's my kind of day.[41]

Sometimes such stories can move beyond being merely interesting and enter the realm of **sensationalism**—coverage of events that is lurid and highly emotional. In the winter of 2006–2007, celebrity starlets Britney Spears, Lindsay Lohan, and Paris Hilton became the big story. The three, famous primarily for being famous, were in the news continually for getting into catfights, being arrested for driving under the influence, and going in and out of rehab. Photos of them flashing various body parts to paparazzi showed up first on celebrity Web sites and in the tabloids. But the stories, if not the photos themselves, soon migrated into the mainstream press, and so we saw stories on them in every media outlet from ABC News to Fox News. Even the *New York Times* ran a bylined story on Spears's "lack of wardrobe" malfunctions.[42] *USA Today* ran a story on when it's appropriate to "go commando." And the *Toronto Star* in Canada gave the apparent trend story a political twist by noting that Margaret Trudeau, the wife of Canada's former prime minister, inadvertently flashed a photographer at Studio 54 back in 1977.

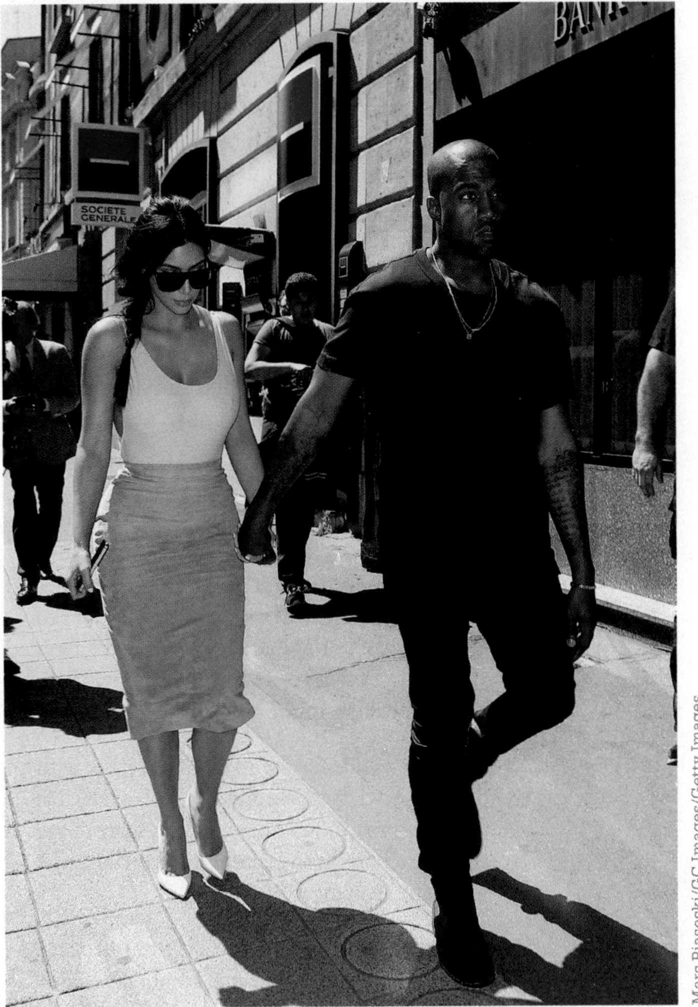

Photos of celebrities like Kim Kardashian and Kanye West often appear in newspapers and magazines to attract attention beyond the actual news value of the image.

Marc Piasecki/GC Images/Getty Images

Sensational news clearly attracts viewers and readers, especially when it's truly out of the norm. When Michael Jackson died unexpectedly in 2009, the coverage of his death and memorial service dominated the media for several weeks, matching the coverage of British princess Diana's death in 1997. And when golfer Tiger Woods had a minor car accident in late 2009, the media coverage began to explode when the news started breaking that Woods had been having affairs with at least eleven different women.[43]

The mainstream media use occasions such as Michael Jackson's death or Tiger Woods's infidelity as an opportunity to engage in **tabloid laundering or tabloidization**, which is when respectable media report on what the tabloids are reporting (without doing the reporting themselves). Journalist and commentator Margaret Carlson says, "We

---

sensationalism: News coverage that panders to audiences with lurid and highly emotional accounts of crime, sex, violence, or celebrity missteps.

tabloid laundering or tabloidization: When respectable media report on what the tabloids are reporting as a way of covering sensationalistic stories on which they might not otherwise report.

take what the tabloids do and write about, and that way get what we wouldn't write about originally into the magazine. And then we run pictures of the pictures to show how terrible the pictures are."[44]

But *Newsweek* editor Mark Whitaker defends his magazine's reporting on the work of the tabloids:

> When the subject of a legitimate news story is the paparazzi phenomenon, and you're running these pictures in a way that's used to illustrate . . . that news story, and not just titillate people with exclusive photographs that have never been seen that you pay a lot of money for, then I think that that is still a defensible and legitimate use of the photographs.[45]

Why has there been such a move toward tabloidization? The editors of the *Columbia Journalism Review* suggest that there are two major reasons for this:

1. Competition—With increased competition and more players in the field, newsmagazines feel compelled to release stories that they might have avoided in the past. Former television reporter Robert MacNeil, speaking in the 1990s, said,

   > I tremble a little for the next sizable crisis with three all-news channels, and scores of other cable and local broadcasters, fighting for a share of the action, each trying to make his twist on the crisis more dire than the next.[46]

2. The Internet—Competition from the Internet has quickened the process by which rumors fly. Because anyone is able to publish, stories move quickly to being "out there." Journalist Jonathan Fenby says, "The Internet has a gun to the head of the responsible media. If you choose not to report a story, the Internet will."[47]

SECRET 4 Although the 1990s saw an unusually high level of tabloid journalism, this wasn't the only period of questionable taste in the news profession. In the 1830s, the biased partisan press ran real or imagined stories about political sex scandals. One paper, for example, claimed that President Andrew Jackson's mother "was a common prostitute, brought to this country by the British soldiers."[48] And the wild stories published by Joseph Pulitzer's and William Randolph Hearst's papers (see Chapter 6) don't seem all that different from the rumors presented today by TMZ or Perez Hilton on the Internet.[49] (This brings to mind Secret Four—Nothing's new: Everything that happened in the past will happen again.)

The ethical problem with sensationalism is multifaceted. First, there is the question of whether it lowers politics, public events, and public discourse to the level of crude entertainment that is not to be taken seriously, as Neil Postman has pointed out.[50] Second, tabloid-style stories can displace significant news—politics, economics, international affairs, war, genocide, famine, environmental issues—about which people need to be concerned. Finally, tabloid stories appeal to people's basest feelings and instincts rather than to their intellect and sense of decency.

When and How Do You Apologize?

Apologies are a hard thing for the media to handle. Too often they take the form of "If anyone was offended, we're sorry you feel that way," which is so weak that it lacks almost all meaning. Other times they can trivialize the seriousness of the error. But sometimes an apology can serve as a springboard for discussion about the original issue.

That's what happened in the fall of 2010, when the *Portland Press Herald* in Maine ran a long, thoughtful story on its front page about the local observance of the end of the Muslim holy month of Ramadan.

What would normally be considered a relatively non-controversial story became extremely controversial because this year the final day of Ramadan fell on September 11. Topping things off for the paper was the fact that it planned on running all of its September 11 anniversary stories in the September 12 Sunday paper.

The response was instantaneous and furious. Letter writers, e-mailers, and callers were uniformly upset that the paper did not have a story on the front page about the 9/11 anniversary. And many were upset that there was a story about Ramadan on the front page that day.

On Sunday, September 12, the day the paper planned to give extensive coverage of the 9/11 anniversary, the paper ran the following apology:

> We made a news decision on Friday that offended many readers and we sincerely apologize for it.
>
> Many saw Saturday's front-page story and photo regarding the local observance of the end of Ramadan as offensive, particularly on the day, September 11, when our nation and the world were paying tribute to those who died in the 9/11 terrorist attacks nine years ago.
>
> We have acknowledged that we erred by at least not offering balance to the story and its prominent position on the front page.
>
> What you are reading today was the planned coverage of the 9/11 events. We believed that the day after the anniversary would be the appropriate occasion to provide extensive new coverage of the events and observances conducted locally and elsewhere.
>
> In hindsight, it is clear that we should have handled this differently and with greater sensitivity toward the painful memories stirred by the anniversary of 9/11.[51]

But the apology wasn't the end of the story. Why not? Because some people read that apology as saying there was some kind of connection between peaceful practitioners of

Web 14.4: Read the *Press Herald* apologies.

Islam in the United States and the terrorists who attacked the nation back in 2001.

That was the central theme of a story that ran soon after on NPR's *On the Media* (*OTM*). In the story, *OTM*'s Bob Garfield had a somewhat confrontational interview with Richard Connor, the *Press Herald*'s editor and publisher. In the interview, Garfield tried to get Connor to acknowledge that the apology made the "connection between Islam and radical Islamic terrorists." Connor refused to do so. If you listen to the program, several things become clear: Connor had obviously had a bad week and was tired of being criticized by all sides about his paper's coverage of the issue, and Garfield was just as clearly trying to hold Connor accountable for what he had to say.[52]

All this led to a follow-up to the September 12 apology that Connor published on September 19 that didn't receive as much attention. Connor wrote:

AP Photo/Pat Wellenbach

The front page of the September 11, 2010, edition of the *Portland Press Herald*, along with the front-page apology for it published the following day.

> I have failed my writing hero, E. B. White, whose guiding principle, outlined in the classic "Elements of Style," was: "Omit needless words."
>
> If I'd followed that rule last week, I would have responded to criticism of our newspaper on 9/11 with this:
>
> "Our coverage of the conclusion of the local Ramadan observance was excellent and we are proud of it. We did not adequately cover 9/11 on the 9/11 anniversary, which also should have been front-page news, in my opinion."
>
> Why would I have omitted the other words in last week's column?
>
> Their lack of precision led to mischaracterization and misunderstanding. They were used to prove the maxim that a lie travels faster than truth. Mostly they allowed those with a personal ax to grind or a political agenda to advance to twist and misinterpret.
>
> I meant to apologize for what we did not print—front-page coverage of 9/11 on the anniversary of a day that stirs deep and unhealed wounds. I was in no way apologizing for what we did print in a deservedly prominent position—a striking photo of our local Muslim community in prayer.[53]

What Connor says here is what he probably should have said the previous week—that the paper did a good job of covering Ramadan and a bad job of covering the September 11 anniversary on September 11. This apology is particularly good because it doesn't talk about "who might have been offended," but rather talks about the quality of judgments made at the paper.

There Is No "They": The Sago Mine Disaster

Few journalistic mistakes have been as cruel as the headlines that ran in newspapers across the country on Wednesday, January 4, 2006. The papers trumpeted that all of the coal miners trapped in West Virginia's Sago Mine had been found alive after having been trapped for two days below ground, when, in reality, all but one of the thirteen had died.

In the early morning hours of Monday, January 2, an explosion, likely triggered by lightning, trapped thirteen miners deep below ground in the Sago Mine. About 9:00 p.m. Tuesday, the first body was discovered in the mine, according to a timeline in the *Washington Post*.[54] At 11:45 p.m., one miner was found alive more than two miles into the tunnel.

At this point, confusion reigned. According to the *Post*, at 12:18 a.m., the rescue command center heard a report from a rescue worker that twelve miners were found alive. Apparently, this early report was overheard and spread instantly through a

Questioning the Media

Should a media outlet always apologize to the public when it makes a mistake? Why or why not? Can a media outlet actually make things worse by apologizing? If you believe so, can you come up with an example of this?

Video 14.5: Watch a panel discussion about the Sago Mine disaster.

The Washington Post

NORTHERN VIRGINIA FINAL

12 Found Alive in W.Va. Coal Mine

Body of 13th Man Was Discovered In Adjacent Area

Abramoff Pleads Guilty to 3 Counts

Lobbyist to Testify About Lawmakers In Corruption Probe

THE NATION'S NEWSPAPER

FINAL SCORES

Wednesday, January 4, 2006

For love of Kenny

USA TODAY

NO. 1 IN THE USA

Sweatin' with the 'Stars'

12 miners found alive

Survivors beat odds in W.Va. after 41 hours; one body found

Paterno wins duel of legends

Newsline

THE NATION'S NEWSPAPER

SPORTS SCORES

Wednesday, January 4, 2006

For love of Kenny

USA TODAY

NO. 1 IN THE USA

Sweatin' with the 'Stars'

12 miners found alive

Amazing discovery in W.Va.; one body found in mine. Story, 3A

The Rose: This game has it all

Newsline

UPSHUR COUNTY, WEST VIRGINIA

BREAKING NEWS

CNN REPORT: 12 MEN FOUND ALIVE

Karen Bleier/AFP/Getty Images

Newspapers and television news outlets across the United States struggled with tight deadlines and inaccurate information during the Sago Mine disaster in West Virginia. Though initial stories reported that all thirteen miners survived, the tragic truth was that twelve of them had died.

crowd that had been praying for a miracle. Church bells started ringing. People cried, sang, and cheered.

According to the *Charleston Daily Mail*, then West Virginia governor Joe Manchin had come out to the mine to wait with family members and had asked for confirmation of the good news. Although he didn't get the confirmation, Manchin said he was quickly caught up by the joyous mood: "We went out with the people and they said, 'They found them.' We got swept up in this celebration. I said, 'The miracle of all miracles has happened.'"[55]

A statement from the governor would seem to signal some level of official confirmation. But within the next half hour, reports started coming into the command center that only one miner was alive—reports that were not passed on to families or the press until nearly 3:00 a.m.

Morning papers, such as the *Charleston Gazette* in West Virginia and Denver's now-defunct *Rocky Mountain News*, started printing around midnight (if not a little earlier). Newspapers have to make really tough calls on a breaking story, and unlike television, they leave a permanent reminder of the times that they get a story wrong. For example, the early edition of the *Rocky Mountain News* carried the headline "They're Alive." The headline was corrected in the final edition.

National papers also had problems with the story. *USA Today*, which has perhaps the best national distribution of any newspaper in the country, devoted one-third of its front page to the rescue story on Wednesday. On Thursday, the press started an intense examination of how the story was botched.

According to industry newsweekly *Editor & Publisher*, the *Inter-Mountain*, an 11,000-circulation afternoon daily out of Elkins, West Virginia, managed to get the story right, not only in its print edition but also on its Web site. *Editor & Publisher* quoted *Inter-Mountain* editor Linda Skidmore's account of the paper's handling of the story: "I feel lucky that we are an afternoon paper and we have the staff that we do. We had a reporter there all night at the scene and I was on the phone with her the whole time." Skidmore also described how the false story started snowballing:

> I was on the phone with [reporter Becky Wagoner] and I was hearing things on CNN and FOX that she was not hearing there. . . . She heard that the miners were alive just before it was broadcast, around midnight. She talked about hearing church bells ringing and people yelling in jubilation—but nothing official.[56]

"We heard that they were found alive through CNN, then it snowballed to ABC, then FOX and it was like a house afire," recalled Wagoner, who said she was at the media information center set up by the mine's operator, International Coal Group Inc., when the reports spread. "A lot of the media left to go to the church where family members were located, but I stayed put because this was where every official news conference was given—and we never got anything official here," she said. "Something was not right. Then we were hearing reports that 12 ambulances had gone in [to the mine area] but only one was coming out. There was so much hype that no one considered the fact that there was no [official] update."[57]

SECRET 7 Then a resident of West Virginia, I went to bed Tuesday night with reports on the Internet announcing that the miners had been found alive. When I sat down to breakfast and my local paper on Wednesday morning, though, it was immediately obvious that something was wrong with the story. The report from the Associated Press read:

> Twelve miners caught in an explosion in a coal mine were found alive Tuesday night, more than 41 hours after the blast, family members and Gov. Joe Manchin III said.
>
> Bells at a church where relatives had been gathering rang out as family members ran out screaming in jubilation.
>
> Relatives yelled, "They're alive!"
>
> Manchin said rescuers told him the miners were found.
>
> "They told us they have 12 alive," Manchin said. "We have some people that are going to need some medical attention."
>
> A few minutes after word came, the throng, several hundred strong, broke into a chorus of the hymn "How Great Thou Art," in a chilly, night air.[58]

What clues tipped me off? How could a reader, reading between the lines, tell there were problems with the story?

There were no official sources cited, other than the governor. Why didn't reporters also quote a source from the coal company?

When the governor made his statement, he noted, "They told us . . ." Not a name—just "they." My high school journalism teacher Judith Funk always took us to task about that word, asking, "Who's 'they'?" And the Sago story is probably one of the saddest examples of Secret Seven—There is no "they."

Later on, the story said, "The company did not immediately confirm the news."

There were no details on the miners' condition or where they were found.

In short, the story read like it was passing along secondhand accounts. How did the press go so wrong with this story?

©iStockphoto.com/dannyfroese

- There was the understandable problem of midnight deadlines. It's very difficult to handle a breaking story under these circumstances. But news organizations certainly could have been clearer in emphasizing the unconfirmed nature of the information in their reports.
- News organizations have gotten way too comfortable passing on unconfirmed stories that originate in the realm of blogs and rumors because they are afraid of being "scooped." No longer does a story have to be true; it just has to be true that the story is out there. When we are dealing with rumors about misconduct by politicians, whose realities are more subject to interpretation, perhaps this is OK (though I don't really think so). But when we are talking about the lives of ordinary people, this irresponsibility just doesn't cut it.
- The facts of the news didn't match the story reporters were looking for. Journalists, especially the national press, were looking for a "miracle story," in which people's prayers would be answered and everything would turn out fine. When reporters thought they found that story, they reported it. Tragically, that wasn't the way the story turned out.

So what can journalists do to make sure this doesn't happen again? *USA Today*'s Mark Memmott, speaking as part of a panel at West Virginia University on the press coverage of Sago, said,

> Our responsibility was to ask a lot of questions and be very, very careful about attributions and sourcing, and to make sure we told people not just about what we knew, but what we didn't know. We hadn't seen anybody come out of that mine. We hadn't really talked to anybody who knew what was going on inside there. We had heard from family members, who had heard from somebody else, who in some cases couldn't even tell reporters on the scene exactly who it was they had heard it from.[59]

Photography

Photos seem to be at the heart of many of the most troubling ethical cases that journalists face. Whether it is showing live television video of the shooting at Columbine High School, moments of private grief following a drunk-driving accident, or the horrors of September 11, 2001, editors have always had to strike a balance between sensitivity toward readers, consideration for sources, and dedication to reporting the news accurately. Now they also have new tools, like Adobe Photoshop, that allow them to manipulate photos digitally, sometimes producing quite different images from those they started with.

How Much Photo Manipulation Is Too Much? Photographs have always been prone to manipulation. Photographers choose their films, lenses, and angles with a particular image in mind. Darkroom techniques extended the photographer's ability

Web 14.5: How truthful is digital manipulation?

Web 14.6: Debating the color of the sky.

to control the image. But now photographs are altered electronically in ways that can be almost undetectable. In fact, all photos published today are manipulated digitally in terms of size, shape, color, and contrast. For example, the light and dark contrasts in many of the photos in this book have been adjusted in preparation for the printing process so that they will look better.

So the question becomes "How much manipulation is too much?" Keep in mind that there are several issues here:

- What is an acceptable level of photo manipulation?
- Should viewers know to what degree a photo has been altered?
- Does intentionally making changes in a photo change the viewer's response to the image?

In 2008, there was an intense discussion on an online photojournalism bulletin board about a college newspaper adviser who insisted that a photographer needed to make the sky bluer in a photo of a Martin Luther King Day march. Most of the photographers on the bulletin board were outraged at the demand, saying that deepening the sky's color would be completely unethical. But how many photographers, seeing the pale winter sky, would have boosted the blue in the sky without a moment's thought? Or if the photo had been taken in the predigital era, how many photographers would have chosen to shoot with Kodak's Kodachrome film, which is known for giving intensely vibrant colors?[60]

On a similar, simple level, a photographer at the *Charleston Gazette* was disciplined for removing a television station's logo from a reporter's microphone. After the altered photo was noticed and commented on by West Virginia radio personality Hoppy Kercheval, the *Gazette* published an apology on Facebook along with the unaltered image:

> A *Gazette* photographer went outside the boundaries of our standards when he obscured the name of a television station on a microphone in today's front-page photo. Other than the photographer, no one at the *Gazette* was aware of what had taken place with the photo. Our photographers know that it is unacceptable to alter reality in news photos. The photographer believed his action helped direct the focus of the photo to the subject. He was wrong to do so. This is a singular incident. Disciplinary action will be taken to ensure it doesn't happen again.[61]

Photo manipulation by magazines first came to the public's attention in 1982, when *National Geographic*'s editors "moved" one of the Egyptian pyramids so that a photo of the pyramids would fit on the magazine's cover. The change had no lasting moral significance—a similar effect could have been created by having the photographer reshoot the picture from a slightly different angle—but it forced the magazine industry to confront the implications of journalists altering images.[62] (See Box 14.1.)

Box 14.1

Standards for Digital Photo Manipulation

The *Charlotte Observer* has put together a very specific set of guidelines for how digital photos can be edited. Among its criteria are the following:

- "Dodging and burning," similar to what could be done in a conventional darkroom, are acceptable.
- Colors can't be changed.
- Backgrounds can't be eliminated or "aggressively toned."
- The original unedited image files need to be downloaded.
- Digital retouching (cloning) can be used only to remove things such as dust spots on the image.
- The only time these rules can be violated is with a photo illustration that is clearly labeled as such and can be clearly seen as an illustration.

Source: Kenny Irby, Charlotte Observer Photo Correction/Editing Guidelines, September 25, 2003, poynter.org/content/content_view.asp?id=46958.

In 1994, *Time* magazine created a furor when it ran what it called a "photo illustration" based on O. J. Simpson's mug shot, taken the week he was arrested as a suspect in the murders of Nicole Brown Simpson and Ron Goldman. *Time* had prepared three covers. One was a straightforward presentation of the mug shot with no manipulation. One was an artist's portrait—an obvious painting. The third was a photo illustration—a computer-manipulated version of the mug shot. In the manipulated photo—which, to *Time*'s credit, was listed as an illustration, not a photo—the prisoner number was reduced, the image was made fuzzier, and the highlights were removed from O. J.'s face. It was the darkening of Simpson's face that was controversial.

In a note to readers the following week, editor James Gaines talked about what had happened:

> I have looked at thousands of covers over the years and chosen hundreds. I have never been so wrong about how one would be received. In the storm of controversy over this cover, several of the country's major news organizations and leading black journalists charged that we had darkened Simpson's face in a racist and legally prejudicial attempt to

Web 14.7: See the before and after images.

make him look more sinister and guilty, to portray him as "some kind of animal," as the NAACP's Benjamin Chavis put it. A white press critic said the cover had the effect of sending him "back to the ghetto." Others objected to the fact that the mug shot had been altered at all, arguing that photographs, particularly news photos, should never be altered.[63]

Conflicts over digital manipulation of photographs emerge on a regular basis. In June 2006, *El Nuevo Herald*, the leading Spanish-language paper in the United States, ran a photo that appeared to show four Cuban prostitutes soliciting tourists in Havana while two police officers looked on. The only problem was that the hookers weren't actually there—they had been added digitally by an editor.[64] In another case, a *Los Angeles Times* photographer was fired in 2003 after he combined two images of an American soldier supervising a group of refugees in Iraq to make the image more dramatic. But sometimes the alterations are on a smaller scale and are intended to help rather than to deceive. After a terrorist bombing of a train in Spain, some newspapers digitally removed a severed arm lying next to the tracks because they felt the image was too horrifying for a family newspaper. (See Chapter 15's "Test Your Visual Media Literacy" box.)

Enforcing Ethics

How should the media address ethical issues? Are such issues the responsibility of the individual journalist? Of his or her editor? Should there be a single person in charge of ethics? Perhaps a code of ethics, applied properly, could provide sufficient guidance. In reality, various methods are used. This section looks briefly at some of the choices for systematically handling ethics issues.

The Ombudsman. The **ombudsman**, also known as the reader's representative or audience advocate, takes the point of view of those who purchase or consume the news. Sanders LaMont, former ombudsman for the *Sacramento Bee*, argues that the ombudsman is an essential part of the journalism ethics process because the ombudsman connects the news consumer with the news outlet, be it a magazine, newspaper, Web site, radio station, or cable news operation.

The term *ombudsman* is derived from the word for a person who mediated between citizens and the government in Sweden in the early 1800s. Since that time it has been used to describe anyone who mediates between two groups. News ombudsmen have a variety of tasks to perform:

- Listening to the concerns of readers or audience members—Readers tend to be enthusiastic about someone taking their point of view, whereas newsroom employees may be less so. Kenneth Starck, a former ombudsman for Iowa's *Cedar Rapids Gazette*, told *American Journalism Review*, "News organizations need individuals who can withdraw from the bustle of the newsroom and get some perspective on performance by communicating—thoughtfully, intelligently, empathetically—with people who care enough to offer their views to the organization."[65]
- Writing a regular column or commentary—The ombudsmen at news outlets such as the *New York Times* and *NPR* have regular commentaries posted online and sometimes within the news pages or broadcast.
- Writing a regular memo for the news staff—The *Washington Post*'s former ombudsman wrote a blog on a regular basis that praises and criticizes the staff; he also wrote a column for the Sunday editorial page.[66]

Until the summer of 2003, the *New York Times* did not have an ombudsman because management believed that the job should be done by the editors. However, following the scandal surrounding reporter Jayson Blair's fabrications, publisher Arthur Sulzberger Jr. appointed two editors to function as ombudsmen and enforce newsroom standards.[67] Although the position of ombudsman has been in a decline in recent years, these internal media critics continue to serve an important function. Poynter's ethicist Kelly McBride points to several examples[68]:

- Arthur Brisbane, writing for the *New York Times* about whether the paper ought to be a "truth vigilante" (discussed back in Chapter 6 on newspapers and the news), drew readers into a major discussion on the role of objectivity in the news.
- ESPN's Don Ohlmeyer discussed *The Decision*, the controversial program the sports channel carried about LeBron James's decision in 2010 to move from Cleveland to Miami.
- NPR's Edward Schumacher-Matos wrote a 35,000-word critique of the network's 2011 investigative series on foster care for Native American children in South Dakota.

---

ombudsman: A representative of a publication's readers who takes the point of view of those who purchase or consume the news; also known as a reader's representative or audience advocate.

Web 14.8: Visit the Web site for the Organization of News Ombudsmen.

TEST YOUR MEDIA LITERACY

Disability and Humor

There's a heartwarming story that circulated on the Internet in the spring of 2012 about President Obama giving a speech on energy policy at Prince George's Community College in Maryland. Stephon—a deaf man—had front-row seating for the event. He got to shake the president's hand after the speech and signed to him, "I am proud of you." To Stephon's surprise, the president signed back at him, "Thank you."[1]

Stephon then posted a YouTube video in which he told the story of what happened in American Sign Language (ASL). The video then spread to several social media sites, along with a transcription for those of us who don't sign.

I first discovered the story through a link on Twitter that took me to the Washington, D.C.–centric blog *District*. The story and video were posted there under the rather clever headline "Sign of the Times."

Then Alex, a former student of mine, mentioned on Facebook that the story had also been posted on the *Huffington Post* site under the considerably less clever headline, "Deaf Student 'Speechless' After Obama Responds to Him in Sign Language."[2]

Alex, who is not deaf, found the headline to be "at least mildly offensive," and he asked me what I thought of it. I read the story and found the following quote from Stephon: "Oh my gosh! I was like wow! He understood me after I said I was proud of him. It was so amazing. . . . I was just speechless."[3]

So my analysis was that the headline was fine. It accurately portrayed what was in the story. But as I read through the other comments on Facebook, I began wondering if the "speechless" pun was in bad taste, referring as it did to someone who communicated primarily (I assumed) through signing.

I did a quick search on the Web, and while I did find criticism of the headline, none of it came from people who identified themselves as being deaf. The only thing I knew for sure to be offensive to the deaf community is when audio or video stories about deafness don't include transcripts or subtitles.[4]

But to really answer the question, I thought I would turn to deaf artist Matt Daigle, who, along with his wife Kay, produces the witty and enlightening Web comic *That Deaf Guy*. Now I don't presume that Matt can speak for the entire deaf community, but he can give us the point of view of someone who takes a humorous look at the issues deaf people and their families face. Here's what he had to say about the story in a series of e-mails:

> I looked over the article and I was not personally offended by the title. Myself as well as many of my deaf friends are aware that the term speechless means in ASL SHOCKED ASTOUNDED. We know that the English language uses figurative language in the form of idioms and metaphors and such so we see those terms and just automatically translate them into meaning—like anyone else.
>
> It is the same concept with the word "hear." Deaf people often sign NEVER HEARD meaning no one told me or I didn't know about that. Within that context the word "hear" has the meaning of KNOW. We don't really think of the literal sense of that word just the meaning.[5]

On a related note, Matt had this to say about media portrayal of deaf people in general:

> The media does misrepresent deaf people often, that is true. We pretty much can agree that the most hated word used in the media concerning deaf people is "Hearing Impaired." Now I say that and yet I know some (very very few) deaf people who preferred to be called Hearing Impaired.[6]

WHO are the sources?

Who is Stephon? Who is Matt Daigle? Who is Alex?

WHAT is the controversy?

Why might the headline from the *Huffington Post* be offensive? To whom would it be offensive?

WHAT evidence is there?

What evidence do you have that the headline was offensive?

WHAT do you and your classmates think about the headline?

Is it all right to make puns or jokes about disability? Why or why not? If so, when is it acceptable? Do you think the *Huffington Post* headline was offensive? Why or why not? Are you deaf, or do you know someone who is deaf? How does that affect how you react to the headline?

---

[1]H. Hoover, "Sign of the Times," *District*, March 20, 2012, distriction.com/2012/03/sign-of-the-times/.

[2]"Deaf Student 'Speechless' After Obama Responds to Him in Sign Language," *Huffington Post*, March 21, 2012, www.huffingtonpost.com/2012/03/21/deaf-student-obama-sign-language_n_1369118.html.

[3]Hoover, "Sign of the Times."

[4]Ralph E. Hanson, "Should Streaming Video About Gallaudet College Be Captioned?" October 18, 2006, ralphehanson.com/blog/archive_06_10.html#101806_questions.

[5]Matt Daigle, personal communication, March 22, 2012.

[6]Ibid.

Video 14.6: Watch the videos about signing with Obama.

Despite the decline in the number of news organizations with ombudsmen, Simon Dumenco, writing in *Advertising Age*, suggests that these reader representatives are less necessary because excellent press criticism sites are available online, including Jim Romenesko's media blog.[69]

THAT DEAF GUY
BY MATT & KAY DAIGLE
YOU GUYS ARE ALREADY DONE WITH "T'WAS THE NIGHT BEFORE CHRISTMAS"?
YEP! DAD DID THE DEAF VERSION.
THE DEAF VERSION?
YEAH... IT'S MUCH SHORTER.
All rights reserved © Matt & Kay Daigle - www.thatdeafguy.com
EARLIER...
"...WHEN OUT ON THE LAWN THERE AROSE SUCH A CLATTER... BUT I DIDN'T SPRING TO MY FEET TO SEE WHAT WAS THE MATTER... AFTER ALL I'M DEAF AND DIDN'T HEAR SANTA DESCEND. HE FILLED OUR STOCKINGS AS I SNORED. MERRY CHRISTMAS. THE END."
©M&K DAIGLE

That Deaf Guy is a weekly Web comic written and drawn by deaf artist Matt Daigle and his hearing wife Kay.

Codes of Ethics. News organizations have a variety of codes of ethics to consider. The Society of Professional Journalists has an extended code of ethics with three main principles:

1. Seek truth and report it as fully as possible.
2. Act independently.
3. Minimize harm.

Beyond those principles and the accompanying code, the organization's ethics handbook contains a series of case studies and a collection of other codes of ethics to help journalists make ethical decisions. In their introduction, the authors argue that ethics are not merely a set of ideals; they are something journalists do that lead to good reporting.[70] Obviously, a single code of ethics cannot cover all the issues encountered by the many different news outlets in the United States. "Can you even hope to have a common set of standards for the *New York Times*, the *National Enquirer*, and *People* magazine?" asks journalism professor Alex S. Jones, writing in the *Columbia Journalism Review*.[71]

If codes of ethics are to be effective, they need to be more than static documents, according to Jeffrey L. Seglin, an ethics columnist for the *New York Times*. A code of ethics must be central to the way the news outlet does business on a daily basis.[72] Unless that is the case, ethics problems will continue to arise, Seglin warns. The *New York Times* management clearly had not followed up on a lower-level editor's complaints about Jayson Blair a year before the young reporter was caught fabricating and plagiarizing stories for the paper.

The *Cincinnati Enquirer* encountered trouble for an exposé it ran on the banana company Chiquita. The story may or may not have been accurate, but the highly critical article about the company's business practices was based on 2,000 voice mail messages the reporter had listened to using stolen access codes. The paper ended up apologizing to the company and paid an out-of-court settlement of $14 million. But prior to writing the story, the reporter had signed a copy of the paper's corporate code of ethics each year.

In these and other cases, the people involved clearly knew that their behavior was wrong and that it violated their publications' codes of ethics.

Ethics and Persuasive Communication

Many of the items we see in the media are not messages created by members of the news staff, but rather persuasive images created by advertising and public relations (PR) professionals seeking to influence people's behavior. The question of what constitutes ethical behavior for people who are attempting to manipulate public opinion then arises.[73] In this section, we examine ethical principles applied in the fields of advertising and public relations.

Advertising

During World War II, the advertising industry formed the Advertising Council in response to charges of unethical behavior. The organization's purpose was to promote both advertising and business in general. One of its first functions was to help build support for wartime austerity. The Ad Council worked on a communication campaign to stop the hoarding of scarce resources, promote the buying of war bonds, and build morale. After the war, it worked on a variety of public interest campaigns to

Web 14.9: Visit Jim Romenesko's blog.

Web 14.7: Watch an interview with the former *New York Times* ombudsman.

Web 14.10: View codes of ethics in the communications industry.

MEDIA TRANSFORMATIONS

Cookie Monsters: Online Privacy and Data Gathering 

We all know (or at least we ought to know) that there's no such thing as a free lunch. That means that when we get media that we don't pay for, such as broadcast television, we know that we're paying for it by being exposed to advertising messages. Now, however, when we go online, we pay in a second, related currency—information. Who are we? Where do we shop? Where do we go? What kind of phone do we use? And the list goes on.

The difficulty is that it isn't always obvious to consumers what kind of information is being collected about us. Think about Facebook. Yes, the social network giant shares its privacy policy, but that policy runs 9,000 words and is read by virtually no one. Geoffrey A. Fowler, writing for the *Wall Street Journal*, notes that Facebook not only tracks what you do on Facebook; it also looks at the cookies (small data files) left behind by other Web sites you've visited and the activity of the apps you use. The thing to remember is that although you don't pay money for accessing Facebook, you do pay with access to your information. And that information, according to the *Wall Street Journal*, is worth about $7 a year per person.[74]

If you know where to look, you actually can see what Facebook thinks you are interested in. There's a small icon in the upper right-hand corner of each ad that will eventually take you to a list of all the

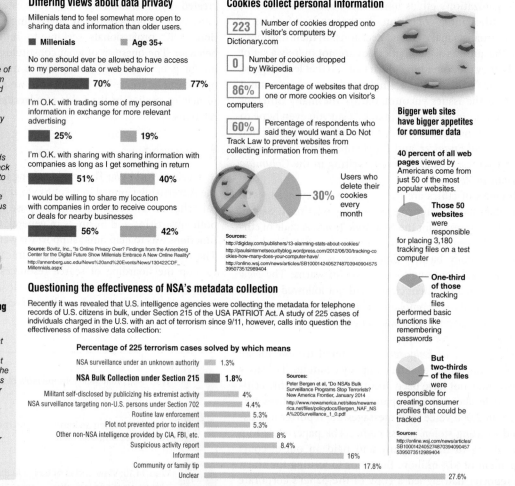

Cookie Monsters: Online Privacy and Data Gathering

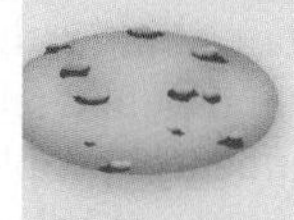

Cookie

A small piece of data sent from a website and stored in a user's web browser. Every time the user loads the website, the browser sends the cookie back to the server to notify the website of the user's previous activity.

Fingerprinting

A newer tracking technique that allows web sites to collect and analyze the characteristics of a computer (plug-ins, software, screen size, time zone, fonts) in order to form a unique signature.

Differing views about data privacy

Millenials tend to feel somewhat more open to sharing data and information than older users.

	Millenials	Age 35+
No one should ever be allowed to have access to my personal data or web behavior	70%	77%
I'm O.K. with trading some of my personal information in exchange for more relevant advertising	25%	19%
I'm O.K. with sharing with sharing information with companies as long as I get something in return	51%	40%
I would be willing to share my location with companies in order to receive coupons or deals for nearby businesses	56%	42%

Source: Bovitz, Inc., "Is Online Privacy Over? Findings from the Annenberg Center for the Digital Future Show Millenials Embrace A New Online Reality"
http://annenberg.usc.edu/News%20and%20Events/News/130422CDF_Millennials.aspx

Cookies collect personal information

223 Number of cookies dropped onto visitor's computers by Dictionary.com

0 Number of cookies dropped by Wikipedia

86% Percentage of websites that drop one or more cookies on visitor's computers

60% Percentage of respondents who said they would want a Do Not Track Law to prevent websites from collecting information from them

30% Users who delete their cookies every month

Sources:
http://digiday.com/publishers/13-alarming-stats-about-cookies/
http://paulsinternetsecurityblog.wordpress.com/2012/06/30/tracking-cookies-how-many-does-your-computer-have/
http://online.wsj.com/news/articles/SB10001424052748703940904575395073512989404

Bigger web sites have bigger appetites for consumer data

40 percent of all web pages viewed by Americans come from just 50 of the most popular websites.

Those 50 websites were responsible for placing 3,180 tracking files on a test computer

One-third of those tracking files performed basic functions like remembering passwords

But two-thirds of the files were responsible for creating consumer profiles that could be tracked

Sources:
http://online.wsj.com/news/articles/SB10001424052748703940904575395073512989404

Questioning the effectiveness of NSA's metadata collection

Recently it was revealed that U.S. intelligence agencies were collecting the metadata for telephone records of U.S. citizens in bulk, under Section 215 of the USA PATRIOT Act. A study of 225 cases of individuals charged in the U.S. with an act of terrorism since 9/11, however, calls into question the effectiveness of massive data collection:

Percentage of 225 terrorism cases solved by which means

NSA surveillance under an unknown authority	1.3%
NSA Bulk Collection under Section 215	**1.8%**
Militant self-disclosed by publicizing his extremist activity	4%
NSA surveillance targeting non-U.S. persons under Section 702	4.4%
Routine law enforcement	5.3%
Plot not prevented prior to incident	5.3%
Other non-NSA intelligence provided by CIA, FBI, etc.	8%
Suspicious activity report	8.4%
Informant	16%
Community or family tip	17.8%
Unclear	27.6%

Sources:
Peter Bergen et al, "Do NSA's Bulk Surveillance Programs Stop Terrorists? New America Frontier, January 2014
http://www.newamerica.net/sites/newamerica.net/files/policydocs/Bergen_NAF_NSA%20Surveillance_1_0.pdf

things that it categorizes you by, and you then have the opportunity to turn off any of the categories you don't want connected to you. For example, my file includes, among many other things, interest in the movie *Blade Runner,* a comparison of *Star Trek* and *Star Wars*, and minimalist music (among several hundred other things).

With consumers spending increasing amounts of their online time using mobile devices, advertisers have moved from wanting to target the right demographic for their product. They now want their carefully targeted ads to reach the "right person, at the right time, in the right place, with the right message."[75] Mobile devices are perfect for this because in addition to the rest of the data they hold about you, they generally know where you are. French carmaker Renault wanted to target adults who are interested in electric cars, so when a targeted consumer is within five miles of a dealership that carries the car, ads start appearing on the shopper's screen. Facebook has even developed technology to target ads based on the particular mode of phone people are using. So, through Facebook, advertisers can target users of an iPhone 5s or a Samsung Galaxy S5.[76]

Media Transformations Questions

- **DO** you ever read the privacy policies of the Web sites or social media sites you use? Have you ever quit using one because of its privacy policy?
- **ARE** you ever troubled by the ads that start showing up on your browser after you've looked at a particular topic online?
- **DOES** it worry you that through mobile technology marketers know not only what you are interested in, but where you've been?
- **DO** marketers do a good job of letting you know what kind of information they are collecting about you? What can you do if you don't like their policies?

maintain the positive image the group had fostered during the war. In recent years, the Ad Council has been responsible for a wide range of memorable public service ads, most notably the "Just Say No" and "This Is Your Brain on Drugs" campaigns.[77]

©iStockphoto.com/Luso

A number of ethical issues concern the advertising industry today, including truth in advertising and the level of control advertisers can expect to have over the news content surrounding their ads.

Truth in Advertising. Snapple claims to make its drinks from the "best stuff on earth." But what is the "best stuff"? Papa John's says "Better Ingredients. Better Pizza." Is this true? Just as important, do consumers expect such claims to be true?

Typically, ads for prescription drugs and medicines are held to high standards of truthfulness, whereas claims that one article of clothing is more fashionable than another are held to a much lower standard of proof. However, a dog food company was once required to prove that dogs really did prefer one brand over another by showing how much of two competing brands dogs would eat.[78]

A number of groups keep tabs on honesty in ads. The Federal Trade Commission (FTC) investigates many complaints. In 2014, the FTC took action against a number of companies making deceptive claims about weight-loss supplements.[79]

The National Advertising Division of the Council of Better Business Bureaus also investigates claims of false advertising. Says council representative Gunnar Waldman, "We care even about the seemingly frivolous or 'less-important' cases. The issues at stake—truth in advertising—are always broader than the products themselves."[80]

Advertising executive Michael Dweck says that claims of being "best" are dangerous: "So the only claims we'd make ought to be sufficiently humorous, exaggerated, and far-fetched that no one will take them seriously."[81] Chris Wall of advertising giant Ogilvy & Mather says that as long as companies are truthful in their ads, they have nothing to worry about: "The most powerful advertising tends to be fundamentally truthful anyway. The trick is finding an honest point of advocacy for a product and then presenting it in a way that moves people, catches their attention, that they remember."[82]

Advertising and Media Control. Sometimes concern about media content comes from advertisers rather than from critics of the media. Advertisers may want to control the kind of material that surrounds their messages, hoping to avoid stories that are critical of their products or simply to associate themselves with high-quality content. For example, a group of car dealers in California pulled all their advertising from the *San Jose Mercury News* after the paper ran an article that explained to buyers how to read the factory invoices on new cars so that they would be in a better negotiating position.[83] At other times, advertising boycotts are driven by advertisers

Questioning the Media

Do advertisers ever produce messages specifically designed to be offensive? Is it proper for the news media to give attention to these offensive ads? Why or why not? Or should the news media just ignore offensive ads to avoid giving them free publicity?

who don't want to be associated with a program's political point of view. In 2012, at least forty-five advertisers pulled their sponsorship from *The Rush Limbaugh Show* when the popular conservative radio talk show host called a law student and birth-control advocate a "slut" over the air.[84]

Magazine editors have long offered warnings to advertisers when potentially offensive articles will be included in a forthcoming issue. *Better Homes and Gardens* warned cigarette makers before running an article on the dangers of secondhand smoke and offered them the option of moving their advertising to another issue. "That's just consideration," said the magazine's editor in chief. "You don't want to purposely slap advertisers in the face."[85] It can also work the other way: Sometimes advertisers are contacted when positive articles are scheduled to appear. An energy company was solicited to advertise in the *National Review* when an article included a favorable mention of the company.

Occasionally companies want to know in advance what kind of content is going to be included in forthcoming issues of magazines so that they can decide whether to include their advertising with it. Some publishers view this simply as a way of keeping important advertisers informed about how their advertising will look. However, the American Society of Magazine Editors warns "that some advertisers may mistake an early warning as an open invitation to pressure the publisher or editor to alter, or even kill, the article in question."[86]

In 1995, Ford pulled all its advertising from the *New Yorker* for six months because one of its ads appeared next to a column by Ken Auletta that quoted an explicit song by Nine Inch Nails. And *Esquire* reportedly canceled a sixteen-page story about gay sex for fear that Chrysler would pull four pages of advertising from the magazine. In 1996, Chrysler sent a letter to one hundred major magazines requiring them to notify the carmaker "in advance of any and all editorial content that encompasses sexual, political, social issues or any editorial that might be construed as provocative or offensive."[87] Chrysler defended its policy in *Advertising Age*:

> We think we have a right to determine how and where we want to place our advertising. . . . We are not trying to get in the way of the editorial integrity of any magazine, but we do have the right to determine the editorial environment where our ads appear.[88]

Advertisers have also attempted to influence programming on television. Finding "family-friendly" shows to sponsor on television, especially broadcast television, is becoming increasingly difficult. The hit program *Friends* delivered a huge audience for NBC, but it did so with racy story lines and risqué humor. Companies such as consumer product giant Johnson & Johnson want to sponsor shows that parents and children can watch together so that they'll see commercials for Band-Aids, baby powder, Motrin, and Mylanta. To combat this problem, Johnson & Johnson, along with companies such as Procter & Gamble, Coca-Cola, and Ford, formed a group called the ANA Alliance for Family Entertainment to promote the development of shows that are acceptable to the entire family (ANA stands for Association of National Advertisers). The group, which began back in 1998 as the Family Friendly Programming Forum, isn't boycotting or criticizing adult-oriented shows; it just wants to promote shows on which its members won't be embarrassed to advertise.

The group funds the development of new shows that will meet these needs; in return, it receives the first right to advertise on them. The companies that belong to the forum control $11 billion worth of advertising, so their voices are important to television networks. In 2000, the first show whose development had been funded by the forum came on the air: *Gilmore Girls*.[89] Since then, the forum has been responsible for the development of shows such as *The New Adventures of Old Christine*, *Ugly Betty*, and *Friday Night Lights*.[90]

Ethics in Public Relations

It is easy to joke about a lack of ethics in public relations, but PR firms ignore ethical behavior at their own peril. The Public Relations Society of America (PRSA), founded in 1948, established its own code of ethics in 1954 not only to improve the profession's behavior, but also to improve the industry's image at a time when practitioners were "generally . . . perceived as slick con artists." In its original form, the code said, "We pledge to conduct ourselves professionally, with truth, accuracy, fairness, and responsibility to the public." The code was substantially revised and clarified in 1999. (See Box 14.2.)

Conducting War Through Public Relations: Citizens for a Free Kuwait. The ethical challenge of balancing the needs of truthfulness, the public interest, and the client's interests became a major issue for one PR firm during the 1991 Persian Gulf War. Foreign governments often hire PR firms to represent their interests in the United States, but few have hired a major firm to promote the nation's involvement in a war.[91]

Hill & Knowlton, the nation's largest PR firm at the time, was hired by Citizens for a Free Kuwait, a group made up of members of the Kuwaiti government. The campaign was designed to create sympathy for Kuwait, opposition to Iraq and Saddam Hussein, and support for U.S. involvement in fighting Iraq. The campaign followed a typical pattern of lobbying Congress, calling press conferences, sending out press releases, and producing video news releases.[92]

What really attracted controversy and raised ethical questions throughout the industry was testimony that Hill & Knowlton arranged to have given before the Congressional Human Rights Caucus. This group of U.S. representatives

Public Relations Society of America's Statement of Professional Values

The following is the Public Relations Society of America's Statement of Professional Values:

> This statement presents the core values of PRSA members and, more broadly, of the public relations profession. These values provide the foundation for the Member Code of Ethics and set the industry standard for the professional practice of public relations. These values are the fundamental beliefs that guide our behaviors and decision-making process. We believe our professional values are vital to the integrity of the profession as a whole.

Advocacy

- We serve the public interest by acting as responsible advocates for those we represent.
- We provide a voice in the marketplace of ideas, facts, and viewpoints to aid informed public debate.

Honesty

- We adhere to the highest standards of accuracy and truth in advancing the interests of those we represent and in communicating with the public.

Expertise

- We acquire and responsibly use specialized knowledge and experience.
- We advance the profession through continued professional development, research, and education.
- We build mutual understanding, credibility, and relationships among a wide array of institutions and audiences.

Independence

- We provide objective counsel to those we represent.
- We are accountable for our actions.

Loyalty

- We are faithful to those we represent, while honoring our obligation to serve the public interest.

Fairness

- We deal fairly with clients, employers, competitors, peers, vendors, the media, and the general public.
- We respect all opinions and support the right of free expression.

held hearings on October 10, 1990, on the Iraqi invasion of Kuwait. The centerpiece of these hearings was the eyewitness testimony of a fifteen-year-old Kuwaiti girl identified only as Nayirah. Nayirah told the caucus that she had personally seen atrocities committed following the invasion:

> While I was there, I saw the Iraqi soldiers come into the hospital with guns, and go into the room where . . . babies were in incubators. They took the babies out of the incubators, took the incubators, and left the babies on the cold floor to die.[93]

Her testimony certainly was effective. President George H. W. Bush mentioned the "twenty-two babies 'thrown on the floor like firewood'" on six separate occasions.[94]

Two years later, journalist John R. MacArthur revealed that Nayirah, who had not previously been identified, was actually the daughter of the Kuwaiti ambassador to the United States, who was a member of the Kuwaiti royal family. MacArthur, and others, charged that the incubator story was not true. Amnesty International found no evidence that the story was true, and ABC News reported that the story was "almost certainly false."[95]

Since Nayirah's testimony had not been given under oath, no questions were raised about the legality of Hill & Knowlton's actions. The firm defended its actions on behalf of Citizens for a Free Kuwait, but the fact remains that it did not investigate Nayirah's claims to see if they were true.[96] Whether true or false, the testimony itself was certainly not enough to send the United States to war with Iraq; rather, it was a well-planned PR effort intended to make Iraq seem evil and Kuwait appear to be a victim in need of assistance.

Whom Do You Serve: The Client or the Public? One of the most difficult ethical problems facing PR practitioners is the conflict between serving the client's interests and serving those of the public. David Martinson, a professor of journalism, argues that PR practitioners can internalize important ethical principles of honesty and serving the public interest by practicing them daily in small ways. Then, when the rare moral dilemmas arise, the practitioner is used to behaving in an ethical manner.[97]

As noted earlier, Aristotle suggested that ethical behavior arises from a golden mean, or balance, between two extremes of behavior or belief. Does this mean that PR practitioners can strike a balance between lying and telling the truth? No. Martinson says that PR practitioners must always be fully committed to the truth, but that it is possible to compromise between serving the public's interests and serving the client's. The PR practitioner must serve the client's best interests, but not to the extent that his or her professional and ethical obligations to the public are compromised.

Chapter SUMMARY

Media ethics are a complex topic because they deal with an institution that must do things that ordinary people in ordinary circumstances would not do. Media ethics draw on a range of philosophical principles, including basic Judeo-Christian values, Aristotle's ideas about virtue and balanced behaviors (the golden mean), Kant's categorical imperative, Mill's principle of utility, Rawls's veil of ignorance, and the Hutchins Commission's social-responsibility ethics. One way contemporary journalists can resolve their ethical problems is by using the Bok model for ethical decision making.

Reporters face a range of ethical issues on a regular basis. Those issues include the following:

Truthfulness—Journalists need to make a commitment to telling the truth. This includes not giving false or made-up reports and telling truthful stories that are not intended to deceive the audience. This may require reporters to provide not only the facts but also the context surrounding them. Truthfulness requires a commitment not only from the journalist but also from the organization he or she works for.

Conflicts of interest—The interests of a corporation that owns a news organization may sometimes be at odds with the nature of the news being reported. Journalists need to be careful not only to portray their parent company in an accurate light, but also to give no special favors to companies connected to the organization's parent company.

Sensationalism—News organizations sometimes emphasize news that is interesting but unimportant. This happens when reporters put more effort into attracting and pleasing an audience than into reporting on the critical issues of the day. This can occur because of the increased pace of the news business brought about by cable television, the Internet, and the parent company's desire for profits.

Authenticity and appropriateness of photographs—Photos can be among the most controversial media materials, both because of their disturbing content and because they can be altered with digital editing tools.

Journalists and their employers can apply a variety of methods for enforcing and implementing ethical behavior. These include employing an ombudsman, requiring a commitment to ethical behavior on the part of all employees, and adhering to a code of ethics.

The advertising industry became concerned with protecting its image during World War II. Among the major ethical issues in advertising are the following:

Truthfulness—How important is it that claims such as "Tastes great" or "It's the best" are demonstrably true?

Taste—Is it appropriate for ads to attract attention by shocking audiences?

Media control—Do advertisers have a right to control the editorial material that surrounds their advertisements?

In the public relations industry, practitioners need to work at balancing their clients' interests against those of the public at large. This can become problematic when a client is attempting to influence the public to support an issue, such as going to war.

Keep up-to-date with content from the author's blog.

Take the chapter quiz.

Key TERMS

morals 356
ethics 356
golden mean 356
categorical imperative 358
principle of utility 358
veil of ignorance 358
sensationalism 363
tabloid laundering or tabloidization 363
ombudsman 369

Concept REVIEW

Ethical principles from Aristotle, Kant, Mill, Rawls, and the Hutchins Commission
The Bok model for ethical decision making
The difference between morals and ethics
Corporate conflict of interest
Digital alteration of photographs
Advertiser influence on media content

Student STUDY SITE

Sharpen your skills with SAGE edge at **edge.sagepub.com/hanson5e**

SAGE edge for Students provides a personalized approach to help you accomplish your coursework goals in an easy-to-use learning environment.

chapter

15

Global Media

Communication Around the World

During the Arab Spring movement of 2011, many Americans turned to the Al Jazeera English Web site to get up-to-the-minute news from the protests in Egypt and other Middle Eastern countries.

Richard Levine/Alamy

When I arrived at my office on the morning of January 28, 2011, I logged into my Twitter account. The news there was flowing fast and furious about the antigovernment rioting taking place in Egypt—protests that would eventually lead to the resignation of President Hosni Mubarak.[1]

American cable news networks were giving spot coverage to the story that was dominated by commentary from American pundits.[2] National media news reporters, such as the *New York Times*'s Brian Stelter (now at CNN) and NPR's David Folkenflik, were pointing their followers to the Al Jazeera English (AJE) Web site for continuous live coverage of the ongoing protests.

I immediately fired up my browser and was greeted by stunning images. AJE was showing protesters throwing tear gas canisters back at police and hurling gasoline bombs at armored personnel carriers, Egyptian national police being knocked down by objects thrown from the crowd, and praying protesters being attacked with spewing fire hoses. The best Western media could do was rebroadcast Al Jazeera's video.

At a time when Western networks had virtually no one available to cover Egypt, AJE had multiple reporters on the ground and numerous video feeds coming in.[3] One of the most fascinating discrepancies was that between an Egyptian television broadcast showing a section of Cairo at peace and AJE video that showed sections of the city in flames. What's more, AJE's access was not limited to Egypt's capital city of Cairo. The network also had reporters on the ground in the Egyptian cities of Suez and Alexandria.

As the protests continued, it became difficult for even Al Jazeera to report the news, as the Egyptian government revoked the network's license to broadcast from Egypt and pulled the accreditation of its reporters.[4]

Along with Al Jazeera, two other major sources of news about the protests were SMS text messages and social media sites such as Twitter and Facebook. Some commentators in Western media emphasized the role of social media in the uprising, calling the protests the "Facebook Revolt." But it's important to remember, as journalist Philip N. Howard points out, that while social networks certainly helped the protesters organize and share information, it was the protesters themselves who put their lives on the line. He wrote: "Overemphasizing the role of information technology diminishes the personal risks that individual protesters took in heading out onto the streets to face tear gas and rubber bullets."[5]

LEARNING OBJECTIVES

After studying this chapter, you will be able to:

1. Discuss different media standards around the world by using four normative theories of the press.
2. Explain the usefulness of a more recent "development theory" for describing the press in the twenty-first century.
3. Explain the importance of social media and other "small media" in the Middle East.
4. Describe the dangers journalists face when reporting from conflict zones.
5. Discuss whether Marshall McLuhan's concept of the "global village" is relevant to the media world today.

In his book *Three Blind Mice*, which is about the American broadcast networks in transition during the 1980s and 1990s, media journalist Ken Auletta talks about how the first Gulf War brought CNN to prominence:

> It wasn't until the war in the Persian Gulf began in January 1991 that the cable revolution became dramatically apparent. Viewers realized that CNN, not the three networks, was a primary source of up-to-the-minute news. And they were getting the news the way they wanted it—instantly and without interruption from soap operas. For as long as the war held their interest, viewers could choose for themselves when to watch the news as easily as they could flick to an HBO movie, an ESPN basketball game, or a Disney cartoon.[6]

Unfortunately for Al Jazeera English, even the 2011 riots and protests in Egypt and the subsequent Arab Spring protest movement were unable to bring permanent increases to the number of American viewers. In 2013, Al Jazeera purchased former vice president Al Gore's Current cable network and rebranded it as Al Jazeera America, thus giving the network access to about 60 percent of American households. But when that happened, cable providers carrying the new channel insisted that Al Jazeera stop making its English-language video feed available for free online. So although Al Jazeera America now had more cable availability, many of the young, digitally literate viewers who viewed the channel online were lost to the network. Ratings from the summer of 2014 showed Al Jazeera America as having a miniscule 17,000 viewers a night.[7]

Timeline

1800

1812 War of 1812 breaks out.
1835 Alexis de Tocqueville publishes *Democracy in America*.
1859 Charles Darwin publishes *On the Origin of Species*.
1861 U.S. Civil War begins.
1869 Transcontinental railroad is completed.
1879 Thomas Edison invents electric light bulb.
1898 Spanish-American War breaks out.

1900

1903 Orville and Wilbur Wright fly first airplane.
1905 Albert Einstein proposes his theory of relativity.

1910

1912 *Titanic* sinks.
1914 World War I begins.
1918 Worldwide influenza epidemic strikes.

1920

1920 Nineteenth Amendment passes, giving U.S. women the right to vote.
1929 U.S. stock market crashes, leading to the Great Depression.

1930

1933 Adolf Hitler is elected chancellor of Germany.
1939 World War II breaks out in Europe.

1940

1941 United States enters World War II.
1945 United States drops two atomic bombs on Japan.
1947 Pakistan and India gain independence from Britain.
1949 Communists establish People's Republic of China.

◀ **1794** First leg of the all-mechanical French State Telegraph system is put into service.

1844 First electric telegraph line using the Morse Code system opens between Baltimore, Maryland, and Washington, D.C.
1852 A channel cable telegraph line connects London and Paris.
1861 The transcontinental telegraph line connects east and west coasts of the United States.
1866 Transatlantic cable connects Europe and North America.
1901 Guglielmo Marconi's wireless telegraph sends a signal across the Atlantic Ocean.

AP Photo

1932 BBC Empire Service launches shortwave radio broadcasts to serve all parts of the British Empire.

Tony Burman, who was the managing director of AJE in 2009, told NPR that part of the challenge has been the lack of awareness within the United States of Al Jazeera English. Obviously, another aspect has been the political stigma that has been attached to Al Jazeera Arabic, and a kind of assumption on the part of some people that what they've heard about Al Jazeera Arabic (a) is true and (b) applies to Al Jazeera's English service.[8]

The notion of being able to print or broadcast almost any kind of news is central to the ideal of free speech in the United States and the democracies of the West. But just because it is legally available doesn't mean that a given channel will actually *be* available. Controls on the marketplace of ideas can come from private industry, as well as the government. Different countries and cultures have differing ideas as to what constitutes the proper form for the media to take. In this chapter, we look at ideals of how the media ought to behave and how the media function in different societies around the world. Finally, we consider what it means to live in a world with such a wide range of media. ■

> "Overemphasizing the role of information technology diminishes the personal risks that individual protestors took in heading out onto the streets to face tear gas and rubber bullets."
>
> —Professor Philip N. Howard

Video 15.1: Read and watch coverage of the Arab Spring revolution.

1950

- **1950** Korean War begins.
- **1953** Francis Crick and James Watson discover structure of DNA.
- **1954** Media coverage of the Army-McCarthy hearings investigating conflicting accusations between Joseph McCarthy and the U.S. Army contributed to McCarthy's decline in popularity
- **1957** Soviet Union launches spacecraft *Sputnik I*

1960

- **1963** Martin Luther King Jr. delivers "I Have a Dream" speech during Washington, D.C., civil-rights march.
- **1969** Neil Armstrong walks on the moon.

1970

- **1974** U.S. president Richard Nixon resigns due to Watergate scandal.
- **1975** Vietnam War ends.
- **1977** Apple II personal computer is introduced.
- **1978** First test-tube baby is born.

1980

- **1983** First HIV/AIDS cases are documented.
  Ozone hole is discovered over Antarctica.
- **1986** Space shuttle *Challenger* explodes.
- **1989** The Berlin Wall falls.

1990

- **1991** Soviet Union disbands.
- **1993** European Union is formed.
- **1994** Nelson Mandela is elected president of South Africa.
- **1997** Diana, Princess of Wales, dies in car accident.

2000-

- **2001** Al Qaida attacks World Trade Center and Pentagon.
- **2003** United States invades Iraq.
- **2008** Barack Obama is elected U.S. president.
- **2011** Earthquake and tsunami hit Japan. United States endseight-year war with Iraq.
- **2012** Superstorm Sandy devastates U.S. eastern seaboard.
- **2014** Russian army invades Ukraine.

- **1956** Siebert, Peterson, and Schramm publish *Four Theories of the Press.*
- **1962** Marshall McLuhan introduces the concept of a "global village" that is linked through media.

- **1985** News media in the Soviet Union experience a brief period of openness during *glasnost,* a policy promoted by Mikhail Gorbachev.

AP Photo/Ira Schwartz

- **1995** John Nerone and his colleagues publish *Last Rights: Revisiting Four Theories of the Press.*
- **2000** There are more than 430 privately owned television stations in Europe.
- **2008** News about the Mumbai terror attacks travels worldwide by social media.
- **2011** Arab Spring protests bring Al Jazeera's English website to American attention.
- **2013** Seventy journalists killed worldwide in "direct connection" to their work, twenty-eight of them in Syria.

Media Ideals Around the World

So far in this book, we have primarily discussed the development of the media in economically developed democracies. But the relationship among politicians, citizens, and the press can take very different forms in other nations, depending on the country's culture, government, and level of development.

In 1956, three journalism professors from the University of Illinois—Fred S. Siebert, Theodore Peterson, and Wilbur Schramm—outlined what they considered to be the major forms the press could take around the world in *Four Theories of the Press*. They built their argument around two basic value-oriented theories of how the press ought to behave: *authoritarian* and *libertarian*. They then created two variations on these: *Soviet/communist* and *social responsibility*.[9]

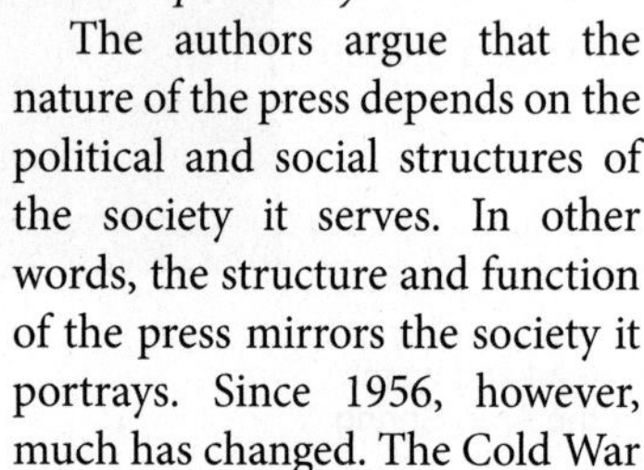

©iStockphoto.com/alengo

The authors argue that the nature of the press depends on the political and social structures of the society it serves. In other words, the structure and function of the press mirrors the society it portrays. Since 1956, however, much has changed. The Cold War has ended, and the Soviet Union has collapsed. We've gone from talking about the influence of the press to talking about the influence of the media. The media industry has come to be dominated by a limited number of large owners. We have seen the rise of the Internet, which allows many more voices to be heard, though they can easily get lost in all the digital noise. And the importance of developing nations is being increasingly recognized.

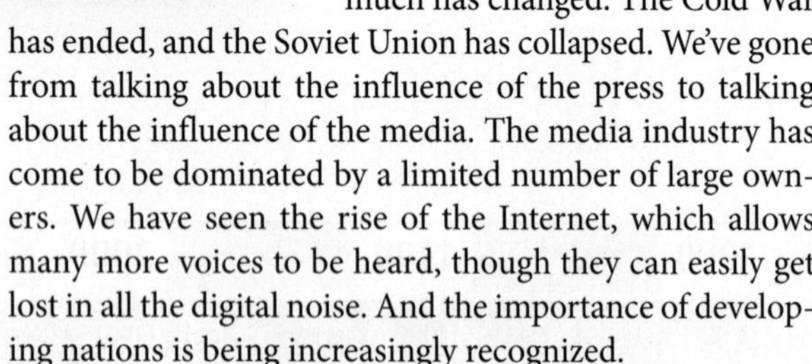

In response to these changes, and many others, scholars started questioning whether the ideas from the book needed to be revisited. John C. Nerone and his contributing authors—also all from the University of Illinois—did just that in 1995 with *Last Rights: Revisiting* Four Theories of the Press. As they pointed out,

> When *Four Theories* was written, many U.S. newspapers carried ads for segregated housing, it was still legal in a number of states for a husband to divorce his wife for being a bad housekeeper, and no one had ever seen what the earth looked like from outer space.[10]

Nerone and his colleagues suggested several things that contemporary readers of *Four Theories* should think about. Most important of these was that the four theories were not a timeless set of categories. Rather, they were a critique set within a particular time period that reflected the politics and economics of the day. Other critics have suggested that there should be a fifth theory of the press—*development theory*—to deal with countries that are in the process of building modern economies.[11] In this section, we look at the four original theories, along with development theory, and see how well they apply to press systems today.

Authoritarian Theory

The **authoritarian theory** is the oldest theory of the press. It says that the role of the press is to be a servant of the government, not a servant of the citizenry. Authoritarian theory has its roots in royal control of societies during the era when the printing press was first developed. Monarchs were believed to derive their authority to rule directly from God, and therefore they had the right and responsibility to control all aspects of society, including the printing press. Rulers felt that the proper role of the press was to provide the public with the information the rulers deemed appropriate. Keep in mind that the reach of the press was still fairly limited because relatively few people were literate. So the monarch gave formal permission to the publisher, who in return had a monopoly on the publishing business.

Today countries that are developing mass media often start by taking an authoritarian approach. Authoritarian rule is also practiced in most totalitarian states, which seek to control the press along with all other aspects of social life.

Authoritarian control of the press is carried out by the following means:

- Giving permits to only certain printers—However, as the number of trained printers grows and an increasingly literate public demands more and more printed materials, the ability of the government to control "outlaw" printers can become problematic.
- Prosecuting anyone who violates generally accepted standards for the press.

Totalitarian governments have been ruthless in controlling the press through arrests, torture, arson, and imprisonment, along with more subtle methods such as controlling the availability of supplies. For example, in the 1990s, Serbian president Slobodan Milošević shut down the capital city's only independent radio station, Radio B92, and the opposition newspaper had trouble publishing because of newsprint shortages—which didn't seem to affect the official state newspaper.[12] Since 2009, strong antiterrorism laws have forced journalists in Ethiopia to self-censor to avoid arrest, and at least two Ethiopian journalists have been imprisoned for more than two and a half years on terrorism charges. In Eritrea, one of the most repressive African countries, there simply is no privately owned media.[13]

Nerone's major critique of authoritarian theory is that it is more a description of the procedures a government uses

authoritarian theory: A theory of appropriate press behavior that says the role of the press is to be a servant of the government, not a servant of the citizenry.

to control the press than a philosophy of press behavior.[14]

Communist Theory

Although the Soviet Union no longer exists, a variety of governments around the world, including those in Cuba and China, continue to hold to communist ideals. The **communist theory** of the press is similar to the authoritarian theory but goes a step further. Instead of just being a servant of the government, the press is run by the government to serve the government's own needs. The communist press is supposedly free to publish the truth. However, in the Soviet Union the press was not free, nor did it speak the truth. The communist view is that there is only one valid political and social philosophy, so there is no need for competing "false" ideals to be portrayed in the media. Moreover, communists argue that the American press is no freer than the communist press because the American media serve the needs of capitalist owners rather than those of society. Communist media theory proposes the following principles:

Mohamed Abdiwahab/AFP/Getty Images

Somalia is a difficult country to practice journalism within. Abdimalik Yusuf (left), head of Shabelle radio, and Mohamed Bashir, a journalist, stand chained near court in Mogadishu. The two journalists have been charged with defamation and insulting state institutions for their work on covering the story of a woman who had been raped.

- The media are an instrument of the government and the Communist Party—An independent press is undesirable and should be suppressed.
- The media should be closely tied to other sources of government power and authority—In the United States, the executive, legislative, and judicial branches of the government serve as checks and balances on each other, all overseen by the press. But communist theory holds that all elements of the state, including the press, should work toward a common goal.
- The media's main purpose is to act as a tool for government propaganda.

The communist notion of absolute right and wrong leaves no room for the media to debate the proper role of government. The press is not a watchdog, but rather a supporter of the Communist Party's efforts to create a perfect state. Since the responsibility for enforcing this truth lies within the leadership of the state, the leadership should control the mass media. So the role of the press is to put forward the official party line. This is almost directly counter to the Western notion of the press as an outside observer keeping watch on the government.[15]

communist theory: A theory of appropriate press behavior that says the press is to be run by the government to serve the government's own needs.

In *Last Rights*, the authors point out that what we've been referring to as "the communist theory" was supposed to represent a generalized Marxist response to libertarian theory (discussed below) but really represented the Soviet approach at a given time.[16] The communist theory of the press was an ideal that Soviet communists never came even close to obtaining. The Soviets may have had an ideal of a communist press, but in reality it was generally just authoritarian controls. The only time the Soviet media came close to acting as a force for the people and not just for those in power was under the leadership of Mikhail Gorbachev in the 1980s during his campaign for *glasnost*, or openness. *Glasnost* allowed citizens and the media to express their opposition to the official government position and to criticize corrupt local leaders. Since then, however, the Russian media have gone back to a level of authoritarian control, as we discuss later in this chapter.

Questioning the Media

If you knew you were going to risk imprisonment or torture, would you still be willing to speak out and criticize your government? Why or why not?

Web 15.1: Read about press freedom around the world at Reporters Without Borders.

Web 15.2: Read about new media and authoritarian regimes.

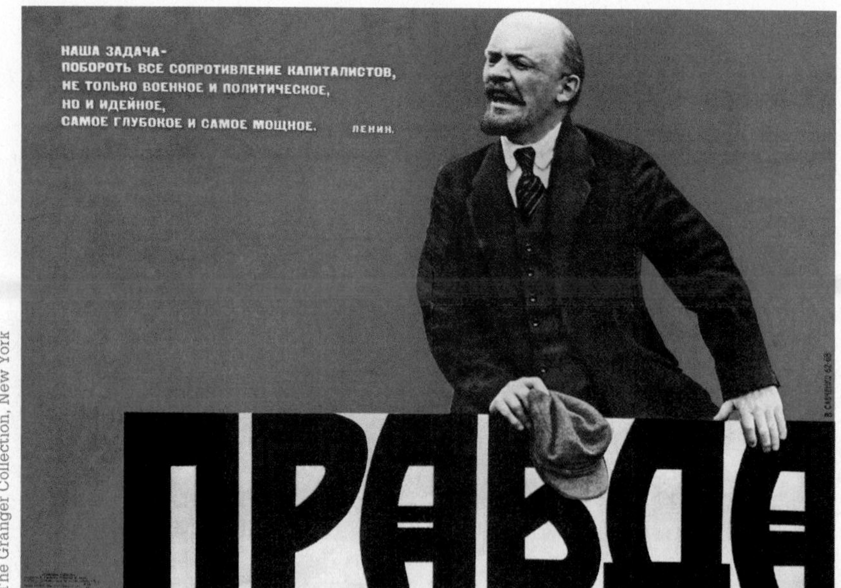

The Granger Collection, New York

This 1968 Soviet propaganda poster depicting Vladimir Ilyich Lenin reads: "Pravda: Our task is to overcome capitalist resistance—not only military and political resistance, but ideological resistance, which is the most profound and powerful."

Libertarian Theory

The opposite of authoritarian theory is **libertarian theory**. In this view, the press does not belong to the government but is instead a separate institution that belongs to the people and serves as an independent observer of the government. Libertarian philosophy views people as moral beings who can tell the difference between truthfulness and falsity. Because of this, they need a free and open press so that they can decide for themselves what is true and what is false. The libertarian theory thus holds that there must be a marketplace of ideas in which both true and false statements can compete for the hearts and minds of audience members. This is the basic idea of the First Amendment to the U.S. Constitution.[17] Libertarian theory is the basis of free speech in the democracies of the West and is the most well developed of the theories in *Four Theories*.[18]

Most noncommunist countries pay at least lip service to the libertarian ideal of the press, although many do not adhere to it. Again, even in the United States, there tends to be much more government control of the broadcast media than of print.

The free press of a libertarian society is based on the following principles:

- People want to know the truth and be guided by it.
- The only way to arrive at the truth is for ideas to be freely and openly discussed.
- Different people will have different opinions, and everyone must be allowed to develop his or her own.
- The most rational ideas will be the most accepted.

Web 15.3: Compare and contrast media outlets.

In the libertarian view, the major functions of the press are to inform, entertain, and advertise (to support itself). Overall, though, the goal of the media is to help people discover the truth. The press should be free of government control, and every idea, no matter how crazy or offensive, should be allowed a forum for expression. As Siebert et al. wrote in *Four Theories*, the ideal is "to let the public at large be subjected to a barrage of information and opinion, some of it possibly true, some of it possibly false, and some of it containing elements of both."[19]

A key problem with libertarian media theory is that it assumes that the primary threat to freedom of speech and communication comes from the government rather than from the marketplace. Under the American system, the voices that are profitable to present will be heard much more loudly than those that do not produce a profit. The ideas that attract advertising revenue and sales draw much more attention from the press than do those about the poor or disenfranchised. Hence we hear more in the news about the stock market than about job programs for the unemployed. *Four Theories* argues that the free market is the ultimate in freedom, rather than media owned by "community groups, nonprofit corporations, universities, religious groups, and municipalities."[20] The debate is framed in terms of external controls rather than access. There is a presumption that the ideal of freedom is corporate or individual ownership with no government intervention. But what about the BBC? Arguably one of the greatest broadcast news operations in the world, it is run with government funding, albeit with a relatively hands-off approach.

Social Responsibility Theory

The **social responsibility theory** of the press is an outgrowth of libertarian theory. This theory is based on the concern that, although the press may be free from interference by the government, the press can still be controlled by corporate interests. For example, in principle, anyone can start up a newspaper, but in reality, it is an expensive and difficult proposition. Moreover, only a limited number of radio and television station licenses are available. So, although the government does not control the press in a free society, the control exercised by a limited number of corporations and

libertarian theory: A theory of appropriate press behavior that says the press does not belong to the government but is instead a separate institution that belongs to the people and serves as an independent observer of the government.

social responsibility theory: A theory of appropriate press behavior based on the concern that, although the press may be free from interference from the government, it can still be controlled by corporate interests. It is an outgrowth of libertarian theory.

individuals can be as effective as that of any government. Social responsibility theory says that the high level of concentrated power in the hands of the media requires that they be socially responsible in covering all sides of controversial issues and providing voters with all the information they need to make considered choices. If the press is not sufficiently vigilant, it is the duty of some representative of the public to force it to be responsible.[21]

Under social responsibility theory, the press is obliged to serve several social functions:

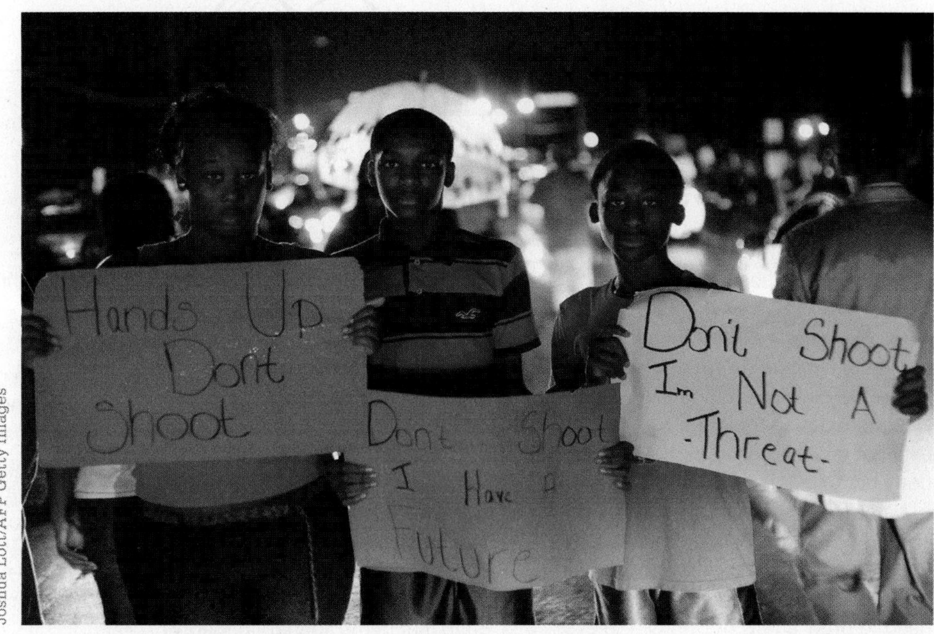

Joshua Lott/AFP Getty Images

In a country with a libertarian theory of the press, journalists are free to cover protests against the government, such as this one in Ferguson, Missouri, where locals were carrying pickets protesting the the killing of local resident Michael Brown.

- Provide the news and information needed to make the political system work.
- Give the public the information needed for self-governance.
- Serve as an overseer of the government.
- Serve the economic function of bringing together buyers and sellers through advertising.
- Provide entertainment.
- Be profitable enough to avoid outside pressures.

Social responsibility theory essentially advocates non-authoritarian media controls. France, Israel, and Sweden all operate under some form of social responsibility controls. The governments own and operate television channels, and the programming tends to promote the government's point of view.[22] The alternative is for the press to be in the hands of private business, which may allow for more political views but limits the media to carrying programming that is profitable. Government ownership frees the media from the constraint of having to make a profit.

The social responsibility theory was a response to the Hutchins Commission report from the late 1940s on the social responsibility of the press, which we discussed in Chapter 14. However, it does describe an approach to the press that is common in the world, for example, in the Israeli press, which we discuss later. The press does not necessarily like the idea that it has responsibilities to go with the freedoms it claims. The question really is, to whom does the freedom of the press belong? Is it to a corporate institution, or is it to people with voices wanting to be heard? Does giving a voice to one limit the voice of the other? Should we automatically favor the rights of those who can afford the press over those who cannot?[23]

Norms for the Press in the Twenty-first Century

Perhaps the biggest problem with these normative theories of the press is that it may take two or more of them to describe a given country's media system. For example, theocratic countries whose media operate under a strong social responsibility theory may incorporate elements of the communist media theory, substituting the values of the state religion for those of the Communist Party.

Several authors have suggested a fifth theory of the press, **development theory**, to address the special needs of emerging nations, whose governments may feel that they need to restrict freedom of the press in order to promote industry, national identity, and partnerships with neighboring nations. Media theorist Denis McQuail writes that less developed societies undergoing the transition from colonial rule to independence have different needs than do developed nations such as those of North America and Western Europe. These developing nations "lack the money, infrastructure, skills, and audiences to sustain a free-market media system."[24] Thus, in many cases, leaders in those nations resort to using authoritarian controls. In May 2007, for example, then Venezuelan president Hugo Chávez revoked the broadcast license of the country's oldest and most watched television network, Radio Caracas Television, or RCTV. The network had been severely critical of Chávez and his administration,

development theory: A theory of appropriate press behavior that states that developing nations may need to implement press controls in order to promote industry, national identity, and partnerships with neighboring nations.

Web 15.4: Read the Hutchins Commission report.

Web 15.5: Read about how former Venezuelan strong man Hugo Chávez silenced Radio Caracas Television.

TEST YOUR MEDIA LITERACY

Updating the Four Theories

John Nerone and the contributing authors of *Last Rights*[1] say that *Four Theories of the Press*[2] was a map of the world's media drawn at a specific time—the mid-1950s. And although it was a good map for its day, it was limited by what could be seen at that time and does not take into account the massive transformations that have taken place since then—the fall of communism, the end of the Cold War, globalization, and media consolidation. So they ask, "Do we need to draw a new map?" Or the even bigger question: "*Can* we draw a new map?"[3] This new map will need to deal with the issues surrounding the press in developing nations, as well as the norms surrounding the controlled press in many Islamic nations.

Reread the section of this chapter describing the four theories, paying particular attention to the critique of the theories, and then answer the questions here.

WHO is the source?

Who is John Nerone? What have he and his colleagues written?

WHAT is he saying?

According to Nerone, what made *Four Theories* such a significant book? What are the major questions he raises about the theories for the current media world? Are there other notions of a free press than that of the libertarian theory?

WHAT evidence is there?

What evidence does Nerone provide that *Four Theories* needs to be updated to apply to the present media world? How do new media—the Internet, Web sites, blogs, and social networking sites—fit within these theories? What other critiques are there of the Four Theories? What evidence is there that the categories are still useful?

WHAT do you and your classmates think?

What role do you think the media should play within society? Should the media be forced to be responsible? If so, who should decide what it means to be responsible? Should the role of the media be to support the government or to be a watchdog over the government? Can they do both?

[1]John C. Nerone, ed., *Last Rights: Revisiting* Four Theories of the Press (Urbana and Chicago: University of Illinois Press, 1995).
[2]Fred S. Siebert, Theodore Peterson, and Wilbur Schramm, *Four Theories of the Press* (Urbana, Ill.: University of Illinois Press, 1956).
[3]Nerone, *Last Rights: Revisiting* Four Theories of the Press.

Web 15.6: Balancing free speech, public safety, and ethnic violence in age of social media.

and lifting the network's broadcast license effectively silenced it. Although the network has been kept off the air since 2007, it has stayed in business at a much smaller level producing programming for other channels.[25]

The Internet in the Twenty-first Century

In *The Victorian Internet*, author Tom Standage argues that the nineteenth-century telegraph was also a significant global development, serving many of the same purposes as the Internet at the end of the twentieth century and the beginning of the twenty-first. According to him, "[The telegraph was] a world-wide communications network whose cables spanned continents and oceans, it revolutionized business practice, gave rise to new forms of crime, and inundated its users with a deluge of information."[26]

The telegraph system was followed by both radio and the telephone as media that could tie large areas of the world together. While the earliest components of the Internet were in use by 1969, the Net was limited largely to interpersonal communication until 1991, when Tim Berners-Lee released the World Wide Web as an easy and uniform way to access material on the Internet. Although the Internet owes a historical debt to the early telegraph and telephone systems, it has grown into a new medium unlike any other because it is the only one that incorporates elements of interpersonal, group, and mass communication. The unique nature of the Internet, especially in a global context, poses new moral dilemmas concerning national boundaries, corporate control, freedom of the press, and the rights of individuals. As you read about global media in different countries later in this chapter, keep in mind some of these issues.

Going Global: Media Standards Around the World

There is a presumption that a direct connection exists between a country's media system and its political system. Central to this presumption is the idea that a free press is essential for a functional democracy. But what constitutes a free press? Broadcasters in countries with commercially run media, such as the United States, presume that the freest press is that run by private-sector corporate control. Broadcasters in countries with strong traditions of public ownership, such as the United Kingdom, might argue that the commercial broadcasters are beholden to stockholders and advertisers and are no freer than the media in totalitarian states.

Alan Wells suggests that the four theories of the press might be replaced by five dimensions over which media could be rated:

- Control—Who controls the media system? This could be the state, a public corporation, a private enterprise, or corporate sponsorship.
- Finance—How do broadcasters pay the bills? Options include license fees, taxes, advertising, private subsidies, subscription charges, or a combination of these.
- Programming goals—What are the media trying to accomplish with their programming? Providing entertainment, educating the audience, selling products, promoting cultural goals, promoting a political ideology, or just putting up the cheapest possible imported material is each a possible programming goal.
- Target audience—For whom are the media producing and distributing content? These could be social or economic elites, the masses, or specialized/targeted audiences.
- Feedback mechanism—How do media organizations hear back from their audiences? Such feedback could be in the form of field reports, audience participation rates, polls and ratings, or response from critics and sponsors.[27]

As you can see, these five properties can be combined in an endless number of ways to describe a wide range of media systems. As we travel around the world looking at the various approaches to running the media, think about how these properties are being applied. You might also consider which of the normative theories of the press discussed previously would apply.

Canada, Western Europe, and Great Britain

Canada, Western Europe, and Britain have liberal democracies that have free speech and media that are relatively free to criticize their governments. But their media differ in significant ways from the media in the United States, if only because the United States has the largest media industry in the world.

Canadian Media. Canada has a free press patterned in part on the United States' model but modified by a desire to preserve Canadian culture in the face of the massive U.S. media industry. Canada can be characterized as a country with a large geographic area offset by a relatively small population, which makes media transmission relatively expensive. Canada's vastness means that it has strongly regional media, amplified by the fact that both English and French are official languages.

SECRET 5 One area of resentment has been the somewhat one-way direction of media influence from the United States. As one major Canadian mass communication text points out,

> In Canada, more American television programming is available to the vast majority of Canadians than is Canadian programming. On most Canadian commercial radio stations, more American material is available to listeners than Canadian material. On virtually all magazine racks in Canada more American magazines are available to the reader than Canadian magazines, in spite of the fact that about 2,000 magazines are published in Canada. More American authors than Canadian authors are read by the average Canadian school child.[28]

The attitudes expressed in this Canadian text might be seen as an example of Secret Five—New media are always scary.

Library of Congress

In the nineteenth century, the telegraph served to transmit news across the United States and around the world far faster than any vehicle could travel. It was the first step toward the creation of global electronic media.

Despite these issues, the Canadian media industry has been seeing growth. Canada's recording industry has been increasing steadily for the past two decades, as has the book publishing industry. The Canadian film industry has benefited from U.S. movie and television productions shooting north of the border, with Canada now being the second-largest producer of television programming in the world, after the United States. The movie and TV industry in western Canada made nearly $1.2 billion in 2011.[29]

In an effort to protect and enhance Canada's media industry, the government has put in place a number of "Canadian content" regulations requiring broadcasters to carry a certain level of Canadian-produced material. For example, programming on Canadian radio must be at least 35 percent domestically produced. Canadian television attracted widespread attention in spring 2007 when the Canadian Broadcasting Corporation put a sitcom on the air called *Little Mosque on the Prairie*, which follows the travails

http://www.cbc.ca/littlemosque

Little Mosque on the Prairie is a popular Canadian television comedy that tells the story of a rural Muslim community in small-town Canada. It's an example of Canadian-produced broadcast programming.

of a rural Muslim community in small-town Canada.[30] (No, I'm not making this up. It was a hit series in Canada that ran six seasons through 2012, and it's recently been available in the United States on Hulu and Hulu Plus.)

These policies put the country at odds with the North American Free Trade Agreement (NAFTA), which calls for products to flow freely across the borders of Canada, the United States, and Mexico. The problem Canada faces is that the United States' largest export is not wheat or steel, but rather media content. Nevertheless, Canada has worked hard at maintaining its cultural production, exporting media content produced by authors such as Margaret Atwood and Douglas Coupland; filmmakers such as James Cameron and Jason Reitman; musicians such as Bryan Adams, Sarah McLachlan, Celine Dion, and Alanis Morissette; actors such as Jim Carrey and Michael J. Fox; and magazine editor Bonnie Fuller (see Chapter 5).[31]

Western Europe and Britain. Western Europe covers a wide range of countries, from Spain and Portugal up through France, Germany, and Scandinavia. These are the countries of the European Union.[32] Cable television is common in some regions, such as Belgium and Germany, while satellite programming is more common in Scandinavia. European broadcasting was dominated by state-run monopolies until the 1980s and 1990s, when commercial alternatives became more common. With this switch, broadcasters started moving away from subsidies to advertising revenues. But even the commercial stations remain heavily regulated and have strong controls and guidelines on the amounts and placement of advertisements. Part of the drive to privatize broadcasting was due to pirate radio stations located offshore on ships that broadcast into the countries.

Broadcasting in France typifies the European approach, with networks having a strong public service obligation and a desire to preserve French culture from foreign encroachment. According to broadcast scholar Matthew Rusher, "Each country in Western Europe seeks to preserve its own culture and language and sees the foreign produced programming on the international channels as a threat to its cultural integrity."[33] These stations want to attract audiences and make money, but they also want to preserve their distinctive national culture.

Globally, the BBC may well be the best-known non-U.S. broadcaster. Britain, a pioneer in broadcasting from its earliest days, used radio to reach out to its far-flung empire, which once covered a quarter of the globe.[34] As we discussed in Chapter 7, this reputation comes from the BBC World Service, much of which is now carried digitally via the Internet. The BBC operates under a public service model in which audience members pay the cost of the programming through equipment licensing fees. Although the BBC is the best known of the British broadcasters, it also competes with several commercial channels, though these channels have not had the worldwide influence of the BBC. Alan Wells argues that the public service orientation of the BBC has helped it deliver more innovative and less bland programming than the American commercial model. (It should, however, be pointed out that international viewers only see the best of the BBC's programming, missing out on the more routine soap operas and game shows.[35])

Media are pervasive throughout Western Europe, with almost every household owning at least one television set and close to half owning two or more. Most homes also have a radio, and two-thirds have VCRs. Computers and the Internet are not as pervasive as in the United States; roughly one-third of homes in Western Europe have a personal computer. The big change in European media is the growth of privately owned television channels.

Video 15.2: Watch an interview about *Little Mosque on the Prairie.*

Web 15.7: Read about BBC programming.

TEST YOUR VISUAL MEDIA LITERACY

REUTERS/El Pais/Landov

Original photo distributed by Reuters news service.

©Telegraph Media Group Limited 2004

Photo as edited by the *Telegraph*.

What's different about these two photos of the 2004 Madrid train bombing? Does one shock or offend you more than the other? Do you even notice the differences? As a news consumer, does it bother you to think the images you see may be edited?

Are There Limits to What Media Images Should Display? 

At first glance, the photo of the terrorist bombing of a Madrid train in 2004 taken by Spanish photographer Pablo Torres Guerrero is disturbing enough, with its visage of carnage and death. But after you look at the original photo for a few moments, you realize that there is a portion of a severed leg in the foreground, bright red with blood.[1]

How was the photo changed to be printed in the British newspaper the *Telegraph*? Do these changes make the photo less graphic? Do these changes make the photo less honest? What else could have been done to tone down the gore in this photo? Or is it wrong to take the horror out of the photo?

The Telegraph wasn't the only newspaper to tone down the graphic image of the train bombing. *The Guardian* (not pictured) left the limb in the photo but took the color out of the limb so it wasn't so graphic. And *The Times* of London took the limb out of the photo all together. Paul Johnson, an editor at *The Guardian,* said that removing the color from the photo was the best compromise the staff could come up with:

> "We could have cropped it out, but someone came up with the suggestion that we bleed out the colour. It is not perfect by any means but I felt it was the best solution all round because it didn't eradicate anything from the picture."[2]

[1]Claire Cozens, "Editors 'Clean Up' Bomb Photo," *Guardian*, March 12, 2004, www.guardian.co.uk/media/2004/mar/12/pressandpublishing.spain.
[2]Ibid.

Web 15.8: Read the *Guardian*'s story on how and why the editors altered the photo.

REUTERS/Benoit Tessier/Landov

The Danish newspaper *Jyllands-Posten* set off a worldwide controversy when culture editor Flemming Rose commissioned a series of cartoons depicting the prophet Muhammad.

As recently as 1990, Europe had only 47 national stations; by 2010, there were more than 9,800, with 300 of them launched in 2010 alone.[36]

As we discussed in Chapters 2 and 6, European newspapers tend to take a more obvious political point of view than the detached, objective approach of U.S. papers. These papers have a clearly understood viewpoint designed to appeal to members of particular political parties.[37] While newspaper readership is higher in Europe than anywhere else in the world, papers in European countries are still facing the same kinds of declines experienced by those in North America.[38]

The Danish Cartoons. The biggest controversy surrounding European newspapers took place in the fall of 2005, at which time Flemming Rose, the culture editor of the Danish newspaper *Jyllands-Posten*, became concerned about what he saw as acts of self-censorship in Europe carried out to avoid offending Muslims. In response, he commissioned a dozen cartoonists to portray the prophet Muhammad in any way that they saw fit.[39]

Web 15.9: Check out more commentary about the Danish cartoons.

The cartoons were drawn in a range of styles. One made fun of the editors of *Jyllands-Posten* for trying to provoke attention, another put a Danish anti-immigration politician in a police lineup, and one portrayed the prophet with a bomb in his turban with a quote from the Koran printed on the front.

At the time the cartoons were published, they drew relatively little attention. But in the winter of 2006, a number of European and American newspapers reprinted the cartoons. Following these reprints came rioting throughout the Middle East that led to dozens of deaths.[40]

So why was half the world infuriated over cartoons published in a conservative Danish newspaper? The answer is both simple and complex. At the heart of the controversy is Islam's prohibition on depicting the prophet Muhammad. According to news accounts, it is a sin for a Muslim to create such an image and the "ultimate sort of insult" for a non-Muslim to do so. The *Washington Post*'s culture critic Philip Kennicott gives a compelling explanation of why the cartoons were so controversial and why he believes that publishing them was a bad idea:

> They were created as a provocation—Islam generally forbids the making of images of its highest prophet—in a conservative newspaper, which wanted to make a point about freedom of speech in a liberal, secular Western democracy. Depending on your point of view, it was a stick in the eye meant to provoke debate, or just a stick in the eye.[41]

He points out that we would be unlikely to see many cartoons quite that offensive toward Christianity in the United States:

> No serious American newspaper would commission images of Jesus that were solely designed to offend Christians. And if one did, the reaction would be swift and certain. Politicians would take to the floors of Congress and call down thunder on the malefactors. Some Christians would react with fury and boycotts and flaming e-mails that couldn't be printed in a family newspaper; others would react with sadness, prayer, and earnest letters to the editor. There would be mayhem, though it is unlikely that semiautomatic weapons would be brandished in the streets.[42]

The response to the cartoons was massive: At least four people were killed when Afghan troops fired on demonstrators, the cartoonists themselves went into hiding for fear of being killed, two Jordanian newspaper editors who reprinted the cartoons were arrested, the cartoons were banned in South Africa and the editor who published them there received death threats, and protesters burned the Danish embassy in Beirut. American commentators have written lengthy pieces on the controversy, the effects of which still linger. As recently as 2012, a Somali man who attacked one of the cartoonists was sentenced to ten years in prison.[43]

SECRET 6 After the debate wore down over whether the *Jyllands-Posten* should have commissioned and run the original cartoons, the question then became whether newspapers and magazines ought to reprint the cartoons so that readers could see for themselves what the controversy was about. It wasn't a question that most major newspapers or newsmagazines could avoid. The cartoons were obviously newsworthy, and they were just as obviously offensive and likely to provoke a violent response somewhere in the world.

William Powers at the *National Journal* raised the question as to what editors stood for. Powers said that it was a question not so much as to whether newspapers *should* publish the cartoons, but as to *why*:

> As I read the various explanations, I was struck by how sensible most of them were—on both sides. Among those who didn't publish the cartoons, the *Boston Globe* offered one of the strongest retorts to those who argued that it was cowardly to withhold the images. "Newspapers," it said in an editorial, "ought to refrain from publishing offensive caricatures of Muhammad in the name of the ultimate Enlightenment value: tolerance."
>
> Yet when I saw the *Austin-American Statesman*'s rationale for publishing the turban-bomb image, I was, frankly, just as impressed. That paper put the cartoon inside, with a front-page note informing readers where to go to "see an example of a drawing that offended Muslims and find out why it has."[44]

Through these arguments, we can see an example of Secret Six—Activism and analysis are not the same thing.

The *Philadelphia Inquirer* did reprint the most offensive of the images. Muslims in the Philadelphia area responded by picketing the paper, thus illustrating the commonsense idea that the proper response to offensive speech is more speech, not less. In fact, *Inquirer* editor Amanda Bennett said of the protesters: "Neither I nor the newspaper meant any disrespect to their religion or their prophet. I told them I was actually really proud of them for exercising their right to freedom of speech."[45] The cartoons also ran in the University of Illinois student paper, the *Daily Illini*, which sparked debate about the issue on the campus and led to peaceful protests.

But far more papers decided against running the cartoons. The *Boston Globe*, in an editorial, explained the paper's reasoning:

> Depicting Mohammed wearing a turban in the form of a bomb with a sputtering fuse is no less hurtful to most Muslims than Nazi caricatures of Jews or Ku Klux Klan caricatures of blacks are to those victims of intolerance. That is why the Danish cartoons will not be reproduced on these pages.[46]

Central and Latin America

Most of Latin American commercial broadcasting is dominated by North American, Mexican, and Brazilian programming. Brazil and Mexico have among the largest and most sophisticated broadcasting operations of any nation in the world. In fact, Mexico and Brazil export culture back to the United States through sports programming and the extremely popular *telenovelas*. Latin American broadcasters tend to follow the American for-profit model rather than the BBC's public-service orientation. One reason for the larger scope of South American broadcasting is that, unlike Africa (which we discuss shortly), Latin America has only two dominant languages to deal with—Spanish and Portuguese.[47]

Since the 1990s, Latin American governments have grown more stable and less repressive, and the economies of these countries have grown. All these factors have contributed to the growth of the media industry in Latin America. Unlike in much of the world, newspaper circulation has been growing in Latin America, with more than 1,000 newspapers being published and daily readership exceeding 100 million.[48] Journalists in Central and South America do face threats of violence, however, coming from organized crime and paramilitary groups, and to a lesser extent from the government.[49]

Islamic Countries and the Middle East

The press in the Middle East seems to straddle the fence between social responsibility and authoritarian media control. For example, although Israel is a modern, liberal democracy, reporters there are required to submit stories on sensitive military issues to the government for approval.[50] During the 1991 Persian Gulf War, all news coming out of Israel via commercial media had to be cleared by military censors. Israeli authorities are also quick to control the dissident Palestinian press.

Even before the terrorist group ISIS (the Islamic State of Iraq and Syria) took over sections of the country, Syria was the world's most dangerous country for journalists, according to the group Reporters Without Borders. Between 2011 and 2013, more than 110 news workers were killed there, and more than sixty journalists were taken prisoner or hostage. Among the highest-profile deaths in Syria was that of American journalist/photographer James Foley, who was beheaded by Islamic State militants in August 2014 after having been held hostage since November 2012. This was not the first time Foley had been taken prisoner. He had previously been held prisoner by Libyan soldiers loyal to Libyan leader Moammar Gadhafi.[51]

Even before the recent revolutions and violence in Syria and Libya, the press there was under authoritarian

Salma Mostafa Salama
4 minutes ago
RT @Beirutiyat: RT @kwasbeb: Uninstalling Mubarak: 100% Complete!
#egypt #jan25 #tahrir #mubarak
h
Kiriel1st
4 minutes ago
RT @ianinegypt: Game over. Arab leaders sleep a little uneasy tonight. #jan25 #egypt
adamwerbach
4 minutes ago
No civil society = no democracy = continued military rule. #jan25
EgyptianMariam
4 minutes ago
YES :D RT: @EmyBin ya ba5t elli fel ta7reeer... #jan25
ukrelic
4 minutes ago
RT @3arabawy: Phone call from Hurghada: All the people r out in the streets celebrating. #Jan25
AmoonaE
4 minutes ago
Renunció Mubarak ("Mubarak resigned" in Spanish) is trending! :D #Egypt #Jan25 (via @RubyYass)
ramy1313
4 minutes ago
RT @demaghmak: انا وطني وطني و بطنطن واتباها بمجدك يا وطنطن..على كل الاوطان متسلطن.. رجالتك طول عمرها رجالة #Jan25 #Tahrir #Egypt
#JAN25
PaulinaLogo
4 minutes ago
RT @25Egypt:
Uninstalling dictator COMPLETE 100%
Installing now: egypt 2.0:
#jan25 #Feb11

http://www.ralphehanson.com/2011/02/11/are-you-watching-this/

Twitter and Facebook were major sources of commentary and news coming out of Egypt during the Arab Spring revolution of 2011. Here is a sample of tweets that appeared on my Twitter feed on February 11, 2011. You might notice the "Uninstalling Dictator" meme that was popular at the time.

control at best. Jordan and Egypt both tightened their controls on the press after the Arab Spring movement in 2011.[52] Along with the official state-controlled media, many Arab nations also have *Al Hayat*, a regional Arabic newspaper published in London, and the Al Jazeera satellite channel, which originates in Qatar. The other alternative is to listen to news from a neighboring Arab state, which will not hesitate to criticize the government of its neighbor. By listening to a range of reports, one can gain a more complete picture of the news.[53]

Satellite and Internet delivery have vastly changed media in the Middle East, and they bypass authoritarian rule. During the 1991 Persian Gulf War, people in the Middle East received news from CNN, which they believed was being censored by the U.S. government. But Western media are not that influential in Arab-speaking countries. First, not everyone speaks English or French, the languages typically spoken on international channels. And the middle class, as well as members of Islamist movements in the Middle East, have an understandable thirst for regional media.[54]

Kai Hafez, a scholar at American University in Cairo, has distinguished three types of press in the Arab world: the "mobilized press," which is controlled by the government to promote the government; the "loyalist press," which is run by private industry but is supportive of people in power, especially those who can control access to resources such as paper and electricity; and finally the "diverse press," which is relatively free.

Many of these countries espouse freedom of the press, and the level of criticism of the government that a country tolerates varies from administration to administration, from year to year. However, even in countries without an Islamist government, it can be a crime to "insult" the country, which puts definite limits on what can be reported.

The Importance of "Small" Media. The question of what passes as mass media is becoming increasingly complicated, however, due to the importance of **small media**. Small media include fax machines, photocopy machines, video cameras, computers, blogs and social media on the Internet, and mobile phone media, such as Twitter and SMS text messages. Hafez has written about the importance of alternative independent media—of which small media are a crucial component—in the Middle East.

Although Palestinian media in the West Bank have been subject to Israeli censorship, Palestinians have been able to use the Web to post accounts and images of demonstrations and violence that bypass government censorship.[55]

SECRET 2 During the Arab Spring protests and revolutions of 2011, social and mobile media were frequently credited as both a source of news about the protests and an organizing tool for the protesters. For more on this, look at the opening vignette for this chapter and the section on long-tail news in Chapter 10.

These small media alternatives have taken the spot formerly occupied by cheaply produced short-run magazines. The alternative-independent media provide for a range of voices, even in countries such as Iran that have strict Islamic control of the mainstream media (which shows us that, even in other parts of the world, Secret Two—There are no mainstream media—still holds).

Religion professor Fred Strickert notes that while the Israelis and Palestinians are still capable of manipulating

Web 15.10: Read more about the dangers of reporting from Syria.

small media: Alternative media, such as fax machines, photocopiers, video cameras, and personal Web sites, which are used to distribute news and information that might be suppressed by the government if published through traditional mass media channels.

the news, the Internet allows for the expression of a wider range of views:

> Yes, the Palestinian Authority can still censor damaging video footage, as it did in the case of the mob lynching of two Israeli soldiers, and the Israeli government can put its spin on the news. But the truth is on the Internet for anyone who cares to find it.[56]

In the Middle East, there is a long tradition of using alternative "small" media to reach out to the public with. The Israeli Defense Forces (IDF) makes extensive use of social media like Twitter to communicate their side of the story during periods of conflict.

Whereas legacy media using Internet and satellite delivery receive a great deal of popular attention, the small media have also done a good job of transmitting messages outside the realm of censorship. Following the disputed Iranian presidential elections in 2009 (discussed in Chapter 10), the Iranian government began to crack down on news media, going so far as to kick reporters out of the country.[57] The government blocked many forms of social media, reduced Internet speed to block online video, shut down mobile phone towers, and threatened retaliation against those who used new media, such as mobile phones and the Internet, to transmit information out of Iran. Legacy media, including CNN, Fox News, MSNBC, and even the BBC, had to turn to online video, blogs, and Twitter feeds of questionable reliability to report on what was happening within Iran. As social media expert Gaurav Mishra points out later on in this chapter, mobile phone–based social media are increasingly going to be the medium through which news breaks.[58]

Television in the Islamic World. Broadcasting in the Arab world is heavily controlled by the government, though the presence of satellite broadcasting is challenging governmental control. Egypt, which is more secular than much of the Arab world, has a large media industry and produces movies, music, and television programming for much of the Arab and Islamic world.[59] Access to television, especially direct broadcast satellite signals, varies significantly throughout the Islamic nations of the Middle East.

The Saudi Arabian monarchy built a substantial television network in the 1960s, in part to respond to anti-Saudi broadcasts coming into the country from Egypt. In March 1994, Saudi Arabia officially banned ownership of satellite receivers to satisfy religious conservatives who objected to Western programming. The ban has not been enforced, however, and both the dishes and the receivers are readily available.

Little is known about television audience behavior in Saudi Arabia, as the government has shown little interest in commercial broadcasting, which would lead to audience measurement.[60] A 2007 Gallup poll found that 82 percent of Saudis relied on pan-Arab satellite television channels to stay informed about their own country, and 93 percent used these cross-border channels to find out what was happening in other countries. As important as satellite television is as a news medium, however, 59 percent of Saudis said word of mouth was a "very important source of information" about their country.[61] According to the survey, the most popular first sources for satellite news were Al Jazeera (30 percent), the Middle East Broadcasting Center (24 percent), and Al Arabiya (23 percent).

Questioning the Media

Can global news operations such as Al Jazeera rely on cell phones and cell phone video to report from war zones around the world? Are Twitter feeds from people in war zones a reliable source of news? Why or why not?

Online censorship in Saudi Arabia has been "relentless" in the words of Reporters Without Borders. In its 2014 World Press Freedom report, the group notes that Saudi blogger Raef Badawi was sentenced to seven years in prison and 600 lashes for "denigrating the religious police." Another columnist was arrested on a number of charges, including criticizing the ban on women drivers.[62]

Al Jazeera. According to a 2007 forum on Arab broadcasting, the average television viewer in the Arab world watches about four hours a day, much of which comes from

Web 15.11: Social media and the Israeli Defense Forces.

Video 15.3: Watch Al Jazeera's coverage of violence during the Arab Spring uprisings.

Video 15.4: Watch the documentary *Control Room.*

REUTERS/LOUAFI LARBI/LANDOV

American photojournalist James Foley (right) had been taken prisoner twice before being murdered by the terrorist group ISIS. He had been held by soldiers loyal to former Libyan leader Moammar Gadhafi before being taken hostage in Syria.

the ten most popular of the 250 free satellite stations. Although there are advertising-supported TV channels, most of the channels rely on state funding.[63] The most significant of these channels is **Al Jazeera**. Broadcast via satellite from the small Arab country of Qatar since 1997, the channel is not censored by the government.[64] Al Jazeera has carried interviews with everyone from Osama bin Laden to Colin Powell and has been criticized for doing so by both the United States and Arab countries. During the current war in Iraq, Al Jazeera came to worldwide attention, presenting an Arab point of view to the fighting between the United States and Iraq. It has a regular audience of 40 million, which dwarfs CNN or Fox in scope.[65]

In the Arab Middle East, satellite news channels that can cross over national borders are clearly the top source of international news, and Al Jazeera is the most popular of the many Arab-language satellite channels. It is the most watched, or perhaps the most important, though many claim to dislike the controversial channel. According to NPR's *On the Media*, a recent survey shows that only 10 percent of Arabs who have access to satellite TV never watch Al Jazeera. In Iraq, the Saudi Arabia–based Al Arabiya is popular. But American channel Alhurra is clearly the last choice, with 53 percent saying they never watch it. Interestingly enough, the Hezbollah channel, Al-Manar, is similarly unpopular.[66]

Although some observers accuse Al Jazeera of being a pro-Arab propaganda channel, others have described it as the CNN of the Arab world. Perhaps neither label is completely fair or completely accurate. It would seem instead that Al Jazeera is committed to presenting an Arab view of the world. That is, it works at telling the news accurately, but it tells it from a clear point of view. (Interestingly enough, taking a page from the American media synergy playbook, there is also an Al Jazeera sports channel.) What makes Al Jazeera interesting is that while its headquarters are in Qatar, it tends to take a broad Arab point of view, rather than that of one particular country. Too often, all Arab or Muslim countries are seen in the West as being the same, rather than having distinctly different views. It's easy for Americans to forget that Iraq and Iran were at war with each other for at least ten years.[67]

Al Jazeera was founded by Sheikh Hamad bin Khalifa al-Thani, the emir of Qatar, in an effort to diversify his nation's economy. He started the satellite news channel following the failure of a 1994 BBC experiment with an Arab-language, Saudi-financed station. Hiring 120 of the unemployed journalists from the project gave Al Jazeera its start. Although Western governments have been highly critical of Al Jazeera, the network has carried criticism of Qatar's government, the Palestinian Authority, the Jordanian government, the Kuwaiti government, and the Israeli government.[68]

Al Jazeera journalists certainly don't receive special treatment by Arab governments. In fact, they are often targeted for the in-depth reporting. Three reporters for Al Jazeera, Peter Greste, Baher Mohamed, and Mohamed Fahmy, were arrested in December 2013, and were convicted of multiple offenses against the Egyptian government in the summer of 2014. As of August 2014, lawyers for Al Jazeera were still trying to get the reporters released from prison.[69]

Africa

The African continent provides a prime example of the range of approaches to development media theory—from a strong social responsibility approach to out-and-out authoritarian controls. The mass media first came to Africa through the European colonial powers; they were

Web 15.12: Explore the BBC's Africa coverage.

Web 15.13: Read the CPJ "Attacks on the Press" report.

Al Jazeera: The largest and most viewed Arabic-language satellite news channel. It is run out of the country of Qatar and has a regular audience of 40 million viewers.

created to serve the needs of the colonists. Newspapers and early broadcast stations covered only white news and ignored black Africans, or else treated them as "subhuman beings."[70] After independence, colonial media continued to exist in some countries, whereas in other countries the press was taken over by the new governments, which did not permit private media. Although the media were serving a new population, they continued to focus on the needs of the elite.

REUTERS/David Rae Morris/Landov

South Africa's vibrant pop music scene has gained fans around the world. Groups such as Mahlathini and the Mahotella Queens, pictured here, and Ladysmith Black Mambazo routinely draw crowds in the United States and Europe.

Africa is still largely rural, and its smaller towns often do not have newspapers. However, according to Tawana Kupe, a media scholar from Zimbabwe and South Africa, most countries have a dominant daily newspaper that is distributed primarily in the capital city. Newspaper circulation is limited by high levels of poverty and illiteracy.[71]

Radio is the most important medium in Africa, but both radios and the batteries to run them are expensive, and transmission equipment often is not good enough to reach an entire country. Television is not available in many countries. Even where there are broadcasts, television can be received only where there is reliable electrical service, primarily in urban areas. Most of the programming consists of old European, American, and Australian reruns. Although many African countries seek to use television and radio to foster development by teaching people how to improve their standard of living, most of the development programming consists of speeches by politicians calling for development.

The Committee to Protect Journalists (CPJ) reports that press freedom varies wildly across the continent, with many of the countries embracing a development theory of the press. A 2011 report from the CPJ notes that many African leaders are claiming that they cannot achieve what they say are contradictory goals of balancing economic and social stability with freedom of the press. This approach goes so far as to shape how sports are covered. A star Cameroonian soccer player complained to a Senegalese reporter after the journalist raised a critical question about the team's play, saying, "You journalists, certain journalists like you, you who do not want Africa to advance, you who do not want Cameroon to advance, you are always negative. Try to change a little."[72] A 2014 update to the report noted that "the insistence on positive news remains a significant threat to press freedom in Africa."[73]

Language continues to be an issue for African media. Many African nations use the former colonial language (typically French or English) in their nation-building efforts, but this tends to be the language of the educated class, not of the majority of the people.[74] Except in Kenya and Tanzania, which have a Swahili press, virtually no major newspapers are published in African languages.

It is tempting in the West to view Africa as something akin to South America, but unlike South America, Africa as a continent does not share common languages or cultures. Africa is exceedingly culturally diverse, with more languages spoken there than on any other continent in the world.[75] Politically, many of the countries are dominated by single-party or military governments, though there are notable exceptions, such as South Africa, Mali, and Ghana.

South Africa was the first country in sub-Saharan Africa to have radio, and today it has the best-developed system in that area of the world. Most of the country's radio is handled by the South African Broadcasting Corporation. Following heavy censorship in South Africa during the apartheid era, the South African press in the early twenty-first century has an organization of publishers, journalists, and members of the public that can reprimand newspapers when necessary. A committee made up of lawyers and media professionals regulates the broadcast industry.[76]

South African television broadcasts in seven different languages: English, Afrikaans, northern and southern Sotho, Tswana, Xhosa, and Zulu. As you can see, language is a big barrier when you consider the linguistic diversity within just a single country—South Africa has eleven language groups. African media expert Osabuohien P. Amienyi recognizes this dilemma: "This plurality [of languages] presents broadcasting with the dilemma of how to fulfill the natural desire of every community to be addressed in its own language or dialect."[77]

If stations hope to reach a large group with a single language, they are likely going to have to transmit in the languages of the colonial whites, typically English, French, Portuguese, or Spanish. This furthers the problem of programming that will be accessible primarily to urban elites and not the rural population who need the service the most.

South Africa has also been a major source of inspiration for Western pop music. Among the Western musicians who have worked at bringing African music to the forefront of American pop culture are Paul Simon, Peter Gabriel, and Talking Heads frontman David Byrne.[78] Simon, a singer and songwriter, was captivated by the sounds of South Africa's township jive and in 1985 traveled to Johannesburg to record there with artists such as Miriam Makeba.[79] This collaboration resulted in the best-selling album *Graceland* and a world tour. Township jive emerged as a style during the apartheid era in South Africa. The music combines traditional African drumming and rhythms with Western instruments to create a unique musical style. Among the South African musicians who have found success in the West are the a cappella men's choir Ladysmith Black Mambazo, the group Mahlathini and the Mahotella Queens, and musician Johnny Clegg and his band Juluka. Groups such as Bongo Maffin have combined the South African pop music style with rhythm and blues, reggae, and rap.[80]

African pop music is no newcomer to the United States. In 1961, the Tokens recorded a hit single, "The Lion Sleeps Tonight," which was based on an African chant.[81]

©iStockphoto.com/FotografiaBasica

One thing that has inhibited world music's popularity in the United States is the language barrier, though language differences have not stopped people in other countries from listening to American music. "People around the world have been listening to American and British music for the last thirty years, very often not understanding the words but enjoying the ways people put things together," says producer D. A. "Jumbo" Vanrenen. "As Third World artists have access to the same recording studios, it's becoming easier to present their music in a clear way. Language becomes less important. People go for the dance rhythms and the fine quality of people's vocals."[82] You can hear this branch of world music on Public Radio International's Afropop Worldwide or on the BBC's world music programming.

Russia and the Former Soviet Republics

Media developed slowly in the old Soviet Union if for no other reason than the vast scale of its empire, which covered one-sixth of the world at its peak, inhibited its development. Along with the more conventional media, such as radio, people in the Soviet Union also made use of alternative media, such as sending broadcasts out over phone lines that would then be played in communities over a loudspeaker system. Under communism, there was no ideal of an independent press. The goal of newspapers and broadcasters was to support the goals of communism, not to be detached and critical external observers. Janis E. Overlock, who specializes in study of the media of the old Soviet empire, describes the problem:

> One of the main problems of the media in the countries of the former Soviet Union is a basic lack of understanding of the role of the media in a democracy. After years of Soviet domination, many of the governments as well as journalists view the media as a propaganda tool for the government.[83]

She further explains that even if the government professes a belief in the free press, that freedom simply doesn't exist within the culture.[84]

Since the collapse of the Soviet Union in 1991, the Russian press has had a troubled existence. Although many of the media are now in private hands, they are not necessarily free of government control, and they experience very high levels of self-censorship. The independent media in Russia are owned by a small group of businesspeople who support the government and want to maintain control of their own media monopolies. As an example, prior to the 2012 Russian presidential election, Kremlin officials warned journalists not to cover antigovernment protests. Editors who did not follow this "suggestion" could find themselves quickly unemployed.[85]

Moscow has at least twenty daily and weekly newspapers that range from communist publications to sensationalistic tabloids.[86] Many of these papers sell article space to the highest bidder—a process that even has a name: *zakazukha*, or "news-by-order." Many newspapers are not truly self-supporting and need a patron, or boss, to provide financial support. In return, the paper supports the boss's political agenda. Papers that are critical of the central government can disappear seemingly overnight with no warning to the journalists who work there.[87]

The government-controlled media are emphatically serving the needs of the ruling party. A reporter for Russian television told an American friend, "Our new executive producer has been going over my copy with a fine-tooth comb. Anything that's in the least bit critical of the government is taken out."[88] As longtime Russian leader Vladimir Putin has restrengthened his position since 2012, "activists, news media and bloggers" have been targeted for trying to report things critical of the government, and defamation has been made a criminal offense, as has publishing "homosexual propaganda."[89]

Audio 15.1: Listen to Afropop Worldwide radio.

Web 15.14: Read the latest on press freedom in Russia.

Asia

Although Asia has many countries and cultures, in most of its nations, the broadcast media are either government controlled or run by public corporations. In

many of these countries, we see a development philosophy for the media, in which broadcasters are expected to work to support the economic and social development goals of the government. China, Japan, and India stand apart from the rest of the continent as major media forces. Communist and former Soviet bloc countries, such as North Korea, continue to operate under the old Soviet-style communist model. Southeast Asia, which includes countries such as Indonesia, Malaysia, and the Philippines, tends to operate under a development philosophy. This can be seen in particular in Malaysia, where the Ministry of Communication and Multimedia sets guidelines on how broadcasters can portray Malaysian education, art, culture, and identity.[90]

Indranil Mukhayee/AFP/Getty Images

During the Mumbai terror attacks of November 29, 2008, the Indian press was cautious with its reporting of the bombings and shootings in order to avoid being shut down by the government.

India. As of 2005, approximately 40 percent of India's households—an astonishing 80 million—had television sets.[91] Residents in about 40 percent of Indian households read a newspaper as well. A handbook on Indian media estimates that 120 million of 220 million households have a radio set. Print media in India are heavily supported by advertising, and hitting a balance between serving the public and making advertisers happy is a major issue.

Newspapers are big business in India, with a daily circulation of 72 million, second only to China, which circulates 85 million copies a day. Whereas the big newspapers face the same sort of competitive pressures from newer media that U.S. papers do, community newspapers dealing with local issues are seen as a growth industry.[92] Journalists in the Kashmir and Chhattisgarh regions face both censorship and physical violence from a variety of sources, including police and security forces, criminal groups, and political party supporters.[93]

All India Radio (AIR) is the dominant radio service and the exclusive source of radio news and public affairs programming. There are broadcast television stations in India, but the television market is dominated by cable and satellite networks. As was discussed at the beginning of the chapter, television is going through a period of growth because of the rise of commercially run satellite channels. Internet access is growing, especially through cybercafés and mobile phones, and India's major newspapers all have significant Web presences.

When a group of terrorists killed 171 people and held the city of Mumbai, India, hostage for more than sixty hours, local journalists had to figure out how to respond to the story.[94]

Arnab Goswami, chief editor of *Times Now*, India's largest satellite news channel, says that the Indian government got very nervous about media coverage of the attacks, fearing that the reports were helping the terrorists. At one point, during the early phases of the attacks, the government shut down television news for forty-five minutes. But Goswami says that when the government cut off the news flow, the response from viewers was

> massive, massive. . . . Every single phone was ringing. People were watching us so closely that if we were off for five seconds they would react, because cable and satellite television is largely the only form of receiving information at a time like this.[95]

Goswami says that he and his reporters often did not report everything they knew for fear of endangering people and drawing government censorship. He told National Public Radio's *On the Media*,

> India has had a largely . . . closed media with only state-run television for 40 years after its independence—that's 1947 to '87. The television media in its present form and private TV channels are only 10 years old. And the power of the television media and news channels is something that sometimes even scares the government. . . . We are fighting for self-regulation, and it is very important that we don't give the opportunity for anyone in the government to accuse us of giving away these kinds of details. That was uppermost in my mind when, on several occasions, I stopped my reporters from giving away such information.[96]

In one case, there were reports of explosives found at a railway station. Near the railway station thousands of people were gathered at the Gateway of India. Goswami said that if the news of the explosives had been televised, there might have been a deadly panic. Instead, he called editors at half a dozen other television stations, and they all agreed not to report it.

China. Until the 1970s and 1980s, the media in China were unapologetically political and propagandistic. The role of the media was not to entertain or market products; instead, they promoted public policies, such as water conservation programs; provided education to rural areas; and mobilized the public after natural disasters or industrial accidents.[97]

Over the past thirty years, Chinese media offerings and availability have changed rapidly. In 1978, China had fewer than one television set per hundred people. By 2007, that number had grown to twenty-five sets per hundred people. Although a wide range of local television stations are available, they are required to carry the China Central Television network's evening newscast. The number of newspapers has similarly expanded, from 42 papers in 1968, most of which were run by the Communist Party, to more than 2,200 newspapers in 2007.[98]

Talk radio is the most open mass medium in China. Prior to the 1990s, radio provided primarily government propaganda. Now lively call-in programs have audience members talking about controversial topics without having to identify themselves. Although party officials have told talk show hosts what they ought to be talking about, the hosts have violated these rules without punishment.[99]

Mobile phones are common in China and serve as a major channel for the flow of news. Chinese phone users tend to upgrade their phones frequently, so new mobile technology spreads through the country fairly rapidly.[100]

Since the 1970s, the press has been freer to criticize the government, though how free the press has been has fluctuated depending on party leadership. For example, in 2012, following a speech by the Communist Party general secretary calling for journalists to contribute to better understanding between China and the rest of the world, the government instituted a crackdown on cyberdissidents, journalists, and bloggers, according to the 2014 Reporters Without Borders report on global freedom of the press.[101]

All media are ultimately subject to control by the Chinese government, from books to newspapers to broadcasting to the Internet. Some American corporations, such as Yahoo and Google, have faced international criticism for cooperating with the Chinese government on censorship efforts. (See Chapter 10 for a description of one such incident.)

Japan. Japan is in many ways the technological heart of our modern media world. Many of our essential electronic

Web 15.15: Read about media censorship in China.

Anais Martane/Corbis

Chinese media tycoon Liu Changle represents the changing face of Chinese media. He is the founder of Phoenix Satellite Television, a privately owned Chinese satellite channel.

media devices come from Japan. Broadcasting started in the country in 1925 and was run by the government for the next twenty-five years. In the era after World War II, American policy helped shape what Japan offered, which became a mix of public and commercial broadcasting.[102] NHK is Japan's public broadcasting corporation, and it provides both domestic and international service. It is financed through a fee that all television owners must pay. Japan has relatively high levels of television broadcast viewership. The biggest difference between Japanese and U.S. broadcasting is that Japan has a much more even balance between commercial and public broadcasting.

The most popular category of magazines in Japan is not fashion, lifestyle, or hobbies; it's manga, or comic books. The word *manga* means comics or amusing drawings, and according to *Publishers Weekly*, the genre accounts for 40 percent of all books and magazines published in Japan. In the United States, manga-style comics are most popular with teenage boys and tend to feature action stories. Some examples are *Yu-Gi-Oh!*, *Pokémon*, and *Sailor Moon*. In Japan, manga cover just about every magazine genre. Douglas Wolk, who has covered manga in the United States, writes, "There are hundreds of manga for girls and for boys, men's manga and women's manga, romance manga, political manga, baseball manga, mah-jongg manga, and more."[103] Plots can range from the story of a teenage girl who becomes a superhero after using magic eye shadow to one that describes the aftermath of the atomic bombing of Hiroshima. There's even one that gives advice on how to get a divorce. Manga targeted at adults often contain violent or pornographic imagery.

Manga started out in the tenth century as illustrated Buddhist scrolls. By the seventeenth century, silk-bound books created using woodblock printing and featuring text

TEST YOUR MEDIA LITERACY

How Free Are the World's Media to Report the News? 

Every year, the group Reporters Without Borders for Freedom of Information issues a report on the state of press freedom around the world. In it, the organization analyzes the degree of freedom that "journalists, news media, and netizens" have in 180 countries around the world. Among the items quantified by the study are cultural pluralism, media independence, self-censorship, legislative framework, transparency, infrastructure, and the level of violence targeted against journalists. Countries gain points for things that discourage or limit freedom of the press, and they have points deducted for behavior that encourages free speech. In the 2014 study, scores ranged from 0 to 179. As of 2014, Finland, the Netherlands, and Norway were ranked in the top three for freedom of speech, all with scores of zero. The countries in last place all had scores in excess of 170, and included Turkmenistan, North Korea, and Eritrea.[104]

And how did the United States score? Take a look at the report's summary. You might be surprised at where it was ranked. (Hint: 2013 was not a good year for freedom of speech or the press in the United States because of the active prosecution of people who leaked government secrets to the press.)

WHO is the source?

Who are Reporters Without Borders? What do they do?

WHAT do they say?

Which three nations had the best records on freedom of the press? Which three nations were at the bottom of the list? Where did the United States fall in the rankings? Was it up or down from the previous year?

WHAT evidence is there?

For each of the countries you've listed above, why did it get the rating it did? How do those countries behave as democracies (or as authoritarian states)?

HOW do you and your classmates feel about the rankings?

How would you describe each of the highest- and lowest-ranked countries' approaches to freedom of speech and of the press? Based on what you have read, how would you describe the United States' approach to freedom of the press? What do you think about the rankings? Are they fair? Why or why not?

Web 15.16: Read the Reporters Without Borders 2014 report.

and drawings about actors and actresses became popular. Current manga can be the size of a small telephone book.[105] Estimates suggest that 95 percent of Japan's population reads manga on a regular basis.[106]

SECRET 3 The United States has been accused of imposing its culture on the world by exporting media products, but the same charges have been leveled against Japan, especially by other Asian countries. However, attempts to keep comics out of those countries have only led to the publication of pirate editions.[107]

Manga are growing in popularity in the United States. They are based primarily on books connected to anime cartoon programs. Featuring characters with spiky hair, big heads, and big eyes, manga are seen by young people as exciting, dynamic, and sexy. Many American translations of Japanese manga are printed to be read from the back of the book to the front, just as they would be in Japan. Why? In part because it's cheaper than redoing the pages in the American front-to-back style, but also because teen readers see the reverse style as cool.[108] Manga characters have also shown up in video games and on a wide range of products, such as clothing and plush toys. Manga's popularity in the United States is also an example of Secret Three—Everything from the margin moves to the center.

Dangers to Journalists

The job of being a journalist around the world can be a dangerous one. The Committee to Protect Journalists reports that worldwide in 2013 seventy journalists were killed "in direct connection" to their work; twenty-eight of them died in Syria. Ten journalists died in Iraq, six in Egypt, five in Pakistan, and four in Somalia. Journalistic deaths peaked at seventy-four in 2012, with thirty-one of those reporters being killed in Syria. The most common cause of death has been deliberate murder, accounting for between 44 and 47 percent; approximately 35 percent of the deaths can be accounted for by being caught in combat crossfire.[109]

War zones are always dangerous places for journalists, especially photographers who need to be out on the front lines to capture combat images. As was mentioned earlier in the chapter, photojournalist James Foley was beheaded by Islamic State militants in August 2014 after having been held hostage since November 2012.[110] British photographer Tim Hetherington and U.S. photographer

MEDIA TRANSFORMATIONS

Are We Really Living in a Media World? 

Marshall McLuhan is often better known for his catchphrases than for what he actually wrote. Aside from "the medium is the message," discussed in Chapter 2, he is best known for popularizing the term *the global village*. He first used it in his 1962 book, *The Gutenberg Galaxy: The Making of Typographic Man*, in which he discusses how electronic media, primarily radio and television, help people live and interact globally. Since the rise of the Internet, it would seem that we are truly living in a world where we can interact with people in any place at any time. But this global village may be largely an illusion.

There is no question that through our media—what McLuhan would call the extension of our senses—we are able to travel to places we could never reach otherwise. In an IMAX theater, we can travel to the bottom of the ocean off the Grand Banks near Newfoundland and visit the wreck of the *Titanic*. Through the photos from the Mars rovers *Curiosity*, *Spirit*, and *Opportunity*, we can see into the craters on a distant planet. On a more down-to-earth scale, our electronic media take us into war zones, into the aftermath of disasters, and to celebrations in cities or countries we would likely never visit. But are we really becoming members of a global village, or are we just sightseers who get a glimpse of something we can't really understand?

Media reporter Ken Auletta, whose work we have discussed extensively elsewhere in this book, suggests that perhaps there is not a single wired global village, but rather hundreds or thousands of them, "each broadcasting in its own language, with its own anchor and news team, its own weather and sports and local slant."[111]

Communications scholar W. Russell Neuman suggests that McLuhan's global village concept is misleading: "McLuhan envisioned Americans seeing what was going on live in an African village. But Americans may not want to watch that. And perhaps vice versa."[112]

Media Transformations Questions

- **HOW** often do you communicate with someone who lives in another country? How often, if ever, do you communicate with someone who doesn't speak English? How do you communicate with that person?
- **DO** you think that having access to a global communication network gives you a better understanding of people who live on the other side of the world?
- **DOES** our new communication technology make the world a better place? Why or why not?

Are we really living in a media world?

In 2001, a United Nations report stated that only about half of the world's population had ever made a phone call. True enough, if you're talking about a landline. Just a decade ago, there were about 1.2 billion landlines worldwide, covering just 19% of the total population. Today, that number has actually declined. Just about 15% of the world's population has a landline. So how connected are we globally?

How are we wired?

The answer is that it depends upon the technology.

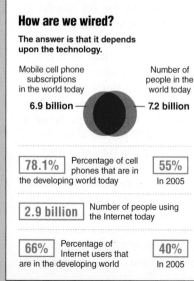

Mobile cell phone subscriptions in the world today: **6.9 billion**

Number of people in the world today: **7.2 billion**

78.1% Percentage of cell phones that are in the developing world today — **55%** In 2005

2.9 billion Number of people using the Internet today

66% Percentage of Internet users that are in the developing world — **40%** In 2005

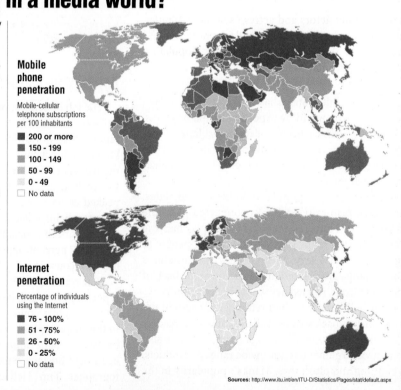

Mobile phone penetration

Mobile-cellular telephone subscriptions per 100 inhabitants

- 200 or more
- 150 - 199
- 100 - 149
- 50 - 99
- 0 - 49
- No data

Internet penetration

Percentage of individuals using the Internet

- 76 - 100%
- 51 - 75%
- 26 - 50%
- 0 - 25%
- No data

Sources: http://www.itu.int/en/ITU-D/Statistics/Pages/stat/default.aspx

Valerie Macon/Getty Images

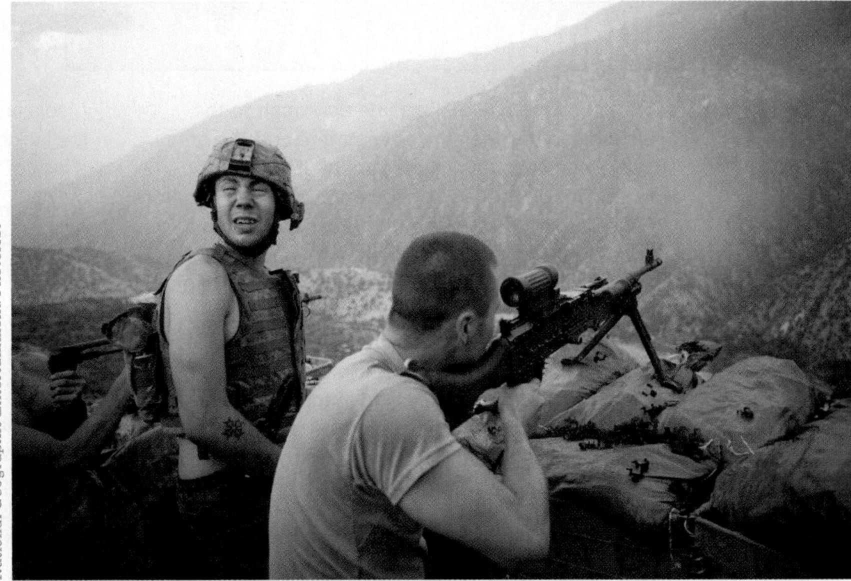

National Geographic Entertainment/Photofest

Photographers Tim Hetherington (smaller photo) and Chris Hondros were killed while covering combat in Libya during the revolution there in 2011. Hetherington, along with reporter Sebastian Junger, had been nominated for an Oscar for co-directing the documentary *Restrepo*, which is about the war in Afghanistan. The larger photo above is a still from *Restrepo* that shows American soldiers fighting in the Korengal Valley region in Afghanistan. Hetherington had faced hostile fire on many occasions while covering war zones around the world.

Chris Hondros were killed by a rocket-propelled grenade while covering fighting near the Libyan city of Misrata in 2011. Two others were injured in the attack. Hetherington was best known for co-directing the Oscar-nominated war documentary *Restrepo*.[113] He was in Libya covering the anti–Moammar Gadhafi rebellion at the time he was killed. This was far from the first time Hetherington had been under attack. Photojournalist Lynsey Addario told the *New York Times* blog *Lens* about a time when she and Hetherington were pinned down by fire in Afghanistan: "We were ambushed from both sides," she said.

> It was a terrifying situation. I was trying to find a place to hide, to shield myself. And I remember looking over and there was Tim—just calmly sitting up, filming the whole ambush on a video camera. And I thought to myself, "Oh my God, I want to be a photographer like him."[114]

Video 15.5: See more about Tim Hetherington and his work.

Death or injuries are not the only risks reporters face. BBC journalist Alan Johnston was held hostage for 114 days in the Gaza Strip, Fox News's Steve Centanni and Olaf Wiig were held hostage in Gaza for thirteen days, and the *Christian Science Monitor*'s Jill Carroll was held hostage for three months in Iraq.[115]

Fox News cameraman Wiig says that the most serious consequence of attacks on journalists is that the stories from war zones won't get told:

> My biggest concern, really, is that as a result of what happened to us, foreign journalists will be discouraged from coming here to tell the story. And that would be a great tragedy for the people of Palestine, and especially for the people of Gaza.[116]

Chapter SUMMARY

Not all countries take the same approach to the relationship between the government and the press. This relationship can take a variety of forms, depending on the form of government and the culture of the country. Theories of the press include the authoritarian, communist, libertarian, social responsibility, and developmental theories. Although these normative theories of the press still have considerable value today, they have to be reexamined in terms of how the world has changed since they were first discussed in the 1950s. An alternative to the normative theories of the press is to look at the media dimensions of control, finance, programming goals, target audience, and feedback mechanisms.

Media in Western democracies generally operate under a combination of libertarian and social responsibility theories. Many countries have free speech as a goal but are concerned about preserving their national cultures from the power of the American media industry.

Latin America has a vibrant media industry, especially in Brazil and Mexico. These countries export Spanish-language programming, especially sports programs and telenovelas, to the United States.

The electronic media have a powerful presence in the Middle East, and satellite television is able to bypass national borders and bring outside content into otherwise closed media systems. The most popular source of news in the Arab-speaking countries of the Middle East is the satellite news channel Al Jazeera. Small media also have a significant presence in the Middle East because of their ability to bypass official government censorship.

Media in Africa face a number of problems, including the lack of a common language, poor economies, and a lack of newsprint and reliable electricity.

While the news media in the old Soviet Union were designed to serve the needs of the government and the Communist Party, they went through a brief period of relative freedom in the 1980s. Since that time, the government has cracked down on free speech, and the press tends to serve the specific goals of its owners.

Media in Asia tend to follow either a social responsibility theory or development theory, depending on the region. The major exception is Japan, which has strong public and private broadcasting businesses. Japan also exports content and media technology to the West and to the rest of the world.

Reporting around the world, and especially in the Iraqi war zone, is dangerous for reporters, with forty-two journalists killed on the job in 2008, including eleven in Iraq. Journalists also face the risks of injury and kidnapping.

Media theorist Marshall McLuhan suggested in the 1960s that the world would become a global village, linked together through electronic media. Although these media have become far more pervasive today than when McLuhan was writing, it is unclear whether they are bringing the world together or breaking it up into a series of disconnected villages.

Keep up-to-date with content from the author's blog.

Take the chapter quiz.

Key TERMS

authoritarian theory 382
communist theory 383
libertarian theory 384
social responsibility theory 384
development theory 385
small media 392
Al Jazeera 394

Concept REVIEW

Normative theories of the press

Analyzing world media systems by control, finance, programming goals, target audience, and feedback mechanisms

How media standards vary among Western democracies

Media standards in the Middle East

The challenge of media in Africa

Having an activist press in countries with no tradition of a free press

The dangers journalists face reporting around the world

The nature of the global village

Student STUDY SITE

Sharpen your skills with SAGE edge at **edge.sagepub.com/hanson5e**

SAGE edge for Students provides a personalized approach to help you accomplish your coursework goals in an easy-to-use learning environment.

Chapter 1

1. Scott Simon, "Astronaut Chris Hadfield's Most Excellent Adventure," May 18, 2013, http://www.npr.org/2013/05/18/184821421/astronaut-chris-hadfields-most-excellent-adventure.
2. Chris Hadfield, *An Astronaut's Guide to Life on Earth: What Going to Space Taught Me About Ingenuity, Determination, and Being Prepared for Anything* (New York: Little, Brown, 2013), p.145.
3. Hadfield, p. 252.
4. Ralph Hanson, interview, March 10, 2014.
5. George Gerbner, "Mass Media and Human Communication Theory," in *Human Communication Theory: Original Essays*, ed. Frank E. X. Dance (New York: Holt, Rinehart, and Winston, 1967).
6. Denis McQuail, *McQuail's Mass Communication Theory*, 5th ed. (London: Sage Publications, 2005).
7. Larry G. Ehrlich, *Fatal Words and Friendly Faces: Interpersonal Communication in the Twenty-First Century* (Lanham, Md.: University Press of America, 2000).
8. Ralph Hanson, interview, September 4, 2009.
9. McQuail, *McQuail's Mass Communication Theory*; Benjamin Compaine et al., eds., *Who Owns the Media?* (White Plains, N.Y.: Knowledge Industry Publications, 1982); Harold Lasswell, "The Structure and Function of Communication in Society," in *Mass Communications*, ed. Wilbur Schramm (Urbana: University of Illinois Press, 1960); Charles R. Wright, *Mass Communication: A Sociological Perspective*, 3rd ed. (New York: Random House, 1986).
10. Ralph Hanson, interview, March 10, 2014.
11. Wright, *Mass Communication: A Sociological Perspective*.
12. Ralph Hanson, personal communication, December 16, 2011.
13. C. W. Mills, *The Power Elite* (New York: Oxford University Press, 1959).
14. Toni Locy, "The Race for the First Report in Legal Journalism," *Jurist*, June 29, 2012, jurist.org/forum/2012/06/toni-locy-ppaca-journalism.php; Adrienne LaFrance, "Anatomy of a Spike: How SCOTUS Blog Dealt With Its Biggest Traffic Day Ever," Nieman Journalism Lab, June 28, 2012, www.niemanlab.org/2012/06/anatomy-of-a-spike-how-scotus-blog-dealt-with-its-biggest-traffic-day-ever/.
15. Brian Steinberg, "Who's Buying What in Super Bowl 2012," *Advertising Age*, February 3, 2011, adage.com/article/special-report-super-bowl/buying-super-bowl-2012/231122/.
16. Stuart Elliott, "Making Every Second, or $100,000, Count," *New York Times*, January 23, 2009.
17. Laurel Wentz, "Super What? World Cup Sponsors Spending $600M on Brazil Network," *Advertising Age*, January 22, 2014, adage.com/article/special-report-2014-sports/super-cup-sponsors-spending-600m-brazil-network/291117/?utm_source=daily_email&utm_medium=newsletter&utm_campaign=adage&ttl=1390947835.
18. W. James Potter, *Media Literacy*, 5th ed. (Thousand Oaks, Calif.: Sage Publications, 2011).
19. Jon Katz, *Virtuous Reality* (New York: Random House, 1997).
20. David Pugliese, "A Mountaineer's Perspective," *Ottawa Citizen,* May 18, 2002, p. A13.
21. Jon Krakauer, *Into Thin Air: A Personal Account of the Mount Everest Disaster* (New York: Villard, 1997), p. 114.
22. Olivia Goldhill, "4G Coverage on Mount Everest," *The Telegraph,* July 5, 2013, www.telegraph.co.uk/technology/mobile-phones/10161553/4G-coverage-on-Mount-Everest.html.
23. Lorena Blas, "Discovery Cancels Everest Live Jump After Tragedy," *USA Today,* April 20, 2014, www.usatoday.com/story/life/tv/2014/04/20/discovery-cancels-everest-jump-live-event/7940935/.
24. Lindsey Bever, "At Least 12 Killed, Others Missing After Mount Everest Avalanche," *The Washington Post,* April 18, 2014, http://www.washingtonpost.com/news/morning-mix/wp/2014/04/18/breaking-6-killed-and-9-still-missing-after-mount-everest-avalanche-officials-say/?tid=hp_mm; Alan Arnette, "Everest 2014: Avalanche Near Camp 1—Sherpa Deaths: Update 9," Alanarnette.com, April 17, 2014, http://www.alanarnette.com/blog/2014/04/17/everest-2014-avalanche-near-camp-1-sherpa-deaths/.
25. McQuail, *McQuail's Mass Communication Theory*.
26. Matthew Palevsky, "Twitter Breaks Record as News of bin Laden's Death Spreads," www.poynter.org/latest-news/mediawire/130585/twitter-sees-highest-sustained-rate-of-tweets-ever-as-news-of-bin-ladens-death-breaks/.
27. Frank Ahrens, "Anti-indecency Forces Opposed," *Washington Post*, March 26, 2005.
28. Shankar Vedantam, "Two Views of the Same News Find Opposite Biases," *TheWashington Post*, July 24, 2006.
29. McQuail, *McQuail's Mass Communication Theory*.
30. Katie Crowe, "Cartoonist Earns Readership, Freelance Deals With 'Girls With Slingshots' Strip," *The Frederick News-Post,*April 26, 2013.
31. Anna Palindrome, "The Transcontinental Disability Choir: Four Ways to Do It Right," November 25, 2009, http://bitchmagazine.org/post/four-ways-to-do-it-right.
32. Crowe, "Cartoonist Earns Readership, Freelance Deals With 'Girls With Slingshots' Strip."
33. Ben H. Bagdikian, *The New Media Monopoly* (Boston: Beacon Press, 2004).

34. George Gerbner, "TV Violence and the Art of Asking the Wrong Question," Center for Media Literacy, www.medialit .org/reading_room/article459.html.
35. Potter, *Media Literacy*.
36. Arthur Asa Berger, *Media Analysis Techniques*, 3rd ed. (Thousand Oaks, Calif.: Sage Publications, 2005).
37. Emma Forrest, "Iconography: Good for What, Exactly, Will Hunting?" *The Guardian*, March 16, 1998.
38. Dwight Garner, "Storm Over Everest," *Ottawa Citizen*, August 23, 1998.
39. Potter, *Media Literacy*.
40. Linda Pershing and Margaret R. Yocom, "The Yellow Ribboning of the USA: Contested Meanings in the Construction of a Political Symbol," *Western Folklore* 55, no. 1 (1996); Jack Santino, "Yellow Ribbons and Seasonal Flags: The Folk Assemblage of War," *The Journal of American Folklore* 105, no. 415 (1992); George Mariscal, "In the Wake of the Gulf War: Untying the Yellow Ribbon," *Cultural Critique*, no. 19 (1991).
41. Brooke Gladstone, "Never the Same Mainstream Twice," NPR, November 24, 2006, www.onthemedia.org/ transcripts/2006/11/24/06.
42. Chris Ariens, "Evening News Ratings: 2012–2013 Season," TVNewser, September 24, 2013, www.mediabistro.com/ tvnewser/evening-news-ratings-2012-2013-season_ b197773; Merrill Knox, "2013 Ratings: HLN Only Cable News Network to Grow From Last Year," TVNewser, January 2, 2014, www.mediabistro.com/tvnewser/2013-ratings-hln-only-cable-news-network-to-grow-from-last-year_b208941; Merrill Knox, "2013 Ratings: CNN Tops MSNBC in Total Day, But Hits 20-Year Low in Primetime," TVNewser, January 2, 2014, www.mediabistro.com/ tvnewser/2013-ratings-cnn-tops-msnbc-in-total-day-but-hits-20-year-low-in-primetime_b208939; Jordan Chariton, "2013 Ratings: MSNBC Stays in Second in Primetime, Falls to Third in Total Day," TVNewser, January 2, 2014, www .mediabistro.com/tvnewser/2013-ratings-msnbc-stays-in-second-in-primetime-falls-to-third-in-total-day_b209001; Merrill Knox, "2013 Ratings: Fox News, #1 for 12 Straight Years, Sheds Viewers Too," TVNewser, January 2, 2014, www.mediabistro.com/tvnewser/2013-ratings-fox-news-1-for-12-straight-years-sheds-viewers-too_b208937.
43. Pew Research Center Project for Excellence in Journalism, "The State of the News Media 2013,"stateofthemedia .org/2013.
44. "Dailykos.com," Quantcast, March 3, 2014, www .quantcast.com/dailykos.com.
45. Gavin O'Malley, "YouTube Streams 4B Videos Daily," Media Post, January 23, 2012, www.mediapost.com/publications/ article/166307/youtube-streams-4b-videos-daily.html.
46. Keith Urbahn, @keithurbahn, May 1, 2011, http://twitter .com/keithurbahn/status/64877790624886784.
47. Joe Weisenthal, "Obama: The U.S. Has Killed Osama bin Laden," Business Insider, May 1, 2011, http://articles. businessinsider.com/2011-05-01/news/30021488_1 _ barack-obama-pakistani-government-firefight.
48. Nicholas Jackson, "Word of Osama bin Laden's Death Spreads Over Twitter," *The Atlantic*, May 1, 2011, www .theatlantic.com/technology/archive/2011/05/word-o f-osama-bin-ladens-death-spreads-over-twitter/238111/.
49. Michelle Jaworski, "Serial Song Theft on 'Glee'? 'Baby Got Back' Wasn't the First," The Daily Dot, January 23, 2013, www.dailydot.com/entertainment/glee-ripping-off-jonathan-coulton-dj-earworm/; Nicola Roberts, "A Collection of Covers *Glee* Borrowed From Other People," Live Journal, January 25, 2013, ontd-glee.livejournal.com/2513279.html.
50. Hal R. Varian, "File-Sharing Is the Latest Battleground in the Clash of Technology and Copyright," *New York Times*, April 7, 2005.
51. Erik Barnouw, *Tube of Plenty: The Evolution of American Television*, 2nd rev. ed. (New York: Oxford University Press, 1990).
52. Shearon A. Lowery and Melvin L. DeFleur, *Milestones in Mass Communication*, 3rd ed. (White Plains, N.Y.: Longman, 1995).
53. Stan Soocher, *They Fought the Law: Rock Music Goes to Court* (New York: Schirmer Books, 1999).
54. Jesse Sheidlower, "If You Seek Amy's Ancestors," *Slate*, March 18, 2009, www.slate.com/id/2214106.
55. Wright, *Mass Communication: A Sociological Perspective*.
56. Ibid.
57. "Rockefeller Bill on Indecency Spurs Action in Congress to Increase Fines on TV Indecency," Sen. Jay Rockefeller, June 16, 2006, rockefeller.senate.gov/press/record. cfm?id=288297.

Chapter 2

1. Glenn Greenwald, *No Place to Hide: Edward Snowden, the NSA, and the U.S. Surveillance State* (New York: Henry Holt and Co., 2014).
2. Janet Reitman, "Snowden and Greenwald: The Men Who Leaked the Secrets," *Rolling Stone,* December 4, 2013, www.rollingstone.com/politics/news/snowden-and-greenwald-the-men-who-leaked-the-secrets-20131204.
3. Greenwald, 2014.
4. Brooke Gladstone, "A Year of Snowden," *On the Media,* June 6, 2014, www.onthemedia.org/story/year-snowden/ transcript/.
5. "Profile: Edward Snowden," BBC News, December 16, 2013, www.bbc.com/news/world-us-canada-22837100.
6. Barton Gellman, Julie Tate, and Ashkan Soltani, "In NSA-Intercepted Data, Those Not Targeted Far Outnumber the Foreigners Who Are," *The Washington Post*, July 5, 2014, www.washingtonpost.com/world/national-security/in-nsa-intercepted-data-those-not-targeted-far-outnumber-the-foreigners-who-are/2014/07/05/8139adf8-045a-11e4-8572-4b1b969b6322_story.html.
7. Peter Schrag, *Test of Loyalty: Daniel Ellsberg and the Rituals of Secret Government* (New York:Simon & Schuster, 1974).
8. "Missing the Point of WikiLeaks," *The Economist*, December 1, 2010, www.economist.com/blogs/ democracyinamerica/2010/12/after_secrets; Marshall Soules, "Harold Adams Innis: The Bias of Communications & Monopolies of Power," 2007, www.media-studies.ca/ articles/innis.htm.
9. W. James Potter, *Media Literacy*, 3rd ed. (Thousand Oaks, Calif.: Sage Publications, 2005).
10. Melvin L. DeFleur and Sandra Ball-Rokeach, *Theories of Mass Communication*, 5th ed. (New York: Longman, 1989); Ferdinand Tönnies, *Gemeinschaft und Gesellschaft*, trans. Charles P. Loomis (East Lansing: Michigan State University Press, 1957).
11. DeFleur and Ball-Rokeach, *Theories of Mass Communication*.
12. Stanley Rothman, "Introduction," in *The Mass Media in Liberal Democratic Societies*, ed. Stanley Rothman (New York: Paragon House, 1992).
13. DeFleur and Ball-Rokeach, *Theories of Mass Communication*.
14. Stephen Ansolabehere, Shanto Iyengar, and Adam Simon, "Shifting Perspectives on the Effects of Campaign Communication," in *Do the Media Govern? Politicians,*

Voters, and Reporters in America, ed. Shanto Iyengar and Richard Reeves (Thousand Oaks, Calif.: Sage Publications, 1997).

15. Paul Lazarsfeld, Bernard Berelson, and Hazel Gaudet, *The People's Choice*, 3rd ed. (New York: Columbia University Press, 1968).
16. Brooke Gladstone, "Trail of Years," *On the Media*, February 23, 2007, www.onthemedia.org/transcripts/2007/02/23/07.
17. Ansolabehere et al., "Shifting Perspectives on the Effects of Campaign Communication."
18. Werner J. Severin and James W. Tankard, *Communication Theories: Origins, Methods, and Uses in the Mass Media*, 5th ed. (New York: Longman, 2001).
19. C. Wright Mills, *The Power Elite* (New York: Oxford University Press, 1959).
20. Ben H. Bagdikian, *The New Media Monopoly* (Boston: Beacon Press, 2004).
21. Frances Martel, "CNN Report: Do Missing White Babies Get More Media Coverage Than Minorities?" October 22, 2011, http://www.mediaite.com/tv/cnn-report-do-missing-white-babies-get-more-media-coverage-than-minorities/; T. L. Stanley, "Nancy Grace Says 'the Devil Is Dancing' at Casey Anthony Verdict," *Los Angeles Times*, July 5, 2011, http://latimesblogs.latimes.com/showtracker/2011/07/nancy-grace-says-the-devil-is-dancing-at-casey-anthony-verdict.html.
22. Mark Memmott, "Spotlight Skips Cases of Missing Minorities," *USA Today*, June 16, 2005.
23. DeFleur and Ball-Rokeach, *Theories of Mass Communication*; Denis McQuail, *McQuail's Mass Communication Theory*, 5th ed. (London: Sage Publications, 2005); Potter, *Media Literacy*.
24. Doris A. Graber, *Processing the News: How People Tame the Information Tide,* 2nd ed. (New York: Longman, 1988).
25. David Hinckley, "Rush and Sean Tops in Talk," *Daily News*, December 10, 2005.
26. Graber, *Processing the News;* Lazarsfeld et al., *The People's Choice*.
27. Jim Rutenberg, "Obama Aims TV Ads at Younger Voters," *New York Times*, October 8, 2008, thecaucus.blogs.nytimes.com/2008/10/08/obama-aims-tv-ads-at-younger-voters; Nicholas Deleon, "Gaming Gets Political: Obama Ads Appear in EA Games," October 15, 2008, TechCrunch Network, www.crunchgear.com/2008/10/15/gaming-gets-political-obama-ads-appear-in-ea-games.
28. Arthur Asa Berger, *Media Analysis Techniques*, 3rd ed. (Thousand Oaks, Calif.: Sage Publications, 2005).
29. Ibid.
30. Potter, *Media Literacy*.
31. "Interview with John Adams About 'On the Transmigration of Souls,'" September 2002, www.earbox.com/W-transmigration.html.
32. Marshall McLuhan, *Understanding Media: The Extensions of Man* (New York: McGraw-Hill, 1964).
33. McQuail, *McQuail's Mass Communication Theory*.
34. Joshua Meyrowitz, "Shifting Worlds of Strangers: Medium Theory and Changes in 'Them' Versus 'Us,'" *Sociological Inquiry* 67, no. 1 (1997): 59–71.
35. Joshua Meyrowitz, *No Sense of Place* (New York: Oxford University Press, 1985).
36. McQuail, *McQuail's Mass Communication Theory*.
37. Jürgen Habermas, *The Theory of Communicative Action,* vol. 1, trans. Thomas McCarthy (Boston: Beacon Press, 1984).
38. Matthew Forney, "Testing Beijing's Limits: In the Quest for China's Lucrative—and Elusive—TV Market, Did Murdoch Bend the Rules?" *Time*, September 5, 2005; Ken Auletta, *Googled: The End of the World as We Know It* (New York: Penguin Press, 2009).
39. Bagdikian, *The New Media Monopoly*.
40. Chris Anderson, *The Long Tail* (New York: Hyperion, 2006).
41. Potter, *Media Literacy*; Shearon A. Lowery and Melvin L. DeFleur, *Milestones in Mass Communication*, 3rd ed. (White Plains, N.Y.: Longman, 1995); McQuail, *McQuail's Mass Communication Theory*.
42. Potter, *Media Literacy*.
43. Elihu Katz, "The Two-Step Flow of Communication," in *Mass Communications*, ed. Wilbur Schramm (Urbana: University of Illinois Press, 1960).
44. Harold Lasswell, "The Structure and Function of Communication in Society," in *Mass Communications*, ed. Wilbur Schramm (Urbana: University of Illinois Press, 1960).
45. Robert K. Merton, *Social Theory and Social Structure*, enlarged ed. (New York: Free Press, 1968).
46. Lasswell, "The Structure and Function of Communication in Society."
47. Charles R. Wright, *Mass Communication: A Sociological Perspective*, 3rd ed. (New York: Random House, 1986).
48. Ibid.
49. Jesse Holcomb, "PEJ News Coverage Index: July 4–10, 2011: Deficit Deliberations and a Surprise Verdict Top the News," Pew Research Center Project for Excellence in Journalism, www.journalism.org/index_report/pej_news_coverage_index_july_4_10_2011.
50. Mark Jurkowitz, "PEJ News Coverage Index: November 7–13, 2011: Two Explosive Scandals Top the News," Pew Research Center Project for Excellence in Journalism, http://www.journalism.org/2011/11/13/pej-news-coverage-index-november-713-2011/.
51. "Investors Now Go Online for Quotes, Advice," Pew Research Center for the People and the Press, June 11, 2000.
52. Wright, *Mass Communication*; Meyrowitz, *No Sense of Place*.
53. Meyrowitz, *No Sense of Place*.
54. Everett M. Rogers, William B. Hart, and James W. Dearing, "A Paradigmatic History of Agenda-Setting Research," in *Do the Media Govern?* ed. Shanto Iyengar and Richard Reeves (Thousand Oaks, Calif.: Sage Publications, 1997).
55. Lowery and DeFleur, *Milestones in Mass Communication*.
56. "PEJ News Coverage Index: January 2–8, 2012: Iowa Caucus Launches 2012 Election Coverage," Pew Research Center Project for Excellence in Journalism, www.journalism.org/index_report/pej_news_coverage_index_january_28_2012.
57. Lowery and DeFleur, *Milestones in Mass Communication*.
58. Elihu Katz, Jay G. Blumler, and Michael Gurevitch, "Utilization of Mass Communication by the Individual," in *The Uses of Mass Communications: Current Perspectives on Gratifications Research,* ed. Jay G. Blumler and Elihu Katz (Beverly Hills, Calif.: Sage Publications, 1974).
59. Berger, *Media Analysis Techniques*.
60. Albert Bandura, "Social Cognitive Theory of Mass Communication," in *Media Effects: Advances in Theory and Research*, ed. Jennings Bryant and Dolf Zillman (Hillsdale, N.J.: Lawrence Erlbaum Associates, 1994).
61. DeFleur and Ball-Rokeach, *Theories of Mass Communication*.
62. George Herbert Mead, *Mind, Self, and Society* (Chicago: University of Chicago Press, 1934).
63. Merton, *Social Theory and Social Structure*.
64. Michael J. Socolow, "The Hyped Panic Over 'War of the Worlds,'" *The Chronicle of Higher Education*, October 24, 2008; Wright, *Mass Communication: A Sociological Perspective*.
65. Elisabeth Noelle-Neumann, "The Contribution of Spiral of Silence Theory to an Understanding of Mass Media," in *The Mass Media in Liberal Democratic Societies*, ed. Stanley Rothman (New York: Paragon House, 1992).
66. Rothman, "Introduction."

67. Huiping Huang, "A Cross-Cultural Test of the Spiral of Silence," *International Journal of Public Opinion Research* 17, no. 13 (2005).
68. Keith Hampton, Lee Rainie, Weixu Lu, Maria Dwyer, Inyoung Shin, and Kristen Purcell, "Social Media and the 'Spiral of Silence,'" Pew Research Internet Project, Auguest 26, 2014, www.pewinternet.org/2014/08/26/social-media-and-the-spiral-of-silence/.
69. David L. Altheide and Robert P. Snow, *Media Worlds in the Postjournalism Era* (Hawthorne, N.Y.: Aldine De Gruyter, 1991).
70. McQuail, *McQuail's Mass Communication Theory*.
71. Joanne Ostrow, "Authority on Media Violence Says Don't Blame TV for Columbine," *Denver Post*, April 25, 1999.
72. George Gerbner et al., "Growing Up With Television: The Cultivation Perspective," in *Media Effects: Advances in Theory and Research*, ed. Jennings Bryant and Dolf Zillman (Hillsdale, N.J.: Lawrence Erlbaum Associates, 1994).
73. Lowery and DeFleur, *Milestones in Mass Communication*.
74. Wilson Biographies, "Gerbner, George," Wilson Web, hwwilsonweb.com.
75. Ibid.
76. Gerbner et al., "Growing Up With Television."
77. Patrick E. Jamieson and Daniel Romer, "Violence in Popular U.S. Prime Time TV Dramas and the Cultivation of Fear: A Time Series Analysis." *Media and Communication* 2, no. 2 (2014), 31–41.
78. Alyssa Rosenberg, "Is TV Making Us More Afraid of Crime? Or Burning Us Out on Violence?" Act Four (*Washington Post*), June 20, 2014, www.washingtonpost.com/news/act-four/wp/2014/06/20/is-tv-making-us-more-afraid-of-crime-or-burning-us-out-on-violence/.
79. Dan Balz and Anne E. Kornblut, "Obama Joins Race With Goals Set High," *Washington Post*, February 11, 2007.
80. Ansolabehere et al., "Shifting Perspectives on the Effects of Campaign Communication."
81. Howard Kurtz, "Media Notes: Big Day or Non-Event?" *Washington Post,* February 19, 2008, www.washingtonpost.com/wp-dyn/content/article/2008/02/19/AR2008021900844.html?referrer= emailarticle.
82. Doris A. Graber, *Mass Media and American Politics*, 7th ed. (Washington, D.C.: CQ Press, 2006).
83. Peter Johnson, "Fox News Enjoys New View—From the Top," *USA Today*, April 4, 2002.
84. Ibid.
85. Ibid.
86. Pew Research Center Project for Excellence in Journalism, "The State of the News Media 2011: Cable TV" (2009), stateofthemedia.org/2011/cable-essay/; Merrill Knox, "Cable Network Ranker: Q2 2014," TVNewser, July 1, 2014, http://www.mediabistro.com/tvnewser/cable-network-ranker-q2-2014_b230729#more-230729.
87. Richard Reeves, "The Question of Media Bias," in *Do the Media Govern?* ed. Shanto Iyengar and Richard Reeves (Thousand Oaks, Calif.: Sage Publications, 1997).
88. "The American Journalist: Party and Party Affiliation," October 6, 2006, www.journalism.org/node/2304.
89. Rothman, "Introduction."
90. Media Matters for America, "O'Reilly Asserted 'Most Journalists Give Money to Democrats'—but Study on Subject Refutes Him," August 24, 2007, mediamatters.org/research/200708240007.
91. Bagdikian, *The New Media Monopoly*.
92. Dana Milbank, "Rove's Reading: Not So Liberal as Leery," *Washington Post*, April 20, 2005.
93. Graber, *Mass Media and American Politics*.
94. Herbert Gans, *Deciding What's News* (New York: Pantheon Books, 1979).
95. Nazila Fathi, "In a Death Seen Around the World, a Symbol of Iranian Protests," *New York Times*, June 23, 2009.
96. James O'Byrne, "Katrina: The Power of the Press Against the Wrath of Nature," September 1, 2006, www.poynter.org/content/content_view.asp?id=106352.
97. Gans, *Deciding What's News*.
98. Rothman, "Introduction."

Chapter 3

1. Henry Barnes, "Spike Lee Raises $1.25m on Kickstarter for 'Bloody, Funny, Sexy' Film," *The Guardian*, August 19, 2013.
2. Ramin Setoodeh, "Spike Lee on 'Da Sweet Blood of Jesus' and Hollywood's Diversity Problem," *Variety*, June 23, 2104, variety.com/2014/film/news/spike-lee-da-sweet-blood-of-jesus-hollywood-diversity-problem-1201243416/.
3. Forrest Wickman, "Spike Lee's Kickstarter Movie Is a Surprise Remake. Will Supporters Get What They Paid For?" *Slate*, June 24, 2014, www.slate.com/blogs/browbeat/2014/06/24/spike_lee_s_kickstarter_movie_da_sweet_blood_of_jesus_is_a_stealth_remake.html?wpisrc=burger_bar.
4. David Carr, "At Sundance, Kickstarter Resembled a Movie Studio, but Without the Egos," Media Decoder (*New York Times*), January 30, 2012, mediadecoder.blogs.nytimes.com/2012/01/30/at-sundance-kickstarter-resembled-a-movie-studio-but-without-the-egos/?_php=true&_type=blogs&_r=0.
5. Barnes, "Spike Lee Raises $1.25m on Kickstarter."
6. Aaron Couch, "Kickstarter Defends Spike Lee's Campaign: 'This Isn't Charity,'" HollywoodReporter.com, August 19, 2013, www.hollywoodreporter.com/news/kickstarter-defends-spike-lees-campaign-609233.
7. Perry Chen, Yancey Strickler, and Charles Adler, "The Truth About Spike Lee and Kickstarter," Kicksatarter Blog, www.kickstarter.com/blog/the-truth-about-spike-lee-and-kickstarter-0.
8. Spike Lee, "The Newest Hottest Spike Lee Joint," Kickstarter.com, August 2013, www.kickstarter.com/projects/spikelee/the-newest-hottest-spike-lee-joint?ref=live.
9. Paul Kendall, "Power to the People: Kickstarter Began as a Website for Complete Strangers to Help Fund Off-beat Ideas. It Worked. But Are Millions of Investors Now Being Short-Changed?" *The Sunday Telegraph*, May 18, 2014.
10. Ben Bagdikian, *The Information Machines: Their Impact on Men and the Media* (New York: Harper & Row, 1971).
11. John Tebbel, *The Media in America* (New York: Thomas Y. Crowell Company, 1974).
12. Ibid.
13. Ibid.
14. Michael Schudson, *The Power of News* (Cambridge, MA: Harvard University Press, 1995).
15. Margaret A. Blanchard, ed., *History of the Mass Media in the United States* (Chicago: Fitzroy Dearborn Publishers, 1998).
16. Schudson, *The Power of News*.
17. Robert Seidman, "DVR Penetration Grows to 39.7% of Households, 42.2% of Viewers," March 23, 2011, tvbythenumbers.zap2it.com/2011/03/23/dvr-penetration-grows-to-39-7-of-households-42-2-of-viewers/; National Cable and Telecommunications Association, "Industry Data," January 17, 2012, www.ncta.com/Statistics.aspx; Satellite Broadcasting and Communications Association, "Satellite Home Entertainment; Industry Overview," www.sbca.com/receiver-network/index.html; Jim Romenesko, "WSJ Remains Largest Circulation U.S. Daily Newspaper," May 4, 2011, www.poynter.org/latest-news/mediawire/

130676/wsj-remains-largest-circulation-daily-newspaper/; Nielsen Company, "How Teens Use Media; A Nielsen Report on the Myths and Realities of Teen Media Trends," June 2009, http://www.nmprevention.org/Project_Docs/Nielsen_HowTeensUseMedia_June2009.pdf.
18. Open Society Institute EU Monitoring and Advocacy Program, *Television Across Europe: Regulation, Policy and Independence*, 2005, http://www.opensocietyfoundations.org/reports/television-across-europe-regulation-policy-and-independence.
19. *Hoover's Company Profile Database: Clear Channel Communications Inc.* (Austin, Texas: Hoover's Inc., 2009); *Hoover's Company Profile Database: Gannett Co. Inc.* (Austin, Texas: Hoover's Inc., 2009).
20. *Hoover's Company Records—In-Depth Records: The Walt Disney Company* (Austin, Texas: Hoover's Inc., 2014).
21. Wilson Biographies, "Walt Disney," vweb.hwwilsonweb.com.
22. Richard Schickel, "Walt Disney," *Time*, December 7, 1998.
23. "The House of the Mouse," *New Internationalist*, December 1998.
24. Suzy Wetlaufer, "Common Sense and Conflict," *Harvard Business Review*, January/February 2000; Wilson Biographies, "Walt Disney."
25. Ken Auletta, *The Highwaymen* (New York: Random House, 1997).
26. *Hoover's Company Records—In-Depth Records: The Walt Disney Company.*
27. Peter Schweizer and Rochelle Schweizer, *Disney: The Mouse Betrayed* (Washington, D.C.: Regnery Publishing, Inc., 1998); Robert F. Hartley, *Marketing Mistakes and Successes*, 7th ed. (New York: Wiley, 1998); Maureen Fan, "A Bumpy Ride for Disneyland in Hong Kong," *Washington Post*, November 20, 2006.
28. Schweizer and Schweizer, *Disney: The Mouse Betrayed*.
29. Richard Verrier, "Disney May Add 2nd China Park," *Los Angeles Times*, July 20, 2002.
30. Walt Disney Company, "The Walt Disney Company 2005 Annual Report," corporate.disney.go.com/investors/annual_reports/2005/index.html.
31. Fan, "A Bumpy Ride for Disneyland in Hong Kong"; *Hoover's Company Records—In-Depth Records: The Walt Disney Company.*
32. "Hong Kong Disneyland Enjoys Fourth Record-Breaking Year," *China Daily*, February 18, 2014.
33. Fan, "A Bumpy Ride for Disneyland in Hong Kong."
34. Brooks Barnes, "Owners to Invest $800 Million More in Shanghai Disneyland," April 29, 2014; *Hoover's Company Records—In-Depth Records: The Walt Disney Company.*
35. Dean Alger, *Megamedia: How Giant Corporations Dominate Mass Media, Distort Competition, and Endanger Democracy* (Lanham, Md.: Rowman & Littlefield, 1998).
36. Shannon Peavey, "Disney Believes It Can Duck Downturn," *Electronic Media*, February 12, 2001; *Hoover's Company Records—In-Depth Records: The Walt Disney Company.*
37. David Lieberman and Laura Petrecca, "Disney, Pixar to Merge in $7.5B Deal," *USA Today*, January 24, 2006; *Hoover's Company Records—In-Depth Records: The Walt Disney Company;* "Biggest Animated Movies," Box Office Mojo, July 9, 2014, http://boxofficemojo.com/showdowns/chart/?id=animationalltime.htm.
38. Wetlaufer, "Common Sense and Conflict."
39. Jon Swartz, "Disney Gets New Comic Heroes With $4 Billion Deal for Marvel," *USA Today*, September 4, 2009.
40. Hoover's Company Records—In-Depth Records: The Walt Disney Company; Georg Szalai, "Analysts Laud Disney's Lucasfilm Acquisition Despite High Price Tag," October 31, 2012, http://www.hollywoodreporter.com/news/analysts-laud-disneys-lucasfilm-acquisition-384719.
41. Auletta, *The Highwaymen*.
42. *Hoover's Company Records—In-Depth Records: News Corporation* (Austin, Texas: Hoover's Inc., 2014); *Hoover's Company Records—In-Depth Records: 21st Century Fox* (Austin, Texas: Hoover's Inc., 2014).
43. Auletta, *The Highwaymen*.
44. Alex Weprin, "The 2011 Cable Network Ranker," December 28, 2011, www.mediabistro.com/tvnewser/the-2011-cable-network-ranker_b104280.
45. *Hoover's Company Records—In-Depth Records: News Corporation.*
46. Pew Research Center Project for Excellence in Journalism, "The State of the News Media 2008: Newspapers," March 15, 2008, pewresearch.org/pubs/767/state-of-the-news-media-2008.
47. *Hoover's Company Records—In-Depth Records: Time Warner Inc.* (Austin, Texas: Hoover's Inc., 2011); *Hoover's Company Records—In-Depth Records: News Corporation; Hoover's Company Records—In-Depth Records: 21stCentury Fox.*
48. *Hoover's Company Records—In-Depth Records: News Corporation.*
49. *Hoover's Company Records—In-Depth Records: 21st Century Fox.*
50. Ken Auletta, *Three Blind Mice: How the TV Networks Lost Their Way* (New York: Random House, 1991).
51. Ibid.
52. *Hoover's Company Records—In-Depth Records: Time Warner Inc.*; *Hoover's Company Records—In-Depth Records: The Walt Disney Company* (Austin, Texas: Hoover's Inc., 2011).
53. *Hoover's Company Records—In-Depth Records: Time Warner Inc.*; Alger, *Megamedia*; AOL Time Warner, "AOL Time Warner 2002 Annual Report," 2002.
54. *Hoover's Company Profile Database: Time Warner Inc.*
55. David Carr and Ravi Somaiya, "Saddled With Debt, Time Inc. Sets a Lonely Course in a Shifting Market," *International New York Times,* June 10, 2014.
56. *Hoover's Company Profile Database: Viacom* (Austin, Texas: Hoover's Inc., 2014); *Hoover's Company Records—In-Depth Records: CBS Corporation* (Austin, Texas: Hoover's Inc., 2014).
57. Devin Leonard, "Who's the Boss?" *Fortune*, April 16, 2001.
58. David Lieberman, "Viacom Plans Split to Spur Growth," *USA Today*, June 14, 2005; *Hoover's Company Records—In-Depth Records: CBS Corporation*; *Hoover's Company Profile Database: Viacom Inc.*; Standard & Poor's, *Standard & Poor's Corporate Descriptions Plus News: Viacom Inc.* (New York: Standard & Poor's, 2011).
59. John Eggerton, "FCC Upholds Viacom Indecency Settlement," *Broadcasting & Cable*, October 17, 2006; Krysten Crawford, "Howard Stern Jumps to Satellite," CNN, October 6, 2004, money.cnn.com/2004/10/06/news/newsmakers/stern_sirius/index.htm?cnn=yes.
60. Ken Auletta, *Googled: The End of the World as We Know It* (New York: Penguin Press, 2009).
61. Ben Bagdikian, *The New Media Monopoly* (Boston: Beacon Press, 2004); *Hoover's Company Records—In-Depth Records: Bertelsmann AG* (Austin, Texas: Hoover's Inc., 2014).
62. Alger, *Megamedia*.
63. "New Chapter," *The Economist*, February 10, 2001; *Hoover's Company Profile Database: Bertelsmann AG.*
64. Jack Ewing, "Bertelsmann's Creed: Inner Growth," *Businessweek*, March 18, 2005, http://www.businessweek.com/stories/2005-03-17/bertelsmanns-creed-inner-growth.
65. Frank Gibney Jr., "Napster Meister," *Time*, November 13, 2000; *Hoover's Company Records—In-Depth Records: Bertelsmann AG.*

66. Jack Ewing, "Bertelsmann's Slimmer Profile Generates Thinner Profits," *Businessweek*, September 6, 2006, www.businessweek.com/globalbiz/content/sep2006/gb20060906_498406.htm.
67. *Hoover's Company Records—In-Depth Records: Bertelsmann AG*.
68. Ewing, "Bertelsmann's Creed: Inner Growth"; Ewing, "Bertelsmann's Slimmer Profile Generates Thinner Profits."
69. *Hoover's Company Records—In-Depth Records: Bertelsmann AG*.
70. *Hoover's Company Records—In-Depth Records: The Walt Disney Company; Hoover's Company Records—In-Depth Records: Comcast Corporation; Hoover's Company Records—In-Depth Records: Google Inc.*(Austin, Texas: Hoover's Inc., 2014), *Hoover's Company Records—In-Depth Records: Apple Inc.*(Austin, Texas: Hoover's Inc., 2014).
71. Alger, *Megamedia*.
72. Auletta, *Three Blind Mice*.
73. Howard Kurtz, "Comcast-NBC Deal Possible," *Washington Post*, October 1, 2009; Paul Tobin, "Vivendi Wants to Exit NBC, Deal Is Complex, CFO Says," November 19, 2009, www.bloomberg.com/apps/news?pid=20601087&sid=anZaSljci4Z4&pos=7; Shira Ovide and Amy Schatz, "Comcast-NBC Deal Would Draw Lengthy Scrutiny in Washington," *Wall Street Journal*, November 16, 2009; Brian Stelter and Tim Arango, "Comcast-NBC Deal Wins Federal Approval," January 18, 2011, http://mediadecoder.blogs.nytimes.com/2011/01/18/f-c-c-approves-comcast-nbc-deal/.
74. Amy Chozick and Brian Stelter, "Comcast Buys Rest of NBC in Early Sale," *New York Times*, February 12, 2013, mediadecoder.blogs.nytimes.com/2013/02/12/comcast-buying-g-e-s-stake-in-nbcuniversal-for-16-7-billion/?_php=true&_type=blogs&smid=tw-share&_r=0.
75. Meg James, "Comcast to Own All of Media Giant," *Los Angeles Times*, February 13, 2013, http://articles.latimes.com/2013/feb/13/business/la-fi-ct-comcast-ge-20130213.
76. Comcast Corp., Form 10-K (Annual Report 2013), February 12, 2014, files.shareholder.com/downloads/CMCSA/3321353799x0xS1193125%2D14%2D47522/1166691/filing.pdf.
77. *Hoover's Company Records—In-Depth Records: Comcast Corporation* (Austin, Texas: Hoover's Inc., 2014); *Hoover's Company Records—In-Depth Records: NBCUniversal Media, LLC* (Austin, Texas: Hoover's Inc., 2011).
78. Brian Stelter and Tim Arango, "Comcast-NBC Deal Wins Federal Approval."
79. "Time Warner Cable Separation Information," Time Warner, 2009, ir.timewarner.com/phoenix.zhtml?c=70972&p=irol-twcseparation.
80. Ken Auletta, "Why Comcast Wants to Buy Time Warner Cable," *The New Yorker*, February 13, 2014, www.newyorker.com/online/blogs/currency/2014/02/why-comcast-wants-to-buy-time-warner-cable.html.
81. Hayley Tsukayama, "Comcast, Time Warner to Merge: What Happens to My Service," *Washington Post,* February 13, 2014, www.washingtonpost.com/business/technology/comcast-time-warner-to-merge-what-happens-to-my-service/2014/02/13/b285f81e-94b4-11e3-83b9-1f024193bb84_story.html.
82. Google, "About Google News," news.google.com/intl/en_us/about_google_news.html.
83. *Hoover's Company Records—In-Depth Records: Google Inc.*
84. Ken Auletta, *Googled: The End of the World as We Know It.*
85. Ben H. Bagdikian, *The New Media Monopoly*.
86. *Hoover's Company Records—In-Depth Records: Google Inc.* (Austin, Texas: Hoover's Inc., 2011); *Hoover's Company Records—In-Depth Records: Comcast Corporation* (Austin, Texas: Hoover's Inc., 2011); *Hoover's Company Records—In-Depth Records: Apple Inc.* (Austin, Texas: Hoover's Inc., 2011).
87. Ken Auletta, *Googled: The End of the World as We Know It.*
88. Apple Inc., Form 10-K (Annual Report 2013), October 29, 2013, investor.apple.com/secfiling.cfm?filingid=1193125-13-416534&cik=.
89. Peter Burrows and Ronald Grover, "Steve Jobs's Magic Kingdom," *Businessweek*, January 26, 2006.
90. Tim Berners-Lee, *Weaving the Web* (New York: HarperCollins, 1999).
91. *Hoover's Company Profile Database: Apple Inc.*; John Markoff, "Oh, Yeah, He Also Sells Computers," *New York Times*, April 25, 2004.
92. Jefferson Graham, "Jobs Has a Knack for Getting His Way," *USA Today*, January 25, 2006.
93. *Hoover's Company Profile Database: Pixar Animation Studios Inc.* (Austin, Texas: Hoover's Inc., 2009).
94. Burrows and Grover, "Steve Jobs's Magic Kingdom."
95. Ken Auletta, *Googled: The End of the World as We Know It.*
96. Brandon Keim, "Twitter Analysis: Massive Global Mourning for Steve Jobs (Infographic)," *Wired*, October 7, 2011, www.wired.com/epicenter/2011/10/global-mourning-for-steve-jobs/.
97. Brian Fung, "Why Apple Is So Interested in Beats: It's Not About the Headphones," May 9, 2014, www.washingtonpost.com/blogs/the-switch/wp/2014/05/09/why-apple-is-so-interested-in-beats-its-not-about-the-headphones/?hpid=z2.
98. *Hoover's Company Records—In-Depth Records: Gannett Co., Inc.* (Austin, Texas: Hoover's Inc., 2014).
99. Alger, *Megamedia*; Bagdikian, *The New Media Monopoly*.
100. *Hoover's Company Records—In-Depth Records: Gannett Co., Inc.*
101. *Hoover's Company Records—In-Depth Records: Clear Channel Communications, Inc.* (Austin, Texas: Hoover's Inc., 2014).
102. Ibid.; Clear Channel, "Know the Facts," www.clearchannel.com/Corporate.
103. Seth Fiegerman, "End of an Era: Clear Channel Rebrands as iHeartMedia," *Mashable*, September 16, 2014, mashable.com/2014/09/16/clear-channel-iheartmedia/.
104. Chris Anderson, *The Long Tail* (New York: Hyperion, 2006).
105. Ibid.
106. Ibid.
107. Ibid.
108. Ibid.
109. Ibid.
110. Michael Liedtke, "Now Starring on the Internet: YouTube.com," *USA Today*, April 9, 2006.
111. Charlie Rose, "Charlie Rose: A Conversation With the YouTube Co-Founders," August 11, 2006, www.charlierose.com/view/interview/271.
112. *Hoover's Company Profile Database: YouTube, LLC* (Austin, Texas: Hoover's Inc., 2009).
113. "Statistics," YouTube Press, July 14, 2014, www.youtube.com/yt/press/statistics.html.
114. "Tops of 2013: Digital," Nielsen, December 16, 2013, www.nielsen.com/us/en/insights/news/2013/tops-of-2013-digital.html.
115. Rose, "Charlie Rose: A Conversation With the YouTube Co-Founders."
116. Diane Mermigas, "Mermigas on Media," *Hollywood Reporter*, October 24, 2006.
117. Ibid.
118. Ibid.
119. Michael Schudson, *The Power of News* (Cambridge, MA: Harvard University Press, 1996).

120. "Future Forum," *Advertising Age*, September 20, 1999.
121. Bagdikian, *The New Media Monopoly*.
122. Jon Bershad, "Disney Bans ABC Affiliates From Talking to Johnny Depp About His New Movie," October 24, 2011, www.mediaite.com/tv/disney-bans-abc-affiliates-from-talking-to-johnny-depp-about-his-new-movie/.
123. Elizabeth Lesly Stevens, "Mouse-ke-fear," *Brill's Content*, January 1999.
124. Ibid.; Todd Gitlin, "Introduction," in *Conglomerates and the Media*, ed. Eric Barnouw (New York: The New Press, 1997).
125. Denis McQuail, *McQuail's Mass Communication Theory*, 5th ed. (London: Sage Publications, 2005).
126. Dave Phillips, "Chrysler Drops Censorship Policy," *Detroit News*, October 14, 1997.
127. Jim Edwards, "Nicetv," *Brill's Content*, March 2001.
128. Johnnie L. Roberts, "All for One, One for AOL," Newsweek, March 13, 2010, http://www.newsweek.com/all-one-one-aol-155987?piano_t=1; Brian Stelter and Tim Arango, "Comcast-NBC Deal Wins Federal Approval."
129. Auletta, *The Highwaymen*.
130. Auletta, *Googled: The End of the World as We Know It*.
131. Ralph Hanson, "Go See What All the Shouting Is About," *Charleston Daily Mail*, February 15, 2006.
132. Herbert Gans, *Deciding What's News* (New York: Pantheon Books, 1979); McQuail, *McQuail's Mass Communication Theory*.
133. Schudson, *The Power of News*.
134. Patrick M. Reilly, "Behind the Covers: How Stars End Up on Those Glossies," *Wall Street Journal*, November 18, 1997.
135. Ben Smith, "Clinton Campaign Kills Negative Story," *Politico*, September 24, 2007, www.politico.com/news/stories/0907/5992.html.
136. Ibid.
137. Alexander Wolff, "Readers Select Eric LeGrand's Return *SI*'s Moment of the Year," *Sports Illustrated*, December 26, 2011, sportsillustrated.cnn.com/2011/magazine/12/20/moment.of.year/index.html.
138. Stephen Galloway, "Test Screenings; Looking to Shore Up Box Office Returns, Studios Have Become Increasingly Dependent on Findings From Research Screenings—Whether Filmmakers Like It or Not," *Hollywood Reporter*, July 25, 2006; "*Little Miss Sunshine*," Box Office Mojo, boxofficemojo.com/movies/?id=littlemisssunshine.htm.
139. Seth Schiesel, "Young Viewers Like Screen Translation," *New York Times*, November 19, 2001.

Chapter 4

1. Rainbow Rowell, "Poverty's Child," *Omaha World Herald*, July 29, 1997.
2. Rainbow Rowell, "Mr. Harvey, Take a Bow," *Omaha World Herald,* July 7, 1997.
3. Rainbow Rowell, "Living With Colorful Name," *Omaha World Herald,* July 21, 1997.
4. Rowell, "Poverty's Child."
5. John Green, "Two Against the World: 'Eleanor & Park,' by Rainbow Rowell," *New York Times*, March 8, 2013, www.nytimes.com/2013/03/10/books/review/eleanor-park-by-rainbow-rowell.html?_r=0.
6. Erin Grace, "Grace: Minnesotans Cancel Rainbow Rowell's Book Visit After Parents' Complaints," *Omaha World Herald,* September 25, 2013, http://www.omaha.com/news/grace-minnesotans-cancel-rainbow-rowell-s-book-visit-after-parents/article_206b548d-01c1-5668-adc4-51a2579b087d.html.
7. "Using 'R Rated' Book Without Asking Parents Was Wrong, School Chair Says," *MPR News,* September 25, 2013, www.mprnews.org/story/2013/09/25/daily-circuit-eleanor-and-park-anoka-hennepin.
8. Grace, "Grace: Minnesotans Cancel Rainbow Rowell's Book Visit."
9. Shannon Prather, "After Anoka County Library Balks, St. Paul Library Invites Author to Speak," *Star Tribune*, October 22, 2013, www.startribune.com/local/north/228805941.html.
10. James D. Hart, *The Popular Book: A History of America's Literary Taste* (New York: Oxford University Press, 1950).
11. Ibid.
12. Ibid.; Bill Katz, *Dahl's History of the Book*, 3rd English ed. (Metuchen, N.J.: Scarecrow Press, 1995).
13. Katz, *Dahl's History of the Book*.
14. Ibid.; John J. Goldman and Eileen V. Quigley, "Gutenberg Bible Is Sold for Record $4.9 Million," *Los Angeles Times*, October 23, 1987, http://articles.latimes.com/1987-10-23/news/mn-10733_1_bids.
15. Katz, *Dahl's History of the Book*.
16. Ibid.
17. Stephen E. Ambrose, *Undaunted Courage* (New York: Simon & Schuster, 1996).
18. Katz, *Dahl's History of the Book*.
19. Hart, *The Popular Book: A History of America's Literary Taste.*
20. Katz, *Dahl's History of the Book.*
21. Ibid.
22. Hart, *The Popular Book: A History of America's Literary Taste*.
23. Ibid.
24. Katz, *Dahl's History of the Book*.
25. Ibid.
26. Chris Anderson, *The Long Tail* (New York: Hyperion, 2006).
27. Katz, *Dahl's History of the Book*.
28. Doreen Carvajal, "Book Publishers Seek Global Reach and Grand Scale," *New York Times*, October 19, 1998.
29. "About Us," Random House, www.randomhouse.com/about/history.html.
30. David Streitfeld, "Book Report," *Washington Post*, March 14, 1999.
31. "The World's 60 Largest Book Publishers, 2013," *Publishers Weekly*, July 19, 2013, www.publishersweekly.com/pw/by-topic/industry-news/financial-reporting/article/58211-the-global-60-the-world-s-largest-book-publishers-2013.html.
32. Florence Shinkle, "University Presses Seize Upon a Silver Lining," *St. Louis Post-Dispatch*, October 12, 1998.
33. Edwin McDowell, "New Best-Selling Novel at Naval Institute Press," *New York Times*, November 1, 1986.
34. Hannah Hess, "Senators Propose Rebranding GPO as Government Publishing Office," *Roll Call*, January 22, 2014, www.rollcall.com/news/senators_propose_rebranding_gpo_as_government_publishing_office-230308-1.html; Steve Vogel, "Marking JFK Anniversary, GPO Releases Digital Warren Commission Report," *The Washington Post*, November 18, 2013, www.washingtonpost.com/blogs/federal-eye/wp/2013/11/18/marking-jfk-anniversary-gpo-releases-digital-warren-commission-report/.
35. Robert Kiely, "Armageddon, Complete and Uncut," *New York Times*, Mary 13, 1990, www.nytimes.com/books/97/03/09/lifetimes/king-stand.html.
36. "Writers and Authors," *Occupational Outlook Handbook,* January 8, 2014, www.bls.gov/ooh/media-and-communication/writers-and-authors.htm.
37. *Hoover's Company Records—In-Depth Records: Ingram Book Company* (Austin, Texas: Hoover's Inc., 2014).

38. James Shapiro, "Wariness Greets the Latest Round in the Publishing Wars," *The Chronicle of Higher Education*, November 27, 1998.
39. *Hoover's Company Records—In-Depth Records: Barnes & Noble Inc.* (Austin, Texas: Hoover's Inc., 2014).
40. Paul Collins, "Chain Reaction; Do Bookstores Have a Future?" *The Village Voice*, May 22, 2006; *Hoover's Company Records—In-Depth Records: American Booksellers Association* (Austin, Texas: Hoover's Inc., 2014).
41. Doreen Carvajal, "Triumph of the Bottom Line; Numbers vs. Words at the Book-of-the-Month Club," *New York Times*, April 1, 1996.
42. Jenna Ross, "It's Textbook Economics: Colleges Fight High Prices; Campuses Across the State Try New Techniques and Technology to Fight Soaring Book Prices," *Star Tribune*, December 29, 2008.
43. *Hoover's Company Records—In-Depth Records: Barnes & Noble Inc.*
44. Associated Press, "Nevada Regents Seek Answers to Rising Textbook Costs," *Las Vegas Sun*, November 6, 2006.
45. Marc Parry, "Students Get Savvier About Textbook Buying," *The Chronicle of Higher Education*, January 27, 2013.
46. Jennifer Howard, "For Many Students, Print Is Still King," *The Chronicle of Higher Education,* January 27, 2013.
47. Associated Press, "Apple Starts Selling Interactive iPad Textbooks," *Wall Street Journal*, January 19, 2012,wsj .com/article/AP07a39a767a3f4ce8a44e07c2d28ef8d1 .html; Brandon Keim, "iPad Textbooks: Reality Less Revolutionary Than Hardware," January 26, 2012, *Wired*, http://www.wired.com/2012/01/ipad-textbooks-learning/all/.
48. Association of American Publishers, "Higher Education Publishing; Charts of Independent Data Sources on Student Spending," www.publishers.org/highered/articles .cfm?ArticleID=45.
49. Hart, *The Popular Book: A History of America's Literary Taste*.
50. Ibid.
51. Katz, *Dahl's History of the Book*.
52. Romance Writers of America, "The Romance Genre: Romance Industry Statistics,"2014, http://www.rwa.org/p/cm/ld/fid=580.
53. Dana Flavelle, "Torstar Eyes Convergence," *Toronto Star*, May 3, 2001.
54. Jeff Ayers, "Janet Evanovich Works Hard at Her Easy-to-Read Stephanie Plum Novels," *Seattle Post-Intelligencer*, June 23, 2006.
55. Allen Pierleoni, "Doubling Up: With Her Wisecracking Heroines Stephanie Plum and Alexandra Barnaby, Novelist Janet Evanovich Is on the Move," *Sacramento Bee*, December 5, 2005.
56. Carol Memmott, "Janet Evanovich by the Numbers," *USA Today*, June 25, 2009; Rachel Donadio, "Promotional Intelligence," *New York Times*, March 21, 2006, www .nytimes.com/2006/05/21/books/review/21donadio .html?pagewanted=all&_r=0.
57. Julie Bosman, "A Classic Turns 50, and Parties Are Planned," *New York Times,* May 25, 2010.
58. Roger Cohen, "In Re: Marketing Parameters for Great American Novel," *New York Times*, March 25, 1990.
59. Jeff Gordinier, "Elvish Lives!," *Entertainment Weekly*, December 14, 2001.
60. Douglas A. Anderson, "Note on the Text," in *The Lord of the Rings*, J. R. R. Tolkien (New York: Houghton Mifflin, 1994); Brian Bethune, "The Lord of the Bookshelves," *Maclean's*, December 23, 2002; Gordinier, "Elvish Lives!"; Lev Grossman et al., "Feeding on Fantasy," *Time*, December 2, 2002; Karen Raugust, "Licensing Hotline," *Publishers Weekly*, July 2, 2001.
61. Carol Memmott and Mary Cadden, "Twilight Series Eclipses Potter Records; Author Meyer Owns Best-Selling Books List," *USA Today*, August 4, 2009.
62. Michelle Dean, "Our Young-Adult Dystopia," *New York Times*, February 2, 2014.
63. Doreen Carvajal, "Booksellers Grab a Young Wizard's Cloaktails," *New York Times*, February 28, 2000.
64. Paul Gray, "Wild About Harry," *Time*, September 20, 1999.
65. "Revised *Times* Children's Bestseller List Creates Room for More Titles," *Book Publishing Report*, September 18, 2000.
66. Martin Bentham, "Harry Potter: The Best Children's Stories Ever: J. K. Rowling's Books About the Schoolboy Wizard Top Survey of British Children, Their Parents," *Sunday Telegraph*, September 23, 2002.
67. The American Library Association, "Frequently Challenged Books of the 21st Century," www.ala.org/advocacy/banned/frequentlychallenged/21stcenturychallenged.
68. Editorial Board, "Lust and Liberties," *Indianapolis Star*, October 5, 1998.
69. "Book Bans Bring Storm of Debate," *Omaha World-Herald*, September 28, 1998.
70. William Breyfogle, "Librarians See Banned Books Week as a Wake-Up Call to Society," *Milwaukee Journal Sentinel*, September 25, 1997.
71. Hart, *The Popular Book: A History of America's Literary Taste*.
72. PBS, "Huck Finn Teacher's Guide: About the Book: *Adventures of Huckleberry Finn*," 2000, www.pbs.org/wgbh/cultureshock/teachers/huck/aboutbook.html.
73. Amy E. Schwartz, "Huck Finn Gets the Revisionist Treatment," *Washington Post*, January 10, 1996.
74. M. L. Lyke, "Blume Explores Her 'Naughty Streak' in 'Sisters,'" *Sacramento Bee*, June 14, 1998.
75. Catherine Flannery, "Still in Blume: What Is It About the Great Judy Blume Novels That All Pre-Teens Want and Need?" *Toronto Sun*, September 21, 1997.
76. Bobbi Battista, "Judy Blume Releases Third Adult Novel," CNN, May 19, 1998, www.cnn.com/books/dialogue/9805/blume/index.html.
77. Paul Vallely, "They Will Not Be Silenced," *The Independent*, February 14, 1998.
78. Barbara Crossette, "Iran Drops Rushdie Death Threat, and Britain Renews Teheran Ties," *New York Times*, September 25, 1998.
79. Douglas Jehl, "New Moves on Rushdie Exposing Iranian Rifts," *New York Times*, October 21, 1998.
80. "Author Banned by British Air," *New York Times*, September 26, 1998.
81. Sarah Lyall, "Rushdie, Free of Threat, Revels in 'Spontaneity,'" *New York Times*, September 26, 1998.
82. Reuters, "Rushdie India Speech Cancelled Amid Death Threats," *Hindustan Times*, January 24, 2012, www .hindustantimes.com/lifestyle/books/rushdie-india-speech-cancelled-amid-death-threats/article1-898405.aspx
83. David Leppard, "Muslim Gang Firebombs Publisher of Allah Novel, Martin Rynja," *Sunday Times*, September 28, 2008; Ron Hogan, "Sherry Jones Reacts to UK *Jewel of Medina* Firebombing," *Galleycat*, September 28, 2008, http://www.mediabistro.com/galleycat/sherry-jones-reacts-to-uk-jewel-of-medina-firebombing_b7802.
84. Vallely, "They Will Not Be Silenced"; "Write and Wrong—Taslima Has the Courage of Conviction," *Statesman* (India), October 22, 1998; Melvyn Bragg, "Forging Links With the Writers in Chains," *Times* (London), February 9, 1998.
85. Anderson, *The Long Tail*.

86. Ibid.
87. Doug Levy, "Amazon.com Amazes: On-Line Gamble Pays off with Rocketing Success," *USA Today*, December 24, 1998; Elisabeth Bumiller, "On-Line Booksellers: A Tale of Two C.E.O.s," *New York Times*, December 8, 1998.
88. Jamie Lendino, "How to Buy an EBook Reader," *PCMag*, December 17, 2003, www.pcmag.com/article2/0,2817,2357102,00.asp.
89. Jim Milliot, "AAP: Book Sales Dipped in 2009," *Publishers Weekly*, April 12, 2010, www.publishersweekly.com/pw/by-topic/industry-news/bookselling/article/42783-aap-book-sales-dipped-in-2009.html.
90. J. Gerry Purdy, "Inside Mobile: Why eBooks and eBook Readers Will Eventually Succeed," *eWeek.com*, October 13, 2008, www.eweek.com/c/a/Mobile-and-Wireless/INSIDE-MOBILE-Why-eBooks-and-eBook-Readers-Will-Eventually-Succeed.
91. Noor Javed, "Digital Reader Meets Skeptics at Literary Fest," *Toronto Star*, September 29, 2008.
92. Jacob Weisberg, "Book End: How the Kindle Will Change the World," March 21, 2009, www.slate.com/id/2214243/.
93. Charlie Rose, "The Charlie Rose Show: A Conversation With Jeff Bezos," February 26, 2009, www.charlierose.com/guest/view/2618.
94. David Pogue, "Some e-Books Are More Equal Than Others," *New York Times*, July 17, 2009, pogue.blogs.nytimes.com/2009/07/17/some-e-books-are-more-equal-than-others/.
95. Anita Singh, "Jonathan Franzen: E-books Are Damaging Society," *Telegraph*, January 29, 2012, www.telegraph.co.uk/culture/hay-festival/9047981/Jonathan-Franzen-e-books-are-damaging-society.html.
96. Jonathan Segura, "No More E-Books vs. Print Books Arguments, OK?," NPR, January 31, 2012, www.npr.org/blogs/monkeysee/2012/01/31/146140663/no-more-e-books-vs-print-books-arguments-ok.
97. Ibid.
98. Ezra Klein, "Will Books Survive eBooks?" *Washington Post*, May 20, 2011, www.washingtonpost.com/blogs/wonkblog/post/will-books-survive-ebooks/2011/05/19/AFHNqz7G_blog.html.
99. Jeffrey P. Bezos, "An Apology From Amazon," July 23, 2009, www.amazon.com/tag/kindle/forum/ref=cm_cd_ef_tft_tp?_encoding=UTF8&cdThread=Tx1FXQPSF67X1IU&displayType=tagsDetail.
100. Anderson, *The Long Tail*.
101. *Hoover's Company Records—In-Depth Records: Ingram Book Group Inc*.

Chapter 5

1. Jessica Coen, "Here Are the Unretouched Images From Lena Dunham's *Vogue* Shoot," *Jezebel*, January 17, 2014, jezebel.com/here-are-the-unretouched-images-from-lena-dunhams-vogu-1503336657; Jodi Kantor, "Debate on Photo Retouching Flares Online, With Roles Reversed," *New York Times,* January 19, 2014, www.nytimes.com/2014/01/20/business/media/debate-on-photo-retouching-flares-online-with-roles-reversed.html.
2. Katy Waldman, "Lena Dunham Responds to the *Vogue* Haters," *Slate,* January 17, 2014, www.slate.com/blogs/xx_factor/2014/01/17/lena_dunham_response_to_vogue_photoshop_criticism_fashion_magazines_are.html.
3. Vanessa Thorpe, "Altered Images: Lena Dunham Defies Her Critics Over 'Doctored' *Vogue* Cover: The *Girls* Writer and Actress Defends Fashion Magazine's Pictures as 'a Beautiful Fantasy,'" *The Observer*, January 19, 20134, Pg. 9.
4. Kathryn Flett, "Focus: White House: Profile: Style Genius Who Frames the Stars," *The Observer*, November 22, 1998.
5. George Lois, "Flashback: Demi Moore," *Vanity Fair*, August 2011, http://www.vanityfair.com/hollywood/features/2011/08/demi-moore-201108.
6. Christine Ledbetter, "Annie Leibovitz Book Signings," *Chicago Sun-Times*, November 16, 1999.
7. James Playsted Wood, *Magazines in the United States*, 3rd ed. (New York: Ronald Press Company, 1971).
8. Ibid.
9. Ibid.
10. Ibid.
11. Michael L. Carlebach, *The Origins of Photojournalism in America* (Washington, D.C.: Smithsonian Institution Press, 1992).
12. *Magazine Media Factbook* 2013/2014 (New York: Association of Magazine Media, 2013).
13. Ibid.
14. Charles P. Daly, Patrick Henry, and Ellen Ryder, *The Magazine Publishing Industry* (Needham Heights, Mass.: Allyn & Bacon, 1997).
15. Jeff Gremillion, "Tough Times for Trades," *Brandweek*, September 20, 1999.
16. Lisa Granatstein, "The Big Deal," *Media Week*, March 6, 2000.
17. Erik Sass, "B2B Ad Pages Down 30%," Media Post Publications, August 26, 2009, http://www.mediapost.com/publications/article/112238/b2b-ad-pages-down-30.html?print.
18. Pew Research Center Project for Excellence in Journalism, "The State of the News Media 2009: Magazines," March 16, 2009, pewresearch.org/pubs/1151/state-of-the-news-media-2009; Matt Kinsman, "The *Atlantic* Posts Profit for First Time in Years," *Folio*, January 6, 2011, www.foliomag.com/2011/atlantic-posts-profit-first-time-years.
19. Jane Sasseen, Katrina-Eva Matsa, and Amy Mitchell, "News Magazines: Embracing Their Digital Future," *The State of the News Media 2013*, stateofthemedia.org/2013/news-magazines-embracing-their-digital-future/#fn-12972-39.
20. Jeff Gargiliano, "Victor Navasky and the State of the *Nation*," *Folio*, September 1, 1998.
21. Ibid.
22. Pew Research Center Project for Excellence in Journalism, "The State of the News Media 2009: Magazines."
23. Bill Eichenberger, "Early Black Authors Featured in Series," *Columbus Dispatch*, January 27, 1999.
24. Larry Bivins, "NAACP Tries to Revive Once-Weighty Magazine," *Detroit News*, April 13, 1997.
25. James Bock, "Revived *Crisis* to Focus on Wide Range of Ideas Publishing: *The Crisis*, the NAACP's Official Publication Founded by W. E. B. Dubois, Is to Reappear in July, and Readers May Be in for Stimulating Experiences," *The Sun*, May 18, 1997; "Timeline," *The Crisis*, 2012, www.thecrisismagazine.com/timeline.html.
26. Wood, *Magazines in the United States*.
27. Louis Joughin, "Introduction," in *The Shame of the Cities*, Lincoln Steffens (New York: Hill and Wang, 1957).
28. Wood, *Magazines in the United States*.
29. Ibid.
30. Vicki Goldberg, *Margaret Bourke-White* (New York: Harper & Row, 1986).
31. Ibid.
32. Ibid.
33. Ibid.

34. "Paid Circulation in Consumer Magazines for Six Months Ended December 31, 2008," *Advertising Age* Data Center, adage.com/datacenter/datapopup.php?article_id=135166.
35. Emily Steel, "Time Warner Pauses Spin-off Plans," *Financial Times,* August 8, 2013.
36. Wood, *Magazines in the United States*.
37. Ibid.; Patricia Okker, *Our Sister Editors: Sarah J. Hale and the Tradition of Nineteenth-Century American Women Editors* (Athens: University of Georgia Press, 1995).
38. Wood, *Magazines in the United States*.
39. Stuart Elliott, "Stuart Elliott in America," *Campaign*, September 27, 2002.
40. Emma Bazilian, "*Ladies' Home Journal* to Cease Monthly Publication [Updated]," *AdWeek*, April 24, 2014, www.adweek.com/news/press/ladies-home-journal-shuts-down-157233.
41. Paula Span, "Between the Covers: As Their Editors Switch Positions, Women's Magazines Unveil a Familiar Look," *Washington Post*, December 30, 1998.
42. Rita Zekas, "The Perfect Cosmo Girl Editor Bonnie Fuller Has It All—Career, Motherhood," *Toronto Star*, June 8, 1997; Fionnuala McHugh, "Penetrating Asia," *South China Morning Post*, April 27, 1997; "Paid Circulation in Consumer Magazines for Six Months Ended June 30, 2013."
43. Zekas, "The Perfect Cosmo Girl Editor Bonnie Fuller Has It All—Career, Motherhood."
44. McHugh, "Penetrating Asia."
45. Shirley Christian, "But Is It Art? Well, Yes: A Trove of Pinups at the University of Kansas Is Admired by All Sorts, Including Feminists," *New York Times*, November 25, 1998.
46. Bill Steigerwald, "Once-Great *Esquire* Is Paying Price for Too Many Silly Articles," *Milwaukee Journal Sentinel*, July 14, 1997; Antonia Zerbisias, "Shriveled *Esquire* Gets Puffed 'n' Fluffed," *Toronto Star*, June 7, 1997; Alasdair Reid, "Have Men's Titles Stalled or Can They Shift Gear?" *Campaign*, February 14, 2002; *Advertising Age* Data Center, February 12, 2012, adage.com/datacenter/.
47. Wood, *Magazines in the United States*.
48. Michael Quintanilla, "Stylemaker/Hugh Hefner: The King of Swingers Reenters the Singles Scene," *Los Angeles Times*, February 5, 1999.
49. Greg Lindsay, "Rethinking a Great American Magazine," *Folio*, November 2002; Keith L. Alexander, "*Playboy* Boots Publishing Executives as Ad Market Wanes," *USA Today*, December 4, 2000; "Paid Circulation in Consumer Magazines for Six Months Ended December 31, 2008"; "Paid Circulation in Consumer Magazines for Six Months Ended June 30, 2013."
50. Alex Kuczynski, "Seeking More Sizzle, *Details* Magazine Hires *Maxim's* Editor," *New York Times*, February 2, 1999; "Maxim's 'Hot Issue' Is All Wrapped Up," *Toronto Star*, April 24 1999; "Paid Circulation in Consumer Magazines for Six Months Ended June 30, 2013"; "Magazine Ad Page Leaders, 4th Quarter 2013," *Advertising Age* Data Center,adage.com/datacenter/datapopup.php?article_id=291966.
51. Alex Kuczynski, "Media: A Magazine for Your 'Inner Guy,'" *New York Times*, October 19, 1998.
52. Kuczynski, "Seeking More Sizzle, *Details* Magazine Hires *Maxim*'s Editor."
53. David Ward, "Men's Lifestyle Magazines—Thriving Market Captures Attention of Younger Men," *PR Week*, April 1, 2002.
54. Janice Turner, "The Trouble with Boys Is They're Just Too Fickle: Janice Turner on Magazines," *The Observer*, March 4, 2007.
55. Jemima Lewis, "From Loaded Lad to Heteropolitan Man," *The Telegraph*, August 15, 2009.
56. Matthew J. Rosenberg, "Media Talk: Men's Journal Encounters Problems on Mount Rainier," *New York Times*, June 29, 1998.
57. Span, "Between the Covers: As Their Editors Switch Positions, Women's Magazines Unveil a Familiar Look."
58. Lisa de Moraes, "Fighting Words from a Bantamweight," *Washington Post*, July 2, 1999; EilsLotozo, "Getting Real: No Skinny Models in *Grace* Magazine," *Hamilton Spectator*, September 5, 2002.
59. Arlene Vigoda, "Calvin Cuts Ties with Kate," *USA Today*, February 24, 1999; Reuters, "British Model Admits 'Losing Plot' on Drink, Drugs," CNN Interactive, customnews.cnn.com/cnews/pna.show_story?p_art_id=3436180&p _ section_name=world.
60. Karen S. Schneider et al., "Mission Impossible: Deluged by Images from TV, Movies, and Magazines, Teenage Girls Do Battle With an Increasingly Unrealistic Standard of Beauty—and Pay a Price," *People*, June 3, 1996.
61. John Leland, Susan Miller, and Carol Hall, "The Body Impolitic," *Newsweek*, June 17, 1996.
62. NanciHellmich, "Do Thin Models Warp Girls' Body Image?" *USA Today*, September 26, 2006.
63. Stuart Elliott, "For Everyday Products, Ads Using the Everyday Woman," *New York Times*, August 17, 2005; Theresa Howard, "Dove Ads Enlist All Shapes, Styles, Sizes," *USA Today*, August 29, 2005; Rebecca Traister, "Move Over, Dove Ads: Nike's Posteriors and Scraped Knees Bring a Greater Dose of Reality to Marketing," *Chicago Sun-Times*, August 23, 2005.
64. Justin Fenner, "PHOTO: *Vogue Italia's* Gorgeous Plus Size Cover," Styleite, June 2, 2011, www.styleite.com/media/vogue-italia-plus-size-cover-june-2011/; Justin Fenner, "PHOTOS: *Vogue Italia's* Very Naked Plus-Sized Spread," Styleite, June 3, 2011, www.styleite.com/media/vogue-italia-plus-sized-spread-photos/; Julia Rubin, "Plus Size Model Poses With Straight Size Model in Controversial Spread," Styleite, January 11, 2012, www.styleite.com/media/plus-size-magazine-weight-statistics/.
65. Madeline Figueroa-Jones, "Plus Size Bodies, What Is Wrong With Them Anyway?" *PLUS Model Magazine*, January 8, 2012, plus-model-mag.com/2012/01/plus-size-bodies-what-is-wrong-with-them-anyway/.
66. Margaret Wheeler Johnson, "Plus Size Magazine 'Reveals' Low Weight Among Models," *Huffington Post*, January 13, 2012, www.huffingtonpost.com/margaret-wheeler-johnson/plus-size-magazine-models-anorexia_b_1205285.html.
67. Jenna Sauers, "*V* Magazine Can't Put a Plus Size Model in Its Pages Without a Straight Size Model for Comparison," *Jezebel*, December 22, 2009, jezebel.com/5432251/v-magazine-cant-put-a-plus-size-model-in-its-pages-without-a-straight-size-model-for-comparison.
68. Sara Ivry, "Liz Hurley, on the Cover and in the Ads," *New York Times*, August 29, 2005.
69. Jen King, "*W* Magazine March Issue Reevaluates Fashion Coverage With Social Media Input," *Luxury Daily*, March 3, 2014, www.luxurydaily.com/90589/.
70. Amy Mitchell, "State of the News Media 2014—Overview," Pew Research Journalism Project, March 26, 2014, http://www.journalism.org/2014/03/26/state-of-the-news-media-2014-overview/.
71. Katherine Rosman, "Stealth Advertising," *Brill's Content*, September 1998.
72. Eric Wemple, "The *Atlantic*'s Scientology Problem, Start to Finish," *Washington Post*, January 15, 2013, www.washingtonpost.com/blogs/erik-wemple/wp/2013/01/15/the-atlantics-scientology-problem-start-to-finish/.
73. Magazine Publishers Association, "Circulation Trends & Data," http://www.magazine.org/insights-resources/research-publications/trends-data/magazine-industry-facts-data/circulation-trends.
74. Joe Hagan, "Cover Creation 2002," *Folio*, February 2002.

75. Ibid.
76. Kathleen Hays, "Why Aren't Minorities on More Magazine Covers?" in *The Biz* (CNNFN, 2002); David Carr, "On Covers of Many Magazines, a Full Racial Palette Is Still Rare," *New York Times*, November 18, 2002.
77. Lauren Duca, "In Statistical Look at Cover Girls of Color, *Maxim* Is the Least Diverse," *Huffington Post*, August 5, 2013, http://www.huffingtonpost.com/2013/08/05/cover-girl-diversity_n_3696327.html.
78. Sophia Kerby, "The State of Women of Color in the United States," *Center for American Progress*, July 17, 2012, www.americanprogress.org/issues/race/report/2012/07/17/11923/the-state-of-women-of-color-in-the-united-states/.
79. Christina Mendez, "Latino Stars on the Cover of *Sports Illustrated* Swimsuit: 50 Years of Our Beautiful," *Latin Trends*, February 4, 2014, http://www.latintrends.com/latinas-on-the-cover-of-sports-illustrated-swimsuit/; Tracie Egan Morrissey, "The 'Evolution' of Sexy: Every *Sports Illustrated* Swimsuit Cover Ever," *Jezebel*, January 15, 2014, jezebel.com/the-evolution-of-sexy-every-sports-illustrated-swims-1501294755.
80. Hagan, "Cover Creation 2002."
81. John Johanek, "Crafting Covers That Sell," *Folio*, February 2002.
82. Span, "Between the Covers: As Their Editors Switch Positions, Women's Magazines Unveil a Familiar Look."
83. Staff, "The Many 'Whys' for Magazines," *MMR*, April 22, 2002.
84. Leara D. Rhodes, "Magazines," in *Mass Media in 2025: Industries, Organizations, People, and Nations*, ed. Erwin K. Thomas and Brown H. Carpenter (Westport, Conn.: Greenwood Press, 2001).
85. "Tablet Edition FAQs," *New Yorker*, November 16, 2011, www.newyorker.com/magazine/apps/faq.
86. Sasseen, Matsa, and Mitchell, "News Magazines: Embracing Their Digital Future."
87. Matt Kinsman, "Study Says Tablet, E-Reader Users Haven't Given Up Print," June 30, 2011, http://www.foliomag.com/2011/study-says-tablet-e-reader-users-haven-t-given-print.
88. Stefanie Botelho, "All 21 Time Inc. Magazines to Have Tablet Editions by Year-End," *Folio*, August 3, 2011, http://www.foliomag.com/2011/all-21-time-inc-magazines-have-tablet-editions-year-end.
89. Ken Doctor, "The Newsonomics of Apple's/Google's/Press+'s Pay-for-All," February 17, 2011, http://newsonomics.com/the-newsonomics-of-applesgooglespresss-pay-for-all/.
90. Rhodes, "Magazines,"
91. Staff, "Historical Subscriptions/Single Copy Sales."
92. Amy Mitchell, "State of the News Media 2014—Overview."
93. Matt Kinsman and Vanessa Voltolina, "The REAL Niche Publishing: Operating as an Independent Magazine in 2010," *Folio*, January 5, 2010, www.foliomag.com/2009/real-niche-publishing-operating-independent-magazine-2010#.Uzb2sFylnll.
94. Tony Case, "Triumph of the Niche: General-Interest Magazines Are Looking for a Place Among the Growing Number of Targeted Titles," *Media Week*, March 4, 2002.
95. Michael Scherer, "Does Size Matter?" *Columbia Journalism Review*, November 2002.
96. Ibid.
97. Katerina-Eva Matsa, Tom Rosentiel, and Paul Moore, "Magazines: A Shakeout for News Weeklies," The Pew Research Center's Project for Excellence in Journalism, 2011, stateofthemedia.org/2011/magazines-essay/; Tina Brown and Baba Shetty, "Turn of the Page for *Newsweek*," October 18, 2012, http://www.thedailybeast.com/articles/2012/10/18/a-turn-of-the-page-for-newsweek.html; Leslie Kaufman and Noam Cohen, "Newsweek Returns to Print and Sets Off a Bitcoin Storm," *New York Times*, March 7, 2014, www.nytimes.com/2014/03/08/business/media/newsweek-returns-to-print-and-sets-off-a-bitcoin-storm.html.
98. Sasseen, Matsa, and Mitchell, "News Magazines: Embracing Their Digital Future."
99. Jeremy W. Peters, "Web Focus Helps Revitalize the *Atlantic*," *New York Times*, December 12, 2010, www.nytimes.com/2010/12/13/business/media/13atlantic.html?.
100. Ibid.
101. Lauren Indvik, "Inside *The Atlantic*: How One Magazine Got Profitable by Going 'Digital First,'" *Mashable Business*, December 19, 2011, mashable.com/2011/12/19/the-atlantic-digital-first/.

Chapter 6

1. Robert Z. Pearlman, "Jeff Bezos' Salvaged Apollo Rocket Engines Reach Shore After Ocean Recovery," Space.com, March 22, 2013, www.space.com/20358-bezos-apollo-rocket-engines-shore.html.
2. Paul Farhi, "*Washington Post* to Be Sold to Jeff Bezos, the Founder of Amazon," *Washington Post*, August 5, 2013, www.washingtonpost.com/national/washington-post-to-be-sold-to-jeff-bezos/2013/08/05/ca537c9e-fe0c-11e2-9711-3708310f6f4d_story.html.
3. Paul Farhi, "Jeffery Bezos, *Washington Post*'s Next Owner, Aims for a New 'Golden Era' at the Newspaper," *Washington Post*, September 3, 2013, www.washingtonpost.com/lifestyle/style/jeffrey-bezos-washington-posts-next-owner-aims-for-a-new-golden-era-at-the-newspaper/2013/09/02/30c00b60-13f6-11e3-b182-1b3bb2eb474c_story.html.
4. Craig Timberg and Jia Lynn Yang, "The Sale of *The Washington Post*: How the Unthinkable Choice Became the Clear Path," *Washington Post*, August 6, 2013, http://www.washingtonpost.com/business/technology/the-sale-of-the-washington-post-how-the-unthinkable-choice-became-the-clear-path/2013/08/06/46216532-fed7-11e2-9711-3708310f6f4d_story.html.
5. Steven Levy, "Jeff Bezos Owns the Web in More Ways Than You Think," *Wired*, November 13, 2011, http://www.wired.com/2011/11/ff_bezos/all/1.
6. Victor Luckerson, "Jeff Bezos Makes His First Major Move at the *Washington Post*," *Time*, March 19, 2014, time.com/30243/jeff-bezos-makes-his-first-major-move-at-the-washington-post/.
7. Michael Calderone, "*Washington Post* Has Hired 50 Staffers in 2014 Amid Bezos-Funded Expansion," *Huffington Post*, May 12, 2014, www.huffingtonpost.com/2014/05/12/washington-post-bezos-50-staffers_n_5310221.html.
8. Farhi, "Jeffery Bezos, *Washington Post*'s Next Owner, Aims for a New 'Golden Era' at the Newspaper."
9. Brian McNair, *News and Journalism in the UK* (London: Routledge, 1994).
10. Bill Katz, *Dahl's History of the Book*, 3rd English ed. (Metuchen, N.J.: Scarecrow Press, 1995).
11. James D. Hart, *The Popular Book: A History of America's Literary Taste* (New York: Oxford University Press, 1950).
12. Michael Schudson, *Discovering the News* (New York: Basic Books, 1978).

13. Katz, *Dahl's History of the Book*, 218.
14. Hazel Dicken-Garcia, *Journalistic Standards in Nineteenth-Century America* (Madison: University of Wisconsin Press, 1989).
15. Schudson, *Discovering the News.*
16. George H. Douglas, *The Golden Age of the Newspaper* (Westport, Conn.: Greenwood Press, 1999).
17. McNair, *News and Journalism in the UK.*
18. Ibid.
19. Schudson, *Discovering the News.*
20. Dicken-Garcia, *Journalistic Standards in Nineteenth-Century America,* 52.
21. Paul H. Weaver, *News and the Culture of Lying* (New York: Free Press, 1994).
22. George Juergens, *Joseph Pulitzer and the New York World* (Princeton, N.J.: Princeton University Press, 1966).
23. Brooke Kroeger, *Nellie Bly: Daredevil, Reporter, Feminist* (New York: Times Books, 1994).
24. Ibid.
25. David Nasaw, *The Chief* (New York: Houghton Mifflin, 2000).
26. Vicki Goldberg, *Margaret Bourke-White* (New York: Harper & Row, 1986).
27. Karin E. Becker, "Photojournalism and the Tabloid Press," in *Journalism and Popular Culture*, ed. Peter Dahlgren and Colin Sparks (London: Sage Publications, 1992).
28. Jon Fine, "Sunday, Bloody Sunday: A New Turn in the Tab Wars," *Columbia Journalism Review*, March/April 1999.
29. Stacy Jones, "Altered Photo Faux Pas," *Editor & Publisher* 130 (1997).
30. William S. Paley, *As It Happened: A Memoir* (Garden City, N.Y.: Doubleday, 1979).
31. Ben H. Bagdikian, *The New Media Monopoly* (Boston: Beacon Press, 2004).
32. Paley, *As It Happened*.
33. Edward Bliss, *Now the News: The Story of Broadcast Journalism* (New York: Columbia University Press, 1991).
34. Richard Zoglin, "Inside the World of CNN: How a Handful of News Executives Make Decisions Felt Round the World," *Time*, January 6, 1992.
35. Ken Auletta, *Three Blind Mice: How the TV Networks Lost Their Way* (New York: Random House, 1991).
36. Peter Johnson, "Fox News Enjoys New View—From the Top," *USA Today*, April 4, 2002.
37. Brian Lowry, "On Cable News, It's All Shoutmanship," *Los Angeles Times*, March 5, 2003.
38. John Maxwell Hamilton and George A. Krimsky, *Hold the Press: The Inside Story on Newspapers* (Baton Rouge: Louisiana State University Press, 1996); Pew Research Center Project for Excellence in Journalism, "The State of the News Media 2009: Newspapers," http://stateofthemedia.org/2009/newspapers-intro/; Newspaper Association of America, "Newspaper Circulation Volume," December 17, 2011, http://www.naa.org/Trends-and-Numbers/Circulation-Volume/Newspaper-Circulation-Volume.aspx; "Number of Newspapers," Pew Research Journalism Project, March 26, 2014, www.journalism.org/media-indicators/number-of-newspapers/.
39. McNair, *News and Journalism in the UK*.
40. *Hoover's Company Profile Database: Gannett Co. Inc*. (Austin, Texas: Hoover's Inc., 2009).
41. Bagdikian, *The New Media Monopoly*.
42. Pew Research Center Project for Excellence in Journalism, "The State of the News Media 2006," www.stateofthemedia.org/2006.
43. "Advertising Revenue vs. Circulation Revenue," Pew Research Journalism Project, March 26, 2014, www.journalism.org/media-indicators/ad-revenue-vs-circulation-revenue/.
44. Rick Edmonds, Emily Guskin, and Tom Rosenstiel, "The State of the News Media 2011: Newspapers: Missed the 2010 Media Rally," 2011, stateofthemedia.org/2011/newspapers-essay/.
45. Johnnie L. Roberts, "The Paperless Paper," *Newsweek*, October 28, 2008.
46. Sinéad O'Brien, "The Last of the Color Holdouts," *American Journalism Review*, December 1997, 15.
47. Average Circulation at the Top 25 U.S. Daily Newspapers, Alliance for Audited Media, March 2013, www.auditedmedia.com/news/research-and-data/top-25-us-newspapers-for-march-2013.aspx.
48. Pew Research Center Project for Excellence in Journalism, "The State of the News Media 2008: Newspapers," www.stateofthemedia.org/2008.
49. James McCartney, "*USA Today* Grows Up," *American Journalism Review*, September 1997.
50. Average Circulation at the Top 25 U.S. Daily Newspapers, Alliance for Audited Media, March 2013, www.auditedmedia.com/news/research-and-data/top-25-us-newspapers-for-march-2013.aspx.
51. Edmonds, Guskin, and Rosentiel, "Notes From State of the News Media 2011: Newspapers: Missed the 2010 Media Rally."
52. McCartney, "*USA Today* Grows Up."
53. John Morton, "Short Term Losses, Long Term Profits," *American Journalism Review*, September 1997.
54. "Brand," *USA Today*, 2014, www.usatoday.com/about/.
55. Daniel Kadlec and Jyoti Thottam, "Extra! Dynasties Duel!" *Time*, November 4, 2002; *Hoover's Company Profile Database: The New York Times Company* (Austin, Texas: Hoover's Inc., 2014).
56. David D. Kirkpatrick, "*International Herald Tribune* Now Run Solely by the *Times*," *New York Times*, January 2, 2003; Lucia Moses, "'IHT': Ads Playing in Prime Time," *Editor & Publisher*, March 19, 2001.
57. Harriett Marsh, "The Battle for Business," *Ad Age Global*, February 2001.
58. Ibid.
59. "The *New York Times* Global Media Kit," www.nytimesglobal.com/; "*Financial Times*: About Us," aboutus.ft.com/corporate-information/ft-company/; "*Wall Street Journal* Media Kit," http://www.wsjmediakit.com/downloads/General_Rate_Card_2012.pdf.
60. Rob Lenihan, "Marking *Times*'s Color Milestone," *Editor & Publisher* 131, no. 39 (1998).
61. O'Brien, "The Last of the Color Holdouts."
62. *Hoover's Company Profile Database: The New York Times Company* (Austin, Texas: Hoover's Inc., 2014).
63. O'Brien, "The Last of the Color Holdouts."
64. Mario R. Garcia, "Color for a New Millennium," *Editor & Publisher* 131, no. 39 (1998).
65. Ben Bradlee, *A Good Life: Newspapering and Other Adventures* (New York: Simon & Schuster, 1995).
66. Ibid.
67. Ken Adelman, "You Can't Have Secrets," *Washingtonian*, August 1994.
68. Alicia C. Shepard, "Ben Bradlee," *American Journalism Review*, March 1995.
69. Charles Rappleye, "Are New Ideas Killing the *L.A. Times*?" *Columbia Journalism Review*, November/December 1994.
70. Katherine Q. Seelye, "The Newspaper Publisher Who Said No to More Cuts," *New York Times*, September 28, 2006; Pew Research Center Project for Excellence in Journalism, "The State of the News Media 2009: Newspapers";

Julie Moos, "More *LA Times* Newsroom Cuts Loom as Editor Exits," December 14, 2011, www.poynter.org/latest-news/mediawire/156056/more-la-times-news room-cuts-loom-as-editor-exits/.
71. Benjamin Mullin, "Target Date for Tribune Publishing Spinoff Set," Poynter.org, June 24, 2014, www.poynter.org/latest-news/mediawire/256708/target-date-for-tribune-publishing-spinoff-set/.
72. Joseph S. Coyle, "Now, the Editor as Marketer," *Columbia Journalism Review*, July/August 1998, 37–41.
73. John Leo, "Quoting by Quota," *U.S. News & World Report*, June 29, 1998.
74. Ibid.
75. Keith Woods, "The Essence of Excellence," Poynter Online, October 16, 2001, www.poynter.org/content/content_view.asp?id=5048.
76. Peter Schrag, "Is Doing the Right Thing Wrong?" *Columbia Journalism Review*, February 2002.
77. "Community Newspaper Facts & Figures," National Newspaper Association, 2014, nnaweb.org/about-nna?articleCategory=community-facts-figures.
78. Charles Bermant, "Hometown Newspapers Use Web to Strengthen Communities," CNN, August 21, 1998, cnn.com/tech/computing/9808/21/hometown.idg/index.html.
79. James O'Byrne, "Katrina: The Power of the Press Against the Wrath of Nature," August 22, 2006, http://www.poynter.org/uncategorized/76853/katrina-the-power-of-the-press-against-the-wrath-of-nature/.
80. Robert E. Park, "The Natural History of the Newspaper," in *Mass Communications*, ed. Wilbur Schramm (Urbana: University of Illinois Press, 1960).
81. George A. Hough, *News Writing*, 4th ed. (Boston: Houghton Mifflin, 1988).
82. Richard M. Cohen, "The Corporate Takeover of News," in *Conglomerates and the Media*, ed. Eric Barnouw (New York: Free Press, 1997).
83. Ibid.
84. Coyle, "Now, the Editor as Marketer."
85. Pew Research Center Project for Excellence in Journalism, "The State of the News Media 2006."
86. Committee to Protect Journalists, "151 Journalists Killed in Iraq Since 1992/Motive Confirmed," February 20, 2012, www.cpj.org/killed/mideast/iraq/.
87. Committee to Protect Journalists, "In Iraq, Journalist Deaths Spike to Record in 2006," December 20, 2006, cpj.org/reports/2006/12/killed-06.php.
88. Patricia Ward Biederman, "Services to Mark Death of Reporter," *Los Angeles Times*, February 19, 2003.
89. Nancy Gibbs, "Death in the Shadow War," *Time*, March 4, 2002.
90. Jim Lehrer, "Mariane Pearl," in *NewsHour with Jim Lehrer* (PBS, 2002).
91. Maya Taal, "CPJ Risk List: Where Press Freedom Suffered," Committee to Protect Journalists, 2014, cpj.org/2014/02/attacks-on-the-press-cpj-risk-list-1.php; "70 Journalists Killed in 2013/Motive Confirmed," Committee to Protect Journalists, 2014, cpj.org/killed/2013/; Mike Brunker, "Richard Engel and NBC News Team Freed From Captors in Syria," NBC News, December 18, 2014, worldnews.nbcnews.com/_news/2012/12/18/15985279-richard-engel-and-nbc-news-team-freed-from-captors-in-syria?lite.
92. Terry Anderson, "He Took a Risk in Pursuit of the Truth," *Los Angeles Times*, February 24, 2002.
93. Charles A. Simmons, *The African American Press* (Jefferson, N.C.: McFarland, 1998).
94. Ibid.
95. Roland E. Wolseley, *The Black Press, U.S.A.*, 2nd ed. (Ames: Iowa State University Press, 1990).
96. Simmons, *The African American Press*.
97. Wolseley, *The Black Press, U.S.A.*
98. Jessica Madore Fitch, "Four Companies Vying for Chicago Defender," *Chicago Sun-Times*, May 1, 2000; Jim Romenesko, "Chicago Defender Lays Off Top Editors, Falls Months Behind on Rent," October 24, 2011, www.poynter.org/latest-news/mediawire/150742/chica go-defender-lays-off-top-editors-falls-months-behind-in-rent/.
99. Wolseley, *The Black Press, U.S.A.*
100. Pew Research Center Project for Excellence in Journalism, "The State of the News Media 2006."
101. Brooke Gladstone, "Tale of Two *Heralds*," NPR, October 6, 2006, www.onthemedia.org/transcripts/2006/10/06/04.
102. Eytan Avriel, "*NY Times* Publisher: Our Goal Is to Manage the Transition From Print to Internet," *Haaretz*, February 8, 2007.
103. "Future Forum," *Advertising Age*, September 20, 1999.
104. Michael Meyer, "Brick by Brick," *Columbia Journalism Review*, June 26, 2014, www.cjr.org/cover_story/washington_post_jeff_bezos.php?page=all.
105. Diana McLellan, "Out in Front," *Washingtonian*, March 1998, 31–35.
106. Richard Pérez-Peña, "*Washington Blade* Newspaper Closes," *New York Times*, November 17, 2009; Erik Sass, "So Over: Window Media Closes," November 16, 2009, http://www.mediapost.com/publications/article/117466/so-over-window-media-closes.html?edition=.
107. "About," *Washington Blade*, 2012, www.washingtonblade.com/contact-us/about/.
108. Pérez-Peña, "*Washington Blade* Newspaper Closes."
109. Tony Case, "Gay Papers Tangle in N.Y.," *Editor & Publisher*, November 8, 1997.
110. Kevin McAuliffe, "No Longer Just Sex, Drugs, and Rock 'n' Roll," *Columbia Journalism Review*, March/April 1999, 40–44.
111. Pew Research Center Project for Excellence in Journalism, "The State of the News Media 2006."
112. Lucia Moses, "Consider the Alternatives: Move to Mainstream Ownership a Sign of the Times," *Editor & Publisher* 132, no. 22 (1999).
113. Howard Kurtz, "The *Village Voice*'s No-Alternative News: Corporate Takeover," *Washington Post,* October 24, 2005, C1.
114. Edmonds, Guskin, and Rosentiel, "Notes From State of the News Media 2011—Newspapers: Missed the 2010 Media Rally," 2011, stateofthemedia.org/2011/newspapers-essay/.
115. Peter Benjaminson, *Death in the Afternoon* (Kansas City, Mo.: Andrews, McMeel & Parker, 1984).
116. Pew Research Center Project for Excellence in Journalism, "The State of the News Media 2006."
117. Roberts, "The Paperless Paper."
119. David Lieberman, "Newspaper Closings Raise Fears About Industry," *USA Today*, March 19, 2009.
119. Agence France-Presse, "Gannett Cuts Staff, *Christian Science Monitor* Drops Print Edition," October 28, 2008, http://www.thefreelibrary.com/Gannett+cuts+staff,+Christian+Science+Monitor+drops+print+edition-a01611685648.

Chapter 7

1. This vignette on Gregg Gillis is based on work originally published on my blog. Ralph Hanson, "Meet Girl Talk's Gregg Gillis," May 24, 2011, www.ralphehanson.com/2011/05/24/meet-girl-talks-gregg-gillis/.

2. Bill Werde, "Defiant Downloads Rise From Underground," *New York Times*, February 25, 2004, www.nytimes.com/2004/02/25/arts/music/25REMI.html.
3. Jamie York, "They Say That I Stole This: Transcript," October 23, 2009, www.onthemedia.org/2009/oct/23/they-say-that-i-stole-this/transcript/.
4. Scott Thill, "Girl Talk's Gregg Gillis Lets It *RiP* on Copyfight, Tour Vlogging," *Wired*, January 8, 2009, www.wired.com/underwire/2009/01/shifting-mass-a/.
5. Will Hodgkinson, "Killing Us Softly With Her Song; Will Hodgkinson Can See Why Dido Has Become a Gentle Voice of Syrian Rebellion," *The Times* (London), March 1, 2013,T28.
6. Angela Watercutter, "*Girl Walk //All Day* Turns Girl Talk Album Into Infectious Dance Marathon," March 9, 2012.
7. Neil Baldwin, *Edison: Inventing the Century* (New York: Hyperion, 1995).
8. Roland Gelatt, *The Fabulous Phonograph* (Philadelphia: L. B. Lippincott, 1955).
9. Baldwin, *Edison: Inventing the Century*.
10. Gelatt, *The Fabulous Phonograph*.
11. Ibid.
12. Charles Hamm, "The Phonograph as Time-Machine" (paper presented at *The Phonograph and Our Musical Life*, Brooklyn College, New York, 1980).
13. Isaac Asimov, *Isaac Asimov's Biographical Encyclopedia of Science and Technology*, rev. ed. (New York: Avon Books, 1972).
14. Ibid.; Kenneth Bilby, *The General: David Sarnoff and the Rise of the Communications Industry* (New York: Harper & Row, 1986).
15. Bilby, *The General*.
16. Ibid.
17. Ibid.
18. Ibid.
19. Burton Paulu, *Television and Radio in the United Kingdom* (Minneapolis: University of Minnesota Press, 1981).
20. Ibid.
21. Lewis J. Paper, *Empire: William S. Paley and the Making of CBS* (New York: St. Martin's Press, 1987).
22. Muriel G. Cantor and Suzanne Pingree, *The Soap Opera*, ed. F. Gerald Kline, The Sage Commtext Series (Beverly Hills, Calif.: Sage, 1983).
23. Ibid.
24. Geoffrey Wheatcroft and Stephen Sandy, "Who Needs the BBC?" *Atlantic Monthly*, March 2001, 53.
25. Mike McGeever, "Commercial Radio Moves Ahead of BBC," *Billboard*, June 7, 1997, 83.
26. "Africa's Dramas Played Out on the Beeb," *Economist*, January 16, 1999, 44.
27. Kim Campbell, "On Media," *Christian Science Monitor*, June 14, 2001, 14.
28. Bob Garfield, "BBC Arabesque," National Public Radio, November 4, 2005, http://www.onthemedia.org/story/129012-bbc-arabesque/transcript/.
29. Julius Lester, "Foreword," in *Playing the FM Band: A Personal Account of the Free Radio*, Steve Post (New York: Viking Press, 1974).
30. James Miller, *Flowers in the Dustbin: The Rise of Rock and Roll, 1947–1977* (New York: Simon & Schuster, 1999).
31. "The Walkman Man," *People Weekly*, October 18, 1999, 132.
32. RiShawn Biddle, "Personal Soundtracks," *Reason*, October 1999, 58–59.
33. Ibid.
34. Ibid.
35. Ronald Byrnside, "The Formation of a Musical Style: Early Rock," in *Contemporary Music and Music Cultures*, ed. Charles Hamm, Bruno Nettl, and Ronald Byrnside (Englewood Cliffs, N.J.: Prentice-Hall, 1975).
36. Miller, *Flowers in the Dustbin*.
37. Gerald Early, *One Nation Under a Groove: Motown and American Culture* (Hopewell, N.J.: Ecco Press, 1995).
38. Miller, *Flowers in the Dustbin*.
39. Ibid.
40. Byrnside, "The Formation of a Musical Style: Early Rock."
41. Miller, *Flowers in the Dustbin*.
42. Ibid.
43. Ibid.
44. Ibid.
45. Ibid.
46. Early, *One Nation Under a Groove*.
47. Ibid.
48. Allan F. Moore, *The Beatles: Sgt. Pepper's Lonely Hearts Club Band* (Cambridge, U.K.: Cambridge University Press, 1997); Patricia Romanowski, Holly George-Warren, and Jon Pareles, eds., *The New Rolling Stone Encyclopedia of Rock & Roll*, completely revised and updated ed. (New York: Rolling Stone Press, 1995).
49. Moore, *The Beatles: Sgt. Pepper's Lonely Hearts Club Band*.
50. Early, *One Nation Under a Groove*.
51. Miller, *Flowers in the Dustbin*.
52. Jon Wilde and David Edwards, "McCartney: I Have Tried Heroin," *Mirror*, June 2, 2004.
53. Moore, *The Beatles: Sgt. Pepper's Lonely Hearts Club Band*.
54. Christopher John Farley, "A Hitmaker and a Gentleman," *Time*, November 11, 1996, 90; "New Babyface/David E. Talbert Musical Set Premiering at Beacon Theater," PR Newswire, May 31, 2001.
55. Romanowski et al., *The New Rolling Stone Encyclopedia of Rock & Roll*.
56. Ibid.
57. Mickey Hess, ed., *Hip Hop in America: A Regional Guide* (New York: Greenwood Press, 2010), viii.
58. Hess, xi.
59. Brian Longhurst, *Popular Music and Society* (Cambridge, U.K.: Polity Press, 1995).
60. Marina Terkourafi, *Language of Global Hip Hop* (London: Continuum International Publishing: 2010).
61. Bob Garfield, "North Africa's Hip Hop Protest Music," *On The Media,* February 11, 2011, www.onthemedia.org/story/133076-north-africas-hip-hop-protest-music/transcript/.
62. Bruce Feiler, "Gone Country," *New Republic*, February 5, 1996, 19–20.
63. Bobby Reed, "'Murder' Numbers; Country Radio Makes a Killing—Is It Killing Country?"*Chicago Sun-Times*, October 8, 2000.
64. Wade Jessen and Gary Trust, "Top 25 Country Artists (1985– 2011)," *Billboard*, www.billboard.com/features/top-25-country-artists-1985-2011-1004095821.story#/features/top-25-country-artists-1985-2010-1004095821.story.
65. Feiler, "Gone Country."
66. Ibid.
67. Brian Longhurst, *Popular Music and Society* (Cambridge, U.K.: Polity Press, 1995).
68. Ken Auletta, *The Highwaymen* (San Diego: Harcourt Brace, 1998).
69. Richard Crawford, "Introduction: The Phonograph and the Scholar" (paper presented at *The Phonograph and Our Musical Life*, Brooklyn College, New York, 1980).
70. Chris Bonastia, "Sucking in the '70s," *New Republic*, January 30, 1995, 11–12.
71. Gelatt, *The Fabulous Phonograph*.
72. Stephanie McKay, "Vinyl Records Get Their Groove Back; Record Store Day Celebrates Format's Return," *Edmonton Journal (Alberta)*, April 20, 2013, D10.
73. Ken C. Pohlmann, "The Last Compact Disc," *Stereo Review*, May 1996.

74. "Katrina's Web," http://www.katrinasweb.com.
75. Jodi Mardesich, "How the Internet Hits Big Music," *Fortune*, May 10, 1999, 96–98.
76. Ted Bridis, "Sony to Suspend Making Antipiracy CDs," *Washington Post*, November 11, 2005.
77. Electronic Frontier Foundation, "*RIAA v. The People*: Two Years Later" (San Francisco: Electronic Frontier Foundation, 2005).
78. Arbitron, "Radio Today 2013: How America Listens to Radio" (Arbitron, 2013).
79. Emily Guskin and Amy Mitchell, "The State of the News Media 2011—Hispanic Media: Faring Better Than the Mainstream Media," March 2012, stateofthemedia.org/2011/hispanic-media-fairing-better-than-the-mainstream-media/.
80. Arbitron, "Hispanic Radio Today," 2011 edition (Arbitron, 2011).
81. Della de Lafuente, "Look Who's Talking: Putting a Face on Hispanic Radio," *Adweek*, September 17, 2007.
82. Walt Albro, "Spanish-Language Ads Sell Comfort," *Bank Marketing*, August 1999.
83. Richard Corliss, "Look Who's Talking," *Time,* January 23, 1995, 22–25.
84. Jennifer Harper, "Big Radio Companies Struggle to Sustain Volume amid Losses," *Washington Times*, March 4, 2009.
85. Judy Rene Sims, "Talk, Talk, Talk: Opinion or Fact?" *Journalism History* 22 (Winter 1997): 173.
86. Corliss, "Look Who's Talking."
87. Brian Stelter, "For Conservative Radio, It's a New Dawn, Too," *New York Times*, December 22, 2008.
88. Kenny Olmstead, Amy Mitchell, and Tom Rosenstiel, "The State of the News Media 2011: Audio: Medium on the Brink of Major Change," March 2012, stateofthemedia.org/2011/audio-essay/.
89. Jonathan Foreman, "Howard's End?" *National Review*, April 7, 1997, 53–54; Jacqui Goddard, "Shock Jocks' Sick Jokes Slay Listeners," *Scotland on Sunday*, November 17, 2002, 26.
90. Paul Farhi, "No Rush to Measure Limbaugh's Ratings," *Los Angeles Times*, March 9, 2009.
91. Jeff Borden, "ESPN Radio Shoots to Rack Up the Score," *Crain's Chicago Business*, September 21, 1998, 1.
92. Joseph P. Kahn, "Macho in the Morning: 'Guy Talk,'" *Boston Globe*, September 7, 1999, A1.
93. Ibid.
94. Nina Huntemann, "Corporate Interference: The Commercialization and Concentration of Radio Post the 1996 Telecommunications Act," *Journal of Communication Inquiry* 23, no. 4 (1999): 390–407.
95. Roy Bragg, "Clear Channel: Owning the Waves," *San Antonio Express-News*, February 4, 2003, 1; Kenneth Creech, *Electronic Media Law and Regulation*, 3rd ed. (Boston: Focal Press, 2000).
96. "House Members Call on FCC Inspector General to Investigate Hidden Studies on Media Consolidation," *US Fed News*, September 21, 2006.
97. L. A. Lorek, "FCC Review Could Clip Clear Channel; Commission Might Limit Ownership of Radio Stations," *San Antonio Express-News*, May 17, 2003, 1.
98. *Hoover's Company Records—In-Depth Records: Clear Channel Communications Inc.* (Austin, Texas: Hoover's Inc., 2014).
99. Seth Fiegerman, "End of an Era: Clear Channel Rebrands as iHeartMedia,"*Mashable*, September 16, 2014, mashable.com/2014/09/16/clear-channel-iheartmedia/.
100. Jeff Smith, "*Radio* Automation," *Radio*, May 1, 2006, 22.
101. Linda Werthheimer, ed., *Listening to America: Twenty-Five Years in the Life of a Nation, as Heard on National Public Radio* (Boston: Houghton Mifflin, 1995).
102. William Buzenberg, "The National Public Radio Idea," *Nieman Reports* 51, no. 2 (1997): 32.
103. Pew Research Journalism Project, "NPR Listenership," 2014, www.journalism.org/media-indicators/average-monthly-unique-visitors-to-npr-org/; NPR, "NPR Stations and Public Media," 2014, www.npr.org/about-npr/178640915/npr-stations-and-public-media.
104. Laura Houston Santhanam, Amy Mitchell, and Tom Rosentiel, "The State of the News Media 2012—Audio: How Far Will Digital Go?" March 2012, stateofthemedia.org/2012/audio-how-far-will-digital-go/.
105. Pew Research Center Project for Excellence in Journalism, "The State of the News Media 2009: Audio."
106. Olmstead, Mitchell, and Rosentiel, "The State of the News Media 2011—Audio: Medium on the Brink of Major Change."
107. Ben Mook, "Two-Year Plan to Balance NPR's Budget Includes Staff Reduction," Current.org, September 27, 2013, www.current.org/2013/09/two-year-plan-to-balance-nprs-budget-includes-staff-reduction/.
108. Buzenberg, "The National Public Radio Idea"; NPR, "Support and Sponsor," 2014, http://www.npr.org/about/support/; Santhanam, Mitchell, and Rosentiel, "The State of the News Media 2012—Audio: How Far Will Digital Go?"
109. Santhanam, Mitchell, and Rosentiel, "The State of the News Media 2012—Audio: How Far Will Digital Go?"; Pew Research Journalism Project, "News Media Indicators Database: Average Monthly Visitors to NPR.org," 2014, www.journalism.org/media-indicators/average-monthly-unique-visitors-to-npr-org/.
110. Catherine Apple Olson, "'Mountain Stage' Brings Roots to Radio," *Billboard*, November 2, 1996, 14.
111. Ibid.
112. John Merli, "AM Holds Its Own in '98: Talk, Personalities to the Rescue," *Broadcasting & Cable*, August 24, 1998, 46.
113. Santhanam, Mitchell, and Rosentiel, "The State of the News Media 2012—Audio: How Far Will Digital Go?"
114. Ibid.
115. Ibid.; *Hoover's Company Records—In-Depth Records: Sirius XM Radio Inc.* (Austin, Texas: Hoover's Inc., 2014).
116. Cecilia Kang, "Liberty Extends $530 Million Loan to Bail Out Sirius XM," *Washington Post*, February 18, 2009; *Hoover's Company Records—In-Depth Records: Liberty Media Corporation* (Austin, Texas: Hoover's Inc., 2012).
117. Ana Marie Cox, "Howard Stern and the Satellite Wars," *Wired*, March 2005.
118. Jacques Steinberg, "Stern Likes His New Censor: Himself," *New York Times*, January 9, 2007, E1.
119. Leonard Wiener, "Radio's Next Wave: 9 Kinds of Latin Music," *U.S. News & World Report*, August 2, 1999, 70.
120. Pew Research Center Project for Excellence in Journalism, "The State of the News Media 2009: Audio."
121. The Infinite Dial 2014: Navigating Digital Platforms" (Triton Digital, Edison Research, 2014), www.edisonresearch.com/home/archives/2014/03/the-infinite-dial-2014.php.
122. Ibid.
123. Byron Acohido, "Radio to the MP3 Degree: Podcasting," *USA Today*, February 9, 2005; Marco R. della Cava, "Podcasting: It's All Over the Dial," *USA Today*, February 9, 2005; Erika Gonzalez, "Podcast Power: Diversity of Free Audio Programs Expands as Technology Catches On," *Rocky Mountain News*, September 23, 2005, 26D.
124. Benny Evangelista, "Jobs Announces iTunes Will Accommodate Podcasts," *San Francisco Chronicle*, May 23, 2005.
125. "The Infinite Dial 2011: Navigating Digital Platforms."
126. Ralph Hanson, interview, January 21, 2007.
127. Ibid.
128. Ibid.

129. Kevin Maney, "If Pirating Grows, It May Not Be the End of Music World," *USA Today*, May 3, 2005.
130. Ibid.
131. Jefferson Graham, "Summer Tours Help Bands Pay Bills," *USA Today*, August 5, 2004.
132. Mike Masnick, "The Future of Music Business Models (and Those Who Are Already There)," TechDirt.com, January 25, 2010, www.techdirt.com/articles/20091119/1634117011/future-music-business-models-those-who-are-already-there.shtml.
133. Mark Glaser, "Music Industry Losing Control Over Album Sales," PBS–Media Shift, January 22, 2007, www.pbs.org/mediashift/2007/01/digital_disruptionmusic_indust.html.

Chapter 8

1. Kenneth Turan, "Review: 'Gravity' Has Powerful Pull Thanks to Sandra Bullock, 3-D," *Lost Angeles Times,* October 3, 2013, www.latimes.com/entertainment/movies/moviesnow/la-et-mn-gravity-movie-review-20131004-story.html#page=1.
2. Dan P. Lee, "The Camera's Cusp: Alfonso Cuaron Takes Filmmaking to a New Extreme With *Gravity,*" *Vulture*, September 22, 2013, www.vulture.com/2013/09/director-alfonso-cuaron-on-making-gravity.html.
3. Ibid.
4. David Salazar, "Exclusive: 'Gravity' Co-Writer Jonas Cuaron Discusses Collaborating With Father Alfonso, Failed Project & 'Desierto'," *Latino Post*, October 7, 2013, http://www.latinospost.com/articles/29211/20131007/exclusive-gravity-co-writer-jonas-cuaron-discusses-collaborating-father-alfonso.htm.
5. Eric Eisenberg, "To 3D or Not to 3D: Buy the Right Gravity Ticket," *CinemaBlend*, n.d., http://www.cinemablend.com/new/3D-Or-3D-Buy-Right-Gravity-Ticket-39663.html.
6. Brent Lang, "George Clooney: 'Gravity' Is an Argument for 3D," The Wrap, October 2, 2013, www.thewrap.com/george-clooney-gravity-is-an-argument-for-3d/.
7. Frazier Tharpe, "Alfonso Cuaron Calls Most 3D Movies 'Crap,' While 'Gravity' Racks Up Rave Reviews for 3D Experience," *Complex*, September 28, 2013, www.complex.com/pop-culture/2013/09/alfonso-cuaron-calls-most-3d-movies-crap.
8. Kenneth Turan, "Review: 'Gravity' Has Powerful Pull Thanks to Sandra Bullock, 3-D," *Los Angeles Times,* www.latimes.com/entertainment/movies/moviesnow/la-et-mn-gravity-movie-review-20131004-story.html#page=1.
9. Brad Bird's Tweets were sent out from @BradBirdA113 in early October 2013. They are curated at "Director Brad Bird Tweets on Gravity," October 11, 2013, www.ralphehanson.com/2013/10/11/director-brad-bird-tweets-on-gravity/.
10. Neil Baldwin, *Edison: Inventing the Century* (New York: Hyperion, 1995).
11. Eadweard Muybridge, "The Attitudes of Animals in Motion (1882)," in *The Movies in Our Midst: Documents in the Cultural History of Film in America*, ed. Gerald Mast (Chicago: University of Chicago Press, 1982).
12. Gerald Mast and Bruce F. Kawin, *A Brief History of the Movies*, 6th ed. (Needham Heights, Mass.: Allyn & Bacon, 1996); John Fell, *A History of Films* (New York: Holt, Rinehart and Winston, 1979).
13. Mast and Kawin, *A Brief History of the Movies*.
14. National Association for the Advancement of Colored People Boston Branch, "Fighting a Vicious Film: Protest Against 'The Birth of a Nation,'" in *The Movies in Our Midst: Documents in the Cultural History of Film in America,* ed. Gerald Mast (Chicago: University of Chicago Press, 1982).
15. Mast and Kawin, *A Brief History of the Movies*.
16. Linda Arvidson Griffith, "When the Movies Were Young (1925)," in *The Movies in Our Midst: Documents in the Cultural History of Film in America*, ed. Gerald Mast (Chicago: University of Chicago Press, 1982).
17. Gerald Mast, "Introduction," in *The Movies in Our Midst: Documents in the Cultural History of Film in America,* ed. Gerald Mast (Chicago: University of Chicago Press, 1982).
18. Mast and Kawin, *A Brief History of the Movies*; Fortune Magazine Staff, "Loew's Inc. (1939)," in *The Movies in Our Midst: Documents in the Cultural History of Film in America,* ed. Gerald Mast (Chicago: University of Chicago Press, 1982); New York Center for Visual History, *American Cinema: The Studio System* (Burlington, Vt.: Annenberg/CBP, 1994), videotape.
19. Steven Bach, *Final Cut: Dreams and Disaster in the Making of "Heaven's Gate"* (New York: William Morrow, 1985).
20. Mast, "Introduction."
21. Fitzhugh Green, "A Soldier Falls," in *The Movies in Our Midst: Documents in the Cultural History of Film in America*, ed. Gerald Mast (Chicago: University of Chicago Press, 1982).
22. Douglas Gomery, "Warner Bros. Innovates Sound: A Business History," in *The Movies in Our Midst: Documents in the Cultural History of Film in America*, ed. Gerald Mast (Chicago: University of Chicago Press, 1982).
23. Harry Geduld, "The Voice of the Vitaphone (1975)," in *The Movies in Our Midst: Documents in the Cultural History of Film in America*, ed. Gerald Mast (Chicago: University of Chicago Press, 1982).
24. Ralph L. Henry, "The Cultural Influence of the 'Talkies'," in *The Movies in Our Midst: Documents in the Cultural History of Film in America*, ed. Gerald Mast (Chicago: University of Chicago Press, 1982).
25. Gilbert Seldes, "Talkies' Progress (1929)," in *The Movies in Our Midst: Documents in the Cultural History of Film in America*, ed. Gerald Mast (Chicago: University of Chicago Press, 1982).
26. *United States v. Paramount Pictures, Inc.*, 334 U.S. 131 (1948).
27. Mast, "Introduction"; Michael Conant, "The Paramount Case and Its Legal Background (1961)," in *The Movies in Our Midst: Documents in the Cultural History of Film in America*, ed. Gerald Mast (Chicago: University of Chicago Press, 1982).
28. House Un-American Activities Committee, "Hearings Regarding the Communist Infiltration of the Motion-Picture-Industry Activities in the United States (1947)," in *The Movies in Our Midst: Documents in the Cultural History of Film in America*, ed. Gerald Mast (Chicago: University of Chicago Press, 1982).
29. Gordon Kahn, "Hollywood on Trial (1948)," in *The Movies in Our Midst: Documents in the Cultural History of Film in America*, ed. Gerald Mast (Chicago: University of Chicago Press, 1982).
30. John Cogley, "Report on Blacklisting," in *The Movies in Our Midst: Documents in the Cultural History of Film in America*, ed. Gerald Mast (Chicago: University of Chicago Press, 1982).
31. Leonard Maltin, ed., *Leonard Maltin's Movie and Video Guide*, 1997 ed. (New York: Signet, 2006).
32. Mast and Kawin, *A Brief History of the Movies*.
33. Daniel Engber, "Will the 3-D Revival Go the Way of Pixar's *Up?*" *Slate*, June 2, 2009, www.slate.com/blogs/blogs/browbeat/archive/2009/06/02/will-the-3d-reviv al-go-the-way-of-pixar-s-up.aspx.

34. Fortune Magazine Staff, "Color and Sound on Film (1930)," in *The Movies in Our Midst: Documents in the Cultural History of Film in America*, ed. Gerald Mast (Chicago: University of Chicago Press, 1982).
35. Garth Jowett, *Movies as Mass Communication*, 2nd ed., vol. 4, The Sage Commtext Series (Newbury Park, Calif.: Sage, 1989).
36. National Association of Theater Owners, "Number of U.S. Movie Screens," www.natoonline.org/statisticsscreens.htm; Elwin Green, "Big Screen Boom Goes Bust; Rash of Theater Closings Raises the Question: What to Do With an Empty Multiplex," *Pittsburgh Post-Gazette*, August 4, 2005, C1.
37. Thomas Schatz, "The Return of the Hollywood Studio System," in *Conglomerates and the Media*, ed. Eric Barnouw (New York: The New Press, 1997).
38. Mast and Kawin, *A Brief History of the Movies*.
39. Brooks Barnes, "Universal Lifts the Veil on a Harry Potter Park," *New York Times*, September 15, 2009, www.nytimes.com/2009/09/16/business/media/16harry.html; Ben Fritz, "Universal Studios Unveils Harry Potter Attraction Plans for L.A.," *Los Angeles Times*, December 7, 2011, articles.latimes.com/2011/dec/07/business/la-fi-ct-potter-park-20111207; Karla Cripps, "Universal Studios Japan's 'Wizarding World of Harry Potter' Opens," *CNN Travel*, July 16, 2014, www.cnn.com/2014/07/16/travel/universal-studios-japan-harry-potter/.
40. "Harry Potter and the Deathly Hallows: Total Lifetime Grosses," *Box Office Mojo*, March 24, 2012, www.boxofficemojo.com/movies/?id=harrypotter72.htm.
41. Leonard Klady, "Tara Torpedoes *Titanic* as the Real B.O. Champ," *Variety*, March 2–8, 1998.
42. Arthur Asa Berger, *Media Analysis Techniques*, 3rd ed. (Thousand Oaks, Calif.: Sage, 2005).
43. Carol Cling, "Room With a View: Audiences Paying for IMAX Experience of Summer Blockbusters," *Las Vegas Review-Journal*, July 17, 2009; Scott Mendelson, "'Gravity' Passes $100M in IMAX," *Forbes*, February 7, 2014, http://www.forbes.com/sites/scottmendelson/2014/02/07/gravity-passes-100m-worldwide-in-imax/2/.
44. Jowett, *Movies as Mass Communication*.
45. MPAA, "Theatrical Market Statistics 2013," March 25, 2014, www.mpaa.org/wp-content/uploads/2014/03/MPAA-Theatrical-Market-Statistics-2013_032514-v2.pdf.
46. Paul Bond, "This Just In: Americans Love DVRs and Streaming Movies Online," *Hollywood Reporter*, January 3, 2012, www.hollywoodreporter.com/news/just-americans-love-dvrs-streaming-277695.
47. Nielsen, "Spoiler Alert: Mobile Moviegoers are the Biggest Movie Enthusiasts," February 12, 2013, www.nielsen.com/us/en/insights/news/2013/spoiler-alert-mobile-moviegoers-are-the-biggest-movie-enthusiasts.html.
48. Maria Bartiromo, "Bartiromo: IMAX CEO Gelfond Has Global Outlook," *USA Today*, July 22, 2014, www.usatoday.com/story/money/columnist/bartiromo/2014/07/21/movies-bartiromo-imax-gelfond/12821501/.
49. J. W. Elphinstone, "Watercooler: DVDs' Popularity Passes VCRs', New Year's Resolutions, Bad Publicity," Associated Press Financial Wire.
50. Dan Frost, "Consumers Changing DVD Buying Habits," *San Francisco Chronicle*, September 5, 2005, E1.
51. Ben Fritz, "Internet to Surpass DVD in Movie Consumption, Not Revenue," *Los Angeles Times*, March 23, 2012, latimesblogs.latimes.com/entertainmentnewsbuzz/2012/03/internet-to-surpass-dvd-in-movie-consumption-not-revenue.html.
52. Scott Bowles, "'Sky Captain' Takes CGI to Limit," *USA Today*, September 14, 2004.
53. William Booth, "The Cyberspace Moviemaker," *Washington Post*, September 15, 2004.
54. Larry Carroll, "Reaching for the Sky," FilmStew.com, January 30, 2004, www.filmstew.com/showArticle.aspx?ContentID=7827.
55. "*Sky Captain and the World of Tomorrow*," *Box Office Mojo*, http://boxofficemojo.com/movies/?id=skycaptain.htm.
56. Duane Dudek, "'Captain' Director May Have Reinvented the Wheel," *Pittsburgh Post-Gazette*, September 17, 2004.
57. "*300*," *Box Office Mojo*, http://boxofficemojo.com/movies/?id=300.htm.
58. Brandon Gray, "Hordes Drive *300* to Record," *Box Office Mojo*, March 12, 2007, http://boxofficemojo.com/news/?id=2268&p=.htm.
59. Archie Thomas, "Half of Screens to Be Digital by 2013," *Variety*, November 12, 2007, www.variety.com/article/VR1117975781.html?categoryid=13&cs=1&nid=2564.
60. Kendrick Macdowell, "Reflections on the Kind of Exhibition Industry That Best Serves Movie Patrons, Makers, and Exhibitors in the Digital Era," http://www.cbgpurchasing.com/PDF/CBG-NATO%20Digital%20for%20Independents%20Essay-Jan-Apr%202009.pdf; MKPE Consulting, "Digital Cinema Technology Frequently Asked Questions (FAQs)," http://mkpe.com/digital_cinema/faqs/tech_faqs.php.
61. Richard Verrier, "End of Film: Paramount First Studio to Stop Distributing Film Prints," *Los Angeles Times*, January 17, 2014, touch.latimes.com/#section/-1/article/p2p-78938624/; Richard Verrier, "Paramount Pictures to Make Some Exceptions to All-Digital Policy," *Los Angeles Times*, January 28, 2014, touch.latimes.com/#section/-1/article/p2p-79073638/.
62. Dade Hayes, "Bombs Away: Biz Disavows Duds," *Variety*, March 20–26, 2000, 7–8.
63. "*Inception*," *Box Office Mojo*, www.boxofficemojo.com/movies/?id=inception.htm.
64. "*The Hunger Games*," *Box Office Mojo*, www.boxofficemojo.com/movies/?id=hungergames.htm.
65. "*John Carter*," *Box Office Mojo*, July 22, 2014, www.boxofficemojo.com/movies/?id=johncarterofmars.htm; Adam B. Vary, "Taylor Kitsch: 'I Would Do "John Carter" Again Tomorrow,'" March 25, 2012, insidemovies.ew.com/2012/03/25/taylor-kitsch-on-john-carter-box-office/.
66. "The Lone Ranger," *Box Office Mojo*, July 22, 2014, www.boxofficemojo.com/movies/?id=loneranger.htm.
67. Ray Subers, "Weekend Report: 'Stars' Align for 'Fault,' Cruise Misses with 'Edge,' *Box Office Mojo*, June 8, 2014, www.boxofficemojo.com/news/?id=3855&p=.htm; "The Fault in Our Stars," *Box Office Mojo*, July 22, 2014, www.boxofficemojo.com/movies/?id=faultinourstars.htm.
68. "*Fireproof*," *Box Office Mojo*, http://boxofficemojo.com/movies/?id=fireproof.htm.
69. Susan Wloszczyna, "What Makes a Film a Phenom?" *USA Today*, May 12, 2006.
70. "*Garden State*," *Box Office Mojo*, http://boxofficemojo.com/movies/?id=gardenstate.htm.
71. Glenn Kenny, "Martin Scorsese and Spike Lee," *Premiere*, October 1999, 74–77.
72. Glenn Kenny, "The Movies That Changed America," *Premiere*, December 1999, 86.
73. Mast, "Introduction."
74. Jowett, *Movies as Mass Communication*.
75. Barbara Mikkelson and David Mikkelson, "The Shirt off His Back," www.snopes.com/movies/actors/gable.htm.
76. Shearon A. Lowery and Melvin L. DeFleur, *Milestones in Mass Communication*, 3rd ed. (White Plains, N.Y.: Longman, 1995).
77. "*Slumdog Millionaire*," Box Office Mojo, boxofficemojo.com/movies/?id=slumdogmillionaire.htm.

78. Victoria Young, "Bolly Good Show," *Sun Herald*, June 30, 2002, 1.
79. Rama Lakshmi, "Hooray for Bollywood: Oscar Bid Lifts Hopes," *Washington Post*, March 24, 2002.
80. Young, "Bolly Good Show."
81. Elham Khatami, "Is Bollywood Coming to Hollywood?" CNN.com, February 23, 2009, www.cnn.com/2009/SHOWBIZ/Movies/02/23/bollywood.hollywood.
82. Roger Ebert, "'Lagaan' Brings Out the Best of Bollywood," *Chicago Sun-Times*, June 7, 2002, 33.
83. Khatami, "Is Bollywood Coming to Hollywood?"
84. Nigeria Surpasses Hollywood as World's Second Largest Film Producer – UN," *UN News Centre*, May 5, 2009, www.un.org/apps/news/story.asp?NewsID=30707#.U869LCh910A; Alexander Bud, "Hooray for Nollywood? Nigeria Isn't the World's Second-Biggest Film Industry After All," *The Conversation*, April 11, 2014, theconversation.com/hooray-for-nollywood-nigeria-isnt-the-worlds-second-biggest-film-industry-after-all-25527.
85. John Collier, "Censorship and the National Board (1915)," in *The Movies in Our Midst*, ed. G. Mast.
86. Ellis Paxson Oberholtzer, "Sex Pictures (1922)," in *The Movies in Our Midst: Documents in the Cultural History of Film in America*, ed. Gerald Mast (Chicago: University of Chicago Press, 1982).
87. J. R. Rutland, "State Censorship of Motion Pictures," in *The Movies in Our Midst: Documents in the Cultural History of Film in America*, ed. Gerald Mast (Chicago: University of Chicago Press, 1982).
88. Mast and Kawin, *A Brief History of the Movies*.
89. Anonymous, "The Sins of Hollywood (1922)," in *The Movies in Our Midst: Documents in the Cultural History of Film in America*, ed. Gerald Mast (Chicago: University of Chicago Press, 1982).
90. Motion Picture Producers and Distributors of America, "The Don'ts and Be Carefuls (1927)," in *The Movies in Our Midst: Documents in the Cultural History of Film in America*, ed. Gerald Mast (Chicago: University of Chicago Press, 1982).
91. Mast, "Introduction."
92. Raymond Moley, "The Birth of the Production Code (1945)," in *The Movies in Our Midst*, ed. G. Mast.
93. Motion Picture Producers and Distributors of America, "The Motion Picture Production Code of 1930s," in *The Movies in Our Midst: Documents in the Cultural History of Film in America*, ed. Gerald Mast (Chicago: University of Chicago Press, 1982); Amy Wallace, "MPAA's Dozen Judge Movies for Millions," *Los Angeles Times*, July 18, 1999, A1.
94. Charles Lyons, *The New Censors: Movies and the Culture Wars* (Philadelphia: Temple University Press, 1997).
95. Sharon Waxman, "Exclusive: Baron Cohen's 'Bruno' Slapped With NC-17," *The Wrap*, March 29, 2009, www.thewrap.com/article/2127?page=1.
96. "Sacha Baron Cohen," August 9, 2012, http://boxofficemojo.com/people/chart/?id=sachabaroncohen.htm.
97. Gary Arnold, "Between PG & R; Valenti Says New Rating Possible by Next Week," *Washington Post*, June 23, 1984, C1.
98. Ibid.
99. Ibid.
100. "Top-Grossing MPAA Ratings 1995 to 2009," *The Numbers*, www.the-numbers.com/market/MPAARatings.
101. Jerome Hellman, "Problems With Movie Ratings Go Beyond Categories," *Los Angeles Times*, August 23, 1999, F3.
102. Wallace, "MPAA's Dozen Judge Movies for Millions."
103. Ibid.
104. Pamela McClintock, "MPAA Tries to Remove NC-17 Stigma," *Variety*, March 10, 2007, www.variety.com/article/VR1117960864.html?categoryid=13&cs=1&query=%22hard+r%2.
105. Brooks Boliek, "Parents Use Film Ratings," *Chicago Sun-Times*, September 10, 1999, 52; Janet Maslin, "Is NC-17 an X in a Clean Raincoat?" *New York Times*, October 21, 1990, sect. 2, 1; "The Silver Screen: Movies Reflect Changes in Society," *USA Today*, December 20, 1990, 13A; David Landis, "NC-17 Rating Bombs With Theaters," *USA Today*, October 7, 1992, 7D.
106. Gray, "'Brokeback Mountain' Most Impressive of Tepid 2005."
107. Michael Medved, "Hollywood's Disconnect," *USA Today*, July 25, 2005.
108. Tim Purtell, "Our Favorite Year," *Entertainment Weekly*, April 29, 1994.
109. "US Movie Market Summary 1995 to 2014," The Numbers, www.the-numbers.com/market.
110. Cogley, "Report on Blacklisting."
111. Schatz, "The Return of the Hollywood Studio System."
112. "*Transformers: Revenge of the Fallen*," Box Office Mojo, http://boxofficemojo.com/movies/?id=transformers2.htm.
113. "Digital Domain Collaborates With Michael Bay on 'Transformers: Revenge of the Fallen' Movie Tie-Ins," CGArena, January 7, 2009, www.cgarena.com/archives/news/transformers_tieins.html.
114. Sarah Mahoney, "Kmart Launches Transformers Tie-In," *Marketing Daily–Media Post News*, June 1, 2009, http://www.mediapost.com/publications/article/107088/kmart-launches-transformers-tie-in.html.
115. Garrett Kessler, "2010 Camaro Stars in Transformers: Revenge of the Fallen, the Game," *Edmunds Inside Line*, June 30, 2009; "Latest Buzz: Chevrolet Unveils Camaro 'Transformers' Edition," *USA Today*, July 22, 2009, http://content.usatoday.com/communities/driveon/post/2009/07/68495117/1.
116. Richard Corliss, "Blair Witch Craft," *Time*, August 16, 1999, 58–64; Timothy L. O'Brien, "The Curse of the Blair Witch," *Talk*, February 2002, 81.
117. Charlotte O'Sullivan, "Film: Hell Is Other People. We Should Know: The Makers of the Blair Witch Project, Ed Sanchez and Daniel Myrick, on the Nightmare of Collective Filmmaking," *The Independent*, October 22, 1999, 13.
118. O'Brien, "The Curse of the Blair Witch."
119. Glenn Whipp, "Searching for 'Blair Witch' a Decade Later," *Los Angeles Times*, July 11, 2009, http://latimesblogs.latimes.com/herocomplex/2009/07/search ing-for-blair-witch-project-a-decade-later.html.
120. Ibid.
121. Chris Anderson, *The Long Tail* (New York: Hyperion, 2006), 110.
122. Chris Anderson, "Briefly Noted From Australia," *The Long Tail*, December 22, 2006, www.longtail.com/the_long_tail/2006/12/briefly_noted_f.html.

Chapter 9

1. Meg James, "Univsion's Jorge Ramos a Powerful Voice on Immigration," *Los Angeles Times*, June 4, 2013, http://www.latimes.com/entertainment/la-et-jorge-ramos-immigration-20130604-dto-htmlstory.html.
2. Ibid.
3. Ibid.
4. Brooke Gladstone, "Hispanic TV's Star Newscaster," On The Media, July 4, 2014, www.onthemedia.org/story/jorge-ramos/transcript/.

5. Reid Cherlin, "Talking TV Ratings, Immigration, and Salsa Sales With Univision Anchor Jorge Ramos," *New York*, May 3, 2014, nymag.com/daily/intelligencer/2014/05/jorge-ramos-on-ratings-and-immigration.html.
6. Gladstone, "Hispanic TV's Star Newscaster."
7. Paul Taylor and Mark Hugo Lopez, "National Latino Leader? The Job Is Open," *Pew Hispanic Center*, November 15, 2010, www.pewhispanic.org/files/reports/131.pdf.
8. Dylan Byers, "Anchor With Attitude: Jorge Ramos Fights for Immigration Reform," *Politico*, May 28, 2014, www.politico.com/story/2014/05/jorge-ramos-fusion-politics-immigration-107124.html.
9. Ibid.
10. David Dugan, "Big Dreams, Small Screen," WGBH Educational Foundation, 1997, www.pbs.org/wgbh/amex/technology/bigdream/bigdreamts.html.
11. Neil Postman, "Philo Farnsworth," *Time*, March 29, 1999, www.time.com/time/time100/scientist/profile/farnsworth.html.
12. Ibid.
13. Erik Barnouw, *Tube of Plenty: The Evolution of American Television*, 2nd rev. ed. (New York: Oxford University Press, 1990).
14. Postman, "Philo Farnsworth."
15. Barnouw, *Tube of Plenty*.
16. John Carman, "The 20 Series That Changed the Tube," *San Francisco Chronicle*, May 24, 1998; Deborah Felder, *The 100 Most Influential Women of All Time: A Ranking Past and Present* (Secaucus, N.J.: Carol Publishing Group, 1996); Douglas McGrath, "The Good, the Bad, the Lucy: A Legacy of Laughs; The Man Behind the Throne: Making the Case for Desi," *New York Times*, October 14, 2001.
17. Fred Kaplan, "Costs of High-Definition TV Make Its Future Look Fuzzy," *Boston Globe*, July 25, 2000.
18. Christopher Carey, "Ready or Not, High-Definition Television Starts on Sunday," *St. Louis Post-Dispatch*, November 1, 1998.
19. Patrick R. Parsons and Robert M. Frieden, *The Cable and Satellite Television Industries* (Needham Heights, Mass.: Allyn & Bacon, 1998).
20. Robert W. Crandall and Harold Furchtgott-Roth, *Cable TV: Regulation or Competition*? (Washington, D.C.: Brookings Institution, 1996).
21. Ibid.
22. Priscilla Painton, "The Taming of Ted Turner," *Time*, January 6, 1992.
23. Ibid.
24. "Prince of the Global Village," *Time*, January 6, 1992.
25. Parsons and Frieden, *The Cable and Satellite Television Industries*.
26. Ken Auletta, *Three Blind Mice: How the TV Networks Lost Their Way* (New York: Random House, 1991).
27. Parsons and Frieden, *The Cable and Satellite Television Industries*.
28. National Cable & Telecommunications Association, "Industry Data," December 2011, http://www.ncta.com/Statistics.aspx.
29. Joseph O'Halloran, "UK Digital TV Inches Upwards to 93% Penetration," *Rapid TV News*, January 18, 2011, http://www.rapidtvnews.com/201101189857/uk-digital-tv-inches-upwards-to-93-penetration.html.
30. Barnouw, *Tube of Plenty*.
31. Satellite Broadcasting & Communications Association, "Facts & Figures," April 10, 2012, http://www.sbca.com/receiver-network/industry-satellite-facts.htm.
32. Sky Italia, *21st Century Fox,* October 16, 2014, www.21cf.com/Sky_Italia.aspx.
33. Mark Dawidziak, "Satellite Television Providers to Include Local Programming," *Plain Dealer*, December 17, 1999.
34. J. W. Elphinstone, "Watercooler: DVDs' Popularity Passes VCRs', New Year's Resolutions, Bad Publicity," Associated Press Financial Wire, December 19, 2006.
35. Richard Mullins, "VCR's Demise Fast Forwards in Brave New World of DVDs," *Tampa Tribune*, December 20, 2006; Wayne Freidman, "As Streaming TV Rises, DVR Penetration Slows," *Media Post*, December 9, 2013, www.mediapost.com/publications/article/215069/as-streaming-tv-rises-dvr-penetration-slows.html.
36. Freidman, "As Streaming TV Rises, DVR Penetration Slows."
37. Joelle Tessler, "Senate OKs 4-Month Delay to Digital TV Changeover," *USA Today*, January 27, 2009; Leslie Cauley, "Switch to Digital Television (DTV) Went Remarkably Well," *USA Today*, June 15, 2009; Associated Press, "800,000 Callers Phone Digital TV Hotline," *USA Today*, June 14, 2009.
38. Paul Farhi, "A Defining Moment for TV? As Digital Broadcast Age Begins, the Outlook Is Far From Clear," *Washington Post*, November 1, 1998.
39. Ibid.
40. Leichtman Research Group, "The Majority of TV Sets Used in U.S. Households Are Now HDTVs," March 7, 2014, www.leichtmanresearch.com/press/030714release.html.
41. Auletta, *Three Blind Mice*.
42. Anthony Smith, "Television as a Public Service Medium," in *Television: An International History*, ed. Anthony Smith (New York: Oxford University Press, 1995).
43. Laurence Jarvik, *PBS: Behind the Scenes* (Rocklin, Calif.: Prima Publishing, 1997).
44. Ibid.
45. Ken Auletta, *The Highwaymen* (San Diego, Calif.: Harcourt Brace, 1998).
46. Gary Levin, "Viewers' Shifting Habits Redefine 'TV Hit,'" *USA Today*, October 23, 2007; Matt Webb Mitovich, "Ratings: You Loved the *Idol* Finale *This* Big—38.6 Million Watch Winner Crowned," *TV Line*, May 26, 2011, http://tvline.com/2011/05/26/ratings-american-idol-finale-modern-family-cougar-town/.
47. "Intro to Nielsen Ratings: Basics and Definitions," *Spotted Ratings*, September 3, 2013, www.spottedratings.com/2013/09/intro-to-nielsen-ratings-basics-and.html.
48. Nicholas Covey, "The State of the Console: Video Game Console Usage Fourth Quarter 2006" (Nielsen Wireless and Interactive Services, 2007); Nielsen Company, "Local Television Market Universe Estimates," 2008.
49. James R. Walker and Douglas A. Ferguson, *The Broadcast Television Industry* (Needham Heights, Mass.: Allyn & Bacon, 1998).
50. Auletta, *Three Blind Mice*.
51. Ibid.
52. Meg James, "Cable TV Networks Feel Pressure of Programming Costs," *Los Angeles Times*, December 8, 2011, articles.latimes.com/2011/dec/08/business/la-fi-ct-cable-economics-20111208.
53. Ibid.
54. Bill Goodykoontz, "Where Have All the 'Good Times' Gone? Networks Skirt Minority Stars," *Arizona Republic*, August 29, 1999.
55. Robert P. Laurence, "NBC Program Executive Says Network Has Lagged on Ethnic Diversity," *San Diego Union-Tribune*, July 31, 1999.
56. Meron Mogos, "Primetime Television: The New Color-Blind Medium?" *HuffPost TV*, January 29, 2013, www.huffingtonpost.com/meron-mogos/diversity-in-primetime-tv_b_2574898.html.
57. Sarah Hughes, "American Television's Real Scandal," *The Guardian*, October 22, 2012, www.theguardian.com/lifeandstyle/2012/oct/22/american-television-real-scandal.

58. Armstrong and Watson, "Diversity in Entertainment."
59. Deboarah Plummer, "Diversity Lessons From Food Network's Chopped," *Huff Post Black Voices*, July 10, 2012, www.huffingtonpost.com/deborah-plummer/linda-green-wins-chopped_b_1655355.html.
60. Meg Sullivan, "Hollywood Failing to Keep Up With Rapidly Increasing Diversity, UCLA Study Warns," February 12, 2014, newsroom.ucla.edu/releases/hollywood-failing-to-keep-up-with-250007.
61. U.S. Census Bureau, "2010 Census Shows America's Diversity," March 24, 2011, www.census.gov/2010census/news/releases/operations/cb11-cn125.html.
62. David Adams, "ABC, CBS, NBC, Fox . . . Univision?" *St. Petersburg Times*, June 5, 2005; Michael Schneider, "Novela Energizes Univision," *Variety*, October 4, 2009.
63. Amanda Kondolojy, "Univision Sets Milestone as No. 4 Network in February Sweeps Ahead of NBC in Key Demos," *TV by the Numbers*, February 27, 2013, tvbythenumbers.zap2it.com/2013/02/27/univision-sets-milestone-as-no-4-network-in-february-sweeps-ahead-of-nbc-in-key-demos/171192/.
64. Lee Romney, "Markets: Univision Shares Drop Over Azteca News," *Los Angeles Times*, September 9, 2000.
65. Meg James, "Univision Demonstrates Its Ratings Steel," *Los Angeles Times*, December 28, 2010, latimesblogs.latimes.com/entertainmentnewsbuzz/2010/12/univision-demonstrates-its-ratings-steel-.html.
66. Scott Collins, "At ABC, a Hopeful Bet on 'Betty'," *Los Angeles Times*, August 14, 2006.
67. "Univision to Produce a Sitcom in the States," *St. Petersburg Times*, May 24, 2000; Juan Tornoe, "2006 World Cup Gives Univision Ratings Boost," *Hispanic Trending*, July 7, 2006, juantornoe.blogs.com/hispanictrending/2006/07/2006_world_cup_.html.
68. Julie Zellinger, "Laverne Cox, 'Orange Is The New Black' Star, on The Necessity of Diverse Female Characters," *Huff Post Women,* August 14, 2013, www.huffingtonpost.com/2013/08/14/laverne-cox-orange-is-the-new-black_n_3750544.html.
69. Roxane Gay, "The Bar for TV Diversity Is Way Too Low," *Salon*, August 22, 2013, www.salon.com/2013/08/22/the_bar_for_tv_diversity_is_way_too_low/.
70. Terry Gross, "Behind 'The New Black': The Real Piper's Prison Story," *NPR Books*, August 12, 2013, www.npr.org/2013/08/12/211339427/behind-the-new-black-the-real-pipers-prison-story.
71. Hollywood Reporter, "Spanish-Language Network Challenges Regis," *Milwaukee Journal Sentinel*, May 21, 2000.
72. Joanne Ostrow, "Risks, Pitfalls Are Plenty When Dubbing TV Shows," *Pittsburgh Post-Gazette*, January 2, 2006.
73. Dennis Hunt, "BET Gambles on Revamped Framework; Network Chief Lists Challenges at Work," *USA Today*, July 28, 2000.
74. Keith L. Alexander, "Placing BET on the Net; Site Part of the CEO's Plan to Expand," *USA Today*, February 10, 2000.
75. Greg Braxton, "BET on the Past and Future of a Dream," *Los Angeles Times*, May 6, 2000.
76. Leona Thompson, "BET Offers 'Blessings' Without Disguise," *Boston Herald*, April 6, 2000.
77. Stuart Elliott, "General Motors Is Significantly Increasing Its Efforts to Aim Pitches at Black Consumers," *New York Times*, September 23, 1999.
78. Laura R. Linder, *Public Access Television: America's Electronic Soapbox* (Westport, Conn.: Praeger Publishers, 1999).
79. Ibid.
80. Ibid.
81. Barnouw, *Tube of Plenty*.
82. Stephen Seplow and Jonathan Storm, "Window to a Culture: The Television Revolution Has Changed Everything, for Better and Worse," *Arizona Republic*, January 4, 1998.
83. Robert Kubey and Mihaly Csikszentmihalyi, *Television and the Quality of Life: How Viewing Shapes Everyday Experience* (Hillsdale, N.J.: Lawrence Erlbaum Associates, 1990).
84. Victoria J. Rideout, Ulla G. Foehr, and Donald F. Roberts, "Generation M2: Media in the Lives of 8–18 Year-Olds" (Henry J. Kaiser Family Foundation, 2010).
85. Kubey and Csikszentmihalyi, *Television and the Quality of Life*.
86. Shearon A. Lowery and Melvin L. DeFleur, *Milestones in Mass Communication*, 3rd ed. (White Plains, N.Y.: Longman, 1995).
87. Terry Gross, "Interview With Mary Tyler Moore," *Fresh Air/NPR*, October 30, 1995, www.npr.org/templates/story/story.php?storyId=1108624.
88. Elizabeth Kolbert, "What's a Network TV Censor to Do?" *New York Times*, May 23, 1993.
89. Warren Berger, "Censorship in the Age of Anything Goes; Where Have You Gone, Standards and Practices?" *New York Times*, September 20, 1998.
90. Stephen Farber, "They Watch What We Watch," *New York Times*, May 7, 1989.
91. David Zurawik, "Ratings Deal Signed; TV: Starting Oct. 1, Symbols Will Give Parents More Clues About Content. Except on NBC," *Baltimore Sun*, July 11, 1997.
92. Berger, "Censorship in the Age of Anything Goes."
93. Associated Press, "A Closer Look at Broadcast Indecency," *First Amendment Center*, March 23, 2004, http://www.firstamendmentcenter.org/a-closer-look-at-broadcast-indecency.
94. Ibid.
95. Brendan Sasso, "Supreme Court Won't Take Up Janet Jackson 'Wardrobe Malfunction' Case," *The Hill*, June 29, 2012, thehill.com/blogs/hillicon-valley/technology/235629-supreme-court-wont-take-up-janet-jackson-case.
96. Frances Martel, "Wardrobe Malfunction! Nancy Graces Lets a Nipple Slip During DWTS Performance (NSFW)," September 26, 2011, www.mediaite.com/tv/wardrobe-malfunction-nancy-grace-lets-a-nipple-slip-during-dwts-performance/.
97. Associated Press, "Some Stations Hesitate to Air 9/11 Documentary," *First Amendment Center*, September 5, 2006, http://www.firstamendmentcenter.org/some-stations-hesitate-to-air-911-documentary.
98. Associated Press, "'Saving Private Ryan' Not Indecent, FCC Rules," *First Amendment Center*, March 1, 2005, http://www.firstamendmentcenter.org/saving-private-ryan-not-indecent-fcc-rules.
99. Adam Sherwin, "Amateur 'Video Bloggers' Under Threat From EU Broadcast Rules," *Times*, October 17, 2006.
100. Gene Policinski, "Censorship in the Name of Decency?" *First Amendment Center*, September 5, 2006, http://www.firstamendmentcenter.org/censorship-in-the-name-of-decency.
101. Crandall and Furchtgott-Roth, *Cable TV: Regulation or Competition*?
102. David Liberman and Laura Petrecca, "Deal Has Some ABC Affiliates Feeling Uneasy," *USA Today*, October 12, 2005, www.usatoday.com/tech/products/services/2005-10-12-abc-ipod-iger_x.htm.
103. *Hoover's Company Records—In-Depth Records: Netflix Inc.* (Austin, Texas: Hoover's Inc., 2012).
104. Jamie Keene, "Tablets the Second Most Popular Way to Watch TV, Says Viacom Study," April 20, 2012, www.theverge.com/2012/4/20/2961964/tablets-tv-growth-viacom-study.

105. "The Digital Consumer," Nielsen Company, February 2014, http://www.nielsen.com/content/dam/corporate/us/en/reports-downloads/2014%20Reports/the-digital-consumer-report-feb-2014.pdf.
106. Jim Romenesko, "My Valentine's Day Break-Up With Comcast," April 17, 2012, jimromenesko.com/2012/04/17/my-valentines-day-break-up-with-comcast/.
107. Auletta, *The Highwaymen*.
108. Freidman, "As Streaming TV Rises, DVR Penetration Slows."
109. Staff, "Tune In, Log On, Go Play," *Newsweek*, April 17, 2000.
110. Ibid.
111. Susan Stellin, "Bad News for Old News," *Media Post*, November 28, 2006, http://www.mediapost.com/publications/article/51695/bad-news-for-old-news.html.

Chapter 10

1. David Thier, "20,000 People Are Watching a Fish Play Pokemon on Twitch," *Forbes*, August 8, 2014, www.forbes.com/sites/davidthier/2014/08/08/20000-people-are-watching-a-fish-play-pokemon/; Jason Koebler, "An Exclusive Interview With the Fish Playing Pokemon," *Motherboard*, August 8, 2014, motherboard.vice.com/read/an-exclusive-interview-with-the-fish-playing-pokemon.
2. Aaron Souppouris, "Playing 'Pokemon' With 78,000 People Is Frustratingly Fun," *The Verge*, February 17, 2014, www.theverge.com/2014/2/17/5418690/play-this-twitch-plays-pokemon-crowdsourced-gaming; thanks are due to my colleague Aaron Blackman who introduced me to Twitch Plays Pokemon and wrote a great guest blog post.
3. Paul Tassi, "Twitch Starts Swinging YouTube-Like Copyright Sledgehammer [Updated]," *Forbes*, August 7, 2014, www.forbes.com/sites/insertcoin/2014/08/07/twitch-starts-swinging-youtube-like-copyright-sledgehammer/.
4. German Lopez, "Why Amazon Spent $970 Million to Buy Twitch," *Vox*, August 26, 2014, www.vox.com/2014/8/26/6067085/amazon-twitch-tv-video-games-live-streaming-league-of-legends-dota-2.
5. Joshua Brustein, "Buying Twitch Gets Google More Than Video Game Spectators," *Bloomberg Businessweek*, July 25, 2014, www.businessweek.com/articles/2014-07-25/buying-twitch-gets-google-more-than-video-game-spectators.
6. "Scientist Who Transformed the Internet," *Irish Times*, June 24, 2000.
7. Peter Grier, "In the Beginning, There Was ARPANET," *Air Force Magazine*, January 1997, 66.
8. Barnaby J. Feder, "Donald W. Davies, 75, Dies; Helped Refine Data Networks," *New York Times*, June 4, 2000.
9. Katie Hafner and Matthew Lyon, *Where Wizards Stay Up Late* (New York: Simon & Schuster, 1996).
10. Ibid.
11. Ibid.
12. Joseph Gallivan, "A Bit More Backbone: Internet II Is in the Wings," *The Independent*, February 25, 1997; Jeffrey R. Young, "Internet2 Spurs Equipment Upgrades, but Use in Research Remains Limited," *Chronicle of Higher Education*, August 13, 1999; University Corporation for Advanced Internet Development, "Frequently Asked Questions About Internet2," http://www.marquette.edu/pdfs/Internet2/i2faq.pdf
13. Stephen Segaller, *Nerds 2.0.1: A Brief History of the Internet* (New York: TV Books, LLC, 1998).
14. Ibid.
15. Ibid.
16. Lawrence K. Grossman, "From Marconi to Murrow to—Drudge?" *Columbia Journalism Review*, July 1999, 17.
17. William J. Mitchell, *City of Bits: Space, Place, and the Infobahn* (Cambridge, Mass.: MIT Press, 1995).
18. Leslie Regan Shade, "Is There Free Speech on the Net? Censorship in the Global Information Infrastructure," in *Cultures of the Internet*, ed. Rob Shields (London: Sage, 1996).
19. Segaller, *Nerds 2.0.1*.
20. Tim Berners-Lee, *Weaving the Web* (New York: Harper Collins, 1999).
21. Anick Jesdanun, "From Two Users to 7 Million, Web's Come a Long Way," Associated Press, December 24, 2000.
22. Segaller, *Nerds 2.0.1*, 288.
23. Ibid., 291.
24. Ibid.
25. M. Chethan and Mohan Ramanathan, "Social Knowledge: The Technology Behind," in *Social Knowledge: Using Social Media to Know What You Know*, ed. John P. Girard and JoAnn L. Girard (Hershey, Pa.: Information Science Reference, 2011).
26. Susannah Fox and Lee Rainie, "The Web at 25 in the U.S," Pew Research Internet Project, February 27, 2014, www.pewinternet.org/2014/02/27/the-web-at-25-in-the-u-s/.
27. "Three Technology Revolutions," Pew Research Internet Project, 2014, www.pewinternet.org/three-technology-revolutions/.
28. Jose Antonio Vargas, "Letter from Palo Alto: The Face of Facebook," September 20, 2010, www.newyorker.com/reporting/2010/09/20/100920fa_fact_vargas.
29. "Social Media Update 2013: Facebook Users," Pew Research Internet Project, December 30, 2013, http://www.pewinternet.org/2013/12/30/social-media-update-2013/facebook-users/; "Facebook: 10 Years of Social Networking, in Numbers," *The Guardian*, February 4, 2014, www.theguardian.com/news/datablog/2014/feb/04/facebook-in-numbers-statistics.
30. Kevin Maney, "Short & Tweet," *Upstart*, February 11, 2009, www.portfolio.com/executives/features/2009/02/11/Twitter-CEO-Evan-Williams-Q-and-A; Britney Fitzgerald, "Twitter Use Is on the Rise, Daily Use Doubles: Pew," *Huffington Post*, June 1, 2012, www.huffingtonpost.com/2012/06/01/twitter-use-stats-growth_n_1559716.html?ref=technology.
31. Jon Swartz, "Twitter Has Millions Tweeting in Public Communication Service," *USA Today*, May 26, 2009.
32. Bob Garfield, "How Tweet It Is," *On the Media*, August 22, 2008, www.onthemedia.org/transcripts/2008/08/22/05.
33. Ibid.
34. Dominic Rushee, "What Makes Twitter Worth a Billion Dollars?" *Sunday Times*, September 27, 2009.
35. Mark Jurkowitz, "Online News Outlets Catch Their Breath; Cyber Slowdown Prompts Rethinking," *Boston Globe*, January 19, 2001.
36. James Fallows, "But Is It Journalism?" *American Prospect*, November 23, 1999.
37. Felicity Barringer, "Rethinking Internet News as a Business Proposition," *New York Times*, January 22, 2001.
38. Richard Morochove, "Cyberpunk Guru Unplugged: When It Comes to the Internet and Computers, Author William Gibson Is Decidedly Low-Tech," *Toronto Star*, June 1, 1995.
39. Gary Gentile, "Hollywood Net Survivor: IFILM Hopes to Build Media Company," *Billings Gazette*, October 24, 2000, http://billingsgazette.com/business/technology/hollywood-net-survivor-ifilm-hopes-to-build-media-company-from/article_d8cf30d6-55c0-5c6b-a648-1e41c31a6f02.html.

40. Hugh Hart, "New Media, Old Methods," *Los Angeles Times*, February 18, 2001.
41. Roger Ebert, "Is '405' a Home Movie?" *Chicago Sun-Times*, November 1, 2000.
42. Jon Healey, "Pay-Per-View Sites Offer New Options for Computer Movie-Viewing," *San Jose Mercury News*, May 21, 2000.
43. Michael Paoletta, "Online Odyssey Stoking Interest in New NIN Album," *Billboard*, March 30, 2007, http://www.billboard.com/articles/news/1053298/online-odyssey-stoking-interest-in-new-nin-album.
44. Fallows, "But Is It Journalism?"
45. Ibid.
46. Segaller, *Nerds 2.0.1*.
47. I would like to thank Charley Reed, a communications graduate student at the University of Nebraska at Omaha, for his research and work on the video game section of this chapter.
48. Andrew Edwards, "Video Games? Microsoft Pitches Xbox 360 as an Entertainment Hub," June 4, 2012, www.siliconvalley.com/news/ci_20779287/video-games-microsoft-pitches-xbox-360-an-entertainment;Paul Tassi, "Twitch Starts Swinging YouTube-Like Copyright Sledgehammer [Updated]."
49. Jim Rutenberg, "Obama Aims TV Ads at Younger Voters," *New York Times*, October 8, 2008, thecaucus.blogs.nytimes.com/2008/10/08/obama-aims-tv-ads-at-younger-voters.
50. Seth Schiesel, "Finding Community in Virtual Town Squares," *New York Times*, November 5, 2005.
51. Derrick J. Lang, "How Iron Man Was Trounced by a Scruffy Car Thief," *USA Today*, May 8, 2008.
52. John Gaudiosi, "Games, Movies Tie the Knot," *Wired*, December 10, 2003, http://archive.wired.com/gaming/gamingreviews/news/2003/12/61358?currentPage=all.
53. Amanda Lenhart et al., "Teens, Video Games and Civics," 2008, www.pewinternet.org/Reports/2008/Teens-Video-Games-and-Civics.aspx?r=1.
54. Amanda Lenhart, Sydney Jones, and Alexandra Macgill, "Pew Internet Project Data Memo: Adults and Video Games," in *Pew Internet and American Life Project* (Pew Foundation, 2008).
55. Grossman, "From Marconi to Murrow to—Drudge?"
56. Segaller, *Nerds 2.0.1*.
57. Stacy Schiff, "Know It All: Can Wikipedia Conquer Expertise?" *New Yorker*, July 31, 2006.
58. David S. Bennahum, "Techno-Paranoia in the White House," *New York Times*, January 25, 1997.
59. Fallows, "But Is It Journalism?"
60. Berners-Lee, *Weaving the Web*.
61. Austin Bunn, "Human Portals," *Brill's Content*, May 2001.
62. Howard Kurtz, "After Blogs Got Hits, CBS Got a Black Eye," *Washington Post*, September 20, 2004; Alessandra Stanley, "The TV Watch; Signing Off, Rather's Wish for Viewers Is Still 'Courage,'" *New York Times*, March 10, 2005.
63. Mark Memmott, "'Milbloggers' Are Typing Their Place in History," *USA Today*, May 12, 2005.
64. Julia Darling, "Julia Darling in Person," September 26, 2002, www.juliadarling.co.uk/weblog/archives/archive-092002.html.
65. Howard Kurtz, "Throw Another Blog on the Fire," *Washington Post*, April 11, 2005.
66. Peter Sayer, "Yahoo's Legal Battle Over Nazi Items Continues," *Infoworld*, August 24, 2004, http://www.infoworld.com/article/2664810/application-development/yahoo-s-legal-battle-over-nazi-items-continues.html.
67. Marc Gunther, "Yahoo's China Problem," *CNN Money*, February 22, 2006, money.cnn.com/2006/02/21/news/international/pluggedin_fortune/?cnn=yes.
68. Nazila Fathi, "In a Death Seen Around the World, a Symbol of Iranian Protests," *New York Times*, June 23, 2009.
69. Ibid.
70. Hiawatha Bray, "Finding a Way Around Iranian Censorship," *Boston Globe*, June 19, 2009.
71. Segaller, *Nerds 2.0.1*.
72. Ibid.
73. Steven Levy, *Hackers* (New York: Penguin Books, 1994); Steven Levy, "The Day I Got Napsterized," *Newsweek*, May 28, 2001.
74. Jamie Portman, "Confronting Cyberspace," *Calgary Herald*, June 11, 1995.
75. Ibid.
76. Douglas Barbour, "Pop Culture on the Cyberfrontier," *Vancouver Sun*, September 14, 1996.
77. Segaller, *Nerds 2.0.1*.
78. Salvador Rodriguez, "60% of World's Population Still Won't Have Internet by the End of 2014," *Los Angeles Times*, May 7, 2014, www.latimes.com/business/technology/la-fi-tn-60-world-population-3-billion-internet-2014-20140507-story.html.
79. Kathryn Zickuhr and Aaron Smith, "Home Broadband 2013," Pew Research Internet Project, August 26, 2013, www.pewinternet.org/2013/08/26/home-broadband-2013/.
80. Berners-Lee, *Weaving the Web*.
81. Shade, "Is There Free Speech on the Net?"
82. David A. Fahrenthold, "SOPA Protests Shut Down Web Sites," *Washington Post*, January 17, 2012, www.washingtonpost.com/politics/sopa-protests-to-shut-down-web-sites/2012/01/17/gIQA4WYl6P_story.html?hpid=z1.
83. Jennifer Martinez, "SOPA and PIPA Dead, for Now," January 20, 2012, www.politico.com/news/stories/0112/71720.html.
84. Brad Plumer, "Now That SOPA's Dead, Five Easy Ways to Reform Copyright Law," *Washington Post*, February 29, 2012, www.washingtonpost.com/blogs/ezra-klein/post/sopa-foes-offer-five-ways-to-fix-online-copy right-law/2012/02/29/gIQAjmeViR_blog.html.
85. Berners-Lee, *Weaving the Web*.
86. Daniel Jacobson, "API Update: New Transcript API and Much More," NPR, July 29, 2009, www.npr.org/blogs/inside/2009/07/api_update_transcript_api_and.html.
87. Frank Ahrens, "2002's News, Yesterday's Sell-Off," *Washington Post*, September 9, 2008.

Chapter 11

1. Kashmir Hill, "How Target Figured Out a Teen Girl Was Pregnant Before Her Father Did," *Forbes*, February 16, 2012, www.forbes.com/sites/kashmirhill/2012/02/16/how-target-figured-out-a-teen-girl-was-pregnant-before-her-father-did/.
2. Charles Duhigg, "How Companies Learn Your Secrets," *New York Times*, February 16, 2012, www.nytimes.com/2012/02/19/magazine/shopping-habits.html.
3. Bob Garfield, "Off Target: Transcript," *On the Media*, October 16, 2009, www.onthemedia.org/2009/oct/16/off-target/transcript/.
4. George E. Belch and Michael A. Belch, *Advertising and Promotion: An Integrated Marketing Communications Perspective* (Boston: Irwin McGraw-Hill, 1998).
5. Pamela Walker Laird, *Advertising Progress* (Baltimore: Johns Hopkins University Press, 1998).
6. James W. Carey, "Advertising: An Institutional Approach," in *Advertising in Society*, ed. Roxanne Hoveland and Gary B. Wilcox (Lincolnwood, Ill.: NTC Business Books, 1989).

7. Laird, *Advertising Progress*.
8. Michael Schudson, "Historical Roots of Consumer Culture," in *Advertising in Society*, ed. Roxanne Hoveland and Gary B. Wilcox (Lincolnwood, Ill.: NTC Business Books, 1989).
9. Laird, *Advertising Progress*.
10. Carey, "Advertising: An Institutional Approach."
11. Schudson, "Historical Roots of Consumer Culture."
12. Laird, *Advertising Progress*.
13. Michael Sebastian, "Ladies' Home Journal Ends Monthly Publication, Lays Off All Staff," *Advertising Age*, April 24, 2014, adage.com/article/media/ladies-home-journal-fold-131-years-print/292839/.
14. James B. Twitchell, *Adcult USA: The Triumph of Advertising in American Culture* (New York: Columbia University Press, 1996).
15. Ibid.
16. Ibid.
17. Ad Council, "Public Service Advertising That Changed a Nation," 2014, www.adcouncil.org/Impact/Research/Public-Service-Advertising-that-Changed-a-Nation.
18. Eugene H. Fram, S. Prakash Sethi, and Nobuaki Namiki, "Newspaper Advocacy Advertising: Molder of Public Opinion," *USA Today Magazine*, July 1993, 90.
19. Belch and Belch, *Advertising and Promotion: An Integrated Marketing Communications Perspective*.
20. Michael Schudson, "Advertising as Capitalist Realism," in *Advertising in Society*, ed. Roxanne Hoveland and Gary B. Wilcox (Lincolnwood, Ill.: NTC Business Books, 1989).
21. Herschell Gordon Lewis, *Advertising Age Handbook of Advertising* (Lincolnwood, Ill.: NTC Business Books, 1999).
22. E. J. Schultz, "'Got Milk' Dropped as National Milk Industry Changes Tactics," *Advertising Age*, February 24, 2014, http://adage.com/article/news/milk-dropped-national-milk-industry-tactics/291819/.
23. Mike Snider, "Hunt for PlayStation 2 Becomes Easier for Shoppers," *USA Today*, March 22, 2001.
24. Nancy Giges, "Coke's Switch a Classic," in *Advertising Age: The Principles of Advertising at Work*, ed. Esther Thorson (Lincolnwood, Ill.: NTC Business Books, 1989).
25. Jack Honomichl, "Missing Ingredients in 'New' Coke's Research," in *Advertising Age: The Principles of Advertising at Work*, ed. Esther Thorson (Lincolnwood, Ill.: NTC Business Books, 1989).
26. Giges, "Coke's Switch a Classic."
27. Stuart Elliott, "Gapo Inc. Puts 'GAP' Back in Logo," *New York Times*, October 12, 2010, mediadecoder.blogs.nytimes.com/2010/10/12/gap-inc-puts-gap-back-in-logo/.
28. Schudson, "Historical Roots of Consumer Culture."
29. Laird, *Advertising Progress*.
30. Lewis, *Advertising Age Handbook of Advertising*.
31. C. Bruce Bartels, "Ad Agencies Must Look to Customers to Change," *Boston Business Journal*, December 30, 1994.
32. Dylan Matthews, "One in Five Beers Sold in America Is a Bud Light," *Vox*, April 16, 2014, www.vox.com/2014/4/16/5620170/one-in-five-beers-sold-in-america-is-a-bud-light; Jeremy Mullman, "In Juvenile Bud Light Lime Spot, This Butt's for You," *Advertising Age*, September 8, 2009, adage.com/article/adages/juvenile-bud-lime-spot-butt-s/138877/.
33. Olivia Bergin, "American Apparel in Trouble Again With Advertising Watchdogs," *The Telegraph*, April 10, 2013, fashion.telegraph.co.uk/news-features/TMG9983620/American-Apparel-in-trouble-again-with-advertising-watchdogs.html.
34. Aaron Taube, "An Incredible New Guinness Ad Breaks Industry Stereotype," *Business Insider*, September 5, 2013, www.businessinsider.com/new-guinness-ad-breaks-the-mold-2013-9.
35. Ibid.
36. David Ogilvy, *Confessions of an Advertising Man* (New York: Atheneum, 1963).
37. Ibid.
38. Ibid.
39. Alf Nucifora, "Advertising 101: How to Get the Best Out of Your Media Buy," *Houston Business Journal*, October 16, 1998.
40. Bradley Johnson, "Revenue, Staffing, Stocks and Digital Show Growth for Agencies in 2014 Report," *Advertising Age*, April 27, 2014, adage.com/article/agency-news/2014-agency-report-revenue-staffing-stocks-digital/292849/.
41. AdAge DataCenter, *Advertising Age Marketing Fact Pack, 2014 Edition,* December 30, 2013, gaia.adage.com/images/bin/pdf/MFPweb_spreadsv2.pdf; Bradley Johnson, "Big U.S. Advertisers Boost 2012 Spending By Slim 2.8% With a Lift From Tech," *Advertising Age*, June 23, 2013, adage.com/article/news/big-u-s-advertisers-boost-2012-spending-slim-2-8/242761/.
42. Bradley Johnson, "Agency Report: U.S. Agency Revenue Jumped 7.7% in 2010," *Advertising Age*, April 25, 2011, http://adage.com/article/agency-news/agency-report-u-s-agency-revenue-jumped-7-7-2010/227162/.
43. Esther Thorson, ed., *Advertising Age: The Principles of Advertising at Work* (Lincolnwood, Ill.: NTC Business Books, 1989).
44. Twitchell, *Adcult USA: The Triumph of Advertising in American Culture*.
45. Rick Edmonds, Emily Guskin, Tom Rosenstiel, and Amy Mitchell, "Newspapers: Building Digital Revenues Proves Painfully Slow," May 1, 2012, stateofthemedia.org/2012/newspapers-building-digital-revenues-proves-painfully-slow/.
46. Pew Research Center's Journalism Project Staff, "Key Indicators in Media & News," State of the News Media 2014, March 26, 2014, www.journalism.org/2014/03/26/state-of-the-news-media-2014-key-indicators-in-media-and-news/.
47. Lewis, *Advertising Age Handbook of Advertising*; Pew Research Center Project for Excellence in Journalism, "The State of the News Media 2009: Newspapers," http://stateofthemedia.org/2009/.
48. Katerina-Eva Matsa, Jane Sasseen, and Amy Mitchell, "Magazines: Are Hopes for Tablets Overdone?" 2012, stateofthemedia.org/2012/magazines-are-hopes-for-tablets-overdone/.
49. Outdoor Advertising Association of America, "About Digital Billboard Technology," www.optecmedia.com/Digital_Billboard_Fact_Sheet.pdf.
50. *Marketing Fact Pack, 2014 Edition*, Advertising Age, 2014, gaia.adage.com/images/bin/pdf/MFPweb_spreadsv2.pdf.
51. Twitchell, *Adcult USA: The Triumph of Advertising in American Culture*; Outdoor Advertising Association of America, "Research and Data," www.oaaa.org/press/ResearchandData.aspx.
52. Louise Story, "Times Sq. Ads Spread via Tourists' Cameras," *New York Times*, December 11, 2006.
53. Michael Learmonth, "Online Advertising Spending Expected to Be Down for 2009," *Advertising Age,* October 19, 2009, adage.com/digital/article?article_id=139785.
54. "Mobile Continues to Steal Share of US Adults' Daily Time Spent With Media," *eMarketer*, April 22, 2014, www.emarketer.com/Article/Mobile-Continues-Steal-Share-of-US-Adults-Daily-Time-Spent-with-Media/1010782.
55. Alex Kantrowitz, "Mobile-Ad Revenue Explodes, Finally," *Advertising Age*, December 16, 2013, adage.com/article/digital/mobile-ad-revenue-explodes-finally/245694/.
56. David Berkowitz, "The Converging Paths of Mobile Advertising," *Advertising Age*, January 22, 2014, http://

adage.com/article/digitalnext/converging-paths-mobile-advertising/291204/.

57. Schudson, "Advertising as Capitalist Realism."
58. Rebecca Piirto Heath, "Psychographics: Q'est-Ce Que C'est," *Marketing Tools*, November/December 1995.
59. Emanuel H. Demby, "Psychographics Revisited: The Birth of a Technique," *Marketing Research* 6, no. 2 (1994).
60. Strategic Business Insights (SBI), "VALS | Strategic Business Insights (SBI)," www.strategicbusinessinsights.com/vals/.
61. Ibid.
62. Joshua Meyrowitz, *No Sense of Place* (New York: Oxford University Press, 1985).
63. Theresa Howard, "Being True to Dew," *Brandweek*, April 24, 2000.
64. Richard Linnett, "A New Dew; A Soft Drink Finds Deliverance," *Print*, November/December 2000.
65. Duane Stanford, "Mountain Dew Wants Some Street Cred,"*Businessweek*, April 26, 2012, www.businessweek.com/articles/2012-04-26/mountain-dew-wants-some-street-cred; Christopher Heine, "Mountain Dew Fiasco Shows Brands Desperately Want Street Cred," *AdWeek*, May 1, 2013, www.adweek.com/news/advertising-branding/mountain-dew-fiasco-shows-brands-desperately-want-street-cred-149079.
66. Barbara Thau, "Courting the Gay Consumer," *HFN*, February 27, 2006.
67. Charles A. Jaffe, "Dealers Say Wooing Gay, Lesbian Customers Is Good Business," *Automotive News*, January 31, 1994.
68. "Marketing to Gay and Lesbian Consumers" (Rivendell Media, 2008).
69. Brett Chase, "Advertisements Land in Gay Publications," *Des Moines Business Record*, August 8, 1994.
70. Thau, "Courting the Gay Consumer"; "Marketing to Gay and Lesbian Consumers."
71. Kate Rockwood, "GLAAD's Helping Hand," *Fast Company*, November 2009.
72. Prime Access Inc., "2007 Gay Press Report" (Rivendell Media Company, 2008).
73. Laura Stampler, "15 Major Brands That Unabashedly Support Gay Marriage," *Business Insider*, March 28, 2013, www.businessinsider.com/major-brands-that-support-gay-marriage-photos-2013-3?op=1; Jim Edwards, "GUTSY: Expedia's Gay Marriage Ad Is Narrated by a Homophobic Father," *Business Insider*, October 17, 2012, www.businessinsider.com/expedias-gay-marriage-ad-2012-10.
74. Ira Teinowitz, "Crazy Horse Brew Incenses Sioux," *Advertising Age*, April 6, 1992.
75. Dirk Johnson, "Complaints by Indians Lead to Bans on a Beer," *New York Times*, December 6, 1995.
76. Associated Press, "No Trademark for Crazy Horse Brew," *Marketing News*, August 28, 1995.
77. Matt Wilson, "Shutterfly Earns Scorn for Mistakenly Sending New-Parent Congratulation," *Ragan.com*, May 15, 2014, www.ragan.com/Main/Articles/48336.aspx#.
78. Kim Rotzoll, James E. Haefner, and Charles H. Sandage, "Advertising and the Classical Liberal World View," in *Advertising in Society*, ed. Roxanne Hoveland and Gary B. Wilcox (Lincolnwood, Ill.: NTC Business Books, 1989).
79. M. Night Shyamalan, *The Sixth Sense: A Conversation With M. Night Shyamalan* (Burbank, Calif.: Hollywood Pictures Home Video, 2000), DVD.
80. Chuck Ross, "NBC Blasts Beyond the 15-Minute Barrier," *Advertising Age*, August 7, 2000.
81. "Network, Cable Messages Buried in Commercial Avalanche," *Chicago Sun-Times*, May 30, 2006.
82. Brian Steinberg, "Spike's Supersized Ad Breaks Buck TV's Clutter-Busting Trend," *Advertising Age*, September 13, 2010, adage.com/article/mediaworks/spike-s-supersized-ad-breaks-buck-tv-s-clutter-busting-trend/145853/.
83. Brian Stelter, "Fox TV's Gamble: Fewer Ads in Break, but Costing More," *New York Times*, February 13, 2009; "Fox Scraps 'Remote-Free TV,'" *New York Times*, May 14, 2009, mediadecoder.blogs.nytimes.com/2009/05/14/fox-scraps-remote-free-tv/.
84. "Numbers Don't Lie," *MediaWeek*, September 12, 2006.
85. Dick Morris, "Break Through the Clutter," *Chain Store Age*, December 2000.
86. Diedtra Henderson, "Rise of Celebrity Testimonials Spurs FDA Scrutiny," *Boston Globe*, October 30, 2005.
87. Martha Rogers and Christine A. Seiler, "The Answer Is No: A National Survey of Advertising Industry Practitioners and Their Clients About Whether They Use Subliminal Advertising," *Journal of Advertising Research* 34, no. 2 (1994).
88. J. Leo, "Hostility Among the Ice Cubes," *U.S. News & World Report*, July 15, 1991; J. Levine and J. L. Aber, "Search and Find," *Forbes*, September 2, 1991.
89. Tom O'Sullivan, "Ridley Scott Returns to Ads With Orange Blitz," *Marketing Week*, April 2, 1998.
90. Bob Garfield, "Breakthrough Product Gets Greatest TV Spot," *Advertising Age*, January 10, 1994.
91. Bradley Johnson, "The Commercial, and the Product, That Changed Advertising," *Advertising Age*, January 10, 1994.
92. Ibid.
93. Lenore Skenazy, "Keep Targeting Kids and the Parents Will Start Targeting You," *Advertising Age,* May 19, 2008.
94. Thorson, ed., *Advertising Age: The Principles of Advertising at Work*; Carole Shifrin, "Ban on TV Ads to Children Is Proposed," *Washington Post*, February 25, 1978.
95. Caroline E. Mayer, "TV Ads Entice Kids to Overeat, Study Finds," *Washington Post*, December 7, 2005.
96. Annys Shin, "Ads Aimed at Children Get Tighter Scrutiny; Firms to Promote More Healthful Diet Choices," *Washington Post*, November 15, 2006.
97. Mayer, "TV Ads Entice Kids to Overeat, Study Finds."
98. "Selling Junk Food to Toddlers," *New York Times*, February 23, 2006.
99. Melanie Warner, "Food Industry Defends Marketing to Children," *New York Times*, July 15, 2005.
100. Mayer, "TV Ads Entice Kids to Overeat, Study Finds."
101. Andrew Martin, "Leading Makers Agree to Put Limits on Junk Food Advertising Directed at Children," *New York Times*, November 15, 2006.
102. Dan Milmo, "Media: That's All, Folks: As ITV Shuts Its Kids Production Unit and with a Ban on Lucrative Junk-Food Advertising Imminent, Producers Say Children's Television Is in Mortal Danger," *The Guardian*, July 31, 2006.
103. Maggie Brown, "Media: When the Chips Are Down: The Ban on Junk-Food Advertising in Kids' Shows Is Expected to Cost the Industry £39m," *The Guardian*, November 20, 2006.
104. Ibid.
105. Dawn Edmiston, "An Examination of Integrated Marketing Communication in U.S. Public Institutions of Higher Education," *International Journal of Educational Advancement* 8, no. 3/4 (2009).
106. David Goetzl, "Denny's Super Bowl Ad Value: 'Incredible,'" February 18, 2009, http://www.mediapost.com/publications/article/100566/dennys-super-bowl-ad-value-incredible.html?edition=.
107. Bruce Horovitz, "2 Million Enjoy Free Breakfast at Denny's," *USA Today*, February 3, 2009.
108. Ibid.
109. Brian Quinton, "Bowl Post-Game Pt. 1: The Drive for Integration," *Chief Marketer Network*, February 18, 2009,

http://www.chiefmarketer.com/blog/big-fat-marketing-blog/bowl-post-game-pt-1-the-drive-for-integration-18022009; John Sternal, "Integrated PR and Marketing; A Grand Slam," *Merit Mile Communication*, March 10, 2009, www.meritmile.com/pr/integrated-pr-and-marketing.
110. Quinton, "Bowl Post-Game Pt. 1: The Drive for Integration"; "Denny's Scores a Promotion Touchdown," *Stradella Road*, February 4, 2009, www.stradellaroad.com.
111. Goetzl, "Denny's Super Bowl Ad Value: 'Incredible.'"
112. Brian Clark, "Don't Waste Your Time With Native Advertising (Do This Instead)," *Say Daily*, February 27, 2014, saydaily.com/2014/02/dont-waste-your-time-with-native-advertising-do-this-instead#awesm=~oFGdbhPAhcdesg.
113. Demian Farnworth, "Copyblogger's 2014 State of Native Advertising Report," *Copyblogger*, April 7, 2014, www.copyblogger.com/native-advertising-2014/.
114. Lucia Moses, "The Washington Post's Native Ads get Editorial Treatment Borrowing From the Newsroom," *Ad Week*, March 3, 2014, www.adweek.com/news/press/washington-posts-native-ads-get-editorial-treatment-156048.
115. Antony Young, "Native Advertising Is Making Media Brands Count for More, Not Less," *Advertising Age*, May 29, 2013, adage.com/article/digitalnext/media-native-good-news/241727/.
116. Demian Farnworth, "12 Examples of Native Ads (and Why They Work)," *Copyblogger*, April 14, 2014, http://www.copyblogger.com/examples-of-native-ads/.
117. Ibid.; Julie Moos, "The Atlantic Publishers Then Pulls Sponsored Content From Church of Scientology," *Poynter.org*, January 15, 2013, www.poynter.org/latest-news/mediawire/200593/the-atlantic-pulls-sponsored-content-from-church-of-scientology/.
118. Jeff Sonderman, "Atlantic Introduces Sponsored Content Guidelines That Address the Scientology Incident," *Poynter.org*, January 30, 2013, www.poynter.org/latest-news/mediawire/202316/atlantic-introduces-sponsored-content-guidelines-that-address-the-scientology-incident/.
119. "Denny's Scores a Promotion Touchdown."
120. Goetzl, "Denny's Super Bowl Ad Value: 'Incredible.'"
121. Robert Seidman, "DVR Penetration Grows to 39.7% of Households, 42.2% of Viewers," March 23, 2011, tvbythenumbers.zap2it.com/2011/03/23/dvr-penetration-grows-to-39-7-of-households-42-2-of-viewers/.
122. Julie Bosman, "TV and Top Marketers Discuss the State of the Medium," *New York Times*, March 24, 2006; Julie Bosman, "A Match Made in Product Placement Heaven," *New York Times*, May 31, 2006.
123. Paul Davidson, "Ad Campaigns for Your Tiny Cellphone Screen Get Bigger: Marketers Leverage Growth in Text Messaging, Wireless Web," *USA Today*, August 9, 2006.
124. Kathryn Koegel, "Unilever Turkey's Cornetto Ice Cream Wins Global Media Awards,"*Advertising Age*, February 15, 2011, adage.com/article/global-news/mobile-marketing-campaigns-u-s/148886/.
125. Stuart Elliott, "More Products Get Roles in Shows, and Marketers Wonder If They're Getting Their Money's Worth," *New York Times*, March 29, 2005.
126. Ibid.
127. Andrew Adam Newman, "Once a Seldom-Heard Word, Pregnancy Is Now in the Spotlight," *New York Times*, April 2, 2009.
128. Doreen Carvajal, "Placing the Product in the Dialog, Too," *New York Times*, January 17, 2006.
129. Learmonth, "Online Advertising Spending Expected to Be Down for 2009"; *Advertising Age,* "100 Leading National Advertisers: 2009 Edition Index."
130. Jefferson Graham, "Google's Adsense a Bonanza for Some Websites," *USA Today*, March 11, 2005.
131. Ken Auletta, *Googled: The End of the World as We Know It* (New York, Penguin Press: 2009).
132. Louise Story, "Marketers Demanding Better Count of the Clicks," *New York Times*, October 30, 2006.
133. Jefferson Graham, "Google to Experiment With Newspaper Ad Sales Online; Search Giant to Offer Print Options to Customer Base," *USA Today*, November 6, 2006.
134. Ibid.

Chapter 12

1. E. J. Schultz, "Dip Dilemma: Is Kraft Running Out of Velveeta?" *AdAge.com*, January 7, 2014, http://adage.com/article/news/dip-dilemma-kraft-running-velveeta/290932/.
2. Jenn Harris, "Kraft Confirms Velveeta Shortage, a.k.a. Cheesepocalypse," *Los Angeles Times*, January 10, 2014 http://www.latimes.com/food/dailydish/la-dd-velveeta-confirms-liquid-gold-cheesepocalypse-shortage-20140110-story.html.
3. "The #Cheesepocalypse Is Real: Your Reactions to the Velveeta Shortage," Great Ideas *People*, January 8, 2014, http://greatideas.people.com/2014/01/08/velveeta-shortage-cheesepocalypse/.
4. Harris; Sandi Moynihan, "#Cheesepocaplypse: Surviving the Super Bowl Without Velveeta," *The Style Blog*, February 1, 2014, http://www.washingtonpost.com/blogs/style-blog/wp/2014/02/01/cheesepocalypse-surviving-the-super-bowl-without-velveeta/.
5. Jack Neff, "How 'Cheesepocalypse' Helped Velveeta Bond With Its Biggest Fans," *Advertising Age*, March 24, 2014, http://adage.com/article/media/cheesepocalypse-helped-velveeta-bond-biggest-fans/292297/?utm_source=daily_email&utm_medium=newsletter&utm_campaign=adage&ttl=1396317492.
6. Eddie Yoon, Steve Carlotti, and Dennis Moore, "Make Your Best Consumers Even Better," *Harvard Business Review*, March 2014, http://hbr.org/2014/03/make-your-best-customers-even-better/ar/1.
7. "Food Marketing 201: Cheesepocalypse Outs Big Velveeta Fans," *ConscienHealth*, March 2014, http://conscienhealth.org/2014/03/food-marketing-201-cheesepocalypse-outs-big-velveeta-fans/.
8. Christie Dedman, "Why the Velveeta Cheesepocalypse Shortage May Be a Good Thing," January 14, 2014, http://blog.al.com/bargain-mom/2014/01/why_the_velveeta_cheesepocalyp.html.
9. Marvin N. Olasky, *Corporate Public Relations: A New Historical Perspective* (Hillsdale, N.J.: Lawrence Erlbaum Associates, 1987).
10. Ibid.
11. Cynthia E. Clark, "Differences Between Public Relations and Corporate Social Responsibility: An Analysis," *Public Relations Review* 26, no. 3 (2000).
12. Olasky, *Corporate Public Relations*.
13. Ibid.
14. H. Frazier Moore and Frank B. Kalupa, *Public Relations: Principles, Cases, and Problems*, 9th ed. (Homewood, Ill.: Richard D. Irwin, Inc., 1985).
15. John C. Stauber and Sheldon Rampton, *Toxic Sludge Is Good for You: Lies, Damn Lies, and the Public Relations Industry* (Monroe, Maine: Common Courage Press, 1995).

16. Olasky, *Corporate Public Relations*.
17. Ray Eldon Hiebert, *Courtier to the Crowd: The Story of Ivy Lee and the Development of Public Relations* (Ames: Iowa State University Press, 1966).
18. Edward L. Bernays, *Public Relations* (Norman: University of Oklahoma Press, 1952).
19. Hiebert, *Courtier to the Crowd*.
20. Ibid.
21. Bernays, *Public Relations*.
22. Stauber and Rampton, *Toxic Sludge Is Good for You*.
23. Bernays, *Public Relations*.
24. Shearon A. Lowery and Melvin L. DeFleur, *Milestones in Mass Communication*, 3rd ed. (White Plains, N.Y.: Longman, 1995).
25. Bernays, *Public Relations*.
26. Moore and Kalupa, *Public Relations: Principles, Cases, and Problems*.
27. Bernays, *Public Relations*.
28. Scott M. Cutlip, Allen H. Center, and Glen M. Broom, *Effective Public Relations* (Upper Saddle River, N.J.: Prentice-Hall, 2000).
29. Raymond Moley, "The Birth of the Production Code (1945)," in *The Movies in Our Midst: Documents in the Cultural History of Film in America*, ed. Gerald Mast (Chicago, Ill.: University of Chicago Press, 1982).
30. Olasky, *Corporate Public Relations*.
31. Kathleen S. Kelly, "Stewardship; The Fifth Step in the Public Relations Process," in *Handbook of Public Relations*, ed. Robert Lawrence Heath and Gabriel M. Vasquez (Thousand Oaks, Calif.: Sage Publications, Inc., 2001).
32. Ibid.
33. Bloomberg News Service, "Anti-Snore Aids Score Big in Super Bowl of Marketing," *Los Angeles Times*, August 20, 1996.
34. Moore and Kalupa, *Public Relations: Principles, Cases, and Problems*.
35. Bloomberg News Service, "Anti-Snore Aids Score Big in Super Bowl of Marketing."
36. Della De Lafuente, "Pros Breathe Life Into Firm's Profits," *Chicago Sun-Times*, January 26, 1996.
37. Melanie Wells, "Small Ad Budgets Don't Stop Super Bowl Play," *USA Today*, January 23, 1996.
38. PR Newswire, "Breathe Right® Celebrates Super Bowl With Commemorative Strips," January 16, 2001, www.thefreelibrary.com/Breathe+Right(R)+Celebrates+Super+Bowl+with+Commemorative+Strips.-a069199900.
39. .Ibid.
40. Joe Drape, "Ruling Clears Way for California Chrome to Run in Belmont," *New York Times*, May 19, 2014, www.nytimes.com/2014/05/20/sports/california-chrome-can-use-nasal-strip-in-the-belmont.html?hpw&rref=sports&_r=0; Paul Walsh, "California Chrome's nasal strip OK has Delano company breathing easier," Star Tribune, May 20, 2014, www.startribune.com/business/259820621.html.
41. "Giants Fans Breathe Right and Love Their Team," *Partnership Activation*, May 10, 2010, http://www.partnershipactivation.com/sportsbiz/2010/5/10/giants-fans-breathe-right-and-love-their-team.html.
42. Moore and Kalupa, *Public Relations: Principles, Cases, and Problems*.
43. Hanson.
44. David P. Bianco, ed., *PR News Casebook: 1,000 Public Relations Case Studies* (Potomac, Md.: Gale Research Inc., 1993).
45. Karleen Murphy, "10 Common Intranet Complaints—and How to Resolve Them," *Ragan.com*, May 14, 2014, http://www.ragan.com/InternalCommunications/Articles/48317.aspx.
46. Hanson, interviews.
47. David E. Williams and Bolanle A. Olaniran, "Exxon's Decision-Making Flaws: The Hypervigilant Response to the *Valdez* Grounding," *Public Relations Review* 20, no. 1 (1994).
48. David McCormack, "Inside Marketing & PR: The Pulling Power of the 'Dark Side,'" *The Guardian*, January 22, 2007.
49. Susanne Courtney, "Measuring PR," *Marketing Magazine*, October 30, 2000.
50. Hanson, interviews.
51. Lazar, "Foot-in-Mouth Disease."
52. Ibid.
53. William J. Small, "Exxon *Valdez*: How to Spend Billions and Still Get a Black Eye," *Public Relations Review* 17, no. 1 (1991).
54. Williams and Olaniran, "Exxon's Decision-Making Flaws: The Hypervigilant Response to the *Valdez* Grounding."
55. Wayne L. Pines, "Myths of Crisis Management," *Public Relations Quarterly* 45, no. 3 (2000).
56. Lazar, "Foot-in-Mouth Disease."
57. Alex Edge, "Yamaha Offers Buyback Option for 2006 R6 Owners," *Motorcycle Daily*, February 14, 2006, http://www.motorcycledaily.com/2006/02/14february06_r6buyback/.
58. John Holusha, "Exxon's Public-Relations Problem," *New York Times*, April 21, 1989.
59. Dana James, "When Your Company Goes Code Blue," *Marketing News*, November 6, 2000.
60. Williams and Olaniran, "Exxon's Decision-Making Flaws: The Hypervigilant Response to the *Valdez* Grounding."
61. N. R. Kleinfield, "Tylenol's Rapid Comeback," *New York Times*, September 17, 1983.
62. Moore and Kalupa, *Public Relations: Principles, Cases, and Problems*.
63. Kleinfield, "Tylenol's Rapid Comeback."
64. Jeff Blyskal and Marie Blyskal, *PR: How the Public Relations Industry Writes the News* (New York: Morrow, 1985).
65. Ibid.; Kleinfield, "Tylenol's Rapid Comeback."
66. Small, "Exxon *Valdez*: How to Spend Billions and Still Get a Black Eye."
67. Holusha, "Exxon's Public-Relations Problem."
68. Williams and Olaniran, "Exxon's Decision-Making Flaws: The Hypervigilant Response to the Valdez Grounding."
69. Holusha, "Exxon's Public-Relations Problem"; Small, "Exxon *Valdez*: How to Spend Billions and Still Get a Black Eye."
70. Williams and Olaniran, "Exxon's Decision-Making Flaws: The Hypervigilant Response to the *Valdez* Grounding."
71. Small, "Exxon *Valdez:* How to Spend Billions and Still Get a Black Eye."
72. Anne C. Mulkern, "BP's PR Blunders Mirror Exxon's, Appear Destined for Record Book," *New York Times*, June 10, 2010, www.nytimes.com/gwire/2010/06/10/10greenwire-bps-pr-blunders-mirror-exxons-appear-destined-98819.html.
73. Jonathan Bernstein, "Crisis Manager University: My Top 5 Internet-Related Crisis Management Tips," www.bernsteincrisismanagement.com/nl/crisismgr070101.html.
74. Carole M. Howard, "Technology and Tabloids: How the New Media World Is Changing Our Jobs," *Public Relations Quarterly* 45, no. 1 (2000).
75. Jonathan Bernstein, "Who Are These Bloggers, and Why Are They Saying Those Terrible Things?" *Associations Now*, October 2006.
76. Leigh Householder, "Pharma Case Study: Epilepsy Advocate," *Ragan's Health Care Communication News*, May 14, 2014, http://healthcarecommunication.com/Main/Articles/12071.aspx#.
77. Pamela Seiple, "How to Leverage Social Media for Public Relations Success," 2012, www.hubspot.com/Portals/53/docs/hubspot_social_media_pr_ebook.pdf.

78. Stephanie Clifford, "Video Prank at Domino's Taints Brand," *New York Times*, April 16, 2009.
79. Emily Bryson York, "What Domino's Did Right—and Wrong—in Squelching Hubbub Over YouTube Video; Pizza Purveyor Faulted for Waiting to Respond but Did Well in the End," *Advertising Age*, April 20, 2009.
80. Ibid.
81. Raymund Flandez, "Domino's Response Offers Lessons in Crisis Management." *Wall Street Journal*, April 20, 2009, http://blogs.wsj.com/independentstreet/2009/04/20/dominos-response-offers-lessons-in-crisis-management/.
82. Bruce Horowitz, "Pizza Hut 'Embarrassed' Over Peeing Video," *USA Today*, February 14, 2014, www.usatoday.com/story/money/business/2014/02/19/pizza-hut-dominos-crisis-management-fast-food/5609225/; Ariel Rothfield, "UPDATE: WV Pizza Hut Permanently Closed After Shocking Video Surfaces on YouTube," WOWKTV.COM, March 13, 2014, http://www.wowktv.com/story/24756182/shocking-video-leads-to-local-pizza-hut-closing-kermit-wv-urine.
83. Alice Gomstyn, "Brown's, Domino's and Beyond: Business Felled by Crime, Scandal," *ABC News*, October 1, 2009, abcnews.go.com/Business/browns-chicken-dominos-crimes-hurt-stores-restaurants/story?id=8706183.
84. Melissa Allison, "Corporations Seek to Clean Up Online Rumors," *Seattle Times*, March 4, 2007.
85. David L. Altheide and Robert P. Snow, *Media Worlds in the Postjournalism Era* (Hawthorne, N.Y.: Aldine De Gruyter, 1991).
86. Blyskal and Blyskal, *PR: How the Public Relations Industry Writes the News*.
87. Dana Harris, "Flack Pack Hits Burnout Track," *Variety*, April 17–23, 2000.
88. "Lobbying Database," OpenSecrets.org, April 28, 2014, www.opensecrets.org/lobby/.
89. Moore and Kalupa, *Public Relations: Principles, Cases, and Problems*; Tim LaPira, "How Much Lobbying Is There in Washington? It's DOUBLE What You Think," *Sunlight Foundation*, November 25, 2013, sunlightfoundation.com/blog/2013/11/25/how-much-lobbying-is-there-in-washington-its-double-what-you-think/.
90. Jeffrey H. Birnbaum, "The Road to Riches Is Called K Street," *Washington Post*, June 22, 2005.
91. Betsy Rothstein, "Capital Living: The Fine Art of Flacking," *The Hill*, February 22, 2006.
92. Ibid.
93. Sarah Lyall, "Trying to Know a Queen (Right Down to the Tupperware)," *New York Times*, September 24, 2006.
94. Moore and Kalupa, *Public Relations: Principles, Cases, and Problems*.
95. Randy Sumpter and James Tankard, "The Spin Doctor: An Alternative View of Public Relations," *Public Relations Review* 20, no. 1 (1994).
96. Ibid.
97. All quotes in this section are from interviews with Ralph Hanson held on October 20, 2009, and April 25, 2012.
98. Daniel Zwerdling, "Fast-Food Deal a Big Win for Small Migrants' Group," NPR, June 16, 2005, www.npr.org/templates/story/story.php?storyId=4706271.
99. David Halberstam, "And Now, Live From Little Rock," *Newsweek*, September 29, 1997.
100. Stephen B. Oates, *Let the Trumpet Sound* (New York: Harper & Row, 1982).
101. Ibid.; Martin Luther King Jr.,*The Autobiography of Martin Luther King Jr.*, ed. Clayborne Carson (New York: Warner Books, 1998); Steven Kasher, *The Civil Rights Movement: A Photographic History, 1954–68* (New York: Abbeville Press, 1996).

Chapter 13

1. Matt Schudel, "A Local Life: Barbara A. Ringer, 83; Force Behind New Copyright Law," *Washington Post*, April 26, 2009.
2. Ibid.
3. Stephen Miller, "She Helped Put Her Stamp on Copyright Law," *Wall Street Journal*, May 9, 2009.
4. Judith Nierman, "Barbara Ringer, 9th Register of Copyrights, Dies," *Copyright Notices*, April 2009.
5. Schudel, "A Local Life: Barbara A. Ringer, 83; Force Behind New Copyright Law."
6. Miller, "She Helped Put Her Stamp on Copyright Law."
7. Matt Schudel, "Barbara Ringer's Untold Story," *Washington Post*, April 29, 2009,
8. voices.washingtonpost.com/postmortem/2009/04/barbara_ringers_untold_story.html.
9. Schudel, "A Local Life: Barbara A. Ringer, 83; Force Behind New Copyright Law"; Nierman, "Barbara Ringer, 9th Register of Copyrights, Dies."
10. Nierman, "Barbara Ringer, 9th Register of Copyrights, Dies."
11. Schudel, "A Local Life: Barbara A. Ringer, 83; Force Behind New Copyright Law."
12. Fred H. Cate, *Privacy in the Information Age* (Washington, D.C.: Brookings Institution, 1997).
13. Ibid.
14. Legal Information Institute, "Legal Information Institute," Cornell Law School, www.law.cornell.edu.
15. Kenneth Creech, *Electronic Media Law and Regulation*, 3rd ed. (Boston: Focal Press, 2000).
16. Ben H. Bagdikian, "Not Just Another Business," University of Arizona, journalism.arizona.edu/.
17. Herbert N. Foerstel, *Banned in the Media* (Westport, Conn.: Greenwood Press, 1998).
18. Creech, *Electronic Media Law and Regulation*; Foerstel, *Banned in the Media*.
19. Harley Geiger, "Issue Brief: Bulk Collection of Records Under Section 215 of the PATRIOT Act," Center for Democracy and Technology, February 10, 2014, cdt.org/blog/issue-brief-bulk-collection-of-records-under-section-215-of-the-patriot-act/.
20. Cindy Cohn and Nadia Kayyali, "Understanding the New USA FREEDOM Act: Questions, Concerns, and EFF's Decision to Support the Bill," Electronic Freedom Foundation, www.eff.org/deeplinks/2014/08/understanding-new-usa-freedom-act-questions-concerns-and-effs-decision-support.
21. Kim Zetter, "Few Companies Fight Patriot Act Gag Orders, FBI Admits," *Wired*, May 10, 2012, www.wired.com/threatlevel/2012/05/nsl-challenges/.
22. "Patriot Act Extension Signed Into Law Despite Bipartisan Resistance in Congress," *Washington Post*, May 27, 2011, www.washingtonpost.com/politics/patriot-act-extension-signed-into-law-despite-bipartisan-resistance-in-congress/2011/05/27/AGbVlsCH_story.html.
23. Rodney A. Smolla, *Law of Defamation* (New York: Clark Boardman Company, 1988).
24. Barbara Dill, *The Journalist's Handbook on Libel and Privacy* (New York: Free Press, 1986).
25. 376 U.S. 254 (1964).
26. Dill, *The Journalist's Handbook on Libel and Privacy*.
27. W. Wat Hopkins, *Actual Malice: Twenty-Five Years After* Times v. Sullivan (New York: Praeger, 1989).
28. Ibid.
29. Ibid.

30. Ibid.
31. 418 U.S. 323 (1974).
32. Ellyn Angelotti, "How Courtney Love and U.S.'s First Twitter Libel Trial Could Impact Journalists," *Poynter*, January 14, 2014, www.poynter.org/latest-news/top-stories/235728/how-courtney-love-and-u-s-s-first-twitter-libel-trial-could-impact-journalists/.
33. Associated Press, "Courtney Love Wins Twitter Libel Case," *CBS News*, January 24, 2014, www.cbsnews.com/news/courtney-love-wins-twitter-libel-case/.
34. Dill, *The Journalist's Handbook on Libel and Privacy*.
35. Cate, *Privacy in the Information Age*.
36. Deckle McLean, *Privacy and Its Invasion* (Westport, Conn.: Praeger Publishers, 1995).
37. Dill, *The Journalist's Handbook on Libel and Privacy*.
38. Ibid.
39. Pember and Calvert, *Mass Media Law*.
40. Ibid.
41. Oscar Dixon, "Jordan Reclaims Richest Athlete Title," *USA Today*, December 1, 1997.
42. Associated Press, "Jennifer Aniston Settles Lawsuit With 'Invasive' Photographer," *Fox News*, September 2, 2006, www.foxnews.com/story/0,2933,211903,00.html?sPage=fnc.entertainment/aniston; "Blogger Sued Over Topless Aniston Photo," *ABC News*, February 21, 2007, abcnews.go.com/Entertainment/wireStory?id=2893926.
43. "Aniston Warns Over Topless Photos," December 5, 2005, www.thesmokinggun.com/archive/1205051aniston1.html.
44. Adrean S. Taylor, "Common Law Invasion of Privacy Claims in Social Media [Guest Post]," Wassom.com, July 2, 2013, www.wassom.com/common-law-invasion-of-privacy-claims-in-social-media-guest-post.html.
45. Dionne Searcey, "A New California Law Places Paparazzi Under the Spotlight," *Wall Street Journal*, October 29, 2009.
46. Christopher Dickey, Mark Hosenball, and Geoffrey Cowley, "A Needless Tragedy," *Newsweek*, September 22, 1997.
47. Larysa Pyk, "Legislative Update: Putting the Brakes on Paparazzi," *Journal of Art and Entertainment Law* 187, no. 9 (1998).
48. Associated Press, "Magazine Fined Over Picture of Diana and Dodi," *Ottawa Citizen*, April 29, 1998.
49. Ester Laushway, "What Price Privacy?" *Europe*, October 1997.
50. "Whose Life Is It Anyway?" *Economist*, March 9, 2002.
51. Jane Kirtley, "Privacy for Sale," *American Journalism Review*, March 2001.
52. Steve Doughty and Richard Simpson, "OK! Magazine Wins Appeal over Zeta-Jones Wedding Photos—but at a Price," *Daily Mail*, May 3, 2007.
53. Dan Tench, "When Uncertainty Takes Precedence: Elton John's Failed Injunction Against a Newspaper Printing a Photo of Him in the Street Highlights Our Hopelessly Confused Privacy Law," *Guardian,* July 24, 2006, 10.
54. Adam Wagner, "Is the Human Rights Act Dead?" *Guardian*, October 3, 2011, www.guardian.co.uk/law/2011/oct/03/is-the-human-rights-act-dead.
55. Laushway, "What Price Privacy?"
56. Matthew D. Bunker, *Justice and the Media: Reconciling Fair Trials and a Free Press* (Mahwah, N.J.: Lawrence Erlbaum Associates, 1997).
57. Ibid.
58. 284 U.S. 333 (1966).
59. 284 U.S. 333 (1966); Kyle Niederpruem, "Big Trials Prompt Judges to Issue More Gag Orders," *Quill*, June 1997.
60. Caitlin Dickson, "This Man Is the Future of Westboro Baptist Church," *The Daily Beast*, March 24, 2014, www.thedailybeast.com/articles/2014/03/24/this-man-is-the-future-of-westboro-baptist-church.html.
61. 752 F. Supp. 1032 (1990).
62. Bunker, *Justice and the Media: Reconciling Fair Trials and a Free Press*.
63. Steven Brill, "Cameras Belong in the Courtroom," *USA Today Magazine*, July 1996.
64. Joshua Sarner, "Comment: Justice, Take Two: The Continuing Debate Over Cameras in the Courtroom," *Seton Hall Constitutional Journal* (2000).
65. "Cameras in the Courtroom," *Quill*, September 1999.
66. Associated Press, "Minnesota Tests Cameras in the Courtroom," March 11, 2012, www.twincities.com/localnews/ci_20147979/pilot-project-tests-photo-coverage-minn-courts.
67. Lisa Balde and Phil Rogers, "Judges Enthusiastic About Cameras in the Courtroom," January 24, 2012, www.nbcchicago.com/news/local/Illinois-Supreme-Court-Approves-Cameras-in-Trial-Courtrooms-137966308.html.
68. Zoe Tillman, "Judges, Attorneys Debate Cameras in the Courtroom," March 28, 2012, legaltimes.typepad.com/blt/2012/03/judges-attorneys-debate-cameras-in-the-courtroom.html.
69. Bunker, *Justice and the Media: Reconciling Fair Trials and a Free Press*.
70. Elliot C. Rothenberg, *The Taming of the Press:* Cohen v. Cowles Media Company (Westport, Conn.: Praeger, 1999).
71. *Cohen v. Cowles Media Company,* 501 U.S. 663 (1991).
72. Lisa de Moraes, "With Appeals Court Ruling, ABC Won't Pay Food Lion's Share," *Washington Post*, October 21, 1999; Sue Anne Pressley, "Food Lion Challenges ABC's Newsgathering; Lawsuit Attacks Hidden Cameras," *Washington Post*, December 12, 1996; James C. Goodale, "Shooting the Messenger Isn't So Easy," *New York Law Journal*, December 3, 1999.
73. Goodale, "Shooting the Messenger Isn't So Easy." See also *Food Lion v. ABC,* 194 F. 3d 505 (4th Cir. 1999).
74. Bunker, *Justice and the Media*; Creech, *Electronic Media Law*. See also *Near v. Minnesota,* 283 U.S. 697 (1931).
75. Sanford J. Ungar, *The Papers and the Papers* (New York: E. P. Dutton, 1972).
76. Ibid.
77. Ben Bradlee, *A Good Life: Newspapering and Other Adventures* (New York: Simon & Schuster, 1995).
78. Ungar, *The Papers and the Papers*.
79. Ibid.
80. 403 U.S. 713 (1971).
81. Peter Schrag, *Test of Loyalty: Daniel Ellsberg and the Rituals of Secret Government* (New York: Simon & Schuster, 1974).
82. Francis Wilkinson, *Essential Liberty: First Amendment Battles for a Free Press* (New York: Columbia University Graduate School of Journalism, 1992).
83. Duncan Campbell, "It's Time to Take Risks," *Guardian,* December 10, 2002, http://www.guardian.co.uk/books/2002/dec/10/biography.usa.
84. Foerstel, *Banned in the Media*.
85. Howard Morland, *The Secret That Exploded* (New York: Random House, 1981).
86. Foerstel, *Banned in the Media*.
87. 484 U.S. 260 (1988).
88. Ibid.
89. Mark Goodman, "Freedom of the Press Stops at the Schoolhouse Gate," *Nieman Reports*, Spring 2001.
90. Ibid.
91. Tara Bahrampour and Lori Aratani, "Teens' Bold Blogs Alarm Area Schools," *Washington Post,* January 17, 2006, A01.
92. "Austin Carroll, Indiana High School Student, Expelled for Tweeting Profanity," *Huffington Post*, March 25, 2012,

www.huffingtonpost.com/2012/03/25/austin-carroll-indiana-hi_n_1378250.html.
93. Case argued before the U.S. Supreme Court, March 19, 2007; 551 U.S. 393 (2007).
94. Robert Barnes, "Justices to Hear Landmark Free-Speech Case," *Washington Post,* March 13, 2007, A03; Charles Lane, "Court Backs School on Speech Curbs,"*Washington Post,* June 26, 2007, A06.
95. Ibid.
96. Cora Currier, "Pressure, Potential for a Federal Shield Law," *Columbia Journalism Review,* June 13, 2014, www.cjr.org/behind_the_news/shield_law_risen_etc.php.
97. Liz Harper, "First Amendment Understanding Lacking," PBS, February 7, 2005, www.pbs.org/newshour/.
98. Zachary M. Seward, "Shield Law: Definition of 'Journalist' Gets Professionalized," Nieman Foundation at Harvard University, September 23, 2009, www.niemanlab.org/2009/09/shield-law-definition-of-journalist-gets-professionalized/.
99. Casey Murray and Kirsten B. Mitchell, "Would a Shield Law Matter?" *The News Media and the Law* 30, no. 3 (2006): 4.
100. Ibid.; Howard Kurtz, "No More Miller Time," *Washington Post*, September 30, 2005, www.washingtonpost.com/wp-dyn/content/blog/2005/09/30/BL2005093000363.html.
101. Ina Fried and Declan McCullagh, "Apple Thwarted in Bid to Unmask Leaker," c|net News, May 26, 2006, news.cnet.com/Apple%20thwarted%20in%20bid%20to%20unmask%20leaker/2100-1047_3-6077547.html?tag=item.
102. Howard Kurtz, "Blogger Makes Deal, Is Released From Jail," *Washington Post,* April 4, 2007, C01.
103. Ibid.
104. Edward Donnerstein, Daniel Linz, and Steven Penrod, *The Question of Pornography* (New York: Free Press, 1987).
105. 354 U.S. 476 (1957).
106. U.S. Supreme Court, *"Samuel Roth, Petitioner v. United States of America, David S. Alberts, Appellant," Communications & the Law* 21, no. 4 (1999).
107. Donnerstein, Linz, and Penrod, *The Question of Pornography*.
108. Ibid.
109. Franklin Mark Osanka and Sara Lee Johann, *Sourcebook on Pornography* (Lexington, Mass.: Lexington Books, 1989).
110. Rieko Mashima, "Problem of the Supreme Court's Obscenity Test Concerning Cyberporn," *The Computer Lawyer* 16, no. 11 (1999).
111. Timothy Egan, "Erotica Inc.—A Special Report; Technology Sent Wall Street Into Market for Pornography," *New York Times*, October 23, 2000.
112. Edward Rothstein, "The Owners of Culture vs. the Free Agents," *New York Times*, January 18, 2003.
113. Amy Harmon, "New Visibility for 1998 Copyright Protection Law, With Online Enthusiasts Confused and Frustrated," *New York Times*, August 13, 2001.
114. Minjeong Kim, "The Creative Commons and Copyright Protection in the Digital Era: Uses of Creative Commons Licenses," *Journal of Computer-Mediated Communication* 13, no. 1 (2007).
115. Creech, *Electronic Media Law and Regulation*.
116. Linda Harowitz, "Laying the Fairness Doctrine to Rest: Was the Doctrine's Elimination Really Fair?" *George Washington Law Review* 58, no. 994 (1990).
117. Kathy E. Gill, "Who Really Owns Your Photos in Social Media?" (Updated 2013 Edition), *MediaShift*, January 25, 2013, www.pbs.org/mediashift/2013/01/who-really-owns-your-photos-in-social-media-updated-2013-edition025/.
118. Kerry O'Shea Gorgone, "Who Owns Your Social Media Content?" *Social Media Explorer*, November 13, 2012, www.socialmediaexplorer.com/media-journalism/who-owns-your-social-media-content/.
119. Creech, *Electronic Media Law and Regulation*.
120. Harowitz, "Laying the Fairness Doctrine to Rest: Was the Doctrine's Elimination Really Fair?"
121. Thomas Blaisdell Smith, "Reexamining the Reasonable Access and Equal Time Provisions of the Federal Communications Act," *Georgetown Law Journal* 74, no. 1491 (1986); Creech, *Electronic Media Law and Regulation*; Dan Fletcher, "The Fairness Doctrine," *Time*, February 20, 2009.
122. Rush Limbaugh, "Mr. President, Keep the Airwaves Free," *Wall Street Journal*, February 20, 2009, online.wsj.com/article/SB123508978035028163.html.
123. Brooks Boliek, "FCC Finally Kills Off Fairness Doctrine," *Politico*, August 22, 2011, www.politico.com/news/stories/0811/61851.html; Dylan Matthews, "Everything You Need to Know About the Fairness Doctrine in One Post," *Washington Post*, August 23, 2011, www.washingtonpost.com/blogs/ezra-klein/post/every thing-you-need-to-know-about-the-fairness-doctrine-in-one-post/2011/08/23/gIQAN8CXZJ_blog.html.
124. Creech, *Electronic Media Law and Regulation*.
125. Ibid.
126. Cecilia Kang, "FCC to Draft Net Neutrality Rules, Taking Step Toward Web Regulation," *Washington Post*, October 23, 2009.
127. Foerstel, *Banned in the Media*.
128. David L. Hudson Jr., "Indecency Online," November 17, 2006, www.firstamendmentcenter.org/.

Chapter 14

1. Richard Drew, text of speech delivered September 11, 2002, to the P.I. Reed School of Journalism, University of West Virginia; Kenny Irby, "Behind the Lens: Part 1," Poynter Institute, October 5, 2001; Jeff Young, interviews with Richard Drew and Richard Pyle, 2002.
2. Kenny Irby, "Behind the Lens: Part 1," Poynter Institute, October 5, 2001.
3. Joe Pompeo, "Photographer Behind 9/11 'Falling Man' Retraces Steps, Recalls 'Unknown Soldier,'" August 29, 2011, news.yahoo.com/photographer-behind-9-11-falling-man-retraces-steps-recalls-unknown-soldier.html.
4. Drew, text of speech.
5. Irby, "Behind the Lens: Part 1."
6. Mac Daniel, "America Prepares Aftermath of Attack/Images of Loss; Families Scan News Photos for Hope," *Boston Globe*, September 20, 2001.
7. Philip Patterson and Lee Wilkins, *Media Ethics, Issues and Cases* (New York: McGraw-Hill, 2002).
8. Doug Underwood, "Secularists or Modern Day Prophets? Journalists' Ethics and the Judeo-Christian Tradition," *Journal of Mass Media Ethics* 16, no. 1 (2001).
9. Franklin Foer, "The Wayward Critic," *New Republic*, May 15, 2000.
10. Larry Z. Leslie, *Mass Communication Ethics* (Boston: Houghton Mifflin, 2000).
11. Patterson and Wilkins, *Media Ethics, Issues and Cases*.
12. David L. Martinson, "Ethical Decision Making in Public Relations: What Would Aristotle Say?" *Public Relations Quarterly* 45, no. 3 (2000).
13. Andrew Sharp, "Robert Griffin III and the Heartbreaking *Washington Post* Sports Page," *SB Nation*, January 7, 2013, www.sbnation.com/nfl/2013/1/7/3845826/robert-griffin-iii-redskins-injury-washington-post.
14. Nick Brincks, Twitter, January 7, 2013, twitter.com/NickBrincks/status/288296830947713026?uid=79253251&iid=d946026a-5679-45a9-b694-68457e81cbc5&nid=4+246.

15. Timothy Burke, "Kevin Ware Suffered Maybe the Most Gruesome Injury in the History of Televised Sports [WARNING: VERY GROSS]," *Deadspin*, March 31, 2013, deadspin.com/kevin-ware-suffered-maybe-the-most-gruesome-injury-in-t-464789219; Sam Amick, "Paul George Injury Ends USA Basketball Scrimmage," *USA Today*, August 2, 2014, www.usatoday.com/story/sports/nba/2014/08/01/paul-george-injury-team-usa/13498731/.
16. Leslie, *Mass Communication Ethics*.
17. Patterson and Wilkins, *Media Ethics, Issues and Cases*.
18. Howard Berkes, Barbara Bradley Hagerty, and Jennifer Ludden, "NBC Defends Release of Va. Tech Gunman Video," NPR, April 19, 2007, www.npr.org/templates/story/story.php?storyId=9604204.
19. Leslie, *Mass Communication Ethics*.
20. Elizabeth Blanks Hindman, "Divergence of Duty: Differences in Legal and Ethical Responsibilities," *Journal of Mass Media Ethics* 14, no. 4 (1999).
21. Patterson and Wilkins, *Media Ethics, Issues and Cases*.
22. Irby, "Behind the Lens: Part 1."
23. Patterson and Wilkins, *Media Ethics, Issues and Cases*.
24. Sissela Bok, *Lying: Moral Choice in Public and Private Life* (New York: Pantheon Books, 1978).
25. Martinson, "Ethical Decision Making in Public Relations: What Would Aristotle Say?"
26. John C. Merrill, "Needed: A More Ethical Press," in *The Media and Morality*, ed. Robert M. Baird, William E. Loges, and Stuart E. Rosenbaum (Amherst, N.Y.: Prometheus Books, 1999).
27. Steven Brill, "Rewind: What Book Reviews Don't Review," *Brill's Content*, August 1999.
28. Paul Tullis and Lorne Manly, "Slipping Past the Fact Checkers: How Magazines Do and Do Not Check Their Stories," *Brill's Content*, July/August 1998.
29. Ann Reilly Dowd, "The Great Pretender: How a Writer Fooled His Readers," *Columbia Journalism Review*, July/August 1998.
30. "Shattered Glass," *Vanity Fair*, October 2007.
31. Tullis and Manly, "Slipping Past the Fact Checkers: How Magazines Do and Do Not Check Their Stories."
32. Dowd, "The Great Pretender: How a Writer Fooled His Readers."
33. Jose Antonio Vargas, "My Life as an Undocumented Immigrant," *New York Times*, June 22, 2011, www.nytimes.com/2011/06/26/magazine/my-life-as-an-undocumented-immigrant.html.
34. Jamil Smith, "Putting a Face to the Name 'Illegal,'" June 29, 2011, www.msnbc.com/rachel-maddow-show/putting-face-the-name-illegal.
35. Frances Martel, "The *Washington Post* Turned Down Jose Vargas's Illegal Immigrant Story," June 22, 2011, www.mediaite.com/online/the-washington-post-turned-down-jose-vargas-illegal-immigrant-story/.
36. Mike Pseca, "Journalist Jose Vargas's Illegal Immigration Revelation," *On the Media*, June 24, 2011, www.onthemedia.org/2011/jun/24/journalist-jose-vargas-illegal-immigration-revelation/transcript/.
37. Phil Bronstein, "I Was Duped by Jose Vargas, Illegal Immigrant," June 22, 2011, blog.sfgate.com/bronstein/2011/06/22/i-was-duped-by-jose-vargas-illegal-immigrant/.
38. Charles Davis and Stephanie Craft, "New Media Synergy: Emergence of Institutional Conflicts of Interest," *Journal of Mass Media Ethics* 15, no. 4 (2000).
39. Staci D. Kramer, "Another Newspaper Buys into a Baseball Team," *Editor & Publisher*, January 6, 1996; Richard Sandomir, "New Owner to Improve Wrigley, and Maybe the Cubs," *New York Times*, October 31, 2009.
40. Lance Morrow, "Journalism After Diana," in *The Media and Morality*, ed. Robert M. Baird, William E. Loges, and Stuart E. Rosenbaum (Amherst, N.Y.: Prometheus Books, 1999).
41. Edna Buchanan, *The Corpse Had a Familiar Face* (New York: Charter Books, 1987).
42. William L. Hamilton, "Low Down; Repulsed, yet Watching All the Same," *New York Times*, December 3, 2006.
43. Jacqueline Sharkey, "The Diana Aftermath," in *The Media and Morality*, ed. Robert M. Baird, William E. Loges, and Stuart E. Rosenbaum (Amherst, N.Y.: Prometheus Books, 1999); Howard Kurtz, "Shakeup at ABC: Coverage of Tiger Woods," CNN.com, December 13, 2009, http://transcripts.cnn.com/TRANSCRIPTS/0912/13/rs.01.html.
44. Sharkey, "The Diana Aftermath."
45. Ibid.
46. Editors, *Columbia Journalism Review*, "What Do We Do Now?" in *The Media and Morality*, ed. Robert M. Baird, William E. Loges, and Stuart E. Rosenbaum (Amherst, N.Y.: Prometheus Books, 1999).
47. Ibid.
48. Adam Goodheart, "Sleaze Journalism? It's an Old Story," in *The Media and Morality*, ed. Robert M. Baird, William E. Loges, and Stuart E. Rosenbaum (Amherst, N.Y.: Prometheus Books, 1999).
49. Ibid.
50. Neil Postman, *Amusing Ourselves to Death: Public Discourse in the Age of Show Business* (New York: Penguin Books, 1985).
51. Richard L. Connor, "A Note of Apology to Readers," *Portland Press Herald*, September 19, 2010, www.pressherald.com/note-of-apology.html.
52. Bob Garfield, "For Some, an Apology Offends," *On the Media*, September 17, 2010, www.onthemedia.org/2010/sep/17/for-some-an-apology-offends/transcript/.
53. Richard L. Connor, "Remembering E. B. White's Sage Advice," September 19, 2010, www.pressherald.com/news/remembering-e_b_-whites-sage-advice_2010-09-19.html.
54. Tamara Jones and Ann Scott Tyson, "After 44 Hours, Hope Showed Its Cruel Side," *Washington Post*, January 5, 2006.
55. "Manchin at a Loss to Explain Rescue Miscommunication: Governor Says He Got Caught up in Families' Celebration," *Charleston Daily Mail*, January 4, 2006.
56. Joe Strupp, "Local W. Va. Paper Says Skepticism Helped It Avoid Mining Story Goof," *Editor & Publisher*, January 4, 2006.
57. Ibid.
58. Vicki Smith, "Family Members Report 12 Trapped Miners Are Alive," *Charleston Gazette*, January 4, 2006.
59. Ralph Hanson, "Searching for a Miracle: Media Lessons From the West Virginia Mine Disaster," *Montana Journalism Review* (2006).
60. "Asked to Do Something Unethical," January 29, 2008, www.sportsshooter.com/*message_display.html?tid=28059*.
61. Ralph Hanson, "Lesson of the Day: Don't Photoshop Details Out of News Photos," *Living in a Media World*, December 3, 2013, www.ralphehanson.com/2013/12/03/lesson-of-the-day-dont-photoshop-details-out-of-news-photos/.
62. Gil Klein, "Computer Graphics Now Allow Subtle Alteration of News Photos," *Christian Science Monitor*, August 1, 1985.
63. James R. Gaines, "To Our Readers," *Time*, July 4, 1994.
64. Chuck Strouse, "Listen Up, McClatchy," *Miami New Times*, July 27, 2006.
65. Jennifer Dorroh, "The Ombudsman Puzzle," *American Journalism Review*, February/March 2005, ajrarchive.org/article.asp?id=3824.
66. Andrew Alexander, "Welcome to the Omblog," *Washington Post*, May 4, 2009, voices.washingtonpost.com/ombudsman-blog/2009/05/welcome_to_the_omblog.html.
67. LaMont, "Lending an Ear."

68. Kelly McBride, "NPR Ombud's Latest Report Raises Important Questions, but It's Not Without Flaws," *Poynter*, August 19, 2013, www.poynter.org/latest-news/creating-a-framework-for-ethical-decision-making-among-journalists-and-those-who-care-about-democracy/221221/npr-ombuds-latest-report-raises-important-questions-but-its-not-without-flaws/.
69. Simon Dumenco, "Is the Newspaper Ombudsman More or Less Obsolete? Five Reasons Why Having a 'Public Editor' at the *Times* and Other Papers No Longer Makes Much Sense," *Advertising Age*, March 24, 2008.
70. Jay Black, Bob Steele, and Ralph Barney, *Doing Ethics in Journalism* (Birmingham, Ala.: EBSCO Media, 1993).
71. Alex S. Jones, "Facing Ethical Challenges: The Integrity/Judgment Grid," *Columbia Journalism Review*, November/December 1999.
72. Jeffrey L. Seglin, "Codes of Ethics: Why Writing Them Is Not Enough," *Media Ethics*, Spring 2002.
73. Robert Jackall and Janice M. Hirota, *Image Makers: Advertising, Public Relations, and the Ethos of Advocacy* (Chicago: University of Chicago Press, 2000).
74. Geoffrey A. Fowler, "What You Can Do About Facebook Tracking," *Wall Street Journal*, August 5, 2014, online.wsj.com/articles/what-you-can-do-about-facebook-tracking-1407263246.
75. Julian Smith, "What Matters in Mobile," *The Drum*, August 4, 2014, www.thedrum.com/opinion/2014/08/04/promise-right-person-right-time-right-place-ad-targeting-becoming-reality-mobile.
76. Gavin O'Malley, "Facebook Improves Mobile Ad Targeting to Specific Devices," *Media Post Mobile Marketing Daily*, July 23, 2014, www.mediapost.com/publications/article/230623/facebook-improves-mobile-ad-targeting-to-specific.html.
77. Patterson and Wilkins, *Media Ethics, Issues and Cases*.
78. Rogier van Bakel, "Tall-Claims Court," *Christian Science Monitor*, February 14, 2000.
79. "Health Claims," Federal Trade Commission, August 20, 2014, www.ftc.gov/news-events/media-resources/truth-advertising/health-claims.
80. Van Bakel, "Tall-Claims Court."
81. Ibid.
82. Ibid.
83. M. L. Stein, "Auto Dealers Banned From Boycotting Calif. Media Outlets," *Editor & Publisher*, April 19, 1995.
84. M. J. Lee, "Rush Limbaugh Loses 45 Advertisers," *Politico*, March 6, 2012, www.politico.com/news/stories/0312/73675.html.
85. Paul D. Colford, "Whose Copy Is It Anyway?" *Los Angeles Times*, June 5, 1997.
86. News Services, "Is *Esquire* Slip a Step up for Mankind?" *Star Tribune*, July 12, 1997.
87. Dave Phillips, "Chrysler Drops Censorship Policy," *Detroit News*, October 14, 1997.
88. Carol Krol, "MPA Joins Editors to Limit Advertiser Interference," *Advertising Age*, September 29, 1997.
89. Jim Edwards, "Nicetv," *Brill's Content*, March 2001.
90. Valerie Kuklenski, "All in the Family; Advertisers Praise—and Fund—Shows for Everyone," *Daily News of Los Angeles*, December 7, 2006; Stuart Elliot, "Marketers, Seeking Family Show, Hold Script Contest," *New York Times*, www.nytimes.com/2012/01/23/business/media/marketers-seeking-family-shows-hold-a-script-contest.html.
91. John C. Stauber and Sheldon Rampton, *Toxic Sludge Is Good for You: Lies, Damn Lies and the Public Relations Industry* (Monroe, Maine: Common Courage Press, 1995).
92. Ibid.; Susanne A. Roschwalb, "The Hill & Knowlton Cases: A Brief on the Controversy," *Public Relations Review* 20, no. 3 (1994).
93. Stauber and Rampton, *Toxic Sludge Is Good for You*.
94. Mary McGrory, "PR Ploy Exaggerated Case Against Iraq," *St. Louis Post-Dispatch*, January 16, 1992.
95. Robert L. Koenig, "Testimony of Kuwaiti Envoy's Child Assailed," *St. Louis Post-Dispatch*, January 9, 1992.
96. Cornelius B. Pratt, "Hill & Knowlton's Two Ethical Dilemmas," *Public Relations Review* 20, no. 3 (1994).
97. Martinson, "Ethical Decision Making in Public Relations: What Would Aristotle Say?"

Chapter 15

1. "Egypt's Mubarak: End of the Great Survivor," *BBC News*, February 11, 2011, www.bbc.co.uk/news/world-middle-east-12416154.
2. Steven L. Taylor, "The Coverage of Egypt and the Fundamental Deficiencies of News in the US," January 30, 2011, www.outsidethebeltway.com/the-coverage-of-egypt-and-the-fundamental-deficiencies-of-news-in-the-us/.
3. Alex Pareene, "Al Jazeera's Egypt Coverage Embarrasses U.S. Cable News Channels," *Salon*, January 28, 2011, www.salon.com/2011/01/28/cable_news_egypt/.
4. "Egypt Shuts Down Al Jazeera Bureau," *Al Jazeera*, January 30, 2011, http://www.aljazeera.com/news/middleeast/2011/01/201113085252994161.html.
5. Philip N. Howard, "The Arab Spring's Cascading Effects," *Pacific Standard*, February 23, 2011, www.psmag.com/politics/the-cascading-effects-of-the-arab-spring-28575/.
6. Ken Auletta, *Three Blind Mice: How the TV Networks Lost Their Way* (New York: Random House, 1991), 4.
7. Dean Starkman, "Al Jazeera America Struggles to Get Off the Margins," *Columbia Journalism Review*, August 20, 2014, http://www.cjr.org/the_audit/al_jazeera_america_struggles_t.php?page=all.
8. David Folkenflik, "Al-Jazeera English Struggles for U.S. Audience," *NPR*, February 4, 2009, www.npr.org/templates/story/story.php?storyId=101071599.
9. Fred S. Siebert, Theodore Peterson, and Wilbur Schramm, *Four Theories of the Press* (Urbana: University of Illinois Press, 1956).
10. John C. Nerone, ed., *Last Rights: Revisiting* Four Theories of the Press (Urbana and Chicago: University of Illinois Press, 1995).
11. Denis McQuail, *McQuail's Mass Communication Theory*, 5th ed. (London: Sage Publications, 2005).
12. "Censorship Has Many Faces," *World Press Review*, April 1997.
13. "World Press Freedom Index 2014," Reporters Without Borders for Freedom of Information, January 31, 2014, rsf.org/index2014/data/index2014_en.pdf.
14. Nerone, ed., *Last Rights: Revisiting* Four Theories of the Press.
15. Siebert, Peterson, and Schramm, *Four Theories of the Press*.
16. Nerone, ed., *Last Rights: Revisiting* Four Theories of the Press.
17. Siebert, Peterson, and Schramm, *Four Theories of the Press*.
18. Nerone, ed., *Last Rights: Revisiting* Four Theories of the Press.
19. Siebert, Peterson, and Schramm, *Four Theories of the Press*.
20. Nerone, ed., *Last Rights: Revisiting* Four Theories of the Press.
21. Siebert, Peterson, and Schramm, *Four Theories of the Press*.

22. Doris Graber, *Mass Media and American Politics*, 7th ed. (Washington, D.C.: CQ Press, 2006).
23. Nerone, ed., *Last Rights: Revisiting* Four Theories of the Press.
24. McQuail, *McQuail's Mass Communication Theory*.
25. Bob Garfield, "Pulling the Plug," *On the Media*, May 18, 2007, onthemedia.org/transcripts/2007/05/18/05; Associated Press, "Anti-Chavez TV Company Struggles to Survive," May 22, 2012, http://www.seattlepi.com/news/article/Anti-Chavez-TV-company-struggles-to-survive-3577895.php.
26. Thomas Standage, *The Victorian Internet* (New York: Berkley Books, 1998), xvii–xviii.
27. Alan Wells, "Introduction," in *World Broadcasting: A Comparative View*, ed. Alan Wells (Norwood, N.J.: Ablex Publishing, 1996).
28. Rowland Lorimer and Mike Gasher, *Mass Communication in Canada*, 5th ed. (Don Mills, Ontario: Oxford University Press, 2004).
29. Ibid.; Brian Morton, "Feature Film Sector Slows as TV Production Ramps Up," *Vancouver Sun*, May 28, 2012, http://www.canada.com/story.html?id=94c7dc72-2cca-4115-8403-a674526ca52f.
30. Bob Garfield, "God Is Great (Funny, Too)," *On the Media*, May 18, 2007, onthemedia.org/transcripts/2007/05/18/08.
31. Ibid.
32. Lorimer and Gasher, *Mass Communication in Canada*.
33. Ibid.
34. Wells, "Introduction."
35. Ibid.
36. Kevin Williams, *European Media Studies* (London: Hodder Arnold, 2005); Association of Commercial Television, "Facts & Figures," 2012, www.acte.be/.
37. Graber, *Mass Media and American Politics*.
38. Williams, *European Media Studies*.
39. Flemming Rose, "Why I Published Those Cartoons," *Washington Post*, February 19, 2006.
40. Daryl Cagle, "Two Kinds of Offensive Cartoonists," *Cagle Cartoons*, February 13, 2006, http://www.caglecartoons.com/column.asp?ColumnID=%7B3FA565D3-2A09-4772-8135-174B4DDF1AD4%7D.
41. Philip Kennicott, "Clash Over Cartoons Is a Caricature of Civilization," *Washington Post*, February 4, 2006.
42. Ibid.
43. Agence France-Presse, "Danish Cartoonist Attacker Has 10-Year Sentence Confirmed," *Vancouver Sun*, May 2, 2012, www.vancouversun.com/.
44. William Powers, "'Toon Terrific," *National Journal*, February 10, 2006.
45. Angela Charlton, "Depictions Put Press Freedoms to the Test," *Star-Ledger*, February 7, 2006.
46. Staff, "Forms of Intolerance," *Boston Globe*, February 4, 2006.
47. Donnalyn Pompper, "Latin America and the Caribbean," in *World Broadcasting: A Comparative View*, ed. Alan Wells (Norwood, N.J.: Ablex Publishing, 1996).
48. Thomas L. McPhail, *Global Communication: Theories, Stakeholders, and Trends* (Malden, Mass.: Blackwell Publishing, 2006).
49. "World Press Freedom Index 2014," Reporters Without Borders for Freedom of Information, January 31, 2014, rsf.org/index2014/data/index2014_en.pdf.
50. Nicole Gaouette, "Mideast's Clash of Images," *Christian Science Monitor*, October 21, 2000.
51. "Journalism in Syria, impossible job?" Reporters Without Borders for Freedom of Information, November 6, 2013, en.rsf.org/syrie-journalism-in-syria-impossible-job-06-11-2013,45424.html; Elle Shearer, "In Syria, Freelancers Like James Foley Covers a Dangerous War Zone With No Front Lines," *The Washington Post*, August 22, 2014, www.washingtonpost.com/opinions/in-syria-freelancers-like-james-foley-covera-dangerous-war-zone-with-no-front-lines/2014/08/22/25e4bfda-295b-11e4-86ca-6f03cbd15c1a_story.html; Karen DeYoung and Adam Goldman, "Islamic State Claims It Executed American Photojournalist James Foley," *Washington Post*, August 20, 2014, www.washingtonpost.com/world/national-security/islamic-state-claims-it-beheaded-american-photojournalist-james-foley/2014/08/19/42e83970-27e6-11e4-86ca-6f03cbd15c1a_story.html.
52. "World Press Freedom Index 2014," Reporters Without Borders for Freedom of Information, January 31, 2014, rsf.org/index2014/data/index2014_en.pdf.
53. Ibid.
54. Kai Hafez, ed., *Mass Media, Politics, and Society in the Middle East* (Cresskill, N.J.: Hampton Press, 2001).
55. Fred Strickert, "War on the Web," *Christian Century*, May 16, 2001.
56. Ibid.
57. I would like to thank Charley Reed, a communications graduate student at University of Nebraska at Omaha, for his research and work on the new media coverage of the Iranian protests section of this chapter.
58. Ali Arouzi, "Iran to Media: No Cameras Allowed," June 16, 2009, http://worldblog.nbcnews.com/_news/2009/06/16/4376296-iran-to-media-no-cameras-allowed; Brian Stelter, "Journalism Rules Are Bent in News Coverage from Iran," *New York Times*, June 29, 2009; Brian Stelter, "In Coverage of Iran, Amateurs Take the Lead," *New York Times*, June 17, 2009, mediadecoder.blogs.nytimes.com/2009/06/17/in-coverage-of-iran-amateurs-take-the-lead; Gaurav Mishra, "The Digital News Lifecycle: Why Breaking News on Twitter Isn't News Anymore," January 18, 2009, https://blogs.commons.georgetown.edu/msfs-556-spring2009/the-digital-news-lifecycle-why-breaking-news-on-twitter-isnt-news-anymore/.
59. Hussein Y. Amin, "The Middle East and North Africa," in *World Broadcasting: A Comparative View*, ed. Alan Wells (Norwood, N.J.: Ablex Publishing, 1996).
60. Khalid Marghalani and Philip Palmgreen, "Direct Broadcast Satellite Television—Saudi Arabia," *Journal of Broadcasting & Electronic Media* 42, no. 3 (1998).
61. Magali Rheault, "International Television Receives High Marks in Saudi Arabia," October 11, 2007, www.gallup.com/poll/101737/international-television-receives-high-marks-saudi-arabia.aspx.
62. "World Press Freedom Index 2014," Reporters Without Borders for Freedom of Information, January 31, 2014, rsf.org/index2014/data/index2014_en.pdf.
63. Peter Feuilherade, "Analysis: Politics Affect Funding of Arab Satellite TV Stations," *BBC Monitoring International Reports* (2007).
64. Christophe Ayad, "Middle East Media Pluralism via Satellite," *UNESCO Courier*, January 2000.
65. Isabel Hilton, "'Al-Jazeera': And Now, the Other News," *New York Times*, March 6, 2005.
66. Brooke Gladstone, "Al-Nielsens," *On the Media*, December 16, 2005, http://www.onthemedia.org/story/128910-al-nielsens/transcript/.
67. Mark Memmott, "Former Marine in Media Glare as He Joins Al-Jazeera," *USA Today*, September 28, 2005.
68. Hilton, "'Al-Jazeera': And Now, the Other News."
69. "Appeal Filed Over Jailed Al Jazeera Staff," *Al Jazeera*, August 21, 2014, www.aljazeera.com/news/middleeast/2014/08/appeal-filed-over-jailed-al-jazeera-staff-2014821123437168213.html.

70. Tawana Kupe, "New Forms of Cultural Identity in an African Society," *Innovation: The European Journal of Social Science* 8, no. 4 (1995).
71. Ibid.
72. Mohamed Keita, "In Africa, Development Still Comes at Freedom's Expense," February 2012, www.cpj.org/2012/02/attacks-on-the-press-in-2011-in-africa-a-return-of.php.
73. Mohamed Keita, "Pressure on Journalists Rises Along With Africa's Prospects," Committee to Protect Journalists, February 2014, www.cpj.org/2014/02/attacks-on-the-press-africa-rising.php.
74. Mohamed Keita, "In Africa, Development Still Comes at Freedom's Expense."
75. Osabuohien P. Amienyi and Gerard Igyor, "Sub-Saharan Africa," in *World Broadcasting: A Comparative View*, ed. Alan Wells (Norwood, N.J.: Ablex Publishing, 1996).
76. Jean Huteau, "Media Self-Control, the South's New Option," *UNESCO Courier*, April 2000.
77. Amienyi and Igyor, "Sub-Saharan Africa."
78. Richard Harrington, "'World Beat' Rattles Pop Music Scene," *Toronto Star*, June 18, 1988.
79. Jim Miller, "Simon's Spirit of Soweto," *Newsweek*, November 17, 1986.
80. Bob Young, "Bongo Maffin Sets Message to Dance Beat," *Boston Herald*, August 16, 2002.
81. Miller, "Simon's Spirit of Soweto."
82. Harrington, "'World Beat' Rattles Pop Music Scene."
83. Janis E. Overlock, "The Former Soviet Union and Eastern Europe," *in World Broadcasting: A Comparative View*, ed. Alan Wells (Norwood, N.J.: Ablex Publishing, 1996).
84. Ibid.
85. Elena Milashina, "Ahead of Elections, Russian Media Are Duly Warned," February 2012, www.cpj.org/blog/2012/03/ahead-of-elections-russian-media-has-been-duly-war.php.
86. Peter Baker and Susan B. Glasser, "Station Break," *New Republic*, April 23, 2001.
87. Mick Paton Walsh, "The Last Stand for Russia's Free Press," *The Guardian*, April 11, 2005.
88. Beth Knobel, "Boris Yeltsin," *Harvard International Journal of Press/Politics* 3, no. 4 (1998).
89. "World Press Freedom Index 2014," Reporters Without Borders for Freedom of Information, January 31, 2014, rsf.org/index2014/data/index2014_en.pdf.
90. Hsiang-Wen Hsiao, "Asia," in *World Broadcasting: A Comparative View*, ed. Alan Wells (Norwood, N.J.: Ablex Publishing, 1996).
91. Uday Sahay, ed., *Making News: Handbook of Media in Contemporary India* (New Delhi: Oxford University Press, 2006).
92. Ibid.
93. "World Press Freedom Index 2014," Reporters Without Borders for Freedom of Information, January 31, 2014, rsf.org/index2014/data/index2014_en.pdf.
94. Gaurav Mishra, "Social Media and Citizen Journalism in the 11/26 Mumbai Terror Attacks: A Case Study," November 28, 2008, www.gauravonomics.com/.
95. Brooke Gladstone, "Detailed Coverage," *On the Media*, December 5, 2008, www.onthemedia.org/transcripts/2008/12/05/01.
96. Ibid.
97. Kenneth C. Petress, "China," in *World Broadcasting: A Comparative View*, ed. Alan Wells (Norwood, N.J.: Ablex Publishing, 1996).
98. Central Intelligence Agency, "The Chinese Media: More Autonomous and Diverse—Within Limits," June 19, 2013, https://www.cia.gov/library/center-for-the-study-of-intelligence/csi-publications/books-and-monographs/the-chinese-media-more-autonomous-and-diverse-within-limits/copy_of_1.htm.
99. Ibid.
100. Sarah Lacy, "Tudou: A Push Towards Mobile Video and Profits," *Washington Post*, November 7, 2009, www.washingtonpost.com/wp-dyn/content/article/2009/11/08/AR2009110801808.html.
101. "World Press Freedom Index 2014," Reporters Without Borders for Freedom of Information, January 31, 2014, rsf.org/index2014/data/index2014_en.pdf.
102. Hiroshi Tokinoya, "Japan," in *World Broadcasting: A Comparative View*, ed. Alan Wells (Norwood, N.J.: Ablex Publishing, 1996).
103. Douglas Wolk, "Manga, Anime Invade the U.S.," *Publishers Weekly*, March 12, 2001.
104. "World Press Freedom Index 2014," Reporters Without Borders for Freedom of Information, January 31, 2014, rsf.org/index2014/data/index2014_en.pdf.
105. Nicole Gaouette, "Get Your Manga Here," *Christian Science Monitor*, January 8, 1999.
106. Milton Mayfield et al., "Manga and the Pirates: Unlikely Allies for Strategic Growth," *Advanced Management Journal* 65, no. 3 (2000).
107. Ibid.
108. Calvin Reid, "Asian Comics Delight U.S. Readers," *Publishers Weekly*, December 23, 2002.
109. Committee to Protect Journalists, "Journalists Killed in 2012," 2013, cpj.org/killed/2012; Committee to Protect Journalists, "Journalists Killed in 2013," 2014, cpj.org/killed/2013.
110. "Journalism in Syria, Impossible job?" Reporters Without Borders for Freedom of Information, November 6, 2013, en.rsf.org/syrie-journalism-in-syria-impossible-job-06-11-2013,45424.html; Elle Shearer, "In Syria, Freelancers Like James Foley Covers a Dangerous War Zone With No Front Lines," *Washington Post*, August 22, 2014, www.washingtonpost.com/opinions/in-syria-freelancers-like-james-foley-covera-dangerous-war-zone-with-no-front-lines/2014/08/22/25e4bfda-295b-11e4-86ca-6f03cbd15c1a_story.html; Karen DeYoung and Adam Goldman, "Islamic State Claims It Executed American Photojournalist James Foley," *Washington Post,* August 20, 2014, www.washingtonpost.com/world/national-security/islamic-state-claims-it-beheaded-american-photojournalist-james-foley/2014/08/19/42e83970-27e6-11e4-86ca-6f03cbd15c1a_story.html.
111. Ken Auletta, *The Highwaymen* (San Diego, Calif.: Harcourt Brace, 1998).
112. Ibid.
113. "Two Photojournalists Killed in Libyan City of Misrata," *BBC News*, April 21, 2011, www.bbc.co.uk/news/uk-13151490.
114. David W. Dunlap, James Estrin, and Kerri Macdonald, "Parting Glance: Time Hetherington," *New York Times*, April 20, 2011, lens.blogs.nytimes.com/2011/04/20/parting-glance-tim-hetherington/.
115. "BBC's Alan Johnston Is Released," BBC News, July 4, 2007, news.bbc.co.uk/2/hi/6267928.stm.
116. Howard Kurtz, "Mission Impossible," *Washington Post*, August 28, 2006, www.washingtonpost.com/wp-dyn/content/blog/2006/08/28/BL2006082800239.html.

Glossary

above the fold: A term used to refer to a prominent story; it comes from placement of a news story in a broadsheet newspaper above the fold in the middle of the front page.

actual malice: A reckless disregard for the truth or falsity of a published account; this became the standard for libel plaintiffs who were public figures or public officials after the Supreme Court's decision in *New York Times Co. v. Sullivan.*

advertising: Defined by the American Marketing Association as "any paid form of nonpersonal communication about an organization, product, service, or idea by an identified sponsor."

advertorials: Advertising materials in magazines designed to look like editorial content rather than paid advertising.

advocacy ads: Advertising designed to promote a particular point of view rather than a product or service. Can be sponsored by a government, corporation, trade association, or nonprofit organization.

agenda-setting theory: A theory of media effects that says that the media tell the public not what to think but rather what to think about—thus the terms of public discourse are set by what is covered in the media.

aggregator site: An organizing Web site that provides surfers with easy access to e-mail, news, online stores, and many other sites.

Alien and Sedition Acts: Laws passed in 1798 that made it a crime to criticize the government of the United States.

Al Jazeera: The largest and most viewed Arabic-language satellite news channel. It is run out of the country of Qatar and has a regular audience of 40 million viewers.

alphabets: A form of writing in which letters represent individual sounds. Sound-based alphabet writing allows any word to be written using only a few dozen unique symbols.

alternative papers: Weekly newspapers that serve specialized audiences ranging from racial minorities, to gays and lesbians, to young people.

American Society of Composers, Authors and Publishers (ASCAP): The original organization that collected royalties on musical recordings, performances, publications, and airplay.

analog recording: An electromechanical method of recording in which a sound is translated into analogous electrical signals that are then applied to a recording medium. Early analog recording media included acetate or vinyl discs and magnetic tape.

ancillary, or secondary, markets: Movie revenue sources other than the domestic box office. These include foreign box office, video rights, and television rights, as well as tie-ins and product placements.

anonymous audience: An audience the sender does not personally know. These are not anonymous, isolated people who have no connection to anyone else; they simply are anonymous in their audience status.

ARPAnet: The Advanced Research Projects Agency Network; the first nationwide computer network, which would become the first major component of the Internet.

authoritarian theory: A theory of appropriate press behavior that says the role of the press is to be a servant of the government, not a servant of the citizenry.

Bay Psalm Book: The first book published in North America by the Puritans in the Massachusetts Bay Colony. The book went through more than fifty editions and stayed in print for 125 years.

Big Four networks: The broadcast landscape we know today: the Big Three networks plus the Fox Network.

the big idea: The goal of every advertising campaign—an advertising concept that will grab people's attention and make them take notice, remember, and take action.

Big Three networks: The original television broadcast networks: NBC, CBS, and ABC.

blacklist: A group of people banned from working in the movie industry in the late 1940s and 1950s because they were suspected of being communists or communist sympathizers. Some of them, such as a few screenwriters, were able to work under assumed names, but others never worked again in the industry.

block bookings: Requiring a theater owner to take a whole series of movies in order to get a few desirable, headliner films. This system was eventually found to violate antitrust laws.

blockbuster era: A period from the late 1970s to the present day when movie studios make relatively expensive movies that have a large, predefined audience. These movies, usually chock full of special effects, are packaged with cable deals and marketing tie-ins, and can be extremely lucrative if they are able to attract large, repeat audiences.

bloggers: People who post their thoughts, typically with the most recent posts at the top of the page, on a regularly updated Web site.

brand image: The image attached to a brand and the associated product that gives the product a personality or identity that makes it stand out from similar products and stick in the mind of the consumer.

brand name: A word or phrase attached to prepackaged consumer goods so that they can be better promoted to the general public through advertising and so that consumers can distinguish a given product from the competition.

breaking news: An ongoing news story that requires frequent updating.

brick-and-mortar stores: Stores that have a physical presence at which you can shop.

British invasion: The British take on classic American rock 'n' roll, blues, and R&B that transformed rock 'n' roll and became internationally popular in the 1960s with groups such as the Beatles and, later, the Rolling Stones and the Who.

broadband networks: High-speed channels for transmitting multimedia content into the home via cable or wireless connections.

broadband service: A high-speed continuous connection to the Internet using a cable modem from a cable television provider or a digital subscriber line from a phone company. Broadband service is also available in many offices through Ethernet lines. Broadband connections are typically ten or more times faster than dial-up services using a modem.

Broadcast Music Inc. (BMI): A competitor of ASCAP that has generally licensed new composers and artists who had not been represented by ASCAP, including a lot of what was known as "minority music"—including blues, country, Latin, and unpublished jazz compositions.

broadsheet newspapers: Standard-sized newspapers, which are generally 17 by 22 inches.

business-to-business (trade) ads: Advertising that promotes products and services directly to other businesses rather than to the general consumer market.

categorical imperative: Kant's idea of a moral obligation that we should act in a way in which we would be willing to have everyone else act; also known as the principle of universality.

chains: Corporations that control a significant number of newspapers and other media outlets.

channel: The medium used to transmit the encoded message.

citizen journalism: Journalism created by people other than professional journalists, often distributed over the Internet.

clutter: The large number of commercials, advertising, and other nonprogramming messages and interruptions that compete for consumer attention on radio and television, and now also on the Internet.

communication: How we socially interact at a number of levels through messages.

communist theory: A theory of appropriate press behavior that says the press is to be run by the government to serve the government's own needs.

community antenna television (CATV): An early form of cable television used to distribute broadcast channels in communities with poor television reception.

community press: Weekly and daily newspapers serving individual communities or suburbs instead of an entire metropolitan area.

compact disc (CD): A digital recording medium that came into common use in the early 1980s. CDs can hold approximately seventy minutes of digitally recorded music.

competitive model: A model of the effects of a political campaign that looks at the campaign as a competition for the hearts and minds of voters.

concept album: An album by a solo artist or group that contains related songs on a common theme or even a story, rather than a collection of unrelated hits or covers.

consumer magazines: Publications targeting an audience of like-minded consumers.

cookies: Tiny files Web sites create to identify visitors and potentially track their actions on the site and the Web.

correlation: The process of selecting, evaluating, and interpreting events to give structure to the news. The media assist the process of correlation by persuasive communication through editorials, commentary, advertising, and propaganda, and by providing cues that indicate the importance of each news item.

country music: Originally referred to as hillbilly or "old-timey" music, this genre evolved out of Irish and Scottish folk music, Mississippi blues, and Christian gospel music, and grew in the 1950s and 1960s with the so-called Nashville sound.

cover lines: Teaser headlines on magazine covers used to shock, intrigue, or titillate potential buyers.

covers: Songs recorded (or covered) by someone other than the original artist. In the 1950s, it was common for white musicians to cover songs originally played by black artists, but now artists commonly cover all genres of music.

CPM: Cost per thousand exposures to the target audience—a figure used in media planning evaluation.

crisis: Any situation that is perceived by the public as being damaging to the reputation or image of an organization. Not all problems develop into crises, but once a situation develops into a crisis, it can be damaging to an organization's reputation even if information behind the crisis is false.

cultivation analysis: An approach to analyzing the effects of television viewing that argues that watching significant amounts of television alters the way an individual views the nature of the surrounding world.

cutting the cord: Replacing traditional paid video services such as cable or satellite television with Internet-based streaming video services.

decoding: The process of translating a signal from a mass medium into a form that the receiver can understand and then interpreting the meaning of the message itself.

demographics: The study of audience members' gender, race, ethnic background, income, education, age, educational attainment, and the like; a method typically used to analyze potential markets for products and programs.

development theory: A theory of appropriate press behavior that states that developing nations may need to implement press controls in order to promote industry, national identity, and partnerships with neighboring nations.

digital-first strategy: An approach to magazine publishing where online and electronic editions are more important than preserving circulation and revenue from print editions.

digital recording: A method of recording sound—for example, that used to create CDs—that involves storing music in a computer-readable format known as binary information.

dime novels: Inexpensive paperback books that sold (despite their name) for as little as five cents and were especially popular during the Civil War era.

direct action message: An advertising message designed to get consumers to go to a particular place to do something specific, such as purchasing a product, obtaining a service, or engaging in a behavior.

direct broadcast satellite (DBS): A low-Earth-orbit satellite that provides television programming via a small, pizza-sized satellite antenna; DBS is a competitor to cable TV.

disco: The name of the heavily produced techno club dance music of the 1970s, which grew out of the urban gay male subculture, with significant black and Latino influences. In many ways, disco defined the look and feel of 1970s pop culture, fashion, and film.

domestic novels: Novels written in the nineteenth century by and for women that told the story of women who overcame tremendous problems to end up in prosperous middle-class homes.

drive time: The morning and afternoon commute in urban areas; the captive audience makes this a popular time to advertise on radio.

e-book reader: A portable device for viewing, and sometimes selling, electronic books and other texts. Among the most popular are the Amazon Kindle and the Barnes & Noble Nook.

economy of abundance: An economy in which there are as many or more goods available as people who want to or have the means to buy them.

electronic mail (e-mail): A message sent from one computer user to another across a network.

encoding: The process of turning the sender's ideas into a message and preparing the message for transmission.

engineering consent: The application of the principles of psychology and motivation to influencing public opinion and creating public support for a particular position.

entertainment: Media communication intended primarily to amuse the audience.

equal time provision: An FCC policy that requires broadcast stations to make equivalent amounts of broadcast time available to all candidates running for public office.

ethics: A rational way of deciding what is good for individuals or society. Ethics provide a way to choose between competing moral principles and help people decide in cases where there is not a clear-cut right or wrong answer.

fairness doctrine: A former FCC policy that required television stations to "afford reasonable opportunity for the discussion of conflicting views on issues of public importance."

false light: Invasion of privacy in which a journalist publishes untrue statements that alter a person's public image in a way that he or she cannot control.

feature-length film: A theatrical movie that runs more than one hour.

Federal Communications Commission (FCC): The federal agency charged with regulating telecommunications, including radio and television broadcasting.

font: All the characters of a typeface in a particular size and style. The term *font* is typically used interchangeably today with the word *typeface*.

format radio: A style of radio programming designed to appeal to a narrow, specific audience. Popular formats include country, contemporary hits, all talk, all sports, and oldies.

45-rpm disc: The record format developed in the late 1940s by RCA. It had high-quality sound but held only about four minutes of music on a side. It was the ideal format for marketing popular hit songs to teenagers, though.

geographics: The study of where people live; a method typically used to analyze potential markets for products and programs.

girl group: A musical group composed of several women singers who harmonize together. Groups such as the Shirelles, the Ronettes, and the Shangri-Las, featuring female harmonies and high production values, were especially popular in the late 1950s and early 1960s.

golden age of radio: A period from the late 1920s until the 1940s, during which radio was the dominant medium for home entertainment.

golden mean: Aristotle's notion that ethical behavior comes from hitting a balance, a "just-right point between excess and defect."

gramophone: A machine invented by Emile Berliner that could play prerecorded sound on flat discs rather than cylinders.

group communication: Communication in which one person is communicating with an audience of two or more people. The roles of communicator and audience can be changing constantly.

hacker ethic: A set of values from the early days of interactive computing that holds that users should have absolute control over their computer systems and free access to all information contained on those computers. The hacker ethic shaped much of the development of the Internet.

halftone: An image produced by a process in which photographs are broken down into a series of dots that appear in shades of gray on the printed page.

HD radio: Sometimes also referred to as high-definition radio, this technology provides listeners with CD-quality sound and the choice of multiple channels of programming but is not yet commonly available in mass-market outlets or as standard equipment in cars.

heterogeneous audience: An audience made up of a mix of people who differ in age, sex, income, education, ethnicity, race, religion, and other characteristics.

high-definition television (HDTV): A standard for high-quality digital broadcasting that features a high-resolution picture, wide-screen format, and enhanced sound.

high fidelity (hi-fi): A combination of technologies that allowed recordings to reproduce music more accurately with higher high notes and deeper bass than was possible with previous recording technologies.

hip-hop: A cultural movement that originated in the 1970s and '80s that features four main elements: MCing, or rapping over music; DJing, playing recorded music from multiple sources; B-boying, a style of dancing; and graffiti art.

Hollywood Ten: A group of ten writers and directors who refused to testify before the House Un-American Activities Committee about their political activities. They were among the first people in Hollywood to be blacklisted.

House Un-American Activities Committee: The congressional committee, chaired by Parnell Thomas, that held hearings on the influence of communism on Hollywood in 1947. These activities mirrored a wider effort to root out suspected communists in all walks of American life.

hypertext: Material in a format containing links that allow the reader to move easily from one section to another and from document to document. The most commonly used hypertext documents are Web pages.

hypertext markup language (HTML): The programming language used to create and format Web pages.

hypertext transfer protocol (http): A method of sending text, graphics, or anything else over the Internet from a server to a Web browser.

ideograph: An abstract symbol that stands for a word or phrase. The written forms of the Chinese, Korean, and Japanese languages make use of ideographs.

indirect action message: An advertising message designed to build the image of and demand for a product, without specifically urging that a particular action be taken at a particular time and place.

industrialization: The movement from work done by hand using muscle or water power in small shops to mass production of goods in factories that used energy sources such as steam power or electricity. It was part of the modernization process.

instant messaging (IM): E-mail systems that allow two or more users to chat with one another in real time, hold virtual meetings that span multiple cities or even countries, and keep track of which of their "buddies" are currently logged on to the system.

integrated marketing communication: An overall communication strategy for reaching key audiences using advertising, public relations, sales promotion, and interactive media.

Internet: "A diverse set of independent networks, interlinked to provide its users with the appearance of a single, uniform network"; the Internet is a mass medium like no other, incorporating elements of interpersonal, group, and mass communications.

interpersonal communication: Communication, either intentional or accidental, between two people. It can be verbal or nonverbal.

intranets: Computer networks designed to communicate with people within an organization. They are used to improve two-way internal communication and contain tools that allow for direct feedback. They are a tool for communicating with internal publics.

intrapersonal communication: Communication you have with yourself. How you assign meaning to the world around you.

intrusion: Invasion of privacy by physical trespass into a space surrounding a person's body or onto property under his or her control.

jazz journalism: A lively, illustrated style of newspapering popularized by the tabloid papers in the 1920s.

kinetoscope: An early peep show–like movie projection system developed by Thomas Edison that could be seen only by an individual viewer.

libel: A published statement that unjustifiably exposes someone to ridicule or contempt; for a statement to be libel, it must satisfy the three elements of defamation, identification, and publication.

libertarian theory: A theory of appropriate press behavior that says the press does not belong to the government but is instead a separate institution that belongs to the people and serves as an independent observer of the government.

Linotype: A typesetting machine that lets an operator type at a keyboard rather than pick each letter out by hand. The Linotype was the standard for typesetting until phototypesetting became common in the 1970s.

listservs: Internet discussion groups made up of subscribers that use e-mail to exchange messages between as few as a dozen people or as many as several thousand.

literary magazines: Publications that focus on serious essays and short fiction.

local advertising: Advertising designed to get people to patronize local stores, businesses, or service providers.

local cable television systems: The companies that provide cable television service directly to consumers' homes.

long-playing record (LP): A record format introduced by Columbia Records in 1948. The more durable LP could reproduce twenty-three minutes of high-quality music on each of two sides and was a technological improvement over the 78-rpm.

long tail: The portion of a distribution curve where a limited number of people are interested in buying a lot of different products.

magazine: A periodical that contains articles of lasting interest. Typically, magazines are targeted at a specific audience and derive income from advertising, subscriptions, and newsstand sales.

mainstreaming: The effort by newspapers such as the *Los Angeles Times* to include quotations by minorities and women in stories that aren't about minority issues.

mass communication: When an individual or institution uses technology to send a message to a large, mixed audience, most of whose members are not known to the sender.

mass media: The technological tools, or channels, used to transmit the messages of mass communication.

mean world syndrome: The perception of many heavy television watchers of violent programs that the world is a more dangerous and violent place than facts and statistics bear out.

media literacy: Audience members' understanding of the media industry's operation, the messages delivered by the media, the roles media play in society, and how audience members respond to these media and their messages.

media logic: An approach to studying the mass media that says the forms the media use to present the world become the forms we use to perceive the world and to create media messages.

media planning: The process central to a successful ad campaign of figuring out which media to use, buying the media at the best rates, and then evaluating how effective the purchase was.

media relations: Two-way interactions between PR professionals and members of the press. These can involve press conferences, press releases, video news releases, or interviews. Typically, media relations involve the placement of unpaid messages within the standard programming or news content of the medium.

message: The content being transmitted by the sender to the receiver.

misappropriation: Invasion of privacy by using a person's name or image for commercial purposes without his or her permission.

modernization: The process of change from a society in which people's identities and roles are fixed at birth to a society where people can decide who they want to be, where they want to live, what they want to do, and how they want to present themselves to the world.

morals: An individual's code of behavior based on religious or philosophical principles. Morals define right and wrong in ways that may or may not be rational.

Mosaic: The first easy-to-use graphical Web browser, developed by a group of student programmers at the University of Illinois at Champaign-Urbana.

MP3: Short for Moving Picture Experts Group audio layer 3; a standard for compressing music from CDs or other digital recordings into computer files that can be easily exchanged on the Internet.

muckrakers: Progressive investigative journalists typically publishing in magazines in the early years of the twentieth century.

multiplex: A group of movie theaters with anywhere from three to twenty screens that share a common box office and concession stand. Largely a suburban phenomenon at first, they replaced the old urban Art Deco movie palaces.

national advertising: Advertising designed to build demand for a nationally available product or service and that is not directing the consumer to local retail and service outlets.

native advertising: Advertising materials mixed in with articles and written by staff writers designed to look like editorial content rather than paid advertising.

Net neutrality: Rules that would require Internet service providers to give equal access to all online content providers.

network: A company that provides common programming to a large group of broadcast stations.

noise: Interference with the transmission of a message. This can take the form of semantic, mechanical, or environmental noise.

non-notated music: Music such as a folk song or jazz solo that does not exist in written form.

obscenity: Sexually explicit material that is legally prohibited from being published.

ombudsman: A representative of a publication's readers who takes the point of view of those who purchase or consume the news; also known as a reader's representative or audience advocate.

open contract: An arrangement that allows advertising agencies to sell space in any publication (and eventually broadcast outlets as well) rather than just a limited few.

opinion leaders: Influential community members who invest substantial amounts of time learning about their own area of expertise, such as politics. Less well-informed friends and family members frequently turn to them for advice about the topic.

opinion leadership: A two-step process of persuasion that uses respected and influential individuals to deliver messages with the hope of influencing members of a community, rather than just relying on the mass media to deliver the message.

packet switching: A method for breaking up long messages into small pieces, or packets, and transmitting them independently across a computer network. Once the packets arrive at their destination, the receiving computer reassembles the message into its original form.

paper: A writing material made from cotton rags or wood pulp; invented by the Chinese between 240 BC and 105 BC.

papyrus: An early form of paper made from the papyrus reed, developed by the Egyptians around 3100 BC.

parchment: An early form of paper made from the skin of goats or sheep, which was more durable than papyrus.

penny press: Inexpensive, widely circulated papers that became popular in the nineteenth century. They were the first American media to be supported primarily through advertising revenue.

PeopleMeter: An electronic box used by the ratings company Nielsen Media Research to record which television shows people watch.

phonograph: An early sound-recording machine invented by Thomas Edison; the recorded material was played back on a cylinder.

phonography: A system of writing in which symbols stand for spoken sounds rather than objects or ideas. Among the most widely used phonographic alphabets are the Latin/Roman used in English and the Cyrillic used for writing Russian.

photojournalism: The use of photographs to portray the news in print.

pictograph: A prehistoric form of writing made up of paintings on rock or cave walls.

plus-sized model: A female fashion model who wears average or larger clothing size.

podcast: An audio program produced as an MP3 compressed music file that can be listened to online at the listener's convenience or downloaded to a computer or an MP3 player. Podcasts sometimes contain video content as well.

Postal Act of 1879: Legislation that allowed magazines to be mailed nationally at a low cost. It was a key factor in the growth of magazine circulation in the late nineteenth century.

press agentry: An early form of public relations that involved sending material from the press agent to the media with little opportunity for interaction and feedback. It often involved conduct that would be considered deceptive and unethical today.

principle of utility: John Stuart Mill's principle that ethical behavior arises from that which will provide the greatest good for the greatest number of people.

print-on-demand: A form of publishing in which the physical book is not printed until it's ordered, or until the distributor of the book prints additional copies in small batches.

prior restraint: A judicial order that stops a media organization from publishing or broadcasting a story or image.

privilege: A legal defense against libel that holds that statements made in government meetings, in court, or in government documents cannot be used as the basis for a libel suit.

producer: The person who puts together the right mix of songs, songwriters, technicians, and performers to create an album; some observers argue that the producer is the key catalyst for a hit album.

product integration: The paid integration of a product or service into the central theme of media content. This is most common in television programming or movies, but it can be found in books, magazine articles, Web pages, or even songs.

Production Code: The industry-imposed rules that controlled the content of movies from the 1930s until the current movie ratings system came into use in 1968.

proofs: The ready-to-print typeset pages sent to book authors for final corrections.

psychographics: A combination of demographics, lifestyle characteristics, and product usage; a method typically used to analyze potential markets for products and programs.

public: Any group of people who share a common set of interests and goals. These include *internal publics*, made up of people within the organization, and *external publics*, consisting of people outside the organization.

public access channels: Local cable television channels that air public affairs programming and other locally produced shows.

Public Broadcasting Service (PBS): A nonprofit broadcast network that provides a wide range of public service and educational programs, which is funded by government appropriations, private industry underwriting, and viewer support.

publicity model: A model of the mass communication process that looks at how media attention can make a person, concept, or thing become important, regardless of what is said about it.

public relations (PR): Public relations is "the management function that establishes and maintains mutually beneficial relationships between an organization and the publics on whom its success or failure depends."

public service ads: Advertising designed to promote the messages of nonprofit institutions and government agencies. The messages are typically produced and run without charge by advertising professionals and the media. Many of these ads are produced by the Ad Council.

publishers: The companies that buy manuscripts from authors, turn them into books, and market them to the public.

race records: A term used by the recording industry prior to 1949 to refer to recordings by popular black artists. It was later replaced by more racially neutral terms such as *R&B*, *soul*, and *urban contemporary*.

Radio Music Box memo: David Sarnoff's 1915 plan, outlining how radio could be used as a popular mass medium.

rap music: This genre arose out of the hip-hop culture in New York City in 1979. It emerged in clubs with DJs playing and remixing different records and sounds and then speaking (or rapping) over the top.

rating point: The percentage of the total potential television audience actually watching a particular show. One rating point indicates an audience of approximately 1.14 million viewers.

receiver: The audience for a mass communication message.

reception model: A critical theory model of the mass communication process that looks at how audience members derive and create meaning out of media content as they decode the messages.

resonance model: A model of political campaign effects that attributes a candidate's success to how well his or her basic message resonates with and reinforces voters' preexisting political feelings.

ritual model: A model of the mass communication process that treats media use as an interactive ritual engaged in by audience members. It looks at how and why audience members (receivers) consume media messages.

rock 'n' roll: A style of music popularized on radio that combined elements of white hillbilly music and black rhythm and blues.

rotary press: A steam-powered press invented in 1814 that could print many times faster than the older, hand-powered flat-bed presses.

satellite radio: The radio service provided by digital signal broadcast from a communications satellite. This service covers a wider area than terrestrial radio, is supported by subscribers, and offers programming that is different from corporate-owned terrestrial stations, but is costly and doesn't provide local coverage, such as traffic and weather reports.

scriptoria: Copying rooms in monasteries where monks prepared early hand-copied books.

Sender Message Channel Receiver (SMCR) or transmission model: A dated model that is still useful in identifying the players in the mass communication process.

sensationalism: News coverage that panders to audiences with lurid and highly emotional accounts of crime, sex, violence, or celebrity missteps.

serial novels: Novels published and sold in single-chapter installments.

service magazines: Magazines that primarily contain articles about how to do things in a better way; such articles include health advice, cooking tips, employment help, or fashion guides.

share: The percentage of television sets in use that are tuned to a particular show.

shield laws: Laws that give journalists special protection from having to testify in court about their stories and sources.

shock jocks: Radio personalities, like Howard Stern, who attract listeners by making outrageous and offensive comments on the air.

short head: The portion of a distribution curve where a large number of people are interested in buying a limited number of products.

small media: Alternative media such as fax machines, photocopiers, video cameras, and personal Web sites used to distribute news and information that might be suppressed by the government if it were published through traditional mass media channels.

soap operas: Serialized daytime dramas targeted primarily at women.

socialization: The process of educating young people and new members about the values, social norms, and knowledge of a group or society.

social learning theory: The process by which individuals learn by observing the behaviors of others and the consequences of those behaviors.

social media: Web sites that allow users to generate content, comment, tag, and network with friends or other like-minded people.

social music: Music that people play and sing for one another in the home or other social settings. In the absence of radio, recordings, and later, television, this was the means of hearing music most readily available to the largest number of people.

social responsibility theory: A theory of appropriate press behavior based on the concern that, although the press may be free from interference from the government, it can still be controlled by corporate interests. It is an outgrowth of libertarian theory.

spiral of silence: A theory that suggests that people want to see themselves as holding a majority opinion and will therefore remain silent if they perceive that they hold a minority opinion. This tends to make the minority opinion appear to be less prevalent than it is.

standard digital television: A standard for digital broadcasting that allows six channels to fit in the broadcast frequency space occupied by a single analog signal.

status conferral: The process by which media coverage makes an individual gain prominence in the eyes of the public.

streaming audio: Audio programming transmitted over the Internet.

studio system: A factory-like way of producing films that involved having all of the talent, including the actors and directors, working directly for the movie studios. The studios also had almost total control of the distribution system.

subliminal advertising: Messages that are allegedly embedded so deeply in an ad that they cannot be perceived consciously. There is no evidence that subliminal advertising is effective.

surveillance: How the media help us extend our senses to perceive more of the world surrounding us.

sweeps: The four times during the year that Nielsen Media Research measures the size of individual television station audiences.

symbolic interactionism: The process by which individuals produce meaning through interaction based on socially agreed-upon symbols.

synchronized soundtrack: Sound effects, music, and voices synchronized with the moving images in a movie.

synergy: Where the combined strength of two items is greater than the sum of their individual strengths. In the media business, synergy means that a large company can use the strengths of its various divisions to successfully market its content.

tabloid laundering or tabloidization: When respectable media report on what the tabloids are reporting as a way of covering sensationalistic stories on which they might not otherwise report.

tabloid newspapers: Newspapers with a half-page (11- by 14-inch) format that usually have a cover rather than a traditional front page like the larger broadsheet papers.

talkie: A movie with synchronized sound; these quickly replaced silent films.

targeting: The process of trying to make a particular product or service appeal to a narrowly defined group. Groups are often targeted using demographics, geographics, and psychographics.

TCP/IP: TCP stands for Transmission Control Protocol, which controls how data are sent out on the Internet; IP stands for Internet Protocol, which provides the address for each computer on the Internet. These protocols provided common rules and translations so that incompatible computers could communicate with each other.

telegraph: The first system for using wires to send messages at a distance; invented by Samuel Morse in 1844.

telenovelas: Spanish-language soap operas popular in both Latin America and the United States.

television network: A company that provides programs to local stations around the country; the local affiliate stations choose which programs to carry.

terrestrial radio: AM and FM broadcast radio stations.

trade books: General-interest fiction and nonfiction books that are sold in hardback or large-format paperback editions.

trade magazines: Magazines published for people who work in a particular industry or business.

typemold: A mold in which a printer would pour molten lead to produce multiple, identical copies of a single letter without hand-carving each.

uniform resource locator (URL): One of the three major components of the Web; the address of content placed on the Web.

university and small presses: Small-scale publishers that issue a limited number of books covering specialized topics. They are often subsidized by a university or an organization.

uses and gratifications theory: An approach to studying mass communication that looks at the reasons why audience members choose to spend time with the media in terms of the wants and needs of the audience members that are being fulfilled.

veil of ignorance: John Rawls's principle of ethics that says that justice comes from making decisions that maximize liberty for all people and without considering which outcome will give us personally the biggest benefit.

vertical integration: Controlling all aspects of a media project, including production, delivery to consumers in multiple formats, and the promotion of the product through other media.

videocassette recorder (VCR): A home videotape machine that allows viewers to make permanent copies of television shows and, thus, choose when they want to watch programs.

video-on-demand: Television channels that allow consumers to order movies, news, or other programs at any time over fiber-optic lines.

Watergate scandal: A burglary authorized by rogue White House staffers of the Democratic National Committee headquarters in the Watergate office and apartment building and its subsequent cover-up led to the resignation of President Richard Nixon in 1974. Bob Woodward and Carl Bernstein, two reporters from the *Washington Post*, covered the Watergate scandal.

Weblog (blog): A collection of links and commentary in hypertext form on the World Wide Web that can be created and posted on the Internet with relatively little effort. Blogs can be public diaries, collections of photos, or commentaries on the news.

wireless telegraph: Guglielmo Marconi's name for his point-to-point communication tool that used radio waves to transmit messages.

World Wide Web: A system developed by Tim Berners-Lee that allows users to view and link documents located anywhere in the world using standard software.

yellow journalism: A style of sensationalistic journalism that grew out of the newspaper circulation battle between Joseph Pulitzer and William Randolph Hearst.

zoned coverage: When a newspaper targets news coverage or advertisements to a specific region of a city or market.

Index